STUDENT TESTED, FACULTY APPROVED

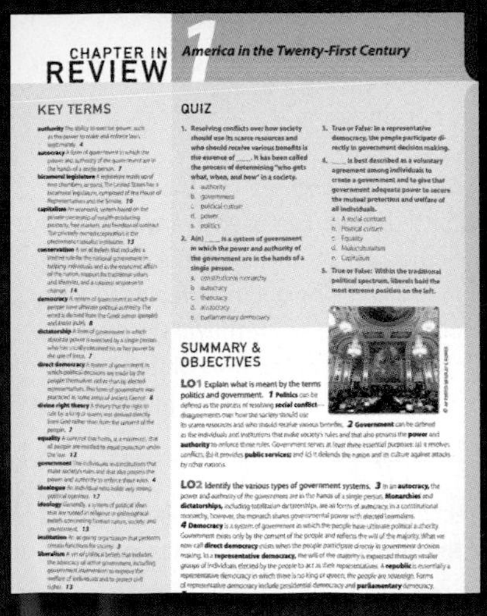

Chapter In Review cards at the back of the Student Edition provide students with a portable study tool containing all of the pertinent information for class preparation.

THE SOLUTION

GOVT Are you in?

ONLINE RESOURCES INCLUDED!

CourseMate **Engaging. Trackable. Affordable.**

CourseMate brings course concepts to life with interactive learning, study, and exam preparation tools that support GOVT3.

FOR INSTRUCTORS:

- First Day of Class Instructions
- Custom options through 4LTR+ Program
- Instructor's Manual
- Test Bank
- PowerPoint Slides
- Tear-out Instructor Prep Cards
- Audio Summaries
- Engagement Tracker

FOR STUDENTS:

- Interactive eBook
- Tutorial Quizzing
- Online Flashcards
- Crossword Puzzles
- PowerPoint Slides
- Videos
- Animated Learning Modules
- Simulations
- Tear-out Student Review Cards
- Web Links
- Audio Summaries

Students sign in at **login.cengagebrain.com**

GOVT[3] California Edition
Edward Sidlow, Beth Henschen,
Larry N Gerston, and Terry Christensen

Publisher: Suzanne Jeans
Executive Editor: Carolyn Merrill
Acquisitions Editor: Anita M. Devine
Development Editor: Rebecca Green
Associate Development Editor: Kate MacLean
Assistant Editor: Laura Ross
Editorial Assistant: Nina Wasserman
Media Editor: Laura Hildebrand
Marketing Manager: Lydia LeStar
Marketing Communications Manager: Heather Baxley
Content Production Manager: Ann Borman
Print Buyer: Fola Orekoya
Photo Researchers: Ann Hoffman, Anne Sheroff
Copy Editor: Mary Berry
Proofreaders: Judy Kiviat and Loretta Palagi
Indexer: Terry Casey
Art Director: Linda Helcher
Interior Design: Ke Design
Cover Design: Lisa Kuhn
Cover Image Credit: © Getty Images
Compositor: Parkwood Composition

Library of Congress Control Number: 2010938093

Student Edition ISBN-13: 978-1-111-34307-1
Student Edition ISBN-10: 1-111-34307-1

Instructor's Edition ISBN-13: 978-1-111-34348-4
Instructor's Edition ISBN-10: 1-111-34348-9

Wadsworth Political Science
20 Channel Center
Boston, MA 02210

Cengage Learning products are represented in Canada by Nelson Education, Ltd.

For your course and learning solutions, visit **www.cengage.com.**

Purchase any of our products at your local college store or at our preferred online store at **www.cengagebrain.com.**

Chapter-Opener Photo Credits:
Ch 1: AP Photo/Bradley C Bower. Ch 2: Steve McAlister/Getty Images. Ch 3: Robyn Beck/AFP/Getty Images. Ch 4: AP Photo/Matt York. Ch 5: Mark Peterson/Redux. Ch 6: AP Photo/Alastair Grant. Ch 7: John Moore/Getty Images. Ch 8: George Frey/Landov. Ch 9: AP Photo/Morry Gash. Ch 10: Kevin Lamarque/Reuters/Landov. Ch 11: Mark Wilson/Getty Images. Ch 12: Mike Theiler/EPA/Landov. Ch 13: AP Photo/Manuel Balce Ceneta. Ch 14: Paul J. Richards/AFP/Getty Images. Ch 15: Kevin Lamarque/Reuters/Landov. Ch 16: AP Photo/Andy Wong. Ch 17: two photos combined, both by Jeff Kravitz/Film Magic/Getty Images. Ch 18: Robyn Beck/AFP/Getty Images. Ch 19: Cheree Ray/Film Magic/Getty Images. Ch 20: Charley Gallay/Getty Images. Ch 21: Justin Sullivan/Getty Images. Ch 22: Paul Sakuma/Getty Images. Ch 23: AP Photo/Chris Carlson. Ch 24: AP Photo/Rich Pedroncelli. Ch 25: David McNew/Getty Images. Ch 26: Mark Ralston/AFP/Getty Images.

Printed in the United States of America

1 2 3 4 5 6 7 14 13 12 11 10

Brief Contents

SIDLOW / HENSCHEN / GERSTON / CHRISTENSEN

GOVT³

CALIFORNIA EDITION

Contents

Chapter 3
Federalism 47

2 *Our Liberties and Rights* 70

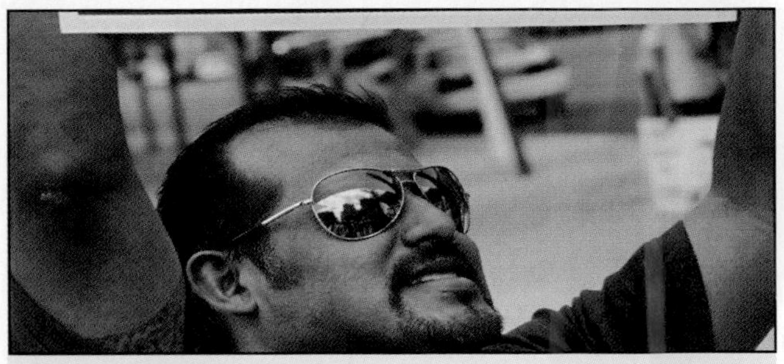

Chapter 4
Civil Liberties 70

Chapter 5
Civil Rights 93

3 *The Politics of Democracy 118*

Chapter 6
Interest Groups 118

Chapter 7
Political Parties 140

Chapter 8
Public Opinion and Voting 162

Chapter 9
Campaigns and Elections 187

Chapter 10
Politics and the Media 209

4 Institutions 230

Chapter 11
Congress 230

Chapter 12
The Presidency 254

Chapter 13
The Bureaucracy 279

Chapter 14
The Judiciary 302

5 Public Policy 325

Chapter 15 *Domestic Policy* 325

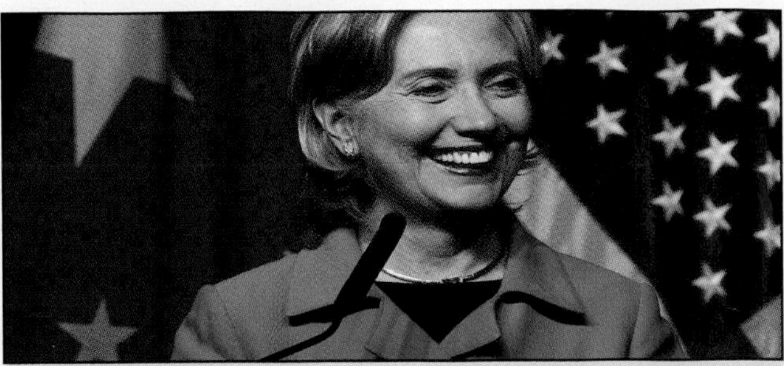

Chapter 16 *Foreign Policy* 345

6 California Government and Politics 367

Chapter 17
California's People, Economy, and Politics 367

Chapter 18
California's Political Parties and Direct Democracy 386

Chapter 19
California Elections, Campaigns, and the Media 404

Chapter 20
California Interest Groups 421

Chapter 21
The Legislature: The Perils of Policy Making 438

Chapter 22
California Law: Courts, Judges, and Politics 457

Chapter 23
The Executive Branch: Coping with Fragmented Authority 472

Chapter 24
Taxing and Spending: Budgetary Politics and Policies 491

Chapter 25
Local Government in California 507

Chapter 26
State-Federal Relations: Conflict, Cooperation, and Chaos 525

Preface

The 2010 congressional elections were expected to be tumultuous and unsettling. They met those expectations, for the Democrats lost a net total of sixty-four seats in the House and six seats in the Senate. Americans—and President Barack Obama among them—find themselves with a divided government. Because the 2010 elections were so important, we have included in this edition a special feature called *Elections 2010*.

Political conflict and divergence of opinion have always characterized our political traditions and way of governing. Nonetheless, our democracy endures, and the U.S. Constitution continues to serve as a model for new democracies around the world. The third edition of GOVT California looks at government and politics in this country as a series of conflicts that have led to compromises.

This text was written with today's generation of students in mind. As such, it does the following:

- Provides the historical context for today's most significant political controversies;
- Presents different perspectives on key issues currently being debated;
- Helps students test their beliefs and assumptions and determine their positions on major political issues;
- Assists students in the process of acquiring informed political values and opinions;
- Fully explains major problems facing the American political system; and
- Looks at the global connections between the American political system and the systems of other countries.

New to This Edition

The entire book—including figures, tables, photos, Web sites, and data—has been updated through 2010.

- In Chapter 1, the recent health-care reform is used as an example to illustrate political ideology.
- Chapter 2 contains a new section, *Defining the Executive,* under *Drafting and Ratifying the Constitution.*
- An updated discussion of same-sex marriage and a new section, *Obama and Federalism,* appear in Chapter 3.
- Chapter 4 includes new subsections under *Personal Privacy and National Security: The USA Patriot Act and The Civil Liberties Debate.*
- Chapter 5 integrates a new section, *The Feminist Movement,* and includes updated discussions of same-sex marriage and affirmative action.
- Chapter 6 contains a new section *The Constitutional Right to Petition the Government,* a revised look at *Why Interests Groups Form,* and a clarified discussion of the free rider problem. In addition, you will find new sections on rating systems, Astroturf lobbying, *Identity Interest Groups,* and *Ideological Interest Groups,* including a discussion of the Tea Party movement and environmental interest groups.
- Chapter 7 now includes sections called *Triumph of the Jeffersonians; Shifting Political Fortunes* (updating the discussion of today's political parties); *Realignment, Dealignment, and Tipping; The Parties Return to Their Roots;* and *Duverger's Law;* as well as an expanded discussion of primaries and selecting candidates.
- A new section, *Types of Polls,* and discussion of the accuracy of polling during the 2010 midterm elections appear in Chapter 8.
- Chapter 9 has been thoroughly revised through the 2010 midterm elections and includes new sections: *Primary Voters, Blanket and "Top Two" Primaries,* and *Citizens United v. Federal Election Commission.*
- Chapter 10 integrates new sections *The Media and the First Amendment, The "Wild West" Migrates to Television,* and *Obama's Difficulties*. There is also a new discussion of narrowcasting and an updated section *Political News and Campaigns on the Web.*
- Updates and analysis of the 112th Congress appear in Chapter 11.
- Chapter 12 has been updated throughout to discuss Obama's presidency.
- Chapter 13, on the bureaucracy, has been streamlined, and the revised section *An Expanding Bureaucracy*

includes the sections *Expanded Government under President Obama* and *A New Spirit in Congress.*

- Court cases through 2010 and the latest Supreme Court appointments are discussed in Chapter 14.
- Chapter 15 includes an updated and completely revised *Health-Care Policy* section discussing the 2010 legislation, and new sections titled *Nuclear Energy, Offshore Drilling,* and *The BP Oil Spill in the Gulf of Mexico.*
- Chapter 16 includes an updated look at *The War on Terrorism* through 2010—including the troop withdrawal in Iraq and updates on Afghanistan—as well as a new subsection called *Toward New Talks* under *The Israeli-Palestinian Conflict* and an updated discussion of North Korea.
- The California chapters 17 through 26 are updated to reflect the 2010 elections results and the latest statistics and propositions.

New Elections 2010 Features

Throughout various chapters, you will find the following *Elections 2010* analyses:

- New Directions for America (Chapter 1)
- Minority Group Members and Women (Chapter 5)
- The Elections and the Parties (Chapter 7)
- Voting by Groups (Chapter 8)
- Campaign Spending (Chapter 9)
- The New Congress (Chapter 11)
- An Island of Stability in a Stormy Nation (Chapter 17)
- The Ballot Proposals (Chapter 18)
- Campaign Finance (Chapter 19)
- Governor Jerry Brown (Chapter 23)

New Our Government Faces a Troubled Economy Features

The Great Recession officially started in December 2007. Officially, it ended in June 2009, when the economy slowly began to grow again. Even though the Great Recession is technically over, the economy is still extremely troubled. The unemployment rate is above 9.5 percent. Each year the federal government deficit exceeds a trillion dollars. Our new feature for this edition of GOVT is appropriately called *Our Government Faces a Troubled Economy.* Almost every chapter in this edition has this new feature. Here are some examples:

- Printing Money to Fight a Recession (Chapter 2)
- Fighting a Recession with Government Spending (Chapter 3)
- Should We Cut Taxes—and How? (Chapter 11)
- Spending More on Health Care—and Less (Chapter 13)
- Red Ink Forever? (Chapter 15)
- Should We Fight China's Cheap Exports? (Chapter 16)
- The Attempt to Roll Back Greenhouse Gas Legislation (Chapter 20)
- Would a New Constitution Help California? (Chapter 23)
- Should California Have Legalized Pot? (Chapter 26)

New *Join the Debate* Features, Too

Most of the popular *Join the Debate* features have been substituted with new debate topics in this edition. Students and instructors will now be able to debate the following:

- Is the Death Penalty a Cruel and Unusual Punishment? (Chapter 2)
- Is Obamacare Constitutional? (Chapter 3)
- Are Admissions to Top Schools Unfair to Asian Americans? (Chapter 5)
- Should D.C. Residents Have a Representative? (Chapter 9)
- Should Judges Be the Ones to Decide Whether Same-Sex Couples Can Marry? (Chapter 14)
- Should Unauthorized Immigrants Be Given a Path to Citizenship? (Chapter 15)
- Do Business Executives Make Better Officeholders? (Chapter 23)
- Should Fees Be Treated Like Taxes? (Chapter 24)

New *America at Odds* Chapter-Opening Features

The majority of chapter-opening *America at Odds* features are new to this edition (and the ones that we have retained have been updated). The new ones include:

- Has Our Government Grown Too Large? (Chapter 1)
- Should the Census Count Be Limited to Citizens? (Chapter 5)
- Is the Republican Party Conservative Enough? (Chapter 7)
- Should Felons Be Allowed to Vote? (Chapter 8)

- Just How Effective Is President Obama? (Chapter 12)
- Do We Send Too Many People to Prison? (Chapter 15)

New *Perception versus Reality* Features

Several of the *Perception versus Reality* features are new to this edition. They include the following:

- Can Congress Really Dig Up Government Corruption? (Chapter 11)
- The Mythical Barack Obama (Chapter 12)
- A United Europe? (Chapter 16)

New *The Rest of the World* Features

Finally, many of *The Rest of the World* features are also new to this edition. They include:

- Fingerprinting 1.1 Billion Citizens of India (Chapter 4)
- Europe's Common Agricultural Policy (Chapter 6)
- Coalition Government in the United Kingdom (Chapter 7)
- Compulsory Voting Elsewhere Improves Voter Turnout (Chapter 9)
- Using Facebook to Organize in Indonesia (Chapter 10)
- The Unusual Role of the French President (Chapter 12)

A Groundbreaking Format

GOVT's daring format has been designed to engage even the most apathetic American government student with its glossy, magazine-style look and dynamic visual appeal. Streamlined, portable, and complete with study resources, this text does more than ever before to accommodate the way students actually use their textbooks. At the same time, our "debate-the-issues" approach effectively involves readers in discussing and debating concepts of American and Californian government. **Chapter Review tear-out cards** at the end of the book provide learning objectives with summaries of key concepts, visuals, and key terms for each chapter—making it easier for students to prepare for class and for exams. And because today's students are technologically savvy, we provide **portable study resources in multiple formats** via this text's CourseMate, accessible through CengageBrain.com. Resources there include flashcards, podcasts, chapter reviews, quizzes, and more that students can download whichever way they prefer (cell phone, computer, MP3 files, and so on) in order to study more efficiently. Access to the site is available at no additional cost when packaged with each student text.

Features That Teach

As exciting as the innovative new GOVT format may be, we have not lost sight of the essential goals and challenges of teaching American and Californian government. Any government text must present the basics of the political process and institutions, and it must excite and draw the student into the *subject.*

Additionally, we present many of today's controversial political issues in special features. Each of the more than one hundred features contained in the text covers a topic of high interest to students. GOVT includes the following different types of features, in addition to the features outlined earlier:

- ***Learning Objectives***—Every chapter-opening page includes a list of three or more Learning Objectives that lets students know what concepts will be covered in the chapter. Each Learning Objective has an identifying number (such as LO1 or LO2). The same number also precedes the major heading of the chapter section in which that topic is presented. This allows students to quickly locate where in the chapter a particular topic is discussed.
- **Chapter-ending *America at Odds* feature**—This feature often opens with a general discussion of the historical evolution of the aspect of government addressed in the chapter. When relevant, the founders' views and expectations relating to the topic are set forth and then compared with the actual workings of our political system in that area today. This part of the feature is designed to indicate how American politics and government currently measure up to the expectations of the founders or to those of today's Americans. Following this discussion, we present questions for debate and discussion. Each question briefly outlines two sides of a current political controversy and then asks the student to identify her or his position on the issue. The feature closes with a "Take Action" section that offers tips to students on what they can do to make a difference in an area of interest to them.
- ***Politics on the Web***—This section gives selected Web sites that students can access for more information on issues discussed in the chapter.

- *CourseMate*—This section directs students to the text's companion Web site, where they can find additional resources for the chapter.

Supplements

Both instructors and students today expect, and indeed require, a variety of accompanying supplements to teach and learn about American and Californian government. GOVT takes the lead in providing the most comprehensive and user-friendly supplements package on the market today.

On **CengageBrain.com** students are able to save up to 60 percent of the cost of their course materials through our full spectrum of options. Students will have the option to rent their textbooks or purchase print textbooks, e-textbooks, or individual e-chapters and audiobooks, all at substantial savings over average retail prices. CengageBrain.com also includes access to Cengage Learning's broad range of homework and study tools, including the student resources discussed here. Follow the URL below to access the book-specific resources.

For further information on any of these supplements, contact your Wadsworth, Cengage Learning sales representative.

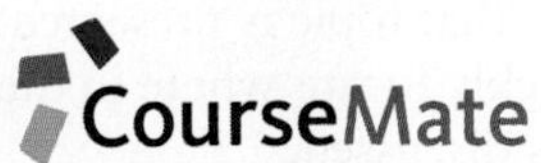

Go to **cengagebrain.com/shop/ISBN/1111343071** to access your *Political Science CourseMate* resources.

- **CourseMate**
  At the beginning and end of every chapter, you will see the CourseMate icon as a reminder to students to use its wealth of online resources to check their understanding of the chapter and further explore its key concepts.

  This media-rich Web site offers a variety of online resources designed to enhance the student learning experience. These resources include video activities, audio summaries, critical-thinking exercises, simulations, animated learning modules, interactive time lines, primary source quizzes, flashcards, learning objectives, glossaries, and crossword puzzles. Chapter resources are correlated to key chapter learning concepts, and users can browse or search for content in a variety of ways.

  NewsNow is a new asset available in CourseMate. It is a combination of weekly new stories from the Associated Press and videos and images that bring current events to life for the student. For instructors, NewsNow includes an additional set of multimedia-rich PowerPoint slides posted each week to the password-protected area of the text's instructor companion Web site. Instructors may use these slides to take a class poll or trigger a lively debate about the events that are shaping the world right now.

  The **Engagement Tracker** assesses student preparation and engagement. Use the tracking tools to see progress for the class as a whole or for individual students. Identify students at risk early in the course. Uncover which concepts are most difficult for your class. Monitor time on task. Keep your students engaged.

  Coursemate also features an **interactive eBook** that has highlighting and search capabilities, along with links to simulations, animated PowerPoints that illustrate concepts, interactive time lines, video activities, primary source quizzes, and flashcards.

- **PowerLecture DVD with JoinIn™ and ExamView®**
  ISBN-10: 1-111-34322-5 | ISBN-13: 978-1-111-34322-4
  This DVD includes two sets of PowerPoint slides—a book-specific and a media-enhanced set; a test bank in both Microsoft Word and ExamView formats; an *Instructor's Manual;* JoinIn "clicker" questions; and a *Resource Integration Guide.*

  - **Interactive book-specific PowerPoint® lectures** make it easy for you to assemble, edit, publish, and present book-specific lectures for your course. You will have access to outlines specific to each chapter of the text, as well as photos, figures, and tables found in the text.
  - **Media-enhanced PowerPoint slides** can be used on their own or easily integrated with the book-specific PowerPoint outlines. Look for audio and video clips depicting both historic and current-day events; animated learning modules illustrating key concepts; tables, statistical charts, and graphs; and photos from the book. Outside sources also are provided at the appropriate places in the chapter.
  - **Test bank in Microsoft® Word and ExamView® computerized testing** offers a large array of well-crafted multiple-choice and essay questions, along with their answers and page references.
  - ***Instructor's Manual*** includes learning objectives, chapter outlines, discussion questions, suggestions for stimulating class activities and projects, tips on integrating media into your class (including step-by-step instructions on how to create your own podcasts), suggested readings and Web

resources, and a section specially designed to help teaching assistants and adjunct instructors.

- **JoinIn™ "clicker" questions** test and track student comprehension of key concepts.
- **Resource Integration Guide** outlines the rich collection of resources available to instructors and students within the chapter-by-chapter framework of the book, suggesting how and when each supplement can be used to optimize learning.

■ **American Government CourseReader**
Printed Text + CourseReader Printed Access Card: ISBN-10: 1-111-65364-X | ISBN-13: 978-1-111-65364-4
This product allows instructors to create a customized reader using a database of hundreds of documents, readings, and videos. Instructors can search by various criteria or browse the collection in order to preview and then select a customized collection to assign to their students. The sources are edited to an appropriate length and include pedagogical support—a headnote describing the document and critical-thinking and multiple-choice questions to verify that the student has read and understood the selection. Students can take notes, highlight, and print content. The CourseReader allows the instructor to select exactly what students will be assigned with an easy-to-use interface and also provides an easily used assessment tool. The sources can be delivered online or in print format.

■ **Instructor Companion Web Site**
The instructor Companion Web site includes the Instructor's Manual; text-specific PowerPoints containing lecture outlines, photos, and figures; and NewsNow PowerPoints.

■ **WebTutor™ on WebCT or Blackboard**
Printed Text + WebCT Printed Access Card: ISBN-10: 1-111-34307-1 | ISBN-13: 978-1-111-34307-1
Printed Text + Blackboard Printed Access Card: ISBN-10: 1-111-34307-1 | ISBN-13: 978-1-111-34307-1
Rich with content for your American government course, this Web-based teaching and learning tool includes course management, study/mastery, and communication tools. Use WebTutor to provide virtual office hours, post your syllabus, and track student progress with WebTutor's quizzing material.

■ **CourseCare**
Available exclusively to Cengage Learning, CourseCare is a revolutionary program designed to provide you and your students an unparalleled user experience with your Cengage Learning digital solution.

CourseCare connects you with a team of training, service, and support experts to help you implement your Cengage Learning Digital Solution. This means real people dedicated to you, your students, and your course from the first day of class through final exams.

■ **Political Theatre 2.0**
ISBN-10: 0-495-79360-4 | ISBN-13: 978-0-495-79360-1
Bring politics home to students with Political Theatre 2.0, which is up-to-date through the 2008 election season. This is the second edition of this three-DVD series and includes real video clips that show American political thought throughout the public sector. Clips include both classic and contemporary political advertisements, speeches, interviews, and more.

■ **JoinIn™ on Turning Point® for Political Theatre**
ISBN-10: 0-495-09550-8 | ISBN-13: 978-0-495-09550-7
For even more interaction, combine Political Theatre with the innovative teaching tool of a classroom response system through JoinIn. Poll your students with questions created for you, or create your own questions.

■ **Wadsworth News Videos for American Government 2012 DVD**
ISBN-10: 1-111-34614-3 | ISBN-13: 978-1-111-34614-0
This collection of three- to six-minute video clips on relevant political issues serves as a great lecture or discussion launcher.

■ **Great Speeches Collection**
Throughout the ages, great orators have stepped up to the podium and used their communication skills to persuade, inform, and inspire their audiences. Studying these speeches can provide tremendous insight into historical, political, and cultural events. The Great Speeches Collection includes the full text of over sixty memorable orations for you to incorporate into your course. Speeches can be collated in a printed reader to supplement your existing course materials or bound into a core textbook.

■ **ABC Video: Speeches by President Barack Obama**
ISBN-10: 1-439-08247-2 | ISBN-13: 9781439082478
This DVD of nine famous speeches by President Barack Obama, from 2004 through his inauguration, includes his speech at the 2004 Democratic National Convention; his 2008 speech on race, "A More Perfect Union"; and his 2009 inaugural address. Speeches are divided into short video segments for easy, time-efficient viewing. This instructor supplement also features critical-thinking questions and answers for each speech, designed to spark classroom discussion.

- **Election 2010: An American Government Supplement**
  Text + Election 2010 supplement: ISBN-10: 1-111-87232-5 | ISBN-13: 978-1-111-87232-8
  Written by John Clark and Brian Schaffner, this booklet addresses the 2010 congressional and gubernatorial races, with both real-time analysis and references.
- **Latino-American Politics Supplement**
  Text + Latino-American Politics supplement: ISBN-10: 1-111-87233-3 | ISBN-13: 978-1-111-87233-5
  This thirty-two-page supplement uses real examples to detail politics related to Latino Americans.
- **Instructor's Guide to YouTube for Political Science**
  Instructors have access to the Instructor's Guide to YouTube, which shows American government instructors where they can look on the Internet to find videos that can be used as learning tools in class. Organized by fifteen topics, the guide follows the sequence of an American government course and includes a Preface with tips on how to use Internet videos in class.

Acknowledgments

A number of political scientists have reviewed GOVT, and we are indebted to them for their thoughtful suggestions on how to create a text that best suits the needs of today's students and faculty.

Anita Anderson
University of Alabama

Kimberly Arvanigian
California State University, Fresno

Yan Bai
Grand Rapids Community College

Janet Barton
Mineral Area College

Catherine Bottrell
Tarrant County College

J. St. Lawrence Brown
Spokane Community College

Michael Ceriello
Clark College

Andrew Civettini
Knox College

Frank DeCaria
West Virginia Northern Community College

Robert De Luna
St. Philip's College

Henry Esparza
University of Texas at San Antonio and Northeast Lakeview College

Shawn Fonville
Western Texas College

Barry D. Friedman
North Georgia College & State University

Michael Gattis
Gulf Coast Community College

Arie Halachmi
Tennessee State University

Jack Hames
Butte College

Jeff Harmon
University of Texas at San Antonio

David M. Head
John Tyler Community College

Steve Hoggard
Chowan University

Kristen Huyck
Mt. San Jacinto Community College, Mira Costa Community College and Anthem Online College

Jose Luis Irizarry
St. Francis College

Jean Gabriel Jolivet
Southwestern College

Michael Kanner
University of Colorado

David R. Katz III
Mohawk Valley Community College

Christine Kelleher
University of Michigan

Sean Kelly
Cal State University Channel Islands

John Kerr
University of Arkansas

Jeffrey Kraus
Wagner College

Kevin Lasher
Francis Marion University

William Lester
Jacksonville State University

William D. Madlock
University of Memphis

Khalil Marrar
DePaul University and The University of Chicago

Matthew McNiece
Howard Payne University

Gay Michele
El Centro College

Amy Miller
Western Kentucky University

Eric Miller
Blinn College–Bryan

Kathleen Murnan
Ozarks Technical Community College

Leah A. Murray
Weber State University

Jalal Nejad
Northwest Vista College

Joseph L. Overton
Kapiolani Community College

James Peterson
Valdosta State University

Daniel Ponder
Drury University

Brett Ramsey
Austin Peay State University

Rob Robinson
University of Alabama–Birmingham

Cy Rosenblatt
University of Mississippi

Robert Sahr
Oregon State University

John Shively
Longview Community College

Susan Siemens
Ozarks Technical Community College

Frank Signorile
Campbell University

Chris Sixta-Rinehart
Francis Marion University

Robert Sullivan
Dallas Baptist University

Gerald Watkins
West Kentucky Community and Technical College

Stephen Wiener
UC Santa Barbara

Donald C. Williams
Western New England College

Bruce M. Wilson
University of Central Florida

Robert S. Wood
University of North Dakota

Mary Young
Southwestern Michigan College

Maryann Zihala
Ozarks Technical Community College

Our styles of teaching and mentoring students were shaped in important ways by our graduate faculty at The Ohio State University. We especially thank Lawrence Baum, Herbert Asher, Elliot Slotnick, and Randall Ripley for lessons well taught. Our colleagues Will McLauchlan (Purdue University) and Barry Pyle (Eastern Michigan University) continue, by their actions, to remind us that the learning environment extends well beyond the classroom. The students we have had the privilege of working with at many fine universities have also taught us a great deal. Of course, we owe an immeasurable debt to our families, whose divergent views on political issues reflect an America at odds.

We thank Jonathan Hulbert, president of Cengage Learning Arts and Sciences, for all of his encouragement and support throughout our work on this project. We were also fortunate to have the editorial advice of Carolyn Merrill, executive editor. We are grateful for the assistance of Rebecca Green, our developmental editor, who supervised all aspects of the text and carefully read the page proofs. We thank Laura Ross, assistant editor, for her coordination of the supplements and related items; Laura Hildebrand and Kate MacLean for their work on the CourseMate; and Nina Wasserman for her editorial assistance. We thank Gregory Scott for his tremendous help in researching the project and for his copyediting and proofreading assistance. We also thank Roxie Lee for her project management and other assistance that ensured a timely and accurate text. The copyediting services of Mary Berry and the proofreading by Judy Kiviat and Lorretta Palagi will not go unnoticed. We are also grateful to Sue Jasin of K&M Consulting.

We are especially indebted to the staff at Parkwood Composition. Their ability to generate the pages for this text quickly and accurately made it possible for us to meet our ambitious schedule. Ann Borman and Ann Sheroff, our cheerful content project managers at Cengage Learning, made sure that all the pieces came together accurately, attractively, and on time. We appreciate the enthusiasm of Lydia LeStar, Heather Baxley, and Josh Hendrick, our hardworking marketing and communications managers and marketing coordinator. We thank Ann Hoffman for her accurate photo research. We would also like to acknowledge Linda Helcher, art director, for her part in producing the most attractive and user-friendly American government text on the market today.

If you or your students have ideas or suggestions, we would like to hear from you. You can e-mail our marketing manager, Lydia, at lydia.lestar@cengage.com, or send us information through Wadsworth, a part of Cengage Learning. Our Web site is **www.cengage.com/political science.**

E.I.S.
B.M.H.
L.N.G.
T.C.

GOVT

America in the Twenty-First Century

1

LEARNING OBJECTIVES

LO1 Explain what is meant by the terms *politics* and *government*.

LO2 Identify the various types of government systems.

LO3 Summarize some of the basic principles of American democracy and the basic American political values.

LO4 Describe how the various topics discussed in this text relate to the "big picture" of American politics and government.

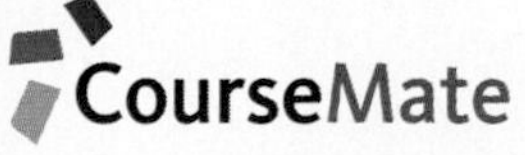

AMERICA AT ODDS

Has Our Government Grown Too Large?

For much of America's history, there was little discussion about whether our government had grown too large. The government, after all, wasn't that big. Since the Great Depression of the 1930s, however, the government has grown by leaps and bounds. Still, only fifteen years ago, President Bill Clinton (1993–2001) pronounced that the "era of big government is over." In fact, the share of U.S. economic activity accounted for by government fell from 1995 through 2000. Today, in contrast, we have seen one of the biggest increases in size of the federal government ever. The value of all federal, state, and local government spending now exceeds 40 percent of the nation's total annual income.

Americans are at odds over the proper size of government. The so-called Tea Party protesters have one basic complaint, expressed in the slogan "Born free, taxed to death." Their opponents, however, believe that the government must be large to address the nation's problems.

Government Must Put On the Golden Straitjacket

Those who oppose the growth of government contend that too much of a good thing can become bad. Every government program to help a specific group starts out with good intentions and certainly does help many people in need of, for example, medical care or better education. The problem is that once government programs are in place, they expand. The result is an "assisted society." Opponents of big government believe that too many people spend too much time seeking government assistance rather than taking care of their problems by themselves or with the help of family and friends.

Conservative economists contend that the growth of government must soon lead to higher taxes. So far, the increases in federal government spending have meant larger budget deficits rather than increased taxes. The government has simply borrowed what it needs. These conservative economists, however, argue that this new government borrowing means that there are fewer funds available for private individuals and businesses to borrow. Moreover, they say, the higher taxes that will eventually be needed will reduce people's incentives to work and to invest, now and in the future. Ultimately, that means less economic growth.

Small May Be Beautiful, but Big Government Is Necessary

Liberal economists believe that these conservative arguments are wrong and that in a recession, government deficits put people back to work. More generally, supporters of an active government say that we have big government for a reason—we are a big country with big problems. Just think of some of them:

- Tens of millions of Americans live below the poverty line.
- Many Americans, especially poor Americans, receive inadequate medical care.
- Unsupervised investment banks created the biggest financial meltdown since the Great Depression.
- Our nation's youth are performing poorly on standardized tests.

How are we to solve these problems and thousands of others? Those who defend government believe that we cannot address these issues by reducing the size of government. If we leave everything to an unregulated, uncontrolled free market, we will have more poor people, more sick people, and more unscrupulous business activities.

Europeans have long understood this. European governments not only have greater control of their economies but also devote more resources to social solidarity. Consequently, they have less income inequality and more fairness. That is where America should be heading.

WHERE DO YOU STAND?

1. **Is big government necessary in times of crisis, such as the terrorist attacks of 9/11, the Great Recession that began in December 2007, and the BP oil catastrophe in the Gulf of Mexico? Explain your answer.**
2. **Would you favor a law that reduced the budget of every federal, state, and local agency by, say, 15 percent? What would be the consequences? Who would gain?**

EXPLORE THIS ISSUE ONLINE

- **The issue of big government divides conservatives and liberals. One of the most prominent conservative Web sites is www.nationalreview.com, sponsored by the magazine *National Review*. For a top liberal site, consider the Daily Kos at www.dailykos.com.**

Introduction

Regardless of how Americans feel about government, one thing is certain: they can't live without it. James Madison (1751–1836) once said, "If men were angels, no government would be necessary." Today, his statement still holds true. People are not perfect. People need an organized form of government and a set of rules by which to live.

Note, though, that even if people were perfect, they would still need to establish rules to guide their behavior. They would somehow have to agree on how to divide up a society's resources, such as its land, among themselves and how to balance individual needs and wants against those of society generally. These perfect people would also have to decide *how* to make these decisions. They would need to create a process for making rules and a form of government to enforce those rules. It is thus not difficult to understand why government is one of humanity's oldest and most universal **institutions.** No society has existed without some form of government. The need for authority and organization will never disappear.

> **"THE ULTIMATE RULERS** of our democracy are . . . the voters of this country."
>
> ~ FRANKLIN D. ROOSEVELT ~
> THIRTY-SECOND PRESIDENT OF THE UNITED STATES
> 1933–1945

As you will read in this chapter, a number of different systems of government exist in the world today. In the United States, we have a democracy in which decisions about pressing issues ultimately are made by the people's representatives in government. Because people rarely have identical thoughts and feelings about issues, it is not surprising that in any democracy citizens are often at odds over many political and social issues, including the very size of government as discussed in the chapter-opening feature. Throughout this book, you will read about contemporary issues that have brought various groups of Americans into conflict with one another.

Differences in opinion are part and parcel of a democratic government. Ultimately, these differences are resolved, one way or another, through the American political process and our government institutions.

LO1 *What Are Politics and Government?*

Politics means many things to many people. To some, politics is an expensive and extravagant game played in Washington, D.C., in state capitols, and in city halls, particularly during election time. To others, politics involves all of the tactics and maneuvers carried out by the president and Congress. Most formal definitions of politics, however, begin with the assumption that **social conflict**—disagreements among people in a society over what the society's priorities should be—is inevitable. Conflicts will naturally arise over how the society should use its scarce resources and who should receive various benefits, such as wealth, status, health care, and higher education. Resolving such conflicts is the essence of **politics.** Political scientist Harold Lasswell perhaps said it best

Demonstrators hold signs at a Tea Party rally at Freedom Plaza on tax day in Washington on April 15, 2010.

ROGER L. WOLLENBERG/UPI/LANDOV

institution An ongoing organization that performs certain functions for society.

social conflict Disagreements among people in a society over what the society's priorities should be when distributing scarce resources.

politics The process of resolving conflicts over how society should use its scarce resources and who should receive various benefits, such as public health care and public higher education. According to Harold Lasswell, politics is the process of determining "who gets what, when, and how" in a society.

government The individuals and institutions that make society's rules and that also possess the power and authority to enforce those rules.

power The ability to influence the behavior of others, usually through the use of force, persuasion, or rewards.

authority The ability to legitimately exercise power, such as the power to make and enforce laws.

public services Essential services that individuals cannot provide for themselves, such as building and maintaining roads, providing welfare programs, operating public schools, and preserving national parks.

> "OUR POLITICAL INSTITUTIONS . . . ARE DESIGNED TO CLANG AGAINST EACH OTHER. THE NOISE IS democracy at work."
>
> ~ MICHAEL NOVAK ~
> JOURNALIST, EDUCATOR; AMERICAN ENTERPRISE INSTITUTE
> B. 1933

when he defined politics as the process of determining "who gets what, when, and how" in a society.[1]

There are also many different notions about the meaning of government. From the perspective of political science, though, **government** can best be defined as the individuals and institutions that make society's rules and that also possess the *power* and *authority* to enforce those rules. Although this definition of government sounds remote and abstract, what the government does is very real indeed. As one scholar put it, "Make no mistake. What Congress does directly and powerfully affects our daily lives."[2] The same can be said for decisions made by state legislators and local government officials, as well as for decisions rendered by the courts—the judicial branch of government.

Of course, a key question remains: How do specific individuals obtain the power and authority to govern? As you will read shortly, the answer to this question varies from one type of political system to another.

To understand what government is, you need to understand what it actually does for people and society. Generally, in any country government serves at least three essential purposes: (1) it resolves conflicts, (2) it provides public services, and (3) it defends the nation and its culture against attacks by other nations.

Resolving Conflicts

Even though people have lived together in groups since the beginning of time, none of these groups has been free of social conflict. As mentioned, disputes over how to distribute a society's resources inevitably arise because valued resources, such as property, are limited, while people's wants are unlimited. To resolve such disputes, people need ways to determine who wins and who loses, and how to get the losers to accept those decisions. Who has the legitimate power—the authority—to make such decisions? This is where government steps in.

Governments decide how conflicts will be resolved so that public order can be maintained. Governments have **power**—the ability to influence the behavior of others. Power is getting someone to do something that he or she would not otherwise do. Power may involve the use of force (often called coercion), persuasion, or rewards. Governments typically also have **authority,** which they can exercise only if their power is legitimate. As used here, the term *authority* means power that is collectively recognized and accepted by society as legally and morally correct. Power and authority are central to a government's ability to resolve conflicts by making and enforcing laws, placing limits on what people can do, and developing court systems to make final decisions.

For example, the judicial branch of government—specifically, the United States Supreme Court—resolved the highly controversial question of whether the Second Amendment to the Constitution grants individuals the right to bear arms. In 2008 and 2010, the Court affirmed that such a right does exist. Because of the Court's stature and authority as a government body, there was little resistance to its decision, even from gun control advocates.

Providing Public Services

Another important purpose of government is to provide **public services**—essential services that many individuals cannot provide for themselves. Governments undertake projects that individuals usually would not or could not carry out on their own, such as building and maintaining roads, providing welfare programs, operating public schools, and preserving national parks. Governments also provide such services as law enforcement, fire protection, and public health and safety programs. As Abraham Lincoln once stated:

> The legitimate object of government is to do for a community of people, whatever they need to have done, but cannot do, *at all*, or cannot, *so well* do, for themselves—in their separate, individual capacities. In all that the people can individually do as well for themselves, government ought not to interfere.[3]

Some public services are provided equally to all citizens of the United States. For example, government services such as national defense and domestic law enforcement allow all citizens, at least in theory, to feel that their lives and property are safe. Laws governing clean air and safe drinking water benefit all Americans. Other services are provided only to citizens who are in need at a particular time, even though they are paid for by all citizens through taxes. Examples of such services include health and welfare benefits, as well as public housing. Laws such as the Americans with Disabilities Act explicitly protect the rights of people with disabilities, although all Americans pay for such protections whether they have disabilities or not.

"In all that the people can individually do as well for themselves, **GOVERNMENT OUGHT NOT TO INTERFERE.**"

~ ABRAHAM LINCOLN ~
SIXTEENTH PRESIDENT OF THE UNITED STATES
1861–1865

One of the most crucial public services that the government is expected to provide is protection from hardship caused by economic recessions or depressions. In recent years, this governmental objective has become more important than almost any other, due to the severity of the recession that began in December 2007. We introduce some of the steps the federal government has taken to combat the recession in this chapter's *Our Government Faces a Troubled Economy* feature on the following page. Additional features throughout the book will supply greater detail.

Defending the Nation and Its Culture

Historically, matters of national security and defense have been given high priority by governments and have demanded considerable time, effort, and expense. The U.S. government provides for the common defense and national security with its Army, Navy, Marines, Air Force, and Coast Guard. The departments of State, Defense, and Homeland Security, plus the Central Intelligence Agency, National Security Agency, and other agencies, also contribute to this defense network.

As part of an ongoing policy of national security, many departments and agencies in the federal government are constantly dealing with other nations. The Constitution gives our national government exclusive power over relations with foreign nations. No individual state can negotiate a treaty with a foreign nation.

Of course, in defending the nation against attacks by other nations, a government helps to preserve the nation's culture, as well as its integrity as an independent unit. Failure to defend successfully against foreign attacks may have significant consequences for a nation's culture. For example, consider what happened in Tibet in the 1950s. When that country was taken over by the People's Republic of China, the conquering Chinese set out on a systematic program, the effective result of which was to destroy Tibet's culture.

Since the terrorist attacks on the World Trade Center and the Pentagon in 2001, defending the homeland against future terrorist attacks has become a priority of our government.

Why Politics Matters to You

As the last few pages have shown, the government performs a wide range of functions that are of extreme importance. From the time we are born until the day we die, we constantly interact with various levels of government. Most (although not all) students attend government-run schools. All of us travel on government-owned streets and highways. Many of us serve in the military—a completely government-controlled environment. A few of us get into trouble and meet up with the government's law enforcement system.

All of us pay substantial sums in taxes. Every citizen can expect the government to help with medical and living expenses after reaching the age of sixty-five. As the new health-care reform system kicks in, the government will eventually ensure that the medical needs of all citizens are met, regardless of age or income.

In a representative democracy such as ours, it is politics that controls what the government decides to do. As discussed in this chapter's opening feature, *America at Odds,* the question is, how big should the government be? What combination of taxes and services is best? Should industries such as agriculture and alternative energy be subsidized? When should our leaders use military force against foreign nations or rebellions in foreign countries? How the nation answers these and many other questions will have a major impact on your life—and participation in politics is the only way you can influence what happens.

LO2 *Different Systems of Government*

Through the centuries, the functions of government just discussed have been performed by many different types of government structures. A government's structure is influenced by a number of factors,

Our Government Faces a Troubled Economy

Making and Fixing an Economic Mess

RAMI HALIM/ISTOCKPHOTO

In recent years, we have witnessed what has been called the Great Recession—the worst economic downturn since the Great Depression of the 1930s. One of the goals of government, as stated in the Preamble to the U.S. Constitution, is "to promote the general Welfare." Maintaining economic prosperity is about as close as you can get to promoting the general welfare.

The Great Depression Was Really Bad

The Great Depression began in 1929. By 1933, the rate of unemployment hit 25 percent, and economic output had dropped by over a third. Republican Herbert Hoover, president until 1933, was voted out of office because the public considered his response to the crisis to be inadequate. The new Democratic president—Franklin D. Roosevelt—undertook a huge number of initiatives, known as the New Deal. Some of these measures helped relieve the suffering of the unemployed and the poor, but they did not pull us out of the Great Depression. That happened later.

Fast-Forward to the Great Recession

From 2002 to 2007, the United States experienced a boom. Credit was easy—Americans with low incomes were able to buy houses with borrowed money at low initial interest rates. But what goes up can come down. The first danger signs appeared in 2006, when housing prices, which had been rising fast, began to fall. By 2007, many people were unable to make payments on their mortgages. Investments based on mortgages lost value. By 2008, major investment firms were failing. On September 15, 2008, Lehman Brothers, a major investment bank, failed. Panic ensued. Banks refused to lend to each other, for fear that they would not get their money back. As the financial markets froze up, our government decided that it had to step in.

Our Modern Government Responds to an Economic Crisis

The government's reaction was far faster than in the 1930s and much more sweeping. Hank Paulson, Treasury secretary under President George W. Bush, obtained $700 billion from Congress for the Troubled Asset Relief Program (TARP), which made large loans to troubled banks—the famous "bank bailout." After Barack Obama became president in 2009, he won from Congress a stimulus package made up of spending increases and tax cuts initially valued at $787 billion.

Ben Bernanke, the head of our central bank—the Federal Reserve, or Fed—also did his part. Bernanke knew that one of the chief causes of the Great Depression was that the Fed let the nation's money supply collapse. This shortage of money choked the life out of the economy. Bernanke once said that he would do anything to prevent another depression, even if it meant shoveling money out of helicopters. This earned him the nickname "Helicopter Ben." After September 2008, Helicopter Ben was true to his word. The Fed loaned out about $1.5 trillion in freshly created money through a dozen new programs.

Were These Responses the Right Way to Go?

The responses were huge, but were they the correct policy? In time, the Great Recession would end. What about the legacy of the government's actions? In 2009, the difference between the federal government's revenues and income—the deficit—jumped by a trillion dollars in one year. By mid-2010, conservative Democrats in Congress, frightened by the deficit, were joining with Republicans to block new spending. Briefly, they even refused to extend unemployment benefits, despite job seekers outnumbering job postings by five to one. One concern was that all the new money might eventually lead to inflation (a sustained rise in prices). There were few signs of such a problem in 2010, though.

You Be the Judge **When economic times are tough, how do you react? Does the federal government react differently? Why or why not?**

such as a country's history, customs, values, geography, resources, and human experiences and needs. No two nations have exactly the same form of government. Over time, however, political analysts have developed ways to classify different systems of government. One of the most meaningful ways is according to *who* governs. Who has the power to make the rules and laws that all must obey?

Rule by One: Autocracy

In an **autocracy,** the power and authority of the government are in the hands of a single person. At one time, autocracy was a common form of government, and it still exists in some parts of the world. Autocrats usually obtain their power either by inheriting it or by force.

MONARCHY One form of autocracy, known as a **monarchy,** is government by a king, queen, emperor, empress, tsar, or tsarina. In a monarchy, the monarch, who usually acquires power through inheritance, is the highest authority in the government.

Historically, many monarchies were *absolute monarchies,* in which the ruler held complete and unlimited power. Until the eighteenth century, the theory of divine right was widely accepted in Europe. The **divine right theory,** variations of which had existed since ancient times, held that God gave those of royal birth the unlimited right to govern other men and women. In other words, those of royal birth had a "divine right" to rule, and only God could judge them. Thus, all citizens were bound to obey their monarchs, no matter how unfair or unjust they seemed to be. Challenging this power was regarded not only as treason against the government but also as a sin against God.

Most modern monarchies, however, are *constitutional monarchies,* in which the monarch shares governmental power with elected lawmakers. Over time, the monarch's power has come to be limited, or checked, by other government leaders and perhaps by a constitution or a bill of rights. Most constitutional monarchs today serve merely as ceremonial leaders of their nations, as in Spain, Sweden, and the United Kingdom (Britain).

DICTATORSHIP Another form of autocracy is a **dictatorship,** in which a single leader rules, although not typically through inheritance. Dictators gain supreme power by using force, often by overthrowing another dictator or leader. Dictators hold absolute power and are not accountable to anyone else.

A dictatorship can also be *totalitarian,* which means that a leader (or group of leaders) seeks to control almost all aspects of social and economic life. The needs of the nation come before the needs of individuals, and all citizens must work for the common goals established by the government. Examples of this form of government include Adolf Hitler's Nazi regime in Germany from 1933 to 1945, Benito Mussolini's rule in Italy from 1923 to 1943, and Joseph Stalin's dictatorship in the Soviet Union from 1929 to 1953. More contemporary examples of totalitarian dictators include Fidel Castro in Cuba, Kim Jong Il in North Korea, and, until his government was dismantled in 2003, Saddam Hussein in Iraq.

KAL, THE ECONOMIST, LONDON, ENGLAND/CARTOON ARTS INTERNATIONAL/THE NEW YORK TIMES SYNDICATE.

autocracy A form of government in which the power and authority of the government are in the hands of a single person.

monarchy A form of autocracy in which a king, queen, emperor, empress, tsar, or tsarina is the highest authority in the government; monarchs usually obtain their power through inheritance.

divine right theory The theory that a monarch's right to rule was derived directly from God rather than from the consent of the people.

dictatorship A form of government in which absolute power is exercised by a single person who usually has obtained his or her power by the use of force.

democracy A system of government in which the people have ultimate political authority. The word is derived from the Greek *demos* ("the people") and *kratia* ("rule").

direct democracy A system of government in which political decisions are made by the people themselves rather than by elected representatives. This form of government was practiced in some parts of ancient Greece.

representative democracy A form of democracy in which the will of the majority is expressed through smaller groups of individuals elected by the people to act as their representatives.

republic Essentially, a representative democracy in which there is no king or queen and the people are sovereign.

Rule by the Many: Democracy

The most familiar form of government to Americans is **democracy,** in which the supreme political authority rests with the people. The word *democracy* comes from the Greek *demos,* meaning "the people," and *kratia,* meaning "rule." The main idea of democracy is that government exists only by the consent of the people and reflects the will of the majority.

THE ATHENIAN MODEL OF DIRECT DEMOCRACY

Democracy as a form of government began long ago. In its earliest form, democracy was simpler than the system we know today. What we now call **direct democracy** exists when the people participate directly in government decision making. In its purest form, direct democracy was practiced in Athens and other ancient Greek city-states about 2,500 years ago. Every Athenian citizen participated in the governing assembly and voted on all major issues. Although some consider the Athenian form of direct democracy ideal because it demanded a high degree of citizen participation, others point out that most residents in the Athenian city-state (women, foreigners, and slaves) were not deemed to be citizens and thus were not allowed to participate in government.

Clearly, direct democracy is possible only in small communities in which citizens can meet in a chosen place and decide key issues and policies. Nowhere in the world does pure direct democracy exist today. Some New England towns, though, and a few of the smaller political subunits, or cantons, of Switzerland still use a modified form of direct democracy.

REPRESENTATIVE DEMOCRACY Although the founders of the United States were aware of the Athenian model and agreed that government should be based on the consent of the governed, they believed that direct democracy would deteriorate into mob rule. They thought that large groups of people meeting together would ignore the rights and opinions of people in the minority and would make decisions without careful thought. They believed that representative assemblies were superior because they would enable public decisions to be made in a calmer and more deliberate manner.

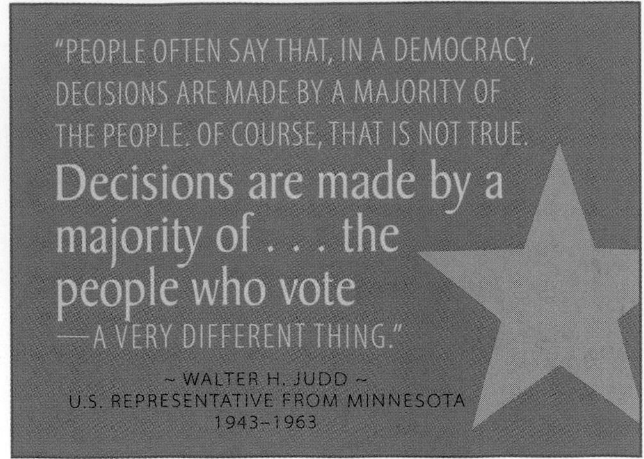

"PEOPLE OFTEN SAY THAT, IN A DEMOCRACY, DECISIONS ARE MADE BY A MAJORITY OF THE PEOPLE. OF COURSE, THAT IS NOT TRUE.
Decisions are made by a majority of . . . the people who vote
—A VERY DIFFERENT THING."
~ WALTER H. JUDD ~
U.S. REPRESENTATIVE FROM MINNESOTA
1943–1963

In a **representative democracy,** the will of the majority is expressed through smaller groups of individuals elected by the people to act as their representatives. These representatives are responsible to the people for their conduct and can be voted out of office. Our founders preferred to use the term **republic,** which means essentially a representative democracy—with one qualification. A republic, by definition, has no king or queen. Rather, the people are sovereign. In contrast, a representative democracy may be headed by a monarch. For example, as Britain evolved into a representative democracy, it retained its monarch as the head of state (but with no real power).

In the modern world, there are basically two forms of representative democracy: presidential and parliamentary. In a *presidential democracy,* the lawmaking and law-enforcing branches of government are separate but equal. For example, in the United States, Congress is charged with the power to make laws, and the president is charged with the power to carry them out. In a *parliamentary democracy,* the lawmaking and law-enforcing branches of government overlap. In Britain, for example, the prime minister and the cabinet are members of the legislature, called Parliament, and are responsible to that body. Parliament thus both enacts the laws and carries them out.

Other Forms of Government

Autocracy and democracy are but two of many forms of government. Traditionally, other types of government have included governments that are ruled "by the few." For example, an aristocracy (from the Greek word *aristos,* or "best") is a government in which a small

AP PHOTO/TOBY TALBOT

These voters are listening to a debate at a town hall meeting in Plainfield, Vermont. Some New England towns use such meetings to engage in a form of direct democracy. Why doesn't the United States as a nation have direct democracy?

privileged class rules. A *plutocracy* is a government in which the wealthy (*ploutos* in Greek means "wealth") exercise ruling power. A *meritocracy* is a government in which the rulers have earned, or merited, the right to govern because of their special skills or talents.

A difficult form of government for Americans to understand is *theocracy*—a term derived from the Greek words meaning "rule by the deity" or "rule by God." In a theocracy, there is no separation of church and state. Rather, the government rules according to religious precepts. In most Muslim countries, government and the Islamic religion are intertwined to a degree that is quite startling to both Europeans and Americans. In Iran, for example, the Holy Koran (or Qur'an), not the national constitution, serves as the basis for the law. The Koran consists of sacred writings that Muslims believe were revealed to the prophet Muhammad by God. In Iran, the Council of Guardians, an unelected group of religious leaders, ensures that laws and lawmakers conform to their interpretation of the teachings of Islam.

CORBIS YELLOW/RF

LO3 *American Democracy*

> This country, with all its institutions, belongs to the people who inhabit it. Whenever they shall grow weary of the existing government, they can exercise their constitutional right to amend it, or their revolutionary right to dismember or overthrow it.[4]

With these words, Abraham Lincoln underscored the most fundamental concept of American government: that the people, not the government, are ultimately in control.

The British Legacy

In writing the U.S. Constitution, the framers incorporated two basic principles of government that had evolved in England: *limited government* and *representative government.* In a sense, then, the beginnings of our form of government are linked to events that occurred centuries earlier in England. They are also linked to the writings of European philosophers, particularly the English political philosopher John Locke. From these writings, the founders of our nation derived ideas to justify their rebellion against Britain and the establishment of a "government by the people."

LIMITED GOVERNMENT At one time, the English monarch claimed to have virtually unrestricted powers. This changed in 1215, when King John was forced by his nobles to accept the Magna Carta, or Great Charter. This monumental document provided for a trial by a jury of one's peers (equals). It prohibited the taking of a free man's life, liberty, or property except through due process of law. The Magna Carta also forced the king to obtain the nobles' approval of any taxes he imposed on them. Government thus became a contract between the king and his subjects.

The importance of the Magna Carta to England cannot be overemphasized, because it clearly established the principle of **limited government**—a

limited government
A form of government based on the principle that the powers of government should be clearly limited either through a written document or through wide public understanding; characterized by institutional checks to ensure that government serves public rather than private interests.

parliament The name of the national legislative body in countries governed by a parliamentary system, such as Britain and Canada.

bicameral legislature A legislature made up of two chambers, or parts. The United States has a bicameral legislature, composed of the House of Representatives and the Senate.

social contract A voluntary agreement among individuals to create a government and to give that government adequate power to secure the mutual protection and welfare of all individuals.

natural rights Rights that are not bestowed by governments but are inherent within every man, woman, and child by virtue of the fact that he or she is a human being.

government on which strict limits are placed, usually by a constitution. Hence, the Magna Carta signaled the end of the monarch's absolute power. Although many of the rights provided under the original Magna Carta applied only to the nobility, the document formed the basis of the future constitutional government for England and eventually the United States.

The principle of limited government was expanded four hundred years later, in 1628, when King Charles I signed the Petition of Rights. Among other things, this petition prohibited the monarch from imprisoning political critics without a jury trial. Perhaps more important, the petition declared that even the king or queen had to obey the law of the land.

In 1689, the English Parliament (described shortly) passed the English Bill of Rights, which further extended the concept of limited government. This document included several important ideas:

- The king or queen could not interfere with parliamentary elections.
- The king or queen had to have Parliament's approval to levy (collect) taxes or to maintain an army.
- The king or queen had to rule with the consent of the people's representatives in Parliament.
- The people could not be subjected to cruel or unusual punishment or to excessive fines.

The English colonists in North America were also English citizens, and thus the English Bill of Rights of 1689 applied to them as well. As a result, virtually all of the major concepts in the English Bill of Rights became part of the American system of government.

REPRESENTATIVE GOVERNMENT In a representative government, the people, by whatever means, elect individuals to make governmental decisions for all of the citizens. Usually, these representatives of the people are elected to their offices for specific periods of time. This group of representatives is often referred to as a **parliament,** which is frequently a **bicameral** (two-house) **legislature.** The English Parliament consists of the House of Lords (upper chamber) and the House of Commons (lower chamber). The English form of government provided a model for Americans to follow. Many of the American colonies had bicameral legislatures—as did, eventually, the U.S. Congress that was established by the Constitution.

POLITICAL PHILOSOPHY—SOCIAL CONTRACTS AND NATURAL RIGHTS Our democracy resulted from what can be viewed as a type of **social contract** among early Americans to create and abide by a set of governing rules. Social-contract theory was developed in the seventeenth and eighteenth centuries by such philosophers as John Locke (1632–1704) and Thomas Hobbes (1588–1679) in England and Jean-Jacques Rousseau (1712–1778) in France. According to this theory, individuals voluntarily agree with one another, in a "social contract," to give up some of their freedoms to obtain the benefits of orderly government. The government is given adequate power to secure the mutual protection and welfare of all individuals. Generally, social-contract theory, in one form or another, provides the theoretical underpinnings of most modern democracies, including that of the United States.

Although Hobbes and Rousseau also posited social contracts as the bases of governments, neither theorist was as influential in America as John Locke was. Locke argued that people are born with **natural rights** to life, liberty, and property. He theorized that the purpose of government was to protect those rights. If it did not, it would lose its legitimacy and need not be obeyed. Locke's assumption that people, by nature, are rational and are endowed with certain rights is an essential component of his theory that people can govern themselves. As you will read in Chapter 2, when the American colonists rebelled against British rule, such concepts as "natural rights" and a government based on a "social contract" became important theoretical tools in justifying the rebellion.

Principles of American Democracy

We can say that American democracy is based on five fundamental principles:

- *Equality in voting.* Citizens need equal opportunities to express their preferences about policies or leaders.

- *Individual freedom.* All individuals must have the greatest amount of freedom possible without interfering with the rights of others.
- *Equal protection of the law.* The law must entitle all persons to equal protection.
- *Majority rule and minority rights.* The majority should rule, while guaranteeing the rights of minorities.
- *Voluntary consent to be governed.* The people who make up a democracy must collectively agree to be governed by the rules laid down by their representatives.

These principles frame many of the political issues that you will read about in this book. They also frequently lie at the heart of America's political conflicts. Does the principle of minority rights mean that minorities should receive preferential treatment in hiring and firing decisions to make up for past mistreatment? Does the principle of individual freedom mean that individuals can express whatever they want on the Internet, including hateful, racist comments? Such conflicts over individual rights and freedoms and over society's priorities are natural and inevitable. Resolving these conflicts is what politics is all about. The key point is that Americans are able to reach acceptable compromises because of their common political heritage.

American Political Values

Historically, as the nations of the world emerged, the boundaries of each nation normally coincided with the boundaries of a population that shared a common ethnic heritage, language, and culture. From its beginnings as a nation, however, America has been defined less by the culture shared by its diverse population than by a set of ideas, or its political culture. A **political culture** can be defined as a patterned set of ideas, values, and ways of thinking about government and politics.

The ideals and standards that constitute American political culture are embodied in the Declaration of Independence, one of the founding documents of this nation, which will be discussed further in Chapter 2 and presented in its entirety in Appendix A. The political values outlined in the Declaration of Independence include natural rights (to life, liberty, and the pursuit of happiness), equality under the law, government by the consent of the governed, and limited government powers. In some ways, the Declaration of Independence defines Americans' sense of right and wrong. It presents a challenge to anyone who might wish to overthrow our democratic processes or deny our citizens their natural rights.

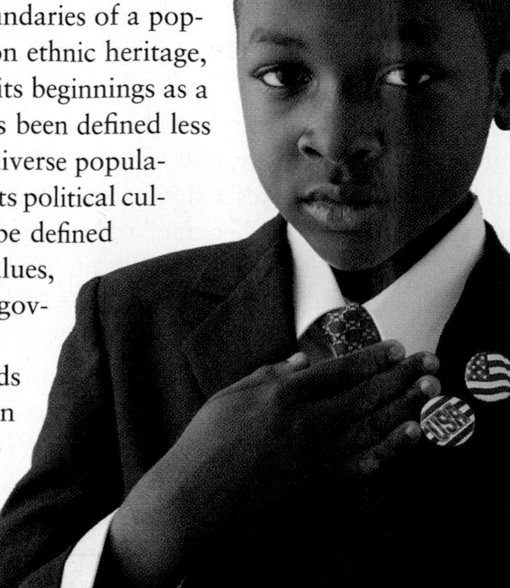

DIGITAL VISION/GETTY IMAGES

The rights to liberty, equality, and property are fundamental political values shared by most Americans. These values provide a basic framework for American political discourse and debate because they are shared, yet individual Americans often interpret their meanings quite differently. Many of our values are shared by other countries, but in some nations they are rejected.

LIBERTY The term **liberty** refers to a state of being free from external controls or restrictions. In the United States, the Constitution sets forth our *civil liberties* (see Chapter 4), including the freedom to practice whatever religion we choose and to be free from any state-imposed religion. Our liberties also include the freedom to speak freely on any topics and issues. Because people cannot govern themselves unless they are free to voice their opinions, freedom of speech is a basic requirement in a true democracy.

Clearly, though, if we are to live together with others, there have to be some restrictions on individual liberties. If people were allowed to do whatever they wished, without regard for the rights or liberties of others, pandemonium would result. Hence, a more accurate definition of liberty would be as follows: *liberty is the freedom of individuals to believe, act, and express themselves as they choose so long as doing so does not infringe on the rights of other individuals in the society.*

political culture The set of ideas, values, and attitudes about government and the political process held by a community or a nation.

liberty The freedom of individuals to believe, act, and express themselves as they choose so long as doing so does not infringe on the rights of other individuals in the society.

ELECTIONS 2010

New Directions for America

In the previous election cycle, the American people put in power a Democratic president, a Democratic-controlled Senate, and a Democratic-controlled House of Representatives. Two years later, the mid-term elections seemed to indicate that the American people had changed its collective mind. Of course, in almost every mid-term election, the party in power loses seats, particularly when the economy is bad. What was less predictable was the largest House shakeup of the past half century. Both new and long-time Democrats were swept out of office. In 2010, the Democrats enjoyed a 255 to 180 majority in the House. As of 2011, the Republican majority was 243 to 192. In the Senate, six seats moved from the Democratic side to the Republican side, leaving the Democrats with a slim majority of fifty-three.

Republicans turned out to vote in large numbers. Also, exit polls confirmed that many independents decided to "punish" Democrats—many of whom they had voted for in 2008—because they felt that the Democratic Party had expanded the size of government too much. Finally, a big shakeup took place at the state level. Republicans garnered a total take of more than 680 state legislative seats—possibly a record. Clearly, the next two years in American politics will see a substantial change in direction.

EQUALITY The goal of **equality** has always been a central part of American political culture. Many of the first settlers came to this country to be free of unequal treatment and persecution. They sought the freedom to live and worship as they wanted. They believed that anyone who worked hard could succeed, and America became known as the "land of opportunity." The Declaration of Independence confirmed the importance of equality to early Americans by stating, "We hold these Truths to be self-evident, that all Men are created equal." Because of the goal of equality, the Constitution prohibited the government from granting titles of nobility. Article I, Section 9, of the Constitution states, "No Title of Nobility shall be granted by the United States." (The Constitution did not prohibit slavery, however—see Chapter 2.)

But what, exactly, does equality mean? Does it mean simply political equality—the right to vote and run for political office? Does it mean that individuals should have equal opportunities to develop their talents and skills? What about those who are poor, suffer from disabilities, or are otherwise at a competitive disadvantage? Should it be the government's responsibility to ensure that such individuals also have equal opportunities? Although most Americans believe that all persons should have the opportunity to fulfill their potential, few contend that it is the government's responsibility to totally eliminate the economic and social differences that lead to unequal opportunities. Indeed, some contend that efforts to achieve equality, in the sense of equal treatment for all, are misguided attempts to create an ideal society that can never exist.

equality A concept that holds, at a minimum, that all people are entitled to equal protection under the law.

PROPERTY As noted earlier, the English philosopher John Locke asserted that people are born with "natural" rights and that among these rights are life, liberty, and *property*. The Declaration of Independence makes a similar assertion: people are born with certain "unalienable" rights, including the right to life, liberty, and the pursuit of happiness. For Americans, property and the *pursuit of happiness* are closely related. Americans place a great value on land ownership, on material possessions, and on their businesses. Property gives its owners political power and the liberty to do what they want—within limits.

Private property in America is not limited to personal possessions such as automobiles and houses. Property also consists of assets that can be used to create and sell goods and services, such as factories, farms, and shops. Private ownership of wealth-producing property is at the heart of our capitalist economic

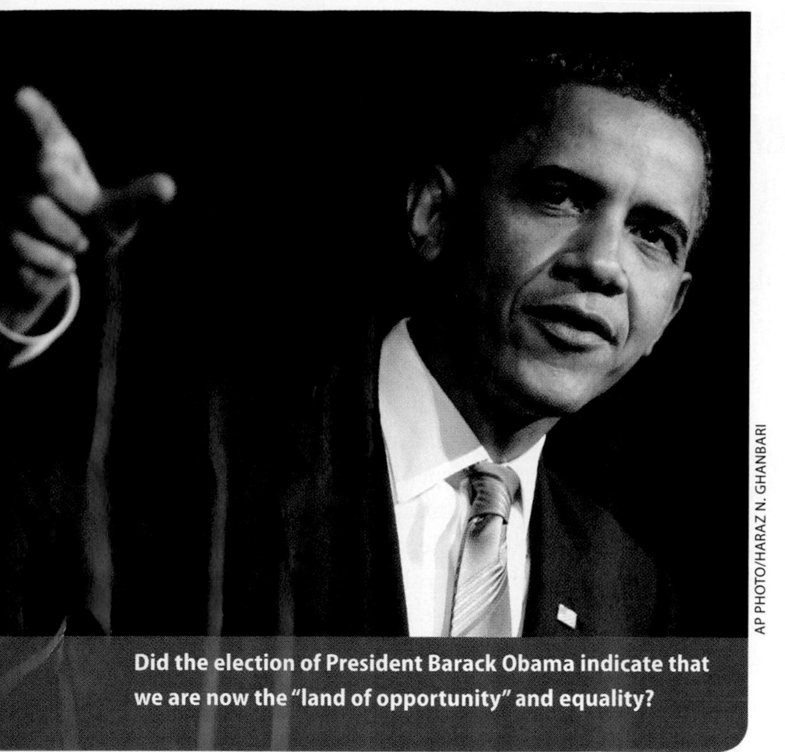

Did the election of President Barack Obama indicate that we are now the "land of opportunity" and equality?

system. **Capitalism** enjoys such widespread support in the United States that we can reasonably call it one of the nation's fundamental political values. In addition to the private ownership of productive property, capitalism is based on *free markets*—markets in which people can freely buy and sell goods, services, and financial investments without undue constraint by the government. Freedom to make binding contracts is another element of the capitalist system. The preeminent capitalist institution is the privately owned corporation.

Political Values in a Multicultural Society

From the earliest English and European settlers to the many cultural groups that today call America their home, American society has always been multicultural. Until recently, most Americans viewed the United States as the world's melting pot. They accepted that American society included numerous ethnic and cultural groups, but they expected that the members of these groups would abandon their cultural distinctions and assimilate the language and customs of earlier Americans. One of the outgrowths of the civil rights movement of the 1960s, however, was an emphasis on *multiculturalism*, the belief that the many cultures that make up American society should remain distinct and be protected—and even encouraged—by our laws.

The ethnic makeup of the United States has changed dramatically in the last two decades and will continue to change (see Figure 1–1 on the following page). Already, non-Hispanic whites are a minority in California. For the nation as a whole, non-Hispanic whites will be in the minority after the year 2050. Some Americans fear that rising numbers of immigrants will threaten traditional American political values and culture. We examine that issue in the feature *Join the Debate: Should We Encourage Immigration?* on page 15.

American Political Ideology

In a general sense, **ideology** refers to a system of political ideas. These ideas typically are rooted in religious or philosophical beliefs about human nature, society, and government. Generally, assumptions as to what the government's role should be in promoting basic values, such as liberty and equality, are important determinants of political ideology.

When it comes to political ideology, Americans tend to fall into two broad political camps: liberals and conservatives. The term *liberal* has been used to refer to someone who advocates change, new philosophies, and new ideas. The term *conservative* has described a person who values past customs and traditions that have proved their value over time. In today's American political arena, however, the terms *liberalism* and *conservatism* have both taken on additional meanings.

LIBERALISM Modern **liberalism** in the United States traces its roots to the administration of Franklin D. Roosevelt (1933–1945). Roosevelt's New Deal programs, launched to counter the effects of the Great Depression, involved the government in the American economic sphere to an extent hitherto unknown. From that time on, the word *liberalism* became associated with the concept of "big government"—that is,

capitalism An economic system based on the private ownership of wealth-producing property, free markets, and freedom of contract. The privately owned corporation is the preeminent capitalist institution.

ideology Generally, a system of political ideas that are rooted in religious or philosophical beliefs concerning human nature, society, and government.

liberalism A set of political beliefs that include the advocacy of active government, including government intervention to improve the welfare of individuals and to protect civil rights.

conservatism A set of beliefs that include a limited role for the national government in helping individuals and in the economic affairs of the nation, support for traditional values and lifestyles, and a cautious response to change.

with government intervention to aid economically disadvantaged groups and to promote equality.

Today's liberals continue to believe that the government has a responsibility to undertake social-welfare programs, at the taxpayers' expense, to assist the poor and the disadvantaged. Further, today's liberals believe that the national government should take steps to ensure that our civil rights and liberties are protected and that the government must look out for the interests of the individual against the majority.

The recently enacted health-care system reform can serve as an example of liberal ideals and policies. True, the package included some measures to limit the growth in spending on Medicare, which funds health care for those over the age of sixty-five. (As a result, the reform was unpopular among the elderly.) Most of the moral fervor behind the health-care legislation, however, was based on the liberal, egalitarian belief that every U.S. citizen should have a right to health-care insurance. Liberals believed that it was a scandal that some Americans could not afford insurance coverage and that others were denied coverage at any price. To remedy this situation, liberals were prepared to impose substantial new regulations on the insurance industry, create a new government spending program, and levy a number of new taxes.

> **"THE THING ABOUT DEMOCRACY,** beloveds, is that it is not neat, orderly or quiet. It requires a certain relish for confusion."
>
> ~ MOLLY IVINS ~
> AMERICAN JOURNALIST
> 1944–2007

Liberals typically believe in the separation of church and state, and generally think that the government should not involve itself in the moral or religious life of the nation. In this area, at least, liberals do not stand for big government, but rather the reverse.

CONSERVATISM Modern **conservatism** in this country can also trace its roots to the Roosevelt administration. Roosevelt gave conservatives a common cause: opposition to the New Deal and to big government. As one author noted, "No factor did more to stimulate

Figure 1–1

Distribution of the U.S. Population by Race and Hispanic Origin, 2000 to 2050

After 2050, minorities will constitute a majority of the U.S. population.

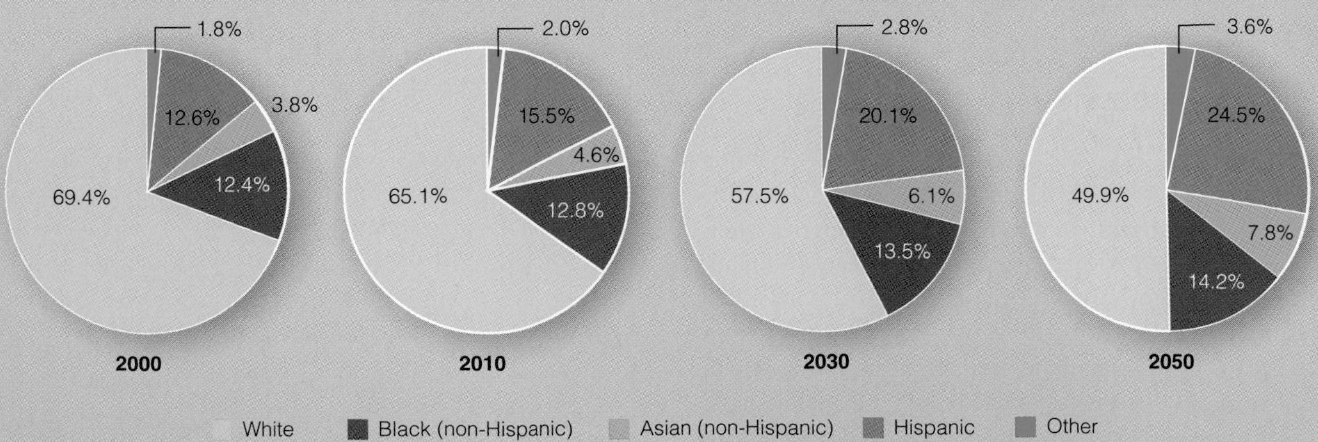

Data for 2010, 2030, and 2050 are projections.

Figures do not necessarily sum to 100%, because of rounding. Hispanics may be of any race. The chart categories "White," "Black," "Asian," and "Other" are limited to non-Hispanics. "Other" consists of the following non-Hispanic groups: "American Indian," "Alaska Native," "Native Hawaiian," "Other Pacific Islander," and "Two or More Races."
Sources: U.S. Bureau of the Census and authors' calculations.

JOIN THE DEBATE

Should We Encourage Immigration?

© CLEO PHOTO/ALAMY

Most discussions about immigration focus on what we should do about illegal immigration, a topic we will address later in this text. For now, the question is about immigration in general. America was founded by immigrants, and few restrictions on immigration existed until the twentieth century. Should the federal government change our immigration laws to allow more foreigners to immigrate legally and eventually become citizens of the United States? Or should we reduce immigration because we already have so many immigrants that they threaten to dilute our national character?

What Was Good Once Is Not Good Now

Those who oppose additional immigration admit that we are a nation founded by immigrants. Immigration opponents say, however, that new immigrants resist assimilation into American society and do not acquire core American values such as individualism and self-reliance. These opponents believe that the loyalty of new immigrants—even well-educated ones—to the United States and its core culture is fragile.

Increased legal immigration will bring in more low-skilled, poorly educated residents. That is not going to help our economy. Some second- and third-generation Latinos, for example, have fallen into the underclass culture. If current immigration patterns hold, in the future we will see decline in U.S. literacy and numeracy. If we want to continue to compete in the global economy, we must have an advanced labor force. If we allow some immigration, we should limit it, as much as possible, to professionals and highly skilled tradespeople.

A Nation Founded by Immigrants Needs More of Them

Immigration supporters believe that we benefit when people flow across borders. Indeed, if we made it easier for talented foreigners to move to this country, America would become even richer than it is now. Immigrants fill jobs, but they also create jobs. A quarter of the engineering and technology companies started in the United States from 1995 to 2005 had at least one founder who was foreign-born. The world's brightest brains and cutting-edge innovators come to the United States to study—and often to stay. Foreign students earn 44 percent of U.S. science and engineering doctorates. Yet many of these students are forced to leave the country after graduation because there are not enough visas available for professionals.

Immigration supporters are aware that many immigrants are unskilled. The United States, however, has jobs available at the bottom as well as the top. Even with unemployment at 10 percent in 2009 and 2010, farmers on the West Coast still could not find U.S. citizens willing to pick fruits and vegetables. And as far as assimilation is concerned, studies have shown that the new immigrants assimilate just as quickly as the old ones did.

For Critical Analysis ***One interesting statistic is that immigrants from Mexico—legal and illegal—have a substantially larger number of children than Mexicans who remain in their homeland. Why might this be so?***

the growth of modern conservatism than the election of Franklin Roosevelt. . . . He is the man conservatives most dislike, for he embodies the big-government ideology they most fear."[5]

As conservative ideology evolved in the latter half of the twentieth century, it incorporated a number of other elements in addition to the emphasis on free enterprise and antipathy toward big government. By the time of Ronald Reagan (1981–1989), conservatives placed a high value on the principles of law and order, states' rights, family values, and individual initiative. Today's conservatives tend to fall into two basic categories: *economic conservatives* (those who seek to minimize government spending and intervention in the economy) and *social conservatives* (those, such as Christian conservatives, who seek to incorporate religious and family values into politics and government).

The health-care reform package was an example of the kind of government program that conservatives typically oppose. Conservatives objected to the additional government spending required by the legislation and to the additional taxes. The new regulations imposed on the insurance industry were, for conservatives, a violation of the free-market principles on which this country was built. Conservatives believe that individuals and families should take responsibility for their own economic circumstances, and if that means that some would go without health-care insurance, so be it.

LIBERALS AND PROGRESSIVES Not all political labels are equally popular, and the term *liberal* has taken a particular beating in the political wars of the last several decades. One result is that most politicians who might have called themselves liberals in the past have abandoned the term and have labeled their philosophy **progressivism** instead. The benefits of the new label are clear. In public opinion polls, voters strongly prefer the term *conservative* to the term *liberal*. In 2009, however, a survey asked Americans to report whether they considered themselves liberal, progressive, conservative, or libertarian. Counting "leaners," the liberals and progressives together were almost as numerous as the conservative/libertarian block.[6]

The term *progressive* dates back to the first years of the twentieth century, when a reforming spirit arose in both major political parties. These "progressives" believed that stronger government was necessary to counterbalance the growing power of large corporations. In the presidential elections of 1912, the two strongest candidates, Theodore Roosevelt and Woodrow Wilson, called themselves progressives, although they disagreed on many issues. Later, the progressive label fell into disuse until it was resurrected in recent years.

progressivism An alternative, more popular term for the set of political beliefs also known as liberalism.

moderate A person whose views fall in the middle of the political spectrum.

radical left Persons on the extreme left side of the political spectrum, who would like major changes in the political order, usually to promote egalitarianism (human equality).

The Traditional Political Spectrum

Traditionally, liberalism and conservatism have been regarded as falling within a political spectrum that ranges from the far left to the far right. As Figure 1–2 on the facing page illustrates, there is a close relationship between those holding conservative views and those identifying themselves politically as Republicans. Similarly, in terms of party affiliation and voting, liberals—or progressives—identify with the Democratic Party.

MODERATES People whose views fall in the middle of the traditional political spectrum are generally called **moderates.** Moderates rarely classify themselves as either liberal or conservative, and they may vote for either Republicans or Democrats. Many moderates do not belong to either major political party and often describe themselves as *independent* (see Chapter 7).

THE EXTREME LEFT AND RIGHT On both ends of the spectrum are those who espouse radical views. The **radical left** consists of those who would like major changes in the political order, usually to promote egalitarianism (human equality). Socialists, who have a significant presence in Europe and elsewhere, generally support democracy and work within established political systems to realize their ideals. Communists,

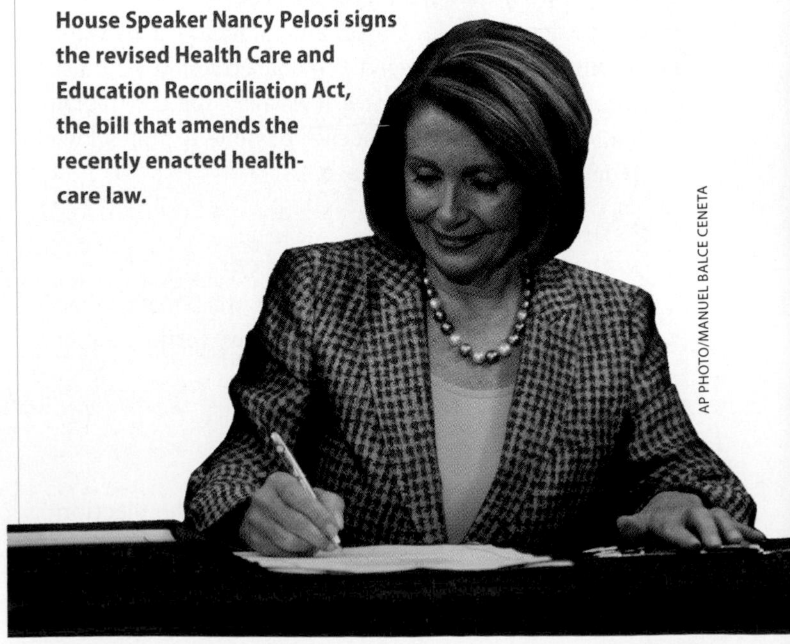
House Speaker Nancy Pelosi signs the revised Health Care and Education Reconciliation Act, the bill that amends the recently enacted health-care law.

AP PHOTO/MANUEL BALCE CENETA

Figure 1–2

The Traditional Political Spectrum

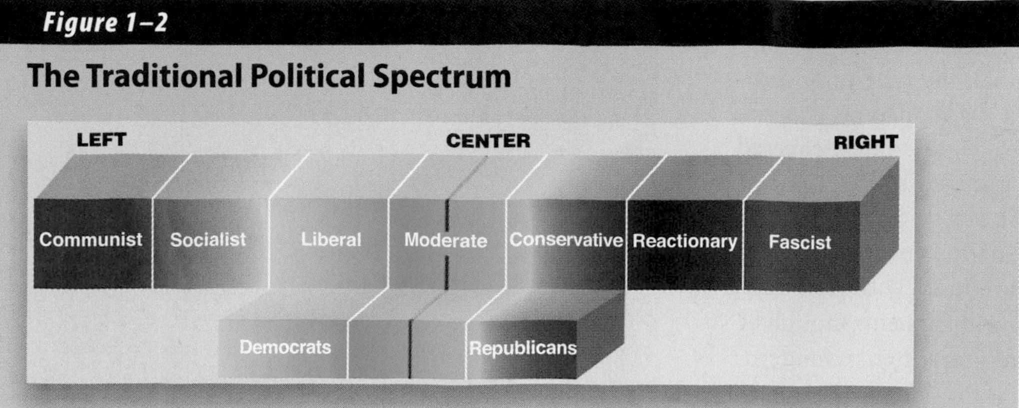

radical right Persons on the extreme right side of the political spectrum. The radical right includes reactionaries (who would like to return to the values and social systems of some previous era) and libertarians (who believe in no regulation of the economy or individual behavior).

ideologue An individual who holds very strong political opinions.

in contrast, have sought to reach their goals through revolutionary violence and totalitarian dictatorships. The political philosopher Karl Marx (1818–1883) is widely considered to be the most important founder of the radical left as it developed in the nineteenth and twentieth centuries.

The **radical right** includes reactionaries, those who wish to turn the clock back to some previous era when, for example, there weren't so many civil rights for the nation's minorities and women. Reactionaries strongly oppose liberal and progressive politics and resist political and social change. Like those on the radical left, members of the radical right may even advocate the use of violence to achieve their goals. This is especially true of fascist movements such as Hitler's Nazi Party. When in power, Fascists have created totalitarian systems based on philosophies of racism or extreme nationalism.

Ideology and Today's Electorate

Those who hold strongly to political ideologies that are well thought out and internally coherent and consistent are called **ideologues.** Ideologues usually fit easily on one side or the other of the political spectrum. Many Americans, though, do not adhere firmly to a particular political ideology. They may not be interested in political issues and may have a mixed set of opinions that do not neatly fit under a liberal or conservative label.

One complication is that many Americans are conservative on economic issues, such as the degree of government intervention in the economy, and at the same time are liberal on social issues, such as abortion. Indeed, the ideology of *libertarianism* favors just this combination. Libertarians oppose government action to regulate the economy, just as they oppose government involvement in issues of private morality. Like the word *liberal,* the term *libertarian* is not particularly popular, and many people who clearly have libertarian beliefs are unwilling to adopt the label. As you will learn later in this book, however, wealthy Americans often have libertarian attitudes.

Many other voters are liberal on economic issues even as they favor conservative positions on social matters. These people favor government intervention to promote both economic "fairness" *and* moral values. Low-income people frequently are social conservatives and economic progressives. A large number of African Americans and Hispanics fall into this camp. While it is widespread within the electorate, this "anti-libertarian" point of view has no agreed-upon name.

In sum, millions of Americans do not fit neatly into the traditional liberal-conservative spectrum. We illustrate an alternative, two-dimensional political classification in Figure 1–3 on the following page.

LO4 *American Democracy at Work*

Even the most divisive issues can be and are resolved through the political process. How does this process work? Who are the key players? These questions will be answered in the remaining chapters of this book. In the meantime, though, it is helpful to have some kind of a "road map" to guide you through these chapters so that you can see how each topic covered in the text relates to the big picture.

The Big Picture

The U.S. Constitution is the supreme law of the land. It sets forth basic governing rules by which Americans, when they ratified the Constitution, agreed to abide. It is appropriate, then, that we begin this text, following this introductory chapter, with a discussion of how and why the Constitution was created, the type of governing structure it established, and the rights and liberties it guarantees for all Americans. These topics, covered in Chapters 2 through 5, are necessarily the point of departure for any discussion of our system of government. As you will see, some of the most significant political controversies today have to do with how various provisions in this founding document should be applied, more than two hundred years later, to modern-day events and issues.

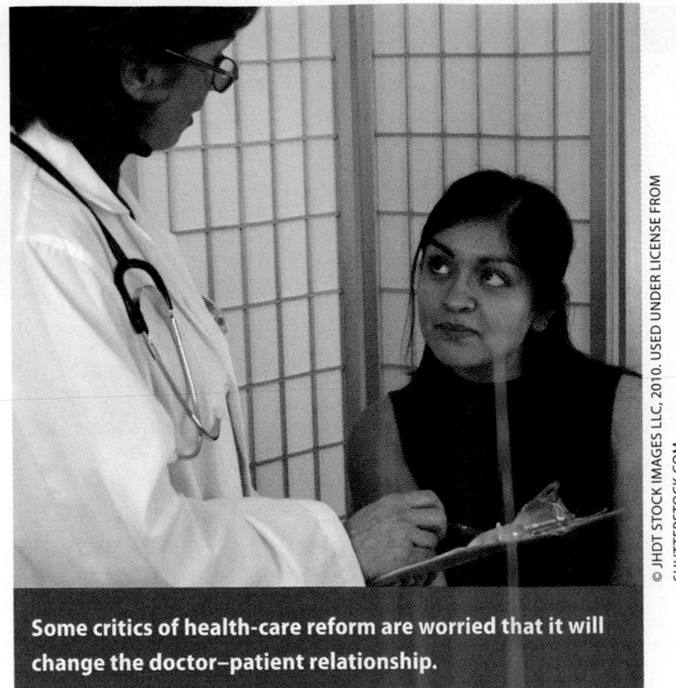

Some critics of health-care reform are worried that it will change the doctor–patient relationship.

Who Governs?

Who acquires the power and authority to govern, and how do they obtain that power and authority? Generally, of course, the "winners" in our political system are the successful candidates in elections. But the electoral process is influenced by more than just the issue positions taken by the candidates. As you read Chapters 6 through 10, keep the following questions in mind: How do interest groups influence elections? How essential are political parties to the electoral process? To what extent do public opinion and voting behavior play a role in determining who the winners and losers will be? Why are political campaigns so expensive, and what are the implications of high campaign costs for our democracy? Finally, what role do the media, including the Internet, play in fashioning the outcomes of campaigns?

Once a winning candidate assumes a political office, that candidate becomes a part of one of the institutions of government. In Chapter 11 and the remaining chapters of this text, we examine these institutions and the process of government decision making. You will learn how those who govern the nation make laws and policies to decide "who gets what, when, and how" in our society. Of course, the topics treated in these chapters are not isolated from the materials covered earlier in the text. For example, when formulating and implementing federal policies, as well as state and local policies, policymakers cannot ignore the wishes of interest groups, particularly those of wealthy groups that can help to fund the policymakers' reelections. And public opinion and the media not only affect election outcomes but also influence which issues will be included on the policymaking agenda.

The political system established by the founders of this nation has endured for more than two hundred years. The challenge facing Americans now is how to make sure that it will continue to endure.

Figure 1–3

A Two-Dimensional Political Classification

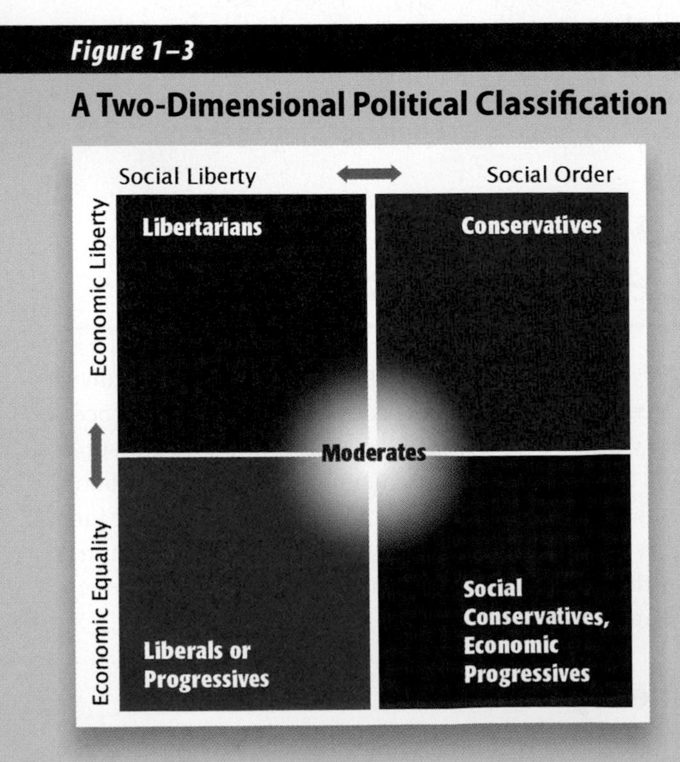

AMERICA AT ODDS Key Conflicts in America in the Twenty-First Century

As you learned in this chapter, Americans are united by a common political culture. At the same time, however, Americans are at odds over how much weight should be given to various fundamental principles. We can summarize these most basic disputes as follows:

- How large should our government be? Should it offer a wide range of services, along with the resulting taxes—or should it provide relatively few services and collect less in taxes?
- Should businesses be strictly regulated to ensure the common good—or should regulation be minimized to promote economic freedom and growth?
- More generally, should we place a greater value on economic liberty and property rights—or on economic egalitarianism and improving the condition of those who are less well-off?
- How active should the government be in promoting moral behavior by Americans? Should the government support traditional values—or place a high value on social liberty?
- Are progressive or liberal policies best for the nation—or does conservatism provide the better answers? Alternatively, is libertarianism the solution—or social conservatism combined with progressive economic policies?

Take Action

Our democratic republic is now more than two hundred years old, and it is easy to assume that it will last forever. It is also easy to forget that the reason we still enjoy the rights and benefits our system provides is that whenever they have been threatened in the past, people spoke out and took action to remove the threat. In the remaining chapters of this book, this *Take Action* section will give examples of how you can take action to make a difference. To function as a free person in our complex society, it is important to know the basic facts about government and politics that are covered in this text. Political science, however, goes well beyond the basics that every citizen ought to know. It is an important field of study in its own right.

Students who major in political science find employment in almost every kind of job imaginable. Naturally, some take employment with government at the federal, state, or local level. Political science is also the most popular major for students who seek to attend law school. Many political science majors also work in law without obtaining a graduate degree—as paralegals, legal assistants, or legal secretaries.

A political science major also can prepare a student for many other jobs. Almost every chapter of this book suggests a possible career. Interest groups? All of them need staff members, and political science can be part of a useful preparation for employment by such groups. Public opinion? Along with statistics, political science is a valuable background for poll takers. The media? Political science makes a good start if you want to go on to study journalism in preparation for a career. Political science can prepare you for jobs in campaign consulting, public relations, or business. Of course, political scientists also teach their subject at the high school and college levels. Regardless of what career they choose, one thing unites all political science majors—they like politics and find it fascinating.

CHIP SOMODEVILLA/GETTY IMAGES

People for the American Way interns make calls to organization members in Louisiana at the organization's "Action Center" in Washington, D.C. Political science majors can start their careers as volunteers.

POLITICS ON THE WEB

PGIAM/iSTOCKPHOTO

Each chapter of *GOVT* concludes with a list of Internet resources and addresses. Once you are on the Internet, you can use the addresses, or uniform resource locators (URLs), listed in the *Politics on the Web* sections in this book to access the ever-growing number of resources available on the Internet relating to American politics and government.

Internet sites tend to come and go, and there is no guarantee that a site included in a *Politics on the Web* feature will be there by the time this book is in print. We have tried, though, to include sites that have so far proved to be fairly stable. If you do have difficulty reaching a site, do not immediately assume that the site does not exist. First, recheck the URL shown in your browser. Remember, you have to type the URL exactly as written. Uppercase and lowercase are sometimes important. If the URL appears to be keyed in correctly, then try the following technique: delete all of the information after the forward slash mark that is farthest to the right in the address, and press "enter." This may allow you to reach a home page, from which you can link to the topic at issue.

A seemingly infinite number of sites on the Web offer information on American government and politics. A list of even the best sites would fill pages. For reasons of space, in this chapter and in those that follow, the *Politics on the Web* sections will include references to only a few selected sites. Following the links provided by these sites will take you to a host of others. The Web sites listed in the next column all provide excellent points of departure for those who wish to learn more about American government and politics today.

- The U.S. government's "official" Web site offers extensive information on the national government and the services it provides for citizens. To access this site, go to **www.usa.gov**
- ThisNation is a nonpartisan site dealing with current political questions. To access this site, go to **www.thisnation.com**
- To find news on the Web, you can go to the site of any major news organization or even your local newspaper. Links to online newspapers, both within the United States and in other countries, are available at **www.newspapers.com**
- Additionally, CNN's Politics Web site offers a wealth of news, news analysis, polling data, and news articles dating back to 1996. Go to **www.cnn.com/POLITICS**
- The Pew Research Center for the People and the Press offers survey data online on a number of topics relating to American politics and government. The URL for the center's site is **people-press.org**
- Yale University Library, one of the great research institutions, has an excellent collection of sources relating to American politics and government. Go to **www.library.yale.edu/socsci**

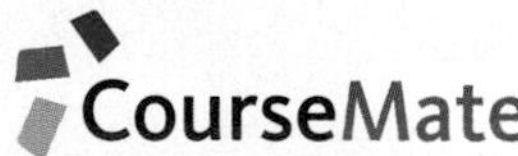

Access CourseMate to review and expand on this chapter through quizzes, flashcards, learning objectives, interactive timelines, a crossword puzzle, audio summaries, video, critical-thinking activities, simulations, and more.

GOVT 2

The Constitution

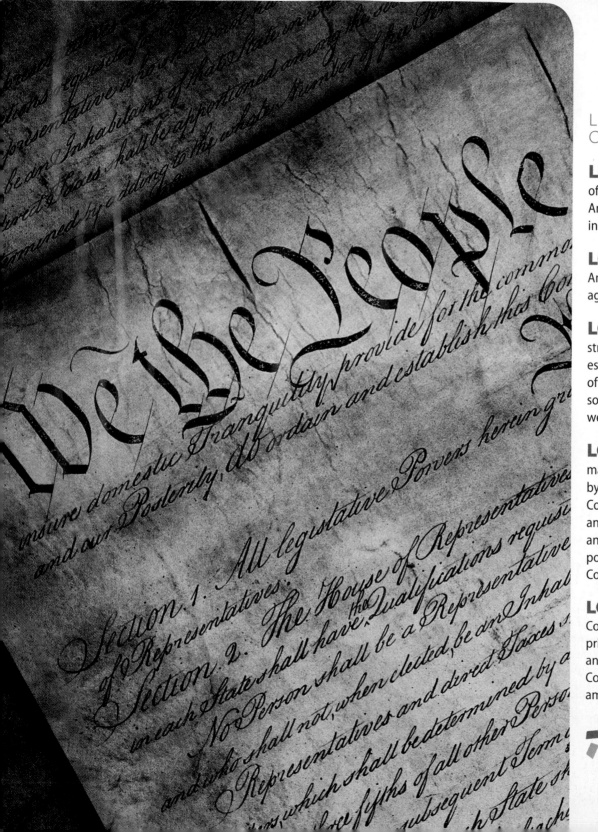

LEARNING OBJECTIVES

LO1 Point out some of the influences on the American political tradition in the colonial years.

LO2 Explain why the American colonies rebelled against Britain.

LO3 Describe the structure of government established by the Articles of Confederation and some of the strengths and weaknesses of the Articles.

LO4 List some of the major compromises made by the delegates at the Constitutional Convention, and discuss the Federalist and Anti-Federalist positions on ratifying the Constitution.

LO5 Summarize the Constitution's major principles of government, and describe how the Constitution can be amended.

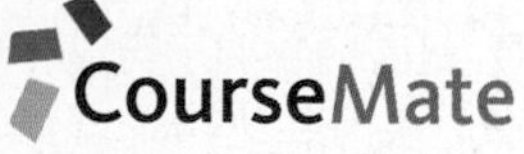

AMERICA AT ODDS

Was the Supreme Court Right to Rule That Individuals Have the Right to Bear Arms?

The Second Amendment to the Constitution of the United States says, "A well regulated Militia, being necessary to the security of a free State, the right of the people to keep and bear Arms, shall not be infringed." It seems clear, doesn't it? Actually, it is not clear. Does this amendment allow any individual in the United States to own a gun? Or does it guarantee the right to bear arms only to those who serve in a militia, such as the National Guard?

For decades, those who oppose gun control have argued that the first statement is correct. Gun control advocates have argued that the second statement is what the founders meant. In 1939, a United States Supreme Court decision seemed to suggest that the right to bear arms is constitutionally protected only when individuals function as part of a state militia. In 2008 and 2010, however, the Court found that the right to bear arms was guaranteed to individuals, not just state militias. The 2008 ruling restricted itself to limiting the actions of the federal government, and therefore it was applicable only in jurisdictions such as the District of Columbia. The 2010 ruling applied to state governments as well.[1] Both cases were decided by narrow, five-to-four margins. Americans are at odds over the question of whether the Court made the right decision.

The Supreme Court's Ruling Has Finally Clarified the Issue

Those who oppose gun control legislation strongly approve of the way the Supreme Court has interpreted the Second Amendment. They argue that the "militia" phrase in the Second Amendment is merely a preamble. James Madison, who drafted it, was providing an explanation of why the amendment was desirable, and not placing a limit on its applicability. The federal government cannot prevent individuals from owning guns, and the states should not have that right either. Sixty million Americans own guns. Barely one-third of Americans believe that the way to combat gun violence is through stricter gun laws.

"If guns are made criminal, only criminals will have guns." Studies conducted in cities where concealed weapons are allowed show that there are fewer robberies and murders than in jurisdictions where concealed weapons are *not* allowed. Washington, D.C., which had a total ban on guns, has one of the nation's highest rates of murder, and 80 percent of these murders are committed with firearms.

Without Gun Control, More Americans Will Die Senselessly

When drafted, the Second Amendment was an accommodation to the Anti-Federalists of the time, who believed that "the people in arms" could serve as an effective fighting force. This notion had already been proved wrong in the Revolutionary War. The current Supreme Court rulings on gun control laws can only have a negative effect on the well-being of Americans. Gun rights advocates will use this decision as a legal tool to strike down effective gun control laws nationwide. More than thirty thousand Americans are killed by guns every year. A third of these deaths are instances of murder. The rest are suicides or accidents.

Those in favor of gun control laws will continue to fight for them. They can do so because the Supreme Court decision did allow for certain types of gun restrictions, particularly bans on gun possession by felons and mentally ill individuals. We know that European nations that have banned almost all gun ownership have much lower homicide rates than we do in the United States. Isn't that enough evidence?

WHERE DO YOU STAND?

1. **The Supreme Court may have thrown out laws that ban the possession of firearms altogether, but the issue of whether and how guns should be regulated remains open. Should guns be registered, as automobiles are? Should citizens be allowed to carry concealed weapons? In either case, why or why not?**
2. **Why do you think so many Americans own firearms?**

EXPLORE THIS ISSUE ONLINE

Given the heat of the gun control controversy, it's no surprise that you can find many Web sites on either side.

- **Web sites that advocate the regulation of firearms are maintained by the Brady Campaign to Prevent Gun Violence at www.bradycampaign.org and the Violence Policy Center at www.vpc.org.**
- **Gun rights sites are maintained by the National Rifle Association at www.nra.org and the Second Amendment Foundation at www.saf.org.**

Introduction

Whether Americans as individuals have a constitutional right to own firearms is just one of many debates concerning the government established by the U.S. Constitution. The Constitution, which was written more than two hundred years ago, continues to be the supreme law of the land. Time and again, its provisions have been adapted to the changing needs and conditions of society. The challenge before today's citizens and political leaders is to find a way to apply those provisions to a society and an economy that could not possibly have been anticipated by the founders. Will the Constitution survive this challenge? Most Americans assume that it will—and with good reason: no other written constitution in the world today is as old as the U.S. Constitution. To understand the principles of government set forth in the Constitution, you have to go back to the beginnings of our nation's history.

LO1 The Beginnings of American Government

When the framers of the Constitution met in Philadelphia in 1787, they brought with them some valuable political assets. One asset was their English political heritage (see Chapter 1). Another was the hands-on political experience they had acquired during the colonial era. Their political knowledge and experience enabled them to establish a constitution that could meet not only the needs of their own time but also the needs of generations to come.

The American colonies were settled by individuals from many nations, including France, Germany, Ireland, the Netherlands, Spain, and Sweden. The majority of the colonists, though, came from England and Scotland. The British colonies in North America were established by private individuals and private trading companies and were under the rule of the British Crown. The colonies, which were located along the Atlantic seaboard of today's United States, eventually numbered thirteen.

Although American politics owes much to the English political tradition, the colonists actually derived most of their understanding of social compacts, the rights of the people, limited government, and representative government from their own experiences. Years before Parliament adopted the English Bill of Rights or John Locke wrote his *Two Treatises on Government* (1690), the American colonists were putting the ideas expressed in those documents into practice.

MARK PETERSON/REDUX

Second Amendment activists gathered at the foot of the Washington Monument in the nation's capital in April. The Supreme Court had just ruled that Americans have a constitutional right to keep guns in their homes for self-defense. Do you think the Supreme Court has ruled often on the issue of gun control?

The First English Settlements

The first permanent English settlement in North America was Jamestown, in what is now Virginia.[2] Jamestown was established in 1607 as a trading post of the Virginia Company of London.[3]

The first New England colony was founded by the Plymouth Company in 1620 at Plymouth, Massachusetts. Most of the settlers at Plymouth were Pilgrims, a group of English Protestants who came to the New World on the ship *Mayflower*. Even before the Pilgrims went ashore, they drew up the **Mayflower Compact,** in which they set up a government and promised to obey its laws. The reason for the compact was that the group was outside the jurisdiction of the Virginia Company, which had arranged for them to settle in Virginia, not Massachusetts. Fearing that some of the passengers might decide that they were no longer subject to any rules of civil order, the leaders on board the *Mayflower* agreed that some form of governmental authority was necessary. The Mayflower Compact, which was essentially a social contract, has historical significance because it was the first of a series of similar contracts among the colonists to establish fundamental rules of government.[4]

The Massachusetts Bay Colony was established as another trading outpost in New England in 1630. In 1639, some of the Pilgrims at Plymouth, who felt that they were being persecuted by the Massachusetts Bay Colony, left Plymouth and settled in what is now Connecticut. They developed America's first written constitution, which was called the Fundamental Orders of Connecticut. This document called for the laws to be made by an assembly of elected representatives from each town. The document also provided for the popular election of a governor and judges. Other colonies, in turn, established fundamental governing rules. The Massachusetts Body of Liberties protected individual rights. The Pennsylvania Frame of Government, passed in 1682, and the Pennsylvania Charter of Privileges of 1701 established principles that were later expressed in the U.S. Constitution and **Bill of Rights** (the first ten amendments to the Constitution). By 1732, all thirteen colonies had been established, each with its own political documents and constitution (see Figure 2–1, above right).

Mayflower Compact A document drawn up by Pilgrim leaders in 1620 on the ship *Mayflower*. The document stated that laws were to be made for the general good of the people.

Bill of Rights The first ten amendments to the U.S. Constitution. They list the freedoms—such as the freedoms of speech, press, and religion—that a citizen enjoys and that cannot be infringed on by the government.

Figure 2–1

The Thirteen Colonies

The thirteen colonies before the American Revolution. The western boundary of the colonies was set by the Proclamation Line of 1763, which banned European settlement in western territories that were reserved for Native Americans.

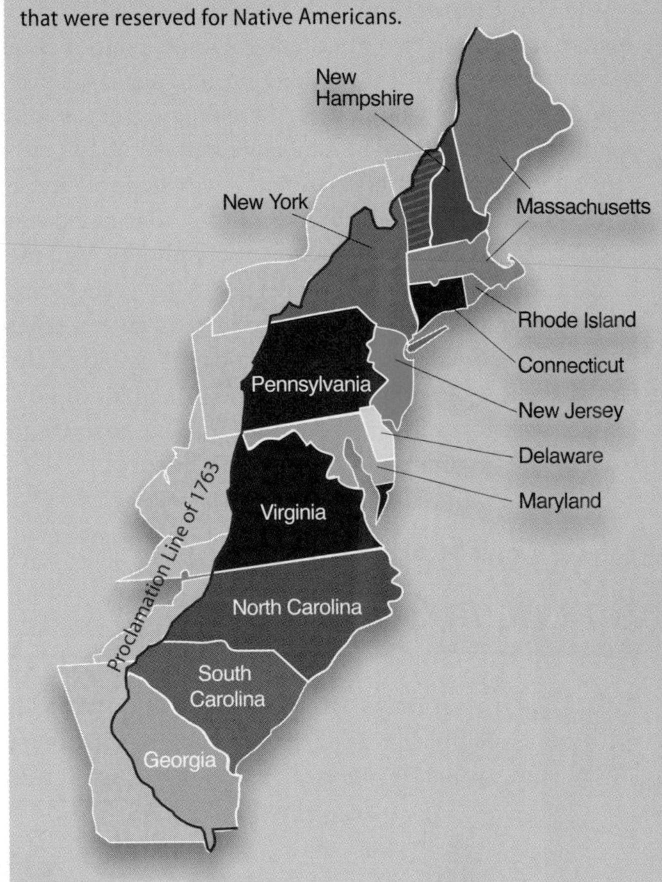

Colonial Legislatures

As mentioned, the British colonies in America were all under the rule of the British monarchy. Britain, however, was thousands of miles away—it took two months to sail across the Atlantic. Thus, to a significant extent, colonial legislatures carried on the "nuts and bolts" of colonial government. These legislatures, or *representative assemblies,* consisted of representatives elected by the colonists. The earliest colonial legislature was the Virginia House of Burgesses, established in 1619. By the time of the American Revolution, all of the colonies had representative assemblies, many of which had been in existence for more than a hundred years.

Through their participation in colonial governments, the colonists gained crucial political experience. Colonial leaders became familiar with the practical problems of governing. They learned how to build coalitions among groups with diverse interests and how to make compromises. Indeed, according to Yale University professor Jon Butler, by the time of the American Revolution in 1776, Americans had formed a complex, sophisticated political system. They had also created a wholly new type of society characterized by, among other things, ethnic and religious diversity.[5] Because of their political experiences, the colonists were quickly able to set up their own constitutions and state systems of government—and eventually a new national government—after they declared their independence from Britain in 1776.

LO2 *The Rebellion of the Colonists*

Scholars of the American Revolution point out that by and large, the American colonists did not want to become independent of Britain. For the majority of the colonists, Britain was the homeland, and ties of loyalty to the British monarch were strong. Why, then, did the colonists revolt against Britain and declare their independence? What happened to sever the political, economic, and emotional bonds that tied the colonists to Britain? The answers to these questions lie in a series of events in the mid-1700s that culminated in a change in British policy toward the colonies. Table 2–1 at right shows the chronology of the major political events in early U.S. political history.

One of these events was the Seven Years' War (1756–1763) between Britain and France, which Americans often refer to as the French and Indian War. The British victory in the Seven Years' War permanently altered the relationship between Britain and its American colonies. After successfully ousting the French from North America, the British expanded their authority over the colonies. To pay its war debts and to finance the defense of its expanded North American empire, Britain needed revenues. The British government decided to obtain some of these revenues by imposing taxes on the American colonists and exercising more direct control over colonial trade. At the same time, Americans were beginning to distrust the expanding British presence in the colonies. Having fought alongside British forces, Americans thought that they deserved more credit for the victory. The British, however, attributed the victory solely to their own war effort.

Furthermore, the colonists began to develop a sense of identity separate from the British. Americans were shocked at the behavior of some of the British soldiers and the cruel punishments meted out to enforce discipline among the British troops. The British, in turn, had little good to say about the colonists alongside whom they had fought. They considered them brutish, uncivilized, and undisciplined. It was during this time that the colonists began to use the word *American* to describe themselves.

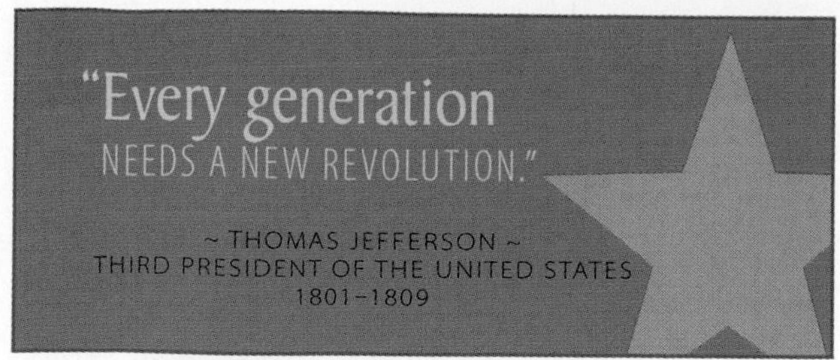

"Every generation
NEEDS A NEW REVOLUTION."
~ THOMAS JEFFERSON ~
THIRD PRESIDENT OF THE UNITED STATES
1801–1809

Table 2–1

Significant Events in Early U.S. Political History

1607	Jamestown established; Virginia Company lands settlers.
1620	Mayflower Compact signed.
1630	Massachusetts Bay Colony set up.
1639	Fundamental Orders of Connecticut adopted.
1641	Massachusetts Body of Liberties adopted.
1682	Pennsylvania Frame of Government passed.
1701	Pennsylvania Charter of Privileges written.
1732	Last of thirteen colonies established (Georgia).
1756	French and Indian War declared.
1765	Stamp Act; Stamp Act Congress meets.
1773	Boston Tea Party.
1774	First Continental Congress.
1775	Second Continental Congress; Revolutionary War begins.
1776	Declaration of Independence signed.
1777	Articles of Confederation drafted.
1781	Last state signs Articles of Confederation.
1783	"Critical period" in U.S. history begins; weak national government until 1789.
1786	Shays' Rebellion.
1787	Constitutional Convention.
1788	Ratification of Constitution.
1791	Ratification of Bill of Rights.

"Taxation without Representation"

In 1764, in an effort to obtain needed revenues, the British Parliament passed the Sugar Act, which imposed a tax on all sugar imported into the American colonies. Some colonists, particularly in Massachusetts, vigorously opposed this tax and proposed a boycott of certain British imports. This boycott developed into a "nonimportation" movement that soon spread to other colonies.

THE STAMP ACT OF 1765 The following year, in 1765, Parliament passed the Stamp Act, which imposed the first direct tax on the colonists. Under the act, all legal documents and newspapers, as well as certain other items, including playing cards and dice, had to use specially embossed (stamped) paper that was purchased from the government.

The Stamp Act generated even stronger resentment among the colonists than the Sugar Act had aroused. James Otis, Jr., a Massachusetts attorney, declared that there could be "no taxation without representation." The American colonists could not vote in British elections and therefore were not represented in the British Parliament. They viewed Parliament's attempts to tax them as contrary to the principle of representative government. The British saw the matter differently. From the British perspective, it was only fair that the colonists pay taxes to help support the costs incurred by the British government in defending its American territories and maintaining the troops that were permanently stationed in the colonies following the Seven Years' War.

In October 1765, nine of the thirteen colonies sent delegates to the Stamp Act Congress in New York City. The delegates prepared a declaration of rights and grievances, which they sent to King George III. This action marked the first time that a majority of the colonies had joined together to oppose British rule. The British Parliament repealed the Stamp Act.

FURTHER TAXES AND THE COERCIVE ACTS Soon, however, Parliament passed new laws designed to bind the colonies more tightly to the central government in London. Laws that imposed taxes on glass, paint, lead, and many other items were passed in 1767. The colonists protested by boycotting all British goods. In 1773, anger over taxation reached a powerful climax at the Boston Tea Party, in which colonists dressed as Mohawk Indians dumped almost 350 chests of British tea into Boston Harbor as a gesture of tax protest.[6]

First Continental Congress A gathering of delegates from twelve of the thirteen colonies, held in 1774 to protest the Coercive Acts.

The British Parliament was quick to respond to the Tea Party. In 1774, Parliament passed the Coercive Acts (sometimes called the "Intolerable Acts"), which closed Boston Harbor and placed the government of Massachusetts under direct British control.

The Continental Congresses

In response to the "Intolerable Acts," New York, Pennsylvania, and Rhode Island proposed a colonial congress. The Massachusetts House of Representatives requested that all colonies select delegates to send to Philadelphia for such a congress.

THE FIRST CONTINENTAL CONGRESS The **First Continental Congress** met on September 5, 1774, at Carpenter's Hall in Philadelphia. Of the thirteen colonies, only Georgia did not participate. The congress decided that the colonies should send a petition to King George III to explain their grievances, which they did. The congress also passed other resolutions calling for a continued boycott of British goods and requiring each colony to establish an army.

During the Boston Tea Party in 1773, the colonists dumped chests of British tea into Boston Harbor as a gesture of tax protest.

TIME LIFE PICTURES/MANSELL/GETTY IMAGES

To enforce the boycott and other acts of resistance against Britain, the delegates to the First Continental Congress urged that "a committee be chosen in every county, city and town, by those who are qualified to vote for representatives in the legislature, whose business it shall be attentively to observe the conduct of all persons." Over the next several months, all colonial legislatures supported this action. The committees of "safety" or "observation," as they were called, organized militias, held special courts, and suppressed the opinions of those who remained loyal to the British Crown. Committee members spied on neighbors' activities and reported to the press the names of those who violated the boycott against Britain. The names were then printed in the local papers, and the transgressors were harassed and ridiculed in their communities.

THE SECOND CONTINENTAL CONGRESS Almost immediately after receiving the petition from the First Continental Congress, the British government condemned the actions of the congress as open acts of rebellion. Britain responded with even stricter and more repressive measures. On April 19, 1775, British soldiers (Redcoats) fought against colonial citizen soldiers (Minutemen) in the towns of Lexington and Concord in Massachusetts, the first battles of the American Revolution.

Less than a month later, delegates from all thirteen colonies gathered in Pennsylvania for the **Second Continental Congress,** which immediately assumed the powers of a central government. The Second Continental Congress declared that the militiamen who had gathered around Boston were now a full army. It also named George Washington, a delegate to the congress who had some military experience, as its commander in chief.

The delegates to the Second Continental Congress still intended to reach a peaceful settlement with the British Parliament. One declaration stated specifically that "we [the congress] have not raised armies with ambitious designs of separating from Britain, and establishing independent States." The continued attempts to effect a reconciliation with Britain, even after the outbreak of fighting, underscore the colonists' reluctance to sever their relationship with the home country. As one scholar put it, "Of all the world's colonial peoples, none became rebels more reluctantly than did Anglo-Americans in 1776."[7]

"THE CONSTITUTION

...is an instrument for the people to restrain the government– lest it come to dominate our lives and interests."

~ PATRICK HENRY ~
AMERICAN STATESMAN AND OPPONENT OF THE CONSTITUTION
1736–1799

Breaking the Ties: Independence

Public debate about the problems with Britain continued to rage, but the stage had been set for declaring independence. One of the most rousing arguments in favor of independence was presented by Thomas Paine, a former English schoolmaster and corset maker, who wrote a pamphlet called *Common Sense*. In that pamphlet, which was published in Philadelphia in January 1776, Paine addressed the crisis using "simple fact, plain argument, and common sense." He mocked King George III and attacked every argument that favored loyalty to the king. He called the king a "royal brute" and a "hardened, sullen-tempered Pharaoh [Egyptian king in ancient times]."[8]

Paine's writing went beyond a personal attack on the king. He contended that America could survive economically on its own and no longer needed its British connection. He wanted the developing colonies to become a model republic in a world in which other nations were oppressed by strong central governments.

None of Paine's arguments was new. In fact, most of them were commonly heard in tavern debates throughout the land. Instead, it was the pungency and eloquence of Paine's words that made *Common Sense* so effective:

> A government of our own is our natural right: and when a man seriously reflects on the precariousness of human affairs, he will become convinced, that it is infinitely wiser and safer, to form a constitution of our own in a cool and deliberate manner, while we have it in our power, than to trust such an interesting event to time and chance.[9]

Many historians regard Paine's *Common Sense* as the single most important publication of the American Revolution. The pamphlet became a best seller; more than 100,000 copies were sold within a few months after its publication.[10] It put independence squarely on the agenda. Above all, *Common Sense* helped sever the remaining ties of loyalty to the British monarch, thus removing the final psychological barrier to independence. Indeed, later John Adams would ask,

> What do we mean by the Revolution? The War? That was no part of the Revolution. It was only an effect and consequence of it. The Revolution was in the minds of the people, and this was effected, from 1760 to 1775, in the course of fifteen years before a drop of blood was drawn at Lexington.[11]

Second Continental Congress The congress of the colonies that met in 1775 to assume the powers of a central government and to establish an army.

Thomas Paine (1737–1809). In addition to his successful pamphlet *Common Sense*, Paine also wrote a series of sixteen pamphlets, under the title *The Crisis*, during the American Revolution. He returned to England and, in 1791 and 1792, wrote *The Rights of Man*, in which he defended the French Revolution. Paine returned to the United States in 1802.

INDEPENDENCE FROM BRITAIN—THE FIRST STEP By June 1776, the Second Continental Congress had voted for free trade at all American ports with all countries except Britain. The congress had also suggested that all colonies establish state governments separate from Britain. The colonists realized that a formal separation from Britain was necessary if the new nation was to obtain supplies for its armies and commitments of military aid from foreign governments. On June 7, 1776, the first formal step toward independence was taken when Richard Henry Lee of Virginia placed the following resolution before the congress:

> RESOLVED, That these United Colonies are, and of right ought to be, free and independent States, that they are absolved from allegiance to the British Crown, and that all political connection between them and the state of Great Britain is, and ought to be, totally dissolved.

The congress postponed consideration of Lee's resolution until a formal statement of independence could be drafted. On June 11, a "Committee of Five" was appointed to draft a declaration that would present to the world the colonies' case for independence.

THE SIGNIFICANCE OF THE DECLARATION OF INDEPENDENCE Adopted on July 4, 1776, the Declaration of Independence is one of the world's most famous documents. Like Paine, Thomas Jefferson, who wrote most of the document, elevated the dispute between Britain and the American colonies to a universal level. Jefferson opened the second paragraph of the declaration with the following words, which have since been memorized by countless American schoolchildren and admired the world over:

> We hold these Truths to be self-evident, that all Men are created equal, that they are endowed by their Creator with certain unalienable Rights, that among these are Life, Liberty, and the Pursuit of Happiness—That to secure these Rights, Governments are instituted among Men, deriving their just Powers from the Consent of the Governed, that whenever any Form of Government becomes destructive of these Ends, it is the Right of the People to alter or to abolish it, and to institute new Government.

The concepts expressed in the Declaration of Independence clearly reflect Jefferson's familiarity with European political philosophy, particularly the works of John Locke.[12] Locke's philosophy, though it did not cause the American Revolution, provided philosophical underpinnings by which the revolution could be justified.

FROM COLONIES TO STATES Even before the Declaration of Independence, some of the colonies had transformed themselves into sovereign states with their own permanent governments. In May 1776, the Second Continental Congress had directed each of the colonies to form "such government as shall . . . best be conducive to the happiness and safety of their constituents [those represented by the government]." Before long, all thirteen colonies had created constitutions. Eleven of the colonies had completely new constitutions. The other

The committee chosen to draft a declaration of independence is shown at work in this nineteenth-century engraving. They are, from the left, Benjamin Franklin, Thomas Jefferson, John Adams, Philip Livingston, and Roger Sherman.

two colonies, Rhode Island and Connecticut, made minor modifications to old royal charters. Seven of the new constitutions contained bills of rights that defined the personal liberties of all state citizens. All constitutions called for limited governments.

REPUBLICANISM Many citizens were fearful of a strong central government because of their recent experiences under the British Crown. They opposed any form of government that resembled monarchy in any way. Consequently, wherever such antiroyalist sentiment was strong, the legislature—composed of elected representatives—became all-powerful. In Pennsylvania and Georgia, for example, **unicameral** (one-chamber) **legislatures** were unchecked by any executive authority. Indeed, this antiroyalist—or *republican*—sentiment was so strong that the executive branch was extremely weak in all thirteen states.

The republican spirit was strong enough to seriously interfere with the ability of the new nation to win the Revolutionary War, for example by failing to adequately supply General Washington's army. Republicans of the Revolutionary Era (not to be confused with supporters of the later Republican Party) were suspicious not only of executive authority in their own states but also of national authority as represented by the Continental Congress. This anti-authoritarian, localist impulse contrasted with the *nationalist* sentiments of many of the nation's founders, especially such leaders as George Washington and Alexander Hamilton. Nationalists favored an effective central authority. Of course, many founders, such as Thomas Jefferson, harbored both republican and nationalist impulses.

Who were the republicans? As with all political movements of the time, the republicans were led by men of "property and standing." Leaders who were strongly republican, however, tended to be less prominent than their nationalist or moderate counterparts. Small farmers may have been the one group that was disproportionately republican. Small farmers, however, were a majority of the voters in every state.

LO3 *The Confederation of States*

Republican sentiments influenced the thinking of the delegates to the Second Continental Congress, who formed a committee to draft a plan of confederation. A **confederation** is a voluntary association of *independent* states (see Chapter 3). The member states agree to let the central government undertake a limited number of activities, such as forming an army, but do not allow the central government to place many restrictions on the states' own actions. The member states typically can still govern most state affairs as they see fit.

On November 15, 1777, the Second Continental Congress agreed on a draft of the plan, which was finally signed by all thirteen colonies on March 1, 1781. The **Articles of Confederation,** the result of this plan, served as this nation's first national constitution and represented an important step in the creation of our governmental system.[13]

The Articles of Confederation established the Congress of the Confederation as the central governing body. This congress was a unicameral assembly of representatives, or ambassadors, as they were called, from the various states. Although each state could send from two to seven representatives to the congress, each state, no matter what its size, had only one vote. The issue of sovereignty was an important part of the Articles of Confederation:

> Each State retains its sovereignty, freedom, and independence, and every power, jurisdiction, and right, which is not by this Confederation expressly delegated to the United States in Congress assembled.

The structure of government under the Articles of Confederation is shown in Figure 2–2 on the following page.

Powers of the Government of the Confederation

Congress had several powers under the Articles of Confederation, and these enabled the new nation to achieve a number of accomplishments (see Figure 2–3 on page 32). The Northwest Ordinance settled states' claims to many of the western lands and established a basic pattern for the government of new territories. Also, the 1783 peace treaty negotiated with Britain granted to the United States all of the territory from the Atlantic Ocean to the Mississippi River and from the Great Lakes and Canada to what is now northern Florida.

In spite of these accomplishments, the central government created

unicameral legislature A legislature with only one chamber.

confederation A league of independent states that are united only for the purpose of achieving common goals.

Articles of Confederation The nation's first national constitution, which established a national form of government following the American Revolution. The Articles provided for a confederal form of government in which the central government had few powers.

Figure 2–2

American Government under the Articles of Confederation

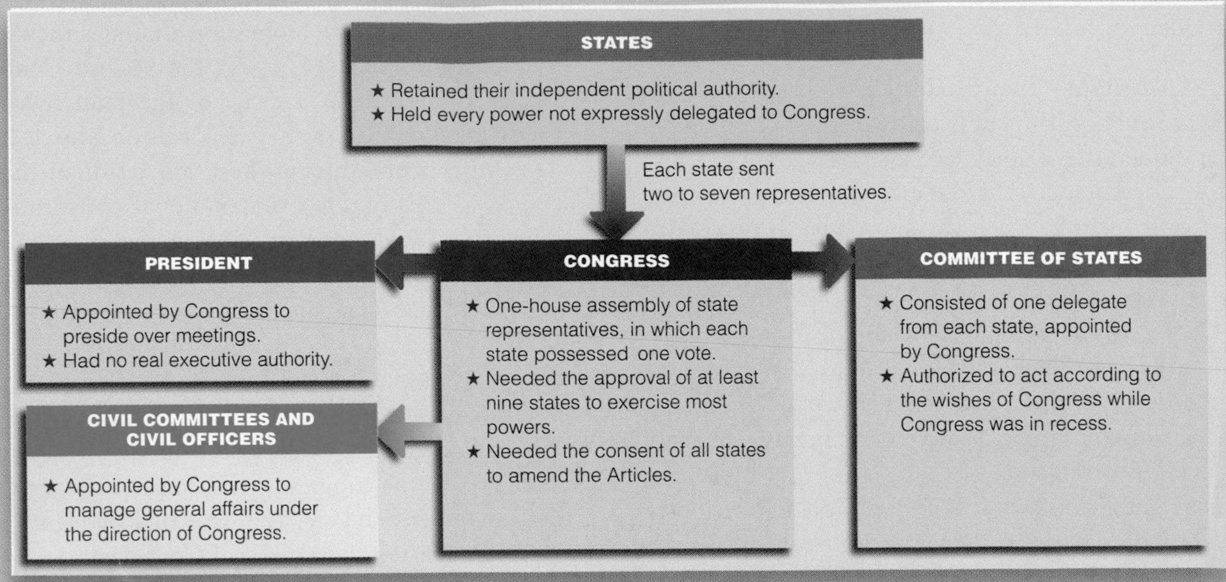

by the Articles of Confederation was quite weak. The Congress of the Confederation had no power to raise revenues for the militia or to force the states to meet military quotas. Essentially, this meant that the new government did not have the power to enforce its laws. Even passing laws was difficult because the Articles of Confederation provided that nine states had to approve any law before it was enacted. Figure 2–4 on page 33 lists these and other powers that the central government lacked under the Articles of Confederation.

STATES
★ Retained their independent political authority.
★ Held every power not expressly delegated to Congress.
Each state sent two to seven representatives.
PRESIDENT
★ Appointed by Congress to preside over meetings.
★ Had no real executive authority.
CIVIL COMMITTEES AND CIVIL OFFICERS
★ Appointed by Congress to manage general affairs under the direction of Congress.
CONGRESS
★ One-house assembly of state representatives, in which each state possessed one vote.
★ Needed the approval of at least nine states to exercise most powers.
★ Needed the consent of all states to amend the Articles.
COMMITTEE OF STATES
★ Consisted of one delegate from each state, appointed by Congress.
★ Authorized to act according to the wishes of Congress while Congress was in recess.

Nonetheless, the Articles of Confederation proved to be a good "first draft" for the Constitution, and at least half of the text of the Articles would later appear in the Constitution. The Articles were an unplanned experiment that tested some of the principles of government that had been set forth earlier in the Declaration of Independence. Some argue that without the experience of government under the Articles of Confederation, it would have been difficult, if not impossible, to arrive at the compromises that were necessary to create the Constitution several years later.

A Time of Crisis—The 1780s

The Revolutionary War ended on October 18, 1781. The Treaty of Paris, which confirmed the colonies' independence from Britain, was signed in 1783. Peace with the British may have been won, but peace within the new nation was hard to find. The states bickered among themselves and refused to support the new central government in almost every way. As George Washington stated, "We are one nation today and thirteen tomorrow. Who will treat [with] us on such terms?"

Indeed, the national government, such as it was, did not have the ability to prevent the various states from entering into agreements with foreign powers, despite the danger that such agreements could completely disrupt the confederation, pitting state against state. When Congress proved reluctant to admit Vermont into the Union, Britain began negotiations with influential Vermonters with the aim of annexing the district to Canada. Likewise, the Spanish governor of Louisiana energetically sought to detach Tennessee and the lands south of it from the United States. Several prominent individuals—including Daniel Boone—accepted Spanish gold.

The states also increasingly taxed each other's imports and at times even prevented trade altogether. By 1784, the new nation was suffering from a serious economic depression. States started printing their own money at dizzying rates, which led to inflation. Banks were calling in old loans and refusing to issue new ones. Individuals who could not pay their debts were often thrown into prison.

SHAYS' REBELLION The tempers of indebted farmers in western Massachusetts reached the boiling point in August 1786. Former Revolutionary War captain Daniel Shays, along with approximately two thousand armed farmers, seized county courthouses and disrupted the debtors' trials. Shays and his men then launched an attack on the national government's arsenal in Springfield. **Shays' Rebellion** continued to grow in intensity and lasted into the winter, when it was finally stopped by the Massachusetts volunteer army, paid by Boston merchants.[14]

Similar disruptions occurred throughout most of the New England states and in some other areas as well. The upheavals, and particularly Shays' Rebellion, were an important catalyst for change. The revolts frightened American political and business leaders and caused more and more Americans to realize that a *true* national government had to be created.

THE ANNAPOLIS MEETING The Virginia legislature called for a meeting of representatives from all of the states at Annapolis, Maryland, on September 11, 1786, to consider extending national authority to issues of commerce. Five of the thirteen states sent delegates, two of whom were Alexander Hamilton of New York and James Madison of Virginia. Both of these men favored a strong central government.[15] They persuaded the other delegates to issue a report calling on the states to hold a convention in Philadelphia in May of the following year.

The Congress of the Confederation at first was reluctant to give its approval to the Philadelphia convention. By mid-February 1787, however, seven of the states had named delegates to the Philadelphia meeting. Finally, on February 21, the congress called on the states to send delegates to Philadelphia "for the sole and express purpose of revising the Articles of Confederation." That Philadelphia meeting became the **Constitutional Convention.**

LO4 *Drafting and Ratifying the Constitution*

Although the convention was supposed to start on May 14, 1787, few of the delegates had actually arrived in Philadelphia on that date. The convention formally opened in the East Room of the Pennsylvania State House on May 25, after fifty-five of the seventy-four delegates had arrived.[16] Only Rhode Island, where feelings were strong against creating a more powerful central government, did not send any delegates.

Who Were the Delegates?

Among the delegates to the Constitutional Convention were some of the nation's best-known leaders. George Washington was present, as were Alexander Hamilton, James Madison, George Mason, Robert Morris, and Benjamin Franklin (who, at eighty-one years old, had to be carried to the convention on a portable chair). Some notable leaders were absent, including Thomas Jefferson and John Adams, who were serving as ambassadors in Europe, and Patrick Henry, who did not attend because he "smelt a rat." (Henry was one of Virginia's most strongly republican leaders.)

For the most part, the delegates were from the best-educated and wealthiest classes. Thirty-three delegates were lawyers, nearly half of the delegates were college graduates, three were physicians, seven were former chief executives of their respective states, six owned large plantations, at least nineteen owned slaves, eight were important business owners, and twenty-one had fought in the Revolutionary War. In other words, the delegates to the convention constituted an elite assembly. No ordinary farmers or merchants were present. Indeed, in his classic work on the Constitution, Charles Beard maintained that the Constitution was produced primarily by wealthy bondholders who had made loans to the government under the Articles and wanted a strong central government that could prevent state governments from repudiating debts.[17] Later historians, however, rejected Beard's thesis, concluding that bondholders played no special role in writing the Constitution.

The Virginia Plan

James Madison had spent months reviewing European political theory before he went to the Philadelphia convention. His Virginia delegation arrived before anybody else, and he immediately put its members to work. On the first day of the convention, Governor Edmund Randolph of Virginia was able to present fifteen resolutions outlining what was to become known as the *Virginia Plan.* This was a masterful political stroke on the part of the Virginia delegation. Its proposals immediately set the agenda for the remainder of the convention.

The fifteen resolutions contained in the Virginia Plan proposed

Shays' Rebellion A rebellion of angry farmers in western Massachusetts in 1786, led by former Revolutionary War captain Daniel Shays. This rebellion and other similar uprisings in the New England states emphasized the need for a true national government.

Constitutional Convention The convention (meeting) of delegates from the states that was held in Philadelphia in 1787 for the purpose of amending the Articles of Confederation. In fact, the delegates wrote a new constitution (the U.S. Constitution) that established a federal form of government to replace the governmental system that had been created by the Articles of Confederation.

Figure 2–3

Powers of the Central Government under the Articles of Confederation

Although the Articles of Confederation were later scrapped, they did allow the early government of the United States to achieve several important goals, including winning the Revolutionary War.

WHAT THE CONGRESS COULD DO	ACCOMPLISHMENT
Congress could establish and control the armed forces, declare war, and make peace.	The United States won the Revolutionary War.
Congress could enter into treaties and alliances.	Congress negotiated a peace treaty with Britain.
Congress could settle disputes among the states under certain circumstances.	Congress passed the Northwest Ordinance, which settled certain states' land claims.
Congress could regulate coinage (but not paper money) and set standards for weights and measures.	Congress carried out these functions, but the inability to regulate paper money proved a major weakness.
Congress could borrow money from the people.	Congress did borrow money, but without the power to tax, it had trouble repaying the loans or obtaining new ones.
Congress could create a postal system, courts to address issues related to ships at sea, and government departments.	Congress created a postal system and departments of foreign affairs, finance, and war.

an entirely new national government under a constitution. The plan, which favored large states such as Virginia, called for the following:

- A bicameral legislature. The lower house was to be chosen by the people. The smaller upper house was to be chosen by the elected members of the lower house. The number of representatives would be in proportion to each state's population (the larger states would have more representatives). The legislature could void any state laws.
- A national executive branch, elected by the legislature.
- A national court system, created by the legislature.

Great Compromise A plan for a bicameral legislature in which one chamber would be based on population and the other chamber would represent each state equally. The plan, also known as the Connecticut Compromise, resolved the small-state/large-state controversy.

"The Constitution only gives people the right to **PURSUE HAPPINESS.** You have to catch it yourself."

~ BENJAMIN FRANKLIN ~
AMERICAN STATESMAN AND SIGNER OF THE CONSTITUTION
1706–1790

The smaller states immediately complained because they would have fewer representatives in the legislature. After two weeks of debate, they offered their own plan—the *New Jersey Plan.*

The New Jersey Plan

William Paterson of New Jersey presented an alternative plan favorable to the smaller states. He argued that because each state had an equal vote under the Articles of Confederation, the convention had no power to change this arrangement. The New Jersey Plan proposed the following:

- Congress would be able to regulate trade and impose taxes.
- Each state would have only one vote.
- Acts of Congress would be the supreme law of the land.
- An executive office of more than one person would be elected by Congress.
- The executive office would appoint a national supreme court.

The Compromises

Most delegates were unwilling to consider the New Jersey Plan. When the Virginia Plan was brought up again, however, delegates from the smaller states threatened to leave, and the convention was in danger of dissolving. On July 16, Roger Sherman of Connecticut broke the deadlock by proposing a compromise plan. Compromises on other disputed issues followed.

THE GREAT COMPROMISE Roger Sherman's plan, which has become known as the **Great Compromise** (or the Connecticut Compromise), called for a legislature with two houses:

- A lower house (the House of Representatives), in which the number of representatives from each state would be determined by the number of people in that state.

Figure 2–4

Powers That the Central Government Lacked under the Articles of Confederation

The government's lack of certain powers under the Articles of Confederation taught the framers of the Constitution several important lessons, which helped them create a more effective government under that new document.

WHAT THE CONGRESS COULD NOT DO	RESULT
Congress could not force the states to meet military quotas.	The central government could not draft soldiers to form a standing army.
Congress could not regulate commerce between the states or with other nations.	Each state was free to set up its own system of taxes on goods imported from other states. Economic quarrels among the states broke out. There was difficulty in trading with other nations.
Congress could enter into treaties, but could not enforce them.	The states were not forced to respect treaties. Many states entered into treaties independent of Congress.
Congress could not directly tax the people.	The central government had to rely on the states to collect and forward taxes, which the states were reluctant to do. The central government was always short of money.
Congress had no power to enforce its laws.	The central government depended on the states to enforce its laws, which they rarely did.
Any amendment to the Articles required all thirteen states to consent.	In practice, the powers of the central government could not be changed.
There was no national judicial system.	Most disputes among the states could not be settled by the central government.
There was no executive branch.	Coordinating the work of the central government was almost impossible.

- An upper house (the Senate), which would have two members from each state; the members would be elected by the state legislatures.

The Great Compromise gave something to both sides: the large states would have more representatives in the House of Representatives than the small states, yet each state would be granted equality in the Senate—because each state, regardless of size, would have two senators. The Great Compromise thus resolved the small-state/large-state controversy.

THE THREE-FIFTHS COMPROMISE A second compromise had to do with how many representatives each state would have in the House of Representatives. Although slavery was legal in parts of the North, most slaves and slave owners lived in the South. Indeed, in the southern states, slaves constituted about 40 percent of the population. Counting the slaves as part of the population would thus greatly increase the number of southern representatives in the House. The delegates from the southern states wanted the slaves to be counted as persons; the delegates from the northern states disagreed. Eventually, the **three-fifths compromise** settled this deadlock: each slave would count as three-fifths of a person in determining representation in Congress. (The three-fifths compromise was eventually overturned in 1868 by the Fourteenth Amendment.)

three-fifths compromise
A compromise reached during the Constitutional Convention by which three-fifths of all slaves were to be counted for purposes of representation in the House of Representatives.

SLAVE IMPORTATION The three-fifths compromise did not satisfy everyone at the Constitutional Convention. Many delegates wanted slavery to be banned completely in the United States. The delegates compromised on this question by agreeing that Congress could prohibit the importation of slaves into the country beginning in 1808. The issue of slavery itself, however, was never really addressed by the delegates to the Constitutional Convention. As a result, the South won twenty years of unrestricted slave trade and a requirement that escaped slaves who had fled to the northern states be returned to their owners. Domestic slave trading was untouched.

BANNING EXPORT TAXES The South's economic health depended in large part on its exports of agricultural products. The South feared that the northern majority in Congress might pass taxes on these exports. This fear led to yet another compromise: the South agreed

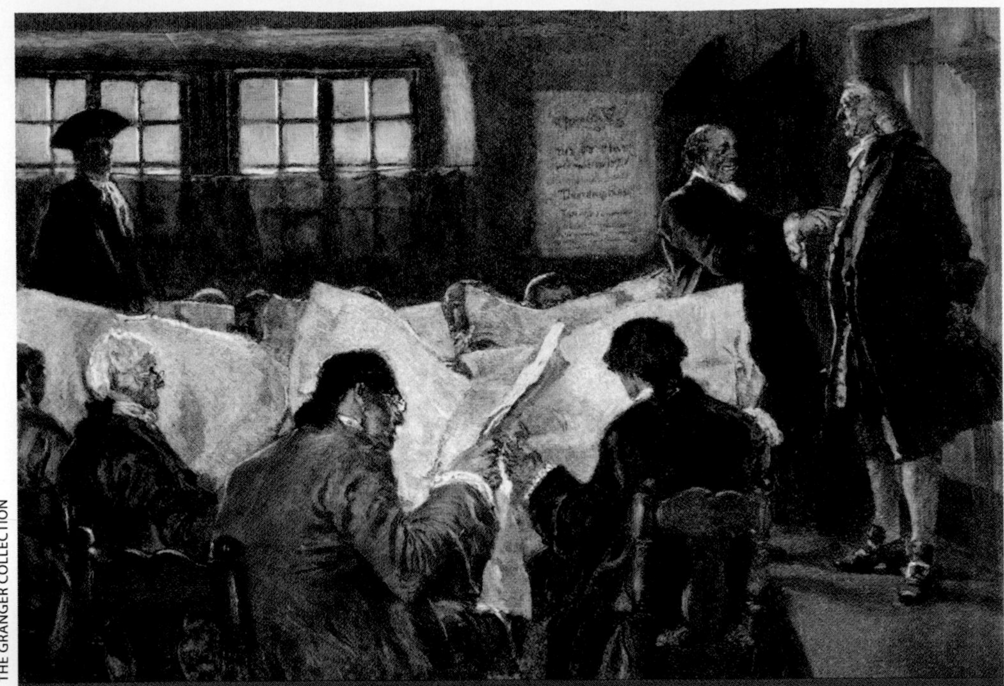

THE GRANGER COLLECTION

The fate of the proposed Constitution was decided in the state ratifying conventions, but it was the subject of intense debates everywhere—in homes, taverns, coffeehouses, and newspapers.

to let Congress have the power to regulate **interstate commerce** as well as commerce with other nations; in exchange, the Constitution guaranteed that no export taxes would ever be imposed on products exported by the states. Today, the United States is one of the few countries that does not tax its exports.

Defining the Executive and the Judiciary

The Great Compromise was reached by mid-July. Still to be determined was the makeup of the executive branch and the judiciary. One of the weaknesses of the Confederation had been the lack of an independent executive authority. The Constitution remedied this problem by creating an independent executive—the president—and by making the president the commander in chief of the army and navy and of the state militias when called into national service. The president was also given extensive appointment powers, although Senate approval was required for certain appointments.

Another problem under the Confederation was the lack of a judiciary that was independent of the state courts. The Constitution established the United States Supreme Court and authorized Congress to establish other "inferior" federal courts.

interstate commerce
Trade that involves more than one state.

To protect against possible wrongdoing, the Constitution also provided for a way to remove federal officials from office—through the impeachment process. The Constitution provides that a federal official who commits "Treason, Bribery, or other high Crimes and Misdemeanors" may be impeached (accused of, or charged with, wrongdoing) by the House of Representatives and tried by the Senate. If found guilty of the charges by a two-thirds vote in the Senate, the official can be removed from office and prevented from ever assuming another federal government post.

The Final Draft Is Approved

A five-man Committee of Detail handled the executive and judicial issues, plus other remaining work. August 6 presented a rough draft to the convention. On September 8, a committee was named to "revise the stile [style] of, and arrange the Articles which had been agreed to" by the convention. The Committee of Style was headed by Gouverneur Morris of Pennsylvania.[18] On September 17, 1787, the final draft of the Constitution was approved by thirty-nine of the remaining forty-two delegates (some delegates left early).

Looking back on the drafting of the Constitution, an obvious question emerges: Why didn't the founders ban slavery outright? Certainly, as already mentioned, many of the delegates thought that slavery was morally wrong and that the Constitution should ban it entirely. Many Americans have since regarded the framers' failure to deal with the slavery issue as a betrayal of the Declaration of Independence, which proclaimed that "all Men are created equal." Others have pointed out how contradictory it was that the framers of the Constitution complained about being "enslaved" by the British yet ignored the problem of slavery in this country.

A common argument supporting the framers' action (or lack of it) with respect to slavery is that they had no alternative but to ignore the issue. If they had taken a stand on slavery, the Constitution certainly would not have been ratified. Indeed, if the antislavery delegates had insisted on banning slavery, the delegates from the southern states might have walked out of the convention—and there would have been no Constitution to ratify.

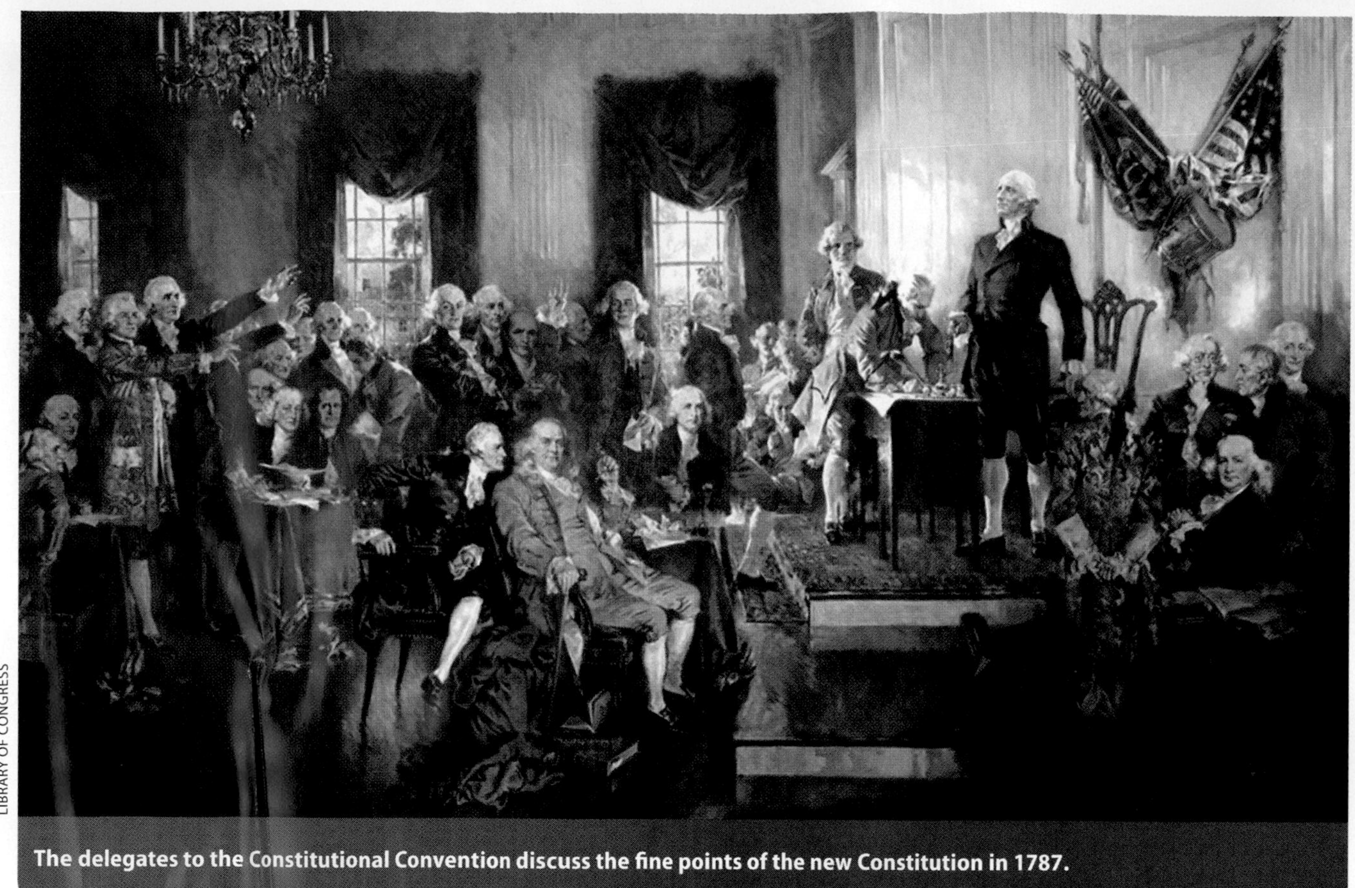
LIBRARY OF CONGRESS

The delegates to the Constitutional Convention discuss the fine points of the new Constitution in 1787.

For another look at this issue, however, see this chapter's *Perception versus Reality* feature on the following page.

The Debate over Ratification

The ratification of the Constitution set off a national debate of unprecedented proportions. The battle was fought chiefly by two opposing groups—the **Federalists** (those who favored a strong central government and the new Constitution) and the **Anti-Federalists** (those who opposed a strong central government and the new Constitution).

In the debate over ratification, the Federalists had several advantages. They assumed a positive name, leaving their opposition with a negative label. (Indeed, the Anti-Federalists could well have called themselves republicans and their opponents nationalists.) The Federalists also had attended the Constitutional Convention and thus were familiar with the arguments both in favor of and against various constitutional provisions.

The Anti-Federalists, in contrast, had no actual knowledge of those discussions because they had not attended the convention. The Federalists also had time, money, and prestige on their side. Their impressive list of political thinkers and writers included Alexander Hamilton, John Jay, and James Madison. The Federalists could communicate with one another more readily because many of them were bankers, lawyers, and merchants who lived in urban areas, where communication was easier. The Federalists organized a quick and effective ratification campaign to elect themselves as delegates to each state's ratifying convention.

THE FEDERALISTS ARGUE FOR RATIFICATION Alexander Hamilton, a leading Federalist, began to answer the Constitution's critics in New York by writing newspaper columns under the pseudonym "Caesar." The Caesar letters appeared to have little effect, so Hamilton switched his pseudonym to "Publius" and enlisted John Jay and James Madison to help him write the papers. In a period of less than a year, these three men wrote a series of eighty-five essays in defense of the Constitution. These essays, which were printed not only in New York newspapers but also in other papers throughout the states, are collectively known as the *Federalist Papers*.

Generally, the papers attempted to allay the fears expressed by the Constitution's critics. One fear was that the rights of those in the minority would not be protected. Another

Federalists A political group, led by Alexander Hamilton and John Adams, that supported the adoption of the Constitution and the creation of a federal form of government.

Anti-Federalists A political group that opposed the adoption of the Constitution because of the document's centralist tendencies and because it did not include a bill of rights.

PERCEPTION VERSUS REALITY | *The Slavery Issue*

TOMML, VISUALFIELD/ISTOCKPHOTO

In the Declaration of Independence, Thomas Jefferson, a Virginia slave owner, pronounced, "all Men are created equal." Jefferson considered slavery a "hideous blot" on America. George Washington, also a southern slave owner, regarded the institution of slavery as "repugnant." Patrick Henry, another southerner, also publicly deplored slavery. Given such views among the leading figures of the era, why didn't the founders stay true to the Declaration of Independence and free the slaves?

The Perception

Most Americans assume that southern economic interests and racism alone led the founders to abandon the principles of equality expressed in the Declaration of Independence. African slaves were the backbone of American agriculture, particularly for tobacco, the most profitable export. Without their slaves, southern plantation owners would not have been able to earn such high profits. Presumably, southerners would not have ratified the Constitution unless it protected the institution of slavery.

The Reality

The third chief justice of the United States Supreme Court, Oliver Ellsworth, declared that "as population increases, poor laborers will be so plenty as to render slaves useless. Slavery in time will not be a speck in our country."[19] He was wrong, of course. But according to Pulitzer Prize–winning historian Gordon S. Wood, Ellsworth's sentiments mirrored those of most prominent leaders in the United States in the years leading up to the creation of our Constitution. Indeed, great thinkers of the time firmly believed that the liberal principles of the Revolution would destroy the institution of slavery.

At the time of the Constitutional Convention, slavery was disappearing in the northern states (it would be eliminated there by 1804). Many founders thought the same thing would happen in the southern states. After all, there were more antislavery societies in the South than in the North. The founders also thought that the ending of the international slave trade in 1808 would eventually end slavery in the United States. Consequently, the issue of slavery was taken off the table when the Constitution was created simply because the founders had a mistaken belief about the longevity of the institution. They could not have predicted at the time that growing cotton would give slavery a new lease on life.[20]

Blog On Slavery and the Constitution is just one of many subjects that you can read about in the Legal History Blog at **legalhistoryblog.blogspot.com.** If you type "slavery" into the box at the top left of the screen and press "enter," you will see the postings on this topic.

---

was that a minority might block the passage of measures that the majority felt were in the national interest. Many critics also feared that a republican form of government would not work in a nation the size of the United States. Various groups, or **factions,** would struggle for power, and chaos would result. Madison responded to the latter argument in *Federalist Paper* No. 10 (see Appendix F), which is considered a classic in political theory. Among other things, Madison argued that the nation's size was actually an advantage in controlling factions: in a large nation, there would be so many diverse interests and factions that no one faction would be able to gain control of the government.[21]

faction A group of persons forming a cohesive minority.

tyranny The arbitrary or unrestrained exercise of power by an oppressive individual or government.

THE ANTI-FEDERALISTS' RESPONSE Perhaps the greatest advantage of the Anti-Federalists was that they stood for the status quo. Usually, it is more difficult to institute changes than it is to keep what is already known and understood. Among the Anti-Federalists were such patriots as Patrick Henry and Samuel Adams. Patrick Henry said of the proposed Constitution: "I look upon that paper as the most fatal plan that could possibly be conceived to enslave a free people."

In response to the *Federalist Papers,* the Anti-Federalists published their own essays, using such pseudonyms as "Montezuma" and "Philadelphiensis." They also wrote brilliantly, attacking nearly every clause of the new document. Many Anti-Federalists contended that the Constitution had been written by aristocrats and would lead the nation to aristocratic **tyranny** (the exercise of absolute, unlimited power). Other Anti-

Federalists feared that the Constitution would lead to an overly powerful central government that would limit personal freedom.[22]

The Anti-Federalists strongly argued that the Constitution needed a bill of rights. They warned that without a bill of rights, a strong national government might take away the political rights won during the American Revolution. They demanded that the new Constitution clearly guarantee personal freedoms. The Federalists generally did not think that a bill of rights was all that important. Nevertheless, to gain the necessary support, the Federalists finally promised to add a bill of rights to the Constitution as the first order of business under the new government. This promise turned the tide in favor of the Constitution.

Ratification

The contest for ratification was close in several states, but the Federalists finally won in all of the state conventions. In 1787, Delaware, Pennsylvania, and New Jersey voted to ratify the Constitution, followed by Georgia and Connecticut early in the following year. Even though the Anti-Federalists were perhaps the majority in Massachusetts, a successful political campaign by the Federalists led to ratification by that state on February 6, 1788.

Following Maryland and South Carolina, New Hampshire became the ninth state to ratify the Constitution on June 21, 1788, thus formally putting the Constitution into effect. New York and Virginia had not yet ratified, however, and without them the Constitution would have no true power. That worry was dispelled in the summer of 1788, when both Virginia and New York ratified the new Constitution. North Carolina waited until November 21 of the following year to ratify the Constitution, and Rhode Island did not ratify until May 29, 1790.

LO5 *The Constitution's Major Principles of Government*

The framers of the Constitution were fearful of the powerful British monarchy, against which they had so recently rebelled. At the same time, they wanted a central government strong enough to prevent the kinds of crises that had occurred under the weak central authority of the Articles of Confederation. The principles of government expressed in the Constitution reflect both of these concerns.

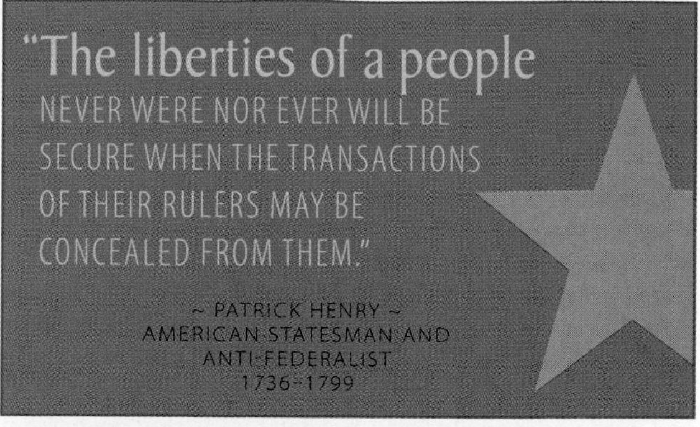

"The liberties of a people
NEVER WERE NOR EVER WILL BE
SECURE WHEN THE TRANSACTIONS
OF THEIR RULERS MAY BE
CONCEALED FROM THEM."
~ PATRICK HENRY ~
AMERICAN STATESMAN AND
ANTI-FEDERALIST
1736–1799

Limited Government and Popular Sovereignty

The Constitution incorporated the principle of limited government, which means that government can do only what the people allow it to do through the exercise of a duly developed system of laws. This principle can be found in many parts of the Constitution. For example, while Articles I, II, and III indicate exactly what the national government *can* do, the first nine amendments to the Constitution list the ways in which the government *cannot* limit certain individual freedoms.

Implicitly, the principle of limited government rests on the concept of popular sovereignty. Remember the phrases that frame the Preamble to the Constitution: "We the People of the United States . . . do ordain and establish this Constitution for the United States of America." In other words, it is the people who form the government and decide on the powers that the government can exercise. If the government exercises powers beyond those granted to it by the Constitution, it is acting illegally. The idea that no one, including government officers, is above the law is often called the **rule of law.**

Ultimately, the viability of a democracy rests on the willingness of the people and their leaders to adhere to the rule of law. A nation's written constitution, such as that of Iraq under the dictator Saddam Hussein, may guarantee numerous rights and liberties for its citizens. Yet, unless the government of that nation enforces those rights and liberties, the law does not rule the nation. Rather, the government decides what the rules will be. Consider the situation in Russia today. After the collapse of the Soviet Union, Russia established a federal republic. By all appearances, though, Vladimir Putin, Russia's leader, is not constrained by the principles set forth in Russia's constitution—see this chapter's *The Rest of the World* feature on the following page for details.

rule of law A basic principle of government that requires those who govern to act in accordance with established law.

THE REST OF THE WORLD

Russia's Short-Lived Flirtation with Democracy

From the Russian Revolution in 1917 to the end of the Soviet Union in 1991, Russians lived under a Communist dictatorship. For centuries prior to 1917, they had lived under an autocracy headed by a tsar. In short, Russians had no experience with democracy before the fall of the Soviet Union.

A Democracy at Last . . .

On December 25, 1993, the Russian Federation (its formal name) saw its first independent constitution. If you read a translation of that constitution, you would conclude that modern Russia is now a democracy. That conclusion seemed to be true for a number of years because Russians freely voted for members of the Duma (the Russian counterpart of our Congress). They voted overwhelmingly in favor of President Vladimir Putin in 2000, too. Western commentators expressed some concern that Putin was formerly the head of the Soviet Union's brutal secret police. Nevertheless, after meeting Putin, President George W. Bush said, "I looked him in the eyes, and I know I can work with this man."

. . . or Not

Perhaps Putin showed his true colors when he referred to the collapse of the Soviet Union as "the greatest geopolitical catastrophe of the twentieth century." Under Putin, freedom of the press all but disappeared—the state simultaneously shut down independent sources of information and expanded government ownership of the media. A formerly promising independent court system all but vanished. In 2005, the election of regional governors was abolished. Governors are now appointed by the president. Beginning in 2006, Putin's administration instituted electoral reforms so that his political party, United Russia, was guaranteed control of the Duma and the presidency. The government won the right to exclude candidates from party slates and to bar parties from running altogether.

Increasingly, Russian authorities arrested and detained public activists. In the economy, the Russian government gradually took control of all oil, natural gas, and other natural resources. Anyone who did not go along with Putin ended up in prison.

The Russian Public's Reaction

Are Russian citizens worried about this reversion to an undemocratic state? Apparently not, for public opinion polls in Russia have shown that more than 80 percent of the Russian people approve of Putin's "strong leadership."

In March 2008, Putin's second term as president came to an end, and under the constitution he could not immediately run again. Instead, he sponsored the election of Dmitry Medvedev, a supporter, as president. Medvedev named Putin as Russia's prime minister, and events soon proved that Putin still held the real power in the government. Putin has hinted that he may return as president in 2012. Given that in that year the presidential term will expand from four years to six, Putin could remain in power until 2024.

For Critical Analysis *Why do you think so many Russians are unconcerned about the erosion of democracy in their country?*

federal system A form of government that provides for a division of powers between a central government and several regional governments. In the United States, the division of powers between the national government and the states is established by the Constitution.

commerce clause The clause in Article I, Section 8, of the Constitution that gives Congress the power to regulate interstate commerce (commerce involving more than one state).

The Principle of Federalism

The Constitution also incorporated the principle of federalism. In a **federal system** of government, the central (national) government shares sovereign powers with the various state governments. Federalism was the solution to the debate over whether the national government or the states should have ultimate sovereignty.

The Constitution gave the national government significant powers—powers that it had not had under the Articles of Confederation. For example, the Constitution expressly states that the president is the nation's chief executive as well as the commander in chief of the armed forces. The Constitution also declares that the Constitution and the laws created by the national government are supreme—that is, they take precedence over conflicting state laws. Other powers given to the national government include the power to coin money, to levy and collect taxes, and to regulate interstate commerce, a power granted by the **commerce clause.** Finally, the national government was authorized to undertake all laws that are "necessary and proper" for carrying out its expressly delegated powers.

The founders granted the federal government exclusive rights over creating money because in previous years, several states had printed excessive quantities of paper money, thus devaluing the currency. How might the founders react to the way in which today's federal government manages the money supply? Consider that question as you read this chapter's *Our Government Faces a Troubled Economy* feature on the following page.

"The truth is that all men having power **OUGHT TO BE MISTRUSTED.**"
~ JAMES MADISON ~
FOURTH PRESIDENT OF THE UNITED STATES
1809–1817

Because the states feared too much centralized control, the Constitution also allowed for many states' rights. These rights include the power to regulate commerce within state borders and generally the authority to exercise any powers that are not delegated by the Constitution to the central government. (See Chapter 3 for a detailed discussion of federalism.)

Separation of Powers

As James Madison once said, after you have given the government the ability to control its citizens, you have to "oblige it to control itself." To force the government to "control itself" and to prevent the rise of tyranny, Madison devised a scheme, the **Madisonian Model,** in which the powers of the national government were separated into different branches: legislative, executive, and judicial.[23] The legislative branch (Congress) passes laws; the executive branch (the president) administers and enforces the laws; and the judicial branch (the courts) interprets the laws. By separating the powers of government, the framers ensured that no one branch would have enough power to dominate the others. This principle of **separation of powers** is laid out in Articles I, II, and III of the Constitution.

Madisonian Model The model of government devised by James Madison, in which the powers of the government are separated into three branches: executive, legislative, and judicial.

separation of powers The principle of dividing governmental powers among the executive, the legislative, and the judicial branches of government.

checks and balances A major principle of American government in which each of the three branches is given the means to check (to restrain or balance) the actions of the others.

veto power A constitutional power that enables the chief executive (president or governor) to reject legislation and return it to the legislature with reasons for the rejection. This prevents or at least delays the bill from becoming law.

Checks and Balances

A system of **checks and balances** was also devised to ensure that no one group or branch of government can exercise exclusive control. Even though each branch of government is independent of the others, it can also check the actions of the others. Look at Figure 2–5 on page 41, and you can see how this is done. As the figure shows, the president checks Congress by holding a **veto power,** which is the ability to return bills to Congress for reconsideration. Congress, in turn, controls taxes and spending, and the Senate must approve presidential appointments. The judicial branch of government can also check the other branches of government through *judicial review*—the power to rule congressional or presidential actions unconstitutional.[24] In turn, the president and the Senate exercise some control over the judiciary through the president's power to appoint federal judges and the Senate's role in confirming presidential appointments.

Among the other checks and balances built into the American system of government are staggered terms of office. Members of the House of Representatives serve for

James Madison (1751–1836). Madison's contributions at the Constitutional Convention in 1787 earned him the title "Master Builder of the Constitution." As a member of Congress from Virginia, he advocated the Bill of Rights. He was secretary of state under Thomas Jefferson (1801–1809) and became our fourth president in 1809.

Our Government Faces a Troubled Economy

Printing Money to Fight a Recession

The U.S. Constitution in Article I, Section 8, gave Congress the power "To borrow Money on the credit of the United States" and "To coin Money [and] regulate the value thereof." The framers of the Constitution would probably be shocked at what the federal government has done with the supply of money in circulation in this country.

What Is Monetary Policy?

Monetary policy involves changing the amount of money in circulation to affect interest rates, credit markets, the rate of inflation, the rate of economic growth, and the rate of unemployment. Monetary policy is not under the direct control of Congress and the president. Instead, it is determined by the Federal Reserve System (the Fed), an independent agency. The Fed is controlled by a board of seven governors, including the very powerful chairperson, currently Ben Bernanke. The president appoints the members of the board of governors, and the Senate must approve the nominations.

The Fed's Response to the Great Depression

The Fed was created to be the "lender of last resort" for the banking system, a bank that could lend to other banks when no one else would. It turns out that as the Great Depression took hold in the 1930s, the Fed acted in the opposite manner. Indeed, many scholars argue that the Fed was responsible for the severity of the Great Depression because it allowed the money supply in circulation to fall by fully one-third by 1933. The result was a severe contraction in economic activity.

Monetary Policy during the Current Economic Crisis

When the Great Recession began in December 2007, the Fed at first appeared not quite sure what to do. When the crisis became acute in September 2008, the Fed went

AP PHOTO/DOUG MILLS

along with the Bush administration's request to Congress to provide a fund of $700 billion to bail out the banks. In an attempt to restart borrowing and lending, the Fed pushed the interest rate on short-term government debt down almost to zero. When this turned out not to be sufficient, the Fed began doing something it had never done before. It started buying huge quantities of debt directly from the private sector—bonds backed up by mortgages, credit-card debt, and student loans. In effect, if banks were reluctant to lend, the Fed would do the lending itself. This practice has been named "quantitative easing." These purchases have the effect of creating new money and expanding the money supply.

What the Future Holds

Some economists fear that by creating money in this way, the Fed has guaranteed that inflation will be a serious problem when the recession comes to an end. True, for the moment, the newly created money simply replaces funds that are "parked by the curb"—that is, pulled out of action by institutions and investors that are afraid to lend. Sooner or later, though, that sidelined money will be put to work again, and that's when inflation becomes a danger. Will the Fed be able to react quickly enough to prevent a big rise in prices? The historical record is not encouraging.

You Be the Judge **Why do you think Congress gave control over monetary policy to an independent body?**

Figure 2–5

Checks and Balances among the Branches of Government

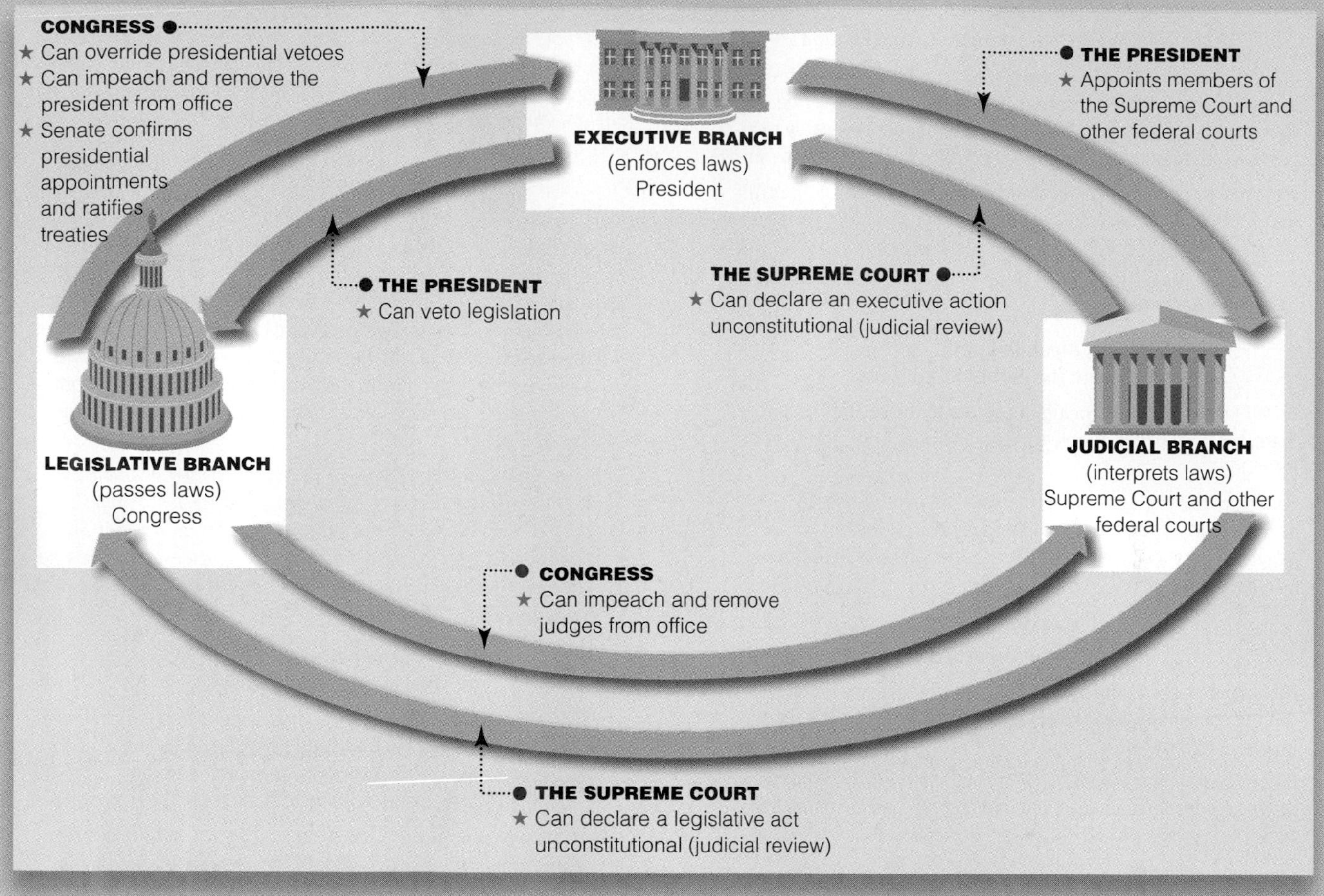

CONGRESS
★ Can override presidential vetoes
★ Can impeach and remove the president from office
★ Senate confirms presidential appointments and ratifies treaties
EXECUTIVE BRANCH
(enforces laws)
President
THE PRESIDENT
★ Appoints members of the Supreme Court and other federal courts
THE PRESIDENT
★ Can veto legislation
THE SUPREME COURT
★ Can declare an executive action unconstitutional (judicial review)
LEGISLATIVE BRANCH
(passes laws)
Congress
JUDICIAL BRANCH
(interprets laws)
Supreme Court and other federal courts
CONGRESS
★ Can impeach and remove judges from office
THE SUPREME COURT
★ Can declare a legislative act unconstitutional (judicial review)

two years, members of the Senate for six, and the president for four. Federal court judges are appointed for life but may be impeached and removed from office by Congress for misconduct. Staggered terms and changing government personnel make it difficult for individuals within the government to form controlling factions. The American system of government also includes numerous other checks and balances, many of which you will read about in later chapters of this book. We look next at another obvious check on the powers of government: the Bill of Rights.

The Bill of Rights

To secure the ratification of the Constitution in several important states, the Federalists had to provide assurances that amendments would be passed to protect individual liberties against violations by the national government. At the state ratifying conventions, delegates set forth specific rights that should be protected. James Madison considered these recommendations as he labored to draft what became the Bill of Rights.

After sorting through more than two hundred state recommendations, Madison came up with sixteen amendments. Congress tightened the language somewhat and eliminated four of the amendments. Of the remaining twelve, two—one dealing with the apportionment of representatives and the other with the compensation of the members of Congress—were not ratified by the states during the ratification process.[25] By 1791, all of the states had ratified the ten amendments that now constitute our Bill of Rights. Table 2–2 on the following page presents the text of the first ten amendments to the Constitution, along with explanatory comments. Note that many phrases in the Bill of Rights are imprecise and call for further judicial interpretation. For example, what exactly did the founders mean by "cruel and unusual punishments" (Eighth Amendment)? We consider that issue in this chapter's *Join the Debate* feature on page 43.

Table 2–2

The Bill of Rights

Amendment I.
Religion, Speech, Press, Assembly, and Petition

Congress shall make no law respecting an establishment of religion, or prohibiting the free exercise thereof; or abridging the freedom of speech, or of the press; or the right of the people peaceably to assemble, and to petition the Government for a redress of grievances.

Congress may not create an official church or enact laws limiting the freedom of religion, speech, the press, assembly, and petition. These guarantees, like the others in the Bill of Rights (the first ten amendments), are not absolute—each may be exercised only with regard to the rights of other persons.

Amendment II.
Militia and the Right to Bear Arms

A well regulated Militia, being necessary to the security of a free State, the right of the people to keep and bear Arms, shall not be infringed.

Each state has the right to maintain a volunteer armed force. Although individuals have the right to bear arms, states and the federal government may regulate the possession and use of firearms by individuals.

Amendment III.
The Quartering of Soldiers

No Soldier shall, in time of peace be quartered in any house, without the consent of the Owner, nor in time of war, but in a manner to be prescribed by law.

Before the Revolutionary War, it had been common British practice to quarter soldiers in colonists' homes. Military troops do not have the power to take over private houses during peacetime.

Amendment IV.
Searches and Seizures

The right of the people to be secure in their persons, houses, papers, and effects, against unreasonable searches and seizures, shall not be violated, and no Warrants shall issue, but upon probable cause, supported by Oath or affirmation, and particularly describing the place to be searched, and the persons or things to be seized.

Here, the word warrant *refers to a document issued by a magistrate or judge indicating the name, address, and possible offense committed. Anyone asking for the warrant, such as a police officer, must be able to convince the magistrate or judge that an offense probably has been committed.*

Amendment V.
Grand Juries, Self-Incrimination, Double Jeopardy, Due Process, and Eminent Domain

No person shall be held to answer for a capital, or otherwise infamous crime, unless on a presentment or indictment of a Grand Jury, except in cases arising in the land or naval forces, or in the Militia, when in actual service in time of War or public danger; nor shall any person be subject for the same offense to be twice put in jeopardy of life or limb; nor shall be compelled in any criminal case to be a witness against himself, nor be deprived of life, liberty, or property, without due process of law; nor shall private property be taken for public use, without just compensation.

There are two types of juries. A grand jury considers physical evidence and the testimony of witnesses and decides whether there is sufficient reason to bring a case to trial. A petit jury hears the case at trial and decides it. "For the same offense to be twice put in jeopardy of life or limb" means to be tried twice for the same crime. A person may not be tried for the same crime twice or forced to give evidence against herself or himself. No person's right to life, liberty, or property may be taken away except by lawful means, called the due process of law. Private property taken for public purposes must be paid for by the government.

Amendment VI.
Criminal Court Procedures

In all criminal prosecutions, the accused shall enjoy the right to a speedy and public trial, by an impartial jury of the State and district wherein the crime shall have been committed, which district shall have been previously ascertained by law, and to be informed of the nature and cause of the accusation; to be confronted with the witnesses against him; to have compulsory process for obtaining witnesses in his favor, and to have the Assistance of Counsel for his defence.

Any person accused of a crime has the right to a fair and public trial by a jury in the state in which the crime took place. The charges against that person must be so indicated. Any accused person has the right to a lawyer to defend him or her and to question those who testify against him or her, as well as the right to call people to speak in his or her favor at trial.

Amendment VII.
Trial by Jury in Civil Cases

In Suits at common law, where the value in controversy shall exceed twenty dollars, the right of trial by jury shall be preserved, and no fact tried by a jury, shall be otherwise re-examined in any Court of the United States, than according to the rules of the common law.

A jury trial may be requested by either party in a dispute in any case involving more than $20. If both parties agree to a trial by a judge without a jury, the right to a jury trial may be put aside.

Amendment VIII.
Bail, Cruel and Unusual Punishment

Excessive bail shall not be required, nor excessive fines imposed, nor cruel and unusual punishments inflicted.

Bail is that amount of money that a person accused of a crime may be required to deposit with the court as a guarantee that she or he will appear in court when requested. The amount of bail required or the fine imposed as punishment for a crime must be reasonable compared with the seriousness of the crime involved. Any punishment judged to be too harsh or too severe for a crime shall be prohibited.

Amendment IX.
The Rights Retained by the People

The enumeration in the Constitution, of certain rights, shall not be construed to deny or disparage others retained by the people.

Many civil rights that are not explicitly enumerated in the Constitution are still held by the people.

Amendment X.
Reserved Powers of the States

The powers not delegated to the United States by the Constitution, nor prohibited by it to the States, are reserved to the States respectively, or to the people.

Those powers not delegated by the Constitution to the federal government or expressly denied to the states belong to the states and to the people. This clause in essence allows the states to pass laws under their "police powers."

JOIN THE DEBATE

Is the Death Penalty a Cruel and Unusual Punishment?

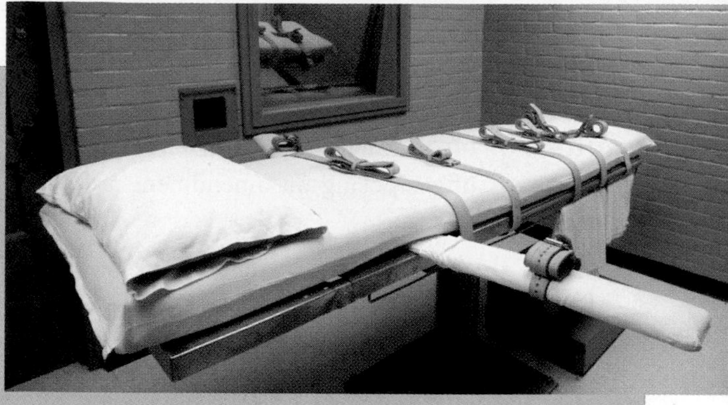
AP PHOTO/PAT SULLIVAN

The Eighth Amendment to the U.S. Constitution explicitly states that the government cannot inflict "cruel and unusual punishments." It is also true that criminals have been executed since the earliest days of the republic.

Even before there were prisons in America, we had the death penalty, also called "capital punishment." In 1608, a man named George Kendall was executed by a firing squad in Virginia on charges of spying for Spain. Since Kendall's time, more than 18,000 Americans have been executed as punishment for their crimes. In addition to murder, a variety of other crimes have been punished by death in this country. In the 1700s, citizens were executed for robbery, forgery, and illegally cutting down trees.

No state executes people for such crimes today. In our modern world, though, is the death penalty itself cruel and unusual, and therefore a violation of the Eighth Amendment?

An Eye for an Eye Makes the Whole World Blind

Some argue that the death penalty is inappropriate even for someone who has committed murder. Violence and death may always be with us, but the law should not encourage violent sentiments. Already in 1764, the Italian jurist Cesare Beccaria asserted that "the death penalty cannot be useful, because of the example of barbarity it gives men."

As United States Supreme Court justice Arthur J. Goldberg once wrote, "The deliberate institutionalized taking of human life by the state is the greatest conceivable degradation of the dignity of a human personality." Face it—capital punishment is barbaric whether it is carried out by a firing squad, an electric chair, a gas chamber, lethal injection, or hanging. Nations other than the United States that permit capital punishment are not ones that we would seek to emulate: they include China, Iran, North Korea, and Saudi Arabia. Almost all of our allies have abolished the practice.

There Is Nothing Cruel and Unusual about Executing a Murderer

Strangely enough, some who are against capital punishment have argued that life in prison without parole is even crueler than death. Prisoners are confined in an environment of violence where they are treated like animals, and the suffering goes on for decades. If you think about it, this is an argument that the death sentence can be merciful. In any event, capital punishment is not cruel and unusual as meant by the Eighth Amendment. Indeed, the current method of execution used in most states—lethal injection—appears quite civilized compared with methods of execution used in England back in the 1700s, which included drawing and quartering and burning at the stake. Practices such as these are what the founders sought to ban.

For Critical Analysis ***Can there be a humane method of extinguishing someone's life? Why or why not?***

Amending the Constitution

Since the Constitution was written, more than eleven thousand amendments have been introduced in Congress. Nonetheless, in the years since the ratification of the Bill of Rights, the first ten amendments to the Constitution, only seventeen proposed amendments have actually survived the amendment process and become a part of our Constitution. It is often contended that members of Congress use the amendment process simply as a political ploy. By proposing an amendment, a member of Congress can show her or his position on an issue, knowing that the odds *against* the amendment's being adopted are high.

One of the reasons there are so few amendments is that the framers, in Article V, made the formal amendment process difficult (although it was easier than it had been under the Articles of Confederation, as just discussed). There are two ways to propose an amendment and two ways to ratify one. As a result, there are four possible ways for an amendment to be added to the Constitution.

METHODS OF PROPOSING AN AMENDMENT The two methods of proposing an amendment are as follows:

1. A two-thirds vote in the Senate and in the House of Representatives is required. All of the twenty-seven existing amendments have been proposed in this way.
2. If two-thirds of the state legislatures request that Congress call a national amendment convention, then Congress must call one. The convention may propose amendments to the states for ratification. There has yet to be a successful amendment proposal using this method.

Independence Hall in Philadelphia.

The notion of a national amendment convention is exciting to many people. Many national political and judicial leaders, however, are very uneasy about the prospect of convening a body that conceivably could do what the Constitutional Convention did—create a new form of government.

In two separate instances, the call for a national amendment convention almost became reality. Between 1963 and 1969, thirty-three state legislatures (out of the necessary thirty-four) attempted to call a convention to amend the Constitution to overturn the Supreme Court's "one person, one vote" decisions (see Chapter 11). Since 1975, thirty-two states have asked for a national convention to propose an amendment requiring that the federal government balance its budget. Generally, the major national convention campaigns have reflected dissatisfaction on the part of conservative and rural groups with the national government's social and economic policies.

METHODS OF RATIFYING AN AMENDMENT There are two methods of ratifying a proposed amendment:

1. Three-fourths of the state legislatures can vote in favor of the proposed amendment. This method is considered the "traditional" ratification method and has been used twenty-six times.
2. The states can call special conventions to ratify the proposed amendment. If three-fourths of the states approve, the amendment is ratified. This method has been used only once—to ratify the Twenty-first Amendment.[26]

You can see the four methods for proposing and ratifying amendments in Figure 2–6 at left. As you can imagine, to meet the requirements for proposal and ratification, any amendment must have wide popular support in all regions of the country.

Figure 2–6

The Process of Amending the Constitution

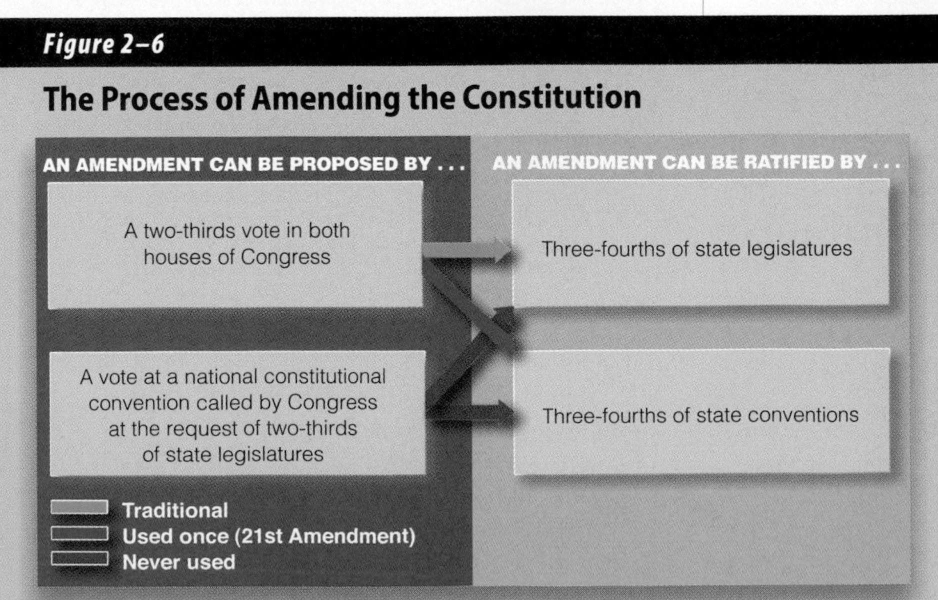
AN AMENDMENT CAN BE PROPOSED BY . . .
AN AMENDMENT CAN BE RATIFIED BY . . .
A two-thirds vote in both houses of Congress
A vote at a national constitutional convention called by Congress at the request of two-thirds of state legislatures
Three-fourths of state legislatures
Three-fourths of state conventions
Traditional
Used once (21st Amendment)
Never used

AMERICA AT ODDS *The Constitution*

Americans engaged in intense disputes about the ratification of the Constitution, as you have learned in this chapter. The most important of these disputes was over the relative power of the states and the national government. This dispute is central to the topic of federalism, which we will take up in Chapter 3. Proposed constitutional amendments have also been the source of many controversies throughout U.S. history. These controversies include the following:

- The Equal Rights Amendment of 1972 stated: "Equality of rights under the law shall not be denied or abridged by the United States or by any state on account of sex." The amendment failed to win approval from enough states. Should it be revived—or are equal rights for women unacceptable because women could not then be exempted from a military draft?
- Members of the Tea Party movement have advocated the repeal of the Seventeenth Amendment, which transferred the election of U.S. senators from state legislatures to the people of the respective states. The argument is that giving the choice of senators back to state legislatures would strengthen the relative power of the states. Is this a good argument—or is popular election of senators the superior system?
- Conservatives have campaigned for a constitutional amendment to ban same-sex marriage. Would such a measure be desirable—or repugnant as the first attempt to write a limit on freedoms into the Constitution?
- What about an amendment to ban the destruction of the American flag as an act of protest? Is such a ban important to the dignity of our fallen soldiers—or would it be an unacceptable limit on free speech?

Take Action

As you have read, the founders envisioned that the Constitution, to remain relevant, would need to be changed over time. You can take action over the Constitution by supporting a proposed constitutional amendment. Currently, two organized efforts seek constitutional amendments—the Tea Party movement and a campaign to limit corporate campaign contributions.

Members of the Tea Party movement could be described as obsessed with the Constitution. Some carry copies of the document with them at all times. Perhaps the best summary of Tea Party ideas is expressed in the "Contract *from* America," which you can find at www.thecontract.org/support. This document has been endorsed by many local Tea Party organizations. The contract endorses "individual liberty, limited government, and economic freedom." The document also calls for amending the Constitution to require a balanced budget and impose a two-thirds-majority requirement for tax increases. If these ideas appeal to you, the Tea Party Patriots Web site provides a long list of local groups at www.teapartypatriots.org.

If you are more concerned about the dangers of big business than big government, several groups support a constitutional amendment to overturn the Supreme Court's 2010 decision *Citizens United v. the Federal Election Commission.* In this ruling, the Court found that corporations (and presumably labor unions) have the same free speech rights as individual persons. The Court therefore overturned decades of legislation governing campaign finance. Many progressives fear that the result will be a tsunami of political corporate cash. Public interest groups opposed to the ruling have organized Free Speech for People, freespeechforpeople.org, which offers a wide range of possible ways to get involved in the campaign. Other active groups are Move to Amend at movetoamend.org and People for the American Way at www.pfaw.org/get-involved/take-action.

SAMUEL PEEBLES/*EL DORADO NEWS-TIMES*/AP

Amendments that would prohibit the burning of the American flag have been proposed in the past, but none has ever been ratified and become a part of the U.S. Constitution.

POLITICS ON THE WEB

- A World Wide Web version of the Constitution provides hypertext links to amendments and other changes. Go to **topics.law.cornell.edu/constitution**
- The National Constitution Center in Philadelphia has a Web page at **www.constitutioncenter.org**. The site offers basic facts about the Constitution plus Constitution puzzles.
- James Madison's notes are one of our most important sources for the debates and exchanges that took place during the Constitutional Convention. These notes are now online at **www.thisnation.com/library/madison**
- An online version of the Anti-Federalist Papers is available at the Web site of the West El Paso Information Network (WEPIN). Go to **wepin.com/articles/afp**
- For information on the effect of new computer and communications technologies on the constitutional rights and liberties of Americans, go to the Center for Democracy and Technology at **www.cdt.org**
- The constitutions of almost all of the states are online. You can find them at **www.findlaw.com/11stategov**
- You can find constitutions of other countries at **www.servat.unibe.ch/icl**

Access CourseMate to review and expand on this chapter through quizzes, flashcards, learning objectives, interactive timelines, a crossword puzzle, audio summaries, video, critical-thinking activities, simulations, and more.

GOVT 3

Federalism

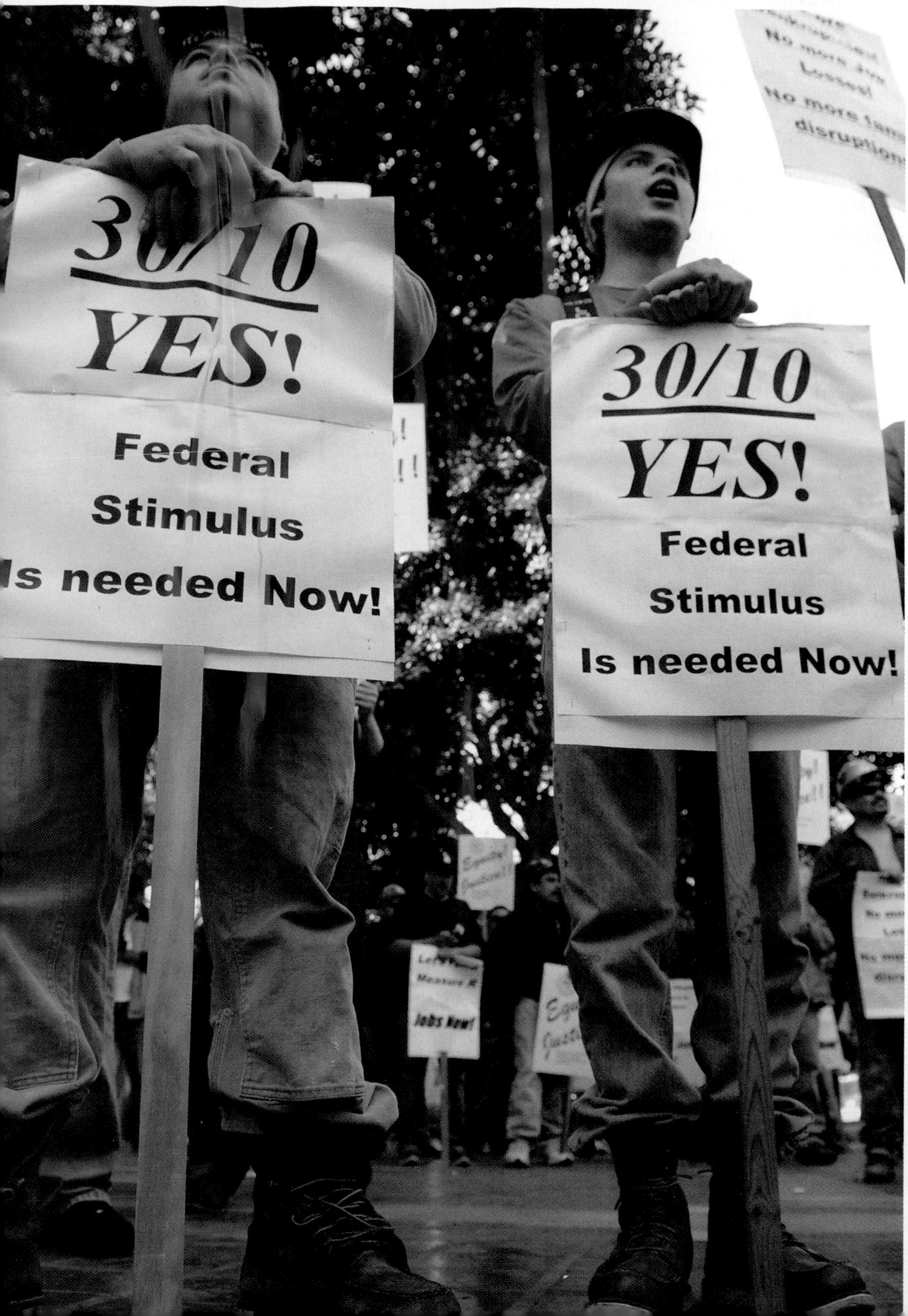

LEARNING OBJECTIVES

LO1 Explain what federalism means, how federalism differs from other systems of government, and why it exists in the United States.

LO2 Indicate how the Constitution divides governing powers in our federal system.

LO3 Summarize the evolution of federal-state relationships in the United States over time.

LO4 Describe developments in federalism in recent years.

LO5 Explain what is meant by the term *fiscal federalism.*

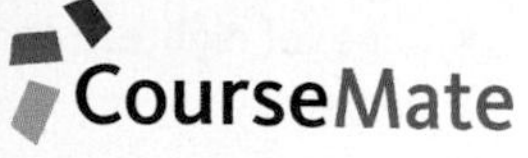

AMERICA AT ODDS

Should the States Lower the Drinking Age?

Our political system is a federal one in which power is shared between the states and the federal government. The Tenth Amendment to the U.S. Constitution reserves all powers not delegated to the national government to the states and to the people. Nonetheless, the federal government has been able to exercise power over matters that traditionally have been under the control of state governments, such as the minimum age for drinking alcoholic beverages. The federal government has been able to do so by its ability to give or withhold federal grants. The provision of grants to the states by the federal government is known as *fiscal federalism,* and these grants give the federal government considerable influence over state policies.

In the 1980s, for example, the national government wanted the states to raise the minimum drinking age to twenty-one years. States that refused to do so were threatened with the loss of federal highway construction funds. The threat worked—it was not long before all of the states had changed their minimum-drinking-age laws. In the 1990s, Congress used the same threat to encourage the states to lower their blood-alcohol limits for drunk driving to 0.08 percent by 2004. Again, states that failed to comply faced reductions in federal highway funds.

It's Time to End This Charade—College Students Still Drink

Underage drinking did not disappear when the minimum-drinking-age requirement was raised to twenty-one years. Indeed, the problem got worse. Millions of young people today are, in effect, criminals, because they are breaking the law by drinking. Moreover, the law encourages young people to binge in secret in order to avoid apprehension and prosecution by the local police. The minimum drinking age of twenty-one years has not reduced drunk driving among teenagers, because it is largely unenforceable. Additionally, it has bred contempt for the law in general among teenagers. That is why a group of 135 U.S. college presidents and chancellors endorsed the Amethyst Initiative, a movement calling for the reconsideration of U.S. drinking-age laws. Prohibition did not work in the 1920s, and prohibiting those under twenty-one from drinking will not work in the twenty-first century. Almost no other country has such a high minimum drinking age. It is time to lower the drinking age everywhere in the United States. Responsible drinking can be taught through role modeling by parents and through educational programs.

Keep the Age-Twenty-One Requirement Because It's Working

Mothers Against Drunk Driving (MADD) leads the opposition to lowering the drinking age. That group contends that the current drinking-age laws have saved more than twenty thousand lives. The National Transportation Safety Board, the American Medical Association, and the Insurance Institute for Highway Safety all agree. After all, young persons' brains are not fully developed, so they are more susceptible to alcohol. When the drinking age limit is twenty-one, it helps to protect young people from being pressured to drink. Teenagers who drink are a danger not only to themselves but also to others—particularly when driving. Young people away at college must deal with enough new responsibilities. They don't need drinking as yet another problem. Fatalities involving eighteen- to twenty-year-old drivers have decreased since the laws establishing the minimum drinking age of twenty-one were enacted. These laws are working as planned, so we should keep them.

WHERE DO YOU STAND?

1. **Is it appropriate to compare what happened during the era of Prohibition, when *all* drinking was illegal, to what is happening to teenagers today, when the minimum drinking age is twenty-one? Why or why not?**
2. **"One can join the military at the age of eighteen and die for this country, so it is absurd not to allow those between the ages of eighteen and twenty-one to drink." Analyze this statement.**

EXPLORE THIS ISSUE ONLINE

- **Professor David Hanson, of the State University of New York at Potsdam, maintains a Web site that explores alcohol-related issues, including the minimum-drinking-age controversy. You can find it at www2.potsdam.edu/hansondj.**
- **You can find an academic study of college-age drinking by researchers at the Harvard School of Public Health at www.hsph.harvard.edu/cas/Documents/underminimum/DrinkingBehavior.pdf.**
- **The Mothers Against Drunk Driving (MADD) site is at www.madd.org. You can find a related organization, Students Against Destructive Decisions (SADD), at www.sadd.org.**

Introduction

The controversy over the drinking age is just one example of how different levels of government in our federal system can be at odds with one another. Let's face it—those who work for the national government based in Washington, D.C., would like the states to fully cooperate with the national government in the implementation of national policies. At the same time, those who work in state government don't like to be told what to do by the national government, especially when the implementation of a national policy is costly for the states. Finally, those who work in local governments would like to run their affairs with the least amount of interference from both their state governments and the national government.

Such conflicts arise because our government is based on the principle of **federalism,** which means that government powers are shared by the national government and the states. When the founders of this nation opted for federalism, they created a practical and flexible form of government capable of enduring for centuries. At the same time, however, they planted the seeds for future conflict between the states and the national government over how government powers should be shared. As you will read in this chapter—and throughout this book—many of today's most pressing issues have to do with which level of government should exercise certain powers. Sometimes two levels of government collaborate. For example, California and the federal government jointly manage the Redwood National Park.

The relationship between the national government and the governments at the state and local levels has never been free of conflict. Indeed, even before the Constitution was adopted, the Federalists and Anti-Federalists engaged in a heated debate over the issue of national versus state powers. As you learned in Chapter 2, the Federalists won the day by convincing Americans to adopt the Constitution. The Anti-Federalists' concern for states' rights, however, has surfaced again and again in the course of our history.

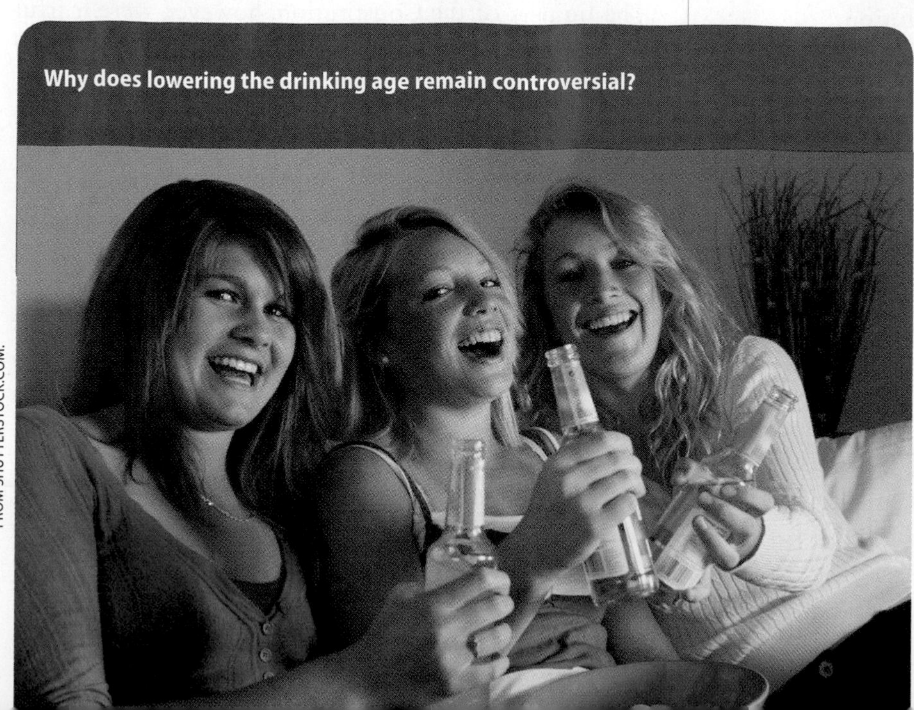

Why does lowering the drinking age remain controversial?

LO1 Federalism and Its Alternatives

There are various ways of ordering relations between central governments and local units. Federalism is one of these ways. Learning about federalism and how it differs from other forms of government is important to understanding the American political system.

What Is Federalism?

Nowhere in the Constitution does the word *federalism* appear. This is understandable, given that the concept of federalism was an invention of the founders. Since the Federalists and the Anti-Federalists argued more than two hundred years ago about what form of government we should have, hundreds of definitions of federalism have been offered. Basically, though, as mentioned in Chapter 2, in a *federal system,* government powers are divided between a central government and regional, or subdivisional, governments.

Although this definition seems straightforward, its application certainly is not. After all, virtually all nations—even the most repressive totalitarian regimes—have some kind of subnational governmental units. Thus, the existence of national and subnational governmental units by itself does not make a system federal. *For a system to be truly federal, the powers of both the national units and the subnational units must be specified and limited.* Under true federalism, individuals are governed by

federalism A system of shared sovereignty between two levels of government—one national and one subnational—occupying the same geographic region.

unitary system A centralized governmental system in which local or subdivisional governments exercise only those powers given to them by the central government.

confederal system A league of independent sovereign states, joined together by a central government that has only limited powers over them.

two separate governmental authorities (national and state authorities) whose expressly designated powers cannot be altered without changing the fundamental nature of the system—for example, by amending a written constitution. Table 3–1 at right lists some of the countries that the Central Intelligence Agency has classified as having a federal system of government.[1]

Table 3–1

Countries That Have a Federal System Today

Country	Population (in Millions)
Argentina	41.3
Australia	21.5
Austria	8.2
Brazil	201.1
Canada	33.8
Ethiopia	88.0
Germany	82.3
India	1,173.1
Malaysia	26.2
Mexico	112.5
Nigeria	152.2
Pakistan	177.3
Switzerland	7.6
United States	310.2
Venezuela	27.2

Source: Central Intelligence Agency, *The World Fact Book;* current edition online at **https://www.cia.gov/library/publications/the-world-factbook.**

Federalism in theory is one thing; federalism in practice is another. As you will read shortly, the Constitution sets forth specific powers that can be exercised by the national government and provides that the national government has the implied power to undertake actions necessary to carry out its expressly designated powers. All other powers are "reserved" to the states. The broad language of the Constitution, though, has left much room for debate over the specific nature and scope of certain powers, such as the national government's implied powers and the powers reserved to the states. Thus, the actual workings of our federal form of government have depended, to a great extent, on the historical application of the broad principles outlined in the Constitution.

To further complicate matters, the term *federal government,* as it is used today, refers to the national, or central, government. When individuals talk of the federal government, they mean the national government based in Washington, D.C. They are *not* referring to the federal *system* of government, which is made up of both the national government and the state governments.

Alternatives to Federalism

Perhaps an easier way to define federalism is to discuss what it is *not.* Most of the nations in the world today have a **unitary system** of government. In such a system, the constitution vests all powers in the national government. If the national government so chooses, it can delegate certain activities to subnational units. The reverse is also true: the national government can take away, at will, powers delegated to subnational governmental units. In a unitary system, any subnational government is a "creature of the national government." The governments of Britain, France, Israel, Japan, and the Philippines are examples of unitary systems. In the United States, because the Constitution does not mention local governments (cities and counties), we say that city and county governmental units are "creatures of state government." That means that state governments can—and do—both give powers to and take powers from local governments.

The Articles of Confederation created a confederal system (see Chapter 2). In a **confederal system,** the national government exists and operates only at the direction of the subnational governments. Few true confederal systems are in existence today, although some people contend that the European Union—a group of twenty-seven European nations that has established many common institutions—qualifies as such a system.

Federalism—An Optimal Choice for the United States?

The Articles of Confederation failed because they did not allow for a sufficiently strong central government. The framers of the Constitution, however, were fearful of tyranny and a too-powerful central government. The outcome had to be a compromise—a federal system.

The appeal of federalism was that it retained state powers and local traditions while establishing a strong national government capable of handling common problems, such as national defense. A federal form of government also furthered the goal of creating a division of powers (to be discussed shortly). There are other reasons why the founders opted for a federal system, and a federal structure of government continues to offer many advantages (as well as some disadvantages) for U.S. citizens.

ADVANTAGES OF FEDERALISM One of the reasons a federal form of government is well suited to the United

Figure 3–1

Governmental Units in the United States Today

The most common type of governmental unit in the United States is the special district, which is generally concerned with a specific issue such as solid waste disposal, mass transportation, or fire protection. Often, the jurisdiction of special districts crosses the boundaries of other governmental units, such as cities or counties. Special districts also tend to have fewer restrictions than other local governments as to how much debt they can incur and so are created to finance large building projects.

THE NUMBER OF GOVERNMENTS IN THE UNITED STATES TODAY

Government	Number
Federal government	1
State governments and District of Columbia	51
Local governments	
Counties	3,034
Municipalities (mainly cities or towns)	19,492
Townships (less extensive powers)	16,519
Special districts (water, sewer, and so on)	37,381
School districts	13,051
Subtotal local governments	89,476
Total	**89,528**

PERCENTAGE OF ALL GOVERNMENTS IN THE UNITED STATES TODAY

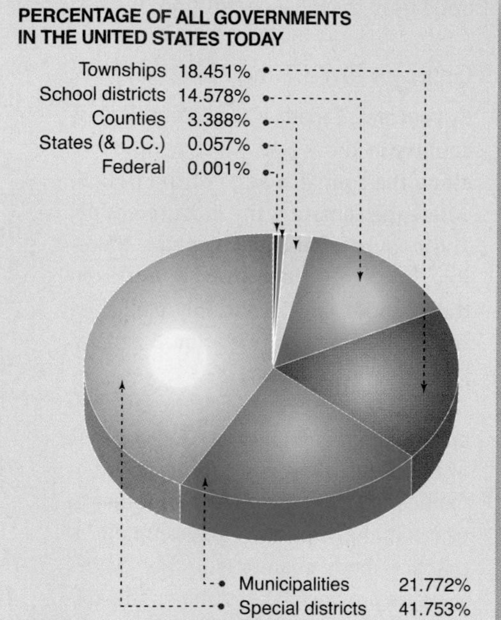

Source: U.S. Census Bureau.

States is our country's large size. Even in the days when the United States consisted of only thirteen states, its geographic area was larger than that of England or France. In those days, travel was slow and communication was difficult, so people in outlying areas were isolated. The news of any particular political decision could take several weeks to reach everyone. Therefore, even if the framers of the Constitution had wanted a more centralized system (which most of them did not), such a system would have been unworkable.

Look at Figure 3–1 above. As you can see, to a great extent the practical business of governing this country takes place in state and local governmental units. Federalism, by providing a multitude of arenas for decision making, keeps government closer to the people and helps make democracy possible.

The existence of numerous government subunits in the United States also makes it possible to experiment with innovative policies and programs at the state or local level. Many observers, including Supreme Court justice Louis Brandeis (1856–1941), have emphasized that in a federal system, state governments can act as "laboratories" for public-policy experimentation. For example, many states have adopted minimum wage laws that establish a higher minimum wage than the one set by national legislation. Several states, including Hawaii and Massachusetts, have experimented with health-care programs that extend coverage to most or all of the states' citizens. Depending on the outcome of a specific experiment, other states may (or may not) implement similar programs. State innovations can also serve as models for federal programs. For instance, California was a pioneer in air-pollution control. Many of that state's regulations were later adapted by other states and eventually by the federal government.

We have always been a nation of different political subcultures. The Pilgrims who founded New England were different from the settlers who established the agricultural society of the South. Both of these groups were different from those who populated the Middle Atlantic states. The groups that founded New England had a religious focus, while those who populated the Middle Atlantic states were more business oriented. Those who settled in the South were more individualistic than the other groups. That is, they were less inclined to act as a collective and more inclined to act independently of each other. A federal system of government allows the political and cultural interests of regional groups to be reflected in the laws governing those groups.

As we noted earlier, nations other than the United States have benefited from the principle of federalism. One of them is Canada, our neighbor to the north. Because federalism permits the expression of varying regional cultures, Canadian federalism naturally differs from the American version, as you will discover in this chapter's *The Rest of the World* feature on the following page.

SOME DRAWBACKS TO FEDERALISM Federalism offers many advantages, but it also has some drawbacks. Consider that although federalism in many ways

THE REST OF THE WORLD

Canadian versus American Federalism

Canada has a federal system similar in some ways to that of the United States—but also with some big differences. When the 1867 Constitution Act created modern Canada, the United States had just concluded the Civil War. Canada's founders blamed that war on the weakness of the U.S. central government. Therefore, the Canadian constitution gave far more power to the central government than did the U.S. Constitution.

The Powers of Lower-Level Governments

Our lower levels of government are called states, whereas in Canada they are called provinces. Right there, the powers of the central government are emphasized. The word *state* implies sovereignty. A *province,* however, is never sovereign and is typically set up for the convenience of the central government. The U.S. Constitution limits the powers of the national government to those listed in Article I, Section 8. In the Canadian constitution, it is the powers of the provinces that are limited by a list. The Tenth Amendment to the U.S. Constitution reserves residual powers to the states or to the people. In Canada, residual powers rest with the national government. Under the 1867 Canadian constitution, the central government could veto any provincial legislation. No such clause appears in the U.S. Constitution.

Changes Over Time

By land area, Canada is the second-largest country in the world. Most people live along the southern edge of the nation, where the climate is the most tolerable. The populated areas of Canada, therefore, are like a ribbon extending from the Atlantic to the Pacific. Physically, the country seems designed for a federal system of government.

Over time, the powers of the U.S. federal government grew at the expense of the states. The opposite happened in Canada. By the end of the nineteenth century, the Canadian government in practice had abandoned the power to veto provincial legislation. The difference between the Canadian and American experiences is well illustrated by the effect of the Great Depression on the federal system. In the United States, the Depression strengthened the federal government. In Canada, it strengthened the provinces.

Two Languages

Another striking difference between Canada and the United States is that Canada has two national languages. A majority of Canadians speak English, but most of the population of Québec speaks French. The Parti Québécois (PQ), which wants Québec to be a separate country, has gained power in that province twice. Both times, it held referenda on whether Québec should demand "sovereignty-association," a euphemism for independence. In 1995, the PQ almost obtained a majority vote for its position. The party has promised to hold another referendum if it returns to power. The possibility exists, therefore, that Canada could actually break apart.

For Critical Analysis *The Canadian constitution is based on the principles of "peace, order, and good government." Contrast that phrase with the Preamble to the U.S. Constitution. How do the statements differ?*

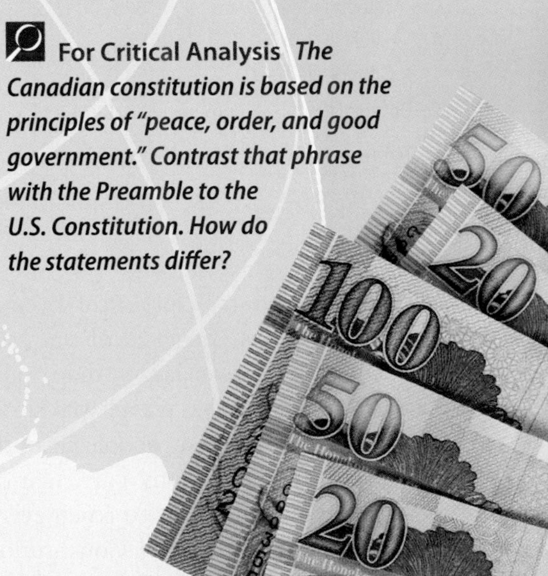

promotes greater self-rule, or democracy, some scholars point out that local self-rule may not always be in society's best interests. These observers argue that the smaller the political unit, the higher the probability that it will be dominated by a single political group, which may or may not be concerned with the welfare of many of the local unit's citizens. For example, entrenched segregationist politicians in southern states denied African Americans their civil rights and voting rights for decades, as we discuss further in Chapter 5.

Powerful state and local interests can block progress and impede national plans. State and local interests often diverge from those of the national government. For example, several of the states have recently been at odds with the national government over how to address the problem of global warming. Finding acceptable solutions to such conflicts has not always been easy. Indeed, as will be discussed shortly, in the 1860s, war—not politics—decided the outcome of a struggle over states' rights.

Federalism has other drawbacks as well. One of them is the lack of uniformity of state laws, which can complicate business transactions that cross state borders. Another problem is the difficulty of coordinating government policies at the national, state, and local levels. Additionally, the simultaneous regulation of business by all levels of government creates red tape that imposes substantial costs on the business community.

Finally, in a federal system, there is always the danger that national power will be expanded at the expense of the states. President Ronald Reagan (1981–1989) once said, "The Founding Fathers saw the federalist system as constructed something like a masonry wall. The States are the bricks, the national government is the mortar. . . . Unfortunately, over the years, many people have increasingly come to believe that Washington is the whole wall."[2]

LO2 *The Constitutional Division of Powers*

The founders created a federal form of government by dividing sovereign powers into powers that could be exercised by the national government and powers that were to be reserved to the states. Although there is no systematic explanation of this **division of powers** between the national and state governments, the original Constitution, along with its amendments, provides statements on what the national and state governments can (and cannot) do.

The Powers of the National Government

The Constitution delegates certain powers to the national government. It also prohibits the national government from exercising certain powers.

POWERS DELEGATED TO THE NATIONAL GOVERNMENT The national government possesses three types of powers: expressed powers, implied powers, and inherent powers. Article I, Section 8, of the Constitution expressly enumerates twenty-seven powers that Congress may exercise. Two of these **expressed powers,** or *enumerated powers,* are the power to coin money and the power to regulate interstate commerce. Constitutional amendments have provided for other expressed powers. For example, the Sixteenth Amendment, added in 1913, gives Congress the power to impose a federal income tax. Article II, Section 2, of the Constitution expressly delegates certain powers to the president. These powers include making treaties and appointing certain federal officeholders. Laws enacted by Congress can also have the effect of creating additional expressed presidential powers.

The constitutional basis for the **implied powers** of the national government is found in Article I, Section 8, Clause 18, often called the **necessary and proper clause.** This clause states that Congress has the power to make "all Laws which shall be necessary and proper for carrying into Execution the foregoing [expressed] Powers, and all other Powers vested by this Constitution in the Government of the United States, or in any Department or Officer thereof." The necessary and proper clause is often referred to as the *elastic clause,* because it gives elasticity to our constitutional system.

The national government also enjoys certain **inherent powers**—powers that governments must have simply to ensure the nation's integrity and survival as a political unit. For example, any national government must have the inherent ability to make treaties, regulate immigration, acquire territory, wage war, and make peace. While some inherent powers are also enumerated in the Constitution, such as the power to wage war and make treaties, others are not. For example, the Constitution does not speak of regulating immigration or acquiring new territory. Although the national government's inherent powers are few, they are important.

POWERS PROHIBITED TO THE NATIONAL GOVERNMENT The Constitution expressly prohibits the national government from undertaking certain actions, such as imposing taxes on exports, and from passing laws restraining certain liberties, such as the freedom of speech or religion. Most of these prohibited powers are listed in Article I, Section 9, and in the first eight amendments to the Constitution. Additionally, the national government is implicitly prohibited from exercising powers, including

division of powers A basic principle of federalism established by the U.S. Constitution, by which powers are divided between the federal and state governments.

expressed powers Constitutional or statutory powers that are expressly provided for by the U.S. Constitution.

implied powers The powers of the federal government that are implied by the expressed powers in the Constitution, particularly in Article I, Section 8.

necessary and proper clause Article I, Section 8, Clause 18, of the Constitution, which gives Congress the power to make all laws "necessary and proper" for the federal government to carry out its responsibilities; also called the *elastic clause.*

inherent powers The powers of the national government that, although not always expressly granted by the Constitution, are necessary to ensure the nation's integrity and survival as a political unit. Inherent powers include the power to make treaties and the power to wage war or make peace.

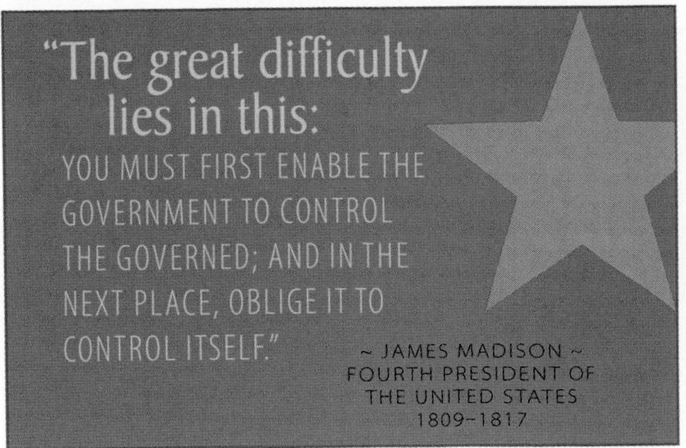

the power to create a national public school system, that are not included among its expressed and implied powers.

The Powers of the States

The Tenth Amendment to the Constitution states that powers that are not delegated to the national government by the Constitution, nor prohibited to the states, "are reserved to the States respectively, or to the people."

POLICE POWERS The Tenth Amendment thus gives numerous powers to the states, including the power to regulate commerce within their borders and the power to maintain a state militia. In principle, each state has the ability to regulate its internal affairs and to enact whatever laws are necessary to protect the health, morals, safety, and welfare of its people. These powers of the states are called **police powers.** The establishment of public schools and the regulation of marriage and divorce have traditionally been considered to be entirely within the purview of state and local governments.

Because the Tenth Amendment does not specify what powers are reserved to the states, these powers have been defined differently at different times in our history. In periods of widespread support for increased regulation by the national government, the Tenth Amendment tends to recede into the background. When the tide turns the other way, the Tenth Amendment is resurrected to justify arguments supporting increased states' rights (see, for example, the discussion of the new federalism later in this chapter). Because the United States Supreme Court is the ultimate arbiter of the Constitution, the outcome of disputes over the extent of state powers often rests with the Court.

police powers The powers of a government body that enable it to create laws for the protection of the health, morals, safety, and welfare of the people. In the United States, most police powers are reserved to the states.

POWERS PROHIBITED TO THE STATES Article I, Section 10, denies certain powers to state governments, such as the power to tax goods that are transported across state lines. States are also prohibited from entering into treaties with other countries. In addition, the Thirteenth, Fourteenth, Fifteenth, Nineteenth, Twenty-fourth, and Twenty-sixth Amendments prohibit certain state actions. (The complete text of these amendments is included in Appendix B.)

Interstate Relations

The Constitution also contains provisions relating to interstate relations. The states have constant commercial and social interactions among themselves, and these interactions often do not directly involve the national government. The relationships among the states in our federal system of government are sometimes referred to as *horizontal federalism.*

The Constitution outlines a number of rules for interstate relations. For example, the Constitution's full faith and credit clause requires each state to honor every other state's public acts, records, and judicial proceedings. The issue of gay marriage, however, has made this constitutional mandate difficult to follow. If a gay couple legally married in Massachusetts moves to a state that bans same-sex marriage, which state's law takes priority? The federal government attempted to answer that question through the 1996 Defense of Marriage Act (DOMA), which provided that no state

During natural disasters, such as this flooding problem in Fargo, North Dakota, local governments will ask for assistance from other cities, the state, and even the federal government.

DANIEL BARRY/REDUX

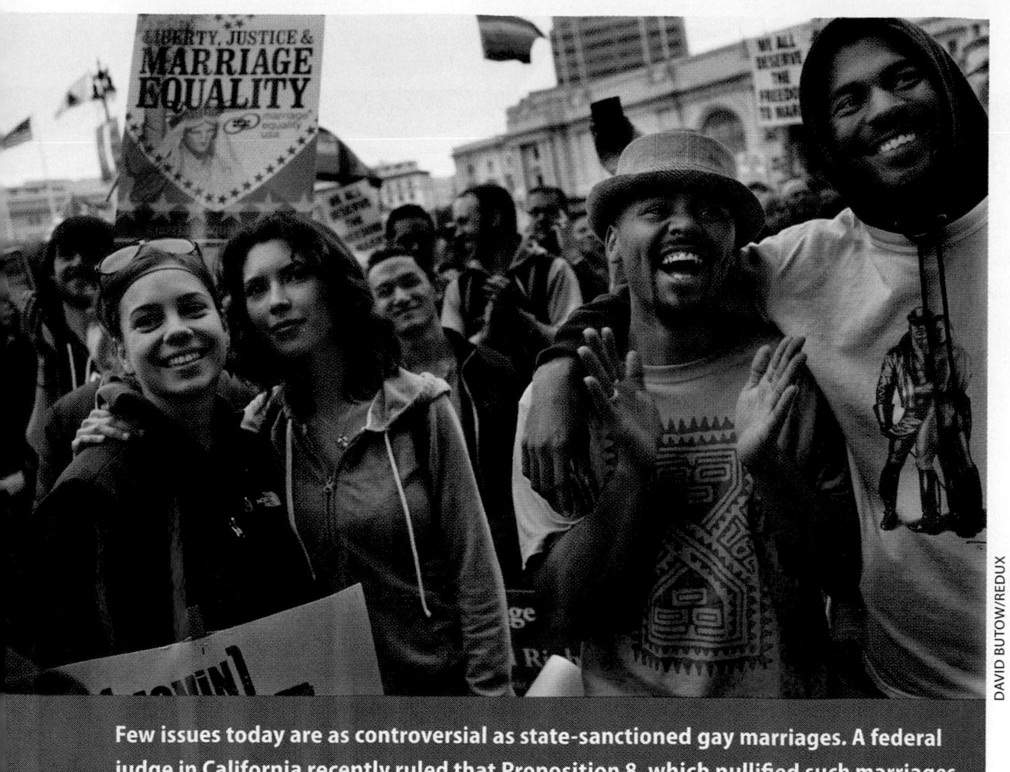

DAVID BUTOW/REDUX

Few issues today are as controversial as state-sanctioned gay marriages. A federal judge in California recently ruled that Proposition 8, which nullified such marriages, was unconstitutional.

is *required* to treat a relationship between persons of the same sex as a marriage, even if the relationship is considered a marriage in another state.

A second part of the law barred the national government from recognizing same-sex marriages in states that legalize them. In July 2010, however, a U.S. district court judge threw out this part of DOMA and ruled that the federal government was required to provide marriage-based benefits to Massachusetts residents who are joined in same-sex marriages. This ruling will certainly be appealed, and ultimately, the United States Supreme Court will have to decide this issue.

Horizontal federalism also includes agreements, known as *interstate compacts,* among two or more states to regulate the use or protection of certain resources, such as water or oil and gas. California and Nevada, for example, have formed an interstate compact to regulate the use and protection of Lake Tahoe, which lies on the border between those states.

Concurrent Powers

Concurrent powers can be exercised by both the state governments and the federal government. Generally, a state's concurrent powers apply only within the geographic area of the state and do not include functions that the Constitution delegates exclusively to the national government, such as the coinage of money and the negotiation of treaties. An example of a concurrent power is the power to tax. Both the states and the national government have the power to impose income taxes—and a variety of other taxes. States, however, are prohibited from imposing tariffs (taxes on imported goods), and as noted, the federal government may not tax articles exported by any state. Figure 3–2 on the following page, which summarizes the powers granted and denied by the Constitution, lists other concurrent powers.

The Supremacy Clause

The Constitution makes it clear that the federal government holds ultimate power. Article VI, Clause 2, known as the **supremacy clause,** states that the U.S. Constitution and the laws of the federal government "shall be the supreme Law of the Land." In other words, states cannot use their reserved or concurrent powers to counter national policies. Whenever state or local officers, such as judges or sheriffs, take office, they become bound by an oath to support the U.S. Constitution. National government power always takes precedence over any conflicting state action.[3]

LO3 *The Struggle for Supremacy*

Much of the political and legal history of the United States has involved conflicts between the supremacy of the national government and the desire of the states to preserve their sovereignty. The most extreme example of this conflict was the Civil War in the 1860s. Through the years, because of the Civil War and several important Supreme Court decisions, the national government has increased its power.

concurrent powers Powers held by both the federal and the state governments in a federal system.

supremacy clause Article VI, Clause 2, of the Constitution, which makes the Constitution and federal laws superior to all conflicting state and local laws.

Figure 3–2

The Constitutional Division of Powers

The Constitution grants certain powers to the national government and certain powers to the state governments, while denying them other powers. Some powers, called *concurrent powers,* can be exercised at either the national or the state level, but generally the states can exercise these powers only within their own borders.

POWERS GRANTED BY THE CONSTITUTION
NATIONAL
★To coin money
★To conduct foreign relations
★To regulate interstate commerce
★To declare war
★To raise and support the military
★To establish post offices
★To admit new states
★Powers implied by the necessary and proper clause
CONCURRENT
★To levy and collect taxes
★To borrow money
★To make and enforce laws
★To establish courts
★To provide for the general welfare
★To charter banks and corporations
STATE
★To regulate intrastate commerce
★To conduct elections
★To provide for public health, safety, welfare, and morals
★To establish local governments
★To ratify amendments to the federal Constitution
★To establish a state militia
POWERS DENIED BY THE CONSTITUTION
NATIONAL
★To tax articles exported from any state
★To violate the Bill of Rights
★To change state boundaries without consent of the states in question
CONCURRENT
★To grant titles of nobility
★To permit slavery
★To deny citizens the right to vote
STATE
★To tax imports or exports
★To coin money
★To enter into treaties
★To impair obligations of contracts
★To abridge the privileges or immunities of citizens or deny due process and equal protection of the laws

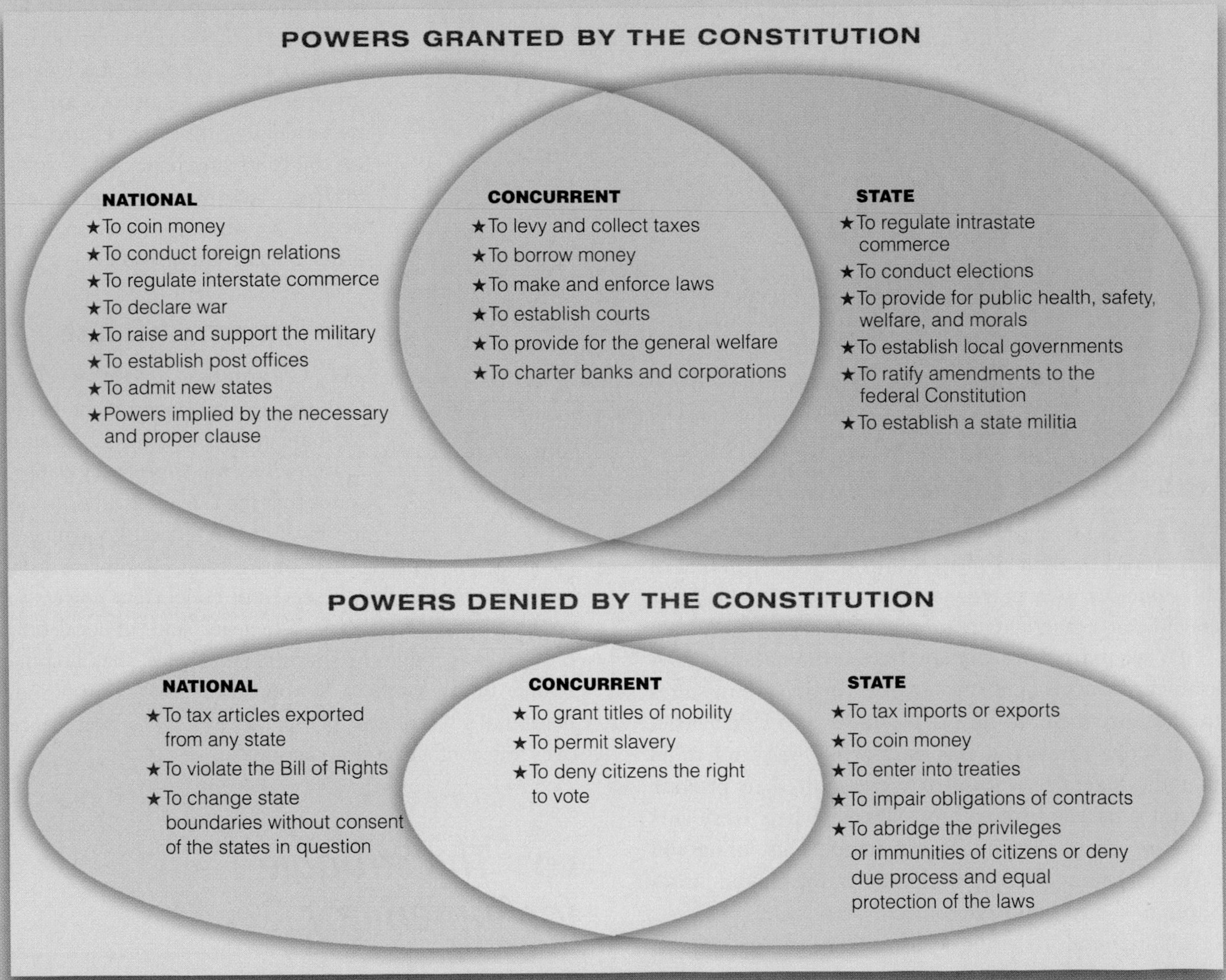

Early U.S. Supreme Court Decisions

Two Supreme Court cases, both of which were decided in the early 1800s, played a key role in establishing the constitutional foundations for the supremacy of the national government. Both decisions were issued while John Marshall was chief justice of the Supreme Court. In his thirty-four years as chief justice (1801–1835), Marshall did much to establish the prestige and the independence of the Court. In *Marbury v. Madison,*[4] he clearly enunciated the principle of judicial review, which has since become an important part of the checks and balances in the American system of government. Under his leadership, the Supreme Court also established, through the following cases, the superiority of federal authority under the Constitution.

***McCULLOCH V. MARYLAND* (1819)** The issue in *McCulloch v. Maryland,*[5] a case decided in 1819, involved both the necessary and proper clause and the supremacy clause. When the state of Maryland imposed a tax on the Baltimore branch of the Second Bank of the United States, the branch's chief cashier, James McCulloch, declined to pay the tax. The state court ruled that McCulloch had to pay it, and the national government appealed to the United States Supreme Court. The case involved much more than a question of taxes. At issue was whether Congress had the authority under the Constitution's necessary and proper clause to charter and contribute capital to the Second Bank of the United States. A second constitutional issue was also involved: If the bank was constitutional, could a state tax it? In other words, was a state action that conflicted with a national government action invalid under the supremacy clause?

Chief Justice Marshall pointed out that no provision in the Constitution grants the national government the *expressed* power to form a national bank. Nevertheless, if establishing such a bank helps the national government exercise its expressed powers, then the authority to do so could be implied. Marshall also said that the necessary and proper clause included "all means that are appropriate" to carry out "the legitimate ends" of the Constitution.

Having established this doctrine of implied powers, Marshall then answered the other important constitutional question before the Court and established the doctrine of national supremacy. Marshall declared that no state could use its taxing power to tax an arm of the national government. If it could, the Constitution's declaration that the Constitution "shall be the supreme Law of the Land" would be empty rhetoric without meaning. From that day on, Marshall's decision became the basis for strengthening the national government's power.

"A LEGISLATIVE ACT contrary to the Constitution is not law."

~ JOHN MARSHALL ~
CHIEF JUSTICE OF THE UNITED STATES SUPREME COURT
1801–1835

John Marshall, chief justice of the United States Supreme Court from 1801 to 1835, was instrumental in establishing the supremacy of the national government.

THE GRANGER COLLECTION

***GIBBONS V. OGDEN* (1824)** As Chapter 2 explained, Article I, Section 8, gives Congress the power to regulate commerce "among the several States." But the framers of the Constitution did not define the word *commerce*. At issue in *Gibbons v. Ogden*[6] was how the *commerce clause* should be defined and whether the national government had the exclusive power to regulate commerce involving more than one state. The New York legislature had given Robert Livingston and Robert Fulton the exclusive right to operate steamboats in New York waters, and Livingston and Fulton licensed Aaron Ogden to operate a ferry between New York and New Jersey. Thomas Gibbons, who had a license from the U.S. government to operate boats in interstate waters, decided to compete with Ogden, but he did so without New York's permission. Ogden sued Gibbons in the New York state courts and won. Gibbons appealed.

Chief Justice Marshall defined *commerce* as including all business dealings, including steamboat travel. Marshall also stated that the power to regulate interstate commerce was an *exclusive* national power and had no limitations other than those specifically found in the Constitution. Since this 1824 decision, the national government has used the commerce clause repeatedly to justify its regulation of virtually all areas of economic activity.

The Civil War—The Ultimate Supremacy Battle

The great issue that provoked the Civil War (1861–1865) was the future of slavery. Because people in different sections of the country had radically different beliefs about slavery, the slavery issue took the form of a dispute over states' rights versus national supremacy. The war brought to a bloody climax the ideological debate that had been outlined by the Federalist and Anti-Federalist factions even before the Constitution was ratified.

As just discussed, the Supreme Court headed by John Marshall interpreted the commerce clause in such a way as to increase the power of the national government at the expense of state powers. By the late 1820s, however, a shift back to states' rights had begun, and the question of the regulation of commerce became one of the major issues in federal-state relations. When the national government, in 1828 and 1832, passed laws imposing tariffs (taxes) on goods imported into the United States, southern states objected, believing that such taxes were against their interests.

One southern state, South Carolina, attempted to *nullify* the tariffs, or to make them void. South Carolina claimed that in conflicts between state governments and the national government, the states should have the ultimate authority to determine the welfare of their citizens. President Andrew Jackson was prepared to use force to uphold national law, but Congress reduced the tariffs. The crisis passed.

"We here highly resolve that . . . **THIS NATION . . . SHALL HAVE A NEW BIRTH OF FREEDOM;** and that government of the people, by the people, for the people, shall not perish from the earth."

~ ABRAHAM LINCOLN ~
GETTYSBURG ADDRESS
1863

Additionally, some Southerners believed that democratic decisions could be made only when all the segments of society affected by those decisions were in agreement. Without such agreement, a decision should not be binding on those whose interests it violates. This view was used to justify the **secession**—withdrawal—of the southern states from the Union in 1860 and 1861.

The defense of slavery and the promotion of states' rights were both important elements in the South's decision to secede, and the two concepts were commingled in the minds of Southerners of that era. Which of these two was the more important remains a matter of controversy even today. Modern defenders of states' rights and those who distrust governmental authority often present southern secession as entirely a matter of states' rights. Liberals and those who champion the rights of African Americans see slavery as the sole cause of the crisis. Economic historians can provide helpful insights into the background to secession, as you will learn in this chapter's *Perception versus Reality* feature on the facing page.

When the South was defeated in the war, the idea that a state has a right to secede from the Union was defeated also. Although the Civil War occurred because of the South's desire for increased states' rights, the result was just the opposite—an increase in the political power of the national government.

Dual Federalism—From the Civil War to the 1930s

Scholars have devised various models to describe the relationship between the states and the national government at different times in our history. These models are useful in describing the evolution of federalism after the Civil War.

The model of **dual federalism** assumes that the states and the national government are more or less equals, with each level of government having separate and distinct functions and responsibilities. The states exercise sovereign powers over certain matters, and the national government exercises sovereign powers over others.

The Civil War is known in the South as the War between the States, but the official Union designation was the War of the Rebellion. The first shot of the Civil War was fired on April 12, 1861, at Fort Sumter, South Carolina.

LIBRARY OF CONGRESS

secession The act of formally withdrawing from membership in an alliance; the withdrawal of a state from the federal Union.

dual federalism A system of government in which the federal and the state governments maintain diverse but sovereign powers.

PERCEPTION VERSUS REALITY

Did the Civil War Destroy the Economy of the South?

The Civil War imposed great destruction on the South. The Union Army burned Atlanta, Columbia, and Richmond. General Philip Sheridan's cavalry famously destroyed the farms and railroads of Virginia's Shenandoah Valley. In addition to the loss of human life, the South lost livestock, houses, barns, railroads, and bridges. In the cities, Union forces destroyed factories, warehouses, and transportation equipment.

The Mississippi in Time of War, circa 1865, by Currier and Ives.

The Perception

The common perception of the South's condition after the Civil War has been heavily influenced by the suffering depicted in *Gone with the Wind* and other popular works. Many Americans have long believed that the destruction of southern wealth by the war made economic recovery impossible. Furthermore, although it was inevitable and proper that the slaves were freed, the North did not compensate the former slave owners for their losses. This immediately destroyed billions of dollars worth of southern capital.

The Reality

The industrial parts of the South actually recovered quite rapidly. For example, by 1867, the railroads between Washington, D.C., and Charleston, South Carolina, were as good as they had been before the war. By 1869, total manufacturing output and investment exceeded their prewar levels.

The South's problem lay in its cotton-based agriculture. You have heard about the huge bubble in housing prices that helped cause the recent Great Recession. There have been many bubbles in the past as well. In the 1850s, the world experienced a cotton bubble. High prices for cotton led to a bubble in the price of slaves. Slave owners believed that even if Abraham Lincoln swore not to interfere with slavery in the states, his presidency still threatened the price of slaves. Secession would serve as a protection. The North could not possibly risk a "war on cotton," and if it did, cotton-dependent Britain would intervene on the side of the South. As a southern lady wrote to her daughters, "civil war was *foreign to the original plan.*"[7]

In fact, just before the war, the price of cotton started to fall due to overproduction of cotton textiles. British per-capita consumption of cotton goods did not exceed 1860 levels until after World War I. As a result, after the Civil War, cotton prices fell until almost the end of the century. The Civil War masked the fact that the cotton bubble had burst. Ultra-low cotton prices—with no good economic alternatives for southern farmers—were the true source of the post–Civil War economic distress, not the devastation caused by the Union Army.

Blog On For a vast collection of Civil War materials, see Shotgun's Home of the American Civil War at **www.civilwarhome.com**. For economic history, try **eh.net**, a Web site supported by the Economic History Association. One of the site's most popular services lets you convert modern prices into those of any past year, or vice versa.

For much of our nation's history, this model of federalism prevailed. Certainly, after the Civil War the courts tended to support the states' rights to exercise their police powers and tended to strictly limit the powers of the federal government under the commerce clause. In 1918, for example, the Supreme Court ruled unconstitutional a 1916 federal law excluding from interstate commerce the products created through the use of child labor. The law was held unconstitutional because it attempted to regulate a local problem.[8] The era of dual federalism came to an end in the 1930s, when the United States was in the depths of the greatest economic depression it had ever experienced.

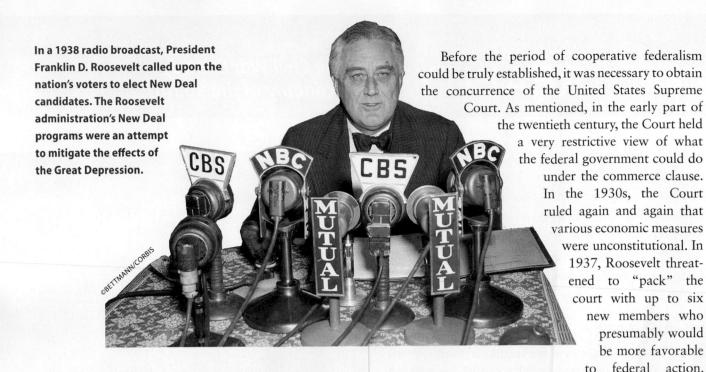

In a 1938 radio broadcast, President Franklin D. Roosevelt called upon the nation's voters to elect New Deal candidates. The Roosevelt administration's New Deal programs were an attempt to mitigate the effects of the Great Depression.

Cooperative Federalism and the Growth of the National Government

The model of **cooperative federalism,** as the term implies, involves cooperation by all branches of government. This model views the national and state governments as complementary parts of a single governmental mechanism, the purpose of which is to solve the problems facing the entire United States. For example, federal law enforcement agencies, such as the Federal Bureau of Investigation, lend technical expertise to solve local crimes, and local officials cooperate with federal agencies.

Cooperative federalism grew out of the need to solve the pressing national problems caused by the Great Depression, which began in 1929. To help bring the United States out of the Depression, President Franklin D. Roosevelt (1933–1945) launched his **New Deal,** which involved many government-spending and public-assistance programs. Roosevelt's New Deal legislation not only ushered in an era of cooperative federalism, which has more or less continued until the present day, but also marked the real beginning of an era of national supremacy.

cooperative federalism The theory that the states and the federal government should cooperate in solving problems.

New Deal The policies ushered in by the Roosevelt administration in 1933 in an attempt to bring the United States out of the Great Depression. The New Deal included many government-spending and public-assistance programs, in addition to thousands of regulations governing economic activity.

picket-fence federalism A model of federalism in which specific policies and programs are administered by all levels of government—national, state, and local.

Before the period of cooperative federalism could be truly established, it was necessary to obtain the concurrence of the United States Supreme Court. As mentioned, in the early part of the twentieth century, the Court held a very restrictive view of what the federal government could do under the commerce clause. In the 1930s, the Court ruled again and again that various economic measures were unconstitutional. In 1937, Roosevelt threatened to "pack" the court with up to six new members who presumably would be more favorable to federal action. This move was widely considered to be an assault on the Constitution, and Congress refused to support it. Clearly, however, the Court got the message: after 1937, it ceased its attempts to limit the scope of the commerce clause.

COOPERATIVE FEDERALISM AND THE WELFARE STATE The 1960s and 1970s saw an even greater expansion of the national government's role in domestic policy. The Great Society legislation of President Lyndon Johnson's administration (1963–1969) created Medicaid, Medicare, the Job Corps, Operation Head Start, and other programs. The Civil Rights Act of 1964 prohibited discrimination in public accommodations, employment, and other areas on the basis of race, color, national origin, religion, or gender. In the 1970s, national laws protecting consumers, employees, and the environment imposed further regulations on the economy. Today, few activities are beyond the reach of the regulatory arm of the national government.

Nonetheless, the massive social programs undertaken in the 1960s and 1970s also precipitated greater involvement by state and local governments. The national government simply could not implement those programs alone. For example, Head Start, a program that provides preschool services to children of low-income families, is administered by local nonprofit organizations and school systems, although it is funded by federal grants. The model in which every level of government is involved in implementing a policy is sometimes referred to as **picket-fence federalism.** In this model, the policy area is the vertical picket on the fence, while the levels of government are the horizontal support boards. America's welfare system has relied on this

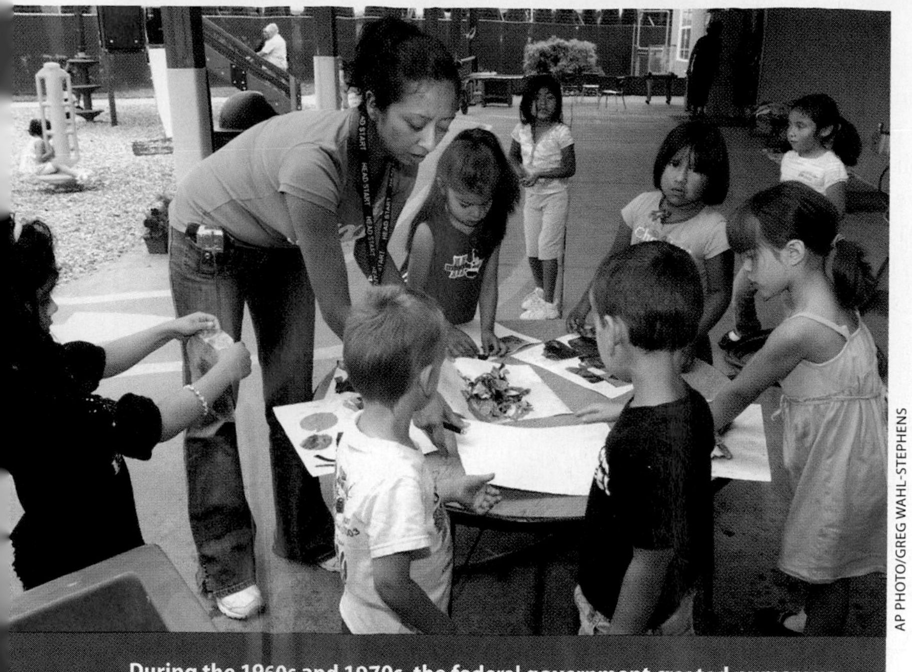

AP PHOTO/GREG WAHL-STEPHENS

During the 1960s and 1970s, the federal government created numerous nationwide programs, such as Head Start, which promotes school readiness for low-income children. State and local governments were called upon to organize and administer these programs, as well as to contribute additional funding. Here, a teacher in a Head Start program in Hillsboro, Oregon, works with preschoolers on an outdoor art project.

model of federalism, although, as you will read, from time to time there have been attempts to give more power to state and local governments.

UNITED STATES SUPREME COURT DECISIONS AND COOPERATIVE FEDERALISM The two United States Supreme Court decisions discussed earlier, *McCulloch v. Maryland* and *Gibbons v. Ogden,* became the constitutional cornerstone of the regulatory powers that the national government enjoys today. From 1937 on, the Supreme Court consistently upheld Congress's power to regulate domestic policy under the commerce clause. Even activities that occur entirely within a state were rarely considered to be outside the regulatory power of the national government. For example, in 1942 the Supreme Court held that wheat production by an individual farmer intended wholly for consumption on his own farm was subject to federal regulation because the home consumption of wheat reduced the demand for wheat and thus could have an effect on interstate commerce.[9]

In 1980, the Supreme Court acknowledged that the commerce clause had "long been interpreted to extend beyond activities actually in interstate commerce to reach other activities that, while wholly local in nature, nevertheless substantially affect interstate commerce."[10] Today, Congress can regulate almost any kind of economic activity, no matter where it occurs. In recent years, though, the Supreme Court has, for the first time since the 1930s, occasionally curbed Congress's regulatory powers under the commerce clause. You will read more about this development shortly.

John Marshall's validation of the supremacy clause of the Constitution has also had significant consequences for federalism. One important effect of the supremacy clause today is that the clause allows for federal **preemption** of certain areas in which the national government and the states have concurrent powers. When Congress chooses to act exclusively in an area in which the states and the national government have concurrent powers, Congress is said to have *preempted* the area. In such cases, the courts have held that a valid federal law or regulation takes precedence over a conflicting state or local law or regulation covering the same general activity.

LO4 *Federalism Today*

By the 1970s, some Americans had begun to question whether the national government had acquired too many powers. Had the national government gotten too big? Had it become, in fact, a threat to the power of the states and the liberties of the people? Should steps be taken to reduce the regulatory power and scope of the national government? Since that time, the model of federalism has evolved in ways that reflect these and other concerns.

The New Federalism—More Power to the States

Starting in the 1970s, several administrations attempted to revitalize the doctrine of dual federalism, which they renamed the "new federalism." The **new federalism** involved a shift from *nation-centered* federalism to *state-centered* federalism. One of the major goals of the new federalism was to return to the states certain powers that had been exercised by the national government since the 1930s. The term

preemption A doctrine rooted in the supremacy clause of the Constitution that provides that national laws or regulations governing a certain area take precedence over conflicting state laws or regulations governing that same area.

new federalism A plan to limit the federal government's role in regulating state governments and to give the states increased power to decide how they should spend government revenues.

devolution—the transfer of powers to political subunits—is often used to describe this process. Although a product of conservative thought and initiated by Republicans, the devolutionary goals of the new federalism were also espoused by the Clinton administration (1993–2001). An example of the new federalism is the welfare reform legislation passed by Congress in 1996, which gave the states more authority over welfare programs.

The Supreme Court and the New Federalism

During and since the 1990s, the Supreme Court has played a significant role in furthering the cause of states' rights. In a landmark 1995 decision, *United States v. Lopez*,[11] the Supreme Court held, for the first time in sixty years, that Congress had exceeded its constitutional authority under the commerce clause. The Court concluded that the Gun-Free School Zones Act of 1990, which banned the possession of guns within one thousand feet of any school, was unconstitutional because it attempted to regulate an area that had "nothing to do with commerce." In a significant 1997 decision, the Court struck down portions of the Brady Handgun Violence Prevention Act of 1993, which obligated state and local law enforcement officers to do background checks on prospective handgun buyers until a national instant check system could be implemented. The Court stated that Congress lacked the power to "dragoon" state employees into federal service through an unfunded **federal mandate** of this kind.[12]

Since then, the Court has continued to limit the national government's regulatory powers. In 2000, for example, the Court invalidated a key provision of the federal Violence Against Women Act of 1994, which allowed women to sue in federal court when they were victims of gender-motivated violence, such as rape. The Court upheld a federal appellate court's ruling that the commerce clause did not justify national regulation of noneconomic, criminal conduct.[13]

In the twenty-first century, the United States Supreme Court has been less noticeably guided by an ideology of states' rights, but some of its decisions have had the effect of enhancing the power of the states. For example, in one case, *Massachusetts v. Environmental Protection Agency*,[14] Massachusetts and several other states sued the Environmental Protection Agency (EPA) for failing to regulate greenhouse-gas emissions. The states asserted that the agency was required to do so by the Clean Air Act of 1990. The EPA argued that it lacked the authority under the Clean Air Act to regulate greenhouse-gas emissions alleged to promote global warming. The Court ruled for the states, holding that the EPA did have the authority to regulate such emissions and should take steps to do so.

devolution The surrender or transfer of powers to local authorities by a central government.

federal mandate A requirement in federal legislation that forces states and municipalities to comply with certain rules. If the federal government does not provide funds to the states to cover the costs of compliance, the mandate is referred to as an *unfunded* mandate.

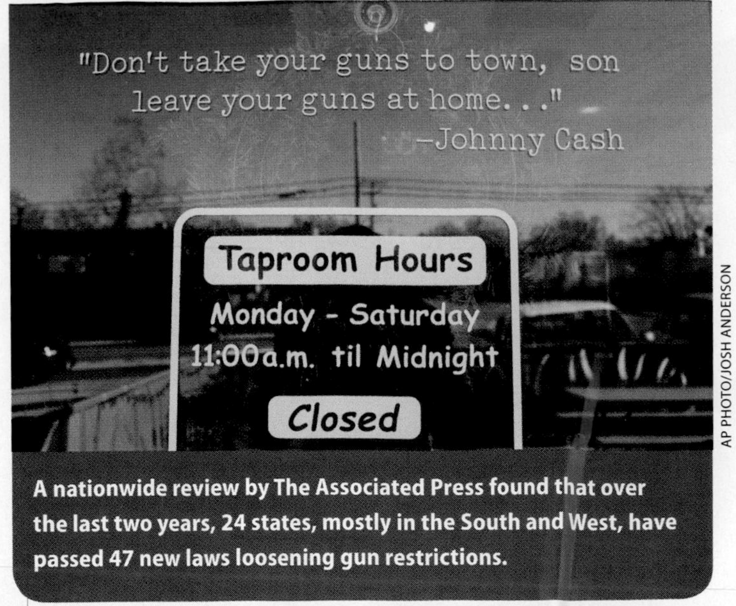

"Don't take your guns to town, son
leave your guns at home. . ."
-Johnny Cash
Taproom Hours
Monday - Saturday
11:00a.m. til Midnight
Closed

AP PHOTO/JOSH ANDERSON

A nationwide review by The Associated Press found that over the last two years, 24 states, mostly in the South and West, have passed 47 new laws loosening gun restrictions.

The Shifting Boundary between Federal and State Authority

Clearly, the boundary between federal and state authority has been shifting. Notably, issues relating to the federal structure of our government, which at one time were not at the forefront of the political arena, have in recent years been the subject of heated debate among Americans and their leaders. The federal government and the states seem to be in a constant tug-of-war over federal regulation, federal programs, and federal demands on the states.

THE POLITICS OF FEDERALISM The Republican Party is often viewed as the champion of states' rights. Certainly, the party has claimed such a role. For example, when the Republicans took control of both chambers of Congress in 1995, they promised devolution—which, as already noted, refers to a shifting of power from the national level to the individual states. Smaller central government and a state-centered federalism have long been regarded as the twin pillars of Republican ideology. In contrast, Democrats usually have sought greater centralization of power in Washington, D.C.

Since the Clinton administration, however, the party tables seem to have turned. As mentioned earlier, it was under Clinton that welfare reform legislation giving more responsibility to the states—a goal that had been endorsed by the Republicans for some time—became a reality. Conversely, the No Child Left Behind Act of 2001, passed at the request of Republican president George W. Bush,

JOIN THE DEBATE

Is Obamacare Unconstitutional?

In 2010, President Obama signed into law the most significant legislation in decades concerning health care. Some were elated by passage of the legislation, nicknamed "Obamacare." Others were aghast. Some who opposed the new law are raising constitutional issues—twenty state attorney generals have joined together in a suit against the federal government. Others, including those who favor Obamacare, are convinced that no constitutional issues are involved.

The Government Can't Force Us to Buy Anything

The reasoning of those who believe Obamacare is unconstitutional runs as follows: It is true that state governments have the right to require, for example, drivers to buy automobile insurance to travel on the public streets. Nothing in the Constitution, in contrast, gives the federal government the right to impose such requirements. The new laws demand that everyone in the United States purchase health-care insurance or be fined. The Internal Revenue Service will enforce this law. While the commerce clause allows the federal government to regulate interstate commerce, it has never been used to *require* citizens to buy any service or good. Another constitutional argument against the reforms is that a requirement to buy insurance violates the Fifth Amendment's right to due process.

Further constitutional challenges are based on states' rights. Some states have passed legislation barring any of their citizens from being required to purchase medical insurance. A suit by Florida claims that the Medicare expansion provided by the law improperly commandeers state officials. The battle between the states and the federal government is not new. Sometimes the Supreme Court has supported states' rights. Sometimes it hasn't.

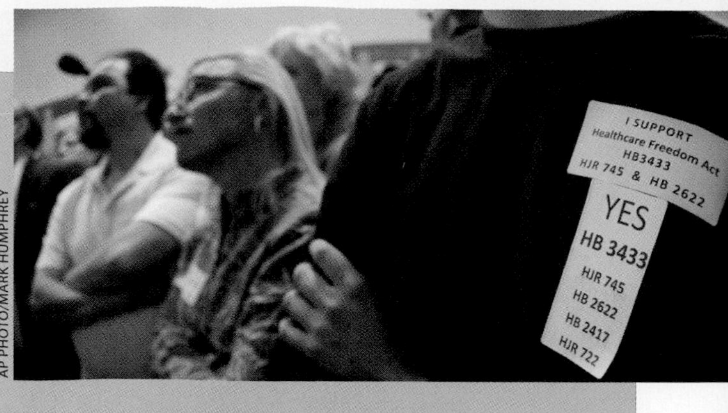

AP PHOTO/MARK HUMPHREY

There Is No Constitutional Basis for a Challenge

Proponents of health-care reform argue that the constitutional challenges to the new legislation are smoke and mirrors. Congress has spoken—all Americans will eventually have access to medical care. For this to occur, almost all Americans will need to have health insurance of one form or another. Otherwise, those who do have health insurance will pay higher premiums to make up for the missing premiums of those that don't have insurance. The "requirement" to buy insurance simply amounts to a tax on those who do not buy it. It's assumed that some people will pay the tax and go without insurance. The courts have always held that Congress can place tax incentives in the Internal Revenue Code.

As for states' rights, that's an old argument brought up every time some people don't like new legislation. In fact, the supremacy of national law was established in 1819 by *McCulloch v. Maryland,* and the breadth of the commerce clause was settled in 1824 by *Gibbons v. Ogden.* (See pages 56 and 57.) If constitutional arguments against the new legislation make it all the way to the United States Supreme Court, they will be rejected—probably on a nine-to-zero vote.

For Critical Analysis ***Who will gain and who will lose because of the new health-care legislation?***

gave the federal government a much greater role in education and educational funding than ever before. Many Republicans also supported a constitutional amendment that would ban same-sex marriages nationwide. Liberals, recognizing that it was possible to win support for same-sex marriages only in a limited number of states, took a states' rights position on this issue. Finally, consider that the Bush administration made repeated attempts to block California's medical-marijuana initiative and Oregon's physician-assisted suicide law.

OBAMA AND FEDERALISM The position of the Obama administration has been more ambiguous. Obama has certainly championed measures that increase the role of government in society, but the new laws have not necessarily shifted power from the states to the federal government. Obama's opponents, however, have frequently invoked states' rights in opposition to such legislation as the health-care reform bills. Officials in a number of states have filed suits claiming that "Obamacare" is unconstitutional. Do these suits have any chance of succeeding? We examine that question in this chapter's *Join the Debate* feature above.

FEDERALISM AND THE "WAR ON TERRORISM" In modern times, terrorism—the use of violence to intimidate or coerce—has become so large-scale and has claimed so many victims that it is hard to consider it an

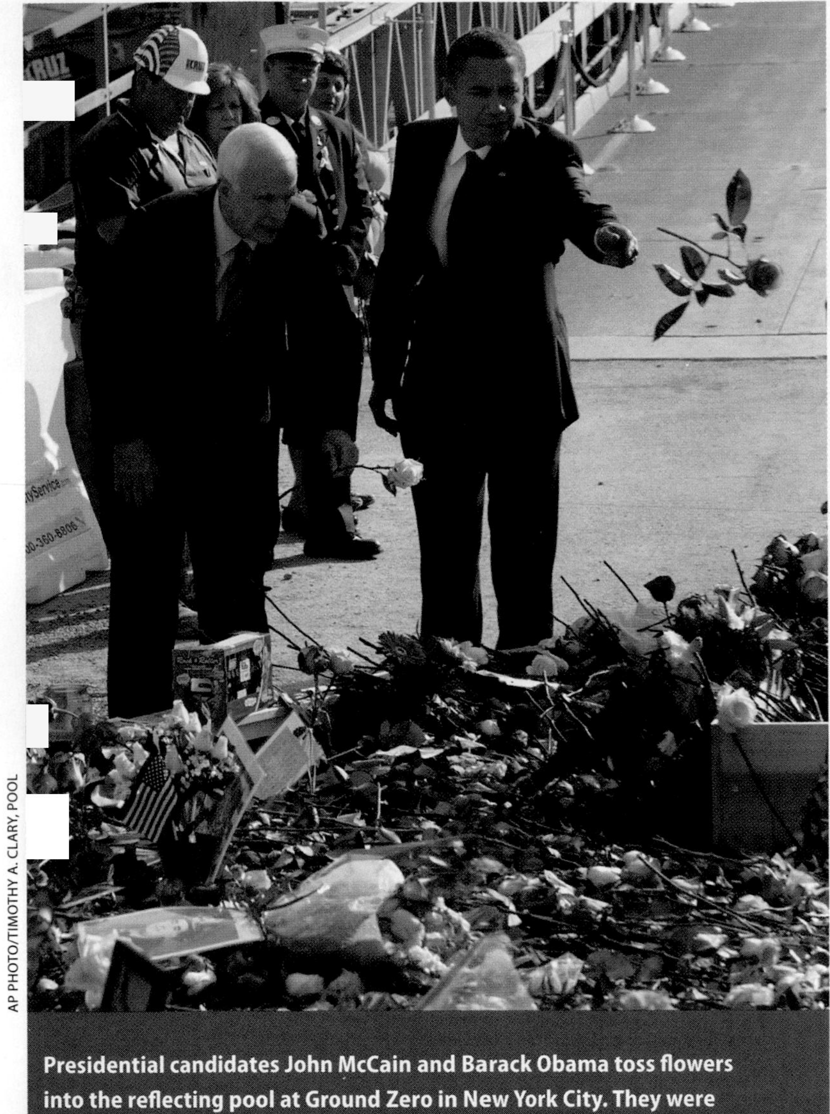

AP PHOTO/TIMOTHY A. CLARY, POOL

Presidential candidates John McCain and Barack Obama toss flowers into the reflecting pool at Ground Zero in New York City. They were commemorating the seventh anniversary of the September 11 terrorist attacks on the World Trade Center towers.

ordinary crime. Terrorism has many of the characteristics of war, not just of crime—hence the term *war on terrorism*. Unlike war, however, terrorism involves nongovernmental actors. Some authorities suggest thinking of terrorism as a "supercrime."[15]

The U.S. Constitution gives Congress the power and authority to provide for the common defense. Nevertheless, most of the burden of homeland defense falls on state and local governments. These governments are the "first responders" to crises, including terrorist attacks. Additionally, state and local governments are responsible for detecting, preparing for, preventing, and recovering from attacks.

After the terrorist attacks of September 11, 2001, the Bush administration increased demands on state and local governments to participate in homeland security. As with the implementation of any national policy, the requirements imposed on the states to support homeland security were costly. Firefighting departments needed more equipment and training. Emergency communications equipment had to be purchased. State and local governments were required to secure ports, ensure water safety and airport security, install new bomb-detecting equipment, and take a multitude of other steps. Since 9/11, almost every state law enforcement agency and about a quarter of local agencies (most of them in larger cities) have formed specialized antiterrorism units. Although the federal government has provided funds to the states to cover some of these expenses, much of the cost of homeland security is borne by the states.

The wars in Afghanistan and Iraq also depleted the ranks of state and local police, firefighters, and other emergency personnel. Many individuals working in these areas were also in the National Guard and were called up to active duty.

FEDERALISM AND THE ECONOMIC CRISIS
Unlike the federal government, state governments are required to balance their budgets. This requirement is written into the constitution of every state except Vermont. Such requirements do not, of course, prevent the states from borrowing money, but typically when a state borrows it must follow a strict series of rules laid down in its constitution. Frequently, a vote of the people is required before a state or local government can go into debt by issuing bonds. In contrast, when the federal government runs a budget deficit, the borrowing that results takes place almost automatically—the U.S. Treasury continually issues new Treasury bonds.

A practical result is that when a major recession occurs, the states are faced with severe budget problems. Because state citizens are earning and spending less, state income and sales taxes fall. At the same time, people who have lost their jobs require more state services. The costs of welfare, unemployment compensation, and Medicaid (health care for low-income persons) all rise. During a recession, state governments may be forced either to reduce spending and lay off staff—or to raise taxes. Either choice helps make the recession worse. State spending patterns tend to make economic booms more energetic and busts more painful—in a word, they are *procyclical.*

Unlike the states, the federal government has no difficulty in spending more on welfare, unemployment compensation, and Medicaid during a recession. Even though revenue raised through the federal income tax may fall, the federal government often cuts tax rates in a recession to spur the economy. It makes up the difference by going further into debt, an option not available to the states. The federal government even has the power to reduce its debt by issuing new money, as you learned in the *Our Government Faces a Troubled Economy* feature in Chapter 2 on page 40. In a recession, the actions of the federal government are normally *anticyclical.*

One method of dealing with the procyclical nature of state spending is to increase federal grants to the states during a recession. For more details on how that can work, see this chapter's *Our Government Faces a Troubled Economy* feature on the following page.

"GIVING MONEY AND POWER TO GOVERNMENT is like giving whiskey and car keys to teenage boys"

~ P.J. O'ROURKE ~
AMERICAN HUMORIST
1947–PRESENT

LO5 *The Fiscal Side of Federalism*

Since the advent of cooperative federalism in the 1930s, the national government and the states have worked hand in hand to implement programs mandated by the national government. Whenever Congress passes a law that preempts a certain area, the states are, of course, obligated to comply with the requirements of that law. As already noted, a requirement that a state provide a service or undertake some activity to meet standards specified by a federal law is called a *federal mandate.* Many federal mandates concern civil rights or environmental protection. Recent federal mandates require the states to provide persons with disabilities with access to public buildings, sidewalks, and other areas; to establish minimum water-purity and air-purity standards; and to extend Medicaid coverage to all poor children.

To help the states pay for some of the costs associated with implementing national policies, the national government gives back some of the tax dollars it collects to the states—in the form of grants. As you will see, the states have come to depend on grants as an important source of revenue. When taxes are collected by one level of government (typically the national government) and spent by another level (typically state or local governments), we call the process **fiscal federalism.**

Federal Grants

Even before the Constitution was adopted, the national government granted lands to the states to finance education. Using the proceeds from the sale of these lands, the states were able to establish elementary schools and, later, *land-grant colleges.* Cash grants started in 1808, when Congress gave money to the states to pay for the state militias. Federal grants were also made available for other purposes, such as building roads and railroads.

Only in the twentieth century, though, did federal grants become an important source of funds to the states. The major growth began in the 1960s, when the dollar amount of grants quadrupled to help pay for the Great Society programs of the Johnson administration. Grants became available for education, pollution control, conservation, recreation, highway construction and maintenance, and other purposes.

There are two basic types of federal grants: categorical grants and block grants. A **categorical grant** is targeted for a specific purpose as defined by federal law—the federal government defines hundreds of categories of state and local spending. Categorical grants give the national government control over how states use the money by imposing certain conditions. For example, a categorical grant may require that the funds not be used for purposes that discriminate against any group or for construction projects that pay below the local prevailing wage. Depending on the project, the government might require that an environmental impact statement be prepared.

In contrast, a **block grant** is given for a broad area, such as criminal justice or mental-health programs. First issued in 1966, block grants now constitute a growing percentage of all federal aid programs. A block grant gives the states more discretion over how the funds

fiscal federalism The allocation of taxes collected by one level of government (typically the national government) to another level (typically state or local governments).

categorical grant A federal grant targeted for a specific purpose as defined by federal law.

block grant A federal grant given to a state for a broad area, such as criminal justice or mental-health programs.

OUR GOVERNMENT FACES A
TROUBLED ECONOMY

Fighting a Recession with Government Spending

In an attempt to prevent the Great Recession from turning into another Great Depression, President Barack Obama called for massive stimulus legislation in 2009. He and his advisers believed that fiscal policy can have profound effects on the nation's economy. Fiscal policy refers to changes in government taxes and spending.

The logic behind fiscal policy is straightforward. When unemployment is rising and the economy is in a recession, fiscal policy should stimulate economic activity by increasing government spending, decreasing tax rates, or both. When unemployment is falling and prices are rising—when there is inflation—the government should curb excessive economic activity by reducing spending, increasing taxes, or both. In other words, the government's budget deficit should rise in a recession and fall in a boom. This view of fiscal policy is based on the theories of the British economist John Maynard Keynes (1883–1946). It's worth noting, by the way, that not all economists agree with Keynes.

Making Grants to the States

It can take a while for the government to realize that a recession has begun. It takes more time for a bill authorizing a tax cut or spending increase to work its way through Congress. It takes still more time for the change in taxation or spending to have an effect. By the time fiscal policy is actually stimulating the economy, the recession may be over. Obama moved quickly, however. He gave the Democrats in Congress almost total freedom to come up with a bill, as long as they did it fast. Indeed, Congress came up with a massive stimulus bill, initially valued at $787 billion, in record time. How could Congress write a bill so quickly?

State and local governments make grant proposals on a continuing basis. Thousands of such proposals from state and local governments were already in hand. Obama therefore promised the American people that the stimulus bill would concentrate on "shovel-ready" projects—state and local projects that were ready to be started immediately upon the receipt of federal funds.

What the Stimulus Really Funded

America has thousands of bridges that need repair, highways that need resurfacing, and other serious infrastructure problems. Of the $787 billion, however, $264 billion was devoted to tax cuts (mostly for individuals), and the rest to spending. Infrastructure received less than $100 billion. Unemployment compensation, food stamps, and other programs totaled more than $100 billion. Health care received about $150 billion—most of it paid to the states—and education received roughly another $100 billion.

Those economists who supported the stimulus believe that it did have a positive effect on the economy. Clearly, however, it did not solve the unemployment problem. By 2010, the unemployment rate was still almost 10 percent. To the extent that the stimulus had an impact on employment, it reduced layoffs rather than creating new jobs. It especially saved the jobs of health-care workers, teachers, and other state government employees. Spending fueled by tax cuts and unemployment compensation presumably saved some jobs as well, but it was impossible to identify who benefited. As a result, the effects of the stimulus were largely invisible. Most voters concluded that the stimulus had no effect.

You Be the Judge **Business tax reductions in the stimulus bill amounted to only $32 billion. Why do you think Obama was reluctant to cut business tax rates further?**

will be spent. Nonetheless, the federal government can exercise control over state decision making through these grants by using *cross-cutting requirements,* or requirements that apply to all federal grants. Title VI of the 1964 Civil Rights Act, for example, bars discrimination in the use of all federal funds, regardless of their source.

Using Federal Grants to Control the States

Grants of funds to the states from the national government are one way that the Tenth Amendment to the U.S. Constitution can be bridged. Remember that the

GARY TRAMONTINA/BLOOMBERG NEWS/VIA GETTY IMAGES

Competitive federalism includes state tax-reduction incentives, through which states offer lower taxes to manufacturing firms that agree to locate in their states. Such an incentive was one reason Toyota opened a plant in Huntsville, Alabama.

Tenth Amendment reserves all powers not delegated to the national government to the states and to the people. You might well wonder, then, how the federal government has been able to exercise control over matters that traditionally have been under the control of state governments, such as the minimum drinking age. The answer involves the giving or withholding of federal grant dollars.

For example, as noted in the *America at Odds* feature at the beginning of this chapter, the national government forced the states to raise the minimum drinking age to twenty-one by threatening to withhold federal highway funds from states that did not comply. The education reforms embodied in the No Child Left Behind (NCLB) Act also rely on federal funding for their implementation. The states receive block grants for educational purposes and, in return, must meet federally imposed standards for testing and accountability. A common complaint, however, is that the existing NCLB Act is an underfunded federal mandate. Critics argue that the national government does not provide sufficient funds to implement it.

The Cost of Federal Mandates

As mentioned, when the national government passes a law preempting an area in which the states and the national government have concurrent powers, the states must comply with that law in accordance with the supremacy clause of the Constitution. Thus, when such laws require the states to implement certain programs, the states must comply—but compliance with federal mandates can be costly. The estimated total cost of complying with federal mandates to the states in the 2000s has been calculated as $29 billion annually. Although Congress passed legislation in 1995 to curb the use of unfunded federal mandates, that legislation was more rhetoric than reality.

Competitive Federalism

The debate over federalism is sometimes reduced to a debate over taxes. Which level of government will raise taxes to pay for government programs, and which will cut services to avoid raising taxes?

How states answer that question gives citizens an option: they can move to a state with fewer services and lower taxes, or to a state with more services but higher taxes. Political scientist Thomas R. Dye calls this model of federalism **competitive federalism.** State and local governments compete for businesses and citizens. If the state of Ohio offers tax advantages for locating a factory there, for example, a business may be more likely to build its factory in Ohio, providing more jobs for Ohio residents. If Ohio has very strict environmental regulations, however, that same business may choose not to build there, no matter how beneficial the tax advantages, because complying with the regulations would be costly. Although Ohio citizens lose the opportunity for more jobs, they may enjoy better air and water quality than citizens of the state where the new factory is ultimately built.

Some observers consider such competition an advantage: Americans have several variables to consider when they choose a state in which to live. Others consider it a disadvantage: a state that offers more social services or lower taxes may experience an increase in population as people "vote with their feet" to take advantage of that state's laws. This population

competitive federalism
A model of federalism devised by Thomas R. Dye in which state and local governments compete for businesses and citizens, who in effect "vote with their feet" by moving to jurisdictions that offer a competitive advantage.

increase can overwhelm the state's resources and force it to cut social services or raise taxes.

It appears likely, then, that the debate over how our federal system functions, as well as the battle for control between the states and the federal government, will continue. The Supreme Court, which has played umpire in this battle, will also likely continue to issue rulings that influence the balance of power.

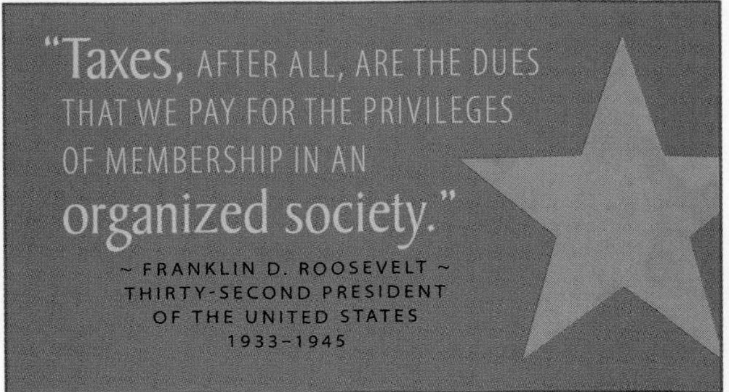

"Taxes, AFTER ALL, ARE THE DUES THAT WE PAY FOR THE PRIVILEGES OF MEMBERSHIP IN AN organized society."
~ FRANKLIN D. ROOSEVELT ~
THIRTY-SECOND PRESIDENT OF THE UNITED STATES
1933–1945

AMERICA AT ODDS Federalism

The topic of federalism raises one of the most enduring disputes in American history—the relative power of the national government versus the governments of the states. As you read in the last two chapters, Americans have been at odds over the strength of the central government since well before the American Revolution. The issue of centralization versus decentralization has taken a number of specific forms:

- Is it right for the national government to use its financial strength to pressure states into taking actions such as raising the drinking age by threatening to withhold subsidies—or are such pressures an abuse of the federal system?
- Should the national government intervene in the issue of legalizing or banning same-sex marriages—or leave such matters strictly to the states?
- Should the commerce clause be interpreted broadly, granting the federal government much power to regulate the economy—or should it be interpreted as narrowly as possible to keep the government from interfering with the rights of business owners?
- Should the federal government have a role in setting national policies for public education—or should that be left entirely to the states?
- Should the federal government establish a national system for funding health care—or should that, too, be left to the states or to the private sector?

Take Action

Many people believe that it's only possible to have a real impact on the problems we face—the economy, poverty, health care, or the environment—at the national level. You can do a lot to address these issues at the state and local level, however. Consider that an individual or a small group can have much more influence on a state government than on the national one, and can make an even bigger impact on a local government.

As the slogan goes, "Think globally, act locally." Your local government controls construction and land-use issues, oversees the police or sheriff's department, and can pass all kinds of local ordinances. Will banning the sale of Styrofoam cups lead to a tidier environment—or is it a ridiculous infringement on personal freedoms? There are hundreds of such issues that you and your friends could take up.

Acting locally does not have to mean political engagement, however. You can also volunteer your services to a cause that concerns you, such as improving the environment or helping the poor or the elderly. Volunteer activities can be very gratifying, and you could make a big difference in the lives that you touch. Try using VolunteerMatch to find volunteer opportunities in your community. Just enter your ZIP code on its Web site (www.volunteermatch.org). Other organizations that work to meet critical needs include AmeriCorps (www.americorps.gov) and the Corporation for National and Community Service (www.nationalservice.gov).

POLITICS ON THE WEB

- You can access the *Federalist Papers,* as well as state constitutions, information on the role of the courts in resolving issues relating to federalism, and information on international federations, at the following site: **www.constitution.org/cs_feder.htm**
- You can find information on state governments, state laws and pending legislation, and state issues and initiatives at **www.statescape.com**
- Supreme Court opinions, including those discussed in this chapter, can be found at the Court's official Web site. Go to **www.supremecourt.gov**
- A good source of information on state governments and issues concerning federalism is the Web site of the Council of State Governments. Go to **www.csg.org**
- The Brookings Institution, the nation's oldest think tank, is a good source for information on emerging policy challenges, including federal-state issues, and for practical recommendations for dealing with those challenges. To access the institution's home page, go to **www.brookings.edu**
- If you are interested in a libertarian perspective on issues such as federalism, you can visit the Cato Institute's Web site at **www.cato.org**
- The Web site of the National Governors Association offers information on many issues affecting the nation, ranging from health-care reform, to education, to new and innovative state programs. You can access information on these issues, as well as many key issues relating to federalism, at **www.nga.org**
- *Governing* magazine, an excellent source of state and local news, can be found online at **www.governing.com**

Access CourseMate to review and expand on this chapter through quizzes, flashcards, learning objectives, interactive timelines, a crossword puzzle, audio summaries, video, critical-thinking activities, simulations, and more.

GOVT

4 Civil Liberties

LEARNING OBJECTIVES

LO1 Define the term *civil liberties,* explain how civil liberties differ from civil rights, and state the constitutional basis for our civil liberties.

LO2 List and describe the freedoms guaranteed by the First Amendment and explain how the courts have interpreted and applied these freedoms.

LO3 Discuss why Americans are increasingly concerned about privacy rights.

LO4 Summarize how the Constitution and the Bill of Rights protect the rights of accused persons.

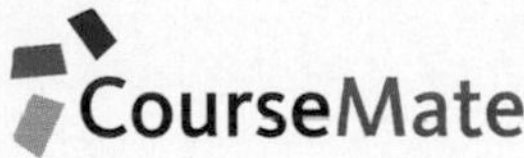

AMERICA AT ODDS

Should Government Entities Enjoy Freedom of Speech?

We all know that the First Amendment to the U.S. Constitution states that Congress shall make no law "abridging the freedom of speech." Indeed, citizens of the United States may enjoy greater freedom of speech than the citizens of any other country. But what about government entities? Do they, too, enjoy freedom of speech? Can government bodies decide without constraint the messages they wish to communicate to the public?

This question becomes important when we consider whether religious displays can be allowed on government property. Until recently, the legal battles over such displays have centered on another part of the First Amendment—the establishment clause, which states: "Congress shall make no law respecting an establishment of religion." On several occasions, the United States Supreme Court has been asked to decide whether Christmas nativity scenes on public property violate the establishment clause. The Court has found that they do, unless equal space is provided for secular displays or the symbols of other religions.

Recently, the Supreme Court grappled with a case in which a small religious group, Summum, wanted to force Pleasant Grove, Utah, to accept a granite monument containing "the Seven Aphorisms of Summum" and place it in a public park. The city had earlier accepted a monument containing the Ten Commandments as one of several dozen displays in the park. Summum claimed that the city had violated the group's free speech rights by refusing to accept its donation. The Court backed the arguments of the city, however, and ruled that "the placement of a permanent monument in a public park is best viewed as a form of government speech and is therefore not subject to scrutiny under the Free Speech Clause." Because it was the city speaking, and not the groups that donated the monuments, none of the organizations could make a free speech claim. In short, government bodies enjoy their own rights to free speech. Is this appropriate?

Obviously, the Government Has a Right to Free Speech

The free speech clause involves government regulation of private speech; it does not regulate government speech. A government entity has the right to "speak for itself" and is entitled to say what it wishes. How could any government body function if it lacked this basic freedom? If citizens had the right to insist that no official paid with public funds could express a view with which that citizen disagreed, debate over issues of public concern would be severely limited. The process of government would be radically transformed. To govern, governments have to say something.

Governments own public land, including parks. Government officials have to decide what expressions of speech should be affixed permanently to public land. If the government did not have the right to decide, every single religious body and special interest group could demand that their monuments be placed on public land. Alongside the Statue of Liberty, New York might be required to erect a "statue of autocracy." In the end, governments would be forced to ban monuments or statues of any description. We cannot take away government bodies' rights to decide in such instances.

It's the Edge of the Wedge

To apply the concept of freedom of speech to governments is asking for trouble. It may be that by accepting a privately financed and donated monument, a government body has exercised a kind of government speech and has implicitly accepted the ideas represented by such monuments. Such thinking raises serious establishment clause issues. If the privately donated monuments are religious in nature, as was true in the Pleasant Grove case, the government is implicitly violating the establishment clause of the First Amendment.

We must make sure that government bodies understand that they cannot even hint at preferring one religion over another. If a government does accept one religious monument, then it had better accept a variety of others. The "government speech doctrine," newly developed by the Supreme Court, must not allow government bodies to escape the establishment clause's ban on discriminating among religious sects or groups. Several Supreme Court justices in the Pleasant Grove case argued that the Court could have ruled for the city without reference to any theory of free speech for governments. The Court's majority should have taken their advice.

WHERE DO YOU STAND?

1. **How can voters hold governments accountable for their decisions about which monuments to display and which not to display?**
2. **Several courts have held that any opinions communicated by specialty license plates are those of the driver, not the state. Why are license plates different from monuments in parks?**

EXPLORE THIS ISSUE ONLINE

- **The FindLaw Web site lets you browse through recent decisions by the Supreme Court on a wide variety of topics. Civil liberties issues are grouped together with civil rights. To locate cases, use the search box at www.findlaw.com/casecode.**
- **Adam Liptak, the Supreme Court correspondent of the *New York Times,* writes a regular column called "Sidebar." To see Liptak's perceptive columns, go to www.nytimes.com and type "sidebar" into the search box.**

CIVIL LIBERTIES are legal and constitutional rights that protect citizens from government actions.

Introduction

The debate over government free speech discussed in the chapter-opening *America at Odds* feature is but one of many controversies concerning our civil liberties. **Civil liberties** are legal and constitutional rights that protect citizens from government actions. For example, the First Amendment to the U.S. Constitution prohibits Congress from making any law that abridges the right to free speech. The First Amendment also guarantees freedom of religion, freedom of the press, and freedom to assemble (to gather together for a common purpose, such as to protest against a government policy or action). These and other freedoms and guarantees set forth in the Constitution and the Bill of Rights are essentially *limits* on government action.

Perhaps the best way to understand what civil liberties are and why they are important to Americans is to look at what might happen if we did not have them. If you were a student in China, for example, you would have to exercise some care in what you said and did. That country prohibits a variety of kinds of speech, notably any criticism of the leading role of the Communist Party. If you criticized the government in e-mail messages to your friends or on your Web site, you could end up in court on charges that you had violated the law—and perhaps even go to prison.

Note that some Americans confuse *civil liberties* (discussed in this chapter) with *civil rights* (discussed in the next chapter) and use the terms interchangeably. Nonetheless, scholars make a distinction between the two. They point out that whereas civil liberties are limitations on government action, setting forth what the government *cannot do*, civil rights specify what the government *must* do—to ensure equal protection under the law for all Americans, for example.

civil liberties Individual rights protected by the Constitution against the powers of the government.

writ of *habeas corpus* An order that requires an official to bring a specified prisoner into court and explain to the judge why the person is being held in prison.

bill of attainder A legislative act that inflicts punishment on particular persons or groups without granting them the right to a trial.

LO1 *The Constitutional Basis for Our Civil Liberties*

The founders believed that the constitutions of the individual states contained ample provisions to protect citizens from government actions. Therefore, the founders did not include many references to individual civil liberties in the original version of the Constitution. Many of our liberties were added by the Bill of Rights, ratified in 1791. Nonetheless, the original Constitution did include some safeguards to protect citizens against an overly powerful government.

Safeguards in the Original Constitution

Article I, Section 9, of the Constitution provides that the writ of *habeas corpus* (a Latin phrase that roughly means "produce the body") will be available to all citizens except in times of rebellion or national invasion. A **writ of *habeas corpus*** is an order requiring that an official bring a specified prisoner into court and show the judge why the prisoner is being kept in jail. If the court finds that the imprisonment is unlawful, it orders the prisoner to be released. If our country did not have such a constitutional provision, political leaders could jail their opponents without giving them the opportunity to plead their cases before a judge. Without this opportunity, many opponents might conveniently disappear or be left to rot away in prison.

The Constitution also prohibits Congress and the state legislatures from passing bills of attainder. A **bill of attainder** is a legislative act that directly punishes a specifically named

Corky Ra is the founder of the group Summum, described on the previous page.

AP PHOTO/SUMMUM, HO

individual (or a group or class of individuals) without a trial. For example, no legislature can pass a law that punishes a named Hollywood celebrity for unpatriotic statements.

Finally, the Constitution also prohibits Congress from passing *ex post facto* laws. The Latin term *ex post facto* roughly means "after the fact." An ***ex post facto* law** punishes individuals for committing an act that was legal when it was committed.

The Bill of Rights

As you read in Chapter 2, one of the contentious issues in the debate over ratification of the Constitution was the lack of protections for citizens from government actions. Although many state constitutions provided such protections, the Anti-Federalists wanted more. The promise of the addition of a bill of rights to the Constitution ensured its ratification.

The Bill of Rights was ratified by the states and became part of the Constitution on December 15, 1791. Look at the text of the Bill of Rights on page 42 in Chapter 2. As you can see, the first eight amendments grant the people specific rights and liberties. The remaining two amendments reserve certain rights and powers to the people and to the states.

Basically, in a democracy, government policy tends to reflect the view of the majority. A key function of the Bill of Rights, therefore, is to protect the rights of those in the minority against the will of the majority. When there is disagreement over how to interpret the Bill of Rights, the courts step in. The United States Supreme Court, as our nation's highest court, has the final say on how the Constitution, including the Bill of Rights, should be interpreted. The civil liberties that you will read about in this chapter have all been shaped over time by Supreme Court decisions. For example, it is the Supreme Court that determines where freedom of speech ends and the right of society to be protected from certain forms of speech begins.

Ultimately, the responsibility for protecting minority rights lies with the American people. Each generation has to learn anew how it can uphold its rights by voting, expressing opinions to elected representatives, and bringing cases to the attention of the courts when constitutional rights are threatened.

The Incorporation Issue

For many years, the courts assumed that the Bill of Rights limited only the actions of the national government, not the actions of state or local governments. In other words, if a state or local law was contrary to a basic freedom, such as the freedom of speech or the right to due process of law, the federal Bill of Rights did not come into play. The founders believed that the states, being closer to the people, would be less likely to violate their own citizens' liberties. Moreover, state constitutions, most of which contain bills of rights, protect citizens against state government actions. The United States Supreme Court upheld this view when it decided, in *Barron v. Baltimore* (1833), that the Bill of Rights did not apply to state laws.[1]

Eventually, however, the Supreme Court began to take a different view. Because the Fourteenth Amendment played a key role in this development, we look next at the provisions of that amendment.

THE RIGHT TO DUE PROCESS In 1868, three years after the end of the Civil War, the Fourteenth Amendment was added to the Constitution. The **due process clause** of this amendment requires that state governments protect their citizens' rights. (A similar requirement, binding on the federal government, was provided by the Fifth Amendment.) The due process clause reads, in part, as follows:

> No State shall . . . deprive any person of life, liberty, or property, without due process of law.

The right to **due process of law** is simply the right to be treated fairly under the legal system. That system and its officers must follow "rules of fair play" in making decisions, in determining guilt or innocence, and in punishing those who have been found guilty.

Procedural Due Process *Procedural* due process requires that any governmental decision to take life, liberty, or property be made equitably. For example, the government must use fair procedures in determining whether a person will be subjected to punishment or have some burden imposed on him or her. Fair procedure has been interpreted as requiring that the person have at least an opportunity to object to a proposed action before an impartial, neutral decision maker (which need not be a judge).

***ex post facto* law** A criminal law that punishes individuals for committing an act that was legal when the act was committed.

due process clause The constitutional guarantee, set out in the Fifth and Fourteenth Amendments, that the government will not illegally or arbitrarily deprive a person of life, liberty, or property.

due process of law The requirement that the government use fair, reasonable, and standard procedures whenever it takes any legal action against an individual; required by the Fifth and Fourteenth Amendments.

establishment clause The section of the First Amendment that prohibits Congress from passing laws "respecting an establishment of religion." Issues concerning the establishment clause often center on prayer in public schools, the teaching of fundamentalist theories of creation, and government aid to parochial schools.

free exercise clause The provision of the First Amendment stating that the government cannot pass laws "prohibiting the free exercise" of religion. Free exercise issues often concern religious practices that conflict with established laws.

Table 4–1

Incorporating the Bill of Rights into the 14th Amendment

Year	Issue	Amendment Involved	Court Case
1925	Freedom of speech	I	*Gitlow v. New York,* 268 U.S. 652.
1931	Freedom of the press	I	*Near v. Minnesota,* 283 U.S. 697.
1932	Right to a lawyer in capital punishment cases	VI	*Powell v. Alabama,* 287 U.S. 45.
1937	Freedom of assembly and right to petition	I	*De Jonge v. Oregon,* 299 U.S. 353.
1940	Freedom of religion	I	*Cantwell v. Connecticut,* 310 U.S. 296.
1947	Separation of church and state	I	*Everson v. Board of Education,* 330 U.S. 1.
1948	Right to a public trial	VI	*In re Oliver,* 333 U.S. 257.
1949	No unreasonable searches and seizures	IV	*Wolf v. Colorado,* 338 U.S. 25.
1961	Exclusionary rule	IV	*Mapp v. Ohio,* 367 U.S. 643.
1962	No cruel and unusual punishments	VIII	*Robinson v. California,* 370 U.S. 660.
1963	Right to a lawyer in all criminal felony cases	VI	*Gideon v. Wainwright,* 372 U.S. 335.
1964	No compulsory self-incrimination	V	*Malloy v. Hogan,* 378 U.S. 1.
1965	Right to privacy	Various	*Griswold v. Connecticut,* 381 U.S. 479.
1966	Right to an impartial jury	VI	*Parker v. Gladden,* 385 U.S. 363.
1967	Right to a speedy trial	VI	*Klopfer v. North Carolina,* 386 U.S. 213.
1969	No double jeopardy	V	*Benton v. Maryland,* 395 U.S. 784.
2010	Right to bear arms	II	*McDonald v. Chicago,* 561 U.S. ___.

Substantive Due Process *Substantive* due process focuses on the content, or substance, of legislation. If a law or other governmental action limits a *fundamental right,* it will be held to violate substantive due process, unless it promotes a *compelling* or *overriding state interest.* All First Amendment rights plus the rights to interstate travel, privacy, and voting are considered fundamental. Compelling state interests could include, for example, the public's safety.

OTHER LIBERTIES INCORPORATED The Fourteenth Amendment also states that no state "shall make or enforce any law which shall abridge the privileges or immunities of citizens of the United States." For some time, the Supreme Court considered the "privileges and immunities" referred to in the amendment to be those conferred by state laws or constitutions, not the federal Bill of Rights.

Starting in 1925, however, the Supreme Court gradually began using the due process clause to say that states could not abridge a civil liberty that the national government could not abridge. In other words, the Court *incorporated* the protections guaranteed by the national Bill of Rights into the liberties protected under the Fourteenth Amendment. As you can see in Table 4–1 above, the Supreme Court was particularly active during the 1960s in broadening its interpretation of the due process clause to ensure that states and localities could not infringe on civil liberties protected by the Bill of Rights. Today, the liberties still not incorporated include the right to refuse to quarter soldiers and the right to a grand jury hearing. The right to bear arms described in the Second Amendment was incorporated only in 2010.

LO2 *Protections under the First Amendment*

As mentioned earlier, the First Amendment sets forth some of our most important civil liberties. Specifically, the First Amendment guarantees the freedoms of religion, speech, the press, and assembly, as well as the right to petition the government. In the pages that follow, we look closely at each of these freedoms and discuss how, over time, Supreme Court decisions have defined their meaning and determined their limits.

Freedom of Religion

The First Amendment prohibits Congress from passing laws "respecting an establishment of religion, or prohibiting the free exercise thereof." The first part of this amendment is known as the **establishment clause.** The second part is called the **free exercise clause.**

AP PHOTO/*SALT LAKE TRIBUNE*/AL HARTMANN

The right to bear arms is included in the Second Amendment to the U.S. Constitution. In 2008, the Supreme Court ruled for the first time that this right applies to individuals, not just state militias. In 2010, the Court ruled that state governments were also required to respect this right.

That freedom of religion was the first freedom mentioned in the Bill of Rights is not surprising. After all, many colonists came to America to escape religious persecution. Nonetheless, these same colonists showed little tolerance for religious freedom within the communities they established. For example, in 1610 the Jamestown colony enacted a law requiring attendance at religious services on Sunday "both in the morning and the afternoon." Repeat offenders were subjected to particularly harsh punishments. For those who twice violated the law, for example, the punishment was a public whipping. For third-time offenders, the punishment was death.

The Maryland Toleration Act of 1649 declared that anyone who cursed God or denied that Jesus Christ was the son of God was to be punished by death. In all, nine of the thirteen colonies had established official religions by the time of the American Revolution.

This context is helpful in understanding why, in 1802, President Thomas Jefferson, a great proponent of religious freedom and tolerance, wanted the establishment clause to be "a wall of separation between church and state." The context also helps to explain why even state leaders who supported state religions might have favored the establishment clause—to keep the national government from interfering in such state matters. After all, the First Amendment says only that *Congress* can make no law respecting an establishment of religion. It says nothing about whether the *states* could make such laws. And, as noted earlier, the protections in the Bill of Rights initially applied only to actions taken by the national government, not the state governments.

THE ESTABLISHMENT CLAUSE The establishment clause forbids the government to establish an official religion. This makes the United States different from countries that are ruled by religious governments, such as the Islamic government of Iran. It also makes us different from nations that have in the past strongly discouraged the practice of any religion at all, such as the People's Republic of China.

What does this separation of church and state mean in practice? For one thing, religion and government, though constitutionally separated in the United States, have never been enemies or strangers. The establishment clause does not prohibit government from supporting religion in *general*. It remains a part of public life.

Most government officials take an oath of office in the name of God, and our coins and paper currency carry the motto "In God We Trust." Clergy of different religions serve in each branch of the armed forces. Public meetings and even sessions of Congress open with prayers. Indeed, the establishment clause often masks the fact that Americans are, by and large, religious and would like their political leaders to be people of faith.

The "wall of separation" that Thomas Jefferson referred to, however, does exist and has been upheld by the Supreme Court on many occasions. An important ruling by the Supreme Court on the establishment clause came in 1947 in *Everson v. Board of Education.*[2] The case involved a New Jersey law that allowed the state to pay for bus transportation of students who attended parochial schools (schools run by churches or other religious groups). The Court stated as follows: "No tax in any amount, large or small, can be levied to support any religious activities or institutions."

The Court upheld the New Jersey law, however, because it did not aid the church *directly* but provided for the safety and benefit of the students. The ruling both affirmed the importance of separating church and state and set the precedent that not *all* forms of state and federal aid to church-related schools are forbidden under the Constitution.

A full discussion of the various church-state issues that have arisen in American politics would fill volumes. Here we examine three of these issues: prayer in the schools, evolution versus creationism or intelligent design, and government aid to parochial schools.

Prayer in the Schools On occasion, some public schools have promoted a general sense of religion without proclaiming allegiance to any particular church or sect. Whether the states have a right to allow this was the main question presented in 1962 in *Engel v. Vitale*,[3] also known as the "Regents' Prayer case." The State Board of Regents in New York had composed a nondenominational prayer (a prayer not associated with any particular church) and urged school districts to use it in classrooms at the start of each day. The prayer read as follows:

> Almighty God, we acknowledge our dependence upon Thee, and we beg Thy blessings upon us, our parents, our teachers, and our Country.

Some parents objected to the prayer, contending that it violated the establishment clause. The Supreme Court agreed and ruled that the Regents' Prayer was unconstitutional. Speaking for the majority, Justice Hugo Black wrote that the First Amendment must at least mean "that in this country it is no part of the business of government to compose official prayers for any group of the American people to recite as a part of a religious program carried on by government."

The First Amendment TO THE CONSTITUTION MANDATES SEPARATION OF CHURCH AND STATE. NONETHELESS, REFERENCES TO GOD ARE COMMON IN PUBLIC LIFE, AS THE PHRASE "IN GOD WE TRUST" ON THIS COIN DEMONSTRATES.

KARY NIEUWENHUIS/ISTOCKPHOTO

Prayer in the Schools—The Debate Continues Since the *Engel v. Vitale* ruling, the Supreme Court has continued to shore up the wall of separation between church and state in a number of decisions. Generally, the Court has had to walk a fine line between the wishes of those who believe that religion should have a more prominent place in our public institutions and those who do not. For example, in a 1980 case, *Stone v. Graham*,[4] the Supreme Court ruled that a Kentucky law requiring that the Ten Commandments be posted in all public schools violated the establishment clause. Many groups around the country opposed this ruling. Today, a number of states have passed or proposed laws permitting (but not *requiring*, as the Kentucky law did) the display of the Ten Commandments on public property, including public schools. Supporters of such displays contend that they will help reinforce the fundamental religious values that are a part of the American heritage. Opponents claim that the displays blatantly violate the establishment clause.

Another controversial issue is whether "moments of silence" in the schools are constitutional. In 1985, the Supreme Court ruled that an Alabama law authorizing a daily one-minute period of silence for meditation and voluntary prayer was unconstitutional. Because the law specifically endorsed prayer, it appeared to support religion.[5] Since then, the lower courts have generally held that a school may require a moment of silence, but only if it serves a clearly secular purpose (such as to meditate on the day's activities).[6] Yet another issue concerns prayers said before public school sporting events, such as football games. In 2000, the Supreme Court held that student-led pregame prayer using the school's public-address system was unconstitutional.[7]

In sum, the Supreme Court has ruled that the public schools, which are agencies of government, cannot

These students at Trey Whitfield School, in Brooklyn, New York—a private school—are engaged in school-organized prayers. Why is it constitutional to allow prayers in private schools but not in public schools?

MARILYNN K. YEE/*NEW YORK TIMES*/REDUX

sponsor religious activities. It has *not,* however, held that individuals cannot pray, when and as they choose, in schools or in any other place. Nor has it held that the schools are barred from teaching *about* religion, as opposed to engaging in religious practices.

Evolution versus Creationism Certain religious groups have long opposed the teaching of evolution in the schools. These groups contend that evolutionary theory, a theory with overwhelming scientific support, directly counters their religious belief that human beings did not evolve but were created fully formed, as described in the biblical story of the creation. In fact, surveys have repeatedly shown that a majority of Americans believe that humans were directly created by God rather than having evolved from other species. The Supreme Court, however, has held that state laws forbidding the teaching of evolution in the schools are unconstitutional.

For example, in *Epperson v. Arkansas,*[8] a case decided in 1968, the Supreme Court held that an Arkansas law prohibiting the teaching of evolution violated the establishment clause because it imposed religious beliefs on students. In 1987, the Supreme Court also held unconstitutional a Louisiana law requiring that the biblical story of the creation be taught along with evolution. The Court deemed the law unconstitutional in part because it had as its primary purpose the promotion of a particular religious belief.[9]

Nevertheless, some state and local groups continue their efforts against the teaching of evolution. Recently, for example, Alabama approved a disclaimer to be inserted in biology textbooks, stating that evolution is "a controversial theory some scientists present as a scientific explanation for the origin of living things." Laws and policies that discourage the teaching of evolution are also being challenged on constitutional grounds. For example, in Cobb County, Georgia, stickers were inserted into science textbooks stating that "evolution is a theory, not a fact" and that "the theory should be approached with an open mind, studied carefully, and critically considered." When Cobb County's actions were challenged in court as unconstitutional, a federal judge held that the stickers conveyed a "message of endorsement of religion," thus violating the First Amendment.

Lemon test A three-part test enunciated by the Supreme Court in the 1971 case of *Lemon v. Kurtzman* to determine whether government aid to parochial schools is constitutional. To be constitutional, the aid must (1) be for a clearly secular purpose; (2) in its primary effect, neither advance nor inhibit religion; and (3) avoid an "excessive government entanglement with religion." The *Lemon* test has also been used in other types of cases involving the establishment clause.

Evolution versus Intelligent Design Some schools have adopted the concept of "intelligent design" as an alternative to the teaching of evolution. Advocates of intelligent design believe that an intelligent cause, and not an undirected process such as natural selection, lies behind the creation and development of the universe and living things. Proponents of intelligent design claim that it is a scientific theory and thus that its teaching should not violate the establishment clause in any way. Opponents of intelligent design theory claim that it is pseudoscience at best and that, in fact, the so-called theory masks its supporters' belief that God is the "intelligent cause."

Aid to Parochial Schools Americans have long been at odds over whether public tax dollars should be used to fund activities in parochial schools—private schools that have religious affiliations. Over the years, the courts have often had to decide whether specific types of aid do or do not violate the establishment clause. Aid to church-related schools in the form of transportation, equipment, or special educational services for disadvantaged students has been held permissible. Other forms of aid, such as funding teachers' salaries and paying for field trips, have been held unconstitutional.

Since 1971, the Supreme Court has held that, to be constitutional, a state's school aid must meet three requirements: (1) the purpose of the financial aid must be clearly secular (not religious), (2) its primary effect must neither advance nor inhibit religion, and (3) it must avoid an "excessive government entanglement with religion." The Court first used this three-part test in *Lemon v. Kurtzman,*[10] and hence it is often referred to as the ***Lemon* test.** In the 1971 *Lemon* case, the Court denied public aid to private and parochial

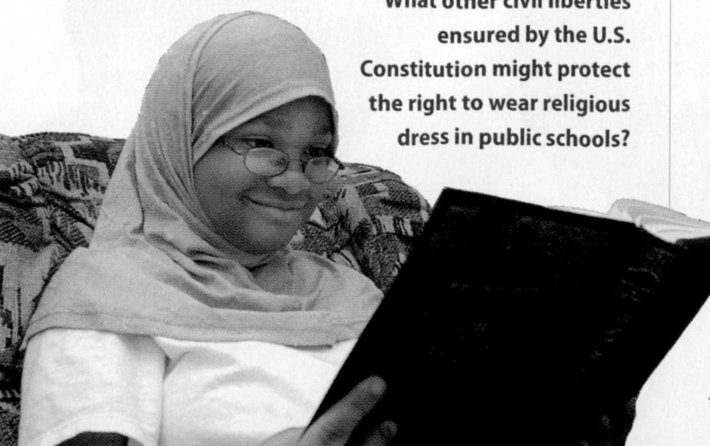
When an Oklahoma school attempted to bar a young Muslim girl from wearing a head scarf to school, the federal government intervened. Why would the U.S. government protect the right to wear religious symbols in public schools? What other civil liberties ensured by the U.S. Constitution might protect the right to wear religious dress in public schools?

AP PHOTO/AMY DEMOSS/MUSKOGEE DAILY PHOENIX

school voucher An educational certificate, provided by a government, that allows a student to use public funds to pay for a private or a public school chosen by the student or his or her parents.

schools for the salaries of teachers of secular courses and for textbooks and instructional materials in certain secular subjects. The Court held that the establishment clause is designed to prevent three main evils: "sponsorship, financial support, and active involvement of the sovereign [the government] in religious activity."

In 2000, the Supreme Court applied the *Lemon* test to a federal law that gives public school districts federal funds for special services and instructional equipment. The law requires that the funds be shared with all private schools in the district. A central issue in the case was whether using the funds to supply computers to parochial schools had a clearly secular purpose. Some groups claimed that it did not, because students in parochial schools could use the computers to access religious materials online. Others, including the Clinton administration (1993–2001), argued that giving high-tech assistance to parochial schools did have a secular purpose and was a religiously neutral policy. The Supreme Court sided with the latter argument and held that the law did not violate the establishment clause.[11]

School Voucher Programs Another contentious issue has to do with the use of **school vouchers**—educational certificates, provided by state governments, that students can use at any school, public or private. In an effort to improve their educational systems, several school districts have been experimenting with voucher systems. Four states now have limited voucher programs under which schoolchildren may attend private elementary or high schools using vouchers paid for by taxpayers' dollars.

In 2002, the United States Supreme Court ruled that a voucher program in Cleveland, Ohio, was constitutional. Under the program, the state provided up to $2,250 to low-income families, who could use the funds to send their children to either public or private schools. The Court concluded that the taxpayer-paid voucher program did not unconstitutionally entangle church and state because the funds went to parents, not to schools. The parents theoretically could use the vouchers to send their children to nonreligious private academies or charter schools, even though 95 percent used the vouchers at religious schools.[12]

Despite the 2002 Supreme Court ruling, several constitutional questions surrounding school vouchers remain unresolved. For example, some state constitutions are more explicit than the federal Constitution in denying the use of public funds for religious education. Even after the Supreme Court ruling in the Ohio case, a Florida court ruled in 2002 that a voucher program in that state violated Florida's constitution.[13]

The public is very closely divided on this issue. About 30 percent of those responding to a public opinion poll on the subject did not have strong feelings one way or the other; those with opinions were evenly split. Support for vouchers tended to come from Catholics and white evangelicals, which is not surprising—a large number of existing private schools represent either the Catholic or evangelical faiths. Public school teacher unions oppose vouchers strongly, and they are a major constituency for the Democratic Party. With the Democrats in control of the presidency, federal support for vouchers is unlikely in the near future.

THE FREE EXERCISE CLAUSE As mentioned, the second part of the First Amendment's statement on religion consists of the free exercise clause, which forbids the passage of laws "prohibiting the free exercise of religion." This clause protects a person's right to worship or believe as he or she wishes without government interference. No law or act of government may violate this constitutional right.

Belief and Practice Are Distinct The free exercise clause does not necessarily mean that individuals can act in any way they want on the basis of their religious beliefs. There is an important distinction between belief and practice. The Supreme Court has ruled consistently

These members of the Texas State Board of Education discuss the teaching of evolution and scientific theory with the state science advisor. What is the controversy?

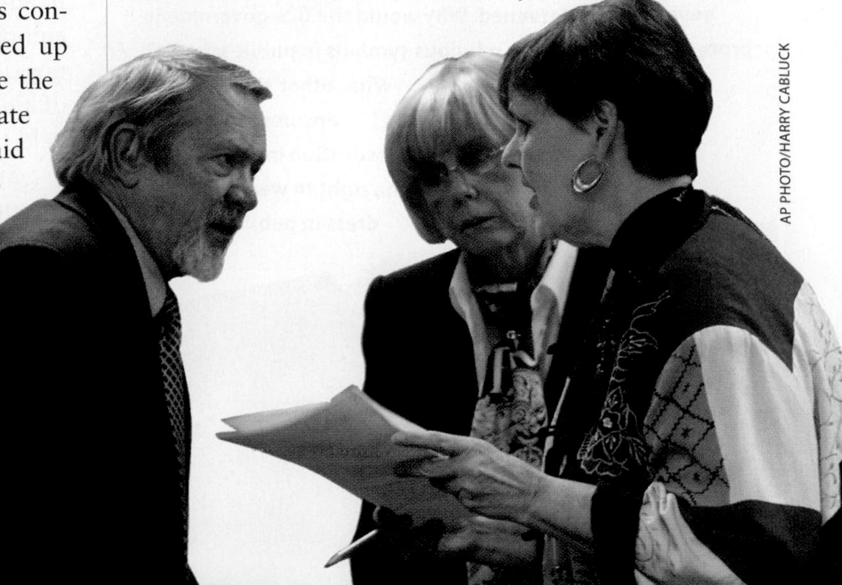

AP PHOTO/HARRY CABLUCK

that the right to hold any *belief* is absolute. The government has no authority to compel you to accept or reject any particular religious belief. The right to *practice* one's beliefs, however, may have some limits. As the Court itself once asked, "Suppose one believed that human sacrifice were a necessary part of religious worship?"

The Supreme Court first dealt with the issue of belief versus practice in 1878 in *Reynolds v. United States.*[14] Reynolds was a Mormon who had two wives. Polygamy, or the practice of having more than one spouse at a time, was encouraged by the customs and teachings of his religion. Polygamy was also prohibited by federal law. Reynolds was convicted and appealed the case, arguing that the law violated his constitutional right to freely exercise his religious beliefs. The Court did not agree. It said that to allow Reynolds to practice polygamy would make religious doctrines superior to the law.

THE FREE EXERCISE CLAUSE protects a person's right to worship or believe as he or she wishes without government interference.

Student religious organizations at colleges and universities have been the subject of a number of civil liberties controversies over the years. One of the most recent cases focused on a free exercise topic. We discuss it in this chapter's feature *Join the Debate: Should We Let Student Religious Groups Bar Gays from Membership?* on the following page.

This proponent of a school voucher program in Cleveland, Ohio, believes that only the students of rich parents have much school choice. Her implicit argument is that school vouchers will give the same school choice to children who are poor as to those who are rich.

Choice is
WIDESPREAD
unless you'RE
Poor

AP PHOTO/RICK BOWMER

Religious Practices and the Workplace The free exercise of religion in the workplace was bolstered by Title VII of the Civil Rights Act of 1964, which requires employers to accommodate their employees' religious practices unless such accommodation causes an employer to suffer an "undue hardship." Thus, if an employee claims that his or her religious beliefs prevent him or her from working on a particular day of the week, such as Saturday or Sunday, the employer must attempt to accommodate the employee's needs.

Several cases have come before lower federal courts concerning employer dress codes that contradict the religious customs of employees. For example, in 1999 the Third Circuit Court of Appeals ruled in favor of two Muslim police officers in Newark, New Jersey, who claimed that they were required by their faith to wear beards and would not shave them to comply with the police department's grooming policy. A similar case was brought in 2001 by Washington, D.C., firefighters.[15] Muslims, Rastafarians, and others have refused to change the grooming habits required by their religions and have been successful in court.

Freedom of Expression

No one in this country seems to have a problem protecting the free speech of those with whom they agree. The real challenge is protecting unpopular ideas. The protection needed is, in Justice Oliver Wendell Holmes's words, "not free thought for those who agree with us but freedom for the thought that we hate." The First Amendment is designed to protect the freedom to express *all* ideas, including those that may be unpopular.

The First Amendment has been interpreted to protect more than merely spoken words. It also protects **symbolic speech**—speech involving actions and other nonverbal expressions. Some common examples include picketing in a labor dispute and wearing a black armband in protest of a government policy. Even burning the American flag as a gesture of protest has been held to be protected by the First Amendment.

symbolic speech The expression of beliefs, opinions, or ideas through forms other than speech or print; speech involving actions and other nonverbal expressions.

JOIN THE DEBATE

AP PHOTO/THE JOPLIN GLOBE, T. ROB BROWN

Should We Let Student Religious Groups Bar Gays from Membership?

The members of campus student organizations often share common beliefs. Young Republicans do not normally seek to join the Democratic club on campus, and vice versa. You don't expect to find many members of the Association of Muslim Law Students who are not Muslims. Many colleges and universities, however, prohibit certain membership restrictions in student organizations. For example, the Student Conduct Code at Eastern Michigan University (EMU) lists the following violation: "*Discrimination by Student Organizations.* Selecting its membership upon the basis of restrictive clauses involving race, religion, color, national origin, gender, age, sexual orientation or disability unless any given student organization's membership restriction is shown to be specifically allowed by law."

Under such rules, EMU's Democratic club could bar Republicans, because political ideology is an acceptable basis for membership. But what about a Christian group that, as a matter of belief, opposes sex outside of marriage between a man and a woman? Can such student religious groups bar gay men and lesbians from membership? If they do, can the school withdraw official recognition?

This question was at the heart of a recent case involving the University of California's Hastings College of the Law. The Christian Legal Society (CLS) at the school excludes from affiliation anyone who engages in "unrepentant homosexual conduct" or holds religious convictions different from those in the group's Statement of Faith. Hastings, however, requires that all recognized student organizations accept *any* student as a member. (At Hastings, unlike EMU, the campus Republicans could *not* formally exclude Democrats.) Hastings therefore refused to grant recognition to the CLS. The organization sued—and lost at every stage, all the way to the Supreme Court.[16]

Government Bodies Must Oppose Discrimination

Those who support the Court's ruling believe that the ruling is as it should be. The Court's ruling did not force the CLS to accept lesbians or gay men as members. It did not ban the group, which continues to meet on campus despite its lack of official status. But why should a student pay mandatory student-activity fees to fund a group that would reject her as a member? A free society must accept all minorities. Whether discrimination is based on religion, sexual orientation, or race, it should not be subsidized by state universities. Groups should be able to believe—and say—whatever they want, but discrimination is an action, not a belief.

What Happened to Freedom of Association?

Opponents of the Court's decision point out that the Bill of Rights grants us freedom of association. Freedom to associate also means freedom *not* to associate. That's why Hastings's ridiculous open membership rule is wrong. Indeed, there's some evidence that Hastings created the rule specifically to apply to the CLS. In effect, the Court's decision denies freedom of expression when that expression offends prevailing standards of political correctness. If campus organizations cannot choose their members, an African American student group will have to admit members of the Ku Klux Klan. Consider one possibility—everyone opposed to the principles of an organization could join that group and then vote to disband. Is this freedom?

For Critical Analysis ***When is it legal for an organization to restrict who may join?***

THE RIGHT TO FREE SPEECH IS NOT ABSOLUTE Although Americans have the right to free speech, not *all* speech is protected under the First Amendment. Our constitutional rights and liberties are not absolute. Rather, they are what the Supreme Court—the ultimate interpreter of the Constitution—says they are. Although the Court has zealously safeguarded the right to free speech, at times it has imposed limits on speech in the interests of protecting other rights of Americans. These rights include security against harm to one's person or reputation, the need for public order, and the need to preserve the government.

Generally, throughout our history, the Supreme Court has attempted to balance our rights to free speech against these other needs of society. As Justice Holmes once said, even "the most stringent protection of free speech would not protect a man in falsely shouting fire in a theatre and causing a panic."[17] We look next at some of the ways that the Court has limited the right to free speech.

EARLY RESTRICTIONS ON EXPRESSION At times in our nation's history, various individuals have opposed our form of government. The government, however, has drawn a fine line between legitimate criticism and the expression of ideas that may seriously harm society. Clearly, the government may pass laws against violent acts. But what about **seditious speech,** which urges resistance to lawful authority or advocates overthrowing the government?

> **"FREE SPEECH** is the whole thing, the whole ball game. Free speech is life itself."
>
> ~ SALMAN RUSHDIE ~
> INDIAN-BORN BRITISH WRITER
> B. 1947

As early as 1798, Congress took steps to curb seditious speech when it passed the Alien and Sedition Acts, which made it a crime to utter "any false, scandalous, and malicious" criticism of the government. The acts were considered unconstitutional by many but were never tested in the courts. Several dozen individuals were prosecuted under the acts, and some were actually convicted. In 1801, President Thomas Jefferson pardoned those sentenced under the acts, and Congress soon repealed them.

During World War I, Congress passed the Espionage Act of 1917 and the Sedition Act of 1918. The 1917 act prohibited attempts to interfere with the operation of the military forces, the war effort, or the process of recruitment. The 1918 act made it a crime to "willfully utter, print, write, or publish any disloyal, profane, scurrilous [insulting], or abusive language" about the government. More than two thousand persons were tried and convicted under this act, which was repealed at the end of World War I.

In 1940, Congress passed the Smith Act, which forbade people from advocating the violent overthrow of the U.S. government. In 1951, the Supreme Court first upheld the constitutionality of the Smith Act in *Dennis v. United States,*[18] which involved eleven top leaders of the Communist Party who had been convicted of violating the act. The Court found that their activities went beyond the permissible peaceful advocacy of change. Subsequently, however, the Court modified its position. Since the 1960s, the Court has defined seditious speech to mean only the advocacy of imminent and concrete acts of violence against the government.[19]

LIMITED PROTECTION FOR COMMERCIAL SPEECH Advertising, or **commercial speech,** is also protected by the First Amendment, but not as fully as regular speech. Generally, the Supreme Court has considered a restriction on commercial speech to be valid as long as the restriction "(1) seeks to implement a substantial government interest, (2) directly advances that interest, and (3) goes no further than necessary to accomplish its objective." Problems arise, though, when restrictions on commercial advertising achieve one substantial government interest yet are contrary to the interest in protecting free speech and the right of consumers to be informed. In such cases, the courts have to decide which interest takes priority.

Liquor advertising is a good illustration of this kind of conflict. For example,

Attorney Patrick Coughlin (center) gives a press conference in front of the Supreme Court. He represented activists who sued Nike for false advertising when it defended itself from attacks against its employment policies in Asia. How much free speech do companies enjoy?

KEVIN LAMARQUE/REUTERS/LANDOV

seditious speech Speech that urges resistance to lawful authority or that advocates the overthrowing of a government.

commercial speech Advertising statements that describe products. Commercial speech receives less protection under the First Amendment than ordinary speech.

libel A published report of a falsehood that tends to injure a person's reputation or character.

slander The public utterance (speaking) of a statement that holds a person up for contempt, ridicule, or hatred.

obscenity Indecency or offensiveness in speech, expression, behavior, or appearance. Whether specific expressions or acts constitute obscenity normally is determined by community standards.

in one case, Rhode Island argued that its law banning the advertising of liquor prices served the state's goal of discouraging liquor consumption (because the ban discouraged bargain hunting and thus kept liquor prices high). The Supreme Court, however, held that the ban was an unconstitutional restraint on commercial speech. The Court stated that the First Amendment "directs us to be especially skeptical of regulations that seek to keep people in the dark for what the government perceives to be their own good."[20]

UNPROTECTED SPEECH Certain types of speech receive no protection under the First Amendment. These types of speech include defamation (libel and slander) and obscenity.

Libel and Slander No person has the right to libel or slander another. **Libel** is a published report of a falsehood that tends to injure a person's reputation or character. **Slander** is the public utterance (speaking) of a statement that holds a person up for contempt, ridicule, or hatred. To prove libel or slander, however, certain criteria must be met. The statements made must be untrue, must stem from an intent to do harm, and must result in actual harm.

The Supreme Court has ruled that public figures (public officials and others in the public limelight) cannot collect damages for remarks made against them unless they can prove the remarks were made with "reckless" disregard for accuracy. Generally, it is believed that because public figures have greater access to the media than ordinary persons do, they are in a better position to defend themselves against libelous or slanderous statements.

Obscenity Obscene speech is another form of speech that is not protected under the First Amendment. Although the dictionary defines **obscenity** as that which is offensive and indecent, the courts have had difficulty defining the term with any precision. Supreme Court justice Potter Stewart's famous statement, "I know it when I see it," certainly gave little guidance on the issue.

One problem in defining obscenity is that what is obscene to one person is not necessarily obscene to another. What one reader considers indecent, another reader might see as "colorful." Another problem is that society's views on obscenity change over time. Major literary works of such great writers as D. H. Lawrence (1885–1930), Mark Twain (1835–1910), and James Joyce (1882–1941), for example, were once considered obscene in most of the United States.

After many unsuccessful attempts to define obscenity, in 1973 the Supreme Court came up with a three-part test in *Miller v. California*.[21] The Court decided that a book, film, or other piece of material is legally obscene if it meets the following criteria:

1. The average person applying contemporary (present-day) standards finds that the work taken as a whole appeals to the prurient interest—that is, tends to excite unwholesome sexual desire.
2. The work depicts or describes, in a patently (obviously) offensive way, a form of sexual conduct specifically prohibited by an antiobscenity law.
3. The work taken as a whole lacks serious literary, artistic, political, or scientific value.

The very fact that the Supreme Court has had to set up such a complicated test shows how difficult defining obscenity is. The Court went on to state that, in effect, local communities should be allowed to set their own standards for what is obscene. What is obscene to many people in one area of the country might be perfectly acceptable to those in another area.

Obscenity in Cyberspace A hugely controversial issue concerning free speech is the question of obscene and pornographic materials in cyberspace. Such materials can be easily accessed by anyone of any age anywhere in the world at countless Web sites. Many people strongly believe that the government should step in to prevent obscenity on the Internet. Others believe, just as strongly, that speech on the Internet should not be regulated.

The issue came to a head in 1996, when Congress passed the Communications Decency Act (CDA). The law made it a crime to transmit "indecent" or "patently offensive" speech or images to minors (those under the age of eighteen) or to make such speech or images available online to minors. Violators of the act could be fined up to $250,000 or imprisoned for up to two years. In 1997, the Supreme Court held that the law's sections on indecent speech were unconstitutional. According to the Court, those sections of the CDA were too broad in their scope and significantly restrained the constitutionally protected free speech of adults.[22] Congress made a further attempt to regulate Internet speech in 1998 with the Child Online Protection Act. The act imposed criminal penalties on those who distribute material that is "harmful to minors" without using some kind of age-verification system to separate adult and minor Web users. In 2004, the Supreme Court barred enforcement of the act, ruling that the act likely violated constitutionally protected free speech, and sent the case back to the district court for a trial.[23] The district court found the act unconstitutional, and in 2008 a federal appellate court upheld the district court's ruling.

Having failed twice in its attempt to regulate online obscenity, Congress decided to try a different approach. In late 2000, it passed the Children's Internet Protection Act (CIPA). This act requires schools and libraries to use Internet filtering software to protect children from pornography or risk losing federal funds for technology upgrades. The CIPA was also challenged on constitutional grounds, but in 2003 the Supreme Court held that the act did not violate the First Amendment. The Court concluded that because libraries can disable the filters for any patrons who ask, the system was reasonably flexible and did not burden free speech to an unconstitutional extent.[24]

FREE SPEECH FOR STUDENTS? America's schools and college campuses experience an ongoing tension between the guarantee of free speech and the desire to restrain speech that is offensive to others. Typically, cases involving free speech in the schools raise the following question: Where should the line between unacceptable speech and merely offensive speech be drawn? Schools at all levels—elementary schools, high schools, and colleges and universities—have grappled with this issue.

Generally, the courts allow elementary schools wide latitude to define what students may and may not say to other students. At the high school level, the Supreme Court has allowed some restraints to be placed on the freedom of expression. For example, as you will read shortly in the discussion of freedom of the press, the Court does allow school officials to exercise some censorship over high school publications. And, in a controversial 2007 case, the Court upheld a school principal's decision to suspend a high school student who unfurled a banner reading "Bong Hits 4 Jesus" at an event off the school premises. The Court sided with the school officials, who maintained that the banner appeared to advocate illegal

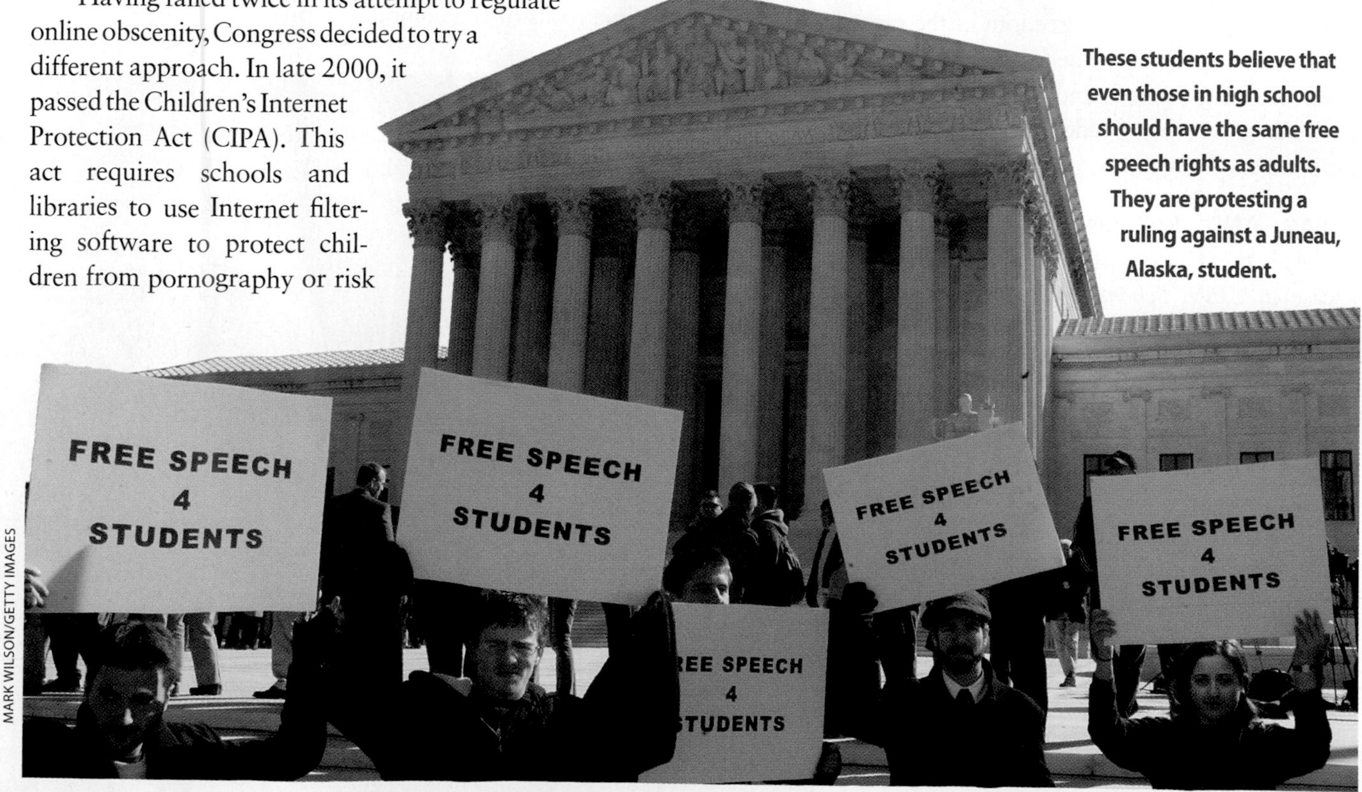

These students believe that even those in high school should have the same free speech rights as adults. They are protesting a ruling against a Juneau, Alaska, student.

MARK WILSON/GETTY IMAGES

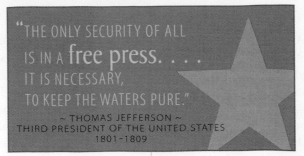

> "THE ONLY SECURITY OF ALL IS IN A **free press.** . . . IT IS NECESSARY, TO KEEP THE WATERS PURE."
>
> ~ THOMAS JEFFERSON ~
> THIRD PRESIDENT OF THE UNITED STATES
> 1801–1809

drug use in violation of school policy. Many legal commentators and scholars strongly criticized this decision.[25]

A difficult question that many universities face today is whether the right to free speech includes the right to make hateful remarks about others based on their race, gender, or sexual orientation. Some claim that allowing people with extremist views to voice their opinions can lead to violence. In response to this question, several universities have gone so far as to institute speech codes to minimize the disturbances that hate speech might cause. Although these speech codes have often been ruled unconstitutional on the ground that they restrict freedom of speech,[26] such codes continue to exist on many college campuses. For example, the student assembly at Wesleyan University passed a resolution in 2002 stating that the "right to speech comes with implicit responsibilities to respect community standards."[27] Campus rules governing speech and expression, however, can foster the idea that "good" speech should be protected, but "bad" speech should not. Furthermore, who should decide what is considered "hate speech"?

Freedom of the Press

The framers of the Constitution believed that the press should be free to publish a wide range of opinions and information, and generally the free speech rights just discussed also apply to the press. The courts have placed certain restrictions on the freedom of the press, however. Over the years, the Supreme Court has developed various guidelines and doctrines to use in deciding whether freedom of speech and the press can be restrained.

CLEAR AND PRESENT DANGER One guideline the Court has used resulted from a case in 1919, *Schenck v. United States.*[28] Charles T. Schenck was convicted of printing and distributing leaflets urging men to resist the draft during World War I. The government claimed that his actions violated the Espionage Act of 1917, which made it a crime to encourage disloyalty to the government or resistance to the draft. The Supreme Court upheld both the law and the convictions. Justice Holmes, speaking for the Court, stated as follows:

> The question in every case is whether the words used are used in such circumstances and are of such a nature as to create a *clear and present danger* that they will bring about the substantive evils that Congress has a right to prevent. It is a question of proximity [closeness] and degree. [Emphasis added.]

Thus, according to the *clear and present danger test,* government should be allowed to restrain speech only when that speech clearly presents an immediate threat to public order. It is often hard to say when speech crosses the line between being merely controversial and being a "clear and present danger," but the principle has been used in many cases since *Schenck.*

The clear and present danger principle seemed too permissive to some Supreme Court justices. Several years after the *Schenck* ruling, in the case of *Gitlow v. New York,*[29] the Court held that speech could be curtailed even if it had only a *tendency* to lead to illegal action. Since the 1920s, however, this guideline, known as the *bad-tendency test,* generally has not been supported by the Supreme Court.

THE PREFERRED-POSITION DOCTRINE Another guideline, called the *preferred-position doctrine,* states that certain freedoms are so essential to a democracy that they hold a preferred position. According to this doctrine, any law that limits these freedoms should be presumed unconstitutional unless the government can show that the law is absolutely necessary. Thus, freedom of speech and the press should rarely, if ever, be diminished, because spoken and printed words are the prime tools of the democratic process.

Brandon Mayfield (left) exits the federal courthouse with his attorney Gerry Spence (right). Mayfield has brought suit against the FBI for wrongful arrest in connection with the Madrid train bombings in 2004.

STEPHEN VOSS/REDUX

PRIOR RESTRAINT Stopping an activity before it actually happens is known as *prior restraint.* With respect to freedom of the press, prior restraint involves *censorship,* which occurs when an official removes objectionable materials from an item before it is published or broadcast. An example of censorship and prior restraint would be a court's ruling that two paragraphs in an upcoming article in the local newspaper had to be removed before the article could be published. The Supreme Court has generally ruled against prior restraint, arguing that the government cannot curb ideas *before* they are expressed.

On some occasions, however, the Court has allowed prior restraint. For example, in a 1988 case, *Hazelwood School District v. Kuhlmeier,*[30] a high school principal deleted two pages from the school newspaper just before it was printed. The pages contained stories on students' experiences with pregnancy and discussed the impact of divorce on students at the school. The Supreme Court, noting that students in school do not have exactly the same rights as adults in other settings, ruled that high school administrators *can* censor school publications. The Court said that school newspapers are part of the school curriculum, not a public forum. Therefore, administrators have the right to censor speech that promotes conduct inconsistent with the "shared values of a civilized social order."

"THE RIGHT TO BE LET ALONE – the most comprehensive of the rights and the right most valued by civilized men."

~ LOUIS BRANDEIS ~
ASSOCIATE JUSTICE OF THE UNITED STATES SUPREME COURT
1916–1939

LO3 The Right to Privacy

Supreme Court justice Louis Brandeis stated in 1928 that the right to privacy is "the most comprehensive of rights and the right most valued by civilized men."[31] The majority of the justices on the Supreme Court at that time did not agree. In 1965, however, in the landmark case of *Griswold v. Connecticut,*[32] the justices on the Supreme Court held that a right to privacy is implied by other constitutional rights guaranteed in the First, Third, Fourth, Fifth, and Ninth Amendments. For example, consider the words of the Ninth Amendment: "The enumeration in the Constitution, of certain rights, shall not be construed to deny or disparage others retained by the people." In other words, just because the Constitution, including its amendments, does not specifically mention the right to privacy does not mean that this right is denied to the people.

Since then, the government has also passed laws ensuring the privacy rights of individuals. For example, in 1966 Congress passed the Freedom of Information Act, which, among other things, allows any person to request copies of any information about her or him contained in government files. In 1974, Congress passed the Privacy Act, which restricts government disclosure of data to third parties. In 1994, Congress passed the Driver's Privacy Protection Act, which prevents states from disclosing or selling a driver's personal information without the driver's consent.[33] In late 2000, the federal Department of Health and Human Services issued a regulation ensuring the privacy of a person's medical information. Health-care providers and insurance companies are restricted from sharing confidential information about their patients.

Although Congress and the courts have acknowledged a constitutional right to privacy, the nature and scope of this right are not always clear. For example, Americans continue to debate whether the right to privacy includes the right to have an abortion or the right of terminally ill persons to commit physician-assisted suicide. Since the terrorist attacks of September 11, 2001, another pressing privacy issue has been how to monitor potential terrorists to prevent another attack without violating the privacy rights of all Americans.

The Abortion Controversy

One of the most divisive and emotionally charged issues being debated today is whether the right to privacy means that women can choose to have abortions.

ABORTION AND PRIVACY In 1973, in the landmark case of *Roe v. Wade,*[34] the Supreme Court, using the *Griswold* case as a precedent, held that the "right of privacy . . . is broad enough to encompass a woman's decision whether or not to terminate her pregnancy." The right is not absolute throughout pregnancy, however. The Court also said that any state could impose certain regulations to safeguard the health of the mother after the first three months of pregnancy and, in the final stages of pregnancy, could act to protect potential life.

Since the *Roe v. Wade* decision, the Supreme Court has adopted a more conservative approach and has upheld restrictive state laws requiring counseling, waiting periods, notification of parents, and other actions prior to abortions.[35] Yet the Court has never overturned the *Roe* decision. In fact, in 1997 and again in 2000, the Supreme Court upheld laws requiring "buffer zones" around abortion clinics to protect those entering the clinics from unwanted counseling or harassment by antiabortion groups.[36] In 2000, the Supreme Court invalidated a Nebraska statute banning "partial-birth" abortions, a procedure used during the second trimester of pregnancy.[37] Undeterred by the fate of the Nebraska law, President George W. Bush signed the Partial Birth Abortion Ban Act in 2003. In a close (five-to-four) and controversial 2007 decision, the Supreme Court upheld the constitutionality of the 2003 act.[38]

Abortion continues to be extremely controversial in the United States. Pro-choice supporters demonstrate their desire that abortion remain legal.

Many were surprised at the Court's decision on partial-birth abortion, given that the federal act banning this practice was quite similar to the Nebraska law that had been struck down by the Court in 2000, just seven years earlier. Since that decision was rendered, however, the Court has become more conservative with the appointment of two new justices by President George W. Bush. Dissenting from the majority opinion in the case, Justice Ruth Bader Ginsburg said that the ruling was an "alarming" departure from three decades of Supreme Court decisions on abortion.

ABORTION AND POLITICS American opinion on the abortion issue is more nuanced than the labels "pro-life" and "pro-choice" would indicate. For example, a 2010 Gallup poll found that 45 percent of the respondents considered themselves pro-choice and 47 percent called themselves pro-life. Yet when respondents were asked whether abortion should be legal or illegal, public opinion was more middle-of-the-road than the attachments to these labels would suggest. About 54 percent thought that abortion should be limited to only certain circumstances, while 19 percent believed it should be illegal in all circumstances, and 24 percent thought that it should be legal in all circumstances.

Do We Have the "Right to Die"?

Whether it is called euthanasia (mercy killing), assisted suicide, or a dignified way to leave this world, it all comes down to one basic question: Do terminally ill persons have, as part of their civil liberties, a right to die and to be assisted in the process by physicians or others? Phrased another way, are state laws banning physician-assisted suicide in such circumstances unconstitutional?

In 1997, the issue came before the Supreme Court, which characterized the question as follows: Does the liberty protected by the Constitution include a right to commit suicide, which itself includes a right to assistance in doing so? The Court's clear and categorical answer to this question was no. To hold otherwise, said the Court, would be "to reverse centuries of legal doctrine and practice, and strike down the considered policy choice of almost every state."[39] Although the Court upheld the states' rights to ban such a practice, the Court did not hold that state laws *permitting* assisted suicide were unconstitutional. In 1997, Oregon became the first state to implement such a law. In 2008, Washington and Montana became the second and third states, respectively, to allow the practice. Oregon's law was upheld by the Supreme Court in 2006.[40]

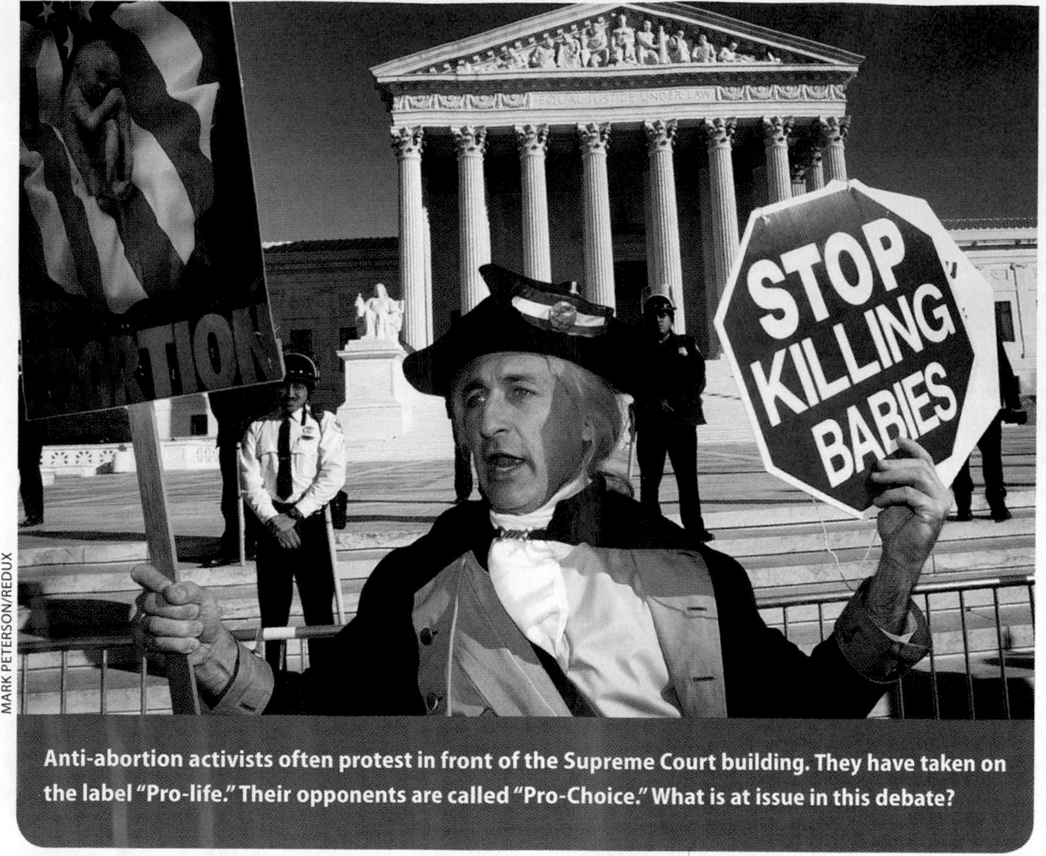

MARK PETERSON/REDUX

Anti-abortion activists often protest in front of the Supreme Court building. They have taken on the label "Pro-life." Their opponents are called "Pro-Choice." What is at issue in this debate?

The Supreme Court's enunciation of its opinion on this topic has not ended the debate, though, just as the debate over abortion did not stop after the 1973 *Roe v. Wade* decision legalizing abortion. Americans continue to be at odds over this issue.

Personal Privacy and National Security

Since the terrorist attacks of September 11, 2001, a common debate in the news media and on Capitol Hill has been how the United States can address the urgent need to strengthen national security while still protecting civil liberties, particularly the right to privacy. As you will read throughout this book, various programs have been proposed or attempted, and some have already been dismantled after public outcry. For example, the Homeland Security Act passed in late 2002 included language explicitly prohibiting a controversial program called Operation TIPS (Terrorism Information and Prevention System). Operation TIPS was proposed to create a national reporting program for "citizen volunteers" who regularly work in neighborhoods and communities, such as postal carriers and meter readers, to report suspicious activity to the government. The public backlash against the program was quick and resolute—neighbors would not spy on neighbors. Indeed, Americans are protective enough of their privacy to reject the idea of national identification cards, even though such cards are common in other countries. We say more about national ID cards in the feature *The Rest of the World: Fingerprinting 1.2 Billion Citizens of India* on the following page.

AP PHOTO/GERALD HERBERT

FBI director Robert Mueller often faces questioning in front of congressional hearings on national security. What limits his decisions?

THE USA PATRIOT ACT Other laws and programs that infringe on Americans' privacy rights were also created in the wake of 9/11 in the interests of protecting the nation's security. For example, the USA Patriot Act of 2001 gave the government broad latitude to investigate people who are only vaguely associated with terrorists. Under this law, the government can access personal information on American citizens to an extent heretofore never allowed by law. The Federal Bureau of Investigation was also authorized to use "National Security Letters" to demand personal information about individuals from private companies (such as banks and phone companies). In one of the most controversial programs, the National Security Agency (NSA) was authorized to monitor certain domestic phone calls without first obtaining a warrant. When Americans learned of the NSA's actions in 2005, the ensuing public furor

Fingerprinting 1.2 Billion Citizens of India

From time to time, persons who are concerned about our national security propose that the United States create a national identity card. That would mean that all 310 million Americans would be required to have an official federal ID card. Now imagine imposing such a requirement on a nation of more than 1.2 billion people. It sounds like quite a task, but the government of India began work on such a project in 2011.

Lots of Precedent

Quite a few countries, including Belgium, France, Germany, and Spain, already require that their residents have national identity cards. In fact, more than a hundred countries require such cards. Why not India? The big problem, of course, is that few countries have to deal with more than a billion fingerprints to create a biometric identity card for every resident.

All for the Good, According to Some

According to Nandan Nilekani, head of India's Unique Identity Authority, providing a national biometric identity card will change his country. "Every person for the first time will be able to prove who he or she is," he said in a recent interview. "If you are going to have all of this economic growth, people who are marginalized should be given a chance." He was referring to the more than 75 million homeless people who do not even have birth certificates. They cannot obtain government aid or register their children for school. They cannot even obtain phone service or open a bank account.

Are Civil Liberties an Issue?

More than one-sixth of the world's population lives in India. If every single man, woman, and child there is registered in a government database, then more than one-sixth of the world's inhabitants can be found by searching that single database. Civil libertarians argue that there will be no oversight mechanism to defend against the surveillance abuses that will be possible with such a large database. The reality, though, is that India already has a gigantic bureaucracy that oversees its citizens. In some regions, residents must have twenty different ID cards—one to vote, one to obtain food ration tickets, and many others for various purposes.

For Critical Analysis *If more than one hundred countries already require a national identity card for every resident, why doesn't the United States do the same?*

forced the Bush administration to agree to henceforth obtain warrants for such monitoring activities.

THE CIVIL LIBERTIES DEBATE Some Americans, including many civil libertarians, are so concerned about the erosion of privacy rights that they wonder why the public outcry has not been even more vehement. They point out that trading off even a few civil liberties, including our privacy rights, for national security is senseless. After all, these liberties are at the heart of what this country stands for. When we abandon any of our civil liberties, we weaken our country rather than defend it. Essentially, say some members of this group, the federal government has achieved what the terrorists were unable to accomplish—the destruction of our freedoms. Other Americans believe that we have little to worry about. Those who have nothing to hide should not be concerned about government surveillance or other privacy intrusions undertaken by the government to make our nation more secure against terrorist attacks. To what extent has the Obama administration revised the policies established under President Bush? We examine that question in this chapter's *Perception versus Reality* feature on page 90.

LO4 *The Rights of the Accused*

The United States has one of the highest murder rates in the industrialized world. It is therefore not surprising that many Americans have extremely strong opinions about the rights of persons accused of criminal offenses. Indeed, some Americans complain that criminal defendants have too many rights.

Why do criminal suspects have rights? The answer is that all persons are entitled to the protections afforded by the Bill of Rights. If criminal suspects were deprived of their basic constitutional liberties, all people would suffer the consequences, because there is nothing to stop the government from accusing anyone of being a criminal. In a criminal case, a state official (such as the district attorney, or D.A.) prosecutes the defendant, and the state has immense resources that it can bring to bear against the accused person. By protecting the rights of accused persons, the Constitution helps to prevent the arbitrary use of power by the government.

The Rights of Criminal Defendants

The basic rights, or constitutional safeguards, provided for criminal defendants are set forth in the Bill of Rights. These safeguards include the following:

- The Fourth Amendment protection from unreasonable searches and seizures.
- The Fourth Amendment requirement that no warrant for a search or an arrest be issued without **probable cause**—cause for believing that there is a substantial likelihood that a person has committed or is about to commit a crime.
- The Fifth Amendment requirement that no one be deprived of "life, liberty, or property, without due process of law." As discussed earlier in this chapter, this requirement is also included in the Fourteenth Amendment, which protects persons against actions by state governments.
- The Fifth Amendment prohibition against **double jeopardy**—being tried twice for the same criminal offense.
- The Fifth Amendment provision that no person can be required to be a witness against (incriminate) himself or herself. This is often referred to as the constitutional protection against **self-incrimination.** It is the basis for a criminal suspect's "right to remain silent" in criminal proceedings.
- The Sixth Amendment guarantees of a speedy trial, a trial by jury, a public trial, and the right to confront witnesses.
- The Sixth Amendment guarantee of the right to counsel at various stages in some criminal proceedings. The right to counsel was strengthened in 1963 in *Gideon v. Wainwright.*[41] The Supreme Court held that if a person is accused of a felony and cannot afford an attorney, an attorney must be made available to the accused person at the government's expense.
- The Eighth Amendment prohibitions against excessive bail and fines and against cruel and unusual punishments.

The Exclusionary Rule

Any evidence obtained in violation of the constitutional rights spelled out in the Fourth Amendment normally is not admissible at trial. This rule, which has been applied in the federal courts since at least 1914, is known as the **exclusionary rule.** The rule was extended to state court proceedings in 1961.[42] The reasoning behind the exclusionary rule is that it forces law enforcement personnel to gather evidence properly. If they do not, they will be unable to introduce the evidence at trial to convince the jury that the defendant is guilty.

The *Miranda* Warnings

In the 1950s and 1960s, one of the questions facing the courts was not whether suspects had constitutional rights—that was not in doubt—but how and when those rights could be exercised. For example, could the right to remain silent (under the Fifth Amendment's prohibition against self-incrimination) be exercised during pretrial interrogation proceedings or only during the trial? Were confessions obtained from suspects admissible in court if the suspects had not been advised of their right to remain silent and other constitutional rights? To clarify these issues, in 1966 the Supreme Court issued a landmark decision in *Miranda v. Arizona.*[43] In that case, the Court enunciated the ***Miranda* warnings** that are now familiar to virtually all Americans:

> Prior to any questioning, the person must be warned that he has a right to remain silent, that any statement he does make may be used against him, and that he has a right to the presence of an attorney, either retained or appointed.

probable cause Cause for believing that there is a substantial likelihood that a person has committed or is about to commit a crime.

double jeopardy The prosecution of a person twice for the same criminal offense; prohibited by the Fifth Amendment in all but a few circumstances.

self-incrimination Providing damaging information or testimony against oneself in court.

exclusionary rule A criminal procedural rule requiring that any illegally obtained evidence not be admissible in court.

***Miranda* warnings** A series of statements informing criminal suspects, on their arrest, of their constitutional rights, such as the right to remain silent and the right to counsel; required by the Supreme Court's 1966 decision in *Miranda v. Arizona.*

PERCEPTION VERSUS REALITY

Obama's Antiterrorism Stance Compared with Bush's

During much of the administration of President George W. Bush, civil libertarians denounced the antiterrorism policies of President Bush and his vice president, Dick Cheney. Certainly, after 9/11, the administration's view of civil liberties, especially those relating to privacy, changed substantially. The USA Patriot Act, which Bush signed into law on October 26, 2001, authorized a major expansion in the "snooping" activities of the federal government. In addition, the National Security Agency (NSA) was allowed to engage in domestic wiretapping without obtaining search warrants.

The Perception

During the Bush administration, Bush and Cheney ran a counterterrorism program that violated the civil liberties of Americans, tortured enemy combatants, and committed a variety of other illegal actions. According to Cheney, these practices saved "thousands, perhaps hundreds of thousands" of lives. They were also "legal, essential, justified, successful and the right thing to do." President Barack Obama made the country "less safe," said Cheney, by eliminating them and by attempting to close the prison holding suspected terrorists at the Guantánamo Bay Naval Base.

In contrast, Obama called the Guantánamo prison a "misguided experiment" that actually increased the threats to American national security. "The problem of what to do with Guantánamo detainees was not caused by my decision to close the facility," Obama said. "The problem exists because of the decision to open Guantánamo in the first place."

The Reality

At most, the excessive antiterrorism policies of the Bush administration lasted for three years following 9/11. This nation had been blindsided—our intelligence officials knew almost nothing about the threats against us. The Bush administration frantically attempted to discover and prevent any further threats. It was in this environment that officials such as Cheney could demand—and obtain—policies that seemed to violate traditional American standards.

By 2005, however, members of the Bush administration were trying to rein in the excesses of the earlier post-9/11 period. Secretary of State Condoleezza Rice, National Security Advisor Stephen Hadley, and other officials sought to wean the administration away from the Cheney approach. In 2007, Rice refused to support an executive order reviving the "enhanced" interrogation program. Throughout Bush's second term, officials tried to close Guantánamo and pleaded with foreign governments to take some of its prisoners.

The most famous "enhanced" interrogation technique—waterboarding—was halted long before Obama came to power. Obama castigated the military-commission system used to try captured enemy combatants, but in fact he revived this system with only cosmetic changes. Harvard law professor Jack Goldsmith puts it this way: "The main difference between the Obama and Bush administrations concerns not the substance of terrorism policy, but rather its packaging." In reality, Obama's policies largely represented a continuation of the policies adopted during Bush's second term. Cheney, Bush, and Obama all had an interest in glossing over that fact.

Blog On National security blogs may outnumber the stars you can see on a cloudless night. We can mention only a few. The *National Journal* offers expert posts at **security.nationaljournal.com.** The Heritage Foundation takes a strongly conservative line at **www.heritage.org/Issues/National-Security-and-Defense.** Finally, this blog defends the rights of Guantánamo detainees: **gtmoblog.blogspot.com.**

The Erosion of *Miranda*

As part of a continuing attempt to balance the rights of accused persons against the rights of society, the Supreme Court has made a number of exceptions to the *Miranda* ruling. In 1986, for example, the Court held that a confession need not be excluded even though the police failed to inform a suspect in custody that his attorney had tried to reach him by telephone.[44] In an important 1991 decision, the Court stated that a suspect's conviction will not be automatically overturned if the suspect was coerced into making a confession. If the other evidence admitted at trial was strong enough to justify the conviction without the confession, then the fact that the confession was obtained illegally can be, in effect, ignored.[45] In yet another case, in 1994 the Supreme Court ruled that a suspect must unequivocally and assertively state his right to counsel in order to stop police questioning. Saying "Maybe I should talk to a lawyer" during an interrogation after being taken into custody is not enough. The Court held that police officers are not required to decipher the suspect's intentions in such situations.[46]

Miranda may eventually become obsolete regardless of any decisions made in the courts. A relatively new trend in law enforcement has been for agencies to digitally record interrogations and confessions. Thomas P. Sullivan, a former U.S. attorney in Chicago, and his staff interviewed personnel in more than 230 law enforcement agencies in thirty-eight states that record interviews of suspects who are in custody. Sullivan found that nearly all police officers said the procedure saved time and money, created valuable evidence to use in court, and made it more difficult for defense attorneys to claim that their clients had been illegally coerced.[47] Some scholars have suggested that recording all custodial interrogations would satisfy the Fifth Amendment's prohibition against coercion and in the process render the *Miranda* warnings unnecessary.

ELENA ROORAID/PHOTOEDIT

This police officer is reading the accused his *Miranda* warnings. Since the 1966 *Miranda* decision, the Supreme Court has relaxed its requirements in some situations, such as when a criminal suspect who is not under arrest enters a police station voluntarily.

AMERICA AT ODDS *Civil Liberties*

Civil liberties is a contentious topic, and Americans are at odds over many of its issues. Almost all Americans claim to believe in individual rights, but how should this freedom be defined? Often, one right appears to interfere with another. Some of the resulting disputes include the following:

- Should the First Amendment's establishment clause be interpreted strictly, so that no one's rights are infringed on by government sponsorship of religion—or should it be interpreted loosely, to recognize that the United States is a very religious country?
- What kinds of religious practices should be allowed under the free exercise clause? In particular, should religious groups that limit or ban participation by gay men and lesbians receive the same government benefits as any other group—or may they be penalized for discrimination?
- Should advertising receive the same free-speech rights as any other kind of speech—or should advertisers be held accountable for making false claims?
- Has the government gone too far in restricting liberties in an attempt to combat terrorism—or are the restrictions trivial compared with the benefits?
- Consider finally the most intense controversy of all. Should women have a privacy right to terminate a pregnancy for any reason—or should abortion be a crime?

Take Action

If you are ever concerned that your civil liberties are being threatened by a government action, you can exercise one of your liberties—the right to petition the government—to object to the action. Often, those who want to take action feel that they are alone in their struggles until they begin discussing their views with others. Brenda Koehler, a writing student attending college in Kutztown, Pennsylvania, relates how one of her friends, whom we will call "Charyn," took action in response to the USA Patriot Act of 2001. Concerned about the extent to which this act infringed on Americans' civil liberties, Charyn began e-mailing her friends and others about the issue. Eventually, a petition against the enforcement of the act in her town was circulated, and the city council agreed to consider the petition. Charyn did not expect anything to come from the review and assumed that the council would dismiss the petition without even reading the three-hundred-page Patriot Act. On the day of the hearing, the council chambers were packed with town citizens who shared Charyn's and her friends' concerns. The council adjourned the meeting for a week so that it could review the act, and when it met the next week, the resolution to oppose enforcing the act was adopted. Although one person's efforts are not always so successful, there will certainly be no successes at all if no one takes action.[48]

POLITICS ON THE WEB

- Almost three dozen First Amendment groups have launched the Free Expression Network, a Web site designed to feature legislation updates, legal briefings, and news on cases of censorship in local communities. Go to **www.freeexpression.org**
- The Web site for the leading civil liberties organization, the American Civil Liberties Union (ACLU), can be found at **www.aclu.org**
- The Liberty Counsel is "a nonprofit religious civil liberties education and legal defense organization established to preserve religious freedom." Its take on civil liberties is definitely right of center. You can access this organization's home page at **www.lc.org**
- For information on the effect of new computer and communications technologies on the constitutional rights and liberties of Americans, go to the Center for Democracy and Technology at **www.cdt.org**
- For information on privacy issues relating to the Internet, go to the Electronic Privacy Information Center's Web site at **www.epic.org/privacy**
- To access United States Supreme Court decisions on civil liberties, go to the Court's official Web site at **www.supremecourt.gov**
- For many people, the YouTube Web site is a favorite destination not only for entertainment but also for information on a host of topics. URLs for locating videos on YouTube take the form of **www.youtube.com/watch?v=** immediately followed by a string of characters that identifies a particular video. Videos on civil liberties topics include **AviKQaEsaDM**, which describes the role of the Jehovah's Witnesses in winning civil liberties cases during the twentieth century. Federal policies on inspecting and seizing laptop computers and MP3 players at the border are described at **rSGDVTk6ra0**.

Access CourseMate to review and expand on this chapter through quizzes, flashcards, learning objectives, interactive timelines, a crossword puzzle, audio summaries, video, critical-thinking activities, simulations, and more.

GOVT 5

Civil Rights

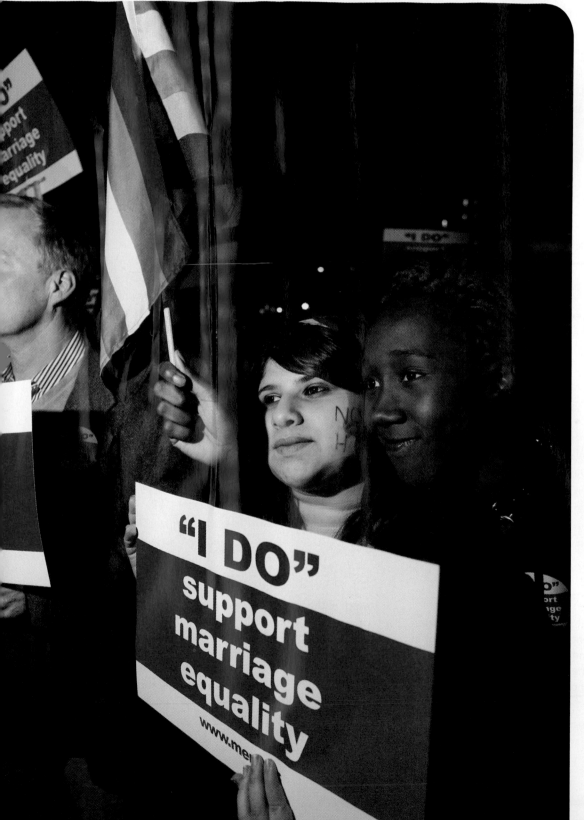

LEARNING OBJECTIVES

LO1 Explain the constitutional basis for our civil rights and for laws prohibiting discrimination.

LO2 Discuss the reasons for the civil rights movement and the changes it caused in American politics and government.

LO3 Describe the political and economic achievements of women in this country over time and identify some obstacles to equality that women continue to face.

LO4 Summarize the struggles for equality that other groups in America experience.

LO5 Explain what affirmative action is and why it has been so controversial.

AMERICA AT ODDS

Should the Census Count Be Limited to Citizens?

The 2010 census was the most expensive ever—it cost about $37 per person counted. The U.S. census, which is taken every ten years, is important in part because the number of persons each state sends to the House of Representatives is based on the most recent census count. In addition, the census determines which communities receive a share of the more than $400 billion in federal funds each year for things such as hospitals; schools; job-training centers; and bridges, tunnels, and other public works projects.

Not surprisingly, who should be counted is an often-debated issue. Should census counters ignore unauthorized immigrants? This question is more than academic. In states with many unauthorized immigrants, such as California, counting them increases the state's representation in Congress. Should everyone be counted? Alternatively, should only citizens and legal permanent residents be counted?

Keep It Simple—Unauthorized Immigrants Need Not Apply

The first Census Act in 1790 provided for a counting of "inhabitants." According to a court ruling, the term *inhabitant* meant "a *bona fide* member of a State, subject to all the requisitions of its laws, and entitled to all of the privileges which they confer." Under such a definition, those who are in the country illegally shouldn't be considered inhabitants.

Naturally, leaders in some states that do not have high numbers of unauthorized immigrants and that will lose one or more seats in the House of Representatives after a census have opposed counting such immigrants. By the time you read this, Louisiana, Massachusetts, Michigan, Ohio, and other states may have already lost one or more seats in the House because of counts based on the 2010 census. Every voter is supposed to have an equal voice. If unauthorized immigrants are counted in determining the apportionment of representatives, voters in areas with large numbers of unauthorized immigrants will be overrepresented.

There is a more fundamental issue at stake, though: Who is an American? Presumably, we want to count the people of the United States in our ten-year census. The "people" should not include those who are living here illegally. This logic seems clear to many.

Follow the Constitution—Count Them All

Those who are against counting unauthorized immigrants forget that the basis of the census, Section 2 of the Fourteenth Amendment to the Constitution, states: "Representatives shall be apportioned among the several States according to their respective numbers, counting the whole number of persons in each State." Apportionment is by *persons*, not *citizens*. The Fourteenth Amendment refers to citizens in some clauses, and persons in others. It distinguishes between the two. Unauthorized immigrants are persons, plain and simple. If California therefore picks up extra seats in the House after a census, so be it. There is nothing unconstitutional about this. Bear in mind the rule for counting slaves in the original Constitution. Three-fifths of the slaves in each state were included when apportioning House seats. This means that the founders were deliberately counting people who weren't citizens and, in the founders' opinion, never would be.

Consider also that cities and states of necessity provide services to unauthorized immigrants. If those people are not counted when dividing up federal funds, citizens in areas with many illegal immigrants won't be adequately compensated by the federal government.

WHERE DO YOU STAND?

1. **Do you think states that have more unauthorized immigrants should consequently have more representatives in the House? Why or why not?**
2. **Why did the authors of the Fourteenth Amendment seek to ensure that persons—and not just citizens—would enjoy certain rights?**

EXPLORE THIS ISSUE ONLINE

Much of the recent debate over counting unauthorized immigrants is based on a *Wall Street Journal* article written by John Baker, a Louisiana State University law professor, and Elliot Stonecipher, a pollster. The *Journal* deleted many of their legal arguments, but you can find a full version of the piece at the Volokh Conspiracy: volokh.com/posts/1250274418.shtml. (Click on a link to pull up the full draft.) You'll also find there a detailed criticism of the Baker/Stonecipher thesis by Eugene Volokh, a law professor at the University of California, Los Angeles.

Introduction

As noted in Chapter 4, people sometimes confuse civil rights with civil liberties. Generally, though, the term **civil rights** refers to the rights of all Americans to equal treatment under the law, as provided for by the Fourteenth Amendment. One of the functions of our government is to ensure—through legislation or other means—that this constitutional mandate is upheld.

All Americans are entitled to **EQUAL TREATMENT UNDER THE LAW** as provided for by the Fourteenth Amendment.

Although the democratic ideal is for all people to have equal rights and equal treatment under the law, and although the Constitution guarantees those rights, this ideal has often remained just that—an ideal. It is people who put ideals into practice, and as James Madison (1751–1836) once pointed out (and as we all know), people are not angels. As you will read in this chapter, the struggle of various groups in American society to obtain equal treatment has been a long one, and it still continues. One such group is made up of immigrants—those here both legally and illegally. We discussed an issue that concerns them in this chapter's opening *America at Odds* feature.

In a sense, the history of civil rights in the United States is a history of discrimination against various groups. Discrimination against women, African Americans, and Native Americans dates back to the early years of this nation, when the framers of the Constitution did not grant these groups rights that were granted to others (that is, to white, property-owning males). During our subsequent history, as peoples from around the globe immigrated to this country at various times and for various reasons, each of these immigrant groups faced discrimination in one form or another. More recently, other groups, including persons with disabilities and gay men and lesbians have struggled for equal treatment under the law.

Central to any discussion of civil rights is the interpretation of the equal protection clause of the Fourteenth Amendment to the Constitution. For that reason, we look first at that clause and at how the courts, particularly the United States Supreme Court, have interpreted it and applied it to civil rights issues.

LO1 The Equal Protection Clause

Equal in importance to the due process clause of the Fourteenth Amendment is the **equal protection clause** in Section 1 of that amendment, which reads as follows: "No State shall . . . deny to any person within its jurisdiction the equal protection of the laws." Section 5 of the amendment provides a legal basis for federal civil rights legislation: "The Congress shall have power to enforce, by appropriate legislation, the provisions of this article."

The equal protection clause has been interpreted by the courts, and especially the Supreme Court, to mean that states must treat all persons in an equal manner and may not discriminate *unreasonably* against a particular group or class of individuals. The task of distinguishing between reasonable

These demonstrators are making sure that the residents of New York City remember the goals of Martin Luther King, Jr.—equality for all minorities in America.

REUTERS/CHIP EAST /LANDOV

civil rights The rights of all Americans to equal treatment under the law, as provided for by the Fourteenth Amendment to the Constitution.

equal protection clause Section 1 of the Fourteenth Amendment, which states that no state shall "deny to any person within its jurisdiction the equal protection of the laws."

fundamental right A basic right of all Americans, such as First Amendment rights. Any law or action that prevents some group of persons from exercising a fundamental right is subject to the "strict-scrutiny" standard, under which the law or action must be necessary to promote a compelling state interest and must be narrowly tailored to meet that interest.

suspect classification A classification, such as race, that provides the basis for a discriminatory law. Any law based on a suspect classification is subject to strict scrutiny by the courts—meaning that the law must be justified by a compelling state interest.

rational basis test A test (also known as the "ordinary-scrutiny" standard) used by the Supreme Court to decide whether a discriminatory law violates the equal protection clause of the Constitution. Few laws evaluated under this test are found invalid.

discrimination and unreasonable discrimination is difficult. Generally, in deciding this question, the Supreme Court balances the constitutional rights of individuals to equal protection against government interests in protecting the safety and welfare of citizens. Over time, the Court has developed various tests, or standards, for determining whether the equal protection clause has been violated.

Strict Scrutiny

If a law or action prevents some group of persons from exercising a **fundamental right** (such as one of our First Amendment rights), the law or action will be subject to the "strict-scrutiny" standard. Under this standard, the law or action must be necessary to promote a *compelling state interest* and must be narrowly tailored to meet that interest. A law based on a **suspect classification,** such as race, is also subject to strict scrutiny by the courts, meaning that the law must be justified by a compelling state interest.

Intermediate Scrutiny

Because the Supreme Court had difficulty deciding how to judge cases in which men and women were treated differently, another test was developed—the "intermediate-scrutiny" standard. Under this standard, laws based on gender classifications are permissible if they are "substantially related to the achievement of an important governmental objective." For example, a law punishing males but not females for statutory rape is valid because of the important governmental interest in preventing teenage pregnancy in those circumstances and because almost all of the harmful and identifiable consequences of teenage pregnancies fall on young females.[1] A law prohibiting the sale of beer to males under twenty-one years of age and to females under eighteen years would not be valid, however.[2]

Generally, since the 1970s, the Supreme Court has scrutinized gender classifications closely and has declared many gender-based laws unconstitutional. In 1979, the Court held that a state law allowing wives to obtain alimony judgments against husbands but preventing husbands from receiving alimony from wives violated the equal protection clause.[3] In 1982, the Court declared that Mississippi's policy of excluding males from the School of Nursing at Mississippi University for Women was unconstitutional.[4] In a controversial 1996 case, *United States v. Virginia,*[5] the Court held that Virginia Military Institute, a state-financed institution, violated the equal protection clause by refusing to accept female applicants. The Court said that the state of Virginia had failed to provide a sufficient justification for its gender-based classification.

The Rational Basis Test (Ordinary Scrutiny)

A third test used to decide whether a discriminatory law violates the equal protection clause is the **rational basis test.** When applying this test to a law that classifies or treats people or groups differently, the justices ask whether the discrimination is rational. In other words, is it a reasonable way to achieve a legitimate government objective? Few laws tested under the rational basis test—or the "ordinary-scrutiny" standard, as it is also called—are found invalid, because few laws are truly unreasonable. A municipal ordinance that prohibits certain vendors from selling their wares in a particular area of the city, for example, will be upheld if the city can meet this rational basis test. The rational basis for the ordinance might be the city's legitimate government interest in reducing traffic congestion in that particular area.

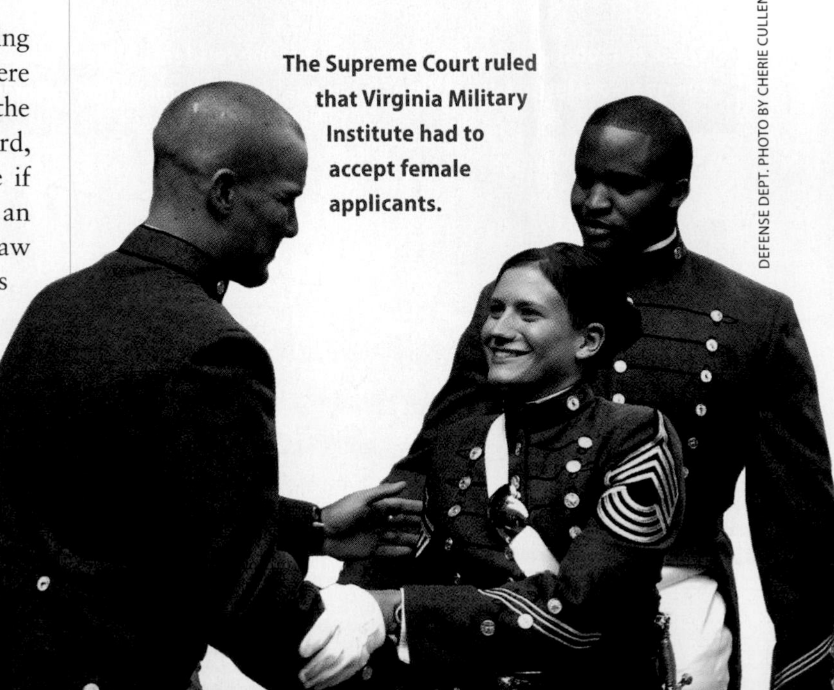

The Supreme Court ruled that Virginia Military Institute had to accept female applicants.

DEFENSE DEPT. PHOTO BY CHERIE CULLEN/RELEASED

LO2 *African Americans*

The equal protection clause was originally intended to protect the newly freed slaves after the Civil War (1861–1865). In the early years after the war, the U.S. government made an effort to protect the rights of blacks living in the former states of the Confederacy. The Thirteenth Amendment (which granted freedom to the slaves), the Fourteenth Amendment (which guaranteed equal protection under the law), and the Fifteenth Amendment (which stated that voting rights could not be abridged on account of race) were part of that effort. By the late 1880s, however, southern legislatures had begun to pass a series of segregation laws—laws that separated the white community from the black community. Such laws were commonly called "Jim Crow" laws (from a song that was popular in minstrel shows that caricatured African Americans). Some of the most common Jim Crow laws called for racial segregation in the use of public facilities, such as schools, railroads, and later, buses. These laws were also applied to housing, restaurants, hotels, and many other facilities.

Separate but Equal

In 1892, a group of Louisiana citizens decided to challenge a state law that required railroads to provide separate railway cars for African Americans. A man named Homer Plessy, who was seven-eighths Caucasian and one-eighth African, boarded a train in New Orleans and sat in the railway car reserved for whites. When Plessy refused to move at the request of the conductor, he was arrested for breaking the law.

separate-but-equal doctrine A Supreme Court doctrine holding that the equal protection clause of the Fourteenth Amendment did not forbid racial segregation as long as the facilities for blacks were equal to those for whites. The doctrine was overturned in the *Brown v. Board of Education of Topeka* decision of 1954.

This man is picketing in front of a variety store in downtown Atlanta in the fall of 1960. What did he mean when he referred to eliminating Jim Crow?

PRESENCE OF
SEGREGATION IS
THE ABSENCE OF
DEMOCRACY
JIM CROW
MUST GO!

AP PHOTO

Four years later, in 1896, the Supreme Court provided a constitutional basis for segregation laws. In *Plessy v. Ferguson*,[6] the Court held that the law did not violate the equal protection clause if *separate* facilities for blacks were *equal* to those for whites. The lone dissenter, Justice John Marshall Harlan, disagreed: "Our Constitution is colorblind, and neither knows nor tolerates classes among citizens." The majority opinion, however, established the **separate-but-equal doctrine,** which was used to justify segregation in many areas of American life for nearly sixty years. Separate facilities for African Americans, when they were provided at all, were in practice almost never truly equal.

In the late 1930s and the 1940s, the United States Supreme Court gradually moved away from this doctrine. The major breakthrough, however, did not come until 1954, in a case involving an African American girl who lived in Topeka, Kansas.

The *Brown* Decisions and School Integration

In the 1950s, Topeka's schools, like those in many cities, were segregated. Mr. and Mrs. Oliver Brown wanted their daughter, Linda Carol Brown, to attend a white school a few blocks from their home instead of an all-black school that was twenty-one blocks away. With the help of lawyers from the National Association for the Advancement of Colored People (NAACP), Linda's parents sued the board of education to allow their daughter to attend the nearby school.

In *Brown v. Board of Education of Topeka*,[7] the Supreme Court reversed *Plessy v. Ferguson*. The Court unanimously held that segregation by race in public education was unconstitutional. Chief Justice Earl Warren wrote as follows:

> Does segregation of children in public schools solely on the basis of race, even though the physical facilities and other "tangible" factors may be equal, deprive the children of the minority group of equal educational opportunities? We believe that it does. . . . [Segregation generates

in children] a feeling of inferiority as to their status in the community that may affect their hearts and minds in a way unlikely ever to be undone. . . . We conclude that in the field of public education the doctrine of "separate but equal" has no place. Separate educational facilities are inherently unequal.

In 1955, in *Brown v. Board of Education*[8] (sometimes called *Brown II*), the Supreme Court ordered desegregation to begin "with all deliberate speed," an ambiguous phrase that could be (and was) interpreted in a variety of ways.

REACTIONS TO SCHOOL INTEGRATION The Supreme Court ruling did not go unchallenged. Bureaucratic loopholes were used to delay desegregation. Another reaction was "white flight." As white parents sent their children to newly established private schools, some formerly white-only public schools became 100 percent black. In Arkansas, Governor Orval Faubus used the state's National Guard to block the integration of Central High School in Little Rock in 1957, which led to increasing violence in the area. A federal court demanded that the troops be withdrawn. Only after President Dwight D. Eisenhower federalized the Arkansas National Guard and sent in troops to help quell the violence did Central High finally become integrated.

By 1970, ***de jure* segregation**—segregation that is established by law—had been abolished by school systems. But that meant only that no public school could legally identify itself as being reserved for all whites or all blacks. It did not mean the end of ***de facto* segregation** (segregation that is not imposed by law but is produced by circumstances, such as the existence of neighborhoods or communities populated primarily by African Americans). Attempts to overcome *de facto* segregation included redrawing school district lines, reassigning pupils, and busing.

***de jure* segregation** Racial segregation that occurs because of laws or decisions by government agencies.

***de facto* segregation** Racial segregation that occurs not as a result of deliberate intentions but because of past social and economic conditions and residential patterns.

busing The transportation of public school students by bus to schools physically outside their neighborhoods to eliminate school segregation based on residential patterns.

BUSING Busing is the transporting of students by bus to schools physically outside their neighborhoods in an effort to achieve racially desegregated schools. The Supreme Court first endorsed busing in 1971 in a case involving the school system in Charlotte, North Carolina.[9] Following this decision, the Court upheld busing in several northern cities.[10] Proponents believed that busing improved the educational and career opportunities of minority children and also enhanced the ability of children from different ethnic groups to get along with one another.

Nevertheless, busing was unpopular with many groups from its inception. By the mid-1970s, the courts had begun to retreat from their former support for busing. In 1974, the Supreme Court rejected the idea of busing children across school district lines.[11] In 1986, the Court refused to review a lower court decision that ended a desegregation plan in Norfolk, Virginia.[12] Today, busing orders to end *de facto* segregation are not upheld by the courts. Indeed, *de facto* segregation in America's schools is still widespread.

The Civil Rights Movement

In 1955, one year after the first *Brown* decision, an African American woman named Rosa Parks, a longtime activist in the NAACP, boarded a public bus in Montgomery, Alabama. When it became crowded, she refused to move to the "colored section" at the rear of the bus. She was arrested and fined for violating local segregation laws. Her arrest spurred the local African American community to organize a year-long boycott of the entire Montgomery bus system. The protest was led by a twenty-seven-year-old Baptist minister, the Reverend Dr. Martin Luther King, Jr. During the protest period,

Martin Luther King Jr. acknowledges the crowd at the Lincoln Memorial for his "I Have a Dream" speech during the March on Washington, D.C., on Aug. 28, 1963.

AP PHOTO

he was jailed and his house was bombed. Despite the hostility and what appeared to be overwhelming odds against them, the protesters were triumphant.

In 1956, a federal court prohibited the segregation of buses in Montgomery, and the era of the **civil rights movement**—the movement by minorities and concerned whites to end racial segregation—had begun. The movement was led by a number of groups and individuals, including Martin Luther King and his Southern Christian Leadership Conference (SCLC). Other groups, such as the Congress of Racial Equality (CORE), the NAACP, and the Student Nonviolent Coordinating Committee (SNCC), also sought to secure equal rights for African Americans.

> "INJUSTICE anywhere is a threat to justice everywhere."
> ~ MARTIN LUTHER KING, JR. ~
> U.S. CIVIL RIGHTS LEADER
> 1929–1968

Civil rights activists were trained in the tools of nonviolence—how to use nonthreatening body language, how to go limp when dragged or assaulted, and how to protect themselves from clubs or police dogs. As the civil rights movement gained momentum, the media images of nonviolent protesters being attacked by police, sprayed with fire hoses, and attacked by dogs shocked and angered Americans across the country. This public backlash led to nationwide demands for reform. The March on Washington for Jobs and Freedom, led by Martin Luther King in 1963, aimed in part to demonstrate the widespread public support for legislation to ban discrimination in all aspects of public life.

NONVIOLENCE AS A TACTIC Civil rights protesters in the 1960s began to apply the tactic of nonviolent **civil disobedience**—the deliberate and public refusal to obey laws considered unjust—in civil rights actions throughout the South. For example, in 1960, in Greensboro, North Carolina, four African American students sat at the "whites only" lunch counter at Woolworth's and ordered food. The waitress refused to serve them, and the store closed early, but more students returned the next day to sit at the counter, with supporters picketing outside. **Sit-ins** spread to other lunch counters across the South. In some instances, students were heckled or even dragged from the store by angry whites. But the protesters never reacted with violence. They simply returned to their seats at the counter, day after day. Within months of the first sit-in, lunch counters began to reverse their policies of segregation.

CIVIL RIGHTS LEGISLATION IN THE 1960s As the civil rights movement demonstrated its strength, Congress began to pass civil rights laws. While the Fourteenth Amendment prevented the *government* from discriminating against individuals or groups, the private sector—businesses, restaurants, and so on—could still freely refuse to employ and serve nonwhites. Therefore, Congress sought to address this issue.

The Civil Rights Act of 1964 was the first and most comprehensive civil rights law. It forbade discrimination on the basis of race, color, religion, gender, and national origin. The major provisions of the act were as follows:

- It outlawed discrimination in public places of accommodation, such as hotels, restaurants, snack bars, movie theaters, and public transportation.
- It provided that federal funds could be withheld from any federal or state government project or facility that practiced any form of discrimination.

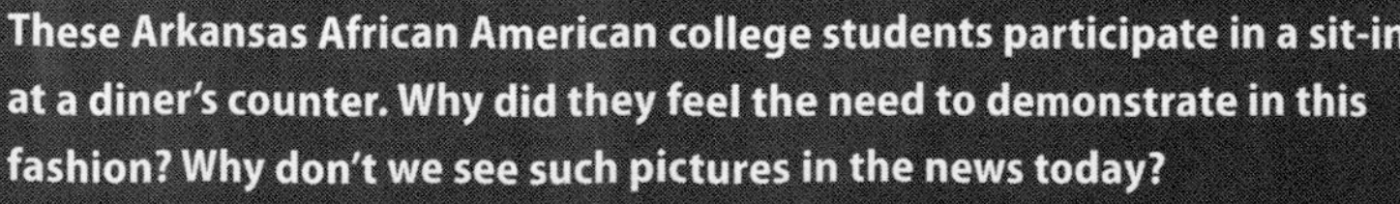
These Arkansas African American college students participate in a sit-in at a diner's counter. Why did they feel the need to demonstrate in this fashion? Why don't we see such pictures in the news today?

MPI/GETTY IMAGES

civil rights movement The movement in the 1950s and 1960s, by minorities and concerned whites, to end racial segregation.

civil disobedience The deliberate and public act of refusing to obey laws thought to be unjust.

sit-in A tactic of nonviolent civil disobedience. Demonstrators enter a business, college building, or other public place and remain seated until they are forcibly removed or until their demands are met. The tactic was used successfully in the civil rights movement and in other protest movements in the United States.

- It banned discrimination in employment.
- It outlawed arbitrary discrimination in voter registration.
- It authorized the federal government to sue to desegregate public schools and facilities.

Other significant laws passed by Congress during the 1960s included the Voting Rights Act of 1965, which made it illegal to interfere with anyone's right to vote in any election held in this country (see Chapter 8 for a discussion of the historical restrictions on voting that African Americans faced), and the Civil Rights Act of 1968, which prohibited discrimination in housing.

THE BLACK POWER MOVEMENT Not all African Americans embraced nonviolence. Several outspoken leaders in the mid-1960s were outraged at the slow pace of change in the social and economic status of blacks. Malcolm X, a speaker and organizer for the Nation of Islam (also called the Black Muslims), rejected the goals of integration and racial equality espoused by the civil rights movement. He called instead for black separatism and black pride. Although he later moderated some of his views, his rhetorical style and powerful message influenced many African American young people.

By the late 1960s, with the assassinations of Malcolm X in 1965 and Martin Luther King in 1968, the era of mass acts of civil disobedience in the name of civil rights had come to an end.

Political Participation

As you will read in Chapter 8, in many jurisdictions African Americans were prevented from voting for years after the Civil War, despite the Fifteenth Amendment (1870). These discriminatory practices persisted in the twentieth century. In the early 1960s, only 22 percent of African Americans of voting age in the South were registered to vote, compared with 63 percent of voting-age whites. In Mississippi, the most extreme example, only 6 percent of voting-age African Americans were registered to vote. Such disparities led to the enactment of the Voting Rights Act of 1965, which ended discriminatory voter-registration tests and gave federal voter registrars the power to prevent racial discrimination in voting.

Today, the percentages of voting-age blacks and whites registered to vote are nearly equal. As a result of this dramatic change, political participation by African Americans has increased, as has the number of African American elected officials.

Today, more than nine thousand African Americans serve in elective office in the United States. At least one congressional seat in each southern state is held by an African American, as are more than 15 percent of the state legislative seats in the South. A number of African Americans have achieved high government office, including Colin Powell, who served as President George W. Bush's first secretary of state, and Condoleezza Rice, his second secretary of state. Of course, in 2008 Barack Obama, a U.S. senator from Illinois, became the first African American president of the United States. Obama's election reflects a significant change in public opinion. Fifty years ago, only 38 percent of Americans said that they would be willing to vote for an African American as president. Today, this number has risen to more than 90 percent. Nonetheless, only two African Americans have been elected to a state governorship, and only a handful of African Americans have been elected to the U.S. Senate since 1900.

Continuing Challenges

Although African Americans no longer face *de jure* segregation, they continue to struggle for income and educational parity with whites. Recent census data show

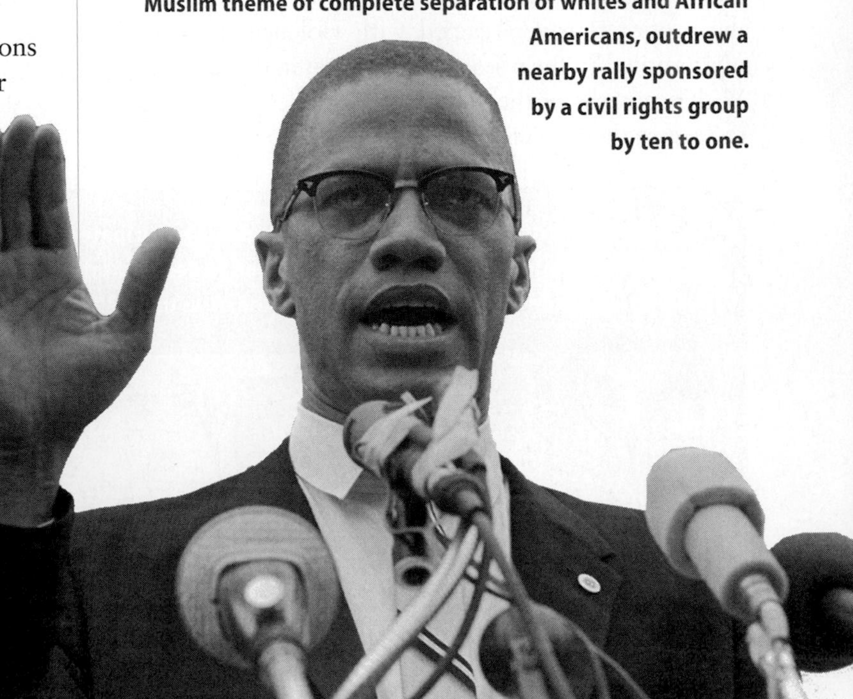

Black Muslim leader Malcolm X speaks to an audience at a Harlem rally in 1963. His talk, in which he restated the Black Muslim theme of complete separation of whites and African Americans, outdrew a nearby rally sponsored by a civil rights group by ten to one.

that incomes in white households are two-thirds higher than those in black households. The poverty rate for blacks is roughly three times that for whites.

The education gap between blacks and whites also persists despite continuing efforts by educators—and by government, through programs such as the federal No Child Left Behind Act—to reduce it. Recent studies show that on average, African American students in high school can read and do math at only the average level of whites in junior high school. While black adults have narrowed the gap with white adults in earning high school diplomas, the disparity has widened for college degrees.

These problems tend to feed on one another. Schools in poorer neighborhoods generally have fewer educational resources available, resulting in lower achievement levels for their students. Thus, some educational experts suggest that it all comes down to money. In fact, many parents of minority students in struggling school districts are less concerned about integration than they are about funds for their children's schools. A number of these parents have initiated lawsuits against their state governments, demanding that the states give poor districts more resources.

Researchers have known for decades that when students enrolled at a particular school come almost entirely from impoverished families, regardless of race, the performance of the students at that school is seriously depressed. When low-income students attend schools where the majority of the students are middle class, again regardless of race, their performance improves dramatically—without dragging down the performance of the middle-class students. Because of this research and recent U.S. Supreme Court rulings that have struck down some racial integration plans, several school systems have adopted policies that integrate students on the basis of socioeconomic class, not race.[13]

LO3 *Women*

In 1848, Lucretia Mott and Elizabeth Cady Stanton organized the first "woman's rights" convention in Seneca Falls, New York. The three hundred people who attended approved a Declaration of Sentiments: "We hold these truths to be self-evident: that all men *and women* are created equal." In the following years, other women's groups held conventions in various cities in the Midwest and the East. With the outbreak of the Civil War, though, women's rights advocates devoted their energies to the war effort.

AP PHOTO/ALEX BRANDON

President Obama often accepts public speaking engagements. While he has stumped for health-care reform, increased regulation of business and of banks, and other causes, he has rarely talked about race relations. Why not?

The Struggle for Voting Rights

The movement for political rights gained momentum again in 1869, when Susan B. Anthony and Elizabeth Cady Stanton formed the National Woman Suffrage Association. **Suffrage**—the right to vote—became their goal. Members of this association, however, saw suffrage as only one step on the road toward greater social and political rights for women. Lucy Stone and other women, who founded the American Woman Suffrage Association, thought that the right to vote should be the only goal. By 1890, the two organizations had joined forces, and the resulting National American Woman Suffrage Association had indeed only one goal—the enfranchisement of women. When little progress was made, small, radical splinter groups took to the streets. Parades, hunger strikes, arrests, and jailings soon followed.

World War I (1914–1918) marked a turning point in the battle for women's rights. The war offered many opportunities for women. Thousands of women served as volunteers, and about a million women joined the workforce, holding jobs vacated by men who entered military service. After the war, President Woodrow Wilson wrote to Carrie Chapman Catt, one of the leaders of the women's movement: "It is high time that [that] part of our debt should be

suffrage The right to vote; the franchise.

acknowledged." Two years later, in 1920, seventy-two years after the Seneca Falls convention, the Nineteenth Amendment to the Constitution was ratified: "The right of citizens of the United States to vote shall not be denied or abridged by the United States or by any State on account of sex."

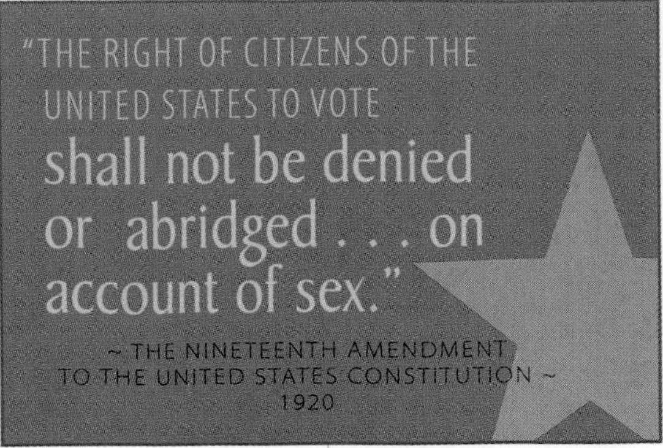
"THE RIGHT OF CITIZENS OF THE UNITED STATES TO VOTE
shall not be denied or abridged . . . on account of sex."
~ THE NINETEENTH AMENDMENT TO THE UNITED STATES CONSTITUTION ~
1920

The Feminist Movement

After winning the right to vote, women engaged in little independent political activity for many years. In the 1960s, however, a new women's movement arose—the feminist movement. Women who faced discrimination in employment and other circumstances were inspired in part by the civil rights movement and the campaign against the war in Vietnam. The National Organization for Women (NOW), founded in 1966, was the most important new women's organization. But the feminist movement also consisted of thousands of small, independent "women's liberation" and "consciousness-raising" groups established on campuses and in neighborhoods throughout the nation. **Feminism,** the goal of the movement, meant full political, economic, and social equality for women.

During the 1970s, NOW and other organizations sought to win passage of the Equal Rights Amendment (ERA) to the Constitution, which would have written equality into the heart of the nation's laws. The amendment did not win support from enough state legislatures, however, and it failed. Campaigns to change state and national laws affecting women were much more successful. Congress and the various state legislatures enacted a range of measures to provide equal rights for women. The women's movement also enjoyed considerable success in legal action. Courts at all levels accepted the argument that *gender discrimination* violated the Fourteenth Amendment's equal protection clause.

Women in American Politics Today

More than ten thousand members have served in the U.S. House of Representatives. Only 1 percent of them have been women, and women continue to face a "men's club" atmosphere in Congress. In 2002, however, a woman, Nancy Pelosi (D., Calif.), was elected minority leader of the House of Representatives. She was the first woman to hold this post. Pelosi again made history when, after the Democratic victories in the 2006 elections, she was elected Speaker of the House of Representatives, the first woman ever to lead the House.

feminism The belief in full political, economic, and social equality for women.

FEDERAL OFFICES Women have been underrepresented when receiving presidential appointments to federal offices. Franklin D. Roosevelt (1933–1945) appointed the first woman to a cabinet post—Frances Perkins, who was secretary of labor from 1933 to 1945. Several women have held cabinet posts in more recent administrations, however. All of the last three presidents have appointed women to the most senior cabinet post—secretary of state. Bill Clinton (1993–2001) appointed Madeleine Albright to this position, George W. Bush (2001–2009) picked Condoleezza Rice for the post in his second term, and most recently, Barack Obama chose New York senator Hillary Clinton to be secretary of state.

These New York protesters hold signs indicating their disagreements with the Catholic Church's official views on abortion and homosexuality.

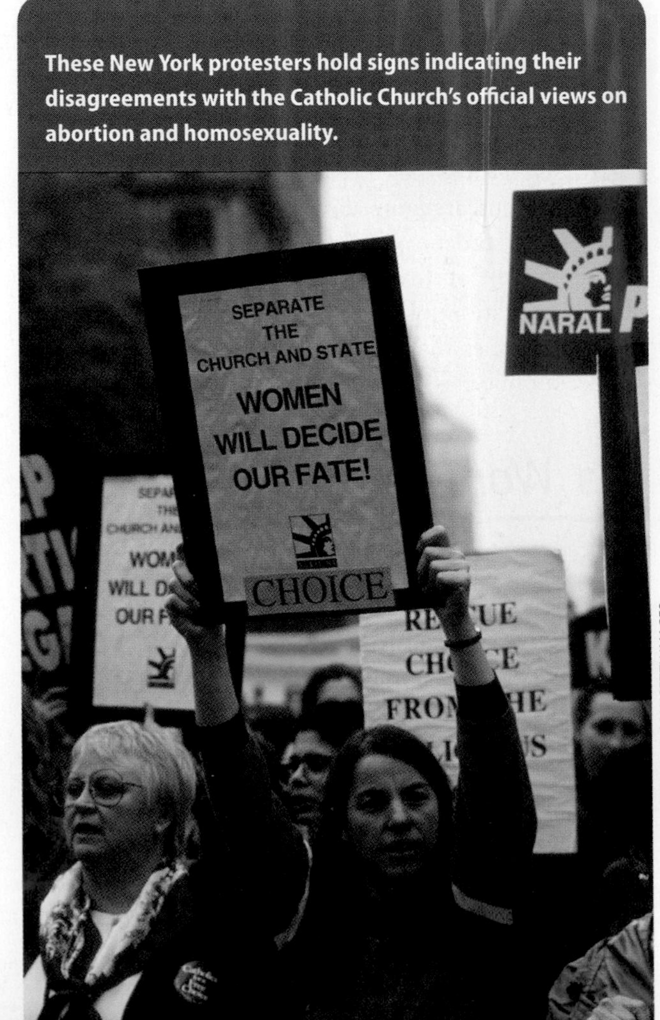
SEPARATE THE CHURCH AND STATE
WOMEN WILL DECIDE OUR FATE!
CHOICE
NARAL

EVAN AGOSTINI/LIAISON/GETTY IMAGES

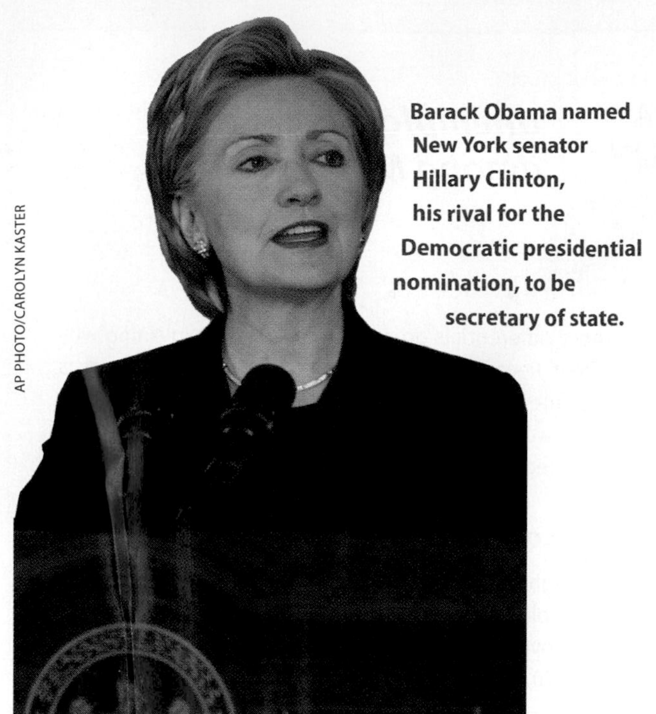

Barack Obama named New York senator Hillary Clinton, his rival for the Democratic presidential nomination, to be secretary of state.

In addition, Ronald Reagan (1981–1989) appointed the first woman to sit on the Supreme Court, Sandra Day O'Connor. Bill Clinton appointed Ruth Bader Ginsburg to the Supreme Court. Barack Obama selected Sonia Sotomayor for the Court in 2009, and Elena Kagan in 2010.

STATE POLITICS Women have made greater progress at the state level, and the percentage of women in state legislatures has been rising steadily. Women now constitute nearly one-fourth of state legislators. Notably, in 1998, women won races for each of the top five offices in Arizona, the first such occurrence in U.S. history. Generally, women have been more successful politically in the western states than elsewhere. In Washington State, more than one-third of the state's legislative seats are now held by women. At the other end of the spectrum are states such as Alabama. In that state, fewer than 10 percent of the lawmakers are women.

Elena Kagan appears just after being sworn in as the 112th justice of the Supreme Court. She is the fourth female named to the Court.

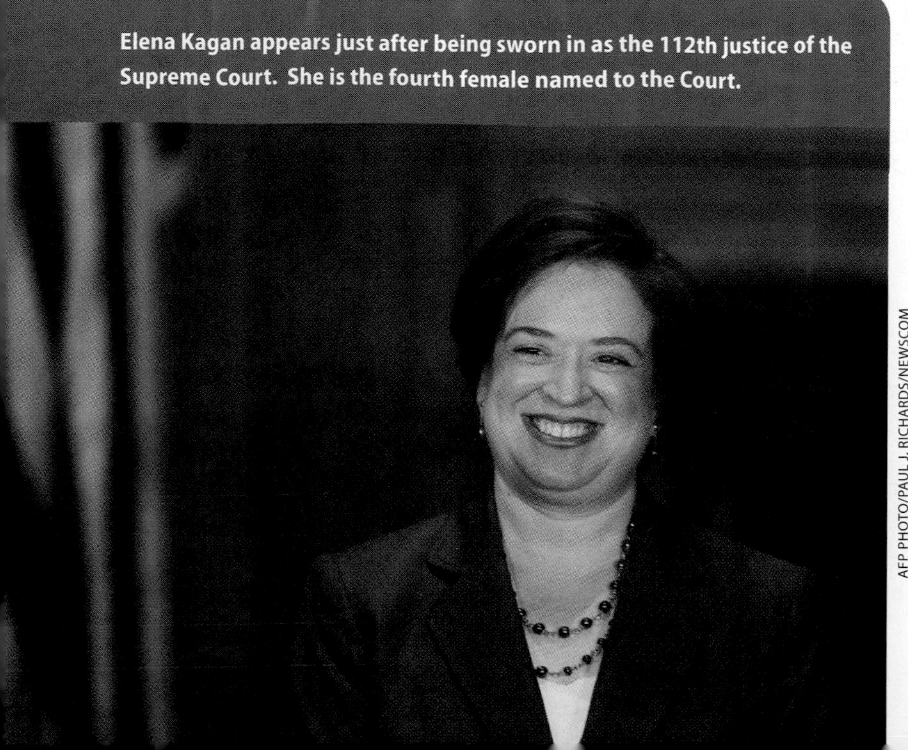

Women in the Workplace

An ongoing challenge for American women is to obtain equal pay and equal opportunity in the workplace. In spite of federal legislation and programs to promote equal treatment of women in the workplace, women continue to face various forms of discrimination.

WAGE DISCRIMINATION In 1963, Congress passed the Equal Pay Act. The act requires employers to pay an equal wage for substantially equal work—males cannot be paid more than females who perform essentially the same job. The following year, Congress passed the Civil Rights Act of 1964, Title VII of which prohibits employment discrimination on the basis of race, color, national origin, gender, and religion. Women, however, continue to face wage discrimination.

It is estimated that for every dollar earned by men, women earn about 80 cents. Although the wage gap has narrowed significantly since 1963, when the Equal Pay Act was enacted (at that time, women earned 58 cents for every dollar earned by men), it still remains. This is particularly true for women in management positions and older women. Female managers now earn, on average, only 70 percent of what male managers earn. And women between the ages of forty-five and fifty-four make, on average, only 73 percent of what men in that age group earn. Notably, when a large number of women are in a particular occupation, the wages that are paid in that occupation tend to be relatively low. On the positive side, women are less likely than men to lose their jobs during a recession. We examine that phenomenon in this chapter's feature *Our Government Faces a Troubled Economy: Unemployment among Men* on the following page.

Even though an increasing number of women now hold business and professional jobs once held only by men, relatively few of these women are able to rise to the top of the career ladder in their firms due to the lingering bias against women in the

OUR GOVERNMENT FACES A
TROUBLED ECONOMY

Unemployment among Men

One of the most far-reaching and painful aspects of any recession is unemployment. Those who are unemployed lose not only their income but also some of their dignity. Continued unemployment was the number-one issue for most voters throughout the Great Recession.

During this period, many people noticed that more men than women were losing their jobs. From December 2007 to October 2009, net employment fell by 5.8 million for men but only 2.5 million for women. As a result, some called the Great Recession a "mancession." At the height of the unemployment crisis, a full one-fifth of the male population of prime working age was, for one or another reason, not working. The only other time in American history when the share of men not working was this large or larger was during the Great Depression of the 1930s.

The Hardest-Hit Industries Were Dominated by Men

The Great Recession started with the collapse of the housing sector. Construction came to an abrupt halt in most of the United States. Men have always dominated the construction industry—up to 88 percent of the jobs in construction are filled by men. Consequently, many more men than women were put out of work in this sector. Manufacturing was hit harder than any sector other than construction, and more than 71 percent of manufacturing jobs are held by men. In contrast, the industries that suffered least were dominated by women. Employment in education and health services actually edged up through the crisis, and more than 77 percent of the workers in those two fields are women.

These differentials go a long way toward explaining why the Great Recession was a mancession. Some economists have pointed out, however, that men have lost many more jobs than women in every recession since World War II. In that sense, all recessions have been mancessions.

In the Long Run

Although the employment picture for men was especially bleak during the recession, male employment has declined over the last forty years in good times and bad. Before 1970, 92 to 95 percent of the men in the prime employment years—ages 25 to 54—were working. On the eve of the Great Recession, the percentage was about 88. Fewer than half of women aged 25 to 54 were working in 1970. In 2000, female employment peaked at about 75 percent.

Women have pulled ahead of men when it comes to education, and that cannot help men get jobs. Consider how many people aged 25 to 29 have college degrees: In 1964, 17 percent of men in this age group had a degree, compared with 9 percent of women. In 2009, 27 percent of men in this age group had a degree—and 35 percent of women had one. Men in their twenties are actually *less* likely to have a college degree today than in 1975.

The Government Reacts

High unemployment rates are very bad news for politicians. They anger voters and can cost officeholders their jobs. In 2009 and 2010, the Democrats attempted to combat the recession and unemployment through stimulus programs and extending unemployment compensation. Subsidies to the states for education and health care may have preserved some jobs in sectors dominated by women. Saving Chrysler and General Motors helped men (auto employment is 80 percent male). At best, though, such measures blunted the effects of the recession. They did not end it.

You Be the Judge **Women continue to receive lower wages than men, on average. What effect might this have on the ability of women to get jobs?**

glass ceiling An invisible but real discriminatory barrier that prevents women and minorities from rising to top positions of power or responsibility.

workplace. This bias has been described as the **glass ceiling**—an invisible but real discriminatory barrier that prevents women (or minorities) from rising to top positions of power or responsibility. Today, less than one-sixth of the top executive positions in the largest American corporations are held by women.

SEXUAL HARASSMENT Title VII's prohibition of gender discrimination has also been extended to prohibit sexual harassment. **Sexual harassment** occurs when job opportunities, promotions, salary increases, or even the ability to retain a job depends on whether an employee complies with demands for sexual favors. A special form of sexual harassment, called hostile-environment harassment, occurs when an employee is subjected to sexual conduct or comments in the workplace that interfere with the employee's job performance or that create an intimidating, hostile, or offensive environment.

The Supreme Court has upheld the right of persons to be free from sexual harassment on the job on a number of occasions. In 1998, the Court made it clear that sexual harassment includes harassment by members of the same sex.[14] In the same year, the Court held that employers are liable for the harassment of employees by supervisors unless the employers can show that (1) they exercised reasonable care in preventing such problems (by implementing antiharassment policies and procedures, for example) and (2) the employees failed to take advantage of any corrective opportunities provided by the employers.[15] The Civil Rights Act of 1991 greatly expanded the remedies available for victims of sexual harassment. Under the act, victims can seek damages as well as back pay, job reinstatement, and other compensation.

LO4 *Securing Rights for Other Groups*

In addition to African Americans and women, a number of other groups in U.S. society have faced discriminatory treatment. To discuss all of these groups would require volumes.

Here, we look first at three significant ethnic groups that have had to struggle for equal treatment—Hispanics, Asian Americans, and Native Americans. Then we examine the struggles of several other groups of Americans—persons with disabilities and gay men and lesbians.

Hispanics

Hispanics, or Latinos, constitute the largest ethnic minority in the United States. Whereas African Americans represent about 13 percent of the U.S. population, Hispanics now constitute more than 15 percent. Each year, the Hispanic population grows by nearly 1 million people, one-third of whom are newly arrived legal immigrants. By 2050, Hispanics are expected to constitute about one-fourth of the U.S. population.

sexual harassment
Unwanted physical contact, verbal conduct, or abuse of a sexual nature that interferes with a recipient's job performance, creates a hostile environment, or carries with it an implicit or explicit threat of adverse employment consequences.

Hispanics can be of any race, and to classify them as a single minority group is misleading. Spanish-speaking individuals tend to identify themselves by their country of origin, rather than as Hispanics. As you can see in Figure 5–1 below, the largest Hispanic group consists of Mexican Americans, who constitute about 66 percent of the Hispanic population living in the United States. About 9 percent of Hispanics are Puerto Ricans, and 3.5 percent are Cuban Americans. Most of the remaining Hispanics are from Central and South American countries.

Economically, Hispanic households are often members of this country's working poor. About 20 percent of Hispanic families live below the poverty line, compared with 8 percent of non-Hispanic white families. Hispanic leaders tend to attribute the low income levels to language problems, lack of job training, and continuing immigration. Immigration disguises statistical progress because language problems and lack of job training are usually more notable among new immigrants than among those who have lived in the United States for many years.

Figure 5–1

Hispanics Living in the United States by Place of Origin

As you can see in this chart, most Hispanics (just under two-thirds) are from Mexico.

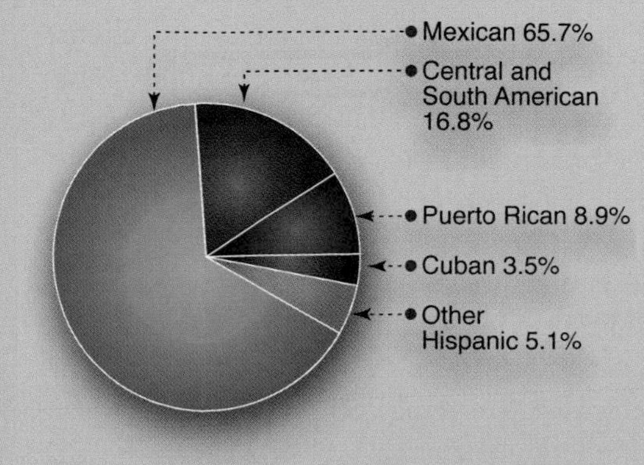

Source: Pew Hispanic Center tabulations of 2008 American Community Survey.

ELECTIONS 2010

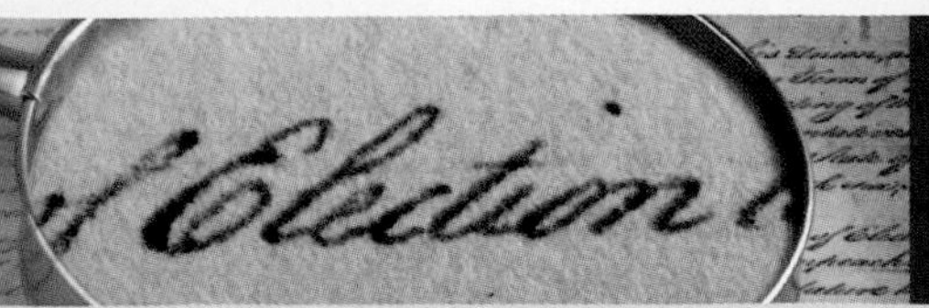

Minority Group Members and Women

The 2010 election saw a large number of minority and female candidates for the Senate, for the House, for governor, and for seats in state legislatures. The total number of minority candidates for the House and Senate was 123. A record number of African-American Republican congressional candidates sought office and two were successful. The number of Latino members of the House and Senate is now a near-record twenty-seven. Five of them are Republican. The number of Asian-American members of the House and Senate will remain at thirteen, while the number of African-Americans will be forty-one, one less than in the previous Congress.

A total of 154 female candidates sought office in the House and Senate. Campaign spending hit new records, and one of them was set by a woman. Republican Meg Whitman spent $140 million of her own money to defeat Democratic rival Jerry Brown for the governorship of California. (She lost nonetheless.) An estimated seventy-two House seats are now held by women, down one from the previous Congress. The number of female senators remained the same at seventeen. At the state level, for the first time ever, two female minority group members won governorships—in New Mexico and South Carolina—bringing the total number of female governors to seven.

PARTY IDENTIFICATION AND ELECTORAL SIGNIFICANCE In their party identification, Hispanics tend to follow some fairly well-established patterns. Traditionally, Mexican Americans and Puerto Ricans identify with the Democratic Party, which has favored more government assistance and support programs for disadvantaged groups. Cubans, in contrast, tend to identify with the Republican Party. This is largely because of a different history. Cuban émigrés fled from Cuba during and after the Communist revolution led by Fidel Castro. The strong anti-Communist sentiments of the Cubans propelled them toward the more conservative party—the Republicans. Today, relations with Communist Cuba continue to be a key political issue for Cuban Americans.

Immigration reform was the subject of heated debate in the months leading up to the 2006 midterm elections, and this debate had a significant impact on Hispanic voters, especially in California. Before the 2006 elections, to appeal to the party base, Republican ads attacked proposed legislation that would have made it possible for unauthorized immigrants to obtain legal status. According to some observers, many Hispanics perceived the ads as attacking all Hispanics and were motivated to vote against Republicans in the 2006 elections. Exit polls conducted during the elections showed that for 69 percent of Hispanic voters, immigration was the number-one priority.

By 2008, immigration had receded as a national issue—it did not come up at all in the presidential debates. For Hispanics, along with everyone else, economic troubles were the number-one issue. In the fall elections, only 31 percent of Hispanic voters chose Republican John McCain, even though he had been a major proponent of immigration reform. This was down sharply from the almost 40 percent of the Hispanic vote won by George W. Bush in 2004.

POLITICAL PARTICIPATION Generally, Hispanics in the United States have a comparatively low level of political participation. This is understandable, given that one-third of Hispanics are below voting age and another one-fourth are not citizens and thus cannot vote. Although voter turnout among Hispanics is

Sonia Sotomayor was grilled by Republicans during her nomination hearing before the Senate Judiciary Committee. (Here you can see that she didn't always feel under pressure.) Her nomination was easily approved by the Senate, making her the first Hispanic to become a Supreme Court justice.

AP PHOTO/J. SCOTT APPLEWHITE

generally low compared with the population at large, the Hispanic voting rate is rising as more immigrants become citizens and as more Hispanics reach voting age. Indeed, when comparing citizens of equal incomes and educational backgrounds, Hispanic citizens' participation rate is higher than average.

Increasingly, Hispanics hold political office, particularly in those states with large Hispanic populations. Today, more than 5 percent of the state legislators in Arizona, California, Colorado, Florida, New Mexico, and Texas are of Hispanic ancestry. Cuban Americans have been notably successful in gaining local political power, particularly in Dade County, Florida.

NEWSCOM

Asian American students routinely score higher on their college-entrance SATs than do other groups. Also, Asian Americans graduate at a higher rate than do other groups. Because they are in a minority, should they nonetheless benefit from affirmative action programs in college admissions and job hiring?

President George W. Bush appointed a number of Hispanics to federal offices, including cabinet positions. For example, he named Alberto Gonzales to head the Justice Department and Carlos Gutierrez as secretary of commerce. Barack Obama appointed Senator Ken Salazar (D., Colo.) to head the Interior Department and Representative Hilda Solis (D., Calif.) as secretary of labor. Hispanics are also increasing their presence in Congress, albeit slowly.

Asian Americans

Asian Americans have also suffered, at times severely, from discriminatory treatment. The Chinese Exclusion Act of 1882 prevented persons from China and Japan from coming to the United States to prospect for gold or to work on the railroads or in factories in the West. After 1900, immigration continued to be restricted—only limited numbers of individuals from China and Japan were allowed to enter the United States. Those who were allowed into the country faced racial prejudice from Americans who had little respect for their customs and culture. In 1906, after the San Francisco earthquake, Japanese American students were segregated into special schools so that white children could use their buildings.

The Japanese bombing of Pearl Harbor in 1941, which launched the entry of the United States into World War II (1939–1945), intensified Americans' fear of the Japanese. Actions taken under an executive order issued by President Franklin D. Roosevelt in 1942 subjected many Japanese Americans to curfews, excluded them from certain "military areas," and evacuated most of the West Coast Japanese American population to internment camps (also called "relocation centers").[16] In 1988, Congress provided funds to compensate former camp inhabitants—$1.25 billion for approximately 60,000 people.

Today, Japanese Americans and Chinese Americans lead other ethnic groups in median income and median education. Indeed, Asians who have immigrated to the United States since 1965 (including immigrants from India) represent the most highly skilled immigrant groups in American history. Nearly 40 percent of Asian Americans over the age of twenty-five have college degrees. The image of Asian Americans as a "model minority" has created certain problems for its members, however. Some argue that leading colleges and universities have discriminated against Asian Americans in admissions because so many of them apply. We discuss that issue in this chapter's *Join the Debate* feature on the following page.

More than a million Indochinese war refugees, most from Vietnam, have immigrated to the United States since the 1970s. Many came with relatives and were sponsored by American families or organizations. Thus, they had support systems to help them get started. Some immigrants from other parts of Indochina, however, have experienced difficulties because they come from cultures that have had very little contact with the practices of developed industrial societies.

Native Americans

When we consider population figures since 1492, we see that the Native Americans experienced one catastrophe after another. We cannot know exactly how many people lived in America when Columbus arrived.

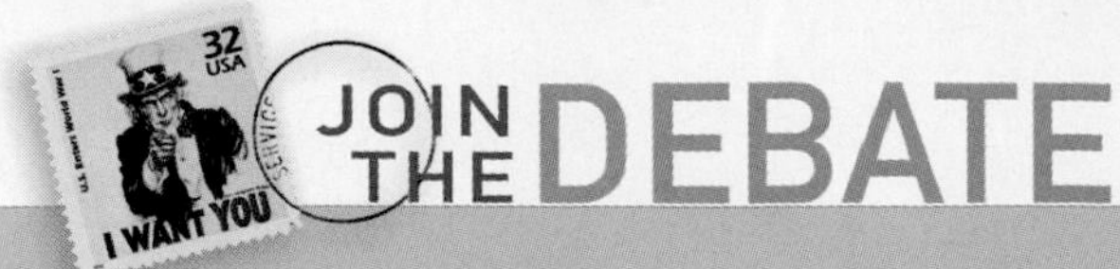

Are Admissions at Top Schools Unfair to Asian Americans?

There are 14 million Asian Americans, about 4.5 percent of the U.S. population. They are a diverse group. Outside of the United States, people from China, India, Japan, and Korea have little in common. Only in America are they lumped together—and in this country, people from East and South Asia do have a few things in common. Their average family income is higher than that of whites. They are also well educated. By one estimate, Asian Americans make up as many as 30 percent of the top college candidates as determined by SAT scores, National Merit and AP Scholar awards, and grades. In the Ivy League, however, Asian admissions have consistently run below 20 percent. In other words, many excellent Asian American students are being turned away.

Colleges Admission Isn't Just about Grades and Test Scores

While it may appear to high-scoring Asian Americans who don't get into their college of choice that they have suffered from discrimination, it is not necessarily true. Universities routinely manage admissions to obtain the freshman classes they wish to have. They try to include the right number of football and basketball players, dancers, minorities, and men (the latter are favored in some universities because otherwise campuses might become "too female"). Only if you believe that high test scores should be the sole basis for admission can you argue that university admission preferences constitute discrimination.

The goal of a diverse freshman class is to expose all students to a mix of races, ethnicities, and viewpoints. Vincent Pan, head of Chinese for Affirmative Action, argues that universities "have a public responsibility to prepare future leaders, and we need to prepare a generation of leaders that will look like America." A freshman class that is, say, 40 percent Asian American does not look like America, just as a class that is 80 percent women does not look like America.

Discrimination Is Discrimination—Period

Lately, Ivy League–level universities have established techniques to limit the number of Asian American students admitted to their institutions. These same techniques were used before World War II (and sometimes even after) to limit the number of Jewish students. The basic scheme, then and now, is to award lots of extra points for being "well-rounded" and then to define well-rounded as everything that young Asian Americans aren't (or that the young Jews weren't). A more labor-intensive method of accomplishing the same goal is through a "holistic" review process for all candidates. Schools using this process rely on admissions officers' subjective views of students, which yields an assessment that supposedly evaluates the "whole person."

There is no need to set Asian Americans in competition with other minorities in admissions. More than 20 percent of the spaces at top private universities are currently set aside for legacy students, children of the rich and famous, and athletes. (Legacy students are the children of alumni or alumnae.) If the number of these unjustified preferences were merely cut in half, there would be enough room for qualified Asian youths.

For Critical Analysis ***Why do some universities reserve spots for the children of their graduates?***

Current research estimates the population of what is now the continental United States to have been anywhere from 3 million to 8 million, out of a total New World population of 40 million to 100 million. The Europeans brought with them diseases to which these Native Americans had no immunity. As a result, after a series of terrifying epidemics, the population of the continental United States was reduced to perhaps eight hundred thousand people by 1600. Death rates elsewhere in the New World were comparable. When the Pilgrims arrived at Plymouth, the Massachusetts coast was lined with abandoned village sites.[17]

In subsequent centuries, the American Indian population continued to decline, bottoming out at about half a million in 1925. These were centuries in which the European American—and African American—populations experienced explosive growth. By 2000, the Native American population had recovered to about 2 million, or about 3.5 million if we count individuals who are only part Indian.

In 1789, Congress designated the Native American tribes as foreign nations so that the government could sign land and boundary treaties with them. As members of foreign nations, Native Americans had no civil rights under U.S. laws. This situation continued until 1924, when the citizenship rights spelled out in the Fourteenth Amendment to the Constitution were finally extended to American Indians.

EARLY POLICIES TOWARD NATIVE AMERICANS The Northwest Ordinance, passed by the Congress of the Confederation in 1787, stated that "the utmost good faith shall always be observed towards the Indians; their lands and property shall never be taken from them without their consent; and in their property, rights, and liberty, they shall never be invaded or disturbed, unless in just and lawful wars authorized by Congress." Over the next hundred years, these principles were violated more often than they were observed.

In the early 1830s, boundaries were established between lands occupied by Native Americans and those occupied by white settlers. In 1830, Congress instructed the Bureau of Indian Affairs (BIA), which Congress had established in 1824 as part of the War Department, to remove all tribes to lands (reservations) west of the Mississippi River in order to free land east of the Mississippi for white settlement.

In the late 1880s, the U.S. government changed its policy. The goal became the "assimilation" of Native Americans into American society. Each family was given a parcel of land within the reservation to farm. The remaining acreage was sold to whites, thus reducing the number of acres in reservation status from 140 million to about 47 million. Tribes that would not cooperate with this plan lost their reservations altogether. The BIA also set up Native American boarding schools for children to remove them from their parents' influence. In these schools, American Indian children were taught to speak English, to practice Christianity, and to dress like white Americans.

Many Native Americans work at locally owned casinos, such as this one in Biloxi, Mississippi. Has gambling on reservations changed the standard of living of all Native Americans? Why or why not?

JUSTIN SULLIVAN/GETTY IMAGES

NATIVE AMERICANS TODAY Native Americans have always found it difficult to obtain political power. In part, this is because the tribes are small and scattered, making organized political movements difficult. Today, American Indians remain fragmented politically because large numbers of their population live off the reservations. Nonetheless, in the 1960s, some Native Americans formed organizations to strike back at the U.S. government and to reclaim their heritage, including their lands.

In the late 1960s, a small group of Indians occupied Alcatraz Island, claiming that the island was part of their ancestral lands. Other militant actions followed. For example, in 1973, supporters of the American Indian Movement took over Wounded Knee, South Dakota, where about 150 Sioux Indians had been killed by the U.S. Army in 1890.[18] The occupation was undertaken to protest the government's policy toward Native Americans and to call attention to the injustices they had suffered.

COMPENSATION FOR INJUSTICES OF THE PAST As more Americans became aware of the sufferings of Native Americans, Congress began to compensate them for past injustices. In 1990, Congress passed the Native American Languages Act, which declared that Native American languages are unique and serve an important role in maintaining Indian culture and continuity. Courts, too, have shown a greater willingness to recognize Native American treaty rights. For example, in 1985, the Supreme Court ruled that three tribes of Oneida Indians could claim damages for the use of tribal land that had been unlawfully transferred in 1795.[19]

The Indian Gaming Regulatory Act of 1988 allows Native Americans to have gambling operations on their reservations. Although the profits from casinos have helped to improve the economic and social status of many Native Americans, some Indians feel that this industry has seriously injured their traditional culture. Poverty and unemployment remain widespread on the reservations.

Obtaining Rights for Persons with Disabilities

Discrimination based on disability crosses the boundaries of race, ethnicity, gender, and religion. Persons with disabilities, especially those with physical deformities or severe mental impairments, have to face social bias. Although attitudes toward persons with disabilities have changed considerably in the last several decades, such persons continue to suffer from discrimination in all its forms.

Persons with disabilities first became a political force in the 1970s, and in 1973, Congress passed the first legislation protecting this group of persons—the Rehabilitation Act. This act prohibited discrimination against persons with disabilities in programs receiving federal aid. The Individuals with Disabilities Education Act (formerly called the Education for All Handicapped Children Act of 1975) requires public schools to provide children with disabilities with free, appropriate, and individualized education in the least restrictive environment appropriate to their needs. Further legislation in 1978 led to regulations for ramps, elevators, and the like in all federal buildings. The Americans with Disabilities Act (ADA) of 1990, however, is by far the most significant legislation protecting the rights of this group of Americans.

THE AMERICANS WITH DISABILITIES ACT The ADA requires that all public buildings and public services be accessible to persons with disabilities. The act also mandates that employers "reasonably accommodate" the needs of workers or job applicants with disabilities who are otherwise qualified for particular jobs unless to do so would cause the employer to suffer an "undue hardship."

The ADA defines persons with disabilities as persons who have physical or mental impairments that "substantially limit" their everyday activities. Health conditions that have been considered disabilities under federal law include blindness, a history of alcoholism, heart disease, cancer, muscular dystrophy, cerebral palsy, paraplegia, diabetes, and acquired immune deficiency syndrome (AIDS). The ADA, however, does not require employers to hire or retain workers who, because of their disabilities, pose a "direct threat to the health or safety" of their co-workers.

LIMITING THE SCOPE OF THE ADA From 1999 to 2002, the Supreme Court handed down a series of rulings that substantially limited the scope of the ADA. The Court found that any limitation that could be remedied by medication or by corrective devices such as eyeglasses did not qualify as a protected disability. According to the Court, even carpal tunnel syndrome was not a disability.[20] In 2008, however, the ADA Amendments Act overturned most of these limits. Carpal tunnel syndrome and other ailments may again qualify as disabilities. (Eyeglasses were not covered by the new law.)

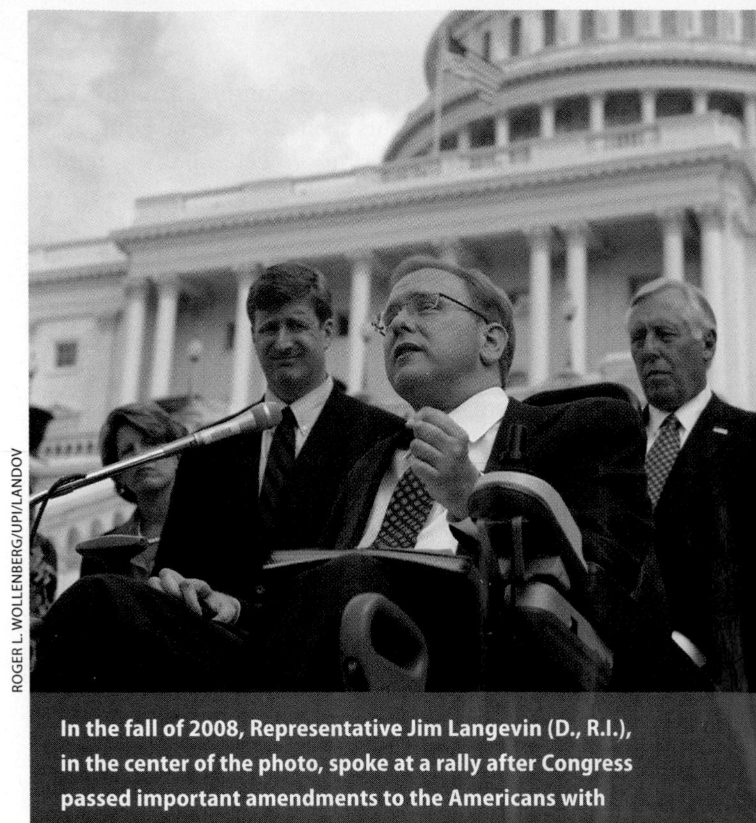
ROGER L. WOLLENBERG/UPI/LANDOV

In the fall of 2008, Representative Jim Langevin (D., R.I.), in the center of the photo, spoke at a rally after Congress passed important amendments to the Americans with Disabilities Act.

In 2001, the Supreme Court reviewed a case raising the question of whether suits under the ADA could be brought against state employers. The Court concluded that states are immune from lawsuits brought to enforce rights under this federal law.[21]

Gay Men and Lesbians

Until the late 1960s and early 1970s, gay men and lesbians tended to keep quiet about their sexual preferences because exposure usually meant facing harsh consequences. This attitude began to change after a 1969 incident in New York City, however. When the police raided the Stonewall Inn—a bar popular with gay men and lesbians—on June 27 of that year, the bar's patrons responded by throwing beer cans and bottles at the police. The riot continued for two days. The Stonewall Inn uprising launched the gay power movement. By the end of the year, gay men and lesbians had formed fifty organizations, including the Gay Activist Alliance and the Gay Liberation Front.

A CHANGING LEGAL LANDSCAPE The number of gay and lesbian organizations has grown from fifty in 1969 to several thousand today. These groups have

> "The liberty protected by the Constitution ALLOWS HOMOSEXUAL PERSONS THE RIGHT TO CHOOSE TO ENTER UPON RELATIONSHIPS IN THE CONFINES OF THEIR HOMES AND THEIR OWN PRIVATE LIVES AND STILL RETAIN THEIR dignity as free persons."
>
> ~ UNITED STATES SUPREME COURT ~
> *LAWRENCE V. TEXAS*, 2003

exerted significant political pressure on legislatures, the media, schools, and churches. In the decades following Stonewall, more than half of the forty-nine states that had sodomy laws—laws prohibiting homosexual conduct and certain other forms of sexual activity—repealed them. In seven other states, the courts invalidated such laws. Then, in 2003, the United States Supreme Court issued a ruling that effectively invalidated all remaining sodomy laws in the country.

In *Lawrence v. Texas,*[22] the Court ruled that sodomy laws violated the Fourteenth Amendment's due process clause. According to the Court, "The liberty protected by the Constitution allows homosexual persons the right to choose to enter upon relationships in the confines of their homes and their own private lives and still retain their dignity as free persons."

Today, twenty-five states and more than 180 cities and counties in the United States have laws prohibiting discrimination against homosexuals in at least some contexts. The laws may prohibit discrimination in housing, education, banking, employment, or public accommodations. In a landmark case in 1996, *Romer v. Evans,*[23] the Supreme Court held that a Colorado constitutional amendment that would have invalidated all state and local laws protecting homosexuals from discrimination violated the equal protection clause of the U.S. Constitution. The Court stated that the amendment would have denied to homosexuals in Colorado—but to no other Colorado residents—"the right to seek specific protection from the law."

A woman holds up a protest placard during a gay rights rally in Hollywood, California, after the state supreme court upheld Proposition 8, which redefined marriage in California as between men and women only.

MARK RALSTON/AFP/GETTY IMAGES

CHANGING ATTITUDES Laws and court decisions protecting the rights of gay men and lesbians reflect social attitudes that are much changed from the 1960s. Liberal political leaders have been supporting gay rights for at least two decades. In 1984, presidential candidate Walter Mondale openly sought the gay vote, as did Jesse Jackson in his 1988 presidential campaign. As president, Bill Clinton strongly supported gay rights.

Even some conservative politicians have softened their stance on the issue. For example, during his 2000 presidential campaign, George W. Bush met with representatives of gay groups to discuss issues important to them. Although Bush stated that he was opposed to gay marriage, he promised that he would not disqualify anyone from serving in his administration on the basis of sexual orientation.

According to a Gallup poll taken in 2009, public support for gay and lesbian rights has continued to rise. The survey showed that 56 percent of respondents believed that gay or lesbian relations between consenting adults should be legal, up from 43 percent in 1978. Support for employment and domestic partnership rights ran even higher. Among those interviewed, 69 percent believed that openly gay or lesbian individuals should be able to serve in the military, and the same number believed that such persons should be allowed to teach children. Giving domestic partners access to health insurance and other employee benefits was endorsed by 67 percent of Americans, and inheritance rights by 73 percent. Only 40 percent of those interviewed endorsed same-sex marriage, but that was up substantially from 27 percent in 1996.

SAME-SEX MARRIAGE Today, same-sex marriage is legal in five states—Connecticut, Iowa, New Hampshire, Massachusetts, and Vermont—and in the District of

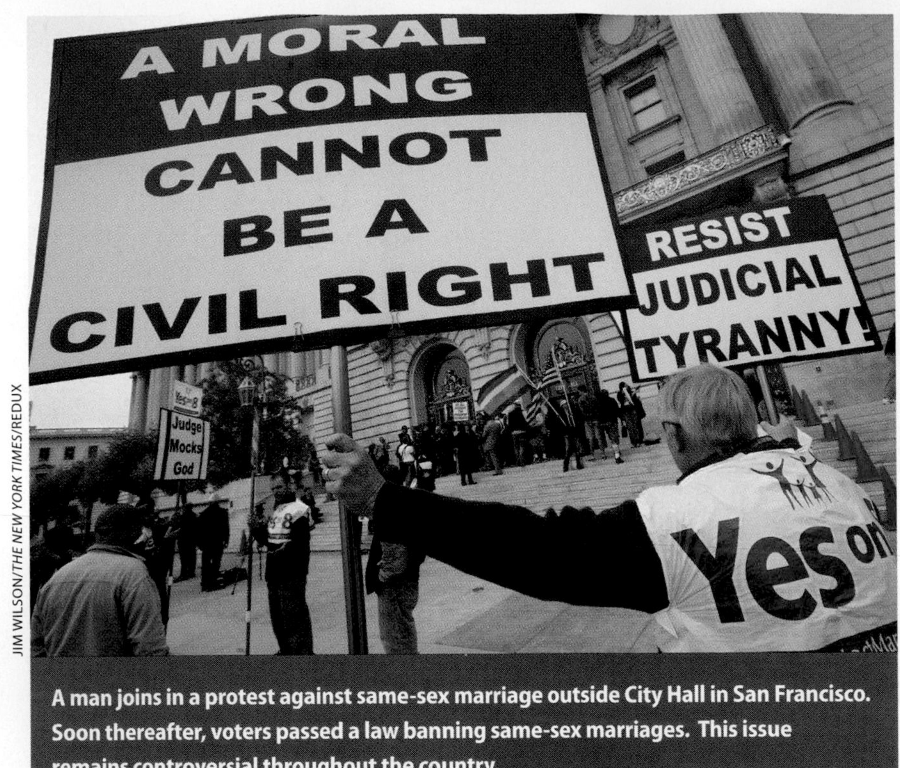

JIM WILSON/THE NEW YORK TIMES/REDUX

A man joins in a protest against same-sex marriage outside City Hall in San Francisco. Soon thereafter, voters passed a law banning same-sex marriages. This issue remains controversial throughout the country.

Columbia. It was temporarily legal in California during part of 2008, between a state supreme court ruling in May that legalized the practice and a constitutional amendment passed by the voters in November that banned it again. California continues to recognize those same-sex couples who married between May and November 2008 as lawfully wedded. New York State and Maryland do not perform same-sex marriages but recognize those performed elsewhere.

A number of states have civil union or domestic partnership laws that grant most of the benefits of marriage to registered same-sex couples. These include California, Nevada, New Jersey, Oregon, and Washington. More limited benefits are provided in Colorado, Hawaii, Maryland, and Wisconsin. Either through a constitutional amendment or through legislation, same-sex marriage is explicitly banned in most states without domestic partnership laws—and even in some of the states just mentioned.

GAYS AND LESBIANS IN THE MILITARY For gay men and lesbians who wish to join the military, one of the battlefields they face is the "Don't ask, don't tell" policy. This policy, which bans openly gay men and lesbians from the military, was implemented in 1993 by President Bill Clinton when it became clear that more liberal alternatives would not be accepted. During his presidential campaign, Barack Obama pledged to abolish the policy. Later, however, gay and lesbian rights activists accused him of "putting the issue on a back burner."

affirmative action A policy calling for the establishment of programs that give special consideration, in jobs and college admissions, to members of groups that have been discriminated against in the past.

Generally, attitudes toward gay men and lesbians in the military divide along party lines, with the Democrats approving and the Republicans in opposition. What do soldiers themselves think about serving alongside gay men and lesbians? In a recent survey, three-quarters of the troops polled said that they would have no problem serving with such people. In October 2010, a federal judge ruled that "don't ask, don't tell was unenforceable. The government will appeal.

LO5 *Beyond Equal Protection—Affirmative Action*

One provision of the Civil Rights Act of 1964 called for prohibiting discrimination in employment. Soon after the act was passed, the federal government began to legislate programs promoting *equal employment opportunity.* Such programs require that employers' hiring and promotion practices guarantee the same opportunities to all individuals. Experience soon showed that minorities often had fewer opportunities to obtain education and relevant work experience than did whites. Because of this, minorities were still excluded from many jobs. Even though discriminatory practices were made illegal, the change in the law did not make up for the results of years of discrimination. Consequently, under President Lyndon B. Johnson (1963–1969), a new policy was developed.

Called **affirmative action,** this policy requires employers to take positive steps to remedy *past* discrimination. Affirmative action programs involve giving special consideration, in jobs and college admissions, to members of groups that have been discriminated against in the past. Until recently, all public and private employers who received federal funds were required to adopt and implement these programs. Thus, the policy of affirmative action has been applied to all agencies of the federal, state, and local governments and to all private employers who sell goods to or perform services for any agency of the federal government. In short, it has covered nearly all of the nation's major employers and many of its smaller ones.

Affirmative Action Tested

The Supreme Court first addressed the issue of affirmative action in 1978 in *Regents of the University of California v. Bakke.*[24] Allan Bakke, a white male, had been denied admission to the University of California's medical school at Davis. The school had set aside sixteen of the one hundred seats in each year's entering class for applicants who wished to be considered as members of designated minority groups. Many of the students admitted through this special program had lower test scores than Bakke. Bakke sued the university, claiming that he was a victim of **reverse discrimination**—discrimination against whites. Bakke argued that the use of a **quota system,** in which a specific number of seats were reserved for minority applicants only, violated the equal protection clause.

The Supreme Court was strongly divided on the issue. Some justices believed that Bakke had been denied equal protection and should be admitted. A majority on the Court concluded that although both the Constitution and the Civil Rights Act of 1964 allow race to be used as a factor in making admissions decisions, race cannot be the *sole* factor. Because the university's quota system was based solely on race, it was unconstitutional. For more on affirmative action problems elsewhere in the world, see *The Rest of the World* feature on the following page.

reverse discrimination Discrimination against those who have no minority status.

quota system A policy under which a specific number of jobs, promotions, or other types of placements, such as university admissions, must be given to members of selected groups.

Any type of affirmative action brings protests from one side or the other. Here, demonstrators oppose a change to current laws that mandate racial integration.

PHOTO BY ALEX WONG/GETTY IMAGES

Strict Scrutiny Applied

In 1995, the Supreme Court issued a landmark decision in *Adarand Constructors, Inc. v. Peña.*[25] The Court held that any federal, state, or local affirmative action program that uses racial classifications as the basis for making decisions is subject to "strict scrutiny" by the courts. As discussed earlier in this chapter, this means that, to be constitutional, a discriminatory law or action must be narrowly tailored to meet a *compelling* government interest. In effect, the *Adarand* decision narrowed the application of affirmative action programs. An affirmative action program can no longer make use of quotas or preferences and cannot be maintained simply to remedy past discrimination by society in general. It must be narrowly tailored to remedy actual discrimination that has occurred, and once the program has succeeded, it must be changed or dropped.

The Diversity Issue

Following the *Adarand* decision, several lower courts faced cases raising the question of whether affirmative action programs designed to achieve diversity on college campuses were constitutional. For example, in a 1996 case, *Hopwood v. State of Texas,*[26] two white law school applicants sued the University of Texas School of Law in Austin, claiming that they had been denied admission because of the school's affirmative action program. The program allowed admissions officials to take racial and other factors into consideration when determining which students would be admitted.

A federal appellate court held that the program violated the equal protection clause because it discriminated in favor of minority applicants. In its decision, the court directly challenged the *Bakke* decision by stating that the use of race even as a means of achieving diversity on college campuses "undercuts the Fourteenth Amendment." In other words, race could never be a factor, even if it was not the sole factor, in such decisions.

In 2003, the United States Supreme Court reviewed two cases involving issues similar to that in the *Hopwood* case. Both cases involved admissions programs at the University of Michigan. In *Gratz v. Bollinger,*[27] two white

India Faces an Affirmative Action Nightmare

Affirmative action in the United States has involved a relatively small number of groups, even if some of them have many members—women, for example, make up more than half the population. In India, however, affirmative action is much more complicated due to the caste tradition. Under this millennia-old system, Indians are grouped into thousands of castes and subcastes. Formerly, some groups were considered outside the caste system altogether—these were the "untouchables," or Dalits. In 1950, after India became independent from Britain, the new constitution abolished the practice of untouchability, or discrimination against Dalits, and established a program of rights and quotas for the former untouchables, now officially called the Scheduled Castes. Discrimination remains widespread in rural India, however.

Quotas for Scheduled Castes

Together with the Scheduled Tribes (generally located in the far east of the country), the Scheduled Castes make up about 25 percent of India's population. Quotas were established to bring members of these groups into universities and government jobs in a program that is now about sixty years old. Several years ago, the government expanded the quota program to include the Other Backward Castes, groups that have suffered impoverishment or discrimination, but not to the degree of the Scheduled Castes and Scheduled Tribes. With the addition of the Other Backward Castes, the favored groups swelled to constitute half of India's population. A nationwide furor resulted.

A Caste of Shepherds Demands to Be Downgraded

In 2007, tens of thousands of members of the Gujjar caste, who traditionally worked as shepherds, blocked the roads in an Indian farming region. The Gujjars were one of the Other Backward Castes, and they were demanding reclassification as one of the Scheduled Castes, or untouchables. Why? The Gujjars realized that if they were classified as Dalits, they would benefit from more generous quotas in schooling and employment, and they would be eligible for more government welfare. This shepherd caste made their demand even though a lower status might result in increased discrimination, such as not being allowed to use the same water pumps as their neighbors.

For Critical Analysis *An Indian sociologist, Dipankar Gupta, commented, "If you play the caste game, you will end up with caste war." What might he have meant?*

These members of India's Gujjar caste are demonstrating in the Indian state of Rajasthan. They wanted their status to be downgraded from "Other Backward Caste" to "untouchable" so that they could benefit from more generous quotas and receive increased welfare benefits.

AP PHOTO/AMAN SHARMA

applicants who were denied undergraduate admission to the university alleged reverse discrimination. The school's policy gave each applicant a score based on a number of factors, including grade point average, standardized test scores, and personal achievements. The system *automatically* awarded every "underrepresented" minority (African American, Hispanic, and Native American) applicant twenty points—one-fifth of the points needed to guarantee admission. The Court held that this policy violated the equal protection clause.

In contrast, in *Grutter v. Bollinger*,[28] the Court held that the University of Michigan Law School's admissions policy was constitutional. In that case, the Court concluded that "[u]niversities can, however, consider race or ethnicity more flexibly as a 'plus' factor in the context of individualized consideration of each and every applicant." The significant difference between the two admissions policies, in the Court's view, was that the law school's approach did not apply a mechanical formula giving "diversity bonuses" based on race or ethnicity. In short, the Court concluded that diversity on college campuses was a legitimate goal and that limited affirmative action programs could be used to attain this goal.

The Supreme Court Revisits the Issue

The Michigan cases were decided in 2003. By 2007, when another case involving affirmative action came before the Court, the Court had a new chief justice, John G. Roberts, Jr., and a new associate justice, Samuel Alito, Jr. Both men were appointed by President George W. Bush, and the conservative views of both justices have moved the Court significantly to the right. Justice Alito replaced Sandra Day O'Connor, who had often been the "swing" vote on the Court, sometimes voting with the more liberal justices and sometimes joining the conservative bloc. Hers was the deciding vote in the five-to-four decision upholding the University of Michigan Law School's affirmative action program.

Some claim that the more conservative composition of today's Court strongly influenced the outcome in a case that came before the Court in 2007: *Parents Involved in Community Schools v. Seattle School District No. 1.*[29] The case concerned the policies of two school districts, one in Louisville, Kentucky, and one in Seattle, Washington. Both schools were trying to achieve a more diversified student body by giving preference to minority students if space in the schools was limited and a choice among applicants had to be made. Parents of white children who were turned away from schools in these districts because of these policies sued the school districts, claiming that the policies violated the equal protection clause. Ultimately, the case reached the Supreme Court, and the Court, in a five-to-four vote, held in favor of the parents, ruling that the policies violated the equal protection clause. The Court's decision did not overrule the 2003 case involving the University of Michigan Law School, however, for the Court did not say that race could *not* be used as a factor in university admissions policies. Nonetheless, some claim that the decision represents a significant change on the Court with respect to affirmative action policies.

State Actions

Beginning in the mid-1990s, some states have taken actions to ban affirmative action programs or replace them with alternative policies. For example, in 1996, by a ballot initiative, California amended its state constitution to prohibit any "preferential treatment to any individual or group on the basis of race, sex, color, ethnicity, or national origin in the operation of public employment, public education, or public contracting."

FURTHER ACTIONS Two years later, voters in the state of Washington approved a ballot measure ending all state-sponsored affirmative action. Florida has also ended affirmative action. In 2006, a ballot initiative in Michigan—just three years after the Supreme Court decisions discussed above—banned affirmative action in that state. In the 2008 elections, Nebraska also banned affirmative action, but voters in Colorado rejected such a measure. The 2008 initiatives were spearheaded by Ward

SUZANNE DECHILLO/*THE NEW YORK TIMES*/REDUX

These high school students are attending a college fair in Queens, New York. Depending on where they are applying, some may benefit from affirmative action admissions policies. There has been a backlash in some states because majority students have argued that affirmative action is equivalent to reverse discrimination.

Connerly, an African American libertarian businessman. In 2010, Arizona also banned affirmative action.

"RACE-BLIND" ADMISSIONS In the meantime, many public universities are trying to find "race-blind" ways to attract more minority students to their campuses. For example, Texas has established a program under which the top students at every high school in the state are guaranteed admission to the University of Texas, Austin. Originally, the guarantee applied to students who were in the top 10 percent of their graduating class. In 2009, the guarantee was limited to students in the top 8 percent of their class.

This policy ensures that the top students at minority-dominated inner-city schools can attend the state's leading public university. It also guarantees admission to the best white students from rural, often poor, communities. Previously, these students could not have hoped to attend the University of Texas. The losers are students from upscale metropolitan neighborhoods or suburbs who have high test scores but are not the top students at their schools. One result is that more students with high test scores enroll in less famous schools, such as Texas Tech University and the University of Texas, Dallas—to the benefit of these schools' reputations.

AMERICA AT ODDS Civil Rights

During the first part of the twentieth century, discrimination against African Americans and members of other minority groups was a social norm in the United States. Indeed, much of the nation's white population believed that the ability to discriminate was a constitutionally protected right. Today, the "right to discriminate" has very few defenders. America's laws—and its culture—now hold that discrimination on the basis of race, gender, religion, national origin, and many other characteristics is flatly unacceptable.

Even if civil rights are now broadly supported and protected by law, however, questions remain as to how far these protections should extend. Americans are at odds over a number of civil rights issues, including the following:

- If unauthorized immigrants have certain rights as *persons* under the Fourteenth Amendment to the Constitution, should these rights be construed broadly—or as narrowly as possible?
- Should same-sex marriages by lesbians and gay men be recognized—or prohibited?
- Should we allow lesbians and gay men to serve openly in the nation's armed forces—or should the "Don't ask, don't tell" policy be retained?
- Is affirmative action still a necessary policy—or should it be abandoned?
- When colleges and universities consider admissions, is it legitimate to promote racial, ethnic, gender, or socioeconomic diversity—or are such considerations just new forms of discrimination?

Take Action

Despite the progress that has been made toward attaining equal treatment for all groups of Americans, much remains to be done. Countless activist groups continue to pursue the goal of equality for all Americans. If you wish to contribute your time and effort toward this goal, there are hundreds of ways to go about it. You can easily find activist opportunities just by going to the Web sites of the groups listed in this chapter's *Politics on the Web* section on the following page. There, you will find links to groups that seek to protect and enhance the rights of African Americans, Latinos, women, persons with disabilities, and more.

Other groups you can contact if you would like to get involved include the Leadership Conference on Civil and Human Rights, which encourages people to contact Congress on matters of interest. Its Web site is www.civilrights.org. If you are interested in the rights of immigrants, a good place to start is the Justice for Immigrants Web site at www.justiceforimmigrants.org, where you can sign up to receive e-mails from the Immigrant Justice Action Network. If there are gatherings or events planned for your neighborhood, such as a demonstration for immigrants' rights, you can participate in them—or volunteer to help organize them. Justice for Immigrants was organized by twenty major Roman Catholic organizations. An additional source of information on Latino issues is the National Council of La Raza at www.nclr.org.

Finally, you can search the Web for blogs on a civil rights issue that particularly interests you, read about what others on that site are saying, and "tell the world" your opinion on the issue.

POLITICS ON THE WEB

- Stanford University's Web site contains primary documents written by Martin Luther King, Jr., as well as secondary documents written about King. The URL for the Martin Luther King, Jr., Research and Education Institute is **mlk-kpp01.stanford.edu**
- If you are interested in learning more about the Equal Employment Opportunity Commission (EEOC), the laws it enforces, and how to file a charge with the EEOC, go to **www.eeoc.gov**
- The home page for the National Association for the Advancement of Colored People (NAACP), which contains extensive information about African American civil rights issues, is **www.naacp.org**
- For information on Hispanics in the United States, the League of United Latin American Citizens is a good source. You can find it at **www.lulac.org**
- The home page of the National Organization for Women (NOW) has links to numerous resources containing information on the rights and status of women both in the United States and around the world. You can find NOW's home page at **www.now.org**
- You can access the Web site of the Feminist Majority Foundation, which focuses on equality for women, at **www.feminist.org**
- For information on the Americans with Disabilities Act, including the text of the act, go to **www.jan.wvu.edu/links/adalinks.htm**
- The Gay and Lesbian Alliance against Defamation has an online news bureau. To find this organization's home page, go to **www.glaad.org**

Access CourseMate to review and expand on this chapter through quizzes, flashcards, learning objectives, interactive timelines, a crossword puzzle, audio summaries, video, critical-thinking activities, simulations, and more.

GOVT

6 Interest Groups

LEARNING OBJECTIVES

LO1 Explain what an interest group is, why interest groups form, and how interest groups function in American politics.

LO2 Indicate how interest groups differ from political parties.

LO3 Identify the various types of interest groups.

LO4 Discuss how the activities of interest groups help to shape government policymaking.

LO5 Describe how interest groups are regulated by government.

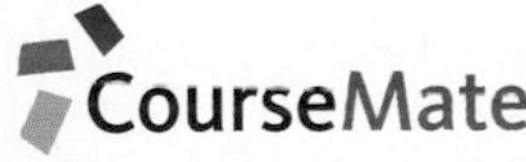

AMERICA AT ODDS

Are Secret Ballots Essential in Union Elections?

The National Labor Relations Act of 1935 established the right of employees to form unions and the right of those unions to engage in collective bargaining—negotiation of contracts for the workers the unions represent—along with the right to strike. The decision on whether or not employees should be represented by a union is typically made though a secret-ballot election.

In the early 2000s, with union membership declining, unions began pressuring members of Congress to pass legislation to help unions organize. The result was the proposed Employee Free Choice Act (EFCA), which has commonly been referred to as "card-check" legislation. The card-check system would in most instances replace privately held, federally supervised secret-ballot voting in collective decisions to form unions. Currently, elections are not mandatory, and an employer may voluntarily recognize a union if the union presents evidence that most employees support unionization. This evidence may include cards signed by a majority of employees. But the employer always has a right to ask for an election in spite of this evidence. Under the proposed law, that would no longer be the case. Organizers would simply need to gather signatures from more than 50 percent of the employees in a workplace. Once 50 percent of the workers had signed those cards, the employer would be required to recognize the union and negotiate with it.

Secret Ballots Are a Democracy's Only Choice

Recently, a group of congressional representatives who were concerned about workers' rights in Mexico wrote to officials in that country stating, "We are writing to encourage you to use the secret ballot in all union recognition elections. . . . We feel that the secret ballot is absolutely necessary in order to ensure that workers are not intimidated into voting for a union they might not otherwise choose." Former Democratic presidential candidate George McGovern had this to say about the card-check legislation: "Workers would lose the freedom to express their will in private, the right to make a decision without anyone peering over their shoulder, free from fear of reprisal."

A major reason why unions spent half a billion dollars in the 2008 elections is because they were unified behind one driving goal—passing card-check legislation. In response to the unions' actions, McGovern stated that "part of being a steward of democracy means telling our friends 'no' when they press for a course that in the long run may weaken labor and disrupt a tried and trusted method for conducting honest elections."

Card-Check Union Organizing Will Level the Playing Field

The late senator Ted Kennedy (D., Mass.) claimed that card-check legislation was necessary to "level the playing field" between unions and management. He argued that there are large loopholes in today's labor laws that allow employers to intimidate their employees prior to and during secret elections. Representative George Miller (D., Calif.) contended that management in nonunion companies can "browbeat" workers about unions anytime and anywhere in the workplace. Union backers point out that it may be illegal to fire an employee for supporting a union drive, but it happens again and again. It is very difficult for an employee to prove that he or she was fired for supporting a union rather than for some other reason.

Proponents of the EFCA agree that it will help increase union membership. They argue that this is good not only for union workers but also for other workers. Workers in general, they say, benefit when some of them strengthen their negotiating positions. Whenever a union effectively organizes another workplace, nonunion workers' bargaining positions are strengthened as well.

WHERE DO YOU STAND?

1. **How important is it for union elections to be held in secret?**
2. **Do you believe that an expansion in union membership can benefit all workers? Why or why not?**

EXPLORE THIS ISSUE ONLINE

- **Employer and conservative groups have organized the Coalition for a Democratic Workplace, a broad umbrella group, to oppose the EFCA card-check legislation. You can find that group's Web site at www.myprivateballot.com.**
- **The two largest union federations support the EFCA, of course. Find out what the American Federation of Labor–Congress of Industrial Organizations (AFL-CIO) says about it at www.aflcio.org/joinaunion/voiceatwork/efca. Change to Win, the nation's second-largest union alliance, argues for the EFCA at www.changetowin.org/issues/workers-rights/freedom-to-join-together-in-unions.html.**

Introduction

The groups supporting and opposing card checks for unionization provide but one example of how Americans form groups to pursue or protect their interests. All of us have interests that we would like to have represented in government: farmers want higher prices for their products, young people want good educational opportunities, and environmentalists want cleaner air and water.

"Politics is about **PEOPLE,** not politicians."
~ SCOTT SIMMS ~
CANADIAN POLITICIAN
B. 1969

The old saying that there is strength in numbers is certainly true in American politics. Special interests significantly influence American government and politics. Indeed, some Americans think that this influence is so great that it jeopardizes representative democracy. Others maintain that interest groups are a natural consequence of democracy. After all, throughout our nation's history, people have organized into groups to protect special interests. Because of the important role played by interest groups in the American system of government, in this chapter we examine such groups. We look at what they are, why they are formed, and how they influence policymaking.

LO1 *Interest Groups and American Government*

An **interest group** is an organized group of people sharing common objectives who actively attempt to influence government policymakers through direct and indirect methods. Whatever their goals—more or fewer social services, higher or lower prices—interest groups pursue these goals on every level and in every branch of government.

On any given day in Washington, D.C., you can see national interest groups in action. If you eat breakfast in the Senate dining room, you might see congressional committee staffers reviewing testimony with representatives from women's groups. Later that morning, you might visit the Supreme Court and watch a civil rights lawyer arguing on behalf of a client in a discrimination suit. Lunch in a popular Washington restaurant might find you listening in on a conversation between an agricultural lobbyist and a congressional representative.

interest group An organized group of individuals sharing common objectives who actively attempt to influence policymakers.

That afternoon you might visit an executive department, such as the Department of Labor, and watch bureaucrats working out rules and regulations with representatives from a business interest group. Then you might stroll past the headquarters of the National Rifle Association (NRA), AARP (formerly the American Association of Retired Persons), or the National Wildlife Federation.

The Constitutional Right to Petition the Government

The right to form interest groups and to lobby the government is protected by the Bill of Rights. The First Amendment guarantees the right of the people "to petition the Government for a redress of grievances." This important right sometimes gets lost among the other, more well-known First Amendment guarantees, such as the freedoms of religion, speech, and the press. Nonetheless, the right to petition the government is as important and fundamental to our democracy as the other First Amendment rights.

The right to petition the government allows citizens and groups of citizens to lobby members of Congress and

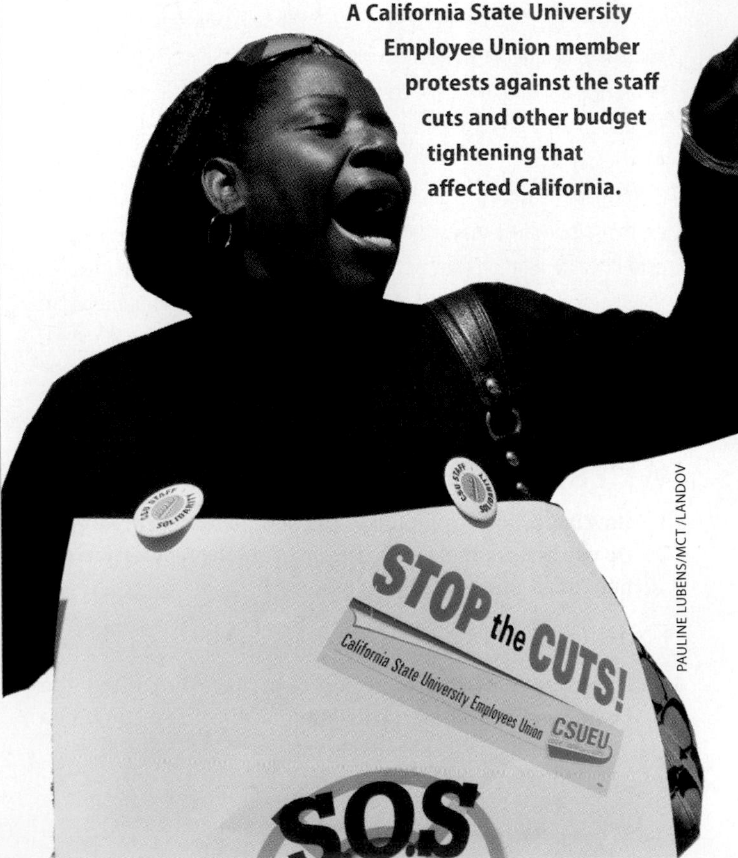

A California State University Employee Union member protests against the staff cuts and other budget tightening that affected California.

other government officials, to sue the government, and to submit petitions to the government. Whenever someone writes to her or his congressional representative for help with a problem, such as not receiving a Social Security payment, that person is petitioning the government.

Why Interest Groups Form

The United States is a vast country of many regions, scores of ethnic groups, and a huge variety of businesses and occupations. The number of potential interests that can be represented is therefore very large. Beyond the sheer size of the country, however, there are a number of specific reasons why the United States has as many interest groups as it does.

It is worth remembering that not all groups are interest groups. A group becomes an interest group when it seeks to affect the policies or practices of the government. Many groups do not meet such a standard. A social group, for example, may be formed to entertain or educate its members, with no broader purpose. Churches, organized to facilitate worship and community, frequently have no political aims. (Indeed, certain political activities, such as campaigning for or against candidates for office, could cost a church its tax-exempt status.)

A group founded with little or no desire to influence the government can become an interest group, however, if its members decide that the government's policies are important to them. Alternatively, lobbying the government may initially be only one of several activities pursued by a group and then grow to become the group's primary purpose. The National Rifle Association (NRA) is an example of this process. From its foundation in 1871 until the 1930s, the group took little part in politics. As late as the 1970s, a large share of the NRA's members joined for reasons that had nothing to do with politics. Many joined solely to participate in firearms training programs or to win marksman certifications. The NRA continues to provide such services today, but it is now so heavily politicized that anyone likely to take out a membership must broadly agree with the NRA's political positions.

MORE GOVERNMENT, MORE INTEREST GROUPS Interest groups may form—and existing groups may become more politically active—when the government expands its scope of activities. More government, in other words, means more interest groups. Prior to the 1970s, for example, the various levels of government were not nearly as active in attempting to regulate the use of firearms as they were thereafter. This change provides one explanation of why the NRA is much more politically active today than it was years ago. Consider another example—AARP, formerly the American Association of

Retired Persons. AARP is a major lobbying force that seeks to preserve or enhance Social Security and Medicare benefits for citizens sixty-five years old and older. Before the creation of Social Security in the 1930s, however, the federal government did not provide income support to the elderly, and there would have been little reason for an organization such as AARP to exist. For more details on the NRA, AARP, and a few other key interest groups, see Figure 6–1 on the following page.

"The health of a
democratic society
MAY BE MEASURED BY THE
QUALITY OF FUNCTIONS
PERFORMED BY PRIVATE CITIZENS."
~ ALEXIS DE TOCQUEVILLE ~
FRENCH HISTORIAN AND POLITICAL SCIENTIST
1805–1859

DEFENDING THE GROUP'S INTERESTS Interest groups also may come into existence in response to a perceived threat to a group's interests. In the example of the NRA, the threat was an increase in the frequency of attempts to regulate or even ban firearms. This increase threatened the interests of gun owners. As another example, the National Right to Life Committee formed in response to *Roe v. Wade,* the United States Supreme Court's decision that legalized abortion. Interest groups can also form in reaction to the creation of other interest groups, thus pitting two groups against each other. Political scientist David B. Truman coined the term *disturbance theory* for his description of this kind of defensive formation of interest groups.[1]

THE IMPORTANCE OF LEADERS Political scientist Robert H. Salisbury provided another analysis of the organization of interest groups that he dubbed *entrepreneurial theory.* This line of thought focuses on the importance of the leaders who establish the organization. The desire of such individuals to guarantee a viable organization is important to the group's survival.[2] AARP is an example of a group with an important founder—Dr. Ethel Percy Andrus, a retired high school principal. Andrus organized the group in 1958 to let older Americans purchase health-care insurance collectively. As with the NRA, AARP did not develop into a lobbying powerhouse until years after it was founded.

INCENTIVES TO JOIN A GROUP The French political observer and traveler Alexis de Tocqueville wrote in 1835 that Americans have a tendency to form "associations" and have perfected "the art of pursuing in common the object of

Figure 6–1

Profiles of Selected Interest Groups

Name: AARP
Founded: 1958
Membership: 40 million working or retired persons 50 years of age or older.
Description: AARP strives to better the lives of older people, especially in the areas of health care, worker equity, and minority affairs. AARP sponsors community crime prevention programs, research on the problems of aging, and a mail-order pharmacy.
Budget: $1,140,000,000
Address: 601 E St. N.W., Washington, DC 20049
Phone: (888) 687-2277 **Web site:** www.aarp.org

Name: U.S. Chamber of Commerce
Founded: 1912
Membership: 3 million businesses.
Description: The Chamber is the world's largest business federation, also representing local chambers and industry associations. More than 96 percent of members are small businesses with 100 employees or fewer. The Chamber fights for free enterprise before Congress, the White House, regulatory agencies, and the courts.
Budget: $150,000,000
Address: 1615 H Street N.W., Washington, DC 20062
Phone: (800) 638-6582 **Web site:** www.uschamber.com

Name: National Education Association (NEA)
Founded: 1857
Membership: 3.2 million elementary and secondary school teachers, college and university professors, academic administrators, and others.
Description: The NEA's committees investigate and take action in the areas of benefits, civil rights, educational support, personnel, higher education, human relations, legislation, minority affairs, and women's concerns. Many NEA locals function as labor unions.
Budget: $307,000,000
Address: 1201 16th St. N.W., Washington, DC 20036
Phone: (202) 833-4000 **Web site:** www.nea.org

Name: National Rifle Association (NRA)
Founded: 1871
Membership: Nearly 4 million persons interested in firearms.
Description: The NRA promotes rifle, pistol, and shotgun shooting, as well as hunting, gun collecting, and home firearm safety. It educates police firearm instructors and sponsors teams to participate in international competitions.
Budget: $200,000,000
Address: 11250 Waples Mill Road, Fairfax, VA 22030
Phone: (800) 672-3888 **Web site:** www.nra.org

Name: The Sierra Club (SC)
Founded: 1892
Membership: 1.3 million.
Description: The Sierra Club protects and conserves natural resources; saves endangered areas; and resolves problems associated with wilderness, clean air, energy conservation, and land use. Its committees are concerned with agriculture, economics, environmental education, hazardous materials, the international environment, Native American sites, political education, and water resources.
Budget: $40,000,000
Address: 85 2d St., 2d Floor, San Francisco, CA 94105
Phone: (415) 977-5500 **Web site:** www.sierraclub.org

their common desires." "In no other country of the world," said Tocqueville, "has the principle of association been more successfully used or applied to a greater multitude of objectives than in America."[3] Of course, Tocqueville could not foresee the thousands of associations that now exist in this country. Surveys show that more than 85 percent of Americans belong to at least one group. Table 6–1 on the facing page shows the percentage of Americans who belong to various types of groups today.

Political scientists have identified various reasons why people join interest groups. Often, people have one or more incentives to join such organizations. If a group

Table 6–1

Percentage of Americans Belonging to Various Groups

Health organizations	16%
Social clubs	17
Neighborhood groups	18
Hobby, garden, and computer clubs	19
PTA and school groups	21
Professional and trade associations	27
Health, sport, and country clubs	30
Religious groups	61

Source: AARP.

stands for something that you believe is very important, you can gain considerable satisfaction from taking action. Such satisfaction is referred to as a **purposive incentive.** Some people enjoy the camaraderie and sense of belonging that comes from associating with other people who share their interests and goals. That enjoyment can be called a **solidary incentive.** Finally, some groups offer their members material incentives for joining, such as discounts on products, subscriptions, or group insurance programs. Each of these could be characterized as a **material incentive.** But sometimes none of these incentives is enough to persuade people to join.

Alexis de Tocqueville (1805–1859) was a well-known French political historian. He lived during a time of political upheaval in France and took a keen interest in the new democracy in America. He toured the United States and Canada as a young man and collected his observations in *Democracy in America,* which was published in 1835.

THE GRANGER COLLECTION

THE FREE RIDER PROBLEM This world in which we live is one of scarce resources that can be used to create *private goods* and *public goods.* Most of the goods and services that you use are private goods. If you consume them, no one else can consume them at the same time. If you eat a sandwich, no one else can have it. With the other class of goods, called public goods, however, your use of a good does not diminish its use by someone else. National defense is a good example. If this country is protected through its national defense system, your protection from enemy invasion does not reduce anybody else's protection.

People cannot be excluded from enjoying a public good, such as national defense, just because they did not pay for it. As a result, public goods are often provided by the government, which can force people to pay for the public good through taxation.

Lobbying, collective bargaining by labor unions, and other forms of representation can also be public goods. If an interest group is successful in lobbying for laws that will improve air quality, for example, everyone who breathes that air will benefit, whether they paid for the lobbying effort or not. The existence of persons who benefit but do not contribute is called the **free rider problem.** Much of what we know about the free rider problem comes from Mancur Olson's classic work of political science, *The Logic of Collective Action.*[4]

In some instances, the free rider problem can be overcome. For example, social pressure may persuade some people to join or donate to a group for fear of being ostracized. For this and other reasons, it is much easier for an interest shared by a relatively small number of people to organize.

The government can also step in to ensure that the burden of lobbying for the public good is shared by all. When the government classifies interest groups as nonprofit organizations, it confers on them tax-exempt status. The groups' operating costs are reduced because they do not have to pay taxes, and the impact of the government's lost revenue is absorbed by all taxpayers.

purposive incentive A reason to join an interest group—satisfaction resulting from working for a cause in which one believes.

solidary incentive A reason to join an interest group—pleasure in associating with like-minded individuals.

material incentive Practical benefits from joining an interest group, such as discounts, subscriptions, or group insurance.

free rider problem The difficulty that exists when individuals can enjoy the outcome of an interest group's efforts without having to contribute, such as by becoming members of the group.

How Interest Groups Function in American Politics

Despite the bad press that interest groups tend to get in the United States, they do serve several purposes in American politics:

- Interest groups help bridge the gap between citizens and government and enable citizens to explain their views on policies to public officials.
- Interest groups help raise public awareness and inspire action on various issues.
- Interest groups often provide public officials with specialized and detailed information that might be difficult to obtain otherwise. This information may be useful in making policy choices.
- Interest groups serve as another check on public officials to make sure that they are carrying out their duties responsibly.

ACCESS TO GOVERNMENT In a sense, the American system of government invites the participation of interest groups by offering many points of access for groups wishing to influence policy. Consider the possibilities at just the federal level. An interest group can lobby members of Congress to act in the interests of the group. If the Senate passes a bill opposed by the group, the group's lobbying efforts can shift to the House of Representatives. If the House passes the bill, the group can try to influence the new law's application by lobbying the executive agency that is responsible for implementing the law. The group might even challenge the law in court, directly (by filing a lawsuit) or indirectly (by filing a brief as an *amicus curiae,*[5] or "friend of the court").

PLURALIST THEORY The **pluralist theory** of American democracy focuses on the participation of groups in a decentralized government structure that offers many points of access to policymakers. According to the pluralist theory, politics is a contest among various interest groups. These groups vie with one another—at all levels of government—to gain benefits for their members. Pluralists maintain that the influence of interest groups on government is not undemocratic because individual interests are indirectly represented in the policymaking process through these groups. Although not every American belongs to an interest group, inevitably some group will represent each individual's interests. Each interest is satisfied to some extent through the compromises made in settling conflicts among competing interest groups.

pluralist theory A theory that views politics as a contest among various interest groups—at all levels of government—to gain benefits for their members.

Pluralists also contend that because of the extensive number of interest groups vying for political benefits, no one group can dominate the political process. Additionally, because most people have more than one interest, conflicts among groups do not divide the nation into hostile camps. Not all scholars agree that this is how interest groups function, however.

LO2 *How Do Interest Groups Differ from Political Parties?*

Although interest groups and political parties are both groups of people joined together for political purposes, they differ in several important ways. As you will read in Chapter 7, a political party is a group of individuals who organize to win elections, operate the government, and determine policy. Interest groups, in contrast, do not seek to win elections or operate the government, although they do seek to influence policy.

Throughout 2009 and 2010, Tea Party supporters called for no new taxes and less government spending.

READ MY LIPSTICK
NO NEW TAXES!!

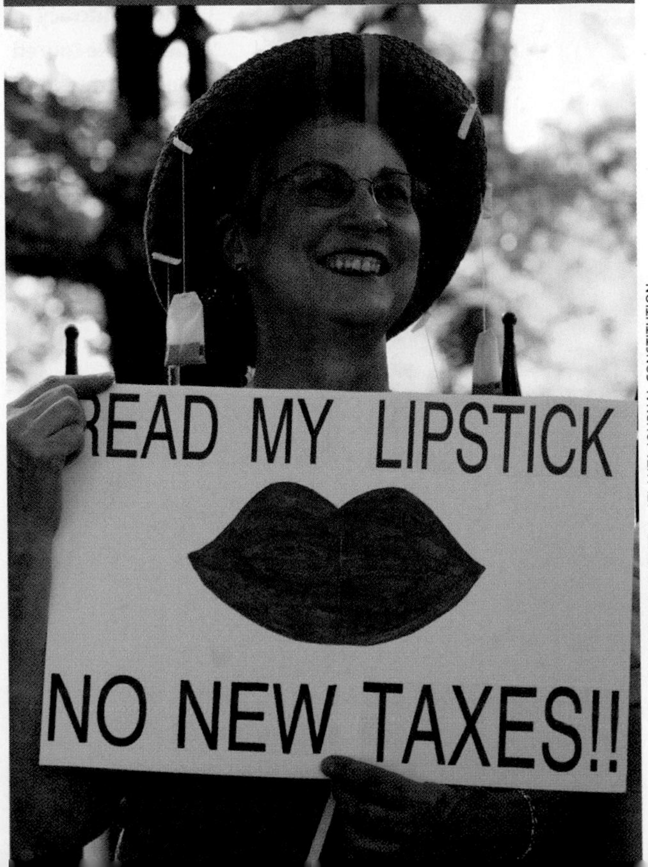

AP PHOTO/CURTIS COMPTON - ATLANTA JOURNAL CONSTITUTION

Interest groups differ from political parties in the following ways:

- Interest groups are often policy *specialists,* whereas political parties are policy *generalists.* Political parties are broad-based organizations that must attract the support of many opposing groups and consider a large number of issues. Interest groups, in contrast, may have only a handful of key policies to push. An environmental group will not be as concerned about the economic status of Hispanics as it is about polluters. A manufacturing group is more involved with pushing for fewer regulations than it is with inner-city poverty.
- Interest groups are usually more tightly organized than political parties. They are often financed through contributions or dues-paying memberships. Organizers of interest groups communicate with members and potential members through conferences, mailings, newsletters, and electronic formats, such as e-mail, Facebook, and Twitter.
- A political party's main sphere of influence is the electoral system. Parties run candidates for political office. Interest groups may try to influence the outcome of elections, but unlike parties, they do not compete for public office. Although a candidate for office may be sympathetic to—or even be a member of—a certain group, he or she does not run for election as a candidate of that group.

LO3 *Different Types of Interest Groups*

American democracy embraces almost every conceivable type of interest group, and the number is increasing rapidly. No one has ever compiled a *Who's Who* of interest groups, but you can get an idea of the number and variety by looking through the annually published *Encyclopedia of Associations.*

Some interest groups have large memberships. AARP, for example, has about 40 million members. Others, such as the Colorado Auctioneers Association, have barely a hundred members. Some, such as the U.S. Chamber of Commerce, are household names and have been in existence for many years, while others crop up overnight. Some are highly structured and are run by full-time professionals, while others are loosely structured and informal.

The most common interest groups are those that promote private interests. These groups seek public policies that benefit the economic interests of their members and work against policies that threaten those interests. Other groups, sometimes called **public-interest groups,** are formed with the broader goal of working for the "public good." The American Civil Liberties Union and Common Cause are examples. Let there be no mistake, though, about the name *public interest.* There is no such thing as a clear public interest in a nation of more than 310 million diverse people. The two so-called public-interest groups just mentioned do not represent all American people but only a relatively small part of the American population. In reality, all lobbying groups, organizations, and other political entities always represent special interests.

public-interest group
An interest group formed for the purpose of working for the "public good." Examples of public-interest groups are the American Civil Liberties Union and Common Cause.

Business Interest Groups

Business has long been well organized for effective action. Hundreds of business groups are now operating in Washington, D.C., in the fifty state capitals, and at the local level across the country. Table 6–2 below lists some top business interests. Two umbrella organizations that include small and large corporations and businesses are the U.S. Chamber of Commerce and the National Association of Manufacturers (NAM). In addition to representing about 3 million individual businesses, the Chamber has more than three thousand local, state, and regional affiliates. It has become a major voice for millions of small businesses.

Table 6–2

Top Business Campaign Donors, 1989–2010

Firm or Group	Total, 1989–2010
1. AT&T Inc.	$45,279,674
2. National Association of Realtors	36,626,273
3. Goldman Sachs (bank)	32,497,752
4. Citigroup Inc. (bank)	27,448,288
5. National Automobile Dealers Assn.	24,968,258
6. United Parcel Service	24,675,166
7. Altria Group (cigarettes)	24,210,766
8. American Bankers Assn.	23,071,721
9. National Assn. of Home Builders	22,655,655
10. National Beer Wholesalers Assn.	21,822,595

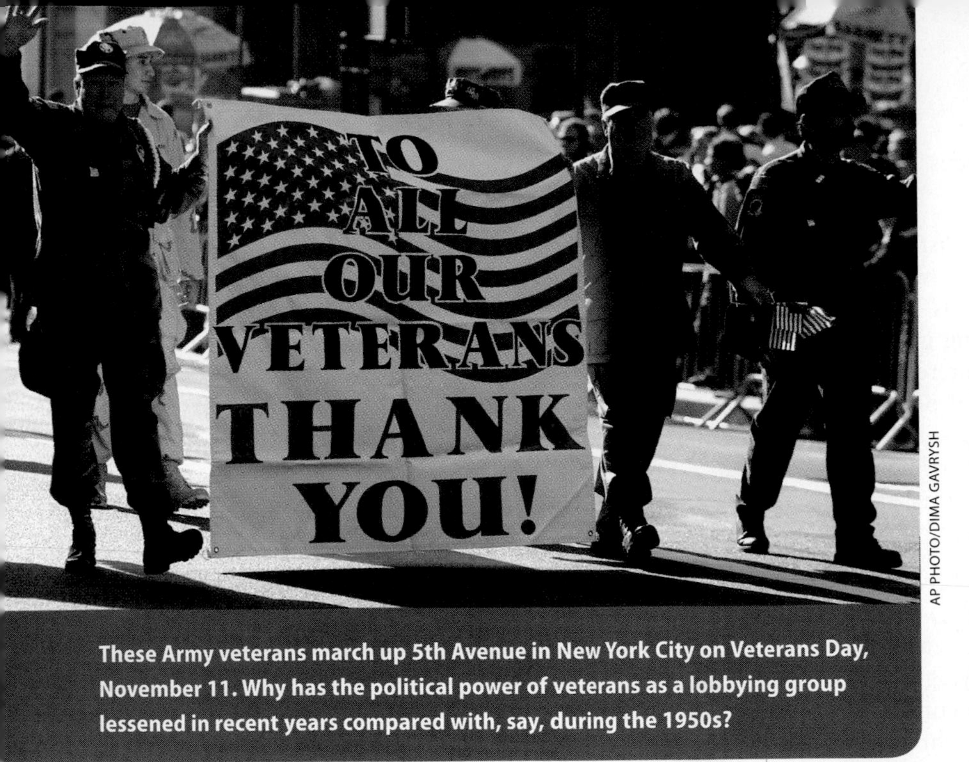

These Army veterans march up 5th Avenue in New York City on Veterans Day, November 11. Why has the political power of veterans as a lobbying group lessened in recent years compared with, say, during the 1950s?

TRADE ORGANIZATIONS The hundreds of **trade organizations** are far less visible than the Chamber of Commerce and the NAM, but they are also important in seeking policies that assist their members. Trade organizations usually support policies that benefit specific industries. For example, people in the oil industry work for policies that favor the development of oil as an energy resource. Other business groups work for policies that favor the development of coal, solar power, and nuclear power. Trucking companies work for policies that would lower their taxes. Railroad companies would, of course, not want other forms of transportation to receive special tax breaks, because that would hurt their business.

HOW BUSINESS INTEREST GROUPS SUPPORT BOTH PARTIES Traditionally, business interest groups have been viewed as staunch supporters of the Republican Party. This is because Republicans are more likely to promote a "hands-off" government policy toward business. Over the last decade, however, donations from corporations to the Democratic National Committee have more than doubled. Why would business groups make contributions to the Democratic National Committee? One reason is that in some fields, business leaders today are more likely to be Democrats than in the past. Financial industry leaders were once almost entirely Republican, but today many of them support the Democrats. Information technology, a new industry, contains both Republicans and Democrats.

trade organization An association formed by members of a particular industry, such as the oil industry or the trucking industry, to develop common standards and goals for the industry. Trade organizations, as interest groups, lobby government for legislation or regulations that specifically benefit their groups.

An additional reason why many business interests support both parties is to ensure that they will benefit regardless of who wins the elections. Fred McChesney, a professor of law and business, offers another reason why business interests might want to contribute to both parties. He argues that campaign contributions are often made not to gain political favors but rather to avoid political disfavor. Just as government officials can take away wealth from citizens (in the form of taxes, for example), politicians can extort from private enterprises payments *not* to damage their business.[6]

Business interests have often wielded great power. In recent years, the financial industry has been especially successful in influencing the government. We discuss that issue in this chapter's *Our Government Faces a Troubled Economy* feature on the following page.

Labor Interest Groups

Interest groups representing labor have been some of the most influential groups in our country's history. They date back to at least 1886, when the American Federation of Labor (AFL) was formed. The largest and most powerful labor interest group today is the AFL-CIO (the American Federation of Labor–Congress of Industrial Organizations), a confederation of fifty-six unions representing 11 million members. Unions not affiliated with the AFL-CIO also represent millions of members. The Change to Win federation consists of seven unions and 6 million workers. Dozens of other unions are independent. Examples include the National Education Association, the United Electrical Workers (UE), and the Major League Baseball Players Association. We list some top labor groups in Table 6–3 on page 128.

UNION GOALS Like labor unions everywhere, American unions press for policies to improve working conditions and ensure better pay for their members. Unions may compete for new members. In many states, for example, the National Education Association and the AFL-CIO's American Federation of Teachers compete fiercely for members.

THE DECLINE OF UNIONS Although unions were highly influential in the 1930s, 1940s, and 1950s, their strength and political power have waned in the last

OUR GOVERNMENT FACES A
TROUBLED ECONOMY

Lobbying by the Financial Industry

From the beginning, helping out the financial industry was a key part of our government's response to the Great Recession. This help was necessary because finance is the lifeblood of our economy. When the crisis became acute in 2008, financial institutions were the ones immediately threatened. Investment banks were among the hardest hit.

A Little History, First

In 2004, the heads of five major investment banks gathered at the Securities and Exchange Commission (SEC). The bankers convinced the SEC to lift a rule that required them to hold reserves as a cushion against losses on their investments. Those five banks, which included Goldman Sachs, then went on an investment spree the likes of which the world had never seen. They created trillions of dollars of mortgage-backed securities and credit derivatives (a form of insurance for investors). The head of Goldman Sachs at that time was Henry M. Paulson, Jr.

Fast-forward four years. All five banks had either gone bankrupt or been bailed out by the federal government. Who made the bailout decisions? None other than Henry M. Paulson, Jr., secretary of the Treasury under President George W. Bush. A huge share of Paulson's $700 billion bank bailout bill helped his friends and colleagues in the investment banking business. Critics complained that Paulson helped bankers, rather than the banking industry.

Reregulating the Financial Industry

The belief that the financial industry caused the Great Recession became nearly universal. Whether that was true or not, calls for financial industry reforms echoed through Congress. The result was the 2,319-page Restoring American Financial Stability Act of 2010. Throughout the months prior to passage of the act, there was intense lobbying in Congress to shape the new legislation.

The Lobbyists Go to Work

Lobbying on tax issues alone is a business worth more than $3.5 billion a year. The financial reform legislation, the most sweeping package of changes since the New Deal, has been called "a Super Bowl for lobbyists." What do interests get for what they pay to lobbyists? Take one example. The new financial reform law contains a rule to keep banks from putting their own funds into risky ventures. The argument was that this rule would limit practices that led to the financial meltdown in 2008. Many beneficiaries of such deals wanted to modify that rule, and their lobbyists went to work. Most mutual-fund companies won complete exemption from the rule. Another provision lets banks invest up to 3 percent of their own capital. Still another change lets banks make investments in small or start-up businesses that "promote the public welfare."

Consumers versus Finance

The Consumer Federation of America fought hard to make sure the new financial reform law benefited consumers, but that group had only three lawyers working on the entire bill. In contrast, according to the legislative director for the Consumer Federation, "the banking industry can have three people working on just a single paragraph." Lobbyists for the banking and financial industries wrote numerous "white papers" to bolster their arguments. These documents provided an unending flow of alternative-language proposals for the new financial reform bill.

Such lobbying typically weakens a bill as it passes through the legislative process. An odd thing happened with the financial reform bill, however. Even while some provisions became more and more generous to the industry, others actually became tougher. As Congressman Barney Frank (D., Mass.) observed, "The more important an issue is to the public, the less important the lobbyists are." Because the financial industry had become so unpopular, legislators could hope to win votes by appearing to be strict with it.

You Be the Judge **Some commentators argue that lobbyists are not the most important reason for the financial industry's influence. Policymakers have simply come to believe that what is good for Wall Street is good for the United States. Many investment bankers go on to become leaders in the executive branch of government. How might such individuals influence policy?**

several decades, as you can see in Figure 6–2 on the following page. Today, members of organized labor make up only 12.4 percent of the **labor force**—defined as all of the people over the age of sixteen who are working or actively looking for jobs.

There are several reasons why the power of organized

labor force All of the people over the age of sixteen who are working or actively looking for jobs.

Table 6–3

Top Labor Campaign Donors, 1989–2010

Union or Group	Total, 1989–2010
1. Amer. Fed. of State, County and Municipal Employees	$42,764,261
2. Intl. Brotherhood of Electrical Workers	32,282,895
3. National Education Assn.	30,606,680
4. Laborers Union	29,604,550
5. Teamsters Union	28,510,684
6. Service Employees International Union	28,461,982
7. Carpenters & Joiners Union	28,386,933
8. American Federation of Teachers	27,711,391
9. Communications Workers of America	27,543,796
10. United Auto Workers	26,241,902

labor has declined in the United States. One is the continuing fall in the proportion of the nation's workforce employed in such blue-collar activities as manufacturing and transportation. These sectors have always been among the most heavily unionized. Another important factor in labor's decline, however, is the general political environment. Forming and maintaining unions is more difficult in the United States than in most other industrial nations. Among the world's wealthy democracies, the United States is one of the most politically conservative, at least on economic issues. Economic conservatives are traditionally hostile to labor unions. Further, many business owners in the United States do not accept unions as legitimate institutions and will do anything within their power to ensure that their own businesses remain unorganized.

The impact of the political environment on labor's organizing ability can be easily seen by comparing rates of unionization in various states. These rates are especially low in conservative southern states. Georgia and North Carolina are both major manufacturing states, but in Georgia, unions represent only 4.6 percent of the workforce, and in North Carolina, only 5 percent. Compare these figures with rates in more liberal states, such as California and New York: unions represent 19.5 percent of the workforce in California and 26.6 percent in New York. One factor that depresses unionization rates in many states is the existence of so-called **right-to-work laws.** These laws ban unions from collecting dues or other fees from workers that they represent but who have not actually joined the union. Such laws create a significant free rider problem for unions. Twenty-two states in the South, Great Plains, and Rocky Mountain region have right-to-work laws.

right-to-work laws Laws that ban unions from collecting dues or other fees from workers that they represent but who have not actually joined the union.

PUBLIC SECTOR UNIONS While labor groups have generally experienced a decline in lobbying power, public employee unions have grown in both numbers and political clout in recent years. Public employees enjoy some of the nation's best health-care and retirement benefits because of the efforts of their labor groups.

Professional Interest Groups

Most professions that require advanced education or specialized training have organizations to protect and promote their interests. These groups are concerned mainly with the standards of their professions, but they also work to influence government policy. Major professional groups include the American Medical Association (AMA), representing physicians; the American Bar Association, representing lawyers; and the American Association for Justice, representing trial lawyers. In addition, there are dozens of less well known and less politically active professional groups, such as the National Association of Social Workers and the American Political Science Association.

Competing interests sometimes divide professional interest groups from one another. For example, consider the issue of tort reform. Advocates of tort reform contend that it is too easy for lawyers to sue physicians, insurance companies, and other businesses, and that generous settlements drive up the cost of health care and other goods. The AMA generally favors tort reform. The American Association for Justice, naturally, opposes it.

Figure 6–2

Union Membership, 1952 to Present

This figure shows the percentage of the workforce who are members of unions from 1952 to the present. As you can see, union membership has declined significantly over the past several decades.

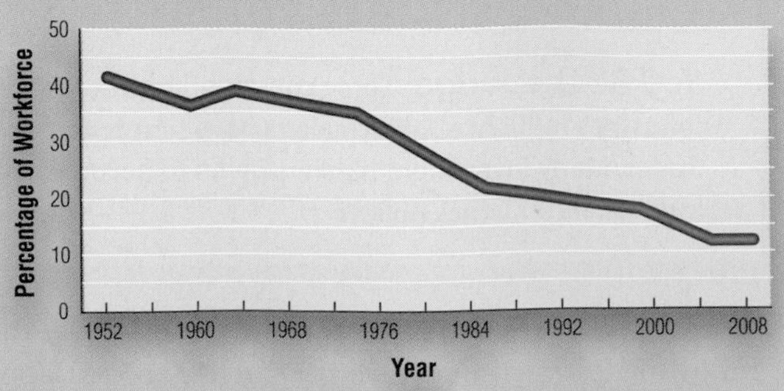

Agricultural Interest Groups

Many groups work for general agricultural interests at all levels of government. Three broad-based agricultural groups represent millions of American farmers, from peanut farmers to dairy producers to tobacco growers. They are the American Farm Bureau Federation (Farm Bureau), the National Grange, and the National Farmers Union. The Farm Bureau, representing more than 5.5 million families (a majority of whom are not actually farm families), is the largest and generally the most effective of the three. Founded in 1919, the Farm Bureau achieved one of its greatest early successes when it helped to obtain government guarantees of "fair" prices during the Great Depression of the 1930s.[7] The Grange, founded in 1867, is the oldest group. It has units in 3,600 communities in thirty-seven states, with a total membership of about 300,000. The National Farmers Union comprises approximately 250,000 farm and ranch families.

AP PHOTO/MICHAEL CONROY

A number of national interest groups protect the rights of farmers. Through their lobbying efforts and campaign contributions, these groups have wielded significant influence in Congress.

Interest groups representing farmers have been spectacularly successful in winning subsidies from the federal government. Farm subsidies cost the taxpayer at least $20 billion per year. Resulting higher prices for food may add another $12 billion to the bill. European farmers, however, have been even more successful in winning subsidies, as we explain in this chapter's feature *The Rest of the World: Europe's Common Agricultural Policy* on the following page.

Producers of various specific farm commodities, such as dairy products, soybeans, grain, fruit, corn, cotton, beef, and sugar beets, have formed their own organizations. These specialized groups, such as the Associated Milk Producers, Inc., also have a strong influence on farm legislation.

Consumer Interest Groups

Groups organized for the protection of consumer rights were very active in the 1960s and 1970s. Some are still active today. The best known and perhaps the most effective are the public-interest groups organized under the leadership of consumer activist Ralph Nader. Another well-known group is Consumers Union, a nonprofit organization started in 1936. In addition to publishing *Consumer Reports,* Consumers Union has been influential in pushing for the removal of phosphates from detergents, lead from gasoline, and pesticides from food. Consumers Union strongly criticizes government agencies when they appear to act against consumer interests.

Consumer groups have been organized in every city. They deal with such problems as poor housing, discrimination against minorities and women, discrimination in the granting of credit, and business inaction on consumer complaints.

Identity Interest Groups

Americans who share the same race, ethnicity, gender, or other characteristic often have important common interests. African Americans, for example, have a powerful interest in combating the racism and racial discrimination that have marked American history from the beginning. Slaves, of course, were not able to form interest groups. For many years after the abolition of slavery, organizing African American interest groups remained impossibly dangerous. Such groups did not come into existence until the twentieth century. The National Association for the Advancement of Colored People was founded in 1909, and the National Urban League was created in 1910. During the civil rights movement of the 1950s and 1960s, African Americans organized a number of new groups, some of which lasted (the Southern Christian Leadership Conference, founded in 1957) and some of which did not (the Student Nonviolent Coordinating Committee, organized in 1960).

THE REST OF THE WORLD

Europe's Common Agricultural Policy

Lobbying efforts by America's farmers have been highly successful—farmers receive tens of billions of dollars of subsidies every year. Consumers in this country pay higher food prices because of such successful lobbying. We are not alone, however. The European Union (EU) doles out agricultural subsidies at an even greater rate than we do.

It's All in the CAP

The EU's agricultural subsidies are part of its Common Agricultural Policy (CAP). The CAP directly pays farmers subsidies for crops and for specific land uses—sometimes for no use at all. The CAP also provides price supports and minimum prices. Specific agricultural goods brought into the EU are taxed, and there are quotas on imports, too. Production quotas limit the supply of certain products such as milk and grain. Not only does the CAP effectively prevent competition from non-European farmers in European markets, but it also injures those farmers by dumping "butter mountains" and "wine lakes" cheaply onto the world market. African and Asian dairy, tomato, and poultry farmers cannot keep up with cheap competition from Europe.

How Successful Are Farm Lobbyists in the EU?

The EU's $130 billion annual budget is paid for by levies on the twenty-seven member nations, which must fund their contributions through taxes. Lobbyists for farming interests have succeeded in capturing 48 percent of this budget. A few brave politicians in Britain and Sweden have called for the abolition of the CAP. The agriculture lobby is strong enough to prevent such a change, however, and farm subsidies in Europe will continue for the foreseeable future.

For Critical Analysis *Farmers make up only about 1 percent of the population in the United States and 5 percent in Europe. Why are they so successful, nonetheless, in winning so many taxpayer dollars?*

The campaigns for dignity and equality of Native Americans, Latinos, women, lesbians and gay men, Americans with disabilities, and many other groups have all resulted in important interest groups. You learned about many of these organizations in Chapter 5. One identity-based group not discussed in that chapter is older Americans. Senior citizens are numerous, are politically active, and have a great deal at stake in debates over certain programs, such as Social Security and Medicare. As a result, groups representing them, such as the AARP, can be a potent political force.

Ideological Interest Groups

Some interest groups are not organized to promote an economic interest or a collective identity but a shared political perspective or ideology. Examples include MoveOn, an Internet-oriented liberal group, and the Club for Growth, a conservative, antitax organization.

The highly decentralized Tea Party movement, which sprang into life in 2009, has been described as an ideological interest group. The activities of the Tea Party movement, however, raise the question of whether it really is an interest group at all. The point is that interest groups, while they are often very concerned about who wins an election and may endorse candidates, do not themselves attempt to gain control of the machinery of government. Most Tea Party leaders claim that the movement is nonpartisan and that it contains not only Republicans but independents, Libertarians, and even some Democrats. Still, some Tea Party groups have attempted to gain control of local Republican Party organizations. It may be only a matter of terminology, but political scientists refer to groups that compete for control of a political party as *factions,* not interest groups. You will learn more about factions in Chapter 7.

Environmental groups have supported pollution controls, wilderness protection, and clean-air legislation. They have opposed strip mining, nuclear power plants, logging activities, chemical waste dumps, and many other potential environmental hazards. In the past, environmental groups have been characterized as single-interest groups, not ideological organizations. Issues such as global warming, however, have led many modern environmental groups to advocate sweeping changes to the entire economy. Groups with such broad agendas could be considered a type of ideological interest group. Environmental interest groups range from traditional organizations such as the National Wildlife Federation, with 4 million members, to more radical groups such as Greenpeace USA, with a membership of 250,000.

Single-Issue Interest Groups

Numerous interest groups focus on a single issue. For example, Mothers Against Drunk Driving (MADD) lobbies for stiffer penalties for drunk driving. Formed in 1980, MADD now boasts more than 3 million members and supporters. The abortion debate has created various single-issue groups, such as the Right to Life organization (which opposes abortion) and NARAL Pro-Choice America (which supports abortion rights). Other examples of single-issue groups are the NRA and the American Israel Public Affairs Committee (a pro-Israel group).

More and more government groups, namely school districts, are using local tax dollars to hire lobbyists. The more the federal government subsidizes state and local activities, the more lobbying by the latter we can expect to occur.

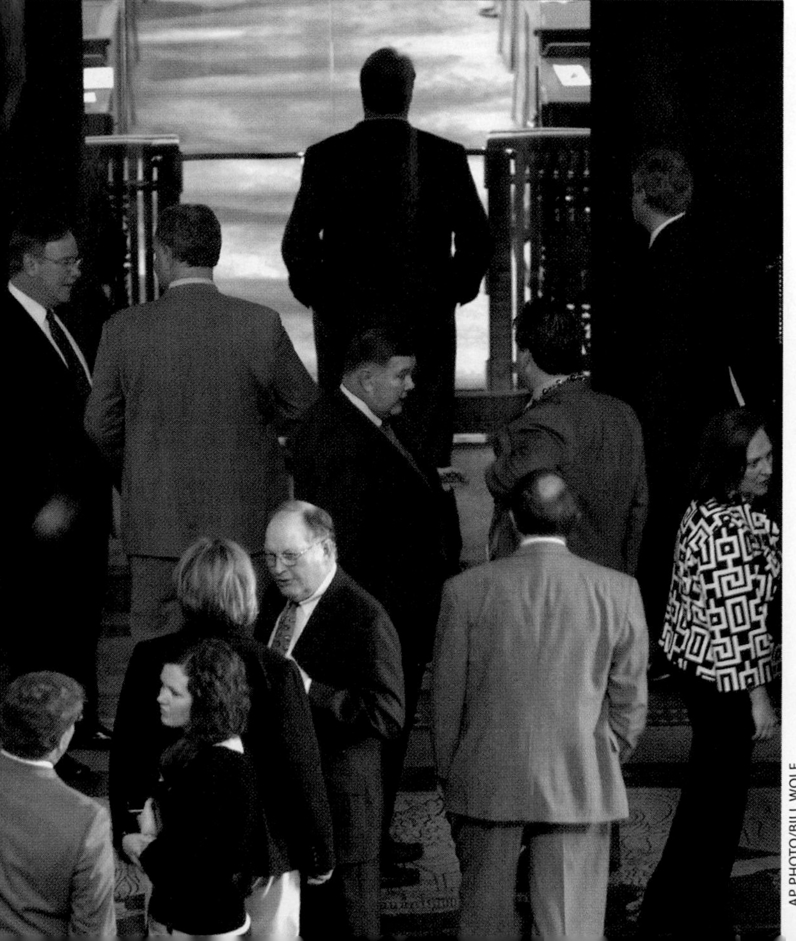

AP PHOTO/BILL WOLF

Government Interest Groups

Efforts by state and local governments to lobby the federal government have escalated in recent years. When states experience budget shortfalls, these governments often lobby in Washington, D.C., for additional federal funds. The federal government has sometimes lobbied in individual states, too. During the 2004 elections, for example, the U.S. Attorney General's office lobbied against medical marijuana use in states that were considering ballot measures on the issue.

direct technique Any method used by an interest group to interact with government officials directly to further the group's goals.

lobbying All of the attempts by organizations or by individuals to influence the passage, defeat, or contents of legislation or to influence the administrative decisions of government.

lobbyist An individual who handles a particular interest group's lobbying efforts.

LO4 *How Interest Groups Shape Policy*

Interest groups operate at all levels of government and use a variety of strategies to steer policies in ways beneficial to their interests. Sometimes, they attempt to influence policymakers directly, but at other times they try to exert indirect influence on policymakers by shaping public opinion. The extent and nature of the groups' activities depend on their goals and their resources.

Direct Techniques

Lobbying and providing election support are two important **direct techniques** used by interest groups to influence government policy.

LOBBYING Today, **lobbying** refers to all of the attempts by organizations or by individuals to influence the passage, defeat, or contents of legislation or to influence the administrative decisions of government. (The term *lobbying* arose because, traditionally, individuals and groups interested in influencing government policy would gather in the foyer, or lobby, of the legislature to corner legislators and express their concerns.) A **lobbyist** is an individual who handles a particular interest group's lobbying efforts. Most of the larger interest groups have lobbyists in Washington, D.C. These lobbyists often include former members of Congress or former employees of executive bureaucracies who are experienced in the methods of political influence and who "know people." Many lobbyists also work at state and local levels. In fact, lobbying at the state level has increased in recent years as states have begun to play a more significant role in policymaking. Table 6–4 at right summarizes some of the basic methods by which lobbyists directly influence legislators and government officials.

Lobbying can be directed at the legislative branch of government, at administrative agencies, and even at the courts. For example, pharmaceutical companies may lobby the Food and Drug Administration to speed up the process of approving new prescription drugs. Lobbying can also be directed at changing international policies. For instance, after political changes had opened up Eastern Europe to business in the late 1980s and early 1990s, intense lobbying by Western business groups helped persuade the United States and other industrial powers to reduce controls on the sale of high-technology products, such as personal computers, to Eastern European countries.

Table 6–4

Direct Lobbying Techniques

Technique	Description
Making Personal Contacts with Key Legislators	A lobbyist's personal contacts with key legislators or other government officials—in their offices, in the halls of Congress, or on social occasions such as dinners, boating expeditions, and the like—are one of the most effective direct lobbying techniques. The lobbyist provides the legislators with information on a particular issue in an attempt to convince them to support the interest group's goals.
Providing Expertise and Research Results for Legislators	Lobbyists often have knowledge and expertise that are useful in drafting legislation, and this expertise can be a major strength for an interest group. Because harried members of Congress cannot possibly be experts on everything they vote on and therefore eagerly seek information to help them make up their minds, some lobbying groups conduct research and present their findings to those legislators.
Offering "Expert" Testimony before Congressional Committees	Lobbyists often provide "expert" testimony before congressional committees for or against proposed legislation. A bill to regulate firearms, for example, might concern several interest groups. The NRA would probably oppose the bill, and representatives from that interest group might be asked to testify. Groups that would probably support the bill, such as law enforcement personnel, might also be asked to testify. Each side would offer as much evidence as possible to support its position.
Providing Legal Advice to Legislators	Many lobbyists assist legislators in drafting legislation or prospective regulations. Lobbyists are a source of ideas and sometimes offer legal advice on specific details.
Following Up on Legislation	Because executive agencies responsible for carrying out legislation can often increase or decrease the scope of the new law, lobbyists may also try to influence the bureaucrats who implement the policy. For example, beginning in the early 1960s, regulations outlawing gender discrimination were broadly outlined by Congress. Both women's rights groups favoring the regulations and interest groups opposing the regulations lobbied for years to influence how those regulations were carried out.

PROVIDING ELECTION SUPPORT Interest groups often become directly involved in the election process. Many interest group members join and work with political parties to influence party platforms and the nomination of candidates. Interest groups provide campaign support for legislators who favor their policies and sometimes encourage their own members to try to win posts in party organizations. Most important, interest groups urge their members to vote for candidates who support the views of the group. They can also threaten legislators with the withdrawal of votes. No candidate can expect to have support from all interest groups, but if the candidate is to win, she or he must have support from many of the strongest ones.

political action committee (PAC)
A committee that is established by a corporation, labor union, or special interest group to raise funds and make contributions on the establishing organization's behalf.

Since the 1970s, federal laws governing campaign financing have allowed corporations, labor unions, and special interest groups to raise funds and make campaign contributions through **political action committees (PACs).** Both the number of PACs and the amount of money PACs spend on elections have grown astronomically in recent years. There were about 1,000 PACs in 1976. Today, there are more than 4,500 PACs. In 1973, total spending by PACs amounted to $19 million. In the 2007–2008 presidential election cycle, total spending by PACs exceeded $400 million. We will discuss PACs in more detail in Chapter 9.

Although campaign contributions do not guarantee that officials will vote the way the groups wish, contributions usually do ensure that the groups will have the ear of the public officials they have helped to elect.

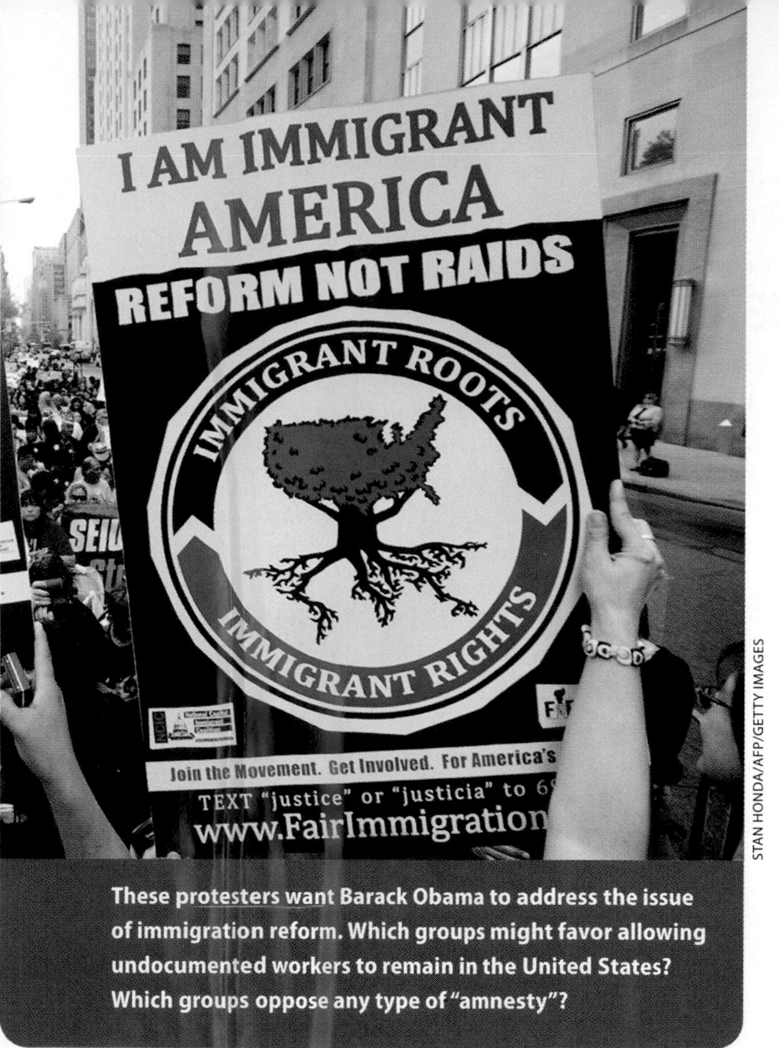

STAN HONDA/AFP/GETTY IMAGES

These protesters want Barack Obama to address the issue of immigration reform. Which groups might favor allowing undocumented workers to remain in the United States? Which groups oppose any type of "amnesty"?

Indirect Techniques

Interest groups also try to influence public policy indirectly through third parties or the general public. The effects of such **indirect techniques** may appear to be spontaneous, but indirect techniques are generally as well planned as the direct lobbying techniques just discussed. Indirect techniques can be particularly effective because public officials are often more impressed by contacts from voters than from lobbyists.

SHAPING PUBLIC OPINION Public opinion weighs significantly in the policymaking process, so interest groups cultivate their public images carefully. If public opinion favors a certain group's interests, then public officials will be more ready to listen and more willing to pass legislation favoring that group. To cultivate public opinion, an interest group's efforts may include online campaigns, television publicity, newspaper and magazine advertisements, mass mailings, and the use of public relations techniques to improve the group's public image.

For example, environmental groups often run television ads to dramatize threats to the environment. Oil companies may respond to criticism about increased gasoline prices with advertising showing their concern for the public welfare. The goal of all these activities is to influence public opinion.

RATING SYSTEMS Some interest groups also try to influence legislators through **rating systems.** A group selects legislative issues that it believes are important to its goals and rates legislators according to the percentage of times they vote favorably on that legislation. For example, a score of 90 percent on the Americans for Democratic Action (ADA) rating scale means that the legislator supported that liberal group's position to a high degree. Other groups tag members of Congress who support (or fail to support) their interests to a significant extent with telling labels. For instance, the Communications Workers of America refers to policymakers who take a position consistent with its views as "Heroes" and those who take the opposite position as "Zeroes." Needless to say, such tactics can be an effective form of indirect lobbying, particularly with legislators who do not want to earn a low ADA score or be placed on the "Zeroes" list.

ISSUE ADS AND "527s" One of the most powerful indirect techniques used by interest groups is the "issue ad"—a television or radio ad taking a position on a particular issue. The Supreme Court has made it clear that the First Amendment's guarantee of free speech protects interest groups' rights to set forth their positions on issues when they are **independent expenditures** that are not coordinated with a candidate's campaign or a political party. Nevertheless, issue advocacy is controversial because the funds spent to air issue ads have had a clear effect on the outcome of elections.

Both parties have benefited from such interest group spending. As you will read in Chapter 9, the Bipartisan Campaign Reform Act of 2002 banned unlimited donations to campaigns and political parties, called *soft money.* In subsequent years, interest groups that had previously given soft money to parties set up new groups called "527s" (after the provision of the tax code that covers them). The 527s engaged

indirect technique Any method used by interest groups to influence government officials through third parties, such as voters.

rating system A system by which a particular interest group evaluates (rates) the performance of legislators based on how often the legislators have voted with the group's position on particular issues.

independent expenditure An expenditure for activities that are independent from (not coordinated with) those of a political candidate or a political party.

in such practices as voter registration, but they also began making large expenditures on issue ads—which were legal so long as the 527s did not coordinate their activities with candidates' campaigns.

In the run-up to the 2008 presidential elections, clever campaign finance lawyers hit upon a new type of group, the 501(c)4 organization, also named after a section of the tax code. Groups such as the Sierra Club and Citizens Against Government Waste have set up special 501(c)4 arms. Lawyers argued that a 501(c)4 group could spend some of its funds on direct campaign contributions as long as most of the group's spending was on issue advocacy. Further, a 501(c)4 group could conceal the identity of its contributors. It was not possible to determine the legality of these claims in time for the 2010 elections. We will discuss this issue in greater depth in Chapter 9.

"Never doubt that a small group of thoughtful, committed citizens can **CHANGE THE WORLD;** indeed, it's the only thing that ever has."

~ MARGARET MEAD ~
AMERICAN ANTHROPOLOGIST
1901–1978

MOBILIZING CONSTITUENTS Interest groups sometimes urge members and other constituents to contact government officials—by letter, e-mail, Facebook, or telephone—to show their support for or opposition to a certain policy. Large interest groups can generate hundreds of thousands of letters, e-mail messages, and phone calls. Interest groups often provide form letters or postcards for constituents to fill out and mail. The NRA has successfully used this tactic to fight strict federal gun control legislation by delivering half a million letters to Congress within a few weeks. Policymakers recognize that such communications are initiated by interest groups, however, and are impressed only when the volume of letters or e-mail communications is very large. Campaigns that masquerade as grassroots mobilizations, but are not, have been given the apt label *Astroturf lobbying.*

GOING TO COURT The legal system offers another avenue for interest groups to influence the political process. In the 1950s and 1960s, civil rights groups paved the way for interest group litigation with major victories in cases concerning equal housing, school desegregation, and employment discrimination. Environmental groups, such as the Sierra Club, have also successfully used litigation to press their concerns. For example, an environmental group might challenge in court an activity that threatens to pollute the environment or that will destroy the natural habitat of an endangered species. The legal challenge forces those engaging in the activity to bear the costs of defending themselves and may delay the project. In fact, much of the success of environmental groups has been linked to their use of lawsuits.

Interest groups can also influence the outcome of litigation without being a party to a lawsuit. Frequently, an interest group files an *amicus curiae* ("friend of the court") brief. The brief states the group's legal argument in support of its desired outcome in a case. For example, in the case *Metro-Goldwyn-Mayer Studios, Inc. v. Grokster, Ltd.*[8]—involving the legality of file-sharing software—hundreds of *amicus* briefs were filed by various groups on behalf of the petitioners. Groups filing *amicus* briefs for the case, which was heard by the Supreme Court in 2005, included the National Basketball Association, the National Football League, the National Association of Broadcasters, the Association of American Publishers, and numerous state governments. Often, interest groups have statistics and research that support their position on a certain issue, and this research can have considerable influence on the judges deciding the case.

DEMONSTRATIONS Some interest groups stage protests to make a statement in a dramatic way. The Boston Tea Party of 1773, in which American colonists dressed as Native Americans and threw tea into Boston Harbor to protest British taxes, is testimony to how long this tactic has been around. Over the years, many groups have organized protest marches and rallies to support or oppose legalized abortion, gay and lesbian rights, the treatment of Native Americans, restrictions on the use of federally owned lands in the West, and the activities of global organizations, such as the World Trade Organization.

Not all demonstration techniques are peaceful. Some environmental groups, for example, have used such dangerous tactics as spiking trees and setting traps on logging roads that puncture truck tires. Pro-life groups have bombed abortion clinics, and members of the Animal Liberation Front have broken into laboratories and freed animals being used for experimentation. Some evidence exists that violent demonstrations can be counterproductive—that is, that they can hurt the demonstrators' cause by angering the public. Historians continue to debate whether violent demonstrations against the Vietnam War (1964–1975) helped or hurt the antiwar cause.

LO5 *Today's Lobbying Establishment*

Without a doubt, interest groups and their lobbyists have become a permanent feature in the landscape of American government. The major interest groups all have headquarters in Washington, D.C., close to the center of government. Professional lobbyists and staff members of various interest groups move freely between their groups' headquarters and congressional offices and committee rooms. Interest group representatives are routinely consulted when Congress drafts new legislation. As already mentioned, interest group representatives are frequently asked to testify before congressional committees or subcommittees on the effect or potential effect of particular legislation or regulations. In sum, interest groups have become an integral part of the American government system.

As interest groups have become a permanent feature of American government, lobbying has developed into a profession. A professional lobbyist—one who has mastered the techniques of lobbying discussed earlier in this chapter—is a valuable ally to any interest group seeking to influence government. Professional lobbyists can and often do represent a number of different interest groups over the course of their careers.

In recent years, it has become increasingly common for those who leave positions with the federal government to become lobbyists or consultants for the private-interest groups they helped to regulate. In spite of legislation and regulations that have been created in an attempt to reduce this "revolving door" syndrome, it is still functioning quite well.

Why Do Interest Groups Get Bad Press?

Despite their importance to democratic government, interest groups, like political parties, are often criticized by both the public and the press. Our image of interest groups and their special interests is not very favorable. You may have run across political cartoons depicting lobbyists standing in the hallways of Congress with briefcases stuffed with money.

These cartoons are not entirely factual, but they are not entirely fictitious either. President Richard Nixon (1969–1974) was revealed to have responded to the campaign contributions of milk producers by authorizing a windfall increase in milk subsidies. In the early 1990s, it was revealed that a number of senators who

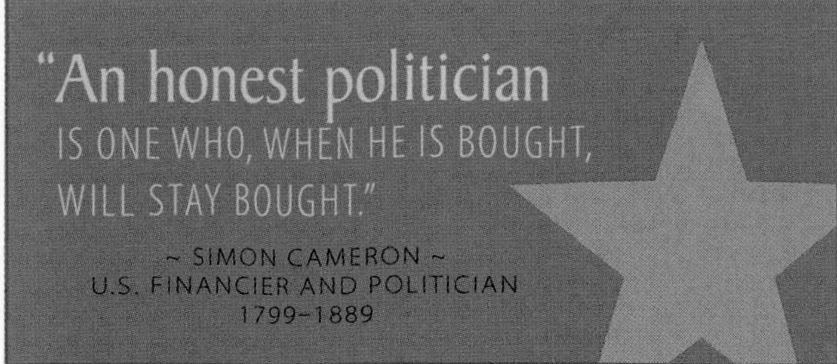

received generous contributions from a particular savings and loan association subsequently supported a "hands-off" policy by savings and loan regulators. The savings and loan association in question later got into financial trouble, costing the taxpayers billions of dollars. (One of the senators criticized for having exercised poor judgment during the savings and loan scandal was John McCain, the 2008 Republican presidential candidate. It may have been this painful experience that inspired McCain to become an ardent advocate of campaign-finance reform.)

Some of the most heated and expensive lobbying in recent years surrounded the health-care reform bills that Congress passed in March 2010. Heavy lobbying may have done its part in causing many Americans to distrust the reforms. Did lobbying damage the health-care legislation? We examine that question in this chapter's *Join the Debate* feature on the following page.

The Regulation of Interest Groups

In an attempt to control lobbying, Congress passed the Federal Regulation of Lobbying Act in 1946. The major provisions of the act are as follows:

- Any person or organization that receives money to influence legislation must register with the clerk of the House and the secretary of the Senate.

"MY GREATEST ASSET IS I'M SO RICH, I CAN'T BE BOUGHT BY ANY INTEREST GROUP."

JOIN THE DEBATE

Did Lobbying Damage the Health-Care Legislation?

Immediately upon taking office in January 2009, President Barack Obama declared that health-care reform "must not wait." One thing that did not wait was perhaps the greatest lobbying spree in American history. Medical interests alone spent almost a billion dollars in lobbying during the following fifteen months. These expenses declined after the passage of the health-care reform legislation, which has been dubbed "Obamacare" by journalists and Republicans. We will, however, see continued lobbying efforts by physicians, the drug industry, and manufacturers of medical products as the government creates thousands of rules and regulations to implement the new policies.

Lobbying Gave Us Imperfect Health-Care Reform

Those who support the reforms contend that every U.S. citizen will soon have the right to obtain health-care insurance at a price she or he can afford, and that this is a blessing. Many supporters, however, believe that lobbying resulted in reforms that were not as good as they could have been. For example, lobbying by the pharmaceutical industry eliminated measures to limit drug prices. Costly brand-name biotech drugs received twelve years of protection against cheaper generic competitors. Pharmaceutical lobbyists also killed a proposal to allow the import of low-cost medicines from abroad.

A major feature of the original plan was a "public option"—a government-sponsored health-care insurance plan that would compete with private insurance companies, presumably holding down their rates. The insurance industry succeeded in eliminating that option. The result of these various lobbying measures was to channel billions of dollars to the pharmaceutical, insurance, and hospital industries. Those sums will come from taxpayers and from everyone who must pay part or all of the cost of their health-care insurance policy.

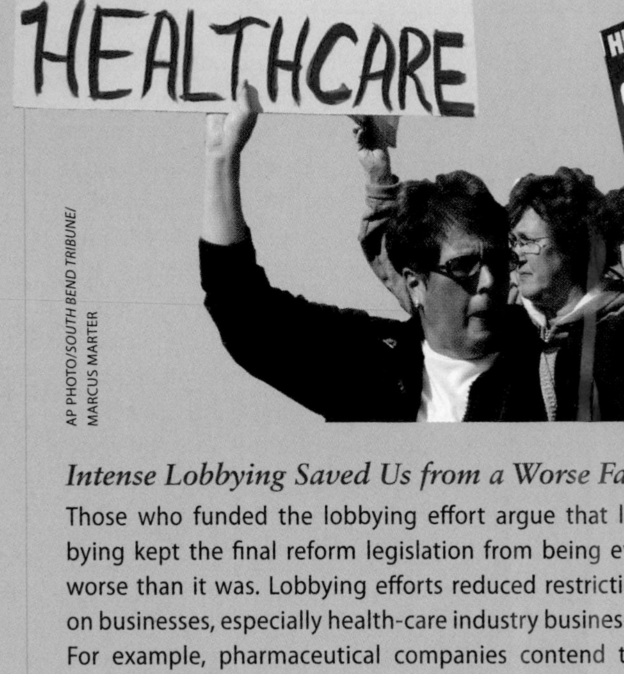

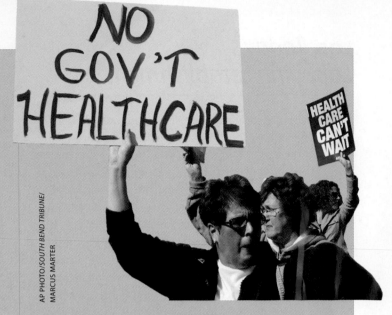

AP PHOTO/SOUTH BEND TRIBUNE/ MARCUS MARTER

Intense Lobbying Saved Us from a Worse Fate

Those who funded the lobbying effort argue that lobbying kept the final reform legislation from being even worse than it was. Lobbying efforts reduced restrictions on businesses, especially health-care industry businesses. For example, pharmaceutical companies contend that price controls on their products would be a disaster. Why? Because controls would lower the profits of pharmaceutical companies—which in turn would force these companies to reduce the sums they spend on research and development. The result would be fewer new drugs.

Opponents of the health-care reform legislation see it as a giant mass of new restrictions on the freedoms of businesses and citizens alike. They see the requirement that everyone must purchase health-care insurance—which did survive the legislative process—as the prime example of such restrictions. Any successes that lobbyists had in limiting the scope of the legislation prevented further erosions of our personal and economic freedoms. That is a plus, not a negative.

For Critical Analysis ***From the very beginning, much of the lobbying paid for by the health-care industries supported the general concept of reform. Why would these interests have taken this position?***

- Any group or person registering must identify their employer, salary, amount and purpose of expenses, and duration of employment.
- Every registered lobbyist must make quarterly reports on his or her activities.
- Anyone violating this act can be fined up to $10,000 and be imprisoned for up to five years.

The act did not succeed in regulating lobbying to any great degree for several reasons. First, the Supreme Court restricted the application of the law to only those lobbyists who sought to influence federal legislation directly.[9] Any lobbyist seeking to influence legislation indirectly through public opinion did not fall within the scope of the law. Second, only persons or organizations whose principal purpose was to influence legislation were required to register. Many groups avoided registration by claiming that their principal function was something else. Third, the act did not cover those whose lobbying was directed at agencies in the executive branch or lobbyists who testified before congressional committees. Fourth, the public was almost totally unaware of the information in the quarterly reports filed by lobbyists. Not until 1995 did Congress finally address those loopholes by enacting new legislation.

The Lobbying Disclosure Act of 1995

In 1995, Congress passed new lobbying legislation—the Lobbying Disclosure Act—that reformed the 1946 act in the following ways:

- Strict definitions now apply to determine who must register with the clerk of the House and the secretary of the Senate as a lobbyist. A lobbyist is anyone who either spends at least 20 percent of his or her time lobbying members of Congress, their staffs, or executive-branch officials, or is paid more than $5,000 in a six-month period for such work. Any organization that spends more than $20,000 in a six-month period conducting such lobbying activity must also register. These amounts have since been altered to $2,500 and $10,000 per quarter, respectively.
- Lobbyists must report their clients, the issues on which they lobbied, and the agency or chamber of Congress they contacted, although they do not need to disclose the names of those they contacted.

Tax-exempt organizations, such as religious groups, were exempted from these provisions, as were organizations that engage in grassroots lobbying, such as a media campaign that asks people to write or call their congressional representative. Nonetheless, the number of registered lobbyists nearly doubled in the first few years of the new legislation.

Lobbying Scandals and Reform Efforts

In 2005, a number of lobbying scandals in Washington, D.C., came to light. A major figure in the scandals was Jack Abramoff, an influential lobbyist who had ties to many Republicans (and a few Democrats) in Congress and to various officials in the Bush administration. Abramoff gained access to the power brokers in the capital by giving them campaign contributions, expensive gifts, and exotic trips. Eventually, Abramoff pleaded guilty to charges of fraud, tax evasion, and conspiracy to bribe public officials. Abramoff received a prison sentence in 2006.

Following the midterm elections of 2006, the new Democratic majority in the Senate and House of Representatives undertook a lobbying reform effort. The goal of the reforms was to force lobbyists to disclose their expenditures on House and Senate election campaigns above and beyond straight campaign contributions.

Bundled campaign contributions, in which a lobbyist arranges for contributions from a variety of sources, would have to be reported. Expenditures on the sometimes lavish parties to benefit candidates would have to be reported as well. (Of course, partygoers were expected to pay for their food and drink with a check written out to the candidate.) The new rules covered PACs as well as registered lobbyists, which led one lobbyist to observe sourly that this wasn't lobbying reform but campaign-finance reform.

President Bush signed the resulting Honest Leadership and Open Government Act in September 2007. The new law increased lobbying disclosure and placed further restrictions on the receipt of gifts and travel by members of Congress paid for by lobbyists and the organizations they represent. The act also included provisions requiring the disclosure of lawmakers' requests for earmarks in legislation. (We discuss earmarks in more depth in Chapter 11.)

Lobbyists and the Obama Administration

During his campaign for the presidency, Barack Obama pledged that "lobbyists won't find a job in my White House." Given how many talented individuals with experience in government have served as lobbyists, that pledge turned out to be unenforceable. Senior administration officials soon included dozens of persons who had served as lobbyists within the past five years.

Appointees signed a pledge not to work on issues for which they had lobbied in the previous two years, but given the positions that many of these appointees filled, such a pledge was probably unworkable as well. Interest groups represented by these former lobbyists included the Campaign for Tobacco-Free Kids, the mortgage giant Fannie Mae, the investment bank Goldman Sachs, Mothers Against Drunk Driving, the National Council of La Raza, the defense industry giant Raytheon, and the Service Employees International Union.

Other restrictions imposed by the new administration included a rule that all communications with lobbyists over economic stimulus projects had to be in writing. Many old hands in Washington considered Obama's policies toward lobbyists absurd and predicted that they would not last.

AMERICA AT ODDS *Interest Groups*

Interest groups are one of the most controversial features of our democratic system. The right to lobby may be protected by the First Amendment, but many people consider lobbying by interest groups to be a source of corruption within the political system. Of course, it is simpler for anyone to see the problems with lobbying when it is done for a cause that they oppose. It is easy to support political action for something you believe in, regardless of what others might think of it. Some of the controversies surrounding interest group lobbying include the following:

- Should labor unions be allowed to organize workplaces by obtaining signed cards—or are secret-ballot elections an essential safeguard?
- Are farm subsidies a valid protection for an important industry—or just another giveaway to the politically powerful?
- Does lobbying always harm legislation—or can lobbying improve it?
- Free riders benefit from a particular activity without paying their share of its costs. Is free riding inherently unfair—or is it only a problem when it is so pervasive that it makes the activity in question (for example, lobbying by consumer groups) unaffordable?
- Are there too many lobbyists—or is the real problem that there aren't enough lobbyists for ordinary people?

Take Action

An obvious way to get involved in politics is to join an interest group whose goals you endorse—perhaps one of the organizations on your campus. You can find lists of interest groups operating at the local, state, and national levels by simply going to an online search engine, such as Google, and keying in the words "interest groups." Alternatively, you can go directly to one of the pages that list interest groups. One is usgovinfo.about.com/blorgs.htm. Another is directory.google.com/Top/Society/Organizations/Advocacy. Almost all interest groups have Web sites, and you'll want to check them out. A very large number of groups have Facebook pages as well—just type the name of the organization into your Facebook search box.

If you have a particular interest or goal that you would like to promote, consider forming your own group, as some Iowa students did when they formed a group called Students Toward Environmental Protection. In the photo at right, students from Grinnell College in Iowa are seen staging a protest rally at the state capitol. The students wanted Iowa's lawmakers to issue tougher regulations governing factory farms and to expand the state's bottle deposit requirements.

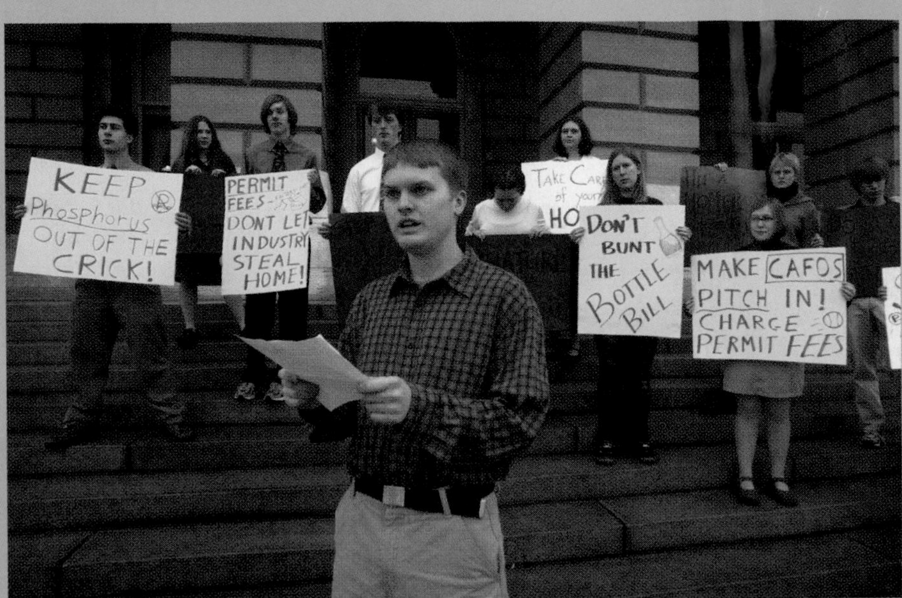

AP PHOTO/CHARLIE NEIBERGALL

POLITICS ON THE WEB

- To find particular interest groups online, a good point of departure is the Internet Public Library Association, which provides links to hundreds of professional and trade associations. Go to **www.ipl.org/div/aon**
- You can access the National Rifle Association online at **www.nra.org**
- AARP's Web site can be found at **www.aarp.org**
- To learn about the activities of the National Education Association, go to **www.nea.org**
- You can find information on environmental issues and the activities of the National Resources Defense Council at **www.nrdc.org**

Access CourseMate to review and expand on this chapter through quizzes, flashcards, learning objectives, interactive timelines, a crossword puzzle, audio summaries, video, critical-thinking activities, simulations, and more.

GOVT

7 Political Parties

LEARNING OBJECTIVES

LO1 Summarize the origins and development of the two-party system in the United States.

LO2 Describe the current status of the two major parties.

LO3 Explain how political parties function in our democratic system.

LO4 Discuss the structure of American political parties.

LO5 Describe the different types of third parties and how they function in the American political system.

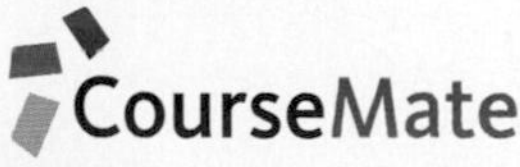

AMERICA AT ODDS

Is the Republican Party Conservative Enough?

The Republican Party lost control of the U.S. House and Senate in 2006, in large part due to the seemingly endless war in Iraq. In 2008, with the economy in crisis, the Republicans lost more seats in Congress and the presidency as well. Not surprisingly, these results touched off a debate within the party. In 2009, a few Republicans argued that their party should moderate its conservatism to attract independent voters. By 2010, however, some Republican activists, many of them part of the Tea Party movement, claimed that incumbent Republican politicians were not conservative enough. Should the Republican Party change its views? And if so, how?

Uncompromising Conservatism Is the Only Way Forward

Uncompromising conservatives believe that the Republicans must steer to the political right. Even though only 29 percent of voters call themselves Republicans, 42 percent say that they are conservatives. In 2009, 39 percent of respondents said that they were becoming more conservative, not less. Support is rising for such conservative positions as the right to bear arms and opposition to abortion. Conservative activists argue that their values are not only popular but also "correct" in a very deep sense. Values such as religious belief, strong families, and individual self-reliance are the foundation of our civilization. Liberalism erodes these values and paves the road to cultural collapse.

Further, as the Tea Party movement has advocated, Republicans must return to their conservative roots on economic issues. Under President George W. Bush, Republicans in Congress abandoned their traditional opposition to government spending. Millions of Americans, including independents, were alarmed at Bush's budget deficits and bank bailouts. They are even more appalled at President Barack Obama's spending programs and his unprecedented federal budget deficits. Americans are starting to rebel against big government and a culture of immorality. If the Republicans don't stand for true conservatism, these Americans won't have anyone to vote for.

Radical Conservatism Spells Disaster in the Long Run

A minority of Republicans argue that the party's improved electoral prospects in 2010 were largely due to Democratic mistakes. The resulting Republican advantage may be only temporary. The face of America is changing. Support for gay rights has risen dramatically. The number of Hispanic voters rises year by year, and after 2050, non-Hispanic whites will be a minority of the U.S. population. Despite these changes, some conservatives seem intent on ensuring that the Republicans are seen as the "nasty party"—the party that hates people. The campaign by leading Republicans against a Muslim cultural center and mosque two blocks from "ground zero" in New York City is an example. In 2000, a majority of Muslims of Middle Eastern background voted Republican because of Islamic cultural conservatism. Today, Muslims are the most Democratic religious group in the nation.

The Republicans must break with the ultraright and stop antagonizing the very people they need to form a majority. Republicans require young voters, but tirades against gays are poison to that constituency. If the vast majority of Latinos come to reject the Republicans because of the party's anti-immigrant rhetoric, eventually the Republicans will fail to carry even Texas. If voters conclude that Republicans see large numbers of their fellow Americans as "the enemy," the party will lose future elections, no matter how well it did in 2010.

WHERE DO YOU STAND?

1. **Pastor Rick Warren, author of *The Purpose Driven Life,* accepts that homosexuality is a sin, but he also emphasizes his belief in God's love for all people. Why might some members of the religious right reject Warren's formula?**
2. **American-style cultural conservatism is not popular in much of Europe. Many of these nations are also facing declines in their populations. Some conservatives would argue that these facts are connected. Is this argument reasonable? Why or why not?**

EXPLORE THIS ISSUE ONLINE

- **Web sites that advocate a more moderate Republican Party include David Frum's www.newmajority.com. For full-throttle conservatism, try www.rushlimbaugh.com.**

Introduction

Political ideology can spark heated debates among Americans, as you read in the chapter-opening *America at Odds* feature. A **political party** can be defined as a group of individuals who organize to win elections, operate the government, and determine policy. Political parties serve as major vehicles for citizen participation in our political system. It is hard to imagine democracy without political parties. Political parties provide a way for the public to choose who will serve in government and which policies will be carried out. Even citizens who do not identify with any political party or who choose not to participate in elections are affected by the activities of parties and their influence on government.

"Both of our political parties . . . agree conscientiously in the same object: **THE PUBLIC GOOD;** but they differ essentially in what they deem the means of promoting that good."

~ THOMAS JEFFERSON ~ IN A LETTER TO ABIGAIL ADAMS 1804

Political parties were an unforeseen development in American political history. The founders defined many other important institutions, such as the presidency and Congress, and described their functions in the Constitution. Political parties, however, are not even mentioned in the Constitution. In fact, the founders decried factions and parties. Thomas Jefferson probably best expressed the founders' antiparty sentiments when he declared, "If I could not go to heaven but with a party, I would not go there at all."[1]

If the founders did not want political parties, though, who was supposed to organize political campaigns and mobilize supporters of political candidates? Clearly, there was a practical need for some kind of organizing group to form a link between citizens and their government. Even our early national leaders, for all their antiparty feelings, realized this. Several of them were active in establishing or organizing the first political parties.

LO1 *A Short History of American Political Parties*

political party A group of individuals who organize to win elections, operate the government, and determine policy.

Throughout the course of our history, several parties have formed, and some have disappeared. Even today, although we have only two major political parties, numerous other parties have been organized, as will be discussed later in this chapter.

The First Political Parties

The founders rejected the idea of political parties because they believed, as George Washington said in his Farewell Address, that the "spirit of party . . . agitates the community with ill-founded jealousies and false alarms, kindles the animosity of one part against another, foments occasionally riot and insurrection."[2] At some point in the future, the founders feared, a party leader might even seize power as a dictator. Nonetheless, two major political factions—the Federalists and Anti-Federalists—were formed even before the Constitution was ratified. Remember from Chapter 2 that the Federalists pushed for the ratification of the Constitution because they wanted a stronger national government than the one that had existed under the Articles of Confederation. The Anti-Federalists argued against ratification. They supported states' rights and feared a too-powerful central government.

These two national factions continued, in somewhat altered form, after the Constitution was ratified. Alexander

John Adams (1735–1826) was the Federalists' candidate to succeed George Washington. Adams defeated Thomas Jefferson in 1796, but lost to him in 1800.

LIBRARY OF CONGRESS

Hamilton, the first secretary of the Treasury, became the leader of the Federalist Party, which was also joined by Vice President John Adams. The Federalists supported a strong central government that would encourage the development of commerce and manufacturing. The Federalists generally thought that a republic should be ruled by its wealthiest and best-educated citizens. Opponents of the Federalists and Hamilton's policies referred to themselves as Republicans. Today, they are often referred to as Jeffersonian Republicans, or Democratic Republicans (a name never used at the time), to distinguish this group from the later Republican Party. The Jeffersonian Republicans favored a more limited role for government. They believed that the nation's welfare would be best served if the states had more power than the central government. In their view, Congress should dominate the government, and government policies should serve farming interests rather than promote commerce and manufacturing.

From 1796 to 1860

The nation's first two parties clashed openly in the elections of 1796, in which John Adams, the Federalists' candidate to succeed George Washington as president, defeated Thomas Jefferson. Over the next four years, Jefferson and James Madison worked to extend the influence of the Jeffersonian Republican Party. In the presidential elections of 1800 and 1804, Jefferson won the presidency, and his party also won control of Congress.

TRIUMPH OF THE JEFFERSONIANS The transition of political power from the Federalists to the Republicans is the first example in American history of what political scientists have called a **realignment.** In a realignment, a substantial number of voters change their political allegiance, which usually also changes the balance of power between the two major parties. In fact, the Federalists never returned to power and thus became the first (but not the last) American party to go out of existence. (See the time line of American political parties in Figure 7–1 on the following page.)

realignment A process in which the popular support for and relative strength of the parties shift and the parties are reestablished with different coalitions of supporters.

Thomas Jefferson (1743–1826) became our third president and served two terms. The Jeffersonian Republicans (not to be confused with the later Republican Party of Abraham Lincoln) dominated American politics for more than two decades.

LIBRARY OF CONGRESS

The Jeffersonian Republicans dominated American politics for the next twenty years. Jefferson was succeeded in the White House by two other members of the party—James Madison and James Monroe. In the mid-1820s, however, the Republicans split into two groups. This was the second realignment in American history. Supporters of Andrew Jackson, who was elected president in 1828, called themselves Democrats. The Democrats appealed to small farmers and the growing class of urbanized workers. The other group, the National Republicans (later the Whig Party), was led by John Quincy Adams, Henry Clay, and the great orator Daniel Webster. It had the support of bankers, business owners, and many southern planters.

THE IMPENDING CRISIS As the Whigs and Democrats competed for the White House throughout the 1840s and 1850s, the two-party system as we know it today emerged. Both parties were large, with well-known leaders and supporters across the nation. Both had

Andrew Jackson (1767–1845) was part of the newly named party of Democrats. Jackson won the presidential election in 1828, defeating the candidate of the National Republicans.

LIBRARY OF CONGRESS

Figure 7–1

A Time Line of U.S. Political Parties

Many of these parties—including the Constitutional Union Party, Henry Wallace's Progressive Party, and the States' Rights Democrats—were important during only one presidential election.

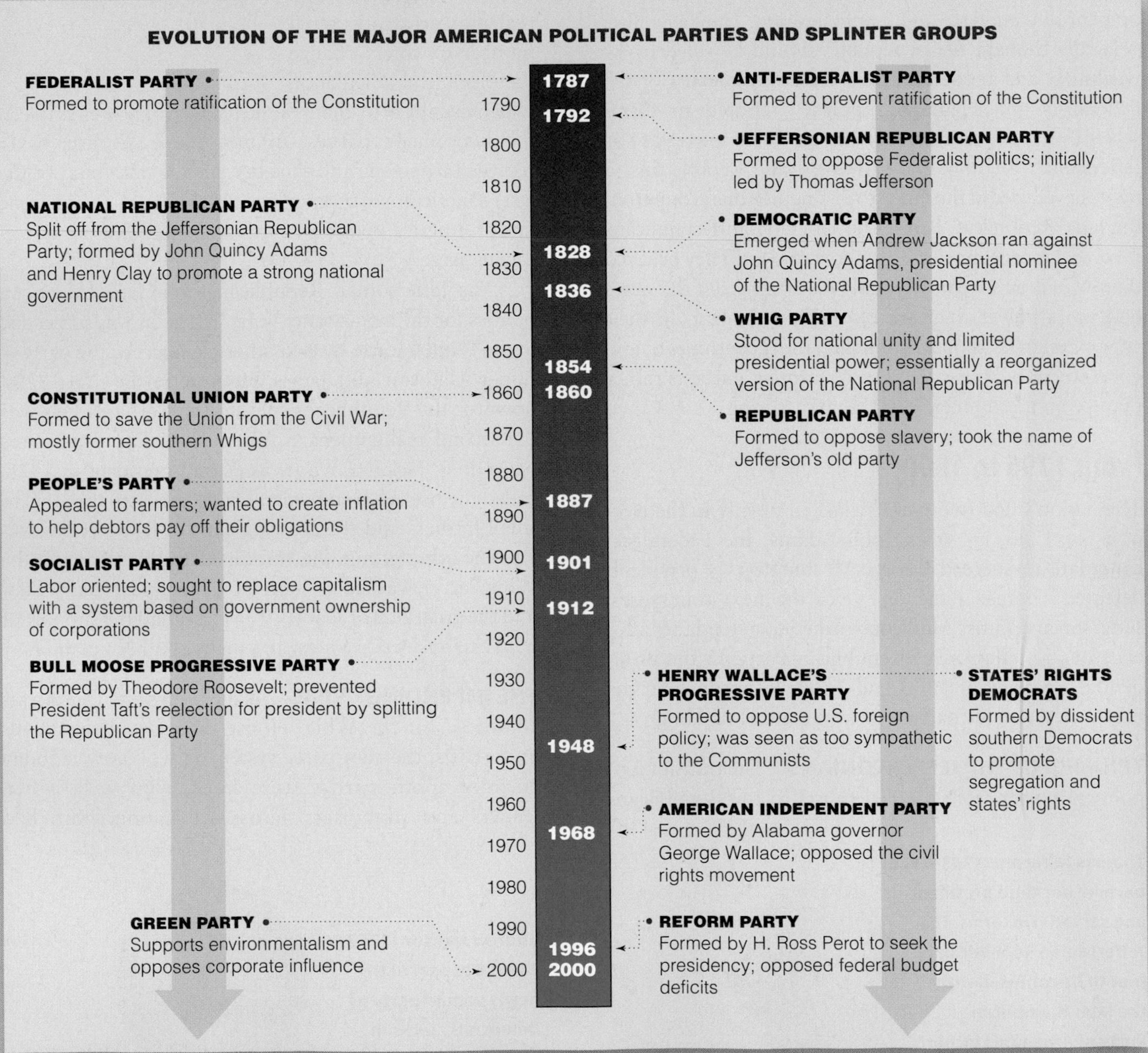

EVOLUTION OF THE MAJOR AMERICAN POLITICAL PARTIES AND SPLINTER GROUPS
FEDERALIST PARTY
Formed to promote ratification of the Constitution
1787
ANTI-FEDERALIST PARTY
Formed to prevent ratification of the Constitution
1790
1792
JEFFERSONIAN REPUBLICAN PARTY
Formed to oppose Federalist politics; initially led by Thomas Jefferson
1800
1810
NATIONAL REPUBLICAN PARTY
Split off from the Jeffersonian Republican Party; formed by John Quincy Adams and Henry Clay to promote a strong national government
1820
DEMOCRATIC PARTY
Emerged when Andrew Jackson ran against John Quincy Adams, presidential nominee of the National Republican Party
1828
1830
1836
WHIG PARTY
Stood for national unity and limited presidential power; essentially a reorganized version of the National Republican Party
1840
1850
1854
REPUBLICAN PARTY
Formed to oppose slavery; took the name of Jefferson's old party
CONSTITUTIONAL UNION PARTY
Formed to save the Union from the Civil War; mostly former southern Whigs
1860
1870
1880
PEOPLE'S PARTY
Appealed to farmers; wanted to create inflation to help debtors pay off their obligations
1887
1890
1900
SOCIALIST PARTY
Labor oriented; sought to replace capitalism with a system based on government ownership of corporations
1901
1910
1912
BULL MOOSE PROGRESSIVE PARTY
Formed by Theodore Roosevelt; prevented President Taft's reelection for president by splitting the Republican Party
1920
1930
HENRY WALLACE'S PROGRESSIVE PARTY
Formed to oppose U.S. foreign policy; was seen as too sympathetic to the Communists
STATES' RIGHTS DEMOCRATS
Formed by dissident southern Democrats to promote segregation and states' rights
1940
1948
1950
1960
AMERICAN INDEPENDENT PARTY
Formed by Alabama governor George Wallace; opposed the civil rights movement
1968
1970
1980
1990
GREEN PARTY
Supports environmentalism and opposes corporate influence
REFORM PARTY
Formed by H. Ross Perot to seek the presidency; opposed federal budget deficits
1996
2000

grassroots organizations of party workers committed to winning as many political offices (at all levels of government) for the party as possible. Both the Whigs and the Democrats tried to avoid the issue of slavery. By the mid-1850s, the Whig coalition had fallen apart, and most northern Whigs were absorbed into the new Republican Party, which opposed the extension of slavery into new territories. Campaigning on this platform, the Republicans succeeded in electing Abraham Lincoln the first president under the banner of the new Republican Party in 1860.

From the Civil War to the Great Depression

When the former Confederate states rejoined the Union after the Civil War, the Republicans and Democrats were roughly even in strength, although the Republicans were

From the election of Abraham Lincoln (shown here) in 1860 until the election of Franklin Delano Roosevelt in 1932, the Republican Party was the more successful party in presidential politics.

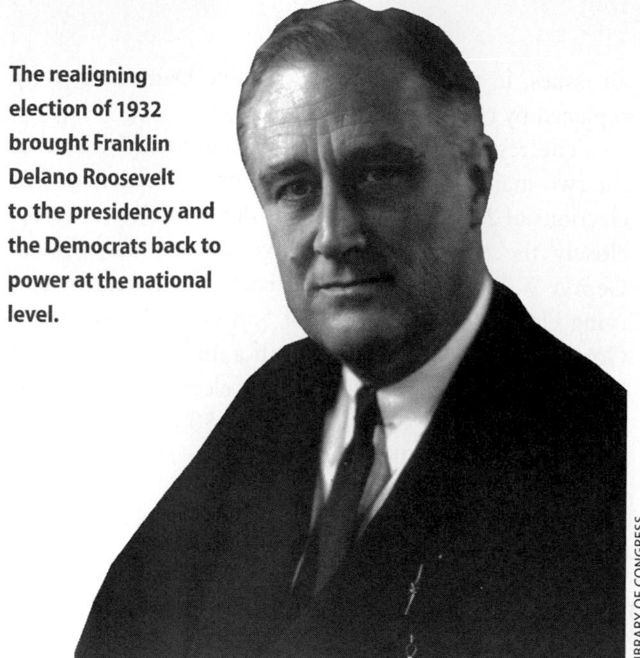

The realigning election of 1932 brought Franklin Delano Roosevelt to the presidency and the Democrats back to power at the national level.

more successful in presidential contests. In the 1890s, however, the Republicans gained a decisive advantage. In that decade, the Democrats allied themselves with the Populist movement, which consisted largely of indebted farmers in the West and South. The Populists—the People's Party—advocated inflation as a way of lessening their debts. Urban workers in the Midwest and East strongly opposed this program, which would erode the value of their paychecks. After the election of 1896, the Republicans established themselves in the minds of many Americans as the party that knew how to manage the nation's economy.

As a result of a Republican split, the Democrats under Woodrow Wilson won power from 1912 to 1920. Otherwise, the Republicans remained dominant in national politics until the onset of the Great Depression.

After the Great Depression

The Great Depression of the 1930s destroyed the belief that the Republicans could better manage the economy and contributed to another realignment in the two-party system. In a realignment, the minority (opposition) party may emerge as the majority party, and this is certainly what happened in 1932. (Realignment can also reestablish the majority party in power with a different coalition of supporters or leave the two parties closely balanced.) The election of 1932 brought Franklin D. Roosevelt to the presidency and the Democrats back to power at the national level. The elections of 1860 and 1896 are also considered to represent realignments.

A CIVIL RIGHTS PLANK Roosevelt's programs to fight the Depression were called the *New Deal*. Those who joined the Democrats during Roosevelt's New Deal included a substantial share of African Americans—Roosevelt's relief programs were open to people of all races. (Until the 1930s, African Americans had been overwhelmingly Republican.) In 1948, for the first time ever, the Democrats adopted a civil rights plank as part of the party platform at their national convention. A number of southern Democrats revolted and ran a separate States' Rights ticket for president.

In 1964, the Democrats, under incumbent president Lyndon Johnson, won a landslide victory, and liberals held a majority in Congress. In the political environment that produced this election result, a coalition of northern Democrats and Republicans crafted the major civil rights legislation that you read about in Chapter 5. The subsequent years were turbulent, with riots and marches in several major cities and student protests against the Vietnam War.

A "ROLLING REALIGNMENT" Conservative Democrats did not like the direction in which their party seemed to be taking them. Under President Richard Nixon, the Republican Party was receptive to these conservative Democrats, and over a period of years, most of them became Republican voters. This was a major alteration in the political landscape, although it was not exclusively associated with a single election. Republican president Ronald Reagan helped cement the new Republican coalition. The Democrats continued to hold majorities in the House and Senate until 1994, but partisan labels were somewhat misleading. During the 1970s and 1980s, a large bloc of Democrats in Congress, mostly from the South, sided with the Republicans on almost all issues. In time, these conservative Democrats were replaced by conservative Republicans.

The result of this "rolling realignment" was that the two major parties were fairly evenly matched. The elections of 2000 were a striking demonstration of how closely the electorate was now divided. Republican George W. Bush won the presidency in that year by carrying Florida with a margin of 538 votes. Democrat Al Gore actually received about half a million more popular votes than Bush. Following the elections, the Senate was made up of 50 Republicans and 50 Democrats. The Republicans controlled the House by a razor-thin margin of seven seats.

LO2 *America's Political Parties Today*

Historically, political parties drew together like-minded individuals. Today, too, individuals with similar characteristics tend to align themselves more often with one or the other major party. Such factors as race, age, income, education, marital status, and geography all influence party identification.

Red States versus Blue States

Geography is one of the many factors that can determine party identification. Examine the national electoral map shown below. In 2008, Republican John McCain did well in the South, on the Great Plains, and in parts of the Mountain West. Democrat Barack Obama did well in the Northeast, in the Midwest, and on the West Coast. Beginning with the presidential elections of 2000, the press has made much of the supposed cultural differences between the "blue" states that vote for the Democratic candidate and the "red" states that vote for the Republican.[3] In reality, though, many states could better be described as "purple"—that is, a mixture of red and blue. These states could give their electoral votes to either party.

For another way to consider the influence of geography, see the map of Ohio on the following page. Most of Ohio is red, and a quick glance might lead you to believe that McCain carried the state. In fact, Obama carried Ohio by a margin of 4.6 percentage points. Ohio looks red because McCain carried almost all of the rural parts of the state. The Obama counties had larger populations. This pattern was seen all over the country: the more urban the county, the more likely it was to vote Democratic.

Shifting Political Fortunes

As noted earlier, by 2000 the two major parties were very closely matched in terms of support. Public opinion polls reported that voters continued to view the parties with roughly equal favor.

TROUBLE FOR THE REPUBLICANS During 2005, however, the partisan deadlock began to break up. The grinding, seemingly endless war in Iraq began to cut into support for the Republicans. By 2006, that party had lost about 5 percentage points in popularity relative to the Democrats, as measured by Gallup. A poll in 2008 found that 51 percent of those surveyed identified with or leaned toward the Democratic Party. Only 37 percent identified with or leaned toward the Republicans. Even before the start of the Great Recession, therefore, the Republicans were in trouble. In 2006, the Democrats regained control of the House and Senate. In 2008, in the shadow of a global financial crisis, the Democrats elected Barack Obama as president.

TROUBLE FOR THE DEMOCRATS Within one year of Obama's inau-

This map shows the 2008 presidential election results by state. Note that Obama won a single electoral vote in Nebraska, which is represented by a symbol.

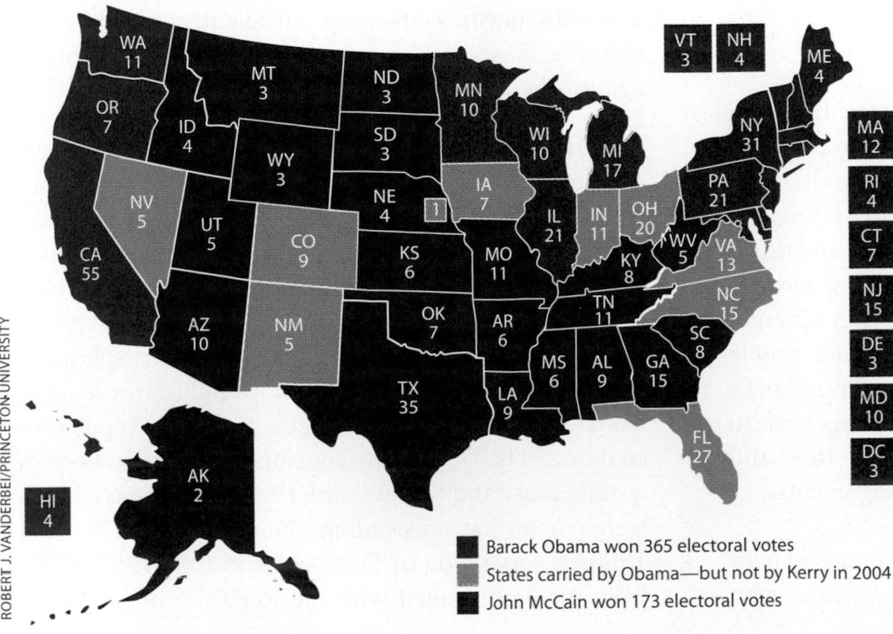

ROBERT J. VANDERBEI/PRINCETON UNIVERSITY

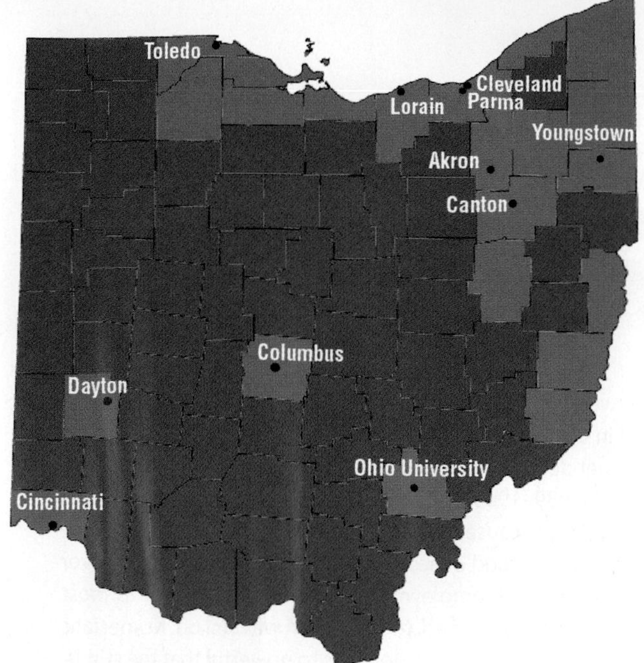

This map displays the Ohio counties carried by Barack Obama (blue) and John McCain (red) in the 2008 presidential elections. The cities shown on the map are the ten most populous municipalities in Ohio. Obama did well in urban and suburban counties, but poorly in nonmetropolitan regions. (Note that one nonmetropolitan county that Obama carried contains a major university.)

guration, the Democratic advantage had vanished. The party's favorability ratings dropped about 5 percentage points during 2009. Both parties were now distinctly less popular than they had been five years earlier. Democratic unpopularity was confirmed in January 2010, when Republican Scott Brown won the Massachusetts Senate seat formerly occupied by Democratic legend Ted Kennedy.

Arguments differ as to why the Democrats lost support. Continued high rates of unemployment were very important. Another reason may have been the dramatic increase in the size and scope of government during Obama's first two years. In February 2009, the Democrats adopted a large economic stimulus package.[4] Then came the bailouts of automobile giants Chrysler and General Motors (GM). In March 2010, Congress passed a massive health-care reform package. Millions of voters concluded that the government was growing too big, too fast.

THE TRIUMPH OF PARTISANSHIP A key characteristic of recent politics has been the extreme partisanship of party activists and members of Congress. As noted earlier, in the 1960s party coalitions contained a variety of factions with differing politics. Many Democrats in Congress were conservatives from the South. Likewise, the Republican Party contained a large liberal faction based in the Northeast. The rolling realignment after the elections of 1968 resulted in parties that were much more homogeneous. Political scientists have calculated that in the 111th Congress (2009–2011), the most conservative Democrat in the House was still to the left of the most moderate Republican.

Ideological uniformity has made it easier for the parties to maintain discipline in Congress. Personal friendships across party lines, once common in Congress, have become rare. The belief has grown that compromise with the other party is a form of betrayal. According to this view, the minority party should not attempt to improve legislation proposed by the majority, but it should oppose majority-party measures in an attempt to make the majority appear ineffective. The Republican Party was able to employ such tactics as early as the 1990s. Democrats soon began to match these capabilities. What impact did extreme partisanship have on the government's attempt to fight the Great Recession? We look at that question in this chapter's *Our Government Faces a Troubled Economy* feature on the following page.

Realignment, Dealignment, and Tipping

Despite the narrowness of the Republican margin after 2000, Republican strategists dreamed of a new realignment that would force the Democrats into the minority. These hopes were not fulfilled. After 2006, many Democrats anticipated a realignment that would benefit the Democrats. These dreams were shattered as well. For a major realignment to take place, a large number of voters must conclude that their party is no longer capable of representing their interests and ideals, and that another party can do better. It is hard to identify large groups of voters who could be swayed to support a different party today.

DEALIGNMENT One political development that may rule out realignment is the growth in the number of independent voters. By 2010, fully 40 percent of the electorate claimed to be independent. True, many of these voters admitted to leaning to the Republicans or the Democrats. Still, anyone claiming to be an independent has a weakened attachment to the parties. Some political scientists argue that with so many independent voters, the concept of realignment becomes irrelevant. Realignment has been replaced by **dealignment.**

TIPPING Realignment is not the only process that can alter the political landscape. What if

dealignment Among voters, a growing detachment from both major political parties.

Our Government Faces a Troubled Economy

No Retreat from Partisan Politics

The Great Recession was America's most serious economic crisis since the Great Depression. You might think that in such a crisis, the major political parties would put partisanship aside to find mutually acceptable solutions. Nothing of the sort happened. When the House took up President Obama's February 2009 stimulus bill, for example, not one Republican voted "yea."

Taxes—and Spending—and More Taxes Still

For many years, the Republicans have beaten the drum for lower taxes. When Republican president George W. Bush took office in 2001, his first major proposal was a series of sweeping tax cuts. Obama's stimulus package did contain some tax cuts. Most of the bill, however, consisted of new spending programs. In contrast, the Republican alternative to the stimulus package consisted entirely of tax cuts. Since that time, Democrats in Congress have enacted a number of tax increases. To pay for universal health care, Congress imposed new taxes on the highest-earning Americans and on the most expensive employer-paid medical plans. In late 2010, Democrats debated whether to let some or all of the Bush tax cuts expire. Republican hostility was severe, given the party's opposition to any tax increase at any time for any reason.

The Mighty, Mighty Deficit

In 2009, Democratic leaders were united in their belief in the necessity of a stimulus program. This belief, based on the theories of John Maynard Keynes, held that the government's budget deficit should rise in a recession and fall in a boom. Between increased government spending and an abrupt fall in tax revenues resulting from the recession, the nation's budget deficit did indeed rise to levels not seen since World War II (1939–1945). By 2010, the sheer size of the deficit was beginning to cause political problems for the Democrats. Few voters understood or accepted Keynesian arguments in favor of the deficit. Unemployment remained high. As far as most people were concerned, the recession was still on. Keynesians contended that the recession was so powerful that the stimulus could only moderate its effects.

A thumping majority of voters, however, concluded that the stimulus had no effects whatsoever—an idea the Republicans endorsed with enthusiasm. Given these attitudes, it was hard for the Democrats even to extend the duration of unemployment benefits, much less consider another stimulus bill.

Freshwater versus Saltwater Economics

While Keynesianism remains the majority view among experts, a different theory has taken hold at many universities. This alternative has been nicknamed "freshwater economics" because many of its advocates work at schools in the Great Lakes states. Likewise, Keynesianism has been dubbed "saltwater economics" because it is popular at many universities on the East and West Coasts. Many leading Republicans now advocate freshwater theories. Freshwater economists reject the proposition that deficits can be beneficial. They argue that sooner or later, all deficits must be paid off in full by the private sector. Freshwater advocates believe that individuals will react to budget deficits by spending less and saving more in preparation for higher taxes in the future. Indeed, saving in the United States is at record levels.

You Be the Judge **If we save more, isn't that good? Could increased savings prolong a recession? If so, how?**

the various types of voters maintain their political identifications—but one type of voter becomes substantially more numerous? This can happen due to migration between states or between counties, or even by changes in education levels and occupations. The result could tip a state from one party to another. Many Democratic strategists believe that such *tipping* will benefit their party greatly in the future.

ELECTIONS 2010

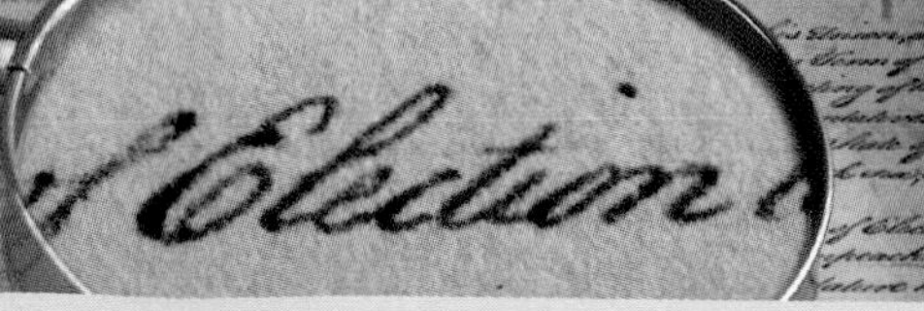

The Parties and the 2010 Elections

As you learned in Chapter 1, the Democratic Party clearly lost support among American voters. That did not mean, though, that the voters had fallen in love with the Republicans. Rather, a large share of those who went to the polls voted *against* the Democratic Party, and by association, against President Obama. Exit polls showed that many voters did not necessarily seek to put the Republicans back into power but rather sought to punish the Democrats. Both parties were viewed with suspicion by more than half of all eligible voters—in fact, the parties were about tied in negative perceptions.

Whatever their reasons, the voters gave the Republican Party a clear majority in the House and reduced the Democratic advantage in the Senate. With the two chambers in the hands of different parties, it was unlikely that the incoming Congress would be able to accomplish much.

At the state level, more than 680 Republicans won legislative seats. The twenty-nine governorships that were now in Republican hands also strengthened that party at the state level. (One new governor is an independent.) The majorities that Republicans obtained in state legislatures, plus the new Republican governors, yielded one important result. The Republicans were now well-placed to gerrymander election districts in their favor during the upcoming reapportionment based on the 2010 Census.

LO3 What Do Political Parties Do?

As noted earlier, the Constitution does not mention political parties. Historically, though, political parties have played a vital role in our democratic system. Their main function has been to link the people's policy preferences to actual government policies. Political parties also perform many other functions.

Selecting Candidates

One of the most important functions of the two political parties is to recruit and nominate candidates for political office. This function simplifies voting choices for the electorate. Political parties take the large number of people who want to run for office and narrow the field. They accomplish this by the use of the **primary,** which is a preliminary election to choose a party's final candidate. This candidate then runs against the opposing party's candidate in the general election.

Voter turnout for primaries is lower than it is for general elections. The voters who do go to the polls are often strong supporters of their party. Indeed, in many states, independents cannot participate in primary elections, even if they lean toward one or the other of the two major parties. As a result, the Republican primary electorate is very conservative, and Democratic primary voters are quite liberal. Candidates often find that they must run to the political right or left during the primaries. Frequently, they then move to the center during the general election campaign. Chapter 9 provides much more detail on primary and general elections.

Informing the Public

Political parties help educate the public about important political issues. In recent years, these issues have included environmental policies, health-care reform, our tax system, education, Social Security, and ways to stimulate the economy. Each party presents its view of these issues through television announcements, newspaper articles or ads, Web site materials, campaign speeches, rallies, debates, and leaflets. These activities help citizens learn about the issues, form opinions, and consider proposed solutions.

Coordinating Policymaking

In our complex government, parties are essential for coordinating policy among the various branches of the government. The political party is usually the major institution through which the executive and legislative branches cooperate with each other. Each president, cabinet head, and member of Congress is normally a member of the Democratic or the Republican Party. The president works through party leaders in Congress to promote the administration's legislative program.

primary A preliminary election held for the purpose of choosing a party's final candidate.

minority party The political party that has fewer members in the legislature than the opposing party.

majority party The political party that has more members in the legislature than the opposing party.

coalition An alliance of individuals or groups with a variety of interests and opinions who join together to support all or part of a political party's platform.

Ideally, the parties work together to fashion compromises—legislation that is acceptable to both parties and that serves the national interest. In recent years, however, there has been little bipartisanship in Congress. (For a more detailed discussion of the role played by political parties in Congress, see Chapter 11.) Parties also act as the glue of our federal structure by connecting the various levels of government—state and national—with a common bond.

Checking the Power of the Governing Party

The party with fewer members in the legislature is the **minority party.** The party with more members is the **majority party.** The party that does not control Congress or a state legislature, or the presidency or a state governorship, also plays a vital function in American politics. The "out party" does what it can to influence the "in party" and its policies, and to check the actions of the party in power. For example, depending on how evenly Congress is divided, the out party, or minority party, may be able to attract to its side some of the members of the majority party to pass or defeat certain legislation. The out party will also work to inform the voters of the shortcomings of the in party's agenda and to plan strategies for winning the next election.

Balancing Competing Interests

Political parties are often described as vast umbrellas under which Americans with diverse interests can gather. Political parties are essentially **coalitions**—individuals and groups with a variety of interests and opinions who join together to support the party's platform, or parts of it.

The Republican Party, for example, includes a number of groups with different views on such issues as health care, immigration, and global warming. The role of party leaders in this situation is to adopt a broad enough view on these issues that the various groups will not be alienated. In this way, different groups can hold their individual views and still come together under the umbrella of the Republican Party. Leaders of both the Democratic Party and the Republican Party modify contending views and arrange compromises among different groups. In so doing, the parties help to unify, rather than divide, their members.

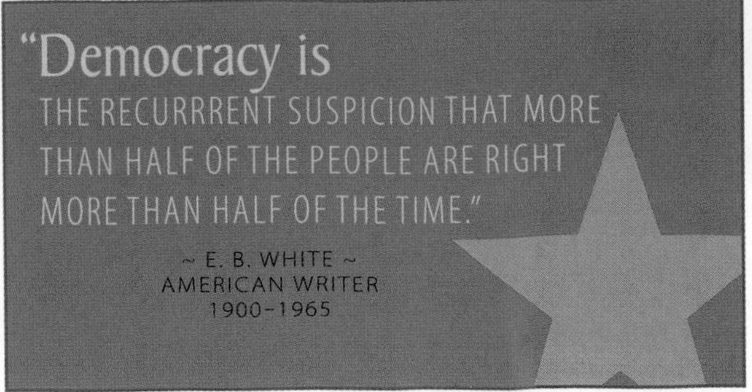

"Democracy is
THE RECURRRENT SUSPICION THAT MORE THAN HALF OF THE PEOPLE ARE RIGHT MORE THAN HALF OF THE TIME."
~ E. B. WHITE ~
AMERICAN WRITER
1900–1965

Running Campaigns

Through their national, state, and local organizations, parties coordinate campaigns. Political parties take care of a large number of small and routine tasks that are essential to the smooth functioning of the electoral process. For example, they work at getting party members registered and at conducting drives for new voters. Sometimes, party volunteers staff the polling places.

LO4 *How American Political Parties Are Structured*

Each of the two major American political parties consists of three components: the party in the electorate, the party organization, and the party in government.

Every political campaign relies on volunteers at the grassroots level, such as these volunteers in Baldwin Park, California. They are tallying votes for their candidate on the evening of election day.

ZUMA PRESS/NEWSCOM

1. The party in the **electorate** is the largest component, consisting of all of those people who describe themselves as Democrats or Republicans. Members of the party in the electorate never need to work on a campaign or attend a party meeting. In most states, they may register as Democrats or Republicans, but registration can be changed at will. Members of parties do not have to work for the party or attend party meetings. Nor must they support the party platform.

2. Each major party has a nationwide organization with national, state, and local offices. As will be discussed later in this section, the party organizations include several levels of people who maintain the party's strength between elections, make its rules, raise money, organize conventions, help with elections, and recruit candidates.

3. The party in government consists of all of the party's candidates who have won elections and now hold public office. Even though members of Congress, state legislators, presidents, and all other officeholders almost always run for office as either Democrats or Republicans, members of any one party do not always agree with each other on government policy. The party in government helps to organize the government's agenda by coaxing and convincing its own party members to vote for its policies. If the party is to translate its promises into public policies, the job must be done by the party in government.

"Under democracy one party always devotes its chief energies to trying to prove that the other party is **UNFIT TO RULE** —and both commonly succeed."

~ H. L. MENCKEN ~
AMERICAN JOURNALIST
1880–1956

The Party in the Electorate

Let's look more closely at the largest component of each party—the party in the electorate. What does it mean to belong to a political party? In many European countries, being a party member means that you actually join a political party. You get a membership card to carry in your wallet, you pay dues, and you vote to select your local and national party leaders. In the United States, becoming a member of a political party is far less involved.

In most states, voters may declare a party preference when they register to vote. This declaration allows them to participate in party primaries. Some states do not register party preferences, however. In short, to be a member of a political party, an American citizen has only to think of herself or himself as a Democrat or a Republican (or a member of a third party, such as the Green Party, the Libertarian Party, or the American Independent Party).

IDENTIFIERS AND ACTIVISTS Generally, the party in the electorate consists of **party identifiers** (those who identify themselves as being members of a particular party) and **party activists**—party members who choose to work for the party and even become candidates for office. Political parties need year-round support from the latter group to survive. During election campaigns in particular, candidates depend on active party members or volunteers to mail literature, answer phones, conduct door-to-door canvasses, organize speeches and appearances, and, of course, donate money.

Between elections, parties also need active members to plan the upcoming elections, organize fund-raisers, and stay in touch with party leaders in other communities to keep the party strong. The major functions of American political parties are carried out by the party activists.

WHY PEOPLE JOIN POLITICAL PARTIES Generally, in the United States people belong to a political party because they agree with many of its main ideas and support some of its candidates. In a few countries, such as the People's Republic of China, people belong to a political party because they are required to do so to get ahead in life, regardless of whether they agree with the party's ideas and candidates.

People join political parties for a multitude of reasons. One reason is that people wish to express their **solidarity,** or mutual agreement, with the views of friends, loved ones, and other like-minded people. People also join parties because they enjoy the excitement of politics.

In addition, many believe they will benefit materially from joining a party through better employment or personal

electorate All of the citizens eligible to vote in a given election.

party identifier A person who identifies himself or herself as being a supporter of a particular political party.

party activist A party member who helps to organize and oversee party functions and planning during and between campaigns.

solidarity Mutual agreement among the members of a particular group.

AP PHOTO/PAUL SANCYA

During the Denver Democratic National Convention in 2008, presidential candidate Barack Obama, then a senator from Illinois, takes center stage with vice-presidential candidate Joe Biden, then a senator from Delaware.

career advancement. The traditional institution of **patronage**—rewarding the party faithful with government jobs or contracts—lives on, even though it has been limited to prevent abuses.[5] Back in the nineteenth century, when almost all government employees got their jobs through patronage, people spoke of it as the "spoils system," as in "the spoils of war."

Finally, some join political parties because they wish to actively promote a set of ideals and principles that they feel are important to American politics and society. As a rule, people join political parties because of their overall agreement with what a particular party stands for. Thus, when interviewed, people may make the following remarks when asked why they support the Democratic Party: "It seems that the economy is better when the Democrats are in control." "The Democrats are for the working people." People might say about the Republican Party: "The Republicans help small businesses more than the Democrats." "The Republicans deal better with foreign policy and defense issues."

The Party Organization

In theory, each of the major American political parties has a standard, pyramid-shaped organization. This theoretical structure is much like that of a large company, in which the bosses are at the top and the employees are at various lower levels.

patronage A system of rewarding the party faithful and workers with government jobs or contracts.

Actually, neither major party is a closely knit or highly organized structure. Both parties are fragmented and *decentralized,* which means there is no central power with a direct chain of command. If there were, the national chairperson of the party, along with the national committee, could simply dictate how the organization would be run, just as if it were Microsoft or General Electric. In reality, state party organizations are all very different and are only loosely tied to the party's national structure. Local party organizations are often quite independent from the state organization. There is no single individual or group who directs all party members. Instead, a number of personalities, frequently at odds with one another, form loosely identifiable leadership groups.

STATE ORGANIZATIONS The powers and duties of state party organizations differ from state to state. In general, the state party organization is built around a central committee and a chairperson. The committee works to raise funds, recruit new party members, maintain a strong party organization, and help members running for state offices.

The state chairperson is usually a powerful party member chosen by the committee. In some instances, however, the chairperson is selected by the governor or a senator from that state.

Then Alaska governor Sarah Palin is shown giving her acceptance speech as candidate for vice president at the Republican National Convention in St. Paul, Minnesota, in 2008.

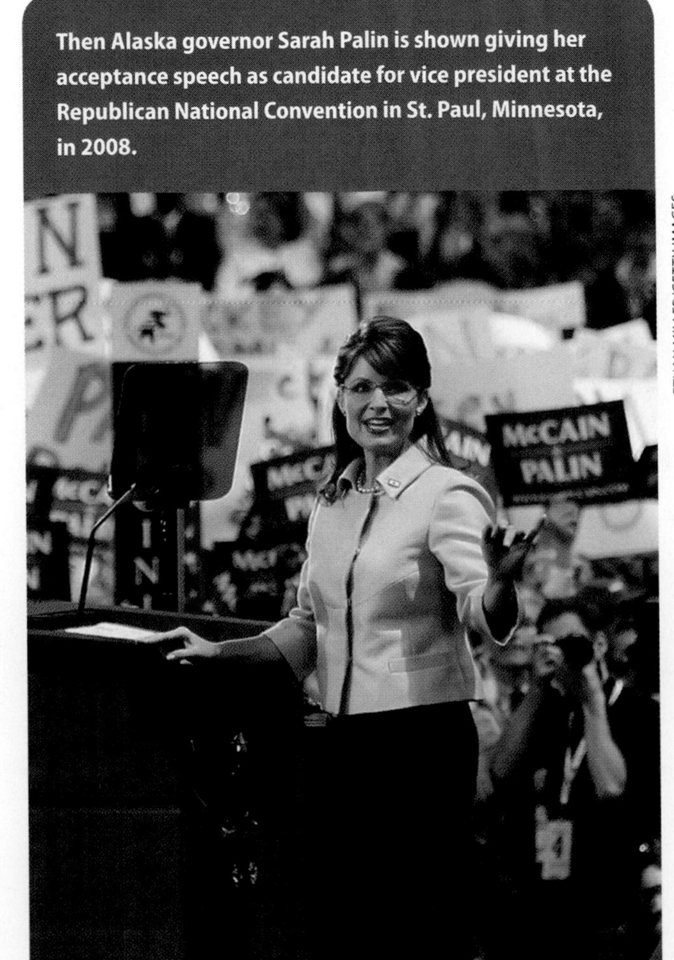

ETHAN MILLER/GETTY IMAGES

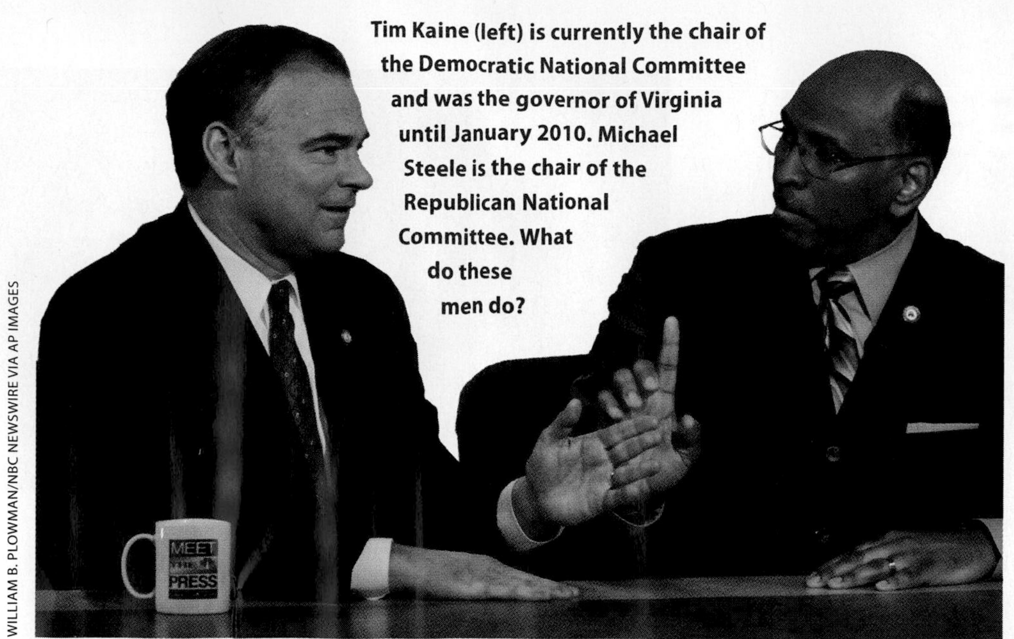

Tim Kaine (left) is currently the chair of the Democratic National Committee and was the governor of Virginia until January 2010. Michael Steele is the chair of the Republican National Committee. What do these men do?

WILLIAM B. PLOWMAN/NBC NEWSWIRE VIA AP IMAGES

ward A local unit of a political party's organization, consisting of a division or district within a city.

precinct A political district within a city, such as a block or a neighborhood, or a rural portion of a county; the smallest voting district at the local level.

national convention The meeting held by each major party every four years to select presidential and vice-presidential candidates, write a party platform, and conduct other party business.

party ticket A list of a political party's candidates for various offices. In national elections, the party ticket consists of the presidential and vice-presidential candidates.

party platform The document drawn up by each party at its national convention that outlines the policies and positions of the party.

national party committee The political party leaders who direct party business during the four years between the national party conventions, organize the next national convention, and plan how to obtain a party victory in the next presidential elections.

national party chairperson An individual who serves as a political party's administrative head at the national level and directs the work of the party's national committee.

LOCAL ORGANIZATIONS Local party organizations differ greatly, but generally there is a party unit for each district in which elective offices are to be filled. These districts include congressional and legislative districts, counties, cities and towns, wards, and precincts.

A **ward** is a political division or district within a city. A **precinct** can be either a political district within a city, such as a block or a neighborhood, or a rural portion of a county. Polling places are located within the precincts. The local, grassroots foundations of politics are formed within voting precincts.

THE NATIONAL PARTY ORGANIZATION On the national level, the party's presidential candidate is considered to be the leader of the party. Well-known members of Congress may also be viewed as national party leaders. In addition to the party leaders, the structure of each party includes four major elements: the national convention, the national committee, the national chairperson, and the congressional campaign committees.

The National Convention Much of the public attention that the party receives comes at the **national convention,** which is held every four years during the summer before the presidential elections. The news media always cover these conventions, and as a result, they have become quite extravagant. Are these extravaganzas worth the cost? We look at that question in this chapter's *Join the Debate* feature on the following page.

The national conventions are attended by delegates chosen by the states in various ways, which we describe in Chapter 9. The delegates' most important job is to choose the party's presidential and vice-presidential candidates, who together make up the **party ticket.** The delegates also write the **party platform,** which sets forth the party's positions on national issues. Essentially, through its platform, the party promises to initiate certain policies if it wins the presidency. Despite the widespread perception that candidates can and do ignore these promises once they are in office, in fact, many of them become law.

The National Committee Each state elects a number of delegates to the **national party committee.** The Republican National Committee and the Democratic National Committee direct the business of their respective parties during the four years between national conventions. The committees' most important duties, however, are to organize the next national convention and to plan how to obtain a party victory in the next presidential elections.

The National Chairperson Each party's national committee elects a **national party chairperson** to serve as administrative head of the national party. The main duty of the national chairperson is to direct the work of the national committee from party headquarters in Washington, D.C. The chairperson is involved in raising

JOIN THE DEBATE

Are National Party Conventions Worth the Cost?

CHUCK KENNEDY-POOL/GETTY IMAGES

For many decades, national party conventions were important to the nomination of each party's presidential candidate. In modern times, however, each party has already chosen its candidates for president and vice president before the conventions begin. Nonetheless, state delegates continue to attend the four-day extravaganzas that each party holds every four years, and so do the media, political commentators, and quite a few entertainers.

At the 2008 Democratic Party convention in Denver, members of Congress were able to hear singer Kanye West, courtesy of the recording industry. Others were given $5,000 to play poker at a tournament that featured actor Ben Affleck. At the 2008 Republican Party convention, some lucky delegates were invited to the Aqua Nightclub in Minneapolis to hear the band Smash Mouth. Both conventions cost over $100 million. Are national party conventions worth the cost?

It's Not Just Flash and Partying

Those who defend the conventions point out that they inspire and mobilize party members throughout the nation. They provide the voters with an opportunity to see and hear the candidates directly, rather than through the filter of the media or through characterizations provided by supporters and opponents. Candidate speeches draw huge audiences. For example, in 2008, more than 38 million people watched the acceptance speeches of Barack Obama and John McCain.

Don't forget the unifying nature of most national party conventions. At the 2008 Democratic convention in Denver, supporters of Hillary Clinton were not necessarily convinced that they should support Barack Obama. By the end of that convention, many of these voters had decided that they could indeed endorse him. At the 2008 Republican convention in St. Paul, a humorous and aggressive acceptance speech by vice-presidential candidate Sarah Palin not only electrified the attending delegates but also served as a way to unify the party behind the ticket. In short, conventions are well worth their costs.

No More Wretched Excess

Who needs multimillion-dollar national conventions to ratify the nominations of presidential and vice-presidential candidates who have already been chosen? What party business is there that cannot be done with less time and expense? In 2008, during a period of economic struggle for many Americans, the spending of millions of dollars on superfluous activities in Denver and St. Paul certainly did not send the right signals.

And where did all that money come from? You guessed it—lobbyists, big business, and labor unions. In spite of new congressional ethics rules designed to curb the influence of these groups, they spent more in 2008 than ever before. Those millions are not spent to further the general welfare—they come from companies and associations that depend on government subsidies, tax breaks, or regulatory favors from Washington, D.C.

For Critical Analysis ***The parties often pick the states that host their national conventions in the hope of enhancing their performance in those states. Do you think that holding a party's convention in a particular state will win votes from its voters? Why or why not?***

funds, providing for publicity, promoting party unity, encouraging the development of state and local organizations, recruiting new voters, and other activities. In presidential election years, the chairperson's attention is focused on the national convention and the presidential campaign.

The Congressional Campaign Committees Each party has a campaign committee, made up of senators and representatives, in each chamber of Congress. Members are chosen by their colleagues and serve for two-year terms. The committees work to help reelect party members to Congress.

The Party in Government: Developing Issues

When a political party wins the presidency or control of one or more chambers of Congress, it has the opportunity to carry out the party platform it developed at its national convention. The platform represents the official party position on various issues, although as just mentioned, neither all party members nor all candidates running on the party's ticket are likely to share these positions exactly.

HOW PRESIDENTS RESPOND TO PARTY PLATFORMS Party platforms do not necessarily tell you what candidates are going to do when they take office. For example, although the Democratic Party generally favors social legislation to help low-income individuals, it was a Democratic president, Bill Clinton, who signed a major welfare reform bill in 1996, forcing many welfare recipients off the welfare rolls. The Democrats usually have the support of labor unions, yet President Clinton approved the North American Free Trade Agreement despite bitter opposition from most of the nation's unions. Additionally, the Democrats have traditionally been associated with "big government" and deficit spending, but under President Bill Clinton there was a budget surplus for several years in a row.

Similarly, although the Republican Party has long advocated "small government" and states' rights, federal government spending was taken to new heights during the George W. Bush administration, budget surpluses disappeared, and legislation such as the No Child Left Behind Act effectively transferred power from the states to the federal government.

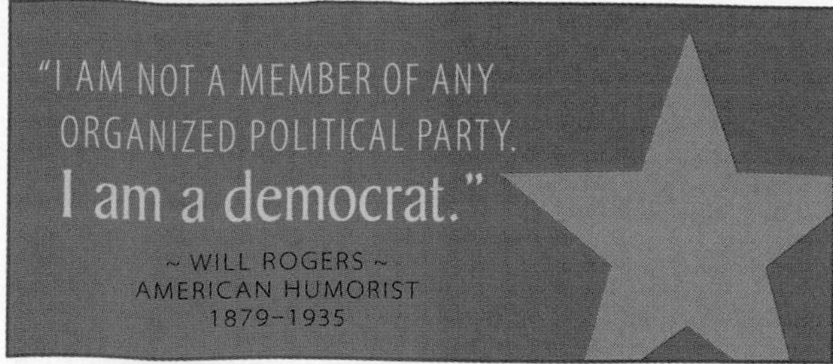

THE PARTIES RETURN TO THEIR ROOTS Following the elections of 2008, the Republican Party appeared to regain its traditional appreciation for states' rights. To a considerable extent, this return to tradition was fueled by the dramatic ambitions of President Obama and the Democratic Party. In reality, the new measures adopted by the Democrats in 2009 and 2010 did not tend to strip power away from the states. Rather, the federal government gained power largely at the expense of the private sector.

Many conservatives, however, saw the states as a force that could counter the federal government. This view led to such actions as state lawsuits challenging the Democrat's health-care reform legislation, discussed in the *Join the Debate* feature in Chapter 3.

Texas delegates at the 2008 Republican Party national convention bow their heads during the invocation on the last day. Do these delegates have any real power to elect their party's presidential candidate when attending this convention?

SARA KRULWICH/*THE NEW YORK TIMES*/REDUX

LO5 *The Dominance of Our Two-Party System*

In the United States, we have a **two-party system.** This means that the two major parties—the Democrats and the Republicans—dominate national politics. Why has the two-party system become so firmly entrenched in the United States? According to some scholars, the first major political division between the Federalists and the Anti-Federalists established a precedent that continued over time and ultimately resulted in the domination of the two-party system.

As noted earlier, about a third of the voters identify themselves as independents (although they may lean toward one party or the other). For these individuals, both of the major parties evidently fail to address issues that are important to them or represent their views. Nonetheless, the two-party system

two-party system A political system in which two strong and established parties compete for political offices.

Most colleges and universities have mascots that represent their athletic teams. So, too, do the two major political parties. On the left, you see the donkey that became the Democratic Party mascot. On the right, you see the elephant that became the Republican Party mascot.[6]

continues to thrive. A number of factors help to explain this phenomenon.

The Self-Perpetuation of the Two-Party System

One of the major reasons for the perpetuation of the two-party system is simply that there is no alternative. Minor parties, called **third parties,**[7] have found it extremely difficult to compete with the major parties for votes. There are many reasons for this, including election laws and institutional barriers.

ELECTION LAWS FAVORING TWO PARTIES American election laws tend to favor the major parties. In many states, for example, the established major parties need relatively few signatures to place their candidates on the ballot, whereas a third party must get many more signatures. The number of signatures required is often based on the total party vote in the last election, which penalizes a new party competing for the first time.

The rules governing campaign financing also favor the major parties. As you will read in Chapter 9, both major parties receive federal funds for presidential campaigns and for their national conventions. Third parties, in contrast, receive federal funds only if they garner 5 percent of the vote, and they receive the funds only *after* the election.

third party In the United States, any party other than one of the two major parties (Republican and Democratic).

INSTITUTIONAL BARRIERS TO A MULTIPARTY SYSTEM The structure of many of our institutions prevents third parties from enjoying electoral success. One of the major institutional barriers is the winner-take-all feature of the electoral college system for electing the president (discussed in more detail in Chapter 9). In a winner-take-all system, which applies in all but two of the states (Maine and Nebraska), the winner of a state's popular vote gets all of that state's electoral votes. Thus, third-party candidates have little incentive to run for president, because they are unlikely to get enough popular votes to receive any state's electoral votes.

Another institutional barrier to a multiparty system is the single-member district. Today, all federal and most state legislative districts are single-member districts—that is, voters elect one member from their district to the House of Representatives and to their state legislature.[8] In most European countries, by contrast, districts are drawn as multimember districts and are represented by multiple elected officials from different parties, according to the proportion of the vote their party received.

DUVERGER'S LAW In nations around the world, the association between multimember districts (or proportional representation) and multiple political parties is strong. So is the association between single-member, first-past-the-post districts and two-party systems. These relationships are firm enough that some scholars have called them a "law" of political science—*Duverger's Law,* named after French political scientist Maurice Duverger.

THE REST OF THE WORLD

Britain's Coalition Government

Coalition governments are impossible in the United States because we do not have a *parliamentary system.* Britain, Canada, Germany, and many other countries do use parliamentary systems, however.

First, a Few Basics

Britain—the United Kingdom—has a typical parliamentary system. Members of Parliament are elected just as we elect members of Congress. Here the similarity ends. British voters do not choose a chief executive, as we do in the United States when we vote for president. Rather, the chief executive is chosen by the *lower house* of Parliament—the House of Commons, analogous to our House of Representatives. (There is an upper house, the House of Lords, but it has little power.)

Each party selects a leader well before the general elections. The leader then chooses other members of Parliament who, if the party wins, will take cabinet posts, such as minister of defense or minister of justice. If one party wins a majority of the seats in the House of Commons, it can name its leader as the *prime minister*—the chief executive of the nation. The Queen then formally appoints the new government.

In the rare event that no party has a majority in the Commons, two options are possible. The largest party can form a "minority government" with the acquiescence of other parties. Alternatively, two or more parties can agree to form a coalition government. Many countries that use the parliamentary system are normally governed by coalitions, although until 2010 Britain had not had one for decades.

The British Parties

Just as in the United States, British legislators are elected in single-member districts. This system makes it difficult for third parties to organize, but over the last century Britain has always had important third parties. In the nineteenth century, the two major parties were the Conservatives and the Liberals. In the early twentieth century, however, the Liberals lost their position as a major party to the Labour Party. The Liberals never vanished entirely. Under the name Liberal Democrats, they are Britain's main third party today. (Other minor parties contest seats only in particular regions.) The Labour Party is the main left-of-center party in Britain. It was originally organized to defend labor unions, but it soon grew into a broader left-wing movement. On the right is the Conservative Party, often called the Tories.

The New British Coalition Government

In 2010, the unthinkable happened in Britain—the first coalition government in sixty-five years was formed. The prime minister is Conservative David Cameron, the youngest person to hold this post in almost two centuries. The deputy prime minister is Liberal Democrat Nick Clegg. Before the elections that led to the coalition, Britain was governed by Labour.

In short order, the coalition government unveiled a plan to make severe cuts to Britain's huge budget deficit. Although some taxes were raised, most of the deficit reduction will come from spending cuts. Except for the National Health Service, every government department will have to shrink by 20 to 30 percent over the next few years. Will the coalition succeed in reducing the size of Britain's government? The future of this "great gamble" is less than clear.

For Critical Analysis *Why don't sitting members of the U.S. Congress ever join the president's cabinet?*

Still, many nations have single-member constituencies and three or more major political parties. Canada and Britain are examples. To guarantee a two-party system, it is probably necessary also to have directly elected executive officers, such as the president and various state governors in the United States. Third parties may be able to elect a few members to a legislature, but winning a nationwide vote for chief executive is typically hopeless. For a closer look at Britain's multiparty system, see the feature *The Rest of the World: Britain's Coalition Government* above.

Third Parties in American Politics

Despite difficulties, throughout American history, third parties have competed for influence in the nation's two-party system. Indeed, as mentioned earlier, third parties have been represented in most of our national elections.

These parties are as varied as the causes they represent, but all have one thing in common: their members and leaders want to challenge the major parties because they believe that certain needs and values are not being properly addressed.

Some third parties have tried to appeal to the entire nation. Others have focused on particular regions, states, or local areas. Most third parties have been short lived. A few, however, such as the Socialist Party (founded in 1901 and disbanded in 1972), lasted for a long time. The number and variety of third parties make them difficult to classify, but most fall into one of the general categories discussed in the following subsections.

> "Let us not seek the Republican answer or the Democratic answer, but the **RIGHT ANSWER.**"
>
> ~ JOHN FITZGERALD KENNEDY ~ THIRTY-FIFTH PRESIDENT OF THE UNITED STATES 1961–1963

ISSUE-ORIENTED PARTIES An issue-oriented third party is formed to promote a particular cause or timely issue. For example, the Free Soil Party was organized in 1848 to oppose the expansion of slavery into the western territories. The Prohibition Party was formed in 1869 to advocate banning the manufacture and use of alcoholic beverages.

Most issue-oriented parties fade into history as the issue that brought them into existence fades from public attention, is taken up by a major party, or is resolved. Some issue-oriented parties endure, however, when they expand their focus beyond a single area of concern. For example, the Green Party was founded in 1972 to raise awareness of environmental issues, but it is no longer a single-issue party. Ralph Nader, the presidential candidate for the Green Party in 2000, campaigned against alleged corporate greed and the major parties' ostensible indifference to a number of issues, including universal health insurance, child poverty, the excesses of globalism, and the failure of the drug war.

IDEOLOGICAL PARTIES As discussed in Chapter 1, a *political ideology* is a system of political ideas rooted in beliefs about human nature, society, and government. An ideological party supports a particular political doctrine or a set of beliefs. For example, a party such as the (still-existing) Socialist Workers Party may believe that our free enterprise system should be replaced by one in which workers own all of the factories in the economy. The party's members may believe that competition should be replaced by cooperation and social responsibility so as to achieve an equitable distribution of income. In contrast, an ideological party such as the Libertarian Party may oppose virtually all forms of government interference with personal liberties and private enterprise.

SPLINTER OR PERSONALITY PARTIES A splinter party develops out of a split within a major party. This split may be part of an attempt to elect a specific person. For example, when Theodore Roosevelt did not receive the Republican Party's nomination for president in 1912, he created the Bull Moose Party (also called the Progressive Party) to promote his candidacy. From the Democrats have come Henry Wallace's Progressive Party and the States' Rights (Dixiecrat) Party, both formed in 1948. In 1968, the American Independent Party was formed to support George Wallace's campaign for president.

Most splinter parties have been formed around a leader with a strong personality, which is why they are sometimes called personality parties. When that person steps aside, the party usually collapses. An example of a personality party is the Reform Party, which was formed in 1996 mainly to provide a campaign vehicle for H. Ross Perot.

The Effects of Third Parties

Although most Americans do not support third parties or vote for their candidates, third parties have influenced American politics in several ways, some of which we examine here.

THIRD PARTIES BRING ISSUES TO THE PUBLIC'S ATTENTION Third parties have brought many political issues to the public's attention. They have exposed

Theodore Roosevelt and his Progressive (Bull Moose) Party changed the outcome of the 1912 election.

BETTMANN/CORBIS

Figure 7–2

The Effect of Third Parties on Vote Distribution, 1848–1992

In eight presidential elections, a third party's candidate received more than 10 percent of the popular vote—and in six of those elections, the incumbent party lost. As shown here, only in 1856 and 1924 did the incumbent party manage to hold on to the White House in the face of a significant third-party showing.

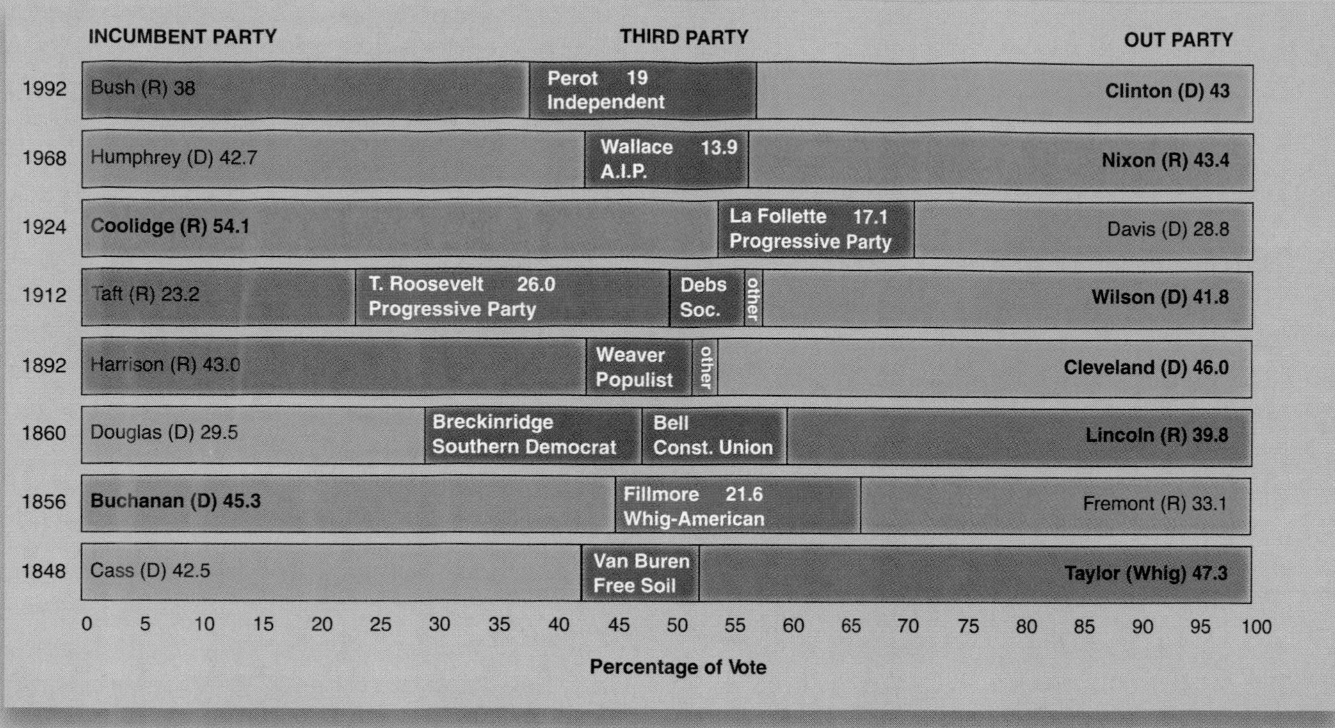

Source: *Congressional Quarterly Weekly Report*, June 13, 1992, p. 1729.

and focused on unpopular or highly debated issues that major parties have preferred to ignore. Third parties are in a position to take bold stands on issues that major parties avoid, because third parties are not trying to be all things to all people. Progressive social reforms such as the minimum wage, women's right to vote, railroad and banking legislation, and old-age pensions were first proposed by third parties. The Free Soilers of the 1850s, for example, were the first true antislavery party, and the Populists and Progressives put many social reforms on the political agenda.

Some people have argued that third parties are often the unsung heroes of American politics, bringing new issues to the forefront of public debate. Some of the ideas proposed by third parties were never accepted, while others were taken up by the major parties as those ideas became increasingly popular.

THIRD PARTIES CAN AFFECT THE VOTE Third parties can also influence election outcomes. Third parties have occasionally taken victory from one major party and given it to another, thus playing the "spoiler" role.

For example, in 1912, when the Progressive Party split off from the Republican Party, the result was three major contenders for the presidency: Woodrow Wilson, the Democratic candidate; William Howard Taft, the regular Republican candidate; and Theodore Roosevelt, the Progressive candidate. The presence of the Progressive Party "spoiled" the Republicans' chances for victory and gave the election to Wilson, the Democrat. Without Roosevelt's third party, Taft might have won. Similarly, some commentators contended that Ralph Nader "spoiled" the chances of Democratic candidate Al Gore in the 2000 elections, because many of those who voted for Nader would have voted Democratic had Nader not been a candidate.

A significant showing by a minor party also reduces an incumbent party's chances of winning the election, as you can see in Figure 7–2 above. In 1992, for example, third-party candidate H. Ross Perot captured about 19 percent of the vote. Had those votes been distributed between the candidates of the major parties, incumbent George H. W. Bush and candidate Bill Clinton, the outcome of the election might have been different.

THIRD PARTIES PROVIDE A VOICE FOR DISSATISFIED AMERICANS Third parties also provide a voice for voters who are frustrated with and alienated from the

Republican and Democratic parties. Americans who are unhappy with the two major political parties can still participate in American politics through third parties that reflect their opinions on political issues. For example, many new Minnesota voters turned out during the 1998 elections to vote for Jesse Ventura, a Reform Party candidate for governor in that state. Ventura won.

Ultimately, third parties find it difficult to break through in an electoral system that perpetuates their own failure. Because third parties normally do not win elections, Americans tend not to vote for them or to contribute to their campaigns, so they continue not to win elections. As long as Americans hold to the perception that third parties can never win big in an election, the current two-party system is likely to persist.

AMERICA AT ODDS *Political Parties*

By their very nature, arguments about the parties are some of the most divisive conflicts in politics. We can list only a sampling of the disputes:

- Is the Republican Party driving off voters that it needs by excessive conservatism—or is it failing to uphold basic conservative values? For that matter, are the Democrats too liberal—or not liberal enough?
- Are political parties desirable and inevitable—or should elections be nonpartisan whenever possible?
- Is it better when the two chambers of Congress and the presidency are held by the same party, thus guaranteeing effective government—or is it better when Congress and the presidency are held by different parties, so that the two parties can check each other?
- Is the increasing importance of political independents a positive development—or is it a sign that citizens are becoming dangerously detached from our political system?
- Is it better to support a third party when you are in greater agreement with its positions than with those of either major party—or should you avoid wasting your vote and always support the major party that is closer to your politics?
- Finally, looking forward, do the Republicans or the Democrats offer the best solutions for our problems?

Take Action

Getting involved in political parties is as simple as going to the polls and casting your vote for the candidate of one of the major parties—or of a third party. If you want to go a step further, you can attend a speech given by a political candidate or even volunteer to assist a political party or a specific candidate's campaign activities.

You can also consider another alternative—becoming a delegate to a party convention. National conventions aren't the only ones that the parties hold. There are state conventions, and most local party units conduct regular conventions as well. Depending on the state, parties may hold conventions by U.S. House district, by county, or by state legislative district. In many states, the lowest-level conventions are open to anyone who shows up.

Voting rights at a convention, however, may be restricted to those who are elected as a precinct delegate in a party primary. In much of the country, precinct delegate slots go unfilled. If this is true in your area, you can become a precinct delegate with a simple write-in campaign. You merely need to write in your own name and persuade a small handful of friends or neighbors to write you in as well. Whether you attend a convention as a voting delegate or as a guest, you'll have a firsthand look at how politics operates. You'll hear debates on resolutions. You might participate in electing delegates to higher-level conventions—perhaps even the national convention if it is a presidential election year. Few exercises are more educational.

VOTE HERE
VOTE AQUI
請在此投票
ĐI BẦU TẠI ĐÂY
7AM - 8PM

AP PHOTO/CHARLES KRUPA

The government provides election materials in a variety of languages other than English.

POLITICS ON THE WEB

- For a list of political Web sites available on the Internet, sorted by country and with links to parties, organizations, and governments throughout the world, go to **www.politicalresources.net**
- Ron Gunzburger's Politics1 Web site contains a vast amount of information on American politics. Click on "Political Parties" in the directory box at the top of the home page to see one of the most complete descriptions of major and minor parties to be found anywhere. Gunzburger's site is at **www.politics1.com**
- The Democratic Party is online at **www.democrats.org**
- The Republican National Committee is online at **www.gop.com**
- The Libertarian Party has a Web site at **www.lp.org**
- The Green Party's Web site can be accessed by going to **www.greenparty.org**

Access CourseMate to review and expand on this chapter through quizzes, flashcards, learning objectives, interactive timelines, a crossword puzzle, audio summaries, video, critical-thinking activities, simulations, and more.

GOVT 8

Public Opinion and Voting

LEARNING OBJECTIVES

LO1 Explain what public opinion is and how it is measured.

LO2 Describe the political socialization process.

LO3 Summarize the history of polling in the United States, and explain how polls are conducted and how they are used in the political process.

LO4 Indicate some of the factors that affect voter turnout, and discuss what has been done to improve voter turnout and voting procedures.

LO5 Discuss the different factors that affect voter choices.

AMERICA AT
ODDS Should Felons Be Allowed to Vote?

Suppose that you commit a crime that is punishable by a prison term. You serve your time and are released. You are now a felon—someone who has been convicted of a serious crime. When you leave prison, the terms people apply to you are not pretty. You are an "ex-con"—an ex-convict. You may believe that you have "repaid your debt to society" by going to prison, but that does not mean that all of your rights are restored after you have served your sentence. In most states, felons do not have the right to vote. Certainly, many people will agree that those who are actually serving time in prison should not be able to vote. But what about those who have rejoined society?

Because America puts more people behind bars than any other nation, the number of ex-cons is staggering. In Florida alone there are more than 120,000 former convicts. At least 13 percent of the nation's African American male population is disenfranchised. The United States takes a much harder line on this issue than most countries. Many of our allies, in fact, allow most people to vote while they are still in prison. Nations that do that include Canada, France, Germany, and many others. In the United States, Maine and Vermont allow prisoners to vote—and so does Puerto Rico. Among our European allies, only Belgium permanently disenfranchises felons. Should such people have the right to vote?

No One Should Be Denied the Right to Vote

Felony disenfranchisement affects almost 6 million persons in the United States. That means that 6 million Americans cannot express their political beliefs by voting. One negative result of this exclusion is racial discrimination. The percentage of African Americans who are felons is much greater than their share of the total population. The result: compared with whites, a disproportionate number of blacks are excluded from the democratic process because of state laws that prevent felons from voting.

Regardless of race, those who are convicted of felonies are disproportionately poor. By excluding many poor persons and minority group members from the voting rolls, we bias the vote against the poor and the historically disadvantaged. Some question how we can call ourselves a fully democratic country if we disenfranchise so many people. Those who want felons to regain the right to vote contend that our current situation is patently unfair.

When You Break the Rules, You Lose Some Rights

No one questions the right of society to incarcerate those convicted of serious crimes. No one questions the need for punishment when individuals violate our accepted rules of behavior. Therefore, why should anyone question each state's right to prevent convicts and former convicts from exercising all of the rights enjoyed by law-abiding citizens? Felons are not the kind of people we want to choose our leaders and the legislators who make our laws.

Some opponents of felon enfranchisement also contend that proponents are making a mountain out of a molehill. When Florida passed a law allowing former convicts to register to vote, the results were not encouraging. Only about 10,000 out of a potential 120,000 former convicts actually registered. Those in favor of allowing felons to vote are misplacing their efforts. They should instead attempt to reduce incentives for Americans to commit crimes.

WHERE DO YOU STAND?

1. **Would you be in favor of allowing individuals currently in prison to be able to register to vote? Why or why not?**
2. **If the millions of former convicts in America could register to vote, would it make any difference? Why or why not?**

EXPLORE THIS ISSUE ONLINE

- **The *New York Times* has covered the issue of felon disenfranchisement in considerable depth. You can find some of its stories by entering their titles into a search engine such as Google. Type in "Voting Behind Bars" for a recent article by Linda Greenhouse that raises the question of whether disenfranchisement is unconstitutional. Enter "States Restore Voting Rights for Ex-Convicts" for details about the Florida experience.**

Introduction

For a democracy to be effective, members of the public must form opinions and openly express them to their elected officials. Only when the opinions of Americans are communicated effectively to elected representatives can those opinions form the basis of government action. As President Franklin D. Roosevelt once said, "A government can be no better than the public opinion that sustains it."

"A government can be no better than the

PUBLIC OPINION

that sustains it."

~ FRANKLIN DELANO ROOSEVELT ~
THIRTY-SECOND PRESIDENT
OF THE UNITED STATES
1933–1945

What exactly is *public opinion*? How do we form our opinions on political issues? How can public opinion be measured accurately? Finally, what factors affect voter participation?

Researchers and scholars have addressed these questions time and again. They are important questions because the backbone of our democracy has always been civic participation—taking part in the political life of the country. Civic participation means many things, but perhaps the most important way that Americans participate in their democracy is through voting—expressing their opinions in the polling places. Who may vote is therefore an important issue, as explained in this chapter's opening *America at Odds* feature.

LO1 What Is Public Opinion?

People hold opinions—sometimes very strong ones—about a variety of issues, ranging from the ethics of capital punishment to the latest trends in fashion. In this chapter, however, we are concerned with only a portion of those opinions. For our purposes here, we define **public opinion** as the sum total of a complex collection of opinions held by many people on issues in the public arena, such as taxes, health care, Social Security, clean-air legislation, and unemployment.

When you hear a news report or read a magazine article stating that "a significant number of Americans" feel a certain way about an issue, you are probably hearing that a particular opinion is held by a large enough number of people to make government officials turn their heads and listen. For example, public opinion surveys in 2008 revealed that the poor state of the economy was the number-one issue for Americans. Polls also showed that the economy was the main issue in 2010, although it hardly took a poll to discover that fact, given that the unemployment rate was above 9 percent and houses were entering foreclosure in huge numbers.

Politicians were forced to react. In 2008, the outgoing Bush administration obtained a $700 billion bank bailout bill from Congress. After January 2009, the incoming Democrats under President Barack Obama undertook a series of expensive steps in an attempt to combat the Great Recession, beginning with an enormous stimulus package in February. These various measures may have reduced the severity of the recession, but they did not halt it. The voters therefore punished the Republicans in 2008—and turned against the Democrats in 2010.

public opinion The views of the citizenry about politics, public issues, and public policies; a complex collection of opinions held by many people on issues in the public arena.

political socialization The learning process through which most people acquire their political attitudes, opinions, beliefs, and knowledge.

agents of political socialization People and institutions that influence the political views of others.

LO2 How Do People Form Political Opinions?

When asked, most Americans are willing to express an opinion on political issues. Not one of us, however, was born with such opinions. Most people acquire their political attitudes, opinions, beliefs, and knowledge through a complex learning process called **political socialization.** This process begins in childhood and continues throughout life.

Most political socialization is informal, and it usually begins during early childhood, when the dominant influence on a child is the family. Although parents normally do not sit down and say to their children, "Let us explain to you the virtues of becoming a Republican," their children nevertheless come to know the parents' feelings, beliefs, and attitudes. The strong early influence of the family later gives way to the multiple influences of school, peers, television, co-workers, and other groups. People and institutions that influence the political views of others are called **agents of political socialization.**

The Importance of Family

As just suggested, most parents or caregivers do not deliberately set out to form their children's political ideas and beliefs. They are usually more concerned with the moral, religious, and ethical values of their offspring. Yet a child first sees the political world through the eyes of his or her family, which is perhaps the most important force in political socialization. Children do not "learn" political attitudes the same way they learn to master in-line skating. Rather, they learn by hearing their parents' everyday conversations and stories about politicians and issues and by observing their parents' actions. They also learn from watching and listening to their siblings, as well as from the kinds of situations in which their parents place them.

The family's influence is strongest when children clearly perceive their parents' attitudes. Parents commonly do communicate their political attitudes to their children. For example, in one study, more high school students could identify their parents' political party affiliation than their parents' other attitudes or beliefs. In many situations, the political party of the parents becomes the political party of the children, particularly if both parents support the same party.

The Schools and Educational Attainment

Education also strongly influences an individual's political attitudes. From their earliest days in school, children learn about the American political system. They say the Pledge of Allegiance and sing patriotic songs. They celebrate national holidays, such as Presidents' Day and Veterans' Day, and learn about the history and symbols associated with them. In the upper grades, young people acquire more knowledge about government and democratic procedures through civics classes and participation in student government and various clubs. They also learn citizenship skills through school rules and regulations. Generally, those with more education have more knowledge about politics and policy than those with less education. The level of education also influences a person's political values, as will be discussed later in this chapter.

Although the schools have always been important agents of political socialization, many Americans today believe that our schools are not fulfilling this mission. Too many students are graduating from high school—and even college—with too little knowledge of the American system of government.

This Native American boy poses with his Cub Scout manual. He hopes to obtain a Cub Scout religious emblem that recognizes his faith in the traditional Navajo spiritual way of life. Both his family and the Cub Scouts are socializing influences on him.

AP PHOTO/NAVAJO NATION, GEORGE HARDEEN

The Media

The **media**—newspapers, magazines, television, radio, and the Internet—also have an impact on political socialization. The most influential of these media is television, which continues to be a leading source of political and public affairs information for most people.

Some contend that the media's role in shaping public opinion has increased to the point at which the media are as influential as the family, particularly among high school students. For example, in her analysis of the media's role in American politics, media scholar Doris A. Graber points out that high school students, when asked where they obtain the information on which they base their attitudes, mention the mass media far more than they mention their families, friends, and teachers.[1] Graber's conclusion takes on added significance in view of a 2006 Gallup poll showing that only about half of the parents polled

media Newspapers, magazines, television, radio, the Internet, and any other printed or electronic means of communication.

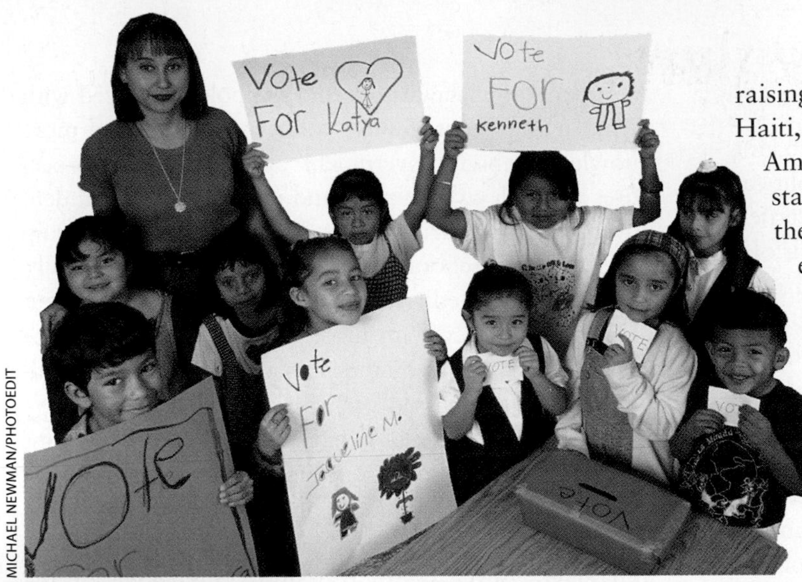

MICHAEL NEWMAN/PHOTOEDIT

Students learn about the political process early on when they participate in class elections.

were concerned about their children's TV-viewing habits, even when their children watched TV "a great deal" or a "fair amount" of time.

Other studies have shown that the media's influence on people's opinions may not be as great as some have thought. Generally, people watch television, read articles, or access online sites with preconceived ideas about the issues. These preconceived ideas act as a kind of perceptual screen that blocks out information that is not consistent with those ideas. For example, if you are already firmly convinced that daily meditation is beneficial for your health, you probably will not change your mind if you watch a TV show that asserts that those who meditate live no longer on average than people who do not. Generally, the media tend to wield the most influence over the views of persons who have not yet formed opinions about certain issues or political candidates. (See Chapter 10 for a more detailed discussion of the media's role in American politics.)

Opinion Leaders

Every state or community has well-known citizens who are able to influence the opinions of their fellow citizens. These people may be public officials, religious leaders, teachers, or celebrities. They are the people to whom others listen and from whom others draw ideas and convictions about various issues of public concern. These opinion leaders play a significant role in the formation of public opinion.

Opinion leaders often include politicians or former politicians. For example, President Barack Obama asked former U.S. presidents George W. Bush (2001–2009) and Bill Clinton (1993–2001) to lead a nationwide fundraising drive following the January 2010 earthquake in Haiti, which destroyed much of that country. Certainly, Americans' attitudes are influenced by the public statements of important government leaders such as the president or secretary of state. Sometimes, however, opinion leaders can fall from grace when they express views radically different from what most Americans believe. This was true for President George W. Bush. His insistence on continuing the widely unpopular war in Iraq was a major factor in causing his approval ratings to dip to historically low levels. Another example is former president Jimmy Carter (1977–1981), who lost much popularity after he published a book that harshly criticized Israel's actions toward the Palestinians.[2] (Most Americans of both parties are strongly pro-Israel.)

Americans do not often look to other countries for opinion leaders, but the president of the United States is frequently an opinion leader in other nations. We examine the impact of a new president on citizens of other countries in this chapter's *The Rest of the World* feature on the facing page.

Senator Ted Kennedy (D., Mass.) is shown here shortly before his death in 2009. Kennedy was a major opinion leader for decades while he served in the Senate. He especially tried to form others' opinions on the need for health-care reform. How does a politician become an opinion leader?

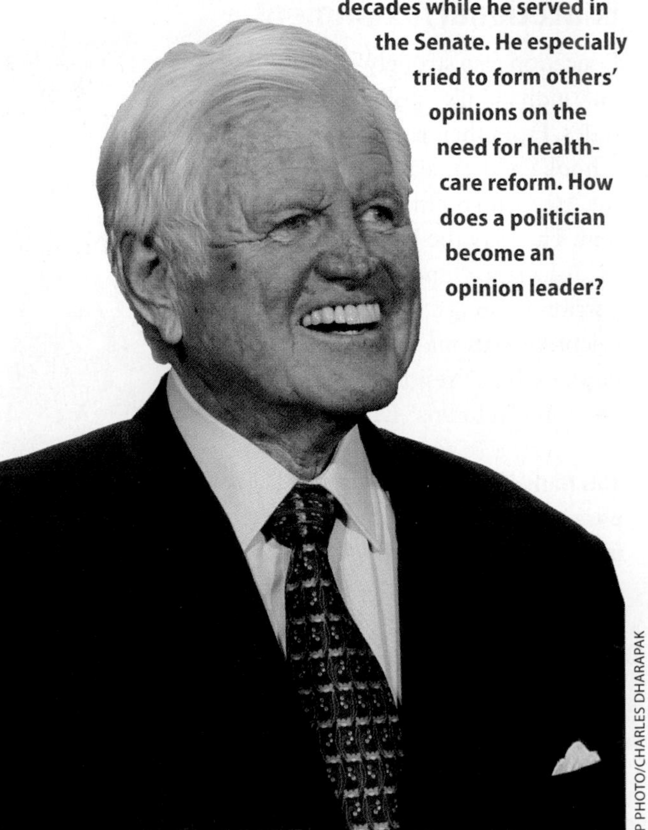

AP PHOTO/CHARLES DHARAPAK

THE REST OF THE WORLD

An Improved Image of the United States Abroad?

During George W. Bush's eight years as president, foreign public opinion about the United States in general and Bush in particular fell dramatically. Since the election of Barack Obama, however, the world's view of the United States has, on average, undergone measurable improvement.

U.S. "Favorability" Ratings

While citizens of most countries have looked at the United States more favorably since President Obama took office, attitudes vary from region to region. In Western Europe, "favorability" ratings have soared. According to the Pew Research Center's Global Attitudes Project, the number of Germans with a favorable opinion of the United States jumped from 31 percent in 2008 to 63 percent in 2010. In France, the number climbed from 42 percent to 73 percent. Opinions of America have also become more positive in many nations of Latin America. An exception is Mexico, where favorable opinions of the United States collapsed after Arizona passed a strict new law in 2010 to control illegal immigration.

It should be understood that in quite a few countries, Bush was never particularly unpopular. These include the nations of Eastern Europe, which for many years were dominated by the Soviet Union. This experience made Eastern Europeans strong supporters of the United States, the longtime rival of the Soviets during the Cold War. By 2008 and 2009, the United States was still popular enough in Eastern Europe that there was little room for improvement. Other nations that did not exhibit strong negativity toward Bush included India, China, South Korea, and Japan.

Bush was actually quite popular in sub-Saharan Africa. Many Americans may not realize that Bush increased foreign aid to Africa dramatically, but Africans know it. Of course, as the son of an African father, Obama has been more popular still.

In contrast, opinions of the United States among Muslims in the Middle East have remained extremely unfavorable. Favorability ratings even fell in Pakistan, probably due to Obama's use of drones to attack Taliban leaders hiding in the border regions of that country. An exception: favorability ratings have gone up substantially in Indonesia, a predominantly Muslim nation. Obama is something of a "favorite son" in that country—he lived there as a boy and has Indonesian relatives. Russian opinions of the United States have risen somewhat, but remain very low.

For Critical Analysis *Will President Obama's Nobel Peace Prize help improve the United States' image in the rest of the world? Why or why not?*

Major Life Events

Often, the political attitudes of an entire generation of Americans are influenced by a major event. For example, the Great Depression (1929–1939), the most severe economic depression in modern U.S. history, persuaded many Americans who lived through it that the federal government should step in when the economy is in decline. A substantial number of voters came to believe that the New Deal programs and policies of President Franklin Roosevelt showed that the Democratic Party was concerned about the fate of ordinary people, and so they became supporters of that party.

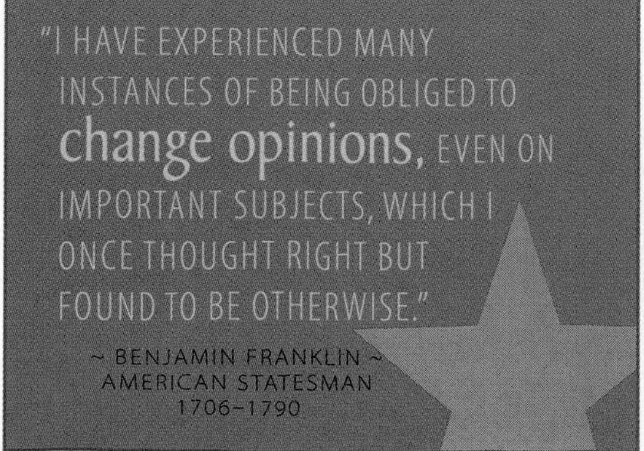

"I HAVE EXPERIENCED MANY INSTANCES OF BEING OBLIGED TO change opinions, EVEN ON IMPORTANT SUBJECTS, WHICH I ONCE THOUGHT RIGHT BUT FOUND TO BE OTHERWISE."
~ BENJAMIN FRANKLIN ~
AMERICAN STATESMAN
1706–1790

The generation that lived through World War II (1939–1945) tends to believe that American intervention in foreign affairs is good. In contrast, the generation that came of age during the Vietnam War (1964–1975) is more skeptical of American interventionism. A national tragedy, such as the terrorist attacks of September 11, 2001, is also likely to influence the political attitudes of a generation, though in what way is difficult to predict. Certainly, the U.S. government's response to 9/11, and particularly the war in Iraq, has elicited

peer group Associates, often close in age to one another; may include friends, classmates, co-workers, club members, or religious group members. Peer group influence is a significant factor in the political socialization process.

public opinion poll A numerical survey of the public's opinion on a particular topic at a particular moment.

sample In the context of opinion polling, a group of people selected to represent the population being studied.

straw poll A nonscientific poll; a poll in which there is no way to ensure that the opinions expressed are representative of the larger population.

biased sample A poll sample that does not accurately represent the population.

deep concern on the part of Americans. Opposition to this war, however, did not lead to the widespread antiwar demonstrations that took place during another unpopular war—in Vietnam—years ago. The recent Great Recession and the financial crisis that struck in September 2008 will surely affect popular attitudes in years to come.

Peer Groups

Once children enter school, the views of friends begin to influence their attitudes and beliefs. From junior high school on, the **peer group**—friends, classmates, co-workers, club members, or religious group members—becomes a significant factor in the political socialization process. Most of this socialization occurs when the peer group is involved in political activities. For example, your political beliefs might be influenced by a peer group with which you are working on a common political cause, such as preventing the clear-cutting of old-growth forests or campaigning for a favorite candidate. Your political beliefs probably would not be as strongly influenced by peers with whom you snowboard regularly or attend concerts.

Economic Status and Occupation

A person's economic status may influence her or his political views. For example, poorer people are more likely to favor government assistance programs. On an issue such as abortion, lower-income people are more likely to be conservative—that is, to be against abortion—than are higher-income groups (of course, there are many exceptions).

Where a person works also affects her or his opinion. Co-workers who spend a great deal of time working together tend to influence one another. For example, labor union members working together for a company may have similar political opinions, at least on issues of government involvement in the economy. Individuals working for a nonprofit agency that depends on government funds will tend to support government spending in that area. Business managers are more likely to favor tax laws helpful to businesses than are factory workers.

LO3 *Measuring Public Opinion*

If public opinion is to affect public policy, then public officials must be made aware of it. They must know which issues are of current concern to Americans and how strongly people feel about those issues. They must also know when public opinion changes. Public officials commonly learn about public opinion through election results, personal contacts, interest groups, and media reports. The only relatively precise way to measure public opinion, however, is through the use of public opinion polls.

A **public opinion poll** is a numerical survey of the public's opinion on a particular topic at a particular moment. The results of opinion polls are most often cast in terms of percentages: 62 percent feel this way, 31 percent do not, and 7 percent have no opinion. Of course, a poll cannot survey the entire U.S. population. Therefore, public opinion pollsters have devised scientific polling techniques for measuring public opinion through the use of **samples**—groups of people who are typical of the general population.

Early Polling Efforts

Since the 1800s, magazines and newspapers have often spiced up their articles by conducting **straw polls** of readers' opinions. Straw polls try to read the public's collective mind by simply asking a large number of people the same question. The early straw polls were mail surveys. Today, some newspapers and magazines still run "mail-in" polls. Increasingly, though, straw polls make use of telephone technology—encouraging people to call "900" numbers, for example—or the Internet. Visitors to a Web page can instantly register their opinions on an issue with the click of a mouse. The problem with straw polls is that the opinions expressed usually represent an atypical subgroup of the population, or a **biased sample.** A survey of those who read the *Reader's Digest* will most likely produce different results than a survey of those who read *Rolling Stone.*

The most famous of all straw-polling errors was committed by the *Literary Digest* in 1936 when it tried to predict the outcome of that year's presidential elections. The *Digest* had accurately predicted the winning candidates in several earlier presidential elections, but in 1936 the *Digest* forecast that Alfred Landon would easily defeat incumbent Franklin Roosevelt. Instead, Roosevelt won by a landslide. The editors of the *Digest* had sent mail-in cards to citizens whose names appeared in telephone directories, to its own subscribers, and to automobile owners—in all, to a staggering 2,376,000 people. In the mid-Depression year of 1936, however, people who owned a car or a telephone or who subscribed to the *Digest* were not representative of the majority of Americans. The vast majority of Americans could not afford such luxuries. Despite the enormous number of people surveyed, the sample was unrepresentative and consequently inaccurate.

Several newcomers to the public opinion poll industry, however, did predict Roosevelt's landslide victory. Two of these organizations are still at the forefront of the polling industry today: the Gallup Organization, started by George Gallup; and Roper Associates, founded by Elmo Roper and now known as the Roper Center.

Voters raise their arms in support of Democratic presidential hopeful Barack Obama as a non-binding straw poll is taken during a caucus in Denver.

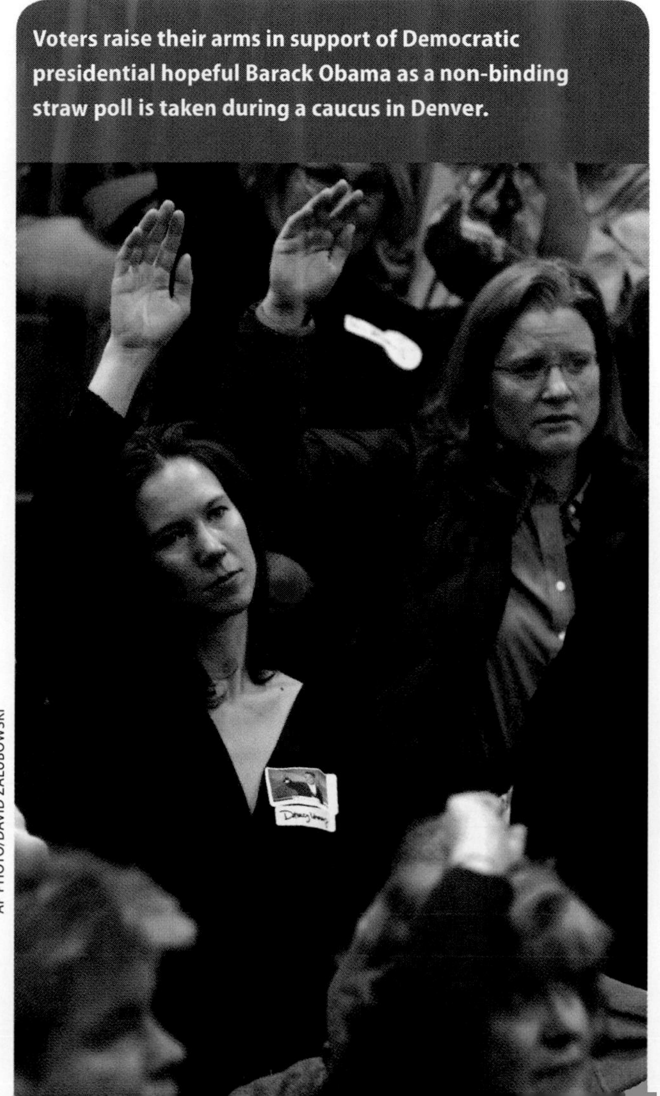

AP PHOTO/DAVID ZALUBOWSKI

Polling Today

random sample In the context of opinion polling, a sample in which each person within the entire population being polled has an equal chance of being chosen.

Today, polling is used extensively by political candidates and policymakers. Politicians and the news media generally place a great deal of faith in the accuracy of poll results. Polls can be remarkably accurate when they are conducted properly. In the last fourteen presidential elections, Gallup polls conducted early in September predicted the eventual winners in eleven of the fourteen races. Even polls taken several months in advance have been able to predict the eventual winner quite well. This success is largely the result of careful sampling techniques.

SAMPLING Today, most Gallup polls sample between 1,500 and 2,000 people. How can interviewing such a small group possibly indicate what millions of voters think? To be successful, a sample must consist of people who are typical of the general population. If the sample is properly selected, the opinions of those in the sample will be representative of the opinions held by the population as a whole. If the sample is not properly chosen, then the results of the poll may not reflect the beliefs of the general population.

The most important principle in sampling is randomness. A **random sample** means that each person within the entire population being polled has an equal chance of being chosen. For example, if a poll is trying to measure how women feel about an issue, the sample should include respondents from all groups within the female population in proportion to their percentage in the entire population. A properly drawn random sample, therefore, would include appropriate numbers of women in terms of age, racial and ethnic characteristics, occupation, geography, household income level, and religious affiliation.

BIAS In addition to trying to secure a random sample, poll takers also want to ensure that there is no bias in their polling questions. How a question is phrased can significantly affect how people answer it. Consider a question about whether high-speed connections to the Internet should be added to the school library's computer center. One way to survey opinions on this issue is simply to ask, "Do you believe that the school district should provide high-speed connections to the Internet?" Another way to ask the same question is, "Are you willing to pay higher property taxes so that the school district can have high-speed connections to the Internet?"

Undoubtedly, the poll results will differ depending on how the question is phrased.

Polling questions also sometimes reduce complex issues to questions that simply call for "yes" or "no" answers. For example, a survey question might ask respondents whether they favor giving aid to foreign countries. A respondent's opinion on the issue might vary depending on the recipient country or the purpose and type of the aid. The poll would nonetheless force the respondent to give a "yes" or "no" answer that does not fully reflect his or her opinion.

> "A popular government without popular information, or the means of acquiring it, is but **A PROLOGUE TO A FARCE OR A TRAGEDY,** or perhaps both."
>
> ~ JAMES MADISON ~
> FOURTH PRESIDENT OF THE UNITED STATES
> 1809–1817

Respondents to such questions sometimes answer "I don't know" or "I don't have enough information to answer," even when the poll does not offer such options. Interestingly, a study of how polling is conducted on the complex issue of school vouchers (school vouchers were discussed in Chapter 4) found that about 4 percent volunteered the answer "I don't know" when asked if they favored or opposed vouchers. When respondents were offered the option of answering "I haven't heard or read enough to answer," however, the proportion choosing that answer jumped to about 30 percent.[3] One current issue on which members of the public often have complicated opinions is health-care reform, as we explain in this chapter's *Our Government Faces a Troubled Economy* feature on the facing page.

TYPES OF POLLS In the earliest days of scientific polling, interviewers typically went door-to-door locating respondents. Such in-person surveys were essential in the mid-twentieth century, when a surprisingly large portion of the population did not have a home telephone. Interviews using telephones only would run the danger of replicating the *Literary Digest* disaster mentioned earlier.

In time, however, the number of homes without phones dwindled, and polling organizations determined that they were able to obtain satisfactory samples of voters through telephone interviews alone. In recent years, poll takers have even replaced human interviewers with prerecorded messages that solicit responses. Such methods allow companies to conduct very large numbers of polls at little cost. Questions have arisen as to whether automated polling is as accurate as polling that uses live interviewers, however. Further complications for telephone poll takers are the increase in the use of cell phones—which not all pollsters bother to call—and the growing number of people who simply refuse to participate in telephone surveys.

sampling error In the context of opinion polling, the difference between what the sample results show and what the true results would have been had everybody in the relevant population been interviewed.

Technological advances have opened up a new possibility—the Internet survey. The Harris Poll now specializes in this type of research. As when telephone interviews were introduced, serious questions exist today as to whether the samples obtained by Harris and other Internet polling firms can be representative. Internet usage has become extremely widespread, but it is still not universal.

RELIABILITY OF POLLS In addition to potential bias, poll takers must also be concerned about the general reliability of their polls. Respondents interviewed may be influenced by the interviewer's personality or tone of voice. They may answer without having any information on the issue, or they may give the answer that they think will please the interviewer. Additionally, any opinion poll contains a **sampling error,** which is the difference between what the sample results show and what the true results would have been had everybody in the relevant population been interviewed. (For a further look at how polling can lead to misleading results, see this chapter's *Perception versus Reality* feature on page 172.)

Opinion polls of voter preferences cannot reflect rapid shifts in public opinion unless they are taken frequently. One example of this problem was the polls taken during the presidential elections of 1980. The candidates in that year were incumbent Democratic president Jimmy Carter and Republican Ronald Reagan. Almost to the end of the campaign, polls showed Carter in the lead. Only the most capable analysts took note of the very large number of undecided voters. In the last week before the elections, these voters broke sharply for Reagan. Few polls were conducted late enough to detect this development.

EXIT POLLS The reliability of polls was also called into question by the use of exit polls in the 2000 presidential elections. The Voter News Service (VNS)—a consortium of news networks that no longer exists—conducted polls of people exiting polling places on Election Day. These

The Public's Complicated Attitude toward Health-Care Reform

During the 2008 campaign for the White House, all the presidential candidates agreed that America's health-care system needed reform. After all, we are currently spending about 17 percent of our total national income on health care, and costs have been rising faster than the rate of inflation. A substantial share of the population also lacks health insurance. On taking office, President Barack Obama served notice that one of his major goals was to reform our health-care system, as quickly as possible. He argued that we cannot have a booming economy unless we change the way medical services are insured and paid for in the United States. In March 2009, about three-quarters of the respondents to a Pew Research poll agreed that the health-care system needed either fundamental changes or a complete rebuilding.

Support for Reform Dwindles

With every step toward turning health-care reform into a reality, however, public support for the process fell. Funding the reform was a major problem—it was likely to cost close to a trillion dollars over a ten-year period. The House proposed to fund the reforms with new taxes on the richest taxpayers. The Senate, in contrast, debated a tax on existing employer-provided benefits. Such a tax was widely considered rational by economists, but not by the public. A poll in July 2009 revealed that increasing taxes on upper-income Americans was strongly or somewhat favored by 58 percent of those polled, but 64 percent opposed taxing employer-provided health insurance. (In the end, most of the new taxes were indeed paid by the rich, and only the most elaborate "Cadillac" employer plans suffered a penalty.)

By the end of July 2009, the nation was split in its view of how well President Obama was handling health-care reform, according to most surveys. This was a significant decline in public approval of Obama's efforts. Polling revealed one problem: While only a minority of Americans believed we have a good health-care system, only 14 percent of those currently insured were dissatisfied with their own plan. Similarly, a majority of those polled believed that reform might help someone else, but not them.

Multiple Sources of Opposition

As the health-care legislation moved toward the finish line in 2010, Republicans argued that a majority of Americans opposed the reforms and that passage would be an affront to democracy. In fact, however, popular attitudes were more complicated than the Republicans were suggesting. It is true that in polls taken early in 2010, a majority of those surveyed opposed the legislation—56 percent were opposed in a March 2010 poll, with 39 percent supporting. That same poll, however, also asked respondents whether they opposed the reforms because they were too liberal or not liberal enough. As it turns out, 13 percent thought the reforms did not go far enough, and only 43 percent thought the reforms went too far. In short, the Republican position on the legislation did not have majority support and was barely more popular than the Democratic one.

Since the passage of the two reform bills in March, public opinion has drifted slightly in favor of the legislation. In several August 2010 polls, just over a third of those surveyed supported repeal of the legislation—a position adopted by most Republican candidates. Majorities either favored the reforms or thought they should be given a chance to work. Polls asking whether the reforms are too liberal or not liberal enough continue to yield results similar to the poll described in the previous paragraph.

You Be the Judge **Those under the age of 65 are much more supportive of the health-care reform legislation than those aged 65 or older. Why might that be so?**

exit polls were used by the news networks to predict the winner of the Florida race—and they were wrong, not just once, but twice. First, they claimed that the Florida vote had gone to Al Gore. Then, a few hours later, they said it had gone to George W. Bush. Finally, they said the Florida race was too close to call.

These miscalls of the election outcome in Florida caused substantial confusion—and frustration—for the

PERCEPTION VERSUS REALITY

The Accuracy of Public Opinion Polls

Today, more than ever before, Americans are bombarded with the results of public opinion polls. If you can think of a political candidate, topic, issue, or concept, chances are that one or more public polling organizations can tell you what "Americans really think" about that candidate or topic. Polling organizations increasingly use telephone interviews and the Internet to conduct their polls. Because these polls are much cheaper to conduct than "feet on the street" polling, it is not surprising that more poll results are available every day. If you subscribe to the online services of the Gallup poll, for example, at least once a week Gallup will send you information on approximately a dozen topics on which that organization has sought to discover Americans' opinions.

The Perception

Americans who hear or read about the results of public opinion polls naturally assume that polling organizations undertook those polls in a scientific way and presented accurate results. Those who know a little bit about polling also assume that the small numbers of people polled represented a random sample.

The Reality

Many polls are not based on a random sample, contrary to popular belief. Consider a poll published by the *Military Times* in 2008, which found that 58 percent of respondents opposed military service by openly gay individuals. Further, 10 percent claimed that they would not reenlist if the ban on openly gay service members were lifted. The press gave this survey widespread coverage without questioning its methodology. One pundit claimed, on the basis of the poll, that gays in the military would "destroy" the institution. In fact, the poll was not based on a random sample but on a self-selected pool of *Military Times* readers, who tended to be older and more conservative than the military as a whole. Further, opinions do not necessarily predict behavior. Before Britain and Canada ended their service bans, polls found widespread resistance to openly gay and lesbian soldiers. Upon integration, however, almost no one actually resigned from service.

Think also about how respondents answer interviewers' questions. In one *New York Times*/CBS News poll, voters were asked if they had voted in a specific presidential election. Although 73 percent said yes, the U.S. Census Bureau later determined that only 64 percent of eligible voters actually voted in that election. Analysts concluded that those who had been interviewed wanted to appear to be "good citizens," so not all of them told the truth.

Do not forget about sampling error. For example, say that two candidates for president are neck and neck in the opinion polls, but the sampling error is 4 percent. That means that either candidate could actually be ahead by 54 percent to 46 percent.

Blog On **Why, in your opinion, do various publications continue to print unscientific pseudopolls?**

candidates, as well as for the voters. They also led to a significant debate over exit polls: Should exit polls be banned, even though they provide valuable information on voter behavior and preferences?

Exit polls again were employed during the 2004 presidential elections. Again the results were troublesome. During the early hours of the elections, exit polls caused the media to conclude that Democratic candidate John Kerry was leading in the race. Preliminary results of exit polls were leaked to the Internet by midafternoon. After the votes were tallied, however, the exit poll results were shown to have inflated Kerry's support by 6.5 percent—the largest margin of error in decades.

In 2008, the television networks were careful about making predictions based on exit polls. It was clear early that Obama was winning, but the networks wanted viewers to keep watching, so they maintained the suspense. Print media exit polls, used to determine the voting preferences of various groups, did better in 2008 than in 2004, when they contained some major errors.

Pollsters had a tough time persuading Americans to participate in surveys leading up to the 2010 elections. Many Americans only use cell phones and therefore are difficult to contact. Nonetheless, the polls were substantially accurate. A survey of polling data from multiple sources predicted that the Democrats would lose fifty-three seats in the House and seven or eight in the Senate. Not a bad prediction—sixty-four Democrats lost in the House and six in the Senate. Polling firms that used real human interviewers had the most accuracy.

MISUSE OF POLLS Today, a frequently heard complaint is that, instead of measuring public opinion, polls can end up creating it. For example, to gain popularity, a candidate might claim that all the polls show that he is ahead in the race. People who want to support the winner may back this candidate despite their true feelings. This is often called the "bandwagon" effect. Presidential approval ratings lend themselves to the bandwagon effect.

The media also sometimes misuse polls. Many journalists take the easy route during campaigns and base their political coverage almost exclusively on poll findings, with no mention of the chance for bias or the margin of error in the poll. A useful checklist for evaluating the quality of opinion polls is presented in Table 8–1 at right. An increasingly common misuse of polls by politicians is the *push poll,* discussed next.

Table 8–1

Checklist for Evaluating Public Opinion Polls

Because public opinion polls are so widely used by the media and policymakers, and their reliability is so often called into question, several organizations have issued guidelines for evaluating polls. Below is a list of questions that you can ask to evaluate the quality and reliability of a poll. You can find the answers to many, if not all, of these questions in the polling organization's report accompanying the poll results.

1. Who conducted the poll, and who sponsored or paid for it?
2. How many people were interviewed for the survey, and what part of the population did they represent (for example, registered voters, likely voters, persons over age eighteen)?
3. How were these people chosen, and how random was the sample?
4. How were respondents contacted and interviewed (by telephone, by mail-in survey)?
5. Who should have been interviewed but was not (what was the "nonresponse" rate—people who should have been part of the random sample but who refused to be interviewed, do not have telephones, or do not have listed telephone numbers, for example)?
6. What is the margin of error for the poll? (The acceptable margin of error for national polls is usually plus or minus 4 percent.)
7. What questions did the poll ask?
8. In what order were the questions asked?
9. When was the poll conducted?
10. What other polls were conducted on this topic, and do they report similar findings?

DEFINING A PUSH POLL One tactic in political campaigns is to use **push polls,** which ask "fake" polling questions that are actually designed to "push" voters toward one candidate or another. The use of push polls has become so prevalent today that many states are taking steps to ban them. The problem with trying to ban push polls, or even to report accurately on which candidates are using them, is that defining a push poll can be difficult.

The National Council on Public Polls describes push polls as outright political manipulation—the spreading of rumors and lies by one candidate about another. For example, a push poll might ask, "Do you believe the rumor that Candidate A misused campaign funds to pay for a family vacation to Hawaii?" Push pollsters usually do not give their name or identify the poll's sponsor. The interviews last less than a minute, whereas legitimate pollsters typically interview a respondent for five to thirty minutes. Based on these characteristics, it is sometimes possible to distinguish a push poll from a legitimate poll conducted by a respected research organization. The checklist in Table 8–1 can also help you distinguish between a legitimate poll and a push poll.

Some researchers argue that identifying a push poll is not that straightforward, however. Political analyst Charlie Cook points out that "there are legitimate polls that can ask push questions, which test potential arguments against a rival to ascertain how effective those arguments might be in future advertising. . . . These are not only legitimate tools of survey research, but any political pollster who did not use them would be doing his or her clients a real disservice."[4] Distinguishing between push polls and push questions, then, can be challenging—which is usually the intent of the push pollsters. A candidate does not want to be accused of conducting push polls, because the public considers them a "dirty trick" and may turn against the candidate who uses them. In several recent campaigns, candidates have accused each other of conducting push polls—accusations that could not always be proved or disproved.

push poll A campaign tactic used to feed false or misleading information to potential voters, under the guise of taking an opinion poll, with the intent to "push" voters away from one candidate and toward another.

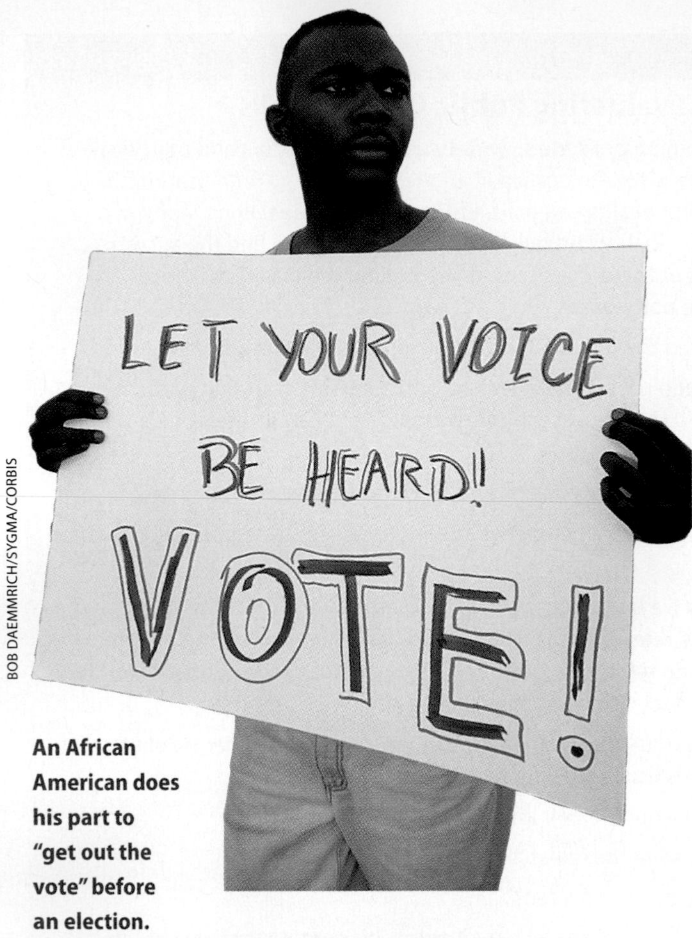

BOB DAEMMRICH/SYGMA/CORBIS

An African American does his part to "get out the vote" before an election. African Americans faced significant restrictions on voting until the 1950s and 1960s, when new laws and policies helped to end both formal and informal barriers to their voting. Voter turnout among African Americans is increasing, and in 2008 their share of the vote rose from 11 percent to 13 percent.

LO4 *Voting and Voter Turnout*

Voting is arguably the most important way in which citizens participate in the political process. Because we do not live in a direct democracy, Americans use the vote to elect politicians to represent their interests, values, and opinions in government. In many states, public-policy decisions—for example, access to medical marijuana—are decided by voters. Our right to vote also helps keep elected officials accountable to campaign promises because they must face reelection.

Factors Affecting Voter Turnout

literacy test A test given to voters to ensure that they could read and write and thus evaluate political information; a technique used in many southern states to restrict African American participation in elections.

If voting is so important, then why do so many Americans fail to exercise their right to vote? Why is voter turnout—the percentage of those eligible to vote who actually turn out to vote—relatively low? As you will read shortly, in the past, legal restrictions based on income, gender, race, and other factors kept a number of people from voting. In the last decades of the twentieth century, these restrictions were almost completely eliminated, and yet voter turnout in presidential elections still hovered around 55 percent, as shown in Figure 8–1 on the facing page. In the last two presidential elections, however, turnout has exceeded 60 percent—a welcome, if modest, improvement.

According to a Pew Research Center survey of voter turnout, one of the reasons for low voter turnout is that many nonvoters (close to 40 percent) do not feel that they have a duty to vote. The survey also found that nearly 70 percent of nonvoters said that they did not vote because they lacked information about the candidates.[5] Finally, some people believe that their vote will not make any difference, so they do not bother to become informed about the candidates and issues or go to the polls.

The Legal Right to Vote

In the United States today, citizens who are at least eighteen years of age and who are not felons have the right to vote. This was not always true, however. Recall from Chapter 5 that restrictions on *suffrage,* the legal right to vote, have existed since the founding of our nation. Expanding the right to vote has been an important part of the gradual democratization of the American electoral process. Table 8–2 on page 176 summarizes the major amendments, Supreme Court decisions, and laws that extended the right to vote to various American groups.

HISTORICAL RESTRICTIONS ON VOTING Those who drafted the Constitution left the power to set suffrage qualifications to the individual states. Most states limited suffrage to adult white males who owned property, but these restrictions were challenged early on in the history of the republic. By 1828, laws restricting the right to vote to Christians were abolished in all states, and property ownership and tax-payment requirements gradually began to disappear as well. By 1850, all white males were allowed to vote. Restrictions based on race and gender continued, however.

The Fifteenth Amendment, ratified in 1870, guaranteed suffrage to African American males. Yet, for many decades, African Americans were effectively denied the ability to exercise their voting rights. Using methods ranging from mob violence to economic restrictions, groups of white southerners kept black Americans from voting. Some states required citizens to pass **literacy tests** and to answer complicated questions about government and history before they could register to vote.

Figure 8–1

Voter Turnout since 1968

The figures in this chart show voter turnout as a percentage of the population that is eligible to vote.

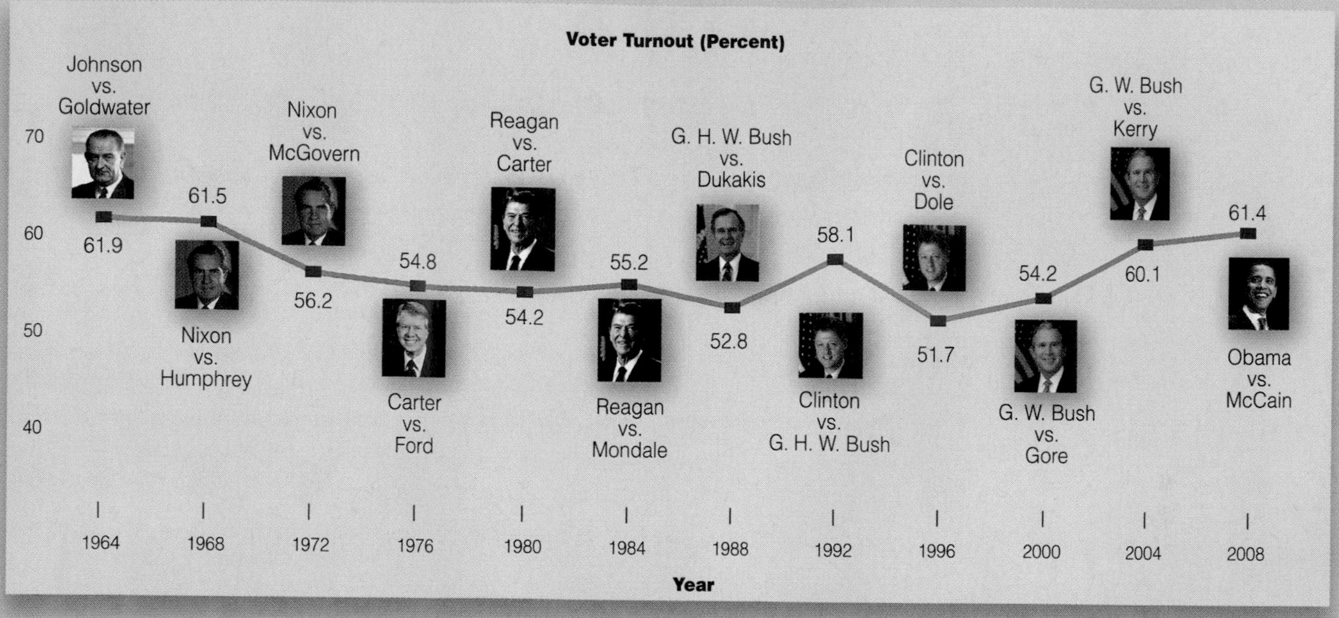

Sources: *Statistical Abstract of the United States,* various issues; the Committee for the Study of the American Electorate; and authors' updates.

Registrars made sure that African Americans would always fail such tests. The **poll tax,** a fee of several dollars, was another device used to prevent African Americans from voting. At the time, this tax was a sizable burden, not only for most blacks but also for poor whites. Another restriction was the **grandfather clause,** which had the effect of restricting voting rights to those whose ancestors had voted before the 1860s. This technique was prohibited by the United States Supreme Court in 1915.[6]

Still another voting barrier was the **white primary**—African Americans were prohibited from voting in the primary elections. The Supreme Court initially upheld this practice on the grounds that the political parties were private entities, not public, and thus could do as they wished. Eventually, in 1944, the Court banned the use of white primaries.[7]

VOTING RIGHTS TODAY Today, these devices for restricting voting rights are explicitly outlawed by constitutional amendments and by the Voting Rights Act of 1965, as discussed in Chapter 5. Furthermore, the Nineteenth Amendment gave women the right to vote in 1920. In 1971, the Twenty-sixth Amendment reduced the minimum voting age to eighteen.

Some restrictions on voting rights still exist. Every state except North Dakota requires voters to register with the appropriate state or local officials before voting. Residency requirements are also usually imposed for voting. Since 1970, however, no state can impose a residency requirement of more than thirty days. Twenty-five states require that length of time, while the other twenty-five states require fewer or no days. Another voting requirement is citizenship. Aliens may not vote in any public election held anywhere in the United States. Most states also do not permit prison inmates, mentally ill people, felons, or election-law violators to vote.

Attempts to Improve Voter Turnout

Attempts to improve voter turnout typically have a partisan dimension. This is because the kinds of people who find it difficult to register to vote tend to be

poll tax A fee of several dollars that had to be paid before a person could vote; a device used in some southern states to prevent African Americans from voting.

grandfather clause A clause in a state law that had the effect of restricting the franchise (voting rights) to those whose ancestors had voted before the 1860s; one of the techniques used in the South to prevent African Americans from exercising their right to vote.

white primary A primary election in which African Americans were prohibited from voting. The practice was banned by the Supreme Court in 1944.

Table 8–2

Extension of the Right to Vote

Year	Action	Impact
1870	Fifteenth Amendment	Discrimination based on race outlawed.
1920	Nineteenth Amendment	Discrimination based on gender outlawed.
1924	Congressional act	All Native Americans given citizenship.
1944	*Smith v. Allwright*	Supreme Court prohibits white primary.
1957	Civil Rights Act of 1957	Justice Department can sue to protect voting rights in various states.
1960	Civil Rights Act of 1960	Courts authorized to appoint referees to assist voter-registration procedures.
1961	Twenty-third Amendment	Residents of District of Columbia given right to vote for president and vice president.
1964	Twenty-fourth Amendment	Poll tax in national elections outlawed.
1965	Voting Rights Act of 1965	Literacy tests prohibited; federal voter registrars authorized in seven southern states.
1970	Voting Rights Act Amendments of 1970	Voting age for federal elections reduced to eighteen years; maximum thirty-day residency required for presidential elections; state literacy tests abolished.
1971	Twenty-sixth Amendment	Minimum voting age reduced to eighteen for all elections.
1975	Voting Rights Act Amendments of 1975	Federal voter registrars authorized in ten more states; bilingual ballots to be used in certain circumstances.
1982	Voting Rights Act Amendments of 1982	Extended provisions of Voting Rights Act amendments of 1970 and 1975; private parties allowed to sue for violations.

disproportionately Democratic in their sympathies. Many, for example, are African Americans, a reliably Democratic voting bloc. As a result, Republicans are generally wary of efforts to make registration easier. For example, most Republicans opposed the passage of the National Voter Registration Act (the "Motor Voter Law") of 1993, which simplified the voter-registration process. The act requires states to provide all eligible citizens with the opportunity to register to vote when they apply for or renew a driver's license. The law also requires that states allow mail-in registration, with forms given at certain public assistance agencies. The law, which took effect on January 1, 1995, has facilitated millions of registrations.

In 1998, Oregon voters approved a ballot initiative requiring that all elections in that state, including presidential elections, be conducted exclusively by mail. In the 2008 presidential elections, 66 percent of Oregonians eligible to vote cast ballots, a figure that is somewhat higher than the national average but not exceptionally so. Some argue that if mail-in voting were allowed nationwide, voter turnout would increase. Others believe that voting by mail has a number of disadvantages, including greater possibilities for voter fraud. We examine whether voter fraud is a serious issue in the *Join the Debate* feature on the following page.

Civil rights protesters, led by Martin Luther King, Jr., march on the road from Selma to Montgomery, Alabama, in March 1965. During the five-day, fifty-mile march, federal troops were stationed every one hundred yards along the route to protect the marchers from violent attacks by segregationists.

MATT HERON/SMITHSONIAN

JOIN THE DEBATE

Voter Fraud—A Real Problem or Much Ado about Nothing?

Cries of voter fraud came from the Democrats in 2000 and again in 2004. The Democrats believed that votes were handled improperly in Florida in 2000 and that this kept Democratic presidential candidate Al Gore from carrying the state and winning the presidency. In 2004, some believed that fraud cost Democratic presidential candidate John Kerry the state of Ohio and the presidency. In 2008, accusations of voter fraud became a major campaign issue when Republican John McCain claimed that a group called Acorn was "on the verge of maybe perpetrating one of the greatest frauds in voter history." Acorn, since dissolved, was a nonprofit group that advocated for the poor. It mounted a voter-registration drive in 2008, and some of its employees handed in registration forms that bore the names of cartoon characters and out-of-state major-league athletes. Strictly speaking, this was not voter fraud, but registration fraud. Voter fraud would occur only if someone using the name Mickey Mouse actually turned up at the polls and tried to vote. Acorn said that it had fired the offending employees and that state laws required it to hand in even obviously bogus registration forms, which it had marked as suspect.

Voter Fraud Is a Myth

Political analyst Harold Meyerson of the *Los Angeles Times* wrote, "Voter fraud is a myth—not an urban or a real myth, as such, but a Republican one." The Justice Department's Ballot Access and Voting Integrity Initiative

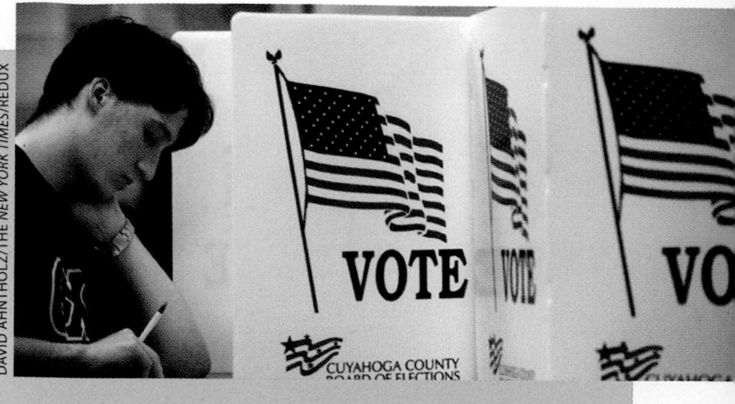

DAVID AHNTHOLZ/THE *NEW YORK TIMES*/REDUX

obtained only eighty-six convictions for voter fraud over a five-year period. Many Americans contend that voter fraud will always exist on a small scale, but it is not a serious problem today. Rather, the Republicans have raised the specter of voter fraud in order to pass laws, such as those requiring photo IDs, that make it harder for disadvantaged persons (mostly Democrats) to vote.

Voter Fraud Is a Real Problem

Other Americans believe that voter fraud is a significant problem. The Election Assistance Commission issued a report indicating that the extent of voter fraud is still open to debate. Lapses in enforcing voting and registration rules continue to occur. Thousands upon thousands of ineligible voters are allowed to vote. Many felons—who are not allowed to vote in most states—end up voting anyway. The only effective method of reducing voter fraud is to require photo IDs at polling places, as is done in states such as Indiana.

For Critical Analysis ***Why might people who find it harder to register and vote tend to support the Democratic Party?***

Attempts to Improve Voting Procedures

Because of serious problems in achieving accurate vote counts in recent elections, particularly in the 2000 presidential elections, steps have been taken to attempt to ensure more accuracy in the voting process. In 2002, Congress passed the Help America Vote Act, which, among other things, provided funds to the states to help them purchase new electronic voting equipment. Concerns about the possibility of fraudulent manipulation of electronic voting machines then replaced the worries over inaccurate vote counts caused by the previous equipment.

PROBLEMS IN 2006 In the 2006 elections, about half of the states that were using new electronic voting systems reported problems. Some systems "flipped" votes from the selected candidate to the opposing candidate. In one Florida district, about eighteen thousand votes apparently were unrecorded by electronic equipment, and this may have changed the outcome of a congressional race. Many experts have demanded that electronic

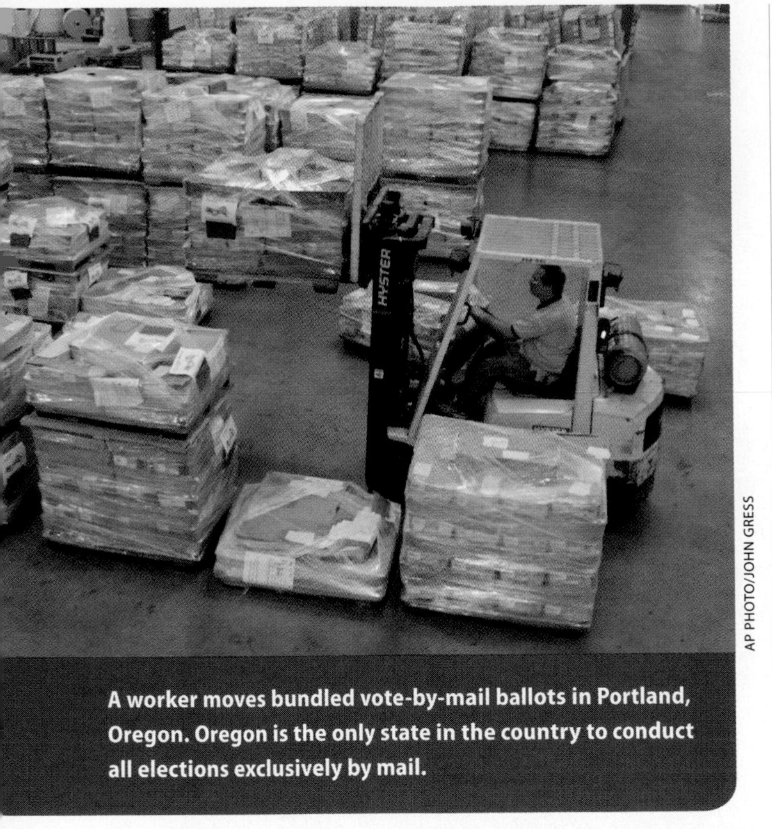
AP PHOTO/JOHN GRESS

A worker moves bundled vote-by-mail ballots in Portland, Oregon. Oregon is the only state in the country to conduct all elections exclusively by mail.

systems create a "paper trail" so that machine errors can be tracked and fixed.

VOTING SYSTEMS IN THE 2008 ELECTIONS Because of problems with electronic systems, fewer polling places used them in 2008. Indeed, more than half of all votes cast in 2008 used old-fashioned paper ballots. As a result, vote counting was slow. One feature of the elections was the large number of states that allowed early voting at polling places that opened weeks before Election Day. A benefit of early voting was that it allowed election workers time to ensure that all systems were working properly by Election Day.

Who Actually Votes

Just because an individual is eligible to vote does not necessarily mean that the person will actually go to the polls on Election Day and vote. Why do some eligible voters go to the polls while others do not? Although nobody can answer this question with absolute conviction, certain factors, including those discussed next, appear to affect voter turnout.

voting-age population
The number of people residing in the United States who are at least eighteen years old.

EDUCATIONAL ATTAINMENT Among the factors affecting voter turnout, education appears to be the most important. The more education a person has, the more likely it is that she or he will be a regular voter. People who graduated from high school vote more regularly than those who dropped out, and college graduates vote more often than high school graduates.

INCOME LEVEL AND AGE Differences in income also lead to differences in voter turnout. Wealthy people tend to be overrepresented among regular voters. Generally, older voters turn out to vote more regularly than younger voters do, although participation tends to decline among the very elderly. Participation likely increases with age because older people tend to be more settled, are already registered, and have had more experience with voting.

MINORITY STATUS Racial and ethnic minorities traditionally have been underrepresented among the ranks of voters. In several recent elections, however, participation by these groups, particularly African Americans and Hispanics, has increased.

It was expected that with an African American running for president on the Democratic ticket in 2008, voter turnout among African Americans would go through the roof. African American turnout was indeed high, but not as high as some had expected. About 20 percent more African Americans voted in 2008 than in 2004, and their share of the vote rose from 11 percent to 13 percent. African Americans were essential to Obama's victories in North Carolina and Virginia.

In part because the number of Hispanic citizens has grown rapidly, the increase in the Hispanic vote—more than 30 percent—was even larger than the increase in the black vote. Hispanics helped Obama carry Colorado, Indiana, Nevada, and New Mexico.

IMMIGRATION AND VOTER TURNOUT The United States has experienced high rates of immigration in recent decades, and that has had an effect on voter turnout figures. In the past, voter turnout was often expressed as a percentage of the **voting-age population,** the number of people residing in the United States who are at least eighteen years old. Due to legal and illegal immigration, however, there are many people of voting age who are not eligible to vote because they are not citizens. Millions more cannot vote because they are felons. Additionally, the voting-age population excludes Americans abroad, who are eligible to cast absentee ballots.

Today, political scientists calculate the **vote-eligible population,** the number of people who are actually entitled to vote in American elections. They have found that there may be 20 million fewer eligible voters than the voting-age population suggests. Therefore, voter turnout is actually greater than the percentages sometimes cited. Some experts have argued that the relatively low levels of voter turnout often reported for the years between 1972 and 2000 were largely due to immigration.[8] Beginning in 2004, voter turnout has improved by any calculation method.

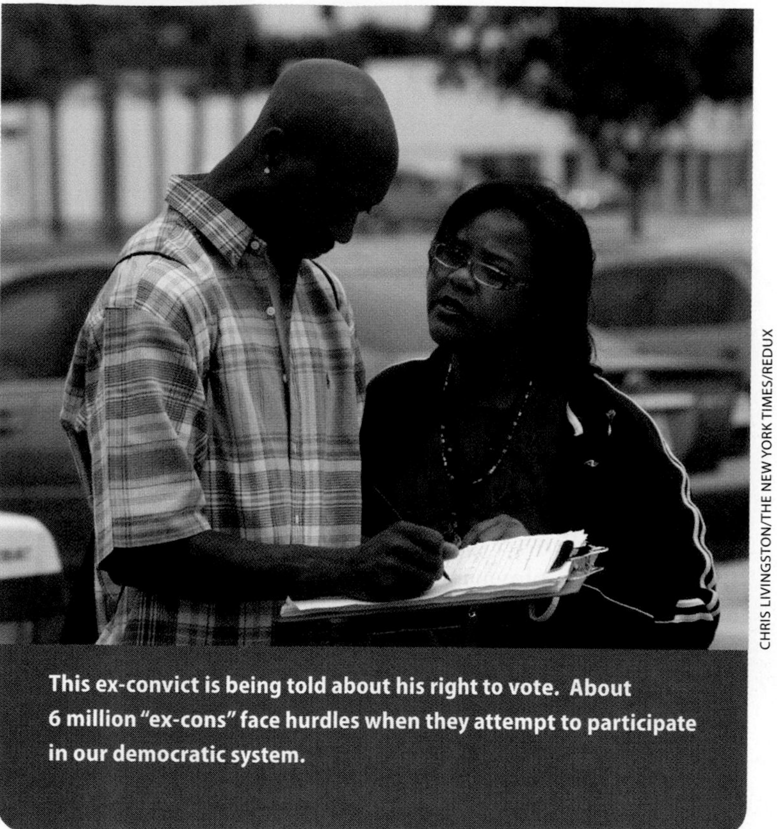
CHRIS LIVINGSTON/THE NEW YORK TIMES/REDUX

This ex-convict is being told about his right to vote. About 6 million "ex-cons" face hurdles when they attempt to participate in our democratic system.

LO5 *Why People Vote as They Do*

What prompts some citizens to vote Republican and others to vote Democratic? What persuades voters to choose certain kinds of candidates? Obviously, more is involved than measuring one's own position against the candidates' positions and then voting accordingly. Voters choose candidates for many reasons. Researchers have collected more information on voting than on any other form of political participation in the United States. These data shed some light on why people decide to vote for particular candidates.

Party Identification

Many voters have a standing allegiance to a political party, or a party identification, although the proportion of the population that does so has fallen in recent decades. For established voters, party identification is one of the most important and lasting predictors of how a person will vote. Party identification is an emotional attachment to a party that is influenced by family, age, peer groups, and other factors that play a role in the political socialization process discussed earlier.

A large number of voters call themselves independents. Despite this label, many independents actually support one or the other of the two major parties quite regularly. Figure 8–2 on the following page shows how those who identified themselves as Democrats, Republicans, and independents voted in the 2008 presidential elections.

Perception of the Candidates

Voters often base their decisions on the perceived character of the candidates rather than on their qualifications or policy positions. Such perceptions were important in the 2008 presidential elections. At first, some observers saw Democrat Barack Obama as aloof or even arrogant. During the economic crisis, however, Obama's calm temperament was viewed as "presidential." Six out of ten voters reported that they had no idea what Obama would do to get the country out of its financial mess, but they were sure he could do it. Republican John McCain sought to portray himself as a fighter for America. Sometimes he simply came across as angry, however. As Republican strategist Karl Rove put it, "When was the last time Americans elected an angry president?" Falling behind in the polls, McCain repeatedly changed direction in an attempt to alter the nature of the race. These moves, however,

vote-eligible population The number of people who are actually eligible to vote in an American election.

played into the impression that he was erratic and unpredictable. His choice of Sarah Palin as a running mate also seemed impulsive.

Policy Choices

When people vote for candidates who share their positions on particular issues, they are engaging in policy voting. If a candidate for senator in your state opposes gun control laws, for example, and you decide to vote for her for that reason, you have engaged in policy voting.

Historically, economic issues have had the strongest influence on voters' choices. When the economy is doing well, it is very difficult for a challenger, particularly at the presidential level, to defeat the incumbent. In contrast, when the country is experiencing inflation, rising unemployment, or high interest rates, the incumbent will likely be at a disadvantage. The main issue in the 2008 presidential elections and the 2010 midterm elections was the financial crisis facing all Americans.

Some of the most heated debates in American political campaigns have involved social issues, such as abortion, gay and lesbian rights, the death penalty, and religion in the schools. Often, presidential candidates prefer to avoid emphasizing their stand on these types of issues, because voters who have strong opinions about such issues are likely to be offended if a candidate does not share their views.

Socioeconomic Factors

Some factors that influence how people vote can be described as socioeconomic. These factors include educational attainment, income level, age, gender, religion, and geographic location. Some of these factors have to do with the circumstances into which individuals are born. Others have to do with personal choices. Figure 8–3 on the facing page shows how various groups voted in the 2008 presidential elections.

EDUCATIONAL ATTAINMENT As a general rule, people with more education are more likely to vote Republican, although in recent years, voters with postgraduate degrees have tended to vote Democratic. Typically, those with less education are also more inclined to vote for the Democratic nominee. Educational attainment, of course, can be linked to income level. Recent studies show that among students from families with income in the bottom fifth of the population, only 12 percent earn a bachelor's degree by the age of twenty-four. In the top fifth, the figure is 73 percent.

OCCUPATION AND INCOME LEVEL Businesspersons tend to vote Republican and have done so for many years. Recently, professionals (such as attorneys, professors, and physicians) have been more likely to vote Democratic than in earlier years. Manual laborers, factory workers, and especially union members are more likely to vote Democratic. In the past, the higher the income, the more likely it was that a person would vote Republican. Conversely, a much larger percentage of low-income individuals voted Democratic. But this pattern is also breaking down, and there are no hard-and-fast rules. Some very poor individuals are

Figure 8–2

Party Identification and Voting Behavior in the 2008 Presidential Elections

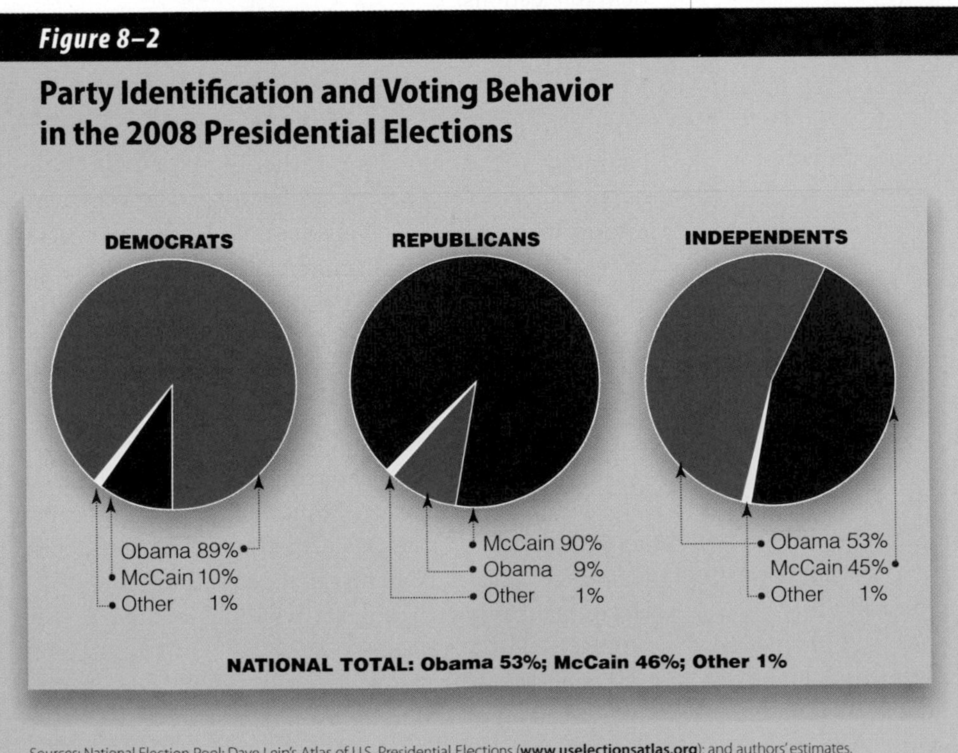

Sources: National Election Pool; Dave Leip's Atlas of U.S. Presidential Elections (**www.uselectionsatlas.org**); and authors' estimates.

Figure 8–3

Voting by Groups in the 2008 Presidential Elections

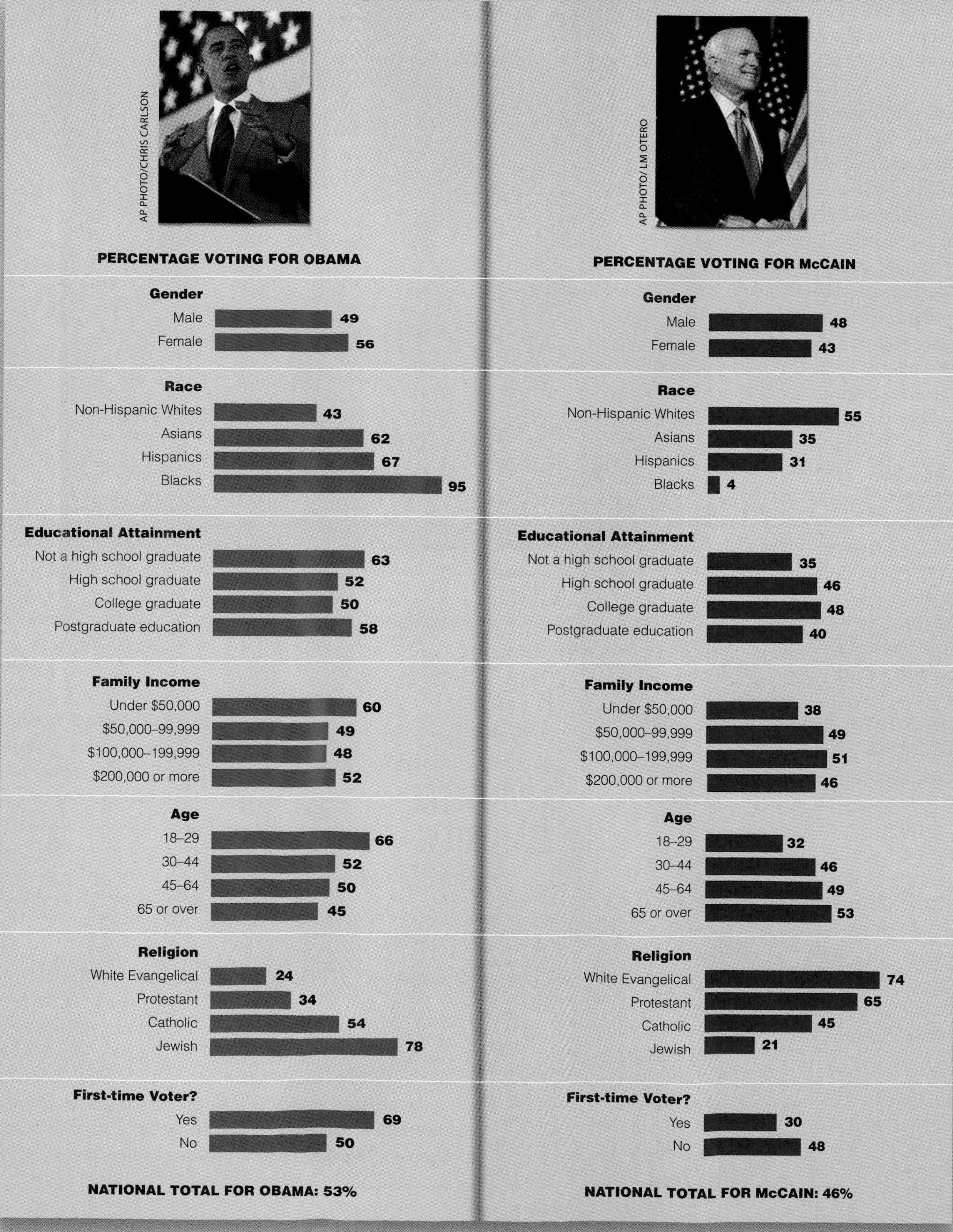

Source: The National Election Pool.

devoted Republicans, just as some extremely wealthy persons are supporters of the Democratic Party.

AGE The conventional wisdom is that the young are liberal and the old are conservative, yet in years past age differences in support for the parties have often been quite small. One age-related effect is that people's attitudes are shaped by the events that unfolded as they grew up. Many voters who came of age during Franklin Roosevelt's New Deal held on to a preference for the Democrats. Voters who were young when Ronald Reagan was president have had a tendency to prefer the Republicans. Younger voters are noticeably more liberal on one set of issues, however—those dealing with the rights of minorities, women, and gay males and lesbians.

EMMANUEL DUNAND/AFP/GETTY IMAGES

Barack Obama supporters hold signs during a "Women's Rally for the Change We Need" in Coral Gables, Florida. Was there a gender gap in 2008 voting?

THE YOUTH VOTE IN THE 2008 ELECTIONS In contrast with past years, age had a striking impact on voters' choices in 2008. Voters under thirty years of age chose Obama by a two-to-one margin. The Obama campaign hoped for a massive increase in the turnout of younger voters. In the end, though, young voters' share of the electorate rose only modestly, from 17 percent to 18 percent. What made the youth vote important was not turnout, but Obama's enormous margin, a result with ominous implications for the Republicans in future years.

"In politics, an organized minority is **A POLITICAL MAJORITY.**"

~ REV. JESSE JACKSON ~
CIVIL RIGHTS ACTIVIST
1941–PRESENT

gender gap The difference between the percentage of votes cast for a particular candidate by women and the percentage of votes cast for the same candidate by men.

GENDER Until about thirty years ago, there seemed to be no fixed pattern of voter preferences by gender in presidential elections. Women and men tended to vote for the various candidates in roughly equal numbers. Some political analysts believe that a **gender gap** became a major determinant of voter decision making in the 1980 presidential elections, however. In that year, Ronald Reagan outdrew Jimmy Carter by 16 percentage points among male voters, whereas women gave about an equal number of votes to each candidate.

THE GENDER GAP IN 2008 In 2008, Barack Obama carried the male vote by one percentage point and the female vote by a 13 percent margin. This gender gap was close to the average seen since 1980. John McCain hoped to make inroads among women by naming Sarah Palin as his running mate. He especially hoped to attract disgruntled supporters of Obama's defeated opponent in the primaries, Hillary Clinton. This strategy does not seem to have worked.

RELIGION AND ETHNIC BACKGROUND A century ago, at least in the northern states, white Catholic voters were likely to be Democrats and white Protestant voters were likely to be Republicans. There are a few places around the country where this pattern continues to hold, but for the most part, white Catholics are now almost as likely as their Protestant neighbors to support the Republicans.

In recent years, a different religious variable has become important in determining voting behavior. Regardless of their denomination, white Christian voters who attend church regularly have favored the Republicans by substantial margins. White voters who attend church rarely or who find religion less important in their lives are more likely to vote Democratic. Jewish voters are strongly Democratic, regardless of whether they attend services.

Most African Americans are Protestants, but African Americans are one of the most solidly Democratic constituencies in the United States. This is a complete reversal of the circumstances that existed a century ago. As noted in Chapter 7, for many years after the Civil War, those African Americans who could vote were overwhelmingly Republican. Not until President Franklin Roosevelt's New Deal did black voters begin to turn to the Democrats. Hispanic voters have supported the Democrats by margins of about two to one, with some exceptions: Cuban Americans are strongly Republican. Asian Americans tend to favor the Democrats, although Vietnamese Americans are strongly Republican.

"Whenever a fellow tells me he is bipartisan, I KNOW HE IS GOING TO VOTE AGAINST ME."

~ HARRY TRUMAN ~
THIRTY-THIRD PRESIDENT
OF THE UNITED STATES
1945–1953

A member of the League of Women Voters participates in a demonstration to protest the lack of voting rights for the citizens of Washington, D.C., on the 90th Anniversary of the 19th Amendment, guaranteeing women the right to vote.

Vote! IT COUNTS
LWV THE LEAGUE OF WOMEN VOTERS

KEVIN DIETSCH/UPI/LANDOV

GEOGRAPHIC REGION In today's presidential contests, states in the South, the Great Plains, and parts of the Rocky Mountains are strongly Republican. The Northeast, the West Coast, and Illinois are firmly Democratic. Many of the swing states that decide elections are located in the Midwest, although several Rocky Mountain states swing between the parties as well. This pattern is an almost complete reversal of the one that existed a century ago. In those years, most white southerners were Democrats, and people spoke of the **Solid South**—solidly Democratic, that is. The Solid South lasted for a century after the Civil War and in large part was the result of southern resentment of the Republicans for their role in the "War between the States" and their support of African Americans in the postwar era. At the end of the nineteenth century, the Republicans were strong in the Northeast and much of the Midwest, while the Democrats were able to find support outside of the South in the Great Plains and the Far West.

The ideologies of the two parties have likewise undergone something of a reversal. One hundred years ago, the

Solid South A term used to describe the tendency of the southern states to vote Democratic after the Civil War.

ELECTIONS 2010

The Vote by Demographic Groups

The 2010 national exit poll was organized ABC, CBS, CNN, Fox, NBC, and the Associated Press, and it contacted more than 17,000 voters in twenty-six states. Some of the results were expected. The gender gap continues to exist—women were six percentage points more likely to vote Democratic than were men. African Americans cast 90 percent of their votes for Democrats. The Hispanic vote was 64 percent Democratic, and Asian Americans voted Democratic by 56 percent. Non-Hispanic whites, however, cast 60 percent of their votes for Republicans. A piece of good news for the Democrats was that the youngest voters, those aged 18 to 29, preferred the Democrats by 57 to 40 percent. Unfortunately for the Democrats, the percentage of youth among the voters who turned out was half what it was in 2008. Voters above the age of 65, in contrast, preferred Republicans by 59 percent to 38 percent. Backing for Republicans among the elderly was 48 percent in 2008—which means the Democrats lost the support of 11 percent of this group in two years. Clearly, the health-care bill, unpopular among seniors, took its toll. The elderly also made up 24 percent of the voters, the highest figure in years. A final point: high family income was a better predictor of Republican support in 2010 than it had been in 2008.

Democrats were seen as *less* likely than the Republicans to support government intervention in the economy. The Democrats were also the party that opposed civil rights. Today, the Democrats are often regarded as the party that supports "big government" and affirmative action programs.

Ideology

Ideology is another indicator of voting behavior. A significant percentage of Americans today identify themselves as moderates. Recent polls indicate that 44 percent of Americans consider themselves to be moderates, 22 percent consider themselves liberals, and 34 percent identify themselves as conservatives.

For many Americans, where they fall in the political spectrum is a strong indicator of how they will vote: liberals vote for Democrats, and conservatives vote for Republicans. The large numbers of Americans who fall in the political center do not adhere strictly to an ideology. In most elections, the candidates compete aggressively for these voters because they know their "base"—on the left or right—is secure.

vital center The center of the political spectrum; those who hold moderate political views. The center is vital because without it, it may be difficult, if not impossible, to reach the compromises that are necessary to a political system's continuity.

THE VITAL CENTER In 1949, historian Arthur Schlesinger, Jr., described the position between the political extremes as the **vital center.** The center is vital because without it, necessary compromises may be difficult, if not impossible, to achieve. One problem with activating the vital center is that voter apathy and low voter turnout are found most commonly among those in the center. The most motivated voters are the "ideologically zealous."[9]

IDEOLOGY IN THE 2008 ELECTIONS According to 2008 exit polls, 89 percent of voters who identified themselves as liberals voted for Barack Obama, who also received the votes of 20 percent of self-identified conservatives. Obama carried self-described moderates by 60 percent to 49 percent, a result that was crucial to his victory.

These figures raise some interesting questions. John McCain tried very hard to portray Obama as "too liberal," and to a certain extent he succeeded. Among all voters, 42 percent thought that Obama was too liberal, compared with 50 percent who thought that his positions were about right. Only 4 percent of those questioned thought that he was too conservative. In another poll, most respondents believed that McCain's ideological positions were closer to their own than Obama's. Still, a majority of these voters supported Obama.

It is clear from these results that there are limits to the power of ideology to determine election outcomes. Many moderate and even some conservative voters supported Obama because they thought he was better suited to be president—regardless of ideology. In this sense, Obama won the support of the vital center.

AMERICA AT ODDS Public Opinion and Voting

Public opinion polls reveal that Americans are in broad agreement on many issues, such as the basic political structure of our nation. Nevertheless, polls also report that Americans are at odds with one another on many other issues. After all, the questions posed by poll takers are typically divisive ones. Issues surrounding who votes and why can also be contentious. Some examples include the following:

- Is the disenfranchisement of felons a form of racial discrimination—or a rational part of the punishment process?
- Given that historical events shape popular attitudes toward the parties, when all is said and done, will the impact of the Great Recession benefit the Republican Party—or will the effects of the recession prove trivial?
- Should legislators follow public opinion as faithfully as they can—or, as the Democrats did on health-care reform, should lawmakers do what they think is best for the country regardless of the polls?
- We discussed *push polls* on page 173. Should push polls be banned—or would that violate First Amendment guarantees of free speech?
- Should voters be most concerned with the policy positions of the presidential candidates—or are the presidential candidates' personalities and personal characteristics of equal or greater concern?

Take Action

"Citizens at the polls are the most powerful agents of change." Thus say political analysts Thomas Mann and Norman Ornstein.[10] But if citizens are not informed about the political issues of the day or the candidates' qualifications, there is little sense in going to the polls. Indeed, as mentioned in this chapter, one of the reasons for the relatively low voter turnout in this country is a sense on the part of some citizens that they lack information. As also noted, peer groups are important in the political socialization process. But just as you might be influenced by your peers, you can also influence them.

If you would like to take action to increase interest in our political life, one thing you might do is host a political salon. This would be a gathering, either in your home or at some other place, that would focus on learning about political issues and opinions. You could invite friends, other students, co-workers, or other persons who might be interested to attend the salon, which could be held weekly, monthly, or at some other interval. At the first meeting, you could set the "rules" for the salon. What topics do you want to discuss? How much time do you want to devote to each topic? What reading or research, if any, should be undertaken before the meetings? Depending on the views and energies of those who attend the salon, you might also devise an activist agenda to increase voter turnout. For example, you could plan a get-out-the-vote drive for the next election.

THIS LITTLE TEST OF YOUR REFLEXES WILL TELL US IF YOU'RE A KNEE-JERK LIBERAL OR KNEE-JERK CONSERVATIVE.
SCHWADRON

©HARLEY SCHWADRON

POLITICS ON THE WEB

- Recent polls conducted and analyzed by the Roper Center for Public Opinion Research can be found at **www.ropercenter.uconn.edu**
- At the Gallup Organization's Web site, you can find the results of recent polls, as well as an archive of past polls and information on how polls are conducted. Go to **www.gallup.com**
- You can find poll data and material on major issues at the following site: **www.publicagenda.org**
- In addition to its enormous collection of recent articles on politics, the Real Clear Politics Web site has one of the most comprehensive collections of election polls available. For the polls, go to **www.realclearpolitics.com/polls**
- Nate Silver gained fame in 2008 for his analysis of polls taken by major firms. His election predictions were outstandingly accurate. Silver and his colleagues at the FiveThirtyEight blog now work under the aegis of the *New York Times*—go to **fivethirtyeight.blogs.nytimes.com**
- You'll find a poll-lover's dream at Mark Blumenthal's Pollster blog site, where readers debate about all the recent polls. Go to **www.pollster.com/blogs**
- Pollster.com's main page is also a trove of information about polls. See it at **www.pollster.com**
- Another site that collects polls and analyzes them is run by Scott Elliott, who is known as the "blogging Caesar." See it at **www.electionprojection.com**

Access CourseMate to review and expand on this chapter through quizzes, flashcards, learning objectives, interactive timelines, a crossword puzzle, audio summaries, video, critical-thinking activities, simulations, and more.

Campaigns and Elections

LEARNING OBJECTIVES

LO1 Explain how elections are held and how the electoral college functions in presidential elections.

LO2 Discuss how candidates are nominated.

LO3 Indicate what is involved in launching a political campaign today, and describe the structure and functions of a campaign organization.

LO4 Describe how the Internet has transformed political campaigns.

LO5 Summarize the laws that regulate campaign financing and the role of money in modern political campaigns.

LO6 Describe what took place during recent presidential elections and what these events tell us about the American electoral system.

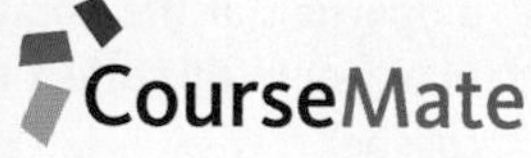

AMERICA AT ODDS

Should We Elect the President by Popular Vote?

When Americans go to the polls every four years to cast their ballots for president, many are unaware that they are not, in fact, voting directly for the candidates. Rather, they are voting for electors—individuals chosen in each state by political parties to cast the state's electoral votes for the candidate who wins that state's popular vote. The system by which electors cast their votes for president is known as the *electoral college.*

Each state is assigned electoral votes based on its number of members in the U.S. Senate and House of Representatives. Each state has the same number of senators in the Senate (two), and the number of representatives a state has in the House is determined by the size of its population. As a result, there are currently 538 electoral votes.[1]

To win in the electoral college, a presidential candidate must win 270 of these 538 electoral votes. Most states have a "winner-take-all" system in which the candidate who receives a plurality of the popular votes (more than any other candidate) in a state receives all of that state's electoral votes, even if the margin of victory is very slight. A candidate who wins the popular vote nationally may yet lose in the electoral college—and vice versa. Many Americans believe that we should let the popular vote, not the electoral college, decide who becomes president.[2] Others are not so sure.

Let the People Elect Our President

In 2000, Democratic candidate Al Gore won the popular vote yet narrowly lost to Republican George W. Bush in the electoral college. Many Americans questioned the legitimacy of Bush's election. In 2004, a 120,000-vote swing in Ohio to Democrat John Kerry would have made him the president, even though Republican George W. Bush had a 2.5 percent lead in the popular vote nationally. If the 2008 presidential elections had been closer than it was, Democrat Barack Obama could easily have been elected with fewer popular votes than Republican John McCain—or McCain could have been elected with fewer votes than Obama.

Opponents decry the electoral college as an outdated invention of the late 1700s. To be sure, among the reasons for the system's original design was to ensure that the interests of smaller states were not totally overshadowed by their more populous neighbors. Yet the electoral college gives the smaller states a disproportionate amount of clout. Consider, for example, that one electoral vote in California now corresponds to roughly 675,000 people, while an electoral vote in more sparsely settled Wyoming represents only about 180,000 individuals. Clearly, the votes of Americans are not weighted equally, and this voting inequality is contrary to the "one person, one vote" principle of our democracy.

The Electoral College Protects the Small States and Ensures Stability

Supporters of the electoral college argue that if the system were abolished, small states would suffer. Because each state has as many electors as its total number of members in Congress, even the smallest states get two votes based on their representation in the Senate. Therefore, the electoral college helps to protect the small states from being overwhelmed by the large states.

The electoral college also helps to maintain a relatively stable and coherent party system. If the president were elected by popular vote, we might have multiple parties vying for the nation's highest office—as occurs in such nations as France, Germany, and Italy. The current system helps to discourage single-issue or regional candidates—candidates who are not focused on the interests of the nation as a whole. To prevail in the electoral college, a candidate must build a national coalition, campaign in Santa Fe as well as New York City, and propose policies that unite, rather than divide, the nation.

Finally, the electoral college vote has diverged from the popular vote in only three elections during our nation's history—in 1876, 1888, and 2000. These exceptions do not justify abolishing the system.

WHERE DO YOU STAND?

1. **Do you believe that a candidate elected by the popular vote would be more representative of the entire nation than a candidate elected by the electoral college? Why or why not?**
2. **Suppose that instead of using the "winner-take-all" system, all states awarded their electoral votes according to the proportion of the popular vote each candidate received. How would this affect the final outcome in the electoral college?**

EXPLORE THIS ISSUE ONLINE

- **For critical views of the electoral college, go to the Web site of the Center for Voting and Democracy at www.fairvote.org/fair-elections and click on "National Popular Vote for President."**
- **For an article making a case for the electoral college, go to the Web site of Accuracy in Media (a conservative media watchdog group) at www.aim.org/briefing/making-a-case-for-the-electoral-college.**

Introduction

During elections, candidates vie to become representatives of the people in both national and state offices. The population of the United States is now more than 310 million. Clearly, all citizens who are eligible to vote cannot gather in one place to make laws and run the government. We have to choose representatives to govern the nation and to act on behalf of our interests. We accomplish this through popular elections.

Campaigning for election has become an arduous task for every politician. As you will see in this chapter, American campaigns are long and expensive undertakings. The rules that govern our elections can be complicated, as you read in the chapter-opening *America at Odds* feature. Yet America's campaigns are an important part of our political process because it is through campaigns that citizens learn about the candidates and decide how they will cast their votes.

LO1 *How We Elect Candidates*

The ultimate goal of a political campaign and the associated fund-raising efforts is, of course, winning the election. The most familiar kind of election is the **general election,** which is a regularly scheduled election held in even-numbered years on the Tuesday after the first Monday in November. During general elections, the voters decide who will be the U.S. president, vice president, and senators and representatives in Congress. The president and vice president are elected every four years, senators every six years, and representatives every two years. General elections are also held to choose state and local government officials, often at the same time as those for national offices. A **special election** is held at the state or local level when the voters must decide an issue before the next general election or when vacancies occur by reason of death or resignation.

Most American citizens still case their ballots in paper form. Why hasn't this technology changed?

DAVID PAUL MORRIS/GETTY IMAGES

Types of Ballots

Since 1888, all states in the United States have used the **Australian ballot**—a secret ballot that is prepared, distributed, and counted by government officials at public expense. As its name implies, this ballot was first developed in Australia in 1856. An Australian innovation that we do not use in this country is compulsory voting, which we describe in this chapter's *The Rest of the World* feature on the following page.

Two variations of the Australian ballot are used today. Most states use the **party-column ballot** (also called the Indiana ballot), which lists all of a party's candidates together in a single column under the party label. In some states, the party-column ballot allows voters to vote for all of a party's candidates for local, state, and national offices by making a single "X" or pulling a single lever. The major parties favor this ballot form because it encourages straight-ticket voting.

Other states use the **office-block ballot** (also called the Massachusetts ballot), which lists together all of the candidates for each office. Parties tend to dislike the office-block ballot because it places more emphasis on the office than on the party and thus encourages split-ticket voting.

general election A regularly scheduled election to choose the U.S. president, vice president, and senators and representatives in Congress. General elections are held in even-numbered years on the Tuesday after the first Monday in November.

special election An election that is held at the state or local level when the voters must decide an issue before the next general election or when vacancies occur by reason of death or resignation.

Australian ballot A secret ballot that is prepared, distributed, and counted by government officials at public expense; used by all states in the United States since 1888.

party-column ballot A ballot (also called the Indiana ballot) that lists all of a party's candidates under the party label. Voters can vote for all of a party's candidates for local, state, and national offices by making a single "X" or pulling a single lever.

office-block ballot A ballot (also called the Massachusetts ballot) that lists together all of the candidates for each office.

Compulsory Voting Elsewhere Improves Voter Turnout

No matter what the election is, no matter what the issues are, and no matter who is running, voter turnout in the United States is low compared with that in many other countries. Obviously, the United States would have higher voter participation if we had a compulsory voting law. Australia is a good example of how such a system works.

Compulsory Voting in Australia

In Australia, citizens over the age of eighteen must register to vote, and they must show up at the polls on Election Day. Otherwise, they are subject to fines. This law has been in effect since 1924. Australia does make voting easier than it is in America, however. Elections are always held on Saturday, not Tuesday. Voters can vote from anywhere in the country. Citizens who live in remote areas can vote before Election Day or send in their ballots by mail.

The Effects of Australia's Law

Before 1924, in a typical year Australia saw a turnout of registered voters that was about on par with the United States—an average of 47 percent. Currently, voter turnout is roughly 95 percent. Candidates or organizations in Australia do not have to engage in "get out the vote" activities. In other words, candidates and their supporters can focus on issues rather than on encouraging voters to go to the polls. In the United States, much effort goes into getting citizens to register and then getting them to go to the polls to vote.

One odd result of compulsory voting is popularly known as the "donkey vote." Citizens who do not care about the elections may simply vote for the first name on a list of candidates. Before 1984, when lists were typically in alphabetical order, candidates could obtain a detectable advantage if their last name began with the letter A. Since that year, however, names have been listed in random order.

Compulsory Voting in Other Countries

Australia is not alone in enforcing compulsory voting. The following nations also do so:

Argentina	Liechtenstein
Brazil	Nauru
Chile	Peru
Congo (Kinshasa)	Singapore
Ecuador	Turkey
Fiji	Uruguay

Twenty other countries have compulsory voting laws but do not attempt to enforce them.

AGENCIA ESTADO VIA AP IMAGES

Like Australia, Brazil has compulsory voting laws. Here voters line up outside an election office in Sao Paulo, Brazil, on the last day of registration to vote in 2010.

For Critical Analysis *Some critics of compulsory voting claim that it is undemocratic. Why do you think they would make this argument?*

Conducting Elections and Counting the Votes

Recall from Chapter 8 that local units of government, such as cities, are divided into smaller voting districts, or precincts. Within each precinct, voters cast their ballots at a designated polling place.

poll watcher A representative from one of the political parties who is allowed to monitor a polling place to make sure that the election is run fairly and to avoid fraud.

An election board supervises the polling place and the voting process in each precinct. The board sets hours for the polls to be open according to the laws of the state and sees that ballots or voting machines are available. In most states, the board provides the list of registered voters and makes certain that only qualified voters cast ballots in each precinct. When the polls close, staff members count the votes and report the results, usually to the county clerk or the board of elections. Representatives from each party, called **poll watchers,** are allowed at each polling place to make sure the election is run fairly and to avoid fraud.

Figure 9–1

State Electoral Votes in 2004 and 2008

This map of the United States is distorted to show the relative weights of the states in terms of their electoral votes in 2004 and 2008, following changes required by the 2000 census. A candidate must win 270 electoral votes, cast by the electors, to become president through the electoral college system.

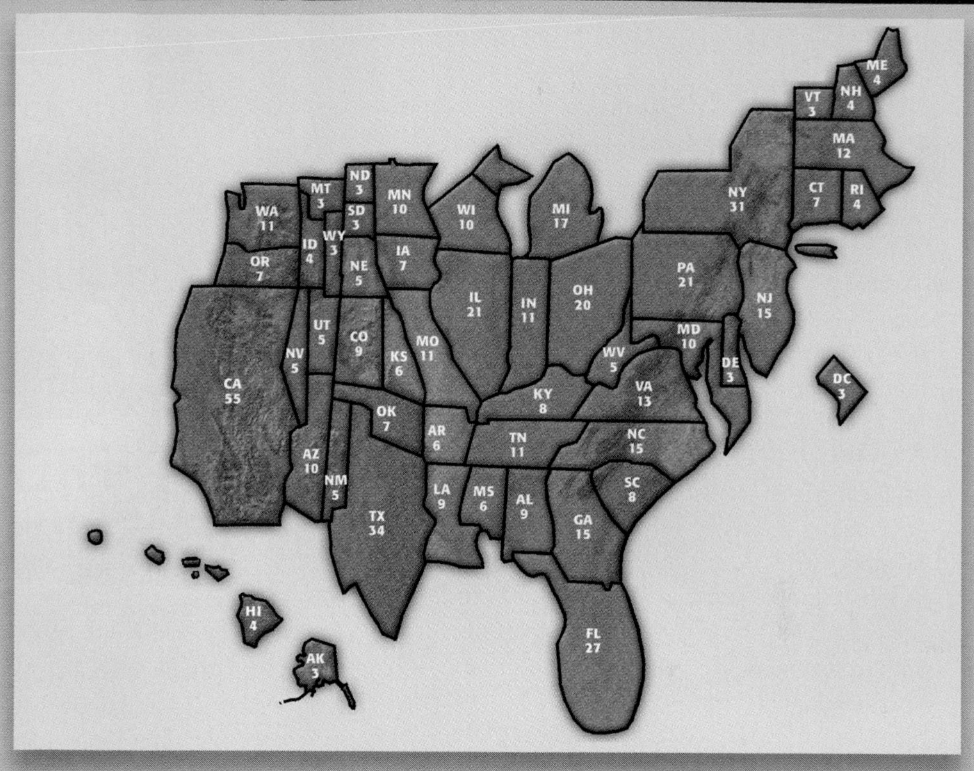

Presidential Elections and the Electoral College

When citizens vote for president and vice president, they are not voting directly for the candidates. Instead, they are voting for **electors** who will cast their ballots in the **electoral college.** The electors are selected during each presidential election year by the states' political parties, subject to the laws of the state. Each state has as many electoral votes as it has U.S. senators and representatives (see Figure 9–1 above). In addition, there are three electors from the District of Columbia, even though it is not a state. Should D.C. also have the right to a representative with a full vote in the House of Representatives? We look at that question in this chapter's *Join the Debate* feature on the following page.

The electoral college system is primarily a **winner-take-all system,** in which the candidate who receives the largest popular vote in a state is credited with all that state's electoral votes. The only exceptions are Maine and Nebraska.[3]

In December, after the general election, electors (either Republicans or Democrats, depending on which candidate has won the state's popular vote) meet in their state capitals to cast their votes for president and vice president. When the Constitution was drafted, the framers intended that the electors would use their own discretion in deciding who would make the best president. Today, however, the electors usually vote for the candidates to whom they are pledged. The electoral college ballots are then sent to the U.S. Senate, which counts and certifies them before a joint session of Congress held early in January. The candidates who receive a majority of the electoral votes are officially declared president and vice president. To be elected, a candidate must receive more than half of the 538 electoral votes available. Thus, a candidate needs 270 votes to win. If no presidential candidate gets an electoral college majority (which has happened twice—in 1800 and 1824), the House of Representatives votes on the candidates, with each state delegation casting only a single vote. If no candidate for vice president gets a majority of

elector A member of the electoral college.

electoral college The group of electors who are selected by the voters in each state to elect officially the president and vice president. The number of electors in each state is equal to the number of that state's representatives in both chambers of Congress.

winner-take-all system A system in which the candidate who receives the most votes wins. In contrast, proportional systems allocate votes to multiple winners.

JOIN THE DEBATE

Should D.C. Residents Have a Representative?

If you are a resident of Washington, D.C., you can vote for president. You also can vote for a delegate who sits in the House of Representatives. That delegate, though, cannot vote on issues that come before the full House. The District of Columbia has no voting representation in Congress.

It's Only Fair

In 2009, Congress debated the D.C. Voting Rights Act. That act would make the District's current delegate a voting member of the House. Such a change seems quite fair, especially to those who live in the District. After all, everybody else who lives in the fifty states is represented by a voting member of the House (and two senators to boot). Whether or not granting full voting privileges to the delegate from the District is fair, one thing is certain. Any representative from D.C. will probably be a Democrat. Why? Because the District has an African American majority, and African Americans for many years have been among the Democrats' most loyal supporters.

Please Respect the Constitution

Others argue that the framers of the Constitution deliberately established the federal capital as a nonstate over which Congress would have exclusive legislative authority. This geographic and political entity has become Washington, D.C., which has been the nation's capital since 1800.

The Constitution requires that House members be elected by the people of the states. The District is not a state, and therefore its residents cannot have a voting member of the House. In other words, the D.C. Voting Rights Act is unconstitutional, and the legislation could never withstand even the first judicial test of its legitimacy.

AP PHOTO/LAUREN BURKE

Why the Real Solution Won't Work

There's an obvious solution to the D.C. representation issue: admit the District as a state. Such a proposal would be perfectly constitutional. It is, in fact, the solution that D.C. residents prefer. If the District became a state, it would join Wyoming as one of the most overrepresented states in the Senate. A second possible solution would be to give the District back to Maryland.[4] The city of Washington would then have enough people to dominate its own House district, and Washington residents could vote for Maryland's U.S. senators.

If the District were a state or part of a state, the national government would still have full authority over all federal facilities, just as it controls such facilities in the states today. What Congress would give up, however, is the right to interfere in the District's business when federal questions are not involved. Clearly, Congress finds that right too precious to lose.

For Critical Analysis ***In what ways might Congress want to interfere with the government of the District?***

electoral votes, the vice president is chosen by the Senate, with each senator casting one vote.

Even when a presidential candidate wins by a large margin in the electoral college and in the popular vote—a *landslide election*—it does not follow that the candidate has won the support of the majority of those eligible to vote. We explore this paradox in this chapter's *Perception versus Reality* feature on page 194.

LO2 *How We Nominate Candidates*

The first step on the long road to winning an election is the nomination process. Nominations narrow the field of possible candidates and limit each political party's choice to one person. For many local government posts, which are often nonpartisan, self-nomination is the most common way to become a candidate. Such a procedure is frequently used in lightly populated areas. A self-proclaimed candidate usually files a petition to be listed on the ballot. Each state has laws that specify how many signatures a candidate must obtain to show that he or she has some public support. An alternative is to be a write-in candidate—voters write the candidate's name on the ballot on Election Day.

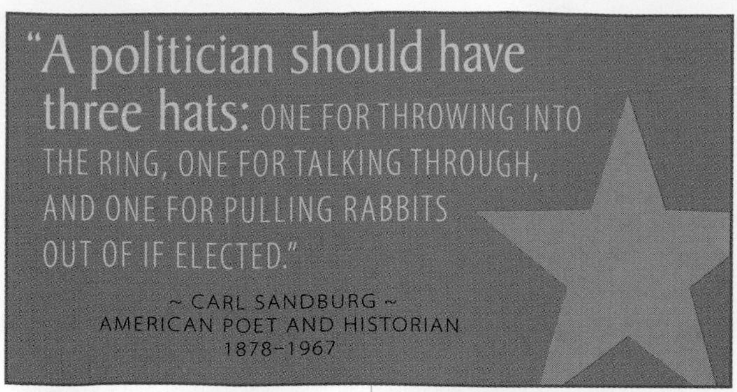

"A politician should have three hats: ONE FOR THROWING INTO THE RING, ONE FOR TALKING THROUGH, AND ONE FOR PULLING RABBITS OUT OF IF ELECTED."
~ CARL SANDBURG ~
AMERICAN POET AND HISTORIAN
1878–1967

Candidates for major offices are rarely nominated in these ways, however. As you read in Chapter 7, most candidates for high office are nominated by a political party and receive considerable support from party activists throughout their campaigns.

Party Control over Nominations

The methods used by political parties to nominate candidates have changed during the course of American history. Broadly speaking, the process has grown more open over the years, with the involvement of ever-greater numbers of local leaders and ordinary citizens. Today, any voter can participate in choosing party candidates. This was not true as recently as 1968, however, and was certainly not possible during the first years of the republic.

George Washington was essentially unopposed in the first U.S. presidential elections in 1789—no other candidate was seriously considered in any state. By the end of Washington's eight years in office, however, political divisions among the nation's leaders had solidified into political parties, the Federalists and the Jeffersonian (or Democratic) Republicans (see Chapter 7). These early parties were organized by gatherings of important persons, who often met in secret. The meetings came to be called **caucuses.**[5] Beginning in 1800, members of Congress who belonged to the two parties held caucuses to nominate candidates for president and vice president. The Republican caucus chose Thomas Jefferson in 1800, as expected, and the Federalist caucus nominated the incumbent president, John Adams. By 1816, the Federalist Party had ceased to exist, and the Jeffersonian Republican congressional caucus was in complete control of selecting the president of the United States.

The congressional caucus system collapsed in 1824.[6] It was widely seen as undemocratic—opponents derided it as "King Caucus." A much-diminished caucus nominated a presidential candidate who then came in third in the electoral vote. The other three major candidates were essentially self-nominated.[7] The four candidates split the electoral vote so completely that the House of Representatives had to decide the contest. It picked John Quincy Adams, even though Andrew Jackson had won more popular and electoral votes.

The Party Nominating Convention

In the run-up to the 1828 elections, two new parties grew up around the major candidates. Adams's supporters called themselves the National Republicans (later known as the Whigs). Jackson's supporters organized as the Democratic Party, which won the election. In 1832, both parties settled on a new method of choosing candidates for president and vice president—the national nominating convention. A number of state parties had already adopted the convention system for choosing state-level candidates. New Jersey held conventions as early as 1800.

A **nominating convention** is an official meeting of a political party to choose its candidates. Those who attend the convention are called **delegates,** and they are chosen to represent the people of a particular geographic area. Conventions can take place at multiple levels. A county convention might choose delegates to attend a state convention. The state convention in turn might select delegates to the national convention. By 1840, the convention system was the most common method of nominating political party candidates at the state and national levels.

While the convention system drew in a much broader range of leaders than had the caucus, it was not a particularly democratic institution. Convention delegates were rarely chosen by a vote of the party's local members. Typically, they were appointed by local party officials, who were usually, with good reason, called bosses. These local leaders often gained

caucus A meeting held to choose political candidates or delegates.

nominating convention An official meeting of a political party to choose its candidates. Nominating conventions at the state and local levels also select delegates to represent the citizens of their geographic areas at a higher-level party convention.

delegate A person selected to represent the people of one geographic area at a party convention.

PERCEPTION VERSUS REALITY | Presidents and the "Popular Vote"

Some presidential contests are very close, such as the 2000 race between Al Gore and George W. Bush. Others are less so, such as the one between Lyndon B. Johnson and Barry Goldwater in 1964. When a presidential candidate wins the race by a wide margin, as Johnson did, we may hear the result referred to as a *landslide election* or a *landslide victory* for the winning candidate.

AP PHOTO

Lyndon B. Johnson came the closest of any candidate ever to winning a majority of the votes of all citizens eligible to cast a ballot.

The Perception

The traditional perception has been that, in general, our presidents are elected by a majority of eligible American voters. A president who has been swept into office by a so-called landslide victory may claim to have received a "mandate from the people" to govern the nation. A president may assert that a certain policy or program she or he endorsed in campaign speeches is backed by popular support simply because she or he was elected to office by a majority of the voters.

The Reality

In reality, the "popular vote" is not all that popular, in the sense of representing the wishes of a majority of American citizens who are eligible to vote. In fact, the president of the United States has never received the votes of a majority of all eligible adults. Lyndon Johnson, in 1964, came the closest of any president in history, and even he won the votes of less than 40 percent of those who were eligible to cast a ballot.

The hotly contested presidential elections of 2000 and 2004 were divisive, leaving the millions of Americans who had voted for the losing candidates unhappy with the results. Indeed, in winning the election of 2000, Bush received the votes of a mere 26.0 percent of those with the right to vote. Nonetheless, Bush assumed that his reelection in 2004 was a signal from the American people to push his controversial domestic ideas, such as Social Security reform, as well as an endorsement of his foreign policy and the war on terrorism. Barack Obama likewise claimed a personal mandate based on his strong performance in 2008, and he parlayed it into a sweeping program of domestic initiatives. Yet Obama had won the support of only 32.9 percent of eligible voters.

It is useful to keep these figures in mind whenever a president claims to have received a mandate from the people. The truth is, no president has ever been elected with sufficient popular backing to make this a serious claim.

Blog On Dave Leip's Atlas of U.S. Presidential Elections provides detailed figures on presidential election results. Find the Atlas at www.uselectionatlas.org.

their positions in ways that were far from democratic. Not until 1972 did ordinary voters in all states gain the right to select delegates to the national presidential nominating conventions.

Primary Elections and the Loss of Party Control

primary election An election in which voters choose the candidates of their party, who will then run in the general election.

The corruption that so often accompanied the convention system led reformers to call for a new way to choose candidates—the **primary election,** in which voters go to the polls to decide among candidates who seek the nomination of their party. Candidates who win a primary election then go on to compete against the candidates from other parties in the general election. The first primary election may have been held in 1842 by Democrats in Crawford County, Pennsylvania. The technique was not widely used, however, until the end of the nineteenth century and the beginning of the twentieth. These were years in which reform was a popular cause.

JIM WILSON/THE NEW YORK TIMES/REDUX

California Republican candidate for governor Meg Whitman, left, and Republican U.S. Senate candidate Carly Fiorina at a rally in Anaheim, Calif. Both candidates were formerly heads of major corporations before turning to politics.

direct primary An election held within each of the two major parties—Democratic and Republican—to choose the party's candidates for the general election. Voters choose the candidate directly, rather than through delegates.

DIRECT AND INDIRECT PRIMARIES The rules for conducting primary elections are highly variable, and a number of different types of primaries exist. One major distinction is between a direct primary and an indirect primary. In a **direct primary,** voters cast their ballots directly for candidates. In an *indirect primary,* voters choose delegates, who in turn choose the candidates. The delegates may be pledged to a particular candidate but sometimes run as *unpledged delegates.* The major parties use indirect primaries to elect delegates to the national nominating conventions that choose candidates for president and vice president. The elections that nominate candidates for Congress and for state or local offices are almost always direct primaries.

THE ROLE OF THE STATES Primary elections are normally conducted by state governments. States set the dates and conduct the elections. They provide polling places, election officials, and registration lists, and they then count the votes. By sponsoring the primaries, state governments have obtained considerable influence over the rules by which the primaries are conducted. The power of the states is limited, however, by the parties' First Amendment right to freedom of association, a right that has been repeatedly confirmed by the United States Supreme Court.[8] On occasion, parties that object to the rules imposed by state governments have opted out of the state-sponsored primary system altogether.[9] Note that third parties typically do not participate in state-sponsored primaries, but hold nominating conventions instead. The major parties rarely opt out of state elections, however, because the financial—and political—costs of going it alone are high. (When primary elections are used to choose candidates for local *nonpartisan* positions, state control is uncontested.)

PRIMARY VOTERS Voter turnout for primaries is lower than it is in general elections. The voters who do go to the polls are often strong supporters of their party. Indeed, as you will learn shortly, independents cannot participate in primary elections in some states, even if they lean toward one or the other of the two major parties. As a result, the Republican primary electorate is very conservative, and Democratic primary voters are quite liberal. Candidates often find that they must run to the political right or left during the primaries. Frequently, they then move to the center during the general election campaign.

New York Democratic candidate for governor, state Attorney General Andrew Cuomo, receives the endorsement of NARAL Pro-Choice New York in the governor's race, at New York's City Hall.

AP PHOTO/RICHARD DREW

INSURGENT CANDIDATES Primary elections were designed to take nominations out of the hands of the party bosses, and indeed, the most important result of the primary system has been to dramatically reduce the power of elected and party officials over the nominating process. Ever since primary elections were established, the insurgent candidate who runs against the party "establishment" has been a common phenomenon. Running against the "powers that be" is often a very effective campaign strategy, and many insurgents have won victories at the local, state, and national levels.

Insurgent campaigns often replace incumbent leaders who are out of touch with the party rank and file, sometimes because the incumbents are too liberal or too conservative. Occasionally, an insurgent's platform is strikingly different from that of the party as a whole. Yet even when an insurgent's politics are abhorrent to the rest of the party—for example, an insurgent might make an outright appeal to racism—the party has no way of denying the insurgent the right to the party label in the general election.

OPEN AND CLOSED PRIMARIES Primaries can be classified as closed or open. In a **closed primary,** only party members can vote to choose that party's candidates, and they may vote only in the primary of their own party. Thus, only registered Democrats can vote in the Democratic primary to select candidates of the Democratic Party. Only registered Republicans can vote for the Republican candidates. A person usually establishes party membership when she or he registers to vote. Some states have a *semiclosed* primary, which allows voters to register with a party or change their party affiliations on Election Day. Regular party workers favor the closed primary because it promotes party loyalty. Independent voters usually oppose it because it forces them to select a party if they wish to participate in the nominating process.

In an **open primary,** voters can vote for a party's candidates regardless of whether they belong to the party. In most open primaries, all voters receive both a Republican ballot and a Democratic ballot. Voters then choose either the Democratic or the Republican ballot in the privacy of the voting booth. In a *semiopen* primary, voters request the ballot for the party of their choice.

closed primary A primary in which only party members can vote to choose that party's candidates.

open primary A primary in which voters can vote for a party's candidates regardless of whether they belong to the party.

The fifty states have developed dozens of variations on the open and closed primary plans. In some states, primaries are closed only to persons registered to another party, and independents can vote in either primary. In several states, an independent who votes in a party primary is automatically enrolled in that party. In other states, the voter remains an independent. The two major parties often have different rules. For example, in two states, the Democrats allow independents to vote in the primaries, but the Republicans do not.

BLANKET AND "TOP TWO" PRIMARIES Until 2000, California and a few other states employed a *blanket primary,* in which voters could choose the candidates of more than one party. A voter might participate in choosing the Republican candidate for governor, for example, and at the same time vote to pick the Democratic candidate for the U.S. Senate. In that year, however, the Supreme Court ruled that the blanket primary violated the parties' right to freedom of association.[10] Similar primary systems in Washington State and Alaska were struck down in later cases.

Louisiana has for many years had a unique system in which all candidates participate in the same primary, regardless of party. The two candidates receiving the most votes then proceed on to the general election. In 2008, Louisiana abandoned this system for the U.S. House and Senate, but kept it for state and local offices.

Even as Louisiana was backing away from this system, however, other states began picking it up. Washington State adopted the Louisiana system in 2004, and in 2008 the Supreme Court ruled that it was constitutional.[11] In June 2010, California voters adopted a system known as the *"top two" primary* that was patterned on the one in Washington State. Political parties continue to have the right to designate preferred candidates, using conventions or other means, but such endorsements do not appear on the ballot. An insurgent Republican and a "regular" Republican, for example, would both be labeled simply "Republican." The California system will go into effect in 2011, and given California's size and importance, its top two primary will be closely watched.

Nominating Presidential Candidates

In some respects, being nominated for president is more difficult than being elected. The nominating process narrows a very large number of hopefuls down to a single candidate from each party. Choosing a presidential candidate is unlike nominating candidates for any other office. One reason for this is that the nomination process combines several different methods.

PRESIDENTIAL PRIMARIES Most of the states hold presidential primaries, beginning early in the election year. For a candidate, a good showing in the early primaries results in plenty of media attention as television networks and newspaper reporters play up the results. Subsequent state primaries tend to serve as contests to eliminate unlikely candidates.

The presidential primaries do not necessarily follow the same rules the states use for nominating candidates for the U.S. Congress or for state and local offices. Often, the presidential primaries are not held on the same date as the other primaries. States frequently hold the presidential primaries early in hopes of exercising greater influence on the outcome.

CAUCUSES The caucus system is an alternative to primary elections. Strictly speaking, the caucus system is a convention system. The caucuses are party conventions held at the local level that elect delegates to conventions at the county or congressional district level. These midlevel conventions then choose the delegates to the state convention, which finally elects the delegates to the national party convention. Unlike the caucuses of two centuries ago, modern caucuses are open to all party members. It is not hard to join a party. At the famous Iowa caucuses, you become a party member simply by attending a local caucus.

Senator John McCain and then-Senator Barack Obama during the presidential campaign.

AP PHOTO/ALEX BRANDON

While some states, such as Iowa and Minnesota, rely on the caucus/convention system to nominate candidates for state and local positions, the system is more frequently used only to choose delegates to the Democratic and Republican national conventions. Most states with presidential caucuses use primaries to nominate state and local candidates. Twelve states choose national convention delegates through caucuses. Four states use caucuses to allocate some of the national convention delegates and use primaries to allocate the others.

PRIMARIES—THE RUSH TO BE FIRST Traditionally, states have held their presidential primaries at various times over the first six months of a presidential election year. In an effort to make their primaries prominent in the media and influential in the political process, however, many states have moved the date of their primary to earlier in the year—a practice known as *front-loading*. In 1988, a group of southern states created a "Super Tuesday" by holding their primaries on the same day in early March. Then, other states moved their primaries to an earlier date, too.

The practice of front-loading primaries has gained momentum over the last decade. The states with later primary dates found that most nominations were decided early in the season, leaving their voters "out of the action." As more states moved up their primary dates, the early primaries became even more important, and other states, to compete, also moved up their primaries.

This rush to be first was particularly notable in the year or so preceding the 2008 presidential primaries. By 2007, about half the states had moved their primaries to earlier dates. Many of these states opted for February 5—or "Super-Super Tuesday," as some called it—as the date for their primaries.

THE IMPACT OF FRONT-LOADING Many Americans worried that with a shortened primary season, long-shot candidates would no longer be able to propel themselves into serious contention by doing well in small, early-voting states, such as New Hampshire and Iowa. Traditionally, a candidate who had a successful showing in the New Hampshire primary had time to obtain enough financial backing to continue in the race. The fear was that an accelerated schedule of presidential primaries would favor the richest candidates.

In practice, front-loading did not have this effect in 2008. On the Republican side, the early primaries might have benefited a front-runner—if there had been a Republican front-runner in January 2008. As it happened, the candidate with the most funds, former Massachusetts governor Mitt Romney, did not win the most votes. After February 5, Arizona senator John McCain had a clear lead. The Republican primaries were mostly conducted on a winner-take-all basis, a rule that allowed McCain to wrap up the nomination on March 4.

The Democrats, however, allocated delegates on a proportional basis, so that each candidate received delegates based on his or her share of the vote. That rule made an early decision impossible, and Barack Obama did not obtain a majority of the Democratic delegates until June 3. As a result, many of the most important Democratic primaries took place late in the season. States that had moved their primaries to February 5 discovered that they were lost in the crowd of early contests. Front-loading, in other words, had become counterproductive.

> **"THERE IS NO EXCITEMENT** anywhere in the world . . . to match the excitement of an American presidential campaign."
>
> ~ THEODORE H. WHITE ~ AMERICAN JOURNALIST AND HISTORIAN 1915–1986

NATIONAL PARTY CONVENTIONS Born in the 1830s, the American national political convention is unique in Western democracies. Elsewhere, candidates for prime minister or chancellor are chosen within the confines of party councils. That is actually closer to the way the framers of the Constitution wanted it done.

At one time, the conventions were indeed often giant free-for-alls. It wasn't always clear who the winning presidential and vice-presidential candidates would be until the delegates voted. As more states opted to hold presidential primaries, however, the drama of national conventions diminished. Today, the conventions have been described as massive pep rallies. Nonetheless, each convention's task remains a serious one. In late summer, two thousand to three thousand delegates gather at each convention to represent the wishes of the voters and political leaders of their home states. They adopt the official party platform and declare their support for the party's presidential and vice-presidential candidates.

On the first day of the convention, delegates hear the reports of the **Credentials Committee,** which inspects each prospective delegate's claim to be seated as a legitimate representative of her or his state. When the eligibility of delegates is in question, the committee decides who will be seated. In the evening, there is usually a keynote speaker to whip up enthusiasm among the delegates. The second day includes committee reports and debates on the party platform. The third day is devoted to nominations and voting. Balloting begins with an alphabetical roll call in which states and territories announce their votes. By midnight, the convention's real work is over, and the presidential candidate has been selected. The vice-presidential nomination and the acceptance speeches occupy the fourth day. We provided more details on the national party conventions in Chapter 7 on pages 153 and 154.

Credentials Committee
A committee of each national political party that evaluates the claims of national party convention delegates to be the legitimate representatives of their states.

LO3 *The Modern Political Campaign*

Once nominated, candidates focus on their campaigns. The term *campaign* originated in the military context. Generals mounted campaigns, using their scarce resources (soldiers and materials) to achieve military objectives. Using the term in a political context is apt. In a political campaign, candidates also use scarce resources (time and funds) in an attempt to defeat their adversaries in the battle for votes.

Responsibilities of the Campaign Staff

To run a successful campaign, the candidate's campaign staff must be able to raise funds for the effort, get media coverage, produce and pay for political ads, schedule the candidate's time effectively with constituent groups and potential supporters, convey the candidate's position on the issues, conduct research on the opposing candidate, and persuade the voters to go to the polls. When party identification was firmer and TV campaigning was still in its infancy, a strong party organization on the local, state, or national level could furnish most of the services and expertise that the candidate needed. Less effort was spent on advertising each candidate's position and character, because the party label communicated that information to many of the voters.

Today, party labels are no longer as important as they once were. In part, this is because fewer people identify with the major parties, as evidenced by the rising number of independent voters. Instead of relying so

Kentucky U.S. Senator Mitch McConnell (right) puts an arm around fellow Republican and senatorial candidate Rand Paul as they wave to the crowd at the Fancy Farm Picnic in Graves County, Ky.

AP PHOTO/THE PADUCAH SUN/JOHN WRIGHT

extensively on political parties, candidates now turn to professionals to manage their campaigns.

The Professional Campaign Organization

With the rise of candidate-centered campaigns in the past two decades, the role of the political party in managing campaigns has declined. Professional **political consultants** now manage nearly all aspects of a presidential candidate's campaign. President Barack Obama, for example, relied heavily on his longtime political adviser David Axelrod in crafting his 2008 election victory. Most candidates for governor, the House, and the Senate also rely on consultants. Political consultants generally specialize in a particular area of the campaign, such as researching the opposition, conducting polls, developing the candidate's advertising, or organizing "get out the vote" efforts. Nonetheless, most candidates have a campaign manager who coordinates and plans the **campaign strategy.** Figure 9–2 on the following page shows a typical presidential campaign organization. The political party also continues to play an important role in recruiting volunteers and getting out the vote.

A major development in contemporary American politics is the focus on reaching voters through effective use of the media, particularly television. At least half of the budget for a major political campaign is consumed by television advertising. Media consultants are therefore pivotal members of the campaign staff. The nature of political advertising is discussed in more detail in Chapter 10.

LO4 *The Internet Campaign*

Over the years, political leaders have benefited from understanding and using new communications technologies. In the 1930s, command of a new medium—radio—gave President Franklin D. Roosevelt an advantage. In 1960, Democratic presidential candidate John F. Kennedy gained an edge on Republican Richard Nixon because Kennedy had a better understanding of the visual requirements of television. Today, the ability to make effective use of e-mail and the Web is essential to a candidate. In the 2008 presidential elections, Barack Obama gained a margin over his rivals in part because of his use of the new technologies. His team relied on the Internet for several tasks, which included fund-raising, targeting potential supporters, and creating local political organizations.

Fund-Raising on the Internet

Internet fund-raising grew out of an earlier technique: the direct-mail campaign. In direct mailings, campaigns send solicitations to large numbers of likely prospects, typically seeking contributions. Developing good lists of prospects is central to an effective direct-mail operation. Postage, printing, and the rental of address lists push the marginal cost of each additional letter well above a dollar. Response rates are low—a 1 percent response rate is a tremendous success. In many direct-mail campaigns, most of the funds raised are used up by the costs of the campaign itself. From the 1970s on, conservative organizations became especially adept at managing direct-mail campaigns. This expertise gave conservative causes and candidates a notable advantage over liberals.

To understand the old system is to recognize the superiority of the new one. The marginal cost of each additional e-mail message is essentially zero. Lists of prospects need not be prepared as carefully, because e-mail sent to unlikely prospects does not waste resources. E-mail fund-raising did face one

political consultant A professional political adviser who, for a fee, works on an area of a candidate's campaign. Political consultants include campaign managers, pollsters, media advisers, and "get out the vote" organizers.

campaign strategy The comprehensive plan developed by a candidate and his or her advisers for winning an election. The strategy includes the candidate's position on issues, slogan, advertising plan, press events, personal appearances, and other aspects of the campaign.

Figure 9–2

A Typical Presidential Campaign Organization

Most aspects of a candidate's campaign are managed by professional political consultants, as this figure illustrates.

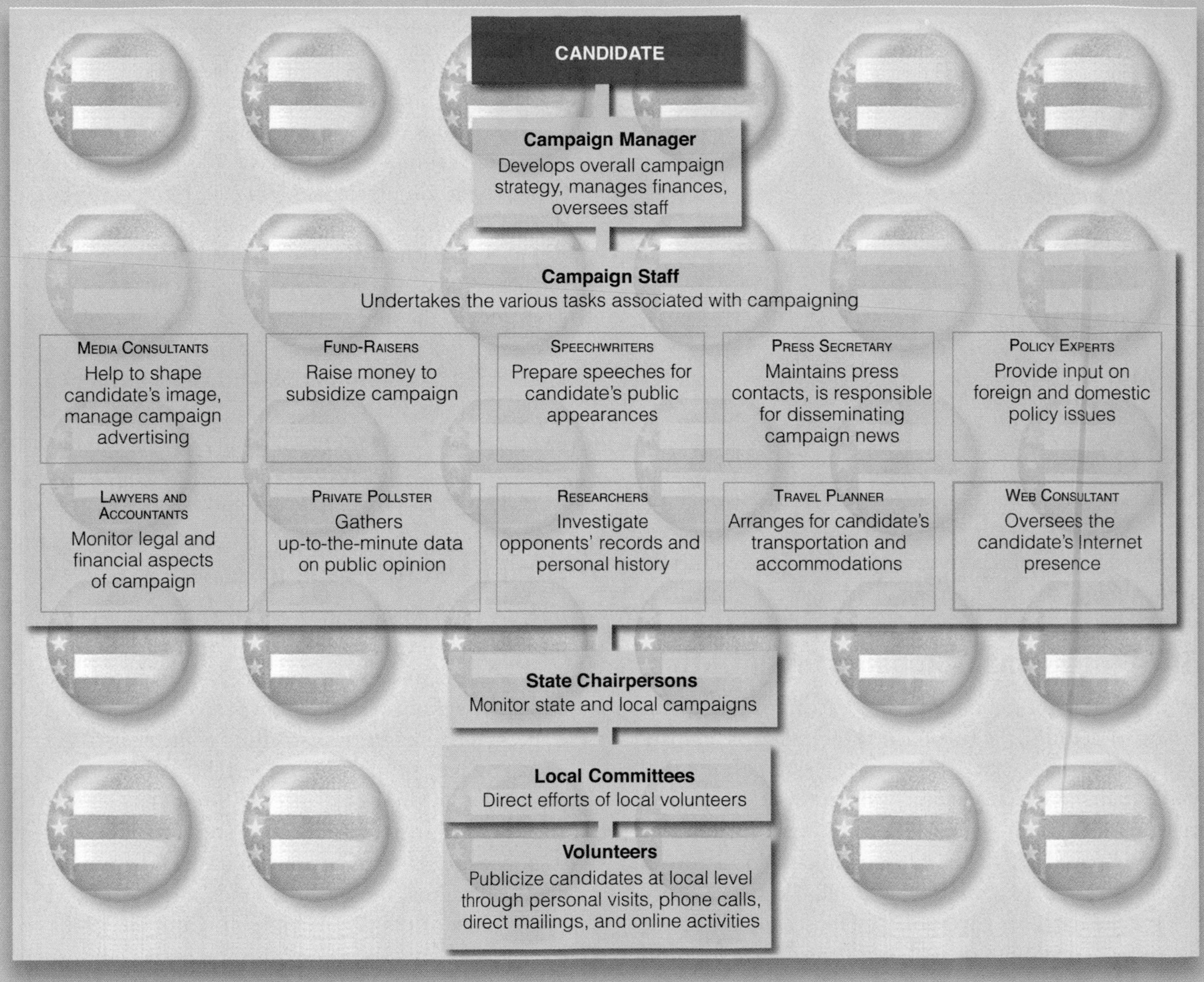

CANDIDATE
Campaign Manager
Develops overall campaign strategy, manages finances, oversees staff
Campaign Staff
Undertakes the various tasks associated with campaigning
MEDIA CONSULTANTS
Help to shape candidate's image, manage campaign advertising
FUND-RAISERS
Raise money to subsidize campaign
SPEECHWRITERS
Prepare speeches for candidate's public appearances
PRESS SECRETARY
Maintains press contacts, is responsible for disseminating campaign news
POLICY EXPERTS
Provide input on foreign and domestic policy issues
LAWYERS AND ACCOUNTANTS
Monitor legal and financial aspects of campaign
PRIVATE POLLSTER
Gathers up-to-the-minute data on public opinion
RESEARCHERS
Investigate opponents' records and personal history
TRAVEL PLANNER
Arranges for candidate's transportation and accommodations
WEB CONSULTANT
Oversees the candidate's Internet presence
State Chairpersons
Monitor state and local campaigns
Local Committees
Direct efforts of local volunteers
Volunteers
Publicize candidates at local level through personal visits, phone calls, direct mailings, and online activities

problem when it was new—many people were not yet online. Today, that issue is no longer so important.

The new technology brought with it a change in the groups that benefited the most. Conservatives were no longer the most effective fund-raisers. Instead, liberal and libertarian organizations enjoyed some of the greatest successes.

Obama Online

Barack Obama took Internet fund-raising to a new level during his 2008 presidential bid. One of the defining characteristics of his fund-raising was its decentralization. The Obama campaign attempted to recruit as many supporters as possible to act as fund-raisers who would solicit contributions from their friends and neighbors. As a result, Obama was spared much of the personal fund-raising effort that consumes the time of most national politicians.

In the first half of 2007, Obama's campaign raised \$58 million, \$16.4 million of which was made up of donations of less than \$200. The total sum was a record, and the small-donation portion was unusually large. In August 2008, the Obama campaign set another record, raising \$66 million—the most ever raised in one month by a presidential campaign. By then, 2.5 million people had donated to Obama's campaign. Most of them had been contacted through the Internet.

Targeting Supporters

In 2004, President George W. Bush's chief political adviser, Karl Rove, pioneered a new campaign technique known as *microtargeting*. The process involves collecting as much information as possible about voters in a gigantic database and then filtering out various groups for special attention. Through microtargeting, for example, the Bush campaign could identify Republican prospects living in heavily Democratic neighborhoods—potential supporters whom the campaign might have neglected because the neighborhood as a whole seemed so unpromising.

> "IN CONSTANT PURSUIT OF MONEY to finance campaigns, the political system is simply unable to function. Its deliberative powers are paralyzed."
>
> ~ JOHN RAWLS ~
> AMERICAN EDUCATOR
> 1921–2000

EXAMPLES OF MICROTARGETING Microtargeting could also reveal groups that might be receptive to specific appeals. For example, the Republican campaign identified a group of education-conscious Hispanic mothers in New Mexico, and it plied them with mailings and phone calls that touted Bush's No Child Left Behind legislation. Although Rove's operation frequently contacted such voters in traditional ways, much of the data necessary for microtargeting was collected through the Internet. In 2004, the Democrats had nothing to match Rove's efforts. By 2008, however, microtargeting was employed by all major candidates.

BEHAVIORAL TARGETING In 2008, both the Democratic and Republican general election campaigns supplemented microtargeting with a new and somewhat controversial targeting method—behavioral targeting. This technique is entirely Web-based. It uses information about people's online behavior, such as the pages they visit and the searches they make, to tailor the advertisements that they see. What is controversial about the practice is that it involves placing a cookie in the cookie folder of a person's computer, without that person's knowledge, to collect information on the person's online behavior. Later, the person may see online advertisements based on what the cookie "knows" about the person's preferences. Behavioral targeting raises privacy concerns, and both Congress and the Federal Trade Commission have held hearings on the practice.

Support for Local Organizing

Perhaps the most effective use of the Internet has been as an organizing tool. One of the earliest Internet techniques was to use the site Meetup.com to organize real-world meetings. In this way, campaigns were able to gather supporters without relying on the existing party and activist infrastructure.

OBAMA'S CAMPAIGN As with fund-raising, Barack Obama took Web-based organizing to a new level. In part, his campaign used existing sites such as Facebook and MySpace. By June 2008, Obama had 953,000 Facebook backers to John McCain's 142,000. He also had 394,000 supporters on MySpace, seven times McCain's total. On YouTube, Obama's videos were viewed 50 million times, compared with 4 million for McCain's. Obama's own Web site was especially important to the campaign. My.BarackObama.com eventually racked up more than a million members.

LOCAL SUPPORT GROUPS By gathering information on large numbers of potential supporters, the Obama campaign was able to create local support groups in towns and counties across the country. For example, the Obama campaign assembled a group of forty volunteers in Avery County, North Carolina, a locality in the Blue Ridge Mountains traditionally carried by Republican presidential candidates at rates of more than three to one. The volunteers were often surprised to discover that neighbors they had known for years were fellow Democrats. Several had thought they were the only Democrats in town. The group coordinated its activities by e-mail, in part because of rugged terrain and poor local cell phone reception.

Obama's national Internet fund-raising success meant that he could field hundreds of paid organizers in North Carolina, some of whom supported local groups of volunteers such as this one. In the end, McCain easily carried Avery County, but Obama carried the state.[12]

LO5 *What It Costs to Win*

The modern political campaign is an expensive undertaking. Candidates must spend huge sums for professional campaign managers and consultants, television and radio ads, the printing of campaign literature, travel, office rent, equipment, and other necessities.

To get an idea of the cost of waging a campaign for Congress today, consider that in the 2010 mid-term election cycle, the average House incumbent raised about $1.7 million. The average House challenger raised close to $700,000. In the Senate, a typical incumbent took in more than $13 million. The average challenger spent almost $5 million. Of course, some contests were much more expensive than the average. Barbara Boxer, the incumbent running for reelection to the Senate from California raised over $26 million, while her challenger, Carly Fiorina, spent over $16 million.

Presidential campaigns are even more costly. In 2004, presidential campaign expenditures amounted to nearly $830 million. In the 2007–2008 election cycle, these costs reached about $2.4 billion, making the 2008 presidential campaigns the most expensive in history.

The high cost of campaigns gives rise to the fear that campaign contributors and special interest groups will try to buy favored treatment from those who are elected to office. In an attempt to prevent these abuses, the government regulates campaign financing.

All campaigns involve supporters and volunteers who make up the grass roots backing for every politician who seriously wishes to win. These volunteers are waiting for the ballot count results during a primary election in St. Paul, Minnesota.

The Federal Election Campaign Act

Congress passed the Federal Election Campaign Act (FECA) of 1971[13] in an effort to curb abuses in the ways political campaigns were financed. The 1971 act placed no limit on overall spending but restricted the amount that could be spent on mass media advertising, including television. It limited the amount that candidates and their families could contribute to their own campaigns and required disclosure of all contributions and expenditures of more than $100. In principle, the 1971 act limited the role of labor unions and corporations in political campaigns. Also in 1971, Congress passed a law that provided for a $1 checkoff on federal income tax returns for general campaign funds to be used by major-party presidential candidates. This law was first applied in the 1976 campaign. (Since then, the amount of the checkoff has been raised to $3.)

AMENDMENTS IN 1974 Amendments to the act passed in 1974 did the following:

- *Created the Federal Election Commission (FEC) to administer and enforce the act's provisions.*
- *Provided public financing for presidential primaries and general elections.* Presidential candidates who raise some money on their own can get funds from the U.S. Treasury to help pay for primary campaigns. For the general election campaign, presidential candidates receive federal funding for almost all of their expenses if they are willing to accept campaign-spending limits.
- *Limited presidential campaign spending.* Candidates accepting federal support must limit spending to amounts set by law.
- *Required disclosure.* Candidates must file periodic reports with the FEC that list the contributors to the campaign and indicate how the funds were spent.
- *Limited contributions.* Limits were placed on how much individuals and groups could contribute to candidates.

A recent development in presidential campaign finance has been the tendency of candidates to reject public funding on the grounds that they can raise larger sums outside the system. By 2008, a majority of the leading Democratic and Republican presidential candidates were refusing public funding for the primaries. That year, Barack Obama became the first major-party candidate in decades to refuse federal funding for the general election as well.

BUCKLEY v. VALEO In a 1976 case, *Buckley v. Valeo*,[14] the United States Supreme Court declared unconstitutional the provision in the 1971 act that limited the amount each individual could spend on his or her own campaign. The Court held that a "candidate, no less than any other person, has a First Amendment right to engage in the discussion of public issues and vigorously and tirelessly to advocate his own election."

THE RISE OF PACS The FECA allows corporations, labor unions, and special interest groups to set up national *political action committees (PACs)* to raise money for candidates. For a PAC to be legitimate, the money must be raised from at least fifty volunteer donors and must be given to at least five candidates in the national elections. PACs can contribute up to $5,000 per candidate in each election, but there is no limit on the total amount of PAC contributions during an election cycle. As discussed in Chapter 6, the number of PACs has grown significantly since the 1970s, as have their campaign contributions. In the 2004 election cycle, about 36 percent of campaign funds spent on House races came from PACs.[15] Since 2004, however, other methods of raising campaign funds have reduced the relative importance of PACs.

Skirting the Campaign-Financing Rules

Individuals and corporations have found **loopholes**—legitimate ways of evading legal requirements—in the federal laws limiting campaign contributions.

SOFT MONEY The biggest loophole in the FECA and its amendments was that they did not prohibit individuals or corporations from contributing to political *parties*.

Senator Ron Wyden, (D., Ore.) and Senator Charles Schumer, right, (D., N.Y.) take part in a campaign finance news conference in front of the Supreme Court in Washington, D.C.

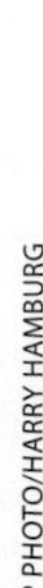

Contributors could make donations to the parties to cover the costs of registering voters, printing flyers, advertising, developing campaigns to "get out the vote," and holding fund-raising events. Contributions to political parties were called **soft money.** Even though soft money clearly was used to support the candidates, it was difficult to track exactly how this was happening.

loophole A legitimate way of evading a certain legal requirement.

soft money Campaign contributions not regulated by federal law, such as some contributions that are made to political parties instead of to particular candidates.

independent expenditure An expenditure for activities that are independent from (not coordinated with) those of a political candidate or a political party.

By 2000, the parties raised nearly $463 million through soft money contributions. Soft dollars became the main source of campaign money in the presidential race until after the 2002 elections, when they were banned, as you will read shortly.

INDEPENDENT EXPENDITURES Another major loophole in campaign-financing laws was that they did not prohibit corporations, labor unions, and special interest groups from making **independent expenditures** in an election campaign. Independent expenditures, as the term implies, are expenditures for activities that are independent from (not coordinated with) those of the candidate or a political party. In other words, interest groups can wage their own "issue" campaigns so long as they do not go so far as to say "Vote for Candidate X."

The problem is, where do you draw the line between advocating a position on a particular issue and contributing to the campaign of a candidate who endorses that position? In addressing this thorny issue, the United States Supreme Court has developed two determinative tests. Under the first test, a group's speech is a campaign "expenditure" only if it explicitly calls for the election of a particular candidate. Using this test, the courts repeatedly have held that interest groups have the right to advocate their positions. For example, the Christian Coalition has the right to publish voter guides informing voters of candidates' positions. The second test applies when a group or organization has made expenditures explicitly for the purpose of endorsing a candidate. Such expenditures are permissible unless they were made in "coordination" with a campaign. According to the Supreme Court, an issue-oriented group has a First Amendment right to advocate the election of its preferred candidates as long as it acts independently.

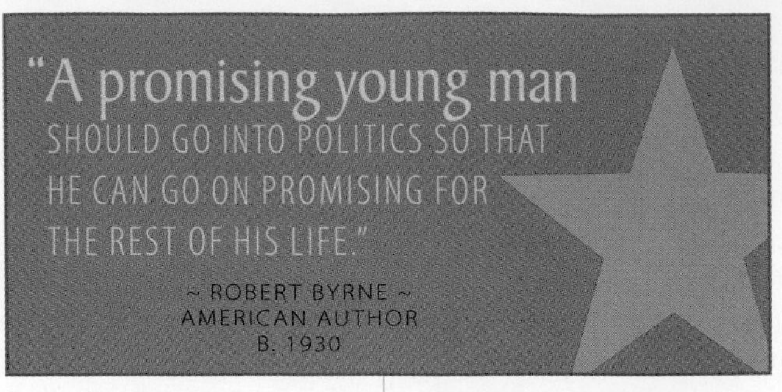

"A promising young man
SHOULD GO INTO POLITICS SO THAT
HE CAN GO ON PROMISING FOR
THE REST OF HIS LIFE."
~ ROBERT BYRNE ~
AMERICAN AUTHOR
B. 1930

In 1996, the Supreme Court held that these guidelines apply to expenditures by political parties as well. Parties may spend money on behalf of candidates if they do so independently—that is, if they do not let the candidates know how, when, or for what the money was spent.[16] As critics of this decision have pointed out, parties generally work closely with candidates, so establishing the "independence" of such expenditures is difficult.

The Bipartisan Campaign Reform Act of 2002

Demand for further campaign-finance reform had been growing for several years, and in 2002, Congress passed, and the president signed, the Bipartisan Campaign Reform Act. The measure is also known as the McCain-Feingold Act after its chief sponsors, senators John McCain (R., Ariz.) and Russell Feingold (D., Wisc.).

The new law banned soft money. It also regulated campaign ads paid for by interest groups and prohibited any such issue advocacy commercials within thirty days of a primary election or sixty days of a general election.

The 2002 act set the amount that an individual can contribute to a federal candidate at $2,000 and the amount that an individual can give to all federal candidates at $95,000 over a two-year election cycle. (Under the law, some individual contribution limits are indexed for inflation and thus may change slightly with every election cycle.) Individuals can still contribute to state and local parties, so long as the contributions do not exceed $10,000 per year per individual. The new law went into effect the day after the 2002 general elections.

CONSTITUTIONAL CHALLENGES TO THE 2002 LAW

Several groups immediately filed lawsuits challenging the constitutionality of the new law. Supporters of the restrictions on campaign ads by special interest groups argued that the large amounts of funds spent on these ads create an appearance of corruption in the political process. In contrast, an attorney for the National Rifle Association (NRA) argued that because the NRA represents "millions of Americans speaking in unison . . . [it] is not a *corruption* of the democratic political process; it *is* the democratic political process."[17] In December 2003, the Supreme Court upheld nearly all of the clauses of the act in *McConnell v. Federal Election Commission.*[18]

In 2007, however, in *Federal Election Commission v. Wisconsin Right to Life, Inc.,* the Supreme Court invalidated a major part of the 2002 law and overruled a portion of its own 2003 decision upholding the act. In the four years since the earlier ruling, Chief Justice John Roberts, Jr., and Associate Justice Samuel Alito, Jr., had been appointed, and both were conservatives. In a five-to-four decision, the Court held that issue ads could not be prohibited in the time period preceding elections (thirty days before primary elections and sixty days before general elections) *unless* they were "susceptible of no reasonable interpretation other than as an appeal to vote for or against a specific candidate."[19] The Court concluded that restricting *all* television ads paid for by corporate or union treasuries in the weeks before an election amounted to censorship of political speech.

INDEPENDENT COMMITTEES AFTER 2002 As you read in Chapter 6, "issue advocacy" groups soon attempted to exploit loopholes in the 2002 act. A major technique was to establish independent 527 committees, named after the provision of the tax code that covers them. Spending by 527s rose rapidly after 2002, and in the 2004 election cycle, the committees spent about $612 million to "advocate positions."

By 2008, the relative importance of 527 committees began to decline. The reason was the creation of a new kind of body, the 501(c)4 organization. According to some lawyers, a 501(c)4 could make limited contributions directly to campaigns and—perhaps more importantly—could conceal the identity of its donors. So far, the Federal Election Commission (FEC) has refused to rule on the legality of this technique.

CITIZENS UNITED v. FEDERAL ELECTION COMMISSION

In January 2010, the Supreme Court took a major step toward freeing up corporate funding of political advertisements. In the *Wisconsin Right to Life* case described earlier, the Court ruled out bans on issue ads placed by corporations and other organizations in the run-up to an election. In the new case, *Citizens United v. FEC,*[20] the Court extended this protection to ads that attack or praise specific candidates, including ads that advise people for whom they should vote in an election. As long as corporations, labor unions, or nonprofit groups do not contribute directly to a candidate's campaign, there is now no limit on their ability to fund advertising. In issuing this decision, the Court not only invalidated key portions of the 2002 act, but also overturned laws dating back to Theodore Roosevelt's presidency (1901–1909).

Republican leaders applauded the ruling as a victory for free speech, but most Democratic leaders were appalled. Their fear was that the ruling would result in a tidal wave of new corporate spending on elections. Presumably, unions and nonprofits are already giving as much as they can, but the ability of corporations to provide new funds for political causes—should they so desire—is vast. Another problem: The Court ruled that it is acceptable to require organizations to disclose the sources of their political spending. Groups such as the 501(c)4 committees mentioned earlier, however, have the right, under current law, to hide the identity of their contributors. Major spenders, in other words, can fund independent ads and conceal such funding from the public.

Table 9–1

Top Industries and Other Groups Contributing Funds in the 2010 Midterm Election Cycle

Industry/Group	Total	To Democrats	To Republicans
1 Retired individuals	$108,971,141	43%	56%
2 Lawyers & law firms	102,839,147	76	22
3 Securities & investment firms	65,799,887	53	46
4 Candidate committees	57,393,283	66	33
5 Real estate	55,449,021	52	46
6 Health professionals	55,002,518	48	50
7 Leadership PACs	32,579,556	50	49
8 Insurance	31,278,892	48	52
9 Business services	24,895,601	61	38
10 Lobbyists	23,545,783	65	34
11 Democratic/liberal	22,670,421	100	0
12 TV, movies & music	21,735,793	72	27
13 Pharm. & health products	19,643,925	54	46
14 Oil & gas	19,588,091	25	73
15 Misc. manufacturing & distrib.	17,757,910	43	57
16 Computers & the Internet	17,219,782	64	36
17 Electric utilities	16,230,025	56	42
18 General contractors	15,601,092	36	62
19 Education	15,431,168	75	23
20 Commercial banks	15,413,738	41	59

The numbers are based on contributions from PACs and individuals giving $200 or more.
Source: Center for Responsive Politics, OpenSecrets.org.

Campaign Contributions and Policy Decisions

Considering the passion on both sides of the debate about campaign-finance reform, one might wonder how much campaign contributions actually influence policy decisions. Table 9–1 above lists leading industries and other groups contributing to either party in the 2010 midterm election cycle. These contributors must want something in return for their dollars, but what, exactly, do their contributions buy? Do these donations influence government policymaking?

Despite popular suspicions, we cannot assume that a member of Congress who received financial contributions from certain groups while campaigning for Congress will vote differently on policy issues than she or he would otherwise vote. After all, many groups make contributions not so much to influence a candidate's views as to ensure that a candidate whose views the group supports will win the elections.

Many groups routinely donate to candidates from both parties so that, regardless of who wins, the groups will have access to the officeholder. Note that many of the groups listed in Table 9–1 contributed to both parties. Not surprisingly, campaign contributors find it much easier than other constituents to get in to see politicians or to get them to return phone calls. Because politicians are more likely to be influenced by those with whom they have personal contacts, access is important for those who want to influence policymaking.

LO6 *The Closeness of Recent Presidential Elections*

The 2000 presidential elections were the first since 1888 in which the electoral college system gave Americans a president who had not won the popular vote. Was the outcome an anomaly? The 2004 elections again were close, but in 2008, the pattern changed.

ELECTIONS 2010

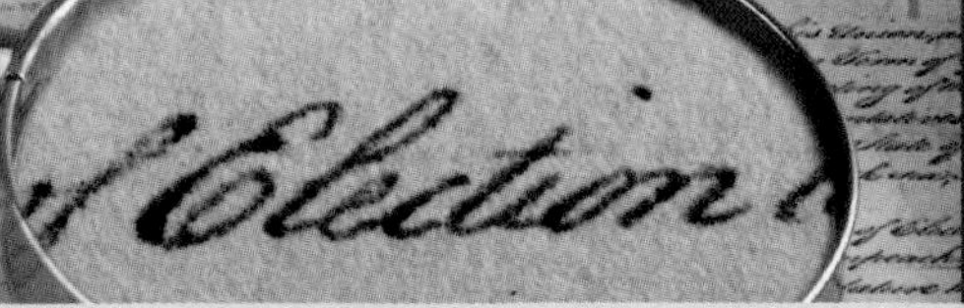

The Campaigns

Two records were broken during the latest election cycle. The first was the amount of spending in a mid-term election. Estimates are not final, but it appears that campaign and independent committees together will have spent almost $4 billion by the time the last dollar is counted. The other record was the share of television campaign ads that were negative.

Some candidates personally spent unprecedented sums in their search for election. As mentioned earlier, Meg Whitman, the former CEO of eBay, spent $140 million of her own funds to become governor of California—an all-time record. Note, though, that none of the five candidates who spent $6 million or more of their own funds, including Whitman, won.

Researchers estimated that about two-thirds of all campaign ads were negative. Back in 2008, Republicans used more ads personally attacking their opponents than the Democrats did. In 2010, the tables were turned, with the Democrats making the larger number of personal attacks. Finally, ads by independent campaign groups set an all-time record. Because they were not, in principle, linked to a particular candidate, they could publicize as much "dirt" as they wanted to—and they did.

The 2000 Presidential Elections

In 2000, then vice president Al Gore won the popular vote by 540,000 votes. Nonetheless, on election night, the outcome in Florida, which would have given Gore the winning votes in the electoral college, was deemed "too close to call." Controversy erupted over the types of ballots used, and some counties in Florida began recounting ballots by hand. This issue ultimately came before the United States Supreme Court: Did manual recounts of some ballots but not others violate the Constitution's equal protection clause? On December 12, five weeks after the election, the Supreme Court ruled against the manual recounts.[21] The final vote tally in Florida gave Bush a 537-vote lead, all of Florida's twenty-five electoral votes, and the presidency.

The 2004 Presidential Elections

The 2004 presidential elections produced another close race, with President Bush edging out Democratic challenger John Kerry by a mere thirty-five electors. In contrast to the situation in 2000, Bush won the popular vote in 2004, defeating Kerry by a 2.5 percentage point margin. Many commentators argued that the elections were decided by the closely contested vote in Ohio.

From early in the 2004 election cycle, Ohio had been viewed as a *battleground state*—a state where voters were not clearly leaning toward either major candidate leading up to the elections. Political analysts and news media outlets placed a great deal of emphasis on the battleground states, arguing that these states could potentially decide the outcome.

At the end of each election, the winning presidential candidate appears with his family for a victory celebration. Here Barack Obama continued the tradition at Grant Park in Chicago on November 4, 2008.

AP PHOTO/PABLO MARTINEZ MONSIVAIS

The 2008 Presidential Elections

At times during the campaign, the 2008 presidential contest appeared to be close. The financial panic that struck on September 15, however, tipped the elections decisively. Barack Obama's victory in 2008 reversed the trend of extremely close elections established in 2000 and 2004. Obama won 365 electoral votes, and his popular-vote margin over John McCain was about 7.2 percentage points, nearly a 10-point swing to the Democrats from the elections of 2004. With approximately 52.9 percent of the total popular vote, Obama was the first Democrat to win an absolute majority (more than 50 percent) of the popular vote since Jimmy Carter did so in 1976. Indeed, Obama won a larger share of the popular vote than any Democrat since Lyndon Johnson's 61 percent victory in 1964.

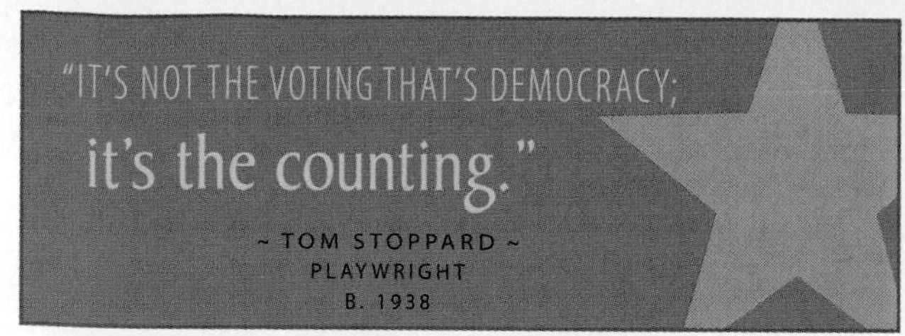

"IT'S NOT THE VOTING THAT'S DEMOCRACY;
it's the counting."
~ TOM STOPPARD ~
PLAYWRIGHT
B. 1938

AMERICA AT ODDS Campaigns and Elections

Some observers believe that if the founders could see how presidential campaigns are conducted today, they would be shocked at how candidates "pander to the masses." Whether they would be shocked at the costliness of modern campaigns is not as clear. After all, the founders themselves were an elitist, wealthy group, as are many of today's successful candidates for high political office. In any event, Americans today are certainly stunned by how much it takes to win an election. Some of the specific controversies concerning campaigns that divide Americans are the following:

- Is the Electoral College a dangerous anachronism—or a force for stability within our political system?
- Should all voters be free to participate in any party primary—or does such a step make it too difficult for the parties to present a coherent group of candidates and policies?
- Should states retain their treasured right to set the dates of their presidential primaries—or should the national parties assume responsibility for establishing a rational primary schedule?
- Are campaign contributions a constitutionally protected form of free speech—or are they too often a thinly veiled method of bribing public officials?
- Should all politically active groups be required to furnish the identities of their major contributors—or should we allow contributors to remain anonymous because they might suffer reprisals due to their contributions?

Take Action

The most obvious way you can take action in political campaigns or elections is to join the campaign of a candidate you support. Any campaign has an insatiable desire for volunteers. Consider that by volunteering, you are in effect making a substantial political contribution that does not have to be reported to anyone. Volunteers can assemble mailings, answer the telephone, or make calls to encourage voters to support their candidate. Even if you have little free time or are not comfortable talking to strangers, most campaigns will be able to find a way in which you can participate.

An alternative is to work for a public-interest group. Many groups have worked toward reforming the way campaign funds are raised and spent in politics today. One nonprofit, nonpartisan, grassroots organization that lobbies for campaign-finance reform is Common Cause. In the photo to the left, a participant in Colorado Common Cause's effort to reform campaign financing displays a mock-up of a TV remote control with a large mute button at a news conference. The group was asking voters to "mute" attack ads directed against a Colorado initiative to amend the state constitution to limit campaign financing and set contribution limits.

AP PHOTO/ED ANDRIESKI

POLITICS ON THE WEB

- Dave Leip's Atlas of U.S. Presidential Elections hosts a major discussion site where hundreds of guests discuss election results. You can find detailed figures to back up your arguments elsewhere on Leip's site, along with an electoral college calculator that lets you figure out how many electoral votes a candidate will receive if he or she carries a particular share of the states. Find the Atlas at **www.uselectionatlas.org**
- You can find out exactly what the laws are that govern campaign financing by accessing the Federal Election Commission's Web site. The commission has provided an online "Citizens' Guide" that spells out what is and is not legal. You can also download actual data on campaign donations from the site. Go to **www.fec.gov**
- To look at data from the Federal Election Commission presented in a more user-friendly way, you can access the following nonpartisan, independent site that allows you to type in an elected official's name and receive large amounts of information on contributions to that official. Go to **moneyline.cq.com/pml/home.do**
- Another excellent source for information on campaign financing, including who's contributing what amounts to which candidates, is the Center for Responsive Politics. You can access its Web site at **www.opensecrets.org**
- Common Cause offers additional information about campaign financing on its Web site at **www.commoncause.org**
- Project Vote Smart offers information on campaign financing, as well as voting, on its Web site at **www.votesmart.org**

Access CourseMate to review and expand on this chapter through quizzes, flashcards, learning objectives, interactive timelines, a crossword puzzle, audio summaries, video, critical-thinking activities, simulations, and more.

Politics and the Media

LEARNING OBJECTIVES

LO1 Explain the role of the media in a democracy.

LO2 Summarize how television influences the conduct of political campaigns.

LO3 Explain why talk radio has been described as the Wild West of the media.

LO4 Describe types of media bias and explain how such bias affects the political process.

LO5 Indicate the extent to which the Internet is reshaping news and political campaigns.

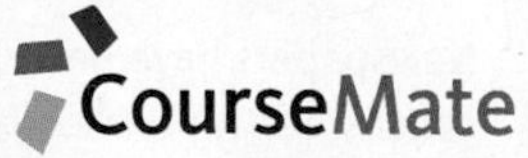

AMERICA AT ODDS

Can We Do without Newspapers?

The *New York Times.* The *Washington Post.* The *Wall Street Journal.* The *Christian Science Monitor.* These and hundreds of other major and minor newspapers have generated and disseminated the nation's news for more than one hundred years. Already in 1783, at the end of the Revolutionary War, America had forty-three newspapers. Not until 1910, though, did all of the essential features that we recognize in today's newspapers become commonplace.

Gradually, radio and television supplanted newspapers as this country's primary information source. Relatively recently, some great newspapers have filed for bankruptcy protection. The following newspapers no longer exist: the *Tucson Citizen,* the *Rocky Mountain News,* the *Baltimore Examiner,* the *Cincinnati Post,* and the *Albuquerque Tribune.* Additional newspapers have reduced their printing schedules or have gone completely online.

The online revolution has certainly changed the newspaper business—and perhaps will eventually eliminate it. The godfather of the U.S. investing community, Warren Buffett, has said that the newspaper business faces "just unending losses." His recommendation to investors—stay away. With newspapers in so much trouble, the question arises: Does it matter if newspapers disappear?

Who Cares about Newspapers When Free Content Is Everywhere?

Those who do not mourn the loss of newspapers—particularly the younger generation—point out the obvious. Americans have more access to more news than ever before. Online news is available and updated day and night. An enormous number of citizen bloggers will help you find out what is happening anywhere in the world anytime you want. So who needs newspapers?

Even if your hometown newspaper shuts down, "hyperlocal" Web sites are increasingly available to deliver local news. Many of these sites are organized by companies such as EveryBlock, Outside.In, Placeblogger, and Patch.

Newspapers have always had a "slant," anyway, and in the past most Americans had to put up with whatever point of view their local newspaper provided. That is no longer the case. You can find the news—presented in whatever way you like—on thousands of Internet news sites and millions of blogs (short for "Web logs"). Variety is the spice of life, and we certainly have more variety in news gathering and presentation than ever before.

Newspapers are dead. Long live the news.

Without Newspapers, the News Is Just Background Noise

The reality of this world is that people have to be paid to do a good job no matter what that job is. Journalists have families to feed. Rarely are they independently wealthy amateurs. Where does all that free content on the Web come from? Most of it can ultimately be traced back to journalists working for the print media. This is true of hyperlocal sites as well. Even today, newspapers employ the overwhelming majority of all journalists. How many bloggers bother to attend city council meetings and report what happens? Precious few do.

A British reporter sums up the entire argument: "The real value that newspapers provide, whether in print or online, is organization, editing, and reputation." The issue is not the survival of the newspaper industry, but the survival of an informed citizenry. If citizens believe that all information, no matter where it comes from—blogs, tweets, Web sites that promote conspiracy theories—is of the same value, then these citizens are in trouble.

We need to change the way newspapers work. We need to figure out ways in which online versions of publications can earn enough revenue to be self-supporting. If we do this, we can ensure that newspapers remain the mainstay of American news gathering and distribution.

WHERE DO YOU STAND?

1. **Most young people rarely, if ever, read a newspaper. Does that mean they are not getting any news? Why or why not?**
2. **How much do you think the reputation of a news source really matters?**

EXPLORE THIS ISSUE ONLINE

- **Newspapers have been harder hit in Michigan than in any other state. Ann Arbor, home of the University of Michigan, with a metro population of almost 350,000, may be the largest urban area in the country to lose its only daily newspaper. Papers in Flint, Saginaw, and Bay City, Michigan, now publish only three times a week. The Detroit papers have drastically cut back their distribution as well. Statewide coverage is now provided by the online service www.mlive.com. For details of how the *Ann Arbor News* came to close its doors, see www.mlive.com/annarbornews.**

Introduction

The debate over the survival of newspapers, described in the chapter-opening *America at Odds* feature, is just one aspect of an important topic: the role of the media in American politics. Strictly defined, the term *media* means communication channels. It is the plural form of *medium,* as in medium of communication. In this strict sense, any method used by people to communicate—including the telephone—is a communication medium. In this chapter, though, we look at the **mass media**—channels through which people can communicate to large audiences. These channels include the **print media** (newspapers and magazines) and the **electronic media** (radio, television, and the Internet).

"The press may not be successful much of the time in telling people what to think, but it is stunningly successful in telling its readers **WHAT TO THINK ABOUT.**"

~ BERNARD C. COHEN ~
AMERICAN POLITICAL SCIENTIST
B. 1926

mass media Communication channels, such as newspapers and radio and television broadcasts, through which people can communicate to large audiences.

print media Communication channels that consist of printed materials, such as newspapers and magazines.

electronic media Communication channels that involve electronic transmissions, such as radio, television, and the Internet.

The media are a dominant presence in our lives largely because they provide entertainment. Americans today enjoy more leisure than at any time in history, and we fill it up with books, movies, Web surfing, and television—a huge amount of television. But the media play a vital role in our political lives as well, particularly during campaigns and elections. Politicians and political candidates have learned—often the hard way—that positive media exposure and news coverage are essential to winning votes.

As you read in Chapter 4, one of the most important civil liberties protected in the Bill of Rights is freedom of the press. Like free speech, a free press is considered a vital tool of the democratic process. If people are to cast informed votes, they must have access to a forum in which they can discuss public affairs fully and assess the conduct and competency of their officials. The

LARRY BUSACCA/WIREIMAGE/GETTY IMAGES

Walter Cronkite was considered the "voice of America" for decades. He presented the *CBS Evening News* from 1962 to 1981. Today, Katie Couric is the CBS News anchor on that show. Why is it harder today for a news anchor to become as well known and influential as was Cronkite?

JIM WATSON/AFP/GETTY IMAGES

THE REST OF THE WORLD

Social Networking Becomes a Political Force in Indonesia

You might be surprised to learn that the Southeast Asian nation of Indonesia has the world's third-largest number of Facebook users. (The United States is first and Britain is second). There are now more than 21 million Facebook users in that country—close to 10 percent of the population. Most Indonesians are too poor to own computers and instead rely on inexpensive cell phones or Internet cafés for online access.

Indonesians are not just using social networking to interact with their friends. Facebook, Twitter, and local social networking systems have become a political power in Indonesia. For example, the government recently erected a statue of Barack Obama as a ten-year-old in a local park in the capital, Jakarta. (Obama lived in that city from the time he was six until he was ten.) Almost sixty thousand online protestors demanded that the statue be taken down, arguing that the park should be limited to honoring Indonesians. City officials soon took down the statue. Protests on Facebook also helped stop an attempt to cripple Indonesia's main anticorruption agency.

Of course, social networking systems such as Facebook are a political force in the United States as well. When Obama sought to build support for his presidential campaign, he got a considerable boost when he began using Facebook. So too did recently elected Senator Scott Brown (R., Mass.) during his campaign.

The Government Is Afraid

Many Indonesians welcome Facebook and Twitter as ways of democratizing the country's often corrupt political system. In contrast, Indonesian politicians worry that social networking will become an unpredictable and perhaps undesirable political force. Indonesia's minister of communication and information technology, Tifatul Sembiring, states that online content should be regulated to preserve "our values, also our culture and also our norms." Online movements have proved unsettling to bureaucrats and politicians because they are an effective way to challenge governmental authority.

The Indonesian government has recently passed laws that can be used against participants in social networking protest movements. More such laws are possible in the future. Under one new law, a person convicted of online defamation can receive a maximum sentence of six years in prison.

China as an Example to Avoid

Internet use is subject to strict control in many countries. For example, Chinese users must contend with what has been called the "Great Firewall of China," which severely limits access to foreign Web sites. Some Indonesians fear that the authorities in their country might emulate China. "I think we are between China and the United States," says Sembiring. "Yes, we are free. But with freedom comes responsibility."

For Critical Analysis *Why might online protests against government corruption be more effective than traditional methods of protest?*

media provide this forum. In contrast, government censorship of the press is common in many nations around the globe. One example is China, where the Web is heavily censored even though China now has more Internet users than any other country on earth. One reason dictatorships fear a free press is that people can use it to organize against the authorities. For an example of how citizens in Indonesia have used new forms of media for such purposes, see this chapter's *The Rest of the World* feature above.

LO1 *The Role of the Media in a Democracy*

What the media say and do has an impact on what Americans think about political issues. But just as clearly, the media also *reflect* what Americans think about politics. Some scholars argue that the media is the fourth "check" in our political system—checking and balancing the power of the president, the Congress, and the courts. The power of the media today is enormous, but how the media use their power is an issue about which Americans are often at odds.

The Media and the First Amendment

As just noted, freedom of the press is essential if the media are to play their role in supporting the democratic process. The concept of freedom of the press has been applied to print media since the adoption of the Bill of Rights. Such freedoms were not, however, immediately extended to other types of media as they came into existence. Film was one of the first types of new media to be considered under the First Amendment, and in 1915 the United States Supreme Court ruled that "as a matter of common sense," freedom of the press did not apply to the movies.[1] Radio received no protection upon its development, and neither did television.

The Court did not extend First Amendment protections to the cinema until 1952.[2] Although the Court has stated that the First Amendment is relevant to broadcast media such as radio and television, to this day it has not granted these media complete protection. For example, the Court has never ruled that the *fairness doctrine,* enforced by the Federal Communications Commission (FCC) from 1949 to 1987, is unconstitutional. Talk radio was essentially impossible until the doctrine was repealed. (You will learn more about the fairness doctrine and talk radio later in this chapter.)

In contrast, the Court extended First Amendment protections to the Internet in 1997, in its first opportunity to rule on the issue.[3] Cable TV received substantial protections in 2000.[4] In recent years, the courts have also shown some willingness to expand the freedoms of broadcast media.

The Agenda-Setting Function of the Media

One of the criticisms often levied against the media is that they play too large a role in determining the issues, events, and personalities that are in the public eye. When people take in the day's top news stories, they usually assume automatically that these stories concern the most important issues facing the nation. In actuality, the media decide the relative importance of issues by publicizing some issues and ignoring others, and by giving some stories high priority and others low priority. By helping to determine what people will talk and think about, the media set the *political agenda*—the issues that politicians will address. In other words, to borrow from Bernard Cohen's classic statement on the media and public opinion, the press (media) may *not* be successful in telling people what to think, but it is "stunningly successful in telling its readers what to think about."[5]

For example, television played a significant role in shaping public opinion about the Vietnam War (1964–1975), which has been called the first "television war." Part of the public opposition to the war in the late 1960s came about as a result of the daily portrayal of the war's horrors on TV news programs. Film footage and narrative accounts of the destruction, death, and suffering in Vietnam brought the war into living rooms across the United States. (To examine whether the press is doing its job, see the *Join the Debate* feature on the following page.)

Events in Iraq were also the subject of constant news coverage. Some believe that the media played a crucial role in influencing public opinion at the outset of the war. Indeed, the media have been sharply criticized by media watchdog groups for failing to do more fact checking prior to the invasion of Iraq. Instead of investigating the Bush administration's assertions that Iraq had weapons of mass destruction and links to al Qaeda, the media just passed this information on to the public. If the media had done their job, claim these critics, there would have been much less public support for going to war with Iraq.

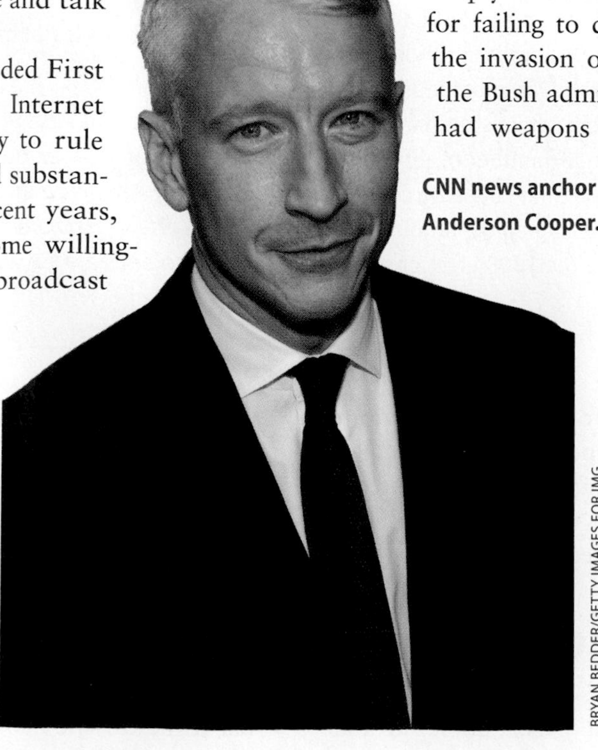

CNN news anchor Anderson Cooper.

BRYAN BEDDER/GETTY IMAGES FOR IMG

The degree to which the media influence public opinion is not always all that clear, however. As you read in Chapter 8, some studies show that people filter the information they receive from the media through their own preconceived ideas

JOIN THE DEBATE

Is the Press Living Up to Its Role as a "Watchdog"?

Thomas Jefferson said in 1787 that he'd rather have newspapers without a government than a government without newspapers. Not surprisingly, the First Amendment to the Constitution upholds the important role of a free press. The news media have been placed in a specially protected position in our complicated country to serve as a watchdog against abuses of government. Some Americans believe that the press has lost its ability to act in this way. Others, however, believe that the government scandals unearthed by the media in years past show that the media are doing their job.

The Press Is Not Doing Its Job

Americans who believe that the media are not acting as proper watchdogs contend that journalists are frequently intimidated by the politicians and public officials that they cover. To write stories that catch the reader's eye, journalists must have access to government officials and political candidates. If the journalists are excessively critical, they may lose this access. Journalists are also addicted to "balanced" coverage that "gives both sides" of an issue. The problem is, sometimes there aren't two sides to a story. If a politician makes a statement that is obviously untrue, reporters do the public no favors by neglecting to point that out. Yet it is very rare for the media to challenge a politician on even the most preposterous falsehoods.

During the run-up to the Iraq War, most journalists were reluctant to dispute the Bush administration's arguments in favor of military action. A number of reporters aferwards admitted that they were afraid of being characterized as "unpatriotic" if they questioned the administration's actions. Later, both before the 2008 elections and after President Barack Obama took office, conservatives argued that mainstream journalists were so personally enamored of Obama that they were giving him a "free ride." For their part, liberals complained that the press had largely failed to challenge a series of obviously false statements that Republican leaders made about Democratic health-care proposals.

The Truth Will Come Out Eventually

Those who take the other side of this debate believe that we still have the freest press in the world. Currently, few regulations control what members of the media can say, report, or film. Even if the traditional media do not do a good job, the truth will come out in the blogosphere. Indeed, bloggers have done a better job of investigating some news stories than have the mainstream media. In some instances, the mainstream press has been forced to publish information on stories that first became big in the blogosphere.

When reporting is erroneous, it is quickly exposed—first by bloggers and then by the established media—and the perpetrators are often punished. Some former media superstars, such as Dan Rather, have been relieved of their duties when critics determined that their news reports were unfounded. Also, let's not forget the role of media watchdog groups. They are numerous and represent both conservative and liberal viewpoints. All in all, it's hard to imagine that with current communications possibilities, our government is not being watched enough.

For Critical Analysis ***We discussed the crisis of the newspaper business in the chapter-opening* America at Odds *feature. What impact might these problems have on the ability of the press to serve as a watchdog?***

about issues. Scholars who try to analyze the relationship between American politics and the media inevitably confront the chicken-and-egg conundrum: Do the media cause the public to hold certain views, or do the media merely reflect views that are formed independently of the media's influence?

The Medium Does Affect the Message

Of all the media, television has the greatest impact. Television reaches into almost every home in the United States. Virtually all homes have televisions. Even outside their homes, Americans can watch television—in airports, shopping malls, golf clubhouses, and medical offices. People can view television shows on their computers, and they can download TV programs to their iPods, iPhones, or Windows Phone 7 and view the programs whenever and wherever they want.

For some time, it was predicted that as more people used the Internet, fewer people would turn to television for news or entertainment. This prediction turned out to be off the mark. Today, Americans watch more television than ever, and it is the primary news source

Figure 10–1

Media Usage by Consumers, 1988 to Present

Hours shown for Internet usage include only those for "pure-play Internet services"—that is, they do not include time spent at the Web sites of TV networks or print media, including e-books. They also do not include hours for Internet services provided by cable TV companies. All of these hours are included in the totals for the traditional media. If they were included with Internet services, the number of Internet hours in 2010 would approximately double. Internet services would then be in the same range as broadcast TV.

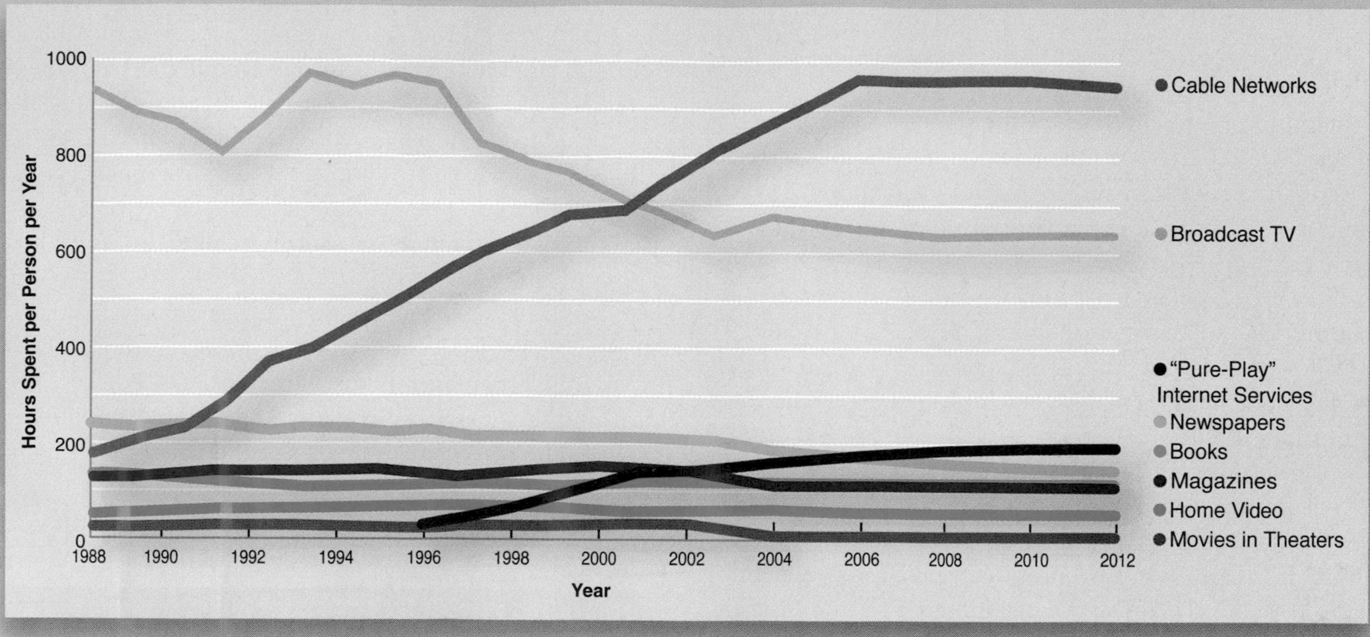

Sources: U.S. Census Bureau, *Statistical Abstract of the United States, 2008* (Washington, D.C.: U.S. Government Printing Office, 2010), and authors' updates.

for more than 65 percent of the citizenry. Figure 10–1 above shows the prominence of television when compared with other media.

As you will read shortly, politicians take maximum advantage of the power and influence of television. But does the television medium alter the presentation of political information in any way? Compare the coverage given to an important political issue by the print media—including the online sites of major newspapers and magazines—with the coverage provided by broadcast and cable TV networks. You will note some striking differences. For one thing, the print media (particularly leading newspapers such as the *Washington Post*, the *New York Times*, and the *Wall Street Journal*) treat an important issue in much more detail. In addition to news stories based on reporters' research, you will find editorials taking positions on the issue and arguments supporting those positions. Television news, in contrast, is often criticized as being too brief and too superficial.

TIME CONSTRAINTS The medium of television necessarily imposes constraints on how political issues are presented. Time is limited. News stories must be reported quickly, in only a few minutes or occasionally in only a **sound bite,** a televised comment lasting for just a few seconds that captures a thought or a perspective and has an immediate impact on the viewers.

A VISUAL MEDIUM Television reporting also relies extensively on visual elements, rather than words, to capture the viewers' attention. Inevitably, the photos or videos selected to depict a particular political event have exaggerated importance. The visual aspect of television contributes to its power, but it also creates a potential bias. Those watching the news presentation do not know what portions of a video being shown have been deleted, what other photos may have been taken, or whether other records of the event exist. This kind of "selection bias" will be discussed in more detail later in this chapter.

TELEVISION IS BIG BUSINESS Today's TV networks compete aggressively with one another to air "breaking news" and to produce interesting news

sound bite A televised comment, lasting for only a few seconds, that captures a thought or a perspective and has an immediate impact on the viewers.

political advertising Advertising undertaken by or on behalf of a political candidate to familiarize voters with the candidate and his or her views on campaign issues; also advertising for or against policy issues.

programs. Competition in the television industry understandably has had an effect on how the news is presented. To make profits, or even stay in business, TV stations need viewers. And to attract viewers, the news industry has turned to "infotainment"—programs that inform and entertain at the same time. Slick sets, attractive reporters, and animated graphics that dance across the television screen are now commonplace on most news programs, particularly on the cable news channels.

TV networks also compete with one another for advertising income. Although the media in the United States are among the freest in the world, their programming nonetheless remains vulnerable to the influence of their advertising sponsors.

Concentrated ownership of media is another concern. Many mainstream media outlets are owned by giant corporations, such as Time Warner, Rupert Murdoch's News Corporation, and even General Electric. Concentrated ownership may be a more serious problem at the local level than at the national level. If only one or two companies own a city's newspaper and its TV stations, these outlets may not present a diversity of opinion. Further, the owners are unlikely to air information that could be damaging either to their advertisers or to themselves, or even to publicize views that they disagree with politically. For example, TV networks have refused to run antiwar commercials created by religious groups. Still, some media observers are not particularly concerned about concentrated ownership of traditional outlets, because the Internet has generated a massive diversification of media.

LO2 *The Candidates and Television*

Given the TV-saturated environment in which we live, it should come as no surprise that candidates spend a great deal of time—and money—obtaining a TV presence through political ads, debates, and general news coverage. Candidates and their campaign managers realize that the time and money are well spent because television has an important impact on the way people see the candidates, understand the issues, and cast their votes.

Political Advertising

Today, televised **political advertising** consumes at least half of the total budget for a major political campaign. In the 2004 election cycle, $1.4 billion was spent for political advertising on broadcast TV. As you can see in Figure 10–2 below, this was almost five times the amount spent in the 1992 election cycle. For the 2006 elections, the figure climbed to $1.7 billion. According to the research firm PQ Media, spending on all forms of political advertising reached $4.5 billion in the 2007–2008 election cycle, including $2.3 billion for broadcast TV in 2008 alone. Even without an expensive presidential race, spending in 2010 substantially surpassed the 2008 figure.

Political advertising first appeared on television during the 1952 presidential campaign. At that time, there were only about 15 million television sets. Today, there are almost as many TV sets as people. Initially, political TV commercials were more or less like any other type of advertising. Instead of focusing on the positive qualities of a product, thirty-second or sixty-second ads focused

Figure 10–2

Political Ad Spending on Broadcast Television, 1992–2010

As you can see in this figure, spending for political advertising has increased steadily during recent elections.

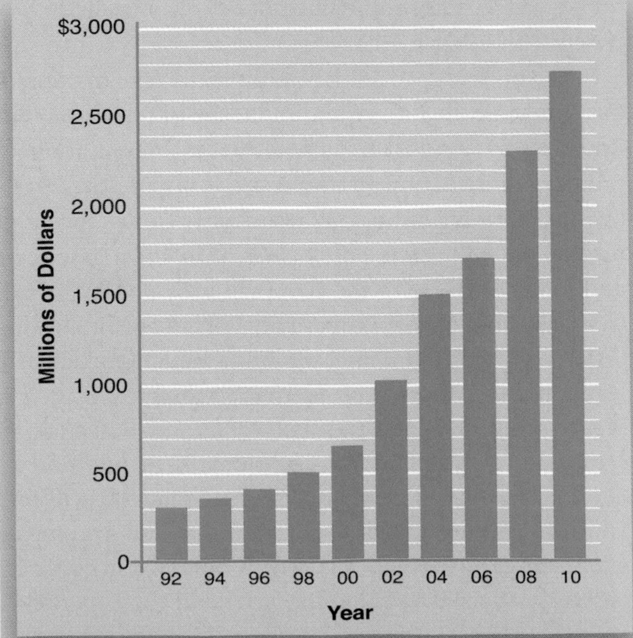

Sources: Television Bureau of Advertising, as presented in Lorraine Woellert and Tom Lowry, "A Political Nightmare: Not Enough Airtime," *Business Week*, November 23, 2000, p. 111; and authors' updates.

on the positive qualities of a political candidate. Within the decade, however, **negative political advertising** began to appear on TV.

ATTACK ADS Despite the barrage of criticism levied against the candidates' use of negative political ads during recent election cycles, such ads are not new. Indeed, **personal attack ads**—advertising that attacks the character of an opposing candidate—have a long tradition. In 1800, an article in the *Federalist Gazette of the United States* described Thomas Jefferson as having a "weakness of nerves, want of fortitude, and total imbecility of character." After the terrorist attacks of September 11, 2001, candidates found that ads involving fear of terrorism resonated with voters. As a result, candidates routinely accused their opponents of lacking the fortitude to wage war on terrorism.

Negative advertising has become a staple in American political campaigns, whether for political races or for issues to be decided by Congress and the president. As much as voters claim that negative ads are offensive, these ads are effective. Why?

In 2008, the Republicans understood that after eight years of President Bush, voters wanted something new. For John McCain to win, voters had to see Democrat Barack Obama as an unacceptable alternative. The McCain campaign therefore aired a series of personal attack ads that portrayed Obama as a dangerous radical with unsavory associates. The ads may have enhanced voter turnout among Republicans at the cost of alienating some independent voters. On the Democratic side, the Obama campaign generally employed issue ads, which were also largely negative.

ISSUE ADS Candidates use negative **issue ads** to focus on flaws in the opponents' positions on issues. Candidates level criticisms at each other's stated positions on various issues, such as health care and the bank-bailout legislation. Candidates also try to undermine their opponents' credibility by pointing to discrepancies between what the opponents say in their campaign speeches and their political records, such as voting records, which are available to the public and thus can easily be verified. As noted in Chapters 6 and 9, issue ads are also used by interest groups to gather support for candidates who endorse the groups' causes.

Issue ads can be even more devastating than personal attacks—as Barry Goldwater learned in 1964 when his opponent in the presidential race, President Lyndon Johnson, aired the "daisy girl" ad. This ad, a new departure in negative advertising, showed a little girl standing quietly in a field of daisies. She held a daisy and pulled off the petals, counting to herself. Suddenly, a deep voice was heard counting: "10, 9, 8, 7, 6, . . ." When the countdown hit zero, the unmistakable mushroom cloud of an atomic explosion filled the screen. Then President Johnson's voice was heard saying, "These are the stakes: to make a world in which all of God's children can live, or to go into the dark. We must either

"The thing to do now, Senator, is to hit back with some negative advertising of our own."

negative political advertising Political advertising undertaken for the purpose of discrediting an opposing candidate in the eyes of the voters. Attack ads are one form of negative political advertising.

personal attack ad A negative political advertisement that attacks the character of an opposing candidate.

issue ad A political advertisement that focuses on a particular issue. Issue ads can be used to support or attack a candidate.

love each other or we must die." A message on the screen then read: "Vote for President Johnson on November 3." The implication, of course, was that Goldwater would lead the country into a nuclear war.[6]

NEGATIVE ADVERTISING—IS IT GOOD OR BAD FOR OUR DEMOCRACY? The debate over the effect of negative advertising on our political system is ongoing. Some observers argue that negative ads can backfire. Extreme ads may create sympathy for the candidate being attacked rather than support for the attacker, particularly when the charges against the candidate being attacked are not credible. Many people fear that attack ads and "dirty tricks" used by both parties during a campaign may alienate citizens from the political process itself and thus lower voter turnout in elections.

Yet candidates and their campaign managers typically assert that they use negative advertising simply because it works. Negative TV ads are more likely than positive ads to grab the viewers' attention and make an impression. Also, according to media expert Shanto Iyengar, "the more negative the ad, the more likely it is to get free media coverage. So there's a big incentive to go to extremes."[7] Others believe that negative advertising is a force for the good because it sharpens public debate, thereby enriching the democratic process. This is the position taken by Vanderbilt University political science professor John Geer. He contends that negative ads are likely to focus on substantive political issues instead of candidates' personal characteristics. Thus, negative ads do a better job of informing the voters about important campaign issues than positive ads do.[8]

Television Debates

Televised debates have been a feature of presidential campaigns since 1960, when presidential candidates Republican Richard M. Nixon and Democrat John F. Kennedy squared off in four great TV debates. Television debates provide an opportunity for voters to find out how candidates differ on issues. They also allow candidates to capitalize on the power of television to improve their images or point out the failings of their opponents.

It is widely believed that Kennedy won the first of the 1960 debates in large part because of Nixon's haggard appearance and poor makeup—many people who heard the debate on the radio thought that Nixon had done well. No presidential debates were held during the general election campaigns of 1964, 1968, or 1972, but the debates have been a part of every election since 1976. The 1992 debates, which starred Republican George H. W. Bush and Democrat Bill Clinton, also included a third-party candidate, H. Ross Perot. Since 1996, however, the Commission on Presidential Debates, which now organizes the events, has limited the participants to candidates of the two major parties.[9] The commission also organizes debates between the vice-presidential candidates.

Many contend that the presidential debates help shape the outcome of the elections. Others doubt that the debates—or the postdebate "spin" applied by campaign operatives and political commentators—have changed many votes. Evidence on this question is mixed.

Gallup polling figures suggest that in 1960 the debates helped Kennedy to victory. In 1980, Republican Ronald Reagan did well in a final debate with Democratic incumbent Jimmy Carter. Reagan impressed many voters with his sunny temperament, which helped dispel fears that he was a right-wing radical. In Gallup's

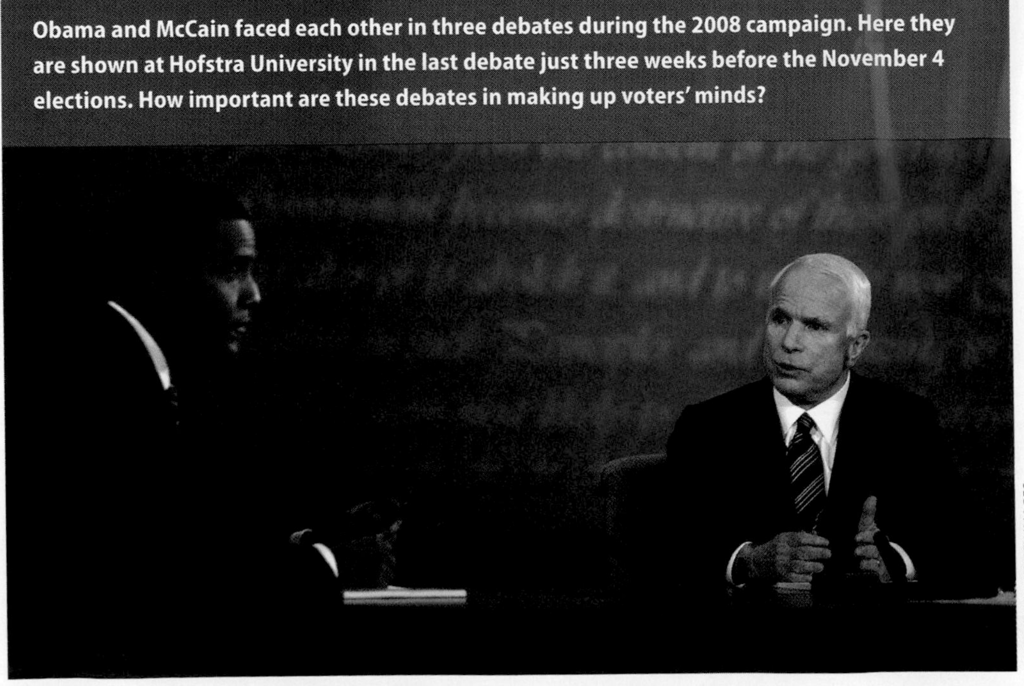
Obama and McCain faced each other in three debates during the 2008 campaign. Here they are shown at Hofstra University in the last debate just three weeks before the November 4 elections. How important are these debates in making up voters' minds?

MARIO TAMA/GETTY IMAGES

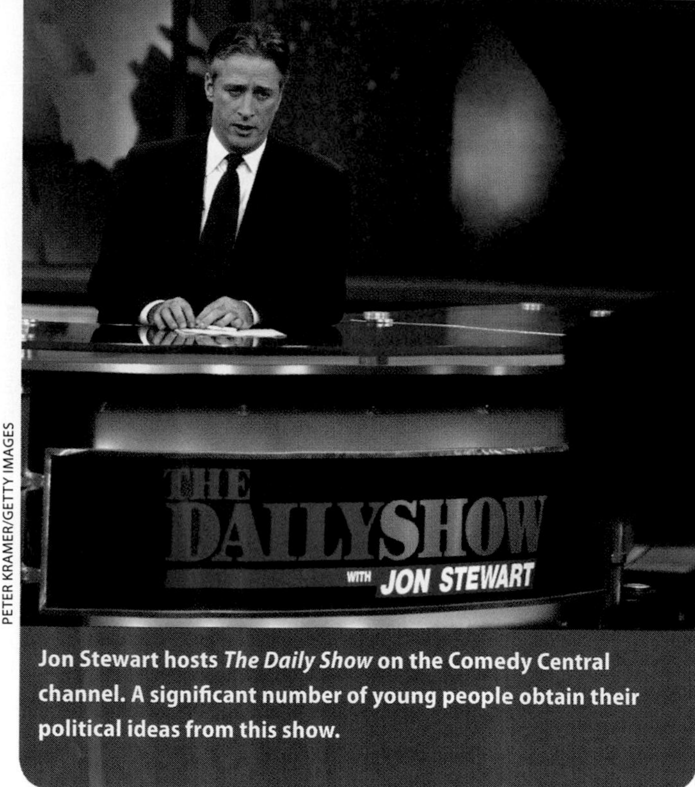

PETER KRAMER/GETTY IMAGES

Jon Stewart hosts *The Daily Show* on the Comedy Central channel. A significant number of young people obtain their political ideas from this show.

opinion, however, Reagan would have won the election even without the debate.

The 2008 Presidential Debates

The first debate between Republican John McCain and Democrat Barack Obama was supposed to focus on foreign policy. It took place, however, in one of the worst weeks of the 2008 financial crisis. Inevitably, much time was spent on economics.

The second debate was steered by questions from undecided voters in a town hall format, which was usually McCain's strong suit. Because the financial meltdown in the economy had gotten worse, many questions related to economics. The debate had a tougher tone than the first one.

In the third and final debate, Obama appeared to be "playing it safe," given that he was so far ahead in the polls. McCain accused Obama of advocating too much redistribution of wealth—in his opinion, a socialist idea. In the end, surveys showed that Obama's performance in all three debates was better received than McCain's.

News Coverage

Whereas political ads are expensive, coverage by the news media is free. Accordingly, the candidates try to take advantage of the media's interest in campaigns to increase the quantity and quality of news coverage. This is not always easy. Often, the media devote the lion's share of their coverage to polls and other indicators of which candidate is ahead in the race.

In recent years, candidates' campaign managers and political consultants have shown increasing sophistication in creating newsworthy events for journalists and TV camera crews to cover. This effort is commonly referred to as **managed news coverage.** For example, typically one of the jobs of the campaign manager is to create newsworthy events that demonstrate the candidate's strong points so that the media can capture this image of the candidate.[10]

Besides considering how camera angles and lighting affect a candidate's appearance, the political consultant plans political events to accommodate the press. The campaign staff attempts to make what the candidate is doing appear interesting. The staff also knows that journalists and political reporters compete for stories and that these individuals can be manipulated. Hence, they often are granted favors, such as exclusive personal interviews with the candidate. Each candidate's press advisers, often called **spin doctors,** also try to convince reporters to give the story or event a **spin,** or interpretation, that is favorable to the candidate.[11]

"Popular" Television

Although not normally regarded as a forum for political debate, television programs such as dramas, sitcoms, and late-night comedy shows often use political themes. For example, the popular courtroom drama *Law & Order* regularly broaches controversial topics such as the death penalty, the USA Patriot Act, and the rights of the accused. For years, the sitcom *Will and Grace* consistently brought to light issues regarding gay and lesbian rights. The dramatic *West Wing* series gave viewers a glimpse into national politics as it told the story of a fictional presidential administration. Late-night shows and programs such as *The Daily Show with Jon Stewart* provide a forum for politicians to demonstrate their lighter sides.

managed news coverage News coverage that is manipulated (managed) by a campaign manager or political consultant to gain media exposure for a political candidate.

spin doctor A political candidate's press adviser, who tries to convince reporters to give a story or event concerning the candidate a particular "spin" (interpretation, or slant).

spin A reporter's slant on, or interpretation of, a particular event or action.

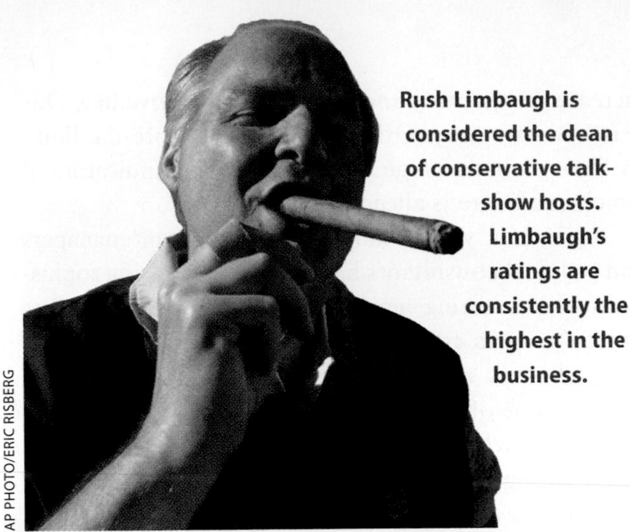
Rush Limbaugh is considered the dean of conservative talk-show hosts. Limbaugh's ratings are consistently the highest in the business.

AP PHOTO/ERIC RISBERG

TV host Glenn Beck addresses the Conservative Political Action Conference (CPAC) in Washington D.C.

AP PHOTO/JOSE LUIS MAGANA

LO3 *Talk Radio—The Wild West of the Media*

Ever since Franklin D. Roosevelt held his first "fireside chats" on radio, politicians have realized the power of that medium. From the beginning, radio has been a favorite outlet for the political right. During the 1930s, for example, the nation's most successful radio commentator was Father Charles Edward Coughlin, a Roman Catholic priest based at the National Shrine of the Little Flower church in Royal Oak, Michigan. Coughlin's audience numbered more than 40 million listeners—this in a nation that had only 123 million inhabitants in 1930. Coughlin started out as a Roosevelt supporter, but he soon moved to the far right, advocating anti-Semitism and expressing sympathy for Adolf Hitler. Coughlin's fascist connections eventually destroyed his popularity.

Modern talk radio took off in the United States during the 1990s. In 1988, there were 200 talk-show radio stations. Today, there are more than 1,200. The growth of talk radio was made possible by the Federal Communications Commission's repeal of the fairness doctrine in 1987. Introduced in 1949, the fairness doctrine required the holders of broadcast licenses to present controversial issues of public importance in a manner that was (in the commission's view) honest, equitable, and balanced. That doctrine would have made it difficult for radio stations to broadcast conservative talk shows exclusively, as many now do. Nine of the top ten talk-radio shows, as measured by Arbitron ratings, are politically conservative. No liberal commentator ranks higher than twentieth place in the ratings. (Several of the shows ranked higher than twentieth, are not political, but deal with subjects such as personal finance and paranormal activities.)

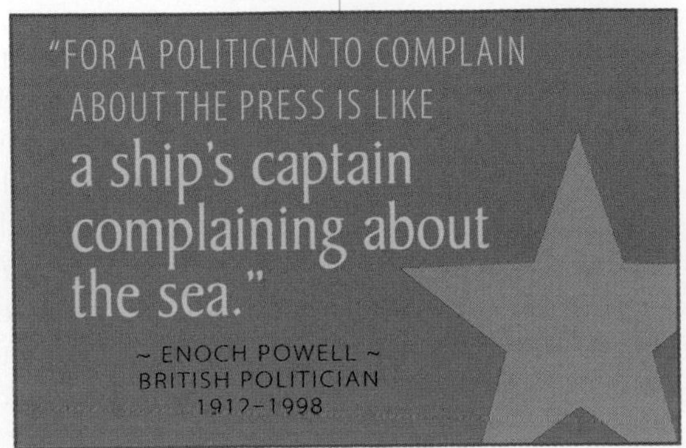

"FOR A POLITICIAN TO COMPLAIN
ABOUT THE PRESS IS LIKE
a ship's captain
complaining about
the sea."
~ ENOCH POWELL ~
BRITISH POLITICIAN
1912–1998

Audiences and Hosts

The Pew Research Center for the People and the Press reports that 17 percent of the public regularly listens to talk radio. This audience is predominantly male, middle-aged, and conservative. Among those who regularly listen to talk radio, 41 percent consider themselves Republicans and 28 percent, Democrats.

Talk radio is sometimes characterized as the Wild West of the media. Talk-show hosts do not attempt to hide their political biases. If anything, they exaggerate them for effect. No journalistic conventions are observed. Leading shows, such as those of Rush Limbaugh, Glenn Beck, Sean Hannity, Andrew Wilkow, and Michael Savage, espouse a brand of conservatism that is robust, even radical. Opponents are regularly characterized as Nazis, Communists, or both at the same time. Limbaugh, for example, consistently refers to feminists as "feminazis." Talk-show hosts appear to care far more about the entertainment value of their statements than whether they are, strictly speaking, true. Hosts often publicize fringe beliefs such as the contention that President Barack Obama was not really born in the United States. The government of Britain actually banned Michael Savage from entry into that country based on his remarks about Muslims.

The Wild West Migrates to Television

Commentators at Fox News have always been predominantly conservative, just as liberals are the rule at the smaller MSNBC network. Still, until recently it was widely seen as inappropriate for television personalities to employ the radical style characteristic of such talk-show hosts as Rush Limbaugh. That understanding began to crumble after October 2008, when Fox News hired conservative commentator Glenn Beck.

Beck's audience is smaller than those of his Fox colleagues Bill O'Reilly and Sean Hannity. In short order, however, Beck transformed himself into one of the nation's most politically polarizing figures. Beck's emotional style—he frequently breaks into tears—his over-the-top statements, and his apocalyptic views were a new development on television. As one example, Beck stated that President Obama had "a deep-seated hatred for white people" and was a racist.

Beck gained further attention by using his on-air pulpit as a political organizing tool. Throughout 2009, Beck promoted the Tea Party movement, and in August 2010 he sponsored the Restoring Honor rally at the Lincoln Memorial in Washington, D.C., which was attended by close to 200,000 people. The apparent aim of the rally was to bring together the Tea Party and Christian conservative movements.

"A nation that is afraid to let its people judge truth and falsehood in an **OPEN MARKET** is a nation that is afraid of its people."

~ JOHN FITZGERALD KENNEDY ~
THIRTY-FIFTH PRESIDENT
OF THE UNITED STATES
1961–1963

The Impact of Talk Radio

The overwhelming dominance of strong conservative voices on talk radio is justified by supporters as a good way to counter what they perceive as the liberal bias in the mainstream print and TV media (we discuss the question of bias in the media in the following section). Supporters say that such shows are simply a response to consumer demand. Those who think that talk radio is good for the country argue that talk shows, taken together, provide a great populist forum. Others are uneasy because they fear that talk shows empower fringe groups, perhaps magnifying their rage.

Certainly, prominent hosts have had great fun organizing potentially disruptive activities. For example, during the 2008 presidential primaries, Limbaugh called for conservatives to reregister as Democrats and vote for Obama. The theory was that Obama would be easier for a Republican to beat than Hillary Clinton. In 2009, Beck (who is on radio as well as television) promoted attempts to shout down Democratic members of Congress at town hall meetings set up to discuss health-care reform.

Those who claim that talk-show hosts go too far ultimately have to deal with the constitutional issue of free speech. While the courts have always given broad support to freedom of expression, broadcast media have been something of an exception, as was explained in Chapter 4. The United States Supreme Court, for example, upheld the fairness doctrine in a 1969 ruling.[12] Presumably, the doctrine could be reinstated. In 2009, after the Democratic victories in the 2008 elections, a few liberals advocated doing just that. President Obama and the Democratic leadership in Congress, however, quickly put an end to this notion. Americans have come to accept talk radio as part of the political environment, and any attempt to curtail it would be extremely unpopular.

LO4 *The Question of Media Bias*

The question of media bias is important in any democracy. After all, for our political system to work, citizens must be well informed. And they can be well informed only if the news media, the source of much of their information, do not slant the news. Today, however, relatively few Americans believe that the news media are unbiased in their reporting. Accompanying this perception is a notable decline in the public's confidence in the news media in recent years.

In a 2010 Gallup poll measuring the public's confidence in various institutions, only 25 percent of the respondents stated that they had "a great deal" or "quite a lot" of confidence in newspapers, and 22 percent had such a degree of confidence in television news. Because of these low percentages, some analysts believe that the media are facing a crisis of confidence.

Partisan Bias

For years, conservatives have argued that there is a liberal bias in the media, and liberals have complained that the media reflect a conservative bias. The majority of Americans think that the media reflect a bias in one direction or another. According to a recent poll, 50 percent of the respondents believed that the news media leaned left, whereas only 22 percent thought that the news media had a conservative bias.

Surveys and analyses of the attitudes and voting habits of reporters have suggested that journalists do indeed hold liberal views. In 2007, MSNBC was able to identify 125 journalists who made political contributions to Democrats or liberal causes, according to Federal Election Commission records. Only 16 gave to Republicans. Two gave to both parties. Still, members of the press are likely to view themselves as moderates. In a 2005 study, the Pew Research Center for the People and the Press found that 64 percent of reporters in both national and local media applied the term "moderate" to themselves. Among journalists working for national outlets, 22 percent described themselves as liberal and only 5 percent as conservative.

In contrast, 14 percent of local reporters called themselves liberals, and 18 percent adopted the conservative label. There is substantial evidence that top journalists working for the nation's most famous newspapers and networks do tend to be liberal. Many journalists themselves perceive the *New York Times* as liberal (although an even larger number view Fox News as conservative).

Nonetheless, a number of media scholars, including Kathleen Hall Jamieson, suggest that even if many reporters hold liberal views, these views are not reflected in their reporting. Based on an extensive study of media coverage of presidential campaigns, Jamieson, director of the Annenberg Public Policy Center of the University of Pennsylvania, concludes that there is no systematic liberal or Democratic bias in news coverage.[13] Media analysts Debra Reddin van Tuyll and Hubert P. van Tuyll have similarly concluded that left-leaning reporters do not automatically equate to left-leaning news coverage. They point out that reporters are only the starting point for news stories. Before any story goes to print or is aired on television, it has to go through a progression of editors and perhaps even the publisher. Because employees at the top of the corporate ladder in news organizations are more right leaning than left leaning, the end result of the editorial and oversight process is more balanced coverage.[14]

The Bias against Losers

Kathleen Hall Jamieson believes that media bias does play a significant role in shaping presidential campaigns and elections, but she argues that it is not a partisan bias. Rather, it is a bias against losers. A candidate who falls behind in the race is immediately labeled a "loser," making it even more difficult for the candidate to regain favor in the voters' eyes.[15]

Jamieson argues that the media use the winner-loser paradigm to describe events throughout the campaigns. Even a presidential debate is regarded as a "sporting match" that results in a winner and a loser. In the days leading up to the 2008 debates, reporters focused on what each candidate had to do to "win" the debate. When the debate was over, reporters immediately speculated about who had "won" as they waited for post-debate polls to answer that question. According to Jamieson, this approach "squanders the opportunity to reinforce learning." The debates are an important source of political information for the voters, and this fact is eclipsed by the media's win-lose focus.

"Selection Bias"

As mentioned earlier, television is big business, and maximizing profits from advertising is a major consideration in what television stations choose to air. After all, a station or network that incurs losses will eventually go bankrupt. The expansion of the media universe to include cable channels and the Internet has also increased the competition among news sources. As a result, news directors *select* programming they believe will attract the largest audiences and garner the highest advertising revenues.

Competition for viewers and readers has become even more challenging in the wake of a declining news audience. A recent survey and analysis of reporters' attitudes conducted by the Pew Research Center's Project for Excellence in Journalism found that all media sectors except two are losing popularity. The two exceptions are the ethnic press, such as Latino newspapers and TV programs, and online sources—and even the online sector has stopped growing.[16]

SELECTION BIAS AND THE BOTTOM LINE The Pew study also indicated that news organizations' struggles to stay afloat are having a notable effect on news coverage. The survey showed that a larger number of reporters than ever before (about 66 percent) agreed that "increased bottom-line pressure is seriously hurting the quality of news coverage." About one-third of the journalists—again, more than in previous surveys—stated that they have felt pressure from either advertisers or corporate owners concerning what to write or broadcast. In other words, these journalists

AP PHOTO/JEFF CHRISTENSEN

Today, news organizations look for special niches around which to build their audiences. Bill O'Reilly hosts *The O'Reilly Factor,* a Fox News cable program where O'Reilly covers news stories and provides commentary on them.

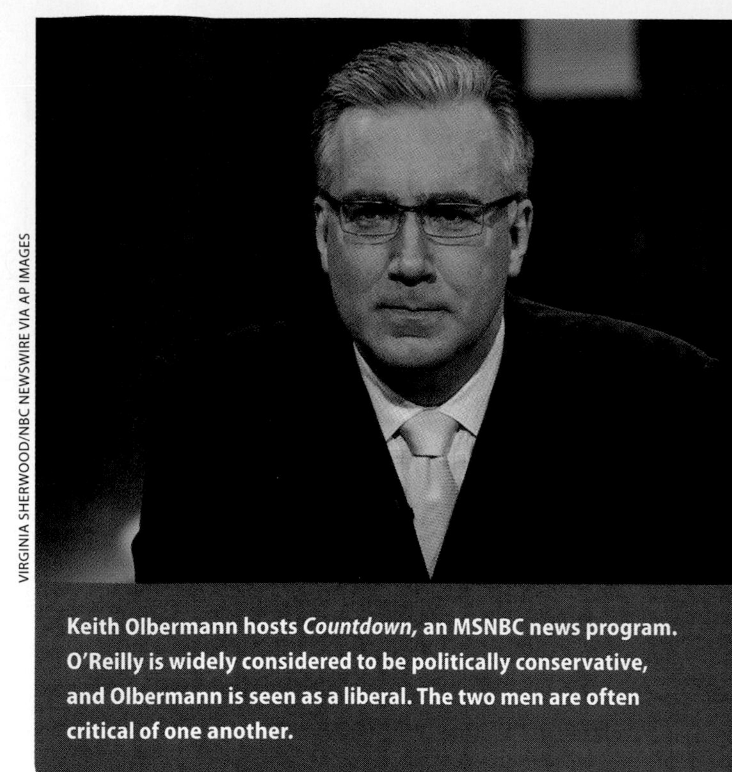

VIRGINIA SHERWOOD/NBC NEWSWIRE VIA AP IMAGES

Keith Olbermann hosts *Countdown,* an MSNBC news program. O'Reilly is widely considered to be politically conservative, and Olbermann is seen as a liberal. The two men are often critical of one another.

believe that economic pressure—the need for revenues—is making significant inroads on independent editorial decision making. Generally, the study found that news reporters are not too confident about the future of journalism.

A CHANGING NEWS CULTURE A number of studies, including the Pew study just cited, indicate that today's news culture is in the midst of change. News organizations are redefining their purpose and increasingly looking for special niches in which to build their audiences. According to the Pew study, for some markets, the niche is *hyperlocalism*—that is, narrowing the focus of news to the local area. For others, it is personal commentary, revolving around highly politicized TV figures such as Bill O'Reilly and Keith Olbermann. In a sense, news organizations have begun to base their appeal less on *how* they cover the news and more on *what* they cover. Traditional journalism—fact-based reporting instead of opinion and punditry—is becoming a smaller part of this mix.

Another development is the move toward highly specific subject matter that appeals strongly to a limited number of viewers. Magazines have always done this—consider the many magazine titles on topics such as model railroading or home decorating. With the large number of cable channels, *narrowcasting* has become important on television as well. Networks now appeal to members of particular ethnic groups (BET—Black Entertainment Television), hobbyists (Cooking Channel), or history buffs (Military Channel).

LO5 *Political News and Campaigns on the Web*

Cyberspace is getting bigger every day. More than one-quarter of the world's inhabitants currently use the Internet, a total of about 2 billion people. According to Technorati, bloggers around the world update their blogs with new posts in eighty-one languages at a rate of almost a million posts every day. Among U.S. Internet users, 77 percent read blogs, and one blog tracker, BlogPulse, has identified more than 146 million blogs. In addition, popular networking sites have enormous numbers of personalized pages—Twitter has 190 million members, and Facebook has more than 500 million.

Not surprisingly, the Internet is now a major source of information for many people. Gone are the days when you and your friends tromped to the library to research a paper. Why should you? You can go online and in a matter of seconds look up practically any subject. Of course, all major newspapers are online, as are

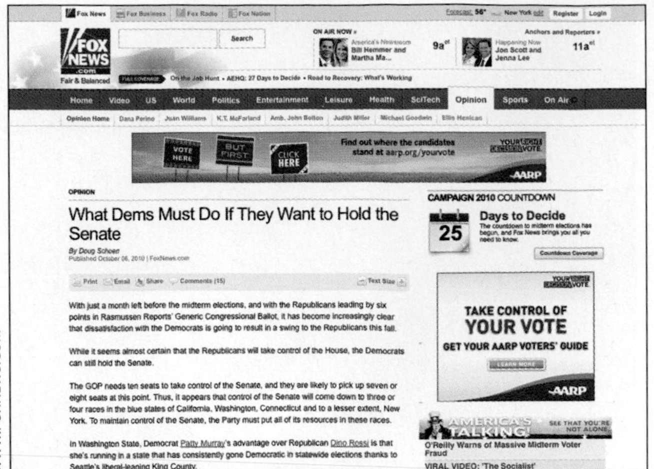

WWW.FOXNEWS.COM

The Fox News site brings the network's conservative take on the news to the Internet.

transcripts of major television news programs. About two-thirds of Internet users consider the Internet to be an important source of news. Certainly, news abounds on the Web, and having an Internet strategy has become an integral part of political campaigning.

News Organizations Online

Almost every major news organization, both print and broadcast, delivers news via the Web. Indeed, an online presence is required to compete effectively with other traditional news companies for revenues. Studies of the media, including the study by the Pew Research Center's Project for Excellence in Journalism mentioned earlier, note that the online share of newspaper company revenues has increased over the years. Today, 12 percent of U.S. newspaper revenues come from online sources.

Web sites for newspapers, such as those of the *Washington Post* and the *New York Times,* have a notable advantage over their printed counterparts. They can add breaking news to their sites, informing readers of events that occurred just minutes ago. Another advantage is that they can link the reader to more extensive reports on particular topics. According to the Pew study, though, many papers shy away from in-text linking, perhaps fearing that if readers leave the news organization's site, they might not return.

Although some newspaper sites simply copy articles from their printed versions, the Web sites for major newspapers, including those for the *Washington Post* and the *New York Times,* offer a different array of coverage and options than their printed counterparts. Indeed, the Pew study noted that the online versions of competing newspapers tend to be much more similar than their printed versions are.

A major problem facing these news organizations is that readers or viewers of online newspapers and news programs are typically the same people who read the printed news editions and view news programs on TV. Web-only readers of a particular newspaper make up a relatively small percentage of those going online for their news. Therefore, investing heavily in online news delivery may not be a solution for news companies seeking to increase readership and revenues.

In fact, the additional revenues that newspapers have gained from their online editions do not come close to making up for the massive losses in advertising revenue suffered by their print editions. In many instances, publications have not sold enough advertising in their online editions even to make up for the additional expense of publishing on the Web.

Blogs and the Emergence of Citizen Journalism

As mentioned earlier, the news culture is changing, and at the heart of this change—and of most innovation in news delivery today—is the blogosphere. There has been a virtual explosion of blogs in recent years. To make their Web sites more competitive and appealing, and to counter the influence of blogs run by private citizens and those not in the news business, the mainstream news organizations have themselves been adding blogs to their Web sites.

Blogs are offered by independent journalists, various scholars, political activists, and the citizenry at large. Anyone who wants to can create a blog and post news or information, including videos, to share with others. Many blogs are political in nature, both reporting political developments and discussing politics. Taken as a whole, the collection, analysis, and dissemination of information online by the citizenry is referred to as **citizen journalism.** Other terms that have been used to

> "The citizen CAN BRING OUR POLITICAL AND GOVERNMENTAL INSTITUTIONS BACK TO LIFE, MAKE THEM RESPONSIVE AND ACCOUNTABLE, AND KEEP THEM HONEST. No one else can."
>
> ~ JOHN GARDNER ~
> AMERICAN NOVELIST
> 1933–1982

citizen journalism The collection, analysis, and dissemination of information online by independent journalists, scholars, politicians, and the general citizenry.

PERCEPTION VERSUS
REALITY

Twitter and Tweets—Much Ado about Nothing?

Back in 2006, Jack Dorsey created Twitter, a free social networking and microblogging service. As just about everyone now knows, Twitter posts—or tweets—are text-based messages that cannot exceed 140 characters. Today, Twitter users can send and receive messages through Twitter.com as well as through other media and applications.

The Perception

What can be more useless than twittering about what you are doing? What can be more superfluous than accessing Paris Hilton's Twitter site to find out that she thinks Jimmy Kimmel is funny, or discovering that Denise Richards just had her breakfast coffee? Twitter appears to be for those who don't value their time very highly—it's even more of a time waster than text messaging and blogging. Just because 90 million tweets are posted every day doesn't mean that it has much value to the world. Some believe that tweeting has simply replaced reading *People* magazine and talking on the phone about, well, nothing.

The Reality

Today, Twitter is an important news and political vehicle. Often, breaking news stories are first reported on Twitter and then picked up by major media sources. In addition, many media outlets use Twitter to measure public sentiment on various issues. And Twitter was used by both candidates in the 2008 U.S. presidential campaign, particularly by Barack Obama.

Look at some of the important messages Twitter made possible. When graduate journalism student James Buck was arrested in Egypt for photographing an antigovernment protest, he used Twitter to get out the message. He was able to send updates about his condition while being detained. He was released the next day. During the 2008 terrorist attacks in Mumbai, India, eyewitnesses twittered every five seconds, letting the rest of the world know what was happening. After the 2009 presidential elections in Iran were deemed fraudulent by many citizens, the Iranian government shut off most Internet outlets. But it wasn't able to shut off Twitter. Indeed, Twitter was almost the only communication medium for protesters in Iran. Much of what the rest of the world saw came through TwitPics.

Blog On You can sign up for Twitter at **twitter.com**. Want to know the demographics of who's on Twitter? The site Quantcast has the answer—go to **www.quantcast.com/twitter.com**. You can follow in-depth reporting on Twitter at **www.telegraph.co.uk/technology/twitter**.

describe the news blogosphere include *people journalism* and *participatory journalism*. When blogs focus on news and developments in a specific community, the term *community journalism* is often applied.

The increase in news blogs and do-it-yourself journalism on the Web clearly poses a threat to mainstream news sources. Compared with the operational costs faced by a major news organization, the cost of creating and maintaining blogs is trivial. How can major news sources adhere to their traditional standards and still compete with this new world of news generated by citizens?

Podcasting the News

Another nontraditional form of news distribution is **podcasting**—the distribution of audio or video files to personal computers or mobile devices, such as iPhones.[17] Though still a relatively small portion of the overall news-delivery system, podcasts are becoming increasingly popular. Almost anyone can create a podcast and make it available for downloading onto computers or mobile devices, and like blogging, podcasting is inexpensive. As you will read next, political candidates are using both blogging and podcasting as part of their Internet campaign strategy.

Still another relatively new Internet technology is Twitter, a method for sending short messages to large numbers of people. How useful is Twitter? We discuss that question in this chapter's *Perception versus Reality* feature above.

Cyberspace and Political Campaigns

Today's political parties and candidates realize the benefits of using the Internet to conduct online campaigns and

podcasting The distribution of audio or video files to a personal computer or a mobile device, such as an iPod.

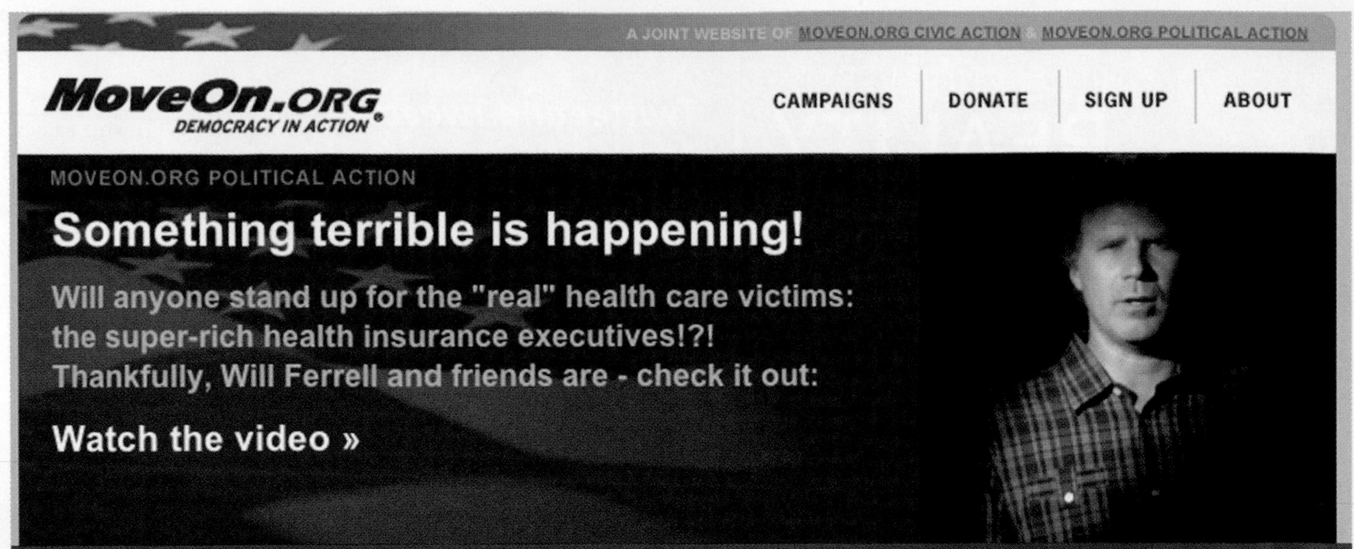

WWW.MOVEON.ORG

MoveOn is a progressive advocacy group. Like other such groups, it uses the Web.

raise funds. Voters also are increasingly using the Web to access information about parties and candidates, promote political goals, and obtain political news. Generally, the use of the Internet is an inexpensive way for candidates to contact, recruit, and mobilize supporters, as well as disseminate information about their positions on issues. In effect, the Internet can replace brochures, letters, and position papers. Individual voters or political party supporters can use the Internet to avoid having to go to special meetings or to a campaign site to do volunteer work or obtain information on a candidate's positions.

That the Internet is now a viable medium for communicating political information and interacting with voters was made clear in the campaigns preceding the 2004, 2006, and 2008 elections. According to a Pew Research Center survey following the 2008 presidential elections, 55 percent of Americans said that they went online for election news—up from 4 percent who did so in the 1996 campaign. Among Internet users, 18 percent posted political comments in a blog or on a social networking site. Fully 45 percent of users watched online videos related to the campaigns. One in three forwarded political content to someone else.

ONLINE FUND-RAISING The Internet can be an effective—and inexpensive—way to raise campaign funds. Fund-raising on the Internet by presidential candidates became widespread after the Federal Election Commission decided, in June 1999, that the federal government could distribute matching funds for credit-card donations received by candidates via the Internet.

In the 2008 presidential contest, however, the candidates took online fund-raising to an entirely new level, especially in the Democratic primaries. The fund-raising effort of Hillary Clinton would have been considered outstanding in any previous presidential election cycle. Yet it was eclipsed by the organization put together by Barack Obama.

Obama's online operation was the heart of his fund-raising success. One of its defining characteristics was its decentralization. The Obama campaign attempted to recruit as many supporters as possible to act as fund-raisers who solicited contributions from their friends and neighbors. As a result, Obama personally was spared much of the fund-raising effort that consumes the time of most national politicians. In the first half of 2007, Obama's campaign raised $58 million, $16.4 million of which was made up of donations of less than $200. The total sum was a record, and the small-donation portion was unusually large. In September 2008, the Obama campaign set another fund-raising record with $150 million, the most ever raised in one month by a presidential campaign. By then, 2.9 million people had donated to Obama's campaign.

THE RISE OF THE INTERNET CAMPAIGN An increasingly important part of political campaigning today is the Internet campaign. Candidates typically hire Web managers to manage their Internet campaigns. The job of the Web manager, or Web strategist, is to create a well-designed, informative, and user-friendly campaign Web site to attract viewers, hold their attention, manage their e-mails, and track their credit-card contributions. The Web manager also hires bloggers to promote the candidate's views, arranges for podcasting of campaign information and updates to supporters, and hires staff to monitor the Web for news about the candidates and to track the online publications of *netroots groups*—online activists who support the candidate but are not controlled by the candidate's organization.

These images are from YouTube videos of campaign advertisements. Which of them does not appear to be an example of negative advertising?

CONTROLLING THE NETROOTS One of the challenges facing candidates today is trying to deliver a consistent campaign message to voters. Netroots groups may publish online promotional ads or other materials that do not represent a candidate's position. Similarly, online groups may attack the candidate's opponent in ways that the candidate does not approve. Yet no candidate wants to alienate these groups, because they can raise significant sums of money and garner votes for the candidate. For example, the group MoveOn.org raised $28 million for Democrats prior to the 2006 elections. Yet MoveOn.org is more left leaning on issues than the most competitive Democratic presidential candidates in 2008 wanted to appear—because those candidates hoped to gain the votes of more moderate voters.

CANDIDATES' 24/7 EXPOSURE Just as citizen journalism, discussed earlier, has altered the news culture, so have citizen videos changed the traditional campaign. For example, a candidate can never know when a comment that she or he makes may be caught on camera by someone with a cell phone or digital camera and published on the Internet for all to see. At times, such exposure can be devastating, as George Allen, the former Republican senator from Virginia, learned in the 2006 midterm elections. He was captured on video making a racial slur about one of his opponent's campaign workers. The video was posted on YouTube, and within a short time the major news organizations picked up the story. Many news commentators claimed that this video exposé gave Allen's Democratic opponent, Jim Webb, enough votes to win the race.

A candidate's opponents may post on YouTube or some other Web site a compilation of video clips showing the candidate's inconsistent comments over time on a specific topic, such as abortion or the health-care reform legislation. The effect can be very damaging by making the candidate's "flip-flopping" on the issue apparent.

This 24/7 exposure also makes it difficult for the candidates to control their campaigns. The potential for citizen videos to destroy a candidate's chances is always there, creating a new type of uncertainty in political campaigning.

OBAMA'S DIFFICULTIES Barack Obama certainly learned about the dangers of 24/7 exposure during his campaign for president. In one incident, while speaking at a gathering of supporters that he believed to be private, Obama described many small towns in Pennsylvania: "Each successive administration has said that somehow these communities are going to regenerate and they have not. And it's not surprising, then, they get bitter, they cling to guns or religion or antipathy to people who aren't like them." When these remarks became public, they were widely criticized as condescending.

A more serious problem surfaced when ABC News downloaded an online collection of sermons preached by the Reverend Jeremiah Wright of Chicago, who had been Obama's personal pastor for twenty years. Some of Wright's comments were highly inflammatory, notably this one: "The government . . . wants us to sing God Bless America. No, no, no, not God Bless America. God damn America . . . for killing innocent people." When these quotes were publicized, support for Obama fell. In a well-regarded speech, Obama repudiated Wright's remarks, but not Wright himself. After further indiscretions by the minister, however, Obama broke with Wright completely and left the Chicago church.

AMERICA AT **ODDS** *Politics and the Media*

Americans love to hate the media, possibly because we spend so much time watching and reading them. Without a doubt, the media are undergoing a revolution today. With the loss of classified ads to the Internet, newspapers are in serious financial jeopardy. Online news sources, meanwhile, have yet to hit upon a reliable method of generating adequate income. In this changing environment, Americans are at odds over a number of media topics:

- Do the difficulties faced by newspapers threaten the existence of competent journalism—or is this not an important problem?
- Is the media's agenda-setting function a vital contribution to the democratic process—or an improper attempt to manipulate viewers?
- Should First Amendment protections be extended to broadcast media without exception—or would such a move threaten the morals of the country and make it impossible for viewers to avoid sexual content?
- Are negative advertisements an inevitable and unremarkable aspect of political campaigns—or should the voters punish politicians who employ them?
- Does talk radio add to the vigor of our political discourse—or is it a corrupting influence that divides the nation?
- Do the mainstream media have a liberal bias—or do they merely publicize facts that do not square with conservative beliefs?

Take Action

Today, the media are wide open for citizen involvement. You, too, can report or comment on the news. Millions of people, especially students, are already halfway to becoming bloggers through their Facebook pages. You might consider turning political discussions on Facebook into an actual blog. Such a project is more easily undertaken if several friends share the responsibility for creating the content. That way, one person does not have to carry the entire load. You can set up links to articles or videos of interest at other sites, but an attractive blog isn't just links but also a place to view unique content.

A variety of other online projects are possible. You can create videos of events that you believe are newsworthy and post them online. You can podcast video or audio coverage of an event from a Web site that you have created. You, by yourself or with others, can set up a "radio station" to spread your views using the Internet. For example, in the photo shown here, two citizens who supported a proposed Tennessee state tax reform set up their own radio station in Nashville to mock local radio personalities who were opposed to the reform. Lining the street nearby are other supporters of the tax reform.

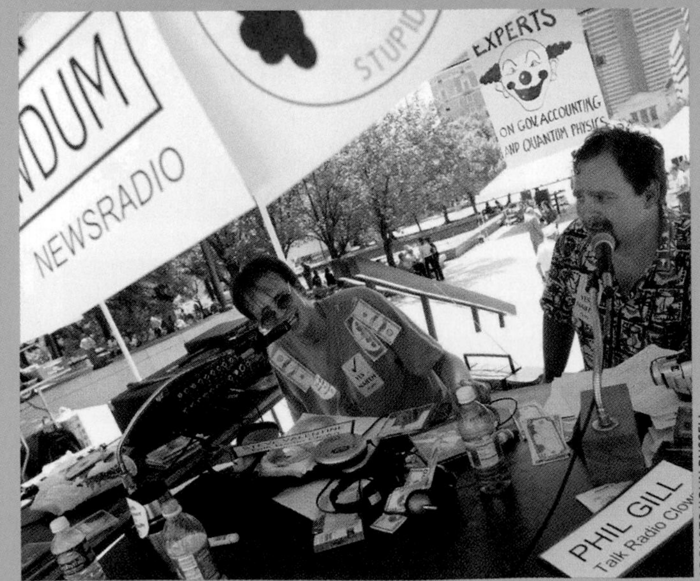

AP PHOTO/JOHN RUSSELL

Local talk-radio and news programs abound. They are often irreverent and operated by young people.

POLITICS ON THE WEB

- Newspapers.com features links to more than ten thousand newspapers nationwide. You can also search by categories, such as business, college newspapers, and industry. Go to **www.newspapers.com**
- A blog search engine with links to blogs in a variety of categories can be accessed at **www.blogsearchengine.com**
- A number of watchdog groups monitor the media in an attempt to expose bias, partisanship, or factual errors. Accuracy in Media is a conservative group. Find it at **www.aim.org**
- Fairness and Accuracy in Reporting is a liberal watchdog group. Its Web site is at **www.fair.org**
- With the growth of YouTube, it is now possible to see historically important political videos of all kinds. These include attack ads, videos of candidates making embarrassing statements, presidential debates, and famous speeches. The easiest way to find a video is to enter a string of descriptive terms into a search engine such as Google. For example, to find the "daisy girl" ad mentioned on pages 217 and 218, enter the following words: **daisy girl video youtube**
- To see an advertisement that Republican presidential candidate George H. W. Bush deployed to great effect against Democratic candidate Michael Dukakis in 1988, enter the following in a search engine: **willie horton ad youtube**
- Quotation marks force a search engine to look for an entire phrase. To see Barack Obama's speech responding to the Jeremiah Wright crisis described on pages 227 and 228, enter **Obama "a more perfect union" full**

Access CourseMate to review and expand on this chapter through quizzes, flashcards, learning objectives, interactive timelines, a crossword puzzle, audio summaries, video, critical-thinking activities, simulations, and more.

GOVT

11 Congress

LEARNING OBJECTIVES

LO1 Explain how seats in the House of Representatives are apportioned among the states.

LO2 Describe the power of incumbency.

LO3 Identify the key leadership positions in Congress, describe the committee system, and indicate some important differences between the House of Representatives and the Senate.

LO4 Summarize the specific steps in the lawmaking process.

LO5 Identify Congress's oversight functions and explain how Congress fulfills them.

LO6 Indicate what is involved in the congressional budgeting process.

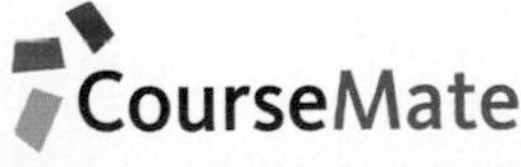

AMERICA AT ODDS

Should It Take Sixty Senators to Pass Important Legislation?

If there is a magic number in politics, it is sixty. Why? Because sixty is the number of Senate votes required to force an end to a filibuster. A filibuster takes place when senators use the chamber's tradition of unlimited debate to block legislation. In years past, filibustering senators would speak for hours—even reading names from the telephone book—to prevent a vote on a proposed bill. In recent decades, however, Senate rules have permitted filibusters in which actual continuous floor speeches are not required. Senators merely announce that they are filibustering. The threat of a filibuster has created an *ad hoc* rule that important legislation needs the support of sixty senators. (There are exceptions. Budget bills are handled using a special "reconciliation" rule that does not permit filibusters.)

If one party can elect sixty or more U.S. senators, assuming they all follow the party line, they can force through any legislation they want by invoking "cloture," which ends filibusters. The Democrats, in fact, enjoyed a supermajority in the Senate for seven months, from July 7, 2009, until February 4, 2010. It began when Al Franken (D., Minn.) joined the Senate after a long-contested race was finally decided in his favor. Shortly after a January 2010 special election, Scott Brown (R., Mass.) was sworn in to a seat formerly held by a Democrat, and that party's supermajority ended.

The question remains, though, whether the magic number of sixty is an appropriate requirement for passing important legislation in the Senate. Should the number be reduced to fifty-five or even to fifty-one—a simple majority of all sitting senators?

Don't Let the Majority Trample on the Minority

The long history of the filibuster in the United States Senate and the consequent need for a supermajority to pass legislation has served us well. Filibusters, or even the threat of filibusters, provide the minority with an effective means of preventing the majority from ramrodding legislation down the throats of American voters.

Rule by a simple majority can be scary. Support for a measure can shift between 49 percent and 51 percent very quickly. Should such small changes be the basis for passing major legislation? A simple majority does not signify an adequate degree of consensus. When it comes to major issues, something more weighty than simple majority rule should prevail.

Many states require supermajorities for passing any legislation that would raise taxes. In California, for example, a tax increase must win two-thirds approval in both chambers of the state legislature. It takes two-thirds of both chambers of Congress to override a veto by the president. That's another supermajority. Changing the Constitution requires a very substantial supermajority—three-quarters of the state legislatures. If these supermajority rules were good enough for the founders, then the principle still is good enough for the Senate.

Don't Let Obstructionists Determine Legislation

Just because supermajorities were required in jury deliberations in classical Rome and for the election of a pope in the Catholic Church does not mean they are necessary in the Senate. Supermajorities make it harder to achieve needed changes. Supermajorities allow a minority to block the preference of the majority. Even James Madison, who worried about the tyranny of the majority over the minority, recognized the opposite possibility. He said that "the fundamental principle of free government" might be reversed by supermajorities. "It would be no longer majority that would rule: the power would be transferred to the minority."

Furthermore, the sixty-vote requirement in the Senate has led to a significant increase in "pork"—that is, special spending provisions inserted into legislation. Senators working on bills find that they must fill them with pork to attract the votes of their colleagues. Without the pork, the bills won't pass. The Senate should reduce the votes required for cloture of a filibuster to fifty-five or even fifty-one. Let's get on with government by the majority, not the supermajority.

WHERE DO YOU STAND?

1. **Why might it be appropriate to require supermajority voting for important legislation?**
2. **Under what circumstances do supermajority voting rules prevent democracy from being fully realized?**

EXPLORE THIS ISSUE ONLINE

William Greider denounces the tradition of the filibuster in the pages of *The Nation,* a strongly liberal publication. See his article at www.thenation.com/article/stop-senator-no. Nick Dranias, a conservative, defends the supermajority concept at www.goldwaterinstitute.org/article/3244.

Introduction

Congress is the lawmaking branch of government. When someone says, "There ought to be a law," at the federal level it is Congress that will make that law. The framers had a strong suspicion of a powerful executive authority. Consequently, they made Congress—not the executive branch (the presidency)—the central institution of American government. Yet, as noted in Chapter 2, the founders created a system of checks and balances to ensure that no branch of the federal government, including Congress, could exercise too much power.

Many Americans view Congress as a largely faceless, anonymous legislative body that is quite distant and removed from their everyday lives. Yet the people you elect to Congress represent and advocate for your interests at the very highest level of power. Furthermore, the laws created by the men and women in the U.S. Congress affect the daily lives of every American in one way or another. Getting to know your congressional representatives and how they are voting in Congress on issues that concern you is an important step toward becoming an informed voter. Even the details of how Congress makes law—such as the Senate rules described in the chapter-opening *America at Odds* feature—should be of interest to the savvy voter.

LO1 The Structure and Makeup of Congress

The framers agreed that the Congress should be the "first branch of the government," as James Madison said, but they did not immediately agree on its organization. Ultimately, they decided on a *bicameral legislature*—a Congress consisting of two chambers. This was part of the Great Compromise, which you read about in Chapter 2.

apportionment The distribution of House seats among the states on the basis of their respective populations.

The framers favored a bicameral legislature so that the two chambers, the House and the Senate, might serve as checks on each other's power and activity. The House was to represent the people as a whole, or the majority. The Senate was to represent the states and would protect the interests of small states by giving them the same number of senators (two per state) as the larger states.

Apportionment of House Seats

The Constitution provides for the **apportionment** (distribution) of House seats among the states on the basis of their respective populations. States with larger populations, such as California, have many more representatives than states with smaller populations, such as Wyoming. California, for example, currently has fifty-three representatives in the House—Wyoming has only one.

Every ten years, House seats are reapportioned based on the outcome of the decennial (ten-year) census conducted by the U.S. Census Bureau. Figure 11–1 on the facing page indicates the states that gained and lost seats based on population changes reported by the 2000 census. This redistribution of seats took effect with the 108th Congress, which was elected in 2002.

Each state is guaranteed at least one House seat, no matter what its population. Today, seven states have only one representative.[1] The District of Columbia, American Samoa, Guam, and the U.S. Virgin Islands all send nonvoting delegates to the House. Puerto Rico, a self-governing possession of the United States, is represented by a nonvoting resident commissioner.

A Senate committee begins work on the health-care reform bill. Most of the work of Congress occurs in committees like this one. Some bills end up being over a thousand pages long. Why do you think they end up being so lengthy?

STEPHEN CROWLEY/*THE NEW YORK TIMES*/REDUX

Congressional Districts

Whereas senators are elected to represent all of the people in a state, representatives are elected by the voters of a particular area known as a **congressional district.** The Constitution makes no provisions for congressional districts, and in the early 1800s each state was given the right to decide whether to have districts at all. Most states set up single-member districts, in which voters in each district elected one of the state's representatives. In states that chose not to have districts, representatives were chosen at large, from the state as a whole. In 1842, however, Congress passed an act that required all states to send representatives to Congress from single-member districts, as you read in Chapter 7.

Figure 11–1

Reapportionment of House Seats following the 2000 Census

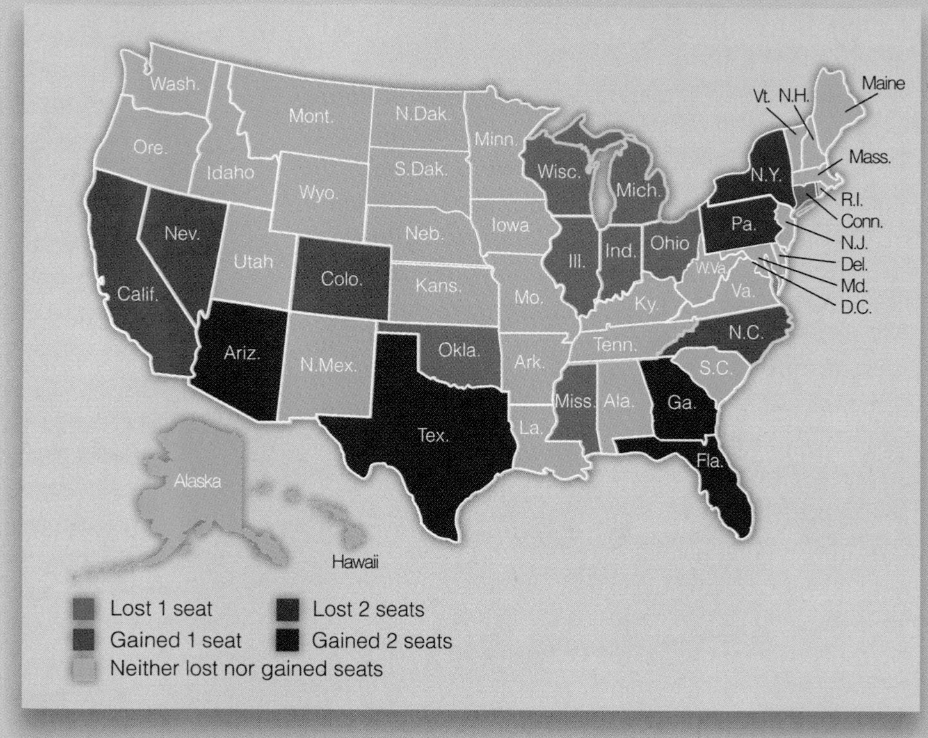

Source: U.S. Bureau of the Census.

For many years, the number of House members increased as the population expanded. In 1929, however, a federal law fixed House membership at 435 members. Thus, today the 435 members of the House are chosen by the voters in 435 separate congressional districts across the country. If a state's population allows it to have only one representative, the entire state is one congressional district. In contrast, states with large populations have many districts. California, for example, because its population entitles it to send fifty-three representatives to the House, has fifty-three congressional districts.

By default, the lines of the congressional districts are drawn by the state legislatures. Alternatively, the task may be handed off to a designated body such as an independent commission. States must meet certain requirements in drawing district boundaries. To ensure equal representation in the House, districts must contain, as nearly as possible, equal numbers of people. Additionally, each district must have contiguous boundaries and must be "geographically compact," although this last requirement is not enforced very strictly.

THE REQUIREMENT OF EQUAL REPRESENTATION

If congressional districts are not made up of equal populations, the value of people's votes is not the same. In the past, state legislators often used this fact to their advantage. For example, traditionally, many state legislatures were controlled by rural areas. By drawing districts that were not equal in population, rural leaders attempted to curb the number of representatives from growing urban centers. At one point in the 1960s, in many states the largest district had twice the population of the smallest district. In effect, this meant that a person's vote in the largest district had only half the value of a person's vote in the smallest district.

For some time, the United States Supreme Court refused to address this problem. In 1962, however, in *Baker v. Carr,*[2] the Court ruled that the Tennessee state legislature's **malapportionment** was an issue that could be heard in the federal courts because it affected the constitutional requirement of equal protection under the law. Two years later, in *Wesberry v. Sanders,*[3] the Supreme Court held that congressional districts must have equal populations. This

congressional district
The geographic area that is served by one member in the House of Representatives.

malapportionment
A condition in which the voting power of citizens in one district is greater than the voting power of citizens in another district.

principle has come to be known as the **"one person, one vote" rule.** In other words, one person's vote has to count as much as another's vote.

GERRYMANDERING Although in the 1960s the Supreme Court ruled that congressional districts must be equal in population, it continued to be silent on the issue of gerrymandered districts. **Gerrymandering** occurs when a district's boundaries are drawn to maximize the influence of a certain group or political party. Where a party's voters are scarce, the boundaries can be drawn to include as many of the party's voters as possible. Where the party is strong, the lines are drawn so that the opponent's supporters are spread across two or more districts, thus diluting the opponent's strength. (The term *gerrymandering* was originally used to describe the district lines drawn to favor the party of Governor Elbridge Gerry of Massachusetts prior to the 1812 elections—see Figure 11–2 on the facing page.)

Although there have been constitutional challenges to political gerrymandering,[4] the practice continues. It was certainly evident following the 2000 census. Sophisticated computer programs can now analyze the partisan leanings of individual neighborhoods and city blocks. District lines are drawn to "pack" the opposing party's voters into the smallest number of districts or "crack" the opposing party's voters into several different districts. Packing and cracking make congressional races less competitive. In 2003, for example, Texas adopted a controversial redistricting plan that was spearheaded by then House majority leader Tom DeLay (R., Tex.). DeLay and Texas Republicans used pack and crack tactics to redraw districts that had formerly leaned toward Democratic candidates. The plan effectively cost four Democratic representatives their seats in the 2004 elections.[5]

Racial Gerrymandering Although political gerrymandering has a long history, gerrymandering to empower minority groups is a relatively new phenomenon. In the early 1990s, the U.S. Department of Justice instructed state legislatures to draw district lines to maximize the voting power of minority groups. As a result, several **minority-majority districts** were created. Many of these districts took on bizarre shapes. For example, North Carolina's newly drawn Twelfth Congressional District was 165 miles long—a narrow strip that, for the most part, followed Interstate 85. Georgia's new Eleventh District stretched from Atlanta to the Atlantic, splitting eight counties and five municipalities. The practice of racial gerrymandering has generated heated argument on both sides of the issue.

Some groups contend that minority-majority districts are necessary to ensure equal representation of minority groups, as mandated by the Voting Rights Act of 1965. They further contend that these districts have been instrumental in increasing the number of African Americans holding political office. Minority-majority districts in the South contain, on average, 45 percent nonblack voters, whereas before 1990, redistricting plans in the South often created only white-majority districts.[6]

Limiting Racial Gerrymandering Opponents of racial gerrymandering argue that such race-based districting is unconstitutional because it violates the equal protection clause. In a series of cases in the 1990s, the Supreme Court agreed and held that when race is the dominant factor in the drawing of congressional district lines, the districts are unconstitutional and must be redrawn.[7]

In 2001, however, the Supreme Court issued a ruling that seemed—at least to some observers—to be out of step with its earlier rulings. North Carolina's Twelfth District, which had been redrawn in 1997, was again challenged in court as unconstitutional, and a lower court agreed. When the case reached the Supreme Court, however, the justices concluded that there was insufficient evidence that race had been the dominant factor in redrawing the district's boundaries.[8]

Elbridge Gerry, governor of Massachusetts, 1810–1812.

"one person, one vote" rule A rule, or principle, requiring that congressional districts have equal populations so that one person's vote counts as much as another's vote.

gerrymandering The drawing of a legislative district's boundaries in such a way as to maximize the influence of a certain group or political party.

minority-majority district A district in which minority groups make up a majority of the population.

Figure 11–2

The First "Gerrymander"

Prior to the 1812 elections, the Massachusetts legislature divided up Essex County in a way that favored Governor Elbridge Gerry's party. The result was a district that looked something like a salamander. A newspaper editor of the time referred to it as a "gerrymander," and the name stuck.

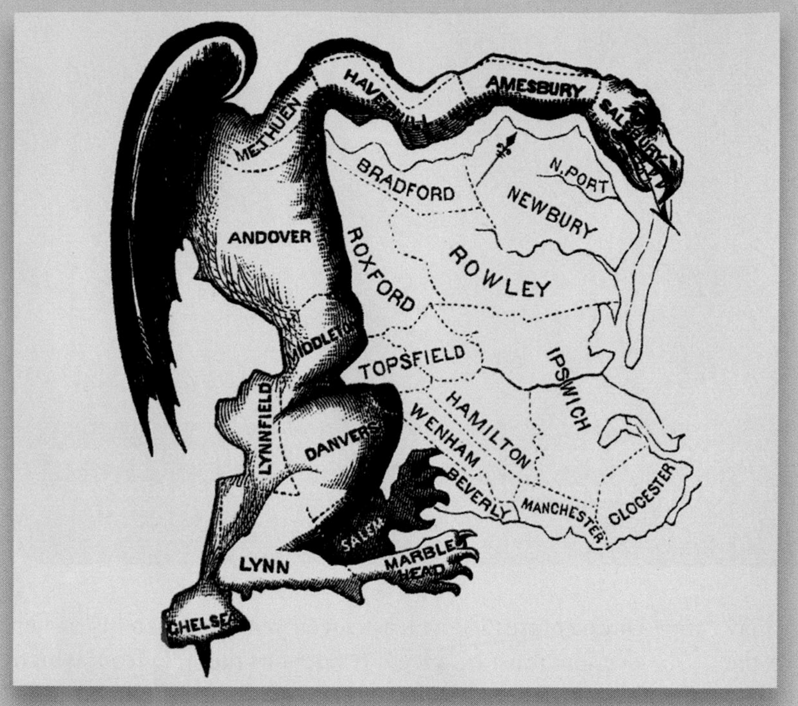

Source: *Congressional Quarterly's Guide to Congress*, 3d ed. (Washington, D.C.: Congressional Quarterly Press, 1982), p. 695.

"When a man assumes a public trust, he should consider himself a **PUBLIC PROPERTY.**"

~ THOMAS JEFFERSON ~
THIRD PRESIDENT OF THE UNITED STATES
1801–1809

The Representation Function of Congress

Of the three branches of government, Congress has the closest ties to the American people. Members of Congress represent the interests and wishes of the constituents in their home states. At the same time, they must also consider larger national issues such as the economy and the environment. Often, legislators find that the interests of their constituents are at odds with the demands of national policy.

For example, limits on emissions of carbon dioxide might help reduce global warming, to the benefit of all Americans and the people of the world generally. Yet members of Congress who come from states where most electricity comes from coal-burning power plants might fear that new laws would hurt the local economy and cause companies to lay off workers. All members of Congress face difficult votes that set representational interests against lawmaking realities. There are several views on how legislators should decide such issues.

THE TRUSTEE VIEW OF REPRESENTATION Some believe that representatives should act as **trustees** of the broad interests of the entire society rather than serving only the narrow interests of their constituents. Under the trustee view, a legislator should act according to her or his conscience and perception of national needs. For example, a senator from North Carolina might support laws regulating the tobacco industry even though the state's economy could be negatively affected.

THE INSTRUCTED-DELEGATE VIEW OF REPRESENTATION In contrast, others believe that members of Congress should behave as **instructed delegates.** The instructed-delegate view requires representatives to mirror the views of their constituents, regardless of their opinions. Under this view, a senator from Nebraska would strive to obtain subsidies for corn growers, and a representative from the Detroit area would seek to protect the automobile industry.

THE PARTISAN VIEW OF REPRESENTATION Because the political parties often take different positions on legislative issues, there are times when members of Congress are very attentive to the wishes of the party leadership. Especially on matters that are controversial, the Democratic members of Congress will be more likely to vote in favor of policies endorsed by a Democratic president, while Republicans will be more likely to oppose them.

THE POLITICO STYLE Typically, members of Congress combine these three approaches in what

trustee A representative who tries to serve the broad interests of the entire society and not just the narrow interests of his or her constituents.

instructed delegate A representative who deliberately mirrors the views of the majority of his or her constituents.

PAUL J. RICHARDS/AFP/GETTY IMAGES

These female members of the House of Representatives wave to the delegates at the Democratic National Convention in Denver in 2008. While women have made serious inroads into the halls of political power, they are still underrepresented relative to their 51 percent share of our population.

is often called the "politico" style. Legislators may take a trustee approach on some issues, adhere to the instructed-delegate view on other matters, and follow the party line on still others.

LO2 *Congressional Elections*

The U.S. Constitution requires that representatives to Congress be elected every second year by popular vote. Senators are elected every six years, also by popular vote (since the ratification of the Seventeenth Amendment). Under Article I, Section 4, of the Constitution, state legislatures control the "Times, Places and Manner of holding Elections for Senators and Representatives." Congress, however, "may at any time by Law make or alter such Regulations." As you read in Chapter 9, control over the process of nominating congressional candidates has largely shifted from party conventions to direct primaries in which the party's supporters select the candidates who will carry that party's endorsement into the general election.

Who Can Be a Member of Congress?

The Constitution sets forth only a few qualifications that those running for Congress must meet. To be a member of the House, a person must have been a citizen of the United States for at least seven years prior to his or her election, must be a legal resident of the state from which he or she is to be elected, and must be at least twenty-five years of age. To be elected to the Senate, a person must have been a citizen for at least nine years, must be a legal resident of the state from which she or he is to be elected, and must be at least thirty years of age. The Supreme Court has ruled that neither the Congress nor the states can add to these three qualifications.[9]

Once elected to Congress, a senator or representative receives an annual salary from the government, $174,000 for rank-and-file members as of 2010. He or she also enjoys certain perks and privileges. Additionally, if a member of Congress wants to run for reelection in the next congressional elections, that person's chances are greatly enhanced by the power that incumbency brings to a reelection campaign.

The Power of Incumbency

The power of incumbency has long been noted in American politics. Typically, incumbents win so often and by such large margins that some observers have claimed that our electoral system involves something similar to a hereditary entitlement. As you can see in Table 11–1 on the facing page, most incumbents in Congress are reelected if they run.

Incumbent politicians enjoy several advantages over their opponents. A key advantage is their fund-

Table 11–1

The Power of Incumbency

	Presidential-Year Elections							Midterm Elections							
House	**1984**	**1988**	**1992**	**1996**	**2000**	**2004**	**2008**	**1982**	**1986**	**1990**	**1994**	**1998**	**2002**	**2006**	**2010**
Number of incumbent candidates	411	409	368	384	403	404	404	393	394	406	387	402	393	405	397
Reelected	392	402	325	361	394	397	381	354	385	390	349	395	383	382	338
Percentage of total	95.4	98.3	88.3	94.0	97.8	98.3	94.3	90.1	97.7	96.0	90.2	98.3	97.5	94.3	85.1
Defeated	19	7	43	23	9	7	23	39	9	16	38	7	10	23	59
Senate															
Number of incumbent candidates	29	27	28	21	29	26	30	30	28	32	26	29	28	29	24
Reelected	26	23	23	19	23	25	26	28	21	31	24	26	24	23	20
Percentage of total	89.6	85.2	82.1	90.5	79.3	96.2	86.7	93.3	75.0	96.9	92.3	89.7	85.7	79.3	83.3
Defeated	3	4	5	2	6	1	4	2	7	1	2	3	4	6	4

Sources: Norman Ornstein, Thomas E. Mann, and Michael J. Malbin, *Vital Statistics on Congress, 2001–2002* (Washington, D.C.: The AEI Press, 2002); and authors' updates.

raising ability. Most incumbent members of Congress have a much larger network of contacts, donors, and lobbyists than their opponents. Incumbents raise, on average, twice as much in campaign funds as their challengers. Other advantages that incumbents can put to work to aid their reelection include:

- *Congressional franking privileges*—members of Congress can mail newsletters and other correspondence to their constituents at the taxpayers' expense.
- *Professional staffs*—members have large administrative staffs both in Washington, D.C., and in their home districts.
- *Lawmaking power*—members can back legislation that will benefit their states or districts, and then campaign on that legislative record in the next election.
- *Access to the media*—because they are elected officials, members have many opportunities to stage events for the press and thereby obtain free publicity.
- *Name recognition*—incumbent members are usually far better known to the voters than challengers are.

Critics argue that the advantage enjoyed by incumbents reduces the competition necessary for a healthy democracy. It also suppresses voter turnout. Voters are less likely to turn out when an incumbent candidate is virtually guaranteed reelection. The solution often proposed to eliminate the power of incumbency is term limits, a topic we discuss shortly.

Congressional Terms and Term Limits

As noted earlier, members of the House of Representatives serve two-year terms, and senators serve six-year terms. This means that every two years, we hold congressional elections: the entire House of Representatives and a third of the Senate are up for election. In January of every odd-numbered year, a "new" Congress convenes (of course, two-thirds of the senators are not new, and most House incumbents are reelected, so they are not new to Congress either). Each Congress has been numbered consecutively, dating back to 1789. The Congress that convened in 2011 is the 112th.

Each congressional term is divided into two regular sessions, or meetings—one for each year. Until about 1940, Congress remained in session for only four or five months, but the complicated rush of legislation and increased demand for services from the public in recent years have forced Congress to remain in session through most of each year.[10] Both chambers, however, schedule short recesses, or breaks, for holidays and vacations. The president may call a *special session* during a recess, but because Congress now meets on nearly a year-round basis, such sessions are rare.

As you will read in Chapter 12, the president can serve for no more than two terms in office, due to the Twenty-second Amendment. There is no limit on the number of terms a senator or representative can serve, however. For example, Strom Thurmond (R., S.C.) served eight terms in the U.S. Senate, from 1955 until he retired, at the age of one hundred, in 2003.

When the Republicans took control of the House after the 2010 elections, former minority leader John Boehner (R., Ohio), left, was the leading candidate for Speaker of the House. Eric Cantor (R., Va.) was the leading contender for House majority leader. It was widely expected that former Speaker Nancy Pelosi (D., Calif.), right, would serve as the House minority leader.

As mentioned, some observers favor term limits for Congress. Persuading incumbent politicians to vote for term limits, however, is difficult. At the national level, the Supreme Court has ruled that state-level attempts to impose term limits on members of the U.S. House or Senate are unconstitutional.[11] Efforts to pass a constitutional amendment that would impose term limits on members of Congress have had little success.

LO3 *Congressional Leadership, the Committee System, and Bicameralism*

The Constitution provides for the presiding officers of both the House and the Senate, and each chamber has added other leadership positions as it has seen fit. Leadership and organization in both chambers are based on membership in the two major political parties. The majority party in each chamber chooses the major officers of that chamber, controls debate on the floor, selects all committee chairpersons, and has a majority on all committees.

Speaker of the House
The presiding officer in the House of Representatives. The Speaker has traditionally been a longtime member of the majority party and is often the most powerful and influential member of the House.

House Leadership

The Constitution states that members of the House are to choose their Speaker and other officers but says nothing more about these positions. Today, important "other officers" include the majority and minority leaders and whips.

SPEAKER OF THE HOUSE Chief among the leaders in the House of Representatives is the **Speaker of the House.** This office is filled by a vote taken at the beginning of each congressional term. The Speaker has traditionally been a longtime member of the majority party who has risen in rank and influence through years of service in the House. The candidate for Speaker is selected by the majority-party caucus. The House as a whole then approves the selection.

As the presiding officer of the House and the leader of the majority party, the Speaker has a great deal of power. In the nineteenth century, the Speaker had even more power and was known as the "king of the congressional mountain." Speakers known by such names as "Uncle Joe Cannon" and "Czar Reed" ruled the House with almost unchallengeable power. A revolt in 1910 reduced the Speaker's powers and gave some of those powers to various committees. Today, the Speaker still has many important powers, including the following:

- The Speaker has substantial control over what bills get assigned to which committees.

ELECTIONS 2010

Control of Congress after the Elections

Following the 2010 elections, President Obama was in a much weaker position to pursue the rest of his legislative agenda. The Republican margin in the House exceeded fifty. In the Senate, the fifty-three Democrats (this includes two Independents who caucus with the Democrats) would have difficulty attaining the sixty votes needed to end a filibuster and force through any additional legislation.

In the House, Democratic Speaker Nancy Pelosi of California had to step aside for Republican John Boehner of Ohio. Pelosi was expected to run for the post of House minority leader. All committee chairs in the House also changed, with Republicans replacing Democrats. The Senate leadership was not expected to change, however. The Democrats retained their control, and Senate majority leader Harry Reid won a close race for re-election against a Tea Party enthusiast.

Numerous observers predicted that Congress would experience legislative gridlock. Many Democratic moderates—those most willing to compromise with Republicans—lost. On the Republican side, the new Tea Party members were philosophically opposed to any compromise with the Democrats. The result was a more liberal set of Democrats and a more conservative set of Republicans, not a good formula for bipartisan consensus. In those states that now have Republican governors and Republican-dominated state legislatures, however, there should be very little gridlock.

- The Speaker may preside over the sessions of the House, recognizing or ignoring members who wish to speak.
- The Speaker votes in the event of a tie, interprets and applies House rules, rules on points of order (questions about procedures asked by members), puts questions to a vote, and interprets the outcome of most of the votes taken.
- The Speaker plays a major role in making important committee assignments, which all members desire.
- The Speaker schedules bills for action.

The Speaker may choose whether to vote on any measure. If the Speaker chooses to vote, he or she appoints a temporary presiding officer (called a Speaker *pro tempore*), who then occupies the Speaker's chair. Under the House rules, the only time the Speaker *must* vote is to break a tie. Otherwise, a tie automatically defeats a bill. The Speaker does not often vote, but by choosing to vote in some cases, the Speaker can actually cause a tie and defeat a proposal.

MAJORITY LEADER The **majority leader** of the House is elected by the caucus of majority party members to act as spokesperson for the party and to keep the party together. The majority leader's job is to help plan the party's legislative program, organize other party members to support legislation favored by the party, and make sure the chairpersons on the many committees finish work on bills that are important to the party. The House majority leader makes speeches on important bills, stating the majority party's position.

MINORITY LEADER The House **minority leader** is the leader of the minority party. Although not as powerful as the majority leader, the minority leader has similar responsibilities. The primary duty of the minority leader is to maintain solidarity within the party. The minority leader persuades influential members of the party to follow its position and organizes fellow party members in criticism of the majority party's policies and programs.

WHIPS The leadership of each party includes assistants to the majority and minority leaders known as **whips.** Whips originated in the British House of Commons, where they were named after the "whipper in," the rider who keeps the hounds together in a fox hunt. The term is applied to assistant party leaders because of the pressure

majority leader The party leader elected by the majority party in the House or in the Senate.

minority leader The party leader elected by the minority party in the House or in the Senate.

whip A member of Congress who assists the majority or minority leader in the House or in the Senate in managing the party's legislative preferences.

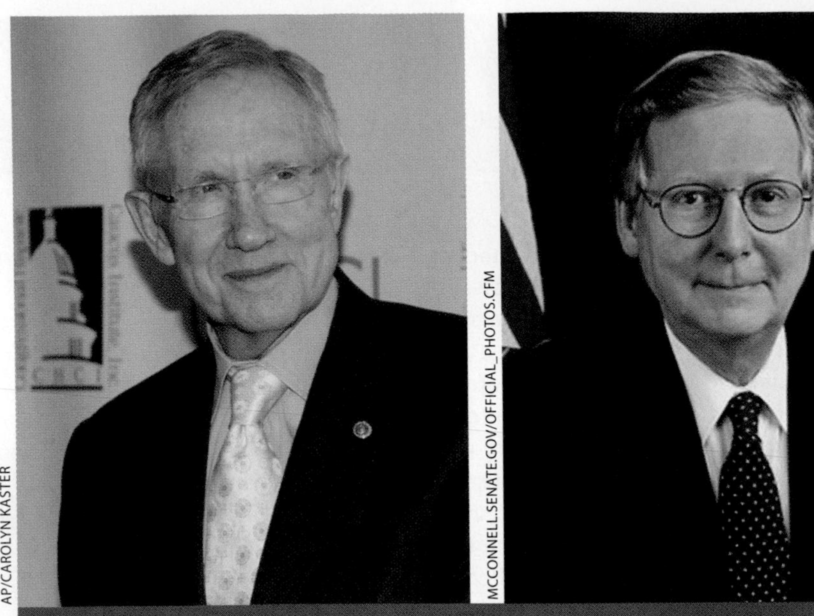

In 2006, Democratic senator Harry Reid of Nevada, left, became the Senate majority leader, and Republican senator Mitch McConnell of Kentucky became Senate minority leader. Both are expected to retain their offices when the new Senate votes on its leaders in late 2010.

that they place on party members to uphold the party's positions. Whips try to determine how each member is going to vote on certain issues and then advise the party leaders on the strength of party support. Whips also try to see that members are present when important votes are to be taken and that they vote with the party leadership. For example, if the Republican Party strongly supports a tax-cut bill, the Republican Party whip might meet with other Republican Party members in the House to try to persuade them to vote with the party.

Senate Leadership

The Constitution makes the vice president of the United States the president of the Senate. As presiding officer, the vice president may call on members to speak and put questions to a vote. The vice president is not an elected member of the Senate, however, and may not take part in Senate debates. The vice president may cast a vote in the Senate only in the event of a tie.

PRESIDENT PRO TEMPORE Because vice presidents are rarely available (or desire) to preside over the Senate, senators elect another presiding officer, the president pro tempore ("pro tem"), who serves in the absence of the vice president. The president pro tem is elected by the whole Senate and is ordinarily the member of the majority party with the longest continuous term of service in the Senate. In the absence of both the president pro tem and the vice president, a temporary presiding officer is selected from the ranks of the Senate, usually a junior member of the majority party.

standing committee
A permanent committee in Congress that deals with legislation concerning a particular area, such as agriculture or foreign relations.

PARTY LEADERS The real power in the Senate is held by the majority leader, the minority leader, and their whips. The majority leader is the most powerful individual and chief spokesperson of the majority party. The majority leader directs the legislative program and party strategy. The minority leader commands the minority party's opposition to the policies of the majority party and directs the legislative strategy of the minority party.

Congressional Committees

Thousands of bills are introduced during every session of Congress, and no single member can possibly be adequately informed on all the issues that arise. The committee system is a way to provide for specialization, or a division of the legislative labor. Members of a committee concentrate on just one area or topic—such as agriculture or transportation—and develop sufficient expertise to draft appropriate legislation when needed. The flow of legislation through both the House and the Senate is determined largely by the speed with which the members of these committees act on bills and resolutions. The permanent and most powerful committees of Congress are called **standing committees;** their names are listed in Table 11–2 on the facing page.

Before any bill can be considered by the entire House or Senate, it must be approved by a majority vote in the standing committee to which it was assigned. As mentioned, standing committees are controlled by the majority party in each chamber. Committee membership is generally divided between the parties according to the number of members in each chamber. In both the House and the Senate, committee *seniority*—the length of continuous service on a particular committee—typically plays a role in determining the committee chairpersons.

Table 11–2

Standing Committees in the 112th Congress, 2011–2013

House Committees	Senate Committees
Agriculture	Agriculture, Nutrition, and Forestry
Appropriations	Appropriations
Armed Services	Armed Services
Budget	Banking, Housing, and Urban Affairs
Education and Labor	Budget
Energy and Commerce	Commerce, Science, and Transportation
Financial Services	Energy and Natural Resources
Foreign Affairs	Environment and Public Works
Homeland Security	Finance
House Administration	Foreign Relations
Judiciary	Health, Education, Labor, and Pensions
Natural Resources	Homeland Security and Governmental Affairs
Oversight and Government Reform	Judiciary
Rules	Rules and Administration
Science and Technology	Small Business and Entrepreneurship
Small Business	Veterans' Affairs
Standards of Official Conduct	
Transportation and Infrastructure	
Veterans' Affairs	
Ways and Means	

Most House and Senate committees also have **subcommittees** with limited areas of jurisdiction. Today, there are more than two hundred subcommittees. There are also other types of committees in Congress. Special, or select, committees, which may be either permanent or temporary, are formed to study specific problems or issues. Joint committees are created by the concurrent action of both chambers of Congress and consist of members from each chamber. Joint committees have dealt with the economy, taxation, and the Library of Congress. There are also conference committees, which include members from both the House and the Senate. They are formed for the purpose of achieving agreement between the House and the Senate on the exact wording of legislative acts when the two chambers pass legislative proposals in different forms. No bill can be sent to the White House to be signed into law unless it first passes both chambers in identical form.

Most of the actual work of legislating is performed by the committees and subcommittees (the "little legislatures"[12]) within Congress. In creating or amending laws, committee members work closely with relevant interest groups and administrative agency personnel. (For more details on the interaction among these groups, see the discussion of "issue networks" and "iron triangles" in Chapter 13.)

The Differences between the House and the Senate

To understand what goes on in the chambers of Congress, we need to look at the effects of bicameralism. Each chamber of Congress has developed certain distinct features. The major differences between the House and the Senate are listed in Table 11–3 on the following page.

SIZE MATTERS Obviously, with 435 voting members, the House cannot operate the same way as the Senate, which has only 100 members. With its larger size, the House needs both more rules and more formality—otherwise, no work would ever get done. The most obvious formal rules have to do with debate on the floor.

The Senate normally permits extended debate on all issues that arise before it. In contrast, the House uses an elaborate system: the House **Rules Committee** normally proposes time limits on debate for any bill, which are accepted or modified by the House. Despite its greater size, as a consequence of its stricter time limits on debate, the House is often able to act on legislation more quickly than the Senate.

IN THE SENATE, DEBATE CAN JUST KEEP GOING AND GOING At one time, both the House and the Senate allowed unlimited debate, but the House ended this practice in 1811. The use of unlimited debate in the Senate to obstruct legislation is called **filibustering**

subcommittee A division of a larger committee that deals with a particular part of the committee's policy area. Most standing committees have several subcommittees.

Rules Committee A standing committee in the House of Representatives that provides special rules governing how particular bills will be considered and debated by the House. The Rules Committee normally proposes time limits on debate for any bill.

filibustering The Senate tradition of unlimited debate undertaken for the purpose of preventing action on a bill.

cloture A method of ending debate in the Senate and bringing the matter under consideration to a vote by the entire chamber.

Table 11–3

Major Differences between the House and the Senate

House*	Senate*
Members chosen from local districts	Members chosen from entire state
Two-year term	Six-year term
Always elected by voters	Originally (until 1913) elected by state legislatures
May impeach (accuse, indict) federal officials	May convict federal officials of impeachable offenses
Larger (435 voting members)	Smaller (100 members)
More formal rules	Fewer rules and restrictions
Debate limited	Debate extended
Floor action controlled	Unanimous consent rules
Less prestige and less individual notice	More prestige and media attention
Originates bills for raising revenues	Power of "advice and consent" on presidential appointments and treaties
Local or narrow leadership	National leadership

*Some of these differences, such as term of office, are provided for in the Constitution, while others, such as debate rules, are not.

(see the chapter-opening feature). The longest filibuster was waged by Senator Strom Thurmond of South Carolina, who held forth on the Senate floor for twenty-four hours and eighteen minutes in an attempt to thwart the passage of the 1957 Civil Rights Act.

Today, under Senate Rule 22, debate may be ended by invoking **cloture**—a method of closing debate and bringing the matter under consideration to a vote in the Senate. Sixteen senators must sign a petition requesting cloture, and then, after two days have elapsed, three-fifths of the entire membership must vote for cloture. Once cloture is invoked, each senator may speak on a bill for no more than one hour before a vote is taken. Additionally, a final vote must take place within one hundred hours after cloture has been invoked.

THE SENATE WINS THE PRESTIGE RACE, HANDS DOWN Because of the large number of representatives, few can garner the prestige that a senator enjoys. Senators have relatively little difficulty in gaining access to the media. Members of the House, who run for reelection every two years, have to survive many reelection campaigns before they can obtain recognition for their activities. Usually, a representative has to become an important committee leader before she or he can enjoy the consistent attention of the national news media.

LO4 *The Legislative Process*

Look at Figure 11–3 on the facing page, which shows the basic process through which a bill becomes law at the national level. Not all of the complexities of the process are shown, to be sure. For example, the figure does not indicate the extensive lobbying and media politics that are often involved in the legislative process. There is also no mention of the informal negotiations and "horse trading" that occur to get a bill passed. Few types of legislation are more contentious than those that set tax rates, as you can see in this chapter's *Our Government Faces a Troubled Economy* feature on page 244.

The basic steps in the process are as follows:

1. ***Introduction of legislation.*** Most bills are proposed by the executive branch, although individual members of Congress or their staffs can come up with ideas for new legislation—so, too, can private citizens or lobbying groups. Only a member of Congress can formally introduce legislation, however. In reality, many bills are proposed, developed, and often written by the White House or an executive agency. Then

Senators Richard Burr of North Carolina, left, and John Thune of South Dakota talk as they leave a Senate Republican lunch in the Mansfield Room of the Capitol.

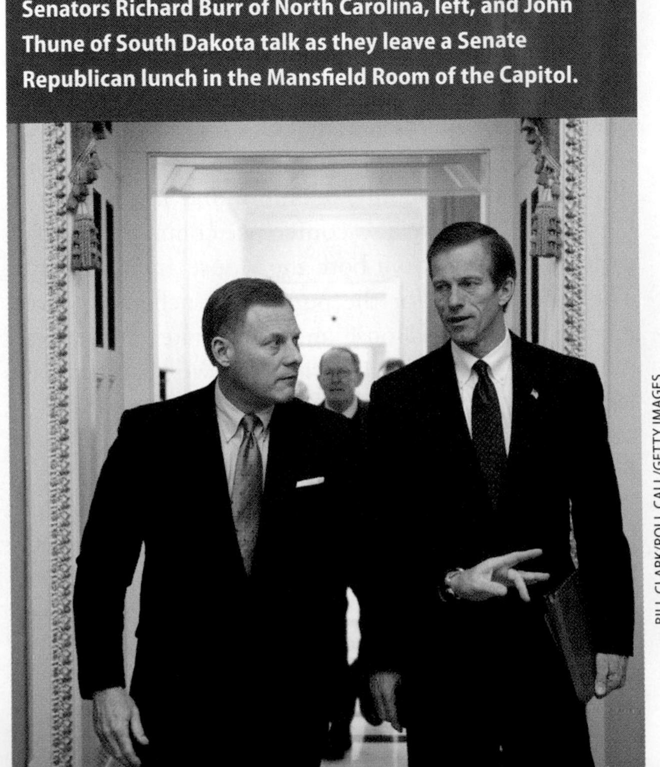

BILL CLARK/ROLL CALL/GETTY IMAGES

Figure 11–3

How a Bill Becomes a Law

This illustration shows the most typical way in which proposed legislation is enacted into law. The process is illustrated with two hypothetical bills, House bill No. 100 (HR 100) and Senate bill No. 200 (S 200). Bills must be passed by both chambers in identical form before they can be sent to the president. The path of HR 100 is traced by an orange line, and that of S 200 by a purple line. In practice, most bills begin as similar proposals in both chambers.

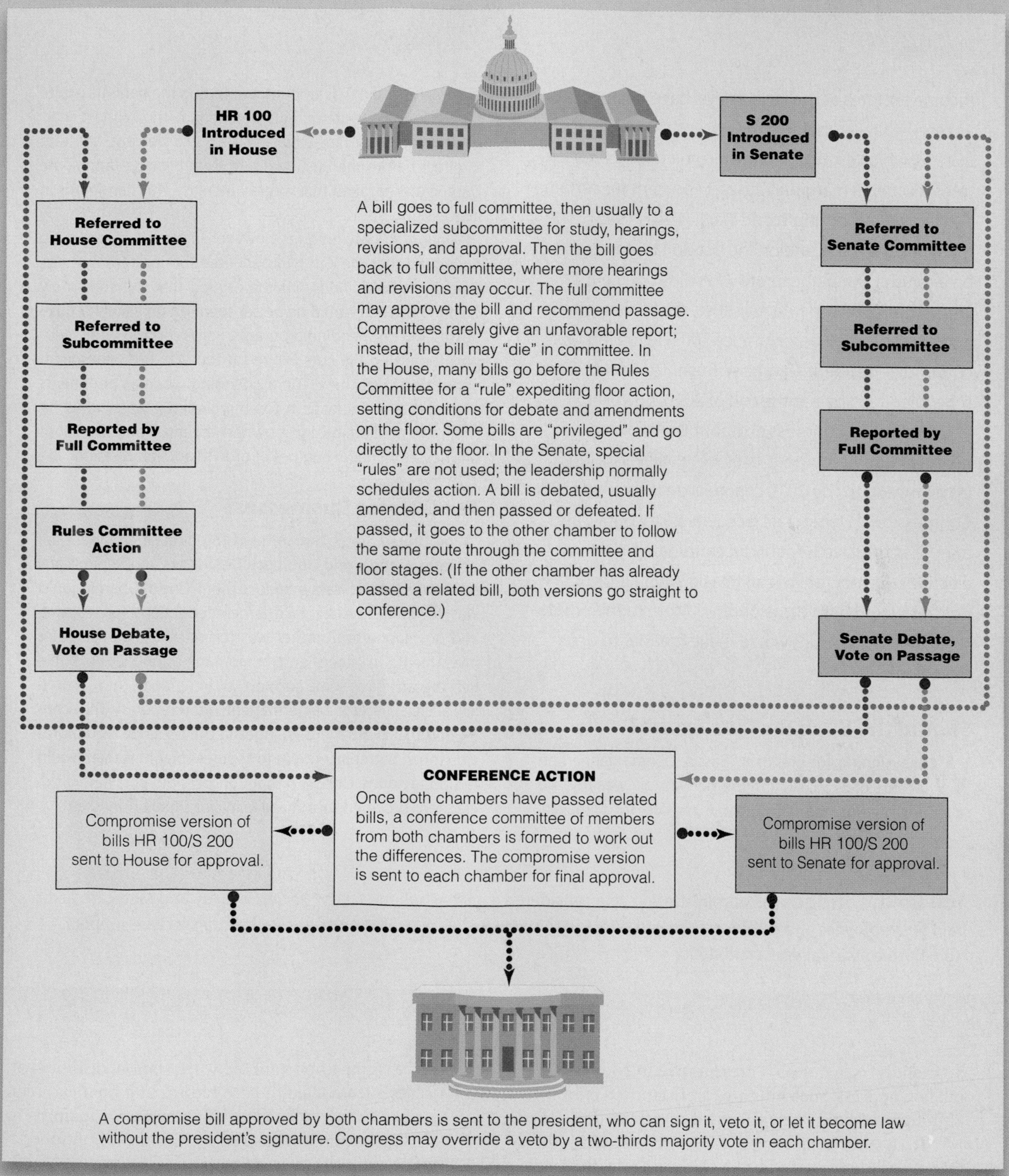

HR 100 Introduced in House
S 200 Introduced in Senate
Referred to House Committee
Referred to Subcommittee
Reported by Full Committee
Rules Committee Action
House Debate, Vote on Passage
Referred to Senate Committee
Referred to Subcommittee
Reported by Full Committee
Senate Debate, Vote on Passage
A bill goes to full committee, then usually to a specialized subcommittee for study, hearings, revisions, and approval. Then the bill goes back to full committee, where more hearings and revisions may occur. The full committee may approve the bill and recommend passage. Committees rarely give an unfavorable report; instead, the bill may "die" in committee. In the House, many bills go before the Rules Committee for a "rule" expediting floor action, setting conditions for debate and amendments on the floor. Some bills are "privileged" and go directly to the floor. In the Senate, special "rules" are not used; the leadership normally schedules action. A bill is debated, usually amended, and then passed or defeated. If passed, it goes to the other chamber to follow the same route through the committee and floor stages. (If the other chamber has already passed a related bill, both versions go straight to conference.)
CONFERENCE ACTION
Once both chambers have passed related bills, a conference committee of members from both chambers is formed to work out the differences. The compromise version is sent to each chamber for final approval.
Compromise version of bills HR 100/S 200 sent to House for approval.
Compromise version of bills HR 100/S 200 sent to Senate for approval.
A compromise bill approved by both chambers is sent to the president, who can sign it, veto it, or let it become law without the president's signature. Congress may override a veto by a two-thirds majority vote in each chamber.

Should We Cut Taxes—and If So, How?

Income tax rates at the federal level have been as low as zero—that was before the Sixteenth Amendment in 1913, which established the income tax. Income tax rates reached a marginal rate of 94 percent for certain rich individuals during World War II (1941–1945). (The *marginal rate* is the rate on the last dollar reported on a return.) The highest rate was still 91 percent as late as 1963. The top rate fell substantially thereafter, and it has been 35 percent since 2003, following tax cuts under President George W. Bush. Those cuts were scheduled to expire at the end of 2010, however.

What would Congress do about the expiring tax cuts? Unemployment rates were still very high in the run-up to the 2010 congressional elections. Congressional Democrats faced an angry public and a set of aggressive Republican candidates in the elections. Democrats began to ask, What kinds of tax policies would help the economy? More to the point, What kinds of policies would make it easier to get reelected?

Should the Bush Tax Cuts Expire?

While running for president, Barack Obama defined an income of $250,000 or more per year as "wealthy." He called for keeping the Bush income tax cuts for taxpayers making less than that amount, but letting the benefits expire for those making more. This meant that the highest marginal income tax rate would rise to 39.6 percent, the rate in effect before the Bush tax cuts. Republicans—and some Democrats—argued that any tax increase was dangerous in a recession.

Obama stuck to his guns, however. In speech after speech, he argued that the rich had benefited too long from reductions in their tax rates. Obama argued that the sums now going to the rich would be better spent on tax relief for businesses and on spending programs. Polls reported public support for letting the cuts expire for the rich, but widespread opposition to any new federal spending. Obama's opponents argued that an increase in top marginal tax rates would hit small and medium business owners the most, and that those businesses were the engines of growth and job creation.

Tax Cuts for Businesses?

The United States has some of the highest corporate tax rates in the world, and both Democrats and Republicans have talked about ways to reduce them. One of Obama's ideas was to let businesses take larger deductions for research and development. Another was to increase deductions for investments in plants and equipment during 2011. While Republicans gave some support to these ideas, they wanted any such changes to be permanent, not temporary. They contended that permanent changes in the tax code would provide much better incentives to business planners than would temporary ones. One plan that Congress did pass before the elections provided subsidized loans for small businesses.

You Be the Judge **The administration also considered a partial holiday on the Social Security and Medicare taxes paid by employees and employers. Obama rejected this idea as too radical. Why might such a plan receive support from both conservatives and liberals?**

a "friendly" senator or representative introduces the bill in Congress. Such bills are rarely ignored entirely, although they are often amended or defeated.

To a degree not seen for some decades, the Obama administration has let Congress take the lead on writing important new legislation dealing with issues such as health-care reform and financial regulation. Even under Obama, however, a majority of the legislation considered by Congress continues to come from the executive branch.

2. *Referral to committees.* As soon as a bill is introduced and assigned a number, it is sent to the appropriate standing committee. In the House, the Speaker assigns the bill to the appropriate committee. In the Senate, the presiding officer assigns the bill to the proper committee. For example, a farm bill in the House would be sent to the Agriculture Committee and a gun control bill would be sent to the Judiciary Committee. A committee chairperson will typically send the bill on to a subcommittee. For example, a Senate bill concerning additional involvement in NATO (the North Atlantic Treaty Organization) in Europe would be sent to the Senate Foreign Relations Subcommittee on European Affairs. Alternatively, the chairperson may decide to put the bill aside and ignore it. Most bills that are pigeonholed in this manner receive no further action.

   If a bill is not pigeonholed, committee staff members go to work researching the bill. The committee may hold public hearings during which people who support or oppose the bill can express their views. Committees also have the power to order witnesses to testify at public hearings. Witnesses may be executive agency officials, experts on the subject, or representatives of interest groups concerned about the bill.

   The subcommittee must meet to approve the bill as it is, add new amendments, or draft a new bill. This meeting is known as the **markup session.** If members cannot agree on changes, a vote is taken. When a subcommittee completes its work, the bill goes to the full standing committee, which then meets for its own markup session. The committee may hold its own hearings, amend the subcommittee's version, or simply approve the subcommittee's recommendations.

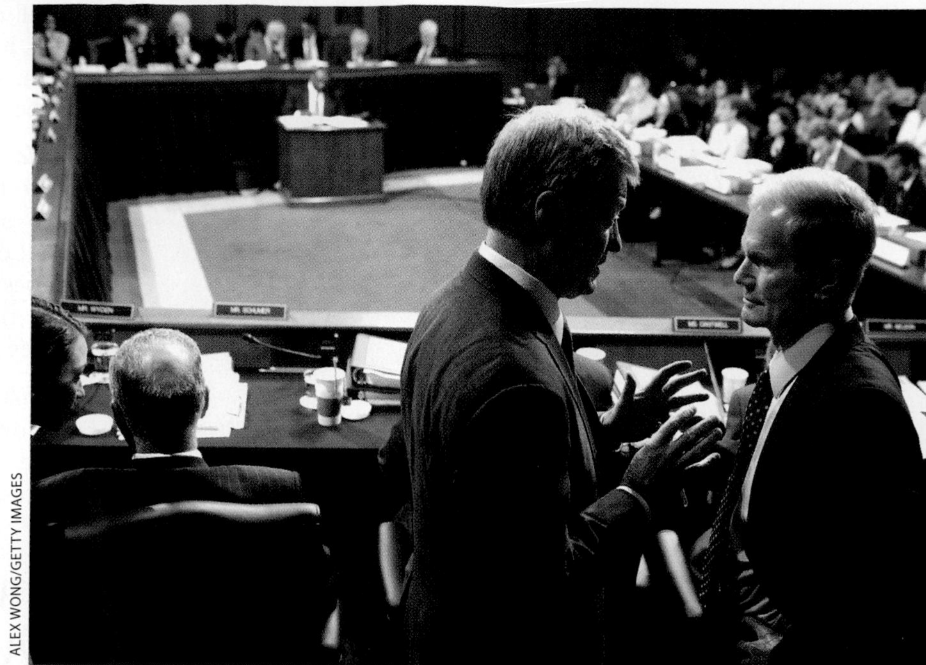

ALEX WONG/GETTY IMAGES

Senator Max Baucus (D., Mont.) on the left discusses pending legislation with Senator Bill Nelson (D., Fla.) during a Finance committee hearing on health-care reform in the fall of 2009. At the same moment, other committees in the House and the Senate were creating their own versions of that legislation.

3. *Reports on a bill.* Finally, the committee will report the bill back to the full chamber. It can report the bill favorably, report the bill with amendments, or report a newly written bill. It can also report a bill unfavorably, but usually such a bill will have been pigeonholed earlier instead. Along with the bill, the committee will send to the House or Senate a written report that explains the committee's actions, describes the bill, lists the major changes made by the committee, and gives opinions on the bill.
4. *The Rules Committee and scheduling.* Scheduling is an extremely important part of getting a bill enacted into law. A bill must be put on a calendar. Typically, in the House the Rules Committee plays a major role in the scheduling process. This committee, along with the House leaders, regulates the flow of the bills through the House. The Rules Committee will also specify the amount of time to be spent on debate and whether amendments can be made by a floor vote.

   In the Senate, a few leading members control the flow of bills. The Senate brings a bill to the floor by "unanimous consent," a motion by which all members present on the floor set aside the formal Senate rules and consider a bill. In contrast to the procedure in the House, individual senators have the power to disrupt work on legislation.
5. *Floor debate.* Because of its large size, the House imposes severe limits on floor debate. The Speaker recognizes those who may speak and can force any member who does not "stick to the subject" to give up the floor. Normally, the chairperson of the standing committee reporting the bill will take charge of the session during which it is debated. You can often watch such debates on C-SPAN.

   Only on rare occasions does a floor debate change

markup session A meeting held by a congressional committee or subcommittee to approve, amend, or redraft a bill.

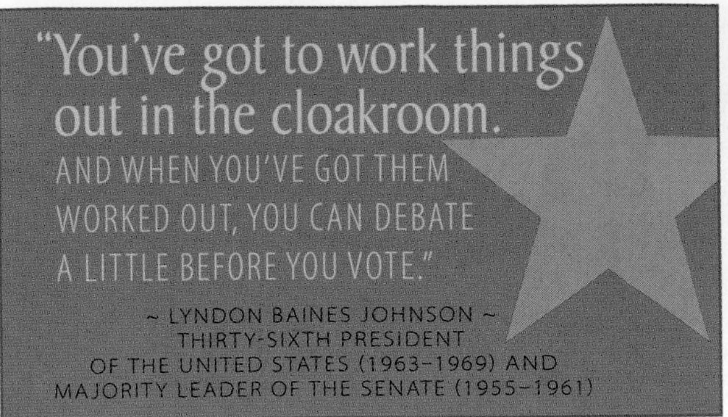

anybody's mind. The written record of the floor debate completes the legislative history of the proposed bill in the event that the courts have to interpret it later on. Floor debates also give the full House or Senate the opportunity to consider amendments to the original version of the bill.

6. *Vote.* In both the House and the Senate, the members present generally vote for or against the bill. There are several methods of voting, including voice votes, standing votes, and recorded votes (also called roll-call votes). Since 1973, the House has had electronic voting. The Senate does not have such a system, however.
7. *Conference committee.* To become a law, a bill must be passed in identical form by both chambers. When the two chambers pass differing versions of the same bill, the measure is turned over to a special committee called a **conference committee**—a temporary committee with members from the two chambers, as mentioned earlier.

   Most members of the committee are drawn from the standing committees that handled the bill in both chambers. In theory, the conference committee can consider only those points in a bill on which the two chambers disagree. No proposals are supposed to be added. In reality, however, the conference committee sometimes makes important changes in the bill or adds new provisions.

   Once the conference committee members agree on the final compromise bill, a **conference report** is submitted to each chamber. The bill must be accepted or rejected by both chambers as it was written by the committee, with no further amendments made. If the bill is approved by both chambers, it is ready for action by the president.
8. *Presidential action.* All bills passed by Congress have to be submitted to the president for approval. The president has ten days to decide whether to sign the bill or veto it. If the president does nothing, the bill goes into effect unless Congress has adjourned before the ten-day period expires. In that case, the bill dies in what is called a **pocket veto.**
9. *Overriding a veto.* If the president decides to veto a bill, Congress can still get the bill enacted into law. With a two-thirds majority vote in both chambers, Congress can override the president's veto.

conference committee A temporary committee that is formed when the two chambers of Congress pass differing versions of the same bill. The conference committee, which consists of members from both the House and the Senate, works out a compromise form of the bill.

conference report A report submitted by a congressional conference committee after it has drafted a single version of a bill.

pocket veto A special type of veto power used by the chief executive after the legislature has adjourned. Bills that are not signed die after a specified period of time.

LO5 *Investigation and Oversight*

Steps 8 and 9 of the legislative process described above illustrate the integral role that the executive and the legislative branches play in making laws. The relationship between Congress and the president is at the core of our system of government, although, to be sure, the judicial branch plays a vital role as well (see Chapter 14).

One of the most important functions of Congress is its oversight (supervision) of the executive branch and its many federal departments and agencies. The executive bureaucracy, which includes the president's cabinet departments, wields tremendous power, as you will read in Chapters 12 and 13. Congress can rein in that power by choosing not to provide the money necessary for the bureaucracy to function (the budgeting process will be discussed later in this chapter).

The Investigative Function

Congress also has the authority to investigate the actions of the executive branch, the need for certain legislation, and even the actions of its own members. The Congressional Research Service and the Congressional Budget Office, for example, provide members of Congress with vital information about policies and economic projections. The numerous congressional committees and subcommittees regularly hold hearings to investigate the actions of the executive branch. Congressional committees receive opinions, reports, and assessments on a broad range of issues. A widely held belief is that

AP PHOTO/DOUG MILLS

In 1998, for only the third time in history, the House Judiciary Committee debated impeachment articles to oust a president. Republicans and Democrats bitterly clashed over articles accusing President Clinton of perjury, obstruction of justice, and abuse of power.

between 2001 and 2007, when Republicans controlled both the two chambers of Congress and the presidency, Congress neglected its oversight function out of deference to President Bush. Some believe that Congress also neglected its oversight function from 2009 to 2011, when the Democrats controlled both chambers of Congress and the presidency. Can oversight also become excessive? We look at this issue in this chapter's *Perception versus Reality* feature on the following page.

"LAWS ARE LIKE SAUSAGES.

It is better if the public does not see how they are made."

~ JOHN GODFREY SAXE ~
AMERICAN POET 1869;
MISATTRIBUTED TO OTTO VON BISMARCK,
CHANCELLOR OF GERMANY
1871–1890

Impeachment Power

Congress has the power to impeach and remove from office the president, vice president, and other "civil officers," such as federal judges. To *impeach* means to accuse a public official of, or charge him or her with, improper conduct in office. The House of Representatives is vested with this power and has exercised it twice against a president—the House voted to impeach Andrew Johnson in 1868 and Bill Clinton in 1998. After a vote to impeach in the full House, the president is then tried in the Senate. If convicted by a two-thirds vote, the president is removed from office. Both Johnson and Clinton were acquitted by the Senate. A vote to impeach President Richard Nixon was pending before the full House of Representatives in 1974 when Nixon chose to resign. Nixon is the only president ever to resign from office.

Congress, as mentioned, can also take action to remove other officials. For example, the House of Representatives voted to impeach Judge Alcee Hastings in 1988, and the Senate removed him from the bench (he was later elected to the House in 1992). Only one United States Supreme Court justice has ever been impeached. The House impeached Samuel Chase in 1804, although he was later acquitted by the Senate.

Senate Confirmation

Article II, Section 2, of the Constitution states that the president may appoint ambassadors, justices of the Supreme Court, and other officers of the United

PERCEPTION VERSUS REALITY

Can Congress Really Dig Up Government Misdeeds?

Our political system relies on checks and balances. One of the checks on the executive branch is congressional oversight. This refers to the supervision and monitoring of federal programs, agencies, and activities, as well as of policy implementation by the executive branch. Congress has dozens of committees through which it carries out its oversight function. These committees and subcommittees routinely hold hearings on various issues that involve the executive branch. While nothing in the U.S. Constitution explicitly gives Congress oversight authority, Congress has taken on this duty as one of its implied powers.

The Perception

While few Americans doubt the value of congressional oversight of the executive branch, many believe that Congress engages in too little of it. Certainly, until 2007, Congress seemed to have "rubber-stamped" the Bush administration's agenda. Americans got the impression that the executive branch was out of control from 2001 until the Democrats took control of Congress in 2007. From 2009, when a Democratic president was matched up with a Democratic Congress, many people believed that Congress went back to sleep.

The Reality

The biggest oversight problem faced by Congress since 2009 has been evaluating the impact of the enormous spending measures advanced by the new administration. Certainly, the Democratic majority had a political interest in putting the best face possible on the Obama administration's proposals. One way in which Congress has "kept itself honest" is by establishing oversight bodies separate from—but responsible to—Congress. These include the Congressional Budget Office (CBO), which evaluates the impact of proposed legislation on the federal budget and the budget deficit. The CBO was much in the news in 2009 due to its "scoring" of the various health-care reform proposals considered by the House and Senate. Members of Congress found themselves tailoring the measures to earn a better score from the CBO.

It is also true that some parts of the executive branch have had so much oversight that they cannot run efficiently. Consider the Department of Homeland Security, which was created by combining more than twenty separate agencies. Each of those agencies had roughly four committees and subcommittees overseeing them. When those agencies were consolidated into one executive department, there was no parallel consolidation of the congressional oversight system. Consequently, about eighty committees and subcommittees now oversee Homeland Security. (Compare this with the Department of Defense, which deals with only four committees on a regular basis.) In a typical year, officials in the Department of Homeland Security must testify in over two hundred congressional hearings. They must also provide more than 2,500 briefings to legislators and their staffs. Much of this time could be used to devise more efficient agency policies.

Blog On Virginia L. Thomas, a conservative, calls for strong oversight of the Internal Revenue Service at **www.heritage.org/press/commentary/ed042899.cfm**. For a left-leaning argument in favor of oversight, see Chuck Collins at **www.thenation.com/blogs/congress2/154082.**

States "with the Advice and Consent of the Senate." The Constitution leaves the precise nature of how the Senate will give this "advice and consent" up to the lawmakers. In practice, the Senate confirms the president's nominees for the Supreme Court, other federal judgeships, and members of the president's cabinet. Nominees appear first before the appropriate Senate committee—the Judiciary Committee for federal judges or the Foreign Relations Committee for the secretary of state, for example. If the individual committee approves the nominee, the full Senate will vote on the nomination.

As you will read further in Chapters 12 and 14, Senate confirmation hearings have been very politicized at times. Judicial appointments often receive the most intense scrutiny by the Senate, because the judges

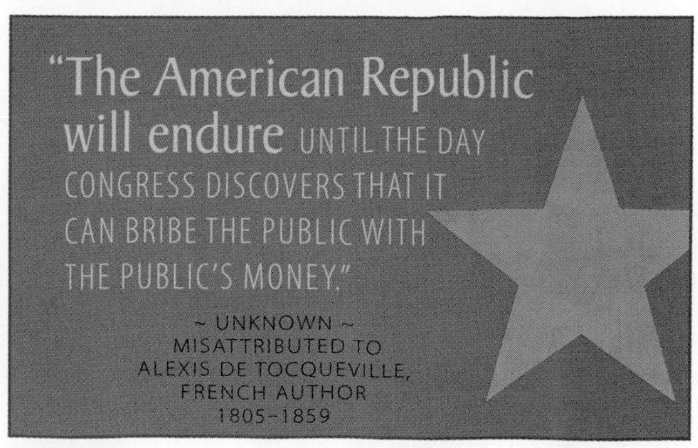

serve on the bench for life. The president has a somewhat freer hand with cabinet appointments, because the heads of executive departments are expected to be loyal to the president. Nonetheless, Senate confirmation remains an important check on the president's power. We will discuss the relationship between Congress and the president in more detail in Chapter 12.

"The American Republic will endure UNTIL THE DAY CONGRESS DISCOVERS THAT IT CAN BRIBE THE PUBLIC WITH THE PUBLIC'S MONEY."
~ UNKNOWN ~
MISATTRIBUTED TO
ALEXIS DE TOCQUEVILLE,
FRENCH AUTHOR
1805–1859

LO6 *The Budgeting Process*

The Constitution makes it very clear that Congress has the power of the purse. Only Congress can impose taxes, and only Congress can authorize expenditures. To be sure, the president submits a budget, but all final decisions are up to Congress.

The congressional budget is, of course, one of the most important determinants of what policies will or will not be implemented. For example, the president might order executive agencies under presidential control to undertake specific programs, but these orders are meaningless if there is no money to pay for their execution. It is Congress that has the power of the "purse strings," and this power is significant. Congress can nullify a president's ambitious program by simply refusing to allocate the necessary money to executive agencies to implement it.

Authorization and Appropriation

The budgeting process is a two-part procedure. **Authorization** is the first part. It involves the creation of the legal basis for government programs. In this phase, Congress passes authorization bills outlining the rules governing the expenditure of funds. Limits may be placed on how much money can be spent and for what period of time.

Appropriation is the second part of the budgeting process. In this phase, Congress determines how many dollars will actually be spent in a given year on a particular set of government activities. Appropriations must never exceed the authorized amounts, but they can be less.

Many **entitlement programs** operate under open-ended authorizations that, in effect, place no limits on how much can be spent. The government is obligated to provide benefits, such as Social Security benefits, veterans' benefits, and the like, to persons who qualify under entitlement laws. The remaining federal programs fall under discretionary spending and can be altered at will by Congress. National defense is the most important item in the discretionary-spending part of the budget. Discretionary spending also includes earmarks, or pork, as described in this chapter's feature *Join the Debate: Should "Earmarks" Be Banned?* on the following page.

authorization A part of the congressional budgeting process that involves the creation of the legal basis for government programs.

appropriation A part of the congressional budgeting process that involves determining how many dollars will be spent in a given year on a particular set of government activities.

entitlement program A government program (such as Social Security) that allows, or entitles, a certain class of people (such as elderly persons) to receive benefits. Entitlement programs operate under open-ended budget authorizations that, in effect, place no limits on how much can be spent.

U.S. Treasury secretary Timothy Geithner testifies during a hearing before the Senate Banking Committee. Geithner testified on international economic and exchange rate policies.

ALEX WONG/GETTY IMAGES

JOIN THE DEBATE

Should "Earmarks" Be Banned?

In recent years, Congress has voted to fund a "bridge to nowhere" in Alaska, a program to combat wild hogs in Missouri, and payment of storage fees for Georgia peanut farmers, among many other special projects. Every year, virtually every bill coming out of Congress includes "earmarked funds" for special projects that are important to individual legislators. This special interest spending is impolitely called *pork-barrel* spending. The term *pork* comes from the idea that members of Congress "bring home the bacon" to their home states, usually in the form of additional federal spending that benefits local businesses and workers. In 2009, earmarks cost taxpayers $16.5 billion. The total for 2010 was estimated to be $11 billion. Should earmarks be banned altogether?

We Must End the Pork

Yes, argue most Americans, it is time to end this unsightly "feeding frenzy" in Congress. Earmarks took off in Congress in the 1990s and rose astronomically thereafter. The bridge to nowhere in Alaska mentioned earlier would have cost more than $200 million. This would have been an obscene use of taxpayers' dollars. (The bridge project was eventually killed.) If pork were banned, legislators would no longer be able to "bribe" other legislators with such requests. In other words, so-called *logrolling* would be much more difficult without earmarks.

Not So Fast

Those in favor of keeping earmarks point out that every member of Congress has constituents who benefit from earmarked funds. Banning earmarks would reduce the value of members of Congress to their constituents and thereby weaken the ties between elected officials and their constituents. Also, without congressional earmarks, Congress would have to accept the decisions of the executive branch as to how each agency or program should allocate its funds among projects. Why should the president and the bureaucracy be the only ones allowed to identify worthy projects?

A less dramatic alternative is to provide for greater disclosure. In the past, the general public often never learned which member of Congress demanded any particular piece of pork. In 2007, Congress changed the rules to require the disclosure of lawmakers' earmark requests. It turns out, however, that many members are quite proud of their pork and want their constituents to know all about it.

AP PHOTO/HALL ANDERSON/KETCHIKAN DAILY NEWS

For Critical Analysis ***Given that pork-barrel spending actually amounts to only a small percentage of the federal government's budget, why are these earmarks so controversial?***

The Actual Budgeting Process

fiscal year A twelve-month period that is established for bookkeeping or accounting purposes. The government's fiscal year runs from October 1 through September 30.

Look at Figure 11–4 on the facing page, which outlines the lengthy budgeting process. The process runs from January, when the president submits a proposed federal budget for the next **fiscal year,** to the start of that fiscal year on October 1. In actuality, about eighteen months prior to October 1, the executive agencies submit their requests to the Office of Management and Budget (OMB), and the OMB outlines a proposed budget. If the president approves it, the budget is officially submitted to Congress.

Figure 11–4

The Budgeting Process

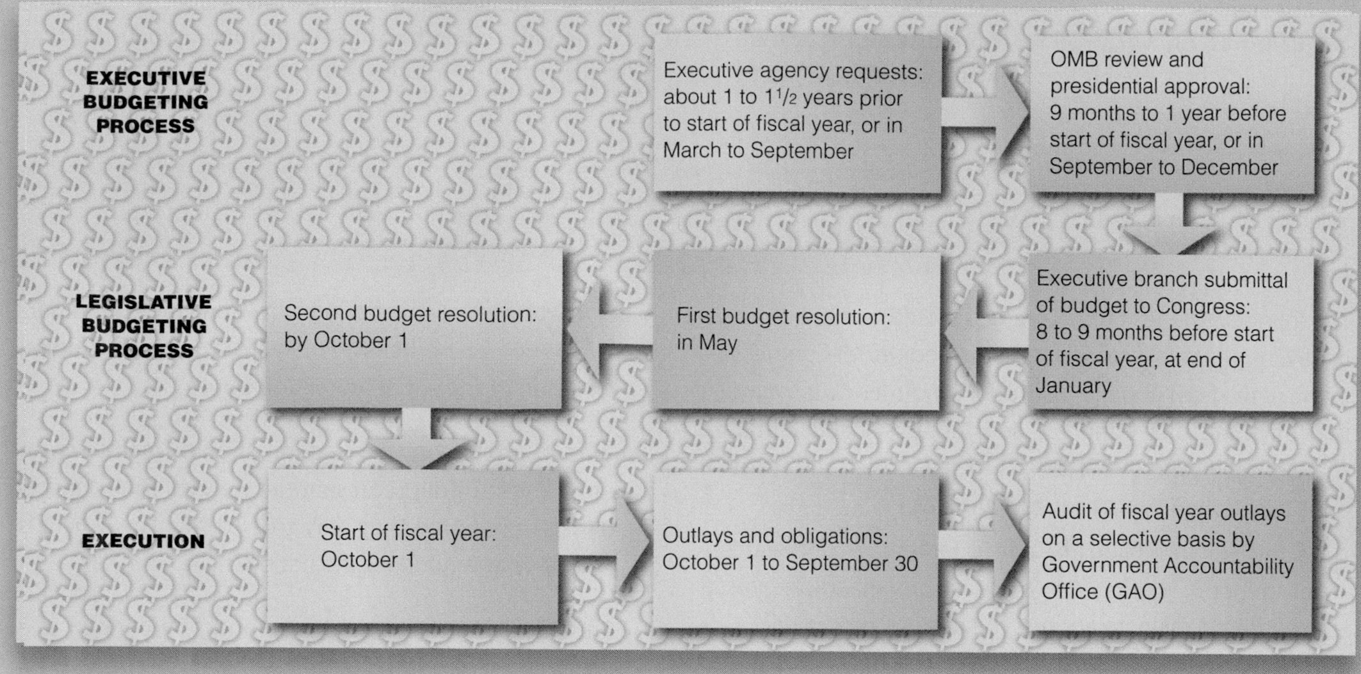

The legislative budgeting process begins eight to nine months before the start of the fiscal year. The **first budget resolution** is supposed to be passed in May. It sets overall revenue goals and spending targets and, by definition, the size of the federal budget deficit or surplus. The **second budget resolution,** which sets "binding" limits on taxes and spending, is supposed to be passed in September, before the beginning of the fiscal year on October 1. Whenever Congress is unable to pass a complete budget by October 1, it passes **continuing resolutions,** which enable the executive agencies to keep on doing whatever they were doing the previous year with the same amount of funding. Even continuing resolutions have not always been passed on time.

The budget process involves making predictions about the state of the U.S. economy for years to come. This process is necessarily very imprecise. Since 1996, both Congress and the president have attempted to make ten-year projections for income (from taxes) and spending, but no one can really know what the financial picture of the United States will look like in ten years. The workforce could grow or shrink, which would drastically alter government revenue from taxes. Any

"WE THE PEOPLE are the rightful masters of both Congress and the courts."

~ ABRAHAM LINCOLN ~
SIXTEENTH PRESIDENT OF THE UNITED STATES
1861–1865

first budget resolution A budget resolution, which is supposed to be passed in May, that sets overall revenue goals and spending targets for the next fiscal year, which begins on October 1.

second budget resolution A budget resolution, which is supposed to be passed in September, that sets "binding" limits on taxes and spending for the next fiscal year.

continuing resolution A temporary resolution passed by Congress when an appropriations bill has not been passed by the beginning of the new fiscal year.

number of emergencies could arise that would require increased government spending—from going to war against terrorists to inoculating federal employees against smallpox.

In any event, when you read about what the administration predicts the budget deficit (or surplus) will be in five or ten years, take such predictions with a grain of salt. There has never been such a long-term prediction that has come close to being accurate. Moreover, most times, the longest-term predictions made by administrations will depend on decisions made when *another* administration is in office later on.

AMERICA AT **ODDS** *Congress*

The founders thought that Congress would be the branch of government that was closest to the people. Yet Congress is one of the least popular institutions in America. It seems that anything that Congress does annoys a substantial share of the electorate. Needless to say, Americans are at odds over Congress on a variety of issues:

- Is the Senate's filibuster rule a legitimate safeguard of minority rights—or a disastrous handicap on Congress's ability to address the nation's problems?
- Is political gerrymandering just a normal part of the political game—or does it deprive voters of their rights?
- Does racial gerrymandering allow the voices of minority groups to be heard—or is it an unconstitutional violation of the equal protection clause?
- When voting on legislation, should members of Congress faithfully represent the views of their constituents—or should they stay true to their own beliefs about what is good for the nation?
- Should legislative earmarks, or "pork," be banned as a waste of taxpayers' resources—or is it appropriate for members of Congress to support specific projects in their own districts?

Take Action

During each session of Congress, your senators and your representative in the House debate the pros and cons of proposed laws, some of which may affect your daily life or the lives of those you care about. If you want to let your voice be heard, you can do so simply by phoning or e-mailing your senators or your representative. You can learn the names and contact information for the senators and the representative from your area by going to the Web sites of the Senate and the House, which are given in this chapter's *Politics on the Web* feature. Your chances of influencing your members of Congress will be greater if you can convince others, including your friends and family members, to do likewise. Citizens often feel that such efforts are useless. Yet members of Congress *do* listen to their constituents and often *do* act in response to their constituents' wishes. Indeed, next to voting, contacting those who represent you in Congress is probably the most effective way to influence government decision making.

KAYTE M. DEIOMA/PHOTOEDIT

Contacting U.S. representatives and senators is much easier today using the Internet. Next to voting, the most effective ways to influence decision making in Washington, D.C., are phoning, writing to, or e-mailing members of Congress.

POLITICS ON THE WEB

- There is an abundance of online information about Congress and congressional activities. The THOMAS site (named for Thomas Jefferson), maintained by the Library of Congress, provides a record of all bills introduced into Congress, information about each member of Congress and how he or she voted on specific bills, and other data. Go to **thomas.loc.gov**
- The U.S. Government Printing Office (GPO) Access on the Web offers information on the Congress in session, bills pending and passed, and a history of the bills at **www.gpoaccess.gov**
- To learn more about how a bill becomes a law, go to **www.vote-smart.org**

  Click on "Political Resources" and scroll down to "Vote Smart Classroom." Select "An Introduction to the U.S. Government," and then choose "How a Bill Becomes Law."
- You can find e-mail addresses and home pages for members of the House of Representatives at **www.house.gov**
- For e-mail addresses and home pages for members of the Senate, go to **www.senate.gov**
- To have your local congressional representative's votes e-mailed to you every week, to post letters online and read what others are saying about elected officials, or to create and post a "soapbox action alert" to get others on your side of an issue, explore your options at **www.congress.org**

Access CourseMate to review and expand on this chapter through quizzes, flashcards, learning objectives, interactive timelines, a crossword puzzle, audio summaries, video, critical-thinking activities, simulations, and more.

GOVT

12 The Presidency

LEARNING OBJECTIVES

LO1 List the constitutional requirements for becoming president.

LO2 Explain the roles that a president adopts while in office.

LO3 Indicate the scope of presidential powers.

LO4 Describe advantages enjoyed by Congress and by the president in their institutional relationship.

LO5 Discuss the organization of the executive branch and the role of cabinet members in presidential administrations.

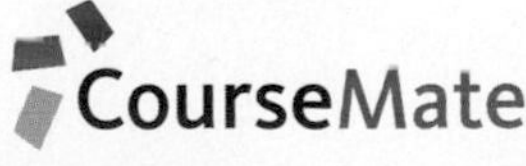

AMERICA AT ODDS

Just How Effective Is President Obama?

During the 2008 presidential campaign, Barack Obama clearly stood to the political left of his Republican opponent, John McCain. Nonetheless, one of Obama's messages was that of uniting this country and avoiding the divisive partisanship that had marked the years of George W. Bush's presidency. Some observers thought that Obama truly did envision a new bipartisan spirit in Washington.

When in office, however, Obama rolled out sweeping domestic policy initiatives, including a giant stimulus bill, an automobile industry bailout, and a huge reform of the health-care system. These programs convinced conservatives that Obama was the most left-wing president in memory, and Obama was able to win almost no Republican votes for his legislation. The administration made compromises—but principally with the most conservative Democrats, not with Republicans. Given these compromises, plus unified Republican opposition, how effective was Obama in carrying out his agenda?

Obama Has Compromised His Progressive Agenda

Liberals soon came to believe that Obama was making too many compromises. For one example, as a candidate Obama promised to close the prison at Guantánamo Bay Naval Base. Two years later, the prison was still in business. Obama also upheld the Bush policy of detaining some prisoners indefinitely without trial.

Health-care reform was the biggest issue of Obama's first two years in office, and progressives grew alarmed at the compromises that the president was willing to make on this issue. Liberals believed that the so-called public option—a government-run health insurance company that would compete with private insurance companies—was key to the reforms. Obama endorsed the public option, but it was not included in the final legislation. True, Republicans opposed the health-care reforms, but the measures that passed actually bore a strong resemblance to plans that many Republicans had supported in earlier years. How progressive was that? Dramatic reform to the nation's energy industry was another key part of Obama's agenda. It died in the Senate. Immigration reform is yet another issue that went nowhere.

Obama's stand on gay rights also disturbed liberals. During his campaign, Obama called for the repeal of the "don't ask, don't tell" policy that prevented lesbians and gay men from serving openly in the armed forces. Unlike closing the Guantánamo prison, this measure enjoyed strong public support. The courts wound up addressing "don't ask, don't tell" before the administration took any actions to repeal it.

Obama's Changes Are Fundamental—and Dangerous

Conservatives paid little attention to liberal criticism of Obama's compromises. They firmly believed that he was indeed the most liberal president we have ever had. Ominously, he was also one of the most successful. Congress passed 96.7 percent of all legislation requested by the president, an all-time record (see page 268). Conservatives argued that Obama wanted to fundamentally change the American social compact. Mainstream conservatives believed that Obama envisioned the kind of social democratic institutions we see in Western Europe. Radical conservatives went so far as to accuse Obama of seeking some kind of dictatorship.

Consider legislative specifics. In the past, stimulus measures had consisted entirely of tax cuts, but the greater share of Obama's stimulus bill was made up of spending programs. This was a sure-fire way of running up the size of the federal government. Obama was willing to make the government (that is, the taxpayers) the owner of banks, insurance companies, and automobile companies. If government ownership of private companies isn't left-wing, then what is?

Conservatives argued that Obama's version of health-care reform was no more than a road to the complete federal takeover of medical care. Yet Obama was able to win the reforms even after the Democrats lost their sixtieth vote in the Senate. That should put to rest any arguments that Obama was somehow ineffective.

WHERE DO YOU STAND?

1. **Has Obama made so many compromises with his original progressive agenda that he could be called a moderate?**
2. **How effective can Obama be during the second half of his term, given the results of the 2010 elections?**

EXPLORE THIS ISSUE ONLINE

- **Dozens of progressive bloggers are prepared to take Obama to task for compromises on health care and other issues. We can name only a few—www.talkingpointsmemo.com, www.dailykos.com, and www.democracyforamerica.com.**
- **A vast number of conservative sites vehemently oppose Obama's programs. Examples include www.americanthinker.com, www.clubforgrowth.org, and www.cwfa.org (Concerned Women for America).**

Introduction

President Lyndon B. Johnson (1963–1969) stated in his autobiography[1] that "of all the 1,886 nights I was President, there were not many when I got to sleep before 1 or 2 A.M., and there were few mornings when I didn't wake up by 6 or 6:30." President Harry Truman (1945–1953) once observed that no one can really understand what it is like to be president: there is no end to "the chain of responsibility that binds him," and he is "never allowed to forget that he is president." These responsibilities are, for the most part, unremitting. Unlike Congress, the president never adjourns.

"No man will ever bring out of the Presidency the reputation which carries him into it. To myself personally, it brings nothing but increasing **DRUDGERY AND DAILY LOSS OF FRIENDS.**"

~ THOMAS JEFFERSON ~
THIRD PRESIDENT OF THE UNITED STATES
1801–1809

Given the demands of the presidency, why would anyone seek the office? There are some very special perks associated with the presidency. The president enjoys, among other things, the use of the White House. The White House has 132 rooms located on 18.3 acres of land in the heart of the nation's capital. At the White House, the president in residence has a staff of more than eighty persons, including chefs, gardeners, maids, butlers, and a personal tailor. Amenities also include a tennis court, a swimming pool, bowling lanes, and a private movie theater. Additionally, the president has at his or her disposal a fleet of automobiles, helicopters, and jets (including *Air Force One,* which costs about $70,000 an hour to run). For relaxation, the presidential family can go to Camp David, a resort hideaway in the Catoctin Mountains of Maryland. Other perks include free dental and medical care.

These amenities are only a minor motivation for wanting to be president of the United States, of course. A greater motivation is that the presidency is at the apex of the political ladder. It is the most powerful and influential political office that any one individual can hold. Presidents can help to shape not only domestic policy but also global developments. Since the demise of the Soviet Union and its satellite Communist countries in the early 1990s, the president of the United States has been the leader of the most powerful nation on earth. The president heads the greatest military force anywhere. Presidents have more power to reach their political objectives than any other players in the American political system. (We discussed President Barack Obama's political agenda in this chapter's opening *America at Odds* feature.) It is not surprising, therefore, that many Americans aspire to attain this office.

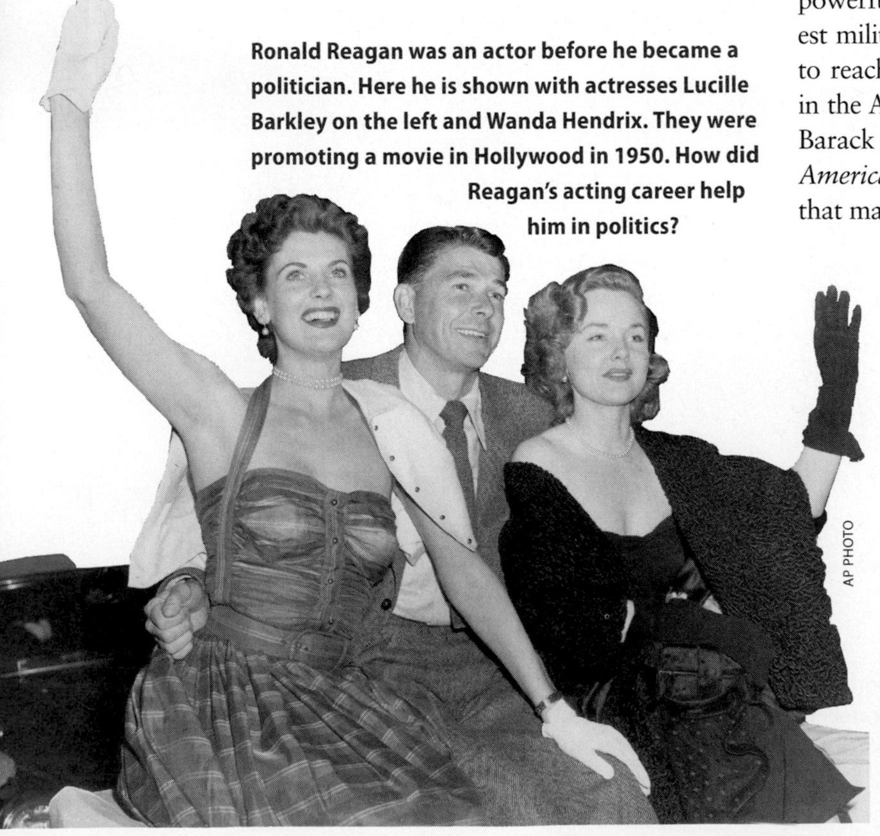

Ronald Reagan was an actor before he became a politician. Here he is shown with actresses Lucille Barkley on the left and Wanda Hendrix. They were promoting a movie in Hollywood in 1950. How did Reagan's acting career help him in politics?

AP PHOTO

LO1 *Who Can Become President?*

The notion that anybody can become president of this country has always been a part of the American mythology. Certainly, the requirements for becoming president set forth in Article II, Section 1, of the Constitution are not difficult to meet:

> No Person except a natural born Citizen, or a Citizen of the United States, at the time of the Adoption of this Constitution, shall be eligible to the Office of President; neither shall any Person be eligible to that Office who shall not

A Foreign-Born President?

As you just read, Article II of the Constitution states that "[n]o Person except a natural born Citizen . . . shall be eligible to the Office of President." This restriction has long been controversial, for it has kept many otherwise qualified Americans from running for president. These persons include California governor Arnold Schwarzenegger, who was born in Austria, and Michigan governor Jennifer M. Granholm, who was born in Canada, both of whom have been U.S. citizens for decades. In all, some 13 million Americans born outside the United States are excluded by this provision. The requirement of native birth has come up most recently because of claims by conspiracy theorists that President Obama was not born in the United States. These individuals claim that Obama's Hawaiian birth certificate was forged, and they are undeterred by the fact that Obama's birth was also announced in Honolulu newspapers.

CERTIFICATION OF LIVE BIRTH

STATE OF HAWAII
HONOLULU

DEPARTMENT OF HEALTH
HAWAII U.S.A.

CERTIFICATE NO.

CHILD'S NAME
BARACK HUSSEIN OBAMA II

DATE OF BIRTH
August 4, 1961

HOUR OF BIRTH
7:24 PM

SEX
MALE

CITY, TOWN OR LOCATION OF BIRTH
HONOLULU

ISLAND OF BIRTH
OAHU

COUNTY OF BIRTH
HONOLULU

MOTHER'S MAIDEN NAME
STANLEY ANN DUNHAM

MOTHER'S RACE
CAUCASIAN

FATHER'S NAME
BARACK HUSSEIN OBAMA

FATHER'S RACE
AFRICAN

DATE FILED BY REGISTRAR
August 8, 1961

OHSM 1.1 (Rev.11/01) LASER

This copy serves as prima facie evidence of the fact of birth in any court proceeding. [HRS 338-13(b), 338-19]

ANY ALTERATIONS INVALIDATE THIS CERTIFICATE

CHICAGO TRIBUNE/MCT/LANDOV

An Obsolete Provision

America is a nation of immigrants, so it strikes some as odd that a foreign-born person would be barred from aspiring to the presidency. Naturalized U.S. citizens are allowed to vote, to serve on juries, and to serve in the military. They are also allowed to serve as secretary of state and represent the nation in foreign affairs. Why can't they run for president? Critics of the Constitution's citizenship requirement think that the requirement should be abolished by a constitutional amendment. They point out that the clause was initially included in the Constitution to prevent European princes from attempting to force the young republic back under monarchical rule in the late 1700s. Clearly, the clause is now obsolete and should no longer apply.

A Requirement Still Valid Today

Other Americans believe that the constitutional ban should remain. They argue that national security could be compromised by a foreign-born president. With the immense power that the president wields, especially in the realm of foreign policy, loyalty is of the utmost concern. The current war on terrorism only heightens the need to ensure that the president does not have divided loyalties.

In addition, the Constitution is quite difficult to amend, requiring support from two-thirds of both chambers of Congress and ratification by three-fourths of the fifty states. The need for an amendment that would allow Schwarzenegger and other immigrants to run for president is hardly as pressing as the need for past antidiscrimination amendments such as those abolishing slavery and giving women the right to vote, opponents argue.

For Critical Analysis ***Some have suggested that a foreign-born president probably would be more nationalistic than a president born in this country. Why might that be so?***

have attained to the Age of thirty-five Years, and been fourteen Years a Resident within the United States. (See this chapter's *Join the Debate* feature above.)

It is true that modern presidents have included a haberdasher (Harry Truman), a peanut farmer (Jimmy Carter), and an actor (Ronald Reagan), although all of these men also had significant political experience before assuming the presidency. If you look at Appendix E, though, you will see that the most common previous occupation of U.S. presidents has been the legal profession. Out of forty-four presidents, twenty-seven have been lawyers. Many presidents have also been wealthy. Additionally, although the Constitution states that anyone who is thirty-five years of age or older can become president, the average age at inauguration has been fifty-five. The youngest person elected president was John F. Kennedy (1961–1963), who assumed the presidency at the age of forty-three (the youngest person to hold the office was Theodore Roosevelt, who was forty-two when he became president after the assassination of William McKinley). The oldest was Ronald Reagan (1981–1989), who was sixty-nine years old when he became president.

For most of American history, all presidential candidates, even those of minor parties, were white, male, and of the Protestant religious tradition. In recent years, however, the pool of talent has expanded. In 1928, Democrat Al Smith became the first Catholic to run for president on a major-party ticket, and in 1960 Democrat John F. Kennedy became the first Catholic president. Among recent unsuccessful Democratic presidential candidates, Michael Dukakis was Greek Orthodox and John Kerry was Catholic. In 2008, the doors swung wide in the presidential primaries as the Democrats chose between a white woman, Hillary Clinton, and an African American man, Barack Obama. By that time, about 90 percent of Americans told pollsters that they would be willing to support an African American for president, and the same number would support a woman.

LO2 *The President's Many Roles*

The president has the authority to exercise a variety of powers. Some of these are explicitly outlined in the Constitution, and some are simply required by the office—such as the power to persuade. In the course of exercising these powers, the president performs a variety of roles. For example, as commander in chief of the armed services, the president can exercise significant military powers. Which roles a president executes successfully usually depends on what is happening domestically and internationally, as well as on the president's personality. Some presidents, including Bill Clinton (1993–2001) during his first term, have shown much more interest in domestic policy than in foreign policy. Others, such as George H. W. Bush (1989–1993), were more interested in foreign affairs than in domestic ones.

chief executive The head of the executive branch of government; in the United States, the president.

Table 12–1 on the facing page summarizes the major roles of the president. An important role is, of course, that of chief executive. Other roles include those of commander in chief, head of state, chief diplomat, chief legislator, and political party leader.

Chief Executive

According to Article II of the Constitution,

> The executive Power shall be vested in a President of the United States of America. . . . [H]e may require the Opinion, in writing, of the principal Officer in each of the executive Departments, upon any Subject relating to the Duties of their respective Offices . . . and he shall nominate, and by and with the Advice and Consent of the Senate, shall appoint . . . Officers of the United States . . . . [H]e shall take Care that the Laws be faithfully executed.

This constitutional provision makes the president of the United States the nation's **chief executive,** or the head of the executive branch of the federal government. When the framers created the office of the president, they created a uniquely American institution. Nowhere else in the world at that time was there a democratically elected chief executive. The executive branch is also unique among the branches of government because it is headed by a single individual—the president.

President Woodrow Wilson throwing out the first pitch on the opening day of the major league baseball season in 1916. This action is part of the president's role as head of state.

NATIONAL PHOTO COMPANY COLLECTION/LIBRARY OF CONGRESS

Table 12–1

Roles of the President

Role	Description	Examples
Chief executive	Enforces laws and federal court decisions, along with treaties signed by the United States	• Can appoint, with Senate approval, and remove high-ranking officers of the federal government • Can grant reprieves, pardons, and amnesty • Can handle national emergencies during peacetime, such as riots or natural disasters
Commander in chief	Leads the nation's armed forces	• Can commit troops for up to ninety days in response to a military threat (War Powers Resolution) • Can make secret agreements with other countries • Can set up military governments in conquered lands • Can end fighting by calling a cease-fire (armistice)
Head of state	Performs ceremonial activities as a personal symbol of the nation	• Decorates war heroes • Dedicates parks and post offices • Throws out first pitch of baseball season • Lights national Christmas tree
Chief diplomat	Directs U.S. foreign policy and is the nation's most important representative in dealing with foreign countries	• Can negotiate and sign treaties with other nations, with Senate approval • Can make pacts (executive agreements) with other heads of state, without Senate approval • Can accept the legal existence of another country's government (power of recognition) • Receives foreign heads of state
Chief legislator	Informs Congress about the condition of the country and recommends legislative measures	• Proposes legislative program to Congress in traditional State of the Union address • Suggests budget to Congress and submits annual economic report • Can veto a bill passed by Congress • Can call special sessions of Congress
Political party leader	Heads political party	• Chooses a vice president • Makes several thousand top government appointments, often to party faithful (patronage) • Tries to execute the party's platform • May attend party fund-raisers • May help reelect party members running for office as mayors, governors, or members of Congress

Commander in Chief

The Constitution states that the president "shall be Commander in Chief of the Army and Navy of the United States, and of the Militia of the several States, when called into the actual Service of the United States." As **commander in chief** of the nation's armed forces, the president exercises tremendous power.

Under the Constitution, war powers are divided between Congress and the president. Congress was given the power to declare war and the power to raise and maintain the country's armed forces. The president, as commander in chief, was given the power to deploy the armed forces. The president's role as commander in chief has evolved over the last century. We will examine this shared power of the president and Congress in more detail later in this chapter.

Head of State

Traditionally, a country's monarch has performed the function of **head of state**—the country's representative to the rest of the world. The United States, of course, has no king or queen to act as

commander in chief The supreme commander of a nation's military force.

head of state The person who serves as the ceremonial head of a country's government and represents that country to the rest of the world.

The Unusual Role of the French President

Earlier in this text, you read about the parliamentary system used by many countries. In that system, the chief executive is chosen by the legislature, not the people. A few countries, however, have a hybrid system that is part parliamentary and part presidential. The best-known example of such a system is France.

The Presidential-Parliamentary System

France has a president, currently Nicolas Sarkozy, and a prime minister. Both represent the "center-right" party in France, the Union for a Popular Movement. In France, the president names the prime minister and the members of the cabinet. The prime minister and the cabinet, though, are responsible to the legislature, not the president. The National Assembly, which is the lower house of Parliament, can force the entire cabinet to resign by passing a motion of no confidence. In other words, "the government"—the prime minister and the other cabinet members—cannot survive politically unless a majority in the National Assembly supports them, regardless of the president's preferences.

The Unique French Practice of Cohabitation

For much of the history of the modern French Republic, the legislature's ability to throw out the government was not important, because the president's party had a majority in the National Assembly. French legislators were willing to let the president—the head of their party—choose the government. In 1981, the French elected a Socialist president for the first time, and they also gave the Socialists a majority in the National Assembly. In the 1986 elections, however, France voted for a center-right Assembly majority. The Socialist president, François Mitterrand, still had two years left in his term of office. The French have a quaint term for the resulting situation: "cohabitation." During cohabitation, the prime minister and the rest of the cabinet are from one party and the president is from another.

Who Does What?

Nowhere in the French constitution is there an explicit statement of the division of powers between the president and the prime minister. The division of duties that exists today has evolved over time. Typically, the president is responsible for foreign policy and the prime minister for domestic policy. This distinction is most carefully observed during periods of cohabitation. When one party is in full control of the government, however, the president tends to take over completely. President Sarkozy meddles in every type of policy. This may be one reason why Sarkozy has become increasingly unpopular since 2007, when he was elected.

For Critical Analysis *Does our president fill too many roles? Would our government work better if a prime minister served under the president?*

President Nicolas Sarkozy is shown with his wife, Carla Bruni, who continues to have a singing career.

AP PHOTO/CHARLES DHARAPAK

head of state. Thus, the president of the United States fulfills this role. The president engages in many symbolic or ceremonial activities, such as throwing out the first pitch to open the baseball season and turning on the lights of the national Christmas tree. The president also decorates war heroes, dedicates parks and post offices, receives visiting heads of state at the White House, and goes on official state visits to other countries. Some argue that presidents should not perform such ceremonial duties because they take time that the president should be spending on "real work." (See this chapter's *The Rest of the World* feature above for more information on how one other country handles this issue.)

Chief Diplomat

A **diplomat** is a person who represents one country in dealing with representatives of another country. In the United States, the president is the nation's **chief diplomat.** The Constitution did not explicitly reserve this role to the president, but since the beginning of this nation, presidents have assumed the role based on their explicit constitutional powers to recognize foreign governments and, with the advice and consent of the Senate, to appoint ambassadors and make treaties. As chief diplomat, the president directs the foreign policy of the United States and is our nation's most important representative.

Chief Legislator

Nowhere in the Constitution do the words *chief legislator* appear. The Constitution, however, does require that the president "from time to time give to the Congress Information of the State of the Union, and recommend to their Consideration such Measures as he shall judge necessary and expedient." The president has, in fact, become a major player in shaping the congressional agenda—the set of measures that actually get discussed and acted on. This was not always the case. In the nineteenth century, some presidents preferred to let Congress lead the way in proposing and implementing policy. Since the administration of Theodore Roosevelt (1901–1909), however, presidents have taken an activist approach. Presidents are now expected to develop a legislative program and propose a budget to Congress every year.

In the past, this shared power has often put Congress and the president at odds. President Bill Clinton's administration, for example, drew up a health-care reform package in 1993 and presented it to Congress almost on a take-it-or-leave-it basis. Congress left it. To avoid such confrontations, President Obama has frequently let Congress determine much of the content of important new legislation, such as the health-care reform bills. In the example of health-care reform, such deference had several negative consequences. These included an unusually large number of earmarks, a protracted and unpopular legislative process, and opportunities for conservatives to mobilize against the reforms. Still, in the end, Obama succeeded where Clinton had failed.

The current and last three presidents are shown in the Oval Office of the White House. What can a president do after she or he leaves office?

DOUG MILLS/THE NEW YORK TIMES/ REDUX

Political Party Leader

The president of the United States is also the *de facto* leader of his or her political party. The Constitution, of course, does not mention this role because, in the eyes of the founders, parties should have no place in the American political system.

As party leader, the president exercises substantial powers. For example, the president chooses the chairperson of the party's national committee. The president can also exert political power within the party by using presidential appointment and removal powers. Naturally, presidents are beholden to the party members who put them in office, and usually presidents indulge in the practice of **patronage**—appointing individuals to government or public jobs to reward those who helped them win the presidential contest. The president may also reward party members with fund-raising assistance (campaign financing was discussed in Chapter 9). The

diplomat A person who represents one country in dealing with representatives of another country.

chief diplomat The role of the president of the United States in recognizing and interacting with foreign governments.

patronage The practice of giving government jobs to individuals belonging to the winning political party.

president is, in a sense, "fund-raiser in chief" for his or her party, and recent presidents, including Bill Clinton, George W. Bush, and Barack Obama, have proven themselves to be prodigious fund-raisers. Understandably, the use of patronage within the party system gives the president extraordinary powers.

LO3 *Presidential Powers*

The president exercises numerous powers. Some of these powers are set forth in the Constitution. Others, known as *inherent powers,* are those that are necessary to carry out the president's constitutional duties. We look next at these powers, as well as at the expansion of presidential powers over time.

The President's Constitutional Powers

As you have read, the constitutional source for the president's authority is found in Article II of the Constitution, which states, "The executive Power shall be vested in a President of the United States of America." The Constitution then sets forth the president's relatively limited constitutional responsibilities. Just how much power should be entrusted to the president was debated at length by the framers of the Constitution. On the one hand, they did not want a king. On the other hand, they believed that a strong executive was necessary if the republic was to survive. The result of their debates was an executive who was granted enough powers in the Constitution to balance those of Congress.

Article II grants the president broad but vaguely described powers. From the very beginning, there were different views as to what exactly the "executive Power" clause enabled the president to do. Nonetheless, Sections 2 and 3 of Article II list the following specific presidential powers. These powers parallel the roles of the president discussed in the previous section:

- To serve as commander in chief of the armed forces and the state militias.
- To appoint, with the Senate's consent, the heads of the executive departments, ambassadors, justices of the Supreme Court, and other top officials.
- To grant reprieves and pardons, except in cases of impeachment.
- To make treaties, with the advice and consent of the Senate.

treaty A formal agreement between the governments of two or more countries.

AP PHOTO

President John F. Kennedy (right) and Prime Minister Harold Macmillan of the United Kingdom stop just outside the White House office in 1961 to discuss problems in Southeast Asia. What role is the president playing here?

- To deliver the annual State of the Union address to Congress and to send other messages to Congress from time to time.
- To call either house or both houses of Congress into special sessions.
- To receive ambassadors and other representatives from foreign countries.
- To commission all officers of the United States.
- To ensure that the laws passed by Congress "be faithfully executed."

In addition, Article I, Section 7, gives the president the power to veto legislation. We discuss some of these powers in more detail below. As you will see, many of these powers are balanced by the powers of Congress. We address the complex relationship between the president and Congress later in this chapter.

PROPOSAL AND RATIFICATION OF TREATIES A **treaty** is a formal agreement between two or more countries. The president has the sole power to negotiate

DAVID HUME KENNERLY/GETTY IMAGES

President Jimmy Carter (center) met with Egyptian president Anwar Sadat (left) and Israeli prime minister Menachem Begin (right) at the White House for the signing of the Camp David Accords on September 18, 1978. Since then, Egypt and Israel have remained at peace with each other.

veto A Latin word meaning "I forbid"; the refusal by an official, such as the president of the United States or a state governor, to sign a bill into law.

and sign treaties with other countries. The Senate, however, must approve a treaty by a two-thirds vote of the members present before it becomes effective. If the treaty is approved by the Senate and signed by the president, it becomes law.

Presidents have not always succeeded in winning the Senate's approval for treaties. Woodrow Wilson (1913–1921) lost his effort to persuade the Senate to approve the Treaty of Versailles,[2] the peace treaty that ended World War I in 1918. Among other things, the treaty would have made the United States a member of the League of Nations. In contrast, Jimmy Carter (1977–1981) convinced the Senate to approve a treaty returning the Panama Canal to Panama by the year 2000 over such objections as those of Senator S. I. Hayakawa, Republican from California, who said, "We stole it fair and square." The treaty was approved by a margin of a single vote.

THE POWER TO GRANT REPRIEVES AND PARDONS The president's power to grant a pardon serves as a check on judicial power. A *pardon* is a release from punishment or the legal consequences of a crime. It restores a person to the full rights and privileges of citizenship. In 1925, the United States Supreme Court upheld an expansive interpretation of the president's pardon power in a case involving an individual convicted for contempt of court. The Court held that the power covers all offenses "either before trial, during trial, or after trial, by individuals, or by classes, conditionally or absolutely, and this without modification or regulation by Congress."[3] The president can grant a pardon for any federal offense, except in cases of impeachment.

One of the most controversial pardons was that granted by President Gerald Ford (1974–1977) to former president Richard Nixon (1969–1974) after the Watergate affair (to be discussed later in the chapter), before any formal charges were brought in court. Sometimes pardons are granted to a class of individuals, as a general amnesty. For example, President Jimmy Carter granted amnesty to tens of thousands of people who had resisted the draft during the Vietnam War by failing to register for the draft or by moving abroad. Just before he left office in 2001, President Bill Clinton pardoned 140 individuals. Some of these pardons were controversial.

A more recent controversy followed President George W. Bush's decision, in 2007, to commute the prison sentence received by Lewis ("Scooter") Libby, Vice President Dick Cheney's chief of staff. Libby was convicted of crimes in connection with a leak to the press that exposed the identity of a Central Intelligence Agency agent. Bush administration critics alleged that the exposure of the agent's identity was an attempt to punish the agent's husband for criticisms of the war in Iraq.

THE PRESIDENT'S VETO POWER As noted in Chapter 11, the president can **veto** a bill passed by Congress. Congress can override the veto with a two-thirds vote by the members present in each chamber. The result of a veto override is that the bill becomes law against the wishes of the president. If the president does not send a bill back to Congress after ten congressional working days, the bill becomes law without the president's signature. If the president refuses to sign the bill and Congress adjourns within ten working days after the bill has been submitted to the president, however, the bill is killed for that session of Congress. As mentioned in Chapter 11, this is called a *pocket veto*.

Presidents used the veto power sparingly until the administration of Andrew Johnson (1865–1869). Johnson vetoed twenty-one bills. Franklin D. Roosevelt (1933–1945) vetoed more bills by far than any of his

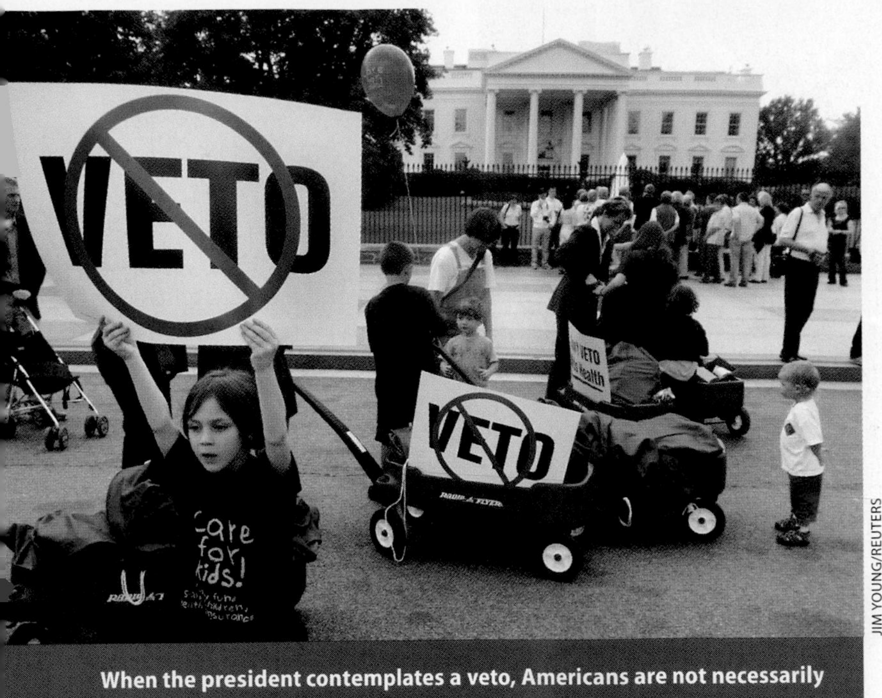

JIM YOUNG/REUTERS

When the president contemplates a veto, Americans are not necessarily in agreement. In 2007, protesters—including these children—asked President George W. Bush not to veto legislation expanding a health-insurance program for low-income children.

predecessors or successors in the presidency. During his administration, there were 372 regular vetoes, 9 of which were overridden by Congress, and 263 pocket vetoes.

The Veto in Recent Administrations President George W. Bush, in contrast, used his veto power very sparingly. Indeed, during the first six years of his presidency, Bush vetoed only one bill—a proposal to expand the scope of stem-cell research. Bush vetoed so few bills, in large part, because the Republican-led Congress during those years strongly supported his agenda. After the Democrats took control of Congress in 2007, however, Bush vetoed eleven bills. Congress overrode four of them.

With a Congress led by his own party, President Obama faced circumstances similar to those enjoyed by George W. Bush during most of his presidency. In his first two years of office, Obama exercised the veto power very rarely.

The Line-Item Veto Many presidents have complained that they cannot control "pork-barrel" legislation—federal expenditures tacked onto bills to "bring home the bacon" to a particular congressional member's district. For example, expenditures on a specific sports stadium might be added to a bill involving crime. The reason is simple: the president would have to veto the entire bill to eliminate the pork—and that might not be feasible politically. Presidents have often argued in favor of a *line-item veto* that would enable them to veto just one (or several) items in a bill. In 1996, Congress passed and President Clinton signed a line-item veto bill. The Supreme Court concluded in 1998 that it was unconstitutional, however.[4]

The President's Inherent Powers

In addition to the powers explicitly granted by the Constitution, the president also has *inherent powers*—powers that are necessary to carry out the specific responsibilities of the president as set forth in the Constitution. The presidency is, of course, an institution of government, but it is also an institution that consists, at any one moment in time, of one individual. That means that the lines between the presidential office and the person who holds that office often become blurred. Certain presidential powers that today are considered part of the rights of the office were simply assumed by strong presidents to be inherent powers of the presidency, and their successors then continued to exercise these powers.

President Woodrow Wilson clearly indicated this interplay between presidential personality and presidential powers in the following statement:

President Bill Clinton used line-item veto powers to eliminate nearly forty projects worth $287 million from a military construction bill in 1997. The line-item veto legislation, passed in 1996, was ruled unconstitutional by the United States Supreme Court in 1998.

AP PHOTO/GREG GIBSON

As chief diplomat, George Washington made foreign policy decisions without consulting Congress. This action laid the ground work for an active presidential role in foreign policy.

By the time Abraham Lincoln gave his Inauguration Day speech, seven southern states had already seceded from the Union. Some scholars believe that Lincoln's skillful and vigorous handling of the Civil War increased the power and prestige of the presidency.

In its attempts to counter the effects of the Great Depression, Franklin D. Roosevelt's administration not only extended the role of the national government in regulating the nation's economic life but also further increased the power of the president.

> The President is at liberty, both in law and conscience, to be as big a man as he can. His capacity will set the limit; and if Congress be overborne by him, it will be no fault of the makers of the Constitution—it will be from no lack of constitutional powers on his part, but only because the President has the nation behind him, and Congress has not.[5]

In other words, because the Constitution is vague as to the actual carrying out of presidential powers, presidents are left to define the limits of their authority—subject, of course, to obstacles raised by the other branches of government.

The Expansion of Presidential Powers

The Constitution defines presidential powers in very general language, and even the founders were uncertain just how the president would perform the various functions. George Washington (1789–1797) set many of the precedents that have defined presidential power. For example, he removed officials from office, interpreting the constitutional power to appoint officials as implying power to remove them as well.[6] He established the practice of meeting regularly with the heads of the three departments that then existed and of turning to them for political advice. He set a precedent for the president to act as chief legislator by submitting proposed legislation to Congress. Abraham Lincoln (1861–1865), confronting the problems of the Civil War during the 1860s, took several important actions while Congress was not in session. He suspended certain constitutional liberties, spent funds that Congress had not appropriated, blockaded southern ports, and banned "treasonable correspondence" from the U.S. mail. Lincoln carried out all of these actions in the name of his power as commander in chief and his constitutional responsibility to "take Care that the Laws be faithfully executed."[7]

Other presidents, including Thomas Jefferson, Andrew Jackson, Woodrow Wilson, Franklin D. Roosevelt, and George W. Bush, also greatly expanded the powers of the president. The power of the president continues to evolve, depending on the person holding the office, the relative power of Congress, and events at home and abroad.

THE PRESIDENT'S EXPANDED LEGISLATIVE POWERS

Congress has come to expect the president to develop a legislative program. From time to time, the president submits special messages on certain subjects. These messages call on Congress to enact laws that the president thinks are necessary. The president also works closely with members of Congress to persuade them to support particular programs. The president writes, telephones, and meets with various congressional leaders to discuss pending bills. The president also sends aides to lobby on Capitol Hill. One study of the legislative process found that "no other single actor in the political system has quite the capability of the president to set agendas in given policy areas." As one lobbyist told a researcher, "Obviously, when a president sends up a bill [to Congress], it takes first place in the queue. All other bills take second place." As noted earlier, however, compared with some recent presidents, Barack Obama has shown a surprising willingness to let Congress determine the details of important legislation.

The Power to Persuade The president's political skills and ability to persuade others play a large role in determining the administration's success. According to Richard Neustadt in his classic work *Presidential Power,* "Presidential power is the power to persuade."[8] For all of the resources at the president's disposal, the president still must rely on the cooperation of others if the administration's goals are to be accomplished. After three years in office, President Harry Truman made this remark about the powers of the president:

> The president may have a great many powers given to him in the Constitution and may have certain powers under certain laws which are given to him by the Congress of the United States; but the principal power that the president has is to bring people in and try to persuade them to do what they ought to do without persuasion. That's what the powers of the president amount to.[9]

Persuasive powers are particularly important when divided government exists. If a president from one political party faces a Congress dominated by the other party, the president must overcome more opposition than usual to get legislation passed.

Going Public The president may also use a strategy known as "going public"[10]—that is, using press conferences, public appearances, and televised events to arouse public opinion in favor of certain legislative programs. The public may then pressure legislators to support the administration's programs. A president who has the support of the public can wield significant persuasive power over Congress. Presidents who are voted into office through "landslide" elections have increased bargaining power because of their widespread popularity. Those with less popular support have less bargaining leverage.

The ability of the president to go public effectively is dependent on popular attitudes toward the president. Such attitudes may be quite rational. For example, voters may rate a president based on the state of the economy. Experts have observed that the president's ability to control the level of economic activity is subject to severe limits. From the public's point of view, however, evaluating its leaders based on results makes good sense. Other views of the president may be highly irrational. We provide an example in this chapter's feature *Perception versus Reality: The Mythical Barack Obama* on the facing page.

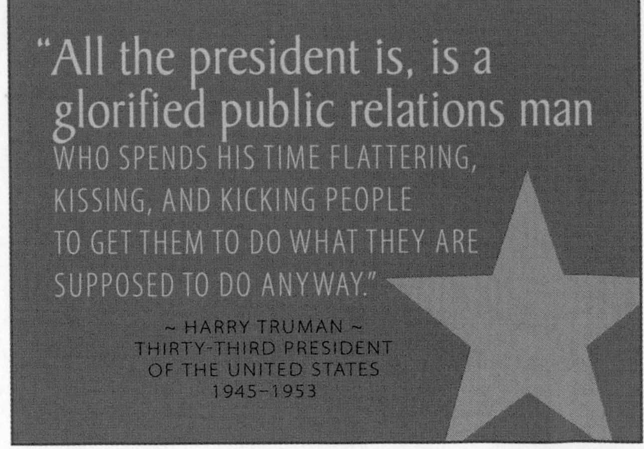

"All the president is, is a
glorified public relations man
WHO SPENDS HIS TIME FLATTERING,
KISSING, AND KICKING PEOPLE
TO GET THEM TO DO WHAT THEY ARE
SUPPOSED TO DO ANYWAY."
~ HARRY TRUMAN ~
THIRTY-THIRD PRESIDENT
OF THE UNITED STATES
1945–1953

The Power to Influence the Economy Some of the greatest expansions of presidential power occurred during Franklin D. Roosevelt's administration. Roosevelt claimed the presidential power to regulate the economy during the Great Depression in the 1930s. Since that time, Americans have expected the president to be actively involved in economic matters and social programs. That expectation becomes especially potent during a major economic downturn, such as the Great Recession that began in December 2007.

Congress annually receives from the president a suggested budget and the *Economic Report of the President.* The budget message suggests what amounts of money the government will need for its programs. The *Economic Report of the President* presents the state of the nation's economy and recommends ways to improve it.

The Legislative Success of Various Presidents Look at Figure 12–1 on page 268. It shows the success records of presidents in getting their legislation passed. Success is defined as how often the president won his way on roll-call votes on which he took a clear position. As you can see, typically a president's success record was very high when he first took office and then gradually declined. This is sometimes attributed to the president's "honeymoon period," when Congress may be most likely to work with the president to achieve the president's legislative agenda. The media often put a great deal of emphasis on how successful a president is during the "first hundred days" in office. Ironically, this is also the period when the president is least experienced in the ways of the White House, particularly if the president was a Washington outsider, such as a state governor, before becoming president.

In 2009, President Obama had the most successful legislative year of any president in half a century. Obama's four years in the Senate may have helped him learn the ways of Washington. Large Democratic majorities in both chambers of Congress were surely

PERCEPTION VERSUS REALITY

The Mythical Barack Obama

When Barack Obama was running for president, his enemies—and there were plenty of them—attempted to "prove" that he could not legally run for president. They contended that Obama was not a native-born citizen, despite ample proof of his birth in Hawaii. Entire Web sites were devoted to creating a perception of Obama as someone who was unfit to become president. One myth propagated by bloggers and radio talk-show hosts was that Obama was a Muslim.

The Perception

In a recent public opinion poll, the number of respondents who said that Obama is a Muslim was 18 percent, up from 12 percent in 2008. Only 34 percent believed that he was a Christian, down from 51 percent. The belief that Obama is a Muslim has increased most sharply among conservative Republicans—up 16 points, to 34 percent. When asked how they learned about Obama's religion, 60 percent cited the media.

One argument employed by bloggers is based on Obama's Kenyan father, who was Muslim by birth (although apparently irreligious later in life). The bloggers argue that in the Muslim world, the father's religion determines the religion of the child. Therefore, Obama is a Muslim, even if he went to a Christian church for most of his adult life.

The Reality

Contrary to the claims of American bloggers, no authority in the Islamic world has ever said that Obama's ancestry makes him a Muslim or a Muslim apostate. Obama lived in Indonesia—a Muslim country—for four years as a young boy, but that proves nothing. As president, he reads a daily Christian devotional message, converses with pastors on the phone, and regularly attends Christian services in a military chapel at Camp David. His mother, who raised him, was an atheist, not a Muslim. Obama was baptized as a Christian in his twenties.

The argument that Obama is not a Christian is odd given that one of his most serious problems during his presidential campaign was his relationship with the Reverend Jeremiah Wright, his longtime pastor. Wright served at Trinity United Church of Christ (UCC) in Chicago. (The UCC, one of America's oldest denominations, is the direct descendent of the church founded by the Puritans.) A key to this contradiction is that a large number of Americans also believe that Wright is a Muslim. Some apparently identify Wright with the Black Muslims because they are both African American, politically radical, and from Chicago.

Of one thing we can probably be certain: as the economy improves, the misperception of Obama's attachment to Islam will decline.

Blog On One of the best sources for debunking rumors and urban legends is snopes.com. For analysis of the Obama-is-a-Muslim legend, see **www.snopes.com/politics/obama/muslim.asp**. To see how talk-show host Rush Limbaugh perpetrates the myth, enter "Rush Limbaugh Obama Muslim" into a search engine such as Google.

even more important in explaining Obama's ability to obtain the legislation that he sought.

THE INCREASING USE OF EXECUTIVE ORDERS As the nation's chief executive, the president is considered to have the inherent power to issue **executive orders,** which are presidential orders to carry out policies described in laws that have been passed by Congress. These orders have the force of law. Presidents have issued executive orders for a variety of purposes, including to establish procedures for appointing noncareer administrators, restructure the White House bureaucracy, ration consumer goods and administer wage and price controls under emergency conditions, classify government information as secret, implement affirmative action policies, and regulate the export of certain items. Presidents issue executive orders frequently, sometimes as many as one hundred a year.

AN UNPRECEDENTED USE OF SIGNING STATEMENTS A **signing statement** is a written statement issued by a president at the time he or she signs a bill into law. James Monroe (1817–1825) was the first president to issue such a statement. For many years, signing statements were rare—prior to the presidency of Ronald

executive order A presidential order to carry out a policy or policies described in a law passed by Congress.

signing statement A written statement, appended to a bill at the time the president signs it into law, indicating how the president interprets that legislation.

Figure 12–1

Presidential Success Records

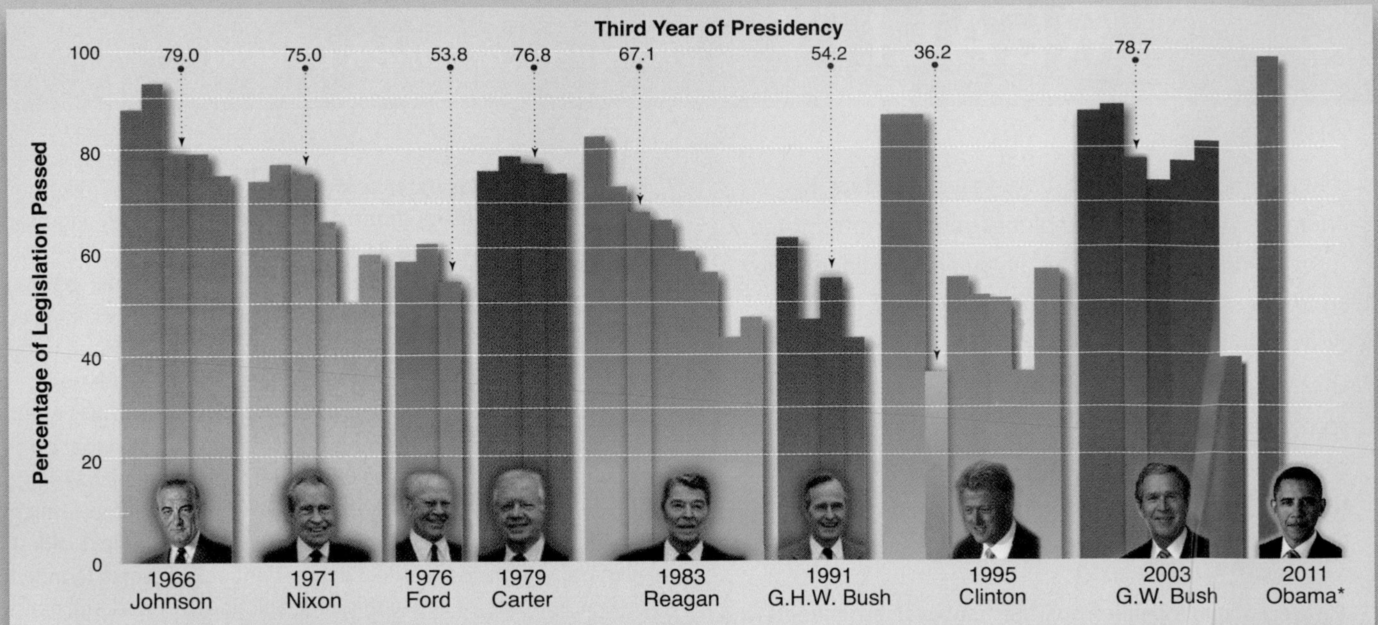

*Obama's first-year success rate (2009) was 96 percent, the highest on record.

Source: *Congressional Quarterly Almanac.*

Reagan, only seventy-five were issued. Most were "rhetorical" in character. They might praise the legislation or the Congress that passed it, or criticize the opposition. On occasion, however, the statements noted constitutional problems with one or more clauses of a bill or provided details as to how the executive branch would interpret legislative language.

Reagan issued a grand total of 249 signing statements. For the first time, each statement was published in the *U.S. Code Congressional and Administrative News,* along with the text of the bill in question. A substantial share of the statements addressed constitutional issues. Reagan staff member Samuel Alito, Jr.—who now sits on the United States Supreme Court—issued a memo in favor of using signing statements to "increase the power of the Executive to shape the law." Reagan's successors George H. W. Bush and Bill Clinton made similar use of the statements.

President George W. Bush took the use of signing statements to an entirely new level. Bush's 161 statements challenged more than 1,100 clauses of federal law—more legal provisions than were challenged by all previous presidents put together. Many legal scholars and members of Congress considered Bush's use of signing statements to be a constitutional crisis. They believed that Bush was attempting by stealth to reinstitute the line-item veto that the Supreme Court had ruled unconstitutional in 1998. The powers that the statements claimed for the president were also alarming. One statement rejected Congress's authority to ban torture. Another affirmed that the president could have anyone's mail opened without a warrant.

As a presidential candidate, Barack Obama criticized Bush's use of signing statements and promised to limit his use of them. As president, he reduced the number of statements substantially during his first

President George W. Bush is shown here approving a signing statement attached to a piece of legislation. During his two terms as president, Bush made unprecedented use of signing statements to assert presidential authority.

AP PHOTO/THE WHITE HOUSE/CHRIS GREENBERG

two years in office, writing only ten of them through October 2010.

EVOLVING PRESIDENTIAL POWER IN FOREIGN AFFAIRS The precise extent of the president's power in foreign affairs is constantly evolving. The president is commander in chief and chief diplomat, but only Congress has the power to formally declare war, and the Senate must ratify any treaty that the president has negotiated with other nations. George Washington laid the groundwork for our long history of the president's active role in foreign policy. For example, when war broke out between Britain and France in 1793, Washington chose to disregard a treaty of alliance with France and to pursue a course of strict neutrality. Since that time, on many occasions presidents have taken military actions and made foreign policy without consulting Congress.

"If one morning I walked on top of the water across the Potomac River, the headline that afternoon would read: **'PRESIDENT CAN'T SWIM.'"**

~ LYNDON B. JOHNSON ~
THIRTY-SIXTH PRESIDENT OF THE UNITED STATES
1963–1969

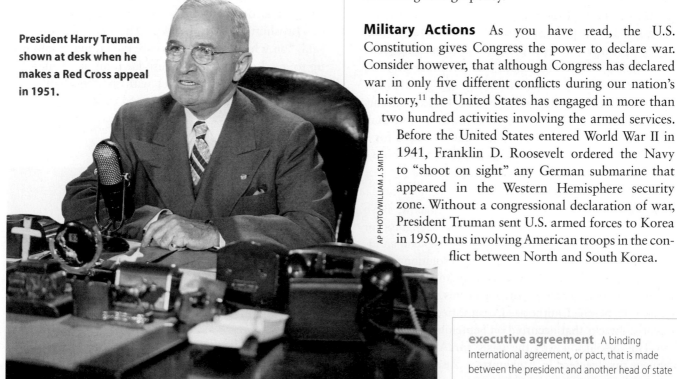

Executive Agreements In foreign affairs, presidential power is enhanced by the ability to make **executive agreements,** which are pacts between the president and other heads of state. Executive agreements do not require Senate approval (even though Congress may refuse to appropriate the necessary money to carry out the agreements), but they have the same legal status as treaties.

Presidents form executive agreements for a wide range of purposes. Some involve routine matters, such as promises of trade or assistance to other countries. Others concern matters of great importance. In 1940, for example, President Franklin D. Roosevelt formed an important executive agreement with British prime minister Winston Churchill. The agreement provided that the United States would lend American destroyers to Britain to help protect that nation and its shipping during World War II. In return, the British allowed the United States to use military and naval bases on British territories in the Western Hemisphere.

To prevent presidential abuse of the power to make executive agreements, Congress passed a law in 1972 that requires the president to inform Congress within sixty days of making any executive agreement. The law did not limit the president's power to make executive agreements, however, and they continue to be used far more than treaties in making foreign policy.

President Harry Truman shown at desk when he makes a Red Cross appeal in 1951.

AP PHOTO/WILLIAM J. SMITH

Military Actions As you have read, the U.S. Constitution gives Congress the power to declare war. Consider however, that although Congress has declared war in only five different conflicts during our nation's history,[11] the United States has engaged in more than two hundred activities involving the armed services. Before the United States entered World War II in 1941, Franklin D. Roosevelt ordered the Navy to "shoot on sight" any German submarine that appeared in the Western Hemisphere security zone. Without a congressional declaration of war, President Truman sent U.S. armed forces to Korea in 1950, thus involving American troops in the conflict between North and South Korea.

executive agreement A binding international agreement, or pact, that is made between the president and another head of state and that does not require Senate approval.

The United States also entered the Vietnam War (1964–1975) without a congressional declaration. President Nixon did not consult Congress when he made the decision to invade Cambodia in 1970. Neither did President Reagan when he sent troops to Lebanon and Grenada in 1983 and ordered American fighter planes to attack Libya in 1986 in retaliation for terrorist attacks on American soldiers. No congressional vote was taken before President George H. W. Bush sent troops into Panama in 1989. Bush did, however, obtain congressional approval to use American troops to force Iraq to withdraw from Kuwait in 1991. Without Congress, President Clinton made the decision to send troops to Haiti in 1994 and to Bosnia in 1995, as well as to bomb Iraq in 1998. In 1999, he also decided on his own authority to send U.S. forces under the command of NATO (North Atlantic Treaty Organization) to bomb Yugoslavia.

In 1991, the United States, along with other nations, used military force to expel Iraqi troops that had invaded Kuwait. Here, President George H. W. Bush (left) meets with General Colin Powell to discuss whether the coalition forces should occupy Baghdad, the capital of Iraq.

The War Powers Resolution As commander in chief, the president can respond quickly to a military threat without waiting for congressional action. This power to commit troops and to involve the nation in a war upset many members of Congress as the undeclared war in Vietnam dragged on for years into the 1970s. Criticism of the president's role in the Vietnam conflict led to the passage of the War Powers Resolution of 1973, which limits the president's warmaking powers. The law, which was passed over President Nixon's veto, requires the president to notify Congress within forty-eight hours of deploying troops. It also prevents the president from sending troops abroad for more than sixty days (or ninety days, if more time is needed for a successful withdrawal). If Congress does not authorize a longer period, the troops must be removed.

The War on Terrorism President George W. Bush did not obtain a declaration of war from Congress for the war against terrorism that began on September 11, 2001. Instead, Congress passed a joint resolution authorizing the president to use "all necessary and appropriate force against those nations, organizations, or persons he determines planned, authorized, committed, or aided the terrorist attacks that occurred on September 11, 2001."

This resolution was the basis for America's subsequent involvement in Afghanistan. Also, in October 2002, Congress passed a joint resolution authorizing the use of U.S. armed forces against Iraq. As a consequence of these resolutions, the president was able to invoke certain emergency wartime measures. For example, through executive order the president created military tribunals for trying terrorist suspects. The president also held American citizens as "enemy combatants," denying them access to their attorneys.

Nuclear Weapons Since 1945, the president, as commander in chief, has been responsible for the most difficult of all military decisions—if and when to use nuclear weapons. In 1945, Harry Truman made the awesome decision to drop atomic bombs on the Japanese cities of Hiroshima and Nagasaki. "The final decision," he said, "on where and when to use the atomic bomb was up to me. Let there be no mistake about it." Today, the president travels at all times with the "football"—the briefcase containing the codes used to launch a nuclear attack.

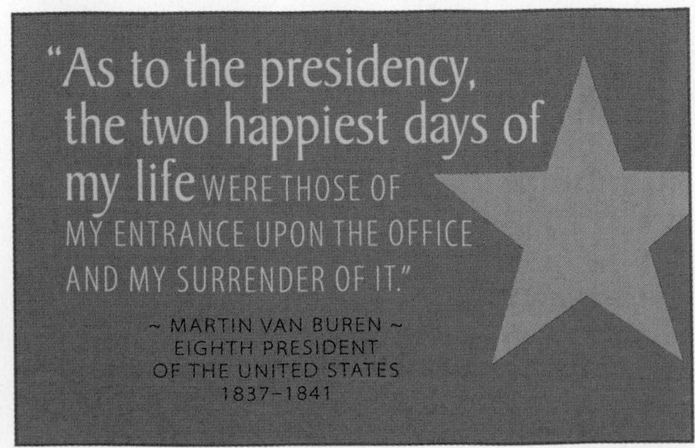

"As to the presidency, the two happiest days of my life WERE THOSE OF MY ENTRANCE UPON THE OFFICE AND MY SURRENDER OF IT."
~ MARTIN VAN BUREN ~
EIGHTH PRESIDENT
OF THE UNITED STATES
1837–1841

LO4 *Congressional and Presidential Relations*

Despite the seemingly immense powers at the president's disposal, the president is limited in what he or she can accomplish, or even attempt. In our system of checks and balances, the president must share some powers with the legislative and judicial branches of government. The president's power is checked not only by these institutions but also by the media, public opinion, and the voters. The founders hoped that this system of shared power would lessen the chance of tyranny.

Some scholars believe the relationship between Congress and the president is the most important one in the American system of government. Congress traditionally has had the upper hand in some areas, primarily in passing legislation. In some other areas, though, particularly in foreign affairs, the president can exert tremendous power that Congress is virtually unable to check.

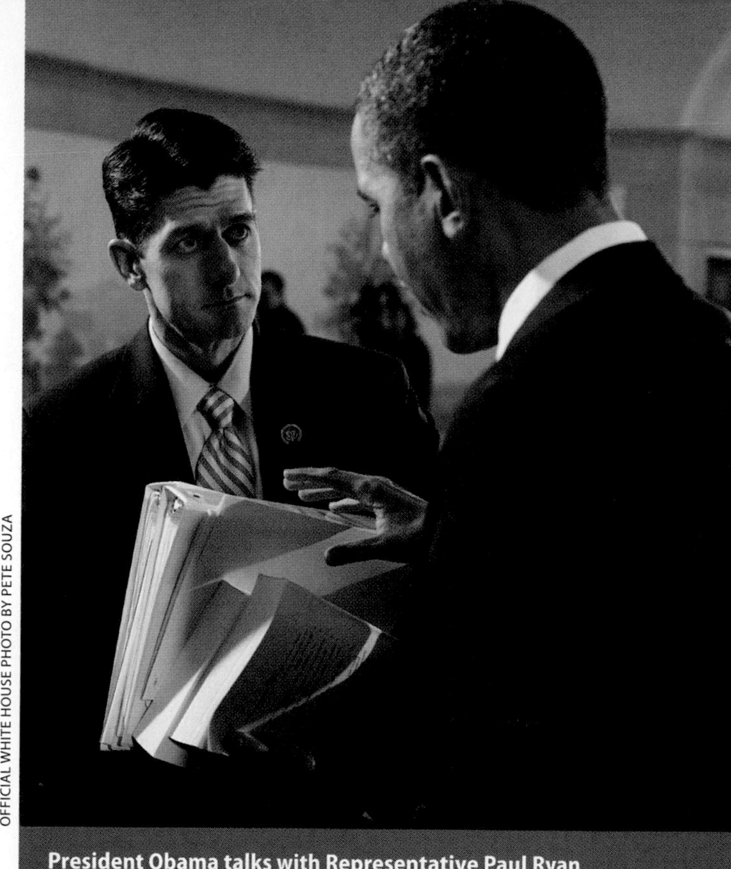

OFFICIAL WHITE HOUSE PHOTO BY PETE SOUZA

President Obama talks with Representative Paul Ryan (R., Wisc.) during a nationally televised bipartisan meeting on health-care reform in February 2010.

Advantage: Congress

Congress has the advantage over the president in the areas of legislative authorization, the regulation of foreign and interstate commerce, and some budgetary matters. Of course, as you have already read, the president today proposes a legislative agenda and a budget to Congress every year. Nonetheless, only Congress has the power to pass the legislation and appropriate the money. The most the president can do constitutionally is veto an entire bill if it contains something that he or she does not like. (As noted, however, recent presidents have frequently used signing statements in an attempt to avoid portions of bills that they did not approve.)

Presidential popularity is a source of power for the president in dealings with Congress. Presidents spend a great deal of time courting public opinion, eyeing the "presidential approval ratings," and meeting with the press. Much of this activity is for the purpose of gaining leverage with Congress. The president can put all of his or her persuasive powers to work in achieving a legislative agenda, but Congress still retains the ultimate lawmaking authority.

DIVIDED GOVERNMENT When government is divided—with at least one house of Congress controlled by a different party than the White House—the president can have difficulty even getting a legislative agenda to the floor for a vote. President Bill Clinton found this to be so after the congressional elections of 1994 brought the Republicans to power in Congress. Clinton's success rate in implementing his legislative agenda dropped to 36.2 percent in 1995, after a high of 86.4 the previous year (see Figure 12–1 on page 268).

President George W. Bush faced a similar problem in 2007, when the Democrats gained a majority in Congress. During his first six years as president, Bush had worked with an extremely cooperative Republican-led Congress.[12] After the Democrats became the majority, however, divided government existed again.

DIFFERENT CONSTITUENCIES Congress and the president have different constituencies, and this fact influences their relationship. Members of Congress represent a state or a local district, and this gives them a regional focus. As we discussed in Chapter 11, members of Congress like to have legislative successes of their own to bring home to their constituents—military bases that remain operative, public-works projects that create local jobs, or trade rules that benefit a big local employer. Ideally, the president's focus should be on the nation as a whole: national defense, homeland security, the national economy. At times, this can put the president at odds even

executive privilege An inherent executive power claimed by presidents to withhold information from, or to refuse to appear before, Congress or the courts. The president can also accord the privilege to other executive officials.

Watergate scandal A scandal involving an illegal break-in at the Democratic National Committee offices in 1972 by members of President Nixon's reelection campaign staff. Before Congress could vote to impeach Nixon for his participation in covering up the break-in, Nixon resigned from the presidency.

with members of his or her own party in Congress.

Furthermore, members of Congress and the president face different election cycles (every two years in the House, every six years in the Senate, and every four years for the president), and the president is limited to two terms in office. Consequently, the president and Congress sometimes feel a different sense of urgency about implementing legislation. For example, the president often senses the need to demonstrate legislative success during the first year in office, when the excitement over the elections is still fresh in the minds of politicians and the public.

Advantage: The President

The president has the advantage over Congress in dealing with a national crisis, in setting foreign policy, and in influencing public opinion. In times of crisis, the presidency is arguably the most crucial institution in government because, when necessary, the president can act quickly, speak with one voice, and represent the nation to the world. George W. Bush's presidency was unquestionably changed by the terrorist attacks of September 11, 2001.

Some scholars have argued that recent presidents have abused the powers of the presidency by taking advantage of crises. Others have argued that there is an unwritten "doctrine of necessity" under which presidential powers can and should be expanded during a crisis. When this has happened in the past, however, Congress has always retaken some control when the crisis was over, in a natural process of institutional give-and-take.

A problem faced during the Bush administration was that the "war on terrorism" had no obvious end or conclusion. It was not clear when the crisis would be over and the nation could return to normal government relations and procedures. In fact, several of Bush's most troubling initiatives, such as support for brutal interrogation methods, were ended during his second term. Many supporters of Barack Obama believed that upon election, he would restore civil liberties lost during Bush's war on terrorism. As it turned out, the Obama administration kept most of Bush's policies in place. (You learned about this issue in greater detail in the Chapter 4 *Perception versus Reality* feature on page 90.)

Executive Privilege

As you read in Chapter 11, Congress has the authority to investigate and oversee the activities of other branches of government. Nonetheless, both Congress and the public have accepted that a certain degree of secrecy by the executive branch is necessary to protect national security. Some presidents have claimed an inherent executive power to withhold information from, or to refuse to appear before, Congress or the courts. This is called **executive privilege,** and it has been invoked by presidents from the time of George Washington to the present.

One of the problems with executive privilege is that it has been used for more purposes than simply to safeguard the national security. President Nixon invoked executive privilege in an attempt to avoid handing over taped White House conversations to Congress during the **Watergate scandal.** President Clinton invoked the privilege in an attempt to keep details of his sexual relationship with Monica Lewinsky a secret.

After the Democrats took control of Congress in 2007 and began to investigate various actions undertaken by the Bush administration, they were frequently blocked in their attempts to obtain information by the claim of executive privilege. For example, during Congress's investigation of the Justice Department's firing of several U.S. attorneys for allegedly political reasons, the Bush administration raised the claim of executive privilege to prevent several people from testifying or submitting requested documents to Congress.

While campaigning, Barack Obama promised that his administration would be much more open than that of President Bush. Many of Obama's own supporters, however, do not believe that he has done enough to carry out that promise.

LO5 *The Organization of the Executive Branch*

In the early days of this nation, presidents answered their own mail, as George Washington did. Only in 1857 did Congress authorize a private secretary for the president, to be paid by the federal government. Even Woodrow Wilson typed most of his correspondence, although by that time several secretaries were assigned to the president. When Franklin D. Roosevelt became president in 1933, the entire staff consisted of thirty-seven employees. Only during Roosevelt's New Deal and World War II did the presidential staff become a sizable organization.

The President's Cabinet

The Constitution does not specifically mention presidential assistants and advisers. The Constitution states only that the president "may require the Opinion, in writing, of the principal Officer in each of the executive Departments." Since the time of our first president, however, presidents have had an advisory group, or **cabinet,** to turn to for counsel. Originally, the cabinet consisted of only four officials—the secretaries of state, treasury, and war and the attorney general.

Today, the cabinet includes fourteen department secretaries, the attorney general, and a number of other officials. (See Table 12–2 at right for the names of the major executive departments represented in the cabinet.) Additional cabinet members vary from one presidency to the next. Typically, the vice president is a member. President Clinton added ten officials to the cabinet, and George W. Bush added five. Barack Obama added the following members in addition to the vice president:

- The administrator of the Environmental Protection Agency.
- The chair of the Council of Economic Advisers.
- The director of the Office of Management and Budget.
- The United States ambassador to the United Nations.
- The United States trade representative.
- The White House chief of staff.

USE OF THE CABINET Because the Constitution does not require the president to consult with the cabinet, the use of this body is purely discretionary. Some presidents have relied on the

Table 12–2

The Major Executive Departments

The heads of all of these departments are members of the president's cabinet.

Department	Year of First Establishment
Department of State	1789
Department of the Treasury	1789
Department of Defense*	1789
Department of Justice (headed by the Attorney General)†	1789
Department of the Interior	1849
Department of Agriculture	1889
Department of Commerce‡	1903
Department of Labor‡	1903
Department of Health and Human Services§	1953
Department of Housing and Urban Development	1965
Department of Transportation	1967
Department of Energy	1977
Department of Education	1979
Department of Veterans Affairs	1989
Department of Homeland Security	2002

*Established in 1947 by merging the Department of War, created in 1789, and the Department of the Navy, created in 1798.
†Formerly the Office of the Attorney General; renamed and reorganized in 1870.
‡Formed in 1913 by splitting the Department of Commerce and Labor, which was created in 1903.
§Formerly the Department of Health, Education, and Welfare; renamed when the Department of Education was spun off in 1979.

cabinet An advisory group selected by the president to assist with decision making. Traditionally, the cabinet has consisted of the heads of the executive departments and other officers whom the president may choose to appoint.

President Barack Obama speaks at the swearing-in of Commerce Secretary Gary Locke and Health and Human Services Secretary Kathleen Sebelius in the East Room of the White House.

CHIP SOMODEVILLA/GETTY IMAGES

counsel of their cabinets. Other presidents solicited the opinions of their cabinets and then did what they wanted to do anyway. After a cabinet meeting in which a vote was seven nays against his one aye, President Lincoln supposedly said, "Seven nays and one aye, the ayes have it."[13] Still other presidents have sought counsel from so-called **kitchen cabinets.** A kitchen cabinet is a very informal group of persons to whom the president turns for advice. The term *kitchen cabinet* originated during the presidency of Andrew Jackson, who relied on the counsel of close friends who allegedly met with him in the kitchen of the White House.

In general, few presidents have relied heavily on the advice of the formal cabinet. The department heads are at times more responsive to the wishes of their own staffs or to their own political ambitions than they are to the president. They may be more concerned with obtaining resources for their departments than with helping presidents achieve their goals.

OBAMA'S CABINET President Obama's response to the need to seek advice has been to centralize the advisory function within the White House Office (discussed below) by appointing a large number of in-house "czars." Each of these White House czars has responsibility for a certain policy area. Critics of the Obama administration believe that the czar system tends to undercut the authority of cabinet members. Congress also loses leverage, because cabinet members must be confirmed by the Senate, whereas czars are responsible only to the president.

kitchen cabinet The name given to a president's unofficial advisers. The term was coined during Andrew Jackson's presidency.

Executive Office of the President (EOP) A group of staff agencies that assist the president in carrying out major duties. Franklin D. Roosevelt established the EOP in 1939 to cope with the increased responsibilities brought on by the Great Depression.

White House Office The personal office of the president. White House Office personnel handle the president's political needs and manage the media.

chief of staff The person who directs the operations of the White House Office and advises the president on important matters.

press secretary A member of the White House staff who holds news conferences for reporters and makes public statements for the president.

The Executive Office of the President

In 1939, President Franklin D. Roosevelt set up the **Executive Office of the President (EOP)** to cope with the increased responsibilities brought on by the Great Depression. Since then, the EOP has grown significantly to accommodate the expansive role played by the national government, including the executive branch, in the nation's economic and social life.

Table 12–3

The Executive Office of the President as of 2010

Department
Council of Economic Advisers
Council on Environmental Quality
Executive Residence
National Security Council and Homeland Security Council
Office of Administration
Office of Management and Budget
Office of National Drug Control Policy
Office of Science and Technology Policy
Office of the U.S. Trade Representative
Office of the Vice President
The White House
White House Office

Source: www.whitehouse.gov.

The EOP is made up of the top advisers and assistants who help the president carry out major duties. Over the years, the EOP has changed according to the needs and leadership style of each president. It has become an increasingly influential and important part of the executive branch. Table 12–3 above lists various offices within the EOP as of 2010. Note that the organization of the EOP is subject to change. Presidents have frequently added new bodies to its membership and subtracted others. President Obama made a number of changes to the EOP's table of organization during his first two years in office.

THE WHITE HOUSE OFFICE Of all of the executive staff agencies, the **White House Office** has the most direct contact with the president. The White House Office is headed by the **chief of staff,** who advises the president on important matters and directs the operations of the presidential staff. A number of other top officials, assistants, and special assistants to the president also aid him or her in such areas as national security, the economy, and political affairs. The **press secretary** (under Obama, Robert Gibbs) meets with reporters and makes public statements for the president. The counsel to the president serves as the White House lawyer and handles the president's legal matters.

The White House staff also includes speechwriters, researchers, the president's physician, and a correspondence secretary. Altogether, the White House Office has more than four hundred employees.

The White House staff has several duties. First, the staff investigates and analyzes problems that require the president's attention. Staff members who are specialists in certain areas, such as diplomatic relations or foreign trade, gather information for the president and suggest solutions. White House staff members also screen the questions, issues, and problems that people present to the president, so matters that can be handled by other officials do not reach the president's desk. Additionally, the staff provides public relations support. For example, the press staff handles the president's relations with the White House press corps and schedules news conferences. Finally, the White House staff ensures that the president's initiatives are effectively transmitted to the relevant government personnel. Several staff members are usually assigned to work directly with members of Congress for this purpose.

The White House Office also includes the staff of the president's spouse. First Ladies have at times taken important roles within the White House. For example, Franklin D. Roosevelt's wife, Eleanor, advocated the rights of women, labor, and African Americans. As First Lady, Hillary Clinton developed an unsuccessful plan for a national health-care system. In 2008, she was a leading contender for the Democratic presidential nomination. Had she won the presidency, Bill Clinton would have become the nation's First Gentleman.

THE OFFICE OF MANAGEMENT AND BUDGET The **Office of Management and Budget (OMB)** was originally the Bureau of the Budget. Under recent presidents, the OMB has become an important and influential unit of the Executive Office of the President. The main function of the OMB is to assist the president in preparing the proposed annual budget, which the president must submit to Congress in January of each year (see Chapter 11 for details). The federal budget lists the revenues and expenditures expected for the coming year. It indicates which programs the federal government will pay for and how much they will cost. Thus, the budget is an annual statement of the public policies of the United States translated into dollars and cents. Making changes in the budget is a key way for presidents to influence the direction and policies of the federal government.

The president appoints the director of the OMB with the consent of the Senate. The director oversees the OMB's work and argues the administration's positions before Congress. The director also lobbies members of Congress to support the president's budget or to accept key features of it. Once the budget is approved by Congress, the OMB has the responsibility of putting it into practice. The OMB oversees the execution of the budget, checking the federal agencies to ensure that they use funds efficiently.

Beyond its budget duties, the OMB also reviews new bills prepared by the executive branch. It checks all legislative matters to be certain that they agree with the president's own positions.

Office of Management and Budget (OMB) An agency in the Executive Office of the President that assists the president in preparing and supervising the administration of the federal budget.

National Security Council (NSC) A council that advises the president on domestic and foreign matters concerning the safety and defense of the nation; established in 1947.

THE NATIONAL SECURITY COUNCIL The **National Security Council (NSC)** was established in 1947 to manage the defense and foreign policy of the United States. Its members are the president, the vice president, and the secretaries of state and defense; it also has several informal advisers. The NSC is the president's link to his or her key foreign and military advisers. The president's special assistant for national security affairs heads the NSC staff.

The Vice Presidency and Presidential Succession

As a rule, presidential nominees choose running mates who balance the ticket or whose appointment rewards or appeases party factions. For example, to balance the ticket geographically, a presidential candidate from the South may solicit a running mate from the West. George W. Bush, who had little experience in national government, picked Dick Cheney, a well-known Republican with extensive political experience in Washington, D.C.

In 2008, unsuccessful Republican candidate John McCain chose as his running mate Alaska governor Sarah Palin. He hoped, in part, to capture a larger share of the female vote. Palin also shored up McCain's support among cultural conservatives. President Barack Obama picked Senator Joe Biden, who had thirty-five years of experience in Congress. Obama wished to counter detractors who claimed that he was too inexperienced.

THE ROLE OF VICE PRESIDENTS For much of our history, the vice president has had almost no responsibilities. Still, the vice president is in a position to become the nation's chief executive should the president die, be impeached, or resign the presidential office. Nine vice presidents have become president because of the death or resignation of the president.

In recent years, the responsibilities of the vice president have grown immensely. The vice president has become one of the most—if not *the* most—important of the president's advisers. The first modern vice president to act as a major adviser was Walter Mondale, who served under Jimmy Carter. Later, Bill Clinton relied heavily on Vice President Al Gore, who shared many of Clinton's values and beliefs.

Without question, however, the most powerful vice president in American history was Dick Cheney, who served under George W. Bush. A consummate bureaucratic strategist, Cheney was able to place his supporters in important positions throughout the government, giving him access to information and influence. This unprecedented delegation of power, of course, would not have been possible without the president's agreement, and Bush clearly approved of it. Vice President Joe Biden is one of President Barack Obama's most important advisers, but not at the level of Cheney.

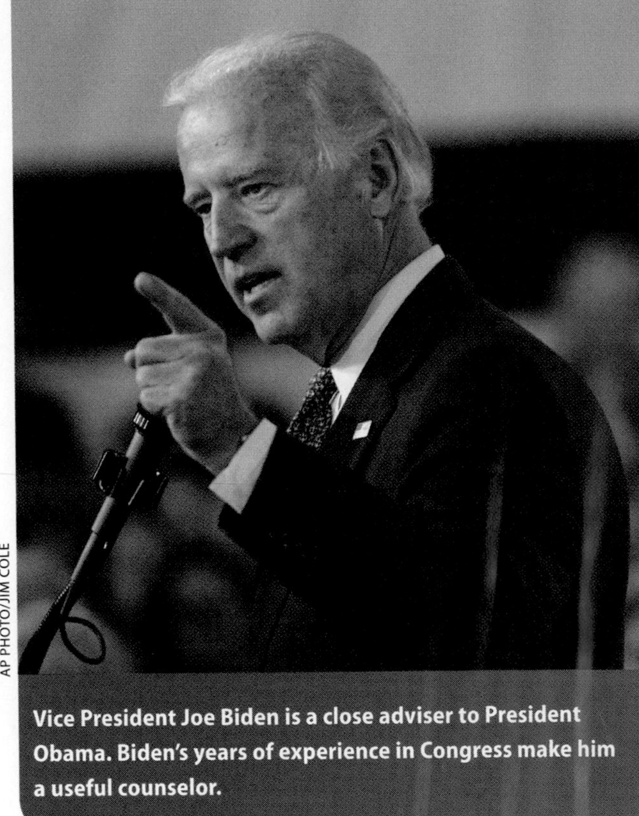
AP PHOTO/JIM COLE

Vice President Joe Biden is a close adviser to President Obama. Biden's years of experience in Congress make him a useful counselor.

PRESIDENTIAL SUCCESSION One of the questions left unanswered by the Constitution was what the vice president should do if the president becomes incapable of carrying out necessary duties while in office. The Twenty-fifth Amendment to the Constitution, ratified in 1967, filled this gap. The amendment states that when the president believes that he or she is incapable of performing the duties of the office, he or she must inform Congress in writing of this fact. Then the vice president serves as acting president until the president can resume his or her normal duties.

Gerald Ford, the 38th president of the United States. He succeeded Richard Nixon after the Watergate scandal, and one of his first public acts was to pardon the former president for his alleged crimes.

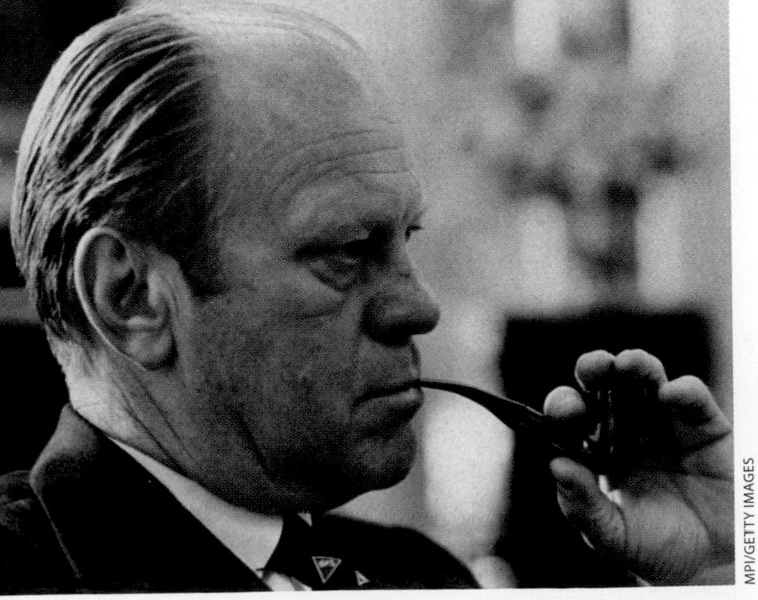
MPI/GETTY IMAGES

When the president is unable to communicate, a majority of the cabinet, including the vice president, can declare that fact to Congress. Then the vice president serves as acting president until the president resumes normal duties. If a dispute arises over the return of the president's ability to discharge the normal functions of the presidential office, a two-thirds vote of both chambers of Congress is required if the vice president is to remain acting president. Otherwise, the president resumes these duties.

The Twenty-fifth Amendment also addresses the question of how the president should fill a vacant vice presidency. Section 2 of the amendment states, "Whenever there is a vacancy in the office of the Vice President, the President shall nominate a Vice President who shall take office upon confirmation by a majority vote of both Houses of Congress."

In 1973, Gerald Ford became the first appointed vice president of the United States after Spiro Agnew was forced to resign. One year later, President Richard Nixon resigned, and Ford advanced to the office of president. President Ford named Nelson Rockefeller as his vice president. For the first time in U.S. history, neither the president nor the vice president had been elected to his position.

What if both the president and the vice president die, resign, or are disabled? According to the Succession Act of 1947, the Speaker of the House of Representatives will then act as president on his or her resignation as Speaker and as representative. If the Speaker is unavailable, next in line is the president pro tem of the Senate, followed by the permanent members of the president's cabinet in the order of the creation of their departments (see Table 12–2 on page 273).

AMERICA AT **ODDS** *The Presidency*

The president is the most conspicuous figure in our political system. Everyone has opinions about what the president should do—and in a presidential election year, who the president should be. To an extent not seen in regard to other offices, the public also has a serious interest in the president's personality and character. The president, after all, represents all of us. Americans are at odds over a variety of questions relating to the presidency. These include the following:

- Should the president try, whenever possible, to compromise with other political players such as the Congress—or should the president generally stand on principle?
- Should the president seek to expand his or her authority so as to deal more effectively with the nation's problems—or should the president try to adhere to a strict constitutional understanding of the powers of the office?
- Is it appropriate for the president to rely primarily on staff members within the White House Office when determining policy—or should the president offer the cabinet a substantial policymaking role?
- Should voters evaluate presidential candidates primarily on the positions they take on the issues—or are the president's character and decision-making style more important considerations?
- Should the president be the "moral leader" of the country and base policies on religious values—or should the president avoid any intermingling of religion and policy?

Take Action

President James Madison (1809–1817) once said, "The citizens of the United States are responsible for the greatest trust ever confided to a political society." Notice that Madison laid the responsibility for this trust on the "citizens," not the "government." Even though it may seem that one person can do little to affect government policymaking and procedures, this assumption has been proved wrong time and again. If you would like to influence the way things are done in Washington, D.C., you can do so by helping to elect a president and members of Congress whose views you endorse and who you think would do a good job of running the country. Clearly, you will want to vote in the next elections. Before then, though, you could join others who share your political beliefs and work on behalf of one of the candidates. You could support a candidate in your home state or join others in "adopting" a candidate from another state who is facing a close race for a congressional seat. You can access that candidate's Web site and offer your services, such as calling voters of the candidate's party and urging them to go to the polls and vote for the candidate. You can also help raise funds for the candidate's campaign and, if you can afford it, even donate some money yourself.

OFFICIAL WHITE HOUSE PHOTO BY PETE SOUZA

President Obama shares a laugh with other world leaders after they posed for the family photo at the G8 Summit in Muskoka, Canada, in June 2010.

POLITICS ON THE WEB

- The White House home page offers links to many sources of information on the presidency. You can access this site at **www.whitehouse.gov**
- If you are interested in reading the inaugural addresses of American presidents from George Washington to Barack Obama, go to **www.bartleby.com/124**. In addition to the full text of the inaugural addresses, this site provides biographical information on the presidents.
- If you would like to research documents and academic resources concerning the presidency, a good Internet site to consult is provided by the University of Virginia's Miller Center of Public Affairs at **millercenter.org/academic/americanpresident**
- To access the various presidential libraries, visit the National Archives site at **www.archives.gov/presidential-libraries**

Access CourseMate to review and expand on this chapter through quizzes, flashcards, learning objectives, interactive timelines, a crossword puzzle, audio summaries, video, critical-thinking activities, simulations, and more.

The Bureaucracy

GOVT 13

LEARNING OBJECTIVES

LO1 Describe the size and functions of the U.S. bureaucracy.

LO2 Discuss the structure and basic components of the federal bureaucracy.

LO3 Indicate when the federal civil service was established and explain how bureaucrats get their jobs.

LO4 Explain how regulatory agencies make rules and how issue networks affect policymaking in government.

LO5 Identify some of the ways in which the government has attempted to curb waste and improve efficiency in the bureaucracy.

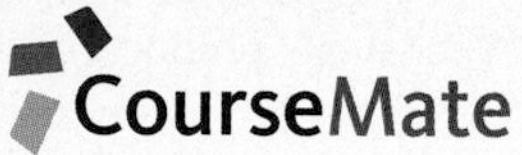

AMERICA AT ODDS

How Much Regulation Do We Need?

Many people believe that the financial crisis of 2008 and 2009 was caused by inadequate regulation of financial enterprises. As a result, these businesses took on far too much risk. It's not surprising, therefore, that in July 2010, Congress imposed a large number of new regulations on the financial industry. Compliance will be costly. The health-care reform legislation adopted earlier in 2010 also involves a substantial body of new regulations.

In the distant past, there was very little government regulation of health care or other industries. One hundred years ago, drugs were not tested before they were put on the market. Hospitals had no uniform standards. Physicians were licensed, but that's about it. Today, the cost of complying with federal rules regulating health care has been estimated at about $350 billion per year.

The Small Business Administration has calculated that the annual cost of all federal regulations is about $1.75 trillion, or 14 percent of the national income. The average cost of regulation for large businesses is $7,755 per employee each year. For small businesses, which do not benefit from economies of scale, the cost is $10,585.

Unbridled Capitalism Is Dead

The law of the capitalist jungle is what got us into the biggest financial crisis since the Great Depression. The events leading up to the credit meltdown in 2008 and the massive federal bailout of banks and insurance companies were caused by unregulated financial entities. Investment banking firms created ever-riskier financial assets, which they sold to unsuspecting individuals and even to local governments as solid, gold-plated investments. In the mortgage industry, unscrupulous salespeople who earned big commissions tricked unsuspecting families into buying homes that were too expensive for their modest means. When house payments went up, those families lost their homes and sometimes their life savings.

We have lived through a time when a president—George W. Bush—scornfully ignored a Supreme Court decision on the regulation of greenhouse gas emissions. Even with something as important as the prescription drugs that we take, the government is not giving us enough protection. Recently, despite its staff members' misgivings, the Food and Drug Administration (FDA) allowed a drug named Avandia to hit the market. That drug turned out to have potential cardiac side effects, and no safety statement on the drug's label warned of them. Regulation is here to stay. Indeed, we need more regulation to protect our lives and our pocketbooks.

Too Much of Anything Is Bad

While no one argues that regulation should be eliminated, many today believe that it is too costly relative to the actual benefits received. Consider the health-care industry regulatory costs mentioned above. By one estimate, the dollar value of the benefits from those regulations is only $170 billion per year. That means that with a total cost of $350 billion, the regulations generate a net cost to society of about $180 billion, or about $1,500 per U.S. household.

Consider another example. We all want safer products, but the Consumer Product Safety Commission now requires that warning labels appear on even common products. A standard ladder has six hundred words of warning pasted on it, including a warning not to place it in front of a swinging door. What are we, idiots? Every toy has a warning that says, "Small parts may cause a choking risk." Parents don't know this? Studies indicate that virtually no one reads warning labels anymore because they are either obvious or too long. What happened to personal responsibility in America? With excessive regulation, the average American no longer appears to be responsible for any of her or his purchases, activities, or actions. Regulation has its place, but it shouldn't control the entire life of a nation.

WHERE DO YOU STAND?

1. **How much do you think you benefit from regulation in our economy? Give some examples.**
2. **Are there any circumstances under which warning labels on consumer products could help you? Give some examples.**

EXPLORE THIS ISSUE ONLINE

1. **For arguments that the FDA is not strict enough in approving medicines, go to the Public Citizen's Health Research Group site at www.citizen.org/hrg.**
2. **The Competitive Enterprise Institute believes the FDA is too slow to approve drugs. See its articles at cei.org/issues/economic-regulation.**

Introduction

Did you eat breakfast this morning? If you did, **bureaucrats**—individuals who work in the offices of government—had a lot to do with that breakfast. If you had bacon, the meat was inspected by federal agents. If you drank milk, the price was affected by rules and regulations of the Department of Agriculture. If you looked at a cereal box, you saw fine print about fat and vitamins, which was the result of regulations made by several other federal agencies, including the Food and Drug Administration. If you ate leftover pizza for breakfast, state or local bureaucrats made sure that the kitchen of the pizza eatery was sanitary and safe. Other bureaucrats ensured that the employees who put together (and perhaps delivered) the pizza were protected against discrimination in the workplace.

GOVERNMENT BUREAUCRACY:

"A marvelous labor-saving device which enables ten men to do the work of one."

~ JOHN MAYNARD KEYNES ~
BRITISH ECONOMIST
1883–1946

Today, the word *bureaucracy* often evokes a negative reaction. For some, it conjures up visions of depersonalized automatons performing chores without any sensitivity toward the needs of those they serve. For others, it is synonymous with government "red tape." A **bureaucracy,** however, is simply a large, complex administrative organization that is structured hierarchically in a pyramid-like fashion.[1] Government bureaucrats carry out the policies of elected government officials. Members of the bureaucracy—government employees—deliver our mail, clean our streets, teach in our public schools, run our national parks, and attempt to ensure the safety of our food and the prescription drugs that we take. Life as we know it would be quite different without the bureaucrats who keep our governments—federal, state, and local—in operation. Still, Americans disagree over how much regulation is necessary, as discussed in the chapter-opening *America at Odds* feature.

The man in the center is a food inspector who is responsible for the quality and safety of what we eat.

MIKE MERGEN/BLOOMBERG NEWS/GETTY IMAGES

LO1 *The Nature and Size of the Bureaucracy*

The concept of a bureaucracy is not confined to the federal government. Any large organization has to have a bureaucracy. In each bureaucracy, everybody (except the head of the bureaucracy) reports to at least one other person. In the federal government, the head of the bureaucracy is the president of the United States, and the bureaucracy is part of the executive branch.[2]

A bureaucratic form of organization allows each person to concentrate on her or his area of knowledge and expertise. In your college or university, for example, you do not expect the basketball coach to solve the problems of the finance department. The reason the federal government bureaucracy exists is that Congress, over time, has delegated certain tasks to specialists. For example, in 1914, Congress

bureaucrat An individual who works in a bureaucracy. As generally used, the term refers to a government employee.

bureaucracy A large, complex, hierarchically structured administrative organization that carries out specific functions.

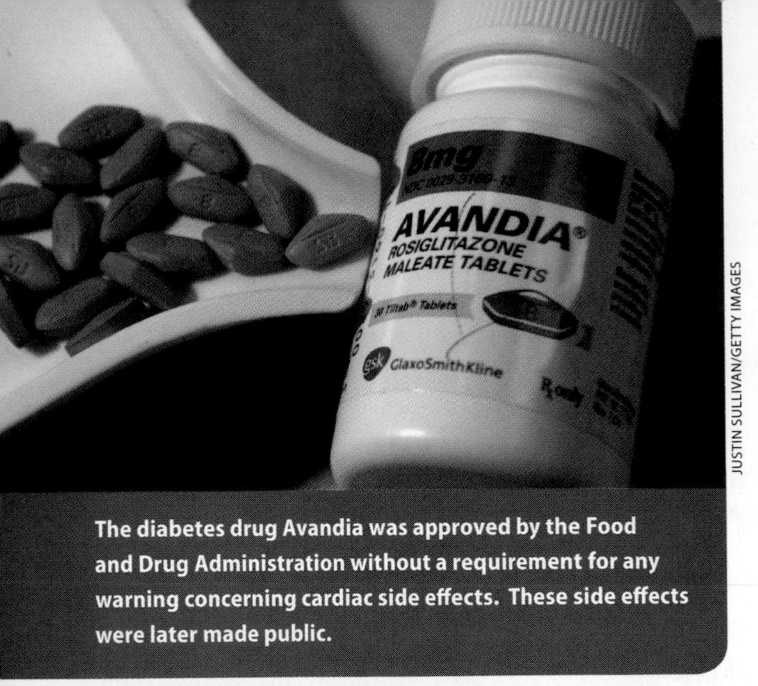

JUSTIN SULLIVAN/GETTY IMAGES

The diabetes drug Avandia was approved by the Food and Drug Administration without a requirement for any warning concerning cardiac side effects. These side effects were later made public.

passed the Federal Trade Commission Act, which established the Federal Trade Commission to regulate deceptive and unfair trade practices. Those appointed to the commission were specialists in this area. Similarly, Congress passed the Consumer Product Safety Act in 1972, which established the Consumer Product Safety Commission to investigate the safety of consumer products. The commission is one of many federal administrative agencies.

Another key aspect of any bureaucracy is that the power to act resides in the *position* rather than in the *person.* In your college or university, the person who is president now has more or less the same authority as any previous president. Additionally, bureaucracies usually entail standard operating procedures—directives on what procedures should be followed in specific circumstances. Bureaucracies normally also have a merit system, meaning that people are hired and promoted on the basis of demonstrated skills and achievements.

The Growth of Bureaucracy

The federal government that existed in 1789 was small. It had three departments, each with only a few employees: (1) the Department of State (nine employees), (2) the Department of War (two employees), and (3) the Department of the Treasury (thirty-nine employees). By 1798, nine years later, the federal bureaucracy was still quite small. The secretary of state had seven clerks. His total expenditures on stationery and printing amounted to $500, or about $8,830 in 2011 dollars. The Department of War spent, on average, a grand total of $1.4 million each year, or about $25.8 million in 2011 dollars.

Times have changed. Figure 13–1 below shows the number of government employees at the local, state, and national levels from 1982 to 2010. Most growth has been at the state and local levels. All in all, the three levels of government employ about 16 percent of the civilian labor force. Today, more Americans are employed by government (at all three levels) than by the entire manufacturing sector of the U.S. economy.

During election campaigns, politicians throughout the nation claim they will "cut big government and red tape" and "get rid of overlapping and wasteful bureaucracies." For the last several decades, virtually every president has campaigned on a platform calling for a reduction in the size of the federal bureaucracy. Yet, at the same time, candidates promise to establish programs that require new employees.

Figure 13–1

Government Employment at the Local, State, and National Levels

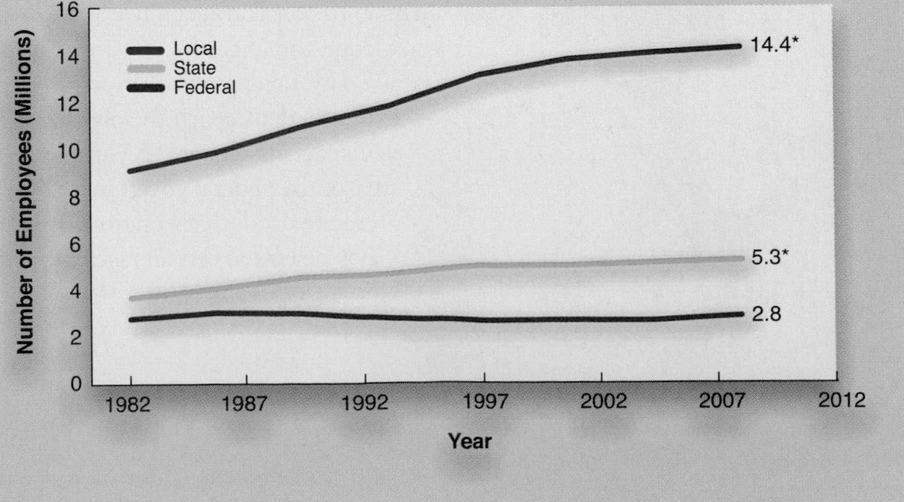

*Estimated
Source: U.S. Census Bureau.

The Costs of Maintaining the Government

The costs of maintaining the government are high and growing. In 1929, government at all levels accounted for about 11 percent of the nation's gross domestic product (GDP). Today, that figure exceeds 40 percent. Average citizens pay a significant portion of their income to federal, state, and local governments. They do this by paying income taxes, sales

Spending More on Health Care—and Less

The heath-care reform bills that President Barack Obama signed into law in March 2010 become effective over a period of several years. The most important parts do not take effect until January 1, 2014. From that day on, subsidies will help citizens purchase health-care insurance if they are not covered by an employer's plan. Individuals and families with incomes up to four times the federal poverty level will be eligible for at least some subsidies. (Currently, the income cutoff would be $88,200 for a family of four, but the exact value will surely change.)

About 32 million Americans who do not have health-care insurance will gain coverage. How will the government pay for that? One method is straightforward—the reforms raise the taxes of the wealthiest taxpayers. Part of the necessary funds, however, come from reducing the growth rate of health-care spending by the federal government. Between the new taxes and the reduced spending, the reforms are expected to shrink the size of the federal budget deficit slightly, thus fulfilling one of President Obama's promises. But what will be cut?

Cost Cutting Is Already Part of the System

In fact, some attempts to restrain spending are built into the existing system. Now, as in the past, most federal health-care spending goes for two programs: Medicare, which provides health-care insurance to those aged sixty-five or older, and Medicaid, which funds health care for the poor. In 2010, a federal agency called the Centers for Medicare and Medicaid Services (CMS) proposed a rate reduction for more than 1 million physicians and non-physician practitioners. This 6.1 percent rate reduction for 2011 applies to everyone paid under the Medical Physician Fee Schedule (MPFS). The MPFS determines Medicare and Medicaid payment rates for seven thousand types of services in physicians' offices and hospitals. Of course, some physicians were not happy about this decision.

Cutting Back on Medicare Advantage

Some of the biggest cuts will come from a program called Medicare Advantage. This program lets seniors use Medicare funds to buy private insurance plans. More than 20 percent of American seniors have already enrolled in Medicare Advantage. The program is somewhat more expensive than standard Medicare, which is a government-administered health-insurance program. Polls also show that Medicare Advantage enrollees are more satisfied with their care than those who are enrolled in the regular Medicare program. In the future, those who wish to continue with Medicare Advantage can expect to pay higher premiums and receive fewer benefits.

Polls show that well over 70 percent of individuals aged sixty-five or over approve of Medicare. A majority consider it to be well run. The question is, will Medicare enrollees continue to report high levels of satisfaction as the government attempts to control the program's costs?

You Be the Judge **Why might persons aged sixty-five and over be more likely than younger Americans to oppose the recent health-care reforms?**

taxes, property taxes, and many other types of taxes and fees. To fully understand the amount of money spent by federal, state, and local governments each year, consider that the same sum of money could be used to purchase all of the farmland in the United States plus all of the assets of the one hundred largest American corporations.

The government is costly, to be sure, but it also provides numerous services for Americans. Cutting back on the size of government inevitably means a reduction in those services. The trade-off between government spending and popular services was central to the debate over health-care reform. Even as the Obama administration advocated substantial new health-care spending, it also tried to limit costs. We discuss that issue in this chapter's *Our Government Faces a Troubled Economy* feature above.

LO2 *How the Federal Bureaucracy Is Organized*

A complete organization chart of the federal government would cover an entire wall. A simplified version is provided in Figure 13–2 below. The executive branch consists of a number of bureaucracies that provide services to Congress, to the federal courts, and to the president directly.

The executive branch of the federal government includes four major types of structures:

- Executive departments.
- Independent executive agencies.
- Independent regulatory agencies.
- Government corporations.

Each type of structure has its own relationship to the president and its own internal workings.

Figure 13–2

The Organization of the Federal Government

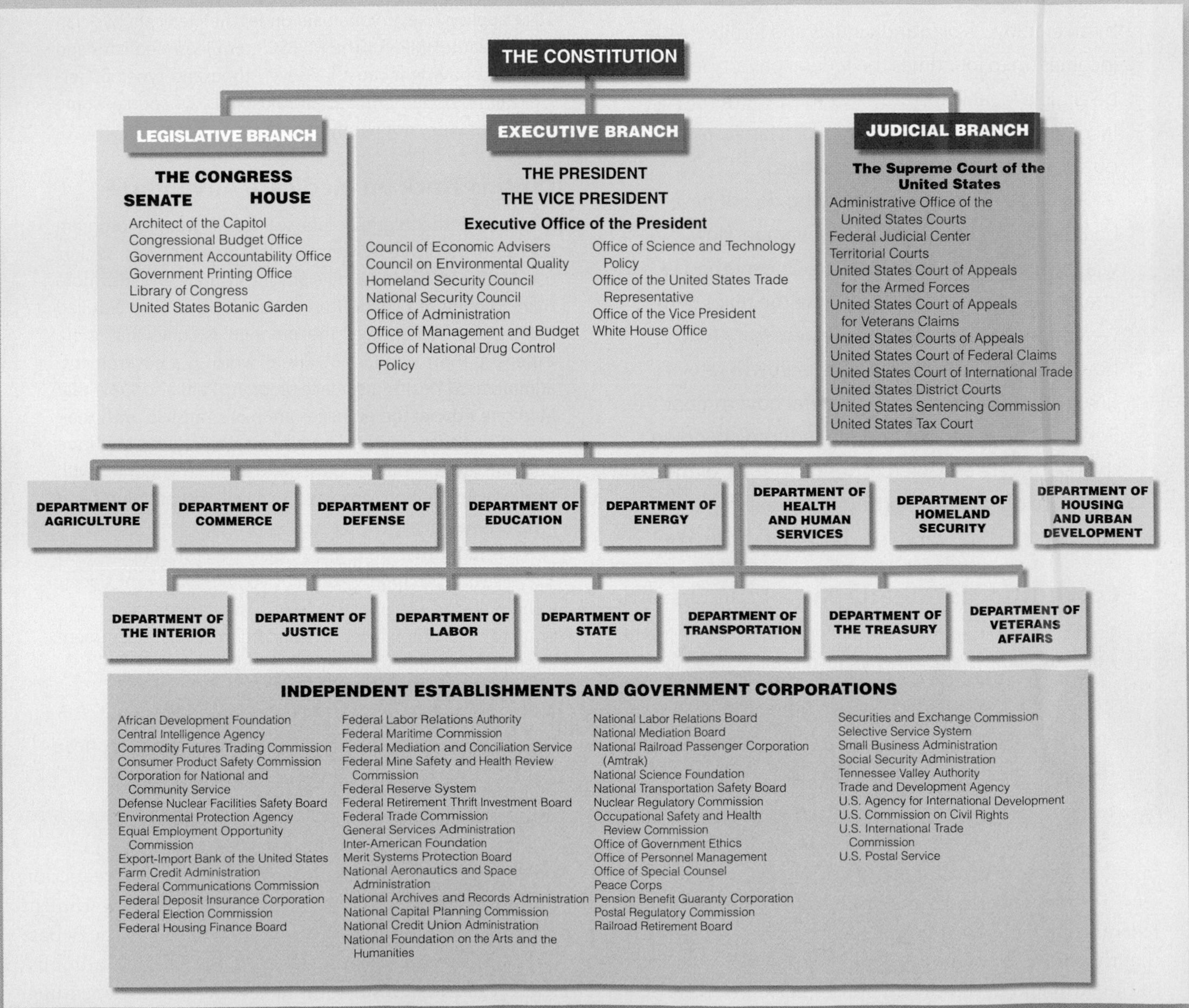

Sources: *United States Government Manual*, 2008–09 (Washington, D.C.: U.S. Government Printing Office, 2008); and **whitehouse.gov**.

The Executive Departments

You were introduced to the various executive departments in Chapter 12, when you read about how the president works with the cabinet and other close advisers. The fifteen executive departments, which are directly accountable to the president, are the major service organizations of the federal government. They are responsible for performing government functions, such as training troops (Department of Defense), printing money (Department of the Treasury), and enforcing federal laws setting minimum safety and health standards for workers (Department of Labor).

Table 13–1 on the following two pages provides an overview of each of the departments within the executive branch. The table lists a few of the many activities undertaken by each department. Because the president appoints the department heads, they are expected to help carry out the president's policy objectives. Often, they attempt to maximize the president's political fortunes as well. Is this a problem when the cabinet member in question is the U.S. attorney general? We discuss that issue in this chapter's *Join the Debate* feature on page 288.

Each executive department was created by Congress as the perceived need for it arose, and each department manages a specific policy area. In 2002, for example, Congress created the Department of Homeland Security to deal with the threat of terrorism. The head of each department is known as the secretary, except for the Department of Justice, which is headed by the attorney general. Each department head is appointed by the president and confirmed by the Senate.

A Typical Departmental Structure

Each cabinet department consists of the department's top administrators (the secretary of the department, deputy secretary, undersecretaries, and the like), plus a number of agencies. For example, the National Park Service is an agency within the Department of the Interior. The Drug Enforcement Administration is an agency within the Department of Justice.

Although there are organizational differences among the departments, each department generally follows a typical bureaucratic structure. The Department of Agriculture provides a model for how an executive department is organized (see Figure 13–3 on page 289).

One aspect of the secretary of agriculture's job is to carry out the president's agricultural policies. Another aspect, however, is to promote and protect the department. The secretary spends time ensuring that Congress allocates enough money for the department to work effectively. The secretary also makes sure that constituents, or the people the department serves—farmers and major agricultural corporations—are happy. In general, the secretary tries to maintain or improve the status of the department with respect to all of the other departments and units of the federal bureaucracy.

The secretary of agriculture is assisted by a deputy secretary and several assistant secretaries and undersecretaries, all of whom are nominated by the president and put into office with Senate approval. The secretary and assistant secretaries have staffs that help with all sorts of jobs, such as hiring new people and generating positive public relations for the Department of Agriculture.

Independent Executive Agencies

Independent executive agencies are federal bureaucratic organizations that have a single function. They are independent in the sense that they are not located within a cabinet department. Rather, independent executive agency heads report directly to the president. A new federal independent executive agency can be created only through cooperation between the president and Congress.

Prior to the twentieth century, the federal government did almost all of its work through the executive departments. In the twentieth century, in contrast, presidents began to ask for certain executive agencies to be kept separate, or independent, from existing departments. Today, there are more than two hundred independent executive agencies.

Sometimes, agencies are kept independent because of the sensitive nature of their functions. At other times, Congress creates independent agencies to protect them from **partisan politics**—politics in support of a particular party. The U.S. Commission on Civil Rights, which was created in 1957, is a case in point. Congress wanted to protect the work of the commission from the influences not only of Congress's own political interests but also of the president. The Central Intelligence Agency (CIA), which was formed in 1947, is another good example. Both Congress and the president know that the intelligence activities of the CIA could be abused if it were not independent. Finally, the General

independent executive agency A federal agency that is not located within a cabinet department.

partisan politics Political actions or decisions that benefit a particular party.

Table 13–1

Executive Departments

DEPARTMENT (Year of Original Establishment)		PRINCIPAL DUTIES	SELECTED SUBAGENCIES
State (1789)		Negotiates treaties; develops our foreign policy; protects citizens abroad.	Passport Services Office; Bureau of Diplomatic Security; Foreign Service; Bureau of Human Rights and Humanitarian Affairs; Bureau of Consular Affairs.
Treasury (1789)		Pays all federal bills; borrows money; collects federal taxes; mints coins and prints paper currency; supervises national banks.	Internal Revenue Service; U.S. Mint.
Defense (1789)*		Manages the armed forces (Army, Navy, Air Force, Marines); operates military bases.	National Security Agency; Joint Chiefs of Staff; Departments of the Air Force, Navy, Army; Defense Intelligence Agency; the service academies.
Justice (1789)†		Furnishes legal advice to the president; enforces federal criminal laws; supervises the federal corrections system (prisons).	Federal Bureau of Investigation; Drug Enforcement Administration; Bureau of Prisons; U.S. Marshals Service.
Interior (1849)		Supervises federally owned lands and parks; operates federal hydroelectric power facilities; supervises Native American affairs.	U.S. Fish and Wildlife Service; National Park Service; Bureau of Indian Affairs; Bureau of Land Management.
Agriculture (1889)		Provides assistance to farmers and ranchers; conducts research to improve agricultural efficiency and to prevent plant disease; works to protect forests from fires and disease.	Soil Conservation Service; Agricultural Research Service; Food Safety and Inspection Service; Federal Crop Insurance Corporation; Forest Service.
Commerce (1903)‡		Grants patents and trademarks; conducts national census; monitors the weather; protects the interests of businesses.	Bureau of the Census; Bureau of Economic Analysis; Minority Business Development Agency; Patent and Trademark Office; National Oceanic and Atmospheric Administration.

Table 13–1

Executive Departments—(Continued)

DEPARTMENT (Year of Original Establishment)		PRINCIPAL DUTIES	SELECTED SUBAGENCIES
Labor (1903)[‡]		Administers federal labor laws; promotes the interests of workers.	Occupational Safety and Health Administration; Bureau of Labor Statistics; Employment Standards Administration; Employment and Training Administration.
Health and Human Services (1953)[§]		Promotes public health; enforces pure food and drug laws; sponsors health-related research.	Food and Drug Administration; Centers for Disease Control and Prevention; National Institutes of Health; Administration for Children and Families; Centers for Medicare and Medicaid Services.
Housing and Urban Development (1965)		Is concerned with the nation's housing needs; develops and rehabilitates urban communities; oversees resale of mortgages.	Government National Mortgage Association; Office of Multifamily Housing Development; Office of Single Family Program Development; Office of Fair Housing and Equal Opportunity.
Transportation (1967)		Finances improvements in mass transit; develops and administers programs for highways, railroads, and aviation.	Federal Aviation Administration; Federal Highway Administration; National Highway Traffic Safety Administration; Federal Transit Administration.
Energy (1977)		Promotes the conservation of energy and resources; analyzes energy data; conducts research and development.	Office of Civilian Radioactive Waste Management; National Nuclear Security Administration; Energy Information Administration.
Education (1979)		Coordinates federal programs and policies for education; administers aid to education; promotes educational research.	Office of Special Education and Rehabilitation Services; Office of Elementary and Secondary Education; Office of Postsecondary Education; Office of Vocational and Adult Education.
Veterans Affairs (1989)		Promotes the welfare of veterans of the U.S. armed forces.	Veterans Health Administration; Veterans Benefits Administration; National Cemetery Administration.
Homeland Security (2002)		Works to prevent terrorist attacks within the United States, control America's borders, and minimize the damage from potential attacks and natural disasters.	U.S. Customs and Border Protection; U.S. Citizenship and Immigration Services; U.S. Coast Guard; Secret Service; Federal Emergency Management Agency.

*Established in 1947 by merging the Department of War, created in 1789, and the Department of the Navy, created in 1798.
†Formerly the Office of the Attorney General; renamed and reorganized in 1870.
‡Formed in 1913 by splitting the Department of Commerce and Labor, which was created in 1903.
§Formerly the Department of Health, Education, and Welfare; renamed when the Department of Education was spun off in 1979.

JOIN THE DEBATE

Should the Attorney General Be Independent of the President?

The attorney general is a member of the president's cabinet. As such, he or she is nominated by the president and must be approved by the Senate before taking office. Traditionally, the attorney general has been a close political ally of the president. Ronald Reagan and Jimmy Carter both named reliable cronies to head up the Justice Department. Richard Nixon's attorney general John Mitchell was even sentenced to prison for corrupt politicization of his office. George W. Bush's attorney general Alberto Gonzales deferred completely to the White House. One result was a politically motivated "midnight massacre" during which eight U.S. attorneys were fired supposedly for purely partisan reasons.

Is it right for the attorney general to be so close to the president? What if it becomes necessary to investigate members of the president's own administration? Shouldn't the nation's chief law enforcement officer be independent and nonpartisan? One way to accomplish this would be to remove the attorney general position from the president's cabinet and appoint that official for a fixed term of years that transcends the term of any one president. That is exactly what we have done with the position of Federal Bureau of Investigation (FBI) director, so why not do it with the position of attorney general?

Yes, Let's Make the Attorney General Independent

We do not need another attorney general like Alberto Gonzales or John Mitchell. Any president needs a personal attorney, but that official should be a member of the White House staff, not the head of the Justice Department. Presidents appoint FBI directors for a fixed term of ten years, which ensures that directors do not serve under a single president. If the FBI director wants to be reappointed, the director must consider that the president making the reappointment could belong to either political party. In the same way, if the attorney general were removed from the cabinet and appointed to a fixed term, the attorney general would have less political allegiance to any one president.

The attorney general should not be the handmaiden of presidential policy. The attorney general should be able to give the White House frank, independent advice whenever the administration is considering actions that might overreach the bounds of what is permitted by law. We should stop allowing our president to appoint cronies to such an important position.

We Don't Want a Nonpolitical Attorney General

Those who accept the current situation argue that we don't want a nonpolitical attorney general. We elect a president based on his or her policy proposals. We expect the agenda of the Justice Department to reflect the policies that got the president elected. If the president is an advocate of civil liberties, those who elected the president expect the attorney general to reflect this position. If a president has made a strong commitment to reduce illegal immigration, voters expect the attorney general to follow through on this pledge.

The comparison with an independent FBI director is not valid. The FBI director is in charge of the closest thing we have to a national police force. We obviously do not want that position to be politicized. The attorney general is a different type of creature. The president should be able to name an attorney general whose views reflect the president's.

For Critical Analysis ***If a president does not like what the attorney general is doing, does the president have any recourse?***

Services Administration (GSA) was created as an independent executive agency in 1949 to provide services and office space for most federal agencies. To serve all parts of the government, it has to be an independent agency.

independent regulatory agency A federal organization that is responsible for creating and implementing rules that regulate private activity and protect the public interest in a particular sector of the economy.

Among the more than two hundred independent executive agencies, a few stand out in importance either because of the mission they were established to accomplish or because of their large size. We list selected independent executive agencies in Table 13–2 on page 290.

Independent Regulatory Agencies

Independent regulatory agencies are responsible for a specific type of public policy. Their function is to create and implement rules that regulate private activity and protect the public interest in a particular sector of the economy. They are sometimes called the "alphabet soup"

Figure 13–3

The Organization of the Department of Agriculture

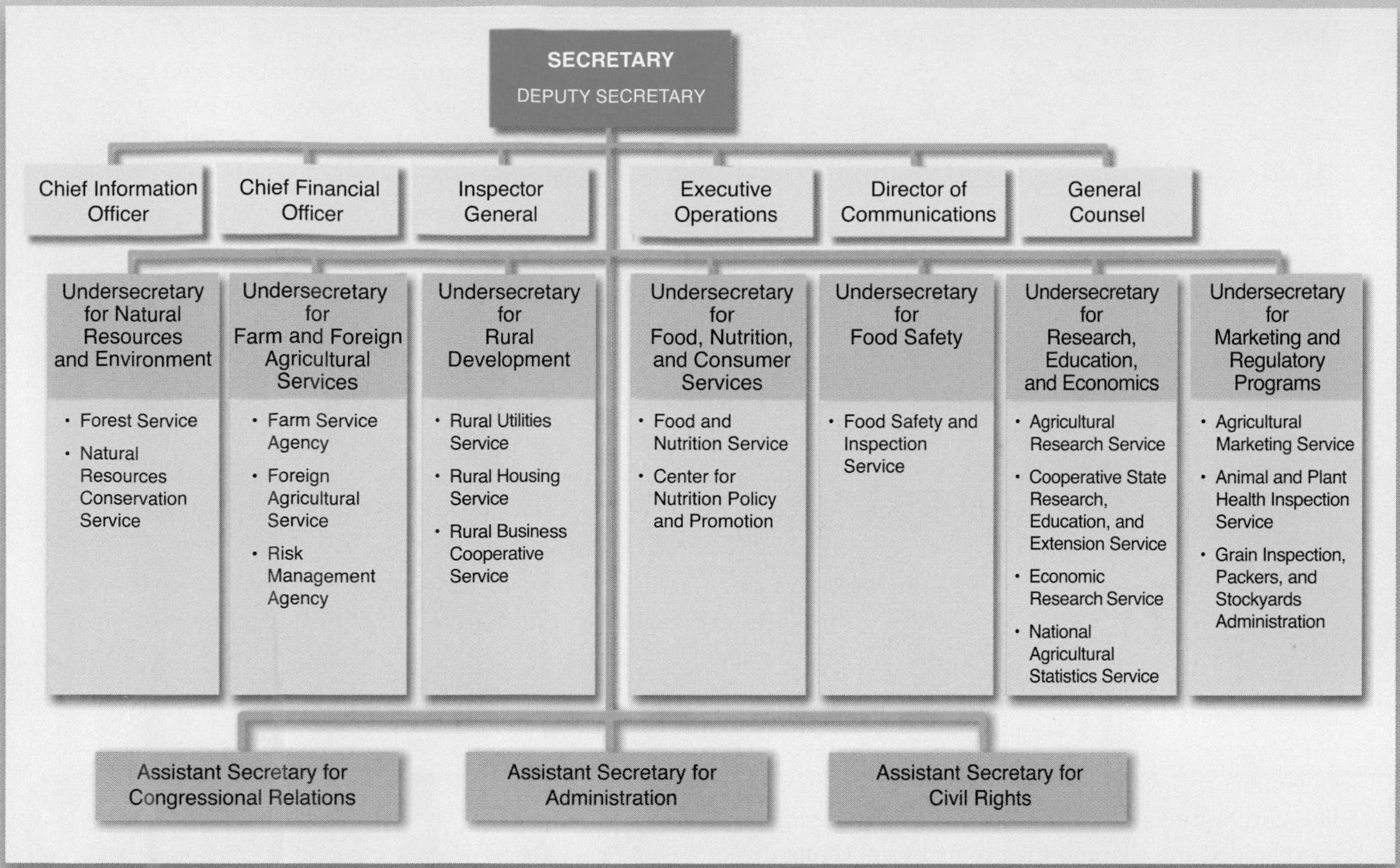

SECRETARY
DEPUTY SECRETARY

- Chief Information Officer
- Chief Financial Officer
- Inspector General
- Executive Operations
- Director of Communications
- General Counsel

Undersecretary for Natural Resources and Environment
- Forest Service
- Natural Resources Conservation Service

Undersecretary for Farm and Foreign Agricultural Services
- Farm Service Agency
- Foreign Agricultural Service
- Risk Management Agency

Undersecretary for Rural Development
- Rural Utilities Service
- Rural Housing Service
- Rural Business Cooperative Service

Undersecretary for Food, Nutrition, and Consumer Services
- Food and Nutrition Service
- Center for Nutrition Policy and Promotion

Undersecretary for Food Safety
- Food Safety and Inspection Service

Undersecretary for Research, Education, and Economics
- Agricultural Research Service
- Cooperative State Research, Education, and Extension Service
- Economic Research Service
- National Agricultural Statistics Service

Undersecretary for Marketing and Regulatory Programs
- Agricultural Marketing Service
- Animal and Plant Health Inspection Service
- Grain Inspection, Packers, and Stockyards Administration

- Assistant Secretary for Congressional Relations
- Assistant Secretary for Administration
- Assistant Secretary for Civil Rights

Source: *United States Government Manual*, 2009–2010 (Washington, D.C.: U.S. Government Printing Office, 2010).

Attorney General Eric Holder, Jr., heads the Department of Justice. Some believe that the attorney general should be insulated from partisan politics, much like the director of the FBI.

DOUG MILLS/THE NEW YORK TIMES/REDUX

of government because most such agencies are known in Washington by their initials.

One of the earliest independent regulatory agencies was the Interstate Commerce Commission (ICC), established in 1887. (This agency was abolished in 1995.) After the ICC was formed, other agencies were created to regulate aviation (the Civil Aeronautics Board, or CAB, which was abolished in 1985), communication (the Federal Communications Commission, or FCC), the stock market (the Securities and Exchange Commission, or SEC), and many other areas of business. Table 13–3 on page 291 lists some major independent regulatory agencies.

Government Corporations

Another form of federal bureaucratic organization is the **government corporation,** a business that is owned by the

government corporation
An agency of the government that is run as a business enterprise. Such agencies engage primarily in commercial activities, produce revenues, and require greater flexibility than most government agencies receive.

Table 13–2

Selected Independent Executive Agencies

Name	Date Formed	Principal Duties
Central Intelligence Agency (CIA)	1947	Gathers and analyzes political and military information about foreign countries so that the United States can improve its own political and military status; conducts covert operations outside the United States.
General Services Administration (GSA)	1949	Purchases and manages property of the federal government; acts as the business arm of the federal government, overseeing federal government spending projects; discovers overcharges in government programs.
National Science Foundation (NSF)	1950	Promotes scientific research; provides grants to all levels of schools for instructional programs in the sciences.
Small Business Administration (SBA)	1953	Promotes the interests of small businesses; provides low-cost loans and management information to small businesses.
National Aeronautics and Space Administration (NASA)	1958	Responsible for the U.S. space program, including building, testing, and operating space vehicles.
Environmental Protection Agency (EPA)	1970	Undertakes programs aimed at reducing air and water pollution; works with state and local agencies to fight environmental hazards.
Social Security Administration (SSA)*	1995	Manages the government's Social Security programs, including Retirement and Survivors Insurance, Disability Insurance, and Supplemental Security Income.

*Separated from the Department of Health and Human Services in 1979 that year; originally established in 1946.

government. Government corporations are not exactly like corporations in which you buy stock, become a shareholder, and share in the profits by collecting dividends. The U.S. Postal Service is a government corporation, but it does not sell shares. If a government corporation loses money in the course of doing business, taxpayers, not shareholders, foot the bill.

Government corporations are like private corporations in that they provide a service that could be handled by the private sector. They are also like private corporations in that they charge for their services, though sometimes they charge less than private-sector corporations charge for similar services. Table 13–4 on the facing page lists selected government corporations.

A number of intermediate forms of organization exist that fall between a government corporation and a private one. In some circumstances, the government can take control of a private corporation. When a company goes bankrupt, for example, it is subject to the supervision of a federal judge until it exits from bankruptcy or is liquidated. The government can purchase stock in a private corporation—the government used this technique to funnel funds into major banks during the financial crisis that began in September 2008. The government can also set up a corporation and sell stock to the public.

The Federal Home Loan Mortgage Corporation (Freddie Mac) and the Federal National Mortgage Association (Fannie Mae) are examples of stockholder-

Homeland Security Secretary Janet Napolitano.

SHAWN THEW/EPA /LANDOV

Table 13–3

Selected Independent Regulatory Agencies

Name	Date Formed	Principal Duties
Federal Reserve System (Fed)	1913	Determines policy with respect to interest rates, credit availability, and the money supply.
Federal Trade Commission (FTC)	1914	Works to prevent businesses from engaging in unfair trade practices and to stop the formation of monopolies in the business sector; protects consumers' rights.
Securities and Exchange Commission (SEC)	1934	Regulates the nation's stock exchanges, where shares of stocks are bought and sold; requires full disclosure of the financial profiles of companies that wish to sell stocks and bonds to the public.
Federal Communications Commission (FCC)	1934	Regulates interstate and international communications by radio, television, wire, satellite, and cable.
National Labor Relations Board (NLRB)	1935	Protects employees' rights to join unions and to bargain collectively with employers; attempts to prevent unfair labor practices by both employers and unions.
Equal Employment Opportunity Commission (EEOC)	1964	Works to eliminate discrimination that is based on religion, gender, race, color, national origin, age, or disability; examines claims of discrimination.
Nuclear Regulatory Commission (NRC)	1974	Ensures that electricity-generating nuclear reactors in the United States are built and operated safely; regularly inspects operations of such reactors.

owned government-sponsored enterprises. Fannie Mae (founded in 1938) and Freddie Mac (created in 1970) buy, resell, and guarantee home mortgages. In September 2008, the government placed the two businesses into a conservatorship—effectively a bankruptcy overseen by the Federal Housing Finance Agency instead of a federal judge. The government also took an 80 percent share of the stock of each firm. Fannie Mae and Freddie Mac had become examples of almost every possible way that the government can intervene in a private company.

Table 13–4

Selected Government Corporations

Name	Date Formed	Principal Duties
Tennessee Valley Authority (TVA)	1933	Operates a Tennessee River control system and generates power for a seven-state region and for U.S. aeronautics and space programs; promotes the economic development of the Tennessee Valley region; controls floods and promotes the navigability of the Tennessee River.
Federal Deposit Insurance Corporation (FDIC)	1933	Insures individuals' bank deposits up to $250,000* and oversees the business activities of banks.
Export/Import Bank of the United States (Ex/Im Bank)	1933	Promotes American-made goods abroad; grants loans to foreign purchasers of American products.
National Railroad Passenger Corporation (AMTRAK)	1970	Provides a national and intercity rail passenger service network; controls more than 23,000 miles of track with about 505 stations.
U.S. Postal Service (formed from the old U.S. Post Office department—the Post Office itself is older than the Constitution)	1971	Delivers mail throughout the United States and its territories. Is the largest government corporation.

*This limit, previously $100,000, was raised in October 2008 in response to the financial crisis of that year.

LO3 How Bureaucrats Get Their Jobs

As already noted, federal bureaucrats holding top-level positions are appointed by the president and confirmed by the Senate. These bureaucrats include department and agency heads, their deputy and assistant secretaries, and so on. The list of positions that are filled by appointments is published after each presidential election in a document called *Policy and Supporting Positions*. The volume is more commonly known as the "Plum Book," because the eight thousand jobs it summarizes are known as "political plums." Normally, these jobs go to those who supported the winning presidential candidate.

The rank-and-file bureaucrats—the rest of the federal bureaucracy—are part of the **civil service** (nonmilitary employees of the government). They obtain their jobs through the Office of Personnel Management (OPM), an agency established by the Civil Service Reform Act of 1978. The OPM recruits, interviews, and tests potential government workers and determines who should be hired. The OPM makes recommendations to individual agencies as to which persons meet relevant standards (typically, the top three applicants for a position), and the agencies then generally decide which of the recommended individuals it will hire. The 1978 act also created the Merit Systems Protection Board (MSPB) to oversee promotions, employees' rights, and other employment matters. The MSPB evaluates charges of wrongdoing, hears employee appeals from agency decisions, and can order corrective action against agencies and employees.

The idea that the civil service should be based on a merit system dates back more than a century. The Civil Service Reform Act of 1883 established the principle of government employment on the basis of merit through open, competitive examinations. Initially, only about 10 percent of federal employees were covered by the merit system. Today, more than 90 percent of the federal civil service is recruited on the basis of merit. Are public employees paid as well as workers in the private sector? For a discussion of this question, see this chapter's *Perception versus Reality* feature on the facing page.

civil service Nonmilitary government employees.

legislative rule An administrative agency rule that carries the same weight as a statute enacted by a legislature.

enabling legislation A law enacted by a legislature to establish an administrative agency. Enabling legislation normally specifies the name, purpose, composition, and powers of the agency being created.

LAWRENCE MIGDALE/STONE/GETTY

LO4 Regulatory Agencies: Are They the Fourth Branch of Government?

In Chapter 2, we considered the system of checks and balances among the three branches of the U.S. government—executive, legislative, and judicial. Recent history, however, shows that it may be time to regard the regulatory agencies as a fourth branch of the government. Although the U.S. Constitution does not mention regulatory agencies, these agencies can and do make **legislative rules** that are as legally binding as laws passed by Congress. With such powers, this administrative branch has an influence on the nation's businesses that rivals that of the president, Congress, and the courts. Indeed, most Americans do not realize how much of our "law" is created by regulatory agencies.

Regulatory agencies have been on the American political scene since the nineteenth century, but their golden age came during the regulatory explosion of the 1960s and 1970s. Congress itself could not have overseen the actual implementation of all of the laws that it was enacting at that time to control pollution and deal with other social problems. It therefore chose (and still chooses) to delegate to administrative agencies the tasks involved in implementing its laws. By delegating some of its authority to an administrative agency, Congress may indirectly monitor a particular area in which it has passed legislation without becoming bogged down in the details relating to the enforcement of that legislation—details that are often best left to specialists. In recent years, the government has been hiring increasing numbers of specialists to oversee its regulatory work.

Agency Creation

To create a federal administrative agency, Congress passes **enabling legislation,** which specifies the name, purpose, composition, and

PERCEPTION VERSUS REALITY

Working for the Government at Low Pay

Most parents do not jump for joy at the thought of their children going to work for the government. Government work in general in the United States has never been considered the road to riches. Indeed, the common picture of government employment is quite negative.

The Perception

It is often assumed that only individuals working in the private sector can hope to receive large paychecks. Even a member of Congress makes far less than most operations officers in midlevel corporations. Top-level staff members in the executive branch of the federal government also make much less than senior executives in the private sector. (This disparity is not really due to low pay for federal executives—it exists because the salaries of private-sector executives have skyrocketed in recent years.) Although even rank-and-file workers in the public sector receive paid-for medical insurance and a generous retirement program, the perception is that these benefits do not make up for the lower pay they earn.

The Reality

The Employee Benefit Research Institute has discovered that overall compensation costs for state and local governments are almost 50 percent higher than for private-sector employers. A recent study showed that a typical hour's work costs state and local governments $26 in wages and salaries, plus more than $13 in benefits. For that same hour of work, on average, a private-sector employer pays only about $19 in wages and salaries, plus $8 in benefits.

Move now to the federal government. The U.S. Bureau of Economic Analysis estimates that federal civilian government workers earn an average of $123,049 a year in total compensation (salaries plus benefits), which is twice the $61,051 in compensation for the average private-sector worker. This is one reason why Washington, D.C.—which is loaded with federal employees—is the fourth richest among this nation's 360 metropolitan areas. The gap between federal and private wages appears to have grown in recent years. Public-sector workers also enjoy pay bonuses amounting to 30 percent more than the bonuses received in the private sector. In addition, federal civil service rules bestow lifetime job security in the sense that it is extremely difficult to fire a federal employee.

One reason why government workers are paid so well is that, on average, they don't do exactly the same kind of work as employees in the private sector. When federal and private salaries are compared on an occupation-by-occupation basis, some of the income disparity goes away. Of course, if many federal employees have jobs that are also well paid in the private sector, that is another reality that contradicts the negative myths concerning government employment.

Blog On Arguments that government employees are overpaid are a constant theme of conservative blogs. Warren Meyer's Coyote Blog pays more attention to the topic than most. Visit it at **www.coyoteblog.com/coyote_blog/government**. The magazine *Government Executive* is a good place to find out how government employees, especially ones in the defense and technological fields, feel about their work. See it at **www.govexec.com.**

powers of the agency being created. The Federal Trade Commission (FTC), for example, was created in 1914 by the Federal Trade Commission Act, as mentioned earlier. The act prohibits unfair and deceptive trade practices. The act also describes the procedures that the agency must follow to charge persons or organizations with violations of the act, and it provides for judicial review of agency orders.

Other portions of the act grant the agency powers to "make rules and regulations for the purpose of carrying out the Act," to conduct investigations of business practices, to obtain reports on business practices from interstate corporations, to investigate possible violations of federal antitrust statutes, to publish findings of its investigations, and to recommend new legislation. The act also empowers the FTC to hold trial-like hearings and to **adjudicate** (formally resolve) certain kinds of disputes that involve FTC regulations or federal antitrust laws. When adjudication takes place, within the FTC or any other regulatory agency, an administrative law judge (ALJ) conducts the hearing and, after weighing

adjudicate To render a judicial decision. In regard to administrative law, it is the process in which an administrative law judge hears and decides issues that arise when an agency charges a person or firm with violating a law or regulation enforced by the agency.

the evidence presented, issues an *order*. Unless it is overturned on appeal, the ALJ's order becomes final.

Enabling legislation makes the regulatory agency a potent organization. For example, the Securities and Exchange Commission (SEC) imposes rules regarding the disclosures a company must make to those who purchase its stock. Under its enforcement authority, the SEC also investigates and prosecutes alleged violations of these regulations. Finally, the SEC sits as judge and jury in deciding whether its rules have been violated and, if so, what punishment should be imposed on the offender (although the judgment may be appealed to a federal court).

Rulemaking

A major function of a regulatory agency is **rulemaking**—the formulation of new regulations. The power that an agency has to make rules is conferred on it by Congress in the agency's enabling legislation. For example, the Occupational Safety and Health Administration (OSHA) was authorized by the Occupational Safety and Health Act of 1970 to develop and issue rules governing safety in the workplace. Under this authority, OSHA has issued various safety standards. For example, OSHA deemed it in the public interest to issue a rule regulating the health-care industry to prevent the spread of certain diseases, including acquired immune deficiency syndrome (AIDS). The rule specified various standards—on how contaminated instruments should be handled, for instance—with which employers in that industry must comply. Agencies cannot just make a rule whenever they wish, however. Rather, they must follow certain procedural requirements, particularly those set forth in the Administrative Procedure Act of 1946.

Agencies must also make sure that their rules are based on substantial evidence and are not "arbitrary and capricious." Therefore, before proposing a new rule, an agency may engage in extensive investigation (through research, on-site inspections of the affected industry, surveys, and the like) to obtain data on the problem to be addressed by the rule. Based on this information, the agency may undertake a cost-benefit analysis of a new rule to determine whether its benefits outweigh its costs. For example, when issuing new rules governing electrical equipment, OSHA predicted that they would cost business $21.7 billion annually but would save 60 lives and eliminate 1,600 worker injuries a year. The agency also estimated that its safety equipment regulations for manufacturing workers would cost $52.4 billion, save 4 lives, and prevent 712,000 lost workdays because of injuries each year.

rulemaking The process undertaken by an administrative agency when formally proposing, evaluating, and adopting a new regulation.

neutral competency The application of technical skills to jobs without regard to political issues.

iron triangle A three-way alliance among legislators, bureaucrats, and interest groups to make or preserve policies that benefit their respective interests.

Don't get the idea that rulemaking is isolated from politics. As you will read shortly, bureaucrats work closely with members of Congress, as well as interest groups, when making rules.

Policymaking

Bureaucrats in federal agencies are expected to exhibit **neutral competency,** which means that they are supposed to apply their technical skills to their jobs without regard to political issues. In principle, they should not be swayed by the thought of personal or political gain. In reality, each independent agency and each executive department is interested in its own survival and expansion. Each is constantly battling the others for a larger share of the budget. All agencies and departments wish to retain or expand their functions and staffs. To do this, they must gain the goodwill of both the White House and Congress.

Although administrative agencies of the federal government are prohibited from directly lobbying Congress, departments and agencies have developed techniques to help them gain congressional support. Each organization maintains a congressional information office, which specializes in helping members of Congress by supplying any requested information and solving casework problems. For example, if a member of the House of Representatives receives a complaint from a constituent that his Social Security checks are not arriving on time, that member of Congress may go to the Social Security Administration and ask that something be done. Typically, requests from members of Congress receive immediate attention.

IRON TRIANGLES Analysts have determined that one way to understand the bureaucracy's role in policymaking is to examine the **iron triangle,** which is a three-way alliance among legislators (members of Congress), bureaucrats, and interest groups. (Iron triangles are also referred to as *subgovernments* or *policy communities*.) Presumably, the laws that are passed and the policies that are established benefit the interests of all three sides of the iron triangle. Iron triangles are well established in almost every part of the bureaucracy.

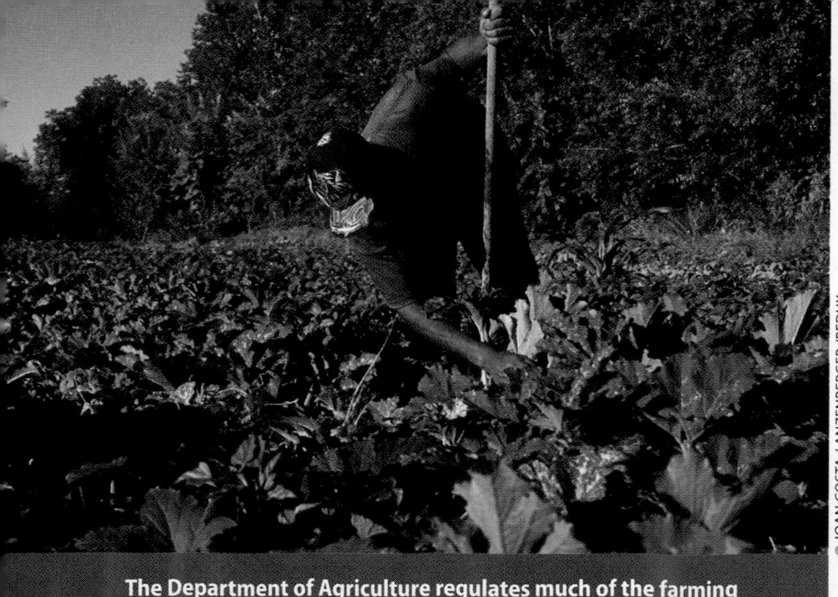

The Department of Agriculture regulates much of the farming sector.

AGRICULTURE AS AN EXAMPLE As an example, consider agricultural policy. Be aware first that the bureaucracy within the Department of Agriculture consists of more than 100,000 individuals working directly for the federal government and thousands of other individuals who work indirectly for the department as contractors, subcontractors, or consultants. Now think about the various interest groups and client groups that are concerned with what the bureaus and agencies in the Agriculture Department can do for them. Some of these groups are the American Farm Bureau Federation, the National Cattlemen's Beef Association, the National Milk Producers Federation, the National Corn Growers Association, and the various regional citrus growers associations. Finally, take a look at Congress, and you will see that two major committees are concerned with agriculture: the House Committee on Agriculture and the Senate Committee on Agriculture, Nutrition, and Forestry. Each committee has several specialized subcommittees.

The bureaucrats, interest groups, and legislators who make up this iron triangle cooperate to create mutually beneficial regulations and legislation. Because of the connections between agricultural interest groups and policymakers within the government, the agricultural industry has benefited greatly over the years from significant farm subsidies.

CONGRESS'S ROLE The Department of Agriculture is headed by the secretary of agriculture, who is nominated by the president (and confirmed by the Senate). But that secretary cannot even buy a desk lamp if Congress does not approve the appropriations for the department's budget. Within Congress, the responsibility for considering the Department of Agriculture's request for funding belongs first to the House and Senate appropriations committees and then to the agriculture subcommittees under them. The members of those subcommittees, most of whom represent agricultural states, have been around a long time and have their own ideas about what is appropriate for the Agriculture Department's budget. They carefully scrutinize the ideas of the president and the secretary of agriculture.

THE INFLUENCE OF INTEREST GROUPS The various interest groups—including producers of farm chemicals and farm machinery, agricultural cooperatives, grain dealers, and exporters—have vested interests in what the Department of Agriculture does and in what Congress lets the department do. Those interests are well represented by the lobbyists who crowd the halls of Congress. Many lobbyists have been working for agricultural interest groups for decades. They know the congressional committee members and Agriculture Department staff extremely well and routinely meet with them.

Issue Networks

The iron triangle relationship does not apply to all policy domains. When making policy decisions on environmental and welfare issues, for example, many members of Congress and agency officials rely heavily on "experts." Legislators and agency heads tend to depend on their staff members for specialized knowledge of rules, regulations, and legislation. These experts have frequently served variously as interest group lobbyists and as public-sector staff members during their careers, creating a revolving-door effect. They often have strong opinions and interests regarding the direction of policy and are thus able to exert a great deal of influence on legislators and bureaucratic agencies.

The relationships among these experts, which are less structured than iron triangles, are often referred to as **issue networks.** Like iron triangles, issue networks are made up of people with similar policy concerns. Issue networks are less interdependent and unified than iron triangles, however, and often include more players, such as media outlets.[3] (See Figure 13–4 on the following page.) A key characteristic of issue networks is that there can be more than one network in a given policy

issue networks Groups of individuals or organizations—which consist of legislators and legislative staff members, interest group leaders, bureaucrats, the media, scholars, and other experts—that support particular policy positions on a given issue.

Figure 13–4

Issue Network: The Environment

Executive Departments and Agencies
- Environmental Protection Agency
- Agriculture Department
- Energy Department
- Department of the Interior
- National Oceanic and Atmospheric Admin.
- Bureau of Land Management
- Army Corps of Engineers

Key Congressional Committees
- **Senate**
  Appropriations; Energy and Natural Resources; Environment and Public Works; Finance; Commerce, Science, and Transportation
- **House of Representatives**
  Agriculture; Appropriations; Natural Resources; Transportation and Infrastructure

Selected Interest Groups
- **Environmental Groups**
  Environmental Defense; Friends of the Earth; National Audubon Society; Clean Water Action; National Wildlife Federation; The Ocean Conservancy; American Forests
- **Industry Groups**
  Citizens for a Sound Economy; Edison Electric Institute; U.S. Chamber of Commerce; National Food Processors Association; International Wood Products Association; National Mining Association; American Resort Development Association

area. To take the example of the environment, one issue network tends to advocate greater environmental regulation, while another network opposes such regulations as undue burdens on businesses and landowners.

LO5 *Curbing Waste and Improving Efficiency*

There is no doubt that our bureaucracy is costly. There is also little doubt that at times it can be wasteful and inefficient. The government has made several attempts to reduce waste, inefficiency, and wrongdoing. For example, federal and state governments have passed laws requiring more openness in government. Other laws encourage employees to report any waste and wrongdoing that they observe.

Despite the difficulties involved in reforming the bureaucracy, our nation at least enjoys a civil service that is relatively impartial and free from corruption. This is not true of many nations. For example, Mexico, our immediate neighbor to the south, has had difficulties that would be almost unimaginable in the United States. We discuss that problem in this chapter's *The Rest of the World* feature on the facing page.

whistleblower In the context of government employment, someone who "blows the whistle" (reports to authorities) on gross governmental inefficiency, illegal action, or other wrongdoing.

Helping Out the Whistleblowers

The term **whistleblower,** as applied to the federal bureaucracy, has a special meaning: it is someone who blows the whistle, or reports, on gross governmental inefficiency, illegal activities, or other wrongdoing. Federal employees are often reluctant to blow the whistle on their superiors, however, for fear of reprisals.

LAWS PROTECTING WHISTLEBLOWERS To encourage federal employees to report government wrongdoing, Congress has passed laws to protect whistleblowers. The 1978 Civil Service Reform Act included some protection by prohibiting reprisals against whistleblowers by their superiors. The act set up the Merit Systems Protection Board as part of this protection. The Whistle-Blower Protection Act of 1989 authorized the Office of Special Counsel (OSC), an independent agency, to investigate complaints of reprisals against whistleblowers. Many federal agencies also have toll-free hotlines that employees can use to anonymously report bureaucratic waste and inappropriate behavior.

WHISTLEBLOWERS CONTINUE TO FACE PROBLEMS In spite of these laws, there is little evidence that whistleblowers are adequately protected against retaliation. According to a study conducted by the Government Accountability Office, 41 percent of the whistleblowers who turned to the OSC for protection during a recent three-year period reported that they were no longer employed by the agencies on which they blew the whistle. Indeed, given how difficult it is to fire a federal employee under normal circumstances, it is amazing how quickly most whistleblowers are "shown the door."

Many federal employees who have blown the whistle say that they would not do so again because it

THE REST OF THE WORLD

Mexico's Security Problem—The Drug Wars

The United States has 225 law enforcement officers for every 100,000 people. Mexico, in contrast, has 370 officers per 100,000 residents. You might think, then, that citizens of our neighbor to the south would enjoy even more personal security than we do in the United States. The reality is quite different. Crime rates in Mexico on average greatly exceed those in the United States.

Why? For one thing, the United States has far more effective, professional, and trustworthy police forces than Mexico. In addition, Mexico is fighting drug cartels that are also fighting each other. Drug cartel enforcers in Mexico have at their disposal the highest-grade, most sophisticated weapons available—almost all purchased in the United States and smuggled across the border. In September 2010, U.S. secretary of state Hillary Clinton characterized Mexico's drug violence as similar to an insurrection.

Estimates of drug cartel earnings range from $14 billion to $50 billion. With this wealth, the cartels have corrupted many of Mexico's customs agents, army commanders, and local police forces. For example, police in the city of Nuevo Laredo have reportedly participated in kidnapping members of the Gulf cartel and handing them over to the Zetas organization. The Zetas then hold them for ransom or torture them for information about drug deals. Mexico's Federal Investigative Agency (AFI) has 7,000 agents in total. Recently, almost 1,500 of these agents were under investigation, and 457 were facing criminal charges. Some agents were believed to work as enforcers for the Sinaloa cartel.[4]

The Mérida Initiative—U.S. Aid for What?

During the last few years, American taxpayers have provided the Mexican government with aid to combat drug trafficking under a program called the Mérida Initiative. Of the $1.4 billion in assistance, however, only about a third is targeted toward repairing Mexico's crumbling law enforcement and judicial systems. Much of the rest goes to equipment. The results have not been encouraging. Let's face it: buying attack helicopters with the funds (as the Mexican government has done) is not going to solve the drug-wars problem.

A House Cleaning

There are signs that some institutional reform may be taking place in Mexico. In the summer of 2009, the Mexican federal government fired all 700 customs agents, a group notorious for corruption and dereliction of duty, and replaced them with 1,400 new personnel. The new agents had to take drug tests and undergo scrutiny to make sure that they did not have criminal records. Seventy percent of the new agents have a college education, compared with only 10 percent of the old group. Customs agents are responsible for curbing the smuggling of arms into the country.

For Critical Analysis *Will it ever be possible to eradicate police corruption in Mexico when bribes can sometimes be ten to twenty times an average officer's annual salary? Why are the bribes so high?*

© DAVID FRANKLIN/ISTOCKPHOTO

was so difficult to get help, and even when they did, the experience was a stressful ordeal. Creating more effective protection for whistleblowers remains an ongoing goal of the government. The basic problem, though, is that most organizations, including federal government agencies, do not like to have their wrongdoings and failings exposed, especially by insiders.

Improving Efficiency and Getting Results

The Government Performance and Results Act, which went into effect in 1997, has forced the federal government to change the way it does business. Since 1997, virtually every agency (except the intelligence agencies) has had to describe its goals and methods for evaluating how well those goals are met. A goal of an agency could be as broad as lowering the number of highway traffic deaths or as narrow as reducing the number of times an agency's phone rings before it is answered.

As one example, consider the National Oceanic and Atmospheric Adminstration (NOAA). It improved the effectiveness of its short-term forecasting services, particularly in issuing warnings of tornadoes. The warning time has increased from seven to nine minutes. This may seem insignificant, but it provides additional critical time for those in the path of a tornado.

President Obama's contribution to the attempt to improve government effectiveness has been to create a chief performance officer. This individual reports directly to the president and works with other economic officials in an attempt to increase efficiency and eliminate waste in government.

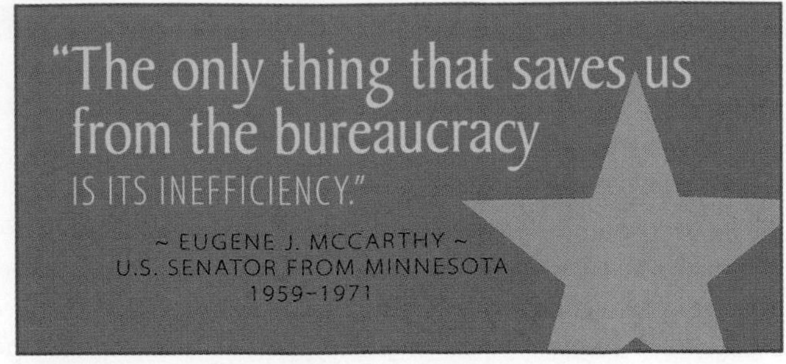

"The only thing that saves us from the bureaucracy
IS ITS INEFFICIENCY."
~ EUGENE J. MCCARTHY ~
U.S. SENATOR FROM MINNESOTA
1959–1971

Another Approach—Pay-for-Performance Plans

For some time, the private sector has used pay-for-performance plans as a means to increase employee productivity and efficiency. About one-third of the major firms in this country use some kind of alternative pay system, such as team-based pay, skill-based pay, profit-sharing plans, or individual bonuses. In contrast, workers for the federal government traditionally have received fixed salaries; promotions and salary increases are given on the basis of seniority, not output.

The federal government has been experimenting with pay-for-performance systems. For example, the U.S. Postal Service has implemented an Economic Value Added program, which ties bonuses to performance. As part of a five-year test of a new pay system, three thousand scientists working in Air Force laboratories received salaries based on actual results. Also, the Department of Veterans Affairs launched a skill-based pay project at its New York regional office.

Many hope that by offering such incentives, the government will be able to compete more effectively with the private sector for skilled and talented employees. Additionally, according to some, pay-for-performance plans will go a long way toward countering the entitlement mentality that has traditionally characterized employment within the bureaucracy.

Privatization

Another idea for reforming government bureaucracies is **privatization,** which means turning over certain types of government work to the private sector. Privatization can take place by contracting out (outsourcing) work to the private sector or by "managed competition," in which the task of providing public services is opened up to competition. In managed competition, both the relevant government agency and private firms can compete for the work. Vouchers are another way in which certain services traditionally provided by government, such as education, can be provided on the open market. The government pays for the vouchers, but the services are provided by the private sector.

State and local governments have been experimenting with privatization for some time. Virtually all of the states have privatized at least a few of their services, and some states, including California, Colorado, and Florida, have privatized more than one hundred activities formerly undertaken by government. In Scottsdale, Arizona, the city contracts for fire protection. In

privatization The transfer of the task of providing services traditionally provided by government to the private sector.

The federal government may pay for additional teaching help in some schools.

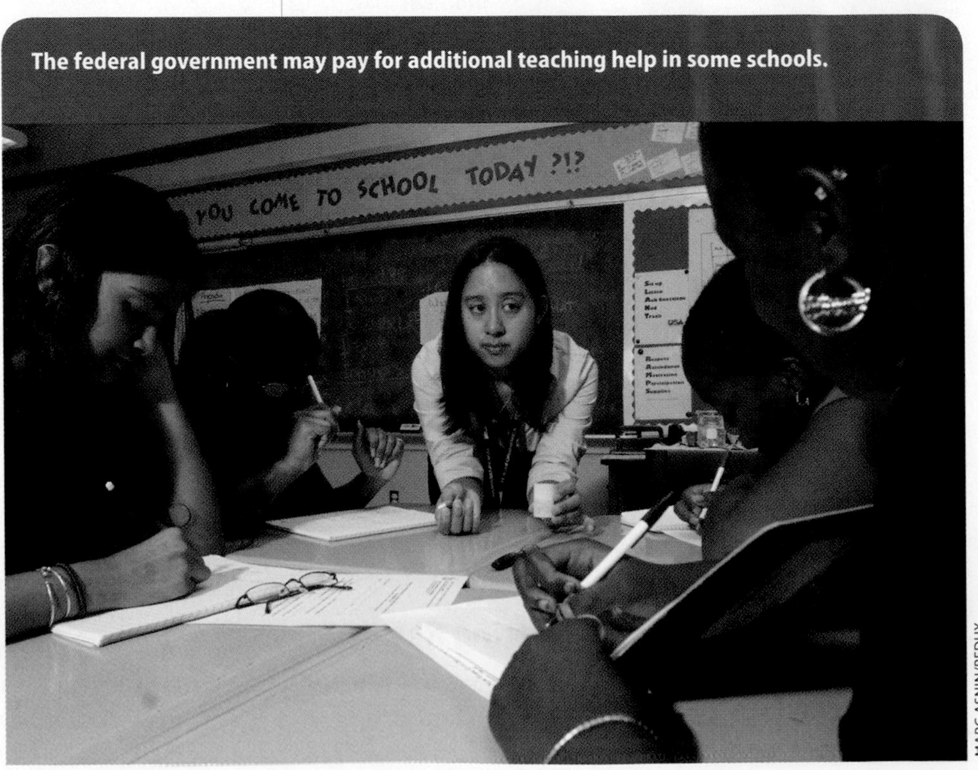

MARC ASNIN/REDUX

Baltimore, Maryland, nine of the city's schools are outsourced to private entities. In other cities, services ranging from janitorial work to management of recreational facilities are handled by the private sector.

Government in the Sunshine

The past four decades saw a trend toward more openness in government. The theory was that because Americans pay for the government, they own it—and they have a right to know what the government is doing with the taxpayers' dollars.

In response to pressure for more government openness and disclosure, Congress passed the Freedom of Information Act in 1966. This act requires federal agencies to disclose any information in agency files, with some exceptions, to any persons requesting it. Since the 1970s, "sunshine laws," which require government meetings to be open to the public, have been enacted at all levels of American government. During the Clinton administration (1993–2001), Americans gained even greater access to government information as federal and state agencies went online.

The trend toward greater openness in government came to an abrupt halt on September 11, 2001. In the wake of the terrorist attacks on the World Trade Center and the Pentagon, the government began tightening its grip on information. In the months following the attacks, hundreds of thousands of documents were removed from government Web sites.

No longer can the public access plans of nuclear power plants, descriptions of airline security violations, or maps of pipeline routes. Agencies were instructed to be more cautious about releasing information in their files and were given new guidelines on what should be considered public information. State and local agencies followed the federal government's lead. Some states barred access to such information as emergency preparedness evacuation plans. Others established commissions or panels whose activities are exempt from state sunshine laws. All in all, the Bush administration made it much more difficult to obtain information about the government than under previous administrations. During the 2008 presidential campaign, Barack Obama championed the restoration of open government. In practice, however, the Obama administration has shown little interest in pursuing this goal.

"BUREAUCRACY DEFENDS THE STATUS QUO long past the time when the QUO has lost its status."

~ LAURENCE J. PETER ~
AMERICAN EDUCATOR
1919–1990

An Expanding Bureaucracy

The Great Recession reached its crisis point on September 15, 2008, while George W. Bush was still president. As a result, the federal government took on substantial new responsibilities even before Barack Obama was sworn in as president. In early October 2008, Congress passed a $700 billion bank bailout bill. The key activity established by this legislation was the Troubled Asset Relief Program, or TARP. New federal staff members were required to administer this program. Oversight personnel were hired to inform Congress whether TARP funds were being loaned out or distributed wisely.

EXPANDED GOVERNMENT UNDER PRESIDENT OBAMA A series of legislative enactments in 2009 and 2010 swelled the rolls of the federal bureaucracy. The stimulus bill of February 2009 was followed by the federal takeover of two automobile manufacturers, Chrysler and General Motors. In March 2010, Congress passed health-care reform. The two reform bills were officially named the Patient Protection and Affordable Care Act and the Health Care and Education Reconciliation Act. Friends of reform shortened this mouthful to the Affordable Care Act. Conservative opponents—and irreverent journalists—dubbed it "Obamacare." Major new regulations covering the financial industry followed in July.

These and other expansions of federal authority had an impact on the bureaucracy. By the middle of 2010, almost every executive department of the federal government had more employees than in 2009. The increased staffing occurred even in departments that were not central to the new legislation. For example, the Department of Agriculture now had 111,987 employees, up from 108,018 in 2009. Across the executive branch, the number of new staff members totaled about 86,000, not counting those hired on a temporary basis to conduct the 2010 census. Layoffs by state and local governments, however, tended to counterbalance the expansion of the federal government as the recession continued to slash state tax receipts.

A NEW SPIRIT IN CONGRESS The 2010 elections dramatically changed the composition of Congress. The new legislators were conspicuously hostile to "big government" and unlikely to support major new programs. As one example, in 2009 the Democrats advocated massive changes to the nation's energy system to reduce the amount of carbon dioxide (CO_2) emitted by American industry. CO_2 emissions are believed to be a major cause of global warming. The bill in question died in the Senate, however, and there seemed to be no chance that any important legislation on this topic could pass the new Congress. The federal government remained on course to hire new bureaucrats to administer programs already created, but additional expansion of the government was no longer on the table.

AMERICA AT **ODDS** *The Bureaucracy*

Although the story is often told about red tape and wasteful spending generated by our bureaucracy, all in all, the U.S. bureaucracy compares favorably with bureaucracies in other countries. Citizens typically overestimate the amount of "government waste" by very large margins. Still, the U.S. government faces the same problems with its bureaucracy—sluggishness, inefficiency, and even incompetence—that large businesses and organizations throughout the country also face. The major difference is the size and scope of the U.S. bureaucracy—and the effect that its actions can have on the daily lives of all Americans. Americans are at odds over a number of issues relating to the bureaucracy, including the following:

- Can new financial regulations eliminate the danger of a catastrophe such as the one we experienced in September 2008—or will clever financiers find ways around any new regulations?
- Do the recent health-care reforms provide vital protection to the citizenry—or are they an example of excessive government meddling in the private sector?
- Are government employees overpaid—or is their pay appropriate given their responsibilities?
- Is the contracting-out of governmental services a way to improve efficiency—or does it mostly serve to hide the true cost and scope of government?
- Should our leaders focus on openness and transparency in government—or are such measures dangerous during the war on terrorism?

Take Action

Although this chapter's focus is on the federal bureaucracy, realize that all levels of government require bureaucracies to implement their goals. In virtually every community, however, there are needs that government agencies cannot meet. Often, agencies simply lack the funds to hire more personnel or to provide assistance to those in need. To help address these needs, many Americans do volunteer work. If you want to take action in this way, check with your local government offices and find out which agencies or offices have volunteer programs. Volunteer opportunities on the local level can range from helping the homeless and mentoring children in a local school to joining a local environmental clean-up effort. Decide where your interests lie, and consider volunteering your time in a local bureaucracy.

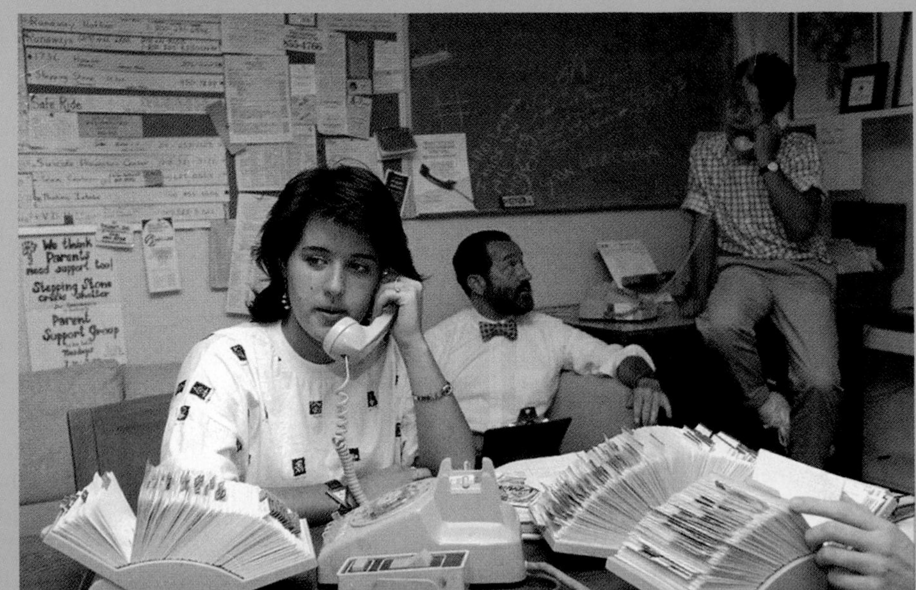

AP PHOTO/LENNOX MCLENDON

Volunteers answer hotlines that teenagers can call when they need help. Many volunteers at such hotline services have found this type of work especially rewarding.

POLITICS ON THE WEB

- For information on the government, including the Web sites for federal agencies, go to the federal government's "gateway" Web site at **www.usa.gov**
- The Web site of the Office of Management and Budget offers information on increasing the government's efficiency—and, of course, on the federal budget. You can access the OMB at **www.whitehouse.gov/omb**
- To learn more about the mission of the General Services Administration (GSA) and its role in managing the federal bureaucracy, go to **www.gsa.gov**
- If you want to see an example of what federal agencies are putting on the Web, you can go to the Department of Commerce's Web site at **www.commerce.gov**
- The *Federal Register* is the official publication for executive-branch documents. This publication, which includes the orders, notices, and rules of all federal administrative agencies, is online at **www.gpoaccess.gov/fr**
- The *United States Government Manual* contains information on the functions, organization, and administrators of every federal department. You can access the most recent edition of the manual online at **www.gpoaccess.gov/gmanual**

Access CourseMate to review and expand on this chapter through quizzes, flashcards, learning objectives, interactive timelines, a crossword puzzle, audio summaries, video, critical-thinking activities, simulations, and more.

GOVT 14

The Judiciary

LEARNING OBJECTIVES

LO1 Summarize the origins of the American legal system and the basic sources of American law.

LO2 Delineate the structure of the federal court system.

LO3 Indicate how federal judges are appointed.

LO4 Explain how the federal courts make policy.

LO5 Describe the role of ideology and judicial philosophies in judicial decision making.

LO6 Identify some of the criticisms of the federal courts and some of the checks on the power of the courts.

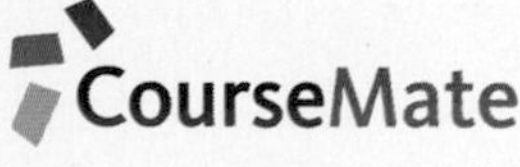

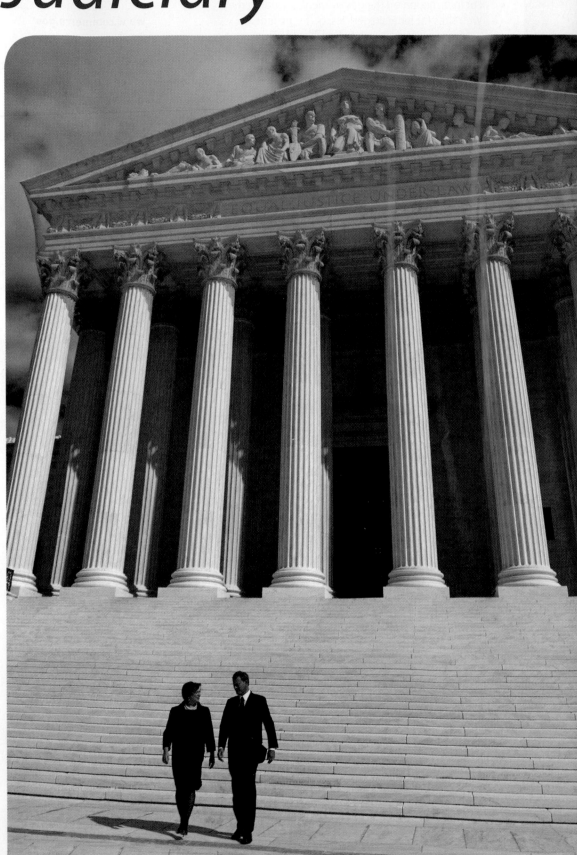

AMERICA AT ODDS

Are There Prisoners We Must Detain without Trial?

After the September 11, 2001, attacks in the United States, the George W. Bush administration interred hundreds of suspected terrorists at the Guantánamo Bay Naval Base in Cuba. Most of them were foreign fighters captured during the war in Afghanistan, a war initiated just after 9/11. A few suspected terrorists from elsewhere ended up at Guantánamo as well. All prisoners were labeled *unlawful enemy combatants* and therefore were afforded neither the legal protections guaranteed to prisoners of war (POWs) under the Geneva Conventions nor the protections required under the conventions for dealing with civilians who commit crimes. Indeed, the Bush administration established the prison at Guantánamo in the belief that the facility would lie outside the reach of American law. President Barack Obama promised to close the Guantánamo prison, but he has failed to do so. Obama furthermore stated that it may be necessary to hold some of the detainees more or less forever without bringing them to trial. There are those who object to this policy, but many who agree with it.

We Release Terrorists at the Civilized World's Peril

Look back over U.S. history. Federal judges never heard cases brought by Confederate prisoners of war held during the Civil War. During World War II, no civilian courts reviewed the cases of the thousands of German prisoners housed in the United States. At the end of that war, the Supreme Court agreed that enemy aliens held by the United States in Europe and Asia had no right to appear in front of an American judge.

Today, if the president deems that certain terrorist prisoners are too dangerous to be tried and perhaps freed, that is the president's prerogative. After all, under our Constitution, the president has wartime decision-making powers. We also have evidence that at least thirty detainees released from the Guantánamo prison rejoined terrorist organizations and have been responsible for the deaths of innocent people overseas.

Who will be responsible for the deaths caused by terrorists if they cannot be convicted and we then let them go? Terrorists do not deserve the civil liberties we offer to fellow Americans. If we cannot be sure that a trial will result in a conviction, we must not let these people stand trial at all.

Indefinite Detention Is Unconstitutional and Damages Our Image Abroad

It is wrong to hold persons deemed "dangerous" by the government indefinitely. How can we know that the government is correct in its allegations against these people? We have learned that some of the Afghans held at Guantánamo and elsewhere were arrested due to false accusations resulting from long-standing feuds between rival families. U.S. officials were reluctant to release these innocents because it meant admitting that the officials had made a mistake.

The way our government has handled prisoners of war (POWs) in the past is irrelevant. Traditional POWs were picked up during battle, on the field, in uniform. The potential for picking up a POW by mistake was minimal. In contrast, the danger of error when picking up an alleged unlawful enemy combatant is enormous. Most of the Guantánamo detainees were arrested nowhere near a battlefield. How can we know whether such detainees are truly dangerous if there is no trial? Furthermore, as the blog site Digby's Hullabaloo puts it: "There are literally tens of thousands of potential terrorists all over the world who could theoretically harm America. We cannot protect ourselves from that possibility by keeping the handful we have in custody locked up forever."

WHERE DO YOU STAND?

1. **Could Congress fashion a law providing a procedure to determine when an alleged terrorist should never be let out of prison? Could such a law withstand Supreme Court review?[1] Why or why not?**
2. **Why is it easier to falsely arrest a purported terrorist than a regular military soldier?**

EXPLORE THIS ISSUE ONLINE

- **The editorial page of the *Wall Street Journal* favors indefinite detention. One of the strongest voices on that page has been John Yoo, who served in President Bush's Justice Department when the detention policies were crafted. You'll find some of Yoo's articles if you perform a Google search on "john yoo wall street journal."**
- **Two of the many bloggers who oppose indefinite detentions are Digby and Glenn Greenwald. You can find their work at digbysblog.blogspot.com and www.salon.com/opinion/greenwald. Digby writes on many topics, and you may need to search his site using "terrorism."**

> "It is confidence IN THE MEN AND WOMEN WHO ADMINISTER THE JUDICIAL SYSTEM that is the true backbone of the rule of law."
>
> ~ JOHN PAUL STEVENS ~
> ASSOCIATE JUSTICE OF THE UNITED STATES SUPREME COURT
> 1975–2010

Introduction

As you read in this chapter's opening *America at Odds* feature, the question of whether certain alleged terrorists should be imprisoned indefinitely without trial has elicited a great deal of controversy. Also controversial is the policymaking function of the United States Supreme Court. After all, when the Court renders an opinion on how the Constitution is to be interpreted, it is, necessarily, making policy on a national level. To understand the nature of this controversy, you first need to understand how the **judiciary** (the courts) functions in this country. We begin by looking at the origins and sources of American law. We then examine the federal court system, at the apex of which is the United States Supreme Court, and consider various issues relating to the courts.

LO1 *The Origins and Sources of American Law*

The American colonists brought with them the legal system that had developed in England over hundreds of years. Thus, to understand how the American legal system operates, we need to go back in time to the early English courts and the traditions they established.

The Common Law Tradition

After the Normans conquered England in 1066, William the Conqueror and his successors began the process of unifying the country under their rule. One of the methods they used was the establishment of the "king's courts," or *curiae regis*. Before the Norman Conquest, disputes had been settled according to the local legal customs and traditions in various regions of the country. The law developed in the king's courts, however, applied to the country as a whole. What evolved in these courts was the beginning of the **common law**—a body of general rules that was applied throughout the entire English realm. Trial by jury is a famous part of the common law tradition. Juries are less common outside the English-speaking world, but some countries with different legal traditions have begun to introduce them, as you will learn in this chapter's *The Rest of the World* feature on the facing page.

THE RULE OF PRECEDENT The early English courts developed the common law rules from the principles underlying judges' decisions in actual legal controversies. Judges attempted to be consistent, and whenever possible, they based their decisions on the principles applied in earlier cases. They sought to decide similar cases in a similar way and considered new kinds of cases with care, because they knew that their decisions would make new law. Each interpretation became part of the law on the subject and served as a legal **precedent**—that is, a decision that furnished an example or authority for deciding subsequent cases involving identical or similar legal principles or facts.

U.S. attorneys are appointed by the president with the advice and consent of the Senate. They serve under the direction of the attorney general.

AP PHOTO/DENNIS COOK

judiciary The courts; one of the three branches of government in the United States.

common law The body of law developed from judicial decisions in English and U.S. courts, not attributable to a legislature.

precedent A court decision that furnishes an example or authority for deciding subsequent cases involving identical or similar facts and legal issues.

THE REST OF THE WORLD

Jury Trials Introduced in Asian Courts

The U.S. Constitution provides for jury trials in Article III and in the Bill of Rights, so most of us take jury trials for granted. Yet juries do not exist in most parts of the world, including many democracies. The right to a jury trial for a criminal defendant seems so obvious that it's hard for us to imagine how greatly the United States differs from many other countries on this issue.

South Korea and Japan Take the Plunge

Until 2008, South Korea had never had a jury trial in a criminal case. The first one was held in the small city of Taegu. It concerned a twenty-seven-year-old man who was charged with the petty criminal offenses of assault and trespass. A dozen South Korean citizens aided the presiding judge. The jury found the defendant guilty.

Until that moment in South Korean judicial history, no one in that country could have imagined that citizens without legal training and with no accountability could decide the fate of a criminal defendant. The South Korean jury system is similar to that in the United States, but with some modifications. The more complex the case, the more jurors there are. Also, jury verdicts are based on majority vote rather than on unanimous decisions, as required in almost all American criminal cases. Finally, at least for the next few years, the vote of the jurors is not binding on the judge.

In 2009, Japan reinstated trials by jury after a sixty-five-year absence. The first individual to be tried under the new system was a seventy-two-year-old man who had confessed to stabbing a neighbor. A panel of ordinary citizens stood in judgment of the accused, alongside professional judges. Despite Japan's tradition of deferring to authority, the citizen judges participated actively, cross-examining the accused and the victim's son. The audience at the trial exceeded two thousand people.

Why the Sudden Desire to Have Jury Trials?

In Japan, those who are prosecuted are almost inevitably convicted—the conviction rate is over 99 percent. Confessions, made in police custody without a lawyer present, are very common. A spate of executions of persons later found to be innocent led to demands for a new system.

Legal scholars analyzing the trend toward jury trials in Asia point out several additional reasons why they are now becoming more common. One is that many of these countries have opened themselves up to a growing influence from the United States.

Another explanation is that some formerly authoritarian countries that are now democracies believe that juries might be a way to foster stronger democratic values. Juries seem to serve as a check on governmental power. They build trust in legal institutions.

For Critical Analysis *In many jurisdictions in the United States, the defendant can waive his or her right to a jury trial. Why might a defendant waive this important right?*

This Japanese judicial officer is attempting to explain the use of juries at a seminar organized by that country's Justice Ministry.

AP PHOTO/KATSUMI KASAHARA

The practice of deciding new cases with reference to former decisions, or precedents, eventually became a cornerstone of the English and American judicial systems. The practice forms a doctrine called ***stare decisis*** ("to stand on decided cases"). Under this doctrine, judges are obligated to follow the precedents established in their jurisdictions. For example, if the Supreme Court of Georgia holds that a state law requiring candidates for state office to pass drug tests is unconstitutional, that decision will control the outcome of future cases on that issue brought before the state

stare decisis A common law doctrine under which judges normally are obligated to follow the precedents established by prior court decisions. Pronounced *ster*-ay dih-*si*-sis.

courts in Georgia. Similarly, a decision on a given issue by the United States Supreme Court (the nation's highest court) is binding on all inferior (lower) courts. For example, if the Georgia case on drug testing is appealed to the United States Supreme Court and the Court agrees that the Georgia law is unconstitutional, the high court's ruling will be binding on *all* courts in the United States. In other words, similar drug-testing laws in other states will be invalid and unenforceable.

DEPARTURES FROM PRECEDENT Sometimes a court will depart from the rule of precedent if it decides that a precedent is simply incorrect or that technological or social changes have rendered the precedent inapplicable. Cases that overturn precedent often receive a great deal of publicity. For example, in 1954, in *Brown v. Board of Education of Topeka,*[2] the United States Supreme Court expressly overturned precedent when it concluded that separate educational facilities for African Americans, which had been upheld as constitutional in many earlier cases under the "separate-but-equal" doctrine[3] (see Chapter 5), were inherently unequal and violated the equal protection clause. The Supreme Court's departure from precedent in *Brown* received a tremendous amount of publicity as people began to realize the political and social ramifications of this change in the law.

More recently, the Supreme Court departed from precedent when it held in a 2003 case, *Lawrence v. Texas,*[4] that a Texas sodomy law (see Chapter 5) violated the U.S. Constitution. In that case, the Court concluded that consensual sexual conduct, including homosexual conduct, was part of the liberty protected by the due process clause of the Fourteenth Amendment. This decision overturned the Court's established precedent on such laws—specifically, its ruling in *Bowers v. Hardwick,*[5] a 1986 case in which the Court upheld a Georgia sodomy statute.

"IT IS BETTER, so the Fourth Amendment teaches, THAT THE GUILTY SOMETIMES GO FREE than that citizens be subject to easy arrest."

~ WILLIAM O. DOUGLAS ~
ASSOCIATE JUSTICE OF THE UNITED STATES SUPREME COURT 1939–1975

primary source of law A source of law that establishes the law. Primary sources of law include constitutions, statutes, administrative agency rules and regulations, and decisions rendered by the courts.

constitutional law Law based on the U.S. Constitution and the constitutions of the various states.

statutory law The body of law enacted by legislatures (as opposed to constitutional law, administrative law, or case law).

Sources of American Law

In any governmental system, the primary function of the courts is to interpret and apply the law. In the United States, the courts interpret and apply several sources of law when deciding cases. We look here only at the **primary sources of law**—that is, sources that *establish* the law—and the relative priority of these sources when particular laws come into conflict.

CONSTITUTIONAL LAW The U.S. government and each of the fifty states have separate written constitutions that set forth the general organization, powers, and limits of their respective governments. **Constitutional law** consists of the rights and duties set forth in these constitutions.

The U.S. Constitution is the supreme law of the land. As such, it is the basis of all law in the United States. Any law that violates the Constitution is invalid and unenforceable. Because of the paramount importance of the U.S. Constitution in the American legal system, the complete text of the Constitution is found in Appendix B.

The Tenth Amendment to the U.S. Constitution reserves to the states and to the people all powers not granted to the federal government. Each state in the union has its own constitution. Unless they conflict with the U.S. Constitution or a federal law, state constitutions are supreme within the borders of their respective states.

STATUTORY LAW Statutes enacted by legislative bodies at any level of government make up another source of law, which is generally referred to as **statutory law.** Federal statutes—laws enacted by the U.S. Congress—apply to all of the states. State statutes—laws enacted by state legislatures—apply only within the state that enacted the law. Any state statute that conflicts with the U.S. Constitution, with federal laws enacted by Congress, or with the state's constitution will be deemed invalid, if challenged in court, and will not be enforced. Statutory law also includes the ordinances (such as local zoning or housing-construction laws) passed by cities and counties, none of which can violate the U.S.

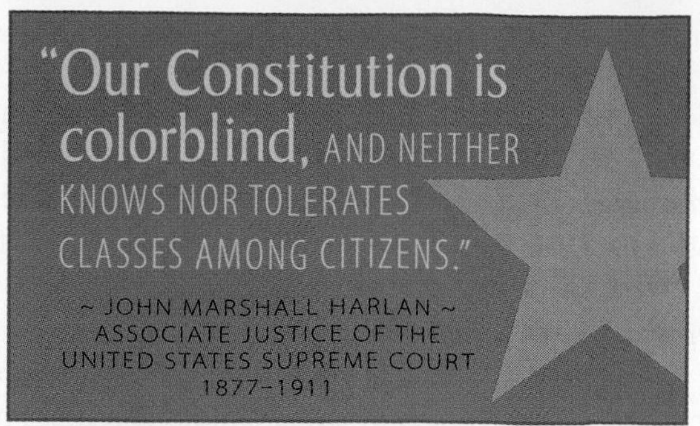

Constitution, the relevant state constitution, or any existing federal or state laws.

ADMINISTRATIVE LAW Another important source of American law consists of **administrative law**—the rules, orders, and decisions of administrative agencies. As you read in Chapter 13, at the federal level, Congress creates executive agencies, such as the Food and Drug Administration and the Environmental Protection Agency, to perform specific functions. Typically, when Congress establishes an agency, it authorizes the agency to create rules that have the force of law and to enforce those rules by bringing legal actions against violators. Rules issued by various government agencies now affect virtually every aspect of our economy. For example, almost all of a business's operations, including the firm's capital structure and financing, its hiring and firing procedures, its relations with employees and unions, and the way it manufactures and markets its products, are subject to government regulation.

Government agencies exist at the state and local levels as well. States commonly create agencies that parallel federal agencies. Just as federal statutes take precedence over conflicting state statutes, federal agency regulations take precedence over conflicting state regulations.

CASE LAW As is evident from the earlier discussion of the common law tradition, another basic source of American law consists of the rules of law announced in court decisions, or **case law.** These rules of law include interpretations of constitutional provisions, of statutes enacted by legislatures, and of regulations issued by administrative agencies. Thus, even though a legislature passes a law to govern a certain area, how that law is interpreted and applied depends on the courts. The importance of case law, or judge-made law, is one of the distinguishing characteristics of the common law tradition.

Civil Law and Criminal Law

All of the sources of law just discussed can be classified in other ways as well. One of the most significant classification systems divides all law into two categories: civil law and criminal law. **Civil law** spells out the duties that individuals in society owe to other persons or to their governments, excluding the duty not to commit crimes. Typically, in a civil case, a private party sues another private party (although the government can also sue a party for a civil law violation). The object of a civil lawsuit is to make the defendant—the person being sued—comply with a legal duty (such as a contractual promise) or pay money damages for failing to comply with that duty.

Criminal law, in contrast, has to do with wrongs committed against the public as a whole. Criminal acts are prohibited by local, state, or federal government statutes. Thus, criminal defendants are prosecuted by public officials, such as a district attorney (D.A.), on behalf of the government, not by their victims or other private parties. In a criminal case, the government seeks to impose a penalty (a fine and/or imprisonment) on a person who has violated a criminal law. For example, when someone robs a convenience store, that person has committed a crime and, if caught and proved guilty, will normally spend time in prison.

Basic Judicial Requirements

A court cannot decide just any issue at any time. Before a court can hear and decide a case, specific requirements must be met. To a certain extent, these requirements act as restraints on the judiciary because they limit the types of cases that courts can hear and decide. Courts also have procedural requirements that frame the judicial process.

JURISDICTION In Latin, *juris* means "law," and *diction* means "to speak." Therefore, **jurisdiction** literally refers to the power "to speak the law." Jurisdiction applies either to the geographic area in which a court has the right and power to decide

administrative law The body of law created by administrative agencies (in the form of rules, regulations, orders, and decisions) in order to carry out their duties and responsibilities.

case law The rules of law announced in court decisions. Case law includes the aggregate of reported cases that interpret judicial precedents, statutes, regulations, and constitutional provisions.

civil law The branch of law that spells out the duties that individuals in society owe to other persons or to their governments, excluding the duty not to commit crimes.

criminal law The branch of law that defines and governs actions that constitute crimes. Generally, criminal law has to do with wrongful actions committed against society for which society demands redress.

jurisdiction The authority of a court to hear and decide a particular case.

cases, or to the right and power of a court to decide matters concerning certain persons, types of property, or subjects. Before any court can hear a case, it must have jurisdiction over the person against whom the suit is brought, the property involved in the suit, and the subject matter.

A state trial court, for example, usually has jurisdictional authority over the residents of a particular area of the state, such as a county or district. (A **trial court** is, as the term implies, a court in which a trial is held and testimony taken.) A state's highest court (often called the state supreme court)[6] has jurisdictional authority over all residents within the state. In some cases, if an individual has committed an offense such as injuring someone in an automobile accident or selling defective goods within the state, the court can exercise jurisdiction even if the individual is a resident of another state. State courts can also exercise jurisdiction over people who do business within the state. A New York company that distributes its products in California, for example, can be sued by a California resident in a California state court.

Because the federal government is a government of limited powers, the jurisdiction of the federal courts is limited. Article III, Section 2, of the Constitution states that the federal courts can exercise jurisdiction over all cases "arising under this Constitution, the Laws of the United States, and Treaties made, or which shall be made, under their Authority." Whenever a case involves a claim based, at least in part, on the U.S. Constitution, a treaty, or a federal law, a federal question arises. Any lawsuit involving a **federal question** can originate in a federal court.

Federal courts can also exercise jurisdiction over cases involving **diversity of citizenship.** Such cases may arise when the parties in a lawsuit live in different states or when one of the parties is a foreign government or a foreign citizen. Before a federal court can take jurisdiction in a diversity case, the amount in controversy must be more than $75,000.

STANDING TO SUE To bring a lawsuit before a court, a person must have **standing to sue,** or a sufficient "stake" in the matter to justify bringing a suit. Thus, the party bringing the suit must have suffered a harm or been threatened with a harm by the action at issue, and the issue must be justiciable. A **justiciable controversy** is one that is real and substantial, as opposed to hypothetical or academic.

The requirement of standing clearly limits the issues that can be decided by the courts. Furthermore, both state and federal governments can specify by law when an individual or group has standing to sue. Variations in state laws have led to some interesting consequences. In New York State, for example, to have standing to sue a lawyer for making a mistake on a legal document, you must be the person who hired the lawyer. As a result, if an attorney makes a mistake when drafting a will, the beneficiaries have no standing to sue. In 2009, a New

trial court A court in which trials are held and testimony taken.

federal question A question that pertains to the U.S. Constitution, acts of Congress, or treaties. A federal question provides a basis for federal court jurisdiction.

diversity of citizenship A basis for federal court jurisdiction over a lawsuit that arises when (1) the parties in the lawsuit live in different states or when one of the parties is a foreign government or a foreign citizen, and (2) the amount in controversy is more than $75,000.

standing to sue The requirement that an individual must have a sufficient stake in a controversy before he or she can bring a lawsuit. The party bringing the suit must demonstrate that he or she has either been harmed or been threatened with a harm.

justiciable controversy A controversy that is not hypothetical or academic but real and substantial; a requirement that must be satisfied before a court will hear a case. *Justiciable* is pronounced jus-*tish*-a-bul.

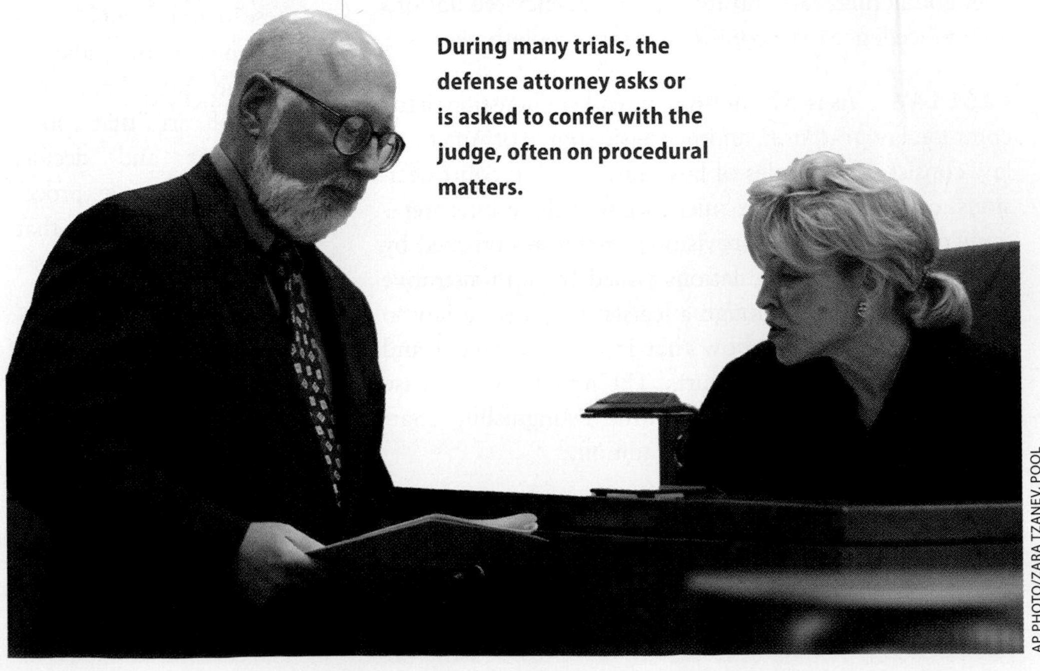

During many trials, the defense attorney asks or is asked to confer with the judge, often on procedural matters.

AP PHOTO/ZARA TZANEV, POOL

Figure 14–1

The Organization of the Federal Court System

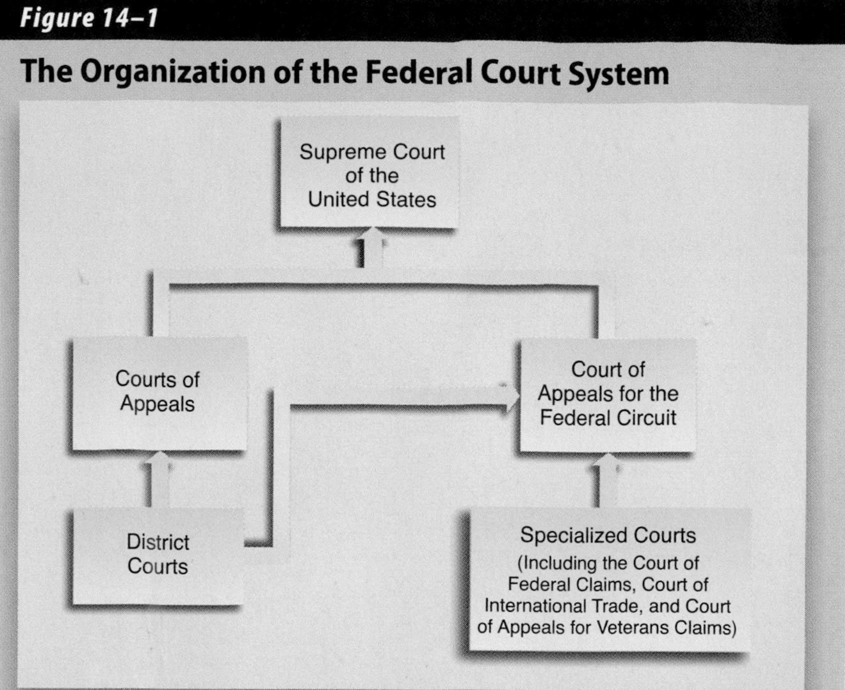

Note: Some specialized courts, such as the Tax Court, are not included in this figure.

York lawyer did in fact make a mistake that cost the beneficiaries of a will millions of dollars, and a state judge affirmed the lawyer's immunity. The court ruled that the only person with standing was the deceased, who was obviously not going to sue anyone.

In complete contrast, the California legislature has placed no restrictions whatsoever on who has standing to file a suit seeking the appointment of a guardian for children. As a result, in 2009, Paul Petersen, a former child actor and head of a child advocacy group called A Minor Consideration, was able to proceed with a lawsuit calling for a guardian to protect the children of Nadya Suleman even though Petersen had no connection at all with the Suleman family. Suleman, also known as the "Octomom," gave birth to octuplets at a time when she was already the mother of six children. Suleman was single, unemployed, and receiving public assistance, and her fitness as a parent was widely questioned in the media.

COURT PROCEDURES Both the federal and the state courts have established procedural rules that apply in all cases. These procedures are designed to protect the rights and interests of the parties, ensure that the litigation proceeds in a fair and orderly manner, and identify the issues that must be decided by the court—thus saving court time and costs. Different procedural rules apply in criminal and civil cases. Generally, criminal procedural rules attempt to ensure that defendants are not deprived of their constitutional rights.

Parties involved in civil or criminal cases must comply with court procedural rules or risk being held in contempt of court. A party who is held in contempt of court can be fined, taken into custody, or both. A court must take care to ensure that the parties—and the court itself—comply with procedural requirements. Procedural errors often serve as grounds for a mistrial or for appealing the court's decision to a higher tribunal.

LO2 *The Federal Court System*

The federal court system is a three-tiered model consisting of U.S. district courts (trial courts), U.S. courts of appeals, and the United States Supreme Court. Figure 14–1 above shows the organization of the federal court system.

Bear in mind that the federal courts constitute only one of the fifty-two court systems in the United States. Each of the fifty states has its own court system, as does the District of Columbia. No two state court systems are exactly the same, but usually each state has different levels, or tiers, of courts, just as the federal system does. Generally, state courts deal with questions of state law, and the decisions of a state's highest court on matters of state law are normally final. If a federal question is involved, however, a decision of a state supreme court may be appealed to the United States Supreme Court. We will discuss the federal court system in the pages that follow.

U.S. District Courts

On the lowest tier of the federal court system are the U.S. district courts, or federal trial courts—the courts in which cases involving federal laws begin. The cases in these courts are decided by a judge or a jury (if it is a jury trial). There is at least one federal district court in every state, and there is one in the District of Columbia. The number of judicial districts varies over time, primarily owing to population changes and corresponding caseloads. Currently, there are ninety-four judicial districts. Figure 14–2 on the following page shows their

Figure 14–2

U.S. Courts of Appeals and U.S. District Courts

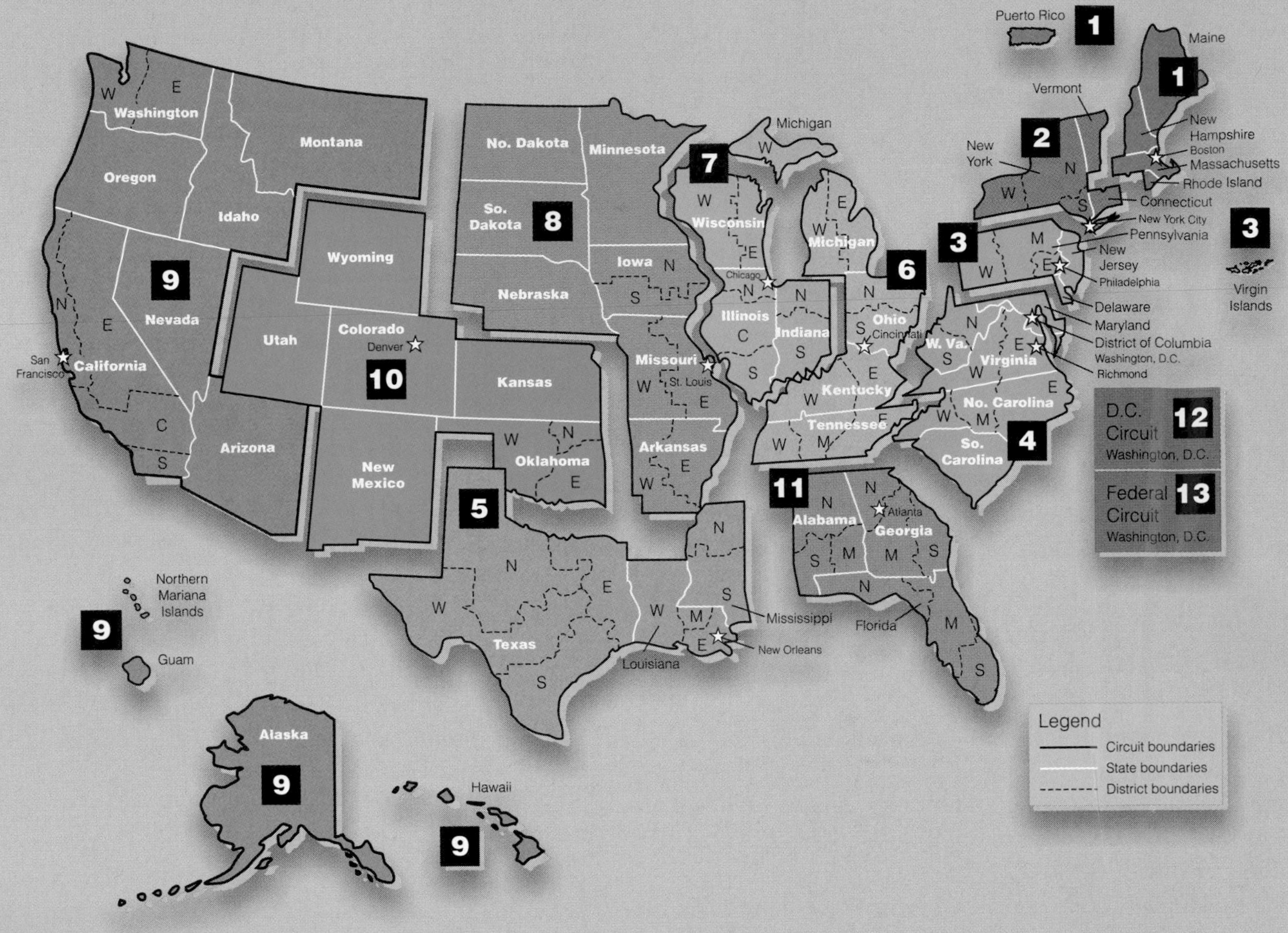

Source: Administrative Office of the United States Courts.

geographic boundaries. The federal system also includes other trial courts, such as the Court of International Trade and others shown in Figure 14–1 on the previous page. These courts have limited, or specialized, subject-matter jurisdiction—that is, they can exercise authority only over certain kinds of cases.

appellate court A court having appellate jurisdiction. An appellate court normally does not hear evidence or testimony but reviews the transcript of the trial court's proceedings, other records relating to the case, and attorneys' arguments as to why the trial court's decision should or should not stand.

U.S. Courts of Appeals

On the middle tier of the federal court system are the U.S. courts of appeals. Courts of appeals, or **appellate courts,** do not hear evidence or testimony. Rather, an appellate court reviews the transcript of the trial court's proceedings, other records relating to the case, and attorneys' arguments as to why the trial court's decision should or should not stand. In contrast to a trial court, where normally a single judge presides, an appellate court consists of a panel of three or more judges. The task of the appellate court is to determine whether the trial court erred in applying the law to the facts and issues involved in a particular case.

There are thirteen federal courts of appeals in the United States. The courts of appeals for twelve of the circuits, including the Court of Appeals for the D.C. Circuit, hear appeals from the U.S. district courts located within their respective judicial circuits (see Figure 14–2 above). Decisions made by federal administrative agencies can in some cases be appealed directly to the U.S. courts of appeals. The Court of Appeals for the Federal Circuit has national jurisdiction over certain types of cases, such as those concerning patent law and some claims against the national government.

The decisions of the federal appellate courts may be appealed to the United States Supreme Court. If a decision is not appealed, or if the high court declines to review the case, the appellate court's decision is final.

Figure 14–3

The Number of Supreme Court Opinions

The number of Supreme Court opinions peaked at 151 in the Court's 1982 term and declined more or less steadily through 1995 and then leveled off. During the 2009 term (ending in June 2010), the Court issued 92 opinions.

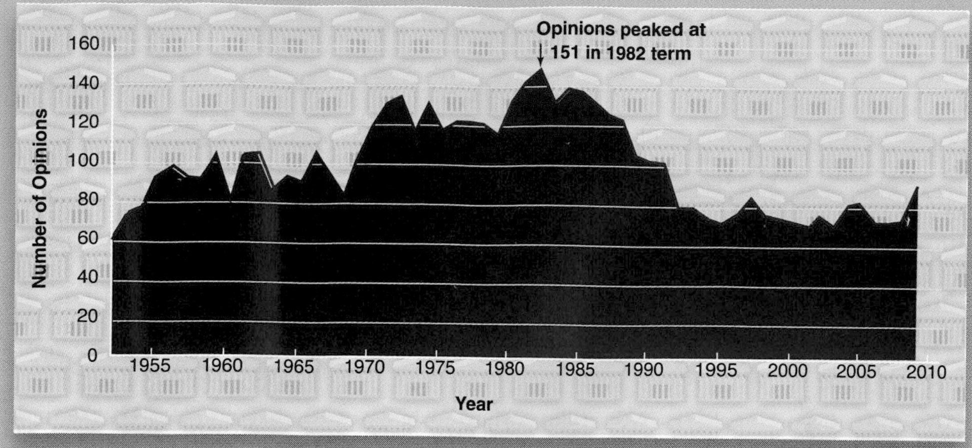

The United States Supreme Court

The highest level of the three-tiered model of the federal court system is the United States Supreme Court. According to Article III of the U.S. Constitution, there is only one national Supreme Court. Congress is empowered to create additional ("inferior") courts as it deems necessary. The inferior courts that Congress has created include the second tier in our model—the U.S. courts of appeals—as well as the district courts and any other courts of limited, or specialized, jurisdiction.

The United States Supreme Court consists of nine justices—a chief justice and eight associate justices—although that number is not mandated by the Constitution. The Supreme Court has original, or trial, jurisdiction only in rare instances (set forth in Article III, Section 2). In other words, only rarely does a case originate at the Supreme Court level. Most of the Court's work is as an appellate court. The Supreme Court has appellate authority over cases decided by the U.S. courts of appeals, as well as over some cases decided in the state courts when federal questions are at issue.

THE WRIT OF *CERTIORARI* To bring a case before the Supreme Court, a party may request that the Court issue a **writ of *certiorari,*** often called "cert.," which is an order that the Supreme Court issues to a lower court requesting the latter to send it the record of the case in question. Parties can petition the Supreme Court to issue a writ of *certiorari,* but whether the Court will do so is entirely within its discretion. The Court will not issue a writ unless at least four of the nine justices approve. In no instance is the Court required to issue a writ of *certiorari.*[7]

Most petitions for writs of *certiorari* are denied. A denial is not a decision on the merits of a case, nor does it indicate that the Court agrees with a lower court's opinion. Furthermore, the denial of a writ has no value as a precedent. A denial simply means that the decision of the lower court remains the law within that court's jurisdiction.

WHICH CASES REACH THE SUPREME COURT? There is no absolute right to appeal to the United States Supreme Court. Although thousands of cases are filed with the Supreme Court each year, on average the Court hears fewer than one hundred. As Figure 14–3 above shows, the number of cases heard by the Court each year has declined significantly since the 1980s. In large part, this has occurred because the Court has raised its standards for accepting cases in recent years.

Typically, the Court grants petitions for cases that raise important policy issues that need to be addressed. In its 2009–2010 term, for example, the Court heard cases involving such pressing issues as the following:

- Whether long-standing campaign finance laws violate the First Amendment free speech rights of corporations and labor unions. (The Court determined that they did.)[8]
- Whether state and local governments are bound to recognize the right to bear arms as an individual right,

writ of *certiorari* An order from a higher court asking a lower court for the record of a case. *Certiorari* is pronounced sur-shee-uh-*rah*-ree.

and not as a right that is limited to state militias. (The Court ruled that state and local governments are so bound.)[9]

- Whether juveniles who commit crimes in which no one is killed may be sentenced to life in prison without the possibility of parole. (The Court found that they may not.)[10]

If the lower courts have rendered conflicting opinions on an important issue, the Supreme Court may review one or more cases involving that issue to define the law on the matter. For example, in 2002 the Court agreed to review two cases raising the issue of whether affirmative action programs (see Chapter 5) violate the equal protection clause of the Constitution. Different federal appellate courts had reached conflicting opinions on this issue.

SUPREME COURT OPINIONS Like other appellate courts, the United States Supreme Court normally does not hear any evidence. The Court's decision in a particular case is based on the written record of the case and the written arguments (legal briefs) that the attorneys submit. The attorneys also present **oral arguments**—spoken arguments presented in person rather than on paper—to the Court, after which the justices discuss the case in **conference.** The conference is strictly private—only the justices are allowed in the room.

When the Court has reached a decision, the chief justice, if in the majority, assigns the task of writing the Court's **opinion** to one of the justices. When the chief justice is not in the majority, the most senior justice voting with the majority assigns the writing of the Court's opinion. The opinion outlines the reasons for the Court's decision, the rules of law that apply, and the judgment.

Often, one or more justices who agree with the Court's decision do so for reasons different from those outlined in the majority opinion. These justices may write **concurring opinions,** setting forth their own legal reasoning on the issue. Frequently, one or more justices disagree with the Court's conclusion. These justices may write **dissenting opinions,** outlining the reasons they feel the majority erred in arriving at its decision.

Although a dissenting opinion does not affect the outcome of the case before the Court, it may be important later. In a subsequent case concerning the same issue, a jurist or attorney may use the legal reasoning in the dissenting opinion as the basis for an argument to reverse the previous decision and establish a new precedent.

oral argument A spoken argument presented to a judge in person by an attorney on behalf of her or his client.

conference In regard to the Supreme Court, a private meeting of the justices in which they present their arguments concerning a case under consideration.

opinion A written statement by a court expressing the reasons for its decision in a case.

concurring opinion A statement written by a judge or justice who agrees (concurs) with the court's decision, but for reasons different from those in the majority opinion.

dissenting opinion A statement written by a judge or justice who disagrees with the majority opinion.

"AS NIGHTFALL DOESN'T COME AT ONCE, NEITHER DOES OPPRESSION. In both instances, . . . we must be aware of change in the air, however slight, lest we become unwitting victims of the darkness."

~ WILLIAM O. DOUGLAS ~
ASSOCIATE JUSTICE OF THE
UNITED STATES SUPREME COURT
1939–1975

LO3 *Federal Judicial Appointments*

Unlike state court judges, who are often elected, all federal judges are appointed. Article II, Section 2, of the Constitution authorizes the president to appoint the justices of the Supreme Court with the advice and consent of the Senate. Laws enacted by Congress provide that the same procedure is to be used for appointing judges to the lower federal courts as well.

Federal judges receive lifetime appointments (because under Article III of the Constitution they "hold their Offices during good Behaviour"). Federal judges may be removed from office through the impeachment process, but such proceedings are extremely rare and are usually undertaken only if a judge engages in blatantly illegal conduct, such as bribery. In the history of this nation, only thirteen federal judges have been

Table 14–1

Backgrounds of United States Supreme Court Justices through 2011

	Number of Justices (112 = Total)
Occupational Position before Appointment	
Private legal practice	25
State judgeship	21
Federal judgeship	31
U.S. attorney general	7
Deputy or assistant U.S. attorney general	2
U.S. solicitor general	3
U.S. senator	6
U.S. representative	2
State governor	3
Federal executive post	9
Other	3
Religious Affiliation	
Protestant	83
Roman Catholic	14
Jewish	7
Unitarian	7
No religious affiliation	1
Age on Appointment	
Under 40	5
41–50	33
51–60	60
61–70	14
Political Party Affiliation	
Federalist (to 1835)	13
Jeffersonian Republican (to 1828)	7
Whig (to 1861)	1
Democrat	46
Republican	44
Independent	1
Education	
College graduate	96
Not a college graduate	16
Gender	
Male	108
Female	4
Race	
White (non-Hispanic)	109
African American	2
Hispanic	1

Sources: *Congressional Quarterly's Guide to the U.S. Supreme Court* (Washington, D.C.: Congressional Quarterly Press, 1997); and authors' updates.

impeached, and only seven of them were removed from office. Normally, federal judges serve until they resign, retire, or die.

Although the Constitution sets no specific qualifications for those who serve on the Supreme Court, those who have done so share one characteristic: all have been attorneys. The backgrounds of the Supreme Court justices have been far from typical of the characteristics of the American public as a whole. Table 14–1 at left summarizes the backgrounds of all of the 112 United States Supreme Court justices through 2011.

The Nomination Process

The president receives suggestions and recommendations as to potential nominees for Supreme Court positions from various sources, including the Justice Department, senators, other judges, the candidates themselves, state political leaders, bar associations, and other interest groups. After selecting a nominee, the president submits her or his name to the Senate for approval. The Senate Judiciary Committee then holds hearings and makes its recommendation to the Senate, where it takes a majority vote to confirm the nomination.

SENATORIAL COURTESY When judges are nominated to the district courts (and, to a lesser extent, the U.S. courts of appeals), a senator of the president's political party from the state where there is a vacancy traditionally has been allowed to veto the president's choice. This practice is known as **senatorial courtesy.** At times, senatorial courtesy even permits senators from the opposing party to veto presidential choices. Because of senatorial courtesy, home-state senators of the president's party may be able to influence the choice of the nominee.

PARTISANSHIP It should come as no surprise that partisanship plays a significant role in the president's selection of nominees to the federal bench, particularly to the Supreme Court, the crown jewel of the federal judiciary. Traditionally, presidents have attempted to strengthen their legacies by appointing federal judges with political and philosophical views similar to their own. In the history of the Supreme Court, fewer than 13 percent of the justices nominated by a president have been from an opposing political party.

senatorial courtesy A practice that allows a senator of the president's party to veto the president's nominee to a federal court judgeship within the senator's state.

That said, presidents have often discovered that the justices they appointed took very different positions than expected. President Dwight D. Eisenhower (1953–1961), for example, had no idea when he appointed Chief Justice Earl Warren that Warren would seek to overturn the system of racial segregation. The Court accomplished this goal through rulings such as *Brown v. Board of Education* (see Chapter 5).[11]

COURTS OF APPEALS Appointments to the U.S. courts of appeals can also have a lasting impact. Recall that these courts occupy the level just below the Supreme Court in the federal court system. Also recall that the decisions rendered by these courts—about 60,000 per year—are final unless overturned by the Supreme Court. Given that the Supreme Court renders opinions in fewer than one hundred cases a year, the decisions of the federal appellate courts have a wide-reaching effect on American society. For example, a decision interpreting the federal Constitution by the U.S. Court of Appeals for the Ninth Circuit, if not overruled by the Supreme Court, establishes a precedent that will be followed in the states of Alaska, Arizona, California, Hawaii, Idaho, Montana, Nevada, Oregon, and Washington.

Confirmation or Rejection by the Senate

The president's nominations are not always confirmed. In fact, almost 20 percent of presidential nominations for the Supreme Court have been either rejected or not acted on by the Senate. The process of nominating and confirming federal judges, especially Supreme Court justices, often involves political debate and controversy. Many bitter battles over Supreme Court appointments have ensued when the Senate and the president have disagreed on political issues.

From 1893 until 1968, the Senate rejected only three Court nominees. From 1968 through 1986, however, two presidential nominees to the highest court were rejected, and two more nominations, both by President Ronald Reagan, failed in 1987. The most significant of these nominees was Robert Bork, who faced hostile questioning about his views on the Constitution during the confirmation hearings. The Bork hearings are often considered to be a turning point after which confirmation hearings became much more contentious.

One of President George H. W. Bush's nominees to the Supreme Court—Clarence Thomas—was also the subject of considerable controversy. The nation watched on television as Anita Hill, a former aide, leveled charges of sexual harassment at Thomas, who nevertheless was confirmed.

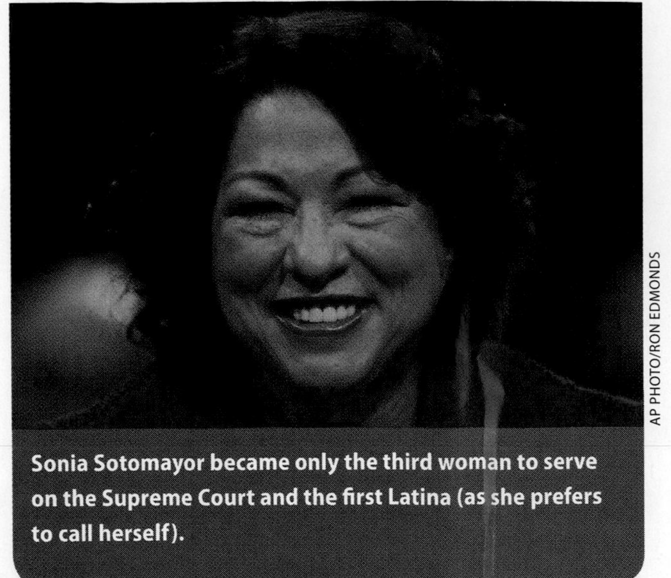

AP PHOTO/RON EDMONDS

Sonia Sotomayor became only the third woman to serve on the Supreme Court and the first Latina (as she prefers to call herself).

GEORGE W. BUSH'S APPOINTMENTS During George W. Bush's second term, Chief Justice William Rehnquist died, and Sandra Day O'Connor, the Court's first woman, retired. These events allowed Bush to nominate John G. Roberts, Jr., to replace Rehnquist and Samuel A. Alito, Jr., to replace O'Connor. Both nominations were confirmed by the Senate with relatively little difficulty. The appointment of Alito in particular changed the character of the Court, because he was distinctly more conservative than O'Connor.

OBAMA'S NOMINEES In May 2009, as a result of a judicial retirement, President Barack Obama named Sonia Sotomayor to the Court. Sotomayor had served for more than a decade as a judge of the U.S. Court of Appeals for the Second Circuit and was the first Hispanic woman ever nominated to the Supreme Court. Due to the large Democratic majority in the Senate, Sotomayor was confirmed without difficulty. Conservatives, however, turned up several statements she had made that they used to challenge the nomination. For example, Sotomayor had said that a "wise Latina woman" might, because of her background, be able to make better decisions in discrimination cases than a white man. On the basis of that remark, talk-show host Rush Limbaugh called Sotomayor a racist.

A second retirement gave Obama an additional chance to pick a nominee in May 2010. He chose Elena Kagan, his solicitor general. At her confirmation hearings, several Republicans seized on an incident that occurred when Kagan was dean of Harvard Law School. In line with Harvard policy, Kagan placed restrictions on military recruiters. The restrictions were in response to the military's "don't ask, don't tell" policy that prevents lesbians and gay men from serving openly. Still, Kagan was confirmed. It was a sign of the increased political polarization in the Senate that neither Sotomayor nor Kagan received more than a handful of votes from Republican senators.

LO4 *The Courts as Policymakers*

In the United States, judges and justices play a major role in government. Unlike judges in some other countries, U.S. judges have the power to decide on the constitutionality of laws or actions undertaken by the other branches of government.

Clearly, the function of the courts is to interpret and apply the law, not to make law—that is the function of the legislative branch of government. Yet judges can and do "make law"; indeed, they cannot avoid making law in some cases because the law does not always provide clear answers to questions that come before the courts. The text of the U.S. Constitution, for example, is set forth in broad terms. When a court interprets a constitutional provision and applies that interpretation to a specific set of circumstances, the court is essentially "making the law" on that issue. Examples of how the courts, and especially the United States Supreme Court, make law abound. Consider privacy rights, which we discussed in Chapter 4. Nothing in the Constitution or its amendments specifically states that we have a right to privacy. Yet the Supreme Court, through various decisions, has established such a right by deciding that it is implied by several constitutional amendments. The Court has also held that this right to privacy includes a number of specific rights, such as the right to have an abortion.

Statutory provisions and other legal rules also tend to be expressed in general terms, and the courts must decide how those general provisions and rules apply to specific cases. The Americans with Disabilities Act of 1990 is an example. The act requires employers to reasonably accommodate the needs of employees with disabilities. But the act does not say exactly what employers must do to "reasonably accommodate" such persons. Thus, the courts must decide, on a case-by-case basis, what this phrase means. Additionally, in some cases there is no relevant law or precedent to follow. In recent years, for example, courts have been struggling with new kinds of legal issues stemming from new communications technologies, including the Internet. Until legislative bodies enact laws governing these issues, it is up to the courts to fashion the law that will apply—and thus make policy.

Solicitor General Elena Kagan testifies at her confirmation hearings on Capitol Hill in Washington during June 2010.

MARY F. CALVERT/THE NEW YORK TIMES/REDUX

The Impact of Court Decisions

As already mentioned, how the courts interpret particular laws can have a widespread impact on society. For example, in 1996, in *Hopwood v. Texas,*[12] the U.S. Court of Appeals for the Fifth Circuit held that an affirmative action program implemented by the University of Texas School of Law in Austin was unconstitutional. The court's decision in *Hopwood* set a precedent for all federal courts within the Fifth Circuit's jurisdiction (which covers Louisiana, Mississippi, and Texas).

Decisions rendered by the United States Supreme Court, of course, have an even broader impact, because all courts in the nation are obligated to follow precedents set by the high court. For example, in 2003 the Supreme Court issued two rulings on affirmative action programs at the University of Michigan. Unlike the appeals court in the *Hopwood* case, the Supreme Court held that diversity on college campuses is a legitimate goal and that affirmative action programs that take race into consideration as part of an examination of each applicant's background do not necessarily violate the equal protection clause of the Constitution.[13] This decision rendered any contrary ruling, including the ruling by the court in the *Hopwood* case, invalid. In 2007, however, the Court retreated somewhat from its position in the University of Michigan cases when it declared that Seattle schools could not use race as a determining factor when assigning students to schools.[14]

Thus, when the Supreme Court interprets laws, it establishes national policy. If the Court deems that a law passed by Congress or a state legislature violates the Constitution, for example, that law will be void and unenforceable in any court within the United States.

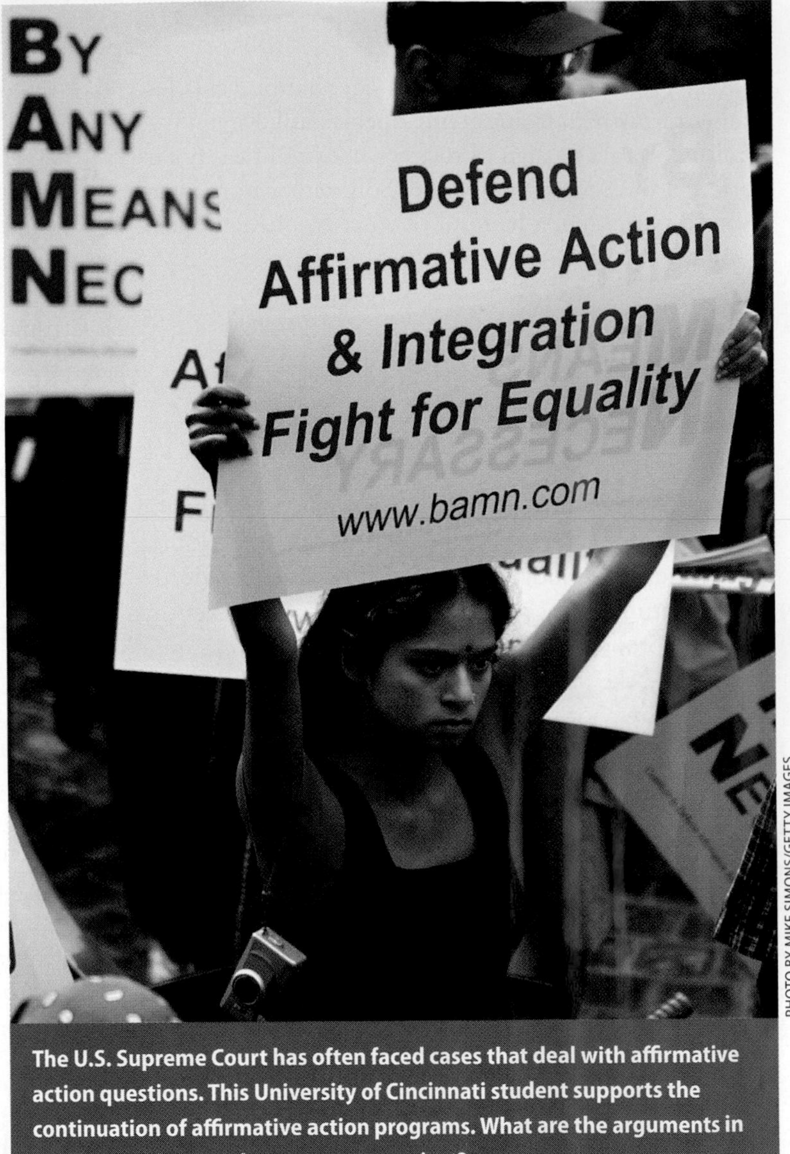

The U.S. Supreme Court has often faced cases that deal with affirmative action questions. This University of Cincinnati student supports the continuation of affirmative action programs. What are the arguments in her favor? What are the arguments against?

The Power of Judicial Review

Recall from Chapter 2 that the U.S. Constitution divides government powers among the executive, legislative, and judicial branches. This division of powers is part of our system of checks and balances. Essentially, the founders gave each branch of government the constitutional authority to check the other two branches. The federal judiciary can exercise a check on the actions of either of the other branches through its power of **judicial review.**

The Constitution does not actually mention judicial review. Rather, the Supreme Court claimed the power for itself in *Marbury v. Madison.*[15] In that case, which was decided by the Court in 1803, Chief Justice John Marshall held that a provision of a 1789 law affecting the Supreme Court's jurisdiction violated the Constitution and was thus void. Marshall declared, "It is emphatically the province and duty of the judicial department [the courts] to say what the law is. . . . If two laws conflict with each other, the courts must decide on the operation of each. . . . So if a law be in opposition to the constitution . . . the court must determine which of these conflicting rules governs the case. This is the very essence of judicial duty."

Most constitutional scholars believe that the framers intended that the federal courts should have the power of judicial review. In *Federalist Paper* No. 78, Alexander Hamilton clearly espoused the doctrine. Hamilton stressed the importance of the "complete independence" of federal judges and their special duty to "invalidate all acts contrary to the manifest tenor of the Constitution." Without judicial review by impartial courts, there would be nothing to ensure that the other branches of government stayed within constitutional limits when exercising their powers, and "all the reservations of particular rights or privileges would amount to nothing." Chief Justice Marshall shared Hamilton's views and adopted Hamilton's reasoning in *Marbury v. Madison.*

judicial review The power of the courts to decide on the constitutionality of legislative enactments and of actions taken by the executive branch.

Judicial Activism versus Judicial Restraint

As already noted, making policy is not the primary function of the federal courts. Yet it is unavoidable that courts do, in fact, influence or even establish policy when they interpret and apply the law. Further, the

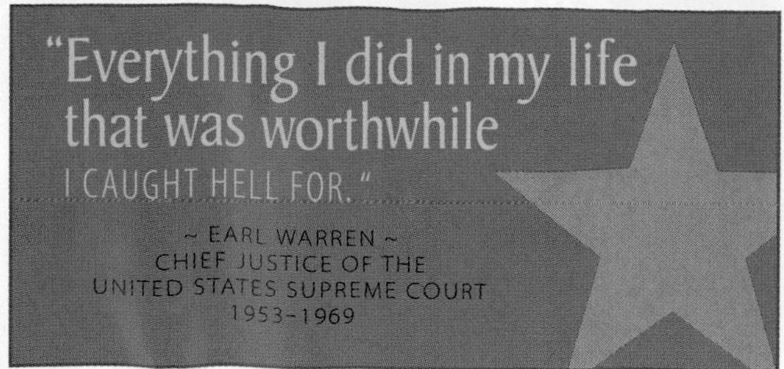

power of judicial review gives the courts, and particularly the Supreme Court, an important policymaking tool. When the Supreme Court upholds or invalidates a state or federal statute, the consequences for the nation can be profound.

"Everything I did in my life that was worthwhile
I CAUGHT HELL FOR."
~ EARL WARREN ~
CHIEF JUSTICE OF THE
UNITED STATES SUPREME COURT
1953–1969

One issue that is often debated is how the federal courts should wield their policymaking power, particularly the power of judicial review. Often, this debate is couched in terms of judicial activism versus judicial restraint.

ACTIVIST VERSUS RESTRAINTIST JUSTICES Although the terms *judicial activism* and *judicial restraint* do not have precise meanings, generally an activist judge or justice believes that the courts should actively use their powers to check the legislative and executive branches to ensure that they do not exceed their authority. A restraintist judge or justice, in contrast, generally assumes that the courts should defer to the decisions of the legislative and executive branches, because members of Congress and the president are elected by the people, whereas federal court judges are not. In other words, the courts should not thwart the implementation of legislative acts unless those acts are clearly unconstitutional.

POLITICAL IDEOLOGY AND JUDICIAL ACTIVISM/RESTRAINT One of the Supreme Court's most activist eras occurred during the period from 1953 to 1969 under the leadership of Chief Justice Earl Warren. The Warren Court propelled the civil rights movement forward by holding, among other things, that laws permitting racial segregation violated the equal protection clause (see Chapter 5).

Because of the activism of the Warren Court, the term *judicial activism* has often been linked with liberalism. Indeed, many liberals are in favor of an activist federal judiciary because they believe that the judiciary can "right" the "wrongs" that result from unfair laws or from "antiquated" legislation at the state and local levels. Neither judicial activism nor judicial restraint is necessarily linked to a particular political ideology, however. In fact, many observers claim that today's Supreme Court is activist on behalf of a conservative agenda.

Still, in handling certain issues, the courts—especially at the state level—have continued to engage in activism that can be characterized as liberal. One such issue is the question of equal rights for lesbians and gay men. Today, the general public supports a variety of rights for such individuals, but the question of same-sex marriage remains extremely controversial. Are the courts an appropriate venue for deciding whether same-sex marriages should be recognized? We address that issue in the *Join the Debate* feature on the following page.

LO5 *Ideology and the Courts*

The policymaking role of the courts gives rise to an important question: To what extent do ideology and personal policy preferences affect judicial decision making? Numerous scholars have attempted to answer this question, especially with respect to Supreme Court justices.

Ideology and Supreme Court Decisions

Few doubt that ideology affects judicial decision making, although, of course, other factors play a role as well. Different courts (such as a trial court and an appellate court) can look at the same case and draw different conclusions as to what law is applicable and how it should be applied. Certainly, there are numerous examples of ideology affecting Supreme Court decisions. As new justices replace old ones and new ideological alignments are formed, the Court's decisions are affected. Yet many scholars argue that there is no real evidence that personal preferences influence Supreme Court decisions to an *unacceptable* extent.

Keep in mind that judicial decision making, particularly at the Supreme Court level, can be very complex. When deciding cases, the Supreme Court often must consider any number of sources of law, including constitutions, statutes, and administrative agency regulations—as well as cases interpreting relevant portions of those sources. At times, the Court may also take demographic data, public opinion, foreign laws, and other factors into account. How much weight is given to each of these sources or factors will vary from justice to justice. After all, reasoning of any kind, including judicial

JOIN THE DEBATE

Should Judges Be the Ones to Decide Whether Same-Sex Couples Can Marry?

Until recently, the idea of marriages by same-sex couples never even entered the consciousness of most people. During the last few decades, however, gay marriage has become a sensitive and newsworthy topic. A few states have passed laws that authorize same-sex marriages. In a few more states, such marriages have been mandated by the state supreme court. A majority of the states, however, have passed laws or adopted constitutional amendments banning the practice.

The California experience is particularly noteworthy. In May 2008, the California Supreme Court ruled that the state constitution required the recognition of same-sex marriages. To overturn this ruling, opponents of gay marriage placed an amendment to the state constitution on the ballot. This was Proposition 8, which passed in November 2008. Same-sex marriage was again illegal in California. Supporters of same-sex marriage then sued to reverse Proposition 8 in a federal district court. In August 2010, Judge Vaughn R. Walker ruled that Proposition 8 violated the U.S. Constitution. The United States Supreme Court may ultimately resolve this conflict. Yet many people have asked, Why should judges be the ones to decide this issue, as opposed to legislators or the people?

Let the People or Their Representatives Decide

Why shouldn't the people of a state or their elected representatives decide whether to legitimize same-sex marriages? The federal government should have no say. Whether same-sex marriages should exist is a political question, not a constitutional one. We have a federal system of government, which means that the states have certain powers that the national government cannot touch. One such power is to create the rules for legal marriages. Whether you are in favor of or against same-sex marriages is irrelevant. The decision on whether to approve such marriages, once made by the people in a referendum or by the legislature in a state capital, must stand as law. There is no reason for judges to intervene and decide whether the people or the legislatures were right or wrong. In the example of California's Proposition 8, the people spoke—against same-sex marriages. As a free people, that was their right.

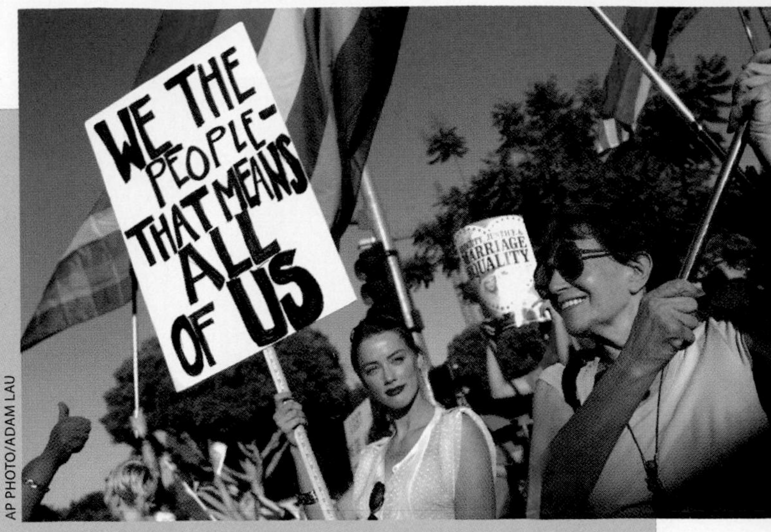

AP PHOTO/ADAM LAU

If Judges Cannot Determine Constitutionality, Who Can?

The interpretation of the Constitution is always a matter for the courts. Individual citizens can have their own opinions, but it is up to the judiciary to carefully assess the constitutionality of any law. Supporters of same-sex marriage argue that the question of whether the Fourteenth Amendment to the U.S. Constitution prohibits states from banning such marriages is a real one.

No level of government may enforce a law that violates the Fourteenth Amendment's equal protection clause unless the law is "rationally related" to a "legitimate" government interest. Satisfying popular prejudices is not a legitimate interest. After careful investigation, Judge Walker found no legitimate interest that justified the banning of same-sex marriages. There will be those who dispute this finding, and they will have a chance to make their arguments through the federal appeals system. However this case turns out, judges ultimately must decide the constitutionality of bans on same-sex marriages. There is no other way.

For Critical Analysis ***Why is it unlikely that the U.S. Congress would pass a law making all same-sex marriages legal?***

reasoning, does not take place in a vacuum. It is only natural that a justice's life experiences, personal biases, and intellectual abilities and predispositions will touch on the reasoning process. Nevertheless, when reviewing a case, a Supreme Court justice does not start out with a conclusion (such as "I don't like this particular law that Congress passed") and then look for legal sources to support that conclusion.

AP PHOTO/CHARLES DHARAPAK

Chief Justice John Roberts, Jr.

AP PHOTO/CHARLES DHARAPAK

Justice Samuel Alito, Jr.

Ideology and the Roberts Court

In contrast to the liberal Supreme Court under Earl Warren, today's Court is generally conservative. The Court began its rightward shift after President Ronald Reagan (1981–1989) appointed conservative William Rehnquist as chief justice in 1986, and the Court moved further to the right as other conservative appointments to the bench were made by Reagan and George H. W. Bush (1989–1993).

Many Supreme Court scholars believe that the appointments of John Roberts (as chief justice) and Samuel Alito (as associate justice) caused the Court to drift even further to the right.[16] Certainly, the five conservative justices on the bench during the Roberts Court's first five terms voted together and cast the deciding votes in numerous cases. The remaining justices held liberal to moderate views and often formed an opposing bloc.

A notable change in the Court occurred when Alito replaced retiring justice Sandra Day O'Connor. O'Connor had often been the "swing" vote on the Court, sometimes voting with the liberal bloc and at other times siding with the conservatives. On the Roberts Court, the swing voter is Justice Anthony Kennedy, who is generally more conservative in his views than O'Connor was. Although Justice Kennedy dislikes being described as a swing voter, he often decides the outcome of a case. In the 2009–2010 term, for example, Kennedy was in the majority in nearly 75 percent of the closely decided cases.

Today's Court is strongly divided ideologically. In the Court term ending in June 2007, one-third of the decisions rendered by the Court were reached by five-to-four votes—the highest share of such votes in more than a decade. In the 2009–2010 term, however, only seventeen out of ninety-two cases were decided by five-to-four votes.[17]

Approaches to Legal Interpretation

It would be a mistake to look at the judicial philosophy of today's Supreme Court solely in terms of the political ideologies of liberalism and conservatism. In fact, some Supreme Court scholars have suggested that other factors are as important as, or even more important than, the justices' political philosophies in determining why they decide as they do. These factors include the justices' attitudes toward legal interpretation and their perceptions of the Supreme Court's role in the federal judiciary.

STRICT VERSUS BROAD CONSTRUCTION Legal scholars have often used the terms *strict* and *broad* construction to describe how judges and justices interpret the law. Generally, strict constructionists look to the letter of the law as written when trying to decipher its meaning, whereas broad constructionists look more to the purpose and context of the law. Broad constructionists believe that the law is an evolving set of standards and is not fixed in concrete. Generally, broad constructionists are more willing to "read between the lines" of a law to serve what they perceive to be the law's intent and purpose.

Strict construction of the law is often linked with conservative views, and broad construction with liberal views. The conservative justices on today's Supreme Court are often labeled strict constructionists because they give great weight to the text of the law. Of course,

AP PHOTO/DAN LOH

Although often considered a conservative when he served on the Rehnquist Court, Justice Anthony Kennedy has typically held the "swing" vote on the closely divided Roberts Court.

AP PHOTO/LAWRENCE JACKSON

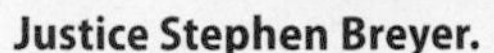
Justice Stephen Breyer.

AP PHOTO/MARK DUNCAN

Justice Antonin Scalia.

AP PHOTO/CHARLES DHARAPAK

Justice Clarence Thomas.

AP PHOTO/EVAN VUCCI

Justice Ruth Bader Ginsburg.

as with judicial activism and judicial restraint, it is possible for these links to be reversed. There have been cases in which the Court appeared to be taking a conservative broad-constructionist or a liberal narrow-constructionist approach.

ORIGINAL INTENT VERSUS MODERNISM The terms *strict construction* and *broad construction* describe different approaches to interpreting the law generally. These approaches may be used when determining the meaning of any law, whether it be a statutory provision, a specific regulation, or a constitutional clause. When discussing *constitutional* interpretation, however, the terms *original intent* and *modernism* are also used to describe the differences in Supreme Court justices' reasoning.

Original Intent Some of the justices believe that to determine the meaning of a particular constitutional phrase, the Court should look to the intentions of the founders. What did the framers of the Constitution themselves intend when they included the phrase in the document? In other words, what was the "original intent" of the phrase? To discern the intent of the founders, the justices should look to sources that shed light on the founders' views. These sources include contemporary writings by the founders, newspaper articles, the *Federalist Papers,* and notes taken during the Constitutional Convention. Justice Antonin Scalia, one of the Court's most conservative justices, gives some insight into this approach to constitutional interpretation in his book *A Matter of Interpretation.*[18] In response to those who maintain that the Constitution is a "living Constitution" and should be interpreted in light of society's needs and practices today, Scalia contends that constitutional principles are fixed, not evolving: "The Constitution that I interpret and apply is not living, but dead."

"THE CONSTITUTION ITSELF SHOULD BE OUR GUIDE, not our own concept of what is fair, decent, and right."

~ HUGO L. BLACK ~
ASSOCIATE JUSTICE OF THE UNITED STATES SUPREME COURT
1937–1971

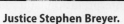

Modernism Other justices, sometimes referred to as "modernists," believe that the Constitution is indeed a living document that evolves to meet changing times and new social needs. Otherwise, how could the Constitution be relevant to today's society? How could the opinions of a small group of white men who drafted the document more than two hundred years ago possibly apply to today's large and diverse population? Moreover, the founders themselves often disagreed on what the Constitution should mean. Additionally, if original intent is the goal, what about the intentions of those who ratified the Constitution? Shouldn't they be taken into consideration also? The modernist approach to constitutional interpretation thus looks at the Constitution in the context of today's society and considers how today's life affects the words in the document. Modernists also defend their approach by stating that the founders intentionally left many constitutional provisions vague so

PERCEPTION VERSUS REALITY

The Supreme Court Legislates from the Bench

Our Constitution gives legislative powers to the Congress exclusively. All executive powers are granted to the president. And all judicial powers are given to the judiciary. The United States Supreme Court is the final arbiter and interpreter of what is and is not constitutional. Because of its power of judicial review, it has the ability to "make law," or so it seems.

The Perception

Using the power of judicial review, the Supreme Court creates new laws. In 1954, the Court determined that racial segregation is illegal, a position that is universally accepted today but was hugely controversial back in the 1950s. The Court has also legalized sexual acts between same-sex adults and, of course, abortion. These decisions, especially the legalization of abortion, remain very controversial today. Such decisions have had a major impact on the nature of American society. Because citizens elect members of Congress and the president only—and not members of the Supreme Court—it is undemocratic to allow these nine justices to determine laws for our nation.

The Reality

The Supreme Court cannot actually write new laws. It can only eliminate old ones. When the Court threw out laws that criminalized adult sexual activity by gay men and lesbians, it was abolishing laws, not creating them. The Court does not have the power to legislate—to create new laws. Consider what would happen if the Court decided that some basic level of health care is a constitutional right—a highly unlikely event. Could the Court establish mechanisms by which such a right could be enforced? It could not. It takes members of Congress months of hard work to craft bills that affect our health-care system. Such legislation fills thousands of pages and can only be developed with the assistance of large numbers of experts and lobbyists. The federal courts could not undertake such projects even if they wanted to.

Supreme Court justice Sonia Sotomayor once said: "The courts of appeals are where policy is made." Indeed, most cases never make it to the Supreme Court, and this fact limits the ability of Supreme Court justices to make policy decisions. More to the point, however, in referring to policy, Sotomayor was speaking of judicial policy, not policy in general. The courts must decide how they will handle the cases that are brought before them. To do so establishes judicial policy. It does not constitute lawmaking.

In any event, we have no alternative to judicial review when it comes to determining what is or is not constitutional. Without the Supreme Court, Congress and the president could make all sorts of laws that violate our Constitution and infringe on our rights, and there would be nothing to stop them. As Chief Justice John Roberts said during his confirmation hearings, "Judges are like umpires. Umpires don't make the rules; they apply them."

Blog On Plenty of bloggers follow the activities of the Supreme Court, but for sophisticated commentary, try **www.scotusblog.com**, produced by the law firm of Akin, Gump, Strauss, Hauer, and Feld. Another choice is **ussc.blogspot.com**, by Paul M. Rashkind, a Florida lawyer.

that future generations could interpret the document in a manner that would meet the needs of a growing nation.

LO6 *Assessing the Role of the Federal Courts*

The federal courts have often come under attack, particularly in the last decade or so, for many reasons. This should come as no surprise in view of the policymaking power of the courts. After all, a Supreme Court decision can establish national policy on such issues as abortion, racial segregation, and gay rights. Critics, especially on the political right, frequently accuse the judiciary of "legislating from the bench." We discuss these criticisms in this chapter's *Perception versus Reality* feature above.

Criticisms of the Federal Courts

Certainly, policymaking by unelected judges and justices in the federal courts has serious implications in a democracy. Some Americans, including many conservatives, contend that making policy from the bench has upset the balance of powers envisioned by the framers of the Constitution. They cite Thomas Jefferson, who once said, "To consider the judges as the ultimate arbiters of all constitutional questions [is] a very dangerous doctrine indeed, and one which would place us under the despotism of an oligarchy."[19] This group believes that we should rein in the power of the federal courts, and particularly judicial activism.

Indeed, from the the mid-1990s until 2007, when the Republicans controlled Congress, a number of bills to restrain the power of the federal judiciary were introduced in Congress. Among other things, it was proposed that Congress, not the Supreme Court, should have the ultimate say in determining the meaning of the Constitution; that judges who ignore the will of Congress or follow foreign precedents should be impeached; that federal courts should not be allowed to decide certain types of cases, such as those involving abortion or the place of religion in public life; and that Congress should be empowered to use its control over the judiciary to punish judges who overstep their authority.

The Case for the Courts

On the other side of the debate over the courts are those who argue in favor of leaving the courts alone. Several federal court judges have sharply criticized congressional efforts to interfere with their authority. They claim that such efforts violate the Constitution's separation of powers. James M. Jeffords, a former independent senator from Vermont, likened the federal court system to a referee: "The first lesson we teach children when they enter competitive sports is to respect the referee, even if we think he [or she] might have made the wrong call. If our children can understand this, why can't our political leaders?"[20]

Others argue that there are already sufficient checks on the courts, some of which we look at next.

JUDICIAL TRADITIONS AND DOCTRINES One check on the courts is judicial restraint. Supreme Court justices traditionally have exercised a great deal of self-restraint. Justices sometimes admit to making decisions that fly in the face of their personal values and policy preferences, simply because they feel obligated to do so in view of existing law. Self-restraint is also mandated by various established judicial traditions and doctrines, including the doctrine of *stare decisis,* which theoretically obligates the Supreme Court to follow its own precedents. Furthermore, the Supreme Court will not hear a meritless appeal just so it can rule on the issue. Finally, more often than not, the justices narrow their rulings to focus on just one aspect of an issue, even though there may be nothing to stop them from broadening their focus and thus widening the impact of their decisions.

OTHER CHECKS The judiciary is subject to other checks as well. Courts may make rulings, but they cannot force federal and state legislatures to appropriate the funds necessary to carry out those rulings. For example, if a state supreme court decides that prison conditions must be improved, the state legislature has to find the funds to carry out the ruling, or the improvements will not take place.

Additionally, legislatures can revise old laws or pass new ones in an attempt to negate a court's ruling. This may happen when a court interprets a statute in a way that Congress did not intend. Congress may also propose amendments to the Constitution to reverse Supreme Court rulings, and Congress has the authority to limit or otherwise alter the jurisdiction of the lower federal courts. Finally, although it is most unlikely, Congress could even change the number of justices on the Supreme Court, in an attempt to change the ideological balance on the Court. (President Franklin D. Roosevelt proposed such a plan in 1937, without success.)

THE PUBLIC'S REGARD FOR THE SUPREME COURT As mentioned, some have proposed that Congress, not the Supreme Court, be the final arbiter of the Constitution. In debates on this topic, one factor is often overlooked: the American public's high regard for the Supreme Court and the federal courts generally. The Court continues to be respected as a fair arbiter of conflicting interests and the protector of constitutional rights and liberties. Even when the Court issued its decision to halt the manual recount of votes in Florida following the 2000 elections, which effectively handed the presidency to George W. Bush, Americans respected the Court's decision-making authority—although many disagreed with the Court's decision. Polls continue to show that Americans have much more trust and confidence in the Supreme Court than they do in Congress.

AMERICA AT **ODDS** *The Judiciary*

A Supreme Court decision can affect the lives of millions of Americans. For example, in 1973, the Supreme Court, in *Roe v. Wade,* held that the constitutional right to privacy included the right to have an abortion. The influence wielded by the Court today is a far cry from the Court's relative obscurity at the founding of this nation. Initially, the Supreme Court was not even included in the plans for government buildings in the national capital. It did not have its own building until 1935. Over time, however, the Court has established a reputation with the public for dispensing justice in a fair and reasonable manner. Still, Americans are at odds over a number of judicial issues:

- Are there terrorist suspects who must be detained indefinitely without trial to protect our safety—or is such an act a violation of our Constitution that does us more damage in the world than a detainee could possibly accomplish if freed?
- Should the United States Supreme Court accept more cases to provide a greater number of definitive rulings—or should it take on relatively few cases so that it can treat each one thoroughly?
- Should senators accept a Supreme Court nomination by a president of the opposing party whenever the nominee appears to have sound judicial temperament—or should senators vote only for those nominees who share their political philosophies?
- Should judges defer to the decisions of legislatures and administrative agencies whenever possible—or should they strictly police the constitutionality of legislative and executive decisions?
- Is it crucial that the Constitution be interpreted in terms of the beliefs of the founders—or should justices take full account of modern circumstances that the founders could not have envisioned?

Take Action

The founders deliberately attempted to insulate the federal judiciary from popular opinion, so it might seem difficult to take action in regard to it. There are points at which the public can exercise leverage, however. One possibility is to lobby senators over judicial appointments. Especially if one or more of your senators is of a different political party than the president, that senator is probably of two minds over a presidential nomination to the Supreme Court or any of the lesser courts. Such senators will pay special attention to letters and e-mail from constituents who oppose or support a nomination. If you have voted for the senator or the senator's party in the past, it is helpful to point that out.

Greater opportunities to take action exist at the state level, especially in the majority of states in which judges are either elected or must face the voters after appointment. An important characteristic of state judicial elections is that most voters typically know nothing about the candidates. You can have a significant impact if you gather information and distribute it. Together with a group of your friends, you could research the candidates and pass on what you have learned, perhaps through an opinion piece in the campus newspaper. You may even be able to get academic credit for such an effort. It is very useful if you can determine who is providing a candidate with campaign funds. A judicial candidate who receives large contributions from businesses such as insurance companies that fear lawsuits may handle cases one way. A candidate who receives most of his or her funds from trial lawyers (who do the suing) may handle cases differently.

Parents confer with a judge during jury deliberations at the trial of their daughter's murderer. He was found guilty and sentenced to death. (He had also killed several other young people.)

AP PHOTO/LARRY KOLVOORD, POOL

POLITICS ON THE WEB

- An excellent Web site for information on the justices of the United States Supreme Court is **www.oyez.org**. This site offers biographies of the justices, links to opinions they have written, and, for justices who have served after 1920, video and audio materials. Oral arguments before the Supreme Court are also posted on this site.
- Another helpful Web site is **www.law.cornell.edu/supct**. This collection of United States Supreme Court cases includes recent Court decisions, as well as selected historic decisions rendered by the Court.
- The Supreme Court makes its opinions available online at its official Web site. Go to **www.supremecourt.gov**
- FindLaw offers a free searchable database of Supreme Court decisions since 1907 at **www.findlaw.com**
- Increasingly, decisions of the state courts are available online. You can search through the texts of state cases that are on the Internet, as well as federal cases, state and federal laws, and the laws of other countries, by accessing WashLaw at **www.washlaw.edu**
- To learn more about the federal court system, go to **www.uscourts.gov**. This is the home page for the federal courts. Among other things, you can follow the path a case takes as it moves through the federal court system.

Access CourseMate to review and expand on this chapter through quizzes, flashcards, learning objectives, interactive timelines, a crossword puzzle, audio summaries, video, critical-thinking activities, simulations, and more.

GOVT 15

Domestic Policy

LEARNING OBJECTIVES

LO1 Explain what domestic policy is and summarize the steps in the policymaking process.

LO2 Discuss the issue of health-care funding and recent legislation on universal health insurance.

LO3 Summarize the issues of energy independence, global warming, and alternative energy sources.

LO4 Describe the two major areas of economic policymaking.

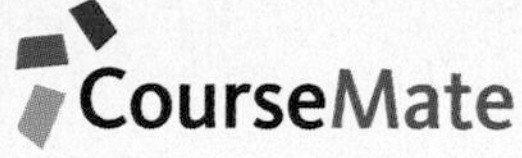

AMERICA AT ODDS

Do We Send Too Many People to Prison?

Currently, there are about 2.4 million U.S. residents in prison or jail. That's roughly one in every one hundred adults. We are setting records—we have twelve times the share of our population in prison as Japan, nine times more than in Germany, and five times more than in Britain. Federal prisons currently hold in excess of 60 percent of their rated capacity. Yet in 1970, the proportion of Americans behind bars—the *incarceration rate*—was only one-fourth of what it is today. Not surprisingly, the number of drug offenders in prison is responsible for much of this increase. Such lockups have multiplied thirteenfold since 1980.

Holding that many prisoners is not cheap. It costs about $50,000 a year to house a convicted criminal in a state prison. As defense attorney Jim Felman of Tampa, Florida, said, America is conducting "an experiment in imprisoning first-time non-violent offenders for periods of time previously reserved only for those who had killed someone." We can expect that more U.S. residents will go to prison in the future. The federal government currently has 4,400 crimes on the books, and that number rises every year. So, do we send too many Americans to prison?

Keep Criminals Behind Bars—It Works

Supporters of aggressive incarceration policies argue that still more criminals should be behind bars. Putting more people in prison reduces crime rates. After all, incentives matter. If potential criminals know that they will be thrown in jail more readily and stay there longer, they will have less incentive to engage in illegal activities. Also, the crime rate is strongly determined by the number of criminals at large. When we remove a criminal from the streets and put that person in prison, the prisoner can no longer commit crimes that harm the public. This effect of removal is called *incapacitation*. The evidence shows that during the 1960s, when incarceration rates fell, the crime rate more than doubled. As incarceration rates rose sharply in the 1990s, the crime rate went steadily down. As a comparison, the risk of criminal punishment in England has been falling. As a consequence, crime rates have risen in England while they have fallen in the United States.

Tough sentencing is effective. We should not turn career criminals loose on the streets.

Too Many Laws and Too Many Prisoners

Those who argue against our high rates of incarceration point out that many individuals are convicted of nonviolent crimes. The government should not be spending $50,000 a year or more to keep such people in prison. Too many acts have been criminalized, particularly at the federal level. Many crimes are so vaguely defined that most Americans would not know if they were breaking the law or not. Granted, hard-core criminals should be behind bars. But what about the casual pot smoker? Or someone convicted under a federal statute designed to protect the environment? Lying to a federal official is a felony. Who can say how many people could be imprisoned based on such an act?

Many states have so-called habitual-offender laws. In California, for example, almost 4,000 individuals are serving life sentences because they were convicted of a third offense—one that was neither violent nor serious. Furthermore, the cost to society of putting drug users behind bars is much greater than the benefits. Wouldn't that money be better spent on rehabilitation?

WHERE DO YOU STAND?

1. **Could other factors underlie the apparent relationship between high incarceration rates and low crime rates? What might they be?**
2. **Why do you think federal, state, and local governments arrest so many drug-law violators?**

EXPLORE THIS ISSUE ONLINE

- **You can find several articles arguing that we imprison too many people in the *Economist*, a British magazine. One such article is at www.economist.com/node/16640389.**
- **The Criminal Justice Legal Foundation is among the few groups that advocate increased rates of incarceration. See its arguments at www.cjlf.org/publctns/ConfiningCriminals.pdf.**

Introduction

Whether we send too many people to prison is just one of the issues that confront our nation's policymakers today. How are questions of national importance, such as this one, decided? Who are the major participants in the decision-making process?

To learn the answers to these questions, we need to delve into the politics of policymaking. Policy, or public policy, can be defined as a plan or course of action taken by the government to respond to a political issue or to enhance the social or political well-being of society. Public policy is the end result of the policymaking process, which will be described shortly. **Domestic policy,** in contrast to foreign policy, consists of public policy concerning issues *within* a national unit.

In this chapter, after discussing how policy is made through the policymaking process, we look at several aspects of domestic policy, including health-care policy, energy policy, and economic policy. We focus on these policy areas because they have been the Obama administration's top priorities. An additional priority for the administration is immigration reform. It is an open question, however, as to when this subject can be addressed. We consider immigration reform in this chapter's *Join the Debate* feature on the following page.

Overcrowding in state and federal prisons, such as this one in California, has placed the issue on the policymaking agenda. One response has been early release of nonviolent offenders.

AP PHOTO/CALIFORNIA DEPARTMENT OF CORRECTIONS

Bear in mind that although the focus here is on policy and policymaking at the national level, state and local governments also engage in policymaking and establish policies to achieve goals relating to activities within their boundaries. This is certainly true in relation to the criminal justice issues discussed in this chapter's opening *America at Odds* feature.

domestic policy Public policy concerning issues within a national unit, such as national policy concerning health care or the economy.

policymaking process The procedures involved in getting an issue on the political agenda; formulating, adopting, and implementing a policy with regard to the issue; and then evaluating the results of the policy.

LO1 *The Policymaking Process*

A new law does not appear out of nowhere. First, the problem addressed by the new law has to become part of the political agenda—that is, the problem must be defined as a political issue to be resolved by government action. Furthermore, once the issue gets on the political agenda, proposed solutions to the problem have to be formulated and then adopted. Issue identification and agenda setting, policy formulation, and policy adoption are all parts of the **policymaking process.** The process does not end there, however. Once the law is passed, it has to be implemented and then evaluated.

Each phase of the policymaking process involves interactions among various individuals and groups. The president and members of Congress are obviously important participants in the process. Remember from Chapter 6 that interest groups also play a key role. Groups that may be affected adversely by a new policy will try to convince Congress not to adopt the policy. Groups that will benefit from the policy will exert whatever influence they can on Congress to do the opposite. Congressional committees and subcommittees may investigate the problem to be addressed by the policy and, in so doing, solicit input from members of various groups or industries.

The participants in policymaking and the nature of the debates involved depend on the particular policy being proposed, formed, or implemented. Whatever the policy, however, debate over its pros and cons occurs during each stage of the policymaking process. Additionally, making policy decisions

Should Unauthorized Immigrants Be Given a Path to Citizenship?

The United States is a land of immigrants. Apart from Native Americans, all of us are either current immigrants or the descendants of immigrants. Yet immigration remains one of the most divisive issues facing Americans and their elected representatives today.

Congress has reacted in various ways to the issue of illegal immigration. At one time, it established an amnesty program to allow unauthorized immigrants who had been working in the United States for five years to obtain legal residency. More recently, it voted in favor of a large, secure fence on the U.S.-Mexican border to keep illegal immigrants out. President Barack Obama's immigration proposals require undocumented immigrants who do not otherwise violate the law to pay a fine, learn English, and go to the back of the line for the opportunity to become citizens. Obama also favors crackdowns on employers who hire illegal immigrants and steps to make legal immigration easier.

Today, there are up to 12 million illegal immigrants living and working in this country. Should they be given a path to citizenship?

How Can Any American Be against Immigration?

Some find the "close the door after me" mentality to be very un-American. Just remember, standards of living in the United States have been improving for decades not in spite of immigration but because of it. It's true that an unauthorized immigrant is not playing by the rules. But that is because the rules are so difficult to follow. We should make it easier for current unauthorized immigrants to become legal. The vast majority of illegal immigrants are working and adding to this nation's well-being. The net taxpayer cost per immigrant is negative. They are normally not eligible to receive welfare benefits. They come here to work, not to receive government handouts.

A Path to Citizenship Sends the Wrong Signals

Illegal immigrants have broken the law. If we give them a path to citizenship or even to legal status, we are sending the wrong signals to the rest of the world. As a result, we will end up with even more illegal immigrants, all of them hoping to find a path to citizenship one day.

Most unauthorized immigrants have few job skills. Immigrants without high school diplomas now head about a third of immigrant households. Certainly, this country can use more high-skilled immigrants—those with scientific degrees and PhDs. Low-skilled immigrants, in contrast, simply take jobs away from Americans. To send the right signals to the rest of the world, we should also crack down on employers who hire illegal immigrants. These employers are making a real contribution to the problem. Then there is the issue of security. We have to protect our borders if we are to prevent terrorists from entering the United States.

For Critical Analysis ***How might we rationalize the inconsistency between our being a country of immigrants and wanting to keep out new ones?***

inevitably involves *trade-offs,* in which policymakers must sacrifice one goal to achieve another because of budget constraints.

Issue Identification and Agenda Setting

If no one recognizes a problem, then no matter how important the problem may be, politically it does not yet really exist. Thus, *issue identification* is part of the first stage of the policymaking process. Some group—whether it be the media, the public, politicians, or even foreign commentators—must identify a problem that can be solved politically. The second part of this stage of the policymaking process involves getting the issue on the political agenda to be addressed by Congress. This is called **agenda setting,** or agenda building.

agenda setting Getting an issue on the political agenda to be addressed by Congress; part of the first stage of the policymaking process.

A problem in society can be identified as an issue and included on the political agenda in a number of different ways. An event or series of events may lead to a call for action. For example, the failure of a major bank may lead to the conclusion that the financial industry is in trouble and that the government should take action to rectify the problem. Dramatic increases

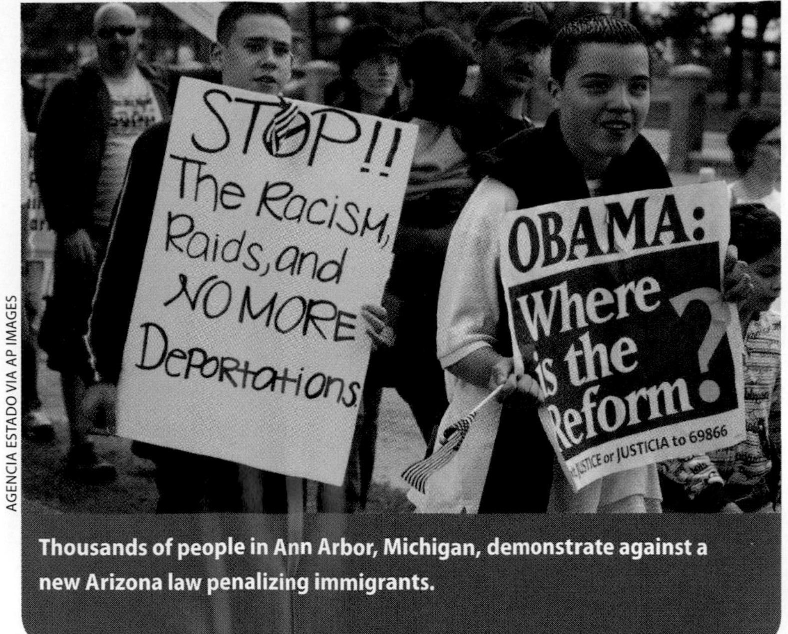

AGENCIA ESTADO VIA AP IMAGES

Thousands of people in Ann Arbor, Michigan, demonstrate against a new Arizona law penalizing immigrants.

in health-care costs may cause the media or other groups to consider health care a priority that should be on the national political agenda. Sometimes, the social or economic effects of a national calamity, such as the Great Depression of the 1930s or the terrorist attacks of September 11, 2001, create a pressing need for government action.

Policy Formulation and Adoption

The second stage in the policymaking process involves the formulation and adoption of specific plans for achieving a particular goal, such as health-care reform. The president, members of Congress, administrative agencies, and interest group leaders typically are the key participants in developing proposed legislation. Remember from Chapter 13 that iron triangles and issue networks work together in forming mutually beneficial policies. To a certain extent, the courts also establish policies when they interpret statutes passed by legislative bodies or make decisions concerning disputes not yet addressed by any law, such as disputes involving new technology.

Note that some issues may get on the political agenda but never proceed beyond that stage of the policymaking process. Usually, this happens when it is impossible to achieve a consensus over what policy should be adopted.

Policy Implementation

Because of our federal system, the implementation of national policies necessarily requires the cooperation of the federal government and the various state and local governments. A case in point is the 1996 Welfare Reform Act. The act required the states to develop plans for implementing the new welfare policy within their borders. The federal government, though, retained some authority over the welfare system by providing that state welfare plans had to be certified, or approved, by the federal government. In addition, successful implementation usually requires the support of groups outside the government. For example, the work requirements of the Welfare Reform Act meant that the business sector would also play a key role in the policy's implementation.

Policy implementation also involves agencies in the executive branch (see Chapter 13). Once Congress establishes a policy by enacting legislation, the executive branch, through its agencies, enforces the new policy. Furthermore, the courts are involved in policy implementation, because the legislation and administrative regulations enunciating the new policy must be interpreted and applied to specific situations by the courts.

Policy Evaluation

The final stage of policymaking involves evaluating the success of a policy during and following its implementation. Once a policy has been implemented, groups both inside and outside the government evaluate the policy. Congress may hold hearings to obtain feedback from different groups on how a statute or regulation has affected them. Scholars and scientists may conduct studies to determine whether a particular law, such as an environmental law designed to reduce air pollution, has actually achieved the desired result—less air pollution. Sometimes, feedback obtained in these or other ways indicates that a policy has failed, and a new policymaking process may be undertaken to modify the policy or create a more effective one.

Policymaking versus Special Interests

The policymaking steps just discussed seem straightforward, but they are not. Every bill that passes through Congress is a compromise. Every bill that passes through Congress is also an opportunity for individual members of Congress to help constituents, particularly those who were kind enough to contribute financially to the members' reelection campaigns.

Consider the Emergency Economic Stabilization Act of 2008, a $700 billion financial rescue plan that the U.S. Treasury Department urgently demanded on

September 19, 2008. After the House defeated the initial "clean" version of the bailout bill, the Senate drafted a second version. This second version included a landmark health-care provision requiring that insurance companies provide coverage for mental health treatment equivalent to that provided for the treatment of physical illnesses. The bill also contained almost $14 billion in tax-break extensions for businesses. Special provisions benefited rural schools, film and television producers, makers of toy wooden arrows, victims of the 1989 *Exxon Valdez* oil spill in Alaska, rum distillers in the Virgin Islands and Puerto Rico, auto racetracks, and wool researchers. The second bill passed the House on October 3. Clearly, policymaking, particularly on the economic front, remains a complicated process.

"THE MORAL TEST OF GOVERNMENT is how it treats those who are in the dawn of life, the children; those who are in the twilight of life, the elderly; and those who are in the shadows of life, the sick, the needy, and the handicapped."

~ HUBERT H. HUMPHREY ~
SENATOR FROM MINNESOTA
1971–1978

LO2 *Health-Care Policy*

In March 2010, Congress passed major health-care reform legislation. The two bills containing the reforms, which President Barack Obama immediately signed, were among the most consequential government initiatives in many years. Health-care reform is one of the most important topics that the government can address. Even before the new legislation was adopted, the federal government was paying the health-care costs of more than 100 million Americans. When President Obama took office, the government was picking up the tab for about 50 percent of the nation's health-care costs. Private insurance was responsible for about a third of all health-care payments, and the rest was met either by patients themselves or by charity. Paying for health-care expenses, in other words, was already a major federal responsibility, and questions about how the government should carry out that function in the future were unavoidable.

Medicare A federal government program that pays for health-care insurance for Americans aged sixty-five years or over.

Medicaid A joint federal-state program that pays for health-care services for low-income persons.

Our system for funding health care suffers from two major problems. One is that health care is expensive. About 17.6 percent of national spending in the United States goes to health care, compared with 10 percent in Canada, 9 percent in Sweden, and 8 percent in Japan. Also, almost 42 million Americans—close to 16 percent of the population—have no health-care insurance. Lack of coverage means that people may neglect preventive care, put off seeing a physician until it is too late, or be forced into bankruptcy due to large medical bills. One study has estimated that 20,000 people each year die prematurely because they lack health insurance.[1] (Others dispute these findings.) All other economically advanced nations provide health insurance to everyone, typically through a government program similar to Social Security or Medicare in the United States.

Before discussing the recently passed health-care reforms, let's first look at the programs that are already in place. The most important of these is **Medicare,** which provides health-care insurance to Americans aged sixty-five or over, and **Medicaid,** which funds health-care coverage for the poor.

Medicaid and Medicare

The federal government pays for health care in a variety of ways. Like many major employers, it buys health-care insurance for its employees. In addition, members of the armed forces, veterans, and Native Americans receive medical services provided directly by the government. Most federal spending on health care, however, is accounted for by Medicare and Medicaid. Both are costly, and each, in its own way, poses a serious financial problem to the government.

MEDICAID A joint federal-state program, Medicaid provides health-care subsidies to low-income persons. The federal government provides about 60 percent of the Medicaid budget, and the states provide the rest. More than 60 million people are in the program, which currently costs all levels of government well over $300 billion per year. The cost of Medicaid has doubled in the last decade, and this has put a considerable strain on the budgets of many states. About 17 percent of the average state general fund budget now goes to Medicaid. Recent cost-containment measures have slowed the growth of Medicaid spending, however. Another program, the **State Children's Health Insurance Program (SCHIP),** covers children in families with incomes that are modest but too high to qualify for Medicaid.

The Great Recession put a considerable strain on the states' ability to pick up their share of Medicaid payments. The Obama administration's February 2009 stimulus package, therefore, included $87 billion to reduce temporarily the Medicaid burden on the states. Congressional Democrats also substantially increased the size of SCHIP within weeks of Obama's inauguration.

MEDICARE Medicare is the federal government's health-care program for persons over the age of sixty-five. Medicare is now the government's second-largest domestic spending program, after Social Security. In 1970, Medicare accounted for only 0.7 percent of total annual U.S. national income (gross domestic product, or GDP). It currently accounts for about 3.2 percent of the GDP, and costs are expected to soar as millions of "baby boomers" retire over the next two decades. By 2030, the sixty-five-and-older population is expected to double. Further, technological developments in health care and the advancement of medical science are driving medical costs up every year. There are simply more things that medical science can do to keep people alive—and Americans naturally want to take advantage of these services.

This senior citizen lives in a nursing home in North Smithfield, Rhode Island. Most of her living and medical expenses are paid for by the government through Medicaid. Rhode Island is one of many states that are facing record Medicaid expenses.

AP PHOTO/STEW MILNE

The Democrats Propose Universal Coverage

As noted earlier, the United States is the only economically advanced nation that does not provide universal health-insurance coverage to its citizens. Universal insurance is not a new idea. German chancellor Otto von Bismarck implemented the first such plan in Germany in 1883. (A staunch conservative, Bismarck sought to use social legislation to "steal the thunder" of the German socialists, who were quite popular.) Democratic president Bill Clinton (1993–2001) and then First Lady Hillary Clinton made a serious push for a universal plan during President Clinton's first term, but the project failed to pass Congress.

Many universal health insurance plans—for example, the systems in Canada and France—involve government monopolies. In these nations, the government is responsible for providing basic health-care insurance to everyone through **national health insurance.** The plan that the United States has adopted, however, provides a larger role for the private sector.

The legislative process began in 2009 with hearings in multiple committees in the House and Senate. Still, all the proposals had common features. All assumed that employer-provided health insurance would continue to be a major part of the system. Large employers

State Children's Health Insurance Program (SCHIP) A joint federal-state program that provides health-care insurance for low-income children.

national health insurance A program, found in many of the world's economically advanced nations, under which the central government provides basic health-care insurance coverage to everyone in the country. Some wealthy nations, such as the Netherlands and Switzerland, provide universal coverage through private insurance companies instead.

who did not offer a plan would be required to pay a penalty. Medicaid would be available to individuals with incomes up to about 1.5 times the federal poverty level. (In 2010, the poverty level for a family of four was $22,050.) A new health-insurance marketplace, the Health Insurance Exchange, would allow individuals and small employers to shop for plans. Insurance companies would not be allowed to deny anyone coverage. Most individuals would be required to obtain coverage or pay an income-tax penalty. This requirement is known as the **individual mandate,** or the *personal mandate.* Those with low-to-middle incomes would receive help in paying their premiums. Subsidies would be phased out for those earning more than four times the federal poverty level.

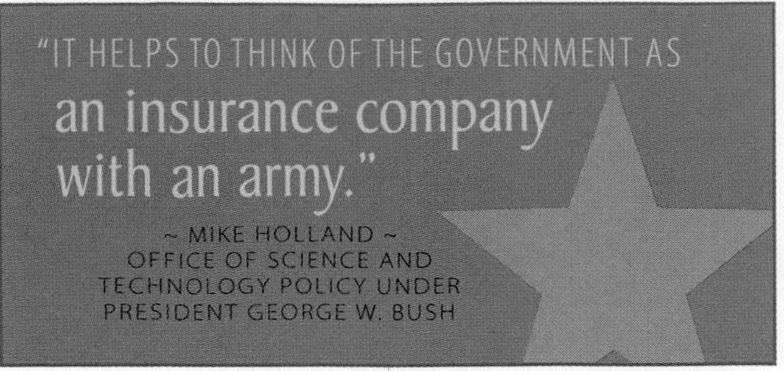

"IT HELPS TO THINK OF THE GOVERNMENT AS
an insurance company
with an army."
~ MIKE HOLLAND ~
OFFICE OF SCIENCE AND
TECHNOLOGY POLICY UNDER
PRESIDENT GEORGE W. BUSH

House legislation called for a government-sponsored insurance plan known as the **public option.** This plan would compete against private plans in the Health Insurance Exchange. The public option, however, was rejected by the Senate. The House passed a plan in November 2009. In December, the Senate version passed with votes from all sixty Democrats and no Republicans.

The Health-Care Debate

Republicans were quite hostile toward the public option. A caucus of conservative Democrats in the House, known as the **Blue Dog Coalition,** also opposed it, as did a half-dozen Democrats in the Senate. Advocates of the public option contended that it would provide needed competition to private plans. Opponents argued that it could lead to the destruction of private-sector health insurance. Polls, however, reported considerable support for the public option.

The individual mandate was also controversial, because it would require all Americans to have health insurance whether they wanted it or not. The mandate would impose a burden on young, healthy persons who chose not to buy insurance. Supporters of reform, however, pointed out that without an individual mandate, reform would not work. Without a mandate, people might wait until they became sick before they purchased insurance. Any system that let healthy people avoid buying insurance would face financial collapse.

SUPPORT AND OPPOSITION The Obama administration won considerable support for reform from interest groups that had opposed universal health-care systems in the past. For the first time, the American Medical Association was on board. Pharmaceutical companies gave general support. The greater part of the opposition came not from interest groups but from conservatives.

Over the course of 2009, conservative hostility to the legislation grew in strength and fervor. Opponents

individual mandate In the context of health-care reform, a requirement that all persons obtain health-care insurance from one source or another. Those failing to do so would pay a penalty.

public option In the context of health-care reform, a government-sponsored health-care insurance program that would compete with private insurance companies.

Blue Dog Coalition A caucus that unites most of the moderate-to-conservative Democrats in the House of Representatives.

Supporters of universal health-care argue that such a system would guarantee that all children receive preventive medical care.

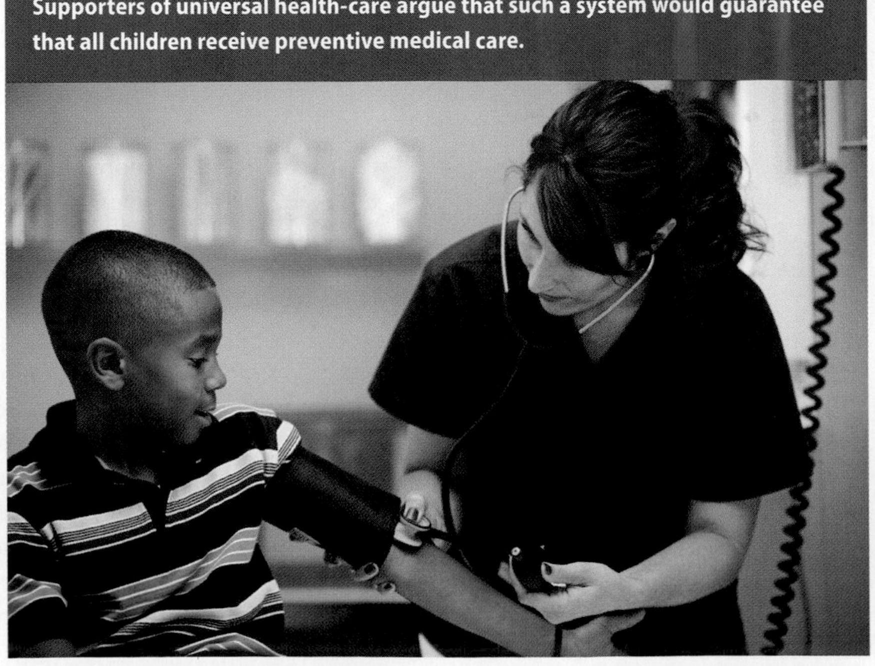

were not only hostile to health-care reform; most were upset over what they saw as the growing power of government in general. They believed that health-care reform was only one of several steps toward a vast federal leviathan that would crush individual freedoms.

In time, a second reason emerged for opposing reform—Democratic plans to curb increases in Medicare spending. Many older persons receiving Medicare were afraid that their benefits would be cut. (See Chapter 13's *Our Government Faces a Troubled Economy* feature on page 283.) By 2010, health-care reform had lost much of its earlier support among the public.

The growing unpopularity of reform was confirmed in January 2010, when Republican Scott Brown won a special election to fill a U.S. Senate seat in Massachusetts. Brown's victory cost the Democrats in the Senate their sixty-vote supermajority.

HOW THE LEGISLATION PASSED Brown's victory came at a time when two different health-care reform bills had passed the House and Senate. Normally, a conference committee of House and Senate leaders would agree to a compromise that would then have to be passed by both chambers. With only fifty-nine votes in the Senate, however, the Democrats would be unable to pass such a bill. Republicans celebrated in the belief that they had successfully killed the health-care legislation. They celebrated too soon, however. If the House passed the Senate version of reform without any changes, no conference committee would be necessary. The bill could go immediately to the president for his signature. House Speaker Nancy Pelosi and President Obama were able to find enough votes in the House to pass the Senate's Patient Protection and Affordable Care Act.

RECONCILIATION The House then passed a second bill, the Health Care and Education Reconciliation Act. **Reconciliation** acts are a special kind of legislation that cannot be filibustered in the Senate. To qualify, an act must deal only in financial matters. This measure amended the Senate's bill in a number of ways. It split the difference between the House and Senate funding mechanisms. Both high-income taxpayers and high-end "Cadillac" health plans would be taxed. The **Congressional Budget Office (CBO),** an agency set up by Congress to evaluate the impact of proposed measures on the federal budget, scored the result as costing $940 billion over ten years and reducing the deficit by $138 billion. The Senate quickly adopted the reconciliation act with fifty-six votes in favor. On Obama's signature, health-care reform was law.

THE CONSERVATIVE REACTION Conservatives argued that the Democrats had ignored the will of the people, who were against the reform legislation. In a typical poll in March 2010, 56 percent of respondents opposed the legislation. That figure was slightly misleading, however. Only 43 percent opposed the reforms because they were "too liberal." Another 13 percent opposed them because they were "not liberal enough."

One last-ditch method of opposing the reforms was to challenge their constitutionality. Attorney generals in twenty states challenged the measure on the basis that the individual mandate violated the Constitution. (See Chapter 3's *Join the Debate* feature on page 63.)

A second method of attack would be to repeal the legislation, and the Republicans made repeal part of their platform for the 2010 elections. Republicans have plenty of time to win repeal, because full universal coverage does not go into effect until 2014. Repeal, however, would require specific legislation passed by Congress and signed by the president. To prevent a veto, a Republican president would be necessary. The Republicans also would have to control the House. Finally, they would need sixty votes in the Senate to override a Democratic filibuster.[2]

LO3 *Energy Policy*

As a priority for the Obama administration, energy policy was second only to health-care policy. Energy policy is important because of two problems: (1) our reliance on imported oil and (2) the possibility of global warming.

The Problem of Imported Oil

Our nation imports about three-fifths of its petroleum supply. Oil imports are a potential problem largely because many of the nations that export oil are not particularly friendly to the United States. Some, such as Iran, are outright adversaries. Other oil exporters that could pose difficulties include Iraq, Libya, Nigeria, Russia, and Venezuela. Even Saudi Arabia, nominally a U.S. friend, is something of a question mark. Most of the terrorists

reconciliation A special kind of legislation not subject to filibuster in the Senate. A reconciliation act must deal only with financial matters.

Congressional Budget Office (CBO) An agency established by Congress to evaluate the impact of proposed legislation on the federal budget.

Corporate Average Fuel Economy (CAFE) standards A set of federal standards under which each manufacturer must meet a miles-per-gallon benchmark averaged across all cars or trucks that it sells.

global warming An increase in the average temperature of the Earth's surface over the last half century and its projected continuation.

greenhouse gas A gas that, when released into the atmosphere, traps the sun's heat and slows its release into outer space. Carbon dioxide (CO_2) is a major example.

who attacked the United States on 9/11 were Saudis, and many Saudis have anti-Western attitudes. A change of regime in Saudi Arabia could spell big trouble. Some exporters, including Iraq, Nigeria, and Venezuela, have recently experienced drops in oil production due to internal disturbances. Fortunately for the United States, half of our oil imports come from Canada and Mexico, stable and friendly neighbors to the north and south. Venezuela, however, is also a major American supplier. In addition, many of our European and Asian allies are dependent on imports from questionable regimes.

THE PRICE OF OIL Until fairly recently, the price of oil was low, and the U.S. government was under little pressure to address our dependence on imports. In 1998, the price per barrel fell below $12. In July 2008, however, on the eve of the collapse of the Lehman Brothers investment bank, the price of oil spiked to more than $125 a barrel, forcing U.S. gasoline prices above $4 per gallon. Thereafter, oil prices fell dramatically when demand collapsed due to the global economic panic. Experts believe, however, that oil prices will rise again as economic activity resumes.

U.S. ENERGY POLICIES The federal government responded to an earlier spurt in oil prices, in the 1970s, by imposing fuel-mileage standards on cars and trucks sold in this country. Under the **Corporate Average Fuel Economy (CAFE) standards,** each manufacturer had to meet a miles-per-gallon benchmark, which was averaged across all cars and trucks that it sold. Under the rules, trucks were allowed to consume more fuel. One unintended result was that when oil prices dropped in the 1980s, Americans began turning away from automobiles and toward pickups and SUVs, which were considered trucks under the standards.

Many economists have long argued that the best way to encourage fuel economy would be to impose a new federal tax on gasoline and diesel fuel, perhaps fifty cents per gallon. The resulting revenues could be used to lower other taxes. European nations have much higher taxes on fuel than the United States does, and as a result, Europeans tend to favor smaller, more fuel-efficient vehicles. Very few American politicians have been willing to endorse such a concept, however. They rightly judged that it would be political poison.

The steep rise in oil prices in 2007 and 2008, plus the election of a Democratic Congress and president, meant that measures to restrain U.S. fuel consumption were on the agenda again. In 2009, President Obama issued higher fuel-efficiency standards for cars and trucks. By 2016, the standards will be thirty-nine miles per gallon for cars and thirty miles per gallon for light trucks. The standards began to take effect in 2010. Because of this government mandate, along with expected high fuel prices, vehicles that are more fuel efficient will almost certainly be part of America's future. Many of the new vehicles will run at least partially on electric power.

Global Warming

Observations collected by agencies such as the National Aeronautics and Space Administration (NASA) suggest that during the last century, average global temperatures increased by about 0.74 degrees Celsius (1.33 degrees Fahrenheit). Figure 15–1 on the facing page illustrates this phenomenon. Most climatologists believe that this **global warming** is the result of human activities, especially the release of **greenhouse gases** into the atmosphere. A United Nations body, the Intergovernmental Panel on Climate Change (IPCC), estimated that during the twenty-first century, global temperatures could rise an additional 1.1 to 6.4 degrees Celsius (2.0 to 11.5 degrees Fahrenheit). Warming may continue in subsequent centuries.

"NATURE PROVIDES A FREE LUNCH but only if we control our appetites."

~ WILLIAM DOYLE RUCKELSHAUS ~
FIRST HEAD OF THE ENVIRONMENTAL PROTECTION AGENCY
1970–1973

The predicted outcomes of global warming vary depending on the climate models on which they are based. If the oceans grow warmer, seawater will expand and polar ice will melt. These two developments will cause sea levels to rise, possibly drowning some coastal areas. Rainfall patterns are expected to change, turning some

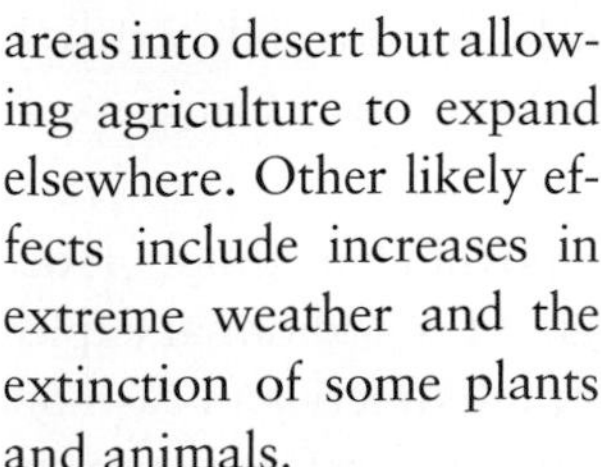

areas into desert but allowing agriculture to expand elsewhere. Other likely effects include increases in extreme weather and the extinction of some plants and animals.

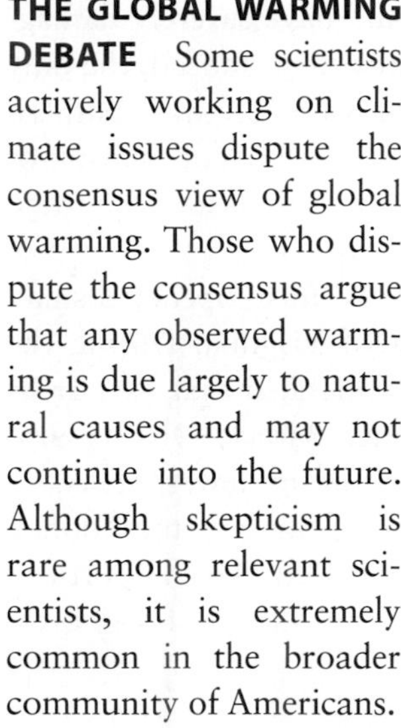

THE GLOBAL WARMING DEBATE Some scientists actively working on climate issues dispute the consensus view of global warming. Those who dispute the consensus argue that any observed warming is due largely to natural causes and may not continue into the future. Although skepticism is rare among relevant scientists, it is extremely common in the broader community of Americans.

A Gallup poll in 2009 revealed that only 49 percent of those with an opinion believed that global warming is the result of human activities. Furthermore, attitudes toward global warming have become highly politicized. Some commentators on the political right contend that global warming is a giant liberal hoax designed to clear the way for increased government control of the economy and society. At the same time, many on the political left believe that the right-wing refusal to accept the existence of global warming threatens the very future of the human race. Members of Congress are influenced by these attitudes even if they do not necessarily share them, and as a result, congressional Republicans and Democrats have almost no common ground on questions of how global warming might be reduced or its effects mitigated.

Figure 15–1

Global Warming

Temperature change in degrees Celsius (°C) from 1951–1980 to 2000–2010.

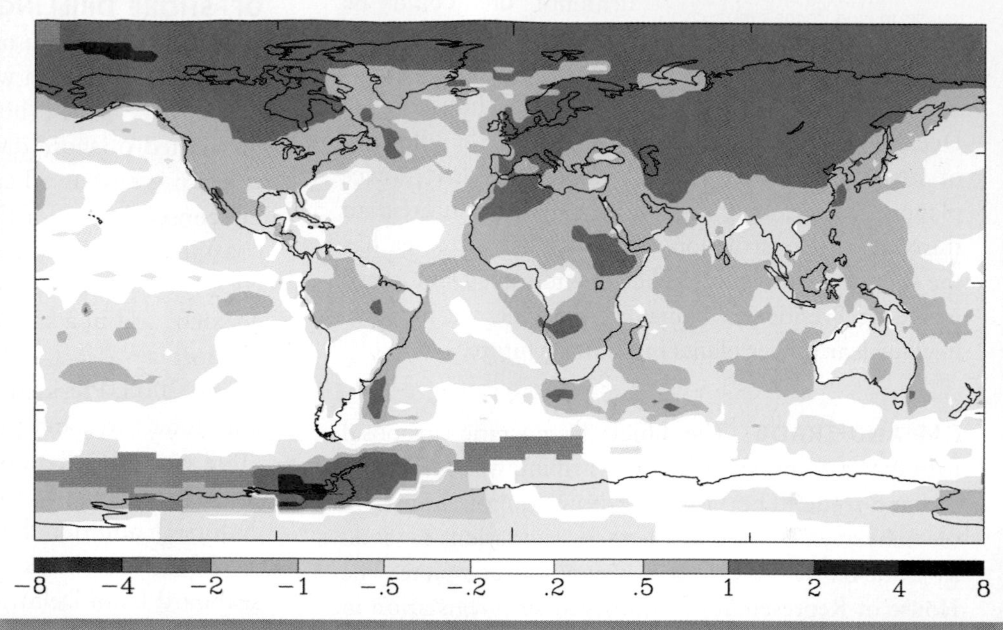

Source: NASA/GISS (Goddard Institute for Space Studies).

RENEWABLE ENERGY Not all methods of supplying the economy with energy depend on burning carbon and thus releasing greenhouse gases into the environment. For example, hydroelectric energy, generated by water flowing through dams, is a widely used technology that employs no coal, natural gas, oil, or other fossil fuels. Energy from such technologies is referred to as **renewable energy,** because it does not rely on extracted resources, such as oil and coal, that can run out. Obviously, the use of renewable energy has many benefits. For one thing, it can be an effective method of reducing potential global warming. The problem is that most existing renewable technologies, such as solar power cells, are expensive. Hydropower is an exception, but the number of feasible locations for new dams in the United States is small, and dams create their own environmental problems.

Wind Energy One renewable technology that is almost as economical as conventional power sources is wind energy, and both the Bush and Obama administrations have subsidized wind power. Windmills are now under construction in many locations. Of course, even if the price is right, wind power suffers from one obvious problem: the wind does not always blow, so wind cannot provide more than a modest share of the nation's electrical needs. Still, Obama's February 2009 stimulus package set aside billions of dollars that could be used for high-tension lines to transport electricity from rural wind farms to major cities.

Nuclear Energy An additional energy source that does not contribute to global warming is nuclear power. This

renewable energy
Energy from technologies that do not rely on extracted resources, such as oil and coal, that can run out.

cap-and-trade A method of restricting the production of a harmful substance. A cap is set on the volume of production, and permits to produce the substance can then be traded on the open market.

technology is not actually renewable, because high-quality deposits of uranium ore could be depleted someday. Still, nuclear power does not release greenhouse gases. Due to concern over possible dangers and the difficulty of storing spent nuclear fuel, no new nuclear power plants have been built in the United States in more than thirty years. Construction of new plants, however, has the support of most Republicans and some Democrats, including President Obama. As a result, we may see new nuclear power plants in the near future.

CAP-AND-TRADE The chief Democratic proposal to respond to possible global warming was known as **cap-and-trade.** The Obama administration hoped to see movement on cap-and-trade legislation as soon as work on health-care legislation was complete. The House of Representatives approved such legislation in June 2009.

Under the bill, the government would establish a cap for CO_2 emissions. Major emitters would need permits, which they could buy and sell—or trade—on the open market. Over time, the cap would decline, resulting in a reduction in emissions. Cap-and-trade died in the Senate, however, and there appears to be no possibility that it could be resurrected during the 2011–2013 Congress.

OFFSHORE DRILLING One possible method of decreasing our reliance on foreign oil is additional exploration and drilling in waters off the American coastline. For twenty years, however, the federal government prohibited offshore drilling in much of the ocean. The concern was that oil spills could have severely damaging consequences for the environment. Indeed, the only coastal areas open to drilling were off the southern coast of Alaska, in the western two-thirds of the Gulf of Mexico, and in a small patch off the coast of Southern California.

In 2008, President George W. Bush opened a small additional area off the coast of Virginia. During the 2008 elections, Republicans demanded that vast areas be made available for drilling. Barack Obama also endorsed additional drilling, but in fewer areas. In March 2010, Obama proposed opening up the Atlantic seaboard from Delaware to northern Florida, portions of the eastern Gulf of Mexico, and waters off the northern coast of Alaska.

THE BP OIL SPILL IN THE GULF OF MEXICO On April 20, 2010, three weeks after Obama's announcement, an offshore drilling platform in the Gulf of Mexico exploded and sank. Eleven workers died, and a torrent of oil and gas began flowing into the Gulf. Before long, tar balls began floating ashore on the Louisiana coast. The drilling platform was leased to BP, formerly known as British Petroleum. BP made multiple attempts to block the undersea leak, all of which failed. A major problem was that the leak was 5,000 feet below the surface. BP also funded a massive cleanup effort by local workers and the federal government.

In May, Obama placed a six-month moratorium on deepwater drilling projects. A federal district court judge ruled the moratorium illegal—so the Department of Interior issued a new one. In June, Obama secured BP's promise to establish a $20 billion fund to pay damage claims. In mid-July, BP was finally able to stop the leak.

During the BP oil spill in the summer of 2010, government and private-sector teams participated in oil cleanup efforts.

AP PHOTO/DAVE MARTIN

The well was permanently plugged via relief wells in September. By that time, 4.9 million barrels of oil had spilled into the sea—the largest oil spill in American history. In October, the government lifted the moratorium one month before it was due to expire.

During the period before the leak was plugged, the federal government was widely derided for its inability to deal with the problem. This criticism was somewhat unfair, because oil leaks and fires had always been the responsibility of the petroleum industry, and thus the federal government had no particular competence in addressing such disasters. It soon became obvious, however, that the federal agency in charge of overseeing drilling safety was fatally corrupt. It was dissolved and replaced with a new one. By the time of the 2010 elections, the oil spill had receded as a national political issue, although it remained powerful in Louisiana and other Gulf states. The negative impact on the offshore oil drilling industry was more long-lasting.

LO4 *Economic Policy*

Economic policy consists of all actions taken by the government to address the ups and downs in the nation's level of business activity. National economic policy is solely the responsibility of the national government.

Federal Reserve chair Ben Bernanke (left) sits with U.S. Treasury secretary Tim Geithner at a meeting of twenty leading nations (the so-called G-20) in 2009. In the past, the Fed and the U.S. Treasury rarely worked together because the Fed is supposed to be an independent agency.

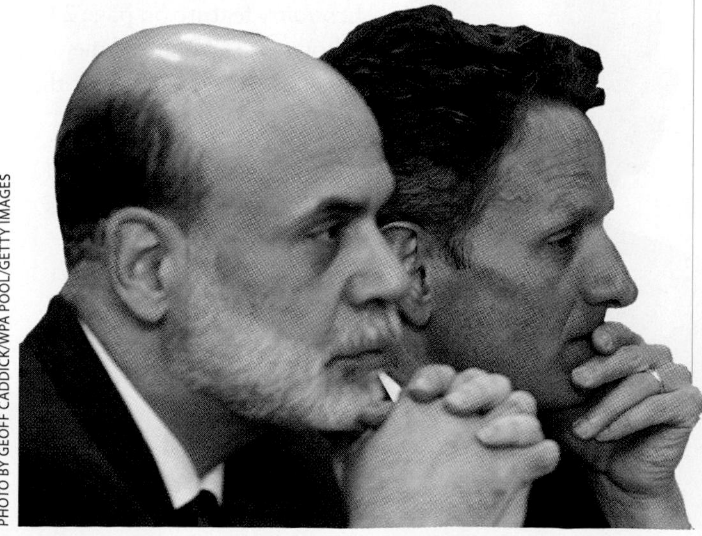

PHOTO BY GEOFF CADDICK/WPA POOL/GETTY IMAGES

One of the tools used in this process is **monetary policy,** which involves changing the amount of money in circulation so as to affect interest rates, credit markets, the rate of inflation, the rate of economic growth, and the rate of unemployment. You read about monetary policy in the *Our Government Faces a Troubled Economy* feature in Chapter 2 (see page 40). There, we explained that monetary policy is under the control of the Federal Reserve System, an independent regulatory agency.

The national government also controls **fiscal policy,** which involves changes in government expenditures and taxes to alter national economic variables. These variables include the rate of unemployment, the total number of those in the labor market, labor force participation rates, and the rate of economic growth.

In this section, we look briefly at the politics of monetary and fiscal policy, as well as the federal tax system and the issue of deficit spending.

economic policy All actions taken by the national government to smooth out the ups and downs in the nation's level of business activity.

monetary policy Actions taken by the Federal Reserve Board to change the amount of money in circulation so as to affect interest rates, credit markets, the rate of inflation, the rate of economic growth, and the rate of unemployment.

fiscal policy The use of changes in government expenditures and taxes to alter national economic variables.

Federal Open Market Committee (FOMC) The most important body within the Federal Reserve System. The FOMC decides how monetary policy should be carried out by the Federal Reserve.

Monetary Policy

The Federal Reserve System (the Fed) was established by Congress as the nation's central banking system in 1913. The Fed is governed by a board of seven governors, including the very powerful chairperson. The president appoints the members of the board of governors, and the Senate must approve the nominations. Members of the board serve for fourteen-year terms. Although the Fed's board of governors acts independently, the Fed has, on occasion, yielded to presidential pressure, and the Fed's chairperson must follow a congressional resolution requiring him or her to report monetary targets over each six-month period. Nevertheless, until recently, the Fed has remained one of the truly independent sources of economic power in the government.

The Fed and its **Federal Open Market Committee (FOMC)** make decisions about monetary policy several times each year. In theory, monetary policy is relatively

easy-money policy A monetary policy that involves stimulating the economy by expanding the rate of growth of the money supply. An easy-money policy supposedly will lead to lower interest rates and induce consumers to spend more and producers to invest more.

Keynesian economics An economic theory proposed by British economist John Maynard Keynes that is typically associated with the use of fiscal policy to alter national economic variables.

straightforward. In periods of recession and high unemployment, we should pursue an **easy-money policy** to stimulate the economy by expanding the rate of growth of the money supply. An easy-money policy supposedly will lead to lower interest rates and induce consumers to spend more and producers to invest more. In periods of rising inflation, the Fed does the reverse: it reduces the rate of growth in the amount of money in circulation. This policy should cause interest rates to rise, thus inducing consumers to spend less and businesses to invest less. In theory, this sounds quite simple. The reality, however, is not simple at all. To give one example, if times are hard enough, people and businesses may not want to borrow even if interest rates go down to zero, and an easy-money policy will have little effect.

An additional difficulty is the length of time it takes for a change in monetary policy to become effective. There is usually a lag of about fourteen months between the time the economy slows down (or speeds up) and the time the economy begins to feel the effects of a policy change. Therefore, by the time a change in policy becomes effective, a different policy may be needed.

Fiscal Policy

The principle underlying fiscal policy, like the one that underlies monetary policy, is relatively simple: when unemployment is rising and the economy is going into a recession, fiscal policy should stimulate economic activity by increasing government spending, decreasing taxes, or both. When unemployment is decreasing and prices are rising (that is, when we have inflation), fiscal policy should curb economic activity by reducing government spending, increasing taxes, or both. In Chapter 3's *Our Government Faces a Troubled Economy* feature (see page 66), we explained that this view of fiscal policy is an outgrowth of the economic theories of the British economist John Maynard Keynes (1883–1946). Keynes's theories were the result of his study of the Great Depression of the 1930s.

Keynesian economics suggests that the forces of supply and demand operate too slowly in recessions, and therefore the government should undertake actions to stimulate the economy during such periods. Keynesian economists maintain that the Great Depression resulted from a serious imbalance in the economy. The public was saving more than usual, and businesses were investing less than usual. According to Keynesian theory, at the beginning of the Depression, the government should have filled the gap that was created when businesses began limiting their investments. The government could have done so by increasing government spending or cutting taxes.

One of the problems with fiscal policy is that, just as with monetary policy, typically a lag exists between the government's decision to institute fiscal policy and the actual implementation of that policy. It is up to Congress, through its many committees, to enact the legislation necessary to implement fiscal policy.

The Federal Tax System

The government raises money to pay its expenses in two ways: through taxes levied on business and personal income and through borrowing. In 1960, individuals paid 52 percent of total federal tax revenues. By 2009, this proportion was more than 80 percent (adding income taxes and Social Security payments together). The American income tax system is progressive—meaning that as you earn more income, you pay a higher tax rate on the additional income earned. The 2010 tax rates are shown in Table 15–1 on the facing page. The tax rates for 2011 will not be known until Congress decides whether to extend some or all of the tax cuts enacted under President George W. Bush in 2003. The cuts were set to expire at the end of 2010. (See Chapter 11's *Our Government Faces a Troubled Economy* feature on page 244.) About 40 percent of American families earn so little that they

WALTER STONEMAN/SAMUEL BOURNE/GETTY IMAGES

British economist John Maynard Keynes developed theories of how to pull the world out of the Great Depression in the 1930s. His work was cited frequently during the Great Recession that started in December 2007.

PERCEPTION VERSUS REALITY

Tax-Rate Cuts Allow the Rich to Pay Lower Taxes

As the saying goes, only two things are certain—death and taxes. In recent years, though, different presidents have instituted a number of tax-rate cuts. The last one occurred in 2003 under the administration of George W. Bush.

The Perception

You often hear or read that the Bush tax-rate cuts favored the rich. After all, it's the rich who received the lion's share of the benefits from these tax-rate cuts.

The Reality

First, we must distinguish between tax rates and taxes paid. It is true that the Bush tax cuts lowered the top marginal tax rate from 39.6 percent to 35 percent and that the long-term capital gains tax rate dropped from 20 percent to 15 percent. Also, the rate applied to dividends fell. Therefore, the tax rates on the highest-income individuals did indeed fall after the tax cuts of 2003 were enacted.

At the same time, though, the percentage of taxes paid by the rich went up, not down. Indeed, the share of individual income tax liabilities paid by the top 1 percent of income earners rose steadily from about 1981 to 2000, dropped off a bit from 2000 to 2003, and has risen ever since. According to the nonpartisan Congressional Budget Office, the top 40 percent of income earners in the United States pay 99.1 percent of all income taxes. The top 10 percent pay more than 70 percent of all income taxes. At the bottom end of the scale, about 40 percent of this nation's households pay no income taxes at all (though they do pay Social Security contributions). Finally, it is true that the rich have been getting richer in the United States. Nevertheless, their share of income has gone up more slowly than their share of individual tax liabilities.

These data give us some indication of what may happen if Congress fails to extend the Bush tax cuts on the upper tax brackets. If these cuts expire, capital gains taxes will rise from 15 percent to 20 percent. The income tax rate for those making more than $250,000 per year will go up from 35 percent to 39.6 percent. What we may see is an ironic reversal in the percentage of taxes (not the tax rate) paid by the rich—it could actually decrease when higher tax rates become reality.

Blog On Scott Adams, creator of the *Dilbert* comic strip, makes hilarious and fresh observations about all sorts of things on his blog. Taxing the rich is just one of his topics—see **dilbertblog.typepad.com/the_dilbert_blog/2007/07/how-to-tax-the-.html.** The blog of Harvard economics professor Greg Mankiw has an interesting discussion at **gregmankiw.blogspot.com/2006/04/are-rich-paying-enough.html.**

Table 15–1

Tax Rates for Single Persons and Married Couples (2010)

Single Persons: Tax Bracket ($)	Single Persons: Marginal Tax Rate (%)	Married Filing Jointly: Tax Bracket ($)	Married Filing Jointly: Marginal Tax Rate (%)
0–8,350	10	0–16,700	10
8,350–33,950	15	16,700–67,900	15
33,950–82,250	25	67,900–137,050	25
82,250–171,550	28	137,050–208,850	28
171,550–372,950	33	208,850–372,950	33
372,950 and higher	35	352,950 and higher	35

Source: Internal Revenue Service.

have no income tax liability at all. (For a discussion of the amount of taxes paid by the rich versus other groups in American society, see this chapter's *Perception versus Reality* feature above.)

THE ACTION-REACTION SYNDROME The Internal Revenue Code consists of thousands of pages, thousands of sections, and thousands of subsections. In other words, our tax system is not simple. Part of the reason for this is that tax policy has always been plagued by the **action-reaction syndrome,** a term describing the following phenomenon: *for every government action, there will be a reaction*

action-reaction syndrome For every government action, there will be a reaction by the public. The government then takes a further action to counter the public's reaction—and the cycle begins again.

by the public. Eventually, the government will react with another action, and the public will follow with further reaction. The ongoing action-reaction cycle is clearly operative in policymaking on taxes.

TAX LOOPHOLES Generally, the action-reaction syndrome means that the higher the tax rate—the action on the part of the government—the greater the public's reaction to that tax rate. Individuals and corporations facing high tax rates will react by making concerted attempts to get Congress to add various loopholes to the tax law that will allow them to reduce their taxable incomes.

Years ago, when Congress imposed very high tax rates on high incomes, it also provided for more loopholes. These loopholes enabled many wealthy individuals to decrease their tax bills significantly. For example, special tax provisions allowed investors in oil and gas wells to reduce their taxable income. Additional loopholes permitted individuals to shift income from one year to the next—which meant that they could postpone the payment of their taxes for one year. Still more loopholes let U.S. citizens form corporations outside the United States in order to avoid some taxes completely.

WILL WE EVER HAVE A TRULY SIMPLE TAX SYSTEM? The Tax Reform Act of 1986 was intended to lower taxes and simplify the tax code—and it did just that for most taxpayers. A few years later, however, large federal deficits forced Congress to choose between cutting spending and raising taxes, and Congress opted to do the latter. Tax increases occurred under the administrations of both George H. W. Bush (1989–1993) and Bill Clinton. In fact, the tax rate for the highest income bracket rose from 28 percent in 1986 to 39.6 percent in 1993. Thus, the effective highest marginal tax rate increased significantly.

In response to this sharp increase in taxes, those who were affected lobbied Congress to legislate special exceptions and loopholes so that the full impact of the rate increase would not be felt by the wealthiest Americans. As a result, the tax code is more complicated than it was before the 1986 Tax Reform Act.

Some people see the complications of our tax code as a limitation on our economic freedom. For a look at the issue of economic freedom around the world, see this chapter's *The Rest of the World* feature on the facing page.

While in principle everyone is for a simpler tax code, in practice Congress rarely is able to pass tax-reform legislation. Why? The reason is that those who now benefit from our complicated tax code will not give up their tax breaks without a fight. These groups include homeowners who deduct interest on their mortgages (and therefore the home-building industry as well), charities that receive tax-deductible contributions, and businesses that get tax breaks for research and development. Two other groups also benefit greatly from the current complicated tax code: tax accountants and tax lawyers.

public debt The total amount of money that the national government owes as a result of borrowing; also called the *national debt*.

The Public Debt

When the government spends more than it receives, it has to finance this shortfall. Typically, it borrows. The U.S. Treasury sells IOUs on behalf of the U.S. government. They are called U.S. Treasury bills, notes, or bonds, depending on how long the funds are borrowed. All are commonly called *treasuries*. The sale of these obligations to corporations, private individuals, pension plans, foreign governments, foreign companies, and foreign individuals is big business. After all, except for a few years in the late 1990s and early 2000s, federal government expenditures have always exceeded federal government revenues.

Every time there is a federal government deficit, there is an increase in the total accumulated **public debt** (also called the *national debt*), which is defined as the total value of all outstanding federal government borrowing. If the existing public debt is $5 trillion and the

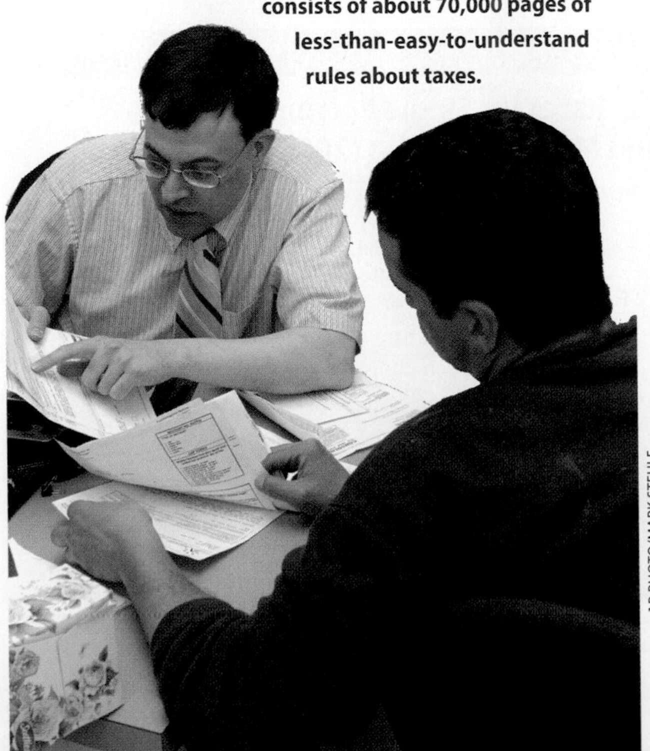

Every year, millions of Americans go see their tax preparers to help them figure out the complicated forms that must be submitted to the Internal Revenue Service. The Tax Code consists of about 70,000 pages of less-than-easy-to-understand rules about taxes.

AP PHOTO/MARK STEHLE

The Relationship between Economic Freedom and Prosperity

For decades, political scientists and economists, as well as sociologists, have examined the key differences between developing countries and developed countries. For decades, the consensus has been that developed countries must transfer more wealth to less developed countries if these poorer nations are to experience economic growth. International institutions such as the World Bank have argued for investments in infrastructure such as roads, sewers, and the like. Some specialists in development argue that impoverished people in developing countries will remain in permanent misery unless the richer countries transfer more wealth to them.

Freedom Enters the Picture

A small but growing band of development specialists see a different path out of misery for the world's poorest countries. They look at the degree of economic freedom and find some powerful correlations. As it turns out, freedom and prosperity are positively related. The freedom we are referring to here is economic freedom, not necessarily political freedom. (Note that in countries where citizens have obtained economic freedom, political freedom often follows after a number of years.)

The 2010 Index of Economic Freedom ranks countries from Hong Kong (number one) to North Korea (last on the list) in terms of how much economic freedom the citizens really have. It turns out that the freest 20 percent of the world's economies have average per-person incomes that are five times greater than those of the least free 20 percent.

Why Economic Freedom Matters

Development specialists who stress the positive relationship between economic freedom and prosperity offer several reasons why such freedom is so important. They believe that the degree of efficiency with which any society uses its scarce resources to produce goods and services is a key element in the speed of economic growth for all citizens. If there is little economic freedom in a society, entrepreneurs face huge barriers to innovation and to starting new businesses. The result is very little economic growth. This analysis holds true for such economically stagnant countries as Belarus, Myanmar (Burma), Cuba, Iran, North Korea, and Zimbabwe. Despite their oil wealth, Russia and Venezuela appear to be headed in this direction as well.

For Critical Analysis *Why do you think multinational agencies such as the World Bank are in favor of massive foreign aid programs for developing countries?*

AP PHOTO

Children eat mangoes in a suburb of Harare, Zimbabwe.

government runs a deficit of $100 billion, then at the end of the year the public debt is $5.1 trillion. Table 15–2 at right shows what has happened to the *net* public debt over time. (The net public debt doesn't count sums that the government owes to itself.)

THE BURDEN OF THE PUBLIC DEBT We often hear about the burden of the public debt. Some even maintain that the government will eventually go bankrupt. As long as the government can collect taxes to pay interest on its public debt, however, that will never happen. What happens instead is that when treasuries come due, they are simply "rolled over," or refinanced. That is, if a $1 million Treasury bond comes due today and is cashed in, the U.S. Treasury pays it off with the money it gets from selling another $1 million bond.

Table 15–2

The Public Debt

Year	Net Public Debt (Billions of Current Dollars)	Year	Net Public Debt (Billions of Current Dollars)
1945	235.2	2003	3,924.1
1950	219.0	2004	4,307.3
1960	236.8	2005	4,601.2
1970	283.2	2006	4,843.1
1980	811.9	2007	5,049.3
1990	2,411.6	2008	5,808.7
1995	3,604.4	2009	7,551.9
2000	3,405.3	2010	9,022.8*
2001	3,339.3	2011	10,120.1*
2002	3,553.2		

*Estimate.
Sources: 1945–1995, U.S. Office of Management and Budget; 2000–2011, U.S. Treasury..

Our Government Faces a Troubled Economy: Red Ink Forever?

A response of the federal government to the Great Recession has been to increase spending. Not since the buildup to World War II has the government increased its spending as fast as it did in late 2008 and in 2009. At the same time, the economy was shrinking, so tax revenues were shrinking, too. Between increased spending and lower revenues, the federal budget deficit shot up. The estimated deficit for 2010 was $1.3 trillion. That was almost 9 percent of the entire economy. For 2011, the estimated deficit was about the same. Take all levels of government together: For every five dollars of spending, three were backed up by tax receipts. The other two were borrowed.

Deficit Spending to Fight the Great Recession

As you read in this chapter, many economists accept the theories of John Maynard Keynes. They advocate government spending and tax cuts to fight a recession, paid for by running up the deficit. When Obama took office, his advisers recommended this solution. Obama's February 2009 stimulus bill was the result. Despite the stimulus, the unemployment rate reached 10 percent in 2009—the highest in decades. Keynesian economists argued that the stimulus had been too small. Not surprisingly, most voters concluded that it was not helping at all.

Short-Term versus Long-Term Deficits

Even if you believe that a Keynesian stimulus doesn't work—and there are economists as well as voters who think that—the deficits are meant to be temporary. Once the recession is over, the government should cut back or even abolish the deficits. No Keynesian economist advises running huge budget deficits until the end of time. But that is what we see in President Obama's budget forecast. Even when the recession is over, the deficit is predicted to remain at $0.7 trillion to $0.8 trillion more or less forever. In a few years, that will run the national debt up past 100 percent of GDP. Peter Orszag, Obama's budget director in 2009 and 2010, admitted that such deficits were "unsustainable." But the Democrats have not shown the courage necessary to address this issue.

A Republican Alternative?

Do the Republicans offer an alternative? They definitely made the deficit a major campaign issue in 2010. Republican policy positions, however, tend to contradict the goal of fixing the long-term deficit. For example, as part of the recent health-care reform legislation, Democrats proposed reducing the rate at which future Medicare spending would rise. Republicans saw the cost curbs as a reason to oppose the program. The Republican platform for the 2010 elections put Medicare, military spending, and Social Security off limits, and it opposed any new taxes. Yet with that much spending "ring-fenced" and with no new revenues, it would have been necessary to shut down the rest of the federal government to balance the budget in 2011 or 2012.

Given the positions of both parties, many citizens wonder: What will happen in the future? How will we pay for these huge deficits? And will the federal government crowd out the rest of the economy?

You Be the Judge **What kind of spending cuts, if any, would you be willing to accept to bring down the long-term deficit? What kind of tax increases, if any?**

The interest on treasuries is paid by federal taxes. Even though much of the interest is being paid to American citizens, the more the federal government borrows to meet these payments, the greater the percentage of its budget that is committed to making interest payments. This reduces the government's ability to supply funds for anything else, including transportation, education, housing programs, and the military.

PUBLIC DEBT EXPLOSION IN 2008 AND 2009 Due to the financial meltdown that began in 2008, Congress passed historic legislation that involved hundreds of billions of dollars in additional spending. Ultimately, the net public debt will rise by trillions of dollars. Just how much trouble is this explosion in public debt likely to cause? We consider that issue in this chapter's *Our Government Faces a Troubled Economy* feature on the facing page.

PERCENTAGE OF THE DEBT HELD BY FOREIGNERS An additional problem with a growing federal debt involves how much non-Americans own. Today, more than 55 percent of the U.S. net public debt is owned by foreign individuals, foreign businesses, and foreign central banks. Some worry that these foreigners might not want to keep all of this U.S. debt. If that were ever to happen, their efforts to sell U.S. government treasuries might lead to a collapse in the markets for government obligations in this country. The result would be much higher interest rates.

There does not appear to be much evidence, however, that such a disaster will happen anytime soon. During the recent economic crises, frightened investors bought more treasuries in the belief that they were the safest possible investment. As a result, the government has been able to borrow at very low interest rates. For example, the September 2010 rate for four-week bills, the shortest-term obligations, dipped below 0.1 percent. (The rate for five-year notes was 1.25 percent and the rate for thirty-year bonds was 3.875 percent.)

AMERICA AT **ODDS** *Domestic Policy*

The Preamble to the U.S. Constitution states that one of the goals of the new government was to "promote the general Welfare." Domestic policy is certainly the main way in which our government seeks to promote the general welfare. But how should this be done? Americans are at odds over many domestic issues. A few of them are listed here:

- Do we send too many people to prison—or do our current incarceration policies protect the public?
- Should unauthorized immigrants be given the opportunity to regularize their position—or would such a measure merely increase the number of illegal immigrants in the future?
- Should universal health-care insurance be a right of all citizens—or does such a program sap individual initiative and lead to an over-mighty government?
- Is global warming a serious problem that must be addressed now—or are the risks overblown and the proposed solutions a danger to our economy?
- Is new offshore drilling essential to our energy independence—or is it an unacceptable threat to the environment?
- Is budgetary stimulus a necessary tool to fight recessions—or does it simply worsen the long-term budget deficit?

Take Action

In 2007, John Kerry and Teresa Heinz Kerry published a book titled *This Moment on Earth: Today's New Environmentalists and Their Vision for the Future.*[3] The book details, in an eminently readable fashion, how numerous individuals and groups have successfully taken action over the years to help protect the health of the environment. If you want to take action to help protect the environment, read through the Kerrys' book. You, like many others, may find the stories of other people's successful actions inspiring. For a list of simple changes you can make in your day-to-day life to preserve energy—from buying energy-efficient appliances to turning off electric lights and electrical appliances when they're not in use—see Appendix B in their book, which is titled "What You Can Do." The appendix also includes a list of environmental groups, with contact information for each group.

AP PHOTO/RICK BOWMER

Linda Ziedrich, author of *The Joy of Pickling,* is shown in her garden in Scio, Oregon.

POLITICS ON THE WEB

- The size of the national debt is a hot topic. You can find out more about the size of the national debt and other subjects at **www.treasurydirect.gov**
- The U.S. Census Bureau provides "USA Statistics in Brief" at **www.census.gov/compendia/statab/brief.html**. If you can't find the data you're looking for here, start with the Census Bureau's home page at **www.census.gov**
- If you are interested in reading the *Economic Report of the President*, go to **www.gpoaccess.gov/eop**
- For a conservative view of domestic policy issues, including economic policy, see the Heritage Foundation site at **www.heritage org**
- Economist Paul Krugman is one of the most readable and entertaining advocates of Keynesian economics and other liberal domestic policies. His blog is at **krugman.blogs.nytimes.com**

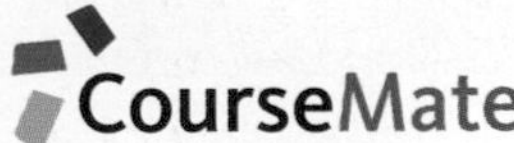

Access CourseMate to review and expand on this chapter through quizzes, flashcards, learning objectives, interactive timelines, a crossword puzzle, audio summaries, video, critical-thinking activities, simulations, and more.

GOVT 16

Foreign Policy

LEARNING OBJECTIVES

LO1 Discuss how foreign policy is made and identify the key players in this process.

LO2 Summarize the history of American foreign policy through the years.

LO3 Identify the foreign policy challenges presented by terrorism and the consequences of the "Bush doctrine" with respect to Iraq.

LO4 Describe the principal issues dividing the Israelis and the Palestinians and the solutions proposed by the international community.

LO5 Outline some of the actions taken by the United States to curb the threat of nuclear weapons.

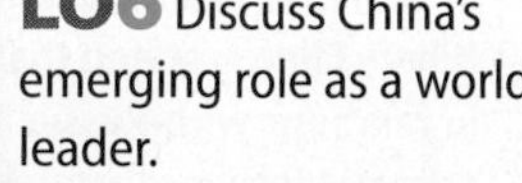

LO6 Discuss China's emerging role as a world leader.

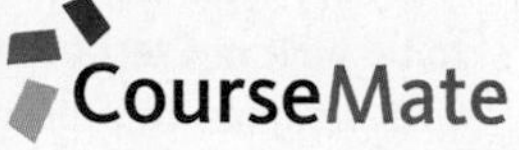

AMERICA AT ODDS

Do Russia's Ambitions Mean Trouble?

In August 2008, the Russian army invaded the small neighboring country of Georgia. The invasion was Russia's first use of troops outside of its own borders since the dissolution of the Soviet Union in 1991. Many people around the world drew the obvious conclusion: the "Russian bear" was back—and it posed a threat to world peace.

During the years of the Cold War, which lasted from the late 1940s until the end of the 1980s, the Russian-dominated Soviet Union clearly was a threat to peace. The Soviets had occupied Eastern Europe. By the 1960s, even the Chinese were worried that the Soviets might attack them. In 1985, the Soviets had more personnel in uniform than any other nation. Its nuclear weapons were at least equal to those of the United States. In 1985, the Soviet Union also had a population of 278 million, compared with 238 million in the United States.

The impact of the Soviet breakup on Russian power was almost beyond belief. With the loss of the fourteen other Soviet republics, Russia stood alone. Its population in 1995 was 150 million. Its economy was in a state of collapse. Its army had only 40 percent as many soldiers as the Soviet army had had, and its inventory of main battle tanks had fallen from 51,000 to 19,500.[1] Russia was unable to prevent its former "satellite states" in Eastern Europe from joining NATO, the American-led alliance originally established to defend the West against the Soviets.

Russia today is nowhere near as formidable as the Soviet Union was—but how much of a threat is it, really? Americans who take an interest in foreign affairs are at odds over this issue.

A Stronger Russia Is Bad News

Those who believe that Russia poses a substantial threat to world peace point to its attack on Georgia, threats made against Ukraine, and the cyberwar it recently launched against the tiny nation of Estonia. Furthermore, Russia is regaining the economic power needed to support a large military. Its economy experienced a substantial recovery during the presidency of Vladimir Putin (2000–2008). Naturally, Putin was popular, and his popularity was not damaged by the way he undermined Russia's democratic institutions.

Russia is the world's largest exporter of natural gas and the second-largest oil exporter. It is Europe's biggest supplier of oil and natural gas, currently providing 33 percent of Europe's oil imports and 38 percent of its natural gas. Ominously, Russia has repeatedly used its energy exports for political purposes. It has temporarily cut off gas supplies to Belarus, the Czech Republic, Georgia, Lithuania, and Ukraine.

Russia's Future as a Great Power Looks Grim

Those who are less worried about the return of the Russian bear point out several factors that may undermine its future as a world power. In many countries, oil wealth has led to gross corruption and inefficiency, and this has happened in Russia. The greatest threat to Russia's future, however, is its collapsing population. Russia's population is now down to 140 million, and the United Nations estimates that it will fall to a mere 109 million by 2050. Many developed nations expect to lose people in forthcoming years. No nation, however, is experiencing losses that come close to what is predicted for Russia. If Russia is no longer one of the world's most populous countries, it will not be able to maintain its position as a great power. Russia not only has a low birth rate, but a very high death rate. The life expectancy of a Russian male is only about fifty-eight years. Experts attribute this in part to extremely high rates of alcoholism among men.

WHERE DO YOU STAND?

1. **What factors might cause Russia to take a belligerent stand toward neighboring countries?**
2. **In 2009, President Barack Obama and Secretary of State Hillary Clinton stated that they would "push the reset button" in relations with Russia, in an attempt to move beyond the negative feelings that had developed during the Bush administration. Later, Obama canceled a missile system scheduled to be built in Czechoslovakia and Poland. While the system was designed to protect Europe from Iranian missiles, the Russians were convinced it was directed at them. Are these steps likely to prove beneficial? Why or why not?**

EXPLORE THIS ISSUE ONLINE

- **You can find a vast amount of information on Russia, much of it written from a relatively sympathetic point of view, at www.russiaprofile.org.**
- **John Bolton is one of America's best-known foreign policy "hawks." For his criticism of Obama's missile decision, see www.aei.org/article/101060.**

Introduction

What we call **foreign policy** is a systematic and general plan that guides a country's attitudes and actions toward the rest of the world. Foreign policy includes all of the economic, military, commercial, and diplomatic positions and actions that a nation takes in its relationships with other countries. Although foreign policy may seem quite removed from the concerns of everyday life, it can and does have a significant impact on the day-to-day lives of Americans.

American foreign policy has been shaped by two principles that are often seen as contradicting each other. One is **moral idealism,** the belief that the most important goal in foreign policy is to do what is right. Moral idealists think that it is possible for nations to relate to each other as part of a rule-based community. Moral idealism appeals to the American belief that our nation is special and should provide an example to the rest of the world.

A contrasting view is **political realism,** the belief that nations are inevitably selfish. Foreign countries, therefore, are by definition dangerous. Foreign policy must be based on protecting our national security, regardless of moral arguments. Although there have been times when one or the other of these two principles has dominated, U.S. foreign policy has usually been a mixture of both.

JOHN MOORE/GETTY IMAGES

Village elders speak with a U.S. Marine in the Korengal Valley of Kunar Province in eastern Afghanistan. The United States has had active troops in this country for almost a decade as part of its attempt to prevent the Taliban from regaining control.

LO1 Who Makes U.S. Foreign Policy?

The framers of the Constitution envisioned that the president and Congress would cooperate in developing American foreign policy. The Constitution did not spell out exactly how this was to be done, though. As commander in chief, the president has assumed much of the decision-making power in the area of foreign policy. Nonetheless, members of Congress, a number of officials, and a vast national security bureaucracy help to shape the president's decisions and to limit the president's powers.

The President's Role

Article II, Section 2, of the Constitution names the president commander in chief of the armed forces. As commander in chief, the president oversees the military and guides defense policies. Presidents have interpreted this role broadly and have sent American troops, ships, and weapons to trouble spots at home and around the world. The Constitution also authorizes the president to make treaties, which must be approved by two-thirds of the Senate. In addition, the president is empowered to form executive agreements—pacts between the president and the heads of other nations. Executive agreements do not require Senate approval. Furthermore, the president's foreign policy responsibilities take on special significance because the president has ultimate control over the use of nuclear weapons.

As head of state, the president also influences foreign policymaking. As the symbolic head of our government, the president represents the United States to the rest of the world. When a serious foreign policy issue or international question arises, the nation expects the president to make a formal statement on the matter.

The Cabinet

Many members of the president's cabinet concern themselves with international problems and recommend policies to deal with them. As U.S. power in the world has grown and as economic

foreign policy A systematic and general plan that guides a country's attitudes and actions toward the rest of the world. Foreign policy includes all of the economic, military, commercial, and diplomatic positions and actions that a nation takes in its relationships with other countries.

moral idealism In foreign policy, the belief that the most important goal is to do what is right. Moral idealists think that it is possible for nations to cooperate as part of a rule-based community.

political realism In foreign policy, the belief that nations are inevitably selfish, and that we should seek to protect our national security regardless of moral arguments.

factors have become increasingly important, the departments of Commerce, Agriculture, Treasury, and Energy have become more involved in foreign policy decisions. The secretary of state and the secretary of defense, however, are the only cabinet members who concern themselves with foreign policy matters on a full-time basis.

"TO BE PREPARED FOR WAR is one of the most effectual means of preserving peace."

~ GEORGE WASHINGTON ~
COMMANDER OF THE CONTINENTAL ARMY AND FIRST PRESIDENT OF THE UNITED STATES
1789–1797

THE DEPARTMENT OF STATE The Department of State is, in principle, the government agency most directly involved in foreign policy. The department is responsible for diplomatic relations with nearly two hundred independent nations around the globe, as well as with the United Nations and other multilateral organizations, such as the Organization of American States. Most U.S. relations with other countries are maintained through embassies, consulates, and other U.S. offices around the world.

As the head of the State Department, the secretary of state has traditionally played a key role in foreign policymaking, and many presidents have relied heavily on the advice of their secretaries of state. Since the end of World War II, though, the preeminence of the State Department in foreign policy has declined dramatically.

THE DEPARTMENT OF DEFENSE The Department of Defense is the principal executive department that establishes and carries out defense policy and protects our national security. The secretary of defense advises the president on all aspects of U.S. military and defense policy, supervises all of the military activities of the U.S. government, and works to see that the decisions of the president as commander in chief are carried out. The secretary advises and informs the president on the nation's military forces, weapons, and bases and works closely with the U.S. military, especially the Joint Chiefs of Staff, in gathering and studying defense information.

The Joint Chiefs of Staff include the chief of staff of the Army, the chief of staff of the Air Force, the chief of naval operations, and the commandant of the Marine Corps. The chairperson of the Joint Chiefs of Staff is appointed by the president for a four-year term. The joint chiefs regularly serve as the key military advisers to the president, the secretary of defense, and the National Security Council (described next). They are responsible for handing down the president's orders to the nation's military units, preparing strategic plans, and recommending military actions. They also propose military budgets, new weapons systems, and military regulations.

Other Agencies

Several other government agencies are also involved in the foreign relations of the United States. Two key agencies in the area of foreign policy are the National Security Council and the Central Intelligence Agency.

THE NATIONAL SECURITY COUNCIL The National Security Council (NSC) was established by the National Security Act of 1947. The formal members of the NSC include the president, the vice president, the secretary of state, and the secretary of defense, but meetings are often attended by the chairperson of the Joint Chiefs of Staff, the director of the Central Intelligence Agency, and representatives from other departments. The national security adviser, who is a member of the president's White House staff, is the director of the NSC. The adviser informs the president, coordinates advice and information on foreign policy, and serves as a liaison with other officials.

Robert M. Gates became Barack Obama's secretary of defense in 2009. He heads one of two departments that focus exclusively on foreign affairs. Our military is ultimately always headed by a civilian.

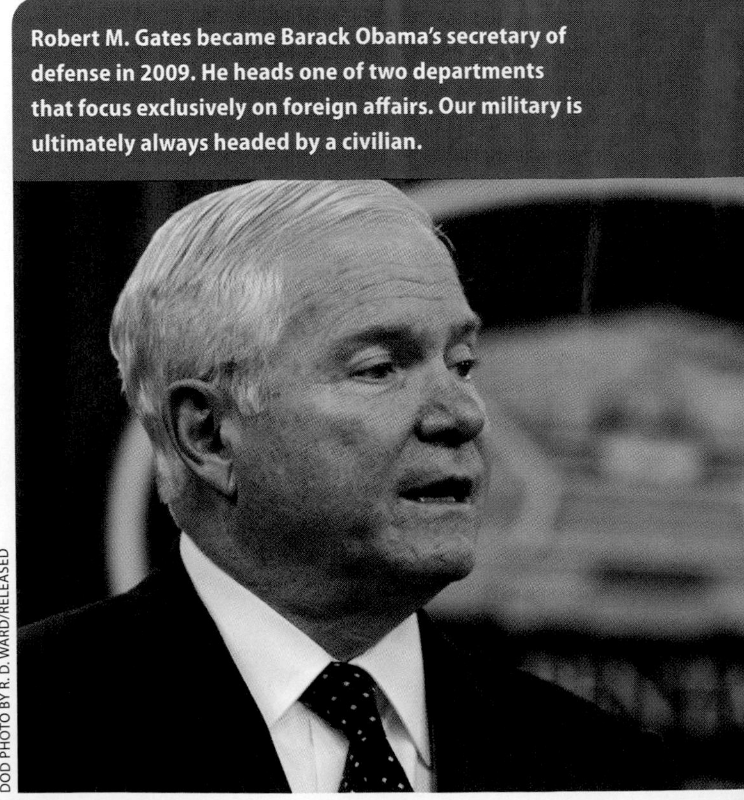
DOD PHOTO BY R. D. WARD/RELEASED

The NSC and its members can be as important and powerful as the president wants them to be. Some presidents have made frequent use of the NSC, whereas others have convened it infrequently. Similarly, the importance of the role played by the national security adviser in shaping foreign policy can vary significantly, depending on the administration and the adviser's identity.

THE CENTRAL INTELLIGENCE AGENCY The Central Intelligence Agency (CIA) was created after World War II to coordinate American intelligence activities abroad. The CIA provides the president and his or her advisers with up-to-date information about the political, military, and economic activities of foreign governments. The CIA gathers much of its intelligence from overt sources, such as foreign radio broadcasts and newspapers, people who travel abroad, the Internet, and satellite photographs. Other information is gathered from covert activities, such as the CIA's own secret investigations into the economic or political affairs of other nations. In addition to its intelligence-gathering functions, the CIA engages in covert operations. It may secretly supply weapons to a force rebelling against an unfriendly government or seize suspected terrorists in a clandestine operation and hold them for questioning.

The CIA has tended to operate autonomously, and the nature of its work, methods, and operating funds is kept secret. Intelligence reform passed by Congress in 2004, however, makes the CIA accountable to a national intelligence director. The CIA is required to cooperate more with other U.S. intelligence agencies and has lost a degree of the autonomy it once enjoyed.

Congress's Powers

Although the executive branch takes the lead in foreign policy matters, Congress also has some power over foreign policy. Remember that Congress alone has the power to declare war. It also has the power to appropriate funds to build new weapons systems, equip the U.S. armed forces, and provide for foreign aid. The Senate has the power to approve or reject the implementation of treaties and the appointment of ambassadors.

In 1973, Congress passed the War Powers Resolution, which limits the president's use of troops in military action without congressional approval. Presidents since then, however, have not interpreted the resolution to mean that Congress must be consulted before military action is taken. On several occasions, presidents have ordered military action and then informed Congress after the fact.

A few congressional committees are directly concerned with foreign affairs. The most important are the Armed Services Committee and the Committee on Foreign Affairs in the House, and the Armed Services Committee and the Foreign Relations Committee in the Senate. Other congressional committees deal with matters, such as oil, agriculture, and imports, that indirectly influence foreign policy.

LO2 *A Short History of American Foreign Policy*

Although many U.S. foreign policy initiatives have been rooted in moral idealism, a primary consideration in U.S. foreign policy has also been national security—the protection of the independence and political integrity of the nation. Over the years, the United States has attempted to preserve its national security in many ways. These ways have changed over time and are not always internally consistent. This is because foreign policymaking, like domestic policymaking, reflects the influence of various political groups in the United States. These groups—including the voting public, interest groups, Congress, and the president and relevant agencies of the executive branch—are often at odds over what the U.S. position should be on particular foreign policy issues.

Isolationism

The nation's founders and the early presidents believed that avoiding political involvement with other nations—**isolationism**—was the best way to protect American interests. The colonies were certainly not yet strong enough to directly influence European developments. As president of the new nation, George Washington did little in terms of foreign policy. Indeed, in his Farewell Address in 1797, he urged Americans to "steer clear of permanent alliances with any portion of the foreign world." During the 1700s and 1800s, the United States generally attempted to avoid conflicts and political engagements elsewhere.

In 1823, President James Monroe proclaimed what became known as the **Monroe Doctrine.** In his message to Congress in December 1823, Monroe stated

isolationism A political policy of noninvolvement in world affairs.

Monroe Doctrine A U.S. policy, announced in 1823 by President James Monroe, that the United States would not tolerate foreign intervention in the Western Hemisphere, and in return, the United States would stay out of European affairs.

STOCK MONTAGE/STOCK MONTAGE/GETTY IMAGES

President James Monroe (1817–1825) said that the United States would not accept foreign intervention in the Western Hemisphere.

that the United States would not tolerate foreign intervention in the Western Hemisphere. In return, promised Monroe, the United States would stay out of European affairs. The Monroe Doctrine buttressed the policy of isolationism toward Europe.

The Beginning of Interventionism

Isolationism gradually gave way to **interventionism** (direct involvement in foreign affairs). The first true step toward interventionism occurred with the Spanish-American War of 1898. The United States fought this war to free Cuba from Spanish rule. Spain lost and subsequently ceded control of several of its possessions, including Guam, Puerto Rico, and the Philippines, to the United States. The United States acquired a **colonial empire** and was acknowledged as a world power.

The growth of the United States as an industrial economy also confirmed the nation's position as a world power. For example, in the early 1900s, President Theodore Roosevelt proposed that the United States could invade Latin American countries when it was necessary to guarantee political or economic stability.

interventionism Direct involvement by one country in another country's affairs.

colonial empire A group of dependent nations that are under the rule of a single imperial power.

neutrality A position of not being aligned with either side in a dispute or conflict, such as a war.

Soviet bloc The group of Eastern European nations that fell under the control of the Soviet Union following World War II.

The World Wars

When World War I broke out in 1914, President Woodrow Wilson initially proclaimed a policy of **neutrality**—the United States would not take sides in the conflict. The United States did not enter the war until 1917, after U.S. ships in international waters were attacked by German submarines that were blockading Britain. Wilson called the war a way to "make the world safe for democracy." In his eyes, Germany was not merely dangerous but evil. Wilson, in short, was our most famous presidential advocate of moral idealism. After World War I ended in 1918, the United States returned to a policy of isolationism. We refused to join the League of Nations, an international body intended to resolve peacefully any future conflicts between nations.

The U.S. policy of isolationism lasted only until the Japanese attacked Pearl Harbor in 1941. The United States joined the Allies—Australia, Britain, Canada, China, France, and the Soviet Union—that fought the Axis nations of Germany, Italy, and Japan. One of the most significant foreign policy actions during World War II was the dropping of atomic bombs on the Japanese cities of Hiroshima and Nagasaki in August 1945.

The Cold War

After World War II ended in 1945, the wartime alliance between the United States and the Soviet Union began to deteriorate quickly. The Soviet Union opposed America's political and economic systems. Many Americans considered Soviet attempts to spread Communist systems to other countries a major threat to democracy. After the war ended, countries in Eastern Europe—Bulgaria, Czechoslovakia, East Germany, Hungary, Poland, and Romania—fell under Soviet domination, forming what became known as the **Soviet bloc.**

THE IRON CURTAIN Britain's wartime prime minister, Winston Churchill, established the tone for a new relationship between the Soviet Union and the Western allies in a famous speech in 1946:

> An iron curtain has descended across the Continent. Behind that line all are subject in one form or another, not only to Soviet influence but to a very high . . . measure of control from Moscow.

Left Photo: The United States entered World War II after the surprise Japanese attack on Pearl Harbor, Hawaii, on December 7, 1941. Right Photo: World War II came to an end shortly after the United States dropped atomic bombs on Hiroshima and Nagasaki, Japan, in 1945.

The reference to an **iron curtain** described the political boundaries between the democratic countries in Western Europe and the Soviet-controlled Communist countries in Eastern Europe.

THE MARSHALL PLAN AND THE POLICY OF CONTAINMENT In 1947, when it appeared that local Communists, backed by the Soviets, would take over Greece and Turkey, President Harry Truman took action. He convinced Congress to appropriate $400 million ($3.9 billion in 2011 dollars) in aid for those countries to prevent the spread of communism. The president also proclaimed what became known as the *Truman Doctrine*. It would be "the policy of the United States to support free peoples who are resisting attempted subjugation by armed minorities or by outside pressures."[2]

The Truman administration also instituted a policy of economic assistance to war-torn Europe, called the **Marshall Plan** after George Marshall, who was then the U.S. secretary of state. During the next five years, Congress appropriated $17 billion (about $160 billion in 2011 dollars) for aid to sixteen European countries. By 1952, the nations of Western Europe, with U.S. help, had recovered and were again prospering.

These actions marked the beginning of a policy of **containment**—a policy designed to contain the spread of communism by offering threatened nations U.S. military and economic aid.[3] To make the policy of containment effective, the United States initiated a program of collective security involving the formation of mutual defense alliances with other nations. In 1949, through the North Atlantic Treaty, the United States, Canada, and ten European nations formed a military alliance—the North Atlantic Treaty Organization (NATO)—and declared that an attack on any member of the alliance would be considered an attack against all members.

Thus, by 1949, almost all illusions of friendship between the Soviet Union and the Western allies had disappeared. The United States became the leader of a bloc of democratic nations in Western Europe, the Pacific, and elsewhere. The tensions between the Soviet Union and the United States became known as the **Cold War**—a war of words, warnings, and ideologies that lasted from the late 1940s through the early 1990s. The term *iron curtain,* from Churchill's speech in 1946, became even more appropriate

iron curtain A phrase coined by Winston Churchill to describe the political boundaries between the democratic countries in Western Europe and the Soviet-controlled Communist countries in Eastern Europe.

Marshall Plan A plan providing for U.S. economic assistance to European nations following World War II to help those nations recover from the war; the plan was named after George C. Marshall, secretary of state from 1947 to 1949.

containment A U.S. policy designed to contain the spread of communism by offering military and economic aid to threatened nations.

Cold War The war of words, warnings, and ideologies between the Soviet Union and the United States that lasted from the late 1940s through the early 1990s.

deterrence A policy of building up military strength for the purpose of discouraging (deterring) military attacks by other nations; the policy of "building weapons for peace" that supported the arms race between the United States and the Soviet Union during the Cold War.

mutually assured destruction (MAD) A phrase referring to the assumption, on which the policy of deterrence was based, that if the forces of two nations are equally capable of destroying each other, neither nation will take a chance on war.

Cuban missile crisis A nuclear standoff that occurred in 1962 when the United States learned that the Soviet Union had placed nuclear warheads in Cuba, ninety miles off the U.S. coast. The crisis was defused diplomatically, but it is generally considered the closest the two Cold War superpowers came to a nuclear confrontation.

détente French word meaning a "relaxation of tensions." Détente characterized the relationship between the United States and the Soviet Union in the 1970s, as the two Cold War rivals attempted to pursue cooperative dealings and arms control.

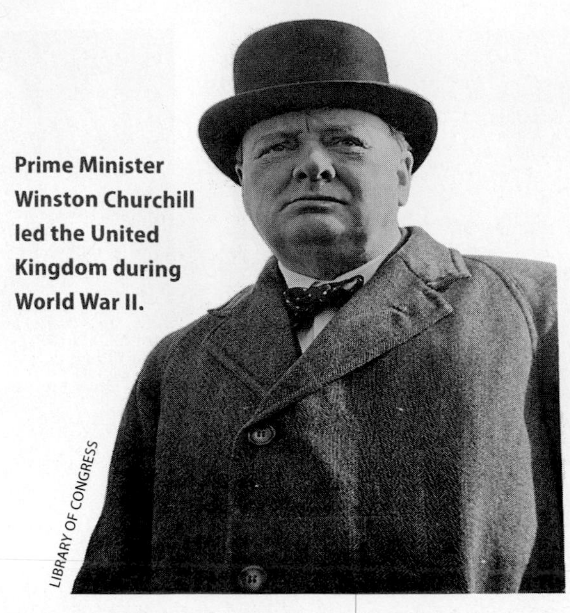
LIBRARY OF CONGRESS
Prime Minister Winston Churchill led the United Kingdom during World War II.

in 1961, when Soviet-dominated East Germany constructed the Berlin Wall, which separated East Berlin from West Berlin.

Although the Cold War was mainly a war of words and belief systems, the wars in Korea (1950–1953) and Vietnam (1964–1975) grew out of the efforts to contain communism.

THE ARMS RACE AND DETERRENCE The tensions induced by the Cold War led both the Soviet Union and the United States to try to surpass each other militarily. They began competing for more and better weapons, particularly nuclear weapons, with greater destructive power. This phenomenon, known as the *arms race,* was supported by a policy of **deterrence**—of rendering ourselves and our allies so strong militarily that our very strength would deter (stop or discourage) any attack on us. Out of deterrence came the theory of **mutually assured destruction (MAD),** which held that if the forces of both nations were equally capable of destroying each other, neither nation would take a chance on war.

THE CUBAN MISSILE CRISIS In 1962, the United States and the Soviet Union came close to a nuclear confrontation in what became known as the **Cuban missile crisis.** The United States learned that the Soviet Union had placed nuclear weapons on the island of Cuba, ninety miles from the coast of Florida. The crisis was defused diplomatically: a U.S. naval blockade of Cuba convinced the Soviet Union to agree to remove the missiles. The United States also agreed to remove some of its missiles near the Soviet border in Turkey. Both sides recognized that a nuclear war between the two superpowers was unthinkable.

DÉTENTE AND ARMS CONTROL In 1969, the United States and the Soviet Union began negotiations on a treaty to limit the number of antiballistic missiles (ABMs) and offensive missiles that each country could develop and deploy. In 1972, both sides signed the Strategic Arms Limitation Treaty (SALT I). This event marked the beginning of a period of **détente,** a French word that means a "relaxation of tensions."

In 1983, President Ronald Reagan (1981–1989) nearly reignited the arms race by proposing a missile defense system known as the strategic defense initiative (SDI, or "Star Wars"). Nonetheless, Reagan and Soviet leader Mikhail Gorbachev pursued arms control agreements, as did Reagan's successor, President George H. W. Bush (1989–1993).

THE DISSOLUTION OF THE SOVIET UNION In the late 1980s, the political situation inside the Soviet Union began to change rapidly. Mikhail Gorbachev had initiated an effort to democratize the Soviet political system and decentralize the economy. The reforms quickly spread to other countries in the Soviet bloc. In 1989, the Berlin Wall, constructed nearly thirty years earlier, was torn down, and East Germany and West Germany were reunited.

In August 1991, a number of disgruntled Communist Party leaders who wanted to reverse the reforms briefly seized control of the Soviet central government. Russian

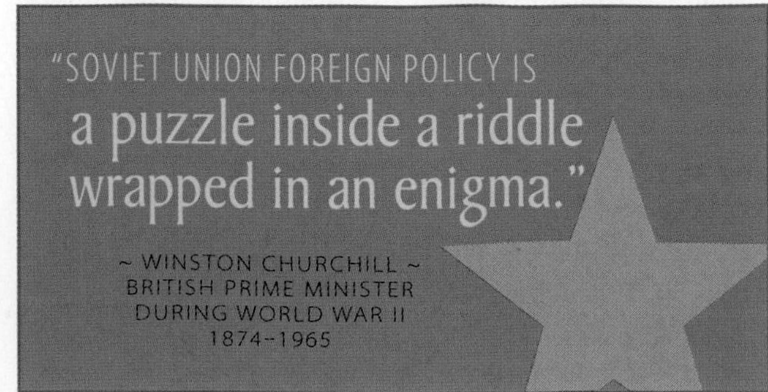
"SOVIET UNION FOREIGN POLICY IS
a puzzle inside a riddle wrapped in an enigma."
~ WINSTON CHURCHILL ~
BRITISH PRIME MINISTER
DURING WORLD WAR II
1874–1965

citizens rose up in revolt and defied those leaders. The democratically elected president of the Russian republic (the largest republic in the Soviet Union), Boris Yeltsin, confronted troops in Moscow that were under the control of the conspirators. The attempted coup collapsed after three days. The Communist Party in the Soviet Union lost virtually all of its power.

The fifteen republics constituting the Soviet Union—including the Russian republic—declared their independence, and by the end of the year, the Union of Soviet Socialist Republics (USSR) no longer existed.

Post–Cold War Foreign Policy

The demise of the Soviet Union altered the framework and goals of U.S. foreign policy. During the Cold War, the moral underpinnings of American foreign policy were clear to all—the United States was the defender of the "free world" against the Soviet aggressor. When the Cold War ended, U.S. foreign policymakers were forced, for the first time in decades, to rethink the nation's foreign policy goals and adapt them to a world arena in which, at least for a time, the United States was the only superpower. Some have argued that the European Union, an economic and political organization of twenty-seven European states, could in time rival the United States. Others are skeptical, as you'll see in the *Perception versus Reality* feature on the following page.

U.S. foreign policymakers have struggled since the end of the Cold War to determine the degree of intervention that is appropriate and prudent for the U.S. military. Should we intervene in a humanitarian crisis, such as a famine? Should the U.S. military participate in peacekeeping missions, such as those instituted after civil or ethnic strife in other countries? Americans have faced these questions in Bosnia, Kosovo, Rwanda, Somalia, and Sudan. Yet no overriding framework emerged in U.S. foreign policy until September 11, 2001. Since that date, our goal has been to capture and punish the terrorists who planned and perpetrated the events of that day and to prevent future terrorist attacks against Americans—even if that means "regime change," which was one of the goals of the second Gulf War against Iraq in 2003.

LO3 *The War on Terrorism*

One of the most difficult challenges faced by governments around the world is how to control terrorism. Terrorism is defined as the use of staged violence, often against civilians, to achieve political goals. International terrorism has occurred in virtually every region of the world. The most devastating terrorist attack in U.S. history occurred on September 11, 2001, when radical Islamist terrorists used hijacked airliners as missiles to bring down the World Trade Center towers in New York City and to destroy part of the Pentagon building in Washington, D.C. A fourth airplane crashed in a Pennsylvania field after passengers fought back against the hijackers. In all, almost three thousand innocent civilians were killed as a result of these terrorist acts.

Terrorist attacks have occurred with increasing frequency during the past three decades. Other examples of terrorist acts include the Palestinian attacks on Israeli Olympic athletes in Munich in 1972; the Libyan suitcase bombing of an American airliner over Lockerbie, Scotland, in 1988; the bombing of two U.S. embassies in Africa in 1998; the bombing of the navy ship USS *Cole* in a Yemeni port in 2000; and coordinated bomb attacks on London's transportation system in 2005.

Somalia has been the battleground for fighting between rival Islamist factions. The United States has supported a United Nations–backed government, but that regime remains almost powerless. The Islamic Party combatants shown here rest after a fully armed conflict exercise.

AP PHOTO/FARAH ABDI WARSAMEH

PERCEPTION VERSUS REALITY

A United Europe?

Decades ago, European leaders had a dream of forging a common European union of nations so that world war would never occur again. To that end, they created the Common Market and later the European Union (EU), which now consists of twenty-seven nations, a third of which are former Communist countries.

The Perception

If you read the newspapers and listen to the TV talk shows in America, you get the impression that the EU represents a bloc of more than 500 million people that acts as a counterweight to America's 310 million citizens. The EU is portrayed as an economic and foreign policy powerhouse today.

The Reality

While the twenty-seven members of the EU have given up some of their sovereignty, particularly over manufacturing standards, food safety, and the like, they are still twenty-seven sovereign nations. This is most evident in the efforts of EU members to protect their own citizens' economic livelihood.

The latest so-called minitreaty among the EU nations, conceived in 2007, is a case in point. France succeeded in removing from the treaty's preamble a statement to the effect that the EU was all about free competition in all countries. Instead, the French substituted the concept that each country must protect its "national champions" and preserve the jobs of its citizens.

In the United States, in contrast, no matter what the individual states would like to do, they cannot raise protectionist walls to prevent job losses due to competition from other states. The U.S. Constitution forbids that.

Europe's disunity, relative to the United States and other full-fledged nations, was clearly revealed by the Great Recession. Of the twenty-seven members of the EU, sixteen use a common currency, the euro. (That eleven countries do not use the euro immediately shows the limits to European unity.)

When the recession struck, it became obvious that in Greece, Ireland, Portugal, and Spain, businesses and individuals had borrowed far too many euros and would now have trouble paying them back. The problem was especially bad in Greece, where the government, as well as the private sector, had borrowed irresponsibly. In 2010, investors became afraid of making additional loans to the Greek government, and the possibility arose that Greece might default on its debts.

"Eurozone" countries with stronger economies, such as France and Germany, were extremely reluctant to help out the Greeks. Germans clearly did not see the Greeks as fellow Europeans, but rather as foreigners. Greece's problems, however, threatened to spread to other troubled economies. In the end, the EU was forced to come up with a huge bailout package to defend Greece and other troubled nations. Compare the situation in the United States, where no state-government crisis could possibly threaten the dollar.

Blog On *The Economist*, published in London, is one of the most highly regarded news magazines in the world. You can find its blogs on Europe at **www.economist.com/blogs**. Politics in Europe generally is tilted further left than in the United States. Find out what left-of-center Europeans are thinking at **www.social-europe.eu.**

Varieties of Terrorism

Terrorists are willing to destroy others' lives and property, and often sacrifice their own lives, for a variety of reasons. Terrorist acts generally fall into one of the three broad categories discussed next.

LOCAL OR REGIONAL TERRORISM Some terrorist acts have been committed by extremists who are motivated by the desire to obtain freedom from a nation or government that they regard as an oppressor. Terrorists have sometimes acted to disrupt peace talks. In Israel, for example, numerous suicide bombings by Palestinians against Israeli civilians have helped to stall efforts to forge a lasting peace between Israel and the Palestinians. The Irish Republican Army, which sought to unite British-governed Northern Ireland with the independent Republic of Ireland, conducted bombings and other terrorist acts in Northern Ireland and England over a period of many years. The attacks came to an end in 1997 as part of a peace process that lasted from 1995 until 2005. Basque separatists in Spain have engaged in terrorism for decades. The separatists were initially—and incorrectly—blamed for bombing a commuter train in Madrid, Spain, on March 11, 2004. That

A hijacked airliner approaches New York's World Trade Center moments before striking the second tower, as seen from downtown Brooklyn on September 11, 2001. The 110-story towers collapsed in a shower of rubble and dust after two hijacked airliners slammed into them. Nearly three thousand people were killed on that day.

terrorist attack, actually perpetrated by Islamic radicals, killed 191 people and injured hundreds of others.

The United States has also been the victim of homegrown terrorists. The bombing of the Oklahoma City federal building in 1995 was the act of vengeful extremists in the United States who claimed to fear an oppressive federal government. Although Timothy McVeigh and Terry Nichols, who were convicted of the crime, were not directly connected to a particular political group, they expressed views characteristic of the extreme right-wing militia movement in the United States.

STATE-SPONSORED TERRORISM Some terrorist attacks have been planned and sponsored by governments. For example, the bombing of Pan Am Flight 103, which exploded over Lockerbie, Scotland, in 1988, killing all 259 people on board and 11 on the ground, was later proved to be the work of an intelligence officer working for Libya. The United Nations imposed economic sanctions against Libya in an effort to force Libyan dictator Muammar Qaddafi to extradite those who were suspected of being responsible for the bombing. More than a decade after the bombing, Libya agreed to hand the men over for trial.

The case of Pan Am Flight 103 illustrates the difficulty in punishing the perpetrators of state-sponsored terrorism. The victim country must first prove who the terrorists were and for whom they were working. Then it must decide what type of retribution is warranted.

FOREIGN TERRORIST NETWORKS A relatively new phenomenon in the late 1990s and early 2000s was the emergence of nonstate terrorist networks, such as al Qaeda. Al Qaeda is the nongovernmental terrorist organization that planned and carried out the terrorist attacks of September 11, 2001. Its leader is the Saudi dissident Osama bin Laden. Throughout the 1990s, al Qaeda conducted training camps in the mountains of Afghanistan, which was ruled by an ultraconservative Islamic faction known as the Taliban. After their training, al Qaeda operatives dispersed into small units across the globe, connected by e-mail and the Internet.

Before September 11, the U.S. government had monitored the activities and movements of al Qaeda operatives and had connected the terrorist attacks on two U.S. embassies in Africa and the bombing of the USS *Cole* to al Qaeda. In 1998, President Bill Clinton (1993–2001) ordered the bombing of terrorist camps in Afghanistan in retaliation for the embassy bombings, but with little effect. Al Qaeda cells continued to operate largely unimpeded until the terrorist attacks of September 11.

In 2004, terrorists detonated explosives in two packed commuter trains in Madrid, Spain. One hundred and ninety-one people were killed, and hundreds of others were injured.

coalition An alliance of nations formed to undertake a foreign policy action, particularly a military action. A coalition is often a temporary alliance that dissolves after the action is concluded.

weapons of mass destruction Chemical, biological, or nuclear weapons that can inflict massive casualties.

preemptive war A war launched by a nation to prevent an imminent attack by another nation.

preventive war A war launched by a nation to prevent the possibility that another nation might attack at some point in the future; not supported by international law.

neoconservatism A philosophy of foreign policy based on moral idealism. Neoconservatives support the use of economic and military power to bring democracy and human rights to other countries.

"FIGHTING TERRORISM IS LIKE BEING A GOALKEEPER. You can make a hundred brilliant saves but the only shot that people remember is the one that gets past you."

~ PAUL WILKINSON ~
BRITISH TERRORISM EXPERT
B. 1937

The U.S. Response to 9/11—The War in Afghanistan

Immediately after the 9/11 terrorist attacks, Congress passed a joint resolution authorizing President George W. Bush to use "all necessary and appropriate force" against nations, organizations, or individuals that the president determined had "planned, authorized, committed, or aided the terrorist attacks." In late 2001, supported by a **coalition** of allies, the U.S. military attacked al Qaeda camps in Afghanistan and the ruling Taliban regime that harbored those terrorists. Once the Taliban had been ousted, the United States helped to establish a government in Afghanistan that did not support terrorism. Instead of continuing the hunt for al Qaeda members in Afghanistan, however, the Bush administration increasingly looked to Iraq as a threat to U.S. security.

The Focus on Iraq

In January 2002, President Bush described Iraq as a regime that sponsored terrorism and that sought to develop **weapons of mass destruction.** In October, Congress authorized Bush to use armed force against Iraq on the grounds that Iraq was seeking to develop weapons of mass destruction and was supporting al Qaeda. (Both of these allegations later proved to be untrue.)

In September, President Bush enunciated a doctrine under which the United States was prepared to strike "preemptively" at Iraq. A **preemptive war** occurs when a nation goes to war against another nation because it believes that an attack from that nation is imminent. When President Bush did go to war against Iraq, though, it was not a preemptive war but a **preventive war**—a war to prevent the possibility that Iraq could attack the United States in the future. International law offers no support for this type of war.

Bush's Iraq policies were bolstered by the philosophy of **neoconservatism** held by many of his advisers. The neoconservatives were moral idealists who supported the use of economic and military power to bring democracy and human rights to other countries. They argued that by occupying Iraq and turning it into a democracy, we could create a positive example for the rest of the Middle East.

BACKGROUND TO INVASION—THE FIRST GULF WAR Back in 1990, Iraqi dictator Saddam Hussein had invaded neighboring Kuwait. Hussein's invasion was a spectacular violation of international law. The United Nations threatened Hussein with sanctions if he did not withdraw his troops. When he failed to do so, U.S.-led coalition forces attacked. Iraqi troops soon withdrew from Kuwait, and the first Gulf War ended. The coalition stopped short of sending troops to Baghdad to unseat Hussein.

The cease-fire that ended the conflict required Iraq to submit to inspections for chemical, biological, and nuclear weapons. In 1998, however, Hussein ceased to cooperate with the inspections. During 2002, the Bush administration sought a resolution from the United Nations on the use of military force in Iraq, but China, France, and Russia blocked the resolution. In March 2003, President Bush gave Saddam Hussein an ultimatum: leave Iraq or face war. Hussein was defiant.

THE SECOND GULF WAR BEGINS On March 20, 2003, U.S. and British forces entered Iraq. President Bush secured the support of several other nations, but most of the world opposed the attack. U.S. forces advanced rapidly, and Iraqi military units crumbled. With the fall of the regime, massive looting and disorder broke out across the country, and coalition troops were unable to restore order immediately. Saddam Hussein was not captured until December 2003. He was convicted of crimes against humanity and executed in 2006.

THE INSURGENCY It soon became clear that many Iraqis opposed the occupation. Opposition was strongest among members of the Sunni branch of Islam, who had been Hussein's staunchest supporters. Iraqi rebels used terrorist tactics to kill occupation forces and Iraqis cooperating with the Americans. Between May 2003 and March 2004, casualty rates for American soldiers averaged more than fifty per month.

In 2005, Iraqi voters chose a new government in the first free elections for half a century. The winning parties represented Shiite Muslims, a sect that formed a majority of Iraq's population, and the Kurds, a minority ethnic group. The Shiites and Kurds had been severely repressed under Saddam Hussein.

The Sunni insurgent groups included al Qaeda in Iraq, which was organized after the U.S. invasion. Al Qaeda attacked not only U.S. and Iraqi government forces but also Shiite civilians, whom it considered apostates (religious traitors). Shiite radicals responded with attacks on Sunnis, and Iraq appeared to be drifting toward interethnic civil war. In reaction to seemingly endless violence, American voters began to turn against the war, and in the 2006 elections they handed Congress over to the Democrats.

Instead of withdrawing U.S. troops in response, however, the Bush administration increased troop levels in 2007 in a program known as the "surge." Under General David Petraeus, American forces for the first time began to employ time-tested counterinsurgency tactics based on protecting the security of ordinary civilians. The tactics were surprisingly successful. Large numbers of Sunnis, who also had been terrorized by al Qaeda, turned against the insurgency and allied with the Americans.

WITHDRAWAL With the insurgency fatally undermined, Iraq was finally on the path to long-term stability. In 2008, Iraqi prime minister Nouri al-Maliki and President Bush set a withdrawal target for the end of 2011. In February 2009, President Barack Obama announced that U.S. combat forces would leave Iraq by the end of August 2010, and the rest of the troops would be out by the end of 2011. In fact, combat forces departed in mid-August 2010, slightly ahead of schedule.

Again, Afghanistan

The war in Iraq tended to draw the Bush administration's attention away from Afghanistan, which was never completely at peace even after the Taliban were ousted from Kabul, the capital. In 2003, NATO took responsibility for coalition military operations in the relatively peaceful central and northern parts of Afghanistan. The hope was that with NATO in charge, European nations would be more willing to supply troops to assist the overstretched Americans. In 2004, Hamid Karzai became the first democratically elected president of Afghanistan, and in 2005, Afghans elected a parliament. By 2006, however, the Taliban had regrouped and were waging a war of insurgency against the new government. The United States remained responsible for the southern areas of the country, in which most of the fighting took place, although in 2006, NATO began to move some forces into the south.

A problem for the coalition forces was that the Taliban were able to take shelter on the far side of the Afghan-Pakistani border, in Pakistan's Federally Administered Tribal Areas. These districts are largely free from central government control. For several years, the United States complained that the government of Pakistan was not doing enough to keep the Taliban out of the Tribal Areas. In 2009, Taliban forces began to take complete control of districts in the Tribal Areas and in adjacent districts of the Northwest Frontier Province. Facing a direct challenge to Pakistan's sovereignty, the Pakistani military began to engage the Taliban forces in what soon became a major struggle.

These Iraqi soldiers march during Army Day celebrations in Baghdad. The Multi-National Force (mainly U.S. troops) handed over control of all parts of the country in late 2010.

AP PHOTO/KARIM KADIM

Palestine Liberation Organization (PLO) An organization formed in 1964 to represent the Palestinian people. The PLO has a long history of terrorism but for some years has functioned primarily as a political party.

DOUG MILLS/*THE NEW YORK TIMES*/REDUX

President Obama looks on as Israeli prime minister Benjamin Netanyahu shakes hands with Mahmoud Abbas, president of the Palestinian Authority in 2009. The United States has been heavily involved in helping Israel and the Palestinians reach a solution to their ongoing conflict. Why would the United States choose to become involved in other countries' political problems?

Barack Obama had opposed the war in Iraq when it was first launched, but he had always supported the U.S. entry into Afghanistan. In February 2009, Obama ordered 17,000 additional troops into the country. In October, the Obama administration launched a major review of its Afghanistan policy. The resulting discussions were intense. It was not known publicly just how heated they became until 2010, when reporter Bob Woodward published an account of the debate.[4] In the end, President Obama ordered an additional 30,000 troops to Afghanistan but pledged to start withdrawing U.S. forces by July 2011. In June 2010, Obama relieved General Stanley McChrystal from command in Afghanistan for insubordination and replaced him with General Petraeus.

LO4 *The Israeli–Palestinian Conflict*

The long-running conflict between Israel and its Arab neighbors has poisoned the atmosphere in the Middle East for more than half a century. Some experts have argued that resolving this conflict is key to solving additional problems, such as terrorism. Others doubt that a resolution would really have that effect. Regardless, the conflict has caused enough bloodshed and heartbreak over the years to deserve attention on its own merits. American presidents dating back at least to Richard Nixon (1969–1974) have attempted to persuade the parties to reach a settlement. Barack Obama is only the latest American leader to address the problem.

The Arab-Israeli Wars

For many years after Israel was founded in 1948, the neighboring Arab states did not accept its legitimacy as a nation. The result was a series of wars between Israel and neighboring states, including Egypt, Jordan, and Syria, waged in 1948, 1956, 1967, and 1973. Following the 1948 Arab-Israeli War, a large number of Palestinians—Arab residents of the Holy Land, known as Palestine until 1948—were forced into exile, adding to Arab grievances. The failure of the Arab states in the 1967 war led to additional Palestinian refugees and the rise of the **Palestine Liberation Organization (PLO),** a nonstate body committed to armed struggle against Israel. In the late 1960s and early 1970s, Palestinian groups launched a wave of terrorist attacks against Israeli targets around the world.

In the 1973 Yom Kippur War, Egyptian armies acquitted themselves well, although Israel successfully repelled the attack. Egyptian president Anwar el Sadat was able to employ the resulting popular support to launch a major peace initiative. He traveled to Israel in 1977 and addressed the Israeli parliament, a major turning point. U.S. president Jimmy Carter (1977–1981) then sponsored intensive negotiations. Egypt and Israel signed a peace treaty in 1979 that marked the end to an era of major wars between Israel and other states. Lower-level conflicts continued, however. On several occasions, Israel launched attacks against nonstate militias in Lebanon in response to incursions across the Israeli-Lebanon border. Israel and Jordan eventually signed a peace treaty in

1994, but no peace treaty between Israel and Syria has yet been negotiated, and the conflict between Israel and the Palestinians has remained.

The Israeli-Palestinian Dispute

Resolving the Israeli-Palestinian dispute has always presented more difficulties than obtaining peace between Israel and neighbors such as Egypt. One problem is that the hostilities between the two parties run deeper. On the Palestinian side, not only had many families lost their homes after the 1948 war, but after the 1967 war, the West Bank of the Jordan River and the Gaza Strip fell under Israeli control. The Palestinians living in these areas became an occupied people.

On the Israeli side, the sheer viciousness of the Palestinian terrorist attacks—which frequently resulted in the deaths of civilians, including children—made negotiations with those responsible hard to imagine. A further complication was the series of Israeli settlements on the West Bank and the Gaza Strip, which the Palestinians considered their own. Settlers living on the West Bank had an obvious interest in opposing any peace deal that required them to move.

Despite the difficulties, the international community, including the United States, was in agreement on several principles for settling the conflict. Lands seized by Israel in the 1967 war should be granted to the Palestinians, who could organize their own independent nation-state there. In turn, the Palestinians would have to not only recognize Israel's right to exist, but also take concrete steps to guarantee Israel's security. The international consensus did not address some important issues. These included what compensation, if any, should go to Palestinians who had lost homes in what was now Israel. A second issue is whether Israel could adjust its pre-1967 borders to incorporate some of the Israeli settlement areas, plus part or all of eastern Jerusalem, which had been under Arab control before 1967.

"The purpose of foreign policy IS NOT TO PROVIDE AN OUTLET FOR OUR OWN SENTIMENTS OF HOPE OR INDIGNATION; it is to shape real events in a real world."

~ JOHN F. KENNEDY ~
THIRTY-FIFTH PRESIDENT
OF THE UNITED STATES
1961–1963

Oslo Accords The first agreement signed between Israel and the PLO; led to the establishment of the Palestinian Authority in the occupied territories.

Negotiations

A long-running uprising in the occupied territories, known as the *Intifada,* broke out in 1987 and helped ensure that the world would not forget the Palestinians. Under the leadership of U.S. president George H. W. Bush, plus Russia and Spain, talks between Israel, Arab nations, and non-PLO Palestinians commenced in Madrid in 1991. In 1993, Israel and the PLO met officially for the first time in Oslo, Norway. The resulting **Oslo Accords** were signed in Washington under the eye of President Bill Clinton. A major result was the establishment of a Palestinian Authority, under Israeli control, on the West Bank and the Gaza Strip.

NEGOTIATIONS COLLAPSE Further attempts to reach a settlement in 2000 at Camp David in Maryland collapsed in acrimony. After the failure of these talks, a second Intifada led to Israeli military incursions into the West Bank and the almost complete collapse of the Palestinian Authority's control over its people. Israeli prime minister Ariel Sharon, concluding that he had no credible peace partner, carried out a plan to unilaterally withdraw from the Gaza Strip in 2005 and also to build an enormous security fence between Israel and the West Bank. The fence came under strong international criticism because it incorporated parts of the West Bank into Israel.

In 2007, Gaza was taken over by Hamas, a radical Islamist party that refuses to recognize Israel. After the imposition of an Israeli blockade, Hamas launched missile attacks on Israel, which in turn briefly occupied the strip in December 2008. The West Bank remained under the control of the PLO-led Palestinian Authority, and so the Palestinians, now politically divided, were in an even worse bargaining position than before. Nevertheless, President Obama sought in 2009 to restart peace talks and appointed a special representative for the region.

TOWARD NEW TALKS Developments in 2010 included an attempt in May by Turkish activists to "run" an Israeli blockade of Gaza with a flotilla of six ships. Israeli commandos seized the ships, but resistance by activists led to the death of nine passengers. The incident drew international attention to the blockade and criticisms of the Israeli ban on many ordinary consumer items. In June, Israel substantially eased the terms of the blockade.

On the West Bank, the Palestinian Authority succeeded in reestablishing itself as an effective government, and the territory entered a period of relative stability and economic growth. The subsequent self-confidence—plus pressure from America and several Arab states—helped bring the West Bank Palestinians back to the bargaining table in September. Confidence between the parties was fragile, however, and the possibility that the talks might break down was constant.

"The risk THAT THE LEADERS OF A ROGUE STATE WILL USE NUCLEAR, CHEMICAL, OR BIOLOGICAL WEAPONS AGAINST US OR OUR ALLIES is the greatest security threat we face."
~ MADELEINE ALBRIGHT ~
U.S. SECRETARY OF STATE
1997–2001

LO5 *Weapons Proliferation in an Unstable World*

Although foreign policy in recent years has focused most visibly on Iraq and Afghanistan, the U.S. government has also had to deal with other threats to U.S. and global security. The Cold War may be over, but the threat of nuclear warfare—which formed the backdrop of foreign policy during the Cold War—has by no means disappeared. The existence of nuclear weapons in Russia and in other countries around the world continues to challenge U.S. foreign policymakers. Concerns about nuclear proliferation mounted in 1998 when India and Pakistan detonated nuclear devices within a few weeks of each other—events that took U.S. intelligence agencies by surprise. Increasingly, American officials have focused on the threat of an attack by a rogue nation or a terrorist group that possesses weapons of mass destruction. Of most concern today are recent developments in North Korea and Iran.

North Korea's Nuclear Program

North Korea signed the Treaty on the Non-Proliferation of Nuclear Weapons in 1985 and submitted to weapons inspections by the International Atomic Energy Agency (IAEA) in 1992. Throughout the 1990s, however, there were discrepancies between North Korean declarations and IAEA inspection findings. In 2002, North Korea expelled the IAEA inspectors.

OPENING NEGOTIATIONS The administration of George W. Bush had been reluctant to engage in diplomatic relations with North Korea. Bush insisted that any talks with North Korea must also include all of North Korea's neighbors—China, Japan, Russia, and South Korea. In 2003, North Korea finally agreed to such talks.

Since that time, it has proved quite difficult to keep North Korea at the bargaining table—its representatives have stormed out of the talks repeatedly, for the most trivial reasons. China is the one power with substantial economic leverage over North Korea, and typically, Chinese leaders have been the ones to lead the North Koreans back to the table.

Tensions heightened in October 2006, when North Korea conducted its first nuclear test. Nevertheless, the Bush administration continued to participate with North Korea's neighbors in multilateral negotiations. In the spring of 2007, North Korea agreed that it would begin to dismantle its nuclear facilities and would allow UN inspectors into the country. In return, the other nations agreed to provide various kinds of aid, and the United States would begin to discuss normalization of relations with North Korea. By mid-2007, North Korea had shut down one of its nuclear reactors and had admitted a permanent UN inspection team into the country.

NEGOTIATIONS COLLAPSE In April 2009, North Korea tested a long-range missile under the guise of attempting to launch a satellite. The UN Security Council unanimously condemned the test. This demonstrated that the Chinese, who have a permanent Security Council seat, were annoyed as well. North Korea then pulled out of the six-party talks and expelled all nuclear inspectors from the country. In May 2009, North Korea tested another nuclear device, to universal disapproval.

In March 2010, tensions rose again after the sinking of a South Korean naval ship, the *Cheonan,* with the loss of forty-six lives. An investigation revealed in May that the sinking was due to a North Korean torpedo. North Korea's aggressive behavior may have been linked to the attempt by its leader, Kim Jong Il, to name a successor in case of his death. The future leader of North Korea is to be Kim Jong Eun, who is Kim Jong Il's third son. Kim Jong Il himself was the son of North Korea's first Communist dictator. North Korea, therefore, is unique in that it is effectively a Communist monarchy.

Iran: An Emerging Nuclear Threat?

For some time, Western intelligence agencies have believed that Iran is attempting to join the ranks of nuclear powers. Investigators for the International Atomic Energy Agency have reported that Iran has initiated a uranium enrichment program for nuclear weapons. U.S. intelligence reports have also found evidence that Iran is working on a missile delivery system for nuclear warheads. Iran has made considerable progress in many aspects of its nuclear program, although Iranian leaders have publicly stated that they have no intention of using their nuclear program for destructive purposes and claim that they are seeking only to develop nuclear energy plants.

Like North Korea, Iran has been openly hostile to the United States. Iran has implemented an extensive terrorism campaign in hopes of undermining U.S. influence in the Middle East. Many analysts have also tied Iran to Iraqi insurgency efforts against American occupation forces. Dealing with a nuclear-equipped Iran would strain already tense relations. Considering Iran's ties to terrorist groups, U.S. national security at home and foreign policy efforts abroad could be significantly endangered.

EUROPE TAKES THE LEAD During the George W. Bush administration, Britain, France, and Germany took the lead in diplomatic efforts to encourage Iran to abandon its nuclear program and engaged in talks with that country. The United Nations has imposed sanctions on Iran in an attempt to curb its nuclear ambitions. The United States has threatened to impose its own sanctions to isolate Iran from the community of nations. Past attempts to strengthen UN sanctions, however, have been frustrated by the opposition of China and Russia.

AMERICA JOINS THE TALKS After a hiatus of over a year, talks with Iran concerning its nuclear program resumed in Geneva on October 1, 2009. Britain, China, France, Germany, Russia, and the United States were at the table. In early discussions, Iran agreed to allow international inspectors access to its facilities. Some observers are hopeful about the talks, but others see them as a way for the Iranians to play for time as they develop their nuclear capabilities. If the Iranians do develop nuclear weapons, what can the United States do about it? We examine that question in this chapter's *Join the Debate* feature on the following page.

LO6 *China— The Next Superpower?*

Following former president Richard Nixon's historic visit to China in 1972, American diplomatic and economic relations with the Chinese gradually improved. Diplomacy with China focused on cultivating a more pro-Western disposition in the former isolationist nation. In 1989, however, when the Chinese

AP PHOTO/OFFICE OF THE SUPREME LEADER

Ayatollah Ali Khamenei is Iran's Supreme Leader— he is the spiritual head of that country. He refused to support those Iranians who contested the flawed reelection of that country's president, Mahmoud Ahmadinejad, in 2009. By fall, many protesters remained in jail and several had been sentenced to death. Why does the United States continue to be concerned about events in Iran?

JOIN THE DEBATE

Can We Tolerate a Nuclear Iran?

On November 4, 1979, militant students in Tehran, Iran, seized the U.S. embassy and took fifty-two American citizens hostage. The crisis lasted 444 days. Ever since, Iran and the United States have been at odds with each other. In the years that followed, the rest of the world discovered that Iran was engaged in a covert nuclear program. It was enriching uranium that could be used in the fabrication of a nuclear bomb. In spite of numerous UN resolutions, Iran is still producing uranium, and at a faster speed. The existence of a second uranium enrichment plant was made public in the fall of 2009. Simultaneously, Iran has been developing missiles that eventually could be capable of carrying a nuclear payload.

We Must Prevent a Nuclear-Armed Iran at All Costs

Repeatedly, the president of Iran, Mahmoud Ahmadinejad, has called for the complete destruction of Israel. Presumably, if he is serious, when Iran has the bomb, it will be used on Israel. Thus, a nuclear Iran carries with it the possibility of a nuclear holocaust. There would be retaliation, and the conflict could lead to massive destruction in the Middle East and elsewhere.

Currently, Iran is the largest state sponsor of terrorism. What if Iran itself does not use the bomb, but rather provides nuclear weapons to a terrorist group? There are many such groups that would have no scruples about killing millions of innocent civilians.

Finally, if Iran obtains a nuclear weapon, oil-rich countries in the Middle East may feel obligated to do so, too. There could be a dangerous arms race on yet another part of this fragile planet. We must stop Iran's production of uranium now. If all else fails, that means bombing Iran's nuclear facilities.

Belligerent Talk Doesn't Mean We Should Go to War

The fact that Ahmadinejad says Israel should not exist does not necessarily mean much. Such crazy talk is mostly for domestic consumption—to strengthen the regime's political position at home by emphasizing Islamic grievances. Further, Ahmadinejad doesn't actually control Iran's military. Supreme Leader Ayatollah Ali Khamenei does.

The United States has two thousand nuclear weapons. We tolerate nuclear weapons in the hands of the Chinese, Indians, Israelis, North Koreans, Pakistanis, and Russians. North Korea is run by a megalomaniac dictator and is arguably a more dangerous supporter of terrorist groups than Iran. So why should Iran be singled out?

Rather than start a war with Iran, if we are worried about Israel's safety, we can do two things. First, we can extend our nuclear deterrence umbrella to that country. Iran will know that if it strikes Israel, the United States will retaliate. Second, we can help Israel build up its missile defenses. In that way, it can effectively defend itself against Iranian missiles as well as deter their use.

For Critical Analysis ***If the United States bombed Iran's uranium enrichment sites, what might be the consequences?***

government brutally crushed a pro-democracy student movement, killing many students and protesters while imprisoning others, Chinese-American relations experienced a distinct chill.

normal trade relations (NTR) status A trade status granted through an international treaty by which each member nation must treat other members at least as well as it treats the country that receives its most favorable treatment. This status was formerly known as *most-favored-nation status.*

Chinese-American Trade Relations

During the Clinton administration, American relations with China began to improve once again. The rapid growth of the Chinese economy, and increasingly close trade ties between the United States and China, helped bring about a policy of diplomatic outreach. Many Americans protested, however, when the U.S. government extended **normal trade relations (NTR) status** to China on a year-to-year basis. Labor groups objected because they feared that American workers would lose jobs that could be performed at lower wages in Chinese factories. Human rights organizations denounced the Chinese government's well-documented mistreatment of its people. Despite this heavy opposition, Congress granted China permanent NTR status in 2000 and endorsed China's application to the World Trade Organization in 2001.

OUR GOVERNMENT FACES A
TROUBLED ECONOMY

Should We Fight China's Cheap Imports?

In the 1960s and 1970s, there was much concern that low-cost imports from Japan were destroying our manufacturing sector, especially the automobile industry. For a time, "Made in Japan" almost became a swearword. Fast-forward to the 2010s, and replace *Japan* with *China*. Some politicians—on both the political left and the right—argue today that China is flooding the U.S. market with its goods and thereby preventing the U.S. economy from enjoying a vigorous recovery from the Great Recession.

The Data Seem to Prove a Point

By the summer of 2010, the U.S. international trade deficit—exports minus imports—was running at more than $50 billion a month. In other words, American consumers are buying more from abroad than foreigners are buying from the United States. China, in contrast, is recording monthly trade surpluses of around $30 billion. That means that China is selling to the rest of the world $30 billion more than its residents are importing. Much of that surplus is coming from the United States. As Chinese goods pile up in America, U.S. dollars pile up in China in the form of treasuries held by the Chinese central bank.

We Buy So Many Chinese Goods Because They Are Cheaper

American consumers are not fools. If they have a choice between goods of equal quality at different prices, they will purchase the ones that are less expensive. For the moment, those goods are frequently from China (as mentioned above, they used to be from Japan). Why are Chinese goods so inexpensive? One obvious reason, of course, is that Chinese workers earn much less than American workers. Another important reason, though, is that the Chinese government maintains a fixed exchange rate between our dollar and the Chinese currency, called the *renminbi* and denominated in *yuan*. When China deliberately keeps the value of its currency low relative to the dollar, its exports become cheaper and its imports more expensive.

A Threat from Congress and the President

Not surprisingly, many members of Congress—and the Obama administration—have demanded that China allow its currency to become more valuable relative to the dollar. Some would like to see the value of the Chinese currency rise by at least 10 to 20 percent. In that way, Chinese imports would no longer be so inexpensive, and we would stop buying so many Chinese goods.

The U.S. Congress does have a weapon if it really wants to reduce China's trade with the United States. It can impose taxes, called *tariffs,* on anything that we buy from China. In so doing, Chinese goods would be more expensive to Americans. Americans would buy fewer of them and buy more domestically produced goods instead. The last time the world saw a major trade war of this type was during the Great Depression, however, and trade restrictions made that economic collapse much worse than it already was.

You Be the Judge **Who benefits and who loses from inexpensive Chinese imports?**

A Future Challenger to American Dominance

Many U.S. observers have warned that China is destined to challenge American global supremacy. With one of the fastest-growing economies in the world, along with a population of 1.3 billion, China's gross domestic product (GDP) could surpass that of the United States by 2039. China's GDP is nearly ten times greater than it was in 1978, when China implemented reforms to make the economy more market oriented. The United States already runs a multibillion-dollar trade deficit with China and could be vulnerable if Chinese economic growth continues at its present pace. How much of a problem do China's cheap exports really pose for the United States? We look at that question in this chapter's feature *Our Government Faces a Troubled Economy* above.

Diplomatic relations between China and the United States have been uneven. China offered its full support of the U.S. war on terrorism following the September 11 attacks, even providing intelligence about terrorist activities. The Chinese did not support the American invasion of Iraq in 2003, however. Although China has not shown ambitions to acquire more territory or become militarily aggressive, it has expressed a desire to take control of the island of Taiwan. China considers Taiwan, a former Chinese province, to be a legal part of China. In practice, however, since 1949 the island has functioned as if it were an independent nation. The United States has historically supported a free and separate Taiwan and has reiterated that any reunion of China and Taiwan must come about by peaceful means. More recently, relations between China and several Western nations have become strained due to criticisms by these nations of Chinese behavior in Tibet. While supposedly autonomous, Tibet is under tight Chinese control.

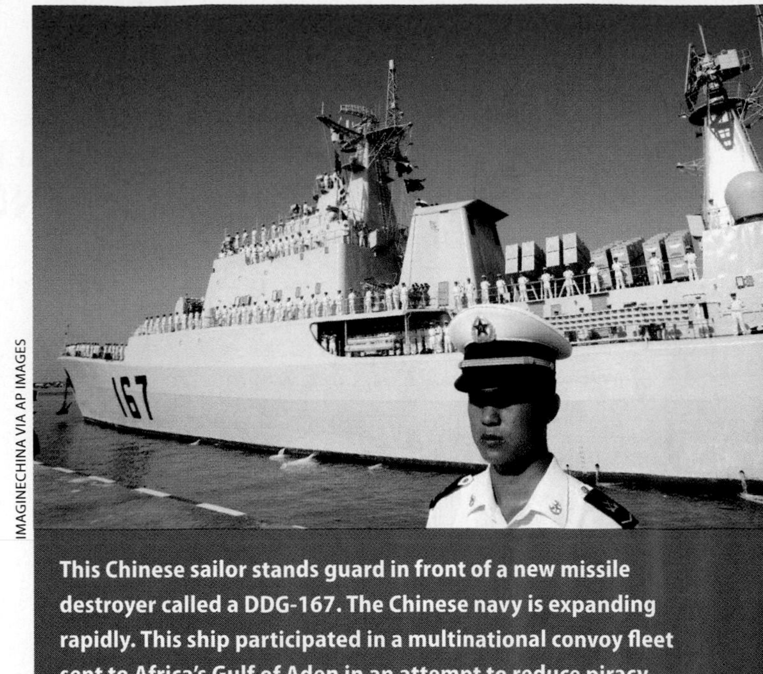

IMAGINECHINA VIA AP IMAGES

This Chinese sailor stands guard in front of a new missile destroyer called a DDG-167. The Chinese navy is expanding rapidly. This ship participated in a multinational convoy fleet sent to Africa's Gulf of Aden in an attempt to reduce piracy.

AMERICA AT **ODDS** *Foreign Policy*

In 1947, Republican senator Arthur Vandenberg of Michigan announced: "Politics stops at the water's edge." By this, Vandenberg, formerly a fierce isolationist, meant that Republicans and Democrats should cooperate in dealing with such foreign policy issues as the Cold War with the Soviet Union. Bipartisanship was never complete even in Vandenberg's day, however, and it is much less common today. True, the two major parties are more likely to cooperate over a foreign policy issue than over domestic policy. Nevertheless, Americans are at odds over many foreign policy issues, and that is reflected in Congress. The following are a few of these issues:

- In foreign policy, is it best to ally with other nations whenever possible—or should America carefully guard its ability to act alone?
- Should the president take complete charge of the foreign policy process, including the use of armed force—or should the president collaborate closely with Congress?
- Should the war on terrorism be the central focus of U.S. foreign policy—or should we devote equal energy to managing our relations with rising powers such as China?
- Is President Obama's plan to withdraw forces from Afghanistan in July 2011 a wise method of putting pressure on the Afghan government—or a recipe for failure in that country?
- In attempting to promote peace between Israelis and Palestinians, should the United States put most of its pressure on the Palestinians—or should it also pressure the Israelis to, for example, suspend the construction of new Jewish settlements on the West Bank?

Take Action

Many Americans of all political persuasions are taking action to help "support the troops" now fighting in Afghanistan. For example, a number of groups are working to help improve the lives of soldiers who have returned from the war. For ideas on what you can do to help, you can contact a veterans' group in your area or visit the Web sites of veterans' groups. For ideas, check out the Web site www.troopssupport.com, which lists more than a hundred organizations seeking to assist our soldiers. These groups represent a wide variety of outlooks and activities. A particular favorite is the Fisher House Foundation at www.fisherhouse.org, which provides housing for family members of hospitalized soldiers.

POLITICS ON THE WEB

- You can find news about international events at an interesting Web site sponsored by the Peterson Institute for International Economics at **www.iie.com**. You can also get access to the group's working papers at this site.
- To learn more about national security policy and defense issues, you can go to the U.S. Department of Defense's site at **www.defense.gov**. For information on the U.S. Department of State and its activities, go to **www.state.gov**
- One of the best resources on the Web for learning about foreign countries is the *World Factbook* of the CIA. You can find it at **www.cia.gov/library/publications/the-world-factbook**
- The Global Legal Information Network (GLIN) provides a database of national laws from countries around the world via the Web server of the U.S. Library of Congress. The site consists of more than 54,000 records of legislation enacted from 1976 to the present. To access this site, go to **www.glin.gov**
- The World Bank's home page offers a wealth of information on international development, research studies containing economic data on various countries, and the like. Go to **www.worldbank.org**
- The Washburn University School of Law offers, among other things, extensive information on international affairs, including United Nations materials. To access this site, go to **www.washlaw.edu**

Access CourseMate to review and expand on this chapter through quizzes, flashcards, learning objectives, interactive timelines, a crossword puzzle, audio summaries, video, critical-thinking activities, simulations, and more.

California's People, Economy, and Politics

GOVT 17

LEARNING OBJECTIVES

LO1 List some of the key events in California's road to statehood.

LO2 Describe the impact railroads had on California's state government.

LO3 Point out the key changes introduced by the Progressives.

LO4 Summarize how the Great Depression and World War II changed California's population and ethnic landscape.

LO5 Explain the factors that influenced postwar political party shifts.

LO6 Discuss how economic, demographic, and technological changes have impacted California politics.

CALIFORNIA AT ODDS

Should California Become Two States? Or Three?

With a population likely to reach 40 million by 2015, California is home to more than six times as many people as the average American state. California extends 770 miles north to south. Surely, if the Mayflower had landed on the California coast, California would be a number of much smaller states today. That is not how history worked itself out. Still, Jose Antonio Carrillo, a delegate to the California Constitutional Convention in 1849, argued that California should be split at San Luis Obispo. Carrillo, three times mayor of Los Angeles and a distinguished fighter for Mexico in the Mexican-American War, proposed that the southern part of California should become a territory, while the north could form a state. Carrillo may have hoped to protect the interests of his fellow Californios, that is, Spanish-speaking former Mexican citizens. His proposal went nowhere, however.

In the following years, at least 27 different proposals were advanced to divide California into two or more states. Most of these notions evaporated quickly. One of the most durable was the State of Jefferson, which was to include counties from Northern California and Southern Oregon. In 1941, residents on both sides of the border enthusiastically endorsed the project as a way of publicizing the failure of the two states to provide the region with roads and other vital services. America's entry into World War II put an abrupt end to the campaign. Still the idea of the State of Jefferson lives on, thanks in part to Jefferson Public Radio, a regional public radio network serving Southern Oregon and Northern California.

The most recent scheme was advanced following the 2008 elections by Citizens for Saving California Farming Industries. This group advocated detaching 13 coastal counties, extending from Marin to Los Angeles counties, into a new heavily urbanized state that presumably would leave the rest of California alone. The farm group was particularly incensed by the passage of Proposition 2, a measure aimed at guaranteeing humane treatment for farm animals. Of course, the chances of this plan succeeding were no greater than for any earlier plan. Still, if dividing California in two were actually possible, would it be a good idea?

California Is Just Too Darn Big

California is too big, too diverse, too divided by competing interest groups to be managed by ordinary mortals, never mind superheros from the movies. State senate districts are larger than the districts used to elect U.S. representatives. How can a state senator possibly keep in touch with his or her constituents, to the degree expected by residents of any other state? What do the citizens of Bakersfield really have in common with the citizens of Marin County? Voters in these regions are not going to want the same kind of state government, nor should they forced to have it.

Let's start by dividing California north-south, with the South getting Santa Barbara, Kern County south of the Tehachapi Mountains, and Inyo County (Owens and Death valleys). San Diego and Imperial counties could reasonably separate from the rest of the South. If ten counties in the San Francisco Bay area and the Wine Country became a fourth new state, the inland farmers could finally be at peace. California would then have eight seats in the U.S. Senate, a much more reasonable representation than today's meager two senators.

Leave Our State Alone

Dividing California is a fun topic for talk show hosts, but the idea off ends the strong state patriotism felt by millions of Californians. Some say that California is ungovernable. Is the Unites States itself ungovernable, with a population eight times that of California? If California is ungovernable, it is not because of its size but because of its laws. In no other state have the voters, through initiatives and referenda, put so much of the state's revenue off -limits to the state government. Only two other states require a two-thirds vote of the legislature to pass a simple budget, even one that doesn't increase taxes. California's voters created these rules and continue to support them. This may make governing California difficult, but the state would continue to face these challenges even if its population were a fraction of what it is today.

WHERE DO YOU STAND?

1. **Do you believe that state government would work better if California were split into two or more states that were more politically and culturally homogeneous? Why or why not?**
2. **Would it be a good idea if the legislature could pass a budget by a majority vote? Explain your reasoning.**

EXPLORE THIS ISSUE ONLINE

- **You can find the Web site of a group that wants to divide California at www.downsizeca.com.**
- **For more information on the mythical State of Jefferson, visit Jefferson Public Radio at www.ijpr.org and click on "state of jefferson."**

Introduction

Is California a failed state? That term is usually applied to collapsed nation-states like Somalia—places that lack a cohesive central government and often are caught up in civil war. But after a decade of budget deficits and gridlock in the California state capital, many observers, including even California loyalists like historian Kevin Starr, were asking that question.[1] To many, California politics seems turbulent and unpredictable. Political leaders rise and fall precipitately. Wealthy candidates and special interests are accused of "buying" elections. The governor and the legislature can't agree on a budget on schedule, as a prolonged recession grips the economy. While state government stalls in gridlock, issues are referred to the voters, who are often confused by complex and sometimes obscure ballot measures. Some say this is democracy gone mad; others have concluded that California is ungovernable. A few have even advocated breaking California into two or more states, as described in the chapter-opening *California at Odds* feature.

But however volatile or dysfunctional California politics may seem, it is serious business that affects us all, and it can be understood by examining the history and present characteristics of our state—especially its changing population and economy. Wave after wave of immigrants have made California a diverse, multicultural society, while new technologies repeatedly transform the state's economy. The resulting disparate demographic and economic interests compete for the benefits and protections conferred by government and thus shape the state's politics. To understand California today—and tomorrow—we need to know a little about its past and about the development of the competing interests within the state.

LO1 *Colonization, Rebellion, and Statehood*

The first Californians probably were immigrants like the rest of us who followed. Archaeologists believe that the ancestors of American Indians crossed an ice or land bridge or traveled by sea from Asia to Alaska thousands of years ago and then headed south. Europeans began exploring the California coast in the early 1500s, but colonization didn't start until 1769, when the Spanish established a string of missions and military outposts. About 300,000 Native Americans were living here then, mostly near the coast.

These native Californians were brought to the missions as Catholic converts and workers, but European diseases and the destruction of the native culture reduced their numbers to about 100,000 by 1849. Disease and massacres wiped out entire tribes, and the Indian population continued to diminish throughout the nineteenth century. Today, less than 1 percent of California's population is Native American, and many feel alienated from a society that has overwhelmed their peoples, cultures, and traditions. Chronic poverty, however, has been alleviated for some by the development of casinos on native lands, a phenomenon that has also made some tribes major players in state politics.

Apart from building missions, the Spaniards did little to develop their faraway possession. Not much changed when Mexico, which included California within its boundaries, declared its independence from Spain in 1822. A few thousand Mexicans quietly raised cattle on vast ranches and continued to build the province's small towns around their central plazas.

Independence and the Gold Rush

Meanwhile, expansionist interests in the United States coveted California's rich lands and access to the Pacific Ocean. When Mexico and the United States went to war over Texas in 1846, Yankee immigrants to California seized the moment and declared independence from Mexico. After the U.S. victory, Mexico surrendered its

The Gold Rush of 1849 lured thousands of people of all colors and creeds.

PERCEPTION VERSUS
REALITY
How Wild Was the Wild West?

When people think of frontier times in the old West, the images that come to mind are largely ones of violence. As the Marshall Tucker Band sang about the California Gold Rush days: "Dance hall girls were the evenin' treat—empty cartridges and blood lined the gutters of the street. Men were shot down for the sake of fun, or just to hear the noise of their forty-four guns." But just how wild was the Wild West in reality?

The Perception

The California mining communities that were swiftly erected in 1848 and 1849 were filled with young men looking for a chance to get rich quick. As saloons, brothels, and gambling dens opened up, trouble inevitably followed. With no regular courts or officers of the law, disputes were often settled by violence. Before long, informal miners' courts were organized, but too often these courts favored the powerful and popular at the expense of the week and unpopular.

The Reality

In time, federal and state governments caught up with the rapid expansion in population and sent in marshals, sheriffs, and judges to provide a more equitable legal system. Even before the arrival of official law and order, however, the camps quickly evolved rules for establishing mining claims and water rights. A considerable degree of cooperation existed, despite the anarchic conditions.

Travel to the mining camps was remarkably peaceful as well. It was dangerous, of course. Thousands of travelers died due to accidents and disease. People starved, fell off horses, drowned, were run over by wagons, or died of dysentery and cholera. Hardly any were killed by fellow travelers or by native Americans. In the West as a whole, many people did carry guns to hunt for food and protect themselves from wild animals. Firearms were banned, however, in many western towns. Larry Schweikart, a conservative historian, once calculated that there were fewer than a dozen bank robberies in the entire frontier West from 1859 to 1900. That's fewer such robberies than Schweikart's home of Dayton, Ohio experienced annually.

The myth of the lawless West was created while the frontier was still open. Writers in the East made up stories about western criminals for dime novels and other publications. Hollywood later fed the myth, creating legends that would draw customers into the theaters. In reality, most settlers, whether they were miners, cowboys, or farmers, were honest and hardworking.

Blog On Buzzle.com hosts a variety of fascinating articles on American history, including a discussion of the Wild West at **www.buzzle.com/articles/the-wild-westof-myth-and-reality.html**. Historian Peter Hill weighs in at **www.perc.org/articles/article572.php**. For lyrics to "Fire on the Mountain," see **www.cowboylyrics.com/lyrics/marshall-tucker-band.html**.

claim to lands extending from Texas to California. By this time, foreigners already outnumbered Californians of Spanish ancestry 9,000 to 7,500.

In 1848 gold was discovered, and the '49ers who started arriving the next year brought the nonnative population to 264,000 by 1852. Many immigrants came directly from Europe. The first Chinese people also arrived to work in the mines, which yielded more than a billion dollars' worth of gold in five years. The mining communities had a reputation for violence. How accurate were the tales about the Wild West? We discuss this question in the *Perception versus Reality* feature above.

Constitution of 1849
California's first constitution, which was copied from constitutions of other states and featured a two-house legislature, a supreme court, and an executive branch including a governor, lieutenant governor, controller, attorney general, and superintendent of public instruction, as well as a bill of rights. Only white males were allowed to vote.

The Structure of Statehood

The surge in population and commerce moved the new Californians to political action. A constitutional convention consisting of forty-eight delegates (only seven of whom were native Californians) threw together the **Constitution of 1849** by cutting and pasting from the constitutions of existing states; the convention requested statehood, which the U.S. Congress quickly granted. The constitutional structure of the new state was remarkably similar to what we have today, with a two-house legislature; a supreme court; and an executive branch consisting of a governor, lieutenant governor, controller, attorney general, and superintendent of public instruction. The constitution also included a bill of rights, but only white males were allowed to vote. California's Chinese, African American, and Native American residents were soon prohibited by law from owning land, testifying in court, or attending public schools.

"**MONEY** is the great tool through whose means labor and skill become universally co-operative."

~ LELAND STANFORD ~
FOUNDER OF STANFORD UNIVERSITY, EIGHTH GOVERNOR OF CALIFORNIA, 1862–1863

THE FIRST STATE GOVERNMENT The voters approved the constitution, and San Jose became the first state capital. With housing in short supply, many newly elected legislators had to lodge in tents, and the primitive living conditions were exacerbated by heavy rain and flooding. Despite these conditions, the partying politicians became known—and discredited—as "the legislature of a thousand drinks." The state capital soon moved on to Vallejo and Benicia, finally settling in 1854 in Sacramento—closer to the gold fields.

LAND OWNERSHIP As the gold rush ended, a land rush began. While small homesteads were common in other states because of federal ownership of land, much of California had been divided into huge tracts by Spanish and Mexican land grants. As early as 1870, a few hundred men owned most of the farmland. Their ranches were the forerunners of the agribusiness corporations of today, and as the mainstay of the state's economy, they exercised even more clout than their modern successors.

In less than fifty years, California had belonged to three different nations. During the same period, its economy and population had changed dramatically as hundreds of thousands of immigrants from all over the world came to claim their share of the "Golden State." The pattern of a rapidly evolving, multicultural polity was set.

Southern Pacific Railroad
A railroad company founded in 1861; developed a political machine that dominated California state politics through the turn of the century.

LO2 *Railroads, Machines, and Reform*

Technology wrought the next transformation in the form of railroads. In 1861 Sacramento merchants Charles Crocker, Mark Hopkins, Collis Huntington, and Leland Stanford founded the railroad that would become the **Southern Pacific Railroad**. They persuaded Congress to provide millions of dollars in land grants and loan subsidies for a railroad linking California with the eastern United States, thus greatly expanding the market for California's products. Stanford, then governor, used his influence to provide state assistance. Cities and counties also contributed—under the threat of being bypassed by the railroad. To obtain workers at cheap rates, the railroad builders imported 15,000 Chinese laborers.

A Political Machine

When the transcontinental track was completed in 1869, the Southern Pacific expanded its system throughout the state by building new lines and buying up existing ones. The railroad crushed competitors by cutting its shipping charges, and by the 1880s it had become the state's dominant transportation company, as well as its largest private landowner, in possession of 11 percent of the entire state. With its business agents doubling as political representatives in almost every California city and county, the Southern Pacific soon developed a formidable political machine. "The Octopus," as novelist Frank Norris called the railroad, placed allies in state and local offices through its control of both the Republican

The Transcontinental Railroad, which linked California to the eastern states, was completed on May 10, 1869, due in large part to the dedication and hard work of thousands of Chinese laborers.

CALIFORNIA STATE LIBRARY

Workingmen's Party
Denis Kearney's anti-railroad, anti-Chinese organization; instrumental in rewriting California's constitution in 1879.

Constitution of 1879
California's second constitution, which retained the basic structures of the Constitution of 1849 but added institutions to regulate railroads and public utilities and to ensure fair tax assessments. Chinese individuals were denied the right to vote, own land, or work for the government.

and Democratic parties. Once there, these officials protected the interests of the Southern Pacific if they wanted to continue in office. County tax assessors who were supported by the political machine set favorable tax rates for the railroad and its allies, while the machine-controlled legislature ensured a hands-off policy by state government.

The Workingmen's Party

People in small towns and rural areas who were unwilling to support the machine lost jobs, business, and other benefits. Some moved to cities, especially San Francisco, where manufacturing jobs were available. Chinese workers who had been brought to California to build the railroad also sought work in the cities when it was completed. But when a depression in the 1870s made jobs scarce, these newcomers faced hostile treatment from earlier immigrants. Led by Denis Kearney, Irish immigrants became the core of the **Workingmen's Party,** a political organization that blamed economic difficulties on the railroad and the Chinese.

Small farmers who opposed the railroad united through the Grange movement. In 1879 the Grangers and the Workingmen's Party called California's second constitutional convention in hopes of breaking the railroad's hold on the state. The **Constitution of 1879** mandated regulation of railroads, utilities, banks, and other corporations. An elected State Board of Equalization was set up to ensure the fairness of local tax assessments on railroads and their friends, as well as their enemies. The new constitution also prohibited the Chinese from owning land, voting, or working for state or local government.

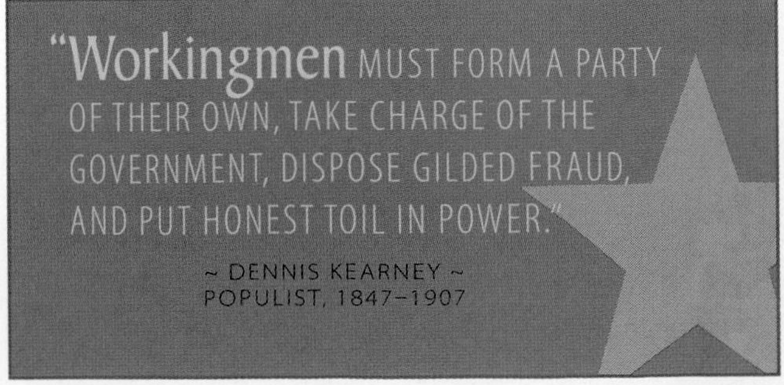

"Workingmen MUST FORM A PARTY OF THEIR OWN, TAKE CHARGE OF THE GOVERNMENT, DISPOSE GILDED FRAUD, AND PUT HONEST TOIL IN POWER."
~ DENNIS KEARNEY ~
POPULIST, 1847–1907

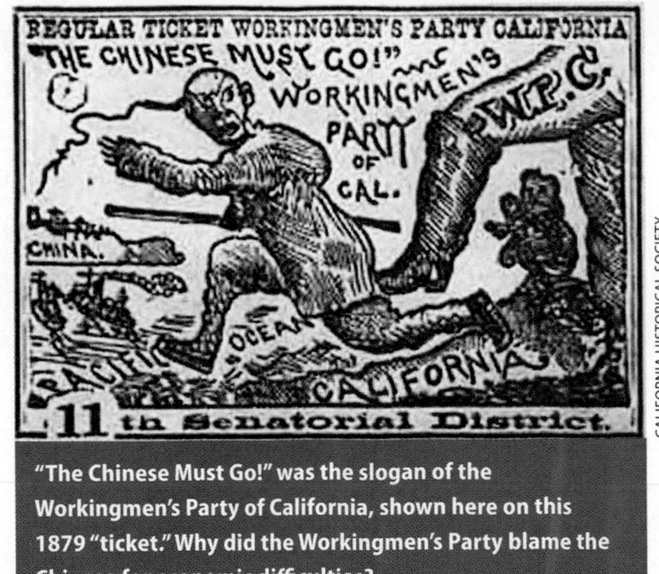

"The Chinese Must Go!" was the slogan of the Workingmen's Party of California, shown here on this 1879 "ticket." Why did the Workingmen's Party blame the Chinese for economic difficulties?

The railroad soon reclaimed power, however, gaining control of the very agencies that were created to regulate it. Nonetheless, the efforts made during this period to regulate big business and control racial relations became recurring themes in California life and politics, and much of the Constitution of 1879 remains intact today.

LO3 *The Progressives*

The growth fostered by the railroad eventually produced a new middle class, encompassing merchants, doctors, lawyers, teachers, and skilled workers, who were not dependent on the railroad. They objected to the corrupt practices and favoritism of the railroad's political machine, which they thought was restraining economic development in their communities. The new middle class demanded honesty and competence, which they called "good government." In 1907 a number of these crusaders established the Lincoln-Roosevelt League, a reform group within the Republican Party, and became part of the national Progressive movement. Their leader, Hiram Johnson, was elected governor in 1910; they also captured control of the state legislature. While the Progressives were certainly advocates of reform in the context of their time, historians have debated how "progressive"—or liberal—the Progressives were by modern standards. We discuss this question in the *Join the Debate* feature on the facing page.

Were the Progressives Really Progressive?

In assessing the Progressives, it helps to understand their backgrounds. Unlike the Populists of the 1890s, who were typically farmers or miners, the Progressives of the early twentieth century were mostly townspeople. Many were lawyers, small businessmen or publishers. Resolutely middle class, the Progressives were alarmed at the enormous power accumulated by great corporations such as the Southern Pacific Railroad. But they also were afraid of radicalism among members of the working class. Labor unions, socialism, and after the Russian Revolution, communism—these too were dangers, alongside the urban political machines and the railroads. As reformers, the Progressives looked not only to the future, but to an idealized American past of yeoman individuals, who did not seek employment by large corporations and who had no need to rebel against them, either. Given this philosophy, was it even possible for the Progressives to be "progressive" in the sense we give the term today? Did they seek to champion the underdog? To improve the condition of the poor and the working class?

Progressive Reforms Were of Great Benefit to Working People

Those who defend the Progressives' record admit that many Progressives shared a deep distrust of the working class. Still, many were highly sympathetic to the problems of working people. Governor Hiram Johnson (1911–1917) had served as an attorney for the Teamsters Union, and he hailed from San Francisco, one of the most organized cities in the nation. Organized labor made some of its greatest legal gains under Johnson. Chief among these victories was a Worker's Compensation Act to benefit employees injured on the job. The first measure, passed in 1911, was weak. It made compensation by employers voluntary. A 1913 law, however, required mandatory compensation.

A minimum wage and an eight-hour day law were established for working women. While modern feminists typically oppose employment legislation that applies only to women, in the belief that such laws can be used to bar women from particular forms of employment, these early California protections were created in response to the demands of Progressive women. Male or female, Progressives were strong advocates of votes for women. Working people, along with almost everyone else, benefited from years of good government and the curbing of the power of the Southern Pacific. On a national level, Progressive leaders such as Theodore Roosevelt even advocated universal health insurance, something the country wouldn't see during the rest of the twentieth century.

But You'd Better Be a White Protestant Worker

Critics of the Progressives point out that many of them were quite hostile to labor. In Los Angeles, Progressives allied with Harrison Otis, the reactionary publisher of the *Los Angeles Times,* to enact anti-picketing and open shop ordinances that crippled the union movement in that city. More generally, almost all of the Progressives were hostile to immigrants, in particular to Catholics such as the Irish and the Italians. Prohibition of the manufacture, sale, and consumption of alcoholic beverages was a major Progressive goal. It finally achieved nationwide success in 1919 through the Eighteenth Amendment to the U.S. Constitution. (Of course, state-level prohibition never triumphed in California, which then as now produced most of the nation's wine.) Prohibition was seen by all concerned as a direct attempt to exercise social control over Catholic working-class communities.

When it came to African Americans or especially Asian Americans, Progressives ventured far beyond simple racism into complete hostility. The 1911 Alien Land Law, which barred Japanese Americans from owning or leasing land, was in effect an attempt to run that community out of the state. Even poor whites might find themselves in danger. Leading Progressives, including both presidential candidates Theodore Roosevelt and Woodrow Wilson, endorsed the eugenics movement, which called for eliminating "unfit" individuals from the gene pool. Poverty was generally taken as a sign of unfitness. Among other things, the eugenics movement called for the sterilization of persons who were mentally handicapped or ill. California passed a compulsory sterilization law in 1909, and in subsequent years it led the nation in the number of sterilizations. These were not policies we would be willing to label "progressive" today.

For Critical Analysis ***The Progressives were hardly the only racists in the early twentieth century. Racist views were almost universal among whites. A majority of whites were also firm believers in Christianity. How might white Americans have accommodated Christian doctrine to racist beliefs?***

AP PHOTO/JEFF CHIU

Aiko (Grace) Obata Amemiya speaks to the University of California Board of Regents about being interned while studying at UC Berkeley in 1942. In 2009, the University of California granted honorary degrees to hundreds of Japanese Americans whose studies were interrupted when they were sent to internment camps during World War II.

The Reform Movement

To break the power of the machine, the **Progressives** introduced a wave of reforms that shape California politics to this day. Predictably, they created a new regulatory agency for the railroads and utilities, the Public Utilities Commission (PUC). Most of their reforms, however, aimed at weakening the political parties as tools of bosses and machines. Instead of party bosses handpicking candidates at party conventions, the voters now were given the power to select their party's nominees for office in primary elections. Cross-filing further diluted party power by allowing candidates to file for and win the nominations of more than one political party. The Progressives removed party labels from the ballot altogether to make city and county elections "nonpartisan." They also created a civil service system to select state employees on the basis of their qualifications rather than their political connections.

Finally, the Progressives introduced direct democracy, which allowed the voters to amend the constitution and create laws through initiatives and referenda and to recall, or remove, elected officials before their terms expired. Supporters of an initiative, referendum, or recall must circulate petitions and collect a specified number of signatures of registered voters before it becomes a ballot measure or proposition.

OTHER PROGRESSIVE MEASURES Like the Workingmen's Party before them, the Progressives were concerned about immigration. Antagonism toward recent Japanese immigrants (who numbered 72,000 by 1910) resulted in Progressive support for a ban on land ownership by aliens and the National Immigration Act of 1924, which effectively halted Asian immigration. Other, more positive changes by the Progressives included giving women the right to vote, passing child labor and workers' compensation laws, and implementing conservation programs to protect natural resources.

Progressives Members of an anti-machine reform movement that reshaped the state's political institutions between 1907 and the 1920s.

Thanks largely to the Progressive reforms, the railroad's political machine eventually died; California's increasingly diverse economy had also weakened the machine, however, as the emerging oil, automobile, and trucking industries gave the state alternative means of transportation and shipping. These and other growing industries ultimately restructured economic and political power in California.

POWER TO THE PEOPLE The reform movement waned in the 1920s, but the Progressive legacy of weak political parties and direct democracy opened up California's politics to its citizens, as well as to powerful interest groups and individual candidates with strong personalities. A long and detailed constitution is also part of the legacy. The Progressives instituted their reforms by amending (and thus lengthening) the Constitution of 1879 rather than calling for a new constitutional convention. Direct democracy subsequently enabled voters and interest groups to amend the constitution, which has become an extraordinarily lengthy document over time.

LO4 *The Great Depression and World War II*

California's population grew by more than 2 million in the 1920s (see Table 17–1). Most of the newcomers headed for Los Angeles, where employment

Table 17–1

California's Population Growth, Selected Decades, 1850–2010

Year	Population	Percentage of U.S. Population
1850	93,000	0.4
1900	1,485,000	2.0
1950	10,643,000	7.0
1960	15,863,000	8.8
1970	20,039,000	9.8
1980	23,780,000	10.5
1990	29,733,000	11.7
2000	33,871,648	12.0
2010	38,648,090	12.6

Source: California Department of Finance and U.S. Census.

> "The private control of credit **IS THE MODERN FORM OF SLAVERY.**"
>
> ~ UPTON SINCLAIR, JR. ~
> AMERICAN NOVELIST
> 1878–1968

opportunities in shipping, filmmaking, and manufacturing (of clothing, automobiles, and aircraft) abounded. Then came the Great Depression of the 1930s, which saw the unemployment rate soar from 3 percent in 1925 to 33 percent by 1933. Even so, more than a million people still came to California, including thousands of poor white immigrants from the "dust bowl" of the drought-impacted Midwest. Many wandered through California's great Central Valley in search of work, displacing Mexicans—who earlier had supplanted the Chinese and Japanese—as the state's farm workers. Racial antagonism ran high, and many Mexicans were arbitrarily sent back to Mexico. Labor unrest reached a crescendo in the early 1930s, as workers on farms, in canneries, and on the docks of San Francisco and Los Angeles fought for higher wages and an eight-hour workday.

The immigrants and union activists of the 1920s and 1930s also changed California politics. Many registered as Democrats, thus challenging the dominant Republicans. The Depression and President Franklin Roosevelt's popular New Deal helped the Democrats become California's majority party in registration, although winning elections proved more difficult. Their biggest boost came from Upton Sinclair, a novelist, a socialist, and the Democratic candidate for governor in 1934.

Sinclair's End Poverty in California (EPIC) movement almost led to an election victory, but the state's conservative establishment spent an unprecedented $10 million to defeat him. The Democrats finally gained the governorship in 1938, but their candidate, Culbert Olson, was the only Democratic winner between 1894 and 1958.

An Economic Boom

World War II revived the economic boom. The federal government spent $35 billion in California between 1940 and 1946, creating 500,000 jobs in defense industries. California's radio, electronics, and aircraft industries grew at phenomenal rates. The jobs brought new immigrants, including many African Americans, whose proportion of the state's population quadrupled during the 1940s. African Americans were nevertheless on the periphery of the state's racial conflicts—unlike Japanese and Mexican Americans. During the war, more than 100,000 Japanese

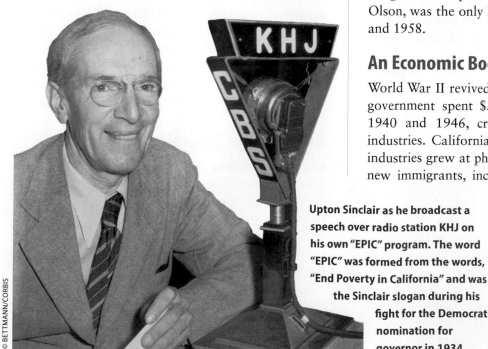

Upton Sinclair as he broadcast a speech over radio station KHJ on his own "EPIC" program. The word "EPIC" was formed from the words, "End Poverty in California" and was the Sinclair slogan during his fight for the Democratic nomination for governor in 1934.

The Central Valley Water Project, part of President Roosevelt's National Recovery Program for California begun in the 1930s, brought thousands of jobs and irrigation to the desert.

Americans, suspected of loyalty to their ancestral homeland, were sent to prison camps (officially called internment centers). Antagonism toward Mexican Americans resulted in the Zoot Suit Riots in Los Angeles in 1943, when Anglo sailors and police attacked Mexican Americans wearing distinctive suits featuring long jackets with wide lapels, padded shoulders, and high-waisted, pegged pants.

While the cities boomed, with defense industries becoming permanent fixtures and aerospace and electronics adding to the momentum, the Central Valley bloomed, thanks to water projects initiated by the state and federal governments during the 1930s. Dams and canals brought water to the desert and reaffirmed agriculture as a mainstay of California's economy.

A New Breed of Moderate

Although the voters chose a Democratic governor during the Great Depression, they returned to the Republican fold as the economy revived. Earl Warren, a new breed of moderate, urbane Republican, was elected governor in 1942, 1946, and 1950, becoming the only individual to win the office three times until Jerry Brown. Warren used cross-filing to win the nominations of both parties and staked out a relationship with the voters that he claimed was above party politics. A classic example of California's personality-oriented politics, Warren left the state in 1953 to become chief justice of the United States Supreme Court.

LO5 *Growth, Change, and Political Turmoil*

In 1958 the Republican Party was in disarray because of infighting. Californians elected a Democratic governor, Edmund G. "Pat" Brown, and a Democratic majority in the state legislature. To prevent Republicans from taking advantage of cross-filing again, the state's new leaders immediately outlawed that electoral device.

In control of both the governor's office and the legislature for the first time in the twentieth century, Democrats moved aggressively to develop the state's infrastructure. Completion of the massive California Water Project, construction of the state highway network, and creation of an unparalleled higher education system were among the advances to accommodate a growing population. Meanwhile, in the 1960s, California's black and Latino minorities became more assertive, pushing for civil rights, desegregation of schools, access to higher education, and improved treatment for California's predominantly Latino farm workers.

The demands of minority groups alienated some white voters, however, and the Democratic programs were expensive. After opening their purse strings during the eight-year tenure of Pat Brown, Californians became more cautious about the state's direction. Race riots precipitated by police brutality in Los Angeles, along with student unrest over the Vietnam War, also turned the voters against liberal Democrats such as Brown.

A Republican Revival

In 1966 Republican Ronald Reagan was elected governor; he moved the state in a more conservative direction before going on to serve as president. His successor as governor, Democrat Edmund G. "Jerry" Brown, Jr., was the son of the earlier governor Brown and a liberal on social issues. Like Reagan, however, the younger Brown led California away from spending on growth-inducing infrastructure, such as highways and schools. In 1978 the voters solidified this change with the watershed tax-cutting initiative, Proposition 13 (see Chapter 24). Although Democrats

ELECTIONS 2010

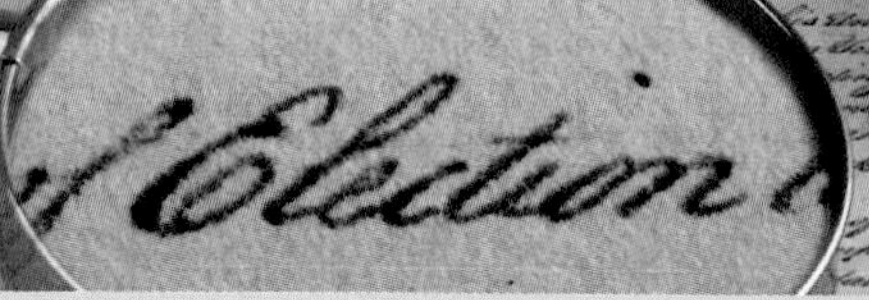

An Island of Stability in a Stormy Nation

Throughout most of the country, the 2010 mid-term elections were a triumph for the Republicans, a "wave" election. California was a conspicuous exception. Democrats prevailed in the top two contests, as Democrat Jerry Brown handily defeated Republican Meg Whitman for governor and Democratic senator Barbara Boxer won against Republican challenger Carly Fiorina. The Democrats also demonstrated strength right down the ticket. While some races were very close, in the end the Republicans failed to gain even a single additional seat in the U.S. House of Representatives.

Democratic candidates won all contests for statewide executive offices, replacing a retiring Republican insurance commissioner with a Democrat. In the state senate, the partisan balance remained exactly the same as before the elections—twenty-five Democrats, thirteen Repulicans, and two vacancies. One Democratic state senator won re-election even though she died shortly before the elections. (A special election was necessary.) The state assembly had two vacancies and one retiring independent going into the elections. As a result, both parties were able to return with larger delegations. The Democrats gained one seat for a total of fifty-two and the Republicans picked up two for a total of twenty-eight.

The voters also determined the fate of several crucial ballot proposals. You'll learn about these proposals in the Chapter 18 *Elections 2010* feature.

have long outnumbered Republicans among California's registered voters, Brown was followed by Republicans George Deukmejian in 1982 and Pete Wilson in 1990, each of whom served two terms in office.

In 1998 California elected Gray Davis, its first Democratic governor in sixteen years. He was reelected in 2002 despite voter concerns about an energy crisis, a recession, and a growing budget deficit. As a consequence of these crises and what some perceived as an arrogant attitude, Davis faced an unprecedented recall election in October 2003. The voters removed him from office and replaced him with Republican Arnold Schwarzenegger, who was reelected in 2006.

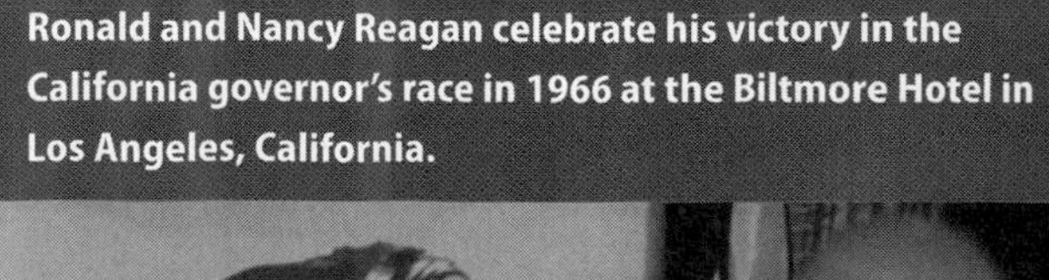

Ronald and Nancy Reagan celebrate his victory in the California governor's race in 1966 at the Biltmore Hotel in Los Angeles, California.

BILL RAY/TIME LIFE PICTURES/GETTY IMAGES

The Voters Lean to the Democrats

In 2010, former governor Jerry Brown attempted a comeback and made history as California's oldest governor when he defeated former eBay chief executive Meg Whitman, a Republican who broke the U.S. campaign spending record for any office other than the presidency.

Democrats have had more consistent success in the state legislature and the congressional delegation, where they have been the dominant party since 1960. California voters have also opted for Democrats in every presidential election since 1988.

The challenges of governing California have been exacerbated by recurring conflicts between a Democratic legislature and Republican governors, as well as by the constitutional requirement for a supermajority to enact the state budget. Meanwhile, the voters have become increasingly involved in policymaking by initiative and referendum (see Chapter 18). Amendments to California's constitution, which require voter approval, appear on almost every state ballot. As a consequence, California's Constitution of 1879 has been amended nearly five hundred times; the U.S. Constitution includes just twenty-seven amendments.

Continued Growth

Throughout these changes the state's population continued to grow, outpacing most other states so much that the California delegation to the U.S. House of Representatives now numbers fifty-three—more than twenty-one other states combined. Much of this growth was the result of a new wave of immigration facilitated by more flexible national immigration laws during the 1960s and 1970s. Immigration from Asia—especially from Southeast Asia after the Vietnam War—increased greatly. A national amnesty for undocumented residents also enabled many Mexicans to gain citizenship and bring their families from Mexico. In all, 85 percent of the 6 million newcomers and births in California in the 1980s were Asian, Latino, or black. Growth slowed in the 1990s, as 2 million more people left the state than came to it from other states, but California's population continued to increase as a result of births and immigration from abroad. In 1990 whites made up 57 percent of the state's population; by 2000 they were 47 percent.

Racial Conflict

Constantly increasing diversity enlivened California's culture and provided a steady flow of new workers, but it also increased tensions. Some affluent Californians retreated to gated communities; others fled the state. Racial conflict broke out between gangs on the streets and in prisons. As in difficult economic times throughout California's history, a recession during the early 1990s led many Californians, including Governor Wilson, to blame immigrants, especially those who were in California illegally. A series of ballot measures raised divisive race-related issues such as illegal immigration, bilingualism, and affirmative action. The issue of immigration enflames California politics to this day, although the increasing electoral clout of minorities and big public demonstrations in support of immigrants have provided some balance.

Demonstrators at a Los Angeles immigrant rights rally in 2006 are being watched by a gang officer. Are immigrants to blame for racial conflict?

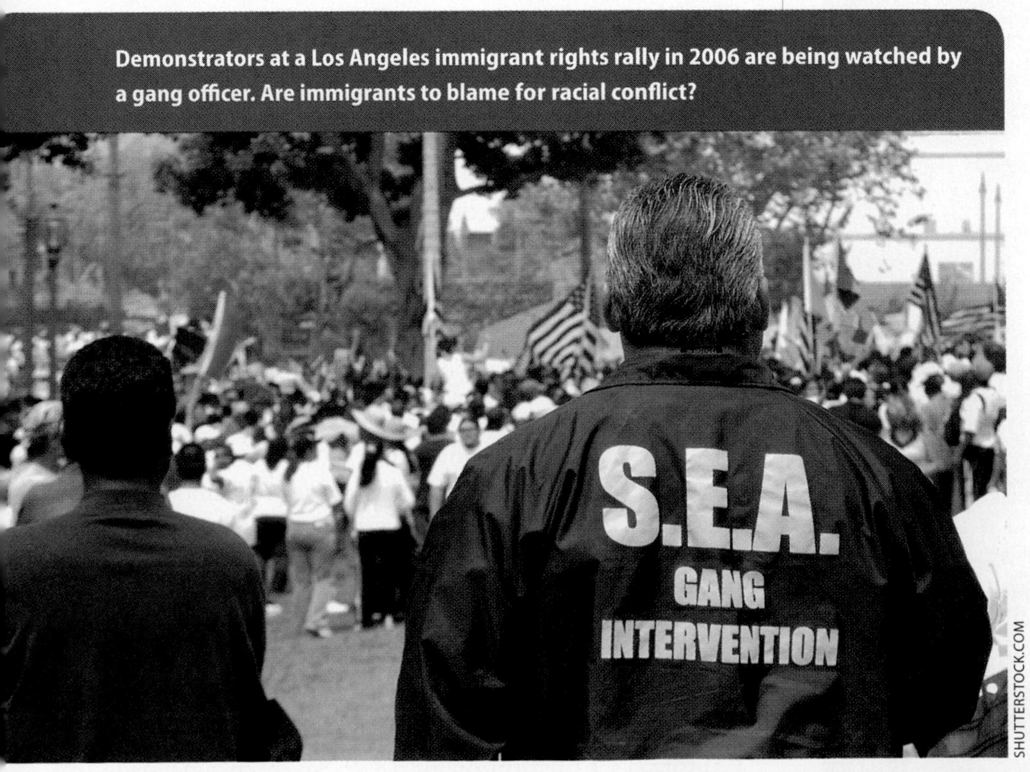

LO6 *California Today*

If California were an independent nation, its economy would rank eighth in the world, with an annual gross domestic product exceeding $1.8 trillion. Much of the state's strength stems from its economic diversity (see Table 17–2). The elements of this diversity also constitute powerful political interests in state politics.

Half of California—mostly desert and mountains—is owned by the state and federal governments. In the rural areas, a few big farm corporations control much of the state's rich farmlands. These enormous corporate farms, known as agribusinesses, make California the nation's leading farm state, producing more than four hundred crops and providing nearly half of the vegetables, fruits, and nuts and a quarter of the dairy products consumed nationally. Grapes and wine are also top products, with 4,600 growers and 2,843 wineries.

California's Agriculture Industry

State politics affects this huge economic force in many ways, but most notably in labor relations, environmental regulation, and water supply. Farmers and their employees have battled for decades over issues ranging from

> "The fight is never about grapes or lettuce
> . . . IT IS ALWAYS ABOUT PEOPLE."
>
> ~ CESAR CHAVEZ ~
> CIVIL RIGHTS ACTIVIST
> AND LABOR ORGANIZER
> 1927–1993

wages to safety. Under the leadership of Cesar Chavez and the United Farm Workers union, laborers organized. Supported by public boycotts of certain farm products, they achieved some improvements in working conditions, but the struggle continues today. California's agricultural industry is also caught up in environmental issues, including the use of pesticides and the pollution of water supplies. In addition, booming growth in the Central Valley has urbanized some farmland, bringing "city" problems such as traffic and crowded schools to once-rural areas. The biggest issue, however, is always water. Most of California's cities and farmlands must import water from other parts of the state. Thanks to government subsidies, farmers claim 80 percent of the state's water supply at prices so low that they have little reason to improve inefficient irrigation systems. Meanwhile, the growth of urban areas is limited by their water supplies. Today, agriculture is in the thick of California politics as the state strives to balance an essential and powerful industry with the interests of its other citizens.

Table 17–2

California's Economy

Industrial Sector	Employees	Amount (in millions)
Professional and business services	2,035,300	$ 260,133
Education and health services	1,766,600	131,067
Leisure and hospitality services	1,483,600	75,639
Other services	477,300	42,196
Information	447,600	112,752
Government	2,482,000	216,764
Trade, transportation, and utilities	2,580,100	299,645
Manufacturing	1,237,200	181,134
Finance, insurance, and real estate	777,800	416,324
Construction	553,800	67,770
Mining and natural resources	24,700	43,333
Agriculture	389,100	36,600
Total, all sectors	14,255,100	$1,883,357

Source: California Employment Development Department, **www.edd.ca.gov** (accessed May 2010); and U.S. Department of Commerce, Bureau of Economic Analysis, *Survey of Current Business,* June 2010.

Cesar Chavez (1927–1993), co-founder of the United Farm Workers of America.

AP PHOTO/ADELE STARR

Economic Diversity

Agriculture is big business, but many more Californians work in manufacturing, especially in the aerospace, defense, and high-tech industries. Employment in manufacturing, however, has been declining in California for some years, especially after the federal government reduced military and defense spending in the 1990s when the collapse of communism in the Soviet Union brought an end to the Cold War. Employment in California shifted to postindustrial occupations such as retail sales, tourism, and services, although jobs in these sectors often pay low wages. Government policies on growth, the environment, and taxation affect all of these employment sectors, and all suffer when any one sector goes into a slump.

HIGH-TECH BOOM But the salvation of California's economy is its innovation, especially in telecommunications, entertainment, medical equipment, international trade, and above all, high-tech businesses spawned by the defense and aerospace companies that withered in the early 1990s. At the peak of the high-tech boom, California hosted one-fourth of the nation's high-tech firms, which provided nearly a million jobs. Half of the nation's computer engineers worked in **Silicon Valley,** named after the silicon chip that revolutionized the computer industry. Running between San Jose and San Francisco, Silicon Valley became a center for innovation in technology from technical instruments, computer chips,

Silicon Valley The top area for high-tech industries; located between San Jose and San Francisco.

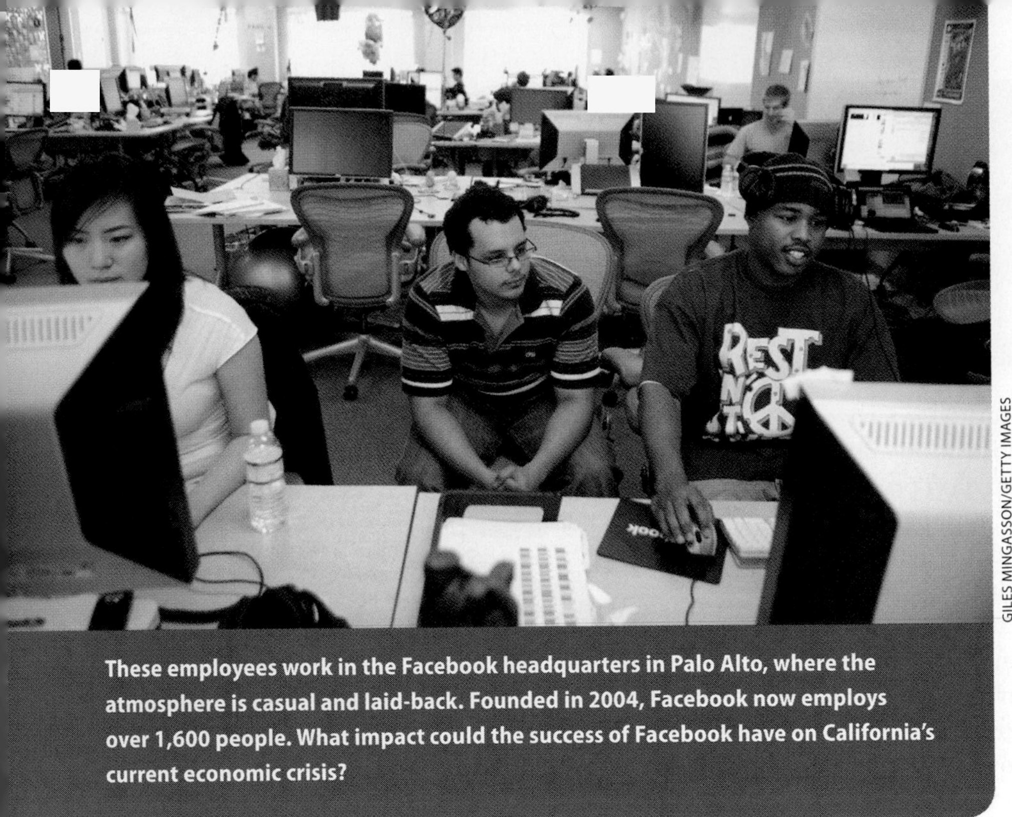

GILES MINGASSON/GETTY IMAGES

These employees work in the Facebook headquarters in Palo Alto, where the atmosphere is casual and laid-back. Founded in 2004, Facebook now employs over 1,600 people. What impact could the success of Facebook have on California's current economic crisis?

networking equipment, workstations, and software to Internet-based dot-com businesses. Biomedical and pharmaceutical companies also proliferated, further contributing to California's transformation.

ENTERTAINMENT AND TOURISM Computer technology also spurred rapid expansion of the entertainment industry, long a key component of California's economy. This growth particularly benefited the Los Angeles area, which had been hit hard by cuts in defense spending. Together, entertainment and tourism provide more than 500,000 jobs for Californians. Half of these are in film and television, but tourism remains a bastion of the economy, with California regularly ranking first among the states in visitors. Along with agriculture, high-tech, telecommunications, and other industries, these businesses have made California a leader in both international and domestic trade. All these industries are part of a globalized economy, which has bolstered and sustained California's economy. Much of this trade goes through the massive port complex of Los Angeles/Long Beach, as well as the San Francisco Bay Port of Oakland; much is also shipped by air.

Economic Decline

The California economy has been on a roller coaster for the past few years, though. It has been in and out of recession—first in the early 1990s, and then again after the stock market collapse of 2000 to 2002, when the California-centered Internet boom went bust as thousands of dot-com companies failed to generate projected profits. High-tech industry went into decline, and tens of thousands of workers lost their jobs, some of which were "off-shored" (moved to other countries). At about the same time, an energy crisis hit California. The state had deregulated energy suppliers in 1996 at the urging of industry, but by 2000, prices for gas and electricity had risen and parts of the state experienced shortages of electrical power. Belatedly, Governor Davis took action to resolve the crisis, but his initial caution and the exorbitant prices the state paid to ensure supplies caused his popularity to slump. All these factors combined to push California into a recession, with unemployment reaching 7 percent statewide and 9 percent in Silicon Valley in 2003 (the national rate was 5.9 percent).

THE IMPACT ON STATE GOVERNMENT When tax revenues rose during the heady days of the dot-coms, Governor Davis and the legislature had expanded programs and cut some fees and taxes. But when the boom ended, tax revenues declined precipitously, producing a state budget deficit that ultimately exceeded $30 billion. The deficit and other issues plunged California into a crisis that continued beyond the recall of Governor Davis in 2003.

THE GREAT RECESSION After a brief resurgence in 2006–2007, California's economy slipped back toward recession as unemployment reached 12.4 percent in 2010 (the U.S. rate was 9.7 percent). California had lost hundreds of thousands of manufacturing jobs since the 1990s as employers migrated to other states. By 2010, however, employment in all sectors, even film and television production, was in decline. The national home finance and foreclosure crisis also hit the California housing market and construction industry hard. Governor Schwarzenegger found himself faced with even bigger budget deficits than his predecessor—and nearly the same low public approval ratings. Why do recessions create more trouble for state governments than for the national government? We examine this issue in the feature *California Faces a Troubled Economy* on the following page.

California Faces a Troubled Economy

Why State Governments Can't Stimulate the Economy

During a recession, individuals and businesses in the private sector reduce the amount that they borrow and spend. In a serious recession, private sector borrowing and spending can collapse. Conventional economic policy is that in a recession, the federal government should run a budget deficit. The borrowing required to fund the deficit—and the spending based on that borrowing—help make up for the reduction in borrowing and spending by the private sector. As a result, the economic downturn is softened, and the economy can right itself sooner. We described this policy recommendation in Chapter 14 and also in the *Our Government Faces a Troubled Economy* feature in Chapter 3.

The federal government is only part of our American system of government, however. We must also consider the states. When we ask how much "the government" borrows and spends, the real answer must include the borrowing and spending of state and local governments. In a recession, the actions taken by these governments can run directly counter to what the federal government is trying to do. The federal government tries to run an "anti-cyclical" fiscal policy that counteracts the economy's booms and busts. State and local policy, however, is typically "pro-cyclical." In California and elsewhere, state borrowing and spending policies tend to make recessions worse than they already are.

Why the States Must Cut Spending

Why is state and local spending pro-cyclical? The answer is that the states, unlike the federal government, do not have an essentially unlimited ability to borrow money. All states except Vermont have a balanced budget requirement written into the state constitution. In California and other states, a recession means that the state's income falls. Indeed, such falling revenues have been a particular problem for California, because the state has relied heavily on a progressive income tax that collects large sums from the state's richest residents. In a recession, the income of the rich actually falls much faster than the income of ordinary people. Much of their income in good years, after all, comes from higher prices of stocks on Wall Street and high business profits. In bad years, these sources of income can experience spectacular declines. Of course, the very rich have plenty of resources to keep the wolf from the door, even in years when they are not doing well. States such as California that live by taxing the variable income of the wealthy, however, can find themselves in big trouble.

Anyone who has followed California politics knows full well that state governments can and do borrow. Students of California government also know that excessive borrowing can get a state into serious financial trouble. Further, in many states, California included, political and legal barriers make borrowing difficult. The inevitable result: in times of crisis, the state must cut its spending to help balance the budget. Even as the federal government is increasing its spending, the states must cut back. It follows that the total government effort to combat a recession is much less effective than you might think if you only look at the actions of the federal government.

Uncle Sam to the Rescue?

One way to counteract pro-cyclical state and local spending is for the federal government to pass funds directly to the states as part of a stimulus plan. In February 2009, the Obama stimulus package indeed allocated $144 billion in fiscal relief to state governments, much of it in the form of support for Medicaid and education programs. Infrastructure spending promised additional sums. California moved quickly to collect its $19 billion allocation. Unfortunately, the federal support was only temporary. Federal stimulus dollars began to dry up in 2010, forcing California and other states to make difficult choices. The budget for fiscal year 2011, adopted in 2010 during Governor Arnold Schwarzenegger's last year in office, assumed that the state would receive $5.3 billion from the federal government. A number of analysts, however, characterized this sum as "beyond optimistic."

You Be the Judge **In your opinion, how tightly should state government borrowing be restrained? Explain your reasoning.**

Adapting through Innovation and Diversity

Throughout its history, California has experienced economic ups and downs like these, recovered, reinvented itself, and moved on thanks to the diversity of its economy and its people and their ability to adapt to change. While some businesses have forsaken California for other states, complaining of burdensome regulation and the high cost of doing business in California, the Public Policy Institute of California reports that the skill and higher productivity of the state's workforce, access to capital, and quality of life compensate for such costs and keep the state attractive to many businesses.[2] Innovation continues to be an economic mainstay as well. Nanotechnology companies, for example, are concentrated in the San Francisco Bay Area, while biotechnology thrives in the San Diego region and green industry (for example, solar power and electric cars) booms throughout California. Small businesses—many of which are minority owned—form the backbone of the California economy, and while many struggle, others thrive. Most other states lack these advantages; some are dependent on a single industry or product, and none can match the energy and optimism brought by California's constant flow of immigrants eager to take jobs in the state's new and old industries.

California's globalized economy consistently attracts more immigrants than any other state; as of 2010, 26.6 percent of the state's population was foreign born, down slightly from a peak of 27.4 percent in 2007.[3] For perspective, the foreign-born share of the U.S. population was 12.2 percent. Fifty-six percent of California's immigrants are from Latin America (mostly Mexico), and 34 percent are from Asia (especially the Philippines, China, Vietnam, India, and Korea). Significantly for the California economy, 75 percent of the state's immigrant population is of working age (twenty-five to sixty-four).[4] An estimated 3 million immigrants are in California illegally. As a consequence of so much immigration, nearly 40 percent of all Californians over the age of five speak a language other than English at home, resulting in a major challenge for California schools. As in past centuries, immigration and language have been hot-button political issues in California in recent years.

The extent of California's ethnic diversity is indicated in Figure 17–1. Although non-Latino whites remain the single largest group, they are no longer a majority. As of 2008, 70.6 percent of students in California's public schools were nonwhite.[5] Overall, the black and white proportions of California's population have decreased, while Asian and Latino numbers have grown rapidly since the 1970s, slowly producing a shift in political power.

Economic Disparity

The realization of the California dream is not shared equally among these groups. Although the median household income as of 2009 was $58,931 according the U.S. Census Bureau, the income of 15.3 percent of Californians fell below the federal poverty level—slightly above the national average—but the state's rate is considerably higher when the cost of living in California is factored in. Over half the students in California schools qualify for free or reduced-price meals.[6] The gap between rich and poor in California is among the largest in the United States and is still growing. Poverty is worst among Latinos, blacks, and Southeast Asians, who tend to hold low-paying service jobs; other Asians, along with Anglos, predominate in the more comfortable professional classes.

Religious leaders join activists angered by Governor Schwarzenegger's veto of a bill that would have allowed undocumented immigrants to drive legally.

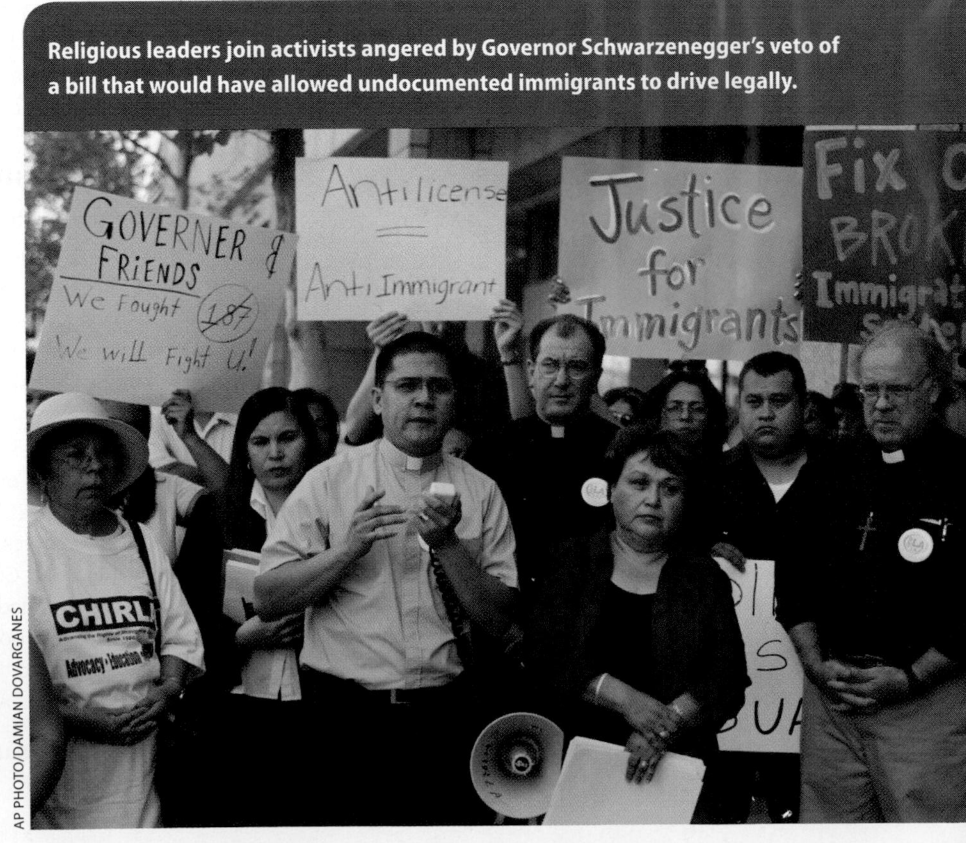

AP PHOTO/DAMIAN DOVARGANES

Figure 17–1

California's Growing Racial and Ethnic Diversity

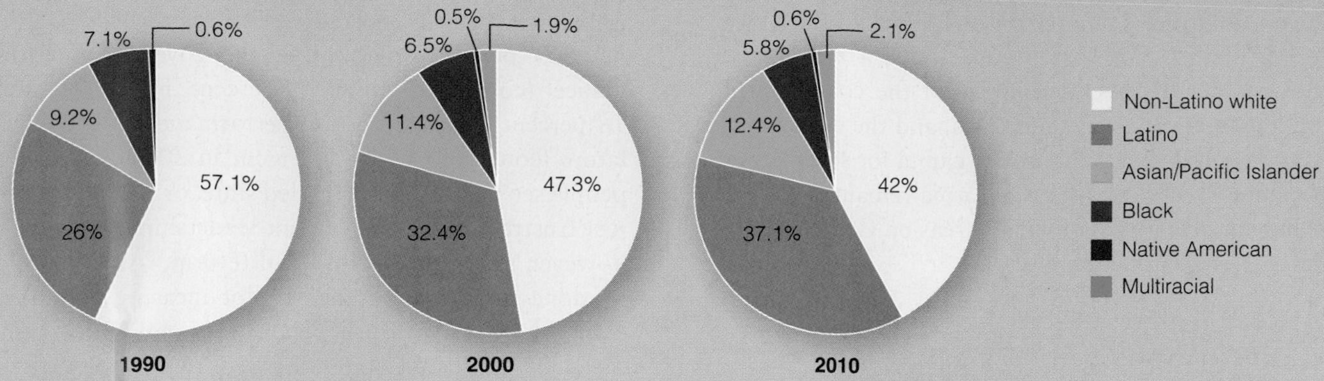

Source: U.S. Census; California Department of Finance, *Population Projections by Race/Ethnicity for California and Its Counties, 2000–2050,* **www.dof.ca.gov** (accessed June 18, 2010).

Decline of the Middle Class

As the poor grow in number, some observers fear that California's middle class is vanishing. Once a majority, many of the middle class have slipped down the economic ladder, and others have simply fled the state. Instead of a class structure with a great bulge in the center, California now exhibits an **"hourglass economy,"** with many people doing very well at the top, many barely getting by at the bottom, and fewer and fewer in the middle. Recent growth has concentrated in low- and high-wage jobs, and the income gap continues to widen.[7]

The costs of housing and health care are at the heart of this problem. The housing crisis of 2008–2009 increased the affordability of home ownership for some families, but many more suffered substantial losses of equity in their homes, and some lost their homes to foreclosure. With a median home price of $306,230 in 2010 compared with the U.S. median of $175,000, Californians still spent more of their income on housing than the national average, and fewer families were able to afford to own homes, especially in the coastal counties from San Diego to San Francisco. Homes were more affordable in inland California, however.[8] Overall, home ownership in California lags well behind the national average, especially for Latinos and blacks. Health care is also a problem for poor and working Californians. Over 24 percent (8.2 million) have no health insurance,[9] although coverage for children was expanded under the state's Healthy Families program established in 2001.

Geographic Divisions

Geographic divisions complicate California's economic and ethnic diversity. In the past, the most pronounced of these divisions was between the northern and southern portions of the state. The San Francisco Bay Area tended to be diverse, liberal, and in elections, Democratic, while Southern California was staunchly Republican and much less diverse. However, with growth and greater diversity, Los Angeles also began voting Democratic. Today, the greatest division is between the coastal and inland regions of the state (see Figure 18–3). Democrats now outnumber Republicans in San Diego, for example, and even notoriously conservative Orange County has elected a Latina Democrat to Congress.

But even as the differences between northern and southern California fade, the contrast between coastal and inland California has increased.[10] The state's vast Central Valley has led the way in population and job growth, with cities from Sacramento to Fresno to Bakersfield gobbling up farmland. The Inland Empire, from Riverside to San Bernardino, has grown even more rapidly since the late 1990s. Although still sparsely populated, California's northern coast, Sierra Nevada, and southern desert regions are also growing, while retaining their own distinct

"CALIFORNIA
is a garden of eden,
a paradise to live in or see;
but believe it or not,
you won't find it so hot
if you ain't got the do re mi."

~ WOODY GUTHRIE ~
AMERICAN SINGER-SONGWRITER
1912–1967

"hourglass economy" The tendency of the California economy to include many people doing very well at the top, many barely getting by at the bottom, and fewer and fewer in the middle; symptomatic of California's vanishing middle class.

identities. Water, agriculture, and the environment are major issues in all these areas. Except for Sacramento, inland California is more conservative than the coastal region of the state. Perhaps ironically, a recent study showed that the liberal counties of the coast contribute more per capita in state taxes, and the conservative inland counties receive more per capita for social service programs.[11] While coastal California remains politically dominant, the impact of inland areas on California politics increases with every election.

California's People, Economy, and Politics

All these elements of California's economic, demographic, and geographic diversity vie with one another for political influence in the context of political structures that were created more than a hundred years ago. Dissatisfaction with this system has resulted in dozens of reforms by ballot measure, a recall election, and more recently, calls for a constitutional convention. Voter frustration is at a peak. As of 2010, only 18 percent of Californians felt the state was "going in the right direction" (compared with 55 percent in 2007); only 23 percent approved of the governor's performance (compared with 57 percent in 2007); and 16 percent approved of the performance of the legislature (compared with 41 percent in 2007).[12] Perhaps people see California as a failed state, or maybe they're just frustrated with the current leadership. A majority, however, support constitutional reform,[13] which could be done piecemeal through ballot measures or more comprehensively through a constitutional convention. A convention can be proposed by a two-thirds vote of the state legislature (which some consider unlikely) and then approved by the voters. In the chapters that follow, we'll see how the diverse interests of our state operate in the current political system and gain an understanding of how it all works, why voters and others may feel frustration, and what some are doing to bring about change even as others resist.

CALIFORNIA AT **ODDS** *California's People, Economy, and Politics*

From a history full of conflicting interests and turbulent change, California has forged unique political institutions, including the ability of the electorate to make policy and recall officeholders through direct democracy. Within these institutions, California's citizens have been at odds over many key questions. These include the following:

- Does the very size of the state make policy-making difficult—or is size an irrelevant factor?
- Is direct democracy, the legacy of the Progressives, an essential ingredient of California's greatness—or an ongoing handicap to effective government?
- California made large investments in water, highways, and higher education under Governor Pat Brown during the early 1960s. Taxes were also high. Was this spending crucial for California's success—or was it excessive, and properly curbed by subsequent governors?
- Have high rates of immigration strengthened California and its economy—or do they constitute an economic penalty that the state can no longer afford?
- Does the changing racial and ethnic composition of California's electorate mean that the Republicans face a future of irrelevance—or do new sources of conservatism exist that may counteract the impact of demography?

Take Action

It's not hard to learn more about California's rich history. All across the state, citizens have organized historical societies to sponsor forums, publications, and museums that tell the California tale. You can visit some of these museums—there are probably several in your area. For example, Kern County is the home of Bakersfield, a large city but not one of the state's very largest. Yet Kern County has at least fifteen historical societies and twenty-four museums. Among the most important is the Kern County Museum, an outdoor facility with fifty-six exhibits located on sixteen acres. Consider also Del Norte County. With fewer than 30,000 inhabitants, it is among California's least populous counties. Nevertheless, its historical society helps support two museums. These include the Battery Point Lighthouse, one of California's more scenic locations. You can visit the lighthouse only at low tide by walking across a sandy beach and some rocks.

POLITICS ON THE WEB

- An online version of the California Constitution can be found on the official Web site for California legislative information. Go to **www.leginfo.ca.gov/const-toc.html**.
- The California Historical Society has created an online historical guide to over three hundred years of California history. You can learn more about key events, personalities, and anecdotes from California's past at **www.californiahistoricalsociety.org/timeline**.
- To learn more about the rich history of San Francisco, visit the virtual museum of the City of San Francisco at **www.sfmuseum.org**. This extensive multimedia Web site can be searched by subject, year, biographies, or you can view their major online exhibits to find text, graphics, and sounds.
- The Demographic Research Unit of the California Department of Finance is designated as the single official source of demographic data for state planning and budgeting. Go to **www.dof.ca.gov/research/demographic**.
- Visit the QuickFacts page of the U.S. Census Bureau's Web site for California to see demographic and business comparisons between California and the United States at **quickfacts.census.gov/qfd/states/06000.html**.
- Calisphere, the University of California's free public gateway to a world of primary sources, contains more than 150,000 digitized items—including photographs, documents, newspaper pages, political cartoons, works of art, diaries, transcribed oral histories, advertising, and other unique cultural artifacts—that reveal the diverse history and culture of California and its role in national and world history. Go to **www.calisphere.universityofcalifornia.edu**.

Access CourseMate to review and expand on this chapter through quizzes, flashcards, learning objectives, interactive timelines, a crossword puzzle, audio summaries, video, critical-thinking activities, simulations, and more.

GOVT 18

California's Political Parties and Direct Democracy

LEARNING OBJECTIVES

LO1 Summarize the impact the Progressives had on political parties.

LO2 Explain the structure and support systems of political parties.

LO3 Describe the different forms of direct democracy.

LO4 Discuss the pros and cons of ballot propositions.

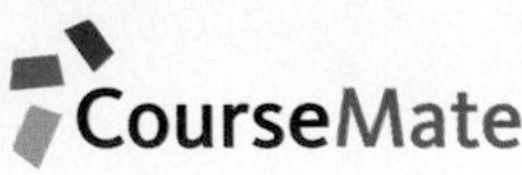

CALIFORNIA AT ODDS

Is the Initiative Process Out of Control?

California provides its citizens with three methods of engaging in direct democracy: the initiative, the referendum, and the recall. The referendum allows voters to override a decision of the state legislature. The recall lets voters remove an elected official from office. Using the initiative, voters can make new laws and amend the constitution without relying on the legislature and the governor. Of these three mechanisms, the initiative is by far the most commonly used. To qualify an initiative for the ballot, petition gatherers must obtain a set number of signatures from registered voters. One important characteristic of the initiative in California is that measures approved by the voters cannot be modified by the legislature. As a result, initiatives are binding on the legislature and on the governor.

Over the years, California voters have decided a very large number of initiatives, more than the voters of most other states. From November 1998 through May 2009, a period of only eleven years, 115 initiatives qualified and the voters endorsed 40. Some Californians believe that the state has had to deal with way too many initiatives, covering far too many subjects. Some even argue that the initiative process is out of control and has helped to dead-lock the state's political process.

Initiatives Are Crippling the State's Politics

Plenty of pundits agree that initiatives are trouble. "Direct democracy provisions of California's constitution have rendered the state ungovernable," stated Laura D'Andrea Tyson in *Business Week.* Voters themselves agree that there are too many ballot proposals and that ballot wording is too complicated. Furthermore, because initiatives are binding on the legislature and governor, if they contain drafting errors that lead to unintended consequences, the state is stuck with the results unless the voters themselves edit their handiwork.

The initiative was originally meant as a way for ordinary citizens to make their voices heard. In reality, however, it is special interests that have the resources to mount initiative campaigns, to pay for the gathering of signatures, and to run effective state-wide advertising efforts. Direct democracy has proven in fact to be highly undemocratic. If Californians don't abolish the initiative altogether, the process should be reformed, perhaps by requiring that signatures be gathered entirely by unpaid volunteers.

The Initiative Is Not Part of the Problem

Some "experts" may think that the initiative is a problem, but ordinary Californians think otherwise. Six out of ten believe that voters make public policy decisions through initiatives that are better than the decisions made by the legislature and the governor. Only one in four believes that the voters make worse decisions. It shouldn't be surprising that the people have confidence in their own handiwork. State legislators are elected from districts that are heavily gerrymandered to favor one or another of the two major parties. As a result, legislators represent the most liberal Democrats or the most conservative Republicans. Moderate voices are absent beneath the Capitol dome. In the electorate, however, moderate voices have their full weight, and in fact a very large share of California's voters are in the political center.

Opponents of the initiative claim that voters have locked up most of the state's spending. Some have claimed that more than two-thirds of the state's budget is earmarked in advance as a result of ballot proposals, and this earmarking makes it impossible for the legislature to balance the budget. Professor John Matsusaka of the University of Southern California, however, believes that the real figure is half that. If the legislature faces political paralysis, Matsuka believes, the fault lies with the parties, not the people.

The initiative is not without its problems, and voters are open to reforms. A majority of those surveyed favor allowing the legislature and an initiative sponsor to negotiate a compromise before the measure is placed on the ballot. Respondents also support a system of review and revision to avoid legal issues and drafting errors. The people of California, however, want to keep their power to make new laws for the state, and they are justified in this desire.

WHERE DO YOU STAND?

1. **What effects might follow if initiative signatures had to be gathered by volunteers? Would this improve the process?**
2. **One commentator believes that initiatives—especially those that amend the state constitution—should be harder to place on the ballot, but referenda should qualify more easily. The theory is that referenda promote dialogue between voters and their elected officials. Is this a valid point? Why or why not?**

EXPLORE THIS ISSUE ONLINE

- **The Center for Governmental Studies has a wealth of information on the California initiative process. To view it, go to www.cgs.org and click on "ballot initiatives" under "State and Local Government."**
- **To see a poll on California initiatives sponsored by the Public Policy Institute of California, visit www.ppic.org/content/pubs/jtf/JTF_InitiativeJTF.pdf.**

Introduction

In many states, political parties are strong organizations that control the selection of their nominees for public office, set out policy agendas based on their political ideologies, and can count on the loyalty of their voters. They link citizens to government, building coalitions of different interests and helping candidates make their case to the voters. This doesn't always happen in California, where party organizations are weak and voters make policy through the initiative process. As we'll learn in Chapter 21, political parties and party discipline are strong in the California state legislature, but that's not usually true of local or statewide party organizations. History tells us why: the Progressive reformers intentionally weakened political parties in order to rid California of the railroad-dominated political machine. In doing so, they unintentionally made candidate personalities, media manipulation, and fat campaign war chests as important in elections as political parties—and sometimes more so.

The Progressives also introduced **direct democracy.** Through the initiative, referendum, and recall, California voters gained the power to make law and even to overrule elected officials or remove them between elections. The reformers' intent was to empower citizens, but in practice, interest groups and politicians are more likely to use—and sometimes abuse—direct democracy.

Weak party organizations and direct democracy are fixtures of the state constitution and modern California politics. Some political observers argue that this combination promotes political disarray, governmental gridlock, and voters who are confused or turned off. Others believe that the system reflects a body of political values that eschews structured authority and maximizes opportunities for democratic decision making. We examine this dispute in the chapter-opening *California at Odds* feature.

direct democracy
Progressive reforms giving citizens the power to make and repeal laws (initiative and referendum) and to remove elected officials from office (recall).

primary elections
Elections to choose nominees for public office; held in June of even-numbered years. Voter turnout is typically low.

general elections
Statewide elections held on the first Tuesday after the first Monday of November in even-numbered years. Voter turnout is higher than in primary elections and highest during presidential elections.

"ALL POLITICAL POWER IS INHERENT IN THE PEOPLE."

ARTICLE 1, SECTION 2
OF THE 1849 AND 1879 CONSTITUTIONS
OF THE STATE OF CALIFORNIA

LO1 The Progressive Legacy

To challenge the dominance of the Southern Pacific Railroad's political machine, Progressive reformers from both the Democratic and Republican parties focused on the machine's control of party conventions, where party leaders picked their candidates for various offices.

Republican reformers scored the first breakthrough in 1908, when they succeeded in electing many anti-railroad candidates to the state legislature. In 1909 the reform legislators replaced party conventions with **primary elections,** in which the registered voters of each party choose the nominee. Candidates who win their party's primary in these elections face the nominees of other parties in the November **general elections.** By instituting this system, the reformers ended the machine's control of the nomination process.

Empowering Voters

In 1910 Progressives won elections for both governor and the legislature. They introduced direct democracy to give policymaking authority to the people. They also

This campaign poster for Senator Hiram W. Johnson in the 1914 governor's race promotes all around support for Johnson from Progressives, Republicans, and Democrats.

CALIFORNIA–
UNANIMOUS FOR
HIRAM JOHNSON!

THE BANCROFT LIBRARY. UNIVERSITY OF CALIFORNIA, BERKELEY

replaced the party column ballot—which had permitted bloc voting for all the candidates of a single party by making just one mark—with separate balloting for each office. In addition, Progressive reformers introduced **cross-filing,** which permitted candidates of one party to seek the nominations of rival parties. Finally, the Progressives instituted **nonpartisan elections,** which eliminated party labels in contests to elect judges, school board members, and local government officials.

The Fallout of Reform

These changes reduced the railroad's control of the political parties, but they also sapped the strength of the party organizations. By allowing the voters to circumvent an unresponsive legislature, direct democracy paved the way for interest groups to dominate policymaking. Deletion of the party column ballot encouraged voters to cast their ballots for members of different parties for different offices (split-ticket voting), increasing the likelihood of a divided-party government (see Chapter 23). Nonpartisan local elections made it difficult for the parties to build their organizations at the grassroots level as well.

Party leaders tried to regain control of nominations by settling on favored candidates before the primary elections. Ultimately, however, such **preprimary endorsements** were also outlawed. Then in 1959, when Democrats gained control of the legislature for the first time in more than forty years, they outlawed cross-filing, which had been disproportionately helpful to Republican incumbents. This marked a return to the system in which candidates file for nomination for their own party only.

LO2 *Party Organization—Structure and Supporters*

Thanks to the Progressive reforms, political parties in California operate under unusual constraints. Although the original reformers have long since departed from the scene, the reform mentality remains very much a part of California's political culture.

Official Party Structures

According to the California State Elections Code, political parties can place candidates on the ballot by registering a number of members equal to 1 percent of the state vote in the most recent gubernatorial election or by submitting a petition with signatures amounting to 10 percent of that vote. After a party is qualified, if it retains the registration of at least 1 percent of the voters or if at least one of its candidates for any statewide office receives 2 percent of the votes cast, that party will be on the ballot in the next election. By virtue of their sizes, the Democratic and Republican parties have been fixtures on the ballot almost since statehood.

cross-filing An election system that allowed candidates to win the nomination of more than one political party; eliminated in 1959.

nonpartisan elections A Progressive reform that removed party labels from ballots for local and judicial offices.

preprimary endorsement Political parties' designation of preferred candidates in party primary elections, thus strengthening the role of party organizations in selecting candidates; banned by state law until 1990.

third parties Minor political parties that capture a small percentages of the vote in the general election but are viewed as important protest vehicles.

THIRD PARTIES Minor parties, sometimes called **third parties,** are another story. Some have been on the ballot for decades; others have had brief political lives. In the 2006 general election, the Green, Libertarian, and Peace and Freedom parties each secured the minimum 2 percent of the vote for one of their statewide candidates, guaranteeing them positions on the ballot in 2010. No statewide candidates for the American Independent Party reached the 2 percent threshold, but enough voters are registered as American Independents to keep the party on the ballot. The total number of parties qualified for the 2010 California ballot, including Democrats and Republicans, was six.

Nonetheless, breaking the hold of the two major political parties has proved difficult. The Democratic and Republican candidates for governor garnered 95 percent of the vote in 2010—slightly less than the 98.2 percent shared by the Democratic and Republican candidates for president in 2008. Among the smaller parties, the Greens have been the most successful at winning elections. They have earned one seat in the state legislature and several seats at the local level.

PARTY REGISTRATION California voters choose their party when they register to vote, which must be done fifteen or more days before the election. In 2010, 75.2 percent were registered as either Democrats or Republicans, 4.6 percent signed up with the other parties, and 20.2 percent declared themselves independent

Figure 18–1

Party Registration in California, 2010

Decline to state
Other (or other parties)
Democrat
Republican
4.6%
20.2%
44.3%
30.9%

Source: (Courtesy of Terry Christensen) California Secretary of State.

(officially known as "decline to state")—see Figure 18–1 above. The independent percentage has more than doubled since 1986, when it was just 9 percent.

For most of its history, California used **closed primary** elections to select the nominees of each party for state elective office and the U.S. Congress. Voters who are registered with a political party cast their ballots in the primary only for that party's nominees for various offices. The winners of each party's primary election face off in the November general election, when all voters are free to cast their ballots for the candidate of any of the parties. But in 2010, voters approved a "top two" or **open primary** system to go into effect in 2012. In an open primary, no matter what their own party, voters may choose their preferred candidate from any party; the top two vote getters face off in the November election, even if they're from the same party. Advocates of this system hope that instead of concentrating their appeals on the core of their own parties (liberals for Democrats and conservatives for Republicans), candidates will reach out to independent and moderate voters and that those elected will be more moderate and thus more willing to compromise when they get to Sacramento. In theory, this system could break the gridlock in the state capital, but whether it will do so remains to be seen. Meanwhile, the political parties have complained that the open primary system takes away the right of voters registered with their party to choose their own candidates, and it will almost certainly mean that candidates of the minor parties never appear on general election ballots. It's likely that the open primary system will be challenged in court.

closed primary An election of party nominees in which only registered party members may participate.

open primary Voters may cast their ballots for any listed candidate for an office irrespective of the voters' party affiliation; the top two vote winners proceed to a runoff in the general election; instituted by a 2010 ballot measure to take effect in 2012.

central committees Political party organizations at county and state levels; weakly linked to one another.

PARTY DOMINANCE Before the Great Depression, California was steadfastly Republican, but during the 1930s a Democratic majority emerged. Since then, the Democrats have dominated in voter registration (see Figure 18–2), although their lead declined from a peak of 60 percent of registered voters in 1942 to a low of 42.7 percent in 2006. Since then, partly due to an exciting presidential election in 2008, Democratic registration has risen slightly—to 44.5 percent in 2010. Meanwhile, Republican registration has slipped to 30.9 percent. The independent percentage, however, has more than doubled since 1986, when it was just 9 percent. Despite their registration margin, the Democrats did not gain a majority in both houses of the state legislature until 1958. Republican candidates have won eight of the last thirteen gubernatorial elections.

PARTY COMMITTEES State law dictates party organization, as it does registration and voting. Today's Democratic and Republican parties have similar structures, although the Democrats elect a few more party officials. The state **central committee** is the highest-ranking body in each party. All party candidates and

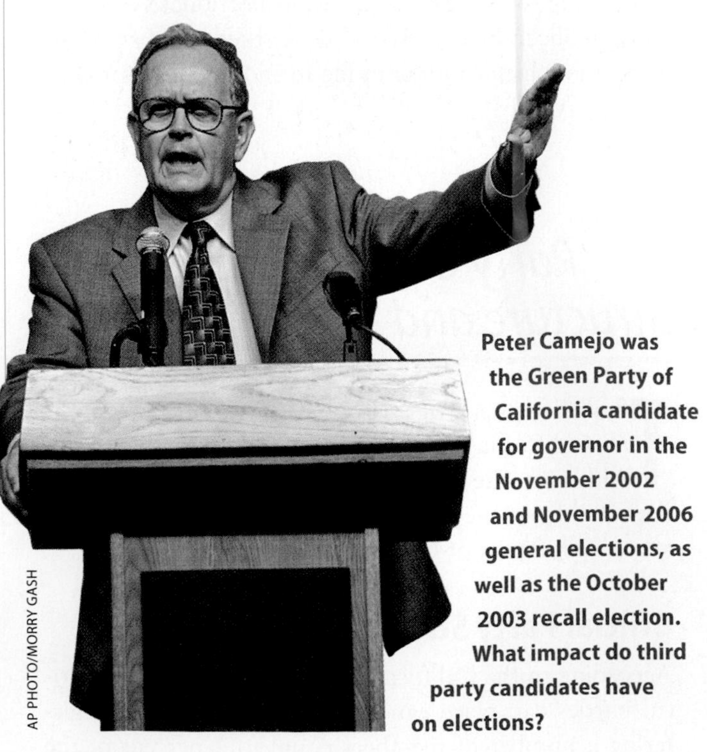

AP PHOTO/MORRY GASH

Peter Camejo was the Green Party of California candidate for governor in the November 2002 and November 2006 general elections, as well as the October 2003 recall election. What impact do third party candidates have on elections?

officeholders are automatically members, along with county chairpersons. Officeholders and nominees of each party also appoint members. In addition, Democratic voters elect members from each assembly district, and Republican county central committees elect or appoint members. Each party's state central committee elects a state chair, who functions mainly as the party spokesperson. Although the position traditionally has been powerless, competition for it is sometimes intense.

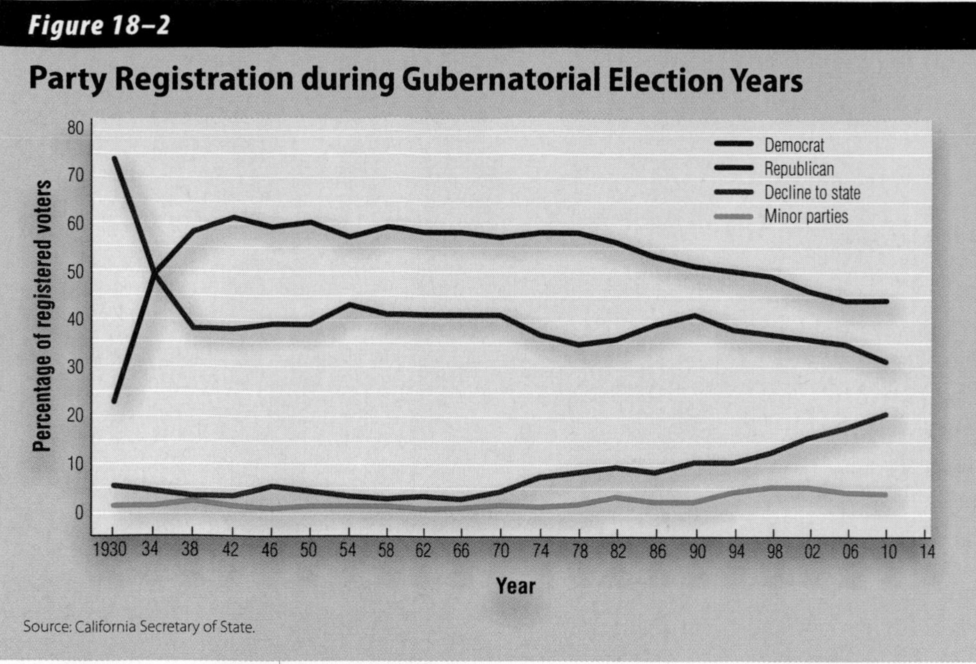

Figure 18–2

Party Registration during Gubernatorial Election Years

Source: California Secretary of State.

COUNTY COMMITTEES Beneath the state central committee are county central committees. The voters registered with each party choose committee members every two years in the primary election. The party's nominees for state legislature are also members, as are those who win election. Critics say this system enables officeholders to dominate the grassroots members, but it also ensures that the two levels of party leadership are linked. The state and county party committees play an important role in generating volunteers and contributions for party candidates. They also draft policy positions for party platforms, although candidates and elected officials often ignore these. Despite their low public profile, county committees are sometimes sites of intense conflict among activists. Liberals usually dominate Democratic county central committees, whereas conservatives rule Republican committees. The religious right gained influence in the Republican Party during the 1990s by taking over a majority of the party's county central committees, but since then, moderate Republicans have regained influence in some counties.

Preprimary Endorsements

California's political parties had an opportunity to strengthen their role in choosing party nominees when the United States Supreme Court overturned the state ban on preprimary endorsements in 1990. California Democrats responded quickly by establishing a preprimary endorsement process that required a candidate to secure at least 60 percent of the delegates at their state convention. The Republican Party declined such endorsements until 2005, when Governor Arnold Schwarzenegger won an early endorsement for reelection and avoided a divisive party primary.

Despite assertions of strengthened party organization, preprimary endorsements don't always matter to California voters. Since the court ruling, Democratic voters have rejected several statewide candidates officially endorsed by their party in primaries, while most party-endorsed candidates who succeeded were incumbents seeking reelection with no opposition in their own party. In 2010, however, the Democratic convention's preprimary endorsement of Assemblyman Dave Jones helped him win the Democratic nomination for state insurance commissioner in an otherwise low-profile race. The influence of such endorsements is limited by the inability of the parties to deliver organizational support to the chosen candidates and by high-spending campaigns and the media, but preprimary endorsements may become more significant when the open primary system goes into effect in 2012.

Party Supporters

Besides the official party organizations, a variety of caucuses and clubs are associated with both major parties. The California Republican Assembly is a staunchly conservative statewide grassroots organization that has dominated the Republican Party, thanks to an activist membership. Republican governor Arnold Schwarzenegger, a moderate, had difficulty with the conservatives in his own party. At the 2007 state party convention, he chastised his fellow California Republicans "for their insularity and narrowness," to which they responded "that they'd rather be ideologically principled

AP PHOTO/ALEX BRANDON

President Barack Obama supports Senator Barbara Boxer at her fundraiser in San Francisco, May 25, 2010.

than pander to moderates."[1] On the Democratic side, liberals dominate through the California Democratic Council, which comprises hundreds of local Democratic clubs organized by geography, gender, race, ethnicity, or sexual orientation. How much of a problem is the domination of the parties by ideological activists? We examine that question in the *Join the Debate* feature on the following page.

Party activists such as these are a tiny percentage of the electorate, however. The remaining support base comes from citizens who designate their party affiliations when they register to vote and usually cast their ballots accordingly. Public opinion polls tell us that voters who prefer the Democratic Party tend to be sympathetic to the poor and immigrants; concerned about health care, education, and the environment; in favor of gay rights, gun control, and abortion rights; and supportive of tax increases to provide public services. Those who prefer the Republican Party are more likely to oppose these views and to worry more about big government and high taxes. Of course, many people mix these positions.[2]

THE DEMOCRATIC PROFILE Both major parties enjoy widespread support, but the more liberal Democratic Party fares better with blacks; city dwellers; union members; and residents of Los Angeles, Sacramento, and the San Francisco Bay Area (see Figure 18–3). Latino voters also favor Democrats, a tendency that was strengthened by Republican support for several statewide initiatives relating to immigration and affirmative action. Voters among most Asian nationalities identify themselves as Democratic, but some (notably Chinese and Vietnamese) lean Republican. Voters with ties to China, India, and Vietnam are also more likely to register as independents than are other Californians. As with Latinos, Asian loyalties to the California Republican Party were weakened by its sponsorship of initiatives perceived as anti-immigrant in the 1990s. Thanks in large part to the failure of Republicans to win support from minority voters, Democrats currently enjoy majorities in the state legislature and congressional delegation, and California is considered a solidly "blue" (Democratic) state—despite occasional Republican victories for statewide offices.

Should Political Parties Matter?

A broad consensus existed among the authors of the U.S. Constitution: the nation would be better off if political parties did not exist. For that reason, parties are mentioned nowhere in the Constitution. The California Progressives, who established many of the institutions and rules that define the state's political framework even today, were almost as hostile to parties as the founders. The Progressives, however, were also more realistic. They did not seek to abolish parties altogether. They did try to weaken the major parties, however, and they had some success. Yet today, at least in the legislature, the parties are stronger than ever. Many Californians believe that the state would be better governed if the parties were not so strong. Other people, however, think that strong parties are a political necessity.

Ideological Parties Are the Root of California's Political Problems

Many of those who favor weakening the major political parties believe that they are the reason why California is "ungovernable." These observers point to the fact that in years past, the two-thirds requirement to pass a budget did not stop legislators from making compromises and passing a budget. Only two other states (Arkansas and Rhode Island) have similar requirements, and they manage not to tie themselves up in knots. Political deadlock occurs because members of the two parties refuse to negotiate agreements. Instead, they stand on principle, no matter what the results may be for the state. Legislators are typically strongly partisan. Highly partisan Republican and Democratic activists have considerable influence in selecting legislative candidates. As a result, the huge and growing portion of the California electorate that considers itself independent or moderate is not adequately represented. California needs new laws that will weaken the power of the parties, or even provide for nonpartisan elections.

The Parties Represent Real People

Those who defend the parties argue that without parties, the people find it impossible to exert any control over their elected leaders. Ordinary voters cannot spare the time to analyze the political positions of legislative candidates in any detail. The party label provides essential information. In states that have elected their legislatures on a nonpartisan basis, such as Minnesota before 1973, prominent local figures often won election even when their politics were completely unrepresentative of their districts. The electorate, in short, was fooled.

Party supporters would admit that Republicans and Democrats in California are partisan and find it hard to reach agreement. Blaming party activists for excessive partisanship, however, misses an important point. While very few people are activists who devote substantial efforts to political campaigns, large numbers of people—probably a majority of the electorate—share the beliefs of the activists. Californians themselves are strongly divided. The state's Democrats and Republicans have seriously contrasting opinions on the role of government. They do not even share a vision of what a good society should look like. The Republican ideal of the autonomous, free individual is completely at odds with the Democratic dream of the caring community. Institutional changes that grant more representation to middle-of-the road points of view may be desirable, but eliminating partisanship altogether would disenfranchise much of the electorate.

For Critical Analysis ***Do you think that a political consensus will ever dominate California's political life, or will politics involve ideological winners and losers more or less indefinitely? Explain your answer.***

THE REPUBLICAN PROFILE The more conservative Republican Party does better with whites, suburbanites, rural voters, and in Orange County, the Central Valley, and inland California, as well as with older, more affluent voters and with Christian conservatives. These constituencies are more likely to turn out to vote than those that support Democrats, which is why Republicans sometimes win statewide elections despite their registration disadvantage. Just how conservative are upscale voters? We discuss that question in the *Perception versus Reality* feature on page 395.

In the past, Republican candidates were also successful because they could often win the support of Democratic voters thanks to cross-filing (until 1958), charismatic candidates, clever campaigns, and split-ticket voting. But in the 1990s, ticket splitting declined, and instead, voters increasingly voted a straight party-line ticket—either all Democratic or all Republican.[3]

Figure 18–3

California's Partisan Division by County, 2010

Source: Author

This includes decline-to-state voters, who, contrary to common wisdom, are not necessarily "independent": 42 percent lean Democratic, and 28 percent lean Republican.[4] Some observers assert that the rightward thrust of the Republican Party drove independent voters to the Democrats and was even more important to the Democratic Party's continued success than was winning over minority voters.[5] Republicans who can present themselves as moderates, as did gubernatorial candidate Arnold Schwarzenegger in 2003 and in 2006, may have proved this thesis by winning the votes of many independents and some Democrats, thus demonstrating that Californians will still indulge in split-ticket voting, at least on occasion.

recall A Progressive reform allowing voters to remove elected officials by petition and majority vote.

LO3 *Direct Democracy*

Party politics is only one way Californians participate in the political process. To counter the railroad machine's control of state and local government, the Progressive reformers also guaranteed the people a say through the mechanisms of direct democracy introduced in Chapter 17: the recall, the referendum, and the initiative. Referenda and initiatives appear on our ballots as "propositions," with numbers assigned by the secretary of state; local measures are assigned letters by the county clerk.

The Recall

The least-used form of direct democracy is the **recall,** by which the voters can remove officeholders at all levels of government between scheduled elections. Advocates circulate a recall petition with a statement of their reasons for wanting the official in question to be removed from office. They must collect a specific number of voter signatures within a specific period. The numbers vary with the office in question. At the local level, for example, the number of signatures required to qualify a recall for the ballot varies between 10 and 30 percent of those who voted in the previous local election; these signatures must be collected over periods that vary between 40 and 160 days. A recall petition for a judge or a legislator requires signatures equaling 20 percent of the vote in the last state election, while for state executive officeholders, the figure is 12 percent. In all these cases, petitioners have 160 days to collect the signatures. If

PERCEPTION VERSUS REALITY

The Rich Are Conservative

One of the enduring beliefs of American—and indeed, world—politics is that the wealthy are conservative and the poor are progressive. Indeed, many people believe that favoring the poor is what defines a policy as progressive. Likewise, measures that favor the rich are conservative by definition. But is this perception entirely true? In particular, is it true in California?

The Perception

The rich must be conservative—the list of California communities with the largest percentage of registered Republicans is topped by upscale enclaves such as Newport Beach, San Marino, and Yorba Linda. Further, if you listen to the rhetoric employed by many liberal California Democrats, you will find it easy to conclude that the political left favors the poor and disdains the wealthy. In 2009, as the reality of the state's budget crisis became unavoidable, Democrats in the California legislature called for increasing the income tax rate on upper-income individuals and families from 10.3 percent to 12 percent. Of course, the Democrats had to know that they didn't have the votes to pass such a tax increase. That they advocated the measure anyway suggests that they saw political benefits in taking such a stand. Consider also that exit polls taken during the 2008 elections show that Californians with family incomes below $15,000 voted for Democrat Barack Obama over Republican John McCain by a margin of 77 to 21 percent—a larger margin than was reported for any other income category.

The Reality

Of course the poor supported Obama. In California, however, Obama carried every income class. He beat McCain 58 to 40 percent among those with incomes in excess of $200,000, a better showing for the Democrats than was turned in by families in the $100,000 to $200,000 income range. We have all heard of wealthy and famous persons who lean well to the left, and these people are no longer limited to Hollywood celebrities. Many executives in high-tech firms are also Democrats. Southern California may still have its wealthy and conservative enclaves, but there is plenty of money in the hills above Berkeley and Oakland, and the percentage of voters who are registered Republicans in those cities is 4.5 and 5.9, respectively.

There are both liberals and conservatives among the rich. Even in today's hard times, class warfare is not on the American agenda, and the cosmopolitan cultural attitudes of the wealthy impel many them towards liberalism. Yes, the Democrats do talk of raising taxes on the rich. It seems that at least some of these people, however, view such proposals with a sense of *noblesse oblige*.

Blog On You can find a slide show that highlights the most Republican and most Democratic cities in California at **www.sacbee.com/1098/story/1853135.html**. You can find exit polls for the 2010 elections at **www.cnn.com/ELECTION/2010/results/polls.** These polls cover not only the vote for candidates, but also the vote for some ballot measures such as California Proposition 19.

enough signatures are collected by advocates and validated by the secretary of state (for a state officeholder) or by the county clerk (for a local officeholder), an election is held. The ballot is simple: "Shall [name] be removed from the office of [title]?" The recall takes effect if a majority of voters vote yes, and then either an election or an appointment—whichever state or local law requires—fills the vacancy for the office. Elected officials who are recalled cannot be candidates in the replacement election.

Recalling state officeholders is easier in California than in the other seventeen states where recall is possible. All but one of these states require more signatures, and while any reason suffices in California, most other states require corruption or malfeasance by the

> "The initiative, the referendum, and the recall ARE NOT THE PANACEA FOR ALL OUR POLITICAL ILLS, YET THEY . . . PLACE IN THE HANDS OF THE PEOPLE THE MEANS BY WHICH THEY MAY PROTECT THEMSELVES."
>
> ~ HIRAM JOHNSON ~
> TWENTY-THIRD GOVERNOR OF CALIFORNIA
> 1866–1945

officeholder. Nevertheless, recalls are rare in California, where the process has been used most extensively and successfully in local government, particularly by parents who are angry with school board members. Even so, only a dozen or so recalls are on local ballots in any given year, and only about half of the officials who face recall are removed from office. Two of California's state senators were recalled in 1913, but no other state officeholders were removed until 1995, when two legislators were recalled during a struggle between Democrats and Republicans over control of the state assembly.

> "It's like the Oakland Raiders saying to Tampa Bay, **WE KNOW YOU BEAT US,** but we want to play the Super Bowl again."
>
> ~ GOVERNOR GRAY DAVIS ~ ON THE RECALL OF 2003

THE RECALL OF GRAY DAVIS Then, spectacularly, Governor Gray Davis was recalled in 2003. Davis had narrowly won reelection in November 2002; three months later, opponents launched their recall petition. Thirty-one previous attempts to recall a California governor had failed to make the ballot, and most political observers assumed that the petitioners would fail to acquire the 897,158 valid signatures required to qualify for an election. But they underestimated voter discontent, not only with Davis but also with the general condition of California politics. Despite his reelection, Davis's approval rating in public opinion polls had sunk to just 24 percent when signature gathering began.[6] His decline in popularity was a result of his cautious leadership during the state's energy crisis in 2001, a recession, a huge budget deficit, and the inability of the legislature and the governor to agree on solutions to these problems.

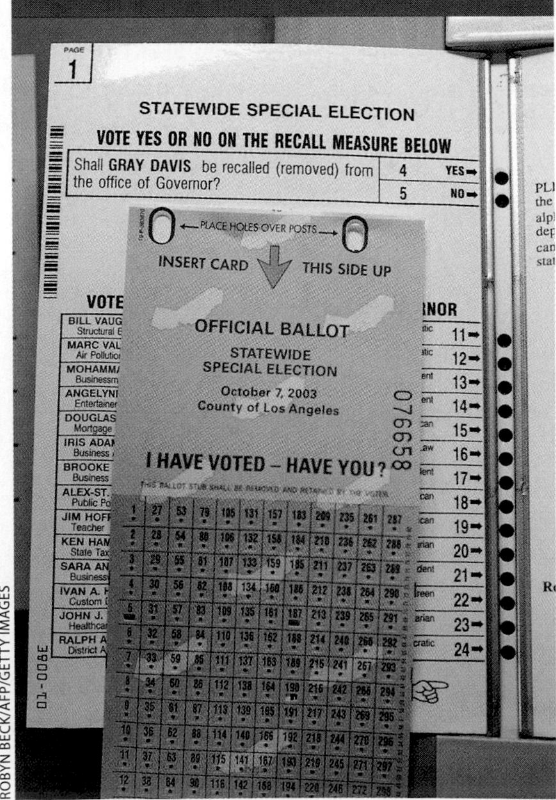

The official ballot for the special recall election of California Governor Gray Davis in 2003. In a historic vote, Californians chose to replace their unpopular governor with action star Arnold Schwarzenegger.

ROBYN BECK/AFP/GETTY IMAGES

Davis's aloof personality also contributed to his problems. His recall opponents discovered a groundswell of support, facilitated by conservative talk radio hosts and the availability of the Internet to circulate petitions. Even so, signature gathering was slow until Republican congressman Darrell Issa contributed $2 million to pay for professionals to assist.

A STAR EMERGES In July 2003, the secretary of state certified that 1.3 million valid signatures had been gathered—far more than required—and the election was set for October. Ultimately, 135 candidates qualified to run, including actor Arnold Schwarzenegger. His seventy-five-day campaign took the state by storm, gaining far more media and public attention than any regular election in recent memory—thanks in part to his status as a movie star. On Election Day, 55.4 percent of the voters said yes to recall, and Schwarzenegger easily outpaced all other replacement candidates with 48.6 percent of the vote. For the first time in California history—and only the second time ever in the United States—a governor had been recalled.

The Referendum

The **referendum** is another form of direct democracy. A referendum allows the voters to nullify acts of the legislature. Referendum advocates have ninety days after the legislature makes a law to collect a number of signatures equal to 5 percent of the votes cast for governor in the previous election (515,116 based on the 2010 vote). Referenda are even rarer than recalls. Of the forty-seven referenda on California ballots since 1912, voters have rejected acts of the legislature twenty-eight times. In 2004, business groups qualified a referendum on health-care legislation approved in Governor Davis's last days in office. The hard-fought campaign

referendum A Progressive reform requiring the legislature to place certain measures before the voters, who may also repeal legislation by petitioning for a referendum.

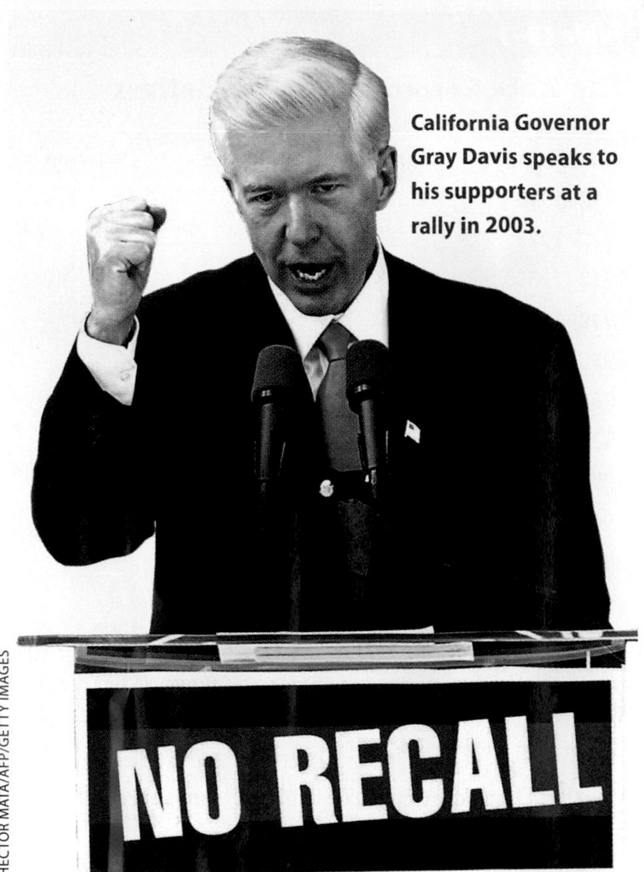

HECTOR MATA/AFP/GETTY IMAGES

California Governor Gray Davis speaks to his supporters at a rally in 2003.

pitted liberals, unions, and Democrats who supported the program against conservatives, business leaders, and Republicans. In the end, the voters narrowly rejected the health-care legislation, even though nearly 20 percent of Californians lacked health insurance. In 2008, competing gambling interests challenged the state's tribal gaming agreements in referenda, but the voters approved the agreements.

The Initiative

Recalls and referenda are reactions to what elected officials do; in contrast, the **initiative** allows citizens to make policy themselves by drafting a new law or a constitutional amendment and then circulating petitions to get it onto the ballot. Qualifying a proposed law requires a number of signatures equal to 5 percent of the votes cast for governor in the last election; constitutional amendments require a number of signatures equal to 8 percent (824,185 based on California's 2010 election). If enough valid signatures are obtained within 150 days, the initiative goes to the voters at the next election or, on rare occasions, in a special election called by the governor.

The subjects of initiatives vary wildly and are often controversial. In the past, voters have approved limits on bilingual education, banned the slaughter of horses for human consumption, and defined marriage as a relationship between a man and a woman only. Other recent propositions have dealt with tribal gambling (repeatedly), redistricting (repeatedly), stem cell research, DNA sampling, and mental health services. In 2010 voters considered legalization of marijuana, redistricting (again), suspension of air-pollution control laws, funding of local governments, and a vehicle license fee to support state parks—and more.

initiative A Progressive device by which people may put laws and constitutional amendments on the ballot after securing the required number of voters' signatures.

Twenty-three other states provide for the initiative, but few rely on it as heavily as California. Initiatives were common between 1912 and 1939, but declined in number during the next four decades (see Table 18–1). Then political consultants, interest groups, and governors rediscovered the initiative, and ballot measures proliferated. The 1988 and 1990 election year ballots witnessed an explosion, with eighteen initiatives on each. In 2010 voters faced a total of fourteen propositions in the primary and general elections, including both citizen-generated and legislative initiatives.

CARLO ALLEGRI/GETTY IMAGES

A man wears a campaign t-shirt supporting gubernatorial candidate Arnold Schwarzenegger in the California recall election. Famous for his role as "The Terminator", what impact did Schwarzenegger's fame as an actor have on his success in winning the election?

Legislative Initiatives, Constitutional Amendments, and Bonds

Propositions can also be placed on the ballot by the state legislature. Such **legislative initiatives** can include new laws that the legislature prefers to put before the voters rather than enact on its own, or proposed **constitutional amendments,** for which voter approval is compulsory. The 2010 open primary measure, for example, was put on the ballot by the legislature as part of a deal to win the vote of a Republican senator for the proposed budget and is discussed in the feature *California Faces a Troubled Economy* on the following page.

Voter approval is also required when the governor or the legislature seeks to issue **bonds** (borrowing money) to finance parks, schools, transportation, or other capital-intensive projects. Few of these proposals are controversial, and more than 60 percent pass with minimal campaigning or spending. In the 2006 and 2008 elections, voters approved $29 billion in bonds for projects ranging from high-speed trains to aid for veterans.

Table 18–1

The Track Record of State Initiatives

Time Period	Number	Number Adopted	Number Rejected
1912–1919	31	8	23
1920–1929	34	10	24
1930–1939	37	10	27
1940–1949	20	7	13
1950–1959	11	1	10
1960–1969	10	3	7
1970–1979	24	7	17
1980–1989	52	25	27
1990–1999	50	20	30
2000–2009	65	20	45
2010	11	4	7
Total	345	115 (33.3%)	230 (66.7%)

Source: California Secretary of State. Citizen-initiated measures; legislatively referred measures not included.

LO4 *The Politics of Ballot Propositions*

The proliferation of ballot propositions is hardly the result of a sudden surge in democratic participation. Rather, it stems largely from the opportunism of special interests, individual politicians, and public relations firms. One man, hoping for cures to diseases suffered by his mother and son, provided the $3 million that funded the initiative to support stem cell research in 2004. Hundreds of millions of dollars have been spent on ballot measures regulating casinos on Native American lands, the most recent of which appeared on the ballot in 2008. In 2010, Pacific Gas and Electric and Mercury Insurance single-handedly funded separate initiatives that were clearly in their self-interest, and both the Chamber of Commerce and the Democratic Party funded measures affecting their own pet causes.

legislative initiatives Propositions placed on the ballot by the legislature rather than by citizen petition.

constitutional amendments May be placed on the ballot by a two-thirds vote of the legislature or through the initiative process; must be approved by a simple majority of the voters.

bonds Subject to voter approval, state and local governments can borrow money by issuing bonds, which are repaid (with interest) from the general fund budget or from special taxes or fees.

Although intended as mechanisms for citizens to shape policy, even the most grassroots-driven initiatives cost half a million dollars to qualify and millions more to mount a successful campaign. "If you pay enough," declared Ronald George, then chief justice of the California Supreme Court, "you can get anything on the ballot. You pay a little bit more and you get it passed."[7] In 2006 the pro and con campaigns on a proposition that would have imposed a modest fee on oil extraction

Women's rights activist Margaret Prescod is shown speaking during a "Yes on K" news conference in San Francisco. Ballot measure Proposition K sought to stop enforcement of laws targeting prostitution, and it was defeated.

CALIFORNIA FACES A
TROUBLED ECONOMY

The "Top Two Candidates" Open Primary Plan

The Great Recession did more than just shred California's budget. It also led, indirectly, to a variety of proposals designed to completely revamp California's elections system. One of these was the plan for a "Top Two Candidates" open primary. The legislature submitted this plan to the voters in June 2010 as Proposition 14, and it passed handily.

Beginning in 2008, as California's budget deficit exploded, Republican legislators united around the demand for no new taxes, and the Democrats early opposed cuts in social services. In early 2009, the Democrats reached a deal with Governor Schwarzenegger, but they needed at least one more Republican vote in the Senate to pass the budget. Moderate Republican senator Abel Maldonado offered to supply the needed vote if lawmakers put an open primary measure on the June 2010 ballot. Reluctantly, the Democratic leadership agreed, and the budget passed.

The goal of the open primary plan is to curb the partisanship that has characterized California politics, especially since the onset of the economic crisis. Proponents of the plan believe that it will lead to more moderate elected officials by reducing the influence of the highly partisan voters who are most likely to vote in the current party primary system. Instead, the plan seeks to empower independent and centrist voters.

What, Exactly, Does the Proposition Do?

Under the new system, all candidates for each state elective office and the U.S. Congress will appear on a single ballot. Candidates are free to indicate their party, but are not required to do so. More than one candidate from each party can appear on the ballot. An insurgent Democratic candidate, for example, can appear on the primary ballot next to the officially endorsed Democrat. The ballot itself will note the party, but it will not say which candidate has the party's endorsement. The two candidates receiving the most votes regardless of party move on to the general election ballot. In the general election, two Republicans may face each other in a conservative district. In a highly Democratic district, the two top finishers could both be Democrats.

Supporters of the new plan believe that in those districts where two members of the same party appear on the November ballot, the voters—who include independents and members of the other party—are likely to choose the more moderate candidate. The Gray Davis recall election provides some evidence for this argument. The winning candidate, Arnold Schwarzenegger, was a Republican who might have had trouble winning a Republican Party primary because he was not considered conservative enough.

As you might imagine, the leaders of the two major parties were not pleased with this concept. "It's a misnomer to call this an open primary," said Ron Nehring, chairman of the California Republican Party. "It is the abolition of primaries." Nehring has a point. The Top Two Candidates primary is not really a partisan primary, because it is not a system through which parties can decide whom to support. Rather, it can be considered as the first half of a two-part general election process.

The Constitutional Problem

California had an open primary in 1998 and 2000, but in 2000 the United States Supreme Court ruled that the system was unconstitutional. In 2008, however, the Court found that the open primary used in Washington State passed muster, and the Top Two Candidates primary was modeled on it.

The issue that bedeviled past attempts at creating an open primary is the First Amendment right of freedom of association. Political parties enjoy this right unless racial discrimination is involved. Freedom of association means that parties have the power to decide who will participate in choosing the candidates that they support. Parties can restrict participation to party members through a closed primary or a convention. They can open the process up to those who are not party members—an open primary. State governments can "bribe" the parties to choose their candidates in a specific way by offering them a state-funded primary mechanism. The parties are not legally required to accept the offer, however, and on rare occasions they have organized their own candidate selection procedures instead.

For this reason, the California ballot proposition made it clear that the state will respect the parties' freedom of association. The parties are free to name the candidates they support, publicize these candidates, and campaign for them. What the parties cannot do, however, is to automatically place their preferred candidates on the November ballot.

You Be the Judge **What do you think the consequences of a Top Two Candidates primary will be in California?**

ELECTIONS 2010

The Ballot Proposals

As is so often the case in California, the proposals on the ballot in November 2010 were as important as the candidates. One measure that passed was Proposition 20, which requires the California Citizens Redistricting Commission to redraw the boundaries of U.S. congressional districts following the results of the 2010 census. The commission already had the task of redrawing the boundaries of state senate and assembly districts. The commission was created to combat *gerrymandering,* that is, the drawing of district boundaries to help one political party and hurt the other. We take a closer look at the measure in a feature in Chapter 20.

The passage of Proposition 25 removed the requirement of a two-thirds majority in both houses of the state legislature to pass a budget—a topic we examine in Chapter 21. The voters kept the two-thirds majority requirement for new or higher taxes, however, and in Proposition 26 they extended the principle to fees and charges. Proposition 22 sought to keep the state from seizing certain local funds, a subject we address in Chapter 25.

Among the measures that failed was Proposition 19, which would have legalized marijuana and let local governments tax it. We discuss it in Chapter 26. Proposition 23 would have postponed state efforts to fight global warming until the unemployment rate fell below 5.5 percent. It failed, and we examine it in Chapter 23. Proposition 21, which would have funded state parks by increasing vehicle license fees, also failed.

spent $152 million, with oil companies spending $93 million on the measure. The campaigns for and against the 2008 proposition banning same-sex marriage spent a total of $83 million—much of it coming from out of state, because California is often seen as setting precedents for campaigns elsewhere. Total spending for proposition campaigns in any given election year now averages nearly $300 million. Much of it comes from corporations and unions. According to the California Fair Political Practices Commission, "These interests have spent hundreds of millions of dollars for and against ballot measures. They often win by spending money to defeat measures, which has the effect of maintaining the status quo. . . . The conclusion is inescapable: A handful of special interests have a disproportionate amount of influence on California elections and public policy."[8]

Politically Driven Initiatives

Besides wealthy individuals such as international financier George Soros (a supporter of drug decriminalization) and high-tech executive Tim Draper (a supporter of school vouchers), politicians have also discovered initiatives as a way to further their own careers or shape public policy. Republican governor Pete Wilson helped secure reelection in 1994 by sponsoring a successful measure on illegal immigration. In 2002 then movie star Arnold Schwarzenegger sponsored an initiative to fund after-school programs, advancing both that cause and his political career. As governor, Schwarzenegger tried to use ballot measures to further his agenda when thwarted by the Democratic majority in the legislature. In a succession of elections, he put forward initiatives addressing political and budget reforms, as well as bond measures. The bond measures passed, but most of the reforms were rejected by the voters, much to the disappointment of the governor.

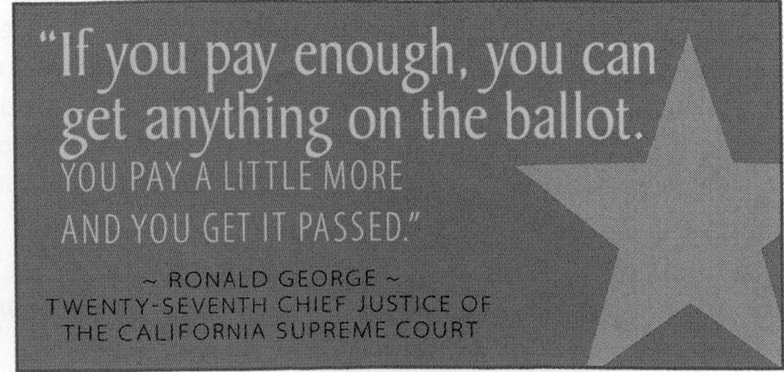

"If you pay enough, you can get anything on the ballot.
YOU PAY A LITTLE MORE
AND YOU GET IT PASSED."
~ RONALD GEORGE ~
TWENTY-SEVENTH CHIEF JUSTICE OF
THE CALIFORNIA SUPREME COURT

Market-Driven Initiatives

Others also take advantage of direct democracy. Public relations firms and political consultants, virtual "guns for hire," have developed lucrative careers managing initiative and referenda campaigns; they offer expertise in public opinion polling, computer-targeted mailing, and television advertising—the staples of modern campaigns. Some firms generate initiatives themselves by conducting test mailings and preliminary polls in hopes of snagging big contracts from proposition sponsors. With millions of dollars in campaign spending hanging in the balance, big economic interests gain an advantage over grassroots efforts—surely not what the Progressives intended.

FARAH NOSH/GETTY IMAGES

Proposition 23 would have postponed the enactment of the Global Warming Solutions Act until California's unemployment rate drops below 5.5%. Supporters called Proposition 23 the California Jobs Initiative, and opponents called for voters to "Stop the Dirty Energy Proposition." The proposition was defeated in the November 2010 election.

Grassroots-driven Initiatives

Nevertheless, direct democracy offers hope to the relatively powerless by enabling them to take their case to the public. In 2004 voters showed sympathy for those with little power when they approved Proposition 63, which increased taxes on the rich to fund mental health programs. In 2008, a proposition on the treatment of farm animals passed, despite the strong opposition of agribusiness. In 2010, environmentalists got a measure to fund state parks on the ballot, and local governments qualified an initiative restricting the state's ability to "take back" local funds at will (see Chapter 25). The former proposition was soundly defeated, but the latter passed easily. Almost every California ballot includes initiatives generated by grassroots groups. Although these initiatives are often defeated by well-funded corporate interests, at least direct democracy provides such groups an opportunity to make their cases.

Proposition 21, defeated in 2010, would have increased vehicle license fees by $18 a year in order to raise roughly $500 million annually in a dedicated fund to support California's 278 state parks.

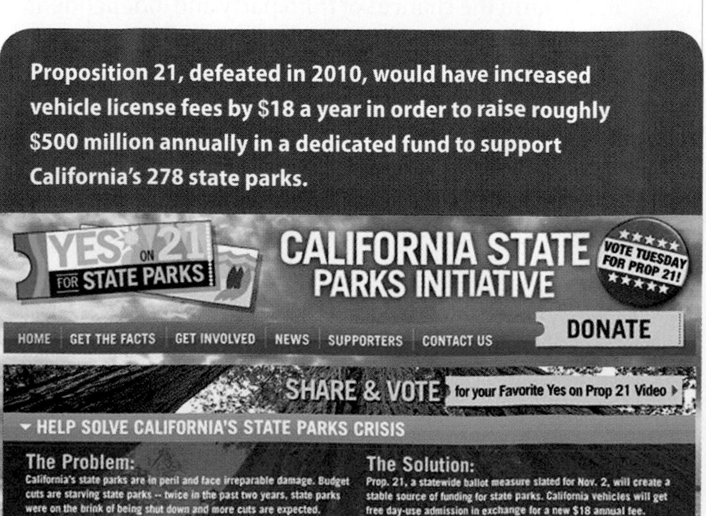

YES ON 21
FOR STATE PARKS
CALIFORNIA STATE PARKS INITIATIVE
VOTE TUESDAY FOR PROP 21!
HOME
GET THE FACTS
GET INVOLVED
NEWS
SUPPORTERS
CONTACT US
DONATE
SHARE & VOTE
for your Favorite Yes on Prop 21 Video
HELP SOLVE CALIFORNIA'S STATE PARKS CRISIS
The Problem:
California's state parks are in peril and face irreparable damage. Budget cuts are starving state parks -- twice in the past two years, state parks were on the brink of being shut down and more cuts are expected.
The Solution:
Prop. 21, a statewide ballot measure slated for Nov. 2, will create a stable source of funding for state parks. California vehicles will get free day-use admission in exchange for a new $18 annual fee.

WWW.YESFORPARKS.COM

Problems with Initiatives

Unfortunately, direct democracy does not necessarily result in good laws. Because self-interested sponsors draft initiatives and media masters run campaigns, careful and rational deliberation is rare. Flaws or contradictions in successful initiatives may take years to resolve. Sometimes this is done through the implementation of the measures by government agencies or through the legislative process. Increasingly, however, disputes about initiatives are resolved in state and federal courts, which must rule on whether the initiatives are consistent with other laws and with the state and federal constitutions. In recent years, courts have overturned all or parts of initiatives dealing with illegal immigration, campaign finance, and same-sex marriage, for example (see Chapter 22). Although such rulings seem to deny the will of the voters, the electorate cannot make laws that contradict the state or federal constitutions.

The increased use of direct democracy has also had an impact on the power of our elected representatives. Although we expect them to make policy, their ability to do so has been constrained by a sequence of initiatives in recent decades. This is particularly the case with the state budget, much of which is dictated by past ballot measures rather than the legislature or the governor.

The proliferation of initiatives, expensive and deceptive campaigns, flawed laws, and court interventions have annoyed voters and policymakers alike. Perhaps as a consequence, two-thirds of all initiatives are rejected (see Table 18–1). Although Californians express anger and frustration with the initiative process, a solid majority of survey respondents support direct democracy in concept. At the same time, a majority favors reforms such as a review of ballot language and legal issues before initiatives are placed on the ballot.[9]

Political Parties and Direct Democracy

Authors Mark Baldassare and Cheryl Katz argue that California has evolved into a unique "hybrid democracy," with power divided between elected representatives and the public.[10] Partisan gridlock in Sacramento, voter distrust, and powerful interest groups (see Chapter 20) have resulted in the increased reliance on direct democracy to resolve issues, albeit often imperfectly. California's political parties can't break the gridlock or even control the choice of their own candidates in an electoral system in which money seems to trump party organization. Once elected, our officials seem unable to resolve the issues that confront us. Direct democracy provides an alternative—for political leaders, moneyed interests, and citizens—yet the proliferation of propositions further confounds voters. Does California have too much democracy? Sometimes it seems so. Some voters feel overwhelmed and turned off, but most manage to sift through complex initiatives and seductive campaigns to find the candidates and policies that suit their preferences.

CALIFORNIA AT **ODDS** *Political Parties and Direct Democracy*

Compared with many other states, California has weak political parties and relies heavily on direct democracy in the form of ballot proposals. California's citizens have long been at odds over the roles that parties and initiatives should play in state politics. Disputes include the following:

- Is it appropriate that voters can amend the state constitution by a simple majority vote—or should such an important step require some type of "supermajority"?
- Is the Democratic Party too far to the left—or are its politics appropriate? How about the Republican Party? Too far to the right—or just right?
- Are bipartisanship and compromise essential to good governance—or is it more important for politicians to stick to their principles?
- Is the Top Two Candidates open primary system a major step forward—or is it unfair to the parties?
- The Top Two Candidates system severely reduces the likelihood that a third party will place its candidate on the November ballot, but third party and independent candidates rarely win anyway. Will the new system really harm the chances of third party and independent candidates—or might it improve their odds of actually winning an election (as opposed to their chances of getting on the November ballot)?

Take Action

Initiative campaigns come and go, but the parties are always with us. In every corner of California, both major parties regularly hold meetings that are open to the general public. Frequently, however, such meetings are not well advertised. The lack of publicity can be advantageous for the student who wants to learn more about one or another of the parties—those present are more likely to speak freely if they think they are talking to other members of the party faithful. You can find out the times and places of meetings by contacting a local party office or by looking on their Web site. For example, if you google "Santa Clara County Republican Party," you'll find all upcoming events listed on their Web site. Who knows? After attending a meeting or two, you might be drawn to become active on behalf of the party of your choice. Alternatively, you might discover new reasons to be glad you are an independent.

POLITICS ON THE WEB

- The Field (California) Poll has operated continuously since 1947 as an independent, non-partisan, media-sponsored public opinion news service and has issued over 2,300 different reports on voter attitudes and party preferences. To read archive reports, visit **www.field.com/fieldpoll**.
- To learn more about the American Independent Party, visit **www.aipca.org**.
- The California Democratic Party is online at **www.cadem.org**.
- The Green Party of California's home page is **www.cagreens.org**.
- The Libertarian Party of California's home page is **www.ca.lp.org**.
- To learn more about the Peace and Freedom Party, go to **www.peaceandfreedom.org**.
- The California Republican Party is online at **www.cagop.org**.
- The Center for Government Studies helps individuals participate more effectively in their communities and governments to strengthen democracy. To learn more, go to **www.cgs.org**.

Access CourseMate to review and expand on this chapter through quizzes, flashcards, learning objectives, interactive timelines, a crossword puzzle, audio summaries, video, critical-thinking activities, simulations, and more.

GOVT

19

California Elections, Campaigns, and the Media

LEARNING OBJECTIVES

LO1 Summarize the profile of California voters and factors involved in non-participation.

LO2 Describe where political candidates come from, how representative they are of the population, and which groups are underrepresented.

LO3 Explain where the money comes from for political campaigns and the laws that regulate campaign financing.

LO4 Discuss how campaigning in California differs from other states, the challenges faced by candidates, and how the recall election of 2003 changed the rules for typical campaigning.

LO5 Indicate the role each form of media plays in California politics.

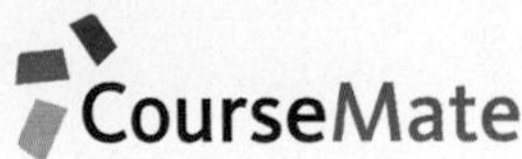

CALIFORNIA AT ODDS

Do Voter Turnout Levels Really Matter?

Voters in the United States are less likely to make it to the polls than voters in most other democratic countries. In the presidential elections of November 2008, only 61.7 percent of eligible Californians voted, and this was one of the highest voter participation rates seen in many years. Coincidentally, the national turnout was also 61.7 percent. (These figures are for eligible voters. Turnout among registered voters is higher.)

Voters are most active when a presidential contest is on the ballot. Turnout in midterm elections, when California elects a governor and members of the U.S. House, is lower. The turnout for the 2010 midterm elections was better than usual, however—45.1 percent of eligible Californians cast a ballot, up almost 5 percent from the previous midterm elections in 2006. Turnout for local or special elections is typically much worse. For purely local elections, turnout rarely reaches 25 percent even of registered voters. For example, when Antonio Villaraigosa was first elected mayor of Los Angeles, turnout almost reached 30 percent, but when he ran for reelection on March 5, 2009, turnout plunged below 15 percent. An exception to the rule that special elections draw few voters was the gubernatorial recall election of 2003, when the voters removed Gray Davis from office and replaced him with Arnold Schwarzenegger. Voters turned out at a rate that was almost 10 percent greater than the rate posted the previous fall, in the regularly scheduled elections of November 2002.

Are low turnout rates a danger to our democracy? Some people believe that they are. Others are not worried.

Low Voter Turnout is Not a Problem

Some observers contend that low rates of voter turnout merely signify that the electorate is satisfied with the status quo. Nonvoters are getting the government—and leaders—they wanted to have anyway. Representative democracy works even if relatively few people vote in most elections. Elected officials must still consider that large numbers of voters could turn out of they became upset with the workings of government. We saw this effect during the Gray Davis recall, when turnout shot up.

Many countries have high voter turnout because there is a serious danger that a bad election result could have serious consequences. In some relatively impoverished countries, election of the wrong candidate could result in businesses being taken over or homes and property seized. This is not anything that Americans need to worry about. In this country, people can concentrate on subjects other than politics. They can devote themselves exclusively to their private lives, their jobs, or their businesses. There is no reason to push people into voting who barely care about the issues. Such people will almost certainly be poorly informed and are likely to be influenced by trivial factors.

Apathy has Destructive Consequences

Those who believe that rates of political participation are too low in California and the nation at large do not consider apathy to be a benign phenomenon. If the voters don't keep an eye on their leaders, the probable consequence will be high levels of corruption. Severe corruption was a major problem in California government in much of the first half of the twentieth century, and we don't want to see that kind of behavior again.

People who do not vote do not receive representation. The poor are less likely to vote than the rich, and when turnout falls off, low-income persons are the ones who will most often stay home. Political scientists at UC San Diego have shown that in cities with low voter turnout, municipal government spends less money on programs that might aid the poor. Instead, such governments fund downtown development and other projects that aid business. Simply put, local governments spend their revenues on those who vote.[1]

Voting is part and parcel of a public-spirited attitude toward life. A recent study shows that people who are socially active, who have many friends and acquaintances, are far more likely to vote.[2] We see high rates of turnout in places with high levels of social satisfaction, such as northern Europe or states such as Minnesota and New Hampshire. High rates of voter turnout are a sign of a healthy society.

WHERE DO YOU STAND?

1. **Voter turnout was higher in 2008 than in any presidential election since the 1960s. What might have driven normally apathetic voters to the polls in the 1960s—and again in 2008?**
2. **Does the fact that the wealthy are among those most likely to vote provide additional evidence that high levels of social integration lead to high voter turnout? Why or why not?**

EXPLORE THIS ISSUE ONLINE

- **The United States Elections Project at George Mason University has excellent materials on voter turnout. You can view the project's work at elections.gmu.edu/voter_turnout.htm.**
- **You can find a small library of articles on increasing voter turnout at nonprofitvote.org/Voter-Turnout-Library.html.**

Introduction

A typical California ballot requires voters to make decisions about more than twenty elective positions and propositions. Even the best-informed citizens sometimes find it difficult to choose among candidates for offices they know little about and to decide on obscure and complicated propositions. Political party labels provide some guidance, but candidates, campaigns, and the media are also crucial in the California elections.

Campaigns and the media are especially important because of the mobility and rootlessness that characterize California society. More than half of all Californians were born elsewhere, and many voters in every California state election are participating for the first time. Residents also move frequently within the state, reducing the political influence of families, friends, and peer groups and boosting that of campaigns and the media.

"THE VOTE is the most powerful instrument ever devised... for breaking down injustice and destroying the terrible walls which imprison men because they are different from other men."

~ LYNDON BAINES JOHNSON ~ THIRTY-SIXTH PRESIDENT OF THE UNITED STATES, 1963–1969

LO1 The Voters

California citizens who are eighteen years or older are eligible to vote unless they are in prison or a mental institution. Those eligible must **register to vote,** which must be done at least fifteen days before an election by completing a form available at post offices, fire stations, libraries, and public places where party activists eagerly solicit new voters. Registration forms are also available with applications for driver's licenses and at social service agencies or online at **www.sos.ca.gov/nvrc/dedform.** Once registered, those who cast their ballots regularly stay on the voter rolls indefinitely. Occasionally, however, voter lists are "purged" of voters who have not participated for some time or who have died or moved.

register to vote Citizens who are over eighteen years of age and who are not incarcerated or in a mental institution are eligible to sign up to vote by completion of a registration form. Nearly 30 percent of those eligible to register in California do not do so and thus cannot participate in elections.

voter turnout The proportion of eligible and/or registered voters who actually participate in an election. When turnout is high, the electorate is usually more diverse and liberal; when it is low, the electorate is usually older, more affluent, and more conservative.

Altogether, nearly 23.4 million Californians are eligible to vote. Only 17 million (72.4 percent) were registered in 2010, however, and as few as 8 million actually vote in some elections—somewhat below the national average. In the gubernatorial election of 2010, **voter turnout** among those registered to vote was 59.6 percent. Turnout is higher in presidential elections. In 2008, 79.4 percent of the state's registered voters participated, a rate that was higher than the national average. In the 2010 primary election, however, only 33.3 percent of those registered actually participated—a record low for a gubernatorial primary election. We discussed the implications of such figures in the chapter-opening *California at Odds* feature.

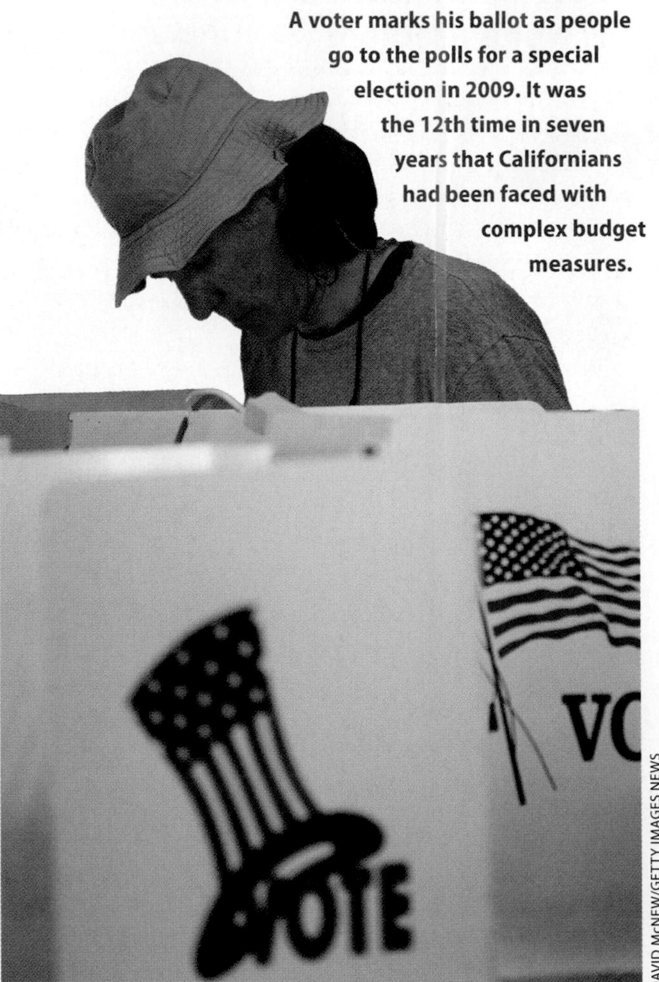

A voter marks his ballot as people go to the polls for a special election in 2009. It was the 12th time in seven years that Californians had been faced with complex budget measures.

DAVID McNEW/GETTY IMAGES NEWS

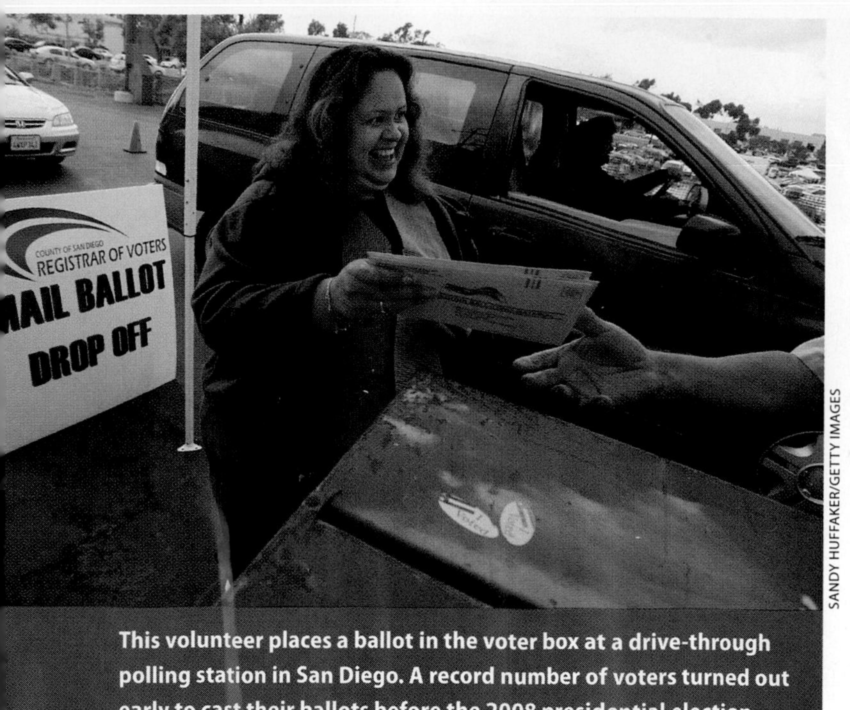

SANDY HUFFAKER/GETTY IMAGES

This volunteer places a ballot in the voter box at a drive-through polling station in San Diego. A record number of voters turned out early to cast their ballots before the 2008 presidential election.

Traditionally, voters go to designated polling places to cast their ballots, but today nearly half **vote by mail,** having requested **absentee ballots** from their county registrar of voters. Those who prefer to cast their ballots this way can sign up as "permanent" absentee voters so that ballots are automatically sent to them for every election. In the 2010 gubernatorial primary election, a record 58 percent of those who voted did so by absentee ballot. Most of these people simply prefer the convenience of voting by mail given their busy lives; many prefer to deal with the complex ballots at their leisure; and still others vote absentee because campaigns push identified supporters to vote by mail to ensure their participation. With so many more people voting absentee—up to three weeks before Election Day—campaigns have had to change their tactics. Rather than a big push in the last few days, they must spread their resources and extend their messages over a longer period.

Factors Affecting Voter Turnout

Voting by mail may have increased participation slightly, but even with this convenience, many Californians choose not to vote. Some don't get around to registering. Millions more who are registered still don't vote. Some are apathetic, some are unaware, and others feel too uninformed to act. Still others believe that voting is a charade because politics "is controlled by special interests." Some people say election information is "too hard to understand," and others are bewildered by all the messages that bombard them during a typical California election. But the reason that people most frequently give for not voting is that they are too busy.[3]

> "One of the penalties FOR REFUSING TO PARTICIPATE IN POLITICS IS THAT YOU END UP BEING GOVERNED BY YOUR INFERIORS."
>
> ~ PLATO ~
> GREEK PHILOSOPHER
> 427–347 BC

Yet political campaigns are designed to motivate voters to support candidates and causes. This task is complicated, though, because those who vote are not a representative cross section of the actual population. Non-Latino whites, for example, make up 42 percent of the population but 65 percent of the electorate. Although Latinos, African Americans, and Asians constitute 58 percent of California's population, they are only 35 percent of the voters in primary and general elections.[4] This disparity in turnout means that California's voting electorate is not representative of the state's population. The lower participation rate among Latinos and Asians is partly explained by the relative youth of these populations (about one-third of Latinos, for example, are too young to vote) and by the fact that many are not yet citizens.

Language, culture, and socioeconomic status may also be barriers to registration and voting among minority groups. This situation is changing, however; Latinos were just 8 percent of the state's registered voters in 1978 but are more than 21 percent today,[5] and the number continues to rise. Still, voter registration lags among Latino citizens, with only about half of those eligible currently registered to vote.[6]

Those Most Likely to Vote

Differences in the levels of voter participation do not end with ethnicity. The people most likely to vote are suburban homeowners and Republicans, who tend to be richer, better educated, and older. Lower levels of participation are usually found among poorer, less educated, and younger inner-city residents and Democrats.[7] According to recent reports,

vote by mail and **absentee ballots** Voters who prefer not to vote at their polling places or who are unable to vote on Election Day may apply to their county registrar of voters for an absentee ballot and vote by mail; nearly half of those who vote in California elections vote by mail.

PERCEPTION VERSUS REALITY

Orange County: Heartland of the Right

California's Orange County has an almost mythic status in the history of American politics. It is often seen as the nation's most important incubator of "movement conservatism." Orange County's population exploded from 216,000 in 1950, to 704,000 in 1960, and 1,421,000 by 1970. The new inhabitants were largely white and midwestern, and many of them were employed by defense industries. Racially and economically homogeneous, Orange County fostered a radical anti-communist conservatism that swept from extremism to respectability through the 1964 presidential nomination of Republican Barry Goldwater and the election of Ronald Reagan as California governor in 1966. This, at least, is the history as described in such accounts as *Suburban Warriors: The Origins of the New American Right,* by Harvard historian Lisa McGirr.[8] This history poses a question: is Orange County still a heartland of movement conservatism today?

The Perception: Orange County Has Changed

The vision of a right-wing Orange County may survive among those with long memories, but among the nation's youth, the perception has been drowned out by a flood of fantasy images based on such cultural artifacts as *The O.C.* and *Real Housewives of Orange County.* While the wealthy individuals portrayed in these largely apolitical productions are poor candidates for liberalism—Newport Beach, supposed home of *The O.C.,* is rated by the *Sacramento Bee* as the second most Republican city in California—these people are not exactly conservative activists, either. And for those who do not equate Orange County entirely with its wealthiest residents, there is always Disneyland, a bit culturally conservative, perhaps, but hardly radical.

In addition, Californians, who know more about Orange County than what is shown on television, are aware of the huge number of Latinos and Asian Americans who have moved into the area in recent years. The Census Bureau reports that as of 2006, non-Hispanic whites were no longer the majority of Orange County's population. Latinos were 33 percent of the population, Asians were 16 percent, and 30 percent of the county's inhabitants were foreign born.

The Reality: But Not That Much

Still, conservatism is alive and well in Orange County. The area remains resolutely Republican, and today's Republican Party is unified around the conservatism that Orange County activists championed in the 1960s and 1970s. Along with Arizona's Maricopa County (Phoenix), Orange County is one of only two populous urbanized counties outside the South to vote for Republican John McCain in 2008. Five of the county's six U.S. representatives, four of its five state senators and seven of its nine state assembly members are Republicans, as are all five members of the County Board of Supervisors. Only four Democrats have carried the county in a statewide race in the last 50 years.

Orange County's ethnic composition can be misleading. The largest Asian group is the Vietnamese, who are strongly conservative in response to the communist takeover of their homeland. Vietnamese Americans who are registered as Republicans outnumber registered Democrats by 55 to 22 percent. Even Latinos in the county are distinctly more conservative than Hispanics elsewhere in California. As a result, conservatism in Orange County may prove surprisingly resistant to future ethnic change. We'll know more about that after the 2010 census and the subsequent redistricting.

Blog On You can get a stiff dose of Orange County conservatism from the opinion pages of the *Orange County Register,* the county's leading newspaper. See it at **www.ocregister.com/sections/opinion**. For a discussion of the Vietnamese American vote, see **www.ocregister.com/articles/vietnamese-188422-community-american.html.**

78 percent of adults over the age of sixty-five are "likely voters," while just 24 percent of adults aged eighteen to twenty-four are "likely to participate in elections."[9] All this adds up to a voting electorate that is more conservative than the population as a whole, which explains how Republicans sometimes win statewide elections despite the Democratic edge in registration and why liberal ballot measures rarely pass. We look at an important Republican heartland in the *Perception versus Reality* feature above.

Of course, voting is only one form of political participation. Many people sign petitions, attend public meetings, write letters or e-mails to officials, and contribute money to campaigns. But as we see in Figure 19–1, the number participating diminishes with each form of engagement, and differences among ethnic groups persist. As with voting, those who participate most are white, older, more affluent, homeowners, and more highly educated. Does the differential in voting and other forms of participation matter? It seems self-evident that elected officials pay more attention to the concerns of those who participate than those who do not.

Figure 19–1

Political Participation by Ethnic Groups

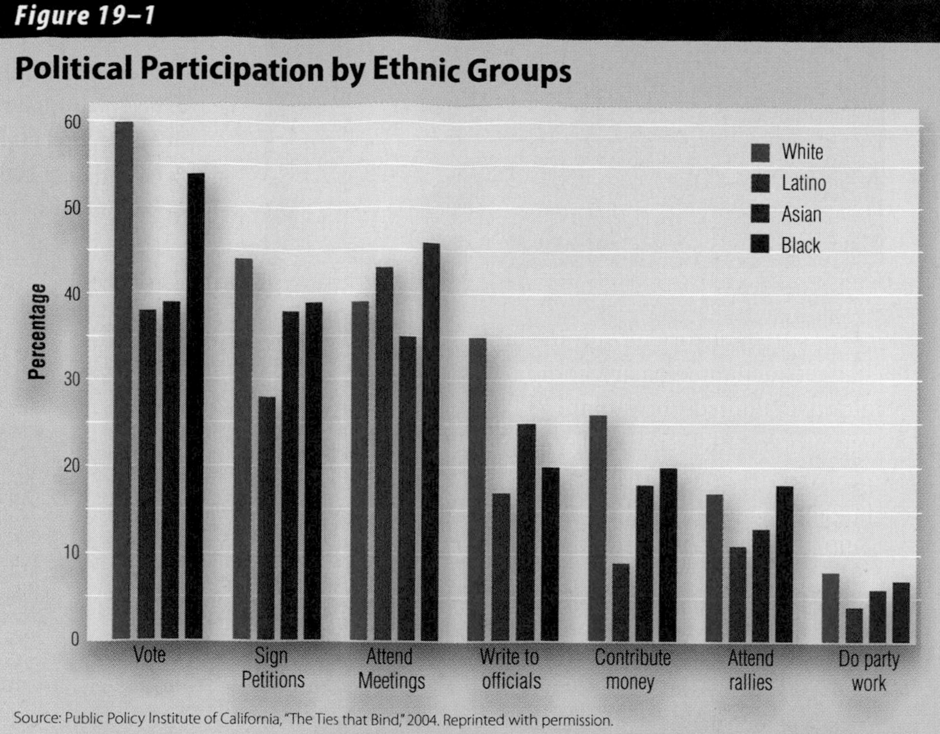

Source: Public Policy Institute of California, "The Ties that Bind," 2004. Reprinted with permission.

LO2 *The Candidates*

When we vote, we choose among candidates, but where do candidates come from? Some are encouraged to run by political parties or interest groups seeking to advance their causes. Political leaders looking for allies recruit others, although weak political parties make such overtures less common in California than elsewhere. Most California candidates are self-starters with an interest in politics who decide to run and then seek support. The rising cost and increasing negativity of campaigns have discouraged some people from running, although wealthy individuals who can fund their own campaigns have frequently appeared as candidates in recent years. Most candidates start at the bottom of the political ladder, running for school board or city council, and work their way up, building support as they go. Others gain experience as staff members for elected officials, eventually running for their boss's job. Wealthy candidates sometimes skip such apprenticeships and run directly for higher office, but the voters are sometimes skeptical about their lack of political experience.

Historically, candidates in California have been even less representative of the population than the electorate. Most have been educated white males of above-average financial means. The 1990s brought change, however. Underrepresented groups such as women, racial and ethnic minorities, and gay men and lesbians grew

Matt Lemcke, a student filmmaker at Cal State Northridge, declared his candidacy for governor of California in the recall election of Governor Gray Davis in 2003. He said he was running for office because he wanted to encourage young people to vote.

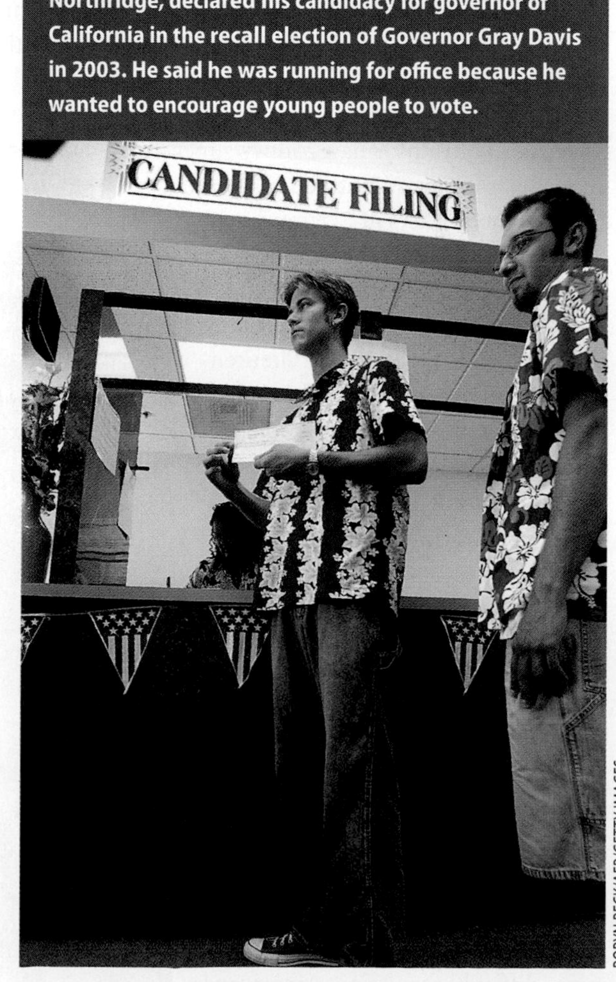

ROBYN BECK/AFP/GETTY IMAGES

> "Elections ARE A GOOD DEAL LIKE MARRIAGES. THERE'S NO ACCOUNTING FOR ANYONE'S TASTE."
>
> ~ WILL ROGERS ~
> AMERICAN HUMORIST, 1879–1935

California Controller John Chiang spoke at an election night celebration in 2008 in Los Angeles.

JEFF VESPA/WIREIMAGES/GETTY IMAGES

in strength and organization, and structural changes facilitated their candidacies. A 1990 initiative limited the number of terms that legislators could serve, thus ensuring greater turnover in the state legislature. In addition, the redistricting decisions after the censuses of 1990 and 2000 resulted in redrawn legislative and congressional districts that gave minority candidates new opportunities at both levels. This could happen again with the redistricting that will follow the 2010 census, when district boundaries will be revised by a citizens' commission created by initiative rather than by the legislators themselves.

Ethnic Representation

Latinos have gained the most from these changes, obtaining a sizable delegation in the state legislature and the California congressional delegation. Latinos have also gained representation at the local level, electing more than 1,200 of California's county supervisors, city council members, mayors, and school board members.[10] Most Latino officeholders are Democrats.

Although a smaller minority, African Americans gained a foothold in state politics earlier, including the statewide positions of lieutenant governor and superintendent of public instruction. Three African Americans have served as speaker of the assembly (its most powerful leader), but overall, black representation has shrunk as that of other minorities has increased.

Asian Americans remain the most underrepresented of California's racial minorities. In the past, Asian Americans have won election to statewide offices, including U.S. senator, secretary of state, and state treasurer. John Chiang, a Democrat of Chinese descent, was elected state controller in 2006 and re-elected in 2010. Electing candidates has been difficult for Asian Americans, however, because many are recent immigrants who are not yet rooted in the state's political system and because of cultural and political differences among the Chinese, Japanese, Vietnamese, Filipinos, Koreans, Indo-Americans, and others. But these groups have generated more candidates in every recent election. Many Asian Americans have won local offices on city councils and school boards, and nine serve in the state legislature.

Sheila James Kuehl was the first woman in California history to be named Speaker pro Tempore of the Assembly during the 1997–98 legislative session. She was also the first openly gay or lesbian person to be elected to the California Legislature. She served eight years in the State Senate and six years in the State Assembly.

WWW.SHEILAKUEHL.ORG

Underrepresented Groups

Women candidates have been more successful. Both of California's U.S. senators are now women. Women have been elected to statewide office in the past as well, although only two, Secretary of State Debra Bowen and Attorney General Kamala Harris, are currently serving. A substantial number of women are in the state legislature, however, including Assembly Speaker pro Tempore Fiona Ma. Many of California's city council members, mayors, and county supervisors also are women.

Lesbians and gay men achieved elected office later than any of these groups. Greater bias may be a factor, and in the past, the closeted status of many homosexuals—including candidates and elected officials—weakened organizing efforts and made gay and lesbian elective successes invisible. Nevertheless, eighty openly gay and lesbian individuals have won election to local offices (including sixteen judges),[11] and seven serve in the state legislature. Some, such as Assembly Speaker John Perez, a Democrat from Los Angeles, have risen to leadership positions.

Racism and sexism partly explain the underrepresentation of all these groups, but other factors contribute as well. Many members of these groups are economically disadvantaged, which makes it hard to participate in politics, let alone to take on the demands of a candidacy. Women, minorities, and gay men and lesbians are usually not plugged in to the network of lobbyists, interest groups, and big donors that provide funds for California's expensive campaigns. Minorities also have difficulty winning support outside their own groups and may alienate their natural constituencies in the process. The fact that minorities are less likely to vote than Anglos further reduces their candidates' potential. Nevertheless, organizations within each of these constituencies work to recruit, train, and support candidates, and the diversity of California candidates and elected officials increases with each election.

AP PHOTO/CHRIS CARLSON

Republican gubernatorial candidate Meg Whitman concedes during her election night party in Los Angeles, Tuesday, Nov. 2, 2010. She lost her bid for governor in spite of spending over $140 million of her personal fortune on the campaign, a new state and national record.

LO3 *The Money*

The introduction of primary elections in 1909 shifted the focus of campaigns from political parties to individual candidates. Political aspirants must raise money, recruit workers, research issues, and plot strategy on their own or with the help of expensive consultants rather than with that of political parties, which contribute little in the way of money or staff. California campaigns thus tend to focus on the personalities of the candidates more than on parties or policies.

Weak parties mean that candidates must promote themselves, so the cost of running for state assembly or senate often exceeds $1 million. Spending on races for the legislature totaled $97.7 million in the 2007–2008 election cycle.[12] Campaigns for statewide offices are even more expensive. The top two candidates for governor together spent more than $210 million in 2010.

> "Politics has become so expensive THAT IT TAKES A LOT OF MONEY EVEN TO BE DEFEATED."
>
> ~ WILL ROGERS ~
> AMERICAN HUMORIST
> 1879–1935

Interest groups, businesses, and wealthy individuals provide the money. Much campaign financing is provided by **political action committees (PACs)**, which interest groups use to direct money to preferred campaigns. Legislative leaders such as the speaker of the assembly and the president pro tem of the senate raise huge sums from such sources and channel the money to their allies in the legislature; individual candidates raise money by asking potential contributors for donations directly and by organizing special fund-raising events, which range from coffees and barbecues to banquets and concerts. They also solicit contributions from specific audiences through targeted mailings and the Internet.

Increasingly, however, it appears that candidates must be wealthy enough to finance their own campaigns. Arnold Schwarzenegger provided more than $10 million for his campaigns in 2003 and 2006, but Republican Meg Whitman broke state and national records by spending $71 million of her own money to win the Republican nomination for governor in 2010 and then splurging another $71 million of her personal fortune in the general election. Voters are skeptical about wealthy candidates who self-finance

political action committees (PACs)
Mechanisms by which interest groups direct campaign contributions to preferred candidates.

Table 19–1

Proposition 34 Limits on Contributions to State Candidates, 2009–2010

Contributor	Legislature	Statewide except Governor	Governor
Person	$3,900	$6,500	$25,000
Small contributor committee	$7,800	$12,900	$25,900
Political party	No limit	No limit	No limit

Source: California Fair Political Practices Commission, www.fppc.ca.gov.

their campaigns, however, and in the past, most such candidates have lost.

Regulating Campaign Finances

Worried about the influence of money and turned off by campaign advertising, Californians have approved a series of initiatives aimed at regulating campaign finance. The **Political Reform Act of 1974** required public disclosure of all donors and expenditures through the **Fair Political Practices Commission (FPPC).** Since then, reformers have tried repeatedly to limit the amount that individuals and groups can contribute, but several initiatives approved by the voters were invalidated by the courts on grounds that they limited free speech. In 2000 voters approved Proposition 34, a legislative initiative setting higher contribution limits for individuals and committees (see Table 19–1).

"Money is the MOTHER'S MILK of politics."

~ JESSE UNRUH ~
FIFTY-FOURTH SPEAKER OF THE CALIFORNIA STATE ASSEMBLY, 1922–1987

Political Reform Act of 1974 An initiative requiring officials to disclose conflicts of interest, campaign contributions, and spending; also requires lobbyists to register with the Fair Political Practices Commission.

Fair Political Practices Commission (FPPC) Established by the Political Reform Act of 1974, this independent regulatory commission monitors candidates' campaign finance reports and lobbyists.

independent expenditures Campaign spending by interest groups and political action committees on behalf of candidates.

Proposition 34 also set voluntary spending limits for candidates (see Table 19–2). Those who accept the limits have their photo and candidate statements published in the official ballot booklets that go to all voters; candidates who decline the limits are excluded from the booklet. Most candidates for the legislature and statewide offices other than governor comply with the spending limits; those who don't lose the moral high ground to those who do, which may influence voters. There is no limit, however, on how much a candidate can contribute to his or her own campaign, which enables candidates such as Whitman to substantially fund their campaigns.

Reform Consequences

Like most reforms, Proposition 34 has had unintended consequences. Money is given to political parties to spend on behalf of candidates rather than to the candidates themselves, which may ultimately increase the power of the parties—and such contributions jumped dramatically after Proposition 34. More significantly, the new spending limits have been subverted by **independent expenditures** by PACs or groups specially organized by political consultants in support of candidates. Since Proposition 34, over $110 million has been spent in this way, including $32 million for the gubernatorial candidates in 2010.[13] Top independent expenditure groups include the prison guards' union, Indian gaming interests, and the California Teachers Association.[14] In some campaigns, independent expenditures exceed those of the candidates. The only restriction on independent expenditures is that they cannot be coordinated with the campaigns of the candidates they support. Because they are not directly associated with the candidates, "independent" mailings and television ads often feature the most vicious attacks on opponents.

Between various loopholes in Proposition 34, independent expenditures, PACs with names that cloak their real purpose and backers, and PACs that contribute to other PACs to obscure the individuals and interests who contribute the money, the Proposition 34 regulations have been condemned as "ineffective hypocrisy,"[15] even

Table 19–2

Voluntary Expenditure Ceilings for Candidates for State Offices, 2009–2010

Office	Primary	General Election
Assembly	$ 518,000	$ 906,000
Senate	777,000	1,165,000
Governor	7,768,000	12,946,000
Other statewide offices	5,178,000	7,768,000

Source: California Fair Political Practices Commission, www.fppc.ca.gov.

ELECTIONS 2010

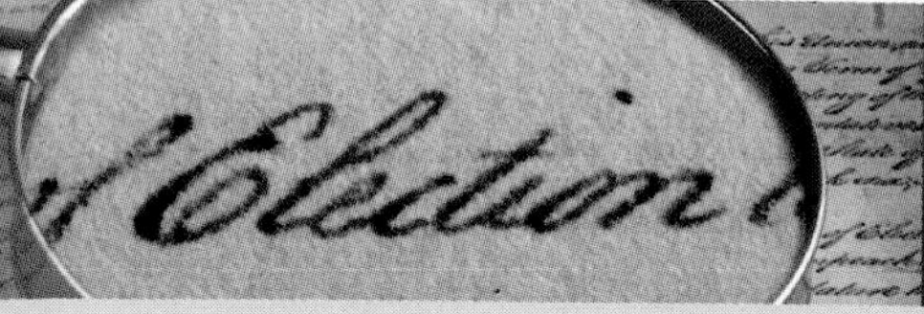

Campaign Finance

The biggest campaign finance story of 2010 was Republican Meg Whitman's run for California governor. With one campaign finance report still out, Whitman had spent $173.2 million, of which $141.6 came out of her own pocket. (These figures are larger than the ones reported immediately after the election.) Democrat Jerry Brown, who won, was not short of funds either. His campaign laid out $40.6 million, and he also benefitted from large independent expenditures. Whitman's run proved that past a certain point, campaign advertising is no longer effective. People already knew Whitman, and additional commercials were merely an annoyance.

Massive sums were also invested in ballot measures, often by wealthy individuals. Charles T. Munger, Jr., a Berkshire Hathaway heir, made the biggest single such contribution—$12.6 million for the anti-gerrymandering Proposition 20. The California Teachers Association spent almost as much on measures such as Proposition 25, which makes it easier to adopt a state budget. Energy companies provided large sums to support Proposition 23, which would postpone action against global warming. Valero Energy of Texas, the leading donor, provided $5.1 billion. These companies were outspent by wealthy environmentalists, however—the family of Thomas Steyer, a hedge fund manager, provided $6.1 million all by itself to oppose Proposition 23.

as reformers seek ways to close the loopholes. Twenty-five other states limit the impact of money on politics by providing some form of public financing for campaigns, but Californians rejected initiatives proposing such a system in the 2006 and 2010 elections.

LO4 *Campaigning California Style*

Campaign contributors hope to elect allies who will support their interests. They also expect their money to buy immediate access and long-term influence. Candidates deny making specific deals, however, insisting that they and their contributors merely share views on key issues. Millions of dollars flow into candidates' coffers through this murky relationship. In the 2010 election, for example, labor unions generously supported Democrat Jerry Brown, while business interests gave to Meg Whitman. Some donors give to candidates of both parties, just to cover their bases.

So much money is needed because California campaigns, whether local or statewide, are highly professionalized. To supplement political party support, candidates hire political consultants and management firms to perform a variety of functions, including recruiting workers, raising money, advertising, conducting public opinion polls, and performing virtually all other campaign activities. These specialists understand the workings of California's volatile electorate and use their knowledge to a candidate's benefit. California's top-ranked political consultants include Gale Kaufman and Garry South, who work for Democratic candidates, and Frank Schubert, who works for Republicans.[16]

Using Media to Reach Voters

Television has made campaign management firms indispensable, allowing candidates instant entry into voters' homes. It also enables candidates to put their message across at the exact moment of their choosing—on broadcast or cable TV, between wrestling bouts, during the local news or *Oprah,* or just after *American Idol,* depending on the targeted audience. The efficacy of the medium is proved repeatedly when relatively unknown candidates spend big money on television commercials and become major contenders, as eBay billionaire Meg Whitman did when she saturated the airwaves beginning in late 2009 in the 2010 race for governor. A statewide advertising buy on television costs at least $1 million—and one round of ads is never enough. Although initially a leader in the Republican race for the U.S. Senate nomination in 2010, former congressman Tom Campbell was effectively eliminated when he lacked funds to compete on television.

More than in smaller, more compact states where people are more connected, Californians rely heavily on television for political information. As a consequence, television advertising accounts for as much as 80 percent of all spending for statewide races in California. In such a big state, it is the only way to reach the mass of voters. At the height of the gubernatorial campaigns, candidates

Mayor Antonio Villaraigosa easily beat his nine opponents for re-election as mayor of Los Angeles in 2009. Voter turnout was low following a low-key election campaign that contrasted sharply to the bitter 2005 race between Villaraigosa and then-incumbent Jim Hahn when Villaraigosa became the first Latino mayor of his native Los Angeles in more than a century.

DAVID McNEW/GETTY IMAGES

run hundreds of ads a day in California's major media markets. Well-funded initiative campaigns also rely almost exclusively on television advertising.

DIRECT MAIL CAMPAIGNS Television is too costly for most candidates for legislative and local offices, however. A thirty-second prime-time spot can cost more than $20,000 in Los Angeles, and because most television stations broadcast to audiences much larger than a legislative district, the message is wasted on many viewers. Advertising during the day or on cable is cheaper, however, and many legislative candidates have turned to these alternatives. Most, however, have found a more efficient way to spend their money: **direct mail.** Computers have revolutionized political mail by enabling campaign strategists to target selected voters with personal messages.

Direct-mail experts develop lists of voters and their characteristics and then send special mailings to people who share particular qualities. In addition to listing voters by party registration and residence, these experts compile data banks that identify various groups, including liberals and conservatives, ethnic voters, retired people, homeowners and renters, union members, women, gay men and lesbians, and those most likely to vote. Campaigns even do data mining on consumer interests that might predict the political or policy concerns of voters so their mailing can be microtargeted. Once the targets have been identified, campaign strategists can develop just the right message to send to them. Conservatives may be told of the candidate's opposition to gay marriage; liberals may be promised action on the environment. For the price of a single thirty-second television spot, local or legislative candidates can send multiple mailings to their selected audiences.

THE NEGATIVE SIDE OF MEDIA CAMPAIGNS Television and direct mail dominate California campaigns because they reach the most voters, but the use of these media is not without problems. Because television and direct mail are expensive, campaign costs have risen, as has the influence of major donors. Candidates who are unable to raise vast sums of money are usually left at the starting gate. Incumbent officeholders, who are masters at fund-raising and are well connected to major contributors, become invincible. Furthermore, these media are criticized for oversimplifying issues and emphasizing the negative. Television commercials for ballot measures reduce complicated issues to emotional thirty-second spots aimed at uninformed voters. Candidates' ads and mailings indulge in the same oversimplification, often in the form of attacks on opponents. When the candidates portray each other negatively, voters may feel that they must choose the lesser evil rather than make a decision on the policies and positive traits of the candidates. Voters have grown skeptical of such attacks, yet they are hard to resist. Campaign consultants, who are usually blamed for the phenomenon, point out that campaigns had a nasty edge even a century ago and that the public pays more attention to negative messages than to positive ones.

direct mail A campaign technique by which candidates communicate selected messages to selected voters by mail.

CAMPAIGNING ONLINE Candidates also take their campaigns to the Internet, with Web sites and e-mail lists to communicate with the media and with supporters. Former eBay executive Meg Whitman, perhaps not surprisingly given her background, spent nearly $3 million on website development and information technology during the 2010 gubernatorial primary, building what was described as the "Cadillac" Web site.[17] The political impact of Internet campaigning is unclear, however. Whereas television and mail enable candidates to reach us whether we're interested or not, voters must initiate contact on the Internet, which limits the audience to those who are already engaged. Interest groups, however, can use e-mail to send campaign messages to their members, and some candidates have targeted e-mails

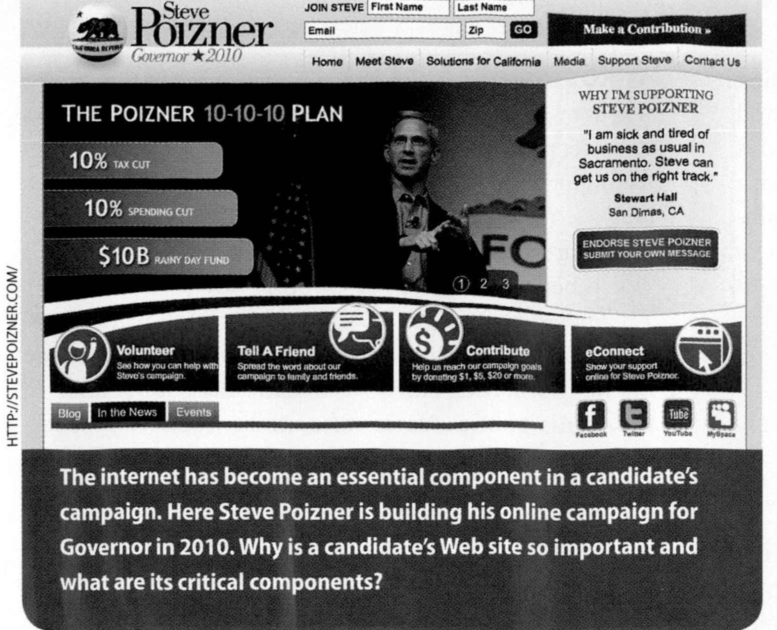

HTTP://STEVEPOIZNER.COM/

The internet has become an essential component in a candidate's campaign. Here Steve Poizner is building his online campaign for Governor in 2010. Why is a candidate's Web site so important and what are its critical components?

to particular constituencies, such as Christian conservatives. The Internet can also help candidates recruit volunteers and solicit donations.

Overall, California's media-oriented campaigns reinforce both the emphasis on candidates' personalities and voter cynicism. Some people blame such campaigns for declining voter turnout. Contemporary campaigns may also depress voter turnout by aiming all their efforts at regular voters and ignoring those who are less likely to vote—often minority voters. Although this is a sensible way to use campaign resources, it is not a way to stimulate democracy.

TAKING IT TO THE STREETS Some candidates try to revive old-fashioned door-to-door or telephone campaigns and get-out-the-vote drives on Election Day. Labor union volunteers have become a force in elections in Los Angeles and San Jose, for example, and the Democratic and Republican parties rely on volunteers to turn out voters for their candidates. Grassroots campaigns have a long and honorable tradition in California, but even in small-scale, local races, they are often up against not only big-money opponents but also the California lifestyle: few people are at home to be contacted, and those who are may let calls go to voice mail or be mistrustful of strangers at their door. For good or ill, candidates need money for their campaigns; those with the most money don't always win, but those with too little rarely even become contenders.

The Seventy-Five Day Campaign

Many of the traditional means of contacting voters were tossed out in the recall election of 2003, when the brevity of the campaign and the candidacy of Arnold Schwarzenegger changed everything. State law required a single election, rather than a primary and a general election, to be held within sixty to eighty days of the certification of the recall petition. Normally, statewide elections sprawl over at least a year, but when the election was set for October 7, Governor Davis and the candidates to replace him had just seventy-five days to make their cases, resulting in the most intense campaign in California history. Candidates who were well known or who could raise funds quickly, such as Democratic lieutenant governor Cruz Bustamante and Republican Arnold Schwarzenegger, had an immediate head start. But Schwarzenegger had another advantage. As an internationally famous and glamorous movie star, he attracted massive—and free—coverage by the news media within California and beyond.

Although media coverage of the brief campaign was different, some elements of the recall were not. The major candidates relied on television ads and mailings more than ever because time was too short to organize more traditional outreach efforts. Even in so short a campaign, more than $85 million was spent. Schwarzenegger ultimately succeeded by appealing to independent voters and many labor and Latino

Arnold Schwarzenegger announces his candidacy for governor in 2003 on the *Tonight Show*. How did Schwarzenegger's celebrity status benefit him in his campaign?

KEVIN WINTER/GETTY IMAGES

Democrats; his campaign balanced the funds going to other candidates, especially from labor unions and tribal gaming interests, with nearly $9 million of his own money and massive free media.[18] Is it a good idea for actors such as Schwarzenegger to serve as candidates? We examine that issue in the *Join the Debate* feature on the following page.

LO5 *The News Media and California Politics*

From candidates and campaigns to public policy, almost everything Californians know about politics—which is not necessarily very much—comes from the news media. They have a profound impact on ideas, issues, and leaders. Until the 1950s, a few family-owned newspapers dominated the media. Then television gave the newspapers some competition while expanding the cumulative clout of the mass media. Today, new media like the Internet and a plethora of ethnic publications also play a role.

Paper Politics

California's great newspapers were founded in the nineteenth century by ambitious men such as Harrison Gray Otis of the *Los Angeles Times,* William Randolph Hearst of the *San Francisco Examiner,* and James McClatchy of the *Sacramento Bee.* These print-media moguls used their newspapers to boost their communities, their political candidates, and their favored causes. Most were like Otis, an ardent conservative who fought labor unions and pushed for growth while making a fortune in land investments. In the heyday of bosses and machines, his *Los Angeles Times* supported the Southern Pacific Railroad's political machine and condemned Progressive leader Hiram Johnson as a demagogue, as did many other newspapers in the state. Other journalists, however, helped found the Lincoln-Roosevelt League and led the campaign for reform.

After reform triumphed over the machine, newspapers continued to play a crucial role in California politics. In Los Angeles, San Francisco, Oakland, San Jose, and San Diego, Republican publishers used the power of the press—on editorial and news pages—to promote their favorite candidates and causes. They were instrumental in keeping Republicans in office long after the Democrats gained a majority of registered voters.

A PROFESSIONAL PRESS Change came in the 1970s, when most of California's family-owned newspapers became part of corporate chains. The new managers brought in more professional editors and reporters. News coverage became more objective, and opinion was more consistently confined to the editorial pages, which became distinctly less conservative.

Such editorials, expressing the opinion of the publisher or, more commonly, an editorial board made up of journalists, have been extremely influential in California politics. Voters often follow editorial recommendations on candidates and issues for lack of alternative sources of advice, especially on lower-profile races and ballot measures. For example, by winning the editorial endorsements of newspapers throughout the state, Larry Aceves, a little-known former school superintendent, beat two prominent legislators to come in first in the 2010 primary election for superintendent of public instruction. Despite these endorsements, however, he was defeated in the November election. Nevertheless, today's editorial pages are less influential than they once were as the number of newspapers and their circulation have declined.

THE DECLINE OF PAPER POLITICS At one time, there were hundreds of newspapers in California, with several competing with one another in most large cities. Today, less than a hundred survive, and most cities have just one. But that's not the only change. As a result of the loss of readers and advertisers to other media, the surviving newspapers have shrunk in both news coverage and staffing. The *Los Angeles Times,* for example, employed more than 1,300 journalists in 1998 but was down to 600 by 2009.[19] As a consequence of these changes, newspaper coverage of California politics is less extensive than it once was. Newspapers now share reporters or rely on the Associated Press or the *Los Angeles Times,* which still maintains the largest and most respected Sacramento bureau. Other media, including television and the Internet, have become more important to many people.

Television Politics

Public opinion surveys report that 47 percent of Californians say they get their news and information about state politics from television, with 15 percent citing newspapers, 12 percent radio, and 17 percent the Internet.[20] But television coverage of California politics leaves a lot to be desired.

Before Arnold Schwarzenegger was elected governor, not one of California's television stations, other

Should Actors Become Politicians?

California is famous around the world for its entertainment industries—movies and television are among California's most important businesses. Top Hollywood actors and actresses are among the most famous people on the planet. A few of these individuals have made the transition from acting to politics. Governor Arnold Schwarzenegger is perhaps the most famous actor to hold office. Ronald Reagan, who began his career as an actor, was governor of California from 1967 to 1975, and he went on to become president of the United States (1981–1989). George Murphy, like Reagan a former head of the Screen Actors' Guild, represented California in the U.S. Senate from 1965 to 1971. Alan Autry, well known from the television series *In the Heat of the Night,* was mayor of Fresno from 2003 to 2009. Musician and entertainer Sonny Bono represented California in the U.S. House from 1995 until his death in a skiing accident in 1998.

It's of some interest that all of these people were Republicans. On the Democratic side, Sheila Kuehl, who starred in the television show *The Many Loves of Dobie Gillis* under the name Sheila James, was an effective member of the state legislature from 1994 to 2008. Rob Reiner, famous from the show *All in the Family,* is an effective campaigner for children's rights and other causes, although he has not actually run for office.

Should a career in acting or entertainment be a legitimate qualification for political office, or should voters reject candidates with such experience? Many people have raised their voices on either side of this issue.

Actors Are Ill-Suited for Public Service

Those who believe that entertainers should not run for public office admit that celebrity status gives such candidates an advantage when seeking election. In fact, the advantage that a celebrity may possess, in name recognition and popularity, is often cited as a reason why such persons should not run. Actors have not gained their fame by doing anything that is relevant to public service. True, they may be good speakers and know how to present themselves. But there is nothing in a Hollywood career that provides expertise in addressing the issues, making laws, or administering a unit of government. Furthermore, anyone with enough fame to leverage it into a political career probably lives in a bubble of yes-men, security staff, and private aircraft. How can such celebrities understand the problems of ordinary voters?

Actors Can Be as Effective in Politics as Anyone Else

Those who would defend actor-politicians observe that only a small number of entertainers have actually taken the plunge. Celebrities such as Angelina Jolie and George Clooney are far more likely to serve as spokespersons for humanitarian causes than as candidates for office. Indeed, it can be argued that given the size and importance of California's entertainment industry, the number of celebrities entering electoral politics has been small. Those who have made the transition usually have had political experience in addition to their entertainment careers. Heading the Screen Actors' Guild—a substantial institution—provided Ronald Reagan and George Murphy with real administrative experience. Governor Schwarzenegger's political résumé is thinner than most; he first made his mark as an advocate for after school programs. Schwarzenegger contemplated running for governor for years, however, and he has long been a close student of the state's politics.

Looking beyond California, Tennessee's Fred Thompson, former U.S. Senator and Republican presidential candidate, was an attorney for many years before he became an actor. Republican Fred Grandy of Iowa, a star of *The Love Boat* who served in the U.S. House, was a congressional staffer before he became an actor. Republicans have argued that Democrat Al Franken, now U.S. senator from Minnesota, was a totally unserious candidate. Franken, however, was always a "policy wonk" in addition to a comedian. His books, such as *Lies and the Lying Liars Who Tell Them: A Fair and Balanced Look at the Right,* may have infuriated conservatives, but they are completely political in content. Franken also spent ten years visiting the troops overseas through the United Service Organizations (USO).

For Critical Analysis ***The politics of many Hollywood celebrities are quite left-wing. Except for Sheila Kuehl and Al Franken, however, every actor elected to office that we have just mentioned was a Republican. Why might successful actor-politicians be more likely to be members of that party?***

than those based in Sacramento, operated a news bureau in the state capital. Television news editors avoided state political coverage because they believed that viewers wanted big national stories or local features. The minimal television coverage of state politics—a tiny percentage of newscast time, according to various studies—was mainly drawn from newspaper articles, wire service stories, or events staged by politicians, who struggled to gain any coverage at all. Even candidates for governor had a hard time making local news broadcasts, and most television stations declined to broadcast live candidate debates out of fear of low ratings. Cynics pointed out that if television doesn't provide news coverage, candidates are forced to buy advertising time—on television. As a consequence, candidate ads take up more time than news coverage of campaigns during the nightly news on California television stations—and provide a major source of revenue for the stations.

Nevertheless, television coverage of state politics has improved somewhat in the twenty-first century. A movie star governor and his carefully staged media events brought the cameras back to Sacramento. Coverage also increased with the advent of transmission by satellite vans, which made it easier for television stations to send reporters to cover breaking news and major events "live from the Capitol!" without the necessity of investing in permanent Sacramento bureaus. Ongoing conflict between the Republican governor and Democratic majorities in the legislature added drama, as did the state's persistent budget crisis.

Californians who prefer their politics raw—without reporters or commentary—can watch their government in action on the California Channel, now available on 114 cable systems.

New Media

The traditional print and broadcast media still dominate, but in recent years more alternative sources of news and information have become available to Californians. Nearly seven hundred ethnic broadcasting outlets and publications now serve Californians in Spanish, Vietnamese, Mandarin, and many other languages.[21] Latino newspapers and television and radio stations reach major audiences, especially in Southern California. Many of these ethnic media are virtually obsessed with politics as their communities generate candidates or factional conflict.

Talk radio has also become a political fixture, especially in a state where people spend so much time in their cars. Fifty percent of Californians say they listen to opinion-filled radio shows "regularly" or "sometimes."[22] Politics is a hot topic on talk radio, which played a crucial role in stirring up the recall of Governor Gray Davis in 2003.

But the medium with the most spectacular recent impact on politics is the Internet. Access to news and information on the Internet has given audiences exponentially more information and sources and diverted audiences and advertisers from more traditional media, especially newspapers. Thousands of Web sites focus on state or local politics and give citizens direct access to their governments. Blogs by political junkies offer news and opinion and often break stories. Listservs and social networking keep members of traditional interest groups in touch with one another and create whole new communities. Seventy-five percent of Californians use a computer at home, work, or school, and 70 percent regularly use the Internet; 55 percent report that they get news on the Internet. Latinos, elders, and

Jerry Brown, right, gestures towards his opponent Meg Whitman, left, during the second of three televised debates leading up to the 2010 gubernatorial election.

AP PHOTO/*THE FRESNO BEE*, ERIC PAUL ZAMORA

lower-income residents are less likely to have access to computers or use the Internet, however, so access is not equally distributed.[23]

Elections, Campaigns, and the Media

The influence of money and the media is greater in California politics than in most other states. Politicians must organize their own campaigns, raise vast sums of money, and then take their cases to the people via direct mail and television. Such campaigns are inevitably personality oriented, with substantive issues taking a back seat to puff pieces or attacks on opponents. The media provide a check of sorts, but declining coverage limits its impact.

All of this takes us back to the issue of declining voter turnout. The recall election of 2003 and the presidential election of 2008 increased turnout, but only momentarily. Turnout in succeeding elections has been much lower. Could stronger parties, more news coverage, and public-financed, issue-oriented campaigns revive voter participation? Maybe, but campaign consultants and the media say they are already giving the public what it wants.

CALIFORNIA AT ODDS *Elections, Campaigns, and the Media*

California's large size affects the nature of campaigning in the state. So does the lengthy ballot, containing as it does so many ballot proposals. Californians are at odds over a variety of issues that relate to election procedures, campaigns and campaign contributions, and the role of the media. Some of these questions include:

- Should California seek to adopt measures that would enhance voter turnout—or are such steps largely a waste of effort?
- Should the political parties play a greater role in locating and encouraging potential candidates for office—or do we have more than enough "self-starters" already?
- Would some form of public financing of elections be a useful way of eliminating the potential for corruption inherent in campaign contributions—or would such financing be an unconscionable raid on taxpayer dollars?
- Are the financial difficulties of many of the state's leading newspapers a threat to the public's ability to learn about politics—or will other forms of journalism pick up the slack?
- Does the Internet play a positive role by giving citizens greater access to politics and government—or does it harm political discourse by allowing liberals and conservatives to live in ideologically pure "bubbles," insulated from dissenting voices?

Take Action

The most fundamental way that you can take action is to vote, and you cannot vote in California if you are not registered. Beyond making sure that you yourself are registered, you can help register your fellow students. Every year, large number of new students arrive on campus, even as others graduate or move on in other ways. For college students, registration is therefore an ongoing issue. In the run-up to major elections, a variety of student organizations regularly canvas the student body on their campuses to promote registration. In some parts of the country, local officials have attempted to dissuade students from registering at their campus addresses, arguing that they should register instead at their parents' addresses. These local officials are providing incorrect information. College students have an established right to vote at their campus addresses. Indeed, the State of California's Donahoe Higher Education Act includes a requirement that institutions of higher education make a "good faith effort" to make mail voter registration forms available to all enrolled students. Campus organizations that have participated in voter registration drives include the California Student Public Interest Group, or CALPIRG, which has branches at many schools.

POLITICS ON THE WEB

- To learn more about elections, political reform, and campaign finance in California, visit the California Secretary of State's website at **www.sos.ca.gov**.
- The California Voter Foundation provides a wealth of voter resources, the latest information on elections, and reliable campaign finance disclosure data at **www.calvoter.org**. This Web site also provides a comprehensive listing of news outlets by region at **www.calvoter.org/voter/politics/camedia.html**.
- Visit the National Institute on Money in State Politics for information on the influence of campaign money on state-level elections and public policy. Go to **www.followthemoney.org** and type in California in the search box to access their campaign-finance database.
- The League of Women Voters, a nonpartisan political organization open to men and women, provides a model of participation in the democratic process at local, regional, state and federal levels. To learn more about the California state league, go to **www.ca.lwv.org**.
- Smart Voter, funded by the League of Women Voters of California, offers extensive background information on candidates in participating counties as well as information on state and local ballot measures. To research candidates and ballot measures prior to an election, visit **www.smartvoter.org**.
- The California Clean Money Campaign's mission is to build statewide support for public funding of election campaigns. To learn more, visit **www.CAclean.org**.
- Visit any of these blogs for political news, analysis, and commentary: **www.calbuzz.com**; **www.flashreport.org; www.calitics.com**; or **www.californiarepublic.org**.
- Visit the online version of *Capitol Weekly,* a newspaper of California government and politics published each Thursday in Sacramento at **www.capitolweekly.net**.
- The *California Report,* a statewide radio news program, provides daily coverage of issues, trends, and public policy decisions affecting California. To listen to the latest news, visit **www.californiareport.org**.

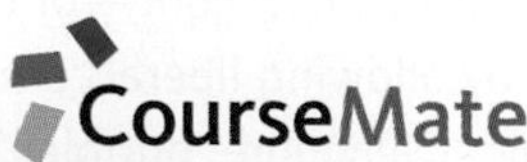

Access CourseMate to review and expand on this chapter through quizzes, flashcards, learning objectives, interactive timelines, a crossword puzzle, audio summaries, video, critical-thinking activities, simulations, and more.

GOVT 20

California Interest Groups

LEARNING OBJECTIVES

LO1 Discuss how the power of interest groups has evolved in California.

LO2 Describe the various types of interest groups.

LO3 Explain the techniques used by interest groups and who they target.

LO4 Summarize how interest groups are regulated.

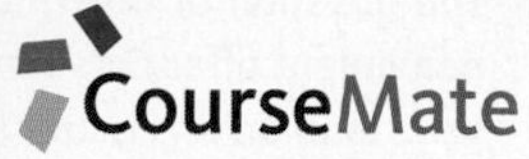

CALIFORNIA AT ODDS

Are California's Prison Guards Mightier than the State Government?

Over the years, the California Correctional Peace Officer's Association (CCPOA) has gained a reputation as perhaps the most potent interest group in the state. CCPOA's influence grew along with California's prison system. In 1980, California had 22,500 prisoners. By 2009, the number of inmates had grown to 154,897. For 25 years, California built an average of one new prison a year. The state spends more than 10 percent of its budget on prisons, a larger share than any other state except Michigan.

In 1980, the average salary of California prison guards was $14,400 a year. By 2008, the average was $63,230. Nationally, the average wage for a prison guard was $41,340. These figures do not include overtime, which increases the pay of California guards by an average of 15 percent. As a result, a substantial number of guards make well over $100,000 annually. Not surprisingly, 130,000 people apply to become California prison guards every year.

It's not just high wages that earned CCPOA its reputation, however. The union also has had enormous success in persuading legislators and the public to increase the number of prison inmates, thus raising the demand for guards. A key victory was the 1994 "Three Strikes" initiative, Proposition 184. This measure imposed a life sentence for third felony convictions, even if the convictions were for relatively minor offenses such as shoplifting.

The Continuing Power of the Prison Guards

CCPOA's influence is based in large part on the union's willingness to raise and spend money. CCPOA donates considerably larger campaign contributions than the California Teachers Association, despite being much smaller. Only the California Medical Association outspends CCPOA. The union's power has been enhanced because no important interests oppose locking up more criminals. Indeed, increased rates of incarceration have been very popular among the voters. For example, in 2008 CCPOA funneled $1.8 million into a campaign to derail Proposition 5, which would have provided drug treatment and rehabilitation programs for many nonviolent drug off enders currently sent to prison. The proposition failed by 60 to 40 percent.

Like other state employees, the prison guards have experienced furloughs and temporary pay cuts as a result of California's budget crisis. CCPOA sued the state over the furloughs, but in October 2010 the California Supreme Court ruled that the legislature had tacitly approved the furloughs in legislation passed in February 2009.

CCPOA's Power May Have Reached Its Limits

Those who argue that CCPOA's power has reached its limits can begin with one basic observation: the union does not have a collective bargaining agreement with the state and has not had one since July 2006. Just how powerful is a union that can't win a contract?

To be sure, in September 2009 CCPOA persuaded Democrats in the state assembly to water down the governor's request for a billion dollars in proposed cuts to the state prison system. The operative words here, however, are "water down." In the old days, the legislature never would have considered any cuts at all. CCPOA, a once-irresistible force, may have met two immovable objects: the state's budget crisis and Governor Schwarzenegger.

CCPOA's power grew in an era when it had no important enemies. It is now at risk of finding that it has no important friends. Liberals may rebel against the union's concept of locking up an ever-larger share of the state's population. Conservatives may view the guards as greedy public employees ripping off the taxpayer.

WHERE DO YOU STAND?

1. **CCPOA's slogan is that its members walk "the toughest beat in the state." Actually, a Los Angeles cop is ten times as likely to be killed in the line of duty as a prison guard. Still, it cannot be doubted that work as a corrections officer is highly unpleasant and stressful. What weight should such factors be given when determining the guards' wages?**
2. **The question of how much prison time is appropriate for nonviolent offenders remains a controversial one. How do you stand on this issue? Explain your position.**

EXPLORE THIS ISSUE ONLINE

- **In exploring this topic, a trip to CCPOA's own Web site is an obvious step. See it at www.ccpoa.org.**
- **For a highly critical look at the California prison system and CCPOA, consult the Web site of Third World Traveler, which has posted a series of excerpts from The Celling of America: An Inside Look at the US Prison Industry.[1] See the excerpts at www.thirdworldtraveler.com/Prison_System/Celling_America.html.**

Introduction

Many people belong to one or more **interest groups**—organizations formed to protect and promote the shared political objectives of their members. Interest groups range from labor unions, ethnic organizations, and business associations to student unions, environmental entities, and automobile clubs. Whatever their differences, interest groups share the same goal of seeing their visions and values incorporated into the actions of public policymakers.

In California, interest groups have prospered and proliferated, and in some cases they have become more important than political parties. That's because weak political parties and the state's election system provide a fertile political environment for organized groups to exercise influence. Weak political parties make candidates dependent on groups for financing, while direct democracy often enables groups to take their issues directly to the voters, circumventing the legislature and other elected policymakers in the process.

Interest groups come in all shapes and sizes. More people pay dues to the California Teachers Association (CTA) or the California Chamber of Commerce, for example, than contribute to the state Republican or Democratic parties. All groups are not equal, however; depending on resources and issues, some are far more successful than others. (We examined one of California's most successful interest groups in the chapter-opening *California at Odds* feature.) Just because groups are large does not automatically mean they are the most successful in having their way.

Besides exercising their influence through campaign contributions and use of direct democracy, interest groups also influence legislators in the lobbies beneath the capitol dome. Some observers view these efforts as assisting the legislative process; others see them as manipulating that process.

LO1 The Evolution of Group Power in California

The astonishing length of California's constitution attests to the historical clout of the state's interest groups. In other states, groups gain advantages such as tax exemptions through acts of the legislature, which can be changed at any time. In California, such protections are often written into the constitution, making alteration difficult because constitutional amendments require the approval of the electorate. Among California's constitutionally favored interests are dozens of crops (protecting organized agriculture), trees less than forty years old (protecting the timber industry), and ships for passengers or freight (protecting the shipping industry). These "safeguards" were not responses to public demands. Instead, interest groups pushed them through for their own benefit either at the time the California Constitution was written or in subsequent elections.

Different interests have benefited throughout California's colorful history. In the early days, the mining industry and ranchers dominated the state's public policy environment. From about 1870 to 1910, the Southern Pacific Railroad monopolized California's economy and politics, with incredible control over both of California's major political parties.[1] Land development, shipping, and horse racing interests next dominated the political landscape through the mid-twentieth century, followed by the automobile and defense industries. Agricultural interests have remained strong through all these periods.

These days, banking and service businesses tower over manufacturing, while high-tech industries have surpassed defense and aerospace. Insurance companies, teachers' associations, physicians' and attorneys' groups, and other vocation-related associations also routinely lobby state government. Agribusiness also remains influential, particularly with respect to water policy and land use. Organized labor and business interests—almost always at odds—continue to battle for preeminence with the legislature and voters. They have been joined by the California Nations Indian Gaming Association, the largest contributor to the 2003 recall campaign and the largest contributor to a series of ballot propositions in 2008 that ratified gaming agreements between the tribes and the state. Single-issue groups, such as Gun Owners of California and Mothers Against Drunk Driving (MADD), have entered the fray, along with evangelical, pro-choice, right-to-life, minority, feminist, and gay and lesbian groups. Public interest groups, such as the League of Women Voters, Common Cause, and The Utility Reform Network (TURN), are also part of the ever-growing interest group mix. Pressured by these many groups and their financial contributions, California politicians often find themselves responding to the demands of interest groups rather than governing them.

interest group An organized group of individuals sharing common political objectives who actively attempt to influence policymakers.

LO2 *The Groups*

Interest groups vary in size, resources, and goals. At one extreme, groups that pursue narrow and targeted economic benefits tend to have relatively small memberships but a great amount of financial resources. At the other end of the spectrum public interest groups often have large memberships but little money. A few, such as the Consumer Attorneys of California (CAC), whose membership consists of 3,000 trial lawyers, have the dual advantage of being both large and well funded. Others, such as the Consumers for Auto Reliability and Safety (CARS), operate on a shoestring.

Economic Groups

Economic groups that seek various financial gains or hope to prevent losses dominate the state's interest group environment. Every major corporation in the state, from Southern California Edison to the California Northern Railroad, is represented in Sacramento either by its own lobbyists or by lobbying firms hired to present the corporation's cases to policymakers. Often, individual corporations or businesses with similar goals form broad-based associations to further their general objectives. These umbrella organizations include the California Manufacturers and Technology Association, the California Business Alliance (for small enterprises), the California Bankers Association, and the California Council for Environmental and Economic Balance (for utilities and oil companies). The California Chamber of Commerce alone boasts 16,000 member companies that employ one-fourth of the private sector workforce in California. One measure promoted by economic interests was Proposition 23 in 2010, which would have frozen California's attempt to curb greenhouse gases. We discuss that ballot proposal in the *California Faces a Troubled Economy* feature on the following page.

Agribusiness is particularly active, because farming depends on the government on issues such as water availability and the regulation of pesticides. The giant farming operations maintain their own lobbyists, but various producer groups also form associations. Most of the state's winemakers, for example, are represented by the 850-member Wine Institute. The California Cotton Ginners Association has only 87 members, yet produces 750 million bales of cotton annually. Broader organizations, such as the California Farm Bureau Federation, one of the state's most powerful lobby groups, speak for agribusiness in general by representing 85,000 members with crops in excess of $36 billion in value.

Recently, high-tech industries have asserted their interests on issues ranging from Internet taxation and H-1B visas for foreign workers to transportation and public education. Organizations such as TechNet, the Silicon Valley Leadership Group, and the American Electronics Association have lobbied for regulatory changes, tax relief, research and development tax credits, "green" incentives in new areas such as solar energy, and other changes. The tech-heavy Silicon Valley Leadership Group alone represents 305 companies that provide $1.1 trillion worth of services and products in the global economy, exceeding the entire gross domestic product of Indonesia.[2]

Then-California governor Arnold Schwarzenegger looks at California's Proposition 14, held by Carl Guardino, CEO of the Silicon Valley Leadership Group. Endorsed by Schwarzenegger and adopted in June 2010, the initiative created the new Top Two Candidates primary system.

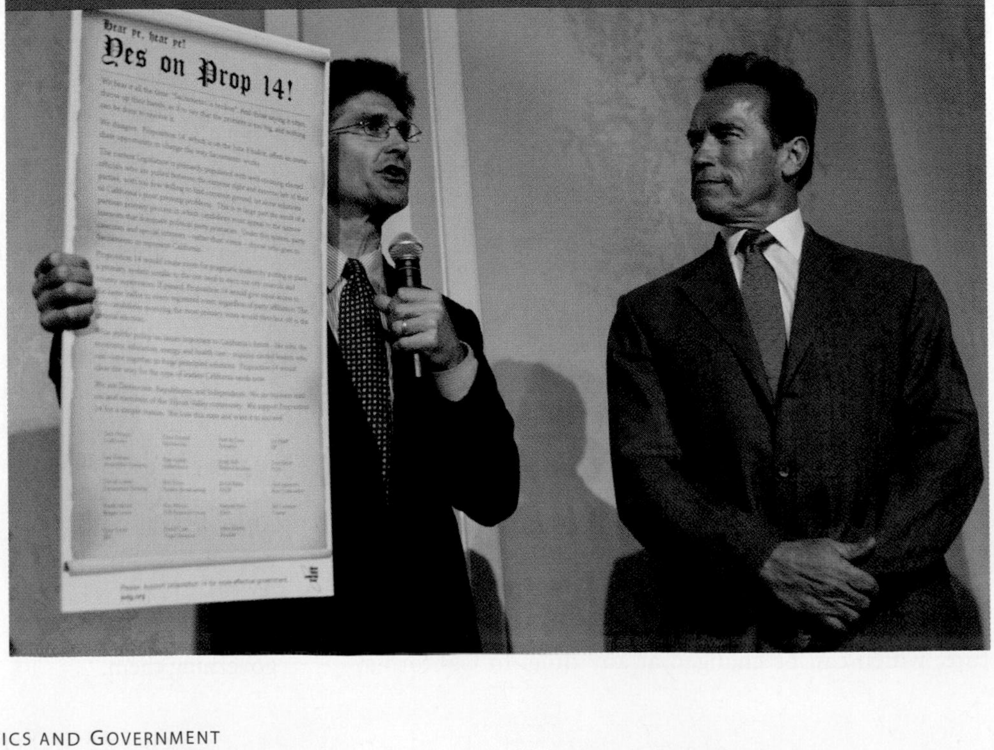

AP PHOTO/PAUL SAKUMA

economic groups Interest groups with sizable financial stakes in the political process who seek to influence legislators and other public policymakers.

CALIFORNIA FACES A
TROUBLED ECONOMY

The Attempt to Roll Back Greenhouse Gas Legislation

Some California interest groups are stronger than others. Typically, business interest groups are among the most effective. Groups are also more successful when they have few opponents, and they often fail when they try to "go it alone." In 2010, for example, the California Teachers Association attempted to repeal a series of state tax breaks worth in excess of $1 billion per year through Proposition 24. The teachers' union argued that California could not afford to sacrifice such revenue when economic hard times had severely unbalanced the state budget. A united front by the business community (and most California newspapers) sank the measure, which in any event was incompatible with the anti-tax spirit of the California electorate. Another business-backed measure, however—Proposition 23—failed dramatically.

Proposition 23

Proposition 23 sought to suspend the Global Warming Solutions Act of 2006, under which California will attempt to lower its greenhouse gas emissions to 1990 levels by 2020. Proposition 23 would have frozen the 2006 act until California's unemployment rate dropped to 5.5 percent for four consecutive quarters. Proponents of the proposition argued that attempts to lower greenhouse gas emissions would destroy thousands of jobs. Like Proposition 24, Proposition 23 was the work of a limited group of interests—independent oil refining companies such as Valero Energy Corporation and Tesoro Corporation, both of which have their headquarters in Texas. Major California energy companies such as Chevron kept away from the initiative. Pacific Gas & Electric (PG&E) actually donated $500,000 to its opponents.

The Environmental Steamroller

At first, Proposition 23 appeared to have a chance. The jobs argument was effective in a year in which the state unemployment rate exceeded 12 percent. Opponents of the measure, however, outspent its supporters three to one. Six individuals or families each donated $1 million or more to defeat it. (One was James Cameron, director of *Avatar*.) Five environmental groups each contributed $1 million or more. The funds purchased television ads claiming that Proposition 23, not the Global Warming Solutions Act, was the real job-killer. The *Los Angeles Times* reported that 3,200 volunteers made 2.8 million phone calls to voters, sent out 3.4 million pieces of mail, made 379,676 on-campus contacts with college students, and operated a sophisticated computerized outreach program that identified and contacted 481,000 voters, and showered voters with 900,000 get-out-the vote phone calls and text messages in the last three days. The opposition campaign was fueled in part by economic interests. California has begun to develop a significant "green economy" based on renewable energy technologies and energy conservation solutions. Wealthy venture capitalists have made large investments in green technology.

Another kind of self-interest was also at work, however. California voters may dislike taxes, but it is easy to persuade them of the benefits of cleaner air. Smog in greater Los Angeles is not what it was years ago, but the region still frequently tops the national charts for air pollution. Curbing CO_2 won't do anything to relieve smog. Still, for many voters, the desirability of curbing greenhouse gas emissions is aligned with their personal experiences.

You Be the Judge **Other than air pollution, what factors might make California citizens more environmentally conscious than the average American?**

Professional Associations and Unions

Professional associations such as the California Medical Association (CMA), the California Association of Realtors (CAR), and the Consumer Attorneys of California (CAOC) are among the state's most active groups, and they are regularly among the largest campaign contributors. Other professionals, such as chiropractors, dentists, and general contractors, also maintain active associations. Because all these professionals serve the public, many promote their concerns as broader than self-interest. Their credibility is further enhanced by expertise in their respective fields and by memberships consisting of affluent, respected individuals.

Teachers' associations and other public employee organizations fall somewhere between business associations and labor unions. Their members view themselves as professionals but in recent years have increasingly resorted to traditional labor union tactics, among them collective bargaining, strikes, and political campaign donations. Other public workers, including the highway patrol and state university professors, have their own organizations. The California State Employees Association (CSEA) is the giant among these, with more than 141,000 members and the ability to raise large campaign war chests for candidates and election issues.

Unions have done reasonably well in California, which ranks sixth among the fifty states in per capita union membership. Unions here represent 18 percent of the workforce, compared with 12 percent nationwide. Traditional labor unions represent nurses, machinists, carpenters, public utility employees, and dozens of other occupations. In 2002 unions worked to persuade the legislature to enact the nation's first paid family leave program, allowing workers to take leave from their jobs for up to six weeks at 55 percent of their salary or a maximum of $728 per week. In 2004 California became the first state in the nation to provide paid paternity leave. The new laws drew the wrath of the California Chamber of Commerce, which predicted that they would create hardship for businesses. Yet, only a fraction of those eligible to participate actually do so.[3]

Perhaps the most controversial union in state politics is the California Correctional Peace Officers Association (CCPOA), which contributed more than $600,000 to the reelection campaign of Governor Gray Davis in 2002, just before the governor signed a three-year pay increase of 35 percent in the midst of a huge state budget deficit. The agreement drew heated criticism of the union and Davis, adding fuel to the recall accusation that Davis was little more than a tool of major contributors.[4] In 2004 Governor Arnold Schwarzenegger renegotiated the contract and won a slight modification in the pay raises, achieving only about one-third of the targeted savings. Still, the CCPOA is adept at looking out for its own interests. In 2008 the union funneled $1.8 million into a campaign to derail Proposition 5, which would have provided drug treatment and rehabilitation programs for many nonviolent drug offenders who otherwise would be sent to prison. The proposition failed, with 60 percent of the elecotrate voting against the measure.

ROBYN BECK/AFP/GETTY IMAGES

Los Angeles teachers' union (UTLA) president A. J. Duffy is arrested in Los Angeles during a protest against proposed budget cuts that would increase class sizes.

demographic groups
Interest groups based on race, ethnicity, gender, or age; usually concerned with overcoming discrimination.

Demographic Groups

Groups that depend more on membership numbers than on money can be described as **demographic groups.** Based on characteristics that distinguish their members from other segments of the population, such as their ethnicity, gender, or age, such groups usually have an interest in overcoming discrimination. Most racial and ethnic organizations fall into this category.

Virtually all of California's minorities have organizations that seek to be their voice. One of the earliest of these was the Colored Convention, which fought for the rights of African Americans in California in the nineteenth century. Today, several such groups advocate for African Americans, Asian Americans, and Native Americans. The United Farm Workers (UFW), GI Forum, Mexican American Legal Defense Fund (MALDEF), and Mexican American Political Association (MAPA) represent Latinos.

The National Organization for Women (NOW), EMILY's List (Early Money Is Like Yeast), and National Women's Political Caucus (NWPC) actively support women candidates and feminist causes. Unlike some of the other statewide organizations, these groups are better organized at the local level than at the state level, however.

Several organizations have become prominent in the struggle for equal rights by lesbians and gay men. Gay rights groups have increased in numbers and voice in recent years, particularly over the issue of same-sex marriage. Equality California, the largest, has worked to elect gay and lesbian legislators, obtain passage of equal rights legislation, and pursue gay marriage through both the courts and the legislative process. These organizations have been opposed by groups like Campaign for California Families, which led the way to declare marriage as an act between a man and a woman in 2000 through **Proposition 22, the California in Defense of Marriage Act.** Californians have been battling over the issue ever since.

Age groups play a smaller part in state politics. California has an aging population heavily dependent on public services, however, so organizations such as AARP (formerly the American Association of Retired Persons), with no fewer than 3.3 million members in California, have achieved a higher profile in state politics, particularly on health-care issues.

Single-Issue Groups

The groups discussed so far tend to have broad bases and deal with a wide range of issues. Another type of interest group operates with a broad base of support for the resolution of narrow issues. **Single-issue groups** push for a specific question to be decided on specific terms. They support only candidates who agree with their particular position on an issue. The California Abortion Rights Action League (CARAL), for example, endorses only candidates who support a woman's right to choose (pro-choice), whereas antiabortion (or pro-life) groups such as the ProLife Council work only for candidates on the opposite side. Likewise, the Howard Jarvis Taxpayers Association evaluates candidates and ballot propositions solely in terms of whether they meet the association's objective of no unnecessary taxes and no wasteful government spending. Each of these groups exercises power on occasion, but their reluctance to compromise limits their effectiveness in the give-and-take of state politics.

Proposition 22, the California Defense of Marriage Act (2000) A ballot initiative that declared marriage an act between a man and a woman.

single-issue groups Organized groups with narrow policy objectives; not oriented toward compromise.

public interest groups Organizations that purport to represent the general good rather than private interests.

A single-interest group's potential ability to deliver a solid bloc of voters on a controversial issue can affect the outcome of a close election and thus enhance its clout, at least on a temporary basis. That's what happened in 1982, when National Rifle Association (NRA) opposition to a proposed gun control initiative brought out sympathizers in droves and led to the defeat of antigun Democratic gubernatorial candidate Tom Bradley, who had been expected to win. An exception occurred in 2008, when antigay groups qualified and campaigned heavily for Proposition 8, a proposed constitutional amendment designed to overturn a state supreme court decision that had legalized same-sex marriage.[5] Advocates urged voters to use presidential candidate positions on the proposition as a guide to their votes. Barack Obama opposed the measure, yet he won California handily as the initiative squeaked by.

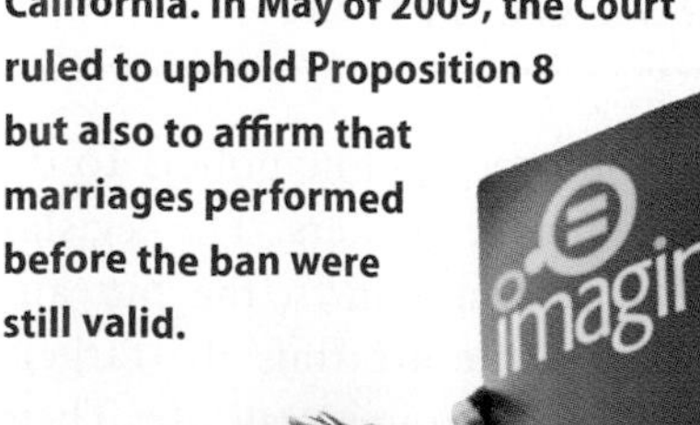

On June 28, 2008, the California Supreme Court ruling that provides a constitutional right to same-sex marriages went into effect. In November 2008, voters overturned that ruling with Proposition 8, which bans gay marriage in California. In May of 2009, the Court ruled to uphold Proposition 8 but also to affirm that marriages performed before the ban were still valid.

MAX WHITTAKER/GETTY IMAGES

Public Interest Groups

Although virtually all organized interest groups claim to speak for the broader public interest, some groups clearly seek no private gain and thus more correctly can claim to be **public interest groups.** These groups are distinguished from other organizations by the fact that they pursue goals to benefit society, not just their members.

Some public interest groups, such as California OneCare, have been instrumental in the fight f or health-care reform. Part of that organization's decade-long struggle was realized when Congress passed the Patient Protection and Affordable Care Act in 2010. Others, such as The Utility Reform Network (TURN), monitor rate requests by the utilities before the state Public Utilities Commission. In 2010 TURN led a coalition of consumer groups against PG&E–sponsored Proposition 16—a proposal that would have made it very difficult for municipalities to purchase renewable power.

Environmental organizations such as the Sierra Club and Friends of the Earth have been very active in California on issues such as water management, offshore oil drilling, air pollution, transportation, and pesticide use. Another important concern of these groups is land use, both for private development in sensitive areas and for public lands, which make up half the state. Surveys have reported that one in nine Californians claims membership in an environmental group.[6] The Sierra Club alone has more than 1.3 million members.

Other public interest groups, such as California Public Interest Research Group (CALPIRG), Common Cause, and the League of Women Voters, focus on governmental reform and voter participation. These groups have been involved in several efforts to reform campaign finance in California. Church groups can be seen as a special kind of public interest group, and we take a look at them in the *Join the Debate* feature on the following page.

A final type of public interest group isn't really a group at all: local governments. Cities, school districts, special districts, and counties all lobby the state government—on whose funds they depend heavily—through the League of California Cities, the California School Boards Association (CSBA), and the California State Association of Counties (CSAC). Dozens of cities and counties employ their own lobbyists in Sacramento, as do other governmental agencies. One study found that local governments collectively spend more on lobbying than organized labor, oil companies, or manufacturing.[7] They also endorse ballot measures that affect their interests and, on rare occasions, even sponsor initiatives. Unlike other groups, cities and counties cannot make campaign contributions or organize their constituents, but they can make themselves heard. In 2010, local governments banded together to promote **Proposition 22, the Local Taxpayers, Public Safety and Transportation Act,** an initiative to keep the state government from borrowing or raiding funds that voters have dedicated to public safety.

Proposition 22, the Local Taxpayers, Public Safety and Transportation Act (2010) An initiative that keeps the state government from taking local government funds dedicated by the voters for public safety.

lobbying Interest group efforts to influence political decision makers, often through paid professionals (lobbyists).

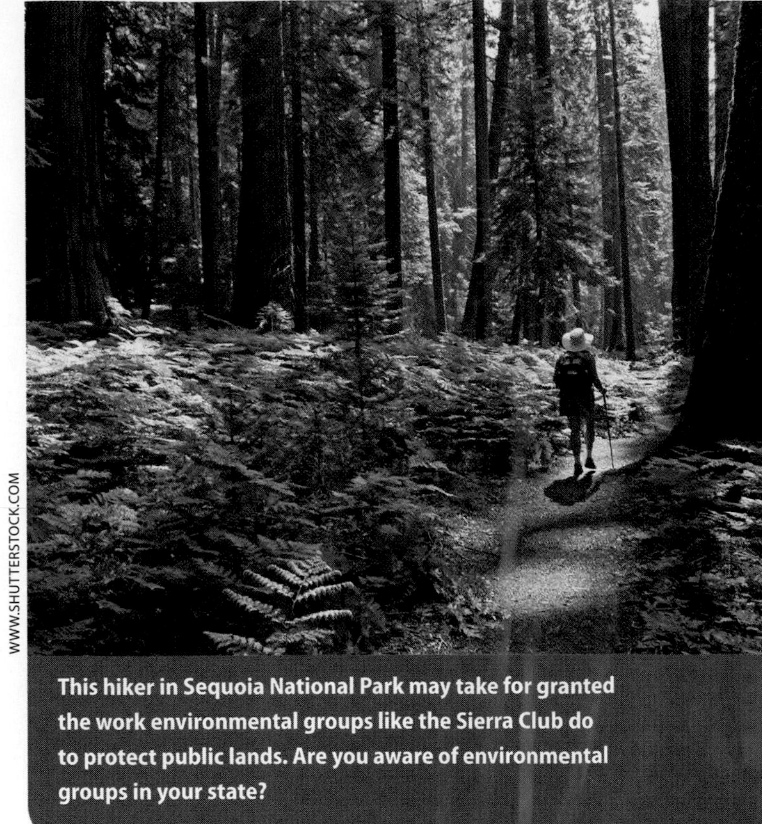
WWW.SHUTTERSTOCK.COM

This hiker in Sequoia National Park may take for granted the work environmental groups like the Sierra Club do to protect public lands. Are you aware of environmental groups in your state?

LO3 *Techniques and Targets: Interest Groups at Work*

Interest groups seek to influence public policy. To do this, they must persuade policymakers. The legislature, the executive branch, the courts, the bureaucracy, and sometimes the people are thus the targets of the various techniques these groups may use. Their primary weapons include lobbying, campaign support, litigation, and direct democracy.

Lobbying

The term **lobbying** refers to the activity that once went on in the lobbies adjacent to the legislative chambers. Advocates for various causes or issues would buttonhole legislators on their way in or out of the legislature

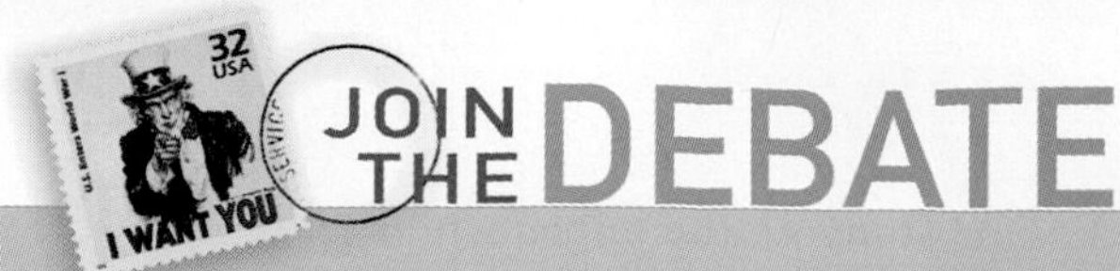

Should Churches Function as Interest Groups?

At the November 2008 general elections, California voters narrowly approved Proposition 8, which amended the state constitution to ban marriages by same-sex couples. A notable feature of the campaign for a "yes" vote was the heavy involvement of church-related groups, particularly those representing the Church of Jesus Christ of Latter Day Saints (LDS, or the Mormons) and the Roman Catholic Church. In June 2008, LDS leaders commanded Mormons "to do all you can" for Proposition 8. LDS leaders throughout California read the church's statement to Mormon congregations, which have more than 750,000 members. LDS volunteers went door-to-door on behalf of Proposition 8. Phone banks to contact California voters were organized not only in California but in other states as well. Contributions to the cause by individual Mormons exceeded $9 million. Conservative Catholics, including the Knights of Columbus, kicked in another $1 million, and other conservative religious organizations, such as James Dobson's Focus on the Family, were generous as well. Some people believe that it is improper for religious organizations to participate in politics in these ways. Others find such involvement perfectly acceptable.

Churches Should Stay Out of Politics, and That Includes Initiatives

Those who oppose participation by church-affiliated groups in initiative campaigns, lobbying, and other political activities often contend that such participation threatens the separation of church and state. Most Americans, especially in California and other western states, do not want churches dominating the political sphere. Another consideration is that churches are tax-exempt organizations. This gives them an unfair advantage relative to other groups. Tax exemption is the reason why churches are not allowed to directly endorse candidates for elective office. Why, then, should they be allowed to participate in initiatives and other ballot proposals, which in California, at least, can be more important than who gets elected to a particular assembly seat? Many people have very passionate opinions on political matters. Religion brings its own passions, and we do not need to inject them into the political arena.

Churches Should Have the Same Rights to Lobby and Campaign as Anyone Else

In California, as in other states, most people are religious. It therefore makes no sense to attempt to bar religious beliefs from the public arena. True, there should be limits on the practices of tax-exempt organizations, religious or otherwise, but religiously motivated individuals ought to be able to set up organizations to serve their political interests. In fact, churches for many years have sponsored organizations that actively lobby in Sacramento. Conservative groups such as the California Family Council are no match in the capital for lobbyists from the mainline churches. These include the California Catholic Conference, the California Council of Churches, Catholic Charities, the Friends Committee on Legislation, Jericho for Justice (an independent Catholic group), and the Lutheran Office of Public Policy.

Most of those who oppose church participation in politics are on the political left. The campaign around Proposition 8, however, may have given progressives a false impression of what issues are most important to religious groups. The current number-one issue for almost all of them is protecting California's programs for the poor and vulnerable from budget cuts. Additionally, the Friends Service Committee has long taken a special interest in California's prison inmates, a group that otherwise has almost no representation in the political system. True, Proposition 8 split the religious lobby. The Catholic Church supported the measure, while most of the mainline Protestant organizations opposed it. Still, most Catholic political activity follows from the church's role as the largest private provider of health care, social services, and education in California. The church has also taken a special interest in the fate of the unauthorized immigrant community—which is not surprising, given that most of these people are Catholic.

For Critical Analysis ***Why might religious lobbying groups take a special interest in the issue of poverty?***

and make their cases. This still goes on in the lobbies and hallways of the capitol, as well as in nearby bars and restaurants and wherever else policymakers congregate. Lobbyists are so integral to the legislative process that they are commonly referred to as members of the "third house," alongside the assembly and senate.

Until the 1950s, lobbying was a crude and completely unregulated activity. Lobbyists lavished food, drink, gifts, and money on legislators in exchange for favorable votes. Today's lobbyists, however, are experts on the legislative process. Many have served as legislators or staff for legislators. Often, they focus on legislative committees and leaders, lobbying the full legislature only as a last resort.

Unlike old-time lobbyists, today's advocates must be well informed to be persuasive. When inexperienced legislators are unable to grasp major issues, lobbyists fill the void, often by actually writing proposed legislation and assembling the coalitions of legislators necessary to pass it.[8] One study during the 2007–2008 legislative session found that 60 percent of the bills that became laws had been introduced by legislators on behalf of lobbyists.[9] Today's lobbyists still use money, but less cavalierly than in the past, instead strategically contributing to campaigns. Legislators and lobbyists alike assert that contributions buy access, not votes, but the tie between money and access can be powerful in its own right. "The bottom line," one strategist states, is that "the system favors the moneyed—and there's been no sign of political reform."[10] All of this makes lobbying not only a highly specialized profession but also an expensive activity. In fact, during 2009 lobby firms spent about $151 million just to influence the legislature alone—that averages out to $1.26 million per legislator.[11]

"I'M THE GOVERNOR OF THE LEGISLATURE; to hell with the governor of California!"

~ ARTHUR "ARTIE" H. SAMISH ~
CALIFORNIA'S MOST INFLUENTIAL LOBBYIST 1897–1974

Although most lobbying activity is focused on the legislature, knowledgeable professionals also target the executive branch, from the governor down to the bureaucracy. The governor not only proposes the budget but also must respond to thousands of bills that await his or her approval or rejection. In the process, the governor frequently meets with lobbyists in an effort to come to terms on proposed legislation before it goes to the legislature.[12]

The roles and responsibilities of bureaucrats do not escape the attention of astute interest groups. The bureaucracy must interpret new laws and make future recommendations to the governor and legislature. Moreover, on questions ranging from tax exemptions to coastal access to energy regulations, bureaucrats often have the final say on how laws will work. One study on the implementation of AB 32, the Global Warming Solutions Act of 2006, found energy interests lobbying the California Air Resources Board more than the governor or legislature to gain favorable regulations. In the words of one energy lobbyist, "I'm not going to say we love the thing (AB 32), but if that's the way the state wants to go . . . we want to make sure that we write regulations that we can comply with and are feasible to do."[13] Sometimes lobbyists will go so far as to offer "talking points" to help bureaucrats justify their decisions on public matters. "It's called 'spoon feeding,'" a lobbyist recently explained to a California coastal commissioner regarding a matter before the commission, "but we're happy to do it."[14]

contract lobbyist An individual or company that represents the interests of clients before the legislature and other policymaking entities.

Lately, the public has become a target of lobbying, too. In media-addicted California, groups have begun making their cases through newspaper and television advertising between elections. Health care, education, Indian gaming, and other issues have been subjects of costly media campaigns with the intent to motivate voters to communicate with state leaders. Are lobbying efforts more of a problem than in the past? We consider that question in the *Perception versus Reality* feature on the following page.

PROFESSIONAL LOBBYISTS Between 1977 and 2007, the number of registered lobbyists in Sacramento nearly doubled, from 582 to 1,074, including about three dozen former legislators. That's about nine lobbyists per legislator. State law prevents former legislators from lobbying for one year after they leave office, but as one legislator has noted, "I would certainly be available to give people political advice."[15]

Most lobbyists represent a particular business, union, organization, or group. Others are **contract lobbyists,** advocates who work for several clients simultaneously. Whether contract or specialized, more and more lobbyists make a career of their professions, accruing vast knowledge and experience. These long-term professionals became even more powerful when term limits eliminated senior legislators with countervailing knowledge, although some lobbyists complain that term limits mean they must constantly reestablish their credibility with new decision makers. One prominent lobbyist, however, explains his lack of concern about term limits or other reforms: "Whatever your rules are, I'm going to win."[16]

PERCEPTION VERSUS
REALITY
Lobbying Just Keeps Getting Worse

When it comes to the gifts that lobbyists give to lawmakers, California's rules are looser than those of many other states, and they are certainly looser than those imposed on the U.S. House and Senate. Legislators are allowed to travel to exotic locations on trips paid for by interest groups—the only restriction is that legislators must show up for the conferences or meetings to which they were invited. Interest groups can give gifts valued at a total of $420 to each lawmaker, official, or staff member. More than 1,200 lobbyists are registered with the state, so $420 per lobbyist can add up fast. In most circumstances, there is no limit whatsoever on gifts to spouses, friends, and relatives. These are generous rules indeed.

The Perception

The *Sacramento Bee* reported that from January 2008 through June 2009, lobbyists gave $610,000 in gifts to legislators, their relatives, and their staff members. An additional $233,000 went to members of the executive branch. California's leaders ate about 8,000 free meals, many of them at the most expensive restaurants in the state, and pocketed about 2,000 free event tickets, many to the Sacramento Kings professional basketball team.[17] This was a period in which California's finances were in freefall, resulting in tax increases and spending cuts that would cause pain all across the state. It would seem that the relationship between lobbyists and elected officials has never been more worrisome.

The Reality

It's a common human failing to believe that things were better in the Good Old Days. Usually, they weren't. Recall from Chapter 17 that the Southern Pacific Railroad ran the state for almost forty years until the Progressives took over in 1910. It's also worth recalling the career of Arthur Samish, lobbyist *extraordinaire.* Elmer R. Rusco, history professor at the University of Nevada, believes that Samish had a stronger political organization during the twenty years between 1930 and 1950 than either the Democratic or Republican parties. When California governor Earl Warren (1943–1953) was asked by *Collier's* magazine whether he or Samish had more influence over the legislature, Warren responded: "On matters that affect his clients, Artie unquestionably has more power than the governor."

It is probably easier for the legislature to resist special interest groups today than in Samish's time. The state's ongoing budget crisis makes major giveaways harder to contemplate—this chapter's opening *California at Odds* feature describes how lawmakers have become more resistant to the demands of the prison guards. A second factor is the ideological polarization of the legislature. Politicians with firm principles may choose to stick to them no matter how much cash is on the table.

Intuit, a major software company, can serve as an example of how partisan politics can frustrate a major interest. Intuit makes TurboTax, the nation's leading federal income tax software. For extra money, you can buy a state version of TurboTax that will prepare your state return. California, as it happens, offers an online program called Ready Return that lets filers with simple returns file their state taxes for free. Since 2001, Intuit has spent more than $1.7 million in an attempt to kill Ready Return. Intuit claims that California filers can use the Free File system supported by Intuit and other software venders. Free File, however, is only a filing system. Unlike Ready Return, it does not fill out returns. To do that, you normally buy software such as TurboTax, and to get a California state module you first have to buy the federal version.

Intuit's fundamental mistake was to funnel almost all of its contributions to Republicans. That helped turn the Ready Return issue into a partisan battle. For now, Ready Return lives. It is possible, however, that in some future budget deal, Democrats might agree to throw Ready Return "under the bus."

The legendary Jesse Unruh, Speaker of the California Assembly from 1961 to 1969, allegedly made a scandalous remark to a worried junior legislator: "Son, if you can't eat their food, drink their whiskey, take their money . . . and then vote against 'em, you don't belong here." Certainly, it would be better if a lawmaker would refuse the food, whiskey, and money and then vote on the merits. Now as in the past, however, elected officials find it hard to take either this advice or Unruh's.

Blog On The Capitol Weekly is an excellent source for following California politics, including the impact of interest groups. See it at **www.capitolweekly.net**. Searching under "archives" for "intuit" will bring up the Ready Return story. The *Los Angeles Times* looks at Samish's career in **articles.latimes.com/2008/feb/03/local/me-then3**.

NONPROFESSIONAL LOBBYISTS Some groups can't afford to hire a lobbyist, so they rely on their members instead. Even groups with professional help use their members on occasion to show elected officials the breadth of their support. Typically, this sort of lobbying is conducted by individuals who live in the districts of targeted legislators, although groups sometimes lobby en masse, busing members to the capitol for demonstrations or concurrent lobbying of many elected officials.

Such grassroots efforts by nonprofessionals have special credibility with legislators, but well-financed groups have learned to mimic grassroots efforts by forming front groups or "Astroturf" organizations that conceal their real interests. In 2008, for example, representatives of pornography filmmakers flooded the capitol for hearings on AB 2914, a bill that would have hiked taxes on the industry from 8 percent to 25 percent, adding $665 million to the beleaguered state coffers. Bill opponents included spokespersons from the Free Speech Coalition (FSC), an adult industry–funded group purportedly concerned with government efforts to limit free speech, regardless of the topic or issue. In this case, the FSC representatives argued that the tax would discriminate against those with different opinions. Through this vehicle, the porn industry appeared less self-serving and provided the logic for legislators to defeat the bill.

Campaign Support

Most groups also try to further their cause by helping sympathetic candidates win election and reelection, commonly through financial contributions to their campaigns. Groups with limited financial resources do so by providing volunteers to go door-to-door or to serve as phone-bank callers for candidates. Labor unions typically fall into this category, along with public education interests.

CONTRIBUTIONS Groups with greater resources make generous campaign contributions. Sometimes such contributions appear to get the groups what they want. Take the issue of consumer protection from cell phone companies. Between 2006 and 2007, the legislature considered nine bills concerning billing transparency, contract grace periods, termination fees, and contract dispute rules. The industry opposed the bills as intrusive and unnecessary. Only one bill was signed to the law by the governor, while the rest never emerged from the legislature or were vetoed. Meanwhile, during the same period, the telecommunications industry pumped more than $7.2 million into political campaigns.[18] Table 20–1 illustrates the top ten interest group contributors in 2008.

Table 20–1

Top Ten Campaign Contributor Groups, 2008

Category	Money
Tribal Governments	$163,223,555
Public Sector Unions	$37,926,398
Electric Utilities	$33,932,562
Oil & Gas	$25,491,497
Party Committees	$24,075,526
Gay/Lesbian Rights & Issues	$21,747,420
Candidate Committees	$18,115,167
General Trade Unions	$17,075,442
Gambling & Casinos	$16,616,687
Real Estate	$15,408,393

Source: Institute on Money in State Politics, **www.followthemoney.org**

Sometimes groups fail, no matter how much they contribute. In 2002 banks, insurance companies, and similar interests contributed more than $20 million in campaign contributions to defeat a bill by state senator Jackie Speier aimed at protecting the financial privacy of consumers.[19] Facing a similar outcome in 2003, Speier organized an initiative campaign and quickly collected 600,000 signatures; the moneyed interests retreated,

Congressman Randy "Duke" Cunningham (center) seen walking into the Federal Courthouse, was found guilty of conspiracy and tax evasion for accepting more than $2.4 million in bribes.

SANDY HUFFAKER/GETTY IMAGES

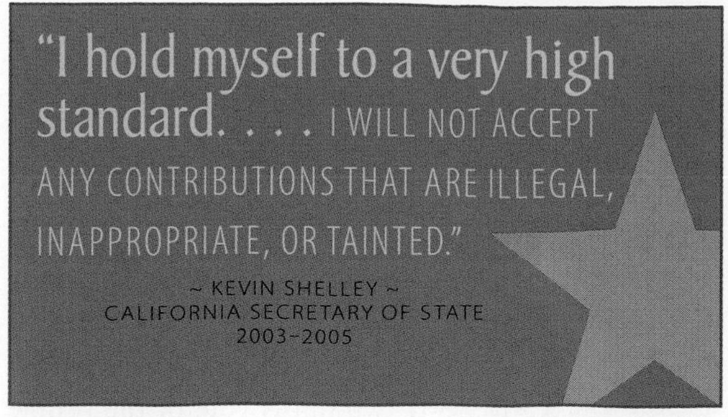

and Speier's bill (SB1) was signed into law by Governor Davis. While they may not always succeed, powerful groups rarely hesitate to use their resources to tilt the outcomes in their favor.

QUID PRO QUO Campaign contributors claim that their money merely buys them access to decision makers. The press and the public often suspect a more conspiratorial process, however, and evidence of money-for-vote trades has emerged in recent years. Federal Bureau of Investigation (FBI) agents posing as businesspeople asked legislators for favors in exchange for campaign contributions, resulting in the 1994 convictions of fourteen people, including five legislators. Their trials revealed the extent to which legislators hustle lobbyists for contributions. In another instance Chuck Quackenbush, California's elected insurance commissioner, was forced to resign in 2000 when it was discovered that he let insurance companies accused of wrongdoing avoid big fines by giving smaller amounts to foundations that subsequently spent the money on polls, ads featuring the commissioner, and other activities. And in 2005 Secretary of State Kevin Shelley resigned from his office after several allegations of illegal activities, including campaign contributions from a company that was awarded a major grant from his office.

As a result of these scandals, politicians and contributors probably exercise greater caution. The high cost of campaigning in California, though, means that candidates continue to ask and lobbyists and interest groups continue to give. Of significance, however, is that the campaign funds come from a variety of interest groups, as well as other sources.

Litigation

Litigation is an option when a group questions the legality of legislation, and in recent years many groups have turned to the courts for a final interpretation of the law. Groups have challenged state laws, regulations, and actions by the executive branch in court. In 2005, for example, the California Nurses Association successfully sued to force Governor Arnold Schwarzenegger to comply with a new state law that reduced the nurse-to-patient ratio. Although the governor lost that battle, he won another when he fended off a court challenge by the powerful California Teachers Association because he rescinded an earlier promise to return $2 billion he had denied the schools the previous year.

litigation An interest group tactic of challenging a law or policy in the courts to have it overruled, modified, or delayed.

direct democracy Progressive reforms giving citizens the power to make and repeal laws (initiative and referendum) and to remove elected officials from office (recall).

Over the years, interest groups have also raised legal challenges to several successful ballot measures—including measures on immigration, affirmative action, campaign finance, bilingual education, and same-sex marriage—hoping that the initiatives would be declared unconstitutional. Even if a group loses its case, it may be able to delay the implementation of a new law or at least establish a principle for debate in the future. In 2001 MALDEF challenged the legislature's redistricting plan, claiming underrepresentation of Latinos. Although the legislature's plan prevailed, MALDEF's tactic kept the issue on the public agenda throughout the decade.

Direct Democracy

In his 1911 inaugural address, Governor Hiram Johnson championed direct democracy to "place in the hands of the people the means by which they may protect themselves." He and his fellow Progressives envisioned the public as the ultimate custodian of the legislative process. A century later, however, only broad-based or well-financed groups have the resources to collect the necessary signatures or to pay for expensive campaigns. **Direct democracy** gives interest groups the opportunity to make policy themselves by promoting their proposals through initiatives and referenda.

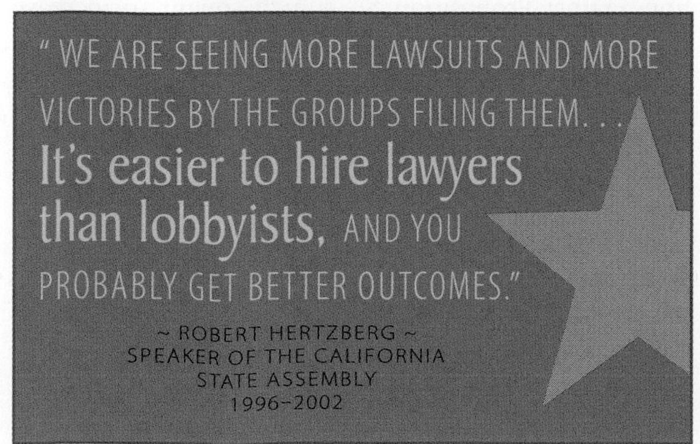

DAVID MCNEW/GETTY IMAGES

The Morongo Casino Resort and Spa near Cabazon is surrounded by property slated for development. Governor Arnold Schwarzenegger convinced the Legislature to allow an expansion of Indian casino gambling in exchange for hundreds of millions of dollars in revenue to the state.

INTEREST GROUPS AND INITIATIVES Sometimes interest groups mobilize to gain passage of a ballot proposition; other times they work to defeat one. In 1998, for example, tribal supporters of gambling on Indian lands spent $10 million qualifying an initiative for the ballot in just thirty days—the most expensive petition campaign in history. The subsequent campaign on the proposition itself also broke records, with the two sides spending a total of $96 million. The voters ultimately approved the initiative. Since then, the costs have gone up. In 2008 the voters were asked to ratify four agreements allowing for 17,000 more slot machines in Indian casinos in addition to the 62,000 already in place, with projected annual taxes for the state at about $450 million. The pro-gaming interests spent more than $150 million on campaign activities—far exceeding the "no" side, which spent less than $40 million. The ballot propositions sailed through.

FIGHTING AGAINST INITIATIVES Big money was spent against two other initiatives in 2006. In one case the tobacco industry marshaled more than $65 million against Proposition 86, which sought to increase tobacco taxes by $2.60 per cigarette package (which would make California the highest tobacco-taxed state in the nation). Similarly, major oil companies spent more than $100 million in opposition to Proposition 87, an effort to tax oil profits with the proceeds used to pursue alternative-energy programs. The campaigns were successful, and the voters rejected both propositions.

Fair Political Practices Commission (FPPC)
Established by the Political Reform Act of 1974, this independent regulatory commission monitors candidates' campaign finance reports and lobbyists.

But big money doesn't always win. For example, utility giant PG&E spent more than $3 million gathering signatures for Proposition 16, the so-called Taxpayers Right to Vote Act. The proposal was actually a thinly veiled effort to change the state constitution to require any municipal power company to get a two-thirds vote of the people before buying renewable energy. PG&E poured more than $46 million into the effort against about $90,000 spent by the "no" side. The proposal was defeated in June 2010, even though the opponents were outspent by a margin of 19,565 to 1.

The recall is also sometimes used by interest groups, usually to remove local elected officials. Teachers' unions, conservative Christians, and minority groups have conducted recall campaigns against school trustees, for example. These efforts, however, pale in comparison with the recall effort against Governor Gray Davis. The People's Advocate, a conservative antitax group, was among the leading forces early in that recall effort. During the campaign, groups ranging from the Howard Jarvis Taxpayers Association to the League of Conservation Voters weighed in on the issue.

LO4 *Regulating Groups*

Free spending by interest groups and allegations of corruption led to the Political Reform Act of 1974 (introduced in Chapter 19), an initiative sponsored by Common Cause. Overwhelmingly approved by the voters, the law requires politicians to report their assets, disclose contributions, and declare how they spend campaign funds. Other provisions compel lobbyists to register with the secretary of state, file quarterly reports on their campaign-related activities, and reveal the beneficiaries of their donations. The measure also established the **Fair Political Practices Commission (FPPC),** an independent regulatory body, to monitor these activities. When the commission finds incomplete or inaccurate reporting, it may fine the violator. Of greater concern than the financial penalty, however, is the bad press for those who incur the commission's reprimand.

The voters approved new constraints in 1996, when they enacted strict limits on interest groups' practice of rewarding supportive legislators with travel and generous fees for speeches. However, this legislation was soon challenged, creating an atmosphere of uncertainty. In 2000 voters approved yet another initiative, **Proposition 34,** which placed new constraints on political action committees and attempted to limit contributions to political campaigns. Yet between self-financed campaigns and the vigorous activities of groups engaged in independent expenditures, any thoughts of reduced spending quickly vanished.

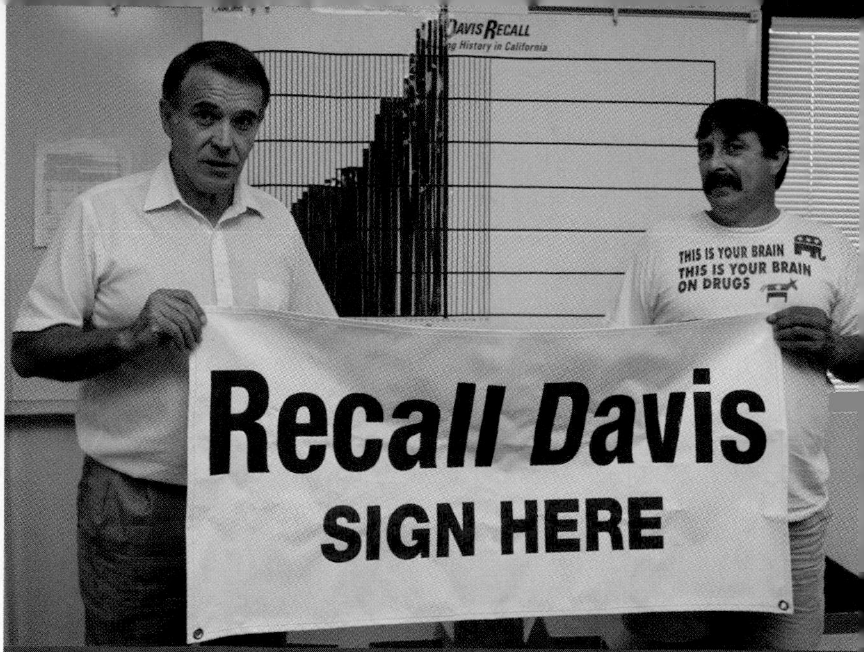

DAVID HUME KENNERLY/GETTY IMAGES

Ted Costa left, head of the political group The People's Advocate, is shown holding a 'Recall Davis' sign at his office in Sacramento, CA. Costa led the effort to recall California Governor Gray Davis in 2003.

Measuring Group Clout: Money, Numbers, and Credibility

Campaign regulations are generally intended to reduce the disproportionate influence of moneyed interests in state politics, but economic groups still have the advantage. Their money makes the full panoply of group tactics available to them and gives them the staying power to outlast the enthusiasm and energy of grassroots groups. The California Chamber of Commerce, for example, contributes lavishly to legislative campaigns and has been a major source of funds for Arnold Schwarzenegger, the first gubernatorial candidate endorsed by the Chamber in its 115-year history. Between 2004 and 2008 the Chamber listed fifty-one "job killer" bills that would be harmful to California business that reached the governor's desk; forty-seven were vetoed by Governor Schwarzenegger. Allan Zaremberg, president of the Chamber, attributes this to the "parallel agendas" of the governor and his organization, but campaign contributions and effective lobbying surely helped.[20] Of course, when Gray Davis was governor, labor unions enjoyed much the same kind of special relationship. Some interest groups are always likely to be more successful than others.

Arnold Schwarzenegger, shown here addressing the California Chamber of Commerce Board of Directors, was the first gubernatorial candidate to be endorsed by the Chamber in its 115-year history. Why would the Chamber break with tradition and endorse Schwarzenegger?

DAVID MCNEW/GETTY IMAGES

Public interest groups and demographic groups, however, gain strength from numbers, credibility, and motives other than self-interest. Occasionally they prevail, such as in 1998, when children's groups and health groups overcame a financial disadvantage to pass Proposition 10, a cigarette tax dedicated to children's health programs, and in 2010, when financially impotent public interest groups won the Proposition 16 battle against PG&E. More commonly, interest groups affected by potentially harmful new costs rise to the occasion, as was the case in 2006, when the oil and tobacco

Proposition 34 A 2000 legislative initiative setting contribution limits for individuals and political action committees; commonly circumvented through independent expenditures.

industries spent nearly $200 million and reversed public opinion—and the votes—on measures to tax oil and increase tobacco taxes.

How powerful are interest groups and their lobbyists? It's hard to tell, but one informal survey of twelve first-time legislators reported that lobbyists wrote 70 percent of the bills they proposed.[21] Whatever the balance among groups, they are central to California politics. In a political environment characterized by weak political parties and direct democracy, California's myriad interests have plenty of opportunity to thrive.

"THE ACTIVITIES OF LOBBYISTS SHOULD BE REGULATED and their finances disclosed in order that improper influences will not be directed at public officials."

~ CALIFORNIA'S POLITICAL REFORM ACT ~ GOVERNMENT CODE SECTION 81002(B)

CALIFORNIA AT ODDS *Interest Groups*

In California as elsewhere, interest groups are both powerful and controversial. It is difficult to accomplish much within the political system without substantial interest group support, and yet such groups are also widely seen as a corrupting influence. Californians disagree on many issues that involve interest groups, including the following:

- Such interest groups as the California prison guards benefit if more people are locked up. Do long prison terms serve to protect the people of the state—or do they perpetuate inequality and injustice?
- Do professional interest groups such as the California Medical Association deserve the credibility they receive due to their expertise—or are they just as self-serving as other interest groups?
- Likewise, do public interest groups truly serve the public—or do they typically represent narrow ideological concerns?
- Are there too many interest groups—or is the real problem that there are not enough groups that represent ordinary people, especially those with lower incomes?
- Are California's laws on lobbying too loose—or would tightening them interfere with constitutionally protected rights?

Take Action

You personally may have a variety of interests that are represented by organized interest groups. Your family might be involved in a profession, type of business, or economic activity that has lobbyists in Sacramento. You might have strong feelings on topics such as the environment, abortion, or gay rights. One interest you almost certainly have if you are reading this textbook, however, is your role as a student. California college students have formed a number of organizations to protect their interests. For example, the University of California Students Association, with more than 200,000 members, advocates on higher education issues important to students at the various U.C. campuses. Its Web site is www.ucsa.org. The California State Student Association provides a voice for the 405,000 students in the California State University system. It has a Legislative Affairs Committee and a Lobby Corps to ensure student representation on legislative matters. Its site is www.csustudents.org. The 2.6 million students at California community colleges are represented by the Student Senate for California Community Colleges—www.studentsenateccc.org. Of course, the California Student Public Interest Group, or CALPIRG, mentioned in Chapter 19, also has a major lobbying presence in the capital.

POLITICS ON THE WEB

- The California Association of Realtors (CAR) covers realtor issues in politics, public policy and legislation on the Governmental Affairs section of their Web site at **www.car.org**.
- Learn more about the lobbying efforts of the California Chamber of Commerce on behalf of California businesses at **www.calchamber.com**.
- Common Cause is a public-interest lobbyist organization. Visit their Web site and select California under the state organizations to find out more at **www.commoncause.org**.
- The California Labor Federation represents the members of more than 1,200 affiliated unions. For more information, visit **www.calaborfed.org**.
- The Howard Jarvis Taxpayers Association is dedicated to the protection of Proposition 13 and the advancement of taxpayers' rights. To learn more, visit **www.hjta.org**.
- You can access the Web site of the League of Women Voters of California, which focuses on governmental reform and voter participation, at **www.ca.lwv.org**.
- The Sierra Club is the oldest and largest grassroots environmental organization in the United States. To learn more about the legislative lobbying arm for the thirteen Sierra Club chapters in California, go to **www.sierraclub.org/ca**.

Access CourseMate to review and expand on this chapter through quizzes, flashcards, learning objectives, interactive timelines, a crossword puzzle, audio summaries, video, critical-thinking activities, simulations, and more.

GOVT 21

The Legislature: The Perils of Policy Making

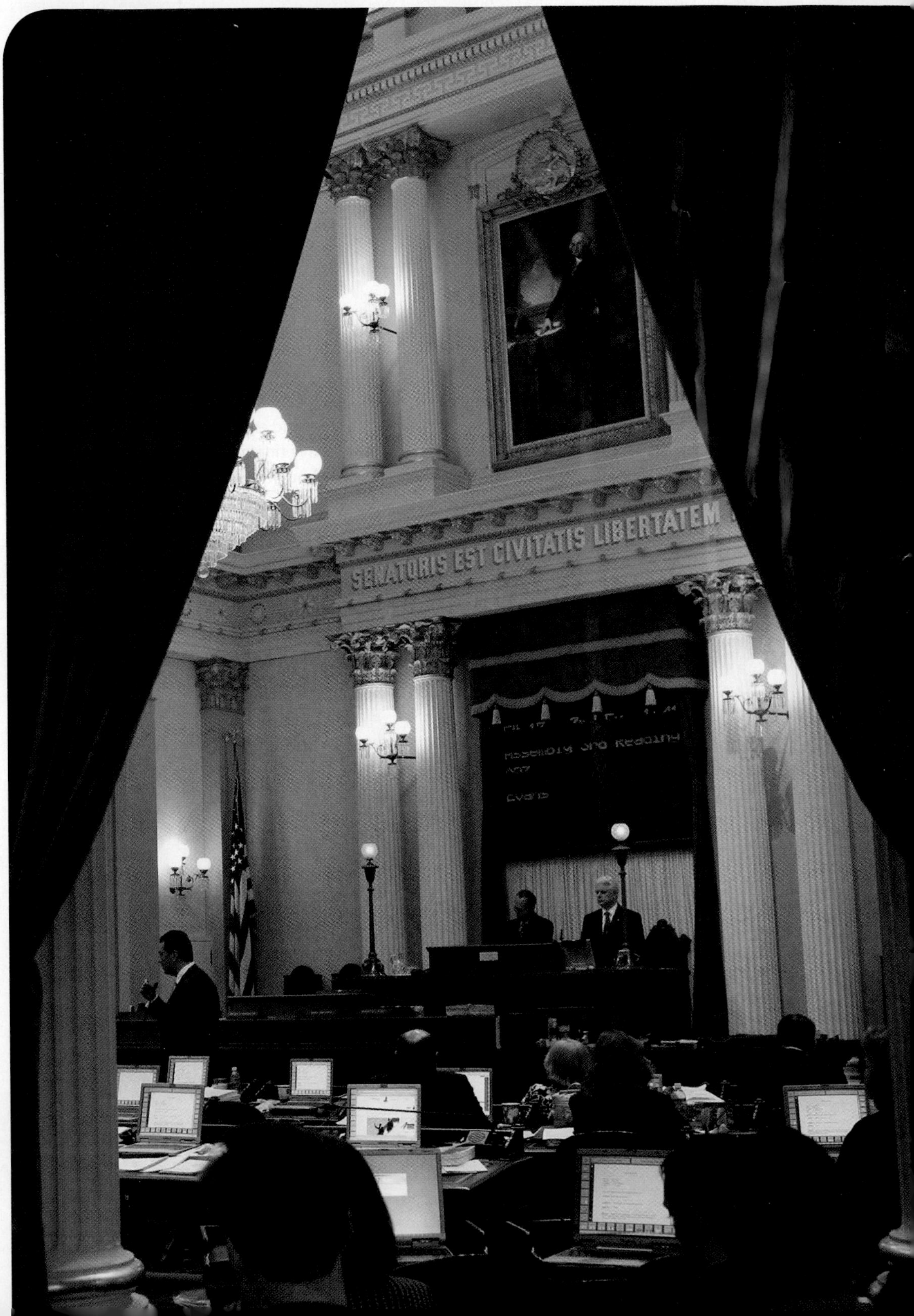

LEARNING OBJECTIVES

LO1 Summarize the evolution of California's legislature, including the impact of redistricting and term limits.

LO2 Characterize the role of leaders and staff members in the legislature.

LO3 Explain how a bill becomes a law through both the formal and informal process.

LO4 Provide examples of the role that personal power plays within the legislature.

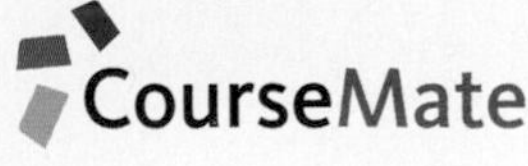

CALIFORNIA AT ODDS

Are Term Limits Good for California?

Proposition 140, passed in 1990, set strict term limits for legislative service in Sacramento. Members of the assembly are limited to six years in office (three two-year terms) over the course of a lifetime; senators are limited to eight years (two four-year terms). In California, many local jurisdictions also have laws that provide for term limits. In contrast, there are no term limits for the U.S. House and Senate, because term limits for members of Congress have been declared unconstitutional. The idea behind term limits is to force entrenched politicians out of office after a predetermined number of years.

Communities around the country have recently had second thoughts about term limits, however. Legislative bodies from New York City to Tacoma, Washington, have tried either to overturn or modify existing term limit legislation. For example, in 2008 the City Council in New York City changed the city's law so that Mayor Michael R. Bloomberg could run for a third term. Governor Schwarzenegger, a long-time supporter of term limits, recently called them "silly." In California, however, voters rejected an attempt to alter the term limit rules—Proposition 93 was defeated in February 2008, possibly because it contained special provisions that benefited a limited number of politicians.

Are term limits good for California? Or do they hinder good governance? Californians are at odds over this issue.

Term Limits Are Doing What They Are Supposed to Do

Backers of term limits point out that at the beginning of this nation, no one expected career politicians. Rather, the framers of our Constitution thought that elected politicians would come from various walks of life, serve their country for several terms, and then go back to doing what they were doing before they entered government. Out of almost forty million Californians, is only a confined, elite class of individuals capable of doing the public's business?

An entrenched set of politicians can do a lot of harm. To fix broken government, we need fresh faces—men and women who are uncorrupted by money and politics. After all, when elected officials can remain in office for only a few terms, special interest groups lose the incentive to spend huge sums. There's little point in influencing people who will soon be gone. Thus, the influence of special interests declines when there are term limits.

It's Time to End Term Limits

Those who are against term limits argue that they break up the institutional memory of the legislature. The longer a legislator is in office, the more competent she or he becomes. Term limits hamper efficient government because they do not allow elected officials enough time to figure out the mechanics of their positions. Furthermore, accountability is lost when a lawmaker has to leave office because of term limits instead of being voted out for cause.

Sacramento Bee columnist Dan Walters calls the new breed a "semi-amateur pack of legislators . . . whose first allegiance is to the outside groups that got them their seats."[1] Walters, in other words, doesn't believe that term limits have curbed the power of special interest groups. The limits have simply changed the identity of the groups with the most influence. Today, after all, lobbyists are often the most knowledgeable people around the capitol building, and this naturally enhances their clout. Term limits also enhance the power of bureaucrats—permanent state employees—who stay in place long after elected officials are "termed out."

WHERE DO YOU STAND?

1. **Given the rules in California, a common career path for a politician is to serve out the six-year term in the assembly, and then move on to eight more years in the senate. As a result, the California Senate has become noticeably more experienced then the assembly. Is this a problem? Does it make the senate conform more closely to what the founders of our country wanted an upper house to look like? Explain your answers.**
2. **Everyone needs to earn a living. Is it really wrong if some people make a career out of public service? Why or why not?**

EXPLORE THIS ISSUE ONLINE

- **Term limits are a movement as well as a law. See the Web site of U.S. Term Limits at www.termlimits.org.**
- **If you'd like a detailed and critical analysis of California term limits, see Sasha Horwitz's *Termed Out,* published by the Center for Governmental Studies in Los Angeles. It's located at www.cgs.org/images/publications/term_limits_final_sm_111907.pdf.**

Introduction

Thousands of bills are introduced in the California legislature every year. Some are narrow in focus, such as requiring egg-laying chickens to have enough room to walk in their cages (passed in 2010) or a truth-in-advertising law about pomegranate juice (passed in 2009). Others, such as sweeping telecommunications legislation (passed in 2010) or mortgage fraud legislation (passed in 2009) attempt to settle disputes between competing industries that have substantial resources at stake. Some of these laws may seem a waste of time to the casual observer, although they usually are critically important to the constituencies they affect.

But along with deciding relatively obscure matters removed from the public eye, the legislature is responsible for solving the state's thorniest problems, including underfunded public education, inadequate revenues, the need for environmental protection, a decaying infrastructure, and an ever-fraying social safety net. Each year the members write thousands of laws and, along with the governor, determine the budget and fund services and programs. As a focal point of power, the legislature is a natural target of public scrutiny, and criticism of it is understandable. Less understandable, however, is its inability to resolve big issues in a contentious political environment.

Of course, the legislature does not act in a policy-making vacuum; rather, it must share power with the other branches of government. Nowhere has there been more disdain for that requirement than in the relationship between the legislature and the governor. For the last twenty-five years, California governors and the legislature have tangled on a regular basis. During that period, the legislature has rarely enacted the state budget before the start of the fiscal year on July 1. In addition, the legislature has suffered internally due to political—and philosophical—battles not only between Democrats and Republicans, but also internally between assembly Democrats and senate Democrats and assembly Republicans and senate Republicans. As one beleaguered assembly member said during lengthy budget negotiations, "More times than not, it seems that we have four political parties in the legislature alone!" Partisanship and ideological schisms shape the legislative process in California in ways rarely observed elsewhere, and these stark divisions often leave the body tied in political knots. Term limits are another complicating factor that we discussed in the chapter-opening *California at Odds* feature.

"THIS IS A FIXED SYSTEM... that rewards legislators for rigid partisanship, and a system that punishes legislators for wanting to come in the middle and go for compromise."

~ ARNOLD SCHWARZENEGGER ~ THIRTY-EIGHTH GOVERNOR OF CALIFORNIA, 2003–2011

bicameral legislature
Organization of the state legislature into two houses: the forty-member senate (elected for four-year terms) and the eighty-member assembly (elected for two-year terms).

Then there's the question of public policy priorities. Some observers have wondered in recent years how the legislature could immerse itself in issues such as tanning salon rules for teenagers and imported kangaroo leather regulations, yet seemingly avoid questions about tax reform, water policy, and universal health insurance. It's no wonder that a 2010 public opinion survey found a whopping 75 percent of likely voters critical of the state legislature—a disapproval rating even higher than that of Governor Arnold Schwarzenegger.[2] Still, the legislature was established as the state institution most directly linking the people with their government. The question is, Does it still do its job in the twenty-first century?

LO1 *The Making and Unmaking of a Model Legislature*

Structurally and numerically, much of today's state legislature parallels its original design and intent. But a series of circumstances in the state's political environment have left the legislative branch considerably different than its national counterpart.

A Little History

California's first constitution, in 1849, provided a **bicameral** (two-house) **legislature** similar to the U.S. Congress. When the constitution was revised thirty years later, the senate was fixed at forty members serving four-year terms (with half the body elected every two years), and the assembly was set at eighty members serving two-year terms. Those numbers and terms of office continue to this day. Throughout the first hundred years of governance, legislators met on a part-time basis, with budgets crafted in two-year increments—characteristics that would change over time.

Beginning in 1926, the organization of the legislature paralleled that of the U.S. Congress. Assembly members, like their counterparts in the U.S. House of Representatives, were elected on the basis of population, and senators were elected by county in the same way that each state has two U.S. senators.[3] The large number of lightly populated counties north of the Tehachapi Mountains enabled the rural north to dominate the state senate despite Southern California's growth. By 1965, twenty-one of the forty state senators in California represented only 10 percent of the population; Los Angeles County, then home to 35 percent of the state's residents, had but a single state senator.

The Shift toward Professionalism

Then came change. The United States Supreme Court's ***Reynolds v. Sims*** decision in 1964 ordered all states to organize their upper houses by population rather than by county or territory.[4] In California, the shift increased urban and southern representation dramatically, with rural and northern representation experiencing a corresponding decline. The revised method of organization produced numerous consequences—some intended, some not. The new legislators were younger, better educated, and more ideological, and more of them were members of racial minorities. More women also were elected. The transition to modernity was completed in 1966, when the voters created a full-time legislature with full-time salaries.

These days, the legislature meets an average of more than two hundred days per year, with full-time salaries to match. As of 2011, their base salary is $95,291—down from the $116,208 that legislators collected until the most recent recession, but still the highest among the fifty states. Perks push annual incomes close to $140,000.[5] Only nine other states have full-time legislatures.[6]

Reynolds v. Sims A 1964 United States Supreme Court decision that ordered redistricting of the upper houses of all state legislatures by population instead of land area.

redistricting Adjustment of legislative district boundaries by the state legislature to keep all districts equal in population; done every ten years after the national census.

Citizens Redistricting Commission Enacted by the voters in Proposition 11 (2009), this commission will assume responsibility for determining the boundaries of state legislative districts and Board of Equalization districts.

An unemployed road worker demonstrates outside the district office of then-Assembly Speaker Karen Bass. When the California Legislature failed to pass a budget in early 2009, work stopped on more than 100 transporation projects statewide.

DAVID MCNEW/GETTY IMAGES

Redistricting: Keeping and Losing Control

By law, every ten years after the national census, the state realigns congressional and state legislative districts so that all have the same population. This process is known as **redistricting.** As of January 1, 2010, the California State Demographics Unit (the state equivalent to the U.S. Census Bureau) estimated California's population at 38,600,000. The state's population grows unevenly. So, during 2011, the state's new fourteen-member **Citizens Redistricting Commission** must realign legislative districts to be equal in size once again—482,500 for each assembly district and 965,000 in each senate district.

Until 2011, redistricting had been left to the legislature, as is the case in most states. But in recent years, critics charged the legislature with being more intent on self-preservation than on providing compact geographic boundaries. After completion of the 2001 redistricting process, one senate district was two hundred miles in length, while others appeared almost as a Rorschach inkblot personality test. Figures 21–1 and 21–2 show examples of the legislature's work. As a result, the partisan compositions of the legislature remained almost identical throughout the decade. Some observers attacked the 2001 redistricting plan as an "incumbency protection plan"

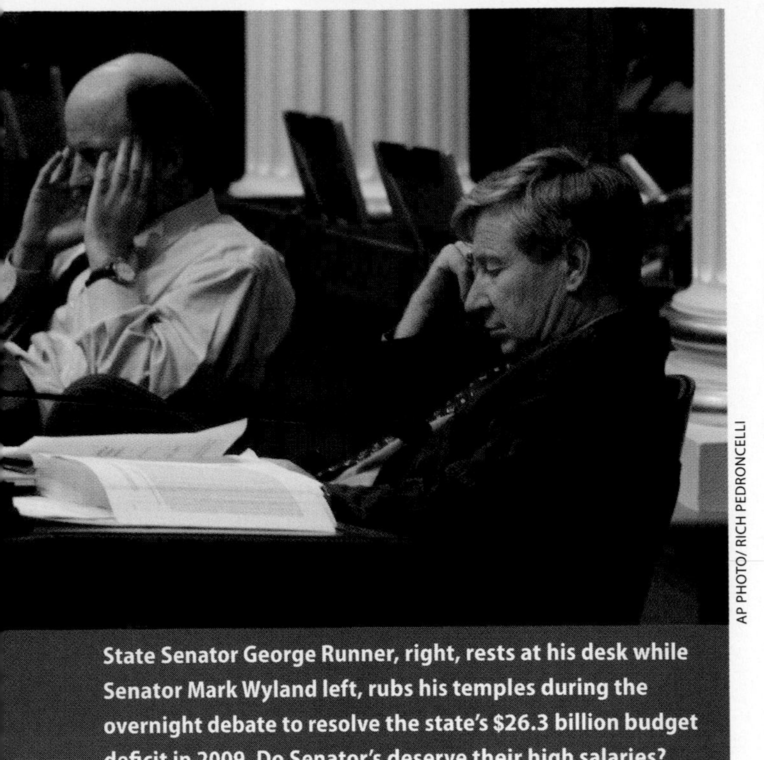

AP PHOTO/ RICH PEDRONCELLI

State Senator George Runner, right, rests at his desk while Senator Mark Wyland left, rubs his temples during the overnight debate to resolve the state's $26.3 billion budget deficit in 2009. Do Senator's deserve their high salaries?

Figure 21–1

Map of State Senate District 15

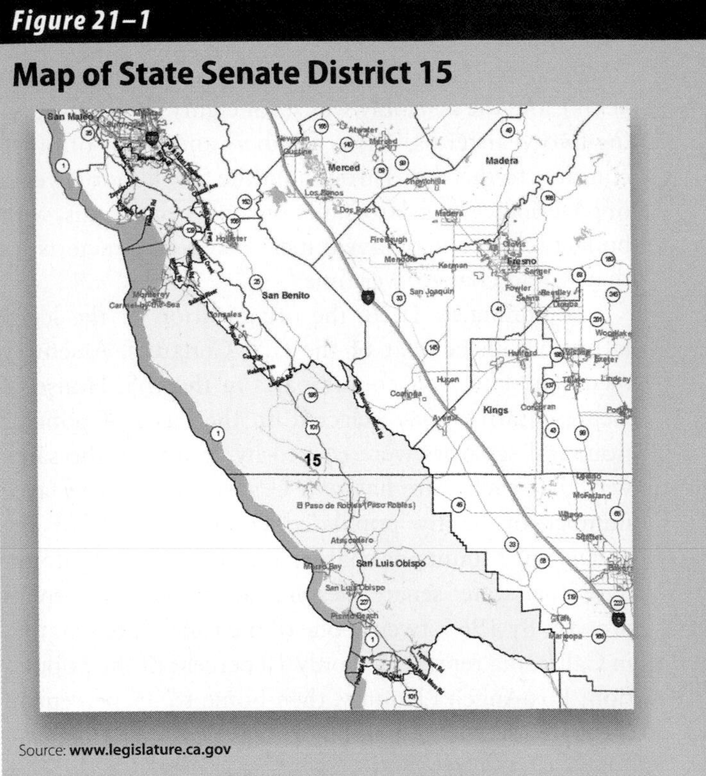

Source: **www.legislature.ca.gov**

that needlessly split cities and ignored natural communities.[7] They argued that packing districts with disproportionate numbers of Democrats or Republicans reduced competition. As one legislator complained, "What happened to drawing lines for the people of the state rather than ourselves?"[8]

PROPOSITION 11 Governor Arnold Schwarzenegger campaigned to establish a redistricting commission of retired judges in a 2005 special election, but the voters soundly rejected his proposal after legislative leaders promised to come up with a better plan. They never did. In 2008, Schwarzenegger joined with Common Cause, the League of Women Voters, and other reform groups to craft **Proposition 11, the Voters FIRST Initiative.** The ballot proposal placed redistricting in the hands of a fourteen-member independent commission. This time, the voters approved the measure, which takes effect before the 2012 state elections. But the redistricting battle has not gone away. Legislative supporters placed the redistricting issue before the voters again in 2010 with Proposition 27, the Financial Accountability in Redistricting Act. However, the voters were content to try the independent commission concept and rejected the proposal. With a new redistricting system in place, it remains to be seen whether the legislature will become less partisan and more effective. Table 21–1 displays the partisan breakdown of the legislature since 1981.

Proposition 11, the Voters FIRST Initiative (2008) An initiative that placed legislative redistricting in the hands of a fourteen-member citizens commission instead of the state legislature.

Figure 21–2

Map of State Assembly District 60

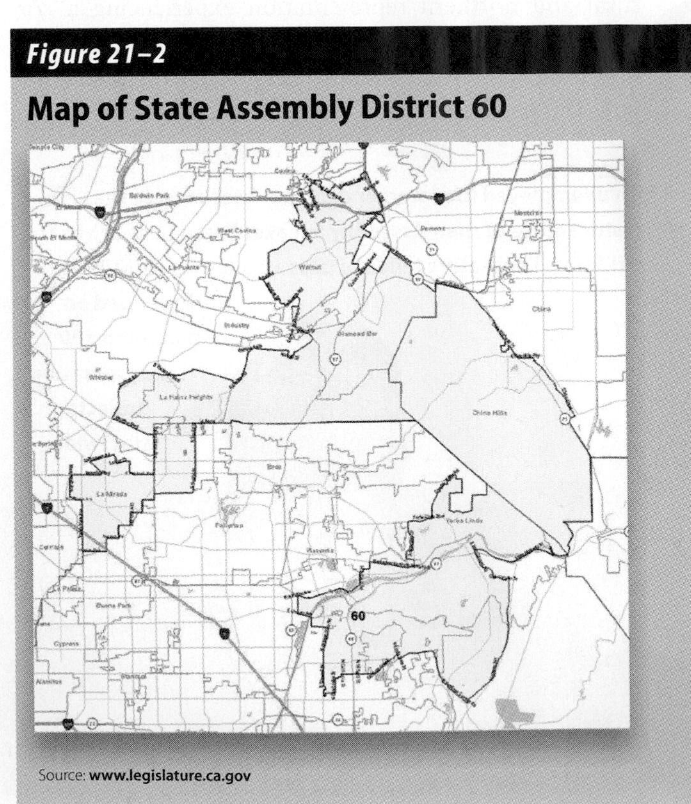

Source: **www.legislature.ca.gov**

Governor Arnold Schwarzenegger speaks out in support of Proposition 11 at a press conference in 2008, along with New York City Mayor Michael Bloomberg.

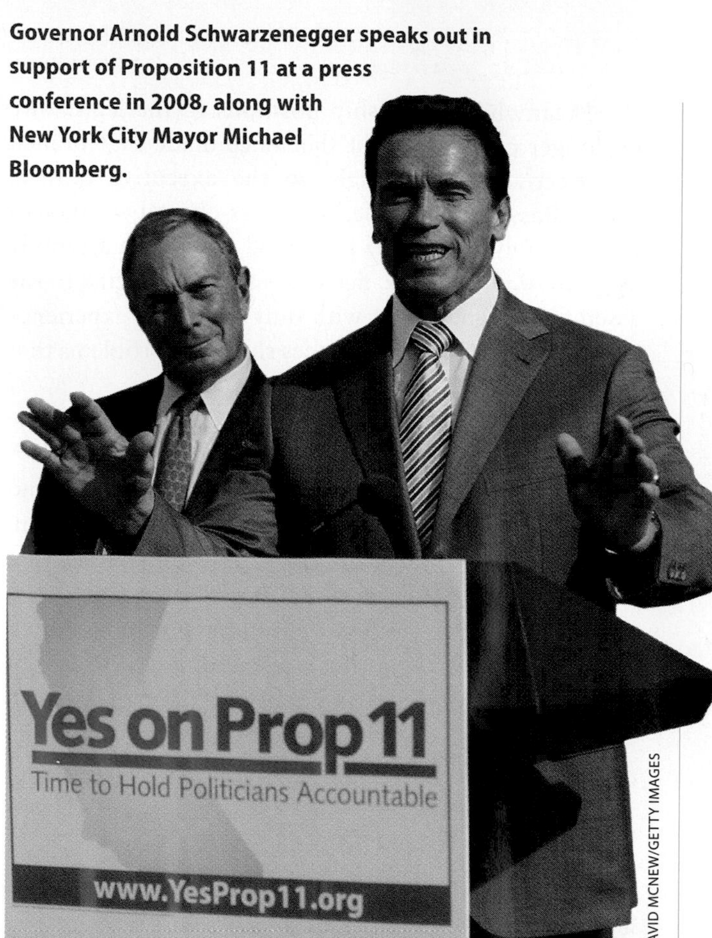

DAVID MCNEW/GETTY IMAGES

Term Limits

Much of the legislature's recent look stems from rising voter antipathy toward incumbents and the near certainty of their perpetual reelection. In 1990 the voters passed **Proposition 140,** an initiative that limited elected executive branch officers and state senators to two 4-year terms and assembly members to three 2-year terms, while reducing the legislature's operating budget (and thus its staff) by 38 percent. Clearly, California voters thought their legislature had become too professional for its own good.

Term-limits advocates envisioned a "turnstile" type of legislature, with members in office for relatively short periods. The system was designed to guarantee new faces, reduce the influence of money, and prevent incumbents from becoming entrenched in excess. Of the fifteen states currently with term-limit legislation in place, California is tied with Arkansas and Michigan for the strictest conditions in the nation. Once legislators complete their terms of service, they may never run for election again.

Some objectives associated with **term limits** have been met, while others show no sign of coming to pass. New faces have certainly appeared—particularly women and minorities in much larger numbers than in the past—but in many cases legislators have simply jumped from one house to the other. And at least one study shows that the most common vocational backgrounds of legislators before term limits—law and business—remain the dominant career patterns in the term-limits era.[9] Those from relatively affluent backgrounds

Table 21–1

Political Parties in the State Legislature, 1981–2011

Legislative Session	Senate Democrats	Senate Republicans	Independents	Assembly Democrats	Assembly Republicans
1981–1982	23	17		48	32
1983–1984	25	14	1	48	32
1985–1986	25	15		47	33
1987–1988	24	15	1	44	36
1989–1990	24	15	1	47	33
1991–1992	27	12	2	47	33
1993–1994	23	15	2	49	31
1995–1996	21	17	2	39	41
1997–1998	22	17	1	42	38
1999–2000	25	15		48	32
2001–2002	26	14		50	30
2003–2004	25	15		48	32
2005–2006	25	15		48	32
2007–2008	25	15		48	32
2009–2010	25	15		50*	30
2011–2012	25	15		52	28

*Juan Arambula (D., Fresno County) became an independent in July 2009.
Source: California Secretary of State.

Proposition 140 (1990) An initiative limiting assembly members to three 2-year terms and senators and statewide elected officials to two 4-year terms and cutting the legislature's budget.

term limits Limits on the number of terms that officeholders may serve; elected executive branch officers and state senators are limited to two 4-year terms, and assembly members are limited to three 2-year terms. Local elected officials are usually limited to two or three 4-year terms.

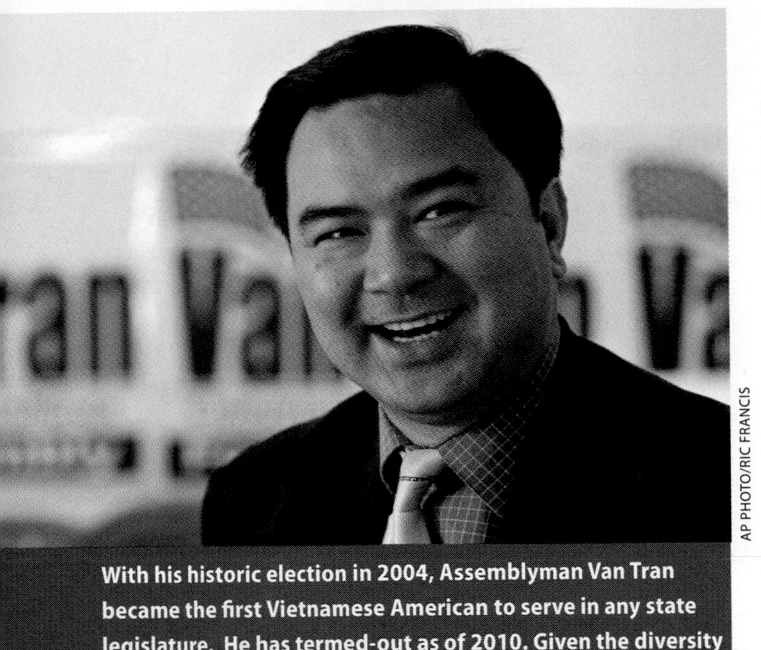

With his historic election in 2004, Assemblyman Van Tran became the first Vietnamese American to serve in any state legislature. He has termed-out as of 2010. Given the diversity of California's population, why are there so few minorities serving in the legislature?

continue be disproportionately elected to the legislature. In this sense, little has changed.

There also have been increasing instances of political "cannibalism." In some cases, termed-out assembly members have challenged senators from their own political party who are eligible to serve another term. In other cases, senators who have a term left in the assembly have attempted to return to that house. In other instances still, termed-out legislators have returned to their counties to run for county supervisor. The term-limits concept in California has spawned the state's version of "musical chairs."

Although the flow of money into campaign coffers has been slowed, the overall costs of campaigning continue to set new records. Research also reveals that another significant impact of term limits has been a considerable decline in the quality of legislation in the postlimits era.[10]

Another criticism of term limits centers on the loss of legislative knowledge because of the rapid turnover. Because legislators have little opportunity to gain expertise, they tend to rely more on the governor and lobbyists,[11] the former because of the governor's access to the bureaucrats who advise him or her and experts who work as aids in the governor's office, and the latter because of the permanence of the lobbyists in the state capital. Legislators may be termed out, but lobbyists are not.

"I always thought term limits were stupid. **PEOPLE CAN VOTE YOU OUT WHENEVER THEY WANT."**

~ JOHN BURTON ~
CHAIRMAN OF THE CALIFORNIA DEMOCRATIC PARTY AND FORMER LEGISLATOR
2009–PRESENT

Meanwhile, leadership positions in the legislature no longer carry the clout that once made that branch an effective counterweight to the executive branch. Karen Bass, for example, who was elected speaker of the assembly in 2008, was termed out of the assembly as of 2010. John Pérez, her successor, was elected to the assembly's highest post with only a year of experience under his belt. Both approaches show the problems that can develop with erratic leadership changes.

Nationwide, the term-limit movement seems to be abating. Mississippi voters rejected the concept in 1999. In 2002, the Idaho legislature removed term limits, and the Oregon Supreme Court found the state law on term limits unconstitutional. In 2003, the Utah state legislature repealed term limits in that state. But in California, the voters continue to favor term limits. A public opinion poll in 2009 found that a resounding 65 percent of Californians supported the concept.[12] We provide an update on the redistricting question in the *California Faces a Troubled Economy* feature on the facing page.

New Rules, New Players

Redistricting, the change from part-time to full-time legislators, higher salaries, and term limits transformed the legislature, albeit unevenly. To be sure, the new framework attracted better-educated and more professional individuals and also made election to office more feasible for women and minorities. Thus, in 2011 the assembly included 19 women, 14 Latinos, 5 African Americans, 7 Asian Americans, and 5 openly gay members; the senate included 13 women, 10 Latinos, 2 African Americans, 2 Asian Americans, and 2 openly gay members (see Figure 21–3).

Despite greater diversity, the legislature has narrowed in terms of vocational backgrounds. During the 1980s, legislative aspirants from the business world were flanked by large numbers of lawyers, local activists, educators, and former legislative aides. But increasingly, the "business candidate" has emerged as the dominant category of self-description. During the 1990s, about half of all legislative candidates on the ballot listed some form of business as their occupation. Beginning in the late 1990s, large numbers of people from city- and county-elected posts also took seats in the legislature.[13] These patterns continue today.[14]

CALIFORNIA FACES A
TROUBLED ECONOMY

An Attempt to Abolish Gerrymandering

In November 2008, California voters narrowly passed Proposition 11, which took the power to redraw the boundaries of state legislative districts away from the state legislature. Various groups tried for many years to get such a measure passed, without success. Why did Proposition 11 win? One new factor may have been popular disgust with the state legislature's response to the budget disaster. Proposition 11 can be seen as one more response to the economic crisis.

In November 2010, opponents of Proposition 11 tried to repeal it through Proposition 27, which was rejected by every county except San Francisco. Voters not only kept Proposition 11, they extended its reach by adopting Proposition 20, which removed the power to set U.S. House districts from the legislature as well. Proposition 20 passed 61 percent to 39 percent.

Redistricting In California

Lawmakers naturally favor redistricting plans that protect incumbents. In most cases, this means making each district as strongly Democratic or Republican as possible.

The state legislature, however, has sometimes lost control of the redistricting process. In 1991, Governor Pete Wilson vetoed a Democratic redistricting plan. The job of redistricting wound up in the lap of the state supreme court, which appointed three retired judges to draw district lines. As a result, the number of competitive districts was increased. In another result, the number of Latinos in the assembly rose from four in 1990 to seventeen in 2000. Previously, as a side effect of protecting the seats of non-Hispanic Democrats, redistricting had tended to block new Latino representation.

In 2001, the legislature, armed with powerful computers, created the most radical incumbent-protection redistricting scheme ever. In 2002, not a single assembly, senate, or U.S. House seat experienced a change in party control. That could only be accomplished by ensuring that every district in the state was solidly Republican or Democratic.

What Propositions 11 and 20 Accomplish

A fourteen-member Redistricting Commission now handles redistricting for assembly, state senate, Board of Equalization, and U.S. House seats. An initial group of sixty candidates—twenty Republicans, twenty Democrats, and twenty independents—is drawn at random from a pool consisting of every eligible citizen who submits an application. (Anyone with a connection to the legislature or a political party's leadership is ineligible.) Legislative leaders can challenge and remove a limited number of candidates. A second lottery then narrows the panel down to three Democrats, three Republicans, and three independents. Finally, these eight choose six additional members. The striking amount of random selection in this process is aimed at reducing the influence of the existing party hierarchies. The commission's plan is subject to approval in a referendum.

Consequences

The hope of the Redistricting Commission's supporters is that a greater number of competitive districts will yield more state lawmakers willing to appeal to the political center, rather than to their party's most ideological members. Such results have been observed in other states that use nonpartisan redistricting boards. Non-partisan redistricting will reinforce the impact of the Top Two Candidates primary described in Chapter 18.

Proposition 20 has national implications. In addition to protecting incumbents, the boundaries of California's U.S. House districts also favor the Democratic Party. Non-partisan redistricting in California, therefore, will probably return several more Republican representatives to Washington in 2012. If this reflects the will of the voters, most people would say that it is fair. A problem, however, is that U.S. House districts in many other large states are gerrymandered to favor the Republicans. Indeed, on a nationwide basis House boundaries exhibit a mild Republican bias. Eliminating a Democratic gerrymander in California threatens to make this national bias even stronger.

You Be the Judge **Cities and counties are often sliced up and shared among multiple districts as a result of gerrymandering. However, the Redistricting Commission is required to respect local government boundaries when possible. What impact might this have on local government officials who are contemplating a run for state office?**

Figure 21–3

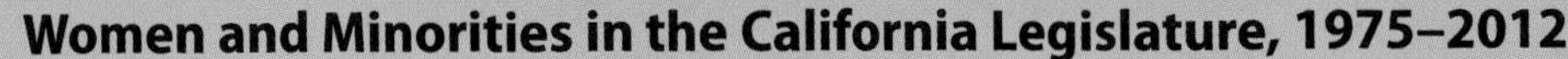

Women and Minorities in the California Legislature, 1975–2012

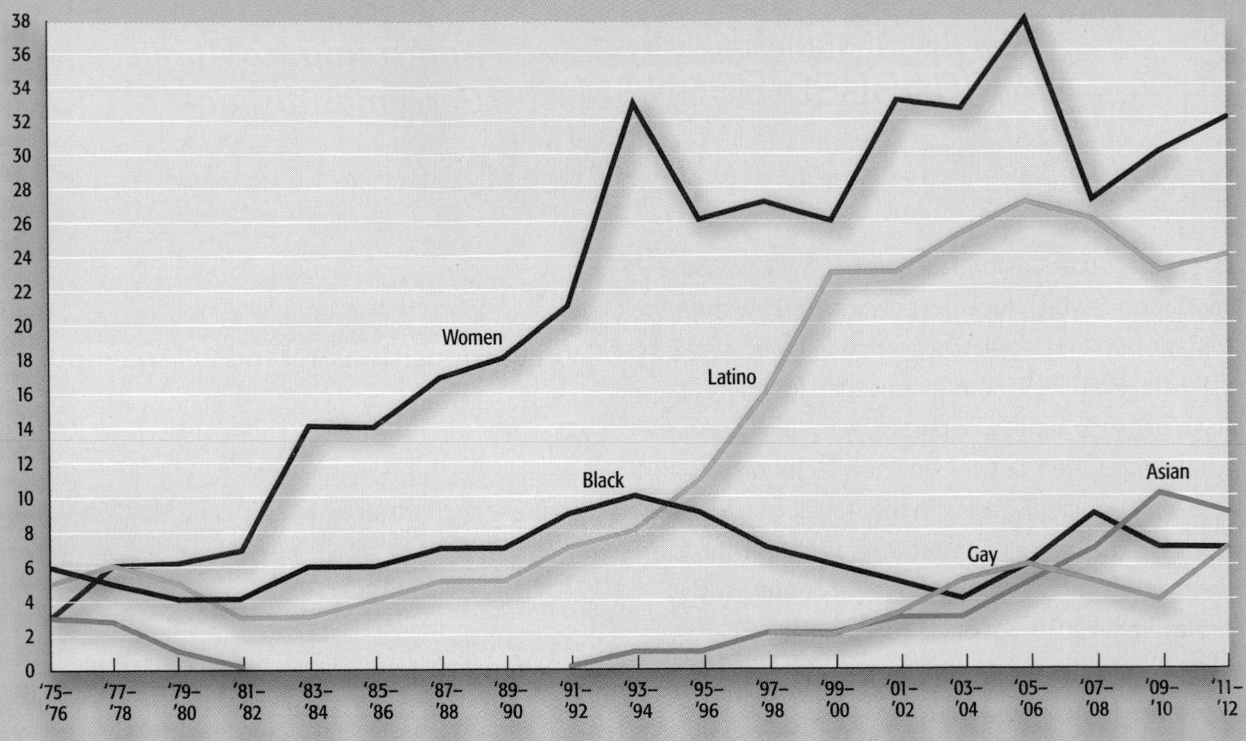

Source: Compiled from *The California Almanac of Government and Politics;* clerks of the assembly and senate.

LO2 *Leaders and Staff Members*

Although the two houses share lawmaking responsibilities, they function differently. Because the assembly is larger, it is more hierarchical in organization.

Speaker of the Assembly

The **speaker of the assembly** is clearly in charge of that body and wields considerable power. The speaker controls the flow of legislation, designation of committee chairs and assignments, and distribution of vast campaign funds to the members of his or her political party. The number of standing, or topical, committees varies each term with the speaker's term in office. For example, there were thirty such committees in the assembly during 2009–2010, one more than in the previous session. Some committees are far more important than others, so the speaker's friendship is of great value to a legislator. The speaker also may carry favor with the governor, especially if the two work well together.

speaker of the assembly The legislative leader of the assembly; selected by the majority party; controls committee appointments and the legislative process.

By tradition, the party with a majority in the assembly chooses the speaker in a closed meeting, or caucus. A vote is then taken by the full assembly, with the choice already known to all. The minority party selects its leader in a similar fashion. Majority and minority floor leaders, as well as their whips (assistants), provide further support for the legislative officers. With solid majorities for most of the past half-century, the Democrats have controlled the speakership for all but four years during the last four decades.

Before the term-limits era, speakers often held their posts for ten years or more. However, since 1996—the year when term limits set in—the tenures of speakers have been limited to between one and three years. The current speaker, John Pérez, may stretch that life span a bit. He was elected to his post in 2009 and may serve through 2014, assuming he is re-elected.

Senate President pro Tem

Prior to the court-ordered redistricting in 1966, the senate emphasized collegiality and cooperation over strong leadership, strict rules, and tight organization. Since the late 1960s, the senate has operated with a level of partisanship closer to that found in the assembly. The most powerful member is the **president pro tem,** who, like the speaker, is elected by the majority party after each general election. The minority party also elects its leader at that time. The key to senate power lies with the five-member **Senate Rules Committee,** which is chaired by the president pro tem and controls all other committee assignments and the flow of legislation. In 2009–2010 the senate had twenty-three standing committees, the same number as the previous session.

AP PHOTO/RICH PEDRONCELLI

Assemblyman John Pérez accompanied by members of the state Assembly, answers questions during a news conference after he was elected as the next leader of the California Assembly, at the Capitol in Sacramento. Pérez will be sworn in as speaker at a later date.

When Democrat John Burton presided as the pro tem, he used the office to raise and dispense large sums of money to grateful fellow Democrats. Burton was president pro tem for six years (1998–2004). More significantly, he had been an assembly member for nearly twenty years, mostly before the term-limits era. Because of his experience, Burton became the legislature's lightning rod against Governor Arnold Schwarzenegger. Many observers viewed him as the legislature's most formidable leader, despite the assembly speaker's traditionally dominant role.

The current president pro tem, Darrell Steinberg, was elected to the position in 2008. He will not be termed out until 2014. Like most others in leadership positions, Steinberg assumed his post with relatively little experience, although he did serve six years in the state assembly.

Although Democrats hold leadership positions in both houses, in recent years they have had as much trouble dealing with one another as they have had with Republican governor Schwarzenegger. Some of this trouble may be due to the differing leadership styles of Senate President Pro Tem Steinberg and Assembly Speaker Pérez. Steinberg has a record of crossing party lines to forge necessary, if distasteful, compromises. Pérez has a reputation for being unwilling to part with core values.[15] Their internal gridlock has taken considerable pressure off the minority Republicans, who have watched internal struggles within the majority party with some glee. Nowhere has this been more evident than in the struggle to balance annual state budgets facing huge deficits. As the legislature grappled with its responsibilities in 2010, interest groups loyal to both sides actually began letter-writing campaigns and purchased television ads—all of which points to the lack of cohesion within the political parties.[16]

Together with the governor, the senate president pro tem, the speaker of the assembly, and the minority leaders in both houses constitute the "big five" who typically take responsibility for negotiating the state budget. We examine this state of affairs in the *Join the Debate* feature on the following page.

Staffing the Professional Legislature

The evolution of the legislature into a full-time body was accompanied by a major expansion of its support staff. In 1990 the number of legislative assistants totaled 2,400—a far cry from the 485 employed by the last part-time legislature in 1966. Reductions from Proposition 140 pared the number of staffers to about 1,750, although increases in the state's population have led to a slow increase in the number of positions. As of 2010, about 2,500 staffers worked for the legislature. Those in the capital usually concentrate on pending legislation and research, whereas staffers in the

president pro tem The legislative leader of the state senate; chairs the Rules Committee; selected by the majority party.

Senate Rules Committee A five-member committee consisting of the senate president pro tem and two other members from each party in the senate; assigns chairs and committee appointments; functions as the gatekeeper of most senate legislation.

Should the "Big Five" Control the Budget Negotiations?

Typically, in most states and at the federal level, the governor or president submits a budget proposal to the legislature. The various items contained in the proposal are examined by legislative standing committees, which may throw out the executive's recommendation altogether and substitute something else. The work of the standing committees then goes to a budget committee in each chamber, which addresses the issue of how to pay for it all, and based on such concerns may make more changes. The budget is then debated, amended, and approved on the floor of each chamber. A conference committee resolves the differences between the two houses before the final budget is ratified and returned to the executive. Once upon a time, this was how budgets were adopted in California.

Since the time of Governor Pete Wilson (1991–1999), however, California has frequently employed a different approach. Committees may debate and vote, but the true work of preparing the budget takes place in negotiations among the "Big Five," the governor along with the speaker of the assembly, the senate president pro tem, and the minority party leaders in each chamber. Big Five negotiations have been especially important whenever the state faces a budget crisis.

Following the 2010 elections, the Big Five include Democratic governor Jerry Brown, plus John A. Pérez of Los Angeles, Democratic speaker of the Assembly and California's first openly gay legislative leader. The other three are Democratic Senate president pro tem Darrell Steinberg of Sacramento, Assembly Republican leader Connie Conway of Tulare, and Senate Republican leader Bob Dutton of Rancho Cucamonga.

Some Californians oppose the Big Five negotiations as the essence of closed, secretive government. Others find the process to be inevitable and necessary.

Big Five Negotiations Are the Only Workable Solution

There is a reason for keeping important budget negotiations secret, especially during a fiscal crisis. If budget negotiations were out in the open, special interests would mobilize against every tough decision, ramp up pressure on lawmakers, and prevent state leaders from reaching a deal that could secure enough votes to pass. Even with the secrecy, interest groups attempted to crack the whip in early 2009. After a few Republicans hinted that they might vote for certain taxes in exchange for business-friendly changes to workplace laws, anti-tax groups and conservative talk-show hosts mounted a campaign to kill any such compromise. On the other side, labor leaders, opposed to any changes to workplace laws, threatened to recall Democratic legislators who voted for such a deal.

Remember, once the leadership reaches an agreement, the whole assembly and the entire senate get to vote on it. The deal can be amended. In July 2009, the legislature rejected a plan to seize almost a billion dollars per year in local gasoline taxes. This forced Governor Schwarzenegger to spend all day on July 27 identifying an additional half-billion in extra budget cuts that he could make with his line-item veto.

Big Five Negotiations are Another California Scandal

"Five Californians are trying to solve the state's budget crisis . . . by keeping the other thirty-eight million residents in the dark." That was the spot-on observation of a *Sacramento Bee* reporter in 2009. Exactly why should the most politically important decision of the year be shielded from the political process? As noted in Chapter 20's *Perception versus Reality* feature, if legislators cannot withstand the pain of being lobbied, they are in the wrong profession. Terry Francke of Californians Aware put it this way: "The thought that to be able to solve this you have to ram it down members' throats just to lock something up before a constituency finds it outrageous is evidence of how bad the process has gotten."[17]

The only reason the Big Five system can work is that the four party caucus leaders have an excessive amount of power over other members of the legislature. The caucus leaders control the party's legislative campaign funds. The majority party leaders control legislative committee and office assignments. This pattern of political centralization is harmful to representative democracy. Power should be decentralized, and budget decisions should once again be made in legislative committees, where they can be discussed openly.

For Critical Analysis ***What changes to the Big Five system are likely now that the voters have abolished the two-thirds rule for passing the state's budget?***

legislators' home district offices spend much of their time responding to constituents' problems. The efforts of these staffers help each legislator to remain in good standing with his or her district.

COMMITTEE STAFF Legislators spend much of their time in committees, the heart of the legislative process. Most committees cover specialized policy areas such as education or natural resources. A few, such as the senate and assembly rules committees, deal with procedures and internal organization. Each committee employs staff consultants who are experts on the committee's subject area and who are politically astute individuals in general—important attributes because they serve at the pleasure of the committee chair. Besides the traditional or standing committees, staffers assist more than sixty select committees that address narrow issues and nine joint committees that coordinate two-house policy efforts.

JUSTIN SULLIVAN/GETTY IMAGES

Democratic State Senate President Pro Tem Darrell Steinberg holds a sign calling for one Republican vote to pass the state's budget on February 18, 2009 in Sacramento. The vote was stalled after the GOP ousted its leader, Dave Cogdill.

OTHER STAFF ROLES Another staff group is even more political. Employed by the Democratic and Republican caucuses and answering to the party leaders in the senate and assembly, these assistants are supposed to deal with possible legislation. However, their real activities usually center on advancing the interests of their party.

In addition to personal, committee, and leadership staffers, legislators have created neutral support agencies. With a staff of fifty-two, the **legislative analyst** (a position created in 1941) provides fiscal expertise, reviewing the annual budget and assessing programs that affect the state's coffers. The **legislative counsel** (created in 1913) employs about eighty attorneys to draft bills for legislators and determine their potential impact on existing legislation. The **state auditor** (created in 1955) assists the legislature by periodically reviewing ongoing programs.

Historically, staffing has enhanced the legislature's professionalism. Yet some staffers, especially those who work for the legislative leaders, clearly spend more time on partisan politics than on legislation. Many have used their positions as apprenticeships to gain knowledge, skills, and contacts for their own campaign efforts. All this, critics point out, is funded by the taxpayers. Defenders of the system counter that this staffing system helps compensate for weak party organizations and the information gaps associated with rapid legislative turnover.

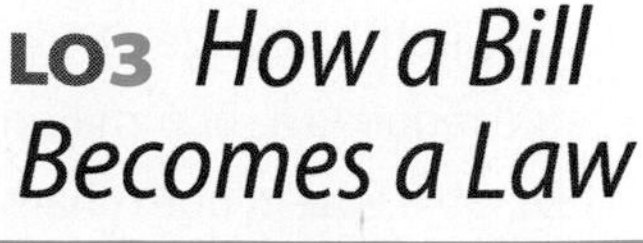

LO3 How a Bill Becomes a Law

The legislature passes laws. It also proposes constitutional amendments, which may be submitted for voter approval after they receive absolute two-thirds majority votes in both houses (the votes of two-thirds of the full membership—that is, twenty-seven votes in the senate and fifty-four in the assembly). The same absolute two-thirds majority votes are required for the legislature to offer bond measures—money borrowed for long-term, expensive state projects. Proposed bond measures must then obtain majority votes at the next election before becoming law.

Most of the legislature's energy, however, is spent on lawmaking. Absolute majorities—twenty-one votes in the senate and forty-one votes in the assembly—are required to pass basic laws intended to take effect the following January, but absolute two-thirds votes in both houses are required for urgency measures (those that become law immediately upon the governor's signature) and overrides of the governor's veto. The process, however, is far from simple.

Many Californians believe that the two-thirds vote requirement to pass a state budget has been responsible for deadlock in the legislature. Now that the public has removed this requirement through 2010's Proposition 25, we will see if that perception is correct. We examine the effects of partisanship and the two-thirds requirement in the *Perception versus Reality* feature on the following page.

legislative analyst An assistant to the legislature who studies the annual budget and proposed programs.

legislative counsel Assists the legislature in preparing bills and assessing their impact on existing legislation.

state auditor An assistant to the legislature who analyzes ongoing programs.

PERCEPTION VERSUS REALITY

The Two-Thirds Vote Rule Caused Deadlock in the Legislature

Until the passage of Proposition 25 in November 2010, moving California's budget through the state legislature required a supermajority—a two-thirds favorable vote in both chambers. Indeed, passage required the support of two thirds of *all* members, not just two thirds of those present for the vote. (The concept of a supermajority was introduced in the *America at Odds* feature in Chapter 11.) California voters first adopted this rule in 1933. The rule only applied, however, to budgets that exceeded the previous year's spending by 5 percent. In 1962, voters extended the two-thirds rule to all budgets. As you learned earlier, Arkansas and Rhode Island are the only states besides California that have required a two-thirds vote in both chambers of the legislature to pass the state's budget.

Figure 21–4

Increased Partisanship in the California Legislature

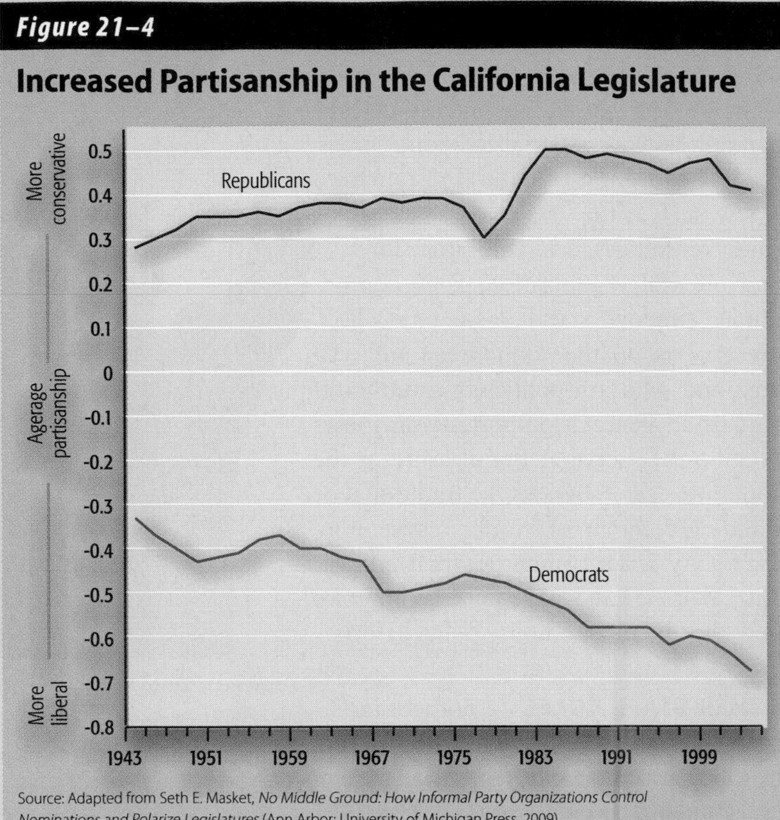

Source: Adapted from Seth E. Masket, *No Middle Ground: How Informal Party Organizations Control Nominations and Polarize Legislatures* (Ann Arbor: University of Michigan Press, 2009).

The Perception

According to the *Los Angeles Times*, "the two-thirds law has warped the budget process, giving an absolute veto to whatever minority can cling to just over 33 percent of seats in either house. . . . That helps make California, once the state of optimism and opportunity, the land of 'no.' "[18] The requirement was supposed to force lawmakers to compromise, but now it leads only to deadlock.

The Reality

The supermajority requirement has not caused nearly as much trouble in Arkansas and Rhode Island as in California. Admittedly, those states are small and have fewer special interests. More to the point, however, the two-thirds majority requirement caused few problems in California itself for most of the 78 years after the voters first approved the rule. In most years, budgets were approved almost unanimously.

In recent years, however, the legislature has regularly deadlocked over budgets. Preventing such deadlocks was the reason that the voters approved Proposition 25, which ensures that budgets can pass by a simple majority vote. Yet before this measure passed, California had the same supermajority requirement as in earlier years. The rules didn't change. What did? One answer is partisanship. The growth in legislative partisanship is clear enough that we can display it in a graph. Political scientist Seth Masket of the University of Denver provides such a graph in Figure 21–4. Masket argues that the members of the legislature are not particularly eager to engage in the ardent partisanship seen in recent years. Rather, local party activists are in effect forcing discipline on the legislators by selecting ideological candidates and threatening to defeat members who do not toe the party line.

The practical effect of Proposition 25 is that the Republican minority in the legislature will no longer be able to force major concessions out of the Democrats in return for passing a budget. (Republican support will still be necessary for any tax rate increases.) The passage of Proposition 25 means that in California, unlike the rest of the country, the 2010 elections were a sweeping Democratic victory.

Blog On **Partisanship data comes from the Voteview project of Professor Keith Poole at the Political Science Department at UC San Diego. Its Web site is voteview.com.**

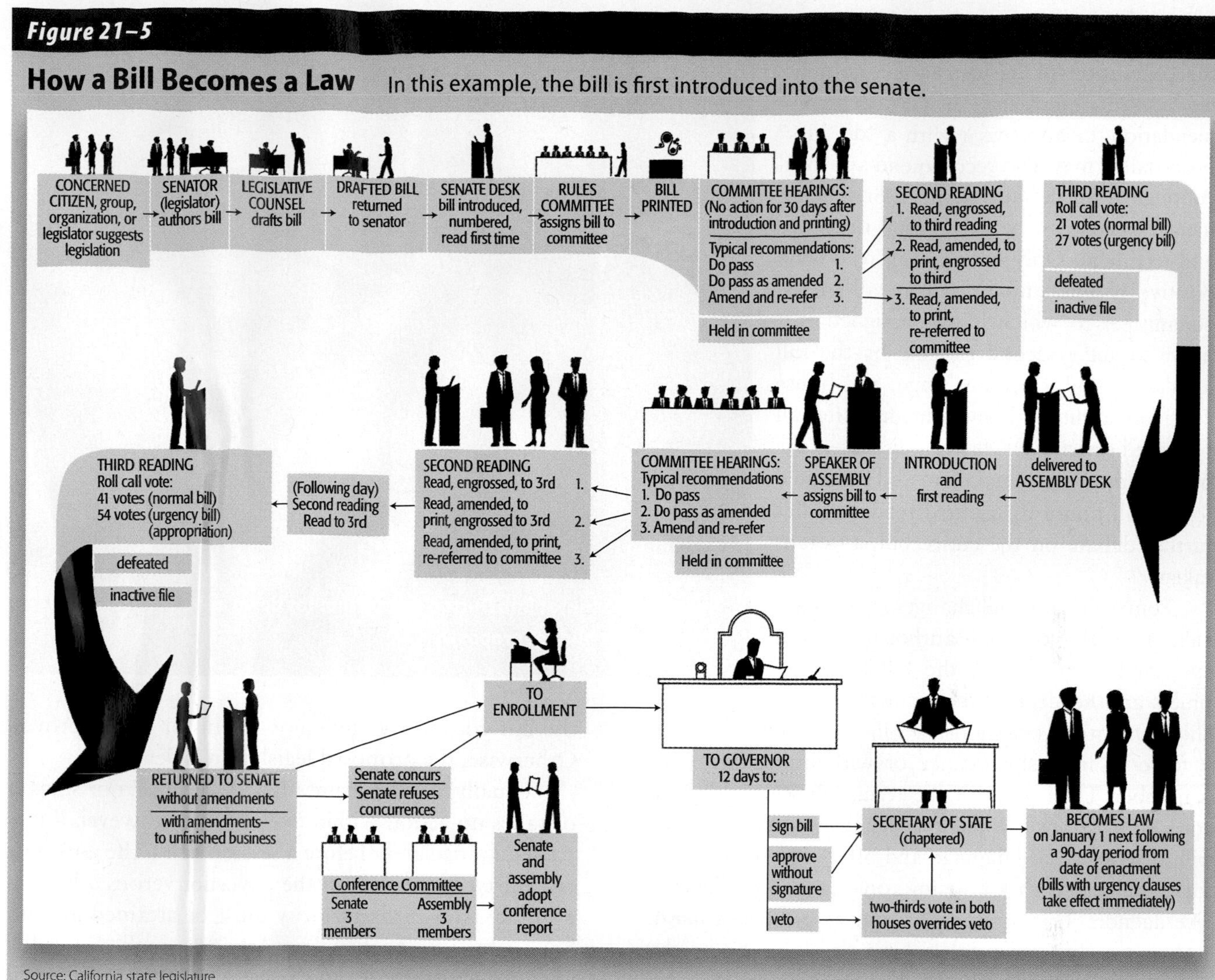

Figure 21–5

How a Bill Becomes a Law In this example, the bill is first introduced into the senate.

Source: California state legislature.

The Formal Process

The legislative process begins when the assembly member or senator sponsoring a bill gives the clerk of the chamber a copy, which is recorded and numbered (see Figure 21–5). The process is known as moving the bill "across the desk" (of the receiving clerk), signifying that the proposed measure is now officially under consideration. The bill then undergoes three readings and several hearings before it is sent to the other house, where the process is repeated. The first reading simply acknowledges the bill's submission.

Depending upon the bill's origin, either the senate Rules Committee or the assembly Rules Committee decides on the route of the bill. The chairs of these important committees can affect a bill's fate by sending it to "friendly" or "hostile" committees and by assigning it a favorable or unfavorable route. Typically, a bill is assigned to two or three committees for careful scrutiny by members who are experts in that bill's subject area. More than half of all bills die in committee, either through a formal vote or because the chair decides not to call for a vote.

More than six thousand bills are introduced during each two-year session, with assembly members limited to fifty proposals and senators limited to sixty-five. With such volume, the **legislative committees** are essential to getting laws passed. They hold hearings, debate, and may eventually vote on each bill delegated to them. Most committees deal in narrow areas, but a few—such as the senate Budget and Fiscal Review Committee and the assembly Committee on Appropriations—focus on the collection and distribution of funds and thus enjoy clout that goes beyond any one policy area.

legislative committees
Small groups of senators or assembly members who consider and make legislation in specialized areas such as agriculture or education.

COMMITTEE RECOMMENDATIONS At the conclusion of its hearings, a committee can kill a bill, release it without recommendation, or approve it with a "do pass" proposal. It may also recommend approval contingent on certain changes or amendments, which can be substantial or minor and technical. Only when a bill receives a positive recommendation from all of the committees to which it was assigned is it likely to get a second reading by the full legislative body. At this stage, the house considers additional amendments. After all proposed revisions have been discussed, the bill is printed in its final form and presented to the full house for a third reading. After further debate on the entire bill, a vote is taken.

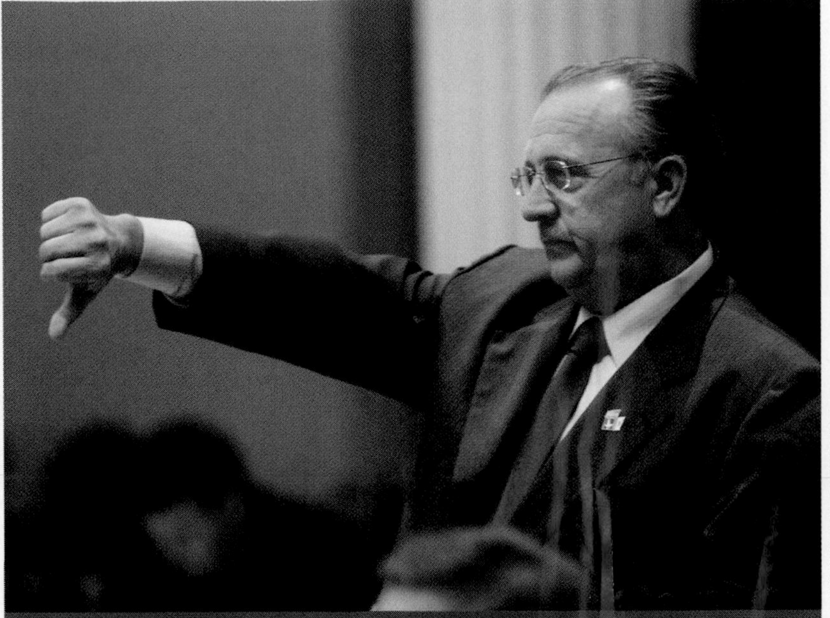
AP PHOTO/RICH PEDRONCELLI

Republican Senator Bob Dutton gives a thumbs down as he votes against a Democratic budget proposal.

Sometimes, the bill changes so dramatically that the original author abandons sponsorship in disgust; the bill then dies unless another legislator assumes sponsorship. On other occasions, a bill is introduced about a topic of little significance or with little more than a number. Then, later in the term, when the deadline for introductions has passed, the author may strip the bill of its original language and offer replacement language to deal with a pressing topic new to the legislative agenda. This strategy, known as **gut-and-amend,** isn't pretty, but gives a legislator flexibility he or she would not have otherwise. It also circumvents the normal legislative process of committee hearings and due deliberation, much to the chagrin of some lobbyists and interest groups.

THE PATH TO APPROVAL If a bill is approved by the members of one house, it goes to the other house, where the process starts anew. Again, the bill may die anywhere along the perilous legislative path. If the two houses pass different versions of the same bill, the versions must be reconciled by a **conference committee.** Senate members are appointed by the Rules Committee; assembly members are chosen by the speaker, yet another sign of the power that comes with that position. If the conference committee agrees on a single version and if both houses approve it by the required margins, the bill goes to the governor for his or her approval. Otherwise, the proposed legislation is dead.

gut-and-amend The process of removing the original provisions from a bill and inserting new, unrelated content.

conference committee A committee of senate and assembly members that meets to reconcile different versions of the same bill.

Usually, a bill becomes law if the governor signs it or takes no action within twelve days. However, if it is passed immediately before a session's end, the governor has thirty days to act. If the governor vetoes a bill, an absolute two-thirds majority must be attained in both houses for it to become law. Attaining such a lopsided vote is next to impossible, so vetoed bills generally fall by the wayside.

The Informal Process

Politics permeates the formal, "textbook" process by which a bill becomes law. This means that every piece of legislation is considered not only on its merits but also on the basis of a variety of factors, including political support, interest group pressure, public opinion, and personal power.

POLITICAL PRESSURES Members of the majority party chair most, if not all, of the committees in any given year. With Democrats in control for most of the last five decades, they have reaped the benefits of the committee chairs (extra staff, procedural advantages, and so forth), secured the best committee assignments, and been assigned the best offices. Likewise, when assembly Republicans briefly held a bare majority in 1996, they assumed control of twenty-five

logrolling A give-and-take process in which legislators trade support for each other's bills.

ghost voting When legislators cast electronic votes in place of assembly members who are not at their posts; this practice is against the law.

MAX WHITTAKER/GETTY IMAGES

A State Assembly member looks at his 'cheat sheet' as they finalize a solution to the state's budget problem on the evening of July 24, 2009 in Sacramento. Should legislators vote on measures they haven't read?

of the twenty-six committees, and the benefits were reversed.

Political support within the legislature is essential to numerous decisions. So many bills flow through the process that members often vote on measures they haven't even read, relying on staff, committee, or leadership recommendations. Sometimes, a bill's fate rests with key legislative leaders, who can use their positions to stifle or speed up a proposal at various points in the legislative process. In the assembly, the speaker may actually appoint extra members to a committee temporarily to move a bill along. Outcomes are also affected by **logrolling,** a give-and-take bargaining process in which legislators agree to support each other's bills. More often than not, legislators give away their votes on matters of little concern to them in hopes of mollifying opponents or pleasing powerful leaders. And on occasion, some members of the assembly have been known to cast the votes of other members by clicking their electronic devices. This illegal activity, called **ghost voting,**[19] can't take place in the senate, where members cast votes by a show of hands.

OUTSIDE PRESSURE Public opinion also affects legislation, sometimes dramatically. Recent statutes on excessive drinking, smoke-free restaurants and bars,

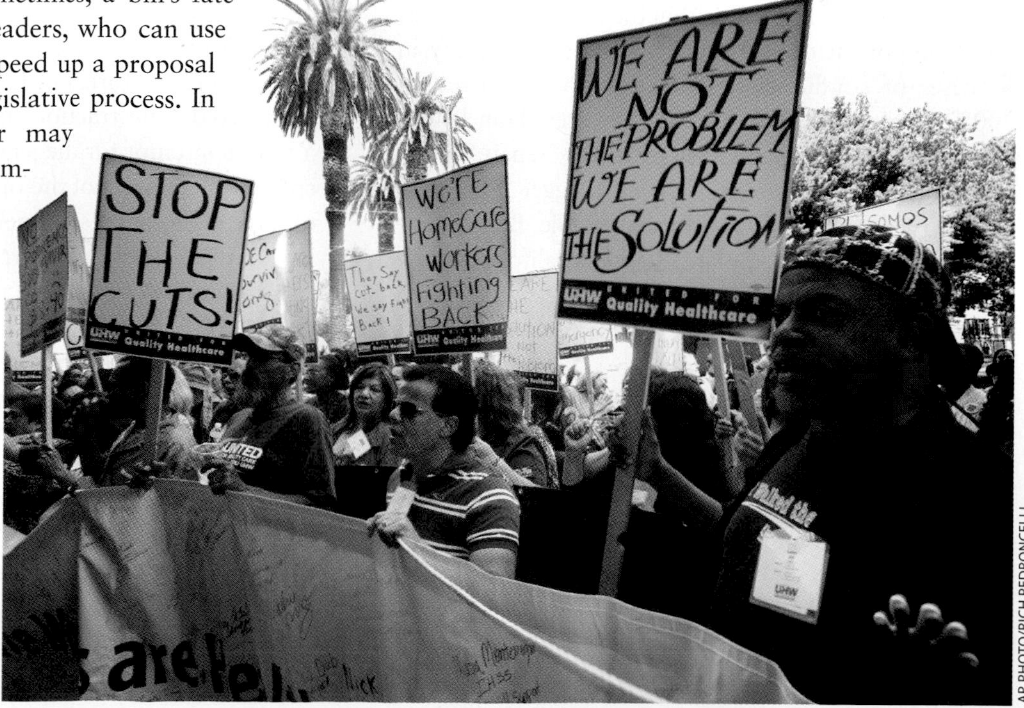

AP PHOTO/RICH PEDRONCELLI

Health care workers and supporters protest Governor Schwarzenegger's proposed 2010–2011 budget, which called for eliminating California's welfare-to-work program in the coming fiscal year.

environmental quality, and longer sentences for repeat felons have been enacted in direct response to public concern.

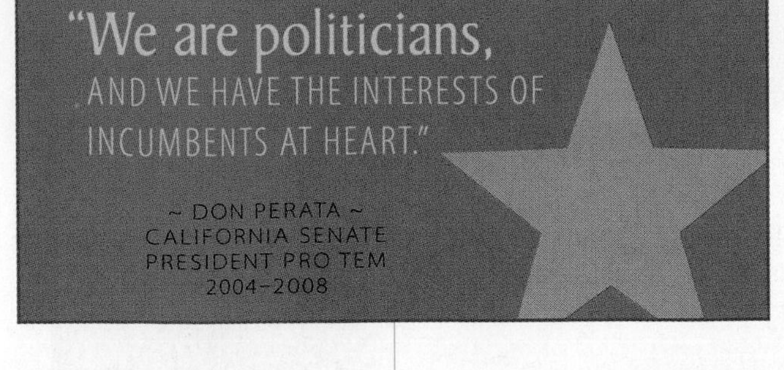

"We are politicians,
AND WE HAVE THE INTERESTS OF INCUMBENTS AT HEART."
~ DON PERATA ~
CALIFORNIA SENATE PRESIDENT PRO TEM
2004–2008

As noted in Chapter 20, pressure from interest groups permeates the legislative process. With the combined cost of legislative campaigns leaping from $7 million in 1966 to $100 million in 1998, candidates welcomed the contributions of these interest groups. Proposition 34, enacted in 2002, attempted to impose some constraints on such fundraising. Thus, in 2002 the cost of state legislative campaigns declined to $76.5 million.[20] Nevertheless, by 2008 the cost of state legislative campaigns had grown by more than 60 percent, to $129.75 million.[21] At just under $1.3 million per seat (eighty assembly, twenty state senate), California's legislative elections were the most expensive in the nation. And given the millions of dollars spent by independent expenditure committees that were not tied officially to any candidate, the total spent on legislative campaigns in the state in all likelihood exceeded $150 million.

LO4 *Other Factors*

Finally, personal power within the legislature remains a component of the political process, especially in cases of conflict. One such example occurred in 2008, when then senate president pro tem Don Perata and the Democratic majority of the senate Rules Committee blocked four Schwarzenegger nominees to the twelve-member California Parole Board. For months, Perata had complained about California's low parole rate, implying that the problem rested with the parole board. This action sent a clear message to both the board and the governor.[22]

Sometimes the mere threat of an initiative spurs the legislature into action that institutional gridlock might otherwise have prevented. In 2003 and 2004, after prodding by governors Davis and Schwarzenegger and the early signature-gathering efforts of an initiative proposal, the legislature reformed the state's workers' compensation program.[23] Conversely, the legislature's work on climate change was nearly undone in November 2010 by a business-sponsored initiative to delay implementation of AB 32. On this occasion, the voters elected to let the controversial law remain in place.

Unfinished Business

Today's legislature faces myriad issues, ranging from a questionable public education system to a deteriorating infrastructure. Faced with revolving participants, the legislature operates with little stability and less tradition. Term limits, restrictions on budget growth (see Chapter 24), and recession for most of the last decade have added to the woes of this policymaking body. Nothing has suffered more than the annual budget, which more times than not emerges well after the start of the next fiscal year. As a result, this outcome can be painful to recipients of services and programs, many of whom are poor, elderly, and sick.

After years in which citizens blamed the legislature for gridlock, voters passed a ballot measure in 2010 that will make it easier to pass budgets by reducing the required support from two-thirds to a majority. Arnold Schwarzenegger tapped into anti-legislature anger early on in his governorship when he casually suggested one day that perhaps the state would be better off with a part-time legislature, but he dropped the proposal after it garnered little traction in state public opinion polls. Yet his contempt for the legislature was rather transparent, although he's not the only California governor ever to have borne such sentiments.

With all these pressures, legislators often seem to react to problems rather than to anticipate or solve them. As a consequence, public policies are made increasingly by initiative, the governor, or the courts. Nevertheless, the legislature continues to grapple with the leading issues of the day, and at least sometimes, lawmakers manage to overcome assorted obstacles in a fractured political environment to enact policies of substance.

CALIFORNIA AT **ODDS** *The Legislature*

The California legislature continues to be one of the least popular political institutions in the state, even though individual legislators typically win general elections by wide margins. The legislature will probably remain highly unpopular as long as the unemployment rate is high. In the next few years, however, California will witness significant changes in the way that voters choose legislators and in the way that the two houses operate—the Top Two Candidates primary, non-partisan redistricting, and the ability to pass a budget by majority vote. It will be interesting to see how much impact these changes actually have, and whether they help make the legislature less unpopular. Californians remain at odds over numerous matters touching on the legislature, including the following:

- Are term limits a good way to keep legislators in touch with their fellow citizens—or do they merely reduce the effectiveness of the legislature in dealing with long-serving lobbyists and bureaucrats?
- In 2004, Governor Schwarzenegger suggested making the California legislature part-time so that lawmakers would not have the time to create so many "strange bills." Is a full-time, professional legislature essential for a large state such as California—or does it result in too many unnecessary laws?
- Is the non-partisan redistricting of U.S. House boundaries a way of ensuring that the people's vote will be heard—or is it a grab for more power by the Republicans?
- Are Big Five negotiations essential to developing an acceptable budget—or do they constitute a fundamentally corrupt system?
- Would abolition of the two-thirds rule for raising taxes resolve the state's fiscal problems—or would it result in the Democrats imposing excessive and burdensome tax increases?

Take Action

Laws passed by the legislature have a direct impact on your life. They can affect the taxes you pay or the number of students that can be admitted into state colleges and universities. As a citizen, you are important. Your influence—and that of your friends and family members—can have an impact on individual members of the California assembly and senate. You can communicate with your legislators or even visit them. If you send a letter or an e-mail message, consider some guidelines for effectiveness:

- **Elected representatives are addressed as "The Honorable" followed by their name.**
- **Your communication should be brief and to the point. Explain what the impact of your proposal will be, and why your legislator should vote as you ask.**
- **Be courteous—no one responds positively to threats.**
- **Finally, timing is important. No matter how good the letter, it won't have much impact if it arrives after the legislature has already voted on the issue.**

© ZENTILIA, 2008. USED UNDER LICENSE FROM SHUTTERSTOCK.COM

POLITICS ON THE WEB

- The Legislative Analyst's Office provides fiscal and policy advice to the legislature, including nonpartisan analyses of the state budget. To learn more about this office and see the latest state budget package, visit **www.lao.ca.gov**.
- To locate and track the status, history, votes, analyses, and veto messages of bills, resolutions, and constitutional amendments, go to **www.leginfo.ca.gov/bilinfo.html**.
- To find your legislator and district, go to **www.legislature.ca.gov**. Click on the "Legislators and Districts" link in the left side navigation bar.
- For a bio and e-mail address of your assembly members, go to **www.assembly.ca.gov**.
- Access the e-mail addresses and home pages of state senators at **www.senate.ca.gov**.
- The National Conference of State Legislatures is a bipartisan organization that provides research, technical assistance and opportunities for policymakers to exchange ideas on the most pressing state issues. To learn more, visit **www.ncsl.org**.
- For a round-up of the day's political and policy-related news, visit **www.rtumble.com**.

Access CourseMate to review and expand on this chapter through quizzes, flashcards, learning objectives, interactive timelines, a crossword puzzle, audio summaries, video, critical-thinking activities, simulations, and more.

GOVT 22

California Law: Courts, Judges, and Politics

LEARNING OBJECTIVES

LO1 Explain the three levels of the California court system and how judges are appointed and fired.

LO2 Describe the work of the courts and the appeals process, including the role of the supreme court.

LO3 Summarize the role of the chief justice and point out some of the more controversial decisions made by the supreme court, including rulings in which initiatives approved by voters were overturned.

LO4 Discuss the supreme court's past rulings on crime and the impact of the three strikes initiative.

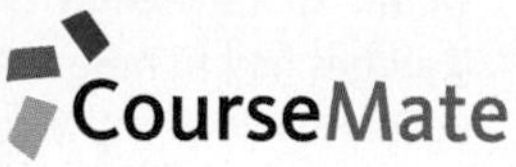

CALIFORNIA AT ODDS

Should the People Elect Judges?

The founders of the American republic were concerned that too great a degree of popular control over the government could lead to "mob rule," and so they sought to insulate various institutions from direct popular elections. Federal judges in particular were to be appointed and serve for life. In contrast, in many states, all judges are popularly elected. As you will learn in this chapter, California employs a mixed system. Superior court judges, those who hear most cases, are theoretically elected on a county-by-county basis. In fact, most are appointed by the governor, and only face the voters if they are challenged at a subsequent election. (An exception—when a judicial position opens up just before an election, candidates compete for the seat and the governor normally does not appoint.) Judges who serve on district courts of appeal or the California Supreme Court—known as justices—are always appointed, although the governor must clear the appointments through the state Commission on Judicial Appointment. These justices may also be required to face the voters. The electorate can retire a justice, but cannot name a replacement—that task is left to the governor.

From time to time, superior court judges are defeated at the polls, but no supreme court justice was ever fired by the people until 1986, when Chief Justice Rose Bird and two of her colleagues failed in their reelection bids. Many voters objected to the consistent reversal of death sentences. Clearly, the most common way to defeat a judge is to accuse that official of being "soft on crime." Some people believe that despite the long prison sentences common in recent years, the judicial system is still too friendly to criminals. Others believe that even the current California system tempts judges to cut corners on civil liberties. Should judges be named exclusively through appointment? Or should California rely more on popular election?

The People Should Rule

Those who favor electing judges do not believe that judges can be insulated from politics. Governors, who do the appointing, are highly political creatures. They tend to appoint supporters of their own party, which means that appointed judges are likely to be noticeably conservative or liberal, rather than hewing to the center. If politics are going to play a role in judicial selection, then the people ought to have their say directly. Let the voters decide whether a judge is tough enough on crime, or too tough on business. We admit ordinary people into the process through juries, and judges should respond to public feeling as well. Officials who do not have to win a popular election may become remote from the people. Living in upscale neighborhoods, they will never experience what it is like to walk home at night fearing for your safety. Instead, they can end up living in a legal never-never land where abstractions matter more than the real world. It takes elections to give us the kinds of judges that we really want.

The Courts Must Be Insulated from Popular Pressure

Many opponents of judicial elections believe that even California's mixed system allows too much opportunity for popular panics and prejudices to influence the process. These Californians believe that the de-selection of Chief Justice Bird and her colleagues set a dangerous precedent. Popular "lock 'em up" attitudes toward criminals do not lead to an optimum strategy for crime reduction. That depends on studying what works and what doesn't. In California, "get tough" policies have led to absurd cases of individuals serving life sentences for trivial offenses. The last thing we need is to place additional pressure on judges by threatening them with removal. Any move toward greater use of elections would bring with it a further problem—the corrupting influence of campaign contributions. Texas elects all judges, and Texas courts are famous for their harsh sentences and enthusiasm for the death penalty. Texan judges also are conspicuously friendly toward the moneyed interests that help get them elected.

WHERE DO YOU STAND?

1. **Los Angeles County has 429 superior court judges. Typically, only a dozen or so of these positions are contested in a given election. If all of them were elected at once, the county might have to be divided into many judicial districts so that voters could keep track of the races. What impact would such a change have on how justice is administered?**
2. **If judges had to raise campaign contributions, what kinds of people would be most likely to contribute? Why?**

EXPLORE THIS ISSUE ONLINE

- **For background information on the California courts, see the California Supreme Court Historical Society site at www.cschs.org.**
- **Arguments over the de-selection of Chief Justice Bird, who died in 1999, are archived at www.rosebirdprocon.org.**

Introduction

Courts are very much a part of the political process. Judges and politicians have always known this, but the public has been slower to understand the political nature of the judiciary. When governors made controversial appointments to the courts during the 1970s and 1980s, however, judicial politics became a very public matter. Later, judicial politics became apparent in court decisions that overturned popular initiatives and, of course, in the appointment and confirmation of justices to the United States Supreme Court. Given these concerns, a debate exists over how judges should be selected, as we explained in the chapter-opening *California at Odds* feature.

What makes the courts political? It's not just controversial judicial decisions or even the involvement of party politicians. Courts are political because their judgments are choices between public policy alternatives. When judges consider cases, they evaluate the issues before them both in terms of existing legislation and in the context of the U.S. and California constitutions. Rulings based on differing judicial interpretations of these documents help some people and hurt others. This is why the courts, like members of the executive and legislative branches, are subject to the attentions and pressures of California's competing interests, and this is why the courts are political. Does the political character of the judiciary mean that judges "legislate from the bench"? We consider that issue in the *Perception versus Reality* feature on the following page.

Figure 22–1

The California Court System

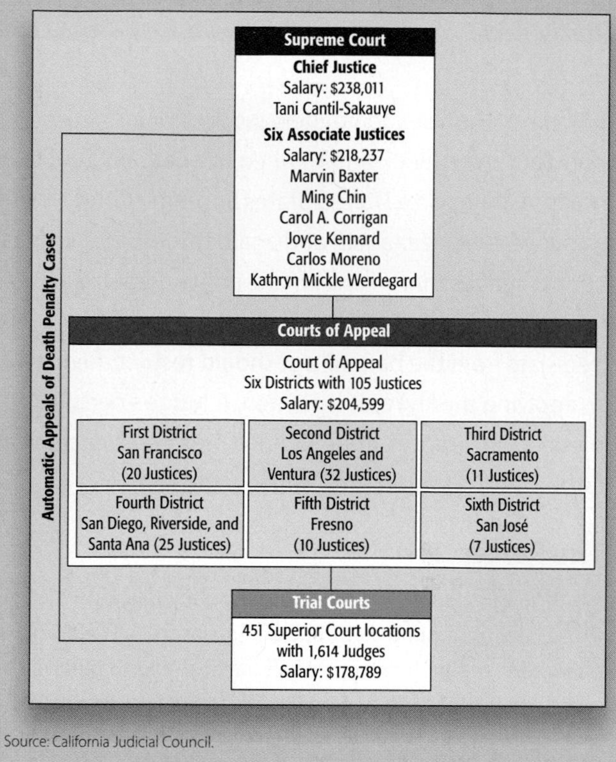

Source: California Judicial Council.

LO1 *The California Court System*

The California court system is the largest in the nation, with more than two thousand judicial officers and nineteen thousand court employees. The three levels within the system are linked, but each has its own responsibilities. Most cases begin and end at the lowest level. Only a few move up the state's judicial ladder through the appeals process (see Figure 22–1), and even fewer end up in the United States Supreme Court.

The Judicial Ladder

The vast majority of cases begin and end in trial courts, the bottom rung of the judicial ladder. In California, **superior courts** in each county are the trial courts, handling misdemeanor cases (minor crimes, including most traffic offenses), felonies (serious crimes subject to sentences of one year or more in state prison), civil suits (noncriminal disputes), divorces, and juvenile cases. Superior courts also operate small claims courts, where individuals can take cases with damage claims up to $7,500 before a judge without attorneys—sort of like television's *Judge Judy.*

Losers in trial courts may ask the court on the next rung of the judicial ladder to review the decision. Most cases aren't appealed, but when major crimes and penalties or big money are involved, the losers in the cases sometimes request a review by one of California's six district **courts of appeal.** As appellate bodies, these courts do not hold trials like the ones we see on television. Lawyers make arguments and submit briefs to panels of three justices, who try to determine whether the original trial was conducted fairly. These justices consider only possible legal errors, not the verdict in the case. If they find errors,

superior courts Lower courts in which criminal and civil cases are first tried.

courts of appeal Three-justice panels that hear appeals from lower courts.

PERCEPTION VERSUS REALITY

Judges Must Never "Legislate from the Bench"

Whenever the selection of new judges comes into popular view—for example, when the national Senate holds hearings on a United States Supreme Court nominee—we hear again and again this refrain: we must choose judges that will not make policy. Republican lawmakers especially argue that judges should never "legislate from the bench," but should restrict themselves to applying the law as it is written. A judge's personal predilections should not influence the court's decision; rather, judges should simply follow the law.

The Perception

Although opposition to "judicial policymaking" has been a mantra among Republican legislators, in California as elsewhere, ordinary citizens of all parties tend to believe that judges go too far in setting policy. The belief is widespread that that judges create new law, as opposed to interpreting existing law, and that this is a bad thing.

The Reality

Lower-level courts, such as California's superior courts, do apply the law as they find it. Judges in such courts have little leeway for making innovative rulings. At the appellate and especially at the California Supreme Court level, however, matters are different. Questions are brought to the supreme court precisely because a dispute exists as to how the law should be interpreted. The supreme court hears cases only when there are strong arguments on both sides.

Furthermore, the belief that the law can be applied "exactly as written" rests on a misunderstanding of what written law looks like. Consider one of the most famous examples, the prohibition in the national Bill of Rights of "cruel and unusual" punishments. What does *cruel* mean? What does *unusual* mean? These words are inevitably subject to interpretation, and interpretations can change as society changes. These are not terms such as "one hundred dollars" or "two years" that have exact, indisputable meanings. It gets worse. In California as elsewhere, the legislature regularly passes bills that contain words such as *reasonable* or *appropriate*. What, exactly, does this terminology refer to? Any bill that contains a word like *reasonable* might as well also contain an explicit clause that states: "The exact meaning of this statute will be left up to the executive and the courts."

Blog On For a broad discussion of policymaking by the courts, see **newtalk.org/2008/07/what-is-the-role-of-the-courts.php.** Lino A. Graglia, a professor of law at the University of Texas, believes his state ought to have a California-style initiative and referendum system precisely to rein in "lawmaking judges." He argues the point at **www.initiativefortexas.org/graglia.html.**

they can send the case back for another trial or even dismiss the charges.

Ultimately, parties to the cases may petition for review by the seven-member state **supreme court,** the top of California's judicial ladder. Few cases reach this level because most are resolved in the lower courts and the high court declines most of the petitions. When the California Supreme Court hears a case, its decision is final unless issues of federal law or the U.S. Constitution arise; the United States Supreme Court may consider such cases.

If a higher court refuses an appeal, the lower court's decision stands. Even when a case is accepted, the justices of the higher court have agreed only to consider the issues. They may or may not overturn the decision of the lower court.

supreme court California's highest judicial body; hears appeals from lower courts.

Judicial Election and Selection

Although the tiered structure of the California courts is similar to that of the federal courts, the selection of judges is not. Federal judges and members of the United States Supreme Court are appointed by the president subject to confirmation by the U.S. Senate. Once appointed, they serve for life. California judges and justices, however, gain office through a more complicated process and regularly face the voters. This periodic scrutiny by the public, the media, and interest groups helps keep judges and their decisions in the news.

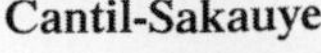

Cantil-Sakauye

Baxter

Chin

Corrigan

Kennard

Moreno

Werdegar

AP PHOTO/PAUL SAKUMA, FILE

Pictured here are California's seven Supreme Court justices, from left to right: Chief Justice Tani Cantil-Sakauye, Associate Justice Marvin R. Baxter, Associate Justice Ming W. Chin, Associate Justice Carol A. Corrigan, Associate Justice Joyce L. Kennard, Associate Justice Carlos R. Moreno, and Associate Justice Kathryn Mickle Werdegar.

runoff election When no candidate receives more than 50 percent of the vote in a nonpartisan primary for trial court judge or local office, the top two candidates face each other in a runoff.

Commission on Judicial Appointments A commission to review and make recommendations on the governor's nominees for appellate and supreme courts; consists of the attorney general, the chief justice of the state supreme court, and the senior presiding judge of the courts of appeal.

Formal qualifications to become a judge are few: candidates must have been admitted to practice law in California for at least ten years. Technically, superior court judges are elected, but most actually gain office through appointment by the governor when a sitting judge dies, retires, or is promoted between elections. The governor also appoints people to the bench when the legislature creates new judgeships. A governor who is elected to two terms of office may appoint as many as half of the state's sitting judges, significantly affecting judicial practices. Governors generally appoint judges who are members of their own political parties, although Republican governor Arnold Schwarzenegger has been more willing than any of his predecessors to appoint judges who are not members of his own political party.[1] Prior service as a district attorney (prosecutor) is common for successful appointees—a fact leading to complaints that judges in general are biased against defendants and defense attorneys.[2]

Appointed judges must run for office when their terms expire, but running as incumbents, they almost always win. Superior court judges can also gain office simply by declaring their candidacy for a specific judicial office and then running. If no candidate wins a majority in the primary election, the two candidates with the most votes face each other in a **runoff election** in November. Superior court judges serve six-year terms and then may run for reelection, usually without opposition. Judges have no term limits.

Appointments and the Higher Courts

Unlike lower court judges, members of the district courts of appeal and the state supreme court attain office only by gubernatorial appointment. The governor's possible nominees are first screened by the state's legal community through its Commission on Judicial Nominees Evaluation. Then the nominees must be approved by the **Commission on Judicial Appointments,** consisting of the attorney general, the chief justice of the state supreme court, and the senior presiding justice of the courts of appeal. The commission may reject a nominee, but it has done so only twice since its creation in 1934.

Once approved by the Commission on Judicial Appointments, the new justices take office, but they must go before the voters at the next gubernatorial election. No opponents or political party labels appear on the ballot; the voters simply check yes or no on the retention of the justices in question. If approved, they serve the remainder of the twelve-year term of the person they have replaced, at which time they can seek voter confirmation for a standard twelve-year term and additional terms after that.

Eleven other states select their supreme court justices in a similar fashion, but twenty-six rely solely on elections. The governor or legislature appoints justices in the remaining twelve states.

Firing Judges

Almost all judges easily win election and reelection, mostly without opposition. Those who designed the system probably intended it to be this way. They wanted to distance judges somewhat from politics and to ensure their independence by giving them relatively long terms, thus also ensuring relatively consistent interpretation of the law. Avoiding costly election campaigns that depend on financial contributors also promotes independence. The framers of the U.S. Constitution put such a high value on judicial continuity and independence that they provided for selection by appointment rather than by election and allowed judges to serve for life. For most of California's history, these values also seemed well entrenched in the political culture, and the state's judges functioned without much criticism or interference. Nevertheless, California's constitution provides several mechanisms of judicial accountability, all of which have been used recently. Judges can be removed through elections, but they can also be reprimanded or removed by the judicial system itself.

REMOVAL BY THE VOTERS Incumbent justices of the California Supreme Court routinely won reelection without serious challenge until 1966, when a backlash against decisions that supported racial integration led to an unsuccessful campaign to unseat justices who were viewed as too liberal. Over the next two decades, several lower court judges faced challenges because critics viewed them as lenient toward criminals, and some were defeated. Although early efforts to oust liberal members of the state supreme court failed, anticourt elements triumphed in 1986, when Chief Justice Rose Bird and two other liberal justices appointed by former Democratic governor Jerry Brown were swept out of office—the only justices removed by the voters in California history. Since then, the anticourt fervor has subsided. Today, sitting judges are rarely challenged.

REMOVAL BY THE COMMISSION Judges also can be removed by the judicial system itself. The **Commission on Judicial Performance** was created in 1960 to investigate charges of misconduct or incompetence. Its members include three judges (appointed by the supreme court), two lawyers (appointed by the governor), and six public members (two each appointed by the governor, the senate Rules Committee, and the speaker of the assembly). Few investigations result in any action, but if the charges are confirmed, the commission may impose censure, removal from office, or forced retirement.

Commission on Judicial Performance The state board empowered to investigate charges of judicial misconduct or incompetence.

Cruz Reynoso, the first Latino to sit on the California Supreme Court, was ousted by voters in 1986 under California's unusual judicial-retention election system. Should voters be able to unseat justices?

MICHAEL SMITH/NEWSMAKERS/GETTY IMAGES

Hundreds of complaints against judges are filed with the commission each year; about one-third are investigated. In the rare cases in which the commission finds a judge to be at fault, it usually issues a warning or reprimand. Even more rarely, the commission may remove a judge from the bench. In recent years, judges have been removed for lying about campaign funds, threatening a district attorney, inappropriate interventions in trials, and in one case, excessive delays and neglect of court orders. Actual removals from the bench are rare, however, because those whose conduct is questionable usually resign before the commission's investigation is completed.

LO2 *The Courts at Work*

In 2007–2008, 9,552,781 cases were filed in California's trial courts. Traffic infractions made up 68.4 percent of these cases. Felony and misdemeanor (criminal) cases numbered 1,252,556 (13.1 percent), and the balance were civil suits (on contract disputes, for example) or divorce and family law cases.[3]

The Legal Process

California's constitution guarantees the right to a jury trial for both criminal and civil cases; if both parties agree, however, a judge alone may hear the case. In jury trials, prospective jurors are drawn from lists of licensed drivers, voters, and property owners, but finding a twelve-member jury is often difficult. Many people avoid jury duty because it takes time away from work and pays only a few dollars a day. Homemakers and retired people are most readily available, but they alone cannot make up a balanced jury. Poor people and minorities tend to be underrepresented because they are less likely to be on the lists from which jurors are drawn and because some avoid participation in a system that they distrust.

The parties in civil cases provide their own lawyers, although legal aid societies sometimes help those who can't afford counsel. In criminal cases, the **district attorney,** an elected county official, carries out the prosecution. Defendants hire their own attorney or are provided with a court-appointed attorney if they cannot afford one. California's larger counties employ a **public defender** to provide such assistance. Well over half of all felony defendants require court-appointed help.

Most cases never go to trial, though. In over 90 percent of all criminal cases, the defendant pleads guilty, often by **plea bargaining,** which results in a pretrial agreement on a plea and a penalty. Plea bargaining reduces the heavy workload of the courts and guarantees some punishment or restitution, but it also allows those charged with a crime to serve shorter sentences than they might have received if convicted of all charges.

"WHETHER BORN FROM EXPERIENCE OR INHERENT PHYSIOLOGICAL OR CULTURAL DIFFERENCES, our gender and national origins may and will make a difference in our judging."

~ SONIA SOTOMAYOR ~
ASSOCIATE JUSTICE OF
THE UNITED STATES SUPREME COURT
2009–PRESENT

district attorney The chief prosecuting officer elected in each county; represents the people against the accused in criminal cases.

public defender A county officer representing defendants who cannot afford an attorney; appointed by the county board of supervisors.

plea bargaining An agreement between the prosecution and the accused in which the latter pleads guilty to a reduced charge and lesser penalty.

Most civil suits are also settled without a trial because the parties to the cases reach an agreement to avoid the high costs and long delays of a trial. Only about 0.1 percent of all cases are tried before a jury (11,218 in 2007–2008); a judge alone hears the others that go to trial.[4]

It is important to note that the judicial system as a whole—including judges, prosecutors, public defenders, lawyers, and juries—does not reflect the diversity of California's people. About 83 percent of California's nearly 170,000 active attorneys are non-Hispanic whites, even though minority group members make up 58 percent of the population. About one-third of the state's attorneys are women, however—a number that is quickly rising.[5] Ethnic representation among California's judges is similar: 71 percent are male, and 73 percent are white.[6] These numbers lead critics to express concern about the fact that a predominantly white judicial system metes out justice to defendants who are, in the majority, nonwhite and that punishment is less severe for whites than for minorities convicted of the same crime.[7] African Americans, and to a lesser extent other minorities, perceive this situation and express deep mistrust of the system. Minority participation as attorneys and court officials has increased over time (Table 22–1 shows increasing diversity in judicial appointments), but considerable disparities remain.

Appeals

When a dispute arises over a trial proceeding or its outcome, the losing party may appeal to a higher court to review the case. Most appeals are refused, but the higher courts may agree to hear a case because of previous procedural problems (for instance, if the defendant was not read his or her rights) or because it raises untested legal issues. Appellate courts do not retry the case or review the facts in evidence; their job is to determine whether the original trial was fair and the law was applied appropriately. In addition to traditional appellate cases, the state supreme court also automatically reviews all death penalty decisions. Although few in number (17 in 2007–2008), these cases take up a substantial amount of the supreme court's time. A few other

Table 22-1

Judicial Appointments by California Governors, 1959–2010

	Male	Female	Non-Hispanic White	Non-Hispanic Black	Hispanic	Asian
Ronald Reagan (R) 1967–1975	97.4% (478)	2.6% (13)	93.1% (457)	2.6% (13)	3.3% (16)	1.0% (5)
Jerry Brown (D) 1975–1983	84.0 (691)	16.0 (132)	75.5 (621)	10.9 (90)	9.4 (77)	4.3 (35)
George Deukmejian (R) 1983–1991	84.8 (821)	15.2 (147)	87.7 (849)	3.6 (35)	5.0 (49)	3.6 (35)
Pete Wilson (R) 1991–1998	74.6 (517)	25.4 (176)	84.4 (585)	5.2 (36)	4.9 (34)	5.5 (38)
Gray Davis (D) 1999–2003	65.8 (237)	34.2 (123)	70.8 (255)	9.25 (33)	12.8 (46)	7.2 (26)
Arnold Schwarzenegger (R) 2003–2010	65.0 (370)	35.0 (199)	73.7 (419)	7.6 (43)	10.7 (61)	8.0 (46)

Source: Governor's Office.

cases come to it directly. Known as *original proceedings,* these include cases involving writs of *mandamus* (ordering a government action) and *habeas corpus* (a request for reasons why someone is in custody). Neither the courts of appeal nor the state supreme court can initiate cases. No matter how eager they are to intervene in an issue, they have to wait for someone else to bring the case to them.

LO3 The Supreme Court

Every year, about 10,000 petitions are filed with the California Supreme Court, mostly requesting reviews of cases decided by the courts of appeal. Each year the members of the court, meeting "in conference," choose about two hundred petitions for consideration, a task that consumes an estimated 40 percent of the court's time. By refusing to hear a case, the court allows the preceding decision to stand. When the court grants a hearing, one of the justices (or a staff member) writes a calendar memo analyzing the case. Attorneys representing the two sides present written briefs and then oral arguments, during which they face rigorous questioning by the justices.

collegiality Deferential behavior among justices as a way of building consensus on issues before the court.

Judicial Council Chaired by the chief justice of the state supreme court and composed of twenty-one judges and attorneys; makes the rules for court procedures, collects data on the courts' operations and workload, and gives seminars for judges.

After hearing the oral arguments, the justices discuss the case in conference and vote in order of seniority; the chief justice casts the final, and sometimes decisive, vote. If the chief justice agrees with the majority, he or she can assign a justice to write the official court opinion; usually this is the same justice who wrote the initial calendar memo. A draft of the opinion then circulates among the justices, each of whom may concur, suggest changes, or write a dissenting opinion. Finally, after many months, the court's decision is made public. The court issued 116 opinions in 2007–2008—about 1 percent of all the cases filed.

This time-consuming process allows plenty of room for politicking among the justices and depends on a high degree of cooperation and deferential behavior among them—what judges call **collegiality**—as a way of building consensus on issues under consideration. With seven independent minds on the court, ongoing negotiations are needed to reach a majority and a decision.

Running the Courts

In addition to deciding cases, the chief justice acts as the administrative head of the California court system. This entails setting procedures for hearings and deliberations, managing public information for the supreme court, and overseeing its staff. The chief justice also assigns cases to specific appellate courts and appoints temporary justices when there are vacancies on the supreme court due to disqualification, illness, or retirement.

As chair of the **Judicial Council,** the chief justice also takes a hand in managing the entire state court system. The Judicial Council has twenty-one members, including fourteen judges (appointed by the chief justice), four attorneys (appointed by the state bar association), and one member from each house of the state legislature. The Judicial Council makes the rules for court procedures, collects data on the operations and workload of the courts, and oversees the Administrative Office of the Courts with 901 employees and a $220 million budget. During the state budget crisis of 2009, the Judicial Council voted to close the courts one day a month, despite an increasing workload.

"Unfortunately, our constitution, which has been amended 512 times since it was written in 1879, has created a system where **NOTHING CAN GET DONE.**"

~ JOHN GRUBB ~
SPOKESPERSON FOR "REPAIR CALIFORNIA"
2009

The High Court as a Political Battleground

The courts are particularly important and powerful in California because of the nature of California's government and politics. California's constitution has been amended more than five hundred times since it was written in 1879, making it both long and elaborately specific, with components addressing all sorts of matters, both major and mundane. The density of California's constitution is reflected in the structures of government it sets out and is increased through constant revision by initiative. In turn, the length, detail, and continually changing complexity of California's constitution give the courts greater power, because they have the job of determining whether laws and public policy are consistent with the constitution. One scholar called the courts a "shadow government"[8] because of their importance in shaping public policy, but others view this as the courts' appropriate constitutional role.

At the top of California's judicial ladder is the state supreme court, the ultimate interpreter of the state constitution (unless issues arise under the U.S. Constitution).

California's former chief justice Ronald M. George, blamed voters and the state's century-old citizens' initiative process for the troubles in Sacramento. In an October 2009 speech, he argued that "frequent amendments—coupled with the implicit threat of more in the future—have rendered our state government dysfunctional." Is direct democracy doing more harm than good?

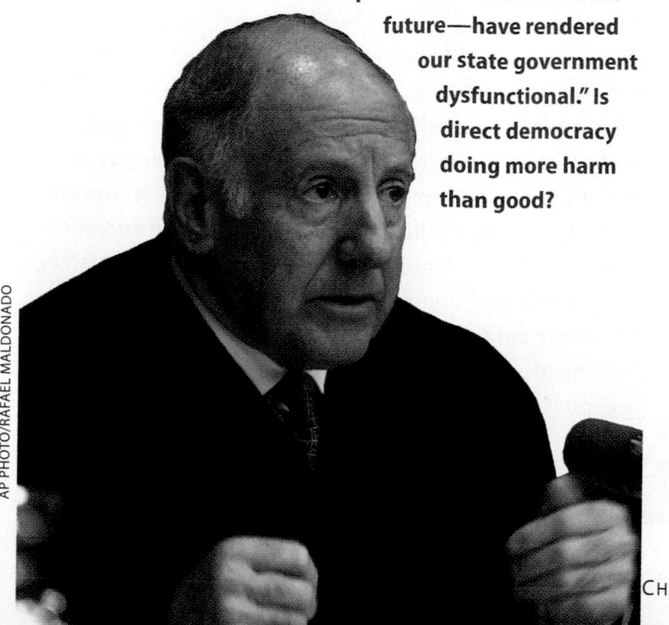

AP PHOTO/RAFAEL MALDONADO

The court's power makes it a center of political interest: governors strive to appoint justices who share their values and pay close attention to the appointment process. As governors have changed, so have the sorts of justices they appoint. And as its membership has changed, the California Supreme Court has moved across the spectrum from liberal to conservative.

Regardless of its collective political values, the court has not backed away from tackling controversial issues, including occasionally overturning decisions of the legislature or the people (as expressed in initiatives). This willingness is less because of interventionist attitudes on the part of the justices than because of a long, complex, and frequently amended constitution and poorly written laws and initiatives.

Governors, Voters, and the Courts

Long dominated by liberals, California's supreme court took a distinct turn toward the right in 1986, after the voters rejected the reelections of three liberal justices, including Rose Bird, the controversial chief justice at the time. Appointed in 1977 by Governor Jerry Brown, Bird and her colleagues waded into controversy with unpopular rulings on busing for school desegregation and Proposition 13 (the popular property tax reduction initiative), as well as consistently reversing death sentences even as public concern about crime increased. When Bird and two other liberal justices were on the ballot in 1986, conservative Republican governor George Deukmejian led a successful campaign to defeat them. With three new openings, Deukmejian transformed the court with conservative appointees, including a new chief justice.

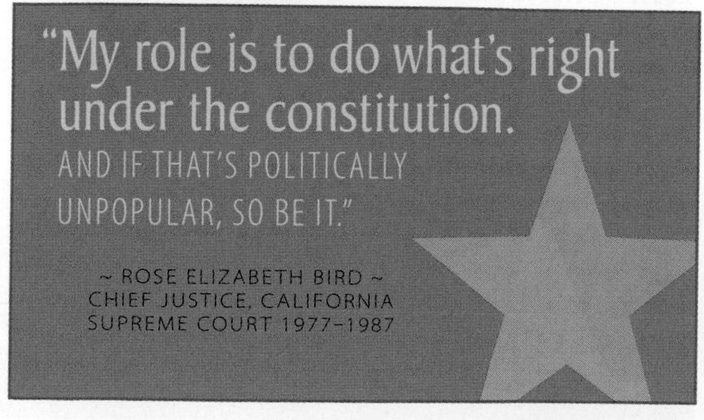
"My role is to do what's right under the constitution.
AND IF THAT'S POLITICALLY UNPOPULAR, SO BE IT."
~ ROSE ELIZABETH BIRD ~
CHIEF JUSTICE, CALIFORNIA SUPREME COURT 1977–1987

judicial activism Making policy through court decisions rather than through the legislative or electoral process.

Proposition 8 (2008) An initiative that amended the state constitution to restrict marriage to opposite-sex couples.

"IT IS A TRAVESTY that the court has, for the first time in California history, permitted a simple majority to use the initiative process to strip a fundamental right from a minority group."

~ RAE CAREY ~
EXECUTIVE DIRECTOR OF THE NATIONAL GAY AND LESBIAN TASK FORCE 2008–PRESENT

Subsequent appointees have maintained the court's conservative majority. Today's court includes Marvin Baxter and Joyce Kennard (both Deukmejian appointees) and Kathryn Werdegar and Ming Chin (appointed by Republican governor Pete Wilson). Governor Gray Davis appointed Carlos Moreno, the court's only Democrat, in 2001. The newest justices are Carol A. Corrigan, a 2006 appointment by Governor Schwarzenegger, and Tani Cantil-Sakauye, appointed chief justice by Schwarzenegger in 2010. Minority members of the court include Cantil-Sakauye (who is Asian), Moreno (who is Latino), Chin (who is Chinese), and Kennard (who is Dutch-Indonesian). Four of the court's seven members are women. All of the current justices have won voter approval, with 65 to 76 percent voting for their retention. Cantil-Sakauye was confirmed for a twelve-year term by the voters in 2010, and Justices Chin and Moreno each won an additional twelve-year term that year.

With a majority of the justices appointed by Republican governors and solidly confirmed by the voters, California's supreme court today is moderately conservative and less controversial than in the past. The court's conservatism is reflected in its tendency to be pro-prosecution in criminal cases and pro-business in economic cases.[9] The court also disappointed local governments seeking new taxes with rulings that rigidly applied a requirement for two-thirds voter approval, a strict interpretation of 1978's Proposition 13 (see Chapter 24).

California Supreme Court Justice Ming W. Chin listens to arguments for and against Proposition 8 in 2009. Chin faced a retention election in 2010; could this have affected his decisions?

PAUL SAKUMA-POOL/GETTYIMAGES

JUDICIAL ACTIVISM Overall, the supreme court avoids **judicial activism** (making policy through court decisions rather than through the legislative or electoral process), but even the current conservative court sometimes asserts its independence, wading into political controversy and significantly affecting state politics. For example, it has followed the Bird court's precedent of approving state-funded abortions, and in 1997 the court ruled against Governor Pete Wilson's plan to privatize the work of the state transportation agency. In 2009, the court rejected a plan by the governor and state legislature to solve their own budget problems by taking transportation and redevelopment funds from local governments.

OVERRULING THE VOTERS Most controversially, the courts sometimes overrule decisions of the voters, as they did when they struck down portions of voter-approved initiatives that required tougher sentences of criminals because the proposals shifted discretion from judges to prosecutors. Probably the highest-profile and most controversial action taken by the supreme court, however, was its 2008 ruling on same-sex marriage. When the City and County of San Francisco licensed such marriages in 2004, the supreme court ruled the marriages illegal on the basis of state law, as approved by the voters in 2002. But the constitutionality of that law was challenged in 2008, and on a four-to-three vote, the court ruled that "the California Constitution properly must be interpreted to guarantee this basic civil right to all Californians, whether gay or heterosexual, and to same-sex couples as well as to opposite-sex couples."[10] Opponents quickly qualified **Proposition 8,** an initiative constitutional amendment to restrict marriage to opposite-sex couples. Voters approved the measure, thus overruling the court. That initiative was subsequently challenged in court, but the California Supreme Court accepted it as a legitimate amendment to the state constitution. Then-chief justice George wrote that the court's decision was not based on whether Proposition 8 "is wise or

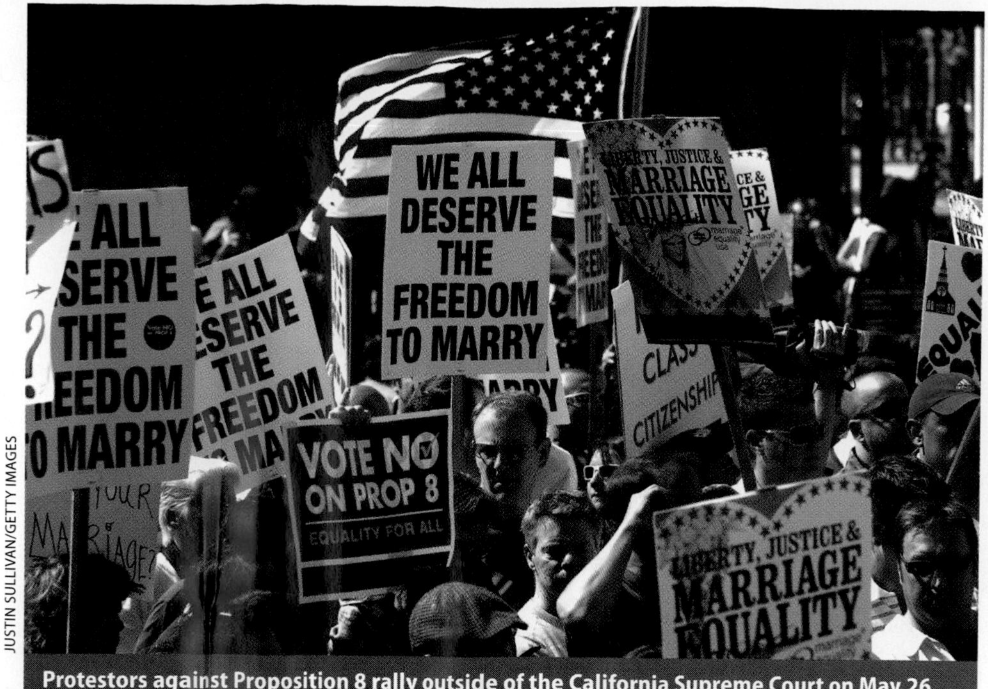

JUSTIN SULLIVAN/GETTY IMAGES

Protestors against Proposition 8 rally outside of the California Supreme Court on May 26, 2009 in San Francisco after the State Supreme Court voted 6–1 to uphold Proposition 8, making it illegal for same-sex couples to marry in the state of California.

sound as a matter of policy," but rather "concerns the right of the people . . . to change or alter the state constitution itself . . . Regardless of our views as individuals on this question of policy, we recognize as judges and as a court our responsibility to confine our consideration to a determination of the constitutional validity and legal effect of the measure in question."[11]

This decision did not put the issue to rest, however. The federal courts are sometimes drawn into battles over California initiatives, too. Since the 1990s, federal courts have overturned initiatives on campaign finance, open primary elections, and limits on public services for immigrants as violations of the U.S. Constitution, which trumps any state law or state constitution. In 2010, proponents of same-sex marriage took their case to a federal district court, arguing that Proposition 8 constituted a denial of equal rights under the U.S. Constitution. The judge in that case ruled in favor of the plaintiffs, thus overriding both the voters of the state of California and the state supreme court. The federal court ruling is being appealed, and the final decision will rest with the United States Supreme Court—or the voters of California when the issue comes back to them in yet another initiative.

Although judicial rulings against voter-approved laws appear undemocratic, the state and federal courts are doing their duty by interpreting these controversial propositions not only for their content but also for their consistency with the California and U.S. constitutions. When the courts find an act of another branch of government or of the voters to be contrary to existing law or to the state or federal constitution, it is their responsibility to overturn that law, even if their decision is unpopular. "When we invalidate one of these initiatives," former chief justice George argued, "what we are doing is not thwarting the public's will. We are adhering to the ultimate expression of the popular will: the Constitution of the United States, or the Constitution of the State of California, which has been adopted by the people and which imposes limits on the initiative process and on lawmaking by legislatures and by the executive."[12] We provide more detail on this controversy in the *Join the Debate* feature on the following page.

As controversial as the California Supreme Court's decisions sometimes are, the court's influence goes well beyond this state. A study of court decisions throughout the country found that courts in other states followed precedents set in California more than precedents set in the courts of any other state.[13] This suggests that the California court is well within the mainstream of jurisprudence in the United States. It's also one reason why the court battle over same-sex marriages was so hard fought.

LO4 *Courts and the Politics of Crime*

Crime topped the list of voter concerns in California and the nation during much of the 1980s and 1990s. Murder, rape, burglary, gang wars, and random violence seemed all too common. Republicans George Deukmejian and Pete Wilson were elected governor at least partly because they were seen as law-and-order candidates.

Capital Punishment

Capital punishment was a key issue in the 1980s, when a liberal supreme court overturned the vast majority of the death penalty cases it reviewed. Since 1986, when the voters rejected these liberals, the supreme court has affirmed most death sentences. The issue has not gone away, however. Law-and-order advocates still condemn

Should Judges Be Able to Overrule Voter Initiatives?

In 2000, by a margin of 62 to 39 percent, California voters approved Proposition 22, which sought to ban same-sex marriages in the state. In February 2004, six couples sued to have Proposition 22 overruled on the basis that it conflicted with the state constitution. The matter eventually wound up before the California Supreme Court. In May 2008, in a four-to-three vote, the court struck down all California statutes limiting marriage to same-sex couples.

Even before this ruling, opponents of same-sex marriage had been circulating petitions for a new initiative. On June 2, Proposition 8 was certified for the November ballot. The language of Proposition 8 was identical to the text of Proposition 22. Unlike the earlier measure, however, the new proposal was an amendment to the state constitution. Backers expected that Proposition 8 would therefore be immune from any court ruling that it was in violation of the constitution.

In November, Proposition 8 passed by a margin of 52 to 48 percent. Backers of same-sex marriage were devastated, but the result provided them with some hope for the future: support for same-sex marriage was clearly growing. In May 2009, the state supreme court upheld Proposition 8, but did not invalidate the same-sex marriages carried out before Election Day.

August 2010 brought a major new development. In that month, a U.S. District Court judge ruled that Proposition 8 violated the U.S. Constitution and should be struck down. The Ninth Circuit Court of Appeals then ruled that Proposition 8 would remain in effect pending its decision on the matter. Clearly, same-sex marriage was now headed for the United States Supreme Court.

These events raise some serious questions. Should judges be allowed to overturn the results of popular initiatives, as they did in the case of Proposition 22? Were there legal grounds on which the California Supreme Court could have rejected Proposition 8, and if so, should the court have done so? Californians are strongly at odds over these questions.

Respect the People's Will

Those who believe that California—and federal—courts should defer to the results of popular initiatives find it bad enough that the California Supreme Court struck down Proposition 22. That in itself was a classic example of legislation from the bench. Striking down a constitutional amendment such as Proposition 8 would be intolerable. It would leave the public with no appeal from an unacceptable judicial decision on a matter that was essentially political.

On the substance of the controversy, it would have been better if the minority had prevailed in May 2008 when the California Supreme Court ruled on same-sex marriage. Writing for the minority, Justice Marvin Baxter stated that the majority "does not have the right to erase, then recast, the age-old definition of marriage, as virtually all societies have understood it, in order to satisfy its own contemporary notions of equality and justice." Baxter noted that in any event, gay rights have gained increasing public support, and the right to same-sex marriage might soon be won through "the ordinary democratic process."[14]

Don't Put Fundamental Rights to a Vote

Those who believe that the courts should have consistently backed same-sex marriage by blocking both Propositions 22 and 8 argue that fundamental rights should never depend on a vote of the people. It is for that reason that the authors of the U.S. and California constitutions entrenched various rights in those documents, where they could not easily be overturned in response to the passions of the day. Indeed, the controversy over same-sex marriage in California can serve as a textbook example of why basic rights should be protected from popular prejudices.

Some long-time observers of California politics draw another conclusion from the various initiatives to amend the California Constitution. They argue that it is absurd to let a simple majority of the voters amend the constitution. These observers contend that amending the constitution ought to be hard, as it is in many jurisdictions.

Arguments exist that the court could have used to overturn Proposition 8. Under the terms of the state constitution, the document can be *amended* by an initiative, but can be *revised* only after the revision wins a two-thirds vote in the assembly and senate. The question of whether something is a revision or an amendment is not dependent on the amount of language involved. Revoking a fundamental right could easily be considered a revision.

For Critical Analysis ***Do you think that the California Supreme Court might have decided that revoking the right to same-sex marriage was a constitutional revision if the right had been in existence for many years, and not just a few months? Explain your reasoning***

the lengthy delays that plague death penalty appeals—up to ten years for the state courts and another ten years for the federal courts—but experts say that much of the delay is because the courts are unable to either find legal counsel for the condemned or handle the workload. A recent report called the system "broken" and "dysfunctional."[15] Neither the proponents nor the opponents of the death penalty are satisfied with its current administration. Meanwhile, forensic methods such as DNA testing have revealed wrongful convictions in death penalty cases so frequently that a moratorium on executions has been proposed.

In 2006 a federal judge took the issue of capital punishment out of the state courts with a ruling suspending executions in California due to concerns about the drugs used for lethal injections and the conditions of outdated prison facilities for executions. Since then, the state has built a new death chamber, but executions remained suspended as of 2010 because the state failed to satisfy the federal court regarding lethal injections.

Three Strikes Initiative

Law-and-order proponents also pushed for tougher sentences for other crimes. Beginning in the 1980s, voters passed a series of initiatives that strengthened penalties for many crimes, and in 1994 the electorate approved the "three-strikes" initiative. The new law reflected the view that liberal judges who were "soft on crime" were letting criminals off with light sentences. **"Three strikes"** required anyone convicted of three felonies to serve a sentence of twenty-five years to life: "three strikes and you're out."

"THE MEDICAL AND MENTAL HEALTH CARE AVAILABLE TO INMATES IN THE CALIFORNIA PRISON SYSTEM IS **woefully and constitutionally inadequate** AND HAS BEEN FOR MORE THAN A DECADE."

~ EXCERPT FROM A 184-PAGE RULING BY THREE FEDERAL JUDGES IN 2009

The three-strikes law quickly increased the state's prison population, as well as its spending on prisons (see Chapter 24). New prisons were built, and operating the state prison system absorbs an ever-growing share of the state budget. With many of the state's worst criminals incarcerated for life, three-strikes prosecutions declined, and so did California's crime rate. Violent crime in California peaked in 1992 (two years before the three-strikes law) and has declined since then. In 2008 the number of violent crimes was about the same as in 1979, even with 14 million more people living in the state.[16] Conservatives attribute this decline to tougher judges and penalties, but many experts argue that the declining crime rate was due to economic prosperity and demographics, with fewer people in the age group that is most commonly associated with criminal activity. Even in the recent recession, crime rates continue to decline. In any case, crime has resonated far less as an issue in recent statewide elections. In the last few years, education, the economy, and health care have outranked crime as the top concerns of California voters.

Several hundred inmates crowd into the gymnasium at San Quentin prison. With the increase in the state's prison population, San Quentin prison, the oldest in the state, had reached a population of 5,300 inmates as of May 2009, more than 2,000 over its maximum capacity design of 2,300.

AP PHOTO/ERIC RISBERG

Meanwhile, the prison population in California remains huge, which means the cost of incarcerating all these men and women is also huge. But despite a massive investment of tax funds, California's prisons are overcrowded and beset by violence and disease. A system built for 84,271 inmates housed 173,479 in 2006 (a historic high) and 168,830 in 2009.[17] Conditions in the prison health-care system were so bad that a class action suit was brought to a federal court, which intervened on grounds that these conditions constituted "cruel and unusual punishment" under the U.S. Constitution. In 2005 a federal

"three strikes" A 1994 law and initiative requiring sentences of twenty-five years to life for anyone convicted of three felonies.

judge put the prison health system in the hands of a court-appointed monitor. In 2009, seeing minimal progress, federal judges gave the state forty-five days to come up with a plan to reduce the prison population—and then rejected the plan submitted by Governor Schwarzenegger, who was unable to persuade the legislature to fund new prisons or approve release of some prisoners (the elderly or low-level offenders, for example). Schwarzenegger appealed the case to the United States Supreme Court, but a ruling was not expected before 2011.

California Law

Crime and other issues discussed in this chapter remind us that the courts play a central role in the politics of our state. Controversies about judicial appointments and decisions make the political nature of the courts apparent, especially when the rulings of the court conflict with the will of the electorate as expressed in initiatives. Yet the courts can never be free of politics. They make policy and interpret the law, and their judgments vary with the values of those who make them.

CALIFORNIA AT ODDS *California Law*

Unlike the legislature, the California courts are well-respected. Still, not everything that the courts do meets with popular approval. California citizens are at odds over a number of judicial issues, including the following:

- Should state judges appear before the voters, thus ensuring that the people have a voice in judicial decisions—or would justice be better served through the system used by the national government, in which judges are appointed and confirmed, and then serve indefinitely?
- Do judges, on a regular basis, improperly intervene in policymaking—or do most rulings on policy result from attempts to interpret vague and imprecise legislation?
- Is plea-bargaining a necessary and appropriate response to heavy court workloads—or is it a scandal that results in light sentences for the guilty and frequently punishes the innocent?
- Is the three-strikes law a useful way to protect the public by keeping career criminals off the streets—or is it a formula for injustice and unaffordably crowded prisons?
- Should the courts respect the results of ballot initiatives as expressions of the popular will—or should judges block any popular initiative that appears to limit fundamental rights?

Take Action

By design, the courts are more thoroughly insulated from popular pressures than are the other two branches of government. It is relatively easy, however, to educate yourself about the normal functioning of the courts. Normally, trials and hearings are open to the public. It may be hard to find a seat at a trial that has received massive attention in the press, but ordinary judicial proceedings almost always have vacant seats. Try attending some sample sessions of a superior court in your area. If you are able to let the court staff know that you are a student who is trying to learn more about the courts, most of them will be pleased with your visit. If you are able to view a series of proceedings, consider any similarities or differences that you may observe. What kinds of people come before the court? Do different kinds of people appear for different reasons? If a defendant is represented by a public defender, how prepared is that attorney? Do any plea bargaining agreements seem appropriate? How does the judge treat the lawyers and citizens who appear in court?

YOUR VOTE COUNTS

POLITICS ON THE WEB

- To learn more about California's court system, visit the California Courts Web site at **www.courtinfo.ca.gov**.
- The State Bar of California has shaped the development of the law, regulated the professional conduct of the state's lawyers, and provided greater access to the justice system for all citizens. To access information about the legal system, visit **www.calbar.org**.
- To learn more about the California Judges Association and access judicial resources, go to **www.caljudges.org**.
- To research legal issues and to find a lawyer, go to **www.avvo.com**.

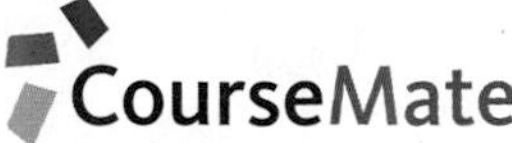

Access CourseMate to review and expand on this chapter through quizzes, flashcards, learning objectives, interactive timelines, a crossword puzzle, audio summaries, video, critical-thinking activities, simulations, and more.

GOVT 23

The Executive Branch: Coping with Fragmented Authority

LEARNING OBJECTIVES

LO1 Explain both the formal and informal powers of the governor.

LO2 Describe the role of the other major members of the executive branch.

LO3 Summarize the makeup and tasks of the bureaucracy, and how it is administered.

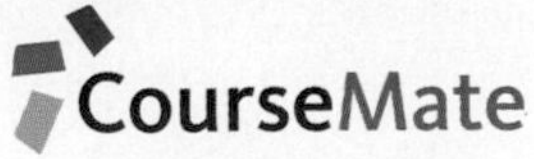

CALIFORNIA AT ODDS

Was Recalling Gray Davis Necessary?

On October 7, 2003, Californians took the unique step of recalling their governor, removing him from office. Gray Davis became the first governor to be recalled in the history of California and only the second in the history of the country. (North Dakota recalled its governor in 1921.) Davis had just been reelected as governor in November 2002—the recall campaign was announced in February 2003, when Davis was one month into his second term of office. Beginning in March, the recall committee had 160 days to collect 897,158 valid signatures of registered voters. It collected 1,363,411.

The resulting ballot had two parts. The first asked whether Davis should be recalled. The second asked which of 135 candidates should replace Davis as governor. If the voters had decided against a recall, the second question would have been irrelevant. In fact, the electorate chose to recall Davis by a margin of 55.4 to 44.6 percent. Republican Arnold Schwarzenegger, a famous actor, was elected governor with 48.6 percent of the vote. Democratic lieutenant governor Cruz Bustamante placed second with 31.5 percent; 131 candidates failed to win even 1 percent.

In some ways, it was surprising that Davis had been reelected in November. He was a singularly uncharismatic politician. The Democratic state attorney general who served with him observed that he "doesn't have any friends." Davis was well known for political opportunism and the relentless pursuit of campaign contributions. Furthermore, voters across the state were angry with him because of the California electricity crisis of 2000–2001, when shortages resulted in rolling blackouts and a tremendous escalation of energy bills. Arguments that the crisis resulted from a flawed deregulation plan championed by the previous Republican governor and that Davis had little power to combat the problem did not satisfy voters. The last straw was Davis's announcement in December following his reelection that California faced a huge budget deficit. At $38.2 billion, the deficit was larger than the deficits of every other state added together.

Should Davis have been recalled? Californians are at odds over this question.

The Recall was Pointless

Those opposed to recalling Davis do not believe that recalls of this type are appropriate, given the legitimacy we accord to elections. How can we justify initiating a recall one month after the voters decide the outcome of a race? If we can recall someone this quickly, we might as well do away with regularly scheduled elections altogether. This whole affair tells us more about how the recall process can be manipulated by well-funded ideologues than it tells us about Gray Davis. Indeed, most of the problems that angered Californians at the time were beyond the governor's control. Recalling Davis did nothing to eliminate California's continuing budget problems. It did nothing to end the perpetual deadlock in the state legislature. What it did do was legitimize the idea of recalling an official simply due to unpopularity, not because of corruption or violation of the law. In the eyes of many recall opponents, the vote only worsened California's besetting political sins: irresponsible majoritarianism, cynicism, and demagoguery.

Davis Had to Go

Defenders of the recall disagree with the idea that a recall election is somehow illegitimate. Rather, they consider it an admirable exercise of popular democracy. California has its problems, but solving them requires more participation by its citizens, not less. True, California's budget problems can't be pinned on Gray Davis alone. Davis, however, was not the right person to serve as governor in a period in which strong leadership was essential. To be sure, California's budget crisis was a tremendous challenge to Governor Schwarzenegger and every other state leader. But could we really have done better with a governor who lacked Schwarzenegger's ability to communicate and persuade? If at times Schwarzenegger failed, could a man with no friends possibly have done better? Recall supporters would say no.

WHERE DO YOU STAND?

1. **Do you think the recall effort could have succeeded if it had not attracted strong gubernatorial candidates such as Schwarzenegger? Why or why not?**
2. **Is it likely that Californians will recall additional officials in years to come, or was the Gray recall relatively unique? Explain your reasoning.**

EXPLORE THIS ISSUE ONLINE

- **Thomas Cronin, political scientist and president of Whitman College in Washington state, criticized the recall effort in the *Seattle Times*. You can find this article and others at search.nwsource.com/search?sort=date&from=ST&byline=Thomas E. Cronin.**
- **The American Homeowners Resource Center was one of the groups campaigning for the recall. See it at www.ahrc.se/new/index.php/src/news/sub/letter/action/ShowMedia/id/535.**

Introduction

The **governor** is California's most powerful public official. He or she shapes the state budget, appoints key policymakers in the executive and judicial branches, and both responds to and shapes public opinion by taking positions on controversial issues. The governor also is the state's chief administrator; the unofficial leader of his or her political party; and liaison to other states, the U.S. government, and other nations. There are times when the governor's powers extend even beyond their normally broad limits to international issues such as immigration or global warming. At times, the governor's performance can generate intense reactions, as evidenced by the vote to recall Governor Gray Davis in 2003. We describe that incident in the chapter-opening *California at Odds* feature. No one in state government is in the spotlight as often the governor.

Unlike the president of the United States, the governor of California shares authority with seven other independently elected executive officers. Occasionally, these other executives clash with the governor over the use of power, as do the legislature and the judiciary. Simply put, the executive branch is anything but a unified body. Endless schisms between officeholders contribute to the state's fragmentation.

There has been one change in the drama among elected officials, however. Term limits, although applicable to both the executive and legislative branches, have left the governor in a stronger position relative to the legislature because of the governor's near certainty of two 4-year terms of office. With legislative leaders ascending to power on much shorter time schedules, the governor's experience has worked to his favor. Would further changes to the state constitution improve governance? We examine that question in the *California Faces a Troubled Economy* feature on the facing page.

Table 23–1

California Governors and Their Parties, 1943–2015

Name	Party	Dates in Office
Earl Warren	Republican*	1943–1953
Goodwin J. Knight	Republican	1953–1959
Edmund G. Brown, Sr.	Democrat	1959–1967
Ronald Reagan	Republican	1967–1975
Jerry Brown	Democrat	1975–1983
George Deukmejian	Republican	1983–1991
Pete Wilson	Republican	1991–1999
Gray Davis	Democrat	1999–November 2003
Arnold Schwarzenegger	Republican	2003–2011
Jerry Brown	Democrat	2011–2015

*Warren cross-filed as both a Republican and a Democrat in 1946 and 1950.
Source: California Secretary of State.

LO1 *The Governor: First Among Equals*

The current governor of California, Democrat Edmund J. ("Jerry") Brown, Jr., was elected in 2010. Brown succeeded Arnold Schwarzenegger, who had been elected after the recall of Gray Davis from office (see Table 23–1). With an annual salary of $206,500, he is the highest-paid chief executive of the fifty states. The governor of New York, second highest in the nation, receives $179,000. Still, this compensation is well below the salaries earned by many other government employees in California, particularly in large cities and counties. Even among state employees, prison wardens, retirement program coordinators, physicians, and university presidents earn considerably more than the governor.

governor California's highest-ranking executive office-holder; elected every four years.

Jerry Brown's election to the governor's office is the latest example of California's bizarre politics. A political fixture in the state since his first election to the Los Angeles Community College District Board of Trustees

California state Controller John Chiang told reporters that he wouldn't write $3.7 billion worth of checks due in 2009 if a budget deal were not in place. What authority does he have to refuse to abide by the governor's order?

HTTP://WWW.SCO.CA.GOV/

CALIFORNIA FACES A
TROUBLED ECONOMY

Would a New Constitution Help California?

In 2009, Governor Schwarzenegger said that he "absolutely" loved the idea of a state constitutional convention to revamp the state's machinery of government. A business group called the Bay Area Council also took an interest in this concept. It sponsored Repair California, a campaign to put a convention call on the November 2010 ballot. Repair California's convention call contained some interesting provisions. One was the method of choosing convention delegates: a substantial share of them would be selected at random, as if from a jury pool.

Let's Start Over

"Our Government has failed us," said Jim Wunderman, president of the Bay Area Council. California once had the nation's best schools, finest infrastructure, and a booming economy. Now the state has the worst bond rating of any of the fifty states. The public schools are ranked near the bottom. California is regularly described as the worst state in the country to do business. The only way to make the comprehensive changes needed to put the state back on track is a constitutional convention.

The movement to call a constitutional convention drew initial support, and played well in public opinion polls. Ultimately, however, Repair California ran out of funds and was unable to place the necessary propositions on the ballot. In October 2010, however, Nicolas Berggruen, a globe-trotting billionaire born in Paris, pledged $20 million toward an effort to restructure the state government. As a result, Californians may hear more about constitutional reform in the near future.

Step-by-Step Is Faster and Safer

Erwin Chemerinsky, dean of the UC Irvine Law School, is a constitutional convention skeptic. He came by his skepticism the hard way, as chair of a commission elected to rewrite the Los Angeles city charter. Every proposed change to the structure of the Los Angeles city government that might have had a real effect proved to be controversial. In the end, the final product was underwhelming.

Chemerinsky believes that the process of writing and implementing a new constitution would take years. The state needs faster solutions. For example, the two-thirds requirement for passage of the state budget should be lowered. In fact, the voters did exactly that in 2010 without waiting for a constitutional convention. Supporters of Proposition 25—mostly unions representing teachers and state employees—proved to be more generous in their support than the business interests behind the constitutional convention plan.

You Be the Judge **Do you think that the public would be more likely to trust constitutional convention delegates selected at random than those chosen through elections? Why or why not?**

in 1969 (that's not a typo!), Brown was elected governor in 1974 and 1978 after serving as the secretary of state. His father, Edmund G. ("Pat") Brown, also was governor in 1958 and 1962. Because his governorship occurred before California adopted term limits in 1990, Jerry Brown was eligible to run again. With his third term, Brown is in rare company. Only Earl Warren was elected to three terms in the pre–term limit era.

Brown's election is significant in another way: He was outspent by a margin of more than 6 to 1, courtesy of Meg Whitman's largely self-funded campaign in which the Republican donated $144 million of her own funds to her ill-fated cause. Indeed, a cornerstone of Brown's campaign was the accusation that Whitman was trying to buy the governorship. Apparently there was no sale.

Formal Powers

Much of the governor's authority comes from formal powers written into the state's constitution and its laws. These responsibilities guide his or her relationships with the legislative and judicial branches, as well as with the

ELECTIONS 2010

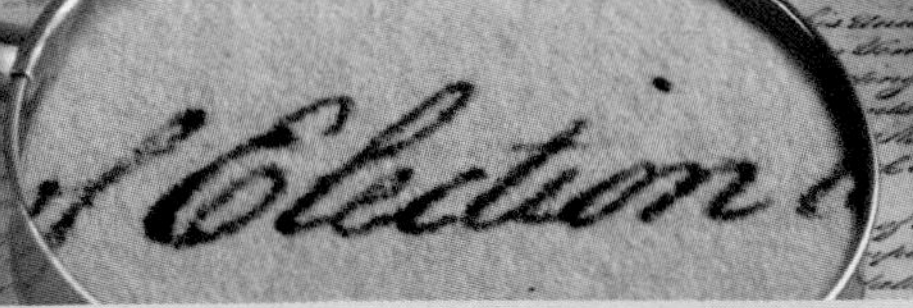

Governor Jerry Brown

Edmund Gerald "Jerry" Brown, Jr., California's new governor, has an unusual background. He was governor before, from 1975 to 1983. Ordinarily, term limits would bar such a candidate from running again, but Brown was governor before the term limits law was adopted. Therefore, his first two terms do not count against the limit. When first elected, Brown was one of California's youngest governors. In 2011, at age 72, he became the oldest. Brown was also California's secretary of state (1971–1975), mayor of Oakland (1999–2007), and the state's attorney general (2007–2011). He sought the Democratic nomination for U.S. president in 1976, 1980, and 1992, but he lost each time.

Brown studied for the Roman Catholic priesthood in the 1950s and has always practiced an austere lifestyle. As governor, he supported environmentalism, opposed the death penalty, named a large number of women to office, and appointed California's first two openly gay judges. His Catholic/Zen philosophy and support for unusual ideas resulted in the nickname "Governor Moonbeam," which stuck.

Brown also practiced budgetary restraint, to a greater extent even than his predecessor, Republican Ronald Reagan. California's tax-cutting Proposition 13 passed on Brown's watch, but by then he had accumulated a budget surplus of $5 billion, which helped offset the effects of the proposition. Given the condition of the state's finances in 2011, Brown will need every ounce of budgetary savvy he may possess.

other officeholders in the executive branch. We examine popular perceptions of the governor's authority in the *Perception versus Reality* feature on the facing page.

SUBMISSION OF AN ANNUAL BUDGET No formal power is more important than the governor's budgetary responsibilities. The budget outlines the sources of state revenues and the programmatic recipients of state funds. According to the state constitution, the governor must recommend a balanced budget to the legislature within the first ten days of each calendar year. Budget work is virtually a year-round task, and it consumes more of the governor's time than just about any other activity except responding to emergencies such as earthquakes or fires. The governor is assisted in this effort by an appointed **director of finance,** the key person in charge of developing the budget document, who spends months with his or her staff gathering data and budget requests from the dozens of departments and agencies that make up the state's bureaucracy. Initial preparations begin on July 1—the start of the fiscal year—and culminate with the governor's submission of a proposal to the legislature the following January (see Chapter 24). Officially, the annual process ends with the signing of the budget document by the governor before the end of the fiscal on June 30, so that the next year can begin with a budget in place. More often than not, however, budget negotiations linger well into summer.

director of finance The state officer primarily responsible for preparation of the budget; appointed by the governor.

VETOES The state constitution requires the legislature to respond to the governor's budget no later than June 15 so that the budget can go into effect by

Former-governor Arnold Schwarzenegger speaks to reporters during his first news conference as governor in November 2003.

JUSTIN SULLIVAN/GETTY IMAGES

PERCEPTION VERSUS REALITY

The Governor Runs the State

The governor is California's most prominent elected official and receives nation-wide publicity even when he or she is not a star of the silver screen. More than anyone else, the governor speaks for the state and represents its people. But how much real power does the governor actually have?

The Perception

The popular impression is that the governor is, or ought to be, in full charge of events. After all, the governor has the power to issue executive orders, declare emergencies, and even call out the militia. Unlike the U.S. president, the governor has a line-item veto that can be used to kill individual spending proposals passed by the legislature. If the state government somehow fails the people, the governor is the first to take the blame.

The Reality

Like most states, California has a fragmented executive. The president of the United States can appoint an attorney general and a secretary of the treasury who will carry out the president's program. Not so in California, where the state attorney general, the state controller, and the state treasurer—along with several other statewide officials—are all independently elected.

Furthermore, the emergency powers of the governor are more limited than many people realize. During the California electricity crisis of 2000 and 2001, Governor Gray Davis came under heavy criticism for his inaction. Davis, however, believed with some justice that state and federal law tied his hands. Davis did declare a state of emergency and authorized the Department of Water Resources to buy power and pass it on to Southern California Edison and Pacific Gas and Electric. These companies were about to go bankrupt because their ability to raise rates was capped even as the cost of the power they had to buy skyrocketed. Even this step was challenged—a state appeals court ruled that it had the power to order the governor to end the state of emergency. (By that time, however, Davis had already done so.)[1]

As this case suggests, the courts in California are more jealous of their authority than in some other states. For example, the California Supreme Court has held that elected officials, the governor included, have no right to consider constitutional issues when performing their statutory duties—that is, they have no right of *executive review.* This issue came up most recently when local officials in San Francisco claimed the right to decide whether it was constitutional to hand out same-sex marriage licenses. The San Francisco officials lost, as they would have in almost any state.[2] In contrast to California, however, courts in Oregon and elsewhere have ruled in favor of executive review when it is exercised by the governor and not limited by the state legislature.[3]

An additional legal peculiarity that California shares with several other states is that the governor's powers pass to the lieutenant governor whenever the governor leaves the state. Normally, this is not important, because there is a "gentlemen's agreement" that the lieutenant governor performs only routine duties while the governor is away. When Democratic governor Jerry Brown left California to run for president in 1979 and 1980, however, the Republican lieutenant governor, Mike Curb, vetoed legislation, appointed judges, and issued executive orders with results that were contrary to Brown's liberal politics. The California Supreme Court later upheld Curb's actions.[4]

Blog On The FindLaw Web site is an invaluable resource for anyone looking for the text of federal and state judicial opinions. You can set up a free account that will let you search for cases by going to **login.findlaw.com/scripts/login.**

July 1—a formidable task because the proposed document is several hundred pages in length. Technically, legislators can disregard any or all parts of the budget package and pass their own version, but usually they stay reasonably close to the governor's proposals. They realize that the governor has the final say, albeit with some limitations. The governor cannot add money, but he or she can reduce or eliminate expenditures through use of the **item veto** before signing the budget into law. An absolute two-thirds vote from each house of the legislature—a near impossibility (see Chapter 21)—is necessary to overturn item vetoes. Accordingly, legislators often attempt to head off vetoes by negotiating with the governor in advance.

item veto The power of the governor to delete or reduce the budget within a bill without rejecting the entire bill or budget; an absolute two-thirds vote of both houses of the state legislature is required to override.

Of course, bills on topics other than budget matters also reach the governor's desk. Whereas the item veto is restricted to appropriations measures, the **general veto** allows the governor to reject any other bill passed by the legislature. It, too, can be overturned only by an absolute two-thirds vote in each house. Over a period of more than twenty years, George Deukmejian, Pete Wilson, and Gray Davis exercised general and item vetoes without a single one being overturned by the legislature.

Arnold Schwarzenegger used the veto even more than Davis, wielding his veto pen with vigor (see Table 23–2). He vetoed more than one-fourth of the bills that reached his desk. More than any governor in history, Schwarzenegger turned the veto into a potent legislative weapon. And, as with his immediate predecessors, he did not suffer any legislative rejections.

Under most circumstances, the governor has twelve days to act after the legislature passes a bill. On the hundreds of bills enacted by the legislature at a session's end, however, the governor has thirty days to act. Only a veto can keep a bill from becoming law. After the governor's time limit has passed, any unsigned or unvetoed bill becomes law the following January (unless the bill is an urgency measure, in which case it takes effect immediately upon signature).

Table 23–2

Vetoes and Overrides, 1967–2010

Governor	Bills Vetoed (%)	Vetoes Overridden
Ronald Reagan (1967–1975)	7.3	1
Jerry Brown (1975–1983)	6.3	13
George Deukmejian (1983–1991)	15.1	0
Pete Wilson (1991–1999)	16.6	0
Gray Davis (1999–November 2003)	17.6	0
Arnold Schwarzenegger (November 2003–2011)	26.4	0

Source: Clerk, California State Senate.

"WE CANNOT AFFORD the programs that we used to be able to afford."

~ ARNOLD SCHWARZENEGGER ~ AFTER USING HIS LINE-ITEM VETO AUTHORITY TO SAVE AN ADDITIONAL $500 MILLION IN 2009

SPECIAL SESSION If the governor believes that the legislature has not addressed an important issue, he or she can take the dramatic step of calling a **special session.** At that time, the lawmakers must discuss only the specific business proposed by the governor. Special sessions often are called to respond to specific crises, as when Governor Schwarzenegger called on the legislature in 2006 to correct a prison system so overcrowded that a federal judge assumed oversight responsibilities.[1] He also called special sessions on health-care reform, water policy, public education, and repeatedly on state budget deficits. Schwarzenegger called sixteen special sessions during his years in office—the most of any governor in state history—leading some to believe that he had diluted the significance of the concept.[2]

general veto The gubernatorial power to reject an entire bill or budget; overruled only by an absolute two-thirds vote of both houses of the state legislature.

special session A legislative session called by the governor; limited to discussion of topics specified by the governor.

executive order The power of the governor to make rules that have the effect of laws; may be overturned by the legislature.

EXECUTIVE ORDER On occasion, the governor can make policy by signing an **executive order,** an action that looks similar to legislation. Governors must exercise this power carefully because such moves often lead to lawsuits over the breadth of their powers. Immediately after taking office in 2003, Arnold Schwarzenegger signed an executive order to repeal the vehicle license fee, a revenue source that had been restored by Governor Gray Davis to reduce the state deficit but that offended many voters. By taking this action, Schwarzenegger honored a crucial campaign promise, although removal of the motor vehicle license fee contributed to a revenue gap almost as large as the one that helped chase Gray Davis from office. Later in his tenure, Schwarzenegger used the executive order to force furloughs on state workers as a means of lessening the state's budget deficit. Here he was only partially successful, as lawsuits overturned the furloughs affecting about one-fourth of the state's workers.[3]

APPOINTMENT POWERS The governor's appointment powers, although substantial, are somewhat more restricted than his or her budgetary authority because others must approve all appointments except personal staff. Moreover, gubernatorial appointees hold only the top policymaking positions in the state system. Before the Progressive reforms, California governors could rely on patronage, or the "spoils" system, to hire friends and political allies. Today, 99 percent of all state employees are not appointed by the governor but rather are selected through a civil service system based on merit. The governor still fills about 2,500 key positions in the executive departments and cabinet agencies, except for the Departments of Justice and Education, whose heads are elected by the public. Together, these appointees direct the state bureaucracy (see Figure 23–1).

The state senate must approve most of the governor's appointees. Generally, senate confirmation is routine, but occasionally the governor's choice for a key post is rejected for reasons other than qualifications. In instances of an opening in the executive branch, both houses must weigh in with positive majorities. In early 2010, the legislature confirmed the selection of Abel Maldonado to fill the lieutenant governor vacancy that resulted from Lieutenant Governor John Garamendi's winning election to a vacated seat in the House of Representatives. After several months of fits and starts, Maldonado was confirmed and ran as the incumbent in the November 2010 general election. (He lost.)

The governor also appoints people to more than three hundred state boards and commissions. Membership on some boards—such as the Arts Council and the Commission on Aging, which have only advisory authority—is largely ceremonial and without pay. Other boards, however, such as the California Energy Commission (CEC), the Public Utilities Commission (PUC), the California Coastal Commission (CCC), and the California Division of Occupational Safety and Health (DOSH; better known as Cal-OSHA), make important policies free from gubernatorial control. Nevertheless, the governor affects key "independent" boards through his or her appointments and manipulation of the budget.

Perhaps the most enduring of all gubernatorial appointments are judgeships. The governor fills both vacancies and new judgeships that are periodically created by the legislature. In his eight years as governor, Pete Wilson filled 693 posts. During his five years in office, Gray Davis appointed 360 judges. Between his election in 2003 and 2010, Arnold Schwarzenegger appointed 545 judges, including two members of the state supreme court. Most judges continue to serve long after those who appointed them have gone. However, the governor's power is checked here to a degree, too, by various judicial commissions and by the voters in future elections. During his tenure as governor, Arnold Schwarzenegger was much less partisan with his judicial appointments than his predecessors (see Chapter 22).

In addition to the major formal authority discussed above, the governor has a wide range of other formal powers. He or she is commander in chief of the California National Guard, which on occasion is sent to help manage local crises in the state on a short-term basis. The governor also has the power to grant pardons, reprieves, or sentence commutations, although such authority is rarely exercised. Finally, the governor is the ceremonial head of state for greeting dignitaries from other countries. Along with the other major functions, these powers keep the governor on a fast track.

Proposition 187 (1994)
An initiative reducing government benefits for illegal immigrants; parts of Proposition 187 were declared unconstitutional by federal courts in 1995.

Proposition 209 (1996)
An initiative that eliminated affirmative action in California.

Proposition 227 (1998)
An initiative limiting bilingual education to no more than one year.

Informal Powers

Formal constraints on the governor can be offset to some extent by a power that is not written into the constitution at all: the governor's popularity. As the top state official, the governor is highly visible. The attention focused on the office provides a platform from which the governor can influence the public and overcome political opponents.

Historically, California's governors have used the prestige of their office to push their own agendas. Republican governor Pete Wilson touted **Proposition 187,** an attempt to reduce government benefits to illegal immigrants that was ultimately declared unconstitutional by the federal courts. In 1996 Wilson championed **Proposition 209,** titled the California Civil Rights Initiative, to eliminate affirmative action. And in 1998 he promoted **Proposition 227,** an initiative restricting bilingual education.

Democratic governor Gray Davis used his executive powers to relax the state's air standards during the 2001 state energy crisis, permitting older, dirtier electricity plants to produce more energy. When Davis was reelected in 2002, energy problems were compounded by a lengthy recession and huge budget shortfalls (see Chapter 24). But his inability to rely upon informal power stemmed from Davis's personality. He attacked the other branches of state government, claiming that state legislators were supposed to implement his vision[4]

Figure 23–1

California State Departments and Agencies

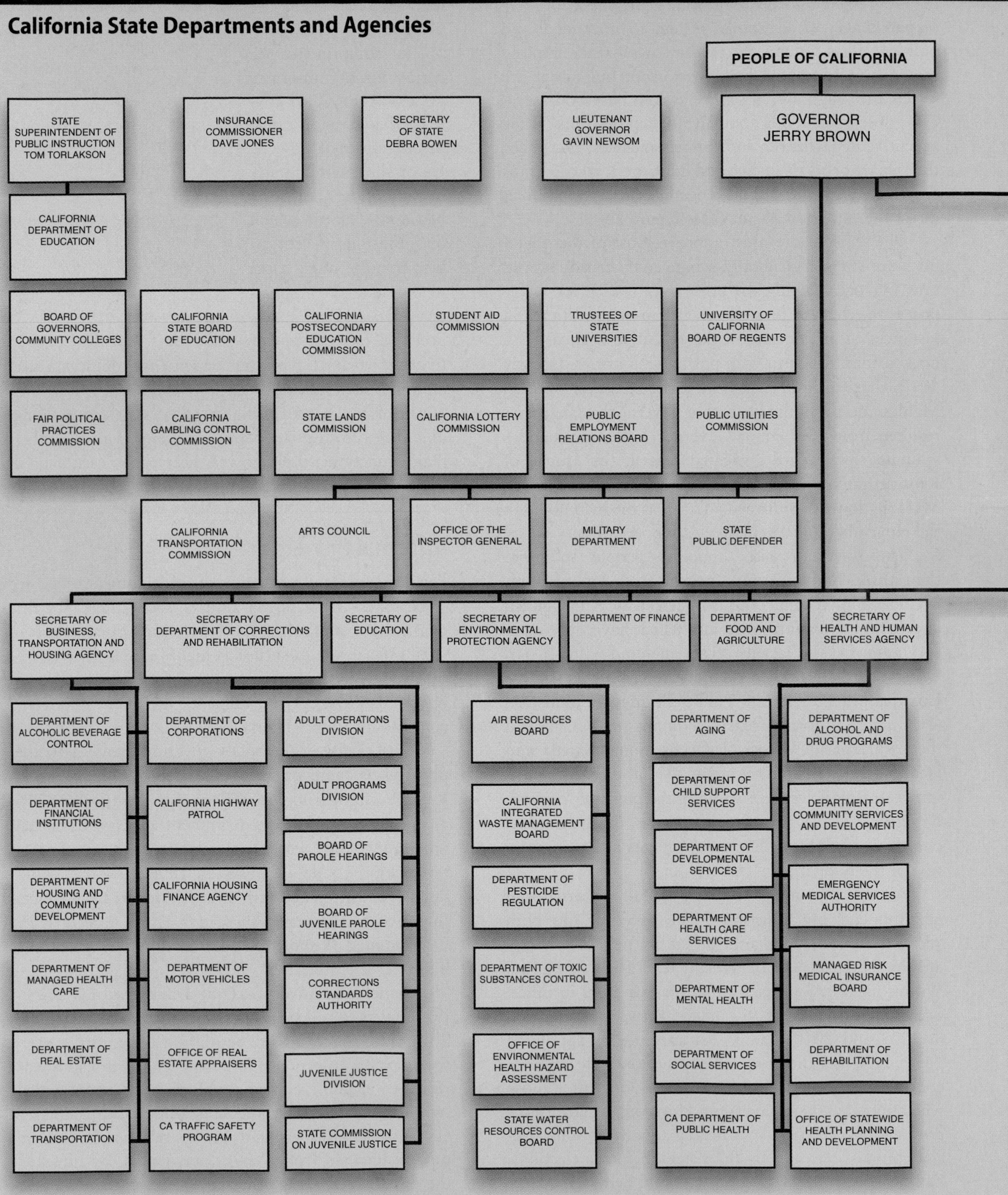
PEOPLE OF CALIFORNIA
GOVERNOR JERRY BROWN
STATE SUPERINTENDENT OF PUBLIC INSTRUCTION TOM TORLAKSON
INSURANCE COMMISSIONER DAVE JONES
SECRETARY OF STATE DEBRA BOWEN
LIEUTENANT GOVERNOR GAVIN NEWSOM
CALIFORNIA DEPARTMENT OF EDUCATION
BOARD OF GOVERNORS, COMMUNITY COLLEGES
CALIFORNIA STATE BOARD OF EDUCATION
CALIFORNIA POSTSECONDARY EDUCATION COMMISSION
STUDENT AID COMMISSION
TRUSTEES OF STATE UNIVERSITIES
UNIVERSITY OF CALIFORNIA BOARD OF REGENTS
FAIR POLITICAL PRACTICES COMMISSION
CALIFORNIA GAMBLING CONTROL COMMISSION
STATE LANDS COMMISSION
CALIFORNIA LOTTERY COMMISSION
PUBLIC EMPLOYMENT RELATIONS BOARD
PUBLIC UTILITIES COMMISSION
CALIFORNIA TRANSPORTATION COMMISSION
ARTS COUNCIL
OFFICE OF THE INSPECTOR GENERAL
MILITARY DEPARTMENT
STATE PUBLIC DEFENDER
SECRETARY OF BUSINESS, TRANSPORTATION AND HOUSING AGENCY
SECRETARY OF DEPARTMENT OF CORRECTIONS AND REHABILITATION
SECRETARY OF EDUCATION
SECRETARY OF ENVIRONMENTAL PROTECTION AGENCY
DEPARTMENT OF FINANCE
DEPARTMENT OF FOOD AND AGRICULTURE
SECRETARY OF HEALTH AND HUMAN SERVICES AGENCY
DEPARTMENT OF ALCOHOLIC BEVERAGE CONTROL
DEPARTMENT OF FINANCIAL INSTITUTIONS
DEPARTMENT OF HOUSING AND COMMUNITY DEVELOPMENT
DEPARTMENT OF MANAGED HEALTH CARE
DEPARTMENT OF REAL ESTATE
DEPARTMENT OF TRANSPORTATION
DEPARTMENT OF CORPORATIONS
CALIFORNIA HIGHWAY PATROL
CALIFORNIA HOUSING FINANCE AGENCY
DEPARTMENT OF MOTOR VEHICLES
OFFICE OF REAL ESTATE APPRAISERS
CA TRAFFIC SAFETY PROGRAM
ADULT OPERATIONS DIVISION
ADULT PROGRAMS DIVISION
BOARD OF PAROLE HEARINGS
BOARD OF JUVENILE PAROLE HEARINGS
CORRECTIONS STANDARDS AUTHORITY
JUVENILE JUSTICE DIVISION
STATE COMMISSION ON JUVENILE JUSTICE
AIR RESOURCES BOARD
CALIFORNIA INTEGRATED WASTE MANAGEMENT BOARD
DEPARTMENT OF PESTICIDE REGULATION
DEPARTMENT OF TOXIC SUBSTANCES CONTROL
OFFICE OF ENVIRONMENTAL HEALTH HAZARD ASSESSMENT
STATE WATER RESOURCES CONTROL BOARD
DEPARTMENT OF AGING
DEPARTMENT OF CHILD SUPPORT SERVICES
DEPARTMENT OF DEVELOPMENTAL SERVICES
DEPARTMENT OF HEALTH CARE SERVICES
DEPARTMENT OF MENTAL HEALTH
DEPARTMENT OF SOCIAL SERVICES
CA DEPARTMENT OF PUBLIC HEALTH
DEPARTMENT OF ALCOHOL AND DRUG PROGRAMS
DEPARTMENT OF COMMUNITY SERVICES AND DEVELOPMENT
EMERGENCY MEDICAL SERVICES AUTHORITY
MANAGED RISK MEDICAL INSURANCE BOARD
DEPARTMENT OF REHABILITATION
OFFICE OF STATEWIDE HEALTH PLANNING AND DEVELOPMENT

Source: Office of the Governor

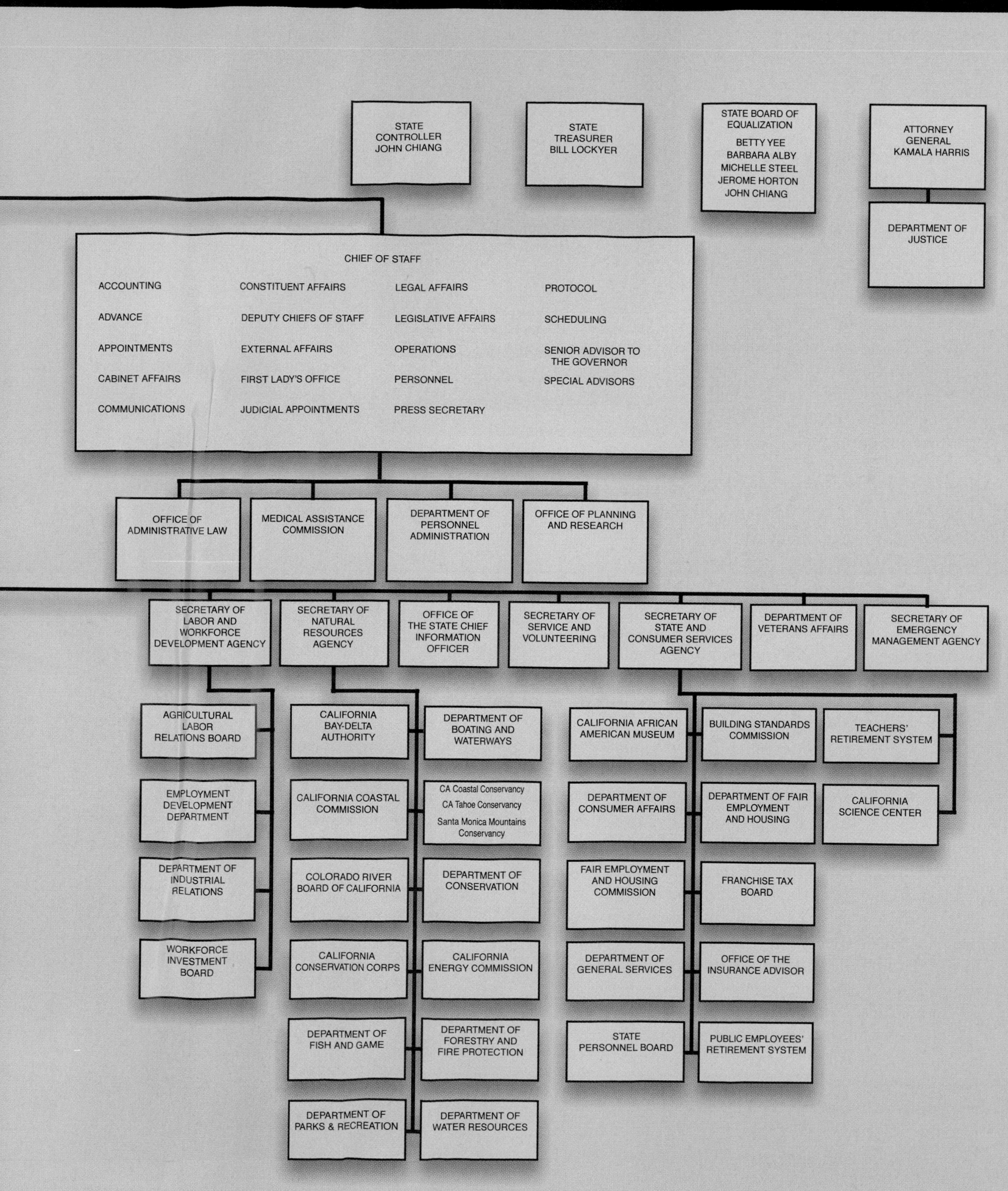
STATE CONTROLLER JOHN CHIANG
STATE TREASURER BILL LOCKYER
STATE BOARD OF EQUALIZATION
BETTY YEE
BARBARA ALBY
MICHELLE STEEL
JEROME HORTON
JOHN CHIANG
ATTORNEY GENERAL KAMALA HARRIS
DEPARTMENT OF JUSTICE
CHIEF OF STAFF
ACCOUNTING
ADVANCE
APPOINTMENTS
CABINET AFFAIRS
COMMUNICATIONS
CONSTITUENT AFFAIRS
DEPUTY CHIEFS OF STAFF
EXTERNAL AFFAIRS
FIRST LADY'S OFFICE
JUDICIAL APPOINTMENTS
LEGAL AFFAIRS
LEGISLATIVE AFFAIRS
OPERATIONS
PERSONNEL
PRESS SECRETARY
PROTOCOL
SCHEDULING
SENIOR ADVISOR TO THE GOVERNOR
SPECIAL ADVISORS
OFFICE OF ADMINISTRATIVE LAW
MEDICAL ASSISTANCE COMMISSION
DEPARTMENT OF PERSONNEL ADMINISTRATION
OFFICE OF PLANNING AND RESEARCH
SECRETARY OF LABOR AND WORKFORCE DEVELOPMENT AGENCY
SECRETARY OF NATURAL RESOURCES AGENCY
OFFICE OF THE STATE CHIEF INFORMATION OFFICER
SECRETARY OF SERVICE AND VOLUNTEERING
SECRETARY OF STATE AND CONSUMER SERVICES AGENCY
DEPARTMENT OF VETERANS AFFAIRS
SECRETARY OF EMERGENCY MANAGEMENT AGENCY
AGRICULTURAL LABOR RELATIONS BOARD
EMPLOYMENT DEVELOPMENT DEPARTMENT
DEPARTMENT OF INDUSTRIAL RELATIONS
WORKFORCE INVESTMENT BOARD
CALIFORNIA BAY-DELTA AUTHORITY
DEPARTMENT OF BOATING AND WATERWAYS
CALIFORNIA COASTAL COMMISSION
CA Coastal Conservancy
CA Tahoe Conservancy
Santa Monica Mountains Conservancy
COLORADO RIVER BOARD OF CALIFORNIA
DEPARTMENT OF CONSERVATION
CALIFORNIA CONSERVATION CORPS
CALIFORNIA ENERGY COMMISSION
DEPARTMENT OF FISH AND GAME
DEPARTMENT OF FORESTRY AND FIRE PROTECTION
DEPARTMENT OF PARKS & RECREATION
DEPARTMENT OF WATER RESOURCES
CALIFORNIA AFRICAN AMERICAN MUSEUM
BUILDING STANDARDS COMMISSION
TEACHERS' RETIREMENT SYSTEM
DEPARTMENT OF CONSUMER AFFAIRS
DEPARTMENT OF FAIR EMPLOYMENT AND HOUSING
CALIFORNIA SCIENCE CENTER
FAIR EMPLOYMENT AND HOUSING COMMISSION
FRANCHISE TAX BOARD
DEPARTMENT OF GENERAL SERVICES
OFFICE OF THE INSURANCE ADVISOR
STATE PERSONNEL BOARD
PUBLIC EMPLOYEES' RETIREMENT SYSTEM

Proposition 58 (2004) A proposition that set broad spending limits on state government and required the state to gradually set aside up to 3 percent of all revenues in a "rainy day" fund.

and that judicial appointees should reflect his views.[5] Further, his obsession with constant fund-raising from individuals and organizations in search of state business added to his image problems. In a July 2003 Field poll, 61 percent of the respondents blamed Davis for the state's problems.[6] Thus, as an unprecedented recall effort moved along during 2003, Davis first lost his public support and informal power, and soon after that, his job.[7]

PHOTO BY DAVID PAUL MORRIS/GETTY IMAGES

California Governor-elect Jerry Brown speaks during a press conference at his campaign headquarters on November 3, 2010 in Oakland, California.

METHODS OF INFLUENCE Arnold Schwarzenegger, in contrast, tried to use his informal powers both by schmoozing with and cajoling legislators and by appealing directly to the public. His record was mixed. He belittled the legislature, calling members "girlie men" for not adopting his budgets.[8] Sending the legislature into special session on sixteen occasions, rarely with any concrete plan, also did not win him friends among Democrats or Republicans. Frustrated, Schwarzenegger often went beyond the legislature to the chagrin of many members, cutting deals directly with organizations and institutions from local governments to universities, prison guards, and Indian gaming interests. Sometimes he prevailed, but other times he did not. Many of his item vetoes of "safety net" programs were overturned by the courts, yet his executive order to furlough state workers because of a budget shortfall was partially successful. And in 2010, Schwarzenegger worked out pension deals with several state employee unions that mandated higher employee contributions—something the legislature had not dared to even tackle.[9] In his own way, although clumsily at times, Schwarzenegger did attempt change.

Like Pete Wilson, Schwarzenegger went directly to the voters, but with mixed results. In March 2004 he barnstormed the state for Proposition 57, described as a $15 billion "recovery" bond, and **Proposition 58,** a measure designed to create more reserves in the future; both measures passed. But in 2005 Schwarzenegger suffered a major defeat, when he asked the voters to approve ballot measures on teacher tenure, union campaign contributions, strict state budget controls, and redistricting. So unpopular was the governor during this time that his standing in the public opinion polls plummeted from 64 percent to 35 percent in ten short months.[10] He never fully recovered.

Still, Schwarzenegger used his personality even in defeat to resurrect his standing with the public. Immediately after the election, he accepted full responsibility for the failed campaign, saying, "The buck stops with me." Using himself as the foil, the governor reflected, "I should have listened to my wife [prominent Democrat Maria Shriver], who said don't do this."[11] That kind of self-effacing approach allowed Schwarzenegger to begin anew with the voters and helped bring about reelection in 2006. But his ballot box success was short-lived. In 2009, Schwarzenegger placed his reputation on the line with support for a series of five budget-related legislative initiatives, all of which failed at the polls.

FORGING RELATIONSHIPS In the end, Schwarzenegger had an uneven relationship with the public. A blend of fiscal conservatism and social liberalism produced an antitax, antilabor governor who simultaneously was pro-choice, pro-health care, and pro-environment. His values may have lacked ideological consistency, but enough of them seemed to mesh with California's contradictory characteristics—especially his strong record on environmental protection. Still, Schwarzenegger's

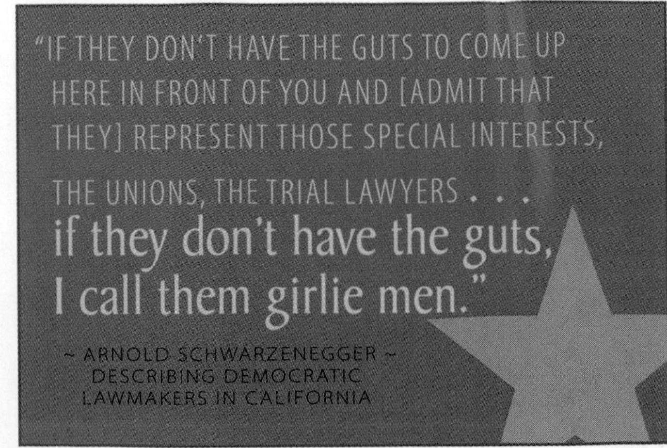

"IF THEY DON'T HAVE THE GUTS TO COME UP HERE IN FRONT OF YOU AND [ADMIT THAT THEY] REPRESENT THOSE SPECIAL INTERESTS, THE UNIONS, THE TRIAL LAWYERS . . .
if they don't have the guts, I call them girlie men."
~ ARNOLD SCHWARZENEGGER ~
DESCRIBING DEMOCRATIC LAWMAKERS IN CALIFORNIA

Meg Whitman, former President and CEO of EBay, speaks at the Republican National Convention in 2008, getting an early jump on her campaign for governor in 2010. Did Whitman have the right experience to run for governor?

AP PHOTO/PAUL SANCYA

vision often exceeded his ability to deliver. In successive years, he declared the "year" of political reform, which ended with the defeat of four Schwarzenegger-tailored ballot measures; the "year" of health-care reform, which fizzled in the legislature; and the "year" of education reform, which sputtered out after he cut public funding several years in a row to leave California near the bottom of the fifty states in per capita spending.

Schwarzenegger's biggest political headache came from a poor relationship with members of his own political party. Particularly on social issues, he and the largely conservative Republican legislators had little agreement. Even on fiscal questions, Schwarzenegger and legislative Republicans had great difficulty forging a unified approach against the Democrats, as witnessed by his support for, and their resistance to, a state-funded health-care program, environmental protection legislation, and prison reform. Out of sync with his own party and never in sync with the Democrats, Arnold Schwarzenegger spent much of his governorship isolated from other leaders.

One argument often made by businessmen and businesswomen who run for governor and other executive positions is that their business experience will be of great benefit in government. The kinds of relationships established in private enterprise, however, are often very different from those forged while running the state, a point we consider in the *Join the Debate* feature on the following page.

LO2 *The Supporting Cast*

If California's executive branch were composed solely of the governor, appointed department heads, and the civil service system, it would parallel the federal executive branch. However, the state's executive branch also includes a lieutenant governor, an attorney general, a secretary of state, a controller, a treasurer, an insurance commissioner, a superintendent of public instruction, and a five-member Board of Equalization. All are elected at the same time and serve four-year terms. Unlike the president and vice president, though, who are elected on the same political party ticket, each of these officeholders runs independently.

Most other states provide for the election of a lieutenant governor, a secretary of state, a treasurer, and an attorney general, but few elect an education officer, a controller, a Board of Equalization, and an insurance regulator. Moreover, most states call for the governor and the lieutenant governor (and others, in some cases) to run as a team, thus providing some executive branch cohesion. Not so in California, where each elected member of the executive branch is beholden to no one.

The consequences can be quite serious. For example, when Governor Schwarzenegger unilaterally withheld \$3.1 billion for the public schools in 2005 in defiance of what many believed were state guarantees, Superintendent of Public Instruction Jack O'Connell sued. Ultimately, O'Connell dropped the suit after the governor and public school officials found agreement. In 2008 and 2010 Governor Schwarzenegger ordered reductions in the salaries of 200,000 state employees to the federal minimum wage (\$6.55 per hour in 2008; \$7.25 in 2010) until the legislature provided a budget. State Controller John Chiang, the individual responsible for issuing checks, refused to abide by the order, which he said exceeded Schwarzenegger's authority. Both times the courts found for the governor in principal, but an antiquated payroll system kept the controller from following through before the budget issue was resolved.

JOIN THE DEBATE

Do Business Executives Make Better Officeholders?

In 2010, the Republican candidates for the top two elective positions in California were both wealthy businesswomen. Meg Whitman was the Republican candidate for governor. In ten years as chief executive officer (CEO) of e-Bay, she successfully took that company from a small startup to a giant with annual revenues approaching $9 billion. Carly Fiorina, Republican candidate for a U.S. Senate seat, was CEO of Hewlett-Packard (HP) for six years. Her time at the top was more controversial than Whitman's. Fiorina was forced out by HP's board of directors in 2005 after the company's stock had lost half of its value.

Both Whitman and Fiorina argued that their experience in business was a valuable qualification for high office, and that as a result they knew how to "create jobs." Whatever the voters may have thought of these claims, they clearly did not find Whitman and Fiorina the best candidates in their respective races—both lost. But what of the argument that experience in business is a qualification for high office? California citizens disagree over whether this proposition is true.

We Need More People with Business Experience in Government

Conservatives frequently argue that we need more people with business experience in government. They offer several reasons for this. First, they contend that government is inherently inefficient and wasteful. People entering government from the private sector are used to an environment in which efficiency is prized. Business people will naturally seek to trim wasteful practices that run counter to what they are used to in private enterprise.

A second argument is that we need business experience in government if governmental bodies are to succeed in promoting economic growth. New jobs come from the private sector, after all, and especially from small businesses. Government agencies are strongly drawn toward new laws and regulations, toward telling people—including businesses—what to do. Rules and regulations create uncertainty, waste time, and interfere with business decisions that promote productivity and create jobs. We need businesspeople in government who really understand how to offer appropriate incentives and to help businesses grow.

Government Is Nothing like the Private Sector

Those who disagree with these arguments admit that it is important for government officials to understand the needs of business, but they also contend that experience as a business leader can easily leave a person completely unfit for public service. CEOs are used to issuing orders in the expectation that they will be obeyed. Indeed, successful entrepreneurs typically exhibit self-confidence bordering on arrogance. Politicians, in contrast, can accomplish nothing unless they assemble coalitions of other officeholders. This is especially true of legislators. Individual senators or representatives exercise command over their own small staffs—and that's it. To do anything constructive, they must negotiate deals with other legislators. A governor or president likewise will accomplish little if she or he cannot assemble a legislative majority or supermajority. An authoritarian approach will also backfire when trying to make changes in a bureaucracy. After all, staff members are hard to fire, and they are well aware that an elected leader may be here today, gone tomorrow.

A successful businessperson will grow the business, as Whitman did at e-Bay. Businesspeople tend to believe, however, that government should shrink. Whitman advocated cutting the state government payroll by 40,000 jobs. She also blamed state employee unions for California's difficulties—and many felt that she was in effect blaming the employees themselves. Smart businesspeople know that you don't foster an effective business organization by demonizing your own employees, but they often seem to forget that truism when it comes to managing government.

For Critical Analysis ***When career politicians try to administer bureaucratic organizations, what difficulties might they face resulting from their past experiences?***

On another occasion, then-state insurance commissioner Steve Poizner sued to stop the sale of the state-run workers' compensation insurance fund, proposed by the governor to help balance the state budget. The issue languished in the courts long after Schwarzenegger and Poizner left office.[12] These examples show the extent to which very public fights can occur between two independently operating officeholders in the executive branch.

The Lieutenant Governor

The **lieutenant governor** is basically an executive-in-waiting with few formal responsibilities. If the governor becomes disabled or is out of the state, the lieutenant governor fills in as acting governor. If the governor leaves office, the lieutenant governor takes over. This has happened seven times in the state's history; the last time was in 1953, when Goodwin Knight replaced Earl Warren, who became chief justice of the United States Supreme Court. The current lieutenant governor, Democrat and former San Francisco Mayor Gavin Newsom, was elected in 2010, displacing Abel Maldonado, who had been appointed to the office earlier in the year.

AP PHOTO/TONY AVELAR

Former San Francisco Mayor Gavin Newsom is the new Lieutenant Governor.

The lieutenant governor heads some units, such as the State Lands Commission and the Commission on Economic Development, and is an *ex officio* (automatic, by virtue of the office) member of the University of California Board of Regents and California State University Board of Trustees. He or she also serves as president of the state senate, but this job, too, is long on title and short on substance. As senate president, the lieutenant governor may vote to break ties, an event that last occurred in 1976. So minimal are the responsibilities of the lieutenant governor that an occupant of the office once quipped that his biggest daily task was to wake up, check the morning newspaper to see whether the governor had died, and then return to bed![13] That description may stretch the point a bit, but not by much. Still, the officeholder can be a nuisance to the governor, if nothing else. After a contentious budget battle in 2009 in which then Democratic lieutenant governor John Garamendi criticized Governor Schwarzenegger's management of the process, Schwarzenegger slashed Garamendi's office budget by 62 percent.

The Attorney General

Despite the lieutenant governor's higher rank, the **attorney general** is usually considered the second-most powerful member of the executive branch. As head of the Department of Justice, the attorney general oversees law enforcement activities, acts as legal counsel to state agencies, represents the state in important cases, and renders opinions on (interprets) proposed and existing laws. The current Attorney General, Democrat Kamala Harris, defeated Republican Steve Cooley in 2010 in a race that separated the two candidates by 50,000 votes of the nearly 9,000,000 cast. Previously, Harris had served as district attorney for San Francisco. She succeeds Jerry Brown, who held the office between 2006 and 2010.

Substantial authority and independent election allow the attorney general to chart a course separate from the governor on important state questions. During his tenure as attorney general, for example, Jerry Brown sued insurance companies for misleading ads, prosecuted businesses for not paying at least the state minimum wage, and petitioned the federal government to regulate greenhouse gases. The same very public platform will allow Harris to pursue themes mapped out earlier in her career as district attorney, such as consumer rights and civil rights. She also has championed innovative anti-recidivism programs and been an outspoken opponent of capital punishment—something that distinguishes her from the majority of Californians.

The Secretary of State

Unlike the U.S. cabinet official who bears the same title, the **secretary of state** of California is basically a records keeper and elections supervisor. The job entails certifying the number and validity of signatures obtained for initiatives, referenda, and recall petitions; producing sample ballots and ballot arguments for the voters; publishing official election results; and keeping the

lieutenant governor The chief executive when the governor is absent from the state or disabled; succeeds the governor in case of death or other departure from office; casts a tiebreaking vote in the senate; is independently elected.

attorney general California's top law enforcement officer and legal counsel; the second most powerful member of the executive branch.

secretary of state An elected state executive who keeps election records and supervises elections.

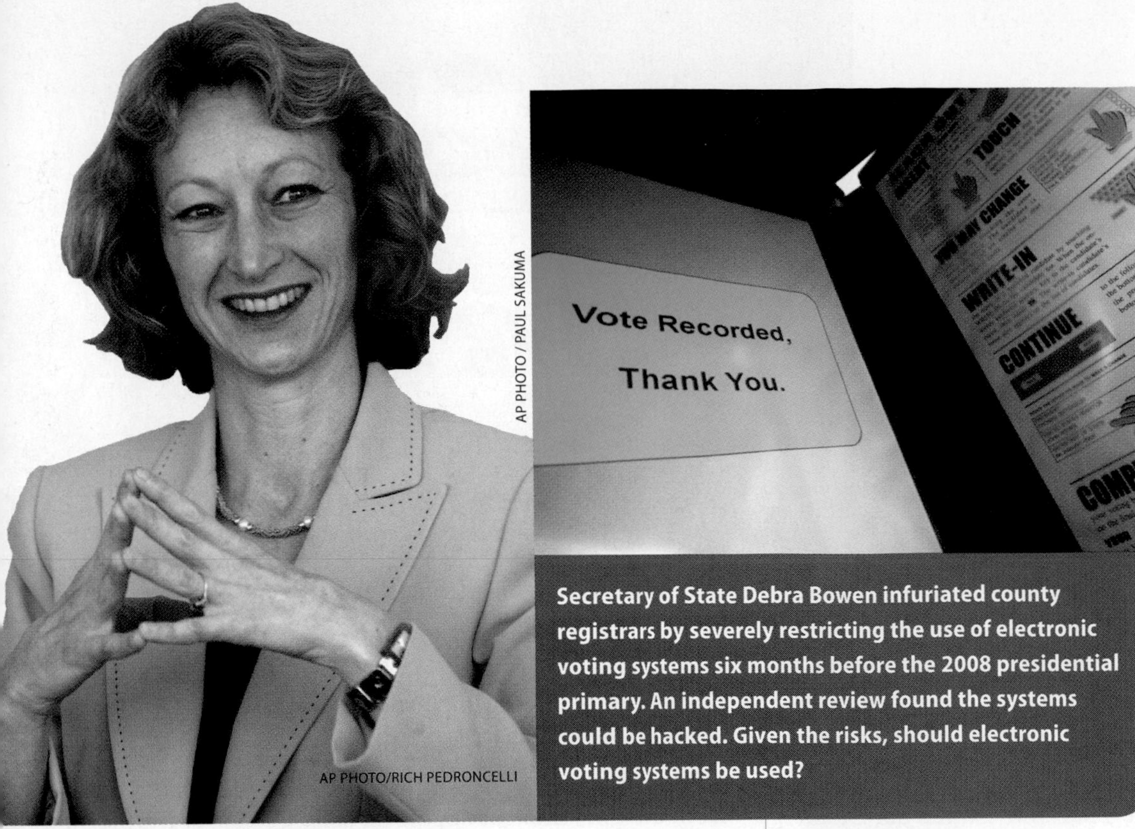

AP PHOTO / PAUL SAKUMA

AP PHOTO/RICH PEDRONCELLI

Secretary of State Debra Bowen infuriated county registrars by severely restricting the use of electronic voting systems six months before the 2008 presidential primary. An independent review found the systems could be hacked. Given the risks, should electronic voting systems be used?

records of the legislature and the executive branch. The current secretary of state, Democrat Debra Bowen, was first elected in 2006. She has brought order to an office that was rocked by scandal in 2005, when then secretary of state Kevin Shelley resigned because of a scandal involving illegal campaign contributions.

Recently, the secretary of state has had responsibility for converting California's election system from paper ballots to electronic voting machines. Bowen, a skeptic about electronic voting, has responsibility for modernizing the machines. She has been in no great hurry. In 2007 she announced a ban on almost all electronic voting machines in thirty-nine counties until it could be demonstrated that the machines are not prone to any viruses or manipulation.[14] This policy has required counties to either invest in new state-certified machines that include paper verification or resort to paper ballots.

The Superintendent of Public Instruction

The **superintendent of public instruction** heads the Department of Education. He or she is the only elected official in the executive branch chosen by nonpartisan ballot. Candidates are identified on the primary ballot only by their name and vocation. Unless one candidate wins a majority, the top two candidates face each other in the November general election. The current superintendent of public instruction, former state senator and assemblyman Tom Torlakson, was elected in 2010. While in the legislature, Torlakson was a champion of public education. During the fall 2010 campaign, he received strong support from the California Teachers' Association, the most powerful education organization in the state.

superintendent of public instruction The elected state executive in charge of public education.

controller An independently elected state executive who oversees taxing and spending.

In general, the electorate knows little about the candidates for superintendent of public instruction, but teachers' unions, education administrators, and other affected groups take great interest in the choice of superintendent because this official oversees California's massive public education system. The superintendent's powers are severely limited, however—funding is determined largely by the governor's budgetary decisions, and policies are closely watched by the governor-appointed state board of education and the education committees of the legislature.

The Money Officers

Perhaps the most fractured part of the executive branch of California government is the group of elected officials who manage the state's money. Courtesy of the Progressive reformers who feared a concentration of power, the controller, the treasurer, and the Board of Equalization have separate but overlapping responsibilities in this area. The **controller** supervises all state and local tax collection and writes checks for the state, including those to state employees. The controller is also an *ex officio* member of several agencies, including the Board of Equalization, the Franchise Tax Board, and the State Lands Commission. Of all the "money officers," the controller is the most powerful, and thus the most prominent. The current controller, Democrat and former Board of Equalization member John Chiang, was elected in 2006 in his first run for statewide office and reelected in 2010. From time to time, he has been outspoken on California's ongoing budget crisis.

The **treasurer** invests state funds raised through taxes and other means until they are needed for expenditures. The treasurer also borrows money for the state by issuing bonds approved by the voters. Typically amounting to several billion dollars, the bonds are sold in financial markets so that the state can finance long-term projects such as highways, water projects, or other infrastructure needs. The state then "redeems" the bonds over time through payments. Democrat Bill Lockyer, former state attorney general, was elected to this office in 2006 and reelected in 2010. Unlike his predecessors, Lockyer has pushed the limits of his office by presenting periodic reports that reflect on the state's financial status with lending institutions that purchase California bonds.

The **Board of Equalization,** also part of California's fiscal system, oversees the collection of excise taxes on sales, gasoline, and liquor. The board also reviews county property assessment practices to ensure uniform calculation methods and practices. The board has five members—four of whom are elected in districts of equal population plus the controller.

Historically, the Board has attracted little attention. That changed in 2007, when the members voted to tax "alcopops"—sweet alcohol drinks often consumed by underage drinkers—at the same rate as hard liquor instead of beer. The change would have raised the tax from 20 cents per gallon to $3.30 per gallon and would have increased the cost of alcopop drinks by about 25 percent. But manufacturers avoided the tax by lowering the alcohol content below beer percentages. Still, the activism on the part of the Board of Equalization portended a new era for the tax agency.

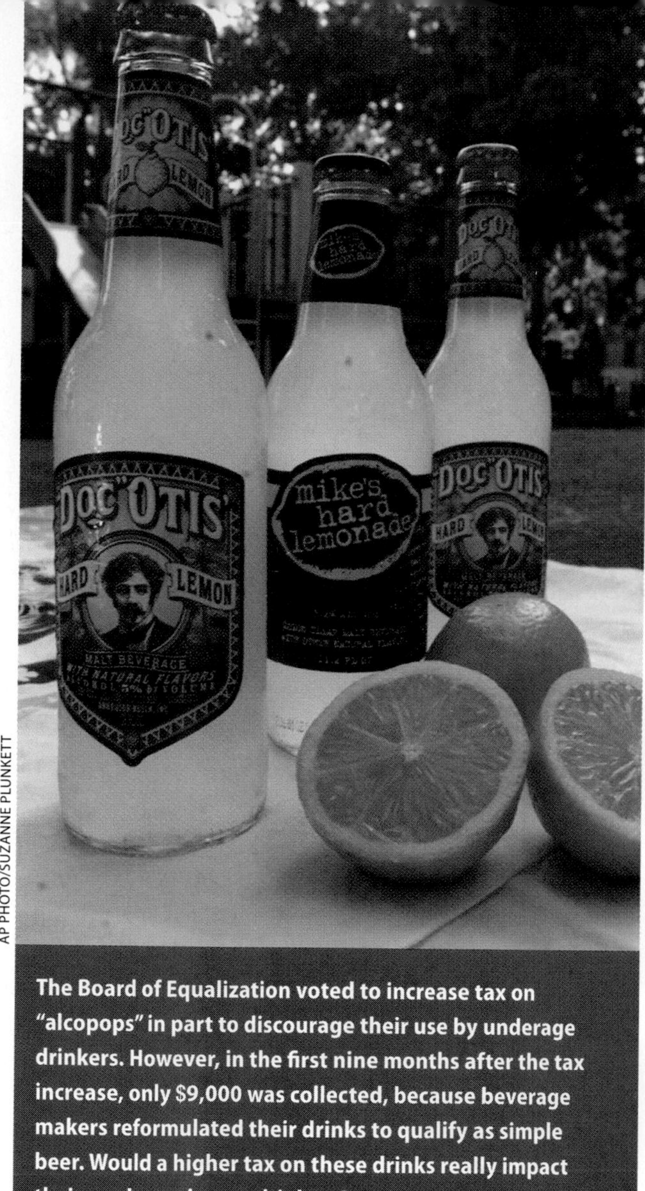

AP PHOTO/SUZANNE PLUNKETT

The Board of Equalization voted to increase tax on "alcopops" in part to discourage their use by underage drinkers. However, in the first nine months after the tax increase, only $9,000 was collected, because beverage makers reformulated their drinks to qualify as simple beer. Would a higher tax on these drinks really impact their use by underage drinkers?

The Insurance Commissioner

The office of **insurance commissioner** exemplifies the persistent reform mentality of California voters. Until 1988, the office was part of the state's Business, Housing, and Transportation Agency. However, with soaring insurance rates, voters approved an initiative that called for 20 percent across-the-board reductions in insurance premiums and created the elected position of insurance commissioner. Consumer Watchdog, the public interest group behind the proposition, claims that the law saved California drivers more than $60 billion during its first twenty years of existence.

Democrat Dave Jones, a termed-out member of the state assembly, was elected to the office of insurance commissioner in 2010, succeeding Steve Poizner, who elected to run for governor instead of seeking a second term. Known as a consumer advocate, Jones was named "2008 Consumer Champion" by the California Consumer Federation. He campaigned on the theme of holding health insurance companies accountable for any rate increases.

The Supporting Cast—Snow White's Seven Dwarfs?

Combined, the seven other elected members of the executive branch (plus the Board of Equalization) present

treasurer The elected state executive responsible for managing state funds between collection and spending.

Board of Equalization The five-member state board that oversees the collection of sales, gasoline, and liquor taxes; members are elected by district; part of the executive branch.

insurance commissioner An elected state executive who regulates the insurance industry; created by a 1988 initiative.

> "Bureaucracy IS THE DEATH OF ALL SOUND WORK."
>
> ~ ALBERT EINSTEIN ~
> THEORETICAL PHYSICIST
> 1879 - 1955

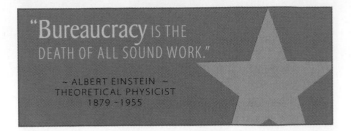

an appearance of tremendous political activity. Still, their efforts often center on narrow policy areas and frequently are in opposition to one another, as well as to the much more powerful governor.

LO3 *The Bureaucracy*

Elected officials are just the most observable part of the state's administrative machinery. Backing them up, implementing their programs, and dealing with citizens on a daily basis are about 335,000 state workers—the **bureaucracy.** Only about 5,000 of these workers are appointed by the governor or by other executive officers. Of the rest, 90,000 work at the University of California and California State University. The remainder are hired and fired through the state's **civil service system** on the basis of their examination results, performance, and job qualifications. The Progressives designed this system to insulate government workers from political influences and to make them more professional than those who might be hired out of friendship.

The task of the bureaucracy is to carry out the programs established by the policymaking institutions—the executive branch, the legislature, and the judiciary, along with a handful of regulatory agencies. However, because bureaucrats are permanent, full-time professionals, they sometimes influence the content of programs and policies, chiefly by advising public officials or by exercising the discretion built into the laws that define bureaucratic tasks. The bureaucracy can also influence policy through the lobbying efforts of its employee organizations (see Chapter 20).

bureaucracy State or local government workers employed through the civil service system rather than appointed by the governor or other elected officials.

civil service system A system for hiring and retaining public employees on the basis of their qualifications or merit; replaced the political machine's patronage, or spoils, system; encompasses 98 percent of state workers.

Administration of the Bureaucracy

State bureaucrats work for various departments and agencies (see Figure 23–1), each run by an administrator who is appointed by the governor and confirmed by the senate. Although civil servants are permanent employees, most administrators serve at the governor's pleasure and must resign at his or her demand. Sometimes, political appointees and civil servants clash over the best ways to carry out state policy. If the bureaucracy becomes too independent, the governor can always use his or her budgetary powers to bring it back into line or, in some cases, dismiss individual employees.

In recent years, California's bureaucrats have been particularly ambitious on climate change. The California Energy Commission has instituted energy efficiency standards for televisions and other electrical appliances. Also, the California Air Resources Board has led the way in regulating greenhouse gas levels. These efforts have kept California's energy consumption flat during the past three decades, compared with a 40 percent increase in energy consumption nationwide.[15] They have also established California as a trendsetting state on the issues of global warming and energy use.

Some observers have criticized California's bureaucracy as unnecessarily inflated and unresponsive, even though the size of the state's system ranks forty-eighth of the fifty states on a per capita basis.[16] Still, there is no denying that slim or not, the state's bureaucracy has grown in recent years under the Schwarzenegger administration, despite his promise to "blow up the boxes" of the bureaucracy shortly after taking office. Between 2004 and 2008 the number of state employees per resident grew from 8.8 per thousand to 9.5 per thousand. Salary costs during the first five years of Schwarzenegger's governorship increased 37 percent, compared with 5 percent for a similar period under his

Security guard Suresh Sonpaki stands in front of a closed Department of Motor Vehicles (DMV) office in San Francisco. The closure is a result of Governor Schwarzenegger's order to furlough state employees on the first and third Fridays of each month until June 2011 to save the state an estimated $1.3 billion.

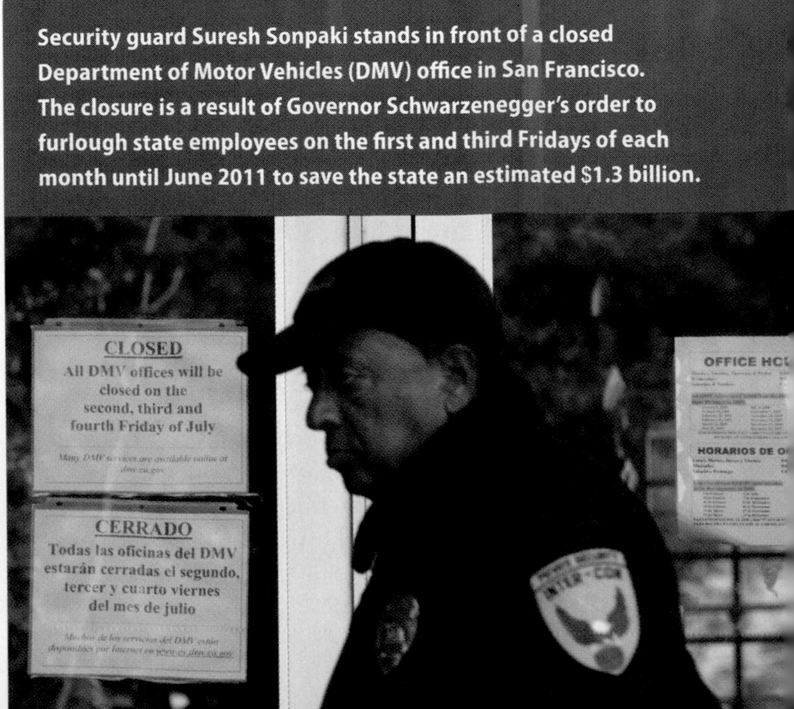

AP PHOTO / JEFF CHIU

predecessor, Gray Davis.[17] Clearly, there were differences between the governor's tough talk and reality.

California's Complex Executive

The executive branch is a hodgepodge of independently elected authorities who serve in overlapping and conflicting institutional positions. Nobody, not even the governor, is really in charge. Each official simply attempts to carry out his or her mission with the hope that passable policy will result. Occasionally, reformers have suggested streamlining the system by consolidating functions and reducing the number of elective offices, but the only recent change has been the addition of yet another office, that of insurance commissioner.

"HELL HATH NO FURY like a bureaucrat scorned."

~ MILTON FRIEDMAN ~
AMERICAN ECONOMIST
1912–2006

Despite these obstacles, the officeholders—most notably governors—have been active policymakers. Pete Wilson waged war against illegal immigrants, affirmative action, and welfare while trumpeting the "law and order" theme. Gray Davis responded to the state's power shortage crisis. Arnold Schwarzenegger was instrumental in environmental reform.

Still, the governor does not operate in a vacuum. He or she must contend with other members of the executive branch, a fractured and suspicious legislature, independent courts, a professional bureaucracy, and most of all, an electorate with a highly erratic collective pulse. Whether these conditions are challenges or impediments, they make the executive branch a fascinating element of California government.

CALIFORNIA AT ODDS *The Executive Branch*

California's executive branch reminds us of a longstanding problem of democratic government: How can we give the executive enough power to do what the people want—without giving it so much power that it will do what the people fear? There may be no good solution to this conundrum. In contemplating the executive branch, Californians are at odds over a number of questions, including the following:

- Was the recall of Gray Davis essential if California was to confront its difficulties—or was it merely an exercise in irresponsibility?
- Does Jerry Brown's record make him uniquely qualified to be governor—or is it a problem? What about the background of Republican candidate Meg Whitman?
- Should we force the governor to spend more time in California by continuing to let the lieutenant governor assume the gubernatorial powers from the instant that the real governor crosses the state line—or is this an absurd anachronism?
- Is it a good idea for California to fill its various executive offices independently of one another—or would government be more effective if these officers had to run as a slate, all of whom won or lost together? What about a slate limited to the governor and lieutenant governor?
- Should more of the state's executive officers be elected on a nonpartisan basis—or would such a step make these officers less responsive politically?

Take Action

You may think of the California governor as someone quite remote from your life. Any governor is a political animal, however, and will always seek to appear accessible to his or her constituents. You can check out the truth of this with a visit to the governor's Web site at **gov.ca.gov**. Here you'll find ways to e-mail the governor, or sign up to follow him on Facebook, Twitter, YouTube, MySpace, or Flickr. If you wish to support Brown politically, you can do so at **my.jerrybrown.org**. Other state officers also have Web sites—visit **ag.ca.gov** for the site of the new attorney general, Kamala Harris.

POLITICS ON THE WEB

- For a snapshot of the daily news on California public policy and politics, visit **www.rtumble.com**.
- To learn more about how the attorney general represents California's people and enforces state laws, visit the Office of the Attorney General at **www.caag.state.ca.us**.
- To read the latest news and information from the Office of the Governor, visit **gov.ca.gov**.
- If you would like to know more about the activities and responsibilities of the lieutenant governor, go to the Office of the Lieutenant Governor at **www.ltg.ca.gov**.
- For the latest on elections, voting, and political reform, visit the Office of the Secretary of State Web site at **www.ss.ca.gov**.
- The Office of the State Board of Equalization home page offers numerous sources of information related to taxes. To learn more, go to **www.boe.ca.gov**.
- As the state's independent fiscal watchdog, the state controller provides fiscal control over more than $100 billion in public funds, as well as uncovering fraud and abuse of taxpayer dollars. To find out more, go to **www.sco.ca.gov**.
- The California Department of Insurance provides licenses and regulates the rates and practices of insurance companies, agents, and brokers in California. Visit the Office of the State Insurance Commissioner's home page at **www.insurance.ca.gov**.
- The office of the state treasurer has broad responsibilities and authority in the areas of investment and finance. To learn more about how taxpayer's money is being invested, go to **www.treasurer.ca.gov**.
- To learn more about the Office of the Superintendent of Public Instruction, visit **www.cde.ca.gov/eo**.

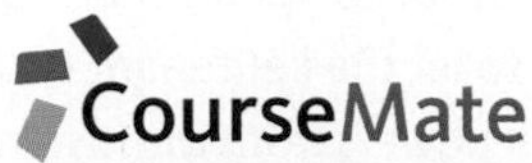

Access CourseMate to review and expand on this chapter through quizzes, flashcards, learning objectives, interactive timelines, a crossword puzzle, audio summaries, video, critical-thinking activities, simulations, and more.

GOVT 24

Taxing and Spending: *Budgetary Politics and Policies*

LEARNING OBJECTIVES

LO1 Explain California's budgetary process and the role of each group of participants.

LO2 Summarize the main sources of revenue used to fund the state's budget.

LO3 Indicate the major areas of spending addressed in the state budget.

CALIFORNIA AT ODDS

Do Initiatives Really Tie Up the State Budget?

As you have learned in previous chapters, California relies heavily on the initiative and referendum process to set state policy. Some people have claimed that use of the initiative, in particular, is out of control. Voters remain supportive of the system, but are open to changes. For example, majorities of those polled support the idea of requiring more than a simple majority vote on initiatives that amend the state constitution.

A key objection to frequent initiatives has been that they tie up the California budget, adding to the state's reputation for ungovernability. Large portions of state revenue are earmarked in advance for various projects, thus reducing the pot of money available for everything else. Many Californians believe that earmarking the budget through initiatives is a major cause of California's budget woes. Others, however, argue that the true problems lie elsewhere.

Initiative Earmarks Make Our Government Dysfunctional

In 2009, the chief justice of the California Supreme Court, Ronald George, stated that initiatives "have rendered our state government dysfunctional, at least in times of severe economic decline."[1] At the time of the Davis recall election, UC Berkeley economist Laura D'Andrea Tyson said: "Direct democracy provisions in California's constitution have rendered the state ungovernable. As a result of several voter initiatives, about 70 percent of state spending is earmarked in advance, limiting the discretion needed to make trade-offs in a crisis."[2] Examples abound:

- Heavily promoted by future governor Arnold Schwarzenegger, Proposition 49 in 2002 earmarked up to $455 million in general fund revenue for before and after-school programs beginning in 2004–2005. This meant that in 2009, after-school program funds could not be touched even though schools were threatening to cut instruction in reading, mathematics, and other fundamentals.
- Proposition 84 in 2006 provided $400 million, funded by state bond sales, to acquire new parks. These dollars, however, cannot be used to keep open existing parks threatened with closure due to the budget crisis.
- Proposition 63 in 2004 placed a 1 percent surtax on incomes of more than $1 million, to be used for new programs to provide mental health services. The new money, however, cannot be transferred to core mental health services that were already provided, which face severe cuts.

Initiative Earmarks Are Not the Problem

Professor John Matsusaka of the University of Southern California believes Laura D'Andrea Tyson's figure of 70 percent of state spending earmarked by initiatives is simply wrong. After reviewing all initiatives approved by voters between 1912 and 2003, Matsusaka finds the real figure to be no more than 32 percent. Modest earmarks approved by the voters in 2004 and 2006 haven't substantially changed the picture. Almost all of the earmarking was done by a single measure—Proposition 98 in 1988, which locked in money for the public schools. Matsusaka believes that this spending would have been appropriated by the legislature anyway, even without an initiative mandate.[3] Considering the shellacking that public education took in the 2009 budget battles, it's hard to argue that Proposition 98 has restrained the legislature unduly. The earmarks mentioned above may be a problem, of course, but the amount of money they have tied up is an order of magnitude less than the size of the state's recent budget deficits.

Even if earmarks on expenditures are not the cause of California's budget woes, however, the voters have certainly created difficulties for the state on the revenue side, as Chief Justice George pointed out in his remarks. True, the voters can't be blamed for the two-thirds majority requirement to pass a budget in the legislature. This limitation was imposed by referenda written by the legislature itself in 1933 and 1962. In both cases, the true effect of the measures was concealed, and the public had no idea what it was really voting on. The voters knew exactly what they were doing in 1978, however, when Proposition 13 slashed property taxes and established a two-thirds requirement for passing any tax increase in the legislature.

WHERE DO YOU STAND?

1. **Is it fair to call Proposition 63 (mental health) an earmark, given that it paid for itself with a new tax? Why or why not?**
2. **Some people say that if you take care of the millions, the billions will take care of themselves. Does this maxim have any application to California's budget? Explain your reasoning.**

EXPLORE THIS ISSUE ONLINE

- **You can find Matsusaka's article at www.iandrinstitute.org/Matsusaka California Budget 2005.pdf. Do you see any problems with his arguments?**
- **UC Hastings College of the Law in San Francisco maintains a database of all California ballot propositions. See it at library.uchastings.edu/library/california-research/ca-ballot-pamphlets.html.**

Introduction

No issue is more critical to Californians than taxation, and no resource is more important to state policymakers than the revenues generated from taxation. Those dollars become the foundation of the annual state budget, the document that determines where and how state funds will be spent.

The connection between taxing and spending can be difficult. Even though most people may agree on taxes in principle, they often disagree on how much should be collected and from whom, as well as who the recipients of those funds should be. When policymakers seem to stray from general public values on budgetary issues, the voters are not shy about using direct democracy to reorder the state's fiscal priorities—and with so many more policy areas of need than dollars available, much is at stake. We examine some of the consequences that follow when voters intervene in the budget in the chapter-opening *California at Odds* feature.

California's Budget Environment

Unlike the national government, which usually operates with a deficit, states are required to balance their budgets. This has been difficult in California, where a steady flow of immigrants, a burgeoning school-aged population, massive attention to crime, and deteriorating infrastructure make for a challenging budget environment. Since a recession in 2002, the state has struggled with one projected state revenue deficit after another regardless of who has been in power. An astronomical projected deficit in 2003 no doubt contributed to the recall of then governor Gray Davis. The state languished in fiscal crisis.

All of that was supposed to change with the fresh approach of Arnold Schwarzenegger. Relying on federal assistance, deferred expenditures, and income sources not even considered by the legislature, Schwarzenegger promised a "balanced" budget. In fact, his first budget was $8 billion out of balance immediately upon signature, according to the state legislative analyst.[4] A temporary economic upswing in 2006 helped the governor and state legislature reach agreement on a balanced, on-time budget for the first time in years. But the joy was short-lived.

By 2008, the state faced a revenue shortfall in excess of $15 billion, once again forcing state leaders to consider drastic cuts, major tax increases, or a combination of the two. In the end, legislators and the governor agreed to a gimmicky document that was "balanced" in name only. In fact, the budget was the most unbalanced in state history. Twice in 2009, the governor and legislature grappled with the deficit. First, they sutured a massive $42 billion hole in March through a combination of new taxes, program cuts, and transfers. Three months later, state leaders had to overcome a new $24 billion gap—this time in program and services cuts only. These events occurred because of a terribly weak state economy, which led to reduced tax revenues and increased demands for social services. Much of the "fix" centered on deferred maintenance, withholding of local government redevelopment funds, and higher withholding of state income taxes. Budget makers even delayed payment of state employee paychecks from June 30 to July 1 so they could "save" $900 million.[5]

The state's economic malaise continued into the 2010–2011 fiscal year, when the weary governor and legislature faced a new $21 billion hole. Again they cut.

As a result, California's state budget has shrunk from about $105 billion in 2005–2006 to $83 billion in 2010–2011, even though the state's population has grown from 36 million to 38.6 million.

> **"THIS IS NOT AN EASY BUDGET, BUT IT IS A NECESSARY BUDGET** that does not raise taxes, solves the $24 billion deficit and includes long-term reforms."
>
> ~ ARNOLD SCHWARZENEGGER ~
> THIRTY-EIGHTH GOVERNOR OF CALIFORNIA, 2003–2011

The voters haven't helped with this ongoing dilemma. Repeatedly, the public has rejected new taxes while embracing new programs and services—the kind of logic that has California in its present-day bind. When two Field polls in March 2010 asked the best way to balance the state budget, respondents who favored spending cuts outnumbered those who favored tax increases by a margin of nearly 4 to 1.[6] Yet when survey respondents were asked where the cuts should be made, majorities could be found in only two of fourteen major public policy areas—prisons and parks.[7] Moreover, over the past quarter century, voters have passed a series of ballot propositions directing the state to spend money on various programs ranging

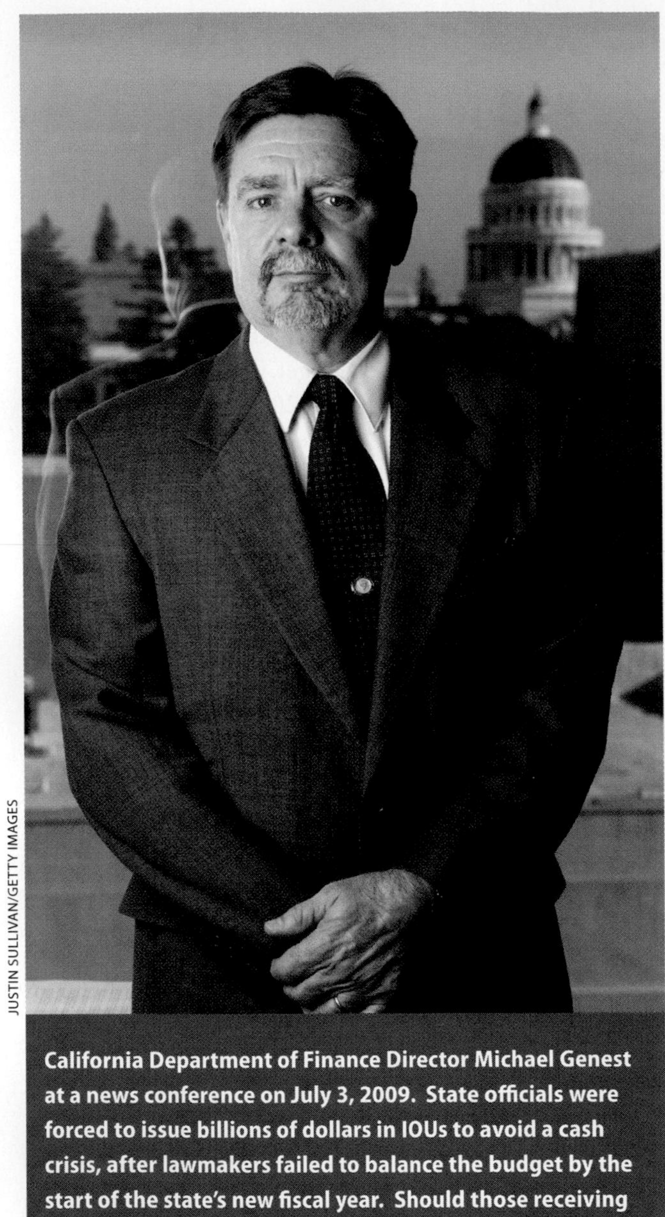
JUSTIN SULLIVAN/GETTY IMAGES

California Department of Finance Director Michael Genest at a news conference on July 3, 2009. State officials were forced to issue billions of dollars in IOUs to avoid a cash crisis, after lawmakers failed to balance the budget by the start of the state's new fiscal year. Should those receiving IOUs be concerned about receiving payment?

from longer prison sentences to more comprehensive public education without providing the funds. This is the political environment in which elected officials must make tough decisions.

LO1 *The Budgetary Process*

Budget making is a complicated and lengthy activity in California. Participants include the governor and various executive-branch departments, the legislature and its support agencies, the public (via initiative and referendum), and increasingly, the courts when judges uphold or overturn commitments made by the other policymakers.

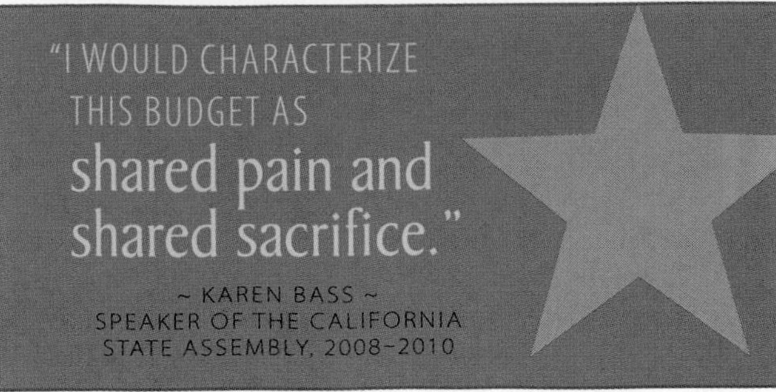

"I WOULD CHARACTERIZE
THIS BUDGET AS
shared pain and
shared sacrifice."
~ KAREN BASS ~
SPEAKER OF THE CALIFORNIA
STATE ASSEMBLY, 2008~2010

The Governor and Other Executive Officers

Preparation of the annual budget is the governor's most important formal power. Other policymakers participate in the budgetary process, but no other individual has as much clout. The governor frames the document before it goes to the legislature and then has additional say afterward through use of the item veto on budget items that he or she opposes. Given this unique power position, legislative leaders often negotiate with the chief executive over what he or she will accept long before the budget lands on the governor's desk.

During the summer and fall, the governor's director of finance works closely with the budget heads of each state agency. Supported by a staff of fiscal experts and researchers, the director of finance gathers and assesses information about the anticipated needs of each department and submits a "first draft" budget to the governor in late fall. The governor presents a refined version of this draft to the legislature the following January. The state constitution gives the legislature until June 15 to respond. The annual budget is supposed to take effect on July 1, but as we learned in Chapter 21, on-time delivery is anything but routine.

Legislative Participants

Upon receiving the budget in January, the legislature's leaders do little more than refer the document to the legislative analyst. Over the next two months, the legislative analyst and his or her staff scrutinize each part of the budget, considering needs, costs, and other factors. Often, the analyst's findings clash with those of the governor, providing the legislature with an independent source of data and evaluation.

Meanwhile, two key legislative units in each house—the appropriations committees and the budget committees—guide the budget proposal through the legislative process. After the staffs of these committees spend about two months going through the entire

THE "BIG FIVE" OF CALIFORNIA GOVERNMENT

Governor **Jerry Brown**

Senate President Pro Tem **Darrell Steinberg**

Speaker of the Assembly **John Pérez**

Senate Minority Leader **Bob Dutton**

Assembly Minority Leader **Connie Conway**

ALL PHOTOS: AP PHOTO/RICH PEDRONCELLI

The Big Five is an informal institution of California state government, consisting of the governor, the Assembly speaker, the Assembly minority leader, the Senate president pro tempore, and the Senate minority leader. Members of the Big Five meet in private to negotiate California's state budget.

document, each house assigns portions to various other committees and their staffs. During this time, lobbyists, individual citizens, government officials, and other legislators testify on the proposed budget before committees and subcommittees. By mid-April, the committees conclude their hearings, combine their portions into a single document, and bring the budget bill to their respective full house for a vote.

As June nears and the two houses hone their versions, a select group of leaders enter into informal negotiations over the document. Known as the **Big Five,** the governor, the speaker of the assembly, the president pro tem of the senate, and the minority party leaders of each house become the nucleus of the final budgetary decisions. In recent years, the Big Five have cast long shadows over just about all of the other players. Should the two houses differ on specifics, the bill goes to a two-house conference committee for reconciliation, after which both houses vote again. Because of a voter-passed initiative in 2010, it now takes a simple majority to pass the budget, a change from the previous long-standing two-thirds requirement. However, inasmuch as a two-thirds vote is still required for revenue increases, the significance of this change is questionable.

The Courts

Sometimes, the courts weigh in on key budget issues to address some of the "quick fixes" to complex budget issues enacted by public policymakers or the voters. Governor Schwarzenegger was humbled in 2005 when a state superior court judge ruled that he was obligated to enforce a new law that reduced the ratio of patients to nurses from 6–1 to 5–1. In 2008, a decision by the U.S. District Court forced the state to spend billions of dollars on improved prison conditions, adding still more to a budget already billions in the red. In 2009 a federal court rejected $500 million in social service cuts as incompatible with federal law, a decision that added to the budget crisis of that year. And even as California attempted to comply with a federal court order to reduce the inmate population of its overcrowded state prisons, a court-appointed receiver rejected the state's effort to reduce costs as excessive. Clearly, the courts have found reason to shape state budgets.[8]

Even the will of the voters has been subject to judicial review on matters relating to the state budget. Particularly significant have been the many cases arising from Proposition 13. Also, decisions on the famous "three strikes and you're out" initiative (see Chapter 22) have added greatly to state incarceration costs.

The Public

On occasion, the public shapes the budget through initiatives or referenda. The voters relied on ballot propositions to approve the sales tax (1933) and repeal the inheritance tax (1982).

In 1993 the voters passed a proposition that increased the state sales tax by 0.5 percent, with new revenues exclusively earmarked for public safety provided by local governments. In 2004 the

Big Five The governor, assembly speaker, assembly minority leader, senate president pro tem, and senate minority leader, who gather together informally to thrash out decisions on the annual budget and other major policy issues.

Proposition 13 (1978) Also known as the Jarvis-Gann initiative; a ballot measure that cut property taxes and significantly reduced revenues for local governments.

voters enacted an initiative that created an additional 1 percent tax bracket for people with taxable incomes of $1 million or more, with the funds designated for mental health programs. The public doesn't always agree to increases, however. The voters soundly rejected a 2006 initiative that would have added an additional tax bracket of 1.7 percent beyond the highest level for individuals with taxable incomes of $400,000 or more, with the revenues earmarked for a statewide preschool program.

In 2009, the governor and legislature strung together five ballot proposals that would simultaneously cap spending and temporarily increase sales taxes (0.25 percent), income taxes (1 percent) and motor vehicle fees (0.50 percent). The ballot proposals also would have earmarked half of any extra revenues to the public schools. The package also would have given the governor new powers to cut programs midyear. The public said no to all five propositions.

Perhaps the most dramatic tax-altering event came in 1978 with the passage of **Proposition 13,** an initiative that reduced local property taxes by 57 percent. Since then, property owners have saved more than $528 billion in taxes,[9] while local governments have become increasingly dependent on the state for relief. As a result, the state has beco me the major funder for local services such as public education, although support has varied with the health of the economy. This uncertainty has brought endless criticism from local government officials.

The bottom line is that there are many more players in the budget process than meet the eye. This complexity both slows down the process and requires near unanimity among the various parties before any major decisions are made.

"Every chamber of commerce, every editorial board, every labor group, every tax-receiver group, **EVERYBODY OPPOSED PROP 13 EXCEPT THE VOTERS."**

~ JON COUPAL ~
PRESIDENT OF THE HOWARD JARVIS TAXPAYERS ASSOCIATION

LO2 *Revenue Sources*

Like most states, California relies on several forms of taxation to fund its general fund budget (that is, the budget exclusive of federal funds). The largest sources of revenue are personal income tax, sales tax, and bank and corporation taxes. Smaller revenue supplies come from motor vehicle, fuel, insurance, tobacco, and alcohol taxes. The state's major revenue sources and expenditures for fiscal year 2010–2011 are shown in Figure 24–1.

Other taxes are levied by local governments. Chief among these is the property tax, although its use was reduced considerably by Proposition 13. This tax is collected by counties rather than by the state, but the state allocates it among the different levels of local government, and it still is a part—directly or indirectly—of the tax burden of all Californians.

All too aware of the state's antitax mood, policymakers have refused to add taxes to cope with burgeoning needs. As a result, the state's commitments to most services have decreased considerably over the past three decades. Individual recipients, school districts, and local governments have been thrown into turmoil.

Figure 24–1

California's Revenue Sources and Expenditures, 2010–2011

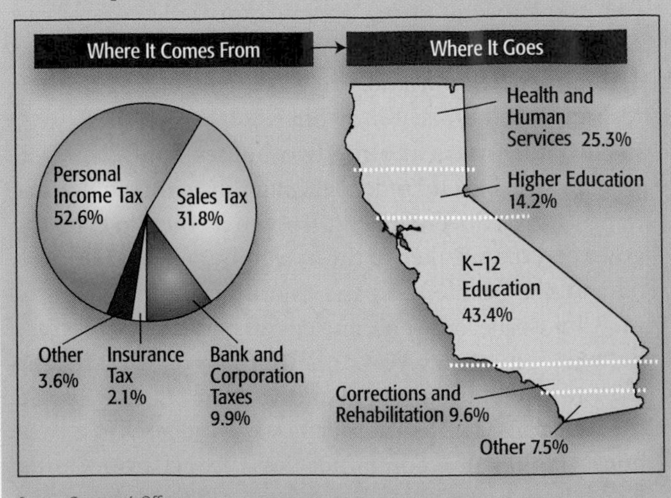

Source: Governor's Office

JUSTIN SULLIVAN/GETTY IMAGES

Blue Sky coffeeshop worker Jon Sarro shows a customer different strains of medical marijuana in Oakland, California where voters overwhelmingly approved a measure for a special tax on sales of medicinal marijuana. The new tax rate will generate an estimated $294,000 for the financially strapped city. Should medical marijuana be taxed locally?

Figure 24–2

California's Tax Burden, 1948–2011

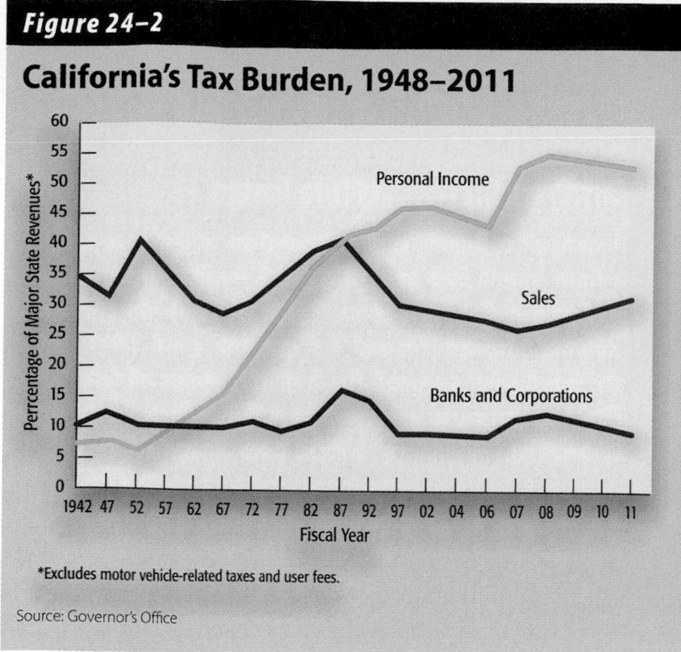

*Excludes motor vehicle-related taxes and user fees.

Source: Governor's Office

Infrastructure work, such as repairs after the 1989 and 1994 earthquakes, and certain highway maintenance programs have been stretched out. Placement of a new earthquake-resistant Oakland–San Francisco Bay bridge will not be complete until 2013, twenty-four years after the earthquake that caused its damage. In fact, a recent study ranks California forty-seventh of the fifty states in per capita highway expenditures.[10]

The Sales Tax

Until the Great Depression of 1929, a relatively small state government garnered funds by relying on minor taxes on businesses and utilities. After the economic crash, however, the state was forced to develop new tax sources to cope with hard times. The first of these, a 2.5 percent **sales tax,** was adopted to provide permanent funding for schools and local governments. Today, the statewide sales tax is 8.25 percent. Of that amount, cities and counties get 2 percent to help meet health and public safety needs. The state keeps the rest. In addition, as much as 1.5 percent is tacked on by counties engaged in state-approved projects, most of which are transportation related.

Occasionally, changes take place in response to economic conditions. In 1991, Governor Pete Wilson and the legislature cut the sales tax by 0.25 percent when the state enjoyed a huge budget surplus. This reduction remained in place until 2002, when the revenue shortfall forced an adjustment upward. In response to the budget crisis in 2004, Governor Schwarzenegger persuaded voters to approve Proposition 57, which provided $15 billion in bonds, or borrowed money, to be repaid over the next decade by diverting 0.25 percent of local governments' share of the sales tax. Today, the sales tax accounts for about 31.8 percent of the state's tax revenues.

The Personal Income Tax

A second major revenue source, the **personal income tax,** was modeled after its federal counterpart to collect greater amounts of money from those residents with greater earnings. Today, the personal income tax varies between 1.0 and 10.3 percent, depending on one's income. The last revision was in 2004, when voters approved a ballot proposition that added a 1 percent tax to those Californians with incomes of $1 million or more. That money is earmarked for mental health programs.

The personal income tax is now the fastest-growing component of state revenue (see Figure 24–2)—a significant fact because Californians ranked tenth among the fifty states in per capita income in 2009. Inasmuch as the tax goes up with increasing incomes, it filled the state coffers in the dramatic economic boom during the later part of the 1990s and slowed just as dramatically in the first few years of the twenty-first

sales tax A statewide tax on most goods and products; adopted in 1933; local governments receive a portion of this tax.

personal income tax A graduated tax on individual earnings adopted in 1935; the largest source of state revenues.

century. As of 2010, the personal income tax accounted for 52.6 percent of the state tax bite.

Bank and Corporation Taxes

Financial industry and corporation income taxes contribute much less to California's budget than do sales and personal income taxes. Taxes on bank and corporate incomes did not exceed 5.5 percent until 1959, when the legislature enacted the first of a series of rate hikes. The last increase occurred in 1980, when, responding to local governments' losses from Proposition 13, the legislature boosted the **bank and corporation tax** from 9.6 percent to 11.6 percent. Between 1987 and 1996, however, the legislature reduced the tax to 8.84 percent, where it remains for corporations today. Since 1996 the corporate tax for banks has been fixed at 10.84 percent. Together, bank and corporation taxes now account for about 9.9 percent of state revenues.

Aside from Proposition 13 and the expanded reliance on **user taxes,** such as those levied on gasoline and cigarettes, California's revenue collection system has undergone gradual adjustments over the past sixty years. Figure 24–2 shows the changing weight of the sales, personal income, and bank and corporation taxes from 1942 to the present. Recent data indicate a steady drift toward increased dependence on the personal income tax and decreased dependence on sales and corporation taxes, although the recession of 2008–2010 pushed income tax receipts down somewhat, while sales taxes increased.

Other Sources

From time to time, state leaders have asked voters to approve bonds, thus obligating the electorate to long-term commitments. These projects, sometimes lasting as long as forty years, finance major infrastructure commitments such as school classroom, transportation, and water projects.

The state has turned to bonds with increasing frequency. In 1991, California ranked thirty-second among the fifty states in indebtedness on a per capita basis. By 2009, the state's bond debt increased to more than $140 billion, $70 billion of which had been enacted during the Schwarzenegger administration alone. That represents a per capita indebtedness of $1,805—well above the national average.

bank and corporation tax A tax on the profits of lending institutions and businesses; the third most important source of state revenue.

user taxes Taxes on select commodities or services "used" by those who benefit directly from them; examples include gasoline taxes and cigarette taxes.

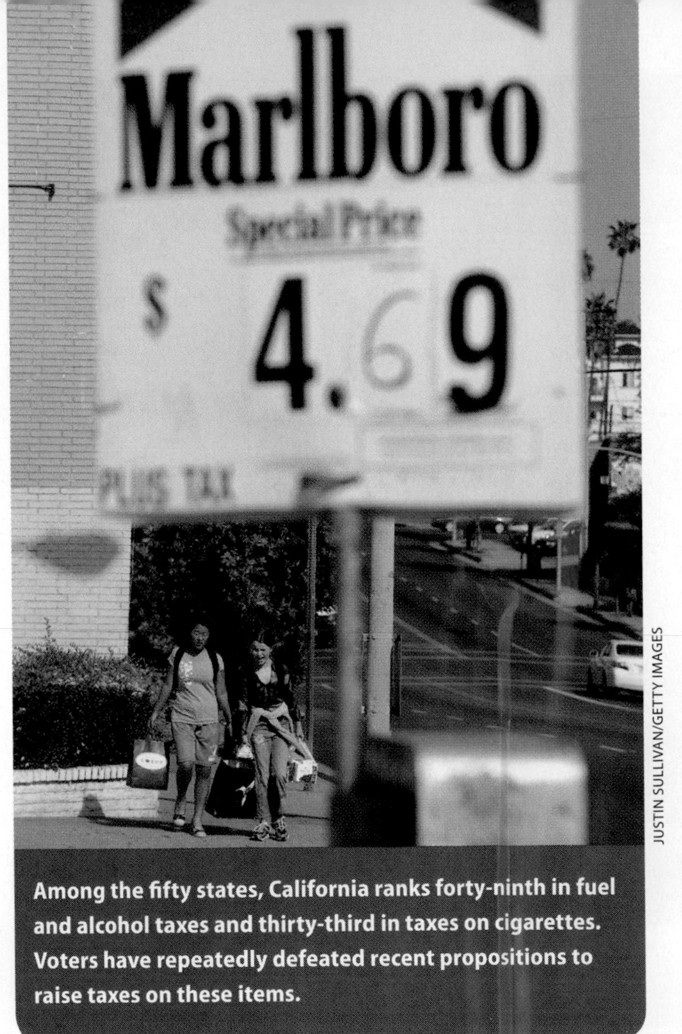

Among the fifty states, California ranks forty-ninth in fuel and alcohol taxes and thirty-third in taxes on cigarettes. Voters have repeatedly defeated recent propositions to raise taxes on these items.

California also gets a small but growing portion of its revenue from fees and charges for services. For example, 90 percent of the operating costs of state parks were funded by taxes in 1982–1983; but within a decade, only 40 percent came from tax revenues, while 57 percent came from fees and concessions. Although Governor Davis and the legislature reduced those fees in 2000, new budget pressures led Governor Schwarzenegger and the legislature to increase them again in 2004 and 2008.

Taxes in Perspective

Viewed in a comparative context, the overall tax burden for California ranks ninth in the nation on a per capita basis, remarkably close to its per capita income ranking. Nevertheless, there have been changes in the state tax blend, with the state becoming increasingly dependent on the personal income tax as its primary source of income.

When calculating state and local taxes as a percentage of personal income, California ranks thirteenth. On a per capita basis, the state ranks seventeenth in sales taxes, eighth in personal income taxes, seventh in bank and corporation taxes, and twenty-ninth in property taxes.[11]

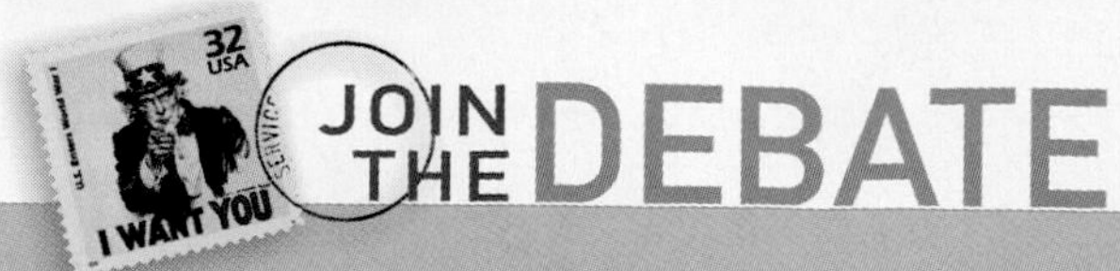

Should Fees Be Treated Like Taxes?

Proposition 26, approved in November 2010, expands the definition of a tax to include so-called *regulatory fees.* These fees are assessed on businesses to recover the costs of regulation. For example, a fee is collected from businesses that make products containing lead. The revenues go to screen children for lead poisoning and to identify sources of lead contamination. After Proposition 26, any new regulatory fee will need two-thirds approval by the state legislature or by local voters. The measure does not apply to user fees such as garbage fees.

Proposition 26 also requires a two-thirds vote on laws that increase taxes on any taxpayer, even if the law does not increase revenues overall. The result is to freeze in place the existing tax code. The legislature is unlikely to cut anyone's taxes if the cut can't be matched by an increase elsewhere. Are these changes a good idea—or a bad one?

Proposition 26 Stops Hidden Tax Increases

Supporters of Proposition 26 argue that it keeps governments from imposing stealth taxes on California businesses, taxes that will be passed on to consumers. One of the arguments used by opponents of the proposition actually makes the case in its favor—that passage of the measure will cost the state billions of dollars in years to come. These are billions of new taxes that the state does not currently collect. Such hidden increases amount to an end-run around the two-thirds majority requirement to increase taxes, a requirement that the overwhelming majority of California voters support. Proposition 26 merely closes a loophole in state law.

Proposition 26 Threatens the Environment

Opponents of Proposition 26 point to the interests that spent the most to support the measure: the Chamber of Commerce, Chevron, the American Beverage Association, and Phillip Morris (the tobacco company). Why do these companies care about Proposition 26? Because they make products that can damage the environment or the health of California's citizens. If companies make things that harm the environment or the public health, it is only fair if they bear some of the costs. That's what regulatory fees are all about.

Proposition 26 also prevents tax reform. For example, in 2010 the legislature cut some taxes on gasoline and raised others by a matching amount. The goal was to free up sums dedicated to roads and use them for the general fund. Proposition 26 reversed this vote and blew a $1 billion hole in the general fund budget.

For Critical Analysis ***Some California cities impose fees on wine and liquor bottles and use the revenue for code and law enforcement, under the principle that alcohol consumption leads to public disorder. Are such laws fair? Why or why not?***

In other areas, California taxes are near the bottom, due largely to the influence of powerful interest groups. For example, the state ranks forty-ninth in both fuel taxes and alcoholic beverage taxes. Reformers attempted to establish oil production taxes of $400 million over ten years via initiative in 2006, but the measure was soundly defeated at the polls. As a result, California is the only one of fourteen major oil-producing states that does not tax oil. With respect to tobacco taxes, California ranks thirty-third in the nation.[12] Had the voters approved a ballot proposition in 2006 increasing the tobacco tax by $2.60 per pack, the state would be collecting an additional $2 billion for children's health care—but that measure, too, was defeated. In 2010's Proposition 26, California voters ensured that state fees and charges were treated as taxes, requiring a two-thirds vote for approval. We look at this ballot measure in the *Join the Debate* feature above. In these and other cases, interest groups have carried great sway with the legislature and public.

LO3 *Spending*

The annual state budget addresses thousands of financial commitments, both large and small. Major areas of expenditure include public education (grades K through 12), health and welfare, higher education, and prisons. Outlays in these four areas account for nearly 90 percent of the general fund. The remainder of the budget (the difference between total expenditures and the general fund) goes to designated long-term projects such as transportation, parks, and veterans' programs, many of which have been authorized by public ballot.

DAVID McNEW/GETTY IMAGES

Teachers rally as the Los Angeles Unified School District Board of Education voted on whether to issue thousands of layoff notices to teachers and other school employees. What impact would these layoffs have on the quality of education in schools?

Since 1979 state spending has been determined more by the public than by the legislature and the governor. Under Proposition 4 (1979) and Proposition 111 (1990), budgets have been determined largely by formulas rather than by need. In 2004—again at the urging of Governor Schwarzenegger—the voters passed **Proposition 58,** which requires the state to gradually set aside up to 3 percent of all revenues in a "rainy day" fund, beginning in 2006. Some critics have characterized the formula approach as a political "straitjacket" that is unresponsive to changing times and needs; others have viewed it as inconsequential, since the state rarely has enjoyed any surplus. Defenders of "formula government" argue that it is the only way to keep state leaders from operating with a blank check.

Push came to shove in 2008. As Democrats and Republicans battled over whether to increase taxes or cut expenditures, the governor waited in frustration for a budget that eventually reached his desk a record eighty days late. Yet all that paled in comparison to the budget crisis in 2009. Confronted with a $42 billion deficit, the governor and legislature asked the voters to help bridge the gap by passing a series of temporary tax increases and tougher spending rules. The voters declined for a variety of reasons. Some argued that they were overtaxed already; others didn't like the extent to which the governor would have had increased budget-making authority with little legislative oversight; others still rejected more creative borrowing, this time through future revenues from the state lottery.[13] The result was that the legislature and governor made massive spending cuts.

More cuts, though less dramatic, were made in 2010 after the budget came in one hundred days late—yet another dubious record. Some observers noted that the damage to education and social welfare programs was not as bad as in the past, but others were quick to point out that the reductions only compounded the cuts that have occurred over the past several years. Some contend that part of the budgetary problem is that California's government is too large. We consider that argument in the *Perception versus Reality* feature on the facing page.

Proposition 58 (2004) A proposition that set broad spending limits on state government and required the state to gradually set aside up to 3 percent of all revenues in a "rainy day" fund.

Public Education: Grades K through 12

The state constitution gives public education a "superior right" to state funds; as such, public schools get the largest share of the state budget. Local school districts periodically add relatively small amounts to education through voter-approved bonds and parcel taxes, but the preponderance of support comes from the state legislature through its annual allocations.

"AT A TIME WHEN OUR NATION SHOULD BE INVESTING IN THE FUTURE OF OUR STUDENTS AS NEVER BEFORE,
this budget cuts education funding for the first time in a decade."
~ JACK O'CONNELL ~
CALIFORNIA SUPERINTENDENT OF PUBLIC INSTRUCTION, 2003–PRESENT

Funding for public education in California has an uneven history. The state ranked among the top-funded states throughout the 1950s and 1960s. Then the pattern changed. During the 1970s and 1980s, the state consistently reduced its per capita support for K through 12 public education, shrinking it to 37 percent of the general fund in 1988. That same year, amid growing concerns about weak funding and poor classroom performance, education reformers secured voter approval

PERCEPTION VERSUS REALITY

California's State Government is Bloated

California's budget crisis raised the question: is state spending out of control? Or is the real problem that tax collections have collapsed? Certainly, California has the largest state budget in the nation, but it also has the largest population. State spending has risen sharply over the years, but so has the state's population, the cost of living, and per capita income. All in all, is California's government bloated?

The Perception

Many people believe that California state government is bloated, and this perception is almost universal among Republicans and conservatives. As one observer put it: "This is a state whose politicians, public sector unions, and advocacy groups have been living in a fantasy world of overspending, investment-deadening taxation, and job-killing regulation."[14] Conservatives argue that the pay of government employees is out of control and that spending on social services is busting the budget. High rates of immigration generate costs that aren't matched by the low taxes paid by poor immigrants. As a result of land-use restrictions, California has the least affordable housing in the nation. In 2005, before the recent budget crisis, California state and local government together were spending $9,578 per resident, 19 percent above the national average. California was fifth in the nation in such spending. Simply put, California suffers from too much government.

The Reality

A look at the rest of the statistics reveals a decidedly more complex picture. By some measures, California does appear to have spent quite freely prior to the 2008–2009 budget crisis. By other measures, the state seems to have been rather tight-fisted. Consider state and local employees. They are indeed among the best-paid in the nation, with pay second only to New Jersey. California school districts pay their teachers the highest average salary in the country. Teachers receive 35 percent more than the national average in wages and benefits—17 percent more when adjusted for the state's higher standard of living. The state's prison guards are unquestionably the nation's best paid, as you learned in Chapter 20.

Although government employees are well paid, there aren't that many of them. California has 95 state employees for every 10,000 residents. Only two states have a smaller ratio. The national average is 143 state employees per 10,000 residents. In other words, California makes do with two workers for every three employed by the average state. The very size of the state may grant California some economies of scale in government, but that cannot explain the entire difference.

If you include local government employees, the differences are less dramatic but still there—California has the fourth smallest workforce with 484 employees per 10,000 residents, compared to a national figure of 544. The picture is the same for public school teachers: again, their salaries are high, but their aren't so many of them. California's average class size is the second-highest in the nation.

For many states, Medicaid, the state-federal health care program for the poor, has been the key financial problem. California enrolls 28 percent of its population in Medi-Cal, the state's Medicaid program. The national average is 19 percent. That ought to spell trouble. California's Medicaid enrollees, however, are younger than average, which is reflected in spending. In 2005, California spent $2,727 on the average Medicaid recipient, compared with a national average of $4,781. As a result, the Medicaid burden per inhabitant of the state was $795.50 compared to a national figure of $931.30 per U.S. resident.

Regardless of whether California's budget has been bloated in the past, the state is looking at a very different future. In the years since Proposition 13, California state government has spent between six and seven dollars per one hundred dollars of residents' income. The 2009-2010 budget proposal cut that to $5.19, the lowest figure in generations. At the state level, California no longer spends substantially more than the U.S. average. When the most recent figures are in, state spending may actually fall below the national average.

Blog On For an excellent poster on the state budget crisis, see **www.mercurynewsphoto.com/graphics/statebudget101.pdf.** For a blog with links to numerous data sources, see **emergentfool.com/2009/05/25/more-on-thecalifornia-state-budget.**

of **Proposition 98,** a measure that established 40 percent as a minimum funding threshold except in times of fiscal emergency. With this mandate, the state poured money into reducing class sizes in grades K through 3 and lengthened the school year from 180 to 190 days. But the upward direction was short lived.

Proposition 98 (1988)
An initiative awarding public education a fixed minimum percentage of the state budget.

Proposition 227 (1998)
An initiative limiting bilingual education to no more than one year.

Table 24–1

California Rankings in Key Education Categories

Category	Rank	Year
Reading, 4th grade	49th	2009
Math, 4th grade	44th	2009
Math, 8th grade	48th	2009
Science, 8th grade	42d	2005*

*Only 44 states participated in the 8th grade science survey.
Source: National Assessment of Education Progress, 2010.

State aid for public education has dropped precipitously with declining state revenues. Between 2008 and 2010 alone, support fell from $50.3 billion to $44.6 billion, a drop of $470 per student; per capita spending dropped more than another $400 after completion of the 2010–2011 budget. At $8,784 per student (2008–2009 figures), California expenditures remain about $1,900 below the national average. According to former state superintendent of public instruction Jack O'Connell, California now ranks forty-sixth of the fifty states in per capita expenditures—despite having one of the highest per capita incomes in the nation (see Figure 24–3).[15] Meanwhile, the school year minimum has fallen to 175 days—three full weeks less classroom instruction than fifteen years ago.

California continues to be near the bottom (forty-ninth) among the states in its student-teacher ratio (a commonly used criterion for assessing education effectiveness) and in reading achievement. The state also ranks forty-seventh in the number of computers per classroom. All this has produced a sorry, if not unexpected, outcome in terms of high school graduation. As of 2010 the state ranked forty-eighth in high school graduation rates.[16] According to studies by the National Assessment of Educational Progress, a well-known nonprofit group, California hovers near the bottom of almost every assessment category. Table 24–1 shows the most recent data available.

Figure 24–3

Personal Income and Public School Spending in California, 1973–2008

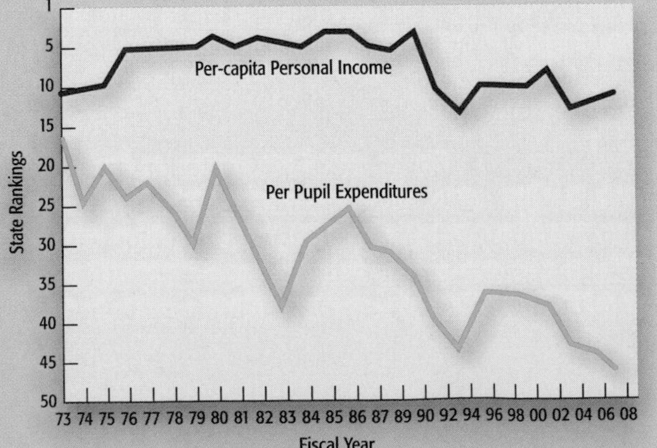

Source: from Terry Christensen and Larry N. Gerston, *Politics in the Golden State: The California Connection*, 2nd ed., Glenview, IL: Scott Foresman, 1988, p 203; Governing: State and Local Source Book, 2006, *EducationWeek*.

Dealing with Diversity

With Latino and Asian American students accounting for 49 percent and 12 percent of the school population, respectively, language-related issues have emerged. In 1998 the passage of **Proposition 227,** a measure limiting bilingual education for non-English–speaking students to one year, added to the debate over how to "mainstream" the diverse California student community. All of this has occurred in a state where one-fourth of all public school students are "English learners" (English is not the first language), compared with 9 percent nationally.

There are chilling consequences from these policies. For starters, California has a high-school dropout rate of 24 percent, or about 125,000 students annually.[17] With few skills, their futures are very limited. At the other end of the spectrum, large numbers of those who do graduate high school are unprepared for college. A recent California State University study found that 55 percent of the incoming freshman class needed remedial instruction in either English or math.[18] Neither of these statistics points to educational excellence.

Nevertheless, the debate goes on. Some reformers have turned to "charter schools"—independent, community-controlled alternatives to what many describe as a broken system. As of 2010 there were about 800 charter schools in California, still a small number compared with the state's 9,700 traditional public schools, although up from 600 in 2008. Other reformers have promoted vouchers—cash payments for parents to use in selecting an educational institution—but the voters have rejected such measures twice in recent years.

The process of fixing California's public education problems will be neither quick nor cheap. In 2007 a 1,700-page report commissioned by Governor Arnold Schwarzenegger declared that it would cost a staggering $1.5 trillion more each year to make all students academically proficient in traditional core knowledge areas such as reading, math, and science.[19] With current state and local expenditures for public education in the neighborhood of $75 billion, even the first step in such a leap would seem highly unlikely.

Higher Education: Colleges and Universities

California's budget woes have cut deeply into support for higher education. Once viewed as the role model for public universities,[20] the higher education system has suffered for a lack of funding and greatly reduced admission slots.

Three components share responsibility for higher education in the state. The state's 110 two-year community colleges enroll about 2.9 million students. Historically, community colleges have been viewed as the entry institutions for students who otherwise did not qualify for, or who could not afford to attend, California's four-year public universities. Funding for these community colleges is connected to the formula for primary and secondary public schools; to that extent, they have benefited from Proposition 98. Still, reduced budget allocations from the state have forced the community colleges to pare back instruction offerings. As a result, during the 2009–2010 academic year, community colleges turned away approximately 140,000 students.[21]

With 222,000 students, the University of California (UC) educates both undergraduate and graduate students at ten campuses throughout the state. Designated as the state's primary research university, UC is the only public institution permitted to award professional degrees (such as medical and law degrees) and doctorates. The California State University (CSU) system, with 433,000 students at twenty-three campuses, concentrates on undergraduate instruction, awarding master's degrees most commonly in such fields as education, engineering, and business.

State support for public universities was fairly constant until the 1990s, holding at about 11 percent of the general-fund budget, and it peaked at 12.7 percent during the 2002–2003 fiscal year. Support eroded considerably during the budget crisis that followed, with the state allocation resting at about 11.7 percent of the general fund in 2008–2009. More significantly, the state's share of the cost of education has decreased dramatically. For example, whereas California provided 90 percent of UC's education costs in 1969–1970, support dropped to 62 percent in 2009–2010. And at CSU, the 90 percent paid by the state in 1969–1970 fell to 69 percent in 2009–2010. Students have been forced to make up much of the shortfall. At both UC and CSU, student fees have more than doubled between 2003–2004 and 2010–2011. Meanwhile, CSU has cut back new enrollments by 40,000; UC has reduced enrollments by 1,500. Between tuition increases and the lack of room, the college participation rate of nineteen-year-olds has fallen precipitously—from 43 percent to 30 percent between 1996 and 2004 alone, dropping California from 17th to 46th place among the 50 states.[22]

MARK RALSTON/AFP/GETTY IMAGES

Assistant Professor Dr. Holli Tonyan, right, talks with a student who can't get classes needed to graduate due to budget cutbacks. The California Faculty Association, which organized this "Vent at the Tent" event, says that more than 40,000 students will be turned away over the next two years.

"In the thirty years I've been watching higher education policy, **I'VE NEVER SEEN A STATE IMPLEMENT BUDGET CUTS OF THIS SIZE AND SCOPE"**

~ TERRY HARTLE ~
SENIOR VICE PRESIDENT OF THE AMERICAN COUNCIL ON EDUCATION

Health and Human Services

Health and human services programs receive the second-largest share of the state budget. The programs accounting for the most significant state commitment include California Work Opportunity and Responsibility to Kids (CalWORKS), Medi-Cal, and the Supplemental Security Income (SSI) program. Medi-Cal provides health-care benefits for the poor, and SSI offers state assistance to the elderly and the disabled. But no program is as politically charged as CalWORKS, the primary welfare program.

"three strikes" law A 1994 law and initiative requiring sentences of twenty-five years to life for anyone convicted of three felonies.

California has sizable welfare costs. With about 12 percent of the nation's population, the state is home to 25 percent of all welfare recipients. In 1990, in contrast, California had 10.5 percent of the nation's population and 12 percent of all welfare recipients.

As welfare numbers have increased, per capita spending has gone down. Changes in state policy began in 1997 after Congress passed the Welfare Reform Act, limiting welfare payments to no more than five years. Shortly thereafter, the legislature passed its CalWORKS legislation, which provides cash grants and welfare-to-work services for needy families with children ten years of age or younger and requires all adults to work at least thirty-two hours per week. As of 2010, about 1.3 million Californians were CalWORKS recipients, two-thirds of whom were children. For the 2010–2011 budget, Governor Schwarzenegger proposed an end to CalWORKS. Elimination would have saved the state budget $1.6 billion annually, although California would have lost $4 billion in matching federal funds. The legislature rejected Schwarzenegger's proposal, although benefits were trimmed. Every other state has a welfare-to-work program.

As of 2010, health and human services programs accounted for about 25 percent of the general fund. Average monthly welfare payments were less than $500 for the typical family of three, down by one-third from five years earlier. Still, with the state scrambling to close a $21 billion budget hole for the coming fiscal year, Governor Schwarzenegger proposed cutting in-home health care for the elderly and disabled by one-third to save $6.037 billion. As with CalWORKS, the legislature greatly tempered the governor's proposal.

Prisons

Of the major state allocation categories, the budgets for prisons and corrections have grown the most in recent years. As with education, the public has played a role in this policy area. Several initiatives have established mandatory prison terms for various crimes and extended the terms for many other crimes. Even more sweeping changes occurred in 1994, when the legislature (and later the voters, through an initiative) enacted a new **"three strikes" law.** This new law required a sentence of twenty-five years to life for anyone convicted of three felonies and added more than 43,000 long-term prisoners to the corrections system between 1994 and 2004.

As a result of the three-strikes law and other policy changes, California's prison population has swelled beyond belief. In 1994 the total prison population was 125,000; it had jumped to 168,000 by 2009—more than double the official capacity. Currently, the costs for incarceration average $49,000 per convict per year. The demographics are equally interesting: 37 percent Latino, 27 percent African American, and 27 percent white. Phenomenal incarceration growth has forced the construction of new prisons, such as the new prison in Delano in 2005. Still, with a soaring inmate population, in 2006 Governor Schwarzenegger asked the legislature to build at least two more state prisons at a cost of $500 million each.[23]

About 10 percent of the state's general fund was used for corrections and rehabilitation during the 2009–2010 fiscal year—once again reflecting the sharpest increase of any major budget category. Meanwhile, lawsuits have led federal court orders requiring the state to release as many as 40,000 prisoners by 2012. Should that occur, the prison budget may moderate.

Other Budget Obligations

California's budget crisis has many sources, some obvious and others not. Clearly, a prolonged recession has contributed mightily to the state's revenue grief. On the expenditure side of the budget ledger, out-of-control prison spending has been of great concern. Two other less known, yet fast-growing, state expenditure categories are payment of bond debt and pension payouts. Together, they now consume more than 10 percent of the state general fund and show little sign of slowing down.

BONDS While voter-approved borrowing through bonds represents an "easy" way to fund major projects over time, cumulatively these bonds are taking a toll on the state. California now ranks tenth in per capita bond debt, up from thirty-second in 1991. Our propensity to rely

A guard watches inmates as they walk down the long hallway on their way out to the recreation yard. Due to overcrowding, the inmates get only four hours of recreation a week at the Deuel Vocational Institution near Tracy.

TONY AVELAR/THE CHRISTIAN SCIENCE MONITOR/GETTY IMAGES

upon bonds has generated the lowest credit rating of any state, which adds to the interest costs to retire the bonds.[24] About 6.7 percent of the state budget now goes to paying interest on the debt. Moreover, State Treasurer Bill Lockyer estimated in 2009 that at present rates, 10 percent or more of the state budget will be dedicated to debt payment by the middle of this decade.[25]

RETIREMENT PENSIONS California's massive public employee pension program, the California Public Employees' Retirement System (CalPERS), covers more than 1.6 million employees, retirees, and their families, or about 4 percent of the state's population. Just under 500,000 are retirees who have worked for various state government agencies. Employees contribute a small portion of their salary to the program, with the state providing the rest as part of the salary compensation package. For years CalPERS gushed with surpluses, thanks to a robust financial market that contained most of the fund's investments. Since the onslaught of the recession in 2008, CalPERS payments have exceeded revenues. By law, the state must make up for any shortfall, and that money comes out of the state budget. In fiscal year 2009–2010, the state was required pay out 5.6 percent of the general fund into CalPERS—up dramatically from a figure that historically averaged 3.4 percent.

California's Budget: Too Little, Too Much, Or Just Right?

Have you ever met anyone who claims that he or she should pay more taxes? Neither have we. Almost everybody dislikes paying taxes, and almost everybody thinks that the money collected is spent incorrectly or unwisely. That seems to be a perennial dilemma in California. However, although most people oppose increased taxes, they also oppose program cuts. It's a modern-day dilemma for state policymakers and the public alike.

Like their counterparts elsewhere, California policymakers have struggled to find a fair system of taxation to pay for needed programs. Given the involvement of so many public and private interests, however, it's difficult to determine what is fair. Moreover, during the last few decades, taxation and budget decisions have been subject to radical change. Somehow, the state's infrastructure has survived, although critics have been less than thrilled with the fiscal uncertainty that has become commonplace in California government.

CALIFORNIA AT **ODDS** *Taxing and Spending*

California's budget embodies the state's priorities. In consequence, California's citizens are inevitably at odds on many budgetary issues, including the following:

- Are ballot initiatives that earmark funds for various purposes or that set levels of taxation an admirable way for California citizens to participate in their own governance—or are they a recipe for a dysfunctional government?
- Is the sales tax a good way to raise revenue because it is imposed on spending, not saving—or is it really a tax on the working class and the poor, who must spend all of what they have to get by?
- Is it appropriate that the state income tax collects such large sums from the state's wealthiest residents—or are "flatter" taxes a fairer way to raise revenue?
- Are poor test results in California schools caused by underfunding—or are such results inevitable in a state with so many recent immigrants?
- Is the "three strikes" law essential to the public's safety—or does it cause prison populations to grow so large that the state cannot afford them?

Take Action

If you want to have an effect on the California budget, you'll need to contact the governor or your representatives in the assembly and senate, as described in earlier chapters. Your comments are likely to be most effective if you have a basic understanding of the budget and the probable impact of the changes that you advocate. Many Web sources provide brief summaries of the budget and associated issues, but it never hurts to go directly to the source. At www.ebudget.ca.gov/pdf/Enacted/BudgetSummary/FullBudgetSummary.pdf you'll find an official analysis of the contents of the most recently enacted budget. Scanning through material such as this may well provide you with new insights.

POLITICS ON THE WEB

- The California Budget Project provides fact-based, nonpartisan analyses of state fiscal and tax policies and their implications for all Californians, especially low- and middle-income residents. To learn more visit **www.cbp.org**.
- For detailed information on the California budget, visit the Department of Finance Web site at **www.dof.ca.gov**.
- The National Center for Education Statistics Web site serves as a comprehensive repository for data related to education. To access, go to **www.nces.ed.gov**.
- The California Taxpayers' Association is a non-partisan, non-profit organization with a mission of protecting taxpayers from unnecessary taxes and promoting government efficiency. To research significant tax and spending issues in the legislative, executive and judicial branches of government, visit **www.caltax.org**.
- As an advocate for fair taxation, the California Tax Reform Association posts the latest news and reports on all tax related issues at **www.caltaxreform.org**.
- The National Governors Association's Web site promotes leadership, best practices, and a unified voice for the nation's governors at **www.nga.org**.

Access CourseMate to review and expand on this chapter through quizzes, flashcards, learning objectives, interactive timelines, a crossword puzzle, audio summaries, video, critical-thinking activities, simulations, and more.

GOVT 25

Local Government in California

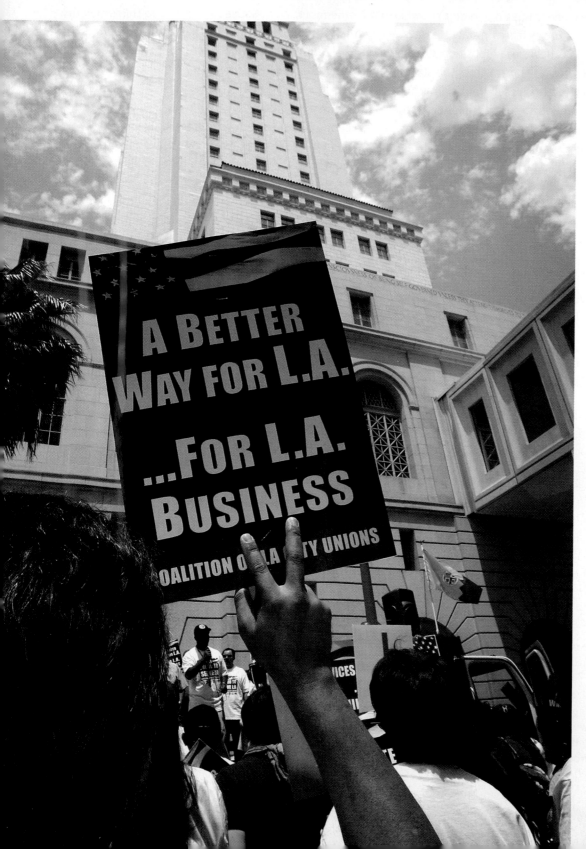

LEARNING OBJECTIVES

LO1 Describe the structure of California's counties and cities, and how they are established.

LO2 Explain who controls California's cities, and how they are elected.

LO3 Identify other forms of local government in California and the services that they provide, and discuss the ways in which direct democracy is used in local politics.

LO4 Summarize how local governments raise and spend money, and the initiatives that have affected revenues.

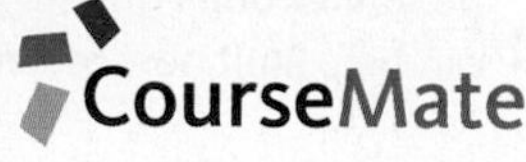

CALIFORNIA AT ODDS

Do We Benefit from Proposition 13?

In 1978, by a margin of 65 to 35 percent, California voters approved Proposition 13, which placed a cap on the real estate tax of 1 percent of assessed value. It also provided that the assessed value could be raised by no more than 2 percent each year unless there is a change of ownership. Furthermore, the initiative required a two-thirds majority in both legislative houses for future increases in state tax rates, and two-thirds support by the voters before local governments could raise special taxes. In 2000, however, Proposition 39 lowered the local threshold for school bonds to 55 percent.

Proposition 13 reduced property taxes across the state by an average of 57 percent. The share of personal income in California taken by state and local taxes fell from as much as 12 percent to about 9.2 percent. California had been a very high-tax state, but for the moment, at least, its taxes didn't exceed the national average.

The new system also introduced distortions into property tax collections. Houses in California frequently have increased in value at rates that exceed 10 percent for many years in a row, so the difference between an owner's taxes and the taxes that a new owner would have to pay has often become quite large. Two houses next door to each other of similar market value could incur dramatically different property taxes.

Proposition 13 had its origins in a series of developments that left homeowners thoroughly alarmed. Explosive population growth and difficulties in building new housing led to skyrocketing house prices. A series of scandals involving county assessors led to a state law that forced assessors to stay close to market value. Previously, assessors had typically valued residential housing more leniently than commercial structures. Many California homeowners therefore experienced drastic increases in assessed value plus rising tax rates on that valuation. Some low-income retired people were forced out of their homes. Subsequently, activists Howard Jarvis and Paul Gann led a "tax revolt" that resulted in Proposition 13. The measure remains popular today. But has it been good for the people of the state?

Proposition 13 Ensures that Tax Rates Are Low and Stable

The Howard Jarvis Taxpayers Association claims that Proposition 13 has saved California taxpayers almost half a trillion dollars over the years. This association, Proposition 13's most ardent advocate, has an interest in quoting the highest possible figure. Surely, however, Proposition 13 has led to lower taxes than would otherwise be the case. Those who believe that California tax rates are still too high naturally find Proposition 13 beneficial. Supporters also say that Proposition 13 has increased community stability by providing predictability for property owners. It has increased predictability for municipalities as well. As a result of property changing hands, the overall tax rate has gone up at a moderate rate. If property taxes reflected market values more closely, local taxes might have shot up during housing booms, only to crash along with the housing market. The existing system has spared local officials the temptation of collecting high, unsustainable taxes.

Proposition 13 Keeps Young Families from Buying Houses

Those who believe that California's schools and other local services have been starved of resources have an obvious reason to oppose Proposition 13. There's another problem with the measure—the distortions it introduces into the housing market. The tax break for long-term owners makes a house more affordable to the current owner than to any potential buyer, so selling makes no economic sense. Of course, that's the point. We don't want to tax grandma out of her home. But this also locks people into place and stifles the free movement of labor. Also, because homeowners don't pay taxes on the increased value of their houses, they have an enhanced interest in anything that will increase the value of their property. In many communities, that can mean opposing new construction—a shortage of housing will drive up property values. Multi-family structures are particularly unwelcome. High house prices transfer prosperity to older, wealthier homeowners and hurt younger, poorer people who want to buy a house. We ought to be able to keep low-income elderly people in their houses without playing Robin Hood in reverse.

WHERE DO YOU STAND?

1. **Do you think that local governments would have raised taxes excessively during the housing boom without Proposition 13? Why or why not?**
2. **Do you or don't you buy the argument that Proposition 13 can help limit new construction? Explain your reasoning.**

EXPLORE THIS ISSUE ONLINE

- **You can find the Howard Jarvis Tax Association at www.hjta.org.**
- **The Public Policy Institute of California provides a large number of short, interesting research pieces. Visit their site at www.ppic.org and see what comes up when you enter "Proposition 13" into the search box.**

Introduction

"YOU ARE FORTUNATE TO LIVE HERE.

If I were your president, I would levy a tax on you for living in San Francisco!"

~ MIKHAIL GORBACHEV ~
FORMER PRESIDENT OF THE SOVIET UNION
1990–1991

counties Local governments and administrative agencies of the state, run by elected boards of supervisors; principal responsibilities include welfare, jails, courts, roads, and elections.

The public and the media tend to focus on state and national politics, but the activities of local governments often have a greater impact on our daily lives. Our city governments make decisions about traffic on our streets; safety in our neighborhoods; and access to parks, libraries, and affordable housing. Our county governments manage transit systems and provide important social services to those most in need, including people who are homeless, mentally ill, and impoverished. Our school districts make decisions about what sorts of teachers are in our classrooms and what our children are taught.

Yet local governments are created by the state, which assigns them their rights and duties, mandating some functions and activities and prohibiting others. The state also allocates taxing powers and shares revenues with local governments. But the state can change the rights and powers granted to local governments, expanding or reducing their tasks, funding, and independence. Cities and counties are infuriated when the state tells them to do things they don't think they can afford or takes away previously committed funds to balance the state budget. School districts depend on the state for funding but are exasperated by burdensome state rules, regulations, and testing requirements. Sometimes, of course, it is the voters rather than the legislature that makes the new rules. An example is Proposition 13, discussed in the chapter-opening *California at Odds* feature.

But local government is also where we—the residents of California—have the greatest influence over our lives, simply because we are closer to it than to Sacramento or Washington, D.C. We can participate directly in local politics precisely because it's local. We can volunteer for candidates, whom we can actually meet and get to know—or we can run for office ourselves. We can lobby elected officials without relying on paid professionals. We can attend city council meetings and testify in person. We can find allies and form interest groups like those described in Chapter 20 (and all those types exist in communities). Local government is the most democratic of all levels of government, and thousands of people participate constantly—go to your own city hall and see for yourself.

San Francisco operates as both a city and a county. City Hall has often been referred to as "The Crown Jewel" of classical architecture in America. It was originally opened in 1915, and is now designated a national landmark.

RAFAEL RAMIREZ LEE / SHUTTERSTOCK.COM

LO1 Counties and Cities

California's 58 counties and 481 cities were created in slightly different ways and perform distinctly different tasks.

Counties

California is divided into counties ranging in size from San Francisco's 49 square miles to San Bernardino County's 20,164, and ranging in population from Alpine County's 1,201 residents to Los Angeles County's 10,393,185. **Counties** function both as local governments and as administrative units of the state. As local governments, counties provide police and fire protection, maintain roads, and perform other services for rural and unincorporated areas (those that are not part of any city). They also run jails, operate transit systems, protect health and sanitation, and keep records on property, marriages, and deaths. As agencies of the state, counties oversee elections, operate the courts, administer the state's welfare system, and collect some taxes.

COUNTY ORGANIZATION State law prescribes the organization of county government. A county's central governing body is a five-member **board of supervisors,** whom voters elect by districts to staggered four-year terms. The board sets county policies and oversees the budget, usually hiring a chief administrator, or **county executive,** to carry out its programs. Besides the members of the board of supervisors, voters elect the sheriff, district attorney, tax assessor, and other department heads (see Figure 25–1). Conflicts often occur as the elected board tries to manage the budget and the elected executives attempt to deliver services. Unlike most of their state counterparts, these local officials are chosen in nonpartisan elections, a Progressive legacy that keeps party labels off the ballot; all serve four-year terms. As of 2010, California's 296 elected county supervisors were overwhelmingly white and male; only 23.5 percent were female, 9.5 percent were Latino, 3.4 percent were Asian, and 1.7 percent were African American. These numbers were roughly the same as in 2002, despite the growth in numbers and political engagement of some of these constituencies.

Although most counties operate under this general-law system, fourteen have used a state-provided option to organize their own governmental structures through documents called **charters.** Most of these charter counties, including Los Angeles, Sacramento, San Diego, and Santa Clara, are highly urbanized. County voters must approve the charter and any proposed amendments. Generally, a "home rule" or **charter county** uses its local option to replace elected executives with appointees of the board of supervisors or to strengthen the powers of the appointed county executive.

San Francisco is unique among California's local governments because it operates as both a city and a county. Most counties have several cities within their boundaries, but the separate city and county governments of San Francisco were consolidated in 1911. San Francisco thus has a board of supervisors with eleven members rather than a city council, but unlike any other county, it has a **mayor.** Should other California cities and counties follow San Francisco's example? We consider that question in the *Join the Debate* feature on the facing page.

board of supervisors The five-member governing body of counties; elected by district to four-year terms.

county executive The top administrative officer in most California counties; appointed by the board of supervisors.

charter The equivalent of a constitution for a local government; includes government structures, election systems, powers of officeholders, conditions for employing local government workers, and often much more.

charter city or county A local government that drafts its own structures and organization through a document like a local constitution (also known as a "home-rule" charter), subject to voter approval.

mayor The ceremonial leader of a city; usually a position that alternates among council members, but in some large cities the mayor is directly elected and given substantial powers.

Figure 25–1

County Government: An Organizational Chart for California's 45 General Law Counties

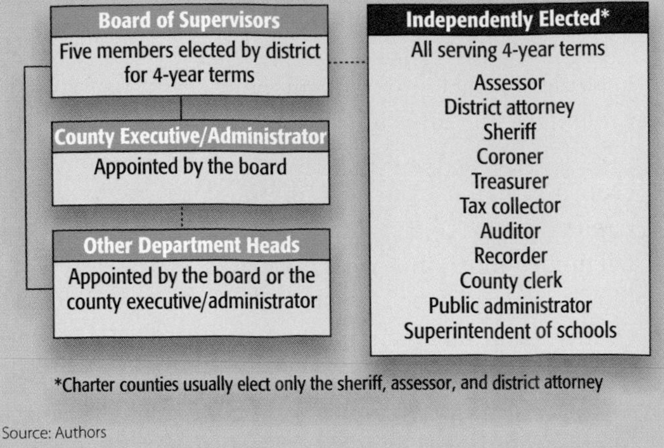

*Charter counties usually elect only the sheriff, assessor, and district attorney

Source: Authors

Downtown San Diego, California's second largest city, as seen from the harbor.

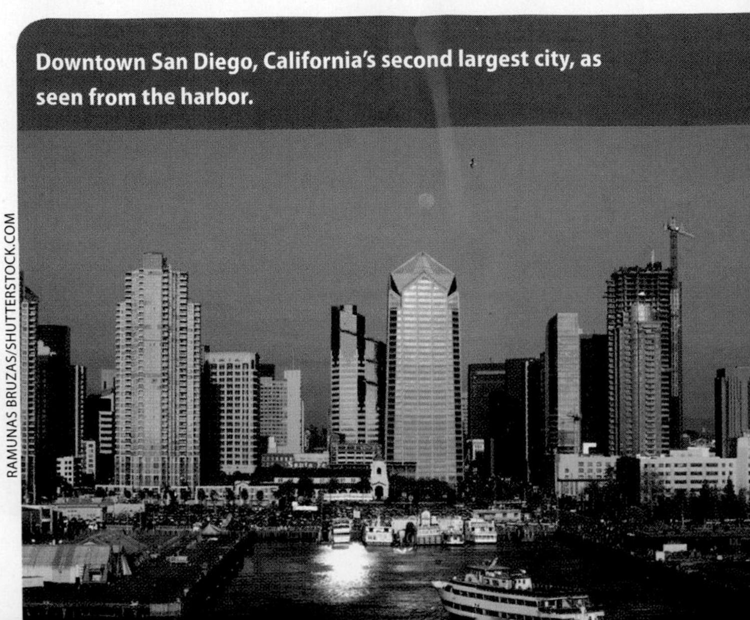

RAMUNAS BRUZAS/SHUTTERSTOCK.COM

Would City-County Consolidation Work in California?

Across the Midwest and the South, a substantial number of metropolitan areas have united the central city and its surrounding county into a consolidated government. Examples include:

- Jacksonville-Duval County in Florida, created when Jacksonville annexed most of the county and the county government was dissolved.
- Louisville Metro, coterminous with the former Jefferson County in Kentucky.
- The Metropolitan Government of Nashville and Davidson County in Tennessee.
- Miami-Dade—formerly Dade County, Florida—formed when Miami and other municipalities ceded most of their responsibilities to the county.
- Unigov, the Indianapolis-Marion County municipal government in Indiana.

These examples, and several dozen others, employ a wide variety of institutional arrangements. What most have in common is that the consolidated government handles most governmental functions, but the municipalities that entered into the merger retain a legal existence and provide a limited number of services. Sometimes, however, pre-existing governments are dissolved—for example, Duval County in Florida and the City of Louisville in Kentucky are no longer in business.

San Francisco has been both a city and a county since 1856, but otherwise California contains no consolidated governments, and consolidation has hardly ever been contemplated. An exception is Sacramento, where city-county consolidation was voted down in 1974 and 1990. Did the people of Sacramento County make the right choice—or should the benefits of consolidation be more widely considered in California?

Consolidation Means Greater Efficiency

California has a huge number of local governments of one kind or another—6,265 by a recent count. These include 4,750-odd special districts. Most citizens cannot keep track of the special districts, do not know who runs them, and even what they do. Such a tangle of administrations is a recipe for inefficiency. It produces unplanned, uncoordinated, and duplicative services. Long-term planning for the metropolitan area as a whole becomes impossible. Urban sprawl becomes a problem as wealthy residents move to outlying areas and central cities experience decay.

California adopted constitutional amendments in 1970 and 1974 to allow local governments to engage in consolidation without asking the state for permission. In 1973, on the request of Sacramento, the legislature established a procedure under which locally inspired consolidation could take place. While the residents of Sacramento County chose not to go ahead with such a merger, there are other communities that can and should consider consolidation.

If It's Not Broken, Don't Fix It

There were good reasons why Sacramento residents turned down consolidation—it did not address any of the real concerns that citizens had with local government. Political scientists Walter Rosenbaum and Gladys Kammerer have posited that three conditions are necessary for a successful consolidation effort: 1) there must be a general climate of crisis, 2) the people must come to believe that current institutions do not work, and 3) a specific triggering event needs to inspire a demand for change.[1] Glen Sparrow, who was part of the 1974 Sacramento consolidation effort, believes that none of these conditions were met in that area. Despite the 128 special districts in the county as of 1970, the voters appeared to feel "an acceptable level of dissatisfaction" with the decentralized system. What really touched off the campaign for consolidation, in Sparrow's opinion, was the large number of energetic young political reformers drawn to Sacramento because it was the state capital. For these people, politics was a sport.[2]

It appears that a majority of California citizens are less concerned about local government efficiency than about the size and scope of government. These concerns would burst into the open a few years later, in 1978, when the electorate adopted Proposition 13. Voters who seek to hobble local government's taxing power are probably not voters who are willing to countenance a new, much larger, government entity. Today, Proposition 13 remains the "third rail" of California politics, and Californians have little interest in consolidation.

For Critical Analysis ***In most states, counties are much smaller geographically than they often are in California. What influence might this fact have on how willing voters are to consider consolidation?***

ANDY Z./SHUTTERSTOCK.COM

Los Angeles is the largest city in the state of California and the second largest city in the United States. Los Angeles is the seat of Los Angeles County, the most populated and one of the most diverse counties in the United States.

No new county has been formed in California since 1907, although in some large counties such as Los Angeles, San Bernardino, and Santa Barbara, rural areas frustrated by urban domination have tried unsuccessfully to break away and form their own jurisdictions. One city in massive San Bernardino County is so far away from the city where county government is headquartered that some residents say they want to "move" to nearby Arizona.

cities Local governments in urban areas, run by city councils and mayors or city managers; principal responsibilities include police and fire protection, land-use planning, street maintenance and construction, sanitation, libraries, and parks.

incorporation The process by which residents of an urbanized area form a city.

local agency formation commission (LAFCO) A county agency set up to oversee the creation and expansion of cities.

general-law city or county A city or county whose organization and structure of government are derived from state law.

city council The governing body of a city; members are elected at large or by district to four-year terms.

city manager The top administrative officer in most California cities; appointed by the city council.

Cities

Whereas counties are created by the state, **cities** are established at the request of their citizens through the process of **incorporation.** Starting with just 8 cities in 1850, California has 481 today. As unincorporated areas urbanize, residents begin to demand more services than their county government can provide. These may include police and fire protection, street maintenance, water, or other services. Residents may also wish to form a city to preserve the identity of their community or to avoid being annexed by some other city. Wealthy areas sometimes incorporate to protect their tax resources or their ethnic homogeneity from the impact of an adjacent big city and its economic and racial problems. California's newest city, incorporated in 2010 with a population of 47,635, is Eastvale, in Riverside County.

The process of incorporation starts with a petition from citizens who live in the area. Then the county's **local agency formation commission (LAFCO)** determines whether the area has a sufficient tax base to support city services and makes sense as an independent entity. If LAFCO approves, the county's board of supervisors holds a hearing, and then the voters of the proposed city approve or reject the incorporation.

GROWING AND SHRINKING Once formed, cities can grow by annexing unincorporated (county) territory. Sometimes, small cities that can't provide adequate services disband themselves by consolidating with an adjacent city. More rarely, residents of an existing city seek to de-annex, or secede. This was the case in the San Fernando Valley, a 222-square-mile section of Los Angeles that contains one-third of the city's population. Residents who felt isolated and ignored agitated to secede from the City of Los Angeles; their proposal was voted on in November 2002, along with a similar proposal for secession by Hollywood. Secession required approval by the voters of both these areas and the city as a whole, however, and while the San Fernando Valley narrowly supported secession, the voters of Los Angeles and Hollywood rejected the plan.

CITY STRUCTURES Like California counties, most California cities operate under the state's general law, which prescribes their governmental structure. **General-law cities** typically have a five-member **city council,** with members elected in nonpartisan elections for four-year terms. The council appoints a **city manager** to supervise daily operations; the manager, in turn, appoints department heads such as the police and fire chiefs (see Figure 25–2).

Cities with populations exceeding 3,500 may choose to write their own charters. A hundred and eighteen

"Los Angeles is 72 suburbs in search of a city."
~ DOROTHY PARKER ~
AMERICAN WRITER AND POET
1893–1967

Figure 25–2

City Government: An Organizational Chart for California's 363 General Law Cities

Source: Authors

California cities have done so. A charter city has more discretion in choosing the structure of its government than a general-law city does, as well as somewhat greater fiscal flexibility and the freedom to set policies, provided that no state law supersedes them. All of California's largest cities have their own charters to enable them to deal with their complex problems.

Whether operating under general law or a home-rule charter, once incorporated a city takes on extensive responsibilities for local services, including police and fire protection, sewage treatment, garbage disposal, parks and recreational services, streets and traffic management, library operation, and land-use planning. The county, however, still provides courts, jails, social services, elections, tax collection, public health, and public transit.

LO2 *Power in the City: Council Members, Managers, and Mayors*

Most of California's cities have five-member city councils with appointed city managers as executives, as set forth by state law. Some cities, particularly older and larger communities, have developed municipal government structures uniquely suited to their own needs and preferences. City councils, for example, may be chosen in a variety of ways or expanded in size to allow for more representation. Los Angeles has fifteen council members, San José ten, and San Diego eight. San Francisco's board of supervisors has eleven members. The executive office also varies among these cities; some opt for a stronger mayor rather than the manager prescribed by the state for general-law cities.

Elections

In most California cities, each council member is chosen by the whole city in **at-large elections.** This system was created by the Progressives to replace **district elections,** in which each council member represents only part of the city. At-large elections were intended to reduce the parochial influence of machine-organized ethnic neighborhoods on the city as a whole. The strategy worked, but as a result, ethnic minority candidates, unable to secure enough votes from the city as a whole to win at large, were rarely elected.

at-large elections City council elections in which all candidates are elected by the community as a whole rather than by districts.

district elections Elections in which candidates are chosen by only one part of the city, county, or state.

As cities grew, citywide campaigns also became extremely costly. The Progressives added to the difficulties of minority candidates and further raised the costs of campaigns by making local elections nonpartisan. This weakened the old party machines, but voters lost the modest cue provided by the listing of parties on the ballot. Furthermore, minority candidates were denied the legitimization of a party label, and campaigns cost more because candidates had to get their messages out without help from a party organization.

The San Bernardino City Council listens to public testimony before voting on a measure that would prohibit the city's landlords from renting to undocumented workers and force day laborers to prove legal residency. Should illegal immigrants be allowed to rent?

DAVID McNEW/GETTY IMAGES

DISTRICT ELECTIONS To increase minority representation and cut campaign costs, some cities have returned to district elections. Los Angeles has used district elections since 1924; Sacramento converted in 1971, followed by San José, Oakland, and later, San Diego and San Francisco. Thirty-eight California cities use some form of district elections. Most are large cities, and most have reverted to district elections through voter-approved charter amendments. District elections increased opportunities for minority candidates in some cities, but minorities remain substantially underrepresented among California's local elected officials. Women have done somewhat better but are also underrepresented. Women and minority candidates, as well as gay and lesbian candidates, have been more successful in local elections than in state elections; they are still held back, however, by discrimination, low participation, at-large elections, high campaign costs, and the lack of party support that results from nonpartisan elections.

In most California cities, especially smaller cities that elect their councils at large, candidates who get the most votes win election even if they don't get a majority. In larger cities and cities that elect their council members by district, if no candidate wins a majority in the primary election, the top two compete in a **runoff election,** ensuring that the winner is elected with a majority of the votes. Critics object to the high cost of such elections—both to taxpayers and in campaign spending. In 2004 San Francisco responded to such criticism with **instant runoff voting,** in which voters rank candidates in order of preference. If no candidate wins a majority, the candidate with the fewest votes is eliminated and those votes are assigned to the voters' second choice—and so on until one candidate attains a majority. Oakland, Berkeley, and San Leandro—all in Northern California—have followed San Francisco's example in hopes of saving time and money and simplifying the task of voting. Other cities and counties are now considering adoption of instant runoff voting. Advocates hope that such simplification will enhance voter participation in local elections, which varies considerably from city to city. Turnout is generally higher in cities with elected mayors and district elections, but the key factor related to turnout is when the elections are held.

VOTER TURNOUT About one-third of California's cities hold their elections separate from state and national elections. Median turnout in these elections is less than 30 percent.[3] Los Angeles, for example, holds its elections separately, and turnout in that city's 2009 city council and mayoral contests was 18 percent. Lower turnout significantly affects outcomes because the composition of the electorate changes along with the number of voters; older, more affluent voters predominate, which usually gives an advantage to more conservative candidates. Research tells us that in cities with low voter turnout, municipal government spends less money on programs that might aid the poor. Instead, such governments fund downtown development and other projects that aid business. In short, local governments spend their revenues on those who vote.[4]

Devastating fires in 2007 that cost the state an estimated $1 billion brought together San Diego Sheriff Bill Kolender, Fire Chief Ruben Grijalva, Governor Arnold Schwarzenegger, President George W. Bush, Senator Dianne Feinstein, and San Diego Mayor Jerry Sanders.

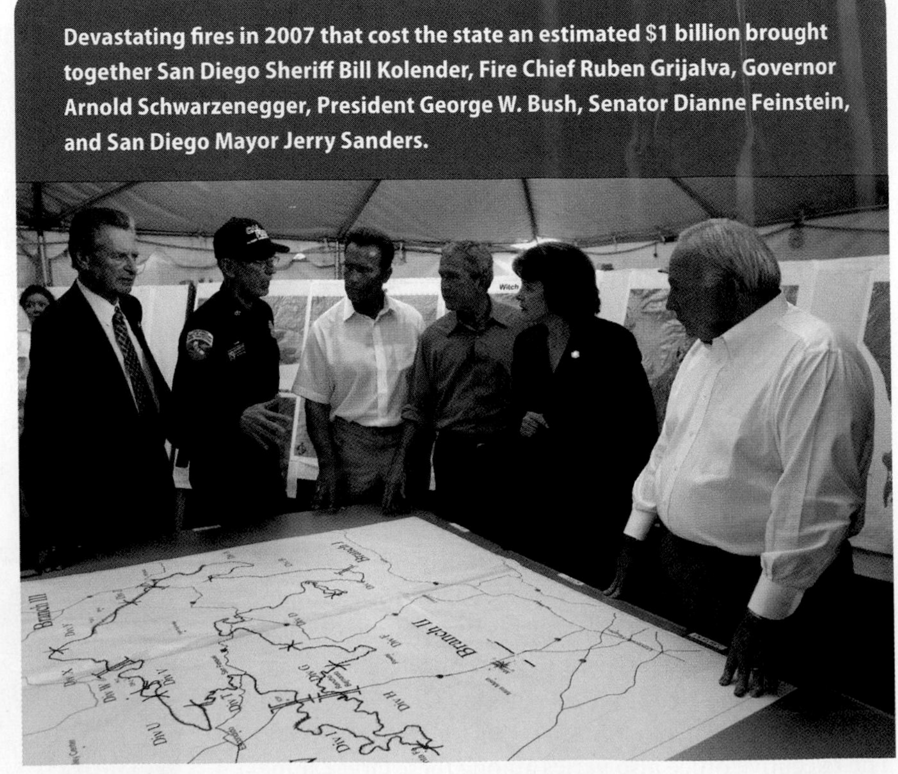

K.C. ALFRED-POOL/GETTY IMAGES

runoff election When no candidate receives more than 50 percent of the vote in a nonpartisan primary for trial court judge or local office, the top two candidates face each other in a runoff.

instant runoff voting Voters rank candidates in order of preference. If no candidate wins a majority, the candidate with the fewest votes is eliminated, and those votes are assigned to the voters' second choice—and so on until one candidate attains a majority.

Turnout in cities that hold their elections concurrently with state and national elections is nearly twice as high.[5] The Silicon Valley city of Santa Clara started holding local elections at the same time as state and national elections in 1988, and voter turnout went from 23–24 percent to 74 percent. Unlike cities, all of California's counties hold their elections at the same time as the state and national elections. Voting for local officials may still be lower, however, due to "drop-off," with some participating voters declining to cast ballots in local races because of lack of interest or information.

AP PHOTO/DAMIAN DOVARGANES

Los Angeles Police Chief Charlie Beck, left, and Los Angeles Mayor Antonio Villaraigosa share a laugh before a City Council panel meeting. Villaraigosa has the authority to appoint forty-four department heads, including the Chief of Police.

SPENDING ON LOCAL CAMPAIGNS As with state-level campaigns, local reformers have been concerned about the costs of city and county races and the influence of money on politics. Spending on local campaigns has risen steadily since the 1980s, when professional campaign consultants and their techniques (see Chapter 19) became common in local races. One hundred and fifty-seven California cities and counties have enacted local campaign-finance laws that require disclosure of contributors and expenditures and sometimes limit the amount of contributions. In most of these cities, the data are available to the public online. Los Angeles also restricts spending and provides limited public financing for campaigns. Long Beach, Sacramento, Oakland, Richmond, and San Francisco are also experimenting with public financing of campaigns.[6] Even in these communities, candidates and interest groups manage to raise and spend substantial sums on campaigns, often through independent expenditures or special campaign committees.[7]

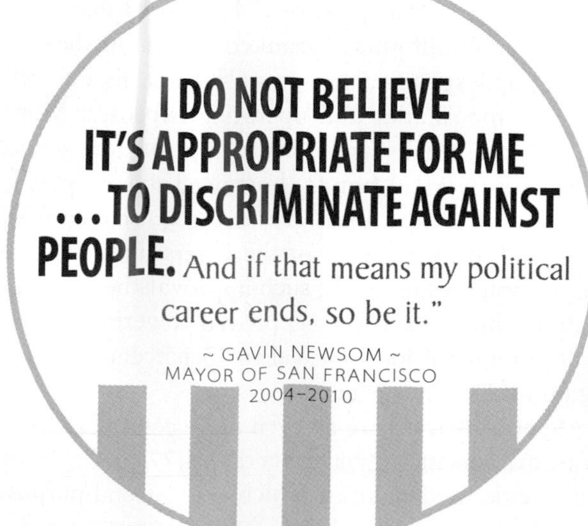

I DO NOT BELIEVE IT'S APPROPRIATE FOR ME ...TO DISCRIMINATE AGAINST PEOPLE. And if that means my political career ends, so be it."
~ GAVIN NEWSOM ~
MAYOR OF SAN FRANCISCO
2004–2010

Executive Power

Most people assume that mayors lead cities and have substantial power, but that's not usually the case in California communities. Because mayors were once connected with political machines, the Progressive reformers stripped away their powers, shifting executive authority to council-appointed city managers who were intended to be neutral, professional administrators. Most California cities use this **council–manager system.** While the manager administers the city's programs, appoints department heads, and proposes the budget, the council members alternate as mayor—a ceremonial post that involves chairing meetings and cutting ribbons.

San Francisco, however, uses a strong-mayor form of government, in which the mayor is elected directly by the people to a four-year term and holds powers similar to those of the president in the national system, including the veto, budget control, and appointment of department heads. Former San Francisco mayor Gavin Newsom exercised his powers to gain a national reputation as a leader on such issues as same-sex marriage and health insurance for all city residents—and as a platform for his candidacy for lieutenant governor in 2010. Los Angeles also has an empowered mayor after voters approved a new charter in 1999 giving the mayor enhanced authority, including the power to appoint forty-four department heads. Mayor Antonio Villaraigosa, elected in 2005 and reelected in

council–manager system A form of government in which an elected council appoints a professional manager to administer daily operations; used by most California cities.

school districts Local governments created by states to provide elementary and secondary education; governed by elected school boards.

bonds Subject to voter approval, state and local governments can borrow money by issuing bonds, which are repaid (with interest) from the general fund budget or from special taxes or fees.

special districts Local government agencies providing a single service, such as fire protection or sewage disposal.

2009, thus exercises more authority than any of his predecessors. Fresno (in 1997), Oakland (in 1998), and San Diego (in 2005) have also switched to a strong-mayor form of government. Sacramento mayor Kevin Johnson has pushed for such a change in his city, but he has failed thus far to persuade the city council to put a charter amendment to the voters.

The Need for Accountability

Many California cities have moved away from the pure council–manager system of government. While retaining their city managers, 149 California cities have revised the system so that the mayor is directly elected and serves a four-year term. Some have also increased the powers of their mayors, although they continue to sit as council members. Even without much authority, being a directly elected mayor brings visibility and influence. Mayors of San José, for example, exercise substantial clout despite their limited official power.

California mayors will probably continue to grow stronger, partly because of media attention but also due to the need for leadership in the tempest of city politics. Elected officials and community groups often complain about the lack of direct accountability inherent in the city manager form, in which the executive is somewhat insulated from the voters. Giving more authority to mayors and council members makes accountability more direct, but it may also decrease the professionalism of local government. We take a closer look at the powers of California mayors in the *Perception versus Reality* feature on the following page.

LO3 *More Governments*

In addition to cities and counties, California has thousands of other, less visible local governments (see Table 25–1). Created by the state or by citizens, they provide designated services and have taxing powers, mostly collecting their revenues as small portions of the property taxes paid by homeowners and businesses or by charging for their services. Yet except for school districts, most of us are unaware of their existence.

Table 25–1

California's Local Governments, 2010

Type	Number
Counties	58
Cities	481
School districts	1,043
Special districts	4,776
TOTAL	6,358

Source: California State Controller, **www.sco.ca.gov**, and Ed-Data, **www.ed-data.ca.us**.

School Districts and Special Districts

In California, 1,043 local governments called **school districts** provide education. They are created and overseen by the state and governed by elected boards, which appoint professional educators as superintendents to oversee day-to-day operations. Except for parents and teachers, whose involvement is intense, voter participation in school elections and politics is low. One challenge for the schools is that while the majority of students are Latino, Asian, or African American, a majority of those who vote in school elections and the majority of school board members are non-Hispanic whites.[8]

Of the $66.7 billion in school spending in 2009–2010, the state supplied 58 percent, the federal government provided 14 percent, and 28 percent came from local property taxes and other local sources.[9] Just two years earlier, local governments provided only 21 percent of school funding, providing a poignant example of how the state's budget crisis has left these governments with more responsibilities. The shift has not been without costs. In 2010, 16 percent of the state's school districts were declared "at risk" because of inadequate funding, and California has ranked low among the states in per-pupil spending for years.[10] These figures refer to funds for salaries and operating expenses. Money for building repairs and construction of new schools comes mostly from **bonds** (borrowed money paid by local taxes), which until recently required approval by a two-thirds majority of the voters. Following the Proposition 13 tax revolt, such approvals became rare; in 2000, however, voters approved lowering the percentage required for approval to 55 percent, and passing bonds became easier.

Special districts are an even more common form of local government, with no fewer than 4,776 in California. Unlike cities and counties, which are "general-purpose"

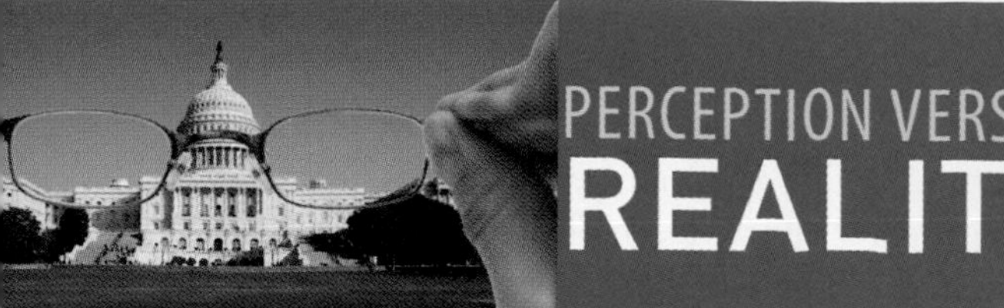

PERCEPTION VERSUS REALITY

Mayors Run Their Cities

We're all familiar with the office of mayor, the person most of us assume is the leader of the city government. In some cities, the mayor is the only official elected by all the voters of the city—members of the city council are frequently elected from wards or districts, electoral subdivisions of the municipality. The power of certain big-city mayors, such as the mayors of Chicago and New York City, is legendary. But how much power do mayors actually have in California?

The Perception

Most people in California know of the mayor of Los Angeles, currently Antonio Villaraigosa. When a problem arises in that city, people tend to look to the mayor for solutions. Even when a community has a city manager in addition to a mayor, many voters are unaware of who the manager is and what that person does.

The Reality

Some mayors in California do have a considerable amount of power. Most do not. In fact, a few California cities do not have a mayor at all. In most smaller municipalities, an elected city council hires a city manager to run departments and administer municipal services. The mayor in these cities is a member of the council, chosen by the council to serve as mayor for one year and with no more power than any of the other city council members, with the sole exception that the mayor chairs the meetings of the council.

During the Progressive era of the early twentieth century, municipal corruption scandals led to the creation of the council-manager system. Power was devolved to the city council, which hired a professional city manager to run day-to-day government operations. Today, California gives cities considerable flexibility of governance, especially if they have adopted charters and do not operate under the general rules provided for "general law" cities. (California has 368 general law cities and 118 charter cities.) As a result, a wide range of systems for municipal governance exists up and down the state.

Typically, the larger the city's population, the more likely it is to have adopted a strong-mayor system. The mayor of Los Angeles, the largest city in California, is among the state's strongest mayors. The current system is the result of a new charter that was adopted in 1999 and went into effect in 2000. There is no city manager—the mayor is the chief executive officer. The mayor can hire and fire department general managers. He or she recommends a budget to the city council, and if the council does not adopt or alter the budget within a specified period of time, the mayor's budget becomes law. Other strong-mayor cities include Oakland and San Francisco.

Fresno voted in a strong-mayor government in 1993, and the system was actually implemented in 1997. San Diego adopted such a system on a five-year trial basis in 2006. Sacramento mayor Kevin Johnson attempted to place a proposal on the June 2010 ballot that would have created the strongest mayor system yet. The mayor would be able to veto council decisions, could hire and fire about 800 staff members including the city manager, and would not face term limits. In January 2010, however, a California Superior Court judge blocked the proposal, ruling that a measure of this type could be placed on the ballot only by the city council. The council then voted against the plan 7 to 2.

For an example of a different style of governance, consider Fullerton, a general law municipality of 126,000 people in Orange County. The city, home of California State University, Fullerton, has a typical council-city manager system. The city council consists of five non-partisan members elected on a citywide basis. Council members elect a chair who serves as mayor, and they hire a professional city manager who exercises almost all administrative authority.

Blog On You can learn a great deal about how California cities really work at **www.publicceo.com**, a site that covers issues important to California city managers.

governments, special districts usually provide a single service. California law provides for fifty-three different types of special districts, ranging from water and waste disposal districts to hospital and cemetery districts. They are created when citizens or governments want a particular function performed but either have no appropriate government agency to perform the service or choose not to delegate it to a city or county. Sometimes special districts are formed when small communities share responsibilities for fire protection, sewage treatment, or other services that can be more efficiently provided on a larger scale. Depending on the nature of the special

contracting for services Smaller cities contract with counties, special districts, or other cities to provide services they cannot efficiently provide themselves.

consolidation The merger of cities, school districts, or special districts; usually requires voter approval.

councils of government (COGs) Regional planning organizations with representation for cities and counties.

district, funding usually comes from property taxes or charges for the service that it provides. The number of special districts increased when Proposition 13 imposed tax constraints on general-purpose local governments, because some services can be funded more easily in this way. Their impacts in terms of taxes and services have been considerable. Altogether, California's special districts spend $39.6 billion a year, while California's cities spend $57 billion and its counties spend $48.4 billion.

A city council or a county board of supervisors governs some special districts, but most are overseen by a commission or board of directors that may be elected or appointed by other officials. Like a school board, this body usually appoints a professional administrator to manage its business. Accountability to the voters and taxpayers is a problem, however, because most of us aren't even aware of these officials.

Regional Governments

The existence of so many sorts of local governments means that many operate in every urban region of California. The vast urban areas between Los Angeles and San Diego or San Francisco and San José, for example, consist of many cities, counties, and special districts, with no single authority in charge of the whole area. Los Angeles County alone hosts eighty-eight cities and two hundred special districts. This fragmentation creates small-scale governments that are accessible to citizens, but that are sometimes too small to provide services efficiently. In addition, problems such as transportation and air pollution go far beyond the boundaries of any one entity.

Many California cities deal with this situation by **contracting for services** from counties, larger cities, or private businesses. Cities in Los Angeles County, for example, may pay the county to provide any of fifty-eight services, from dog catching to tree planting. Small cities commonly contract with the county sheriff for police protection rather than fund their own forces. Contracting allows such communities to provide needed services while retaining local control, although some see the system as unfair because wealthy communities can afford more than poor ones.

Another solution to urban fragmentation is **consolidation,** or the merger of existing governmental entities. With voter approval, small school districts, special districts, or even cities can unite to provide services more efficiently. In the past consolidation has occurred mostly with school districts, but proposals for consolidations have become more common lately due to California's prolonged budget crisis.[11]

Special districts are yet another way to address fragmentation and regional problems—particularly problems, such as air pollution and transportation, that extend beyond the boundaries of existing cities or counties. For example, California has forty-seven transit districts that run bus and rail systems. Most are countywide, but some, including the Bay Area Rapid Transit (BART) system, cover several counties.

Councils of Government

Twenty of California's urban areas also have **councils of government (COGs),** in which all of the cities and counties in the region are represented. The biggest COGs are the six-county Southern California Association of Governments (SCAG) and the nine-county Association of Bay Area Governments (ABAG) in Northern California. These regional bodies focus on land-use planning and development. Because they can't force their plans on cities and counties, though, they serve mainly as forums for communication and coordination among the jurisdictions they encompass.

As regional problems have grown and competition among cities has increased, the need for regional planning has also grown. The state has asserted its authority over local governments to require the implementation of regional plans through agencies such as ABAG and SCAG. Other state-created agencies, such as the Metropolitan Water District and the South Coast Air Quality Management Board in Southern California, exercise great power. Reformers sometimes advocate the creation of multipurpose regional governments, perhaps by merging existing regional special districts, to provide government capable of dealing with area-wide issues including transportation, air quality, and growth; however, existing cities firmly oppose any loss of local control.

Direct Democracy in Local Politics

Direct democracy is used even more locally than statewide. Between 1995 and 2008 an average of 428 local ballot measures were voted on by Californians each year.[12] All charter changes—such as increasing the powers of the mayor or introducing district council elections—are subject to voter approval by referendum. Voters must also approve proposals for local governments to introduce or raise taxes or to borrow money by issuing bonds. Charter changes require a simple majority, but a supermajority of two-thirds is required for most taxes. Resulting from a series of statewide initiatives, these requirements have severely restricted the ability of local governments to raise money, because voter approval on funding issues is difficult to win.

Most local measures are placed on the ballot by a city council, county board of supervisors, or school board. They include tax measures and charter amendments, but the most common measures have to do with education (usually seeking additional funding). Citizens also put proposals to the voters through the initiative process, although initiatives constitute only a tiny percentage of local measures. Most often, the initiatives are attempts to control growth or amend charters. Some are frivolous, like the 2008 San Francisco initiative that proposed renaming the city sanitation facility the "George W. Bush Sewage Plant," but most are more serious. District elections, for example, were introduced in some cities by initiative, as were **term limits** (usually restricting elected officials to two four-year terms). Several California counties and over forty cities now limit the terms of elected officials. As a last resort, voters may express their dissatisfaction with elected officials through recall elections. Recalls of local officials are rare, however, averaging fewer than a dozen a year, even after the dramatic recall of the governor in 2003.[13]

Land Use: Coping with Growth

One of the most frequent uses of direct democracy in California cities and counties is by citizens seeking to control growth. Deciding how land can be used is a major power assigned to local governments by the state. The way they use this power affects us all. If local governments encourage growth in the form of housing, industry, or shopping centers, for example, the economy may boom, but streets may become clogged, schools overcrowded, sewage treatment plants strained, and police and fire protection stretched too thin. When this happens, environmentalists or residents who merely expect adequate services may grow frustrated and demand controls on growth. If the city council or county board of supervisors is unresponsive, discontented groups may take their case to the voters through an initiative.

Since 1971, when development became a major local issue, almost all California communities have enacted some form of growth control. The battle typically pits a grassroots coalition with little money against big-spending developers and builders. The recent recession brought growth to a halt in most communities, decreasing the salience of this issue, but even so the cities of Buellton, Pleasanton, and San Juan Capistrano approved growth limits and protections for open space in 2008.

term limits Limits on the number of terms that officeholders may serve. Local elected officials are usually limited to two or three 4-year terms.

property tax A tax on land and buildings; until the passage of Proposition 13 in 1978, the primary source of revenues for local governments.

Proposition 13 (1978) Also known as the Jarvis-Gann initiative; a ballot measure that cut property taxes and significantly reduced revenues for local governments.

LO4 *Taxing and Spending*

The way local governments raise and spend money reveals a great deal, not only about what they do but also about the limits they face in doing it.

The biggest single source of money for California's local governments was once the **property tax,** an annual assessment based on the value of land and buildings. Then, in 1978, taxpayers revolted with **Proposition 13,** a statewide initiative that cut property tax revenues by 57 percent. Cities adjusted by cutting jobs and services to save money. Many

AP PHOTO

Paul Gann (left) and Howard Jarvis celebrate their victory in 1978 with the passage of their initiative, Proposition 13. When California voters overwhelmingly passed Proposition 13, which put a cap on property taxes, it was seen as the biggest tax revolt in modern American history.

charges for services
Local government fees for services such as sewage treatment, trash collection, building permits, and the use of recreational facilities; a major source of income for cities and counties since the passage of Proposition 13 in 1978.

fiscalization of land use
When cities and counties, in making land-use decisions, opt for the alternative that produces the most revenue.

introduced or increased **charges for services** such as sewage treatment, trash collection, building permits, and the use of recreational facilities. Such charges are now the largest source of income for most cities (see Figure 25–3), followed by the sales tax, which returns 2 percent of the state's basic 8.25 percent sales tax to the city or county where the sale occurs. Some counties add to the base sales tax to fund transportation. Some cities and counties have also added taxes on hotel rooms, utilities, or other things. In 2009 voters in Oakland approved a tax on the sale of medical marijuana, undoubtedly setting a precedent for other cities.

The shift from property taxes to other sources of revenue also affects local land-use decisions. When a new development is proposed, most cities now prefer retail businesses to housing or industry because of the sales taxes that such businesses generate. This trend has been labeled the **fiscalization of land use** because instead of choosing the best use for the land, cities opt for the one that produces the most revenue.

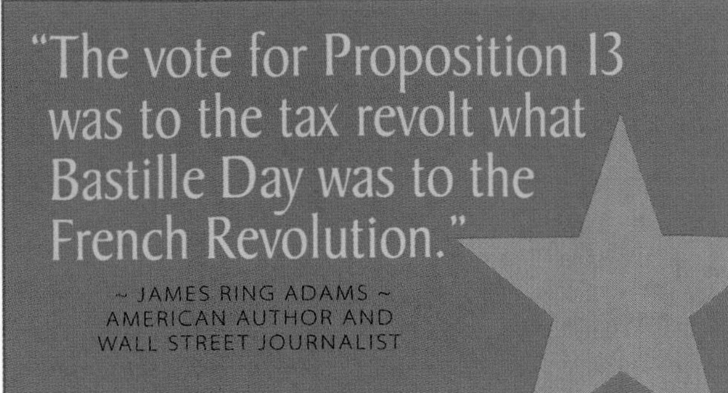

"The vote for Proposition 13 was to the tax revolt what Bastille Day was to the French Revolution."
~ JAMES RING ADAMS ~
AMERICAN AUTHOR AND
WALL STREET JOURNALIST

Staying Alive

With more legal constraints on their taxing powers, counties had an even rougher time after Proposition 13. State aid to counties increased slightly, but with no alternative local taxes readily available after the passage of Proposition 13, most counties cut spending deeply. Years later, they are still struggling to provide essential services. Like cities, most counties increased charges and fees for services.

Over half of county revenues come from the state and federal governments (32.5 percent and 19.4 percent, respectively), but this money must be spent on required programs such as social services, health care, and the courts. Even so, state and federal aid does not cover the cost of these mandatory services, leaving counties with little money to spend as they choose.

Figure 25–3

Revenues and Expenditures of California Cities and Counties, 2007–2008

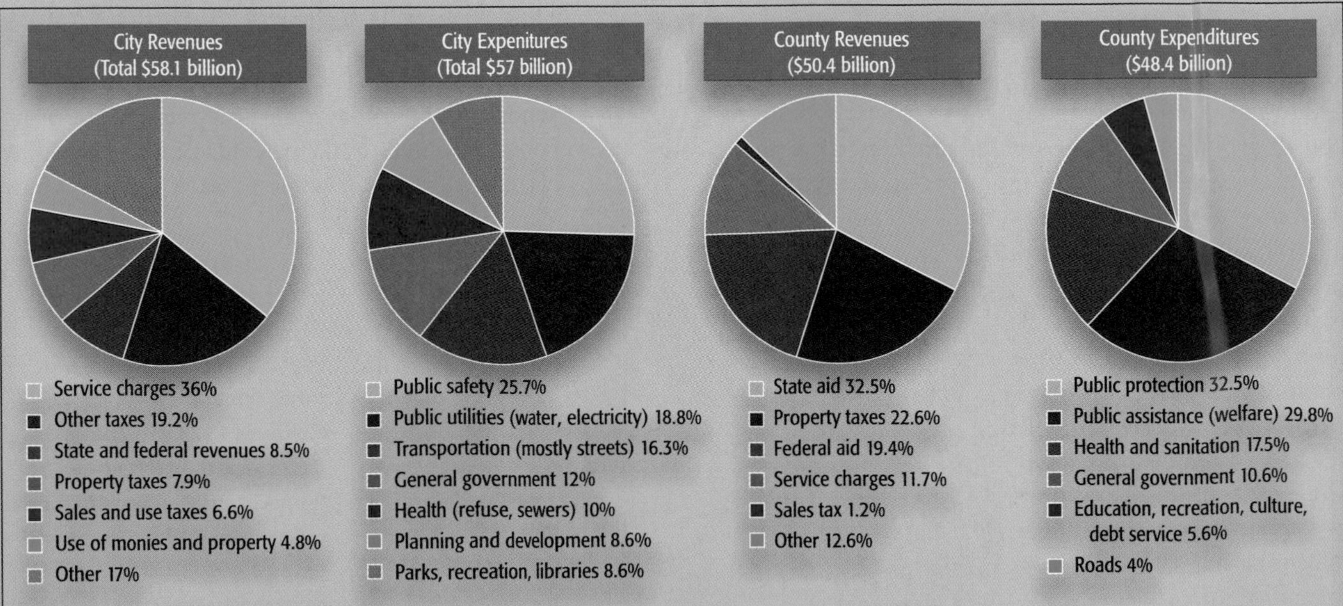

Source: California State Controller (**www.sco.ca.gov**), 2010

State Constraints

Just as the revenue sources of cities and counties differ, so do their spending patterns, largely because the state assigns them different responsibilities. As you can see in Figure 25–3, public safety is the biggest expenditure for California cities, whereas welfare is a major county expenditure.

"In the heady years before the passage of Proposition 13, **CALIFORNIA HAD BEEN A HIGH-TAX STATE.** In 1968, it was second in the nation in state and local tax collection as a percentage of personal income."

~ PETER SCHRAG ~
AUTHOR AND FORMER EDITOR, THE SACRAMENTO BEE

Proposition 1A A 2004 ballot measure designed to prevent the state from taking revenues from local governments in times of fiscal stress.

Proposition 22, the Local Taxpayers, Public Safety and Transportation Act (2010) An initiative that keeps the state government from taking local government funds dedicated by the voters.

Although Proposition 13 is much loved by homeowners for reducing property tax bills, the initiative caused serious fiscal problems for local governments by cutting property tax revenues and making approval of new taxes or tax increases more difficult. That combination necessitated severe budget cuts for cities and counties. Beyond that, Proposition 13 gave the state the responsibility to allocate property taxes among local governments even as Proposition 98 (see Chapter 24) mandated allocation of a fixed percentage of the state budget to education. As a consequence, a portion of property taxes that had previously gone to cities and counties was shifted to schools—putting even further pressure on city and county budgets and resulting in further cuts in services. Moreover, cities and counties, which previously had some control of their own revenues, became dependent on the state for property and sales tax revenues, a significant loss of local control.[14]

These problems were compounded when successive recessions hit California in the early 1990s and again in 2001–2003 and 2009–2010. Facing massive deficits, the state balanced its budget by "take-backs" of local property tax revenues totaling billions of dollars. In 2004 Governor Arnold Schwarzenegger exacerbated circumstances for local governments by reducing vehicle license fees, which had previously been a significant source of local revenues.

Cities were so frustrated by all this that they pushed for a way to lock in their revenues through a constitutional amendment to guarantee future revenues and prevent such state take-backs. Voters approved **Proposition 1A** in 2004. Local governments hoped it would give them greater financial security in the future, but in the 2009 fiscal crisis, the state diverted nearly $4 billion in local property taxes from schools, cities, counties, and redevelopment agencies. Under Proposition 1A the state must eventually repay these funds, but in the short term the action only worsened the fiscal problems of local governments. Cities and counties responded in 2010 with **Proposition 22, the Local Taxpayers, Public Safety and Transportation Act** banning state borrowing from local governments, and won voter approval. The voters' steps to prevent state raiding of local budgets is discussed in the *California Faces a Troubled Economy* feature on the following page.

The City of Vallejo, California filed for Chapter 9 bankruptcy protection in May of 2008 after administrators and leaders were unable to cut the budget enough to meet a nearly $17 million shortfall.

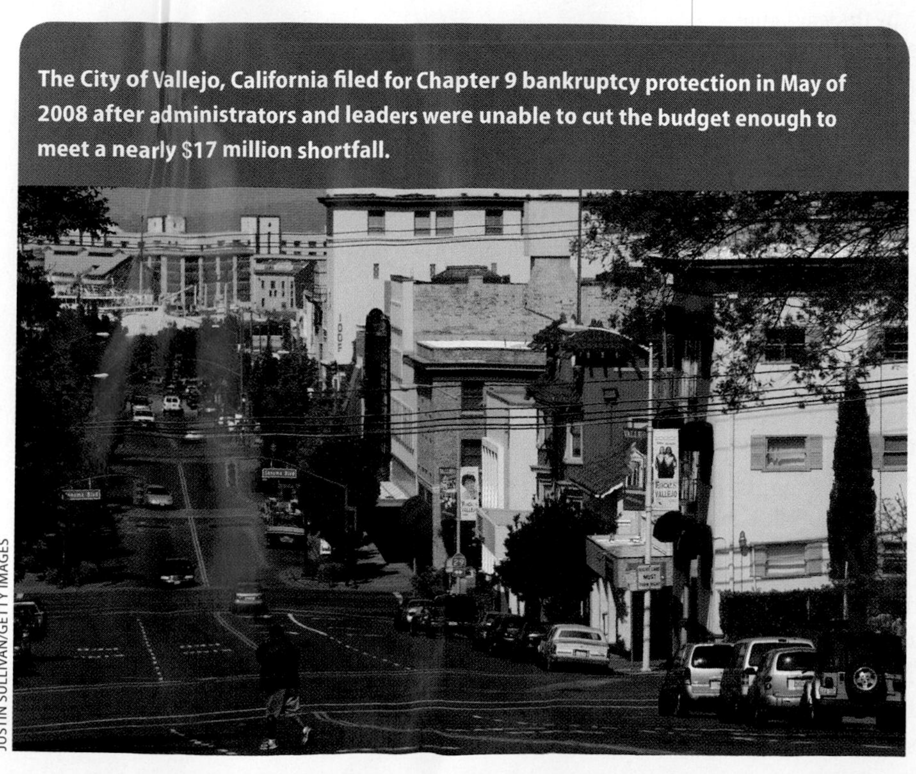

JUSTIN SULLIVAN/GETTY IMAGES

CALIFORNIA FACES A
TROUBLED ECONOMY

The State Raids Local Government Funds

One effect of Proposition 13 was to give the state government a substantial degree of control over local finances. This transfer of control took place because the state stepped in to supply funding to local schools and other projects that lost support with the passage of the proposition. With the state in control of a major share of local funding, however, the possibility arose that the state might seize some of these revenues if its own financial position became precarious. This actually happened in the 1990s and again in 2004. In response, California voters approved Proposition 1A in 2004, a measure designed to protect funding for public safety, health, libraries, parks, and other locally delivered services. Proposition 1A prohibits the state from reducing local governments' property tax proceeds.

The Seizures that Apparently Were Legal

Proposition 1A was a referendum written by the legislature to head off an initiative on the same topic. It was successful; the initiative failed. As a compromise measure, however, 1A contained an escape clause: its provisions could be suspended if the governor declared a fiscal emergency and a two-thirds vote of both houses of the legislature approved the suspension. In July 2009, the state duly exercised this option. Under the Proposition 1A suspension, the state took 8 percent of the property tax revenue of cities, counties, and special districts to help balance the 2009–2010 state budget. The loan was to be paid back in three years. Statewide, the enforced loan amounted to $1.9 billion.

The Ones that Probably Weren't

The legislature also passed, and the governor approved, several other raids on local funds that amounted to approximately $5 billion. About $1 billion came from local transit projects. Roughly $2 billion was taken from local redevelopment funds. The seizure of the transit funds was part of a financial gimmick that had been going on for several years. The California Transit Association sued for the return of the funds, and in June 2009, a state appellate court ruled that the takings were illegal. In October, the California Supreme Court refused to hear the case, leaving the appellate court ruling intact. In addition to the $1 billion taken for 2009–2010, the state faced paying back an additional $2.8 billion diverted in previous years.

Also in 2009, the California Redevelopment Association sued for return of the $2 billion in redevelopment money on the basis that the seizure violated multiple clauses of the state constitution. The Redevelopment Association had won an earlier, similar case in 2008, but in 2010 a Superior Court judge ruled against the association. The case is now on appeal.

Proposition 22

In response to these various takings, a coalition of local governments and citizens' groups launched a ballot initiative to unambiguously stop the state from borrowing local property or gasoline tax revenues. Proposition 22 passed in November 2010. It was criticized by some newspapers and by a number of business and labor groups, who saw it as another initiative earmark that would strip the legislature of badly needed flexibility.

You Be the Judge **One reason that some people both on the political left and right opposed Proposition 22 is that many of the funds taken by the state came from redevelopment agencies. For these persons, cutting the budgets of such agencies was "not a bug but a feature." Why might some groups oppose redevelopment?**

Meanwhile, California cities and counties have been pushed to the fiscal brink. Vallejo (near San Francisco) declared bankruptcy in 2008 when tax revenues dropped and the city couldn't meet its commitments to employee salaries and benefits. In 2010 Oakland laid off over 10 percent of its police force, despite its high crime rate. Facing a $529 million deficit, Los Angeles mayor Antonio Villaraigoso, usually an ally of public employees, proposed layoffs and demanded salary concessions from the city's unions.

Maywood, in Southern California, laid off all its city employees, including police officers, and contracted with other cities for some services and with Los Angeles County for police protection. "We will become 100 percent a contracted city," said Maywood's interim city manager.[15] Other cities also considered contracting for services. Redding, in Northern California, and Santa Clarita, in Southern California, for example, contracted with a private company to provide library services. Still other cities considered merging police or fire departments with neighboring cities. In some areas, reformers called for consolidation of small school districts, special districts, and cities as a partial solution to budget problems.

Cities from San Diego to San José, along with many other local agencies, also faced fiscal strain due to the pensions and other benefits they had offered their employees when their budgets were flush with cash. Now unable to meet these commitments but bound by contracts, local governments, like the state (see Chapter 24), are seeking to renegotiate the contracts to win concessions from current employees or to move to a two-tier pension system, preserving benefits for current workers but reducing them for future hires.

Despite their fiscal trials, local governments remain a major component of the California economy, with nearly 1.3 million employees (half are in education)[16] and combined budgets totaling over $212 billion. Local governments cost a lot, but they also do a lot.

Local Government

The state limits what local governments can do, as demonstrated by Proposition 13 and ongoing budget battles. Some may dispute such interventions, but the state's authority remains supreme. At the same time, local governments can lead the way to innovations in public policy, as illustrated by San Francisco's health insurance policy, Long Beach's public financing for campaigns, and Oakland's tax on medical marijuana. California's political system gives residents many opportunities to decide what sort of communities they want, and many Californians take advantage of these opportunities by engaging in local politics.

CALIFORNIA AT **ODDS** *Local Government*

Voters often tend to neglect what happens at the local government level, but local decisions have an immediate and intimate affect on people's lives. Therefore, California citizens are at odds over various local government issues, including the following:

- Was Proposition 13 a vital protection for taxpayers—or a fiscal disaster that has crippled the state?
- Does California have too many local governments—or would consolidation of special districts and other units serve to erode local democracy?
- Are nonpartisan elections at the local level a good way of keeping partisan disputes out of local government—or do they deprive the voters of important information about the beliefs of local candidates?
- Does a strong mayor system enhance political accountability—or lead to autocratic behavior on the part of local leaders?
- Do controls on development enhance the local quality of life—or do they merely redistribute wealth from the poor to the rich and from the young to the old?

Take Action

Local government can affect your life in very direct ways, and participation is relatively easy. Candidates and officials are not hard to meet. It's simple to attend meetings of city councils, county boards, school boards, or the boards of special districts. In order to attend such meetings, however, you have to know where they are and when they are scheduled. Counties and cities have Web sites you can visit to find this information, and so do many special districts. For a directory of Web sites, visit State and Local Government on the Net at www.statelocalgov.net/state-ca.cfm. Here you'll find a list of county and city Web sites. For special district sites, try the membership directory of the California Special Districts Association at www.csda.net. The Membership Directory is under the heading Featured Sections. You can find a list of additional special district associations under Resource Links.

POLITICS ON THE WEB

- The League of California Cities is an association of California city officials who work together to enhance their knowledge and skills, exchange information, and combine resources so that they may influence policy decisions that affect cities. The association's Web site provides a wealth of resources and answers to most frequently asked questions about California cities at **www.cacities.org**.
- The primary purpose of the California State Association of Counties is to represent county government before the California legislature, its administrative agencies, and the federal government. The association's Web site offers a wealth of county information as well as links to county Web sites at **www.csac.counties.org**.
- The California Elections Data Archive (CEDA) summarizes candidate and ballot measure results for county, city, community college, and school district elections in more than 6,000 jurisdictions throughout California. To find information about local elections, visit **www.csus.edu/isr/reports/california_elections**.
- Instant runoff voting (IRV) is a voting system for single-winner elections that guarantees majority winners in a single round of voting. To learn more about how IRV works and what cities use it, go to **www.instantrunoff.com**.
- The Public Policy Institute of California's mission is to inform and improve public policy in California through independent, objective, nonpartisan research on major social, economic, and political issues. To access data on California, visit **www.ppic.org**.
- The Association of Bay Area Governments (ABAG) is the official comprehensive planning agency for the San Francisco Bay region. ABAG's mission is to strengthen cooperation and coordination among local governments. In doing so, ABAG addresses social, environmental, and economic issues that transcend local borders. To learn more about the Bay Area, go to **www.abag.org**.
- As a designated Metropolitan Planning Organization, the Southern California Association of Governments is mandated by the federal government to research and draw up plans for transportation, growth management, hazardous waste management, and air quality. Find out more about SCAG at **www.scag.ca.gov**.
- For a list of state and local publications and online news sources in California, visit **www.abyznewslinks.com/uniteca.htm**.

Access CourseMate to review and expand on this chapter through quizzes, flashcards, learning objectives, interactive timelines, a crossword puzzle, audio summaries, video, critical-thinking activities, simulations, and more.

GOVT 26

State-Federal Relations: Conflict, Cooperation, and Chaos

LEARNING OBJECTIVES

LO1 Describe the relationship California has had with the nation's recent presidents.

LO2 Explain the power California has within Congress and the conflicts that divide their representatives.

LO3 Summarize California's responsibility in fighting terrorism.

LO4 Discuss the impact of immigration on California.

LO5 Identify some of the issues involved in California's relationship with the EPA.

LO6 Indicate how California has worked with the federal government to deal with the issue of water.

LO7 Point out some of the issues involved in sharing resources between California and the federal government.

CALIFORNIA AT ODDS

Should Grants-in-Aid be Awarded to States Strictly by Population?

Federal-to-state revenue transfers are larger than some people realize. In fiscal year 2010, the U.S. government gave an estimated $517 billion to state and local governments—more than half a trillion dollars. California's share was in excess of $55 billion. Federal money supports a vast range of programs, notably in education, welfare, and transportation. The largest program, however, is Medicaid, the state-federal program to fund health care for the poor. (California's Medicaid program is called Medi-Cal.) In fiscal year 2010, the federal government gave the states about $269 billion for Medicaid. That's half of all of the federal aid. State governments are required to put up matching funds according to a formula based on state per capita income. Before 2009, states with a high average income—such as California—had to come up with one dollar for every dollar provided by the federal government. A poor state such as Mississippi received three dollars from Washington for each dollar it raised itself. President Obama's 2009 stimulus package, however, temporarily increased the federal share of Medi-Cal from 50 percent to 61.59 percent.

Medicaid is not the only program to distribute funds based on a formula. Most grant programs employ formulas, some of which are extremely complicated. Often, Congress writes the formula into the legislation that establishes the program. Sometimes it delegates the formula-setting role to an executive agency or department. In a few cases, Congress has simply written the percentages to be received by each state into the legislation. When Congress controls the formulas, they are inevitably politicized. Every senator and member of the House is acutely aware of the impact of each formula on his or her state.

An obvious question is whether these formulas give California its fair share of the revenue. The structure of the federal government suggests that it might not. After all, each state, no matter how large or small, fills exactly two seats in the U.S. Senate. California has 12 percent of the nation's population and 12 percent of the seats in the U.S. House. It has 2 percent of the Senate. We might expect that the Senate would be biased against a big state such as California. Some have suggested that instead of using formulas, Congress should simply distribute funds to each state based on its population. This would keep politics out of the process and ensure fairness to everyone. Others disagree and defend the current system.

The Current System is Unfair to California

California gets 78 cents back from the federal government for every dollar it pays in taxes—it ranks forty-third in the size of its payback. What more do we need to know? The current formula system is unfair to California. Consider also the Medicaid formula just described. It is based on per capita state income, not the number of low-income people eligible for Medicaid. But California has a disproportionately high share of the nation's poor. On that basis, it should receive more federal money for Medi-Cal. The reason the state has such a high average income is that the extremely rich prefer to live here. That distorts the state's income picture completely. (New York has the same problem, and Medicare also discriminates against it.) Let's get politics out of the allocation business and distribute funds strictly by population.

The Answer to Distribution Problems is Better Formulas

California's wealthy residents certainly do distort the statistics—such as the one about getting only 78 cents back on the dollar. That figure is low because California's rich pay a lot of taxes to the federal government. In fact, California's share of federal grants-in-aid is within 3 percent of what it ought to be according to a pure population formula. As for Medi-Cal, an earlier feature noted that California's poor tend to be healthy young immigrants who require less health care than Medicaid recipients in most other states. If California received Medicaid reimbursements based on the number of people in poverty, it would be overpaid. True, formulas set by Congress have a political dimension. Still, a typical formula takes account of reasonable factors such as the number of persons at risk, the local cost of living, and similar characteristics. If there is a problem with any formula, we can adjust it. Incremental improvements are best.

WHERE DO YOU STAND?

1. **Is it fair to provide larger federal grants-in-aid to states with low average incomes? Why or why not?**
2. **Would an executive agency be more likely to come up with a good formula than a Congressional committee—or not? Explain your reasoning.**

EXPLORE THIS ISSUE ONLINE

- **To see what each state gets back in return for its federal taxes, check out www.taxfoundation.org/research/show/266.html.**
- **For details on how the 2010 census affected representation in the U.S. House, go to the U.S. Census Bureau home page at www.census.gov.**

Introduction

California's uniqueness stems in part from its position as the nation's most populated state; it also emanates from the state's vast resources, size, diversity, and engagement in thorny issues. We see problems and their outcomes on a scale here that is unequaled elsewhere. And so it is with the state's relationship with the federal government, which can be described as wary, uneven, and often fraught with controversy.

Sometimes state and national leaders differ about how California should be managed. Public education reform is one such controversial policy area, with the federal government and state legislature at odds over the definition of *reform*. On other issues, such as water policy, however, officials from the two governments have worked well together. There are also instances where California has moved forward with its own response to national issues, with the federal government eventually moving into line; nowhere is this more obvious than with environmental protection. Deciding the best responses to problems that affect both the nation and state can be a challenge because, like its forty-nine counterparts, California is both a self-governing entity and a member of the larger national government.

Matters become even more complicated when attempts are made to determine financial responsibility for costly issues such as massive transportation projects, immigration control, or homeland security, to name a few. Because the state is so large and complex, federal assistance almost always seems inadequate. When federal aid or programs are cut, California seems to suffer disproportionately compared with other states, as we explain in the chapter-opening *California at Odds* feature.

Nevertheless, when the state confronts a complex issue, its internal battle is often the harbinger of similar concerns likely to affect the rest of the nation. The women's right to choose movement, gun control, political reform, the tax revolt, medical marijuana, stem cell research, and same-sex marriage all had early beginnings—and in some cases, origins—in California. California's innovations do not always result in a comfortable relationship with the national government, as you will learn in the *California Faces a Troubled Economy* feature on the following page.

In this chapter we review California's impact on national policymaking and policy actors. We also explore some of the critical policy areas that test California's relationship with the federal government: immigration, greenhouse gas emissions, and the distribution of federal resources to the state of California. Each topic touches on the delicate balance between state autonomy and national objectives—perspectives in federalism that are not always viewed the same ways by state and federal government leaders. These issues are important not only because of their present urgency but also because of their effects on California's people, economy, and political values.

LO1 California's Clout With the President

Despite its size and huge bloc of Electoral College votes, California hasn't figured prominently in presidential elections in recent years, largely because the state has been predictably secure for Democratic candidates in every election since 1992. As a consequence, we don't see as much of the candidates in California as voters do in other states. Republican presidential candidates do not invest significant resources on California because they don't see much return, and Democrats stay away because of their need to pursue electoral votes in more competitive states. But California is important to both national political parties in one major respect—namely, as the top state for campaign contributions. That alone keeps candidates coming, albeit infrequently, to places such as Orange County, Silicon Valley, and Hollywood.

President Barack Obama greets Arnold Schwarzenegger at an event announcing new fuel and emission standards for cars and trucks at the White House in May 2009.

AP PHOTO/CHARLES DHARAPAK

CALIFORNIA FACES A
TROUBLED ECONOMY

Should California Have Legalized Pot?

By 2009, California's budget crisis led some citizens to come up with seriously creative methods for addressing the state's budget problems. One proposal was to legalize—and tax—recreational marijuana. By the fall of 2009, the leading initiative, soon to become Proposition 19, was easily on pace to make the November 2010 ballot. Proposition 19 would make the sale and taxation of marijuana an option for local governments. Tax officials estimated that the measure could bring in about $1.4 billion per year. Law enforcement officials across the state were opposed to any change to the law, but fully expected a major battle for public opinion in 2010.

Current Marijuana Law

Pending any change to the law, marijuana remains illegal. California authorities arrested 78,500 people on marijuana charges in 2008. Seizures of marijuana planted in public forests and parks, often by Mexican gangsters, reached an all-time high in 2009. Still, California legalized marijuana for medical purposes in 1996. The drug is dispensed—ostensibly for medical use—at almost a thousand locations in Los Angeles alone. The city of Oakland passed a measure to tax medical marijuana in July 2009.

The Federal Angle

The Bush administration made it clear that it had no tolerance for medical marijuana, and federal authorities were prepared to arrest anyone involved in the business on federal charges. The United States Supreme Court backed up the administration's position in 2005 when it ruled that Congress may ban the use of marijuana even where a state approves its use for medical purposes. The case involved homegrown medical marijuana that was legal under California law. The Court based its reasoning on the Constitution's interstate commerce clause.[1] Many legal observers found this basis odd because the marijuana in question 1) never left California and 2) was never bought or sold. The suggestion was made that some conservative justices were allowing their dislike of marijuana to override their constitutional principles.

In October 2009, however, the Obama administration announced that it would not prosecute users and providers of medical marijuana who obey state law. The Justice Department reiterated, however, that recreational use of marijuana was off-limits. October 2010, in the run-up to the November elections, U.S. Attorney General Eric Holder warned that the federal government would "vigorously enforce" national laws against marijuana even if the drug were legalized at the state level. An attempt by California to legalize and tax marijuana was therefore guaranteed to create a truly major state-federal confrontation.

Proposition 19 Fails

While Proposition 19 led in early polls, it ultimately went down by 54 percent to 45 percent. One factor in its failure was the decriminalization of marijuana by the legislature—Governor Schwarzenegger signed the new legislation in October 2010, immediately before the election. The new law made possession of small amounts of the drug a civil infraction similar to a traffic ticket, punishable by a $100 fine.

You Be the Judge **Sponsors of the legalization initiative claimed that people's attitudes toward marijuana were shifting. Others suggested that voters were mostly attracted by the chance to tax something they didn't use personally. Which do you think was most important? Also, do you think the figure of $1.4 billion in taxes is too generous—or too conservative?**

California has had an uneven relationship with the nation's presidents. Democrat Bill Clinton, who benefitted from California's then fifty-four electoral votes in 1992 and 1996, funneled discretionary federal funds to California, particularly in the areas of high-tech research and defense industry projects. Clinton was also pro-choice, pro–gun control, and environmentally sensitive—themes that resonate with most

Californians. None of this was lost on the California electorate, which supported Democratic candidates Al Gore in 2000 and John Kerry in 2004 over the winner, Republican George W. Bush.

Republican president George W. Bush approached California with a different point of view than Clinton, largely due to his general hands-off attitude on domestic policy issues. For example, the Bush administration rejected California's claim of illegal electricity price hikes in 2001, although the courts eventually found otherwise. Other areas in which the president lacked interest included agriculture, border patrol assistance, and terrorism funding. Even the election of fellow Republican Arnold Schwarzenegger in 2003 failed to bond the two Republican leaders except in the most cosmetic fashion. Given the clash of cultural and political values between most Californians and the conservative Republican president, it's easy to see why the distance between the state and the president was more than a matter of miles. Bush visited California fewer than two dozen times during his presidency, compared with seventy visits by Clinton in his eight years in office.

"We now have a president [who is] **NOT HOSTILE TO THE STATE OF CALIFORNIA.**"

~ ADAM SCHIFF ~
DEMOCRATIC MEMBER OF THE U.S. HOUSE OF REPRESENTATIVES FROM CALIFORNIA'S 29TH DISTRICT

The administration of Democrat Barack Obama falls somewhere between Clinton's "love fest" for and Bush's seeming indifference to California. On the one hand, Obama has been sensitive to the role of technology in California and called for extension of the soon-to-expire $74 billion research and development tax credit immediately upon assuming office. The Obama administration has also embraced California's strict rules on automobile exhaust emissions, a move completely opposite to the approach of George W. Bush. On the other hand, the Obama administration has been willing to compensate California for only a fraction of the hundreds of millions of dollars spent on the incarceration of illegal immigrants awaiting transport to their home countries. And California was unsuccessful in wresting any of the $4.35 billion in Obama's "Race to the Top" education improvement funds at a time when public education has been gasping for support. During the first two years of his administration, Obama visited California on eleven occasions.

Nancy Pelosi has represented California's 8th District since 1987. She first made history in November 2002 when House Democrats elected her the first woman to serve as House Democratic leader. How has her national leadership position boosted California's prominence in Washington?

AP PHOTO/SUSAN WALSH

LO2 *California's Clout With Congress*

As the nation's most populated state, California has fifty-three members in the House of Representatives, dwarfing the delegations of every other state. Texas and New York are second and third, with thirty-two and twenty-nine members, respectively. The majority party in each house of Congress chooses committee chairs who, in turn, control the flow of national legislation. Republicans possessed a majority of seats between 1995 and 2007, resulting in the accumulation of considerable power. By 2005 Californians held a record six chairmanships of the twenty-one standing committees. Then the political winds shifted.

In 2006 growing discontent with the war in Iraq, an uneven national economy, and political corruption in Congress led the nation's voters to elect a Democratic majority to the House of Representatives. San Francisco's Nancy Pelosi, elected in 2002 to the post of minority leader of the House, was chosen to be Speaker. With that election, she assumed the highest national leadership position ever held in the United States by a woman. As a result of the election outcome, several prominent California Democrats assumed key committee chairmanships by virtue of their years of seniority in the House.

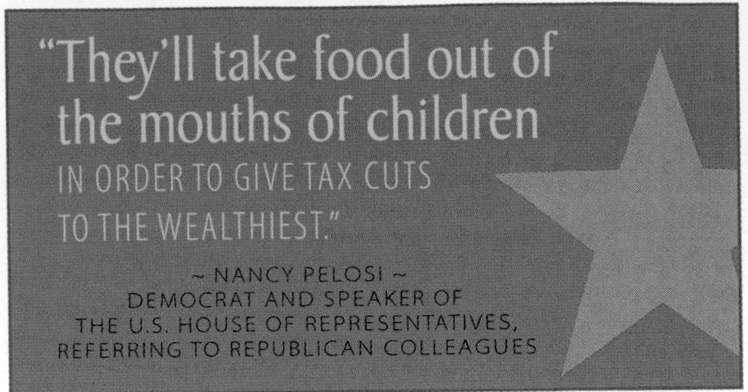

Political party fortunes took a turn in 2010 when the Republicans captured control of the House and increased the size of their minority in the Senate. As of 2011, California Republicans were poised to gain at least three chairmanships: Oversight and Governmental Reform (Darrell Issa); Armed Services (Howard "Buck" McKeon; and Appropriations (Jerry Lewis). Also, Kevin McCarthy was elected majority whip, the third highest party post after speaker and majority leader.

The political winds have shifted similarly in the U.S. Senate, but not as much as in the House. Although the upper chamber is a bit less partisan than the lower one, the majority party still controls all committee chairmanships, and therefore the flow of legislation. In 2006 the off-year revolution produced a slim 51-to-49 Democratic majority, thanks to the cooperation of two independents who promised their loyalty to the Democratic side of the aisle. Suddenly, Senators Dianne Feinstein and Barbara Boxer, both first elected in 1992, emerged as key players on issues dealing with the environment, foreign relations, and the judiciary. By 2009 the Democratic majority hit 60, a number large enough to cut off filibusters. Within a year, however, the supermajority was lost with the death of Massachusetts senator Ted Kennedy.

Democrats in California enjoy a comfortable margin of 34–19 over Republicans in the House of Representatives. In other respects California's congressional makeup is as diverse as the rest of the state. As of 2011, the delegation includes seven Latinos, four African Americans, and three Asians; nineteen women are members of the delegation. Both of California's U.S. senators are women as well.

The Republican ascendancy to power in the House opens the way for a new chapter in governance at the national level. With divided government, Republicans and Democrats find themselves with tough choices: either cooperate on major issues in the name of consensus or hold out with gridlock as the outcome. Consideration of each strategy is important, given the upcoming national election in 2012.

congressional delegation Members of the House of Representatives and Senate representing a particular state.

Divisiveness

One other fact must be added to the discussion of Californians in Washington: historically, the state's **congressional delegation** has been notoriously fractured in its responses to key public policy issues affecting California. Much of the conflict stems from the makeup of the districts. North/south, urban/suburban/rural, and coastal/valley/mountain divisions separate the state geographically. Other differences exist, too, in terms of wealth, ethnicity, and basic liberal/conservative distinctions. To be sure, no congressional district is completely homogeneous, yet most members of Congress tend to protect their districts' interests more than those of the state as a whole. Thus, on issues ranging from desert protection to immigration, California's representatives have often canceled each other's votes, leaving states such as Texas far more powerful because of their relatively unified stances. Even on foreign trade, members from California often have worked at cross-purposes, depending on the industries, interest groups, and demographic characteristics of their districts.

Democratic Senator Dianne Feinstein is Chairman of the Senate Select Committee on Intelligence, where she oversees the nation's sixteen intelligence agencies—the first female Senator to hold that position.

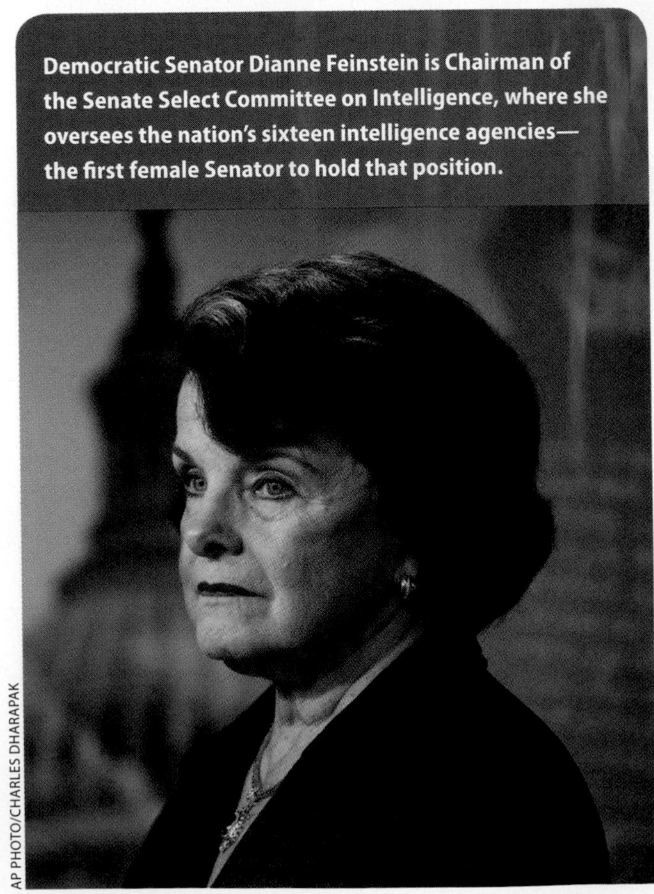

AP PHOTO/CHARLES DHARAPAK

Only on the question of offshore oil drilling have most members of the state's delegation voted the same way. In 2008, with gasoline prices hitting record levels, President Bush called for an end to the twenty-seven–year federal moratorium on offshore drilling. Almost the entire California delegation opposed the proposal, and the damaging Gulf of Mexico offshore oil blowout in 2010 silenced any further discussion.

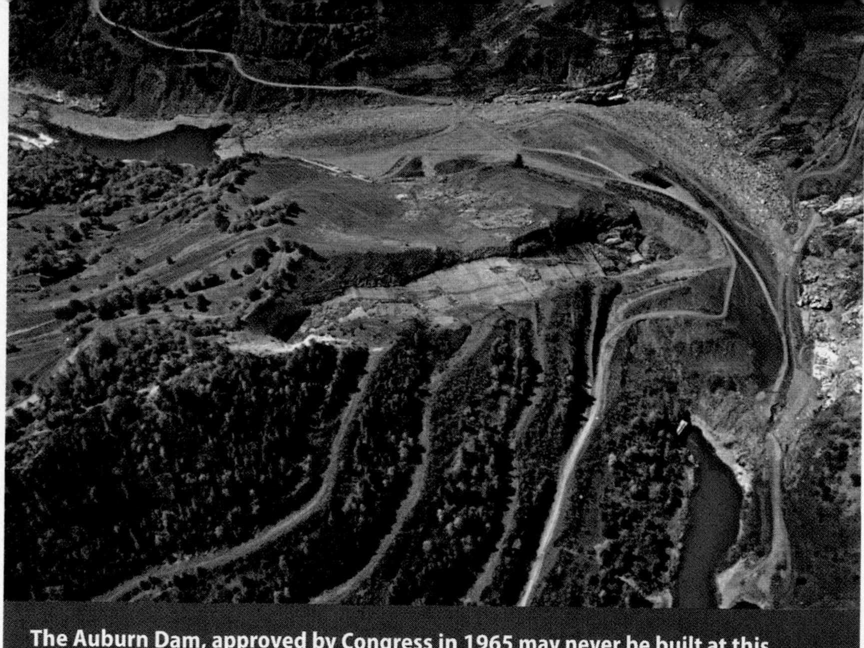

AP PHOTO/SACRAMENTO BEE/JAY MATHER

The Auburn Dam, approved by Congress in 1965 may never be built at this site on the American River, thirty-five miles northeast of Sacramento. The U.S. Bureau of Reclamation halted construction more than thirty years ago because of safety concerns and, in 2008, the state water board revoked the water rights it granted to the federal government nearly forty years ago.

CONTROVERSY OVER THE PROPOSED AUBURN DAM The struggle over the proposed Auburn Dam in Northern California is a current case in point. California hungers for more water, but the real debate has been over the best ways to get it and at what cost. The massive $9.6 billion proposal has been considered in Congress since 1960. Federal agencies have spent $325 million just on feasibility studies. Yet California lawmakers in Washington have remained paralyzed over the issue, due in no small part to the conflicting objectives of environmentalists and farmers. The various sides struck a compromise in 2003 by upgrading another dam downstream. But concerns over California's weakened levee system led House Republican Dan Lungren to pursue the idea yet again in 2007 after the release of a 152-page report by the U.S. Department of the Interior.[2] Meanwhile, Democrats Pete Stark and George Miller have used their clout with the majority to thwart consideration of the project as an environmentally unsound proposal. The issue of whether the project is a boondoggle or a vital flood-control program is not as significant as the fact that it has polarized the California congressional delegation. As a result, while Californians have fussed among themselves over this vexing question, representatives from other states have worked in bipartisan ways to garner federal dollars for their projects.

LO3 *Terrorism*

September 11, 2001, represented a turning point in American history. Never before had terrorists penetrated onto American soil in such a punishing way. As expected, the federal government took the lead in responding to this unprecedented event. With passage of the USA Patriot Act on October 26, 2001, the national government assumed expanded powers to search out terrorism and terrorist-related activities in the areas of hazardous substances, money laundering, illegal immigration, cyber crime, fraud, and other areas. Acting under these new powers, the U.S. attorney general asked states and local governments to help in detaining and questioning suspicious persons; the new Transportation Security Administration assumed security responsibilities at the nation's airports; and the U.S. Border Patrol increased its vigilance against illegal entry. Statewide, between 2002 and 2010, the Governor's Office of Homeland Security distributed more than $1.3 billion in federal funds for state and local equipment and training.

Although the federal government has picked up much of the tab, the states have been burdened with significant costs, too, and are likely to see those costs continue well into the future. From transportation systems and port security to water pipelines and canals to electricity lines, California's infrastructure now requires additional protection against terrorists. As a result, the state has absorbed major security obligations without federal funding. For example, the Real ID Act, a federal law requiring states to issue universal driver's licenses, has an estimated price tag in California of $500 million to $750 million between 2008 and 2013, yet only a small fraction of the cost was funded by the federal government.[3] Such costs are difficult for governments to

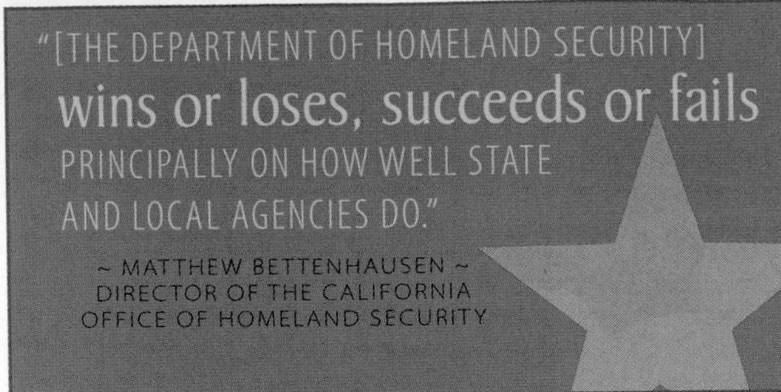

swallow in good economic times, and with California plagued by out-of-balance budgets for most of the time between 2002 and 2011, they have made a major dent in available resources.

Allocation of Funds

The state's surge in congressional chairmanships has somewhat helped California's position with the federal government on homeland security allocations. Following the September 11 terrorist attacks on the United States, the federal government made antiterrorism funds available to all fifty states. With $5.03 per capita for the 2004–2005 fiscal year, California ranked last despite its coastal location, huge seaports, nuclear power plants, massive power line grids, and other targets that are ripe for terrorist attacks. Meanwhile, Wyoming ranked first with $37.94 per capita, followed by Vermont ($31.56 per capita), North Dakota ($30.81 per capita), and Alaska ($30.42 per capita). Hard work by Senator Feinstein and California House Republican leaders produced a new method of allocation at the Department of Homeland Security. Thus, for the 2006–2007 fiscal year, California climbed to twenty-first place, with $6.81 per capita. Meanwhile, Vermont took over first place, with $20.03 per capita; Wyoming dropped to second, with $18.06.[4] Since then, the Obama administration has promised to review the funding formula in recognition of high-risk states such as California, but serious economic issues have prevented the development of new legislation.

LO4 *Immigration*

California has long been a magnet for those in search of opportunity. And they have come—first the Spanish; then Yankee, Irish, and Chinese immigrants during the nineteenth century; followed by Japanese, Eastern European, African American, and Vietnamese immigrants beginning in the 1970s; Asian Indians in the 1990s; and more Latinos throughout the last half century (see Table 26–1). But over the past two decades, several independent events have converged to influence the moods of the state's residents and would-be residents. Lack of opportunity in other nations has led millions to choose California as an alternative; meanwhile, an overburdened and underfunded infrastructure has led many of those

Table 26–1

California's Immigrants: Leading Countries of Origin, 2006

Country	Number
Mexico	4,396,000
Philippines	750,000
China	659,000
Vietnam	446,000
El Salvador	396,000
Korea	323,000
India	303,000
Guatemala	241,000
Iran	182,000
Taiwan	163,000
Canada	134,000
United Kingdom	126,000

Source: U.S. Census, 2005.

A man is shown here walking along the border fence between the United States and Mexico in Ciudad Juarez, Mexico. Many immigrants cross illegally into the United States from this area because houses are close to the border on the south side and the highway is close to the north side.

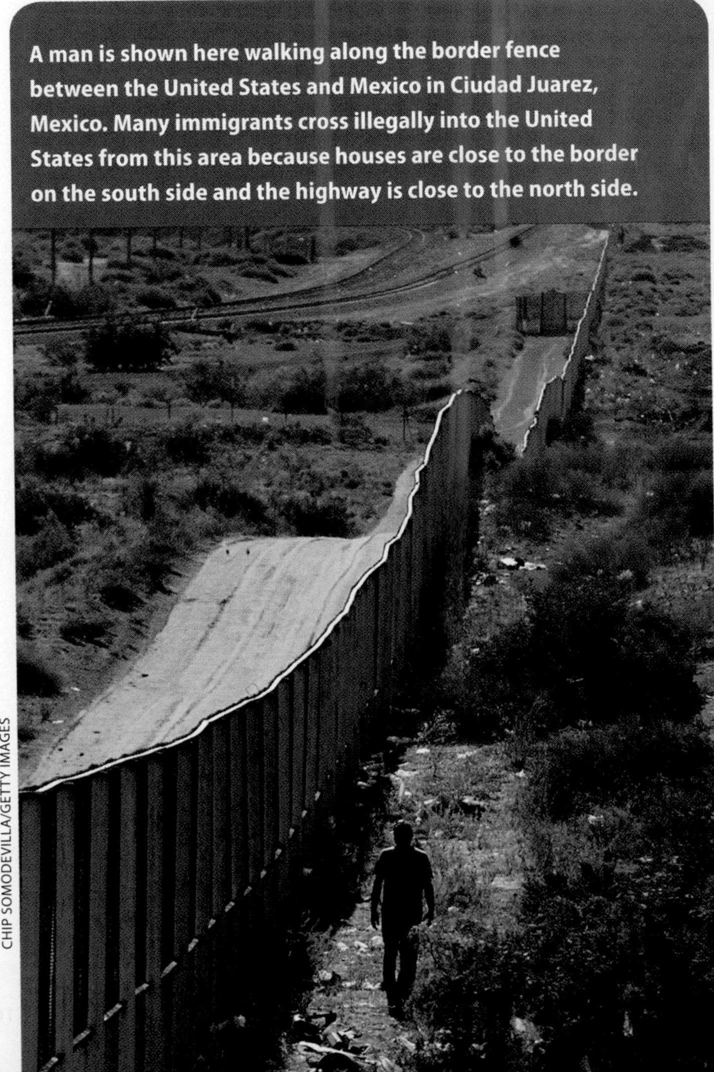

CHIP SOMODEVILLA/GETTY IMAGES

Figure 26–1

Population of Foreign-Born Residents, California and United States Compared

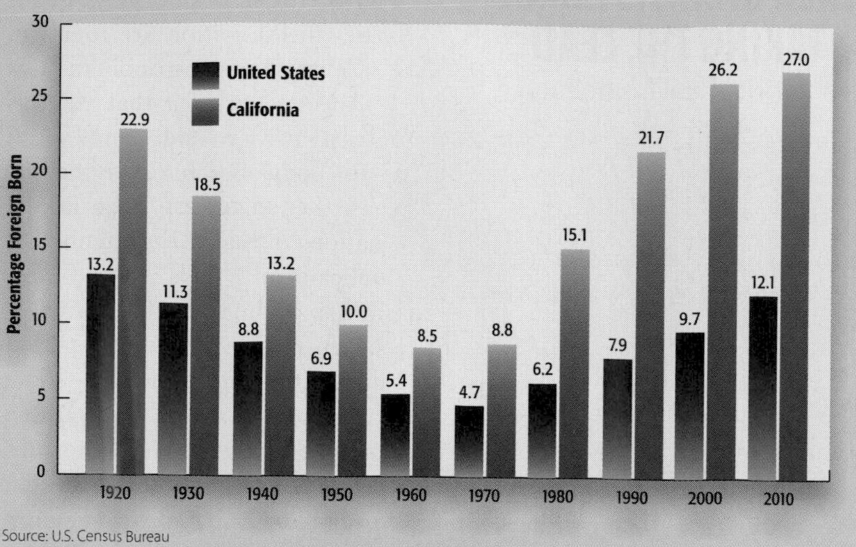

Source: U.S. Census Bureau

already here to oppose further immigration. Much of the antipathy has been directed at Latinos—particularly those from Mexico—but anger has also been aimed at Asians.

The numbers are substantial. Whereas 15.1 percent of California's population were foreign born in 1980, 27 percent fell within that category in 2010, with projections showing that percentage remaining in place through 2030.[5] During the same period, the percentage of foreign-born residents of the United States as a whole edged up from 6.2 to 12.1 percent (see Figure 26–1). Between 1990 and 2005 California's population grew by between 500,000 and 600,000 annually, and more than 40 percent of that number came from foreign immigration. In 2010 the Pew Hispanic Center estimated that there were between 11.4 million and 12.4 million illegal immigrants nationwide, with between 2.5 million and 2.85 million of them in California.[6] Between 1990 and 2008 the percentage of illegal immigrants living in California dropped from 42 percent to 22 percent, indicating greater movement to other states.[7]

This young woman joins a candle-light procession and vigil in support of the Federal DREAM Act in downtown Los Angeles. The Development, Relief and Education for Alien Minors Act, which Congress defeated in late 2010, would have allowed the legalization of people who illegally entered the United States before they turned 16, who have been here for at least five years, and who complete at least two years of college, or join the military, among other requirements.

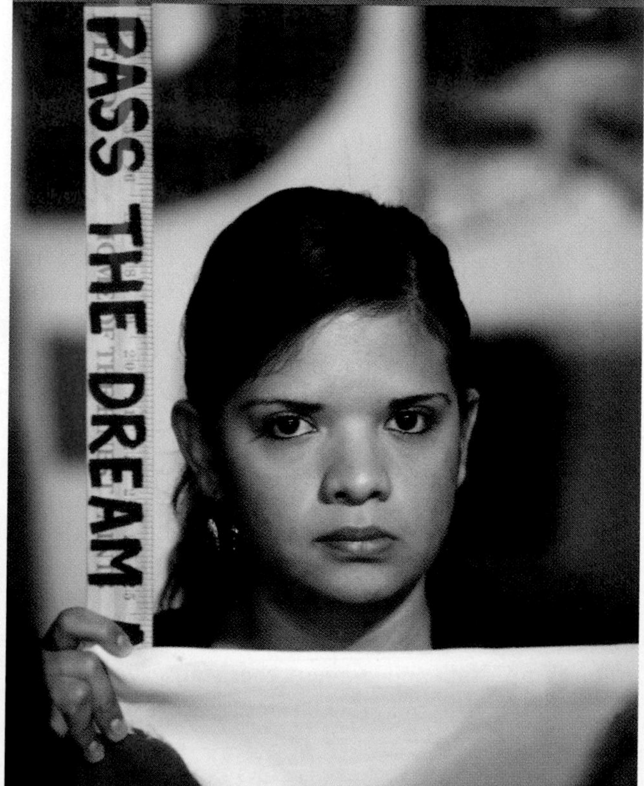

AP PHOTO/DAMIAN DOVARGANES

Benefits for Immigrants

With these dramatic events reshaping California, experts have argued about whether the immigrants help or harm the state's economy. For example, one recent study finds that only about one-third of recent immigrants have health insurance, suggesting a financial burden for public health institutions and services.[8] At the same time, other studies show that immigrants—legal and illegal combined—are very similar in economic makeup to the rest of America.[9] Moreover, in some industries, such as California farming, illegal immigrants are critical to harvests, making up as much as 90 percent of the workforce. To the extent that these workers are prevented from laboring in the fields, California's $36 billion agriculture industry could suffer irreparable damage.[10] All these findings suggest a growing ambivalence toward the illegal immigration issue in California.

The Costs of Illegal Immigration

None of this has stopped the federal government from moving on immigration, although observers disagree about the appropriate level of federal involvement. In 2008 the Bush administration increased surveillance

Environmental Protection Agency (EPA) The federal government body charged with carrying out national environmental policy objectives.

"I am pleased to see **CALIFORNIA IS AGAIN TAKING THE LEAD** on critical environmental challenges."

~ JANE HARMAN ~
DEMOCRATIC MEMBER OF THE U.S. HOUSE OF REPRESENTATIVES FROM CALIFORNIA'S 36TH DISTRICT

of U.S. companies with illegal immigrant employees, leading to fines for employers, imprisonment for undocumented workers, and workforce shortages in some industries.[11] At the same time, between a more vigilant border protection system and a declining U.S. economy, the number of attempted border crossings by illegal immigrants declined.[12]

The largest issue related to immigration is determining which level of government should assume responsibility for its costs. While the federal government has long established the criteria for immigration and the conditions for enforcement, it leaves the states responsible for meeting the needs of immigrants. Nowhere does this contradiction ring louder than in California. Among unauthorized immigrants alone, recent estimates cite health-care costs of $1 billion, education costs for 400,000 of their children at $1 billion, and incarceration costs for 18,000 illegal immigrants at $500 million.[13] Few of these costs have been picked up by the federal government, yet their day-to-day impact is a reality.

Controversy continues over how much responsibility California should assume for stemming the tide of illegal immigration. In 2006 President Bush asked Governor Schwarzenegger to send 2,500 members of the National Guard to Arizona and New Mexico to help U.S. Border Patrol agents. The governor dispatched only 1,000 troops, arguing that the rest were needed at home to assist in cases of wildfires, earthquakes, or other unanticipated calamities.[14] Clearly, the role of each government in managing the immigration question remains a tough issue to sort out.

LO5 *Climate Change*

California and the federal government have had a rocky relationship with respect to climate change. At times, the state has fought national objectives; at others, California has taken the lead. No example of state resistance is more obvious than the issue of air quality. According to the U.S. **Environmental Protection Agency (EPA),** the ten smoggiest counties in the nation are found in California. Metropolitan Los Angeles, an area that extends east to Riverside and south to Long Beach, tops the list as the smoggiest area in the nation. Actually, the number of "unhealthful" days in the L.A. basin has declined from an average of 189.6 during the 1996–1998 period to 141.8 during the period of 2006–2008, according to the American Lung Association, although progress has stopped since 2004.[15] Statewide, the costs have been great. One recent study finds that annual losses in California from unhealthy air amount to $28 billion in the form of premature deaths, illness, and lost productivity in the workplace.[17]

Congress and the EPA have been unhappy with the inability of the state to move forward on clean air. But given the state's dependence on manufacturing, particularly in the vast Los Angeles basin, it has been difficult to meet national standards without choking off the local economy. In 1992 state regulators in Southern California established the Regional Clean Air Incentives Market Program (RECLAIM), a program in which manufacturers buy and sell emissions permits as a means of encouraging emissions reduction. The program has led to substantial reductions in environmental decay,[17] although the region remains far from healthy.

Auto Emissions

The state has enjoyed more success in the area of auto emissions, although at times the road has been bumpy for other reasons. California has a history of leading the nation in reducing auto emissions, which account for 28 percent of the state's greenhouse gases. Since the passage of the original Clean Air Act of 1970, state environmental regulators have asked for and received forty-four waivers from the EPA to establish standards beyond federal requirements. That's what happened until 2007, when the Bush administration's EPA ruled that there was no evidence suggesting that auto emissions contained greenhouse gases,[18] to the amazement of most scientists in the United States and worldwide. Since the agency gave no scientific explanation for its ruling, California and sixteen other states sued the EPA for not carrying out its mandate. The United States

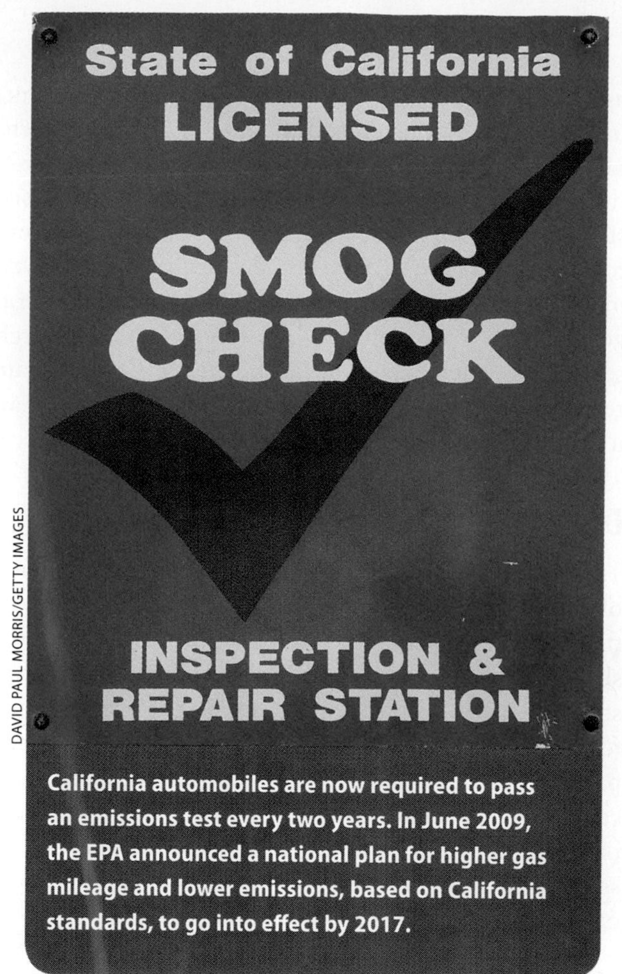
State of California
LICENSED
SMOG
CHECK
INSPECTION &
REPAIR STATION

DAVID PAUL MORRIS/GETTY IMAGES

California automobiles are now required to pass an emissions test every two years. In June 2009, the EPA announced a national plan for higher gas mileage and lower emissions, based on California standards, to go into effect by 2017.

Supreme Court agreed, and thus began another chapter in the struggle for control over emissions standards.

The political environment regarding auto emissions changed dramatically with the election of Barack Obama to the presidency in 2008. Early in 2009 he asked his new EPA administrator to review previous decisions on California's waiver petitions. In June 2009 the EPA approved California's proposal and announced a new national policy on higher gasoline mileage and lower emissions by 2017, based on California's standards. On this occasion, at least, California set the trend for the rest of the nation.

LO6 *Water*

Not all of California's jurisdictional disputes have occurred with the federal government. In several areas, the state has tangled with other states. The storage of nuclear waste and agriculture rules are two such examples of interstate fights, but no argument has as much significance as California's struggle for freshwater. Three-quarters of California's water comes from north of Sacramento. Three-quarters of the water

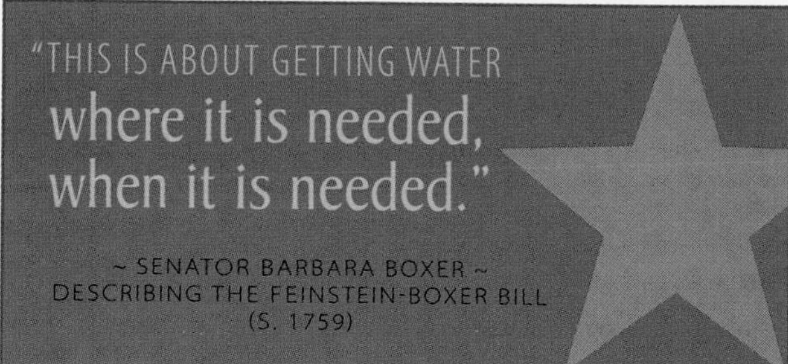
"THIS IS ABOUT GETTING WATER
where it is needed,
when it is needed."
~ SENATOR BARBARA BOXER ~
DESCRIBING THE FEINSTEIN-BOXER BILL
(S. 1759)

is consumed south of the capital. For this transfer to work, water must move, and it does so thanks to two giant systems. The federal Central Valley Project, which dates from 1937, supplies the farmers of the southern Central Valley. The State Water Project, begun in 1960, largely supplies southern urban areas. Both systems intercept freshwater near the Sacramento–San Joaquin Delta before it can flow out to the ocean through San Francisco's Golden Gate. Given the state's huge population and pivotal role in agriculture, water is a resource that California can ill afford to do without, and that fact has led to ugly entanglements.

The Colorado River

The linchpin of the water dispute between California and other states is the Colorado River, the freshwater source that begins in Colorado and winds through six other states. Under a 1922 multistate agreement, California is entitled to 4.4 million acre-feet, or 59 percent, of the lower basin river annually. Yet according to some critics, California exceeded its share by as much as 800,000 acre-feet per year, enough to provide for the annual water needs of 1.6 million households in rapidly growing nearby states such as Arizona and Nevada.[19]

Fearing an all-out water war that would spill into Congress, officials from seven states held talks for eighteen months to resolve the problem. In 2000 they agreed to a formula that would allow California to gradually reduce its consumption of the excess over a fifteen-year period. During the transition, officials from Arizona offered to "bank" surplus water for California, should the state require it. But with Arizona, Nevada, and other western states growing faster than any other parts of the nation, it remains to be seen how long the fragile agreement will remain in play. At least for the time being, the seven western states have solved a troublesome issue without federal participation.

The Battle for Water Supplies

Meanwhile, the federal government's Department of the Interior and the state of California worked to resolve the ongoing three-way battle among agribusiness (responsible for 80 percent of the state's water

federalism The distribution of power, resources, and responsibilities among the national and state governments.

grants-in-aid Payments from the national government to states to assist in fulfilling public policy objectives.

consumption), environmentalists seeking to preserve rivers and deltas, and urban areas in need of water to grow. Under the auspices of CalFed, a joint federal and state water agency, the two governments developed a plan in 2000 to expand existing federal reservoirs in California, improve drinking water quality, and develop a creative water recycling program. Most of the $8.5 billion price tag will be borne by the federal government, with Californians providing $825 million from the passage of Proposition 50 in 2002. In 2004 Congress reauthorized CalFed, with a commitment of $10 billion over thirty years to improve the quality of water flowing into the Sacramento Delta and San Francisco Bay.

Uncertainties remain, however. In 2002 the U.S. Department of the Interior modified a plan previously favored by environmentalists. The new plan sent more water from the Central Valley Project to farmers, rather than using it for ecosystem restoration. Still, water can only be distributed to customers if it is available, and recent droughts in California and the West have left the region thirsty. The issue has become so important that in 2007, responding to a record-low snowpack in the Sierra Nevada Mountains and concern for the welfare of endangered species, a federal court judge reduced deliveries of Northern California water to Southern California by 25 percent. The impact of the order put Southern California governments on notice: until water supplies could be assured, major construction projects in that portion of the state would be put on hold.[20] So the battle over water continues, not only between California and the federal government but also between farmers, environmentalists, and developers. We take a closer look at the water supply issue in the *Perception versus Reality* feature on the facing page.

LO7 *Shared Resources*

The word **federalism** refers to the multifaceted political relationship that binds the state and national governments. One aspect of that relationship centers on financial assistance that wends its way from federal coffers to state and local treasuries, and that amounted to about $550 billion in fiscal year 2010. The preponderance of this assistance comes in the form of **grants-in-aid,** amounting to about 20 percent of all state and local government revenues. This assistance is the result of more than six hundred federal programs designed to assist states in areas ranging from agricultural development to high-tech research. For decades, California received more than its fair share of grants-in-aid from the federal government. With defense- and space-related research serving as a huge economic magnet, the Golden State received more money from the federal government than it sent in.

Declining Federal Support

That has changed. In 1983 California had 10 percent of the national population but received 22 percent of the national government's expenditures. Then came the slide: with a pared defense budget, cutbacks in infrastructure work, and the push for a balanced budget, federal contributions have shrunk considerably over the past two decades. As of 2007 California had 12.1 percent of the nation's population but received 11.8 percent of the nation's federal funds. The state now ranks thirty-seventh in the distribution of federal spending on a per capita basis—down sharply from twentieth in 1990.[21]

There is another way to appreciate the changing relationship between the federal government and California. Because of the state's massive growth and receipt of federal assistance in highway and water projects and environmental protection, California had a

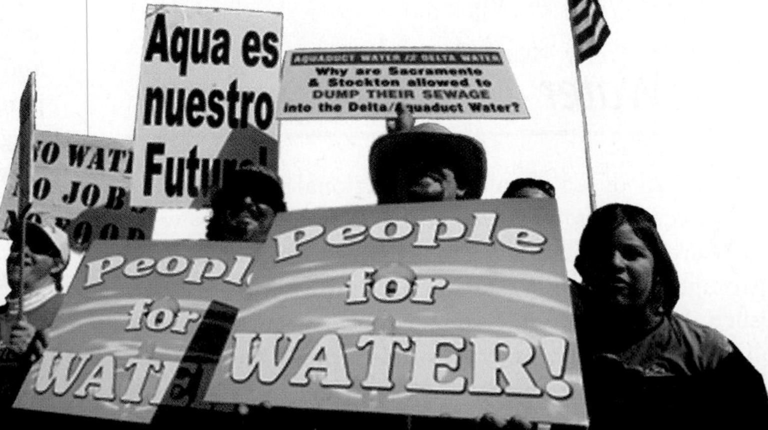

Farmers, farm workers, and supporters hold a march through the Central Valley to bring attention to the California water crisis. The year 2010 marked the fourth year of a worsening California drought, resulting in extreme water shortages, job losses, and significant drops in crop production.

DAVID McNEW/GETTY IMAGES

PERCEPTION VERSUS REALITY

The Federal Government Caused the Water Shortages

Three-quarters of California's water comes from north of Sacramento. Three-quarters of the water is consumed south of the capital. For this to work, water must move, and it does so thanks to two giant systems. The federal Central Valley Project, which dates from 1937, supplies the farmers of the southern Central Valley. The State Water Project, begun in 1960, largely supplies southern urban areas. Both systems intercept fresh water in the Sacramento-San Joaquin Delta before it can flow out to the ocean through San Francisco's Golden Gate.

Beginning in 2007, California entered a multi-year drought, and the amount of water available through the Delta fell by one-third. This spelled trouble for the 25 million Californians who depend on the system for their drinking water and for the farms in the Central Valley that produce half of the nation's fruits and vegetables.

Still, despite the drought, there were signs that California might have enough water if it were managed properly. The Westlands Water District, an agricultural water contractor west of Fresno, was cut back to 10 percent of its normal allocation, yet neighboring agricultural contractors received 100 percent of their water. Water use restrictions were imposed in southern cities, but California continued to grow thirsty crops. In 2008, farmers did cut the number of acres planted in cotton—a crop that needs plenty of water—by two-fifths. Yet production of rice, an even more water-intensive crop, was not affected at all. California, the nation's second-largest rice-producing state, harvests four billion pounds of the grain every year.

Still, in some parts of the Central Valley, unemployment reached 40 percent. Central Valley farmers were convinced that their real problem was a man-made, "regulatory" drought caused by strict environmental regulations. Were they right?

The Perception

Central Valley leaders contend that way too much water goes to environmental purposes. Farmers were particularly incensed over the delta smelt, a tiny endangered fish. Lawsuits filed on behalf of the fish by environmental groups triggered restrictions on pumping imposed by a federal court. Farmers demanded that the federal government convene a "God squad" to pull the smelt off the endangered species list. Then the state could turn on the pumps full blast.

The Reality

California water rights are shared out on the principle of "first in time, first in rights." Whoever signed up for a water contract first got the best guarantees. Latecomers have junior rights. That is the real problem faced by the Westlands Water District. It is last in line for the water, and therefore the first customer to be cut off. True, water diverted for environmental purposes hurt the Central Valley in 2009. About one-quarter of the deficiency was the result of diversion. Three-quarters was due to the fact that it didn't rain.

Further, the delta smelt was not the only environmental issue. There were sturgeon, salmon, steel-head trout. The U.S. Department of the Interior described the Delta as "in a state of full environmental collapse," even with the diverted water. Even so, the 2009 diversion ended on June 30, and the pumps were on again. The year 2010 turned out to be a normal water year, and most customers received 100 percent allocations. Westlands, however, still received only 30 percent.

California suffers from a basic problem: the state has pledged several times as much water to title-holders as exists in nature. All water consumers need to take sustainability seriously. That includes both agricultural districts with senior water rights and urban consumers. For example, city dwellers can use "gray water" outflows from washing machines, showers, and bathroom sinks to irrigate household lawns and gardens. Unfortunately, state officials, asked to draw up regulations for such systems, responded with unnecessary restrictions that are almost impossible to meet.

A more controversial solution is to create new infrastructure—the existing pipes and levies are in any event dangerously old. A major proposal is to build a peripheral canal around the Delta. Such a system could increase water flows while restoring the Delta's ecology. In 2009, the legislature placed an $11 billion bond issue on the November 2010 ballot. The measure contained sums for building new dams, restoring the Delta, monitoring groundwater use, and a variety of other projects. It also established a mechanism for considering whether to build a peripheral canal. In August 2010, however, the legislature postponed a vote on the measure until 2012. The argument was that the state might be better placed to afford the bond issue at a future date.

Blog On For an account of how water shortages are hurting the western San Joaquin Valley, see **www.newsweek.com/id/211381**. For the U.S. Department of the Interior's take on the water crisis, go to **www.cacoastkeeper.org/document/california-water-reality-check.pdf.**

long history of getting more dollars from the federal government than it contributed. Beginning in 1986, however, California became a "donor" state. Ever since, California has contributed more money to the national treasury than it has received, and the disparity is increasing every year. In 1992, for every dollar California sent to Washington, D.C., the state received 93 cents in federal goods and services. In 2005, for every dollar California sent to Washington, only 78 cents came back in goods and services, leaving the state in forty-third place in per capita federal spending (see Table 26-2). No matter how you slice it, California is getting less of the federal "pie" today than in the past.

Table 26–2

Federal Expenditures per Dollar of Taxes, Fiscal Years 1992 and 2005—California and Selected States

	Expenditures per Dollar of Taxes		Ranking	
	FY1992	FY2005	FY1992	FY2005
New Mexico	$2.08	$2.03	11	1
Maryland	$1.27	$1.30	15	18
Kansas	$1.05	$1.12	27	22
Texas	$ .93	$ .94	37	35
Massachusetts	$1.01	$ .82	31	40
California	$ .93	$ .78	38	43
New Jersey	$ .66	$ .61	50	50

Source: Tax Foundation.

Equity in Numbers?

But there is more to the story than just numbers; it's the kind of numbers that make a huge difference. Data compiled in 2006 found that if the cost of living is added to the mix, more than 16 percent of all Californians fall under the poverty line, compared with about 12 percent nationwide.[22] And when we consider that the state's immigrant population is more than twice the national average on a per capita basis, it becomes clear that the state's needs fare particularly poorly when it comes to federal funding.

The data presented here fly in the face of the political posturing that has emerged from both Congress and the presidency in recent years. Instead, they show a California with unlimited potential, and a California that has been much better for some than others. They reveal a state that in recent years has given much more to the federal government in taxes than it has received in programs and services. They also reflect the fragmentation that has haunted the state's congressional delegation on virtually every issue except offshore oil drilling. As a result, California's "Golden State" nickname has a different meaning in Washington than in California—namely, sizable economic resources that have landed disproportionately in the federal treasury.

California Today: Golden State or Fool's Gold?

Is today's California still the state with unlimited potential or the state with too many burdens to survive? When it comes to relations with the federal government, perhaps the answer is a little of both. California is king when it comes to campaign contributions for national candidates, research and development, the center of agriculture, and auto emissions standards. At the same time, California is a pauper in matters of dealing with a perpetual state budget deficit, a dilapidated infrastructure, and a frayed social safety net. Once upon a time, the state would have looked to the federal government for rescue, and the federal government would have been happy to help. That relationship has been replaced by one in which the state and federal government are often at odds, and occasionally in sync.

Some of the shift has been because of the ebb and flow of national politics. By most accounts, California is a "blue" (Democratic) state when it comes to national elections. Thus, during the Clinton years, the state benefitted

A solar energy field under construction near Sacramento. Governor Schwarzenegger signed an executive order here in 2009, giving California the nation's most aggressive energy standards.

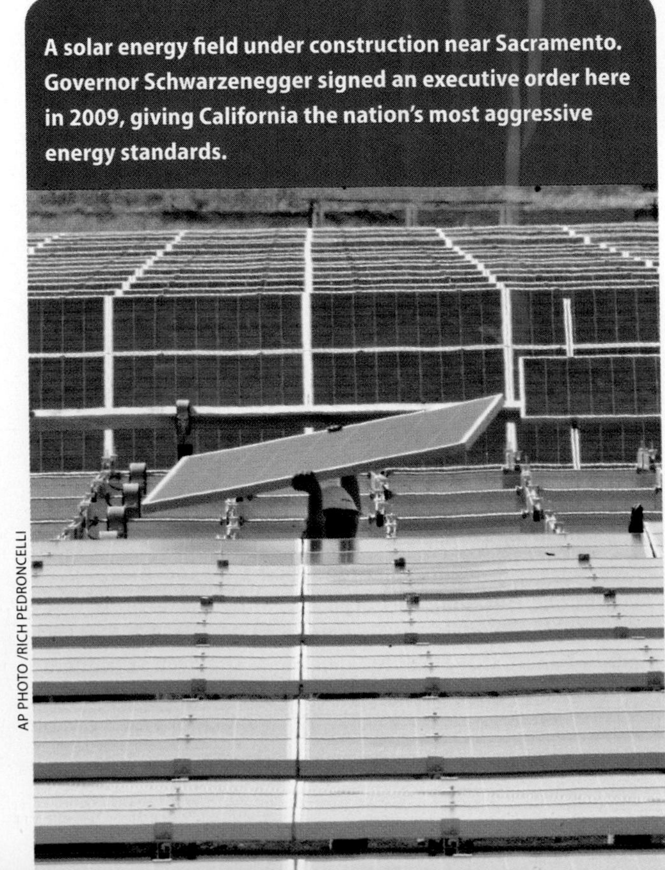

AP PHOTO/RICH PEDRONCELLI

Is California Still the American Future?

The American dream was always a vision of perpetual improvement. Common people from the overcrowded, class-ridden Old World could come to a land of infinite possibilities. Perhaps the most powerful version of this dream has been the California Dream. Newcomers could reinvent themselves here. The California Dream helped propel the state from a semi-frontier commonwealth of 1.5 million people in 1900 to the urbanized giant of 38 million that it is today.

For some, the dream was simply a decent job and a taste of the good life. For the ambitious, the dream meant new industries to dominate—film, then aerospace, and most recently information technology. Economic innovation flourished. The state was rich enough to build the world's best publicly supported system of higher education. California's infrastructure—including its state park system and its vast grid of freeways—was unmatched anywhere.

But is the dream over? Is California now too crowded, too polyglot, and too wracked by the competing demands of radical environmentalists and anti-tax zealots, neopagans and fundamentalists, intellectual snobs and the proudly ignorant? Does the future lie in gated communities surrounded by slums? Will California really fall into the sea? Some people seem to think so. Others believe that California is still America's future.

California Is a Mess

California certainly provides plenty of material for pessimists, both liberal and conservative. The state has earthquakes, forest fires, and droughts. Economic disasters match the ecological ones. The state's cities have become unbearably crowded. Housing prices rose to the point where young families could no longer afford to buy homes—and then crashed in a wave of foreclosures and bankruptcies. Illegal immigration is out of control. Gangs rule the streets. Citizens now flee to other states. Businesses also are fleeing the state, driven out by regulation and high taxes.

The state's educational system is failing fast. The public schools are now among the nation's worst, and the prized higher educational system is crumbling for lack of funds. California is increasingly separating the haves from have-nots. The children of the haves are getting good educations, even if they must attend private schools. The children of the have-nots are dropping out. Those with means are not affected by California's deterioration—those without are the ones who suffer. That's a reason that many have lost the dream. And let's not even mention the state's dysfunctional politics and government. No, California won't really fall into the sea, but if earthquakes destroy the levies around Sacramento and in the Sacramento-San Joaquin Delta, suburbs could drown in twenty-foot floods and the water supply of half the state's people could be cut off. Time to pack up; time to move to Arizona, Nevada, or Oregon.

But It Is Still America's Future

California's defenders might begin by noting some flaws in the previous litany of pessimism. Yes, California's political system has tied itself in knots, but even that problem may be solved as some of the reforms mentioned in previous chapters are adopted. The rest of the state—the nonpolitical part—is in surprisingly good shape. California's crime rates are at the lowest level since 1963. The murder rate hasn't been this low for 40 years. And one side effect of the recent recession is that illegal immigration has essentially stopped.

More importantly, the economy remains strong despite current high rates of unemployment. "Good business climate" figures are based on such things as low wages, but that's not California's strong suit. Low wages imply low productivity and low rates of innovation, but the "new new thing" has always been where California triumphed. Creativity and high pay go hand-in-hand. This, after all, is the state that gave us not only blue jeans, Hollywood, and McDonalds, but Hewlett-Packard, Apple, Intel, and Google. All this in a "hostile business climate."

In 2010, California attracted as much venture capital as the rest of the nation combined, and much of that money is flowing into "green" technology. Already, the state consumes half as much carbon per capita as the rest of the country. California is the home of the nation's solar power industry, the digitized energy grid, and research on fuel from algae. California firms are developing green materials, advanced batteries, electric cars, and zero-emission homes. The state is crowded and racially diverse—and also green, prosperous, and above all, creative. In all these ways, California today is America tomorrow.

For Critical Analysis ***Unlike the older East Coast states, California looks out across the Pacific toward Asia. In what ways might a Pacific orientation have helped shape the state's character?***

from extra federal attention on research and development tax credits, H1-B visas, and even some defense contracts. During the Bush years, California didn't fare so well, as attested by the administration's disregard for the state's immigration issues, antiterrorism concerns, and exorbitant electricity bills.

We're still sifting the relationship with Democratic president Barack Obama, although there are some early hints of an uptick in the relationship. The Obama administration has backed off on prosecuting for marijuana possession, supported continuation of the research and development tax credit, and sent hundreds of millions of federal dollars to help California homeowners deal with foreclosure issues. At the same time, California has not fared well in capturing a chunk of federal dollars in the Race to the Top education reform program. Moreover, the state did not do so well in capturing a large share of the $787 billion in economic stimulus funds provided in the American Recovery and Reinvestment Act passed in 2009. Whereas the state had the fourth highest unemployment rate, it ranked eighteenth in per capita funding.

If nothing else, California operates more independently of the federal government today than in the times of heavy government defense spending. To this extent the state has been weaned of federal dependence. The process may not have been enjoyable, but the state has become more self-reliant as a result. To that end, California's growing autonomy may be the hallmark of the state's direction in the coming years. Whatever the future, it will be an interesting experiment. Will California still be America's future? We address this question in the *Join the Debate* feature on the previous page.

CALIFORNIA AT **ODDS** *State-Federal Relations*

The federal system in the United States inevitably leads to tensions between the state and national governments. California has experienced its share of such tensions, and as a result, its people have been at odds over a number of issues, including the following:

- Is California subject to discrimination resulting from the formulas used by the federal government to distribute grants-in-aid—or is the distribution of federal dollars basically fair?
- Has California's delegation in Washington done all that can be reasonably expected on behalf of the state—or has it fallen down on the job?
- Even if taxing marijuana were a good idea in the abstract, would it be worth tangling with the national government over the issue—or would that simply be a waste of effort?
- Does the U.S. government provide the state with enough support in resolving problems resulting from legal and illegal immigration—or has it left California in the lurch?
- Is the national government to blame, in whole or in part, for California's water woes—or are water shortages chiefly the state's own fault?

Take Action

Contacting your representative or senator is a time-honored method of affecting the political process. To undertake such an action, however, you need to know who your representative is. Given how convoluted congressional district boundaries can be as a result of gerrymandering, this can be harder than you'd think. One easy solution is to visit Congress Merge at www.congressmerge.com/onlinedb. This commercial site sells data products, but it also supplies free information to the general public. Here, you can type your address into a form, and the database will immediately provide you with the matching U.S. senators and member of the House. You can obtain telephone numbers and addresses for e-mail and the U.S. Postal Service.

POLITICS ON THE WEB

- To research information on federal taxes and arguments for conservative tax policy at both the state and federal levels, visit the Web site for The Tax Foundation at **www.taxfoundation.org**.
- The California Institute for Federal Policy Research serves as a resource for information on federal policy and California. To learn more, visit **www.calinst.org**.
- Learn more about the issues, governing laws, and regulations of the Environmental Protection Agency at **www.epa.gov**.
- The School of International Relations and Pacific Studies (IR/PS) in San Diego is the University of California's only professional school of international relations. To read more about their programs and centers, visit **www.irps.ucsd.edu**.

Access CourseMate to review and expand on this chapter through quizzes, flashcards, learning objectives, interactive timelines, a crossword puzzle, audio summaries, video, critical-thinking activities, simulations, and more.

Appendix A

THE DECLARATION OF INDEPENDENCE

IN CONGRESS, JULY 4, 1776

A Declaration by the Representatives of the United States of America, in General Congress assembled. When in the Course of human Events, it becomes necessary for one People to dissolve the Political Bands which have connected them with another, and to assume among the Powers of the Earth, the separate and equal Station to which the Laws of Nature and of Nature's God entitle them, a decent Respect to the Opinions of Mankind requires that they should declare the causes which impel them to the Separation.

We hold these Truths to be self-evident, that all Men are created equal, that they are endowed by their Creator with certain unalienable Rights, that among these are Life, Liberty, and the Pursuit of Happiness—That to secure these Rights, Governments are instituted among Men, deriving their just Powers from the Consent of the Governed, that whenever any Form of Government becomes destructive of these Ends, it is the Right of the People to alter or to abolish it, and to institute new Government, laying its Foundation on such Principles, and organizing its Powers in such Forms, as to them shall seem most likely to effect their Safety and Happiness. Prudence, indeed, will dictate that Governments long established should not be changed for light and transient Causes; and accordingly all Experience hath shewn, that Mankind are more disposed to suffer, while Evils are sufferable, than to right themselves by abolishing the Forms to which they are accustomed. But when a long Train of Abuses and Usurpations, pursuing invariably the same Object, evinces a Design to reduce them under absolute Despotism, it is their Right, it is their Duty, to throw off such Government, and to provide new Guards for their future Security. Such has been the patient Sufferance of these Colonies; and such is now the Necessity which constrains them to alter their former Systems of Government. The History of the present King of Great-Britain is a History of repeated Injuries and Usurpations, all having in direct Object the Establishment of an absolute Tyranny over these States. To prove this, let Facts be submitted to a candid World.

He has refused his Assent to Laws, the most wholesome and necessary for the public Good.

He has forbidden his Governors to pass Laws of immediate and pressing Importance, unless suspended in their Operation till his Assent should be obtained; and when so suspended, he has utterly neglected to attend to them.

He has refused to pass other Laws for the Accommodation of large Districts of People, unless those People would relinquish the Right of Representation in the Legislature, a Right inestimable to them, and formidable to Tyrants only.

He has called together Legislative Bodies at Places unusual, uncomfortable, and distant from the Depository of their Public Records, for the sole Purpose of fatiguing them into Compliance with his Measures.

He has dissolved Representative Houses repeatedly, for opposing with manly Firmness his Invasions on the Rights of the People.

He has refused for a long Time, after such Dissolutions, to cause others to be elected; whereby the Legislative Powers, incapable of Annihilation, have returned to the People at large for their exercise; the State remaining in the mean time exposed to all the Dangers of Invasion from without, and Convulsions within.

He has endeavoured to prevent the Population of these States; for that Purpose obstructing the Laws for Naturalization of Foreigners; refusing to pass others to encourage their Migrations hither, and raising the Conditions of new Appropriations of Lands.

He has obstructed the Administration of Justice, by refusing his Assent to Laws for establishing Judiciary Powers.

He has made Judges dependent on his Will alone, for the Tenure of their offices, and the Amount and payment of their Salaries.

He has erected a Multitude of new Offices, and sent hither Swarms of Officers to harrass our People, and eat out their Substance.

He has kept among us, in Times of Peace, Standing Armies, without the consent of our Legislatures.

He has affected to render the Military independent of, and superior to the Civil Power.

He has combined with others to subject us to a Jurisdiction foreign to our Constitution, and unacknowledged by our Laws; giving his Assent to their Acts of pretended Legislation:

For quartering large Bodies of Armed Troops among us:

For protecting them, by a mock Trial, from Punishment for any Murders which they should commit on the Inhabitants of these States:

For cutting off our Trade with all Parts of the World:

For imposing Taxes on us without our Consent:

For depriving us, in many cases, of the Benefits of Trial by Jury:

For transporting us beyond Seas to be tried for pretended Offences:

For abolishing the free System of English Laws in a neighbouring Province, establishing therein an arbitrary Government, and enlarging its Boundaries, so as to render it at once an Example and fit Instrument for introducing the same absolute Rule into these Colonies:

For taking away our Charters, abolishing our most valuable Laws, and altering fundamentally the Forms of our Governments:

For suspending our own Legislatures, and declaring themselves invested with Power to legislate for us in all Cases whatsoever.

He has abdicated Government here, by declaring us out of his Protection and waging War against us.

He has plundered our Seas, ravaged our Coasts, burnt our towns, and destroyed the Lives of our People.

He is, at this Time, transporting large Armies of foreign Mercenaries to compleat the works of Death, Desolation, and Tyranny, already begun with circumstances of Cruelty and Perfidy, scarcely paralleled in the most barbarous Ages, and totally unworthy the Head of a civilized Nation.

He has constrained our fellow Citizens taken Captive on the high Seas to bear Arms against their Country, to become the Executioners of their Friends and Brethren, or to fall themselves by their Hands.

He has excited domestic Insurrections amongst us, and has endeavoured to bring on the Inhabitants of our Frontiers, the merciless Indian Savages, whose known Rule of Warfare, is an undistinguished Destruction, of all Ages, Sexes and Conditions.

In every state of these Oppressions we have Petitioned for Redress in the most humble Terms: Our repeated Petitions have been answered only by repeated Injury. A Prince, whose Character is thus marked by every act which may define a Tyrant, is unfit to be the Ruler of a free People.

Nor have we been wanting in Attentions to our British Brethren. We have warned them from Time to Time of Attempts by their Legislature to extend an unwarrantable Jurisdiction over us. We have reminded them of the Circumstances of our Emigration and Settlement here. We have appealed to their native Justice and Magnanimity, and we have conjured them by the Ties of our common Kindred to disavow these Usurpations, which, would inevitably interrupt our Connections and Correspondence. They too have been deaf to the Voice of Justice and of Consanguinity. We must, therefore, acquiesce in the Necessity, which denounces our Separation, and hold them, as we hold the rest of Mankind, Enemies in War, in Peace, Friends.

We, therefore, the Representatives of the UNITED STATES OF AMERICA, in General Congress Assembled, appealing to the Supreme Judge of the World for the Rectitude of our Intentions, do, in the Name, and by the Authority of the good People of these Colonies, solemnly Publish and Declare, That these United Colonies are, and of Right ought to be, Free and Independent States; that they are absolved from all Allegiance to the British Crown, and that all political Connection between them and the State of Great-Britain, is and ought to be totally dissolved; and that as Free and Independent States, they have full Power to levy War, conclude Peace, contract Alliances, establish Commerce, and to do all other Acts and Things which Independent States may of right do. And for the support of this declaration, with a firm Reliance on the Protection of divine Providence, we mutually pledge to each other our lives, our Fortunes, and our sacred Honor.

THE CONSTITUTION OF THE UNITED STATES

PREAMBLE

We the People of the United States, in Order to form a more perfect Union, establish Justice, insure domestic Tranquility, provide for the common defence, promote the general Welfare, and secure the Blessings of Liberty to ourselves and our Posterity, do ordain and establish this Constitution for the United States of America.

ARTICLE I

SECTION 1. All legislative Powers herein granted shall be vested in a Congress of the United States, which shall consist of a Senate and House of Representatives.

SECTION 2. The House of Representatives shall be composed of Members chosen every second Year by the People of the several States, and the Electors in each State shall have the Qualifications requisite for Electors of the most numerous Branch of the State Legislature.

No Person shall be a Representative who shall not have attained to the Age of twenty five Years, and been seven Years a Citizen of the United States, and who shall not, when elected, be an Inhabitant of that State in which he shall be chosen.

Representatives and direct Taxes shall be apportioned among the several States which may be included within this Union, according to their respective Numbers, which shall be determined by adding to the whole Number of free Persons, including those bound to Service for a Term of Years, and excluding Indians not taxed, three fifths of all other Persons. The actual Enumeration shall be made within three Years after the first Meeting of the Congress of the United States, and within every subsequent Term of ten Years, in such Manner as they shall by Law direct. The Number of Representatives shall not exceed one for every thirty Thousand, but each State shall have at Least one Representative; and until such enumeration shall be made, the State of New Hampshire shall be entitled to chuse three, Massachusetts eight, Rhode Island and Providence Plantations one, Connecticut five, New York six, New Jersey four, Pennsylvania eight, Delaware one, Maryland six, Virginia ten, North Carolina five, South Carolina five, and Georgia three.

When vacancies happen in the Representation from any State, the Executive Authority thereof shall issue Writs of Election to fill such Vacancies.

The House of Representatives shall chuse their Speaker and other Officers; and shall have the sole Power of Impeachment.

SECTION 3. The Senate of the United States shall be composed of two Senators from each State, chosen by the Legislature thereof, for six Years; and each Senator shall have one Vote.

Immediately after they shall be assembled in Consequence of the first Election, they shall be divided as equally as may be into three Classes. The Seats of the Senators of the first Class shall be vacated at the Expiration of the second Year, of the second Class at the Expiration of the fourth Year, and of the third Class at the Expiration of the sixth Year, so that one third may be chosen every second Year; and if Vacancies happen by Resignation, or otherwise, during the Recess of the Legislature of any State, the Executive thereof may make temporary Appointments until the next Meeting of the Legislature, which shall then fill such Vacancies.

No Person shall be a Senator who shall not have attained to the Age of thirty Years, and been nine Years a Citizen of the United States, and who shall not, when elected, be an Inhabitant of that State for which he shall be chosen.

The Vice President of the United States shall be President of the Senate, but shall have no Vote, unless they be equally divided.

The Senate shall chuse their other Officers, and also a President pro tempore, in the Absence of the Vice President, or when he shall exercise the Office of President of the United States.

The Senate shall have the sole Power to try all Impeachments. When sitting for that Purpose, they shall be on Oath or Affirmation. When the President of the United States is tried, the Chief Justice shall preside: And no Person shall be convicted without the Concurrence of two thirds of the Members present.

Judgment in Cases of Impeachment shall not extend further than to removal from Office, and disqualification to hold and enjoy any Office of honor, Trust, or Profit under the United States: but the Party convicted shall nevertheless be liable and subject to Indictment, Trial, Judgment, and Punishment, according to Law.

SECTION 4. The Times, Places and Manner of holding Elections for Senators and Representatives, shall be prescribed in each State by the Legislature thereof; but the Congress may at any time by Law make or alter such Regulations, except as to the Places of chusing Senators.

The Congress shall assemble at least once in every Year, and such Meeting shall be on the first Monday in December, unless they shall by Law appoint a different Day.

SECTION 5. Each House shall be the Judge of the Elections, Returns, and Qualifications of its own Members, and a Majority of each shall constitute a Quorum to do Business; but a smaller Number may adjourn from day to day, and may be authorized to compel the Attendance of absent Members, in such Manner, and under such Penalties as each House may provide.

Each House may determine the Rules of its Proceedings, punish its Members for disorderly Behavior, and, with the Concurrence of two thirds, expel a Member.

Each House shall keep a Journal of its Proceedings, and from time to time publish the same, excepting such Parts as may in their Judgment require Secrecy; and the Yeas and Nays of the Members of either House on any question shall, at the Desire of one fifth of those Present, be entered on the Journal.

Neither House, during the Session of Congress, shall, without the Consent of the other, adjourn for more than three days, nor to any other Place than that in which the two Houses shall be sitting.

SECTION 6. The Senators and Representatives shall receive a Compensation for their Services, to be ascertained by Law, and paid out of the Treasury of the United States. They shall in all Cases, except Treason, Felony and Breach of the Peace, be privileged from Arrest during their Attendance at the Session of their respective Houses, and in going to and returning from the same; and for any Speech or Debate in either House, they shall not be questioned in any other Place.

No Senator or Representative shall, during the Time for which he was elected, be appointed to any civil Office under the Authority of the United States, which shall have been created, or the Emoluments whereof shall have been increased during such time; and no Person holding any Office under the United States, shall be a Member of either House during his Continuance in Office.

SECTION 7. All Bills for raising Revenue shall originate in the House of Representatives; but the Senate may propose or concur with Amendments as on other Bills.

Every Bill which shall have passed the House of Representatives and the Senate, shall, before it become a Law, be presented to the President of the United States; If he approve he shall sign it, but if not he shall return it, with his Objections to the House in which it shall have originated, who shall enter the Objections at large on their Journal, and proceed to reconsider it. If after such Reconsideration two thirds of that House shall agree to pass the Bill, it shall be sent together with the Objections, to the other House, by which it shall likewise be reconsidered, and if approved by two thirds of that House, it shall become a Law. But in all such Cases the Votes of both Houses shall be determined by Yeas and Nays, and the Names of the Persons voting for and against the Bill shall be entered on the Journal of each House respectively. If any Bill shall not be returned by the President within ten Days (Sundays excepted) after it shall have been presented to him, the Same shall be a Law, in like Manner as if he had signed it, unless the Congress by their Adjournment prevent its Return in which Case it shall not be a Law.

Every Order, Resolution, or Vote, to which the Concurrence of the Senate and House of Representatives may be necessary (except on a question of Adjournment) shall be presented to the President of the United States; and before the Same shall take Effect, shall be approved by him, or being disapproved by him, shall be repassed by two thirds of the Senate and House of Representatives, according to the Rules and Limitations prescribed in the Case of a Bill.

SECTION 8. The Congress shall have Power To lay and collect Taxes, Duties, Imposts and Excises, to pay the Debts and provide for the common Defence and general Welfare of the United States; but all Duties, Imposts and Excises shall be uniform throughout the United States;

To borrow Money on the credit of the United States;

To regulate Commerce with foreign Nations, and among the several States, and with the Indian Tribes;

To establish an uniform Rule of Naturalization, and uniform Laws on the subject of Bankruptcies throughout the United States;

To coin Money, regulate the Value thereof, and of foreign Coin, and fix the Standard of Weights and Measures;

To provide for the Punishment of counterfeiting the Securities and current Coin of the United States;

To establish Post Offices and post Roads;

To promote the Progress of Science and useful Arts, by securing for limited Times to Authors and Inventors the exclusive Right to their respective Writings and Discoveries;

To constitute Tribunals inferior to the supreme Court;

To define and punish Piracies and Felonies committed on the high Seas, and Offenses against the Law of Nations;

To declare War, grant Letters of Marque and Reprisal, and make Rules concerning Captures on Land and Water;

To raise and support Armies, but no Appropriation of Money to that Use shall be for a longer Term than two Years;

To provide and maintain a Navy;

To make Rules for the Government and Regulation of the land and naval Forces;

To provide for calling forth the Militia to execute the Laws of the Union, suppress Insurrections and repel Invasions;

To provide for organizing, arming, and disciplining, the Militia, and for governing such Part of them as may be employed in the Service of the United States, reserving to the States respectively, the Appointment of the Officers, and the Authority of training the Militia according to the discipline prescribed by Congress;

To exercise exclusive Legislation in all Cases whatsoever, over such District (not exceeding ten Miles square) as may, by Cession of particular States, and the Acceptance of Congress, become the Seat of the Government of the United States, and to exercise like Authority over all Places purchased by the Consent of the Legislature of the State in which the Same shall be, for the Erection of Forts, Magazines, Arsenals, dock-Yards, and other needful Buildings;—And

To make all Laws which shall be necessary and proper for carrying into Execution the foregoing Powers, and all other Powers vested by this Constitution in the Government of the United States, or in any Department or Officer thereof.

SECTION 9. The Migration or Importation of such Persons as any of the States now existing shall think proper to admit, shall not be prohibited by the Congress prior to the Year one thousand eight hundred and eight, but a Tax or duty may be imposed on such Importation, not exceeding ten dollars for each Person.

The privilege of the Writ of Habeas Corpus shall not be suspended, unless when in Cases of Rebellion or Invasion the public Safety may require it.

No Bill of Attainder or ex post facto Law shall be passed.

No Capitation, or other direct, Tax shall be laid, unless in Proportion to the Census or Enumeration herein before directed to be taken.

No Tax or Duty shall be laid on Articles exported from any State.

No Preference shall be given by any Regulation of Commerce or Revenue to the Ports of one State over those of another: nor shall Vessels bound to, or from, one State be obliged to enter, clear, or pay Duties in another.

No Money shall be drawn from the Treasury, but in Consequence of Appropriations made by Law; and a regular Statement and Account of the Receipts and Expenditures of all public Money shall be published from time to time.

No Title of Nobility shall be granted by the United States: And no Person holding any Office of Profit or Trust under them, shall, without the Consent of the Congress, accept of any present, Emolument, Office, or Title, of any kind whatever, from any King, Prince, or foreign State.

SECTION 10. No State shall enter into any Treaty, Alliance, or Confederation; grant Letters of Marque and Reprisal; coin Money; emit Bills of Credit; make any Thing but gold and silver Coin a Tender in Payment of Debts; pass any Bill of Attainder, ex post facto Law, or Law impairing the Obligation of Contracts, or grant any Title of Nobility.

No State shall, without the Consent of the Congress, lay any Imposts or Duties on Imports or Exports, except what may be absolutely necessary for executing its inspection Laws: and the net Produce of all Duties and Imposts, laid by any State on Imports or Exports, shall be for the Use of the Treasury of the United States; and all such Laws shall be subject to the Revision and Controul of the Congress.

No State shall, without the Consent of Congress, lay any Duty of Tonnage, keep Troops, or Ships of War in time of Peace, enter into any Agreement or Compact with another State, or with a foreign Power, or engage in War, unless actually invaded, or in such imminent Danger as will not admit of delay.

ARTICLE II

SECTION 1. The executive Power shall be vested in a President of the United States of America. He shall hold his Office during the Term of four Years, and, together with the Vice President, chosen for the same Term, be elected, as follows:

Each State shall appoint, in such Manner as the Legislature thereof may direct, a Number of Electors, equal to the whole Number of Senators and Representatives to which the State may be entitled in the Congress; but no Senator or Representative, or Person holding an Office of Trust or Profit under the United States, shall be appointed an Elector.

The Electors shall meet in their respective States, and vote by Ballot for two Persons, of whom one at least shall not be an Inhabitant of the same State with themselves. And they shall make a List of all the Persons voted for, and of the Number of Votes for each; which List they shall sign and certify, and transmit sealed to the Seat of the Government of the United States, directed to the President of the Senate. The President of the Senate shall, in the Presence of the Senate and House of Representatives, open all the Certificates, and the Votes shall then be counted. The Person having the greatest Number of Votes shall be the President, if such Number be a Majority of the whole Number of Electors appointed; and if there be more than one who have such Majority, and have an equal Number of Votes, then the House of Representatives shall immediately chuse by Ballot one of them for President; and if no Person have a Majority, then from the five highest on the List the said House shall in like Manner chuse the President. But in chusing the President, the Votes shall be taken by States, the Representation from each State having one Vote; A quorum for this Purpose shall consist of a Member or Members from two thirds of the States, and a Majority of all the States shall be necessary to a Choice. In every Case, after the Choice of the President, the Person having the greater Number of Votes of the Electors shall be the Vice President. But if there should remain two or more who have equal Votes, the Senate shall chuse from them by Ballot the Vice President.

The Congress may determine the Time of chusing the Electors, and the Day on which they shall give their Votes; which Day shall be the same throughout the United States.

No person except a natural born Citizen, or a Citizen of the United States, at the time of the Adoption of this Constitution, shall be eligible to the Office of President; neither shall any Person be eligible to that Office who shall not have attained to the Age of thirty five Years, and been fourteen Years a Resident within the United States.

In Case of the Removal of the President from Office, or of his Death, Resignation or Inability to discharge the Powers and Duties of the said Office, the same shall devolve on the Vice President, and the Congress may by Law provide for the Case of Removal, Death, Resignation or Inability, both of the President and Vice President, declaring what Officer shall then act as President, and such Officer shall act accordingly, until the Disability be removed, or a President shall be elected.

The President shall, at stated Times, receive for his Services, a Compensation, which shall neither be increased nor diminished during the Period for which he shall have been elected, and he shall not receive within that Period any other Emolument from the United States, or any of them.

Before he enter on the Execution of his Office, he shall take the following Oath or Affirmation: "I do solemnly swear (or affirm) that I will faithfully execute the Office of President of the United States, and will to the best of my Ability, preserve, protect and defend the Constitution of the United States."

SECTION 2. The President shall be Commander in Chief of the Army and Navy of the United States, and of the Militia of the several States, when called into the actual Service of the United States; he may require the Opinion, in writing, of the principal Officer in each of the executive Departments, upon any Subject relating to the Duties of their respective Offices, and he shall have Power to grant Reprieves and Pardons for Offenses against the United States, except in Cases of Impeachment.

He shall have Power, by and with the Advice and Consent of the Senate to make Treaties, provided two thirds of the Senators present concur; and he shall nominate, and by and with the Advice and Consent of the Senate, shall appoint Ambassadors, other public Ministers and Consuls, Judges of the supreme Court, and all other Officers of the United States, whose Appointments are not herein otherwise provided for, and which shall be established by Law; but the Congress may by Law vest the Appointment of such inferior Officers, as they think proper, in the President alone, in the Courts of Law, or in the Heads of Departments.

The President shall have Power to fill up all Vacancies that may happen during the Recess of the Senate, by granting Commissions which shall expire at the End of their next Session.

SECTION 3. He shall from time to time give to the Congress Information of the State of the Union, and recommend to their Consideration such Measures as he shall judge necessary and expedient; he may, on extraordinary Occasions, convene both Houses, or either of them, and in Case of Disagreement between them, with Respect to the Time of Adjournment, he may adjourn them to such Time as he shall think proper; he shall receive Ambassadors and other public Ministers; he shall take Care that the Laws be faithfully executed, and shall Commission all the Officers of the United States.

SECTION 4. The President, Vice President and all civil Officers of the United States, shall be removed from Office on Impeachment for, and Conviction of, Treason, Bribery, or other high Crimes and Misdemeanors.

ARTICLE III

SECTION 1. The judicial Power of the United States, shall be vested in one supreme Court, and in such inferior Courts as the Congress may from time to time ordain and establish. The Judges, both of the supreme and inferior Courts, shall hold their Offices during good Behaviour, and shall, at stated Times, receive for their Services a Compensation, which shall not be diminished during their Continuance in Office.

SECTION 2. The judicial Power shall extend to all Cases, in Law and Equity, arising under this Constitution, the Laws of the United States, and Treaties made, or which shall be made, under their Authority;—to all Cases affecting Ambassadors, other public Ministers and Consuls;—to all Cases of admiralty and maritime Jurisdiction;—to Controversies to which the United States shall be a Party;—to Controversies between two or more States;—between a State and Citizens of another State;—between Citizens of different States;—between Citizens of the same State claiming Lands under Grants of different States, and between a State, or the Citizens thereof, and foreign States, Citizens or Subjects.

In all Cases affecting Ambassadors, other public Ministers and Consuls, and those in which a State shall be a Party, the supreme Court shall have original Jurisdiction. In all the other Cases before mentioned, the supreme Court shall have appellate Jurisdiction, both as to Law and Fact, with such Exceptions, and under such Regulations as the Congress shall make.

The Trial of all Crimes, except in Cases of Impeachment, shall be by Jury; and such Trial shall be held in the State where the said Crimes shall have been committed; but when not committed within any State, the Trial shall be at such Place or Places as the Congress may by Law have directed.

SECTION 3. Treason against the United States, shall consist only in levying War against them, or, in adhering to their Enemies, giving them Aid and Comfort. No Person shall be convicted of Treason unless on the Testimony of two Witnesses to the same overt Act, or on Confession in open Court.

The Congress shall have Power to declare the Punishment of Treason, but no Attainder of Treason shall work Corruption of Blood, or Forfeiture except during the Life of the Person attainted.

ARTICLE IV

SECTION 1. Full Faith and Credit shall be given in each State to the public Acts, Records, and judicial Proceedings of every other State. And the Congress may by general Laws prescribe the Manner in which such Acts, Records and Proceedings shall be proved, and the Effect thereof.

SECTION 2. The Citizens of each State shall be entitled to all Privileges and Immunities of Citizens in the several States.

A Person charged in any State with Treason, Felony, or other Crime, who shall flee from Justice, and be found in another State, shall on Demand of the executive Authority of the State from which he fled, be delivered up, to be removed to the State having Jurisdiction of the Crime.

No Person held to Service or Labour in one State, under the Laws thereof, escaping into another, shall, in Consequence of any Law or Regulation therein, be discharged from such Service or Labour, but shall be delivered up on Claim of the Party to whom such Service or Labour may be due.

SECTION 3. New States may be admitted by the Congress into this Union; but no new State shall be formed or erected within the Jurisdiction of any other

State; nor any State be formed by the Junction of two or more States, or Parts of States, without the Consent of the Legislatures of the States concerned as well as of the Congress.

The Congress shall have Power to dispose of and make all needful Rules and Regulations respecting the Territory or other Property belonging to the United States; and nothing in this Constitution shall be so construed as to Prejudice any Claims of the United States, or of any particular State.

SECTION 4. The United States shall guarantee to every State in this Union a Republican Form of Government, and shall protect each of them against Invasion; and on Application of the Legislature, or of the Executive (when the Legislature cannot be convened) against domestic Violence.

ARTICLE V

The Congress, whenever two thirds of both Houses shall deem it necessary, shall propose Amendments to this Constitution, or, on the Application of the Legislatures of two thirds of the several States, shall call a Convention for proposing Amendments, which, in either Case, shall be valid to all Intents and Purposes, as part of this Constitution, when ratified by the Legislatures of three fourths of the several States, or by Conventions in three fourths thereof, as the one or the other Mode of Ratification may be proposed by the Congress; Provided that no Amendment which may be made prior to the Year One thousand eight hundred and eight shall in any Manner affect the first and fourth Clauses in the Ninth Section of the first Article; and that no State, without its Consent, shall be deprived of its equal Suffrage in the Senate.

ARTICLE VI

All Debts contracted and Engagements entered into, before the Adoption of this Constitution shall be as valid against the United States under this Constitution, as under the Confederation.

This Constitution, and the Laws of the United States which shall be made in Pursuance thereof; and all Treaties made, or which shall be made, under the Authority of the United States, shall be the supreme Law of the Land; and the Judges in every State shall be bound thereby, any Thing in the Constitution or Laws of any State to the Contrary notwithstanding.

The Senators and Representatives before mentioned, and the Members of the several State Legislatures, and all executive and judicial Officers, both of the United States and of the several States, shall be bound by Oath or Affirmation, to support this Constitution; but no religious Test shall ever be required as a Qualification to any Office or public Trust under the United States.

ARTICLE VII

The Ratification of the Conventions of nine States shall be sufficient for the Establishment of this Constitution between the States so ratifying the Same.

AMENDMENT I [1791]

Congress shall make no law respecting an establishment of religion, or prohibiting the free exercise thereof; or abridging the freedom of speech, or of the press; or the right of the people peaceably to assemble, and to petition the Government for a redress of grievances.

AMENDMENT II [1791]

A well regulated Militia, being necessary to the security of a free State, the right of the people to keep and bear Arms, shall not be infringed.

AMENDMENT III [1791]

No Soldier shall, in time of peace be quartered in any house, without the consent of the Owner, nor in time of war, but in a manner to be prescribed by law.

AMENDMENT IV [1791]

The right of the people to be secure in their persons, houses, papers, and effects, against unreasonable searches and seizures, shall not be violated, and no Warrants shall issue, but upon probable cause, supported by Oath or affirmation, and particularly describing the place to be searched, and the persons or things to be seized.

AMENDMENT V [1791]

No person shall be held to answer for a capital, or otherwise infamous crime, unless on a presentment or indictment of a Grand Jury, except in cases arising in the land or naval forces, or in the Militia, when in actual service in time of War or public danger; nor shall any person be subject for the same offense to be twice put in jeopardy of life or limb; nor shall be compelled in any criminal case to be a witness against himself, nor be deprived of life, liberty, or property, without due process of law; nor shall private property be taken for public use, without just compensation.

AMENDMENT VI [1791]

In all criminal prosecutions, the accused shall enjoy the right to a speedy and public trial, by an impartial jury of the State and district wherein the crime shall have been committed, which district shall have been previously ascertained by law, and to be informed of the nature and cause of the accusation; to be confronted with the witnesses against him; to have compulsory process for obtaining witnesses in his favor, and to have the Assistance of Counsel for his defence.

AMENDMENT VII [1791]

In Suits at common law, where the value in controversy shall exceed twenty dollars, the right of trial by jury shall be preserved, and no fact tried by a jury, shall be otherwise re-examined in any Court of the United States, than according to the rules of the common law.

AMENDMENT VIII [1791]

Excessive bail shall not be required, nor excessive fines imposed, nor cruel and unusual punishments inflicted.

AMENDMENT IX [1791]

The enumeration in the Constitution, of certain rights, shall not be construed to deny or disparage others retained by the people.

AMENDMENT X [1791]

The powers not delegated to the United States by the Constitution, nor prohibited by it to the States, are reserved to the States respectively, or to the people.

AMENDMENT XI [1798]

The Judicial power of the United States shall not be construed to extend to any suit in law or equity, commenced or prosecuted against one of the United States by Citizens of another State, or by Citizens or Subjects of any Foreign State.

AMENDMENT XII [1804]

The Electors shall meet in their respective states, and vote by ballot for President and Vice-President, one of whom, at least, shall not be an inhabitant of the same state with themselves; they shall name in their ballots the person voted for as President, and in distinct ballots the person voted for as Vice-President, and they shall make distinct lists of all persons voted for as President, and of all persons voted for as Vice-President, and of the number of votes for each, which lists they shall sign and certify, and transmit sealed to the seat of the government of the United States, directed to the President of the Senate;—The President of the Senate shall, in the presence of the Senate and House of Representatives, open all the certificates and the votes shall then be counted;—The person having the greatest number of votes for President, shall be the President, if such number be a majority of the whole number of Electors appointed; and if no person have such majority, then from the persons having the highest numbers not exceeding three on the list of those voted for as President, the House of Representatives shall choose immediately, by ballot, the President. But in choosing the President, the votes shall be taken by states, the representation from each state having one vote; a quorum for this purpose shall consist of a member or members from two-thirds of the states, and a majority of all states shall be necessary to a choice. And if the House of Representatives shall not choose a President whenever the right of choice shall devolve upon them, before the fourth day of March next following, then the Vice-President shall act as President, as in the case of the death or other constitutional disability of the President.—The person having the greatest number of votes as Vice-President, shall be the Vice-President, if such number be a majority of the whole number of Electors appointed, and if no person have a majority, then from the two highest numbers on the list, the Senate shall choose the Vice-President; a quorum for the purpose shall consist of two-thirds of the whole number of Senators, and a majority of the whole number shall be necessary to a choice. But no person constitutionally ineligible to the office of President shall be eligible to that of Vice-President of the United States.

AMENDMENT XIII [1865]

SECTION 1. Neither slavery nor involuntary servitude, except as a punishment for crime whereof the party shall have been duly convicted, shall exist within the United States, or any place subject to their jurisdiction.

SECTION 2. Congress shall have power to enforce this article by appropriate legislation.

AMENDMENT XIV [1868]

SECTION 1. All persons born or naturalized in the United States, and subject to the jurisdiction thereof, are citizens of the United States and of the State wherein they reside. No State shall make or enforce any law which shall abridge the privileges or immunities of citizens of the United States; nor shall any State deprive any person of life, liberty, or property, without due process of law; nor deny to any person within its jurisdiction the equal protection of the laws.

SECTION 2. Representatives shall be apportioned among the several States according to their respective numbers, counting the whole number of persons in each State, excluding Indians not taxed. But when the right to vote at any election for the choice of electors for President and Vice President of the United States, Representatives in Congress, the Executive and Judicial officers of a State, or the members of the Legislature thereof, is denied to any of the male inhabitants of such State, being twenty-one years of age, and citizens of the United States, or in any way abridged, except for participation in rebellion, or other crime, the basis of representation therein shall be reduced in the proportion which the number of such male citizens shall bear to the whole number of male citizens twenty-one years of age in such State.

SECTION 3. No person shall be a Senator or Representative in Congress, or elector of President and Vice President, or hold any office, civil or military, under the United States, or under any State, who having previously taken an oath, as a member of Congress, or as an officer of the United States, or as a member of any State legislature, or as an executive or judicial officer of any State, to support the Constitution of the United States, shall have engaged in insurrection or rebellion against the same, or given aid or comfort to the enemies thereof. But Congress may by a vote of two-thirds of each House, remove such disability.

SECTION 4. The validity of the public debt of the United States, authorized by law, including debts incurred for payment of pensions and bounties for services in suppressing insurrection or rebellion, shall not be questioned. But neither the United States nor any State shall assume or pay any debt or obligation incurred in aid of insurrection or rebellion against the United States, or any claim for the loss or emancipation of any slave; but all such debts, obligations and claims shall be held illegal and void.

SECTION 5. The Congress shall have power to enforce, by appropriate legislation, the provisions of this article.

AMENDMENT XV [1870]

SECTION 1. The right of citizens of the United States to vote shall not be denied or abridged by the United States or by any State on account of race, color, or previous condition of servitude.

SECTION 2. The Congress shall have power to enforce this article by appropriate legislation.

AMENDMENT XVI [1913]

The Congress shall have power to lay and collect taxes on incomes, from whatever source derived, without apportionment among the several States, and without regard to any census or enumeration.

AMENDMENT XVII [1913]

SECTION 1. The Senate of the United States shall be composed of two Senators from each State, elected by the people thereof, for six years; and each Senator shall have one vote. The electors in each State shall have the qualifications requisite for electors of the most numerous branch of the State legislatures.

SECTION 2. When vacancies happen in the representation of any State in the Senate, the executive authority of such State shall issue writs of election to fill such vacancies: Provided, That the legislature of any State may empower the executive thereof to make temporary appointments until the people fill the vacancies by election as the legislature may direct.

SECTION 3. This amendment shall not be so construed as to affect the election or term of any Senator chosen before it becomes valid as part of the Constitution.

AMENDMENT XVIII [1919]

SECTION 1. After one year from the ratification of this article the manufacture, sale, or transportation of intoxicating liquors within, the importation thereof into, or the exportation thereof from the United States and all territory subject to the jurisdiction thereof for beverage purposes is hereby prohibited.

SECTION 2. The Congress and the several States shall have concurrent power to enforce this article by appropriate legislation.

SECTION 3. This article shall be inoperative unless it shall have been ratified as an amendment to the Constitution by the legislatures of the several States, as provided in the Constitution, within seven years from the date of the submission hereof to the States by the Congress.

AMENDMENT XIX [1920]

SECTION 1. The right of citizens of the United States to vote shall not be denied or abridged by the United States or by any State on account of sex.

SECTION 2. Congress shall have power to enforce this article by appropriate legislation.

AMENDMENT XX [1933]

SECTION 1. The terms of the President and Vice President shall end at noon on the 20th day of January, and the terms of Senators and Representatives at noon on the 3d day of January, of the years in which such terms would have ended if this article had not been ratified; and the terms of their successors shall then begin.

SECTION 2. The Congress shall assemble at least once in every year, and such meeting shall begin at noon on the 3d day of January, unless they shall by law appoint a different day.

SECTION 3. If, at the time fixed for the beginning of the term of the President, the President elect shall have died, the Vice President elect shall become President. If the President shall not have been chosen before the time fixed for the beginning of his term, or if the President elect shall have failed to qualify, then the Vice President elect shall act as President until a President shall have qualified; and the Congress may by law provide for the case wherein neither a President elect nor a Vice President elect shall have qualified, declaring who shall then act as President, or the manner in which one who is to act shall be selected, and such person shall act accordingly until a President or Vice President shall have qualified.

SECTION 4. The Congress may by law provide for the case of the death of any of the persons from whom the House of Representatives may choose a President whenever the right of choice shall have devolved upon them, and for the case of the death of any of the persons from whom the Senate may choose a Vice President whenever the right of choice shall have devolved upon them.

SECTION 5. Sections 1 and 2 shall take effect on the 15th day of October following the ratification of this article.

SECTION 6. This article shall be inoperative unless it shall have been ratified as an amendment to the Constitution by the legislatures of three-fourths of the several States within seven years from the date of its submission.

AMENDMENT XXI [1933]

SECTION 1. The eighteenth article of amendment to the Constitution of the United States is hereby repealed.

SECTION 2. The transportation or importation into any State, Territory, or possession of the United States for delivery or use therein of intoxicating liquors, in violation of the laws thereof, is hereby prohibited.

SECTION 3. This article shall be inoperative unless it shall have been ratified as an amendment to the Constitution by conventions in the several States, as provided in the Constitution, within seven years from the date of the submission hereof to the States by the Congress.

AMENDMENT XXII [1951]

SECTION 1. No person shall be elected to the office of the President more than twice, and no person who has held the office of President, or acted as President, for more than two years of a term to which some other person was elected President shall be elected to the office of President more than once. But this Article shall not apply to any person holding the office of President when this Article was proposed by the Congress, and shall not prevent any person who may be holding the office of President, or acting as President, during the term within which this Article becomes operative from holding the office of President or acting as President during the remainder of such term.

SECTION 2. This article shall be inoperative unless it shall have been ratified as an amendment to the Constitution by the legislatures of three-fourths of the several States within seven years from the date of its submission to the States by the Congress.

AMENDMENT XXIII [1961]

SECTION 1. The District constituting the seat of Government of the United States shall appoint in such manner as the Congress may direct:

A number of electors of President and Vice President equal to the whole number of Senators and Representatives in Congress to which the District would be entitled if it were a State, but in no event more than the least populous state; they shall be in addition to those appointed by the states, but they shall be considered, for the purposes of the election of President and Vice President, to be electors appointed by a state; and they shall meet in the District and perform such duties as provided by the twelfth article of amendment.

SECTION 2. The Congress shall have power to enforce this article by appropriate legislation.

AMENDMENT XXIV [1964]

SECTION 1. The right of citizens of the United States to vote in any primary or other election for President or Vice President, for electors for President or Vice President, or for Senator or Representative in Congress, shall not be denied or abridged by the United States, or any State by reason of failure to pay any poll tax or other tax.

SECTION 2. The Congress shall have power to enforce this article by appropriate legislation.

AMENDMENT XXV [1967]

SECTION 1. In case of the removal of the President from office or of his death or resignation, the Vice President shall become President.

SECTION 2. Whenever there is a vacancy in the office of the Vice President, the President shall nominate a Vice President who shall take office upon confirmation by a majority vote of both Houses of Congress.

SECTION 3. Whenever the President transmits to the President pro tempore of the Senate and the Speaker of the House of Representatives his written declaration that he is unable to discharge the powers and duties of his office, and until he transmits to them a written declaration to the contrary, such powers and duties shall be discharged by the Vice President as Acting President.

SECTION 4. Whenever the Vice President and a majority of either the principal officers of the executive departments or of such other body as Congress may by law provide, transmit to the President pro tempore of the Senate and the Speaker of the House of Representatives their written declaration that the President is unable to discharge the powers and duties of his office, the Vice President shall immediately assume the powers and duties of the office as Acting President.

Thereafter, when the President transmits to the President pro tempore of the Senate and the Speaker of the House of Representatives his written declaration that no inability exists, he shall resume the powers and duties of his office unless the Vice President and a majority of either the principal officers of the executive department or of such other body as Congress may by law provide, transmit within four days to the President pro tempore of the Senate and the Speaker of the House of Representatives their written declaration that the President is unable to discharge the powers and duties of his office. Thereupon Congress shall decide the issue, assembling within forty-eight hours for that purpose if not in session. If the Congress, within twenty-one days after receipt of the latter written declaration, or, if Congress is not in session, within twenty-one days after Congress is required to assemble, determines by two-thirds vote of both Houses that the President is unable to discharge the powers and duties of his office, the Vice President shall continue to discharge the same as Acting President; otherwise, the President shall resume the powers and duties of his office.

AMENDMENT XXVI [1971]

SECTION 1. The right of citizens of the United States, who are eighteen years of age or older, to vote shall not be denied or abridged by the United States or by any State on account of age.

SECTION 2. The Congress shall have power to enforce this article by appropriate legislation.

AMENDMENT XXVII [1992]

No law, varying the compensation for the services of the Senators and Representatives, shall take effect, until an election of Representatives shall have intervened.

Supreme Court Justices Since 1900

Chief Justices

Name	Years of Service	State App'd from	Appointing President	Age App'd	Political Affiliation	Educational Background*
Fuller, Melville Weston	1888–1910	Illinois	Cleveland	55	Democrat	Bowdoin College; studied at Harvard Law School
White, Edward Douglass	1910–1921	Louisiana	Taft	65	Democrat	Mount St. Mary's College; Georgetown College (now University)
Taft, William Howard	1921–1930	Connecticut	Harding	64	Republican	Yale; Cincinnati Law School
Hughes, Charles Evans	1930–1941	New York	Hoover	68	Republican	Colgate University; Brown; Columbia Law School
Stone, Harlan Fiske	1941–1946	New York	Roosevelt, F.	69	Republican	Amherst College; Columbia
Vinson, Frederick Moore	1946–1953	Kentucky	Truman	56	Democrat	Centre College
Warren, Earl	1953–1969	California	Eisenhower	62	Republican	University of California, Berkeley
Burger, Warren Earl	1969–1986	Virginia	Nixon	62	Republican	University of Minnesota; St. Paul College of Law (Mitchell College)
Rehnquist, William Hubbs	1986–2005	Virginia	Reagan	62	Republican	Stanford; Harvard; Stanford University Law School
Roberts, John G., Jr.	2005–present	District of Columbia	G. W. Bush	50	Republican	Harvard; Harvard Law School

*Source: Educational background information derived from Elder Witt, *Guide to the U.S. Supreme Court*, 2d ed. (Washington, D.C.: Congressional Quarterly Press, Inc., 1990). Reprinted with the permission of the publisher.

Associate Justices

Name	Years of Service	State App'd from	Appointing President	Age App'd	Political Affiliation	Educational Background*
Harlan, John Marshall	1877–1911	Kentucky	Hayes	61	Republican	Centre College; studied law at Transylvania University
Gray, Horace	1882–1902	Massachusetts	Arthur	54	Republican	Harvard College; Harvard Law School
Brewer, David Josiah	1890–1910	Kansas	Harrison	53	Republican	Wesleyan University; Yale; Albany Law School
Brown, Henry Billings	1891–1906	Michigan	Harrison	55	Republican	Yale; studied at Yale Law School and Harvard Law School
Shiras, George, Jr.	1892–1903	Pennsylvania	Harrison	61	Republican	Ohio University; Yale; studied law at Yale and privately
White, Edward Douglass	1894–1910	Louisiana	Cleveland	49	Democrat	Mount St. Mary's College; Georgetown College (now University)
Peckham, Rufus Wheeler	1896–1909	New York	Cleveland	58	Democrat	Read law in father's firm

Associate Justices (Continued)						
Name	Years of Service	State App'd from	Appointing President	Age App'd	Political Affiliation	Educational Background*
McKenna, Joseph	1898–1925	California	McKinley	55	Republican	Benicia Collegiate Institute, Law Dept.
Holmes, Oliver Wendell, Jr.	1902–1932	Massachusetts	Roosevelt, T.	61	Republican	Harvard College; studied law at Harvard Law School
Day, William Rufus	1903–1922	Ohio	Roosevelt, T.	54	Republican	University of Michigan; University of Michigan Law School
Moody, William Henry	1906–1910	Massachusetts	Roosevelt, T.	53	Republican	Harvard; Harvard Law School
Lurton, Horace Harmon	1910–1914	Tennessee	Taft	66	Democrat	University of Chicago; Cumberland Law School
Hughes, Charles Evans	1910–1916	New York	Taft	48	Republican	Colgate University; Brown University; Columbia Law School
Van Devanter, Willis	1911–1937	Wyoming	Taft	52	Republican	Indiana Asbury University; University of Cincinnati Law School
Lamar, Joseph Rucker	1911–1916	Georgia	Taft	54	Democrat	University of Georgia; Bethany College; Washington and Lee University
Pitney, Mahlon	1912–1922	New Jersey	Taft	54	Republican	College of New Jersey (Princeton); read law under father
McReynolds, James Clark	1914–1941	Tennessee	Wilson	52	Democrat	Vanderbilt University; University of Virginia
Brandeis, Louis Dembitz	1916–1939	Massachusetts	Wilson	60	Democrat	Harvard Law School
Clarke, John Hessin	1916–1922	Ohio	Wilson	59	Democrat	Western Reserve University; read law under father
Sutherland, George	1922–1938	Utah	Harding	60	Republican	Brigham Young Academy; one year at University of Michigan Law School
Butler, Pierce	1923–1939	Minnesota	Harding	57	Democrat	Carleton College
Sanford, Edward Terry	1923–1930	Tennessee	Harding	58	Republican	University of Tennessee; Harvard; Harvard Law School
Stone, Harlan Fiske	1925–1941	New York	Coolidge	53	Republican	Amherst College; Columbia University Law School
Roberts, Owen Josephus	1930–1945	Pennsylvania	Hoover	55	Republican	University of Pennsylvania; University of Pennsylvania Law School
Cardozo, Benjamin Nathan	1932–1938	New York	Hoover	62	Democrat	Columbia University; two years at Columbia Law School
Black, Hugo Lafayette	1937–1971	Alabama	Roosevelt, F.	51	Democrat	Birmingham Medical College; University of Alabama Law School
Reed, Stanley Forman	1938–1957	Kentucky	Roosevelt, F.	54	Democrat	Kentucky Wesleyan University; Foreman Yale; Columbia University
Frankfurter, Felix	1939–1962	Massachusetts	Roosevelt, F.	57	Independent	College of the City of New York; Harvard Law School
Douglas, William Orville	1939–1975	Connecticut	Roosevelt, F.	41	Democrat	Whitman College; Columbia University Law School
Murphy, Frank	1940–1949	Michigan	Roosevelt, F.	50	Democrat	University of Michigan; Lincoln's Inn, London; Trinity College
Byrnes, James Francis	1941–1942	South Carolina	Roosevelt, F.	62	Democrat	Read law privately

Associate Justices (Continued)						
Name	**Years of Service**	**State App'd from**	**Appointing President**	**Age App'd**	**Political Affiliation**	**Educational Background***
Jackson, Robert Houghwout	1941–1954	New York	Roosevelt, F.	49	Democrat	Albany Law School
Rutledge, Wiley Blount	1943–1949	Iowa	Roosevelt, F.	49	Democrat	University of Wisconsin; University of Colorado
Burton, Harold Hitz	1945–1958	Ohio	Truman	57	Republican	Bowdoin College; Harvard University Law School
Clark, Thomas Campbell	1949–1967	Texas	Truman	50	Democrat	University of Texas
Minton, Sherman	1949–1956	Indiana	Truman	59	Democrat	Indiana University College of Law; Yale Law School
Harlan, John Marshall	1955–1971	New York	Eisenhower	56	Republican	Princeton; Oxford University; New York Law School
Brennan, William J., Jr.	1956–1990	New Jersey	Eisenhower	50	Democrat	University of Pennsylvania; Harvard Law School
Whittaker, Charles Evans	1957–1962	Missouri	Eisenhower	56	Republican	University of Kansas City Law School
Stewart, Potter	1958–1981	Ohio	Eisenhower	43	Republican	Yale; Yale Law School
White, Byron Raymond	1962–1993	Colorado	Kennedy	45	Democrat	University of Colorado; Oxford University; Yale Law School
Goldberg, Arthur Joseph	1962–1965	Illinois	Kennedy	54	Democrat	Northwestern University
Fortas, Abe	1965–1969	Tennessee	Johnson, L.	55	Democrat	Southwestern College; Yale Law School
Marshall, Thurgood	1967–1991	New York	Johnson, L.	59	Democrat	Lincoln University; Howard University Law School
Blackmun, Harry A.	1970–1994	Minnesota	Nixon	62	Republican	Harvard; Harvard Law School
Powell, Lewis F., Jr.	1972–1987	Virginia	Nixon	65	Democrat	Washington and Lee University; Harvard Law School
Rehnquist, William H.	1972–1986	Arizona	Nixon	48	Republican	Stanford; Harvard; Stanford University Law School
Stevens, John Paul	1975–present	Illinois	Ford	55	Republican	University of Colorado; Northwestern University Law School
O'Connor, Sandra Day	1981–2006	Arizona	Reagan	51	Republican	Stanford; Stanford University Law School
Scalia, Antonin	1986–present	Virginia	Reagan	50	Republican	Georgetown University; Harvard Law School
Kennedy, Anthony M.	1988–present	California	Reagan	52	Republican	Stanford; London School of Economics; Harvard Law School
Souter, David Hackett	1990–present	New Hampshire	Bush, G. H. W.	51	Republican	Harvard; Oxford University
Thomas, Clarence	1991–present	District of Columbia	Bush, G. H. W.	43	Republican	Holy Cross College; Yale Law Columbia School
Ginsburg, Ruth Bader	1993–present	District of Columbia	Clinton	60	Democrat	Cornell University; Columbia Law School
Breyer, Stephen G.	1994–present	Massachusetts	Clinton	55	Democrat	Stanford; Oxford University; Harvard Law School
Alito, Samuel Anthony, Jr.	2006–present	New Jersey	G. W. Bush	55	Republican	Princeton University; Yale Law School
Sotomayor, Sonia	2009–present	New York	Obama	55	Democrat	Princeton University; Yale Law School
Kagan, Elena	2010–present	District of Columbia	Obama	50	Democrat	Princeton and Oxford Universities; Harvard Law School

Appendix D

PARTY CONTROL OF CONGRESS SINCE 1900

Congress	Years	President	Majority Party in House	Majority Party in Senate
57th	1901–1903	T. Roosevelt	Republican	Republican
58th	1903–1905	T. Roosevelt	Republican	Republican
59th	1905–1907	T. Roosevelt	Republican	Republican
60th	1907–1909	T. Roosevelt	Republican	Republican
61st	1909–1911	Taft	Republican	Republican
62d	1911–1913	Taft	Democratic	Republican
63d	1913–1915	Wilson	Democratic	Democratic
64th	1915–1917	Wilson	Democratic	Democratic
65th	1917–1919	Wilson	Democratic	Democratic
66th	1919–1921	Wilson	Republican	Republican
67th	1921–1923	Harding	Republican	Republican
68th	1923–1925	Coolidge	Republican	Republican
69th	1925–1927	Coolidge	Republican	Republican
70th	1927–1929	Coolidge	Republican	Republican
71st	1929–1931	Hoover	Republican	Republican
72d	1931–1933	Hoover	Democratic	Republican
73d	1933–1935	F. Roosevelt	Democratic	Democratic
74th	1935–1937	F. Roosevelt	Democratic	Democratic
75th	1937–1939	F. Roosevelt	Democratic	Democratic
76th	1939–1941	F. Roosevelt	Democratic	Democratic
77th	1941–1943	F. Roosevelt	Democratic	Democratic
78th	1943–1945	F. Roosevelt	Democratic	Democratic
79th	1945–1947	Truman	Democratic	Democratic
80th	1947–1949	Truman	Republican	Democratic
81st	1949–1951	Truman	Democratic	Democratic
82d	1951–1953	Truman	Democratic	Democratic
83d	1953–1955	Eisenhower	Republican	Republican
84th	1955–1957	Eisenhower	Democratic	Democratic
85th	1957–1959	Eisenhower	Democratic	Democratic
86th	1959–1961	Eisenhower	Democratic	Democratic
87th	1961–1963	Kennedy	Democratic	Democratic
88th	1963–1965	Kennedy/Johnson	Democratic	Democratic
89th	1965–1967	Johnson	Democratic	Democratic
90th	1967–1969	Johnson	Democratic	Democratic
91st	1969–1971	Nixon	Democratic	Democratic
92d	1971–1973	Nixon	Democratic	Democratic
93d	1973–1975	Nixon/Ford	Democratic	Democratic
94th	1975–1977	Ford	Democratic	Democratic
95th	1977–1979	Carter	Democratic	Democratic
96th	1979–1981	Carter	Democratic	Democratic
97th	1981–1983	Reagan	Democratic	Republican
98th	1983–1985	Reagan	Democratic	Republican
99th	1985–1987	Reagan	Democratic	Republican
100th	1987–1989	Reagan	Democratic	Democratic
101st	1989–1991	G. H. W. Bush	Democratic	Democratic
102d	1991–1993	G. H. W. Bush	Democratic	Democratic
103d	1993–1995	Clinton	Democratic	Democratic
104th	1995–1997	Clinton	Republican	Republican
105th	1997–1999	Clinton	Republican	Republican
106th	1999–2001	Clinton	Republican	Republican
107th	2001–2003	G. W. Bush	Republican	Democratic
108th	2003–2005	G. W. Bush	Republican	Republican
109th	2005–2007	G. W. Bush	Republican	Republican
110th	2007–2009	G. W. Bush	Democratic	Democratic
111th	2009–2011	Obama	Democratic	Democratic
112th	2011–2013	Obama	Republican	Democratic

Appendix E

Information on U.S. Presidents

	Term of Service	Age at Inauguration	Party Affiliation	College or University	Occupation or Profession
1. George Washington	1789–1797	57	None		Planter
2. John Adams	1797–1801	61	Federalist	Harvard	Lawyer
3. Thomas Jefferson	1801–1809	57	Democratic-Republican	William and Mary	Planter, Lawyer
4. James Madison	1809–1817	57	Democratic-Republican	Princeton	Lawyer
5. James Monroe	1817–1825	58	Democratic-Republican	William and Mary	Lawyer
6. John Quincy Adams	1825–1829	57	Democratic-Republican	Harvard	Lawyer
7. Andrew Jackson	1829–1837	61	Democrat		Lawyer
8. Martin Van Buren	1837–1841	54	Democrat		Lawyer
9. William H. Harrison	1841	68	Whig	Hampden-Sydney	Soldier
10. John Tyler	1841–1845	51	Whig	William and Mary	Lawyer
11. James K. Polk	1845–1849	49	Democrat	U. of N. Carolina	Lawyer
12. Zachary Taylor	1849–1850	64	Whig		Soldier
13. Millard Fillmore	1850–1853	50	Whig		Lawyer
14. Franklin Pierce	1853–1857	48	Democrat	Bowdoin	Lawyer
15. James Buchanan	1857–1861	65	Democrat	Dickinson	Lawyer
16. Abraham Lincoln	1861–1865	52	Republican		Lawyer
17. Andrew Johnson	1865–1869	56	National Union†		Tailor
18. Ulysses S. Grant	1869–1877	46	Republican	U.S. Mil. Academy	Soldier
19. Rutherford B. Hayes	1877–1881	54	Republican	Kenyon	Lawyer
20. James A. Garfield	1881	49	Republican	Williams	Lawyer
21. Chester A. Arthur	1881–1885	51	Republican	Union	Lawyer
22. Grover Cleveland	1885–1889	47	Democrat		Lawyer
23. Benjamin Harrison	1889–1893	55	Republican	Miami	Lawyer
24. Grover Cleveland	1893–1897	55	Democrat		Lawyer
25. William McKinley	1897–1901	54	Republican	Allegheny College	Lawyer
26. Theodore Roosevelt	1901–1909	42	Republican	Harvard	Author
27. William H. Taft	1909–1913	51	Republican	Yale	Lawyer
28. Woodrow Wilson	1913–1921	56	Democrat	Princeton	Educator
29. Warren G. Harding	1921–1923	55	Republican		Editor
30. Calvin Coolidge	1923–1929	51	Republican	Amherst	Lawyer
31. Herbert C. Hoover	1929–1933	54	Republican	Stanford	Engineer
32. Franklin D. Roosevelt	1933–1945	51	Democrat	Harvard	Lawyer
33. Harry S Truman	1945–1953	60	Democrat		Businessman
34. Dwight D. Eisenhower	1953–1961	62	Republican	U.S. Mil. Academy	Soldier
35. John F. Kennedy	1961–1963	43	Democrat	Harvard	Author
36. Lyndon B. Johnson	1963–1969	55	Democrat	Southwest Texas State	Teacher
37. Richard M. Nixon	1969–1974	56	Republican	Whittier	Lawyer
38. Gerald R. Ford‡	1974–1977	61	Republican	Michigan	Lawyer
39. James E. Carter, Jr.	1977–1981	52	Democrat	U.S. Naval Academy	Businessman
40. Ronald W. Reagan	1981–1989	69	Republican	Eureka College	Actor
41. George H. W. Bush	1989–1993	64	Republican	Yale	Businessman
42. William J. Clinton	1993–2001	46	Democrat	Georgetown	Lawyer
43. George W. Bush	2001–2009	54	Republican	Yale	Businessman
44. Barack Obama	2009–	47	Democrat	Columbia	Lawyer

*Church preference; never joined any church.
†The National Union Party consisted of Republicans and War Democrats. Johnson was a Democrat.
**Inaugurated Dec. 6, 1973, to replace Agnew, who resigned Oct. 10, 1973.
‡Inaugurated Aug. 9, 1974, to replace Nixon, who resigned that same day.
§Inaugurated Dec. 19, 1974, to replace Ford, who became president Aug. 9, 1974.

Religion	Born	Died	Age at Death	Vice President	
1. Episcopalian	Feb. 22, 1732	Dec. 14, 1799	67	John Adams	(1789–1797)
2. Unitarian	Oct. 30, 1735	July 4, 1826	90	Thomas Jefferson	(1797–1801)
3. Unitarian*	Apr. 13, 1743	July 4, 1826	83	Aaron Burr	(1801–1805)
				George Clinton	(1805–1809)
4. Episcopalian	Mar. 16, 1751	June 28, 1836	85	George Clinton	(1809–1812)
				Elbridge Gerry	(1813–1814)
5. Episcopalian	Apr. 28, 1758	July 4, 1831	73	Daniel D. Tompkins	(1817–1825)
6. Unitarian	July 11, 1767	Feb. 23, 1848	80	John C. Calhoun	(1825–1829)
7. Presbyterian	Mar. 15, 1767	June 8, 1845	78	John C. Calhoun	(1829–1832)
				Martin Van Buren	(1833–1837)
8. Dutch Reformed	Dec. 5, 1782	July 24, 1862	79	Richard M. Johnson	(1837–1841)
9. Episcopalian	Feb. 9, 1773	Apr. 4, 1841	68	John Tyler	(1841)
10. Episcopalian	Mar. 29, 1790	Jan. 18, 1862	71		
11. Methodist	Nov. 2, 1795	June 15, 1849	53	George M. Dallas	(1845–1849)
12. Episcopalian	Nov. 24, 1784	July 9, 1850	65	Millard Fillmore	(1849–1850)
13. Unitarian	Jan. 7, 1800	Mar. 8, 1874	74		
14. Episcopalian	Nov. 23, 1804	Oct. 8, 1869	64	William R. King	(1853)
15. Presbyterian	Apr. 23, 1791	June 1, 1868	77	John C. Breckinridge	(1857–1861)
16. Presbyterian*	Feb. 12, 1809	Apr. 15, 1865	56	Hannibal Hamlin	(1861–1865)
				Andrew Johnson	(1865)
17. Methodist*	Dec. 29, 1808	July 31, 1875	66		
18. Methodist	Apr. 27, 1822	July 23, 1885	63	Schuyler Colfax	(1869–1873)
				Henry Wilson	(1873–1875)
19. Methodist*	Oct. 4, 1822	Jan. 17, 1893	70	William A. Wheeler	(1877–1881)
20. Disciples of Christ	Nov. 19, 1831	Sept. 19, 1881	49	Chester A. Arthur	(1881)
21. Episcopalian	Oct. 5, 1829	Nov. 18, 1886	57		
22. Presbyterian	Mar. 18, 1837	June 24, 1908	71	Thomas A. Hendricks	(1885)
23. Presbyterian	Aug. 20, 1833	Mar. 13, 1901	67	Levi P. Morton	(1889–1893)
24. Presbyterian	Mar. 18, 1837	June 24, 1908	71	Adlai E. Stevenson	(1893–1897)
25. Methodist	Jan. 29, 1843	Sept. 14, 1901	58	Garret A. Hobart	(1897–1899)
				Theodore Roosevelt	(1901)
26. Dutch Reformed	Oct. 27, 1858	Jan. 6, 1919	60	Charles W. Fairbanks	(1905–1909)
27. Unitarian	Sept. 15, 1857	Mar. 8, 1930	72	James S. Sherman	(1909–1912)
28. Presbyterian	Dec. 29, 1856	Feb. 3, 1924	67	Thomas R. Marshall	(1913–1921)
29. Baptist	Nov. 2, 1865	Aug. 2, 1923	57	Calvin Coolidge	(1921–1923)
30. Congregationalist	July 4, 1872	Jan. 5, 1933	60	Charles G. Dawes	(1925–1929)
31. Friend (Quaker)	Aug. 10, 1874	Oct. 20, 1964	90	Charles Curtis	(1929–1933)
32. Episcopalian	Jan. 30, 1882	Apr. 12, 1945	63	John N. Garner	(1933–1941)
				Henry A. Wallace	(1941–1945)
				Harry S Truman	(1945)
33. Baptist	May 8, 1884	Dec. 26, 1972	88	Alben W. Barkley	(1949–1953)
34. Presbyterian	Oct. 14, 1890	Mar. 28, 1969	78	Richard M. Nixon	(1953–1961)
35. Roman Catholic	May 29, 1917	Nov. 22, 1963	46	Lyndon B. Johnson	(1961–1963)
36. Disciples of Christ	Aug. 27, 1908	Jan. 22, 1973	64	Hubert H. Humphrey	(1965–1969)
37. Friend (Quaker)	Jan. 9, 1913	Apr. 22, 1994	81	Spiro T. Agnew	(1969–1973)
				Gerald R. Ford**	(1973–1974)
38. Episcopalian	July 14, 1913	Dec. 26, 2006	93	Nelson A. Rockefeller[§]	(1974–1977)
39. Baptist	Oct. 1, 1924			Walter F. Mondale	(1977–1981)
40. Disciples of Christ	Feb. 6, 1911	June 5, 2004	93	George H. W. Bush	(1981–1989)
41. Episcopalian	June 12, 1924			J. Danforth Quayle	(1989–1993)
42. Baptist	Aug. 19, 1946			Albert A. Gore	(1993–2001)
43. Methodist	July 6, 1946			Dick Cheney	(2001–2009)
44. United Church of Christ	August 4, 1961			Joe Biden	(2009–)

FEDERALIST PAPERS NO. 10 AND NO. 51

The founders completed drafting the U.S. Constitution in 1787. It was then submitted to the thirteen states for ratification, and a major debate ensued. As you read in Chapter 2, on the one side of this debate were the Federalists, who urged that the new Constitution be adopted. On the other side of the debate were the Anti-Federalists, who argued against ratification.

During the course of this debate, three men well known for their Federalist views—Alexander Hamilton, James Madison, and John Jay—wrote a series of essays in which they argued for immediate ratifcation of the Constitution. The essays appeared in the New York City Independent Journal *in October 1787, just a little over a month after the Constitutional Convention adjourned. Later, Hamilton arranged to have the essays collected and published in book form. The articles filled two volumes, both of which were published by May 1788. The essays are often referred to collectively as the* Federalist Papers.

Scholars disagree as to whether the Federalist Papers *had a significant impact on the decision of the states to ratify the Constitution. Nonetheless, many of the essays are masterpieces of political reasoning and have left a lasting imprint on American politics and government. Above all, the Federalist Papers shed an important light on what the founders intended when they drafted various constitutional provisions.*

Here we present just two of these essays, Federalist Paper No. 10 *and* Federalist Paper No. 51*. Each essay was written by James Madison, who referred to himself as "Publius." We have annotated each document to clarify the meaning of particular passages. The annotations are set in italics to distinguish them from the original text of the documents.*

#10

Federalist Paper No. 10 *is a classic document that is often referred to by teachers of American government. Authored by James Madison, it sets forth Madison's views on factions in politics. The essay was written, in large part, to counter the arguments put forth by the Anti-Federalists that small factions might take control of the government, thus destroying the representative nature of the republican form of government established by the Constitution. The essay opens with a discussion of the "dangerous vice" of factions and the importance of devising a form of government in which this vice will be controlled.*

Among the numerous advantages promised by a well-constructed Union, none deserves to be more accurately developed than its tendency to break and control the violence of faction. The friend of popular governments never finds himself so much alarmed for their character and fate as when he contemplates their propensity to this dangerous vice. He will not fail, therefore, to set a due value on any plan which, without violating the principles to which he is attached, provides a proper cure for it. The instability, injustice, and confusion introduced into the public councils have, in truth, been the mortal diseases under which popular governments have everywhere perished, as they continue to be the favorite and fruitful topics from which the adversaries to liberty derive their most specious declamations. The valuable improvements made by the American constitutions on the popular models, both ancient and modern, cannot certainly be too much admired; but it would be an unwarrantable partiality to contend that they have as effectually obviated the danger on this side, as was wished and expected. Complaints are everywhere heard from our most considerate and virtuous citizens, equally the friends of public and private faith and of public and personal liberty, that our governments are too unstable, that the public good is disregarded in the conflicts of rival parties, and that measures are too often decided, not according to the rules of justice and the rights of the minor party, but by the superior force of an interested and overbearing majority. However anxiously we may wish that these complaints had no foundation, the evidence of known facts will not permit us to deny that they are in some degree true. It will be found, indeed, on a candid review of our situation, that some of the distresses under which we labor have been erroneously charged on the operation of our governments; but it will be found, at the same time, that other causes will not alone account for many of our heaviest misfortunes; and, particularly, for that prevailing and increasing distrust of public engagements and alarm for private rights which are echoed from one end of the continent to the other. These must be chiefly, if not wholly, effects of the unsteadiness and injustice with which a factious spirit has tainted our public administration.

In the following paragraph, Madison clarifies for his readers his understanding of what the term faction *means.*

By a faction I understand a number of citizens, whether amounting to a majority or minority of the whole, who are united and actuated by some common impulse of passion, or of interest, adverse to the rights of other citizens, or the permanent and aggregate interests of the community.

In the following passages, Madison looks at the two methods of curing the "mischiefs of factions." One of these methods is removing the causes of faction. The other is to control the effects of factions.

There are two methods of curing the mischiefs of faction: the one, by removing its causes; the other, by controlling its effects.

There are again two methods of removing the causes of faction: the one, by destroying the liberty which is essential to its existence; the other, by giving to every citizen the same opinions, the same passions, and the same interests.

It could never be more truly said than of the first remedy that it was worse than the disease. Liberty is to faction what air is to fire, an aliment without which it instantly expires. But it could not be a less folly to abolish liberty, which is essential to political life, because it nourishes faction than it would be to wish the annihilation of air, which is essential to animal life, because it imparts to fire its destructive agency.

The second expedient is as impracticable as the first would be unwise. As long as the reason of man continues fallible, and his is at liberty to exercise it, different opinions will be formed. As long as the connection subsists between his reason and his self-love, his opinions and his passions will have a reciprocal influence on each other; and the former will be objects to which the latter will attach themselves. The diversity in the faculties of men, from which the rights of property originate, is not less an insuperable obstacle to a uniformity of interests. The protection of these faculties is the first object of government. From the protection of different and unequal faculties of acquiring property, the possession of different degrees and kinds of property immediately results; and from the influence of these on the sentiments and views of the respective proprietors ensues a division of the society into different interests and parties.

The latent causes of faction are thus sown in the nature of man; and we see them everywhere brought into different degrees of activity, according to the different circumstances of civil society. A zeal for different opinions concerning religion, concerning government, and many other points, as well of speculation as of practice; an attachment to different leaders ambitiously contending for pre-eminence and power; or to persons of other descriptions whose fortunes have been interesting to the human passions, have, in turn, divided mankind into parties, inflamed them with mutual animosity, and rendered them much more disposed to vex and oppress each other than to co-operate for their common good. So strong is this propensity of mankind to fall into mutual animosities that where no substantial occasion presents itself the most frivolous and fanciful distinctions have been sufficient to kindle their unfriendly passions and excite their most violent conflicts. But the most common and durable source of factions has been the various and unequal distribution of property. Those who hold and those who are without property have ever formed distinct interests in society. Those who are creditors, and those who are debtors, fall under a like discrimination. A landed interest, a manufacturing interest, a mercantile interest, a moneyed interest, with many lesser interests, grow up of necessity in civilized nations, and divide them into different classes, actuated by different sentiments and views. The regulation of these various and interfering interests forms the principal task of modern legislation and involves the spirit of party and faction in the necessary and ordinary operations of government.

No man is allowed to be a judge in his own cause, because his interest would certainly bias his judgment, and, not improbably, corrupt his integrity. With equal, nay with greater reason, a body of men are unfit to be both judges and parties at the same time; yet what are many of the most important acts of legislation but so many judicial determinations, not indeed concerning the rights of single persons, but concerning the rights of large bodies of citizens? And what are the different classes of legislators but advocates and parties to the causes which they determine? Is a law proposed concerning private debts? It is a question to which the creditors are parties on one side and the debtors on the other. Justice ought to hold the balance between them. Yet the parties are, and must be, themselves the judges; and the most numerous party, or in other words, the most powerful faction must be expected to prevail. Shall domestic manufacturers be encouraged, and in what degree, by restrictions on foreign manufacturers? Are questions which would be differently decided by the landed and the manufacturing classes, and probably by neither with a sole regard to justice and the public good. The apportionment of taxes on the various descriptions of property is an act which seems to require the most exact impartiality; yet there is, perhaps, no legislative act in which greater opportunity and temptation are given to a predominant party to trample on the rules of justice. Every shilling with which they overburden the inferior number is a shilling saved to their own pockets.

It is in vain to say that enlightened statesmen will be able to adjust these clashing interests and render them all subservient to the public good. Enlightened statesmen will not always be at the helm. Nor, in many cases, can such an adjustment be made at all without taking into view indirect and remote considerations, which will rarely prevail over the immediate interest which one party may find in disregarding the rights of another or the good of the whole.

The inference to which we are brought is that the causes of faction cannot be removed and that relief is only to be sought in the means of controlling its effects.

In the preceding passages, Madison has explored the causes of factions and has concluded that they cannot "be removed" without removing liberty itself, which is one of the causes, or altering human nature. He now turns to a discussion of how the effects of factions might be controlled.

If a faction consists of less than a majority, relief is supplied by the republican principle, which enables the majority to defeat its sinister views by regular vote. It may clog the administration, it may convulse the society; but it will be unable to execute and mask its violence under the forms of the Constitution. When a majority is included in a faction, the form of popular government, on the other hand, enables it to sacrifice to its ruling passion or interest both the public good and the rights of other citizens. To secure the public good and private rights against the danger of such a faction, and at the same time to preserve the spirit and the form of popular government, is then the great object to which our inquiries are directed. Let me add that it is the great desideratum by which alone this form of government can be rescued from the opprobrium under which it has so long labored and be recommended to the esteem and adoption of mankind.

According to Madison, one way of controlling the effects of factions is to make sure that the majority is not able to act in "concert," or jointly, to "carry into effect schemes of oppression."

By what means is this object attainable? Evidently by one of two only. Either the existence of the same passion or interest in a majority at the same time must be prevented, or the majority, having such coexistent passion or interest, must be rendered, by their number and local situation, unable to concert and carry into effect schemes of oppression. If the impulse and the opportunity be suffered to coincide, we well know that neither moral nor religious motives can be relied on as an adequate control. They are not found to be such on the injustice and violence of individuals, and lose their efficacy in proportion to the number combined together, that is, in proportion as their efficacy becomes needful.

From this view of the subject it may be concluded that a pure democracy, by which I mean a society consisting of a small number of citizens, who assemble and administer the government in person, can admit of no cure for the mischiefs of faction. A common passion or interest will, in almost every case, be felt by a majority of the whole; a communication and concert results from the form of government itself; and there is nothing to check the inducements to sacrifice the weaker party or an obnoxious individual. Hence it is that such democracies have ever been spectacles of turbulence and contention; have ever been found incompatible with personal security or the rights of property; and have in general been as short in their lives as they have been violent in their deaths. Theoretic politicians, who have patronized this species of government, have erroneously supposed that by reducing mankind to a perfect equality in their political rights, they would at the same time be perfectly equalized and assimilated in their possessions, their opinions, and their passions.

In the following six paragraphs, Madison sets forth some of the reasons why a republican form of government promises a "cure" for the mischiefs of factions. He begins by clarifying the difference between a republic and a democracy. He then describes how in a large republic, the elected representatives of the people will be large enough in number to guard against factions—the "cabals," or concerted actions, of "a few." On the one hand, representatives will not be so removed from their local districts as to be unacquainted with their constituents' needs. On the other hand, they will not be "unduly attached" to local interests and unfit to understand "great and national objects." Madison concludes that the Constitution "forms a happy combination in this respect."

A republic, by which I mean a government in which the scheme of representation takes place, opens a different prospect and promises the cure for which we are seeking. Let us examine the points in which it varies from pure democracy, and we shall comprehend both the nature of the cure and the efficacy which it must derive from the Union.

The two great points of difference between a democracy and a republic are: first, the delegation of the government, in the latter, to a small number of citizens elected by the rest; secondly, the greater number of citizens and greater sphere of country over which the latter may be extended.

The effect of the first difference is, on the one hand, to refine and enlarge the public views by passing them through the medium of a chosen body of citizens, whose wisdom may best discern the true interest of their country and whose patriotism and love of justice will be least likely to sacrifice it to temporary or partial considerations. Under such a regulation it may well happen that the public voice, pronounced by the representatives of the people, will be more consonant to the public good than if pronounced by the people themselves, convened for the purpose. On the other hand, the effect may be inverted. Men of factious tempers, of local prejudices, or of sinister designs, may, by intrigue, by corruption, or by other means, first obtain the suffrages, and then betray the interests of the people. The question resulting is, whether small or extensive republics are most favorable to the election of proper guardians of the public weal; and it is clearly decided in favor of the latter by two obvious considerations.

In the first place it is to be remarked that however small the republic may be the representatives must be raised to a certain number in order to guard against the cabals of a few; and that however large it may be they must be limited to a certain number in order to guard against the confusion of a multitude. Hence, the number of representatives in the two cases not being in proportion to that of the constituents, and being proportionally greatest in the small republic, it follows that if the proportion of fit characters be not less in the large than in the small republic, the former will present a greater option, and consequently a greater probability of a fit choice.

In the next place, as each representative will be chosen by a greater number of citizens in the large than in the small republic, it will be more difficult for unworthy candidates to practice with success the vicious arts by which elections are too often carried; and the suffrages of the people being more free, will be more likely to center on men who possess the most attractive merit and the most diffusive and established characters.

It must be confessed that in this, as in most other cases, there is a mean, on both sides of which inconveniencies will be found to lie. By enlarging too much the number of electors, you render the representative too little acquainted with all their local circumstances and lesser interests; as by reducing it too much, you render him unduly attached to these, and too little fit to comprehend and pursue great and national objects. The federal Constitution forms a happy combination in this respect; the great and aggregate interests being referred to the national, the local and particular to the State legislatures.

In the remaining passages of this essay, Madison looks at another "point of difference" between a republic and a democracy. Specifically, a republic can encompass a larger territory and a greater number of citizens than a democracy can. This fact, too, argues Madison, will help to control the influence of factions because the interests that draw people together to act in concert are typically at the local level and would be unlikely to affect or dominate the national government. As Madison states, "The influence of factious leaders may kindle a flame within their particular States but will be unable to spread a general conflagration through the other States." Generally, in a large republic, there will be numerous factions, and no particular faction will be able to "pervade the whole body of the Union."

The other point of difference is the greater number of citizens and extent of territory which may be brought within the compass of republican than of democratic government; and it is this circumstance principally which renders factious combinations less to be dreaded in the former than in the latter. The smaller the society, the fewer probably will be the distinct parties and interests composing it; the fewer the distinct parties and interests, the more frequently will a majority be found of the same party; and the smaller the number of individuals composing a majority, and the smaller the compass within which they are placed, the more easily will they concert and execute their plans of oppression. Extend the sphere and you take in a greater variety of parties and interests; you make it less probable that a majority of the whole will have a common motive to invade the rights of other citizens; or if such a common motive exists, it will be more difficult for all who feel it to discover their own strength and to act in unison with each other. Besides other impediments, it may be remarked that, where there is a consciousness of unjust or dishonorable purposes, communication is always checked by distrust in proportion to the number whose concurrence is necessary.

Hence, it clearly appears that the same advantage which a republic has over a democracy in controlling the effects of faction is enjoyed by a large over a small republic—is enjoyed by the Union over the States composing it. Does this advantage consist in the substitution of representatives whose enlightened views and virtuous sentiments render them superior to local prejudices and to schemes of injustice? It will not be denied that the representation of the Union will be most likely to possess these requisite endowments. Does it consist in the greater security afforded by a greater variety of parties, against the event of any one party being able to outnumber and oppress the rest? In an equal degree does the increased variety of parties comprised within the Union increase this security. Does it, in fine, consist in the greater obstacles opposed to the concert and accomplishment of the secret wishes of an unjust and interested majority? Here again the extent of the Union gives it the most palpable advantage.

The influence of factious leaders may kindle a flame within their particular States but will be unable to spread a general conflagration through the other States. A religious sect may degenerate into a political faction in a part of the Confederacy; but the variety of sects dispersed over the entire face of it must secure the national councils against any danger from that source. A rage for paper money, for an abolition of debts, for an equal division of property, or for any other improper or wicked project, will be less apt to pervade the whole body of the Union than a particular member of it, in the same proportion as such a malady is more likely to taint a particular county or district than an entire State.

In the extent and proper structure of the Union, therefore, we behold a republican remedy for the diseases most incident to republican government. And according to the degree of pleasure and pride we feel in being republicans ought to be our zeal in cherishing the spirit and supporting the character of federalists.

Publius
(James Madison)

#51

Federalist Paper No. 51, *which was also authored by James Madison, is one of the classics in American political theory. Recall from Chapter 2 that a major concern of the founders was to create a relatively strong national government but one that would not be capable of tyrannizing over the populace. In the following essay, Madison sets forth the theory of "checks and balances." He explains that the new Constitution, by dividing the national government into three branches (executive, legislative, and judicial), offers protection against tyranny.*

To what expedient, then, shall we finally resort, for maintaining in practice the necessary partition of power among the several departments as laid down in the Constitution? The only answer that can be given is that as all these exterior provisions are found to be inadequate the defect must be supplied, by so contriving the interior structure of the government as that its several constituent parts may, by their mutual relations, be the means of keeping each other in their proper places. Without presuming to undertake a full development of this important idea I will hazard a few general observations which may perhaps place it in a clearer light, and enable us to form a more correct judgment of the principles and structure of the government planned by the convention.

In the following two paragraphs, Madison explains that to ensure that the powers of government are genuinely separated, it is important that each of the three branches of government (executive, legislative, and judicial) should have a "will of its own." Among other things, this means that persons in one branch should not depend on persons in another branch for the "emoluments annexed to their offices" (pay, perks, and privileges). If they did, then the branches would not be truly independent of one another.

In order to lay a due foundation for that separate and distinct exercise of the different powers of government, which to a certain extent is admitted on all hands to be essential to the preservation of liberty, it is evident that each department should have a will of its own; and consequently should be so constituted that the members of each should have as little agency as possible in the appointment of the members of the others. Were this principle rigorously adhered to, it would require that all the appointments for the supreme executive, legislative, and judiciary magistracies should be drawn from the same fountain of authority, the people, through channels having no communication whatever with one another. Perhaps such a plan of constructing the several departments would be less difficult in practice than it may in contemplation appear. Some difficulties, however, and some additional expense would attend the execution of it. Some deviations, therefore, from the principle must be admitted. In the constitution of the judiciary department in particular, it might be inexpedient to insist rigorously on the principle: first, because peculiar qualifications being essential in the members, the primary consideration ought to be to select that mode of choice which best secures these qualifications; second, because the permanent tenure by which the appointments are held in that department must soon destroy all sense of dependence on the authority conferring them.

It is equally evident that the members of each department should be as little dependent as possible on those of the others for the emoluments annexed to their offices. Were the executive magistrate, or the judges, not independent of the legislature in this particular, their independence in every other would be merely nominal.

One of the striking qualities of the theory of checks and balances as posited by Madison is that it assumes that persons are not angels but driven by personal interests and motives. In the following two paragraphs, which are among the most widely quoted of Madison's writings, he stresses that the division of the government into three branches helps to check personal ambitions. Personal ambitions will naturally arise, but they will be linked to the constitutional powers of each branch. In effect, they will help to keep the three branches separate and thus serve the public interest.

But the great security against a gradual concentration of the several powers in the same department consists in giving to those who administer each department the necessary constitutional means and personal motives to resist encroachments of the others. The provision for defense must in this, as in all other cases, be made commensurate to the danger of attack. Ambition must be made to counteract ambition. The interest of the man must be connected with the constitutional rights of the place. It may be a reflection on human nature that such devices should be necessary to control the abuses of government. But what is government itself but the greatest of all reflections on human nature? If men were angels, no government would be necessary. If angels were to govern men, neither external nor internal controls on government would be necessary. In framing a government which is to be administered by men over men, the great difficulty lies in this: you must first enable the government to control the governed; and in the next place oblige it to control itself. A dependence on the people is, no doubt, the primary control on the government; but experience has taught mankind the necessity of auxiliary precautions.

This policy of supplying, by opposite and rival interests, the defect of better motives, might be traced through the whole system of human affairs, private as well as public. We see it particularly displayed in all the subordinate distributions of power, where the constant aim is to divide and arrange the several offices in such a manner as that each may be a check on the other—that the private interest of every individual may be a sentinel over the public rights. These inventions of prudence cannot be less requisite in the distribution of the supreme powers of the State.

In the next two paragraphs, Madison first points out that the "legislative authority necessarily predominates" in a republican form of government. The "remedy" for this lack of balance with the other branches of government is to divide the legislative branch into two chambers with "different modes of election and different principles of action."

But it is not possible to give to each department an equal power of self-defense. In republican government, the legislative authority necessarily predominates. The remedy for this inconveniency is to divide the legislature into different branches; and to render them, by different modes of election and different principles of action, as little connected with each other as the nature of their common functions and their common dependence on the society will admit. It may even be necessary to guard against dangerous encroachments by still further precautions. As the weight of the legislative authority requires that it should be thus divided, the weakness of the executive may require, on the other hand, that it should be fortified. An absolute negative on the legislature appears, at first view, to be the natural defense with which the executive magistrate should be armed. But perhaps it would be neither altogether safe nor alone sufficient. On ordinary occasions it might not be exerted with the requisite firmness, and on extraordinary occasions it might be perfidiously abused. May not this defect of an absolute negative be supplied by some qualified connection between this weaker department and the weaker branch of the stronger department, by which the latter may be led to support the constitutional rights of the former, without being too much detached from the rights of its own department?

If the principles on which these observations are founded be just, as I persuade myself they are, and they be applied as a criterion to the several State constitutions, and to the federal Constitution, it will be found that if the latter does not perfectly correspond with them, the former are infinitely less able to bear such a test.

In the remaining passages of this essay, Madison discusses the importance of the division of government powers between the states and the national government.

This division of powers, by providing additional checks and balances, offers a "double security" against tyranny.

There are, moreover, two considerations particularly applicable to the federal system of America, which place that system in a very interesting point of view.

First. In a single republic, all the power surrendered by the people is submitted to the administration of a single government; and the usurpations are guarded against by a division of the government into distinct and separate departments. In the compound republic of America, the power surrendered by the people is first divided between two distinct governments, and then the portion allotted to each subdivided among distinct and separate departments. Hence a double security arises to the rights of the people. The different governments will control each other, at the same time that each will be controlled by itself.

Second. It is of great importance in a republic not only to guard the society against the oppression of its rulers, but to guard one part of the society against the injustice of the other part. Different interests necessarily exist in different classes of citizens. If a majority be united by a common interest, the rights of the minority will be insecure. There are but two methods of providing against this evil: the one by creating a will in the community independent of the majority—that is, of the society itself; the other, by comprehending in the society so many separate descriptions of citizens as will render an unjust combination of a majority of the whole very improbable, if not impracticable. The first method prevails in all governments possessing an hereditary or self-appointed authority. This, at best, is but a precarious security; because a power independent of the society may as well espouse the unjust views of the major as the rightful interests of the minor party, and may possibly be turned against both parties. The second method will be exemplified in the federal republic of the United States. Whilst all authority in it will be derived from and dependent on the society, the society itself will be broken into so many parts, interests and classes of citizens, that the rights of individuals, or of the minority, will be in little danger from interested combinations of the majority. In a free government the security for civil rights must be the same as that for religious rights. It consists in the one case in the multiplicity of interests, and in the other in the multiplicity of sects. The degree of security in both cases will depend on the number of interests and sects; and this may be presumed to depend on the extent of country and number of people comprehended under the same government. This view of the subject must particularly recommend a proper federal system to all the sincere and considerate friends of republican government, since it shows that in exact proportion as the territory of the Union may be formed into more circumscribed Confederacies, or States, oppressive combinations of a majority will be facilitated; the best security, under the republican forms, for the rights of every class of citizen, will be diminished; and consequently the stability and independence of some member of the government, the only other security, must be proportionally increased. Justice is the end of government. It is the end of civil society. It ever has been and ever will be pursued until it be obtained, or until liberty be lost in the pursuit. In a society under the forms of which the stronger faction can readily unite and oppress the weaker, anarchy may as truly be said to reign as in a state of nature, where the weaker individual is not secured against the violence of the stronger; and as, in the latter state, even the stronger individuals are prompted, by the uncertainty of their condition, to submit to a government which may protect the weak as well as themselves; so, in the former state, will the more powerful factions or parties be gradually induced, by a like motive, to wish for a government which will protect all parties, the weaker as well as the more powerful. It can be little doubted that if the State of Rhode Island was separated from the Confederacy and left to itself, the insecurity of rights under the popular form of government within such narrow limits would be displayed by such reiterated oppressions of factious majorities that some power altogether independent of the people would soon be called for by the voice of the very factions whose misrule had proved the necessity of it. In the extended republic of the United States, and among the great variety of interests, parties, and sects which it embraces, a coalition of a majority of the whole society could seldom take place on any other principles than those of justice and the general good; whilst there being thus less danger to a minor from the will of a major party, there must be less pretext, also, to provide for the security of the former, by introducing into the government a will not dependent on the latter, or, in other words, a will independent of the society itself. It is no less certain than it is important, notwithstanding the contrary opinions which have been entertained, that the larger the society, provided it lie within a practicable sphere, the more duly capable it will be of self-government. And happily for the *republican cause,* the practicable sphere may be carried to a very great extent by a judicious modification and mixture of the *federal principle.*

Publius
(James Madison)

Appendix G

How to Read Case Citations and Find Court Decisions

Many important court cases are discussed in references in endnotes throughout this book. Court decisions are recorded and published. When a court case is mentioned, the notation that is used to refer to, or to cite, the case denotes where the published decision can be found.

State courts of appeals decisions are usually published in two places, the state reports of that particular state and the more widely used *National Reporter System* published by West Group. Some states no longer publish their own reports. The *National Reporter System* divides the states into the following geographic areas: Atlantic (A. or A.2d, where *2d* refers to *Second Series*), South Eastern (S.E. or S.E.2d), South Western (S.W., S.W.2d, or S.W.3d), North Western (N.W. or N.W.2d), North Eastern (N.E. or N.E.2d), Southern (So. or So.2d), and Pacific (P., P.2d, or P.3d).

Federal trial court decisions are published unofficially in West's *Federal Supplement* (F.Supp. or F.Supp.2d), and opinions from the circuit courts of appeals are reported unofficially in West's *Federal Reporter* (F., F.2d, or F.3d). Opinions from the United States Supreme Court are reported in the *United States Reports* (U.S.), the *Lawyers' Edition of the Supreme Court Reports* (L.Ed.), West's *Supreme Court Reporter* (S.Ct.), and other publications. The *United States Reports* is the official publication of United States Supreme Court decisions. It is published by the federal government. Many early decisions are missing from these volumes. The citations of the early volumes of the *U.S. Reports* include the names of the actual reporters, such as Dallas, Cranch, or Wheaton. *McCulloch v. Maryland,* for example, is cited as 17 U.S. (4 Wheat.) 316. Only after 1874 did the present citation system, in which cases are cited based solely on their volume and page numbers in the *United States Reports,* come into being. The *Lawyers' Edition of the Supreme Court Reports* is an unofficial and more complete edition of Supreme Court decisions. West's *Supreme Court Reporter* is an unofficial edition of decisions dating from October 1882. These volumes contain headnotes and numerous brief editorial statements of the law involved in the case.

State courts of appeals decisions are cited by giving the name of the case; the volume, name, and page number of the state's official report (if the state publishes its own reports); the volume, unit, and page number of the *National Reporter;* and the volume, name, and page number of any other selected reporter. Federal court citations are also listed by giving the name of the case and the volume, name, and page number of the reports. In addition to the citation, this textbook lists the year of the decision in parentheses. Consider, for example, the case *United States v. Curtiss-Wright Export Co.,* 299 U.S. 304 (1936). The Supreme Court's decision of this case may be found in volume 299 of the *United States Reports* on page 304. The case was decided in 1936.

Today, many courts, including the United States Supreme Court, publish their opinions online. This makes it much easier for students to find and read cases, or summaries of cases, that have significant consequences for American government and politics. To access cases via the Internet, use the URLs given in the *Politics on the Web* section at the end of Chapter 14.

Notes

Chapter 1

1. Harold Lasswell, *Politics: Who Gets What, When, and How* (New York: McGraw-Hill, 1936).
2. Charles Lewis, *The Buying of Congress* (New York: Avon Books, 1998), p. 346.
3. As quoted in Paul M. Angle and Earl Schenck Miers, *The Living Lincoln* (New York: Barnes & Noble, 1992), p. 155.
4. Martin J. Wade and William F. Russell, *The Short Constitution* (Iowa City: American Citizen Publishing, 1920), p. 38.
5. John W. Dean, *Conservatives without Conscience* (New York: Penguin, 2007), p. 11.
6. John Halpin and Karl Agne, *State of American Political Ideology, 2009: A National Study of Political Values and Beliefs* (Washington, D.C.: Center for American Progress, 2009).

Chapter 2

1. *U.S. v. Miller,* 307 U.S. 174 (1939), *District of Columbia v. Heller,* 128 S.Ct. 2783 (2008), and *McDonald v. Chicago,* 561 U.S. ___ (2010).
2. The first *European* settlement in today's United States was St. Augustine, Florida (a city that still exists), which was founded on September 8, 1565, by the Spaniard Pedro Menéndez de Ávilés.
3. Archaeologists recently discovered the remains of a colony at Popham Beach, on the southern coast of what is now Maine, that was established at the same time as the colony at Jamestown. The Popham colony disbanded after thirteen months, however, when the leader, after learning that he had inherited property back home, returned—with the other colonists—to England.
4. John Camp, *Out of the Wilderness: The Emergence of an American Identity in Colonial New England* (Middleton, Conn.: Wesleyan University Press, 1990).
5. Jon Butler, *Becoming America: The Revolution before 1776* (Cambridge, Mass.: Harvard University Press, 2000).
6. Ironically, the colonists were in fact protesting a tax reduction. The British government believed that if tea were cheaper, Americans would be more willing to drink it, even though it was still taxed. The Americans viewed the tax reduction as an attempt to trick them into accepting the principle of taxation. If the tea had been expensive, it would have been easy to organize a boycott. Because the tea was cheap, the protesters destroyed it so that no one would be tempted to buy it. (Also, many of the protesters were in the business of smuggling tea, and they would have been put out of business by the cheap competition.)
7. Paul S. Boyer *et al., The Enduring Vision: A History of the American People* (Lexington, Mass.: D. C. Heath, 1996).
8. Much of the colonists' fury over British policies was directed personally at King George III, who had ascended the British throne in 1760 at the age of twenty-two, rather than at Britain or British rule *per se.* If you look at the Declaration of Independence in Appendix A, you will note that much of that document focuses on what "He" (George III) has or has not done. George III's lack of political experience, his personality, and his temperament all combined to lend instability to the British government at this crucial point in history.
9. *The Political Writings of Thomas Paine,* Vol. 1 (Boston: J. P. Mendum Investigator Office, 1870), p. 46.
10. The equivalent in today's publishing world would be a book that sells between 9 million and 11 million copies in its first year of publication.
11. As quoted in Winthrop D. Jordan *et al., The United States,* 6th ed. (Englewood Cliffs, N.J.: Prentice Hall, 1987).
12. Some scholars feel that Locke's influence on the colonists, including Thomas Jefferson, has been exaggerated. For example, Jay Fliegelman states that Jefferson's fascination with the ideas of Homer, Ossian, and Patrick Henry "is of greater significance than his indebtedness to Locke." Jay Fliegelman, *Declaring Independence: Jefferson, Natural Language, and the Culture of Performance* (Stanford, Calif.: Stanford University Press, 1993).
13. Well before the Articles were ratified, many of them had, in fact, already been implemented. The Second Continental Congress and the thirteen states conducted American military, economic, and political affairs according to the standards and form specified later in the Articles of Confederation. See Robert W. Hoffert, *A Politics of Tensions: The Articles of Confederation and American Political Ideas* (Niwot, Colo.: University Press of Colorado, 1992).
14. Shays' Rebellion was not merely a small group of poor farmers. The participants and their supporters represented whole communities, including some of the wealthiest and most influential families of Massachusetts. Leonard L. Richards, *Shays' Rebellion: The American Revolution's Final Battle* (Philadelphia: University of Pennsylvania Press, 2003).
15. Madison was much more "republican" in his views—that is, less of a centralist—than Hamilton. See Lance Banning, *The Sacred Fire of Liberty: James Madison and the Founding of the Federal Republic* (Ithaca, N.Y.: Cornell University Press, 1995).
16. The State House was later named Independence Hall. The East Room was the same room in which the Declaration of Independence had been signed eleven years earlier.
17. Charles A. Beard, *An Economic Interpretation of the Constitution of the United States* (New York: Macmillan, 1913; New York: Free Press, 1986).
18. Morris was partly of French descent, which is why his first name may seem unusual. Note, however, that naming one's child *Gouverneur* was not common at the time in any language, including French.
19. Quoted in J. J. Spengler, "Malthusianism in Late Eighteenth-Century America," *American Economic Review* 25 (1935), p. 705.
20. For further detail on Wood's depiction of the founders' views, see Gordon S. Wood, *Revolutionary Characters: What Made the Founders Different* (New York: Penguin Press, 2006).
21. Some scholarship suggests that the *Federalist Papers* did not play a significant role in bringing about the ratification of the Constitution. Nonetheless, the papers have lasting value as an authoritative explanation of the Constitution.
22. The papers written by the Anti-Federalists are online (see the *Politics on the Web* section at the end of Chapter 2 for the Web URL). For essays on the positions, arranged in topical order, of both the Federalists and the Anti-Federalists in the ratification debate, see John P. Kaminski and Richard Leffler, *Federalists and Antifederalists: The Debate over the Ratification of the Constitution,* 2d ed. (Madison, Wis.: Madison House, 1998).
23. The concept of the separation of powers generally is credited to the French political philosopher Montesquieu (1689–1755), who included it in his monumental two-volume work entitled *The Spirit of the Laws,* published in 1748.
24. The Constitution does not explicitly mention the power of judicial review, but the delegates at the Constitutional Convention probably assumed that the courts would have this power. Indeed, Alexander Hamilton, in *Federalist Paper* No. 78, explicitly outlined the concept of judicial review. In any event, whether the founders intended for the courts to exercise this power is a moot point, because in an 1803 decision, *Marbury v. Madison,* the Supreme Court successfully claimed this power for the courts—see Chapter 14.
25. Eventually, Supreme Court decisions led to legislative reforms relating to apportionment. The amendment concerning compensation of members of Congress became the Twenty-seventh Amendment to the Constitution when it was ratified 203 years later, in 1992.
26. The Twenty-first Amendment repealed the Eighteenth Amendment, which had prohibited the manufacture or sale of alcoholic beverages nationwide (Prohibition). Special conventions were necessary because prohibitionist forces controlled too many state legislatures for the standard ratification method to work.

Chapter 3

1. The federal models used by the German and Canadian governments provide interesting comparisons with the U.S. system. See Arthur B. Gunlicks, *Laender and German Federalism* (Manchester, England: Manchester University Press, 2003); and Jennifer Smith, *Federalism* (Vancouver: University of British Columbia Press, 2004).
2. Text of an address by the president to the National Conference of State Legislatures, Atlanta, Georgia (Washington, D.C.: The White House, Office of the Press Secretary, July 30, 1981).
3. An excellent illustration of this principle was President Dwight Eisenhower's disciplining of Arkansas governor Orval Faubus when Faubus refused to allow a Little Rock high school to be desegregated in 1957. Eisenhower federalized the National Guard to enforce the court-ordered desegregation of the school.
4. 5 U.S. 137 (1803).
5. 17 U.S. 316 (1819).
6. 22 U.S. 1 (1824).
7. As quoted in Gavin Wright, *The Political Economy of the Cotton South: Households, Markets, and Wealth in the Nineteenth Century* (New York: W. W. Norton & Co., 1978), p. 147.
8. *Hammer v. Dagenhart,* 247 U.S. 251 (1918). This decision was overruled in *United States v. Darby,* 312 U.S. 100 (1941).
9. *Wickard v. Filburn,* 317 U.S. 111 (1942).
10. *McLain v. Real Estate Board of New Orleans, Inc.,* 444 U.S. 232 (1980).
11. 514 U.S. 549 (1995).
12. *Printz v. United States,* 521 U.S. 898 (1997).
13. *United States v. Morrison,* 529 U.S. 598 (2000).
14. 549 U.S. 497 (2007).
15. See George P. Fletcher, "The Indefinable Concept of Terrorism," *Journal of International Criminal Justice,* November 2006, pp. 894–911.

Chapter 4

1. 32 U.S. 243 (1833).
2. 330 U.S. 1 (1947).
3. 370 U.S. 421 (1962).
4. 449 U.S. 39 (1980).
5. *Wallace v. Jaffree,* 472 U.S. 38 (1985).
6. See, for example, *Brown v. Gwinnett County School District,* 112 F.3d 1464 (1997).

7. *Santa Fe Independent School District v. Doe,* 530 U.S. 290 (2000).
8. 393 U.S. 97 (1968).
9. *Edwards v. Aguillard,* 482 U.S. 578 (1987).
10. 403 U.S. 602 (1971).
11. *Mitchell v. Helms,* 530 U.S. 793 (2000).
12. *Zelman v. Simmons-Harris,* 536 U.S. 639 (2002).
13. Holmes v. Bush (Fla.Cir.Ct. 2002). For details about this case, see David Royse, "Judge Rules School Voucher Law Violates Florida Constitution," *USA Today,* August 6, 2002, p. 7D.
14. 98 U.S. 145 (1878).
15. *Christian Legal Society v. Martinez,* 561 U.S. ___ (2010).
16. For more information on this case, see Bill Miller, "Firefighters Win Ruling in D.C. Grooming Dispute," *The Washington Post,* June 23, 2001, p. B01.
17. *Schenck v. United States,* 249 U.S. 47 (1919).
18. 341 U.S. 494 (1951).
19. *Brandenburg v. Ohio,* 395 U.S. 444 (1969).
20. *Liquormart v. Rhode Island,* 517 U.S. 484 (1996).
21. 413 U.S. 15 (1973).
22. *Reno v. American Civil Liberties Union,* 521 U.S. 844 (1997).
23. *Ashcroft v. American Civil Liberties Union,* 542 U.S. 656 (2004). The district court, located in Philadelphia, made its second ruling on the case in 2007. On July 22, 2008, the U.S. Court of Appeals for the Third Circuit upheld the decision in *American Civil Liberties Union v. Mukasey,* 534 F.3d 181 (3d Cir. 2008).
24. *United States v. American Library Association,* 539 U.S. 194 (2003).
25. *Morse v. Frederick,* 551 U.S. 393.
26. See, for example, *Doe v. University of Michigan,* 721 F.Supp. 852 (1989).
27. "Meeting Minutes of the Wesleyan Student Assembly Meeting, 2002–2003," October 2, 2002, p. 10.
28. 249 U.S. 47 (1919).
29. 268 U.S. 652 (1925).
30. 484 U.S. 260 (1988).
31. Brandeis made this statement in a dissenting opinion in *Olmstead v. United States,* 277 U.S. 438 (1928).
32. 381 U.S. 479 (1965).
33. The state of South Carolina challenged the constitutionality of this act, claiming that the law violated states' rights under the Tenth Amendment. The Supreme Court, however, held that Congress had the authority, under its commerce power, to pass the act because drivers' personal information had become articles of interstate commerce. *Reno v. Condon,* 528 U.S. 141 (2000).
34. 410 U.S. 113 (1973). Jane Roe was not the real name of the woman in this case. It is a common legal pseudonym used to protect a party's privacy.
35. See, for example, the Supreme Court's decision in *Lambert v. Wicklund,* 520 U.S. 1169 (1997). The Court held that a Montana law requiring a minor to notify one of her parents before getting an abortion was constitutional.
36. *Schenck v. ProChoice Network,* 519 U.S. 357 (1997); and *Hill v. Colorado,* 530 U.S. 703 (2000).
37. *Stenberg v. Carhart,* 530 U.S. 914 (2000).
38. *Gonzales v. Carhart,* 127 S.Ct. 1610 (2007).
39. *Washington v. Glucksberg,* 521 U.S. 702 (1997).
40. *Gonzales v. Oregon,* 546 U.S. 243 (2006).
41. 372 U.S. 335 (1963).
42. *Mapp v. Ohio,* 367 U.S. 643 (1961).
43. 384 U.S. 436 (1966). In 1968, Congress passed legislation including a provision that reinstated the previous rule that statements made by defendants can be used against them as long as the statements were made voluntarily. This provision was never enforced, however, and only in 1999 did a court try to enforce it. The case ultimately came before the Supreme Court, which held that the *Miranda* rights were based on the Constitution and thus could not be overruled by legislative act. See *Dickerson v. United States,* 530 U.S. 428 (2000).
44. *Moran v. Burbine,* 475 U.S. 412 (1986).
45. *Arizona v. Fulminante,* 499 U.S. 279 (1991).
46. *Davis v. United States,* 512 U.S. 452 (1994).
47. Thomas P. Sullivan, *Police Experiences with Recording Custodial Interrogations* (Chicago: Northwestern University School of Law Center on Wrongful Convictions, Summer 2004), p. 4.
48. This example is drawn from Brenda Koehler, "Respond Locally to National Issues," in *50 Ways to Love Your Country* (Maui, Hawaii: Inner Ocean Publishing, 2004), pp. 110–111.

Chapter 5

1. *Michael M. v. Superior Court,* 450 U.S. 464 (1981).
2. See, for example, *Craig v. Boren,* 429 U.S. 190 (1976).
3. *Orr v. Orr,* 440 U.S. 268 (1979).
4. *Mississippi University for Women v. Hogan,* 458 U.S. 718 (1982).
5. 518 U.S. 515 (1996).
6. 163 U.S. 537 (1896).
7. 347 U.S. 483 (1954).
8. 349 U.S. 294 (1955).
9. *Swann v. Charlotte-Mecklenburg Board of Education,* 402 U.S. 1 (1971).
10. *Keyes v. School District No. 1,* 413 U.S. 189 (1973).
11. *Milliken v. Bradley,* 418 U.S. 717 (1974).
12. *Riddick v. School Board of City of Norfolk,* 627 F.Supp. 814 (E.D.Va. 1984).
13. Emily Bazelon, "The Next Kind of Integration," *The New York Times Magazine,* July 20, 2008.
14. *Oncale v. Sundowner Offshore Services,* 523 U.S. 75 (1998).
15. *Faragher v. City of Boca Raton,* 524 U.S. 775 (1998).
16. The Supreme Court upheld these actions in *Hirabayashi v. United States,* 320 U.S. 81 (1943); and *Korematsu v. United States,* 323 U.S. 214 (1944).
17. Historians in the early and mid-twentieth century gave much smaller figures for the pre-Columbian population—as low as 14 million people for the entire New World. Today, 40 million is considered a conservative estimate, and an estimate of 100 million has much support among demographers. If 100 million is correct, the epidemics that followed the arrival of the Europeans killed one out of every five people alive in the world at that time. See Charles C. Mann, *1491* (New York: Vintage, 2006).
18. The 1890 siege was the subject of Dee Brown's best-selling book *Bury My Heart at Wounded Knee* (New York: Holt, Rinehart & Winston, 1971).
19. *County of Oneida, New York v. Oneida Indian Nation,* 470 U.S. 226 (1985).
20. *Sutton v. United Airlines,* 527 U.S. 471 (1999); and *Toyota v. Williams,* 534 U.S. 184 (2002).
21. *Board of Trustees of the University of Alabama v. Garrett,* 531 U.S. 356 (2001).
22. 539 U.S. 558 (2003).
23. 517 U.S. 620 (1996).
24. 438 U.S. 265 (1978).
25. 515 U.S. 200 (1995).
26. 84 F.3d 720 (5th Cir. 1996).
27. 539 U.S. 244 (2003).
28. 539 U.S. 306 (2003).
29. 551 U.S. 701 (2007).

Chapter 6

1. David Bicknell Truman, *The Governmental Process: Political Interests and Public Opinion,* 2d rev. ed. (New York: Alfred A. Knopf, 1971). This work is a classic of political science.
2. Robert H. Salisbury, *Interests and Institutions: Substance and Structure in American Politics* (Pittsburgh: University of Pittsburgh Press, 1992).
3. *Democracy in America,* Vol. 1, ed. Phillip Bradley (New York: Knopf, 1980), p. 191.
4. Mancur Olson, *The Logic of Collective Action: Public Goods and the Theory of Groups,* rev. ed. (Cambridge, Mass.: Harvard University Press, 1971).
5. Pronounced ah-*mee*-kus *kure*-ee-eye.
6. Fred McChesney, *Money for Nothing: Politicians, Rent Extraction and Political Extortion* (Cambridge, Mass.: Harvard University Press, 1997).
7. The Agricultural Adjustment Act of 1933 (declared unconstitutional) was replaced by the 1937 Agricultural Adjustment Act, which later was changed and amended several times.
8. 545 U.S. 913 (2005).
9. *United States v. Harriss,* 347 U.S. 612 (1954).

Chapter 7

1. Letter to Francis Hopkinson written from Paris while Jefferson was minister to France, as cited in John P. Foley, ed., *The Jeffersonian Cyclopedia* (New York: Russell & Russell, 1967), p. 677.
2. The U.S. Senate presents the text of the address at **www.access.gpo.gov/congress/senate/farewell/sd106-21.pdf**.
3. The association of red with the Republicans and blue with the Democrats is barely a decade old. The terms *red* and *blue* are derived from the colors used by the major television networks to show the states carried by the Republican and Democratic presidential candidates. This use of colors deliberately reverses a traditional pattern. In most European countries, the right-of-center party uses blue, while the left-of-center party employs red. The use of red originated in the socialist movement, from which most European left-of-center parties descend. From time to time, Republicans have accused Democrats of socialism. U.S. television networks thus assigned red to the Republicans precisely so that the networks would not appear to be endorsing that accusation.
4. By August 2010, the cost of the stimulus package was reestimated as \$814 billion.
5. For an interesting discussion of the pros and cons of patronage from a constitutional perspective, see the majority opinion versus the dissent in the Supreme Court case *Board of County Commissioners v. Umbehr,* 518 U.S. 668 (1996).
6. Thomas Nast, the cartoonist who drew these images, was a Republican. "Copperhead" was a derisive term for northern Democrats who sympathized with the South during the Civil War, and in the first cartoon Nash condemned Democratic newspapers for abusing Edwin Stanton, Lincoln's secretary of war, following Stanton's death. The elephant in the second cartoon referred to the large size of the Republican vote in the North. Nash depicted the elephant as stampeded into a pit by a jackass dressed in a lion skin. This referred to the *New York Herald,* a Democratic newspaper, which made accusations against Republican president Ulysses S. Grant that caused Republicans to panic.
7. The term *third party,* although inaccurate (because sometimes there have been fourth parties, fifth parties, and even more), is commonly used to refer to a minor party.
8. Today, twelve states have multimember districts for their state houses, and a handful also have multimember districts for their state senates.

Chapter 8

1. Doris A. Graber, *Mass Media and American Politics,* 7th ed. (Washington, D.C.: CQ Press, 2005).
2. Jimmy Carter, *Palestine: Peace Not Apartheid* (New York: Simon & Schuster, 2007).
3. John M. Benson, "When Is an Opinion Really an Opinion?" *Public Perspective,* September/October 2001, pp. 40–41.
4. As quoted in Karl G. Feld, "When Push Comes to Shove: A Polling Industry Call to Arms," *Public Perspective,* September/October 2001, p. 38.
5. Pew Research Center for the People and the Press, survey conducted September 21–October 4, 2006, and reported in "Who Votes, Who Doesn't, and Why," released October 28, 2006.
6. *Guinn v. United States,* 238 U.S. 347 (1915).
7. *Smith v. Allwright,* 321 U.S. 649 (1944).
8. The argument about the vote-eligible population was first made by Michael P. McDonald and Samuel L. Popkin, "The Myth of the Vanishing Voter," *American Political Science Review,* Vol. 95, No. 4 (December 2001), p. 963.

9. As quoted in Owen Ullman, "Why Voter Apathy Will Make a Strong Showing," *BusinessWeek*, November 4, 1996.
10. Thomas E. Mann and Norman J. Ornstein, *The Broken Branch: How Congress Is Failing America and How to Get It Back on Track* (New York: Oxford University Press, 2006), p. 277.

Chapter 9

1. Today, there are 100 senators in the Senate and 435 members of the House of Representatives. In addition, the District of Columbia has 3 electoral votes, as provided for by the Twenty-third Amendment to the Constitution.
2. This group includes those who support the National Popular Vote movement, a proposed interstate compact that would cast the electoral votes of each participating state for the candidate who won the national popular vote. The compact would go into effect if participating states controlled a majority of the votes in the electoral college.
3. These states award one electoral vote to the candidate who wins the popular vote in a congressional district and an additional two electoral votes to the winner of the statewide popular vote. Other states have considered similar plans.
4. The Maryland legislature would probably have to vote to accept the return of the District, because under the Constitution, state boundaries cannot be altered without state consent.
5. The word *caucus* apparently was first used in the name of a men's club, the Caucus Club of colonial Boston, sometime between 1755 and 1765. (Many early political and government meetings took place in pubs.) We have no certain knowledge of the origin of the word, but it may be from an Algonquin term meaning "elder" or from the Latin name of a drinking vessel.
6. Today, the Democratic and Republican caucuses in the House and Senate (the Republicans now use the term *conference* instead of caucus) choose each party's congressional leadership and sometimes discuss legislation and legislative strategy.
7. Due to the customs of the time, none of the candidates could admit that he had made a personal decision to run. All claimed to have entered the race in response to popular demand.
8. Parties cannot use their freedom-of-association rights to practice racial discrimination in state-sponsored elections: *Smith v. Allwright,* 321 U.S. 649 (1944). When racial discrimination is not involved, the parties have regularly won freedom-of-association suits against state governments. Examples are *Tashjian v. Republican Party of Connecticut,* 479 U.S. 208 (1986), and *California Democratic Party v. Jones,* 530 U.S. 567 (2000).
9. In Washington, the state government holds presidential primaries for both parties. The Democratic Party, however, ignores the Democratic primary and chooses its national convention delegates through a caucus/convention system. In 1984, following a dispute with the state of Michigan over primary rules, the state Democratic Party organized a presidential primary election that was run completely by party volunteers. In 2008, after a similar dispute with its state, the Virginia Republican Party chose its candidate for the U.S. Senate at its state party convention instead of through the Virginia primary elections.
10. The case was *California Democratic Party v. Jones,* cited in footnote 8.
11. *Washington State Grange v. Washington State Republican Party et al.,* 552 U.S. 442 (2008).
12. Christopher Rhoads, "Candidates Try New Web Tactics in Battle to Tap Fresh Supporters," *The Wall Street Journal,* October 30, 2008, p. 16.
13. This act is sometimes referred to as the Federal Election Campaign Act of 1972 because it became effective in that year. The official date of the act, however, is 1971.
14. 424 U.S. 1 (1976).
15. This figure is from the Center for Responsive Politics.
16. *Colorado Republican Federal Campaign Committee v. Federal Election Commission,* 518 U.S. 604 (1996).
17. Quoted in George Will, "The First Amendment on Trial," *The Washington Post,* December 1, 2002, p. B7.
18. 540 U.S. 93 (2003).
19. 551 U.S. 449 (2007).
20. 558 U.S. 50 (2010).
21. *Bush v. Gore,* 531 U.S. 98 (2000).

Chapter 10

1. *Mutual Film Corporation v. Industrial Commission of Ohio,* 236 U.S. 230 (1915).
2. *Joseph Burstyn, Inc. v. Wilson,* 343 U.S. 495 (1952).
3. *Reno v. American Civil Liberties Union,* 521 U.S. 844 (1997).
4. *United States v. Playboy Entertainment Group,* 529 U.S. 803 (2000).
5. Bernard Cohen, *The Press and Foreign Policy* (Princeton, N.J.: Princeton University Press, 1963), p. 81.
6. Interestingly, in the 2000 campaigns, a Texas group supporting George W. Bush's candidacy paid for a remake of the "daisy" commercial, but the target in the new ad was Al Gore.
7. As quoted in Michael Grunwald, "The Year of Playing Dirtier," *The Washington Post,* October 27, 2006, p. A1.
8. John G. Geer, *In Defense of Negativity: Attack Ads in Presidential Campaigns* (Chicago: University of Chicago Press, 2006).
9. The commission's action was upheld by a federal court. See *Perot v. Federal Election Commission,* 97 F.3d 553 (D.C.Cir. 1996).
10. For more details on how political candidates manage news coverage, see Doris A. Graber, *Mass Media and American Politics,* 7th ed. (Washington, D.C.: CQ Press, 2005).
11. For suggestions on how to dissect spin and detect when language is steering one toward a conclusion, see Brooks Jackson and Kathleen Hall Jamieson, *unSpun: Finding Facts in a World of Disinformation* (New York: Random House, 2007).
12. *Red Lion Broadcasting Co. v. FCC,* 395 U.S. 367 (1969).
13. Kathleen Hall Jamieson, *Everything You Think You Know about Politics . . . and Why You're Wrong* (New York: Basic Books, 2000), pp. 187–195.
14. Debra Reddin van Tuyll and Hubert P. van Tuyll, "Political Partisanship," in William David Sloan and Jenn Burleson Mackay, eds., *Media Bias: Finding It, Fixing It* (Jefferson, N.C.: McFarland, 2007), pp. 35–49.
15. Jamieson, *Everything You Think You Know about Politics,* pp. xiii–xiv.
16. Pew Research Center for the People and the Press and the Project for Excellence in Journalism, *The State of the News Media 2007: An Annual Report on American Journalism.*
17. The term *podcasting* is used for this type of information delivery because initially podcasts were downloaded onto Apple's iPods.

Chapter 11

1. These states are Alaska, Delaware, Montana, North Dakota, South Dakota, Vermont, and Wyoming.
2. 369 U.S. 186 (1962).
3. 376 U.S. 1 (1964).
4. See, for example, *Davis v. Bandemer,* 478 U.S. 109 (1986).
5. The plan was controversial because it was not implemented in response to the 2000 census. Rather, it was a "midterm" redistricting—held between censuses—that overturned what had been the postcensus redistricting plan in Texas.
6. *Amicus curiae* brief filed by the American Civil Liberties Union (ACLU) in support of the appellants in *Easley v. Cromartie,* 532 U.S. 234 (2001).
7. See, for example, *Shaw v. Reno,* 509 U.S. 630 (1993); *Miller v. Johnson,* 515 U.S. 900 (1995); *Shaw v. Hunt,* 517 U.S. 899 (1996); and *Bush v. Vera,* 517 U.S. 952 (1996).
8. *Easley v. Cromartie,* 532 U.S. 234 (2001).
9. *Powell v. McCormack,* 395 U.S. 486 (1969).
10. Some observers maintain that another reason Congress *can* stay in session longer is the invention of air-conditioning. Until the advent of air-conditioning, no member of Congress wanted to stay in session during the hot and sticky late spring, summer, and early fall months.
11. *U.S. Term Limits, Inc. v. Thornton,* 514 U.S. 779 (1995).
12. A term used by Woodrow Wilson in *Congressional Government* (New York: Meridian Books, 1956 [first published in 1885]).

Chapter 12

1. Lyndon B. Johnson, *The Vantage Point: Perspectives of the Presidency, 1963–1969* (New York: Henry Holt & Co., 1971).
2. Versailles, located about twenty miles from Paris, is the name of the palace built by King Louis XIV of France. It served as the royal palace until 1793 and was then converted into a national historical museum, which it remains today. The preliminary treaty ending the American Revolution was signed by the United States and Britain at Versailles in 1783.
3. *Ex parte Grossman,* 267 U.S. 87 (1925).
4. *Clinton v. City of New York,* 524 U.S. 417 (1998).
5. As cited in Lewis D. Eigen and Jonathan P. Siegel, *The Macmillan Dictionary of Political Quotations* (New York: Macmillan, 1993), p. 565.
6. The Constitution does not grant the president explicit power to remove from office officials who are not performing satisfactorily or who do not agree with the president. In 1926, however, the Supreme Court prevented Congress from interfering with the president's ability to fire those executive-branch officials whom he had appointed with Senate approval. See *Myers v. United States,* 272 U.S. 52 (1926).
7. Ironically, Lincoln believed that the actions of the president ought to be strictly limited when war powers were not concerned. He therefore left most domestic issues that did not involve the war entirely to Congress. In doing so, Lincoln was true to the ideas of his former party, the Whigs. That party advocated a limited role for the presidency in reaction to the sweeping assumption of authority by President Andrew Jackson, their great opponent. See David Donald's classic essay "Abraham Lincoln: Whig in the White House," in *Lincoln Reconsidered: Essays on the Civil War Era,* 3d ed. (New York: Vintage, 2001), pp. 133–147.
8. Richard E. Neustadt, *Presidential Power: The Politics of Leadership* (New York: John Wiley, 1960), p. 10.
9. As quoted in Richard M. Pious, *The American Presidency* (New York: Basic Books, 1979), pp. 51–52.
10. A phrase coined by Samuel Kernell in *Going Public: New Strategies of Presidential Leadership,* 2d ed. (Washington, D.C.: Congressional Quarterly Press, 1992).
11. Congress used its power to declare war in the War of 1812, the Mexican War (1846–1848), the Spanish-American War (1898), and World War I (U.S. involvement lasted from 1916 until 1918) and on six different occasions during World War II (U.S. involvement lasted from 1941 until 1945).
12. Actually, the Republicans had some difficulty controlling the Senate during Bush's first term. After the 2000 elections, the Senate was split 50–50 and the Republicans gained control only when Vice President Dick Cheney cast a tie-breaking vote. Four months later, Senator Jim Jeffords of Vermont left the Republicans to caucus with the Democrats, granting that party control of the chamber. In the 2002 elections, however, the Republicans picked up two net seats and regained control of the Senate, 51–49.
13. As quoted in Thomas E. Cronin, *The State of the Presidency,* 2d ed. (Boston: Little, Brown, 1980), p. 11.

Chapter 13

1. This definition follows the classic model of bureaucracy put forth by German sociologist Max Weber. See Max Weber, *Theory of Social and Economic Organization,* ed. Talcott Parsons (New York: Oxford University Press, 1974).

2. It should be noted that although the president is technically the head of the bureaucracy, the president cannot always control the bureaucracy—as you will read later in this chapter.
3. For an insightful analysis of the policymaking process in Washington, D.C., and the role played by various groups in the process, see Morton H. Halperin and Priscilla A. Clapp, with Arnold Kanter, *Bureaucratic Politics and Foreign Policy,* 2d ed. (Washington, D.C.: The Brookings Institution, 2006). Although the focus of the book is on foreign policy, the analysis applies in many ways to the general policymaking process.
4. Colleen W. Cook, *CRS Report for Congress: Mexico's Drug Cartels* (Washington, D.C.: Congressional Research Service, 2008).

Chapter 14

1. *Boumediene v. Bush,* 128 S.Ct. 2229 (2008).
2. 347 U.S. 483 (1954).
3. See *Plessy v. Ferguson,* 163 U.S. 537 (1896).
4. 539 U.S. 558 (2003).
5. 478 U.S. 186 (1986).
6. Although a state's highest court is often referred to as the state supreme court, there are exceptions. In the New York court system, for example, the supreme court is a trial court, and the highest court is called the New York Court of Appeals.
7. Between 1790 and 1891, Congress allowed the Supreme Court almost no discretion over which cases to decide. After 1925, in almost 95 percent of appealed cases the Court could choose whether to hear arguments and issue an opinion. Beginning in October 1988, mandatory review was virtually eliminated.
8. *Citizens United v. Federal Election Commission,* 558 U.S. 50 (2010).
9. *McDonald v. Chicago,* 561 U.S. ___ (2010).
10. *Graham v. Florida,* 560 U.S. ___ (2010).
11. 347 U.S. 483 (1954).
12. 84 F.3d 720 (5th Cir., 1996).
13. *Grutter v. Bollinger,* 539 U.S. 306 (2003); and *Gratz v. Bollinger,* 539 U.S. 244 (2003).
14. *Parents Involved in Community Schools v. Seattle School District No. 1,* 127 S.Ct. 2738 (2007).
15. 5 U.S. 137 (1803). The Supreme Court had considered the constitutionality of an act of Congress in *Hylton v. United States,* 3 U.S. 171 (1796), in which Congress's power to levy certain taxes was challenged. That particular act was ruled constitutional, rather than unconstitutional, however, so this first federal exercise of judicial review was not clearly recognized as such. Also, during the decade before the adoption of the federal Constitution, courts in at least eight states had exercised the power of judicial review.
16. For an analysis of the Roberts Court's first term by a Georgetown University law professor, see Jonathan Turley, "The Roberts Court: Seeing Is Believing," *USA Today,* July 6, 2006, p. 11A.
17. Erwin Chemerinsky, "Roberts and Kennedy Were Most Often in the Supreme Court Majority in Term 2009," *California Bar Journal,* August 2010.
18. Antonin Scalia, *A Matter of Interpretation* (Ewing, N.J.: Princeton University Press, 1997).
19. Letter by Thomas Jefferson to William C. Jarvis, 1820, in Andrew A. Lipscomb and Albert Ellery Bergh, *The Writings of Thomas Jefferson,* Memorial Edition (Washington, D.C.: Thomas Jefferson Memorial Association of the United States, 1904).
20. As quoted in Carl Hulse and David D. Kirkpatrick, "DeLay Says Federal Judiciary Has 'Run Amok,' Adding Congress Is Partly to Blame," *The New York Times,* April 8, 2005, p. 5.

Chapter 15

1. Stan Dorn, *Uninsured and Dying Because of It: Updating the Institute of Medicine Analysis on the Impact of Uninsurance on Mortality* (Washington, D.C.: Urban Institute, 2008).
2. An alternative possibility would be to change the Senate rules so that sixty votes would no longer be necessary to pass legislation. Changing the rules, however, could easily prove more difficult than assembling sixty votes.
3. John Kerry and Teresa Heinz Kerry, *This Moment on Earth: Today's New Environmentalists and Their Vision for the Future* (New York: PublicAffairs, 2007).

Chapter 16

1. David L. Rousseau, *Identifying Threats and Threatening Identities: The Social Construction of Realism and Liberalism* (Palo Alto, Calif.: Stanford University Press, 2006), p. 154.
2. *Public Papers of the Presidents of the United States: Harry S. Truman, 1947* (Washington, D.C.: U.S. Government Printing Office, 1963), pp. 176–180.
3. The containment policy was outlined by George F. Kennan, the chief of the policy-planning staff for the Department of State at that time, in an article that appeared in *Foreign Affairs,* July 1947, p. 575. The author's name was given as "X."
4. Bob Woodward, *Obama's Wars* (New York: Simon & Schuster, 2010).

Chapter 17

1. Quoted in Paul Harris, "Will California Become America's First Failed State?" *Guardian.co.uk,* October 5, 2009, **www.guardian.co.uk/world/2009/oct/04/california-failing-state-debt** (accessed June 14, 2010). See also **www.newsweek.com/2010/01/25/california-america-s-first-failed-state.html** (accessed June 14, 2010). Googling "California as a failed state" produces 2,870,000 hits.
2. Jed Kolko, "California Economy: Planning for a Better Future," July 2009, **www.ppic.org** (accessed June 18, 2010).
3. USC Population Dynamics Research Group, School of Policy, Planning and Development, "The New Place of Birth Profile of Los Angeles and California Residents in 2010," **www.usc.edu/schools/sppd/research/popdynamics/futures** (accessed June 18, 2010).
4. Public Policy Institute of California, "Just the Facts: Immigrants in California," June 2008, **www.ppic.org** (accessed June 21, 2010).
5. Southern Education Foundation, January 31, 2010, **www.southerneducation.org/pdf/New%20Diverse%20Majority-Summary.pdf** (accessed June 21, 2010).
6. *Ibid.*
7. California Budget Project, "A Generation of Widening Inequality," August 2007, **www.cpb.org** (accessed June 21, 2010); and California Budget Project, "Policy Points: New Data Show That California's Income Gaps Continue to Widen," June 2009, **www.cpb.org** (accessed June 21, 2010).
8. For information about regional variation in housing costs, see the National Association of Home Builders (NAHB)/Wells Fargo Housing Opportunity Index (HOI), **www.nahb.org/reference_list.aspx?sectionID=135** (accessed June 13, 2010).
9. UCLA Center for Health and Policy Research, reported in "The Uninsured," *San Jose Mercury News,* March 17, 2010, p. A1.
10. See Frederick Douzet and Kenneth P. Miller, "California's East-West Divide," in *The New Political Geography of California,* ed. Frederick Douzet, Thad Kousser, and Kenneth P. Miller (Berkeley: Berkeley Public Policy Press, Institute of Governmental Studies, University of California, 2008).
11. Report from the Legislative Analyst's Office cited in "California's Unequal Give and Take," *San Jose Mercury News,* June 21, 2010.
12. Public Policy Institute of California, "Statewide Survey Time Trends," **www.ppic.org** (accessed June 21, 2010).
13. Public Policy Institute of California, "Statewide Survey," September 9, 2009. Thirty-three percent supported major constitutional change, 36 percent supported minor changes, 24 percent thought California's constitution was fine as is, and 7 percent don't know.

Chapter 18

1. Peter Schrag, "On Race and Gender, the GOP's Tent Is Teeny," *Sacramento Bee,* September 19, 2007.
2. See Public Policy Institute of California, "California Voter and Party Profiles," *Just the Facts,* September 2009, **www.ppic.org** (accessed June 24, 2010); and past reports of the PPIC Statewide Survey, also at **www.ppic.org.**
3. See Gary C. Jacobson, "Partisanship and Ideological Polarization in the California Electorate," *State Politics and Policy Quarterly* 4 (2004): 113–139.
4. Public Policy Institute of California, "California's Likely Voters," *Just the Facts,* September 2009, **www.ppic.org** (accessed June 24, 2010).
5. Morris P. Fiorina and Samuel J. Abrams, "Is California Really a Blue State?" in *The New Political Geography of California,* ed. Frederick Douzet, Thad Kousser, and Kenneth P. Miller (Berkeley: Berkeley Public Policy Press, Institute of Governmental Studies, University of California, 2008).
6. "State of the Golden State," Public Policy Institute of California, San Francisco: Public Policy Institute of California, August 2003, **www.ppic.org.**
7. Ronald George, "Promoting Judicial Independence," *The Commonwealth,* February 2006, p. 9.
8. California Fair Political Practices Commission, *Big Money Talks,* March 2010, p. 6, **www.fppc.ca.gov/reports/Report38104.pdf** (accessed June 25, 2010).
9. Public Policy Institute of California, "Californians and Their Government," Statewide Survey, December 2008, **www.ppic.org** (accessed June 25, 2010).
10. Mark Baldassare and Cheryl Katz, *The Coming Age of Direct Democracy* (New York: Rowman & Littlefield, 2008).

Chapter 19

1. Jessica Trounstine and Zoltan Hajnal, "Low Voter Turnout Does Matter: Spending Priorities in Local Politics" (paper presented at the annual meeting of the Midwest Political Science Association, Chicago, April 2004).
2. James H. Fowler and Christopher T. Dawes, "Two Genes Predict Voter Turnout," *Journal of Politics,* Vol. 70, No. 3, July 2008. Fowler and Dawes are also at UC San Diego.
3. California Voter Foundation, "California Voter Participation Survey," March 2005, **www.calvoter.org.**
4. "The Changing California Electorate," *California Opinion Index,* August 2009, **www.fieldpoll.com** (accessed June 27, 2010).
5. *Ibid.*
6. Ricardo Ramirez and Luis Fraga, "Continuity and Change: Latino PoliticalIncorporation in California since 1990," in *Racial and Ethnic Politics in California,* ed. Sandra Bass and Bruce E. Cain (Berkeley: Berkeley Public Policy Press, Institute of Governmental Studies, University of California, 2008).
7. Public Policy Institute of California, "California's Likely Voters," *Just the Facts,* September 2009, **www.ppic.org.**
8. Lisa McGirr, *Suburban Warriors: The Origins of the New American Right* (Princeton, N.J.: Princeton University Press, 2002).
9. Public Policy Institute of California, "The Age Gap in California Politics," *Just the Facts,* August 2008, **www.ppic.org.**
10. National Association of Latino Elected Officials, "2010 Latino Electoral Profile: California State Primary Election," **www.naleo.org** (accessed June 28, 2010).
11. Gay and Lesbian Leadership Institute, **www.glli.org/leadership** (accessed June 27, 2010).
12. California Fair Political Practices Commission, "The Billion Dollar Money Train," April 2009, **www.fppc.ca.gov** (accessed June 29, 2010).
13. *Ibid.*

14. California Fair Political Practices Commission, "Independent Expenditures: The Giant Gorilla in Campaign Finance," June 2008, **www.fppc.ca.gov** (accessed June 29, 2010).
15. Dan Walters, "Proposition 34 Only Gave the Appearance of Reform," *San Jose Mercury News,* June 6, 2010. For more on how PACs shuffle funds and obscure sources, see "Campaign Spending Harder to Track," *San Jose Mercury News,* June 28, 2010.
16. "Capitol Weekly's Top 100 List, Parts I and II," *Capitol Weekly,* April 16 and 23, 2009, **www.capitolweekly.net** (accessed June 29, 2010).
17. "Whitman Digs Deep into Tech's Toolbox," *San Jose Mercury News,* July 2, 2010, p. 1A.
18. For a full discussion of the recall campaign, see Larry N. Gerston and Terry Christensen, *Recall! California's Political Earthquake* (Armonk, N.Y.: M. E. Sharpe, 2004).
19. "As Cities Downsize from Two Newspapers to Just One, Some Talk of Zero," *New York Times,* March 12, 2009.
20. Public Policy Institute of California, "Californians' News and Information Sources," *Just the Facts,* September 2007, **www.ppic.org.**
21. Marcelo Ballve et al., *Profiles of Ethnic Media: California's New Civic Communicators* (San Francisco: New California Media, 2002).
22. Public Policy Institute of California, *Statewide Survey,* October 2004, **www.ppic.org.**
23. Public Policy Institute of California, *Statewide Survey,* June 2008, **www.ppic.org.**

Chapter 20

1. See Stephanie S. Pincetl, *Transforming California: A Political History of Land Use and Development* (Baltimore, MD: The Johns Hopkins University Press, 1999), pp. 20–22.
2. "The World in 2011," *The Economist* special edition, December 2010, pp. 115–123.
3. *California Business Issues, 2004* (Sacramento: California Chamber of Commerce, 2004), p. 77; also see "Few Take State's Family Leave," *San Jose Mercury News,* July 4, 2006, pp. 1C, 9C.
4. See Larry N. Gerston and Terry Christensen, *Recall! California's Political Earthquake* (Armonk, NY: M. E. Sharpe), p. 22.
5. The ruling was *In re Marriage Cases,* S147999.
6. Public Policy Institute of California, *Statewide Survey,* June 2000, **www.ppic.org.**
7. "Cities, Counties, Pay Price for Capitol Clout," *Los Angeles Times,* September 10, 2007, pp. B1, B4.
8. See "Bumper Crop of Clout," *Los Angeles Times,* September 22, 2004, pp. A1, A22, A23.
9. "How Our Laws Are Really Made," *San Jose Mercury News,* July 11, 2010, pp. A1, A6, A7.
10. "Special Interests: How They Get around Voter-Approved Limits on Campaign Contributions," *San Francisco Chronicle,* February 11, 2008, pp. A1, A6.
11. "End of Session Money Rains Down on Candidates," press release, California Fair Political Practices Commission, September 16, 2009.
12. See "A Lobbyist by Any Other Name?" *San Jose Mercury News,* May 20, 2005, pp, 1A, 17A.
13. "Lobbyists Heat up over Climate Law," *Sacramento Bee,* July 12, 2010, pp. A1, A10.
14. "E-mails Put California Coastal Commissioner in an Awkward Spot," *Los Angeles Times,* July 10, 2010, p. AA3.
15. "Elective Office Improves a Resume," *Los Angeles Times,* November 24, 2006, pp. B1, B11.
16. Douglas Foster, "The Lame Duck State," *Harper's,* February 1994.
17. Phillip Reese, "Amid Budget Crisis, California Legislators Still Wined and Dined on Lobbyists' Dime," *Sacramento Bee,* September 13, 2009, p. 1A.
18. See "Cell Phone Lobby Thwarts Reform Efforts," *San Jose Mercury News,* September 18, 2007, pp. 1A, 15A.
19. "$20 Million Tab to Defeat a Privacy Bill," *San Francisco Chronicle,* September 7, 2002, pp. A1, A11.
20. "Business Czar Delivers Major Cash to Governor," *San Jose Mercury News,* February 22, 2005, pp. 1A, 12A; also see "Business Sees an Ally in Governor," *Los Angeles Times,* October 18, 2004, pp. B1, B7.
21. Foster, *op. cit.*

Chapter 21

1. As quoted in Randy Bayne, "Time to End Term Limits," California Progress Report, **www.californiaprogressreport.com/2009/01/time_to_end_ter.html.**
2. *Californians and Their Government,* Public Policy Institute of California Statewide Survey (San Francisco: PPIC, January 2010).
3. In general, the plan provided one senator per county. In a few cases, two low-populated counties shared a senator, and in one case, three low-populated counties—Alpine, Inyo, and Mono—shared a senator.
4. 377 U.S. 533 (1964).
5. Legislators receive monthly allowances for cars (including gasoline and maintenance); life, health, dental, vision, and disability insurance; and a daily housing allowance when they are in session in Sacramento. On average these benefits amount to about $42,000 annually, almost all of which is nontaxable. For an interesting critique, see Dan Walters, "Legislative Per Diem Boondoggle," *Sacramento Bee,* July 7, 2007, p. A3.
6. The other full-time legislatures are Alaska, Florida, Massachusetts, Michigan, New Jersey, New York, Ohio, Pennsylvania, and Wisconsin.
7. "Plan to Redraw Districts Passes," *Los Angeles Times,* September 14, 2001, p. B8.
8. *Ibid.*
9. Rene Bukovichik Van Vechten, "Taking the Politics Out of Politics? State Legislative Politics and Institutional Reform in Twentieth Century California" (Ph.D. diss., University of California, Irvine 2002), 203–213.
10. *Ibid,* p. 21.
11. "Report Chronicles Downside of Term Limits," Stateline.org, August 16, 2006, **www.stateline.org/live/details/story?contentId=134247.**
12. Public Policy Institute of California, *Californians and Their Government,"* (San Francisco: PPIC, September 10, 2009), p. 7.
13. Kathleen Les, "Mr. Mayor Goes to the Capitol," *California Journal* 30, no. 10 (October 1999): 36–38.
14. See Bruce E. Cain and That Kousser, *Adapting to Term Limits: Recent Experiences and New Directions* (San Francisco: Public Policy Institute of California, 2004), p. 15.
15. "Choosing Sides in State Budget Fiasco," *Los Angeles Times,* June 26, 2010, pp. A1, A14.
16. *Ibid.*
17. Kevin Yamamura, "State's Big Five Keep Talks Secret for Fear of Dooming Budget Deal," *Sacramento Bee,* Feb. 4, 2009, p. 1A.
18. "End of the Supermajority," *Los Angeles Times,* (Dec. 23, 2008).
19. See "Ghost Voting: A Long History," *San Francisco Chronicle,* June 10, 2008, pp. A1, A16.
20. "What Limits? New Law Can't Stop Big Money," *Los Angeles Times,* September 3, 2003, pp. A1, A18.
21. Institute on Money and State Politics, "State Elections Overview, 2008," Helena, Mont., April 2010, **www.followthemoney.org/database/StateGlance/state_candidates.phtml?s=CA&y=2008&f=0&so=a&p=7#sorttable** (accessed April 2010).
22. "Dems Reject Two of Schwarzenegger's Parole Appointees," *Sacramento Bee,* June 26, 2008, p. A3.
23. "State Fund Posts 9.9% Dip in Comp Rates," *Los Angeles Times,* June 5, 2004, pp. C1, C2.

Chapter 22

1. "Forum Sheds Light on How Judges Are Screened, Chosen," *San Jose Mercury News,* June 4, 2006. As of 2006, 54 percent of Schwarzenegger's appointees were Republican, 34 percent were Democrats, and 12 percent had "unstated" party affiliations.
2. Rodney F. Kingsnorth, "Change How We Appoint Judges," in *Remaking California,* ed. R. Jeffrey Lustig (Berkeley, Calif.: Heyday Books, 2010), pp. 226–227.
3. Judicial Council, *2009 Court Statistics Report,* **www.courtinfo.ca.gov** (accessed July 7, 2010).
4. *Ibid.*
5. California Bar Association, "The State Bar of California: What Does It Do? How Does It Work?" 2006, **www.calbar.org** (accessed August 12, 2008).
6. Judicial Council of California, "Demographic Data Provided by Justices and Judges Relative to Gender and Race/Ethnicity," **www.courtinfo.ca.gov** (accessed July 7, 2010).
7. Elsa Y. Chen, "Cumulative Disadvantage and Racial and Ethnic Disparities in California Federal Sentencing," in *Racial and Ethnic Politics in California,* ed. Sandra Bass and Bruce M. Cain (Berkeley: Public Policy Press, Institute of Governmental Studies, University of California, 2008).
8. Charles Price, "Shadow Government," *California Journal,* October 1997, p. 38.
9. See Preble Stolz, Gerald F. Uelmen, and Susan Rasky, "The California Supreme Court," in *Governing California,* ed. Gerald C. Lubenow, 2d ed. (Berkeley: Public Policy Press, Institute of Governmental Studies, University of California, 2006), p. 103.
10. *In re Marriage Cases,* S147999.
11. *Strauss v. Horton,* S168047; *Tyler v. State of California,* S168066; and *City and County of San Francisco v. Horton,* S168078, **www.courtinfo.ca.gov/courts/supreme.**
12. Ronald George, "Promoting Judicial Independence," *The Commonwealth,* February 2006, p. 10.
13. Jake Dear and Edward W. Jesson, "Followed Rates and Leading Cases, 1940–2005," *University of California, Davis, Law Review* 41 (April 2007): 683.
14. Bob Egelko, "State's Top Court Strikes Down Marriage Ban," *San Francisco Chronicle,* May 16, 2008.
15. California Commission on the Fair Administration of Justice, "Fair Administration of the Death Penalty," June 30, 2008, **www.ccfaj.org** (accessed August 1, 2008).
16. "California Crime Rates, 1960-2008," **www.disastercenter.com/crime/cacrime.htm** (accessed July 9, 2010).
17. Department of Corrections, "Population Reports," **www.cdcr.ca.gov** (accessed July 9, 2010).

Chapter 23

1. "Gov. Calls for New Spending on Prisons," *Los Angeles Times,* June 27, 2006, pp. A1, A7.
2. "Special Sessions Define Schwarzenegger," Sign on San Diego, October 22, 2009, **http://signonsandiego.printthis.clickability.com/pt/cpt?action=cpt&tit.**
3. "Judge Halts Many State Furloughs," *San Francisco Chronicle,* March 25, 2010, pp. A1, A12.
4. "Tensions Flare between Davis and His Democrats," *Los Angeles Times,* July 22, 1999, pp. A1, A28.
5. "Davis Comments Draw Fire," *San Jose Mercury News,* March 1, 2000, p. 14A.
6. *The Field Poll,* Release #2074, July 15, 2003.
7. For an account of how Davis fell from power, see Larry N. Gerston and Terry Christensen, *Recall! California's Political Earthquake* (Armonk, N.Y.: M. E. Sharpe, 2004).

8. "Gov. Criticizes Legislators as 'Girlie Men,'" *Los Angeles Times,* July 18, 2004, pp. B1, B18.
9. "Governor Slashes Workers' Pay," *San Francisco Chronicle,* July 2, 2010, pp. C1, C6.
10. "Schwarzenegger's Popularity Slide," *Los Angeles Times,* October 28, 2005, p. B2.
11. "Schwarzenegger Says the Fault Is His," *New York Times,* November 11, 2006, p. A14.
12. "Plan to Sell Portion of State Fund Collapses," *Los Angeles Times,* December 30, 2009, pp. B1, B5.
13. "The Most Invisible Job in Sacramento," *Los Angeles Times,* May 10, 1998, pp. A1, A20.
14. "Touch Vote Machine Ban Hurts Counties, *San Francisco Chronicle,* August 7, 2007, p. B3.
15. "California Imposes Rule for Efficiency on Some TVs," *New York Times,* November 19, 2009, p. A16.
16. "Looking for Waste," *Economist,* May 1, 2010, p. 33.
17. "Soaring Payroll Stymies 'Reform' Governor," *San Francisco Chronicle,* May 28, 2008, pp. A1, A6.

Chapter 24

1. "Debt Remains in Governor's Budget Plan," *San Jose Mercury News,* July 1, 2004, pp. 1A, 17A.
2. "Deal Puts State in Hole for Next Year," *San Francisco Chronicle,* July 26, 2009, pp. A1, A17.
3. Field Poll, Release No. 2329, March 2, 2010.
4. Field Poll, Release No. 2335, March 24, 2010.
5. "California Finding That Prisons Costs Aren't So Easy to Cut," *San Jose Mercury News,* March 24, 2010, pp. B1, B9.
6. Howard Jarvis Taxpayers Association, 2009, **www.hjta.org/index.php.**
7. "Highway Spending," in *Governing: State and Local Sourcebook* (Washington, D.C.: Congressional Quarterly, 2006), pp. 32–36.
8. "Finance," in *Governing: State and Local Government Sourcebook* (Washington, D.C.: Congressional Quarterly, 2006), pp. 32–36.
9. "State Cigarette Excise Tax Rates and Rankings, 2010," **www.tobaccofreekids.org.**
10. See "Ballot Battle to Follow Wrangling over Budget," *San Francisco Chronicle,* February 17, 2009, pp. A1, A14; and "Traditional Foes Team Up over Prop. 1A," *San Francisco Chronicle*, April 6, 2009, pp. A1, A7.
11. Testimony before Assembly Budget Subcommittee No. 2, March 11, 2008.
12. See *Just the Facts* (Albany: Public Policy Institute of New York State, 2007).
13. "State Education Rankings: Graduation Rates for High School, College and Grad/Professional School," Associated Content, July 21, 2010, **www.associatedcontent.com/article/5562698/state_education_rankings_graduation.html.**
14. "CSU Freshmen Face Challenges," *Los Angeles Times,* March 15, 2006, p. B9.
15. "No Quick, Cheap Fix for State's Schools," *Los Angeles Times,* March 15, 2007, pp. B1, B10.
16. See James Richardson, "What Price Glory?" *UCLA Magazine,* February 1997, p. 30; also see "A Crown Jewel of Education Struggles with Cuts in California," *New York Times,* November 20, 2009, pp. A1, A25.
17. "Community Colleges Make Concerted Effort to Meet Demand," press release issued by the California Community Colleges Chancellor's Office, Sacramento, June 3, 2010.
18. Christopher Neufeld and Stanton Glantz, "Ending the California Dream," op-ed in *San Francisco Chronicle,* July 14, 2009, p. A11.
19. "Gov. Calls for New Spending on Prisons," *Los Angeles Times,* June 27, 2006, pp. A1, A7.
20. "Rising Debt a Threat to State General Fund," *San Francisco Chronicle,* November 24, 2009, p. C3.
21. "California Bond Rating Now Lowest of Any State," *Los Angeles Times,* February 4, 2009, pp. A1, A11

Chapter 25

1. 1. Walter A. Rosenbaum and Gladys M. Kammerer, *Against Long Odds: The Theory and Practice of Successful Government Consolidation* (Beverly Hills, Calif.: Sage, 1974).
2. Glen W. Sparrow, "Consolidation, West-Coast Style: Sacramento, California," *Case Studies of City-County Consolidation: Reshaping the Local Government Landscape,* Suzanne M. Leland and Kurt Thurmaier, eds. (Armonk, N.Y.: M.E. Sharpe, 2004).
3. Zoltan L. Hajnal, Paul G. Lewis, and Hugh Louch, "Municipal Elections in California: Turnout, Timing, and Competition," Public Policy Institute of California, March 2002, **www.ppic.org.**
4. Jessica Trounstine and Zoltan Hajnal, "Low Voter Turnout Does Matter: Spending Priorities in Local Politics" (paper presented at the annual meeting of the Midwest Political Science Association, Chicago, April 2004).
5. Hajnal, Lewis, and Louch, *op. cit.*
6. Jessica Levinson, "Local Public Financing Charts" (Los Angeles: Center for Governmental Studies, May 2009), **www.cgs.org** (accessed July 13, 2010).
7. See Center for Governmental Studies, *Money and Power in the City of Angels,* July 2010, **www.cgs.org** (accessed July 16, 2010).
8. Belinda I. Reyes, "Demographic Change and the Politics of Education in California," in *Racial and Ethnic Politics in California,* ed. Sandra Bass and Bruce M. Cain (Berkeley: Berkeley Public Policy Press, Institute of Governmental Studies, University of California, 2008), pp. 236, 241.
9. EdSource, **www.edsource.org** (accessed July 14, 2010).
10. California Department of Education, **www.cde.ca.gov** (accessed July 14, 2010). For California's rank among the states on education spending, see Public Policy Institute of California, *California 2025,* **www.ppic.org** (accessed July 14, 2010), or California Budget Project, "School Finance Facts," June 2010, **www.cbp.org** (accessed July 14, 2010).
11. For more on regional fragmentation and special districts, see Brian, P. Janiskee, "The Problem of Local Government in California," in *California Republic,* ed. Brian P. Janiskee and Ken Masugi (Lanham, Md.: Rowman and Littlefield, 2004).
12. California Elections Data Archive, Institute for Social Research, California State University, Sacramento, **www.csus.edu/isr** (accessed July 15, 2010).
13. *Ibid.*
14. For further discussion of these effects of Proposition 13, see John Decker, *California in the Balance* (Berkeley, Calif.: Berkeley Public Policy Press, 2009), pp. xi, 116, 137–138.
15. "Maywood to Lay Off All City Employees, Dismantle Police Department," June 22, 2010, **www.latimesblogs.latimes.com/lanow/2010/06.**
16. U.S. Census, **www.census.gov/govs/apes** (accessed July 16, 2010).

Chapter 26

1. *Gonzales v. Raich,* 545 U.S. 1 (2005).
2. U.S. Department of Interior, "Reclamation: Managing Water in the West, Auburn-Folsom South Unit Special Report," December 2006.
3. For example, for fiscal 2009 the entire federal commitment to all fifty states plus the District of Columbia was $48, 575,000, of which California received a small percentage. See Department of Homeland Security, "Driver's License Security Program," **www.dhs.gov/files/programs/gc_1214423542432.shtm.**
4. Dowell Myers, John Pitkin, and Julie Park, *California Demographic Features* (Los Angeles: School of Policy, Planning, and Development, University of Southern California, February 2005), p. ix.
5. U.S. Census Bureau, *Statistical Abstract of the United States: 2009* (Washington, D.C.: Government Printing Office, 2008), p. 19.
6. "Report: One in 10 Workers in California Is Illegal," *Sacramento Bee,* April 15, 2010, pp. A1, A20.
7. "Illegal Immigrants Become Subject of Coverage Debate," *San Francisco Chronicle,* September 11, 2009, pp. A1, A18.
8. *The Size and Characteristics of the Unauthorized Migrant Population in the U.S.* (Washington, D.C.: Pew Hispanic Center, 2006), p. 9.
9. "Immigrants in the Work Force: Study Belies Image," *New York Times,* April 10, 2010, pp. A1, A3.
10. "Border Policy Is Pinching Farmers," *Los Angeles Times,* September 22, 2005, pp. C1, C2.
11. See "Bush Orders Some Firms to Show Workers' Status," *Wall Street Journal,* June 10, 2008, p. A6; and "Shortage of Skilled Workers Looms in U.S.," *Los Angeles Times,* April 21, 2008, p. A1, A7.
12. "Crossings by Migrants Slow as Job Picture Dims," *Wall Street Journal,* April 9, 2008, pp. A1, A12.
13. "These data are cited in Bernard L. Hyink and David H. Provost, *Politics and Government in California,* 16th ed. (New York: Pearson Longman, 2004), p. 233.
14. "Gov. Refuses Bush Request for Border Troops," *Los Angeles Times,* June 24, 2006, pp. A1, A18.
15. "Smog in L.A. Still Tops in Nation," *Los Angeles Times,* April 28, 2010, pp. AA1, AA6.
16. California Healthline, November 13, 2008, **www.californiahealthline.org.**
17. See Daniel A. Mazmanian, "Achieving Air Quality: The Los Angeles Experience" (unpublished paper, University of Southern California, March 2006), p. 28.
18. "E.P.A. Says 17 States Can't Set Greenhouse Gas Rules for Cars," *New York Times,* December 20, 2007, pp. A1, A30.
19. "California Water Users Miss Deadline on Pact for Sharing," *New York Times,* January 1, 2003. The six states in addition to California are Arizona, Colorado, Nevada, New Mexico, Utah, and Wyoming.
20. "Enforcing Recent Water Laws May Throttle State's Growth," *Los Angeles Times,* January 14, 2008, pp. B1, B8.
21. U.S. Census Bureau, *op. cit.,* table 467.
22. Deborah Reed, "Poverty In California," *California Counts* 7, no. 4 (May 2006), **www.ppic.org.**

Glossary

A

Absentee ballots Voters who prefer not to vote at their polling places or who are unable to vote on Election Day may apply to their county registrar of voters or an absentee ballot and vote by mail; nearly half of those who vote in California elections vote by mail.

Action-reaction syndrome For every government action, there will be a reaction by the public. The government then takes a further action to counter the public's reaction—and the cycle begins again.

Adjudicate To render a judicial decision. In regard to administrative law, the process in which an administrative law judge hears and decides issues that arise when an agency charges a person or firm with violating a law or regulation enforced by the agency.

Administrative law The body of law created by administrative agencies (in the form of rules, regulations, orders, and decisions) in order to carry out their duties and responsibilities.

Affirmative action A policy calling for the establishment of programs that give special consideration, in jobs and college admissions, to members of groups that have been discriminated against in the past.

Agenda setting Getting an issue on the political agenda to be addressed by Congress; part of the first stage of the policymaking process.

Agents of political socialization People and institutions that influence the political views of others.

Anti-Federalists A political group that opposed the adoption of the Constitution because of the document's centralist tendencies and because it did not include a bill of rights.

Appellate court A court having appellate jurisdiction. An appellate court normally does not hear evidence or testimony but reviews the transcript of the trial court's proceedings, other records relating to the case, and attorneys' arguments as to why the trial court's decision should or should not stand.

Apportionment The distribution of House seats among the states on the basis of their respective populations.

Appropriation A part of the congressional budgeting process that involves determining how many dollars will be spent in a given year on a particular set of government activities.

Articles of Confederation The nation's first national constitution, which established a national form of government following the American Revolution. The Articles provided for a confederal form of government in which the central government had few powers.

At-large elections City council elections in which all candidates are elected by the community as a whole rather than by districts.

Attorney general California's top law enforcement officer and legal counsel; the second most powerful member of the executive branch.

Australian ballot A secret ballot that is prepared, distributed, and counted by government officials at public expense; used by all states in the United States since 1888.

Authority The ability to legitimately exercise power, such as the power to make and enforce laws.

Authorization A part of the congressional budgeting process that involves the creation of the legal basis for government programs.

Autocracy A form of government in which the power and authority of the government are in the hands of a single person.

B

Bank and corporation tax A tax on the profits of lending institutions and businesses; the third most important source of state revenue.

Biased sample A poll sample that does not accurately represent the population.

Bicameral legislature A legislature made up of two chambers, or parts. The United States has a bicameral legislature, composed of the House of Representatives and the Senate.

Big Five The governor, assembly speaker, assembly minority leader, senate president pro tem, and senate minority leader, who gather together informally to thrash out decisions on the annual budget and other major policy issues.

Bill of attainder A legislative act that inflicts punishment on particular persons or groups without granting them the right to a trial.

Bill of Rights The first ten amendments to the U.S. Constitution. They list the freedoms—such as the freedoms of speech, press, and religion—that a citizen enjoys and that cannot be infringed on by the government.

Block grant A federal grant given to a state for a broad area, such as criminal justice or mental-health programs.

Blue Dog Coalition A caucus that unites most of the moderate-to-conservative Democrats in the House of Representatives.

Board of Equalization The five-member state board that oversees the collection of sales, gasoline, and liquor taxes; members are elected by district; part of the executive branch.

Board of supervisors The five-member governing body of counties; elected by district to four-year terms.

Bonds Subject to voter approval, state and local governments can borrow money by issuing bonds, which are repaid (with interest) from the general fund budget or from special taxes or fees.

Bureaucracy A large, complex, hierarchically structured administrative organization that carries out specific functions.

Bureaucrat An individual who works in a bureaucracy. As generally used, the term refers to a government employee.

Busing The transportation of public school students by bus to schools physically outside their neighborhoods to eliminate school segregation based on residential patterns.

C

Cabinet An advisory group selected by the president to assist with decision making. Traditionally, the cabinet has consisted of the heads of the executive departments and other officers whom the president may choose to appoint.

Campaign strategy The comprehensive plan developed by a candidate and his or her advisers for winning an election. The strategy includes the candidate's position on issues, slogan, advertising plan, press events, personal appearances, and other aspects of the campaign.

Cap-and-trade A method of restricting the production of a harmful substance. A cap is set on the volume of production, and permits to produce the substance can then be traded on the open market.

Capitalism An economic system based on the private ownership of wealth-producing property, free markets, and freedom of contract. The privately owned corporation is the preeminent capitalist institution.

Case law The rules of law announced in court decisions. Case law includes the aggregate of reported cases that interpret judicial precedents, statutes, regulations, and constitutional provisions.

Categorical grant A federal grant targeted for a specific purpose as defined by federal law.

Caucus A meeting held to choose political candidates or delegates.

Central committees Political party organizations at county and state levels; weakly linked to one another.

Charges for services Local government fees for services such as sewage treatment, trash collection, building permits, and the use of recreational facilities; a major source of income for cities and counties since the passage of Proposition 13 in 1978.

Charter The equivalent of a constitution for a local government; includes government structures, election systems, powers of officeholders, conditions for employing local government workers, and often much more.

Charter city or county A local government that drafts its own structures and organization through a document like a local constitution (also known as a "home-rule" charter), subject to voter approval.

Checks and balances A major principle of American government in which each of the three branches is given the means to check (to restrain or balance) the actions of the others.

Chief diplomat The role of the president of the United States in recognizing and interacting with foreign governments.

Chief executive The head of the executive branch of government; in the United States, the president.

Chief of staff The person who directs the operations of the White House Office and who advises the president on important matters.

Cities Local governments in urban areas, run by city councils and mayors or city managers; principal responsibilities include police and fire protection, landuse planning, street maintenance and construction, sanitation, libraries, and parks.

Citizen journalism The collection, analysis, and dissemination of information online by independent journalists, scholars, politicians, and the general citizenry.

Citizens Redistricting Commission Enacted by the voters in Proposition 11 (2009), this commission will assume responsibility for determining the boundaries of state legislative districts and Board of Equalization districts.

City council The governing body of a city; members are elected at large or by district to four-year terms.

City manager The top administrative officer in most California cities; appointed by the city council.

Civil disobedience The deliberate and public act of refusing to obey laws thought to be unjust.

Civil law The branch of law that spells out the duties that individuals in society owe to other persons or to their governments, excluding the duty not to commit crimes.

Civil liberties Individual rights protected by the Constitution against the powers of the government.

Civil rights The rights of all Americans to equal treatment under the law, as provided for by the Fourteenth Amendment to the Constitution.

Civil rights movement The movement in the 1950s and 1960s, by minorities and concerned whites, to end racial segregation.

Civil service Nonmilitary government employees.

Civil service system A system for hiring and retaining public employees on the basis of their qualifications or merit; replaced the political machine's patronage, or spoils, system; encompasses 98 percent of state workers.

Closed primary A primary in which only party members can vote to choose that party's candidates.

Cloture A method of ending debate in the Senate and bringing the matter under consideration to a vote by the entire chamber.

Coalition An alliance of individuals or groups with a variety of interests and opinions who join together to support all or part of a political party's platform. Also an alliance of nations formed to undertake a foreign policy action, particularly a military action. A coalition is often a temporary alliance that dissolves after the action is concluded.

Cold War The war of words, warnings, and ideologies between the Soviet Union and the United States that lasted from the late 1940s through the early 1990s.

Collegiality Deferential behavior among justices as a way of building consensus on issues before the court.

Colonial empire A group of dependent nations that are under the rule of a single imperial power.

Commander in chief The supreme commander of a nation's military force.

Commerce clause The clause in Article I, Section 8, of the Constitution that gives Congress the power to regulate interstate commerce (commerce involving more than one state).

Commercial speech Advertising statements that describe products. Commercial speech receives less protection under the First Amendment than ordinary speech.

Commission on Judicial Appointments A commission to review and make recommendations on the governor's nominees for appellate and supreme courts; consists of the attorney general, the chief justice of the state supreme court, and the senior presiding judge of the courts of appeal.

Commission on Judicial Performance The state board empowered to investigate charges of judicial misconduct or incompetence.

Common law The body of law developed from judicial decisions in English and U.S. courts, not attributable to a legislature.

Competitive federalism A model of federalism devised by Thomas R. Dye in which state and local governments compete for businesses and citizens, who in effect "vote with their feet" by moving to jurisdictions that offer a competitive advantage.

Concurrent powers Powers held by both the federal and the state governments in a federal system.

Concurring opinion A statement written by a judge or justice who agrees (concurs) with the court's decision, but for reasons different from those in the majority opinion.

Confederal system A league of independent sovereign states, joined together by a central government that has only limited powers over them.

Confederation A league of independent states that are united only for the purpose of achieving common goals.

Conference In regard to the Supreme Court, a private meeting of the justices in which they present their arguments concerning a case under consideration.

Conference committee A temporary committee that is formed when the two chambers of Congress pass differing versions of the same bill. The conference committee, which consists of members from both the House and the Senate (or senate and assembly in California state government) works out a compromise form of the bill.

Conference report A report submitted by a congressional conference committee after it has drafted a single version of a bill.

Congressional Budget Office (CBO) An agency established by Congress to evaluate the impact of proposed legislation on the federal budget.

Congressional delegation Members of the House of Representatives and Senate representing a particular state.

Congressional district The geographic area that is served by one member in the House of Representatives.

Conservatism A set of beliefs that include a limited role for the national government in helping individuals and in the economic affairs of the nation, support for traditional values and lifestyles, and a cautious response to change.

Consolidation The merger of cities, school districts, or special districts; usually requires voter approval.

Constitution of 1849 California's first constitution, which was copied from constitutions of other states and featured a two-house legislature, a supreme court, and an executive branch including a governor, lieutenant governor, controller, attorney general, and superintendent of public instruction, as well as a bill of rights. Only white males were allowed to vote.

Constitution of 1879 California's second constitution, which retained the basic structures of the Constitution of 1849 but added institutions to regulate railroads and public utilities and to ensure fair tax assessments. Chinese individuals were denied the right to vote, own land, or work for the government.

Constitutional amendments May be placed on the ballot by a two-thirds vote of the legislature or through the initiative process; must be approved by a simple majority of the voters.

Constitutional Convention The convention (meeting) of delegates from the states that was held in Philadelphia in 1787 for the purpose of amending the Articles of Confederation. In fact, the delegates wrote a new constitution (the U.S. Constitution) that established a federal form of government to replace the governmental system that had been created by the Articles of Confederation. In state government, an occasion for extensive revision or reform of the state constitution. A two-thirds vote of the California state legislature is required to put a proposal for a convention on the ballot. If voters approve, delegates are elected by district.

Constitutional law Law based on the U.S. Constitution and the constitutions of the various states.

Containment A U.S. policy designed to contain the spread of communism by offering military and economic aid to threatened nations.

Continuing resolution A temporary resolution passed by Congress when an appropriations bill has not been passed by the beginning of the new fiscal year.

Contract lobbyist An individual or company that represents the interests of clients before the legislature and other policymaking entities.

Contracting for services Smaller cities contract with counties, special districts, or other cities to provide services they cannot efficiently provide themselves.

Controller An independently elected state executive who oversees taxing and spending.

Cooperative federalism The theory that the states and the federal government should cooperate in solving problems.

Corporate Average Fuel Economy (CAFE) standards A set of federal standards under which each manufacturer must meet a miles-per-gallon benchmark averaged across all cars or trucks that it sells.

Council–manager system A form of government in which an elected council appoints a professional manager to administer daily operations; used by most California cities.

Councils of government (cogs) Regional planning organizations with representation for cities and counties.

Counties Local governments and administrative agencies of the state, run by elected boards of supervisors; principal responsibilities include welfare, jails, courts, roads, and elections.

County executive The top administrative officer in most California counties; appointed by the board of supervisors.

Courts of appeal Three-justice panels that hear appeals from lower courts.

Credentials Committee A committee of each national political party that evaluates the claims of national party convention delegates to be the legitimate representatives of their states.

Criminal law The branch of law that defines and governs actions that constitute crimes. Generally, criminal law has to do with wrongful actions committed against society for which society demands redress.

Cross-filing An election system that allowed candidates to win the nomination of more than one political party; eliminated in 1959.

Cuban missile crisis A nuclear stand-off that occurred in 1962 when the United States learned that the Soviet Union had placed nuclear warheads in Cuba, ninety miles off the U.S. coast. The crisis was defused diplomatically, but it is generally considered the closest the two Cold War superpowers came to a nuclear confrontation.

D

***De facto* segregation** Racial segregation that occurs not as a result of deliberate intentions but because of past social and economic conditions and residential patterns.

***De jure* segregation** Racial segregation that occurs because of laws or decisions by government agencies.

Dealignment Among voters, a growing detachment from both major political parties.

Delegate A person selected to represent the people of one geographic area at a party convention.

Democracy A system of government in which the people have ultimate political authority. The word is derived from the Greek demos ("the people") and kratia ("rule").

Demographic groups Interest groups based on race, ethnicity, gender, or age; usually concerned with overcoming discrimination.

Détente French word meaning a "relaxation of tensions." Détente characterized the relationship between the United States and the Soviet Union in the 1970s, as the two Cold War rivals attempted to pursue cooperative dealings and arms control.

Deterrence A policy of building up military strength for the purpose of discouraging (deterring) military attacks by other nations; the policy of "building weapons for peace" that supported the arms race between the United States and the Soviet Union during the Cold War.

Devolution The surrender or transfer of powers to local authorities by a central government.

Dictatorship A form of government in which absolute power is exercised by a single person who usually has obtained his or her power by the use of force.

Diplomat A person who represents one country in dealing with representatives of another country.

Direct democracy A system of government in which political decisions are made by the people themselves rather than by elected representatives. This form of government was practiced in some areas of ancient Greece.

Direct mail A campaign technique by which candidates communicate selected messages to selected voters by mail.

Direct primary An election held within each of the two major parties—Democratic and Republican— to choose the party's candidates for the general election. Voters choose the candidate directly, rather than through delegates.

Direct technique Any method used by an interest group to interact with government officials directly to further the group's goals.

Director of finance The state officer primarily responsible for preparation of the budget; appointed by the governor.

Dissenting opinion A statement written by a judge or justice who disagrees with the majority opinion.

District attorney The chief prosecuting officer elected in each county; represents the people against the accused in criminal cases.

District elections Elections in which candidates are chosen by only one part of the city, county, or state.

Diversity of citizenship A basis for federal court jurisdiction over a lawsuit that arises when (1) the parties in the lawsuit live in different states or when one of the parties is a foreign government or a foreign citizen, and (2) the amount in controversy is more than $75,000.

Divine right theory The theory that a monarch's right to rule was derived directly from God rather than from the consent of the people.

Division of powers A basic principle of federalism established by the U.S. Constitution, by which powers are divided between the federal and state governments.

Domestic policy Public policy concerning issues within a national unit, such as national policy concerning health care or the economy.

Double jeopardy The prosecution of a person twice for the same criminal offense; prohibited by the Fifth Amendment in all but a few circumstances.

Dual federalism A system of government in which the federal and the state governments maintain diverse but sovereign powers.

Due process clause The constitutional guarantee, set out in the Fifth and Fourteenth Amendments, that the government will not illegally or arbitrarily deprive a person of life, liberty, or property.

Due process of law The requirement that the government use fair, reasonable, and standard procedures whenever it takes any legal action against an individual; required by the Fifth and Fourteenth Amendments.

E

Easy-money policy A monetary policy that involves stimulating the economy by expanding the rate of growth of the money supply. An easy-money policy supposedly will lead to lower interest rates and induce consumers to spend more and producers to invest more.

Economic groups Interest groups with sizable financial stakes in the political process who seek to influence legislators and other public policymakers.

Economic policy All actions taken by the national government to smooth out the ups and downs in the nation's level of business activity.

Elector A member of the electoral college.

Electoral college The group of electors who are selected by the voters in each state to elect officially the president and vice president. The number of electors in each state is equal to the number of that state's representatives in both chambers of Congress.

Electorate All of the citizens eligible to vote in a given election.

Electronic media Communication channels that involve electronic transmissions, such as radio, television, and the Internet.

Enabling legislation A law enacted by a legislature to establish an administrative agency. Enabling legislation normally specifies the name, purpose, composition, and powers of the agency being created.

Entitlement program A government program (such as Social Security) that allows, or entitles, a certain class of people (such as elderly persons) to receive special benefits. Entitlement programs operate under open-ended budget authorizations that, in effect, place no limits on how much can be spent.

Environmental Protection Agency (EPA) The federal government body charged with carrying out national environmental policy objectives.

Equal protection clause Section 1 of the Fourteenth Amendment, which states that no state shall "deny to any person within its jurisdiction the equal protection of the laws."

Equality A concept that holds, at a minimum, that all people are entitled to equal protection under the law.

Establishment clause The section of the First Amendment that prohibits Congress from passing laws "respecting an establishment of religion." Issues concerning the establishment clause often center on prayer in public schools, the teaching of fundamentalist theories of creation, and government aid to parochial schools.

***Ex post facto* law** A criminal law that punishes individuals for committing an act that was legal when the act was committed.

Exclusionary rule A criminal procedural rule requiring that any illegally obtained evidence not be admissible in court.

Executive agreement A binding international agreement, or pact, that is made between the president and another head of state and that does not require Senate approval.

Executive Office of the President (EOP) A group of staff agencies that assist the president in carrying out major duties. Franklin D. Roosevelt established the EOP in 1939 to cope with the increased responsibilities brought on by the Great Depression.

Executive order A presidential order to carry out a policy or policies described in a law passed by Congress. In state government, the power of the governor to make rules that have the effect of laws; may be overturned by the legislature.

Executive privilege An inherent executive power claimed by presidents to withhold information from, or to refuse to appear before, Congress or the courts. The president can also accord the privilege to other executive officials.

Expressed powers Constitutional or statutory powers that are expressly provided for by the Constitution.

F

Faction A group of persons forming a cohesive minority.

Fair Political Practices Commission (FPPC) Established by the Political Reform Act of 1974, this independent regulatory commission monitors candidates' campaign finance reports and lobbyists.

Federal mandate A requirement in federal legislation that forces states and municipalities to comply with certain rules. If the federal government does not provide funds to the states to cover the costs of compliance, the mandate is referred to as an unfunded mandate.

Federal Open Market Committee (FOMC) The most important body within the Federal Reserve System. The FOMC decides how monetary policy should be carried out by the Federal Reserve.

Federal question A question that pertains to the U.S. Constitution, acts of Congress, or treaties. A federal question provides a basis for federal court jurisdiction.

Federal system A form of government that provides for a division of powers between a central government and several regional governments. In the United States, the division of powers between the national government and the states is established by the Constitution.

Federalism A system of shared sovereignty between two levels of government—one national and one subnational—occupying the same geographic region.

Federalists A political group, led by Alexander Hamilton and John Adams, that supported the adoption of the Constitution and the creation of a federal form of government.

Feminism The belief in full political, economic, and social equality for women.

Filibustering The Senate tradition of unlimited debate undertaken for the purpose of preventing action on a bill.

First budget resolution A budget resolution, which is supposed to be passed in May, that sets overall revenue goals and spending targets for the next fiscal year, which begins on October 1.

First Continental Congress A gathering of delegates from twelve of the thirteen colonies, held in 1774 to protest the Coercive Acts.

Fiscal federalism The allocation of taxes collected by one level of government (typically the national government) to another level (typically state or local governments).

Fiscal policy The use of changes in government expenditures and taxes to alter national economic variables.

Fiscal year A twelve-month period that is established for bookkeeping or accounting purposes. The government's fiscal year runs from October 1 through September 30.

Fiscalization of land use Cities and counties, when making land-use decisions, opt for the alternative that produces the most revenue.

Foreign policy A systematic and general plan that guides a country's attitudes and actions toward the rest of the world. Foreign policy includes all of the economic, military, commercial, and diplomatic positions and actions that a nation takes in its relationships with other countries.

Free exercise clause The provision of the First Amendment stating that the government cannot pass laws "prohibiting the free exercise" of religion. Free exercise issues often concern religious practices that conflict with established laws.

Free rider problem The difficulty that exists when individuals can enjoy the outcome of an interest group's efforts without having to contribute, such as by becoming members of the group.

Fundamental right A basic right of all Americans, such as First Amendment rights. Any law or action that prevents some group of persons from exercising a fundamental right is subject to the "strict-scrutiny" standard, under which the law or action must be necessary to promote a compelling state interest and must be narrowly tailored to meet that interest.

G

Gender gap The difference between the percentage of votes cast for a particular candidate by women and the percentage of votes cast for the same candidate by men.

General election A regularly scheduled election to choose the U.S. president, vice president, and senators and representatives in Congress, as well as state offices. General elections are held in even-numbered years on the Tuesday after the first Monday in November.

General veto The gubernatorial power to reject an entire bill or budget; overruled only by an absolute two-thirds vote of both houses of the state legislature.

General-law city or county A city or county whose organization and structure of government are derived from state law.

Gerrymandering The drawing of a legislative district's boundaries in such a way as to maximize the influence of a certain group or political party.

Ghost voting When legislators cast electronic votes in place of assembly members who are not at their posts; this practice is against the law.

Glass ceiling An invisible but real discriminatory barrier that prevents women and minorities from rising to top positions of power or responsibility.

Global warming An increase in the average temperature of the Earth's surface over the last half century and its projected continuation.

Government The individuals and institutions that make society's rules and that also possess the power and authority to enforce those rules.

Government corporation An agency of the government that is run as a business enterprise. Such agencies engage in primarily commercial activities, produce revenues, and require greater flexibility than that permitted in most government agencies.

Governor California's highest-ranking executive officeholder; elected every four years.

Grandfather clause A clause in a state law that had the effect of restricting the franchise (voting rights) to those whose ancestors had voted before the 1860s; one of the techniques used in the South to prevent African Americans from exercising their right to vote.

Grants-in-aid Payments from the national government to states to assist in fulfilling public policy objectives.

Great Compromise A plan for a bicameral legislature in which one chamber would be based on population and the other chamber would represent each state equally. The plan, also known as the Connecticut Compromise, resolved the small-state/large-state controversy.

Greenhouse gas A gas that, when released into the atmosphere, traps the sun's heat and slows its release into outer space. Carbon dioxide (CO_2) is a major example.

Gut-and-amend The process of removing the original provisions from a bill and inserting new, unrelated content.

H

Head of state The person who serves as the ceremonial head of a country's government and represents that country to the rest of the world.

"Hourglass" economy The tendency of the California economy to include many people doing very well at the top, many barely getting by at the bottom, and fewer and fewer in the middle; symptomatic of California's vanishing middle class.

I

Ideologue An individual who holds very strong political opinions.

Ideology Generally, a system of political ideas that are rooted in religious or philosophical beliefs concerning human nature, society, and government.

Implied powers The powers of the federal government that are implied by the expressed powers in the Constitution, particularly in Article I, Section 8.

Incorporation The process by which residents of an urbanized area form a city.

Independent executive agency A federal agency that is not located within a cabinet department.

Independent expenditure An expenditure for activities that are independent from (not coordinated with) those of a political candidate or a political party.

Independent expenditures Campaign spending by interest groups and political action committees on behalf of candidates.

Independent regulatory agency A federal organization that is responsible for creating and implementing rules that regulate private activity and protect the public interest in a particular sector of the economy.

Indirect technique Any method used by interest groups to influence government officials through third parties, such as voters.

Individual mandate In the context of health-care reform, a requirement that all persons obtain health-care insurance from one source or another. Those failing to do so would pay a penalty.

Inherent powers The powers of the national government that, although not always expressly granted by the Constitution, are necessary to ensure the nation's integrity and survival as a political unit. Inherent powers include the power to make treaties and the power to wage war or make peace.

Initiative A Progressive device by which people may put laws and constitutional amendments on the ballot after securing the required number of voters' signatures.

Instant runoff voting Voters rank candidates in order of preference. If no candidate wins a majority, the candidate with the fewest votes is eliminated, and those votes are assigned to the voters' second choice—and so on until one candidate attains a majority.

Institution An ongoing organization that performs certain functions for society.

Instructed delegate A representative who deliberately mirrors the views of the majority of his or her constituents.

Insurance commissioner An elected state executive who regulates the insurance industry; created by a 1988 initiative.

Interest group An organized group of individuals sharing common objectives who actively attempt to influence policymakers.

Interstate commerce Trade that involves more than one state.

Interventionism Direct involvement by one country in another country's affairs.

Iron curtain A phrase coined by Winston Churchill to describe the political boundaries between the democratic countries in Western Europe and the Soviet-controlled Communist countries in Eastern Europe.

Iron triangle A three-way alliance among legislators, bureaucrats, and interest groups to make or preserve policies that benefit their respective interests.

Isolationism A political policy of noninvolvement in world affairs.

Issue ad A political advertisement that focuses on a particular issue. Issue ads can be used to support or attack a candidate.

Issue networks Groups of individuals or organizations—which consist of legislators and legislative staff members, interest group leaders, bureaucrats, the media, scholars, and other experts—that support particular policy positions on a given issue.

Item veto The power of the governor to delete or reduce the budget within a bill without rejecting the entire bill or budget; an absolute two-thirds vote of both houses of the state legislature is required to override.

J

Judicial activism Making policy through court decisions rather than through the legislative or electoral process.

Judicial Council Chaired by the chief justice of the state supreme court and composed of twenty-one judges and attorneys; makes the rules for court procedures, collects data on the courts' operations and workload, and gives seminars for judges.

Judicial review The power of the courts to decide on the constitutionality of legislative enactments and of actions taken by the executive branch.

Judiciary The courts; one of the three branches of government in the United States.

Jurisdiction The authority of a court to hear and decide a particular case.

Justiciable controversy A controversy that is not hypothetical or academic but real and substantial; a requirement that must be satisfied before a court will hear a case. Justiciable is pronounced jus-tish-a-bul.

K

Keynesian economics An economic theory proposed by British economist John Maynard Keynes that is typically associated with the use of fiscal policy to alter national economic variables.

Kitchen cabinet The name given to a president's unofficial advisers. The term was coined during Andrew Jackson's presidency.

L

Labor force All of the people over the age of sixteen who are working or actively looking for jobs.

Legislative analyst An assistant to the legislature who studies the annual budget and proposed programs.

Legislative committees Small groups of senators or assembly members who consider and make legislation in specialized areas such as agriculture or education.

Legislative counsel Assists the legislature in preparing bills and assessing their impact on existing legislation.

Legislative initiatives Propositions placed on the ballot by the legislature rather than by citizen petition.

Legislative rule An administrative agency rule that carries the same weight as a statute enacted by a legislature.

***Lemon* test** A three-part test enunciated by the Supreme Court in the 1971 case of *Lemon v. Kurtzman* to determine whether government aid to parochial schools is constitutional. To be constitutional, the aid must (1) be for a clearly secular purpose; (2) in its primary effect, neither advance nor inhibit religion; and (3) avoid an "excessive government entanglement with religion." The Lemon test has also been used in other types of cases involving the establishment clause.

Libel A published report of a falsehood that tends to injure a person's reputation or character.

Liberalism A set of political beliefs that include the advocacy of active government, including government intervention to improve the welfare of individuals and to protect civil rights.

Liberty The freedom of individuals to believe, act, and express themselves as they choose so long as doing so does not infringe on the rights of other individuals in the society.

Lieutenant governor The chief executive when the governor is absent from the state or disabled; succeeds the governor in case of death or other departure from office; casts a tiebreaking vote in the senate; is independently elected.

Limited government A form of government based on the principle that the powers of government should be clearly limited either through a written document or through wide public understanding; characterized by institutional checks to ensure that government serves public rather than private interests.

Literacy test A test given to voters to ensure that they could read and write and thus evaluate political information; a technique used in many southern states to restrict African American participation in elections.

Litigation An interest group tactic of challenging a law or policy in the courts to have it overruled, modified, or delayed.

Lobbying All of the attempts by organizations or by individuals to influence the passage, defeat, or contents of legislation or to influence the administrative decisions of government.

Lobbyist An individual who handles a particular interest group's lobbying efforts.

Local agency formation commission (LAFCO) A county agency set up to oversee the creation and expansion of cities.

Logrolling A give-and-take process in which legislators trade support for each other's bills.

Loophole A legitimate way of evading a certain legal requirement.

M

Madisonian Model The model of government devised by James Madison, in which the powers of the government are separated into three branches: executive, legislative, and judicial.

Majority leader The party leader elected by the majority party in the House or in the Senate.

Majority party The political party that has more members in the legislature than the opposing party.

Malapportionment A condition in which the voting power of citizens in one district is greater than the voting power of citizens in another district.

Managed news coverage News coverage that is manipulated (managed) by a campaign manager or political consultant to gain media exposure for a political candidate.

Markup session A meeting held by a congressional committee or subcommittee to approve, amend, or redraft a bill.

Marshall Plan A plan providing for U.S. economic assistance to European nations following World War II to help those nations recover from the war; the plan was named after George C. Marshall, secretary of state from 1947 to 1949.

Mass media Communication channels, such as newspapers and radio and television broadcasts, through which people can communicate to large audiences.

Material incentive Practical benefits from joining an interest group, such as discounts, subscriptions, or group insurance.

Mayflower Compact A document drawn up by Pilgrim leaders in 1620 on the ship *Mayflower*. The document stated that laws were to be made for the general good of the people.

Mayor The ceremonial leader of a city; usually a position that alternates among council members, but in some large cities the mayor is directly elected and given substantial powers.

Media Newspapers, magazines, television, radio, the Internet, and any other printed or electronic means of communication.

Medicaid A joint federal-state program that provides health-care services for low-income persons.

Medicare A federal government program that pays for health-care insurance for Americans aged sixty-five years or over.

Minority leader The party leader elected by the minority party in the House or in the Senate.

Minority party The political party that has fewer members in the legislature than the opposing party.

Minority-majority district A district in which minority groups make up a majority of the population.

***Miranda* warnings** A series of statements informing criminal suspects, on their arrest, of their constitutional rights, such as the right to remain silent and the right to counsel; required by the Supreme Court's 1966 decision in *Miranda v. Arizona*.

Moderate A person whose views fall in the middle of the political spectrum.

Monarchy A form of autocracy in which a king, queen, emperor, empress, tsar, or tsarina is the highest authority in the government; monarchs usually obtain their power through inheritance.

Monetary policy Actions taken by the Federal Reserve Board to change the amount of money in circulation so as to affect interest rates, credit markets, the rate of inflation, the rate of economic growth, and the rate of unemployment.

Monroe Doctrine A U.S. policy, announced in 1823 by President James Monroe, that the United States would not tolerate foreign intervention in the Western Hemisphere, and in return, the United States would stay out of European affairs.

Moral idealism In foreign policy, the belief that the most important goal is to do what is right. Moral idealists think that it is possible for nations to cooperate as part of a rule-based community.

Mutually assured destruction (MAD) A phrase referring to the assumption, on which the policy of deterrence was based, that if the forces of two nations are equally capable of destroying each other, neither nation will take a chance on war.

N

National convention The meeting held by each major party every four years to select presidential and vice-presidential candidates, write a party platform, and conduct other party business.

National health insurance A program, found in many of the world's economically advanced nations, under which the central government provides basic health-care insurance coverage to everyone in the country. Some wealthy nations, such as the Netherlands and Switzerland, provide universal coverage through private insurance companies instead.

National party chairperson An individual who serves as a political party's administrative head at the national level and directs the work of the party's national committee.

National party committee The political party leaders who direct party business during the four years between the national party conventions, organize the next national convention, and plan how to obtain a party victory in the next presidential elections.

National Security Council (NSC) A council that advises the president on domestic and foreign matters concerning the safety and defense of the nation; established in 1947.

Natural rights Rights that are not bestowed by governments but are inherent within every man, woman, and child by virtue of the fact that he or she is a human being.

Necessary and proper clause Article I, Section 8, Clause 18, of the Constitution, which gives Congress the power to make all laws "necessary and proper" for the federal government to carry out its responsibilities; also called the elastic clause.

Negative political advertising Political advertising undertaken for the purpose of discrediting an opposing candidate in the eyes of the voters. Attack ads are one form of negative political advertising.

Neoconservatism A philosophy of foreign policy based on moral idealism. Neoconservatives support the use of economic and military power to bring democracy and human rights to other countries.

Neutral competency The application of technical skills to jobs without regard to political issues.

Neutrality A position of not being aligned with either side in a dispute or conflict, such as a war.

New Deal A program ushered in by the Roosevelt administration in 1933 in an attempt to bring the United States out of the Great Depression. The New Deal included many government-spending and public assistance programs, in addition to thousands of regulations governing economic activity.

New federalism A plan to limit the federal government's role in regulating state governments and to give the states increased power to decide how they should spend government revenues.

Nominating convention An official meeting of a political party to choose its candidates. Nominating conventions at the state and local levels also select delegates to represent the citizens of their geographic areas at a higher-level party convention.

Nonpartisan elections A Progressive reform that removed party labels from ballots for local and judicial offices.

Normal trade relations (NTR) status A trade status granted through an international treaty by which each member nation must treat other members at least as well as it treats the country that receives its most favorable treatment. This status was formerly known as most-favored-nation status.

O

Obscenity Indecency or offensiveness in speech, expression, behavior, or appearance. Whether specific expressions or acts constitute obscenity normally is determined by community standards.

Office of Management and Budget (OMB) An agency in the Executive Office of the President that assists the president in preparing and supervising the administration of the federal budget.

Office-block ballot A ballot (also called the Massachusetts ballot) that lists together all of the candidates for each office.

"One person, one vote" rule A rule, or principle, requiring that congressional districts have equal populations so that one person's vote counts as much as another's vote.

Open primary A primary in which voters can vote for a party's candidates regardless of whether they belong to the party.

Opinion A written statement by a court expressing the reasons for its decision in a case.

Oral argument A spoken argument presented to a judge in person by an attorney on behalf of her or his client.

Oslo Accords The first agreement signed between Israel and the PLO; led to the establishment of the Palestinian Authority in the occupied territories.

P

Palestine Liberation Organization (PLO) An organization formed in 1964 to represent the Palestinian people. The PLO has a long history of terrorism but for some years has functioned primarily as a political party.

Parliament The name of the national legislative body in countries governed by a parliamentary system, such as Britain and Canada.

Partisan politics Political actions or decisions that benefit a particular party.

Party activist A party member who helps to organize and oversee party functions and planning during and between campaigns.

Party identifier A person who identifies himself or herself as being a member of a particular political party.

Party platform The document drawn up by each party at its national convention that outlines the policies and positions of the party.

Party ticket A list of a political party's candidates for various offices. In national elections, the party ticket consists of the presidential and vice-presidential candidates.

Party-column ballot A ballot (also called the Indiana ballot) that lists all of a party's candidates under the party label. Voters can vote for all of a party's candidates for local, state, and national offices by making a single "X" or pulling a single lever.

Patronage A system of rewarding the party faithful and workers with government jobs or contracts; giving government jobs to individuals belonging to the winning political party.

Peer group Associates, often close in age to one another; may include friends, classmates, co-workers, club members, or religious group members. Peer group influence is a significant factor in the political socialization process.

Personal attack ad A negative political advertisement that attacks the character of an opposing candidate.

Personal income tax A graduated tax on individual earnings adopted in 1935; the largest source of state revenues.

Picket-fence federalism A model of federalism in which specific policies and programs are administered by all levels of government—national, state, and local.

Plea bargaining An agreement between the prosecution and the accused in which the latter pleads guilty to a reduced charge and lesser penalty.

Pluralist theory A theory that views politics as a contest among various interest groups—at all levels of government—to gain benefits for their members.

Pocket veto A special type of veto power used by the chief executive after the legislature has adjourned. Bills that are not signed die after a specified period of time.

Podcasting The distribution of audio or video files to a personal computer or a mobile device, such as an ipod.

Police powers The powers of a government body that enable it to create laws for the protection of the health, morals, safety, and welfare of the people. In the United States, most police powers are reserved to the states.

Policymaking process The procedures involved in getting an issue on the political agenda; formulating, adopting, and implementing a policy with regard to the issue; and then evaluating the results of the policy.

Political action committee (PAC) A committee that is established by a corporation, labor union, or special interest group to raise funds and make contributions on the establishing organization's behalf.

Political advertising Advertising undertaken by or on behalf of a political candidate to familiarize voters with the candidate and his or her views on campaign issues; also advertising for or against policy issues.

Political consultant A professional political adviser who, for a fee, works on an area of a candidate's campaign. Political consultants include campaign managers, pollsters, media advisers, and "get out the vote" organizers.

Political culture The set of ideas, values, and attitudes about government and the political process held by a community or a nation.

Political party A group of individuals who organize to win elections, operate the government, and determine policy.

Political realism In foreign policy, the belief that nations are inevitably selfish, and that we should seek to protect our national security regardless of moral arguments.

Political Reform Act of 1974 An initiative requiring officials to disclose conflicts of interest, campaign contributions, and spending; also requires lobbyists to register with the Fair Political Practices Commission.

Political socialization The learning process through which most people acquire their political attitudes, opinions, beliefs, and knowledge.

Politics The process of resolving conflicts over how society should use its scarce resources and who should receive various benefits, such as public health care and public higher education. According to Harold Lasswell, politics is the process of determining "who gets what, when, and how" in a society.

Poll tax A fee of several dollars that had to be paid before a person could vote; a device used in some southern states to prevent African Americans from voting.

Poll watcher A representative from one of the political parties who is allowed to monitor a polling place to make sure that the election is run fairly and to avoid fraud.

Power The ability to influence the behavior of others, usually through the use of force, persuasion, or rewards.

Precedent A court decision that furnishes an example or authority for deciding subsequent cases involving identical or similar facts and legal issues.

Precinct A political district within a city, such as a block or a neighborhood, or a rural portion of a county; the smallest voting district at the local level.

Preemption A doctrine rooted in the supremacy clause of the Constitution that provides that national laws or regulations governing a certain area take precedence over conflicting state laws or regulations governing that same area.

Preemptive war A war launched by a nation to prevent an imminent attack by another nation.

Preprimary endorsement Political parties' designation of preferred candidates in party primary elections, thus strengthening the role of party organizations in selecting candidates; banned by state law until 1990.

President pro tem The legislative leader of the state senate; chairs the Rules Committee; selected by the majority party.

Press secretary A member of the White House staff who holds news conferences for reporters and makes public statements for the president.

Preventive war A war launched by a nation to prevent the possibility that another nation might attack at some point in the future; not supported by international law.

Primary A preliminary election held for the purpose of choosing a party's final candidate.

Primary election An election in which voters choose the candidates of their party, who will then run in the general election.

Primary elections Elections to choose nominees for public office; held in June of even-numbered years. Voter turnout is typically low.

Primary source of law A source of law that establishes the law. Primary sources of law include constitutions, statutes, administrative agency rules and regulations, and decisions rendered by the courts.

Print media Communication channels that consist of printed materials, such as newspapers and magazines.

Privatization The transfer of the task of providing services traditionally provided by government to the private sector.

Probable cause Cause for believing that there is a substantial likelihood that a person has committed or is about to commit a crime.

Progressives In California, members of an anti-machine reform movement that reshaped the state's political institutions between 1907 and the 1920s.

Progressivism An alternative, more popular term for the set of political beliefs also known as liberalism.

Property tax A tax on land and buildings; until the passage of Proposition 13 in 1978, the primary source of revenues for local governments.

Proposition 1A A 2004 ballot measure designed to prevent the state from taking revenues from local governments in times of fiscal stress.

Proposition 8 (2008) An initiative that amended the state constitution to restrict marriage to opposite-sex couples.

Proposition 11, the Voters first initiative (2008) An initiative that placed legislative redistricting in the hands of a fourteen-member citizens commission instead of the state legislature.

Proposition 13 (1978) Also known as the Jarvis-Gann initiative; a ballot measure that cut property taxes and significantly reduced revenues for local governments.

Proposition 22, the California Defense of Marriage Act (2000) A ballot initiative that declared marriage an act between a man and a woman.

Proposition 22, the Local Taxpayers, Public Safety and Transportation Act (2010) An initiative that keeps the state government from taking local government funds dedicated by the voters for public safety.

Proposition 34 A 2000 legislative initiative setting contribution limits for individuals and political action committees; commonly circumvented through independent expenditures.

Proposition 58 (2004) A proposition that set broad spending limits on state government and required the state to gradually set aside up to 3 percent of all revenues in a "rainy day" fund.

Proposition 98 (1988) An initiative awarding public education a fixed percentage of the state budget.

Proposition 140 (1990) An initiative limiting assembly members to three 2-year terms and senators and statewide elected officials to two 4-year terms and cutting the legislature's budget.

Proposition 187 (1994) An initiative reducing government benefits for illegal immigrants; parts of Proposition 187 were declared unconstitutional by federal courts in 1995.

Proposition 209 (1996) An initiative that eliminated affirmative action in California.

Proposition 227 (1998) An initiative limiting bilingual education to no more than one year.

Public debt The total amount of money that the national government owes as a result of borrowing; also called the *national debt.*

Public defender A county officer representing defendants who cannot afford an attorney; appointed by the county board of supervisors.

Public interest groups Organizations that purport to represent the general good rather than private interests.

Public opinion The views of the citizenry about politics, public issues, and public policies; a complex collection of opinions held by many people on issues in the public arena.

Public opinion poll A numerical survey of the public's opinion on a particular topic at a particular moment.

Public option In the context of health-care reform, a government-sponsored health-care insurance program that would compete with private insurance companies.

Public services Essential services that individuals cannot provide for themselves, such as building and maintaining roads, providing welfare programs, operating public schools, and preserving national parks.

Public-interest group An interest group formed for the purpose of working for the "public good." Examples of public-interest groups are the American Civil Liberties Union and Common Cause.

Purposive incentive A reason to join an interest group—satisfaction resulting from working for a cause in which one believes.

Push poll A campaign tactic used to feed false or misleading information to potential voters, under the guise of taking an opinion poll, with the intent to "push" voters away from one candidate and toward another.

Q

Quota system A policy under which a specific number of jobs, promotions, or other types of placements, such as university admissions, must be given to members of selected groups.

R

Radical left Persons on the extreme left side of the political spectrum, who would like major changes in the political order, usually to promote egalitarianism (human equality).

Radical right Persons on the extreme right side of the political spectrum. The radical right includes reactionaries (who would like to return to the values and social systems of some previous era) and libertarians (who believe in no regulation of the economy or individual behavior).

Random sample In the context of opinion polling, a sample in which each person within the entire population being polled has an equal chance of being chosen.

Rating system A system by which a particular interest group evaluates (rates) the performance of legislators based on how often the legislators have voted with the group's position on particular issues.

Rational basis test A test (also known as the "ordinary-scrutiny" standard) used by the Supreme Court to decide whether a discriminatory law violates the equal protection clause of the Constitution. Few laws evaluated under this test are found invalid.

Realignment A process in which the popular support for and relative strength of the parties shift and the parties are reestablished with different coalitions of supporters.

Recall A Progressive reform allowing voters to remove elected officials by petition and majority vote.

Reconciliation A special kind of legislation not subject to filibuster in the Senate. A reconciliation act must deal only with financial matters.

Redistricting Another term for reapportionment, the adjustment of legislative districts by population every ten years.

Referendum A Progressive reform requiring the legislature to place certain measures before the voters, who may also repeal legislation by petitioning for a referendum.

Register to vote Citizens who are over eighteen years of age and who are not incarcerated or in a mental institution are eligible to sign up to vote by completion of a registration form. Nearly 30 percent of those eligible to register in California do not do so and thus cannot participate in elections.

Renewable energy Energy from technologies that do not rely on extracted resources, such as oil and coal, that can run out.

Representative democracy A form of democracy in which the will of the majority is expressed through smaller groups of individuals elected by the people to act as their representatives.

Republic Essentially, a representative democracy in which there is no king or queen and the people are sovereign.

Reverse discrimination Discrimination against those who have no minority status.

Reynolds v. Sims A 1964 United States Supreme Court decision that ordered redistricting of the upper houses of all state legislatures by population instead of land area.

Right-to-work laws Laws that ban unions from collecting dues or other fees from workers that they represent but who have not actually joined the union.

Rule of law A basic principle of government that requires those who govern to act in accordance with established law.

Rulemaking The process undertaken by an administrative agency when formally proposing, evaluating, and adopting a new regulation.

Rules Committee A standing committee in the House of Representatives that provides special rules governing how particular bills will be considered and debated by the House. The Rules Committee normally proposes time limits on debate for any bill.

Runoff election When no candidate receives more than 50 percent of the vote in a nonpartisan primary for trial court judge or local office, the top two candidates face each other in a runoff.

S

Sales tax A statewide tax on most goods and products; adopted in 1933; local governments receive a portion of this tax.

Sample In the context of opinion polling, a group of people selected to represent the population being studied.

Sampling error In the context of opinion polling, the difference between what the sample results show and what the true results would have been had everybody in the relevant population been interviewed.

School districts Local governments created by states to provide elementary and secondary education; governed by elected school boards.

School voucher An educational certificate, provided by the government, that allows a student to use public funds to pay for a private or a public school chosen by the student or his or her parents.

Secession The act of formally withdrawing from membership in an alliance; the withdrawal of a state from the federal Union.

Second budget resolution A budget resolution, which is supposed to be passed in September, that sets "binding" limits on taxes and spending for the next fiscal year.

Second Continental Congress The congress of the colonies that met in 1775 to assume the powers of a central government and to establish an army.

Secretary of state An elected state executive who keeps election records and supervises elections.

Seditious speech Speech that urges resistance to lawful authority or that advocates the overthrowing of a government.

Self-incrimination Providing damaging information or testimony against oneself in court.

Senate Rules Committee A five-member committee consisting of the senate president pro tem and two other members from each party in the senate; assigns chairs and committee appointments; functions as the gatekeeper of most senate legislation.

Senatorial courtesy A practice that allows a senator of the president's party to veto the president's nominee to a federal court judgeship within the senator's state.

Separate-but-equal doctrine A Supreme Court doctrine holding that the equal protection clause of the Fourteenth Amendment did not forbid racial segregation as long as the facilities for blacks were equal to those for whites. The doctrine was overturned in the Brown v. Board of Education of Topeka decision of 1954.

Separation of powers The principle of dividing governmental powers among the executive, the legislative, and the judicial branches of government.

Sexual harassment Unwanted physical contact, verbal conduct, or abuse of a sexual nature that interferes with a recipient's job performance, creates a hostile environment, or carries with it an implicit or explicit threat of adverse employment consequences.

Shays' Rebellion A rebellion of angry farmers in western Massachusetts in 1786, led by former Revolutionary War captain Daniel Shays. This rebellion and other similar uprisings in the New England states emphasized the need for a true national government.

Signing statement A written statement, appended to a bill at the time the president signs it into law, indicating how the president interprets that legislation.

Silicon Valley The top area for high-tech industries; located between San Jose and San Francisco.

Single-issue groups Organized groups with narrow policy objectives; not oriented toward compromise.

Sit-in A tactic of nonviolent civil disobedience. Demonstrators enter a business, college building, or other public place and remain seated until they are forcibly removed or until their demands are met. The tactic was used successfully in the civil rights movement and in other protest movements in the United States.

Slander The public utterance (speaking) of a statement that holds a person up for contempt, ridicule, or hatred.

Social conflict Disagreements among people in a society over what the society's priorities should be when distributing scarce resources.

Social contract A voluntary agreement among individuals to create a government and to give that government adequate power to secure the mutual protection and welfare of all individuals.

Soft money Campaign contributions not regulated by federal law, such as some contributions that are made to political parties instead of to particular candidates.

Solid South A term used to describe the tendency of the southern states to vote Democratic after the Civil War.

Solidarity Mutual sympathy among the members of a particular group.

Solidary incentive A reason to join an interest group—pleasure in associating with like-minded individuals.

Sound bite A televised comment, lasting for only a few seconds, that captures a thought or a perspective and has an immediate impact on the viewers.

Southern Pacific Railroad A railroad company founded in 1861; developed a political machine that dominated California state politics through the turn of the century

Soviet bloc The group of Eastern European nations that fell under the control of the Soviet Union following World War II.

Speaker of the assembly The legislative leader of the assembly; selected by the majority party; controls committee appointments and the legislative process.

Speaker of the House The presiding officer in the House of Representatives. The Speaker has traditionally been a longtime member of the majority party and is often the most powerful and influential member of the House.

Special districts Local government agencies providing a single service, such as fire protection or sewage disposal.

Special election An election that is held at the state or local level when the voters must decide an issue before the next general election or when vacancies occur by reason of death or resignation.

Special session A legislative session called by the governor; limited to discussion of topics specified by the governor.

Spin A reporter's slant on, or interpretation of, a particular event or action.

Spin doctor A political candidate's press adviser, who tries to convince reporters to give a story or event concerning the candidate a particular "spin" (interpretation, or slant).

Standing committee A permanent committee in Congress that deals with legislation concerning a particular area, such as agriculture or foreign relations.

Standing to sue The requirement that an individual must have a sufficient stake in a controversy before he or she can bring a lawsuit. The party bringing the suit must demonstrate that he or she has either been harmed or been threatened with a harm.

Stare decisis A common law doctrine under which judges normally are obligated to follow the precedents established by prior court decisions. Pronounced *ster*-ay dih-*si*-*sis*.

State auditor An assistant to the legislature who analyzes ongoing programs.

State Children's Health Insurance Program (SCHIP) A joint federal-state program that provides health-care insurance for low-income children.

Statutory law The body of law enacted by legislatures (as opposed to constitutional law, administrative law, or case law).

Straw poll A nonscientific poll; a poll in which there is no way to ensure that the opinions expressed are representative of the larger population.

Subcommittee A division of a larger committee that deals with a particular part of the committee's policy area. Most standing committees have several subcommittees.

Suffrage The right to vote; the franchise.

Superintendent of public instruction The elected state executive in charge of public education.

Superior courts Lower courts in which criminal and civil cases are first tried.

Supremacy clause Article VI, Clause 2, of the Constitution, which makes the Constitution and federal laws superior to all conflicting state and local laws.

Supreme court Highest federal court, and in state government, California's highest judicial body; hears appeals from lower courts.

Suspect classification A classification, such as race, that provides the basis for a discriminatory law. Any law based on a suspect classification is subject to strict scrutiny by the courts—meaning that the law must be justified by a compelling state interest.

Symbolic speech The expression of beliefs, opinions, or ideas through forms other than speech or print; speech involving actions and other nonverbal expressions

T

Term limits Limits on the number of terms that officeholders may serve; elected executive branch officers and state senators are limited to two 4-year terms, and assembly members are limited to three 2-year terms. Local elected officials are usually limited to two or three 4-year terms.

Term limits Limits on the number of terms that officeholders may serve; Local elected officials are usually limited to two or three 4-year terms.

Third party In the United States, any party other than one of the two major parties (Republican and Democratic).

"Three strikes" law A 1994 law and initiative requiring sentences of twenty-five years to life for anyone convicted of three felonies.

Three-fifths compromise A compromise reached during the Constitutional Convention by which three-fifths of all slaves were to be counted for purposes of representation in the House of Representatives.

Trade organization An association formed by members of a particular industry, such as the oil industry or the trucking industry, to develop common standards and goals for the industry. Trade organizations, as interest groups, lobby government for legislation or regulations that specifically benefit their groups.

Treasurer The elected state executive responsible for managing state funds between collection and spending.

Treaty A formal agreement between the governments of two or more countries.

Trial court A court in which trials are held and testimony taken.

Trustee A representative who tries to serve the broad interests of the entire society and not just the narrow interests of his or her constituents.

Two-party system A political system in which two strong and established parties compete for political offices.

Tyranny The arbitrary or unrestrained exercise of power by an oppressive individual or government.

U

Unicameral legislature A legislature with only one chamber.

Unitary system A centralized governmental system in which local or subdivisional governments exercise only those powers given to them by the central government.

User taxes Taxes on select commodities or services "used" by those who benefit directly from them; examples include gasoline taxes and cigarette taxes.

V

Veto A Latin word meaning "I forbid"; the refusal by an official, such as the president of the United States or a state governor, to sign a bill into law.

Veto power A constitutional power that enables the chief executive (president or governor) to reject legislation and return it to the legislature with reasons for the rejection. This prevents or at least delays the bill from becoming law.

Vital center The center of the political spectrum; those who hold moderate political views. The center is vital because without it, it may be difficult, if not impossible, to reach the compromises that are necessary to a political system's continuity.

Vote by mail Voters who prefer not to vote at their polling places or who are unable to vote on Election Day may apply to their county registrar of voters or an absentee ballot and vote by mail; nearly half of those who vote in California elections vote by mail.

Vote-eligible population The number of people who are actually eligible to vote in an American election.

Voter turnout The proportion of eligible and/or registered voters who actually participate in an election. When turnout is high, the electorate is usually more diverse and liberal; when it is low, the electorate is usually older, more affluent, and more conservative.

Voting-age population The number of people residing in the United States who are at least eighteen years old.

W

Ward A local unit of a political party's organization, consisting of a division or district within a city.

Watergate scandal A scandal involving an illegal break-in at the Democratic National Committee offices in 1972 by members of President Nixon's reelection campaign staff. Before Congress could vote to impeach Nixon for his participation in covering up the break-in, Nixon resigned from the presidency.

Weapons of mass destruction Chemical, biological, or nuclear weapons that can inflict massive casualties.

Whip A member of Congress who assists the majority or minority leader in the House or in the Senate in managing the party's legislative preferences.

Whistleblower In the context of government employment, someone who "blows the whistle" (reports to authorities)

on gross governmental inefficiency, illegal action, or other wrongdoing.

White House Office The personal office of the president. White House Office personnel handle the president's political needs and manage the media.

White primary A primary election in which African Americans were prohibited from voting. The practice was banned by the Supreme Court in 1944.

Winner-take-all system A system in which the candidate who receives the most votes wins. In contrast, proportional systems allocate votes to multiple winners.

Workingmen's Party Denis Kearney's anti-railroad, anti-Chinese organization; instrumental in rewriting California's constitution in 1879.

Writ of *certiorari* An order from a higher court asking a lower court for the record of a case. *Certiorari* is pronounced sur-shee-uh-*rah*-ree.

Writ of *habeas corpus* An order that requires an official to bring a specified prisoner into court and explain to the judge why the person is being held in prison.

Index

A

C

D

E

G

H

I

J

K

L

M

N

O

P

Q

R

S

T

U

V

W

Y

Z

CHAPTER IN
REVIEW

1 America in the Twenty-First Century

KEY TERMS

authority The ability to exercise power, such as the power to make and enforce laws, legitimately. *4*

autocracy A form of government in which the power and authority of the government are in the hands of a single person. *7*

bicameral legislature A legislature made up of two chambers, or parts. The United States has a bicameral legislature, composed of the House of Representatives and the Senate. *10*

capitalism An economic system based on the private ownership of wealth-producing property, free markets, and freedom of contract. The privately owned corporation is the preeminent capitalist institution. *13*

conservatism A set of beliefs that includes a limited role for the national government in helping individuals and in the economic affairs of the nation, support for traditional values and lifestyles, and a cautious response to change. *14*

democracy A system of government in which the people have ultimate political authority. The word is derived from the Greek *demos* (people) and *kratia* (rule). *8*

dictatorship A form of government in which absolute power is exercised by a single person who has usually obtained his or her power by the use of force. *7*

direct democracy A system of government in which political decisions are made by the people themselves rather than by elected representatives. This form of government was practiced in some areas of ancient Greece. *8*

divine right theory A theory that the right to rule by a king or queen was derived directly from God rather than from the consent of the people. *7*

equality A concept that holds, at a minimum, that all people are entitled to equal protection under the law. *12*

government The individuals and institutions that make society's rules and that also possess the power and authority to enforce those rules. *4*

ideologue An individual who holds very strong political opinions. *17*

ideology Generally, a system of political ideas that are rooted in religious or philosophical beliefs concerning human nature, society, and government. *13*

institution An ongoing organization that performs certain functions for society. *3*

liberalism A set of political beliefs that includes the advocacy of active government, including government intervention to improve the welfare of individuals and to protect civil rights. *13*

QUIZ

1. Resolving conflicts over how society should use its scarce resources and who should receive various benefits is the essence of _____. It has been called the process of determining "who gets what, when, and how" in a society.

a. authority
b. government
c. political culture
d. power
e. politics

2. A(n) _____ is a system of government in which the power and authority of the government are in the hands of a single person.

a. constitutional monarchy
b. autocracy
c. theocracy
d. aristocracy
e. parliamentary democracy

3. True or False: In a representative democracy, the people participate directly in government decision making.

4. _____ is best described as a voluntary agreement among individuals to create a government and to give that government adequate power to secure the mutual protection and welfare of all individuals.

a. A social contract
b. Political culture
c. Equality
d. Multiculturalism
e. Capitalism

5. True or False: Within the traditional political spectrum, liberals hold the most extreme position on the left.

© AP PHOTO/BRADLEY C BOWER

SUMMARY & OBJECTIVES

LO1 Explain what is meant by the terms politics and government. ***1*** **Politics** can be defined as the process of resolving **social conflict**—disagreements over how the society should use its scarce resources and who should receive various benefits. ***2*** **Government** can be defined as the individuals and institutions that make society's rules and that also possess the **power** and **authority** to enforce those rules. Government serves at least three essential purposes: (a) it resolves conflicts; (b) it provides **public services;** and (c) it defends the nation and its culture against attacks by other nations.

LO2 Identify the various types of government systems. ***3*** In an **autocracy,** the power and authority of the government are in the hands of a single person. **Monarchies** and **dictatorships,** including totalitarian dictatorships, are all forms of autocracy. In a constitutional monarchy, however, the monarch shares governmental power with elected lawmakers.
4 **Democracy** is a system of government in which the people have ultimate political authority. Government exists only by the consent of the people and reflects the will of the majority. What we now call **direct democracy** exists when the people participate directly in government decision making. In a **representative democracy,** the will of the majority is expressed through smaller groups of individuals elected by the people to act as their representatives. A **republic** is essentially a representative democracy in which there is no king or queen; the people are sovereign. Forms of representative democracy include presidential democracy and **parliamentary** democracy.
5 An aristocracy is a government in which a small privileged class rules. Other forms of government characterized by "rule by the few" include plutocracy (the wealthy exercise ruling power) and

meritocracy (rulers have earned the right to govern because of their special skills or talents). Theocracy is a form of government in which there is no separation of church and state. The government rules according to religious precepts.

LO3 Summarize some of the basic principles of American democracy and the basic American political values. ***6*** In writing the U.S. Constitution, the framers incorporated two basic principles of government that had evolved in England: **limited government** and representative government. Our democracy resulted from a type of **social contract** among early Americans to create and abide by a set of governing rules. Social-contract theory was developed in the seventeenth and eighteenth centuries by such philosophers as John Locke, Thomas Hobbes, and Jean-Jacques Rousseau. ***7*** The fundamental principles of American democracy are (a) equality in voting, (b) individual freedom, (c) equal protection of the law, (d) majority rule and minority rights, and (e) collectively voluntary consent to be governed. ***8*** From its beginnings as a nation, America has been defined less by the culture shared by its diverse population than by a patterned set of ideas, values, and ways of thinking about government and politics—its political culture. The rights to **liberty, equality,** and property are fundamental political values shared by most Americans. ***9*** Generally, assumptions as to what the government's role should be in promoting basic values, such as liberty and equality, are important determinants of political **ideology.** When it comes to political ideology, Americans tend to fall into two broad camps: **liberals** and **conservatives.** Liberals, or **progressives,** often identify with the Democratic Party, and conservatives tend to identify politically as Republicans. People whose views fall in the middle of the traditional political spectrum are generally called **moderates.** On both ends of the spectrum are those who espouse **radical** views. ***10*** Many Americans do not adhere firmly to a particular political ideology. They may not be interested in all political issues and may have a mixed set of opinions that do not fit neatly under a liberal or conservative label.

LO4 Describe how the various topics discussed in this text relate to the "big picture" of American politics and government. ***11*** The U.S. Constitution is the supreme law of the land. It sets forth basic governing rules by which Americans agreed to abide. Some of the most significant political controversies today have to do with how various provisions in this founding document should be applied to modern-day events and issues. ***12*** Generally, those who acquire the power and authority to govern in our political system are the successful candidates in elections. The electoral process is influenced by interest groups, political parties, public opinion, voting behavior, campaign costs, and the media. ***13*** Those persons who have been selected for public office become part of one of the institutions of government. They make laws and policies to decide "who gets what, when, and how" in our society. Interest groups, public opinion, and the media not only affect election outcomes but also influence the policymaking process.

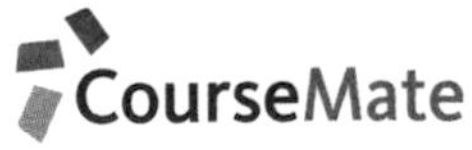

Find more practice tests and study tools for this chapter on CourseMate.

liberty The freedom of individuals to believe, act, and express themselves as they choose so long as doing so does not infringe on the rights of other individuals in the society. *11*

limited government A form of government based on the principle that the powers of government should be clearly limited either through a written document or through wide public understanding; characterized by institutional checks to ensure that government serves public rather than private interests. *9*

moderate A person whose views fall in the middle of the political spectrum. *16*

monarchy A form of autocracy in which a king, queen, emperor, empress, tsar, or tsarina is the highest authority in the government; monarchs usually obtain their power through inheritance. *7*

natural rights Rights that are not bestowed by governments but are inherent within every man, woman, and child by virtue of the fact that he or she is a human being. *10*

parliament The name of the national legislative body in countries governed by a parliamentary system, such as Britain and Canada. *10*

political culture The set of ideas, values, and attitudes about government and the political process held by a community or a nation. *11*

politics The process of resolving conflicts over how society should use its scarce resources and who should receive various benefits, such as public health care and public higher education. According to Harold Lasswell, politics is the process of determining "who gets what, when, and how" in a society. *3*

power The ability to influence the behavior of others, usually through the use of force, persuasion, or rewards. *4*

progressivism An alternative, more popular term for the set of political beliefs also known as liberalism. *16*

public services Essential services that individuals cannot provide for themselves, such as building and maintaining roads, providing welfare programs, operating public schools, and preserving national parks. *4*

radical left Persons on the extreme left side of the political spectrum who would like major changes to the political order, usually to promote egalitarianism (human equality). *16*

radical right Persons on the extreme right side of the political spectrum. The radical right includes reactionaries (who would like to return to the values and social systems of some previous era) and libertarians (who believe in no regulation of the economy and individual behavior, except for defense and law enforcement). *17*

representative democracy A form of democracy in which the will of the majority is expressed through smaller groups of individuals elected by the people to act as their representatives. *8*

republic Essentially, a term referring to a representative democracy in which there is no king or queen and the people are sovereign. The people elect smaller groups of individuals to act as the people's representatives. *8*

social conflict Disagreements among people in a society over what the society's priorities should be with respect to the use of scarce resources *3*

social contract A voluntary agreement among individuals to create a government and to give that government adequate power to secure the mutual protection and welfare of all individuals. *10*

Quiz Answers: 1. e; 2. b; 3. False; 4. a; 5. False

CHAPTER IN REVIEW 2 *The Constitution*

KEY TERMS

Anti-Federalists A political group that opposed the adoption of the Constitution because of the document's centralist tendencies and because it did not include a bill of rights ***35***

Articles of Confederation The nation's first national constitution, which established a national form of government following the American Revolution. The Articles provided for a confederal form of government in which the central government had few powers. ***29***

Bill of Rights The first ten amendments to the U.S. Constitution. They list the freedoms—such as the freedoms of speech, press, and religion—that a citizen enjoys and that cannot be infringed on by the government. ***24***

checks and balances A major principle of American government in which each of the three branches is given the means to check (to restrain or balance) the actions of the others. ***39***

commerce clause The clause in Article I, Section 8, of the Constitution that gives Congress the power to regulate interstate commerce (commerce involving more than one state). ***38***

confederation A league of independent states that are united only for the purpose of achieving common goals. ***29***

Constitutional Convention The convention (meeting) of delegates from the states that was held in Philadelphia in 1787 for the purpose of amending the Articles of Confederation. In fact, the delegates wrote a new constitution (the U.S. Constitution) that established a federal form of government to replace the governmental system that had been created by the Articles of Confederation. ***31***

faction A group of persons forming a cohesive minority. ***36***

Federalists A political group, led by Alexander Hamilton and John Adams, that supported the adoption of the Constitution and the creation of a federal form of government. ***35***

federal system A form of government that provides for a division of powers between a central government and several regional governments. In the United States, the division of powers between the national government and the states is established by the Constitution. ***38***

First Continental Congress A gathering of delegates from twelve of the thirteen colonies, held in 1774 to protest the Coercive Acts. ***26***

Great Compromise A plan for a bicameral legislature in which one chamber would be based on population and the other chamber would represent each state equally. The plan, also known as the Connecticut Compromise, resolved the small-state/large-state controversy. ***32***

QUIZ

1. **True or False: The American colonists were anxious to declare their independence from Britain as soon as they arrived in North America.**
2. **True or False: One of the most rousing arguments in favor of independence was written by Alexander Hamilton, John Jay, and James Madison. In the Federalist Papers they contended that America could survive economically on its own and no longer needed its British connection.**
3. **Shays' Rebellion _____.**
   a. was one of the first battles of the American Revolution
   b. was a protest against the imposition of a tax on all sugar imported into American colonies
   c. was a response to the Coercive Acts (sometimes called the "Intolerable Acts")
   d. was an uprising of indebted farmers in western Massachusetts in 1786 and was a catalyst for changing the government that had been established under the Articles of Confederation
   e. led to the Boston Tea Party of 1773, in which colonists dumped almost 350 chests of British tea into Boston Harbor
4. **In the debate over ratification, the Anti-Federalists strongly argued that the Constitution needed a(n) _____.**
   a. system of checks and balances
   b. powerful judiciary
   c. bill of rights to guarantee personal freedoms
   d. independent executive
   e. strong central government
5. **True or False: The veto is a "check" on legislative power.**

© STEVE MCALISTER/GETTY IMAGES

SUMMARY & OBJECTIVES

LO1 Point out some of the influences on the American political tradition in the colonial years. ***1*** American politics owes much to the English political tradition, but the colonists derived most of their understanding about governing from their own experiences. The Pilgrims founded the first New England colony at Plymouth in 1620. Before going ashore, they drew up the **Mayflower Compact,** in which they set up a government and promised to obey its laws. Connecticut colonists developed America's first written constitution, the Fundamental Orders of Connecticut. Under it, an elected assembly made laws, and a governor and judges were popularly elected. The Pennsylvania Charter of Privileges of 1701 established principles later expressed in the Constitution and **Bill of Rights.** ***2*** By participating in colonial governments, the colonists became familiar with the practical problems of governing. They learned how to build coalitions and make compromises.

LO2 Explain why the American colonies rebelled against Britain. ***3*** Initially, most colonists were strongly loyal to Britain. After the British victory in the Seven Years' War (1756–1763), however, the British Parliament sought to pay its war debts and to finance the defense of North America by imposing taxes on the colonists and controlling colonial trade. ***4*** In response, the colonists set up the **First Continental Congress** and petitioned the king, explaining their grievances. Americans boycotted British goods and established colonial armies. Britain responded with even more repressive measures. **5** In 1775, British soldiers fought colonial citizen soldiers in the first battles of the American Revolution. Delegates gathered for the **Second Continental Congress,** which assumed the powers of a central government. **6** The congress adopted the Declaration of Independence on July 4, 1776.

LO3 **Describe the structure of government established by the Articles of Confederation and some of the strengths and weaknesses of the Articles.**
7 The **Articles of Confederation,** the country's first national constitution, established a Congress as the central governing body. It was a **unicameral** assembly in which each state had only one vote. Congress could declare war, enter into treaties, and settle certain disputes among the states. **8** In spite of several accomplishments, the central government created by the Articles was weak. Congress had no power to raise revenues for the militia or to force the states to meet military quotas. It could not regulate commerce between the states or with other nations. There was no national judicial system and no executive branch.

LO4 **List some of the major compromises made by the delegates at the Constitutional Convention, and discuss the Federalist and Anti- Federalist positions with respect to ratifying the Constitution.** **9** Dissatisfaction with the Articles and disruptions such as **Shays' Rebellion** persuaded American leaders that a true national government was necessary. Congress called for delegates to a meeting in Philadelphia in 1787 that became the **Constitutional Convention.** **10** Delegates resolved the small/large-state controversy with the **Great Compromise.** In one chamber of a bicameral legislature, the number of representatives from each state would be determined by the number of people in that state. The other chamber would have two members from each state. The **three-fifths compromise** settled a deadlock on how slaves would be counted to determine representation in the House of Representatives. The delegates also agreed that Congress could prohibit the importation of slaves into the country beginning in 1808. The South agreed to give Congress the power to regulate both **interstate commerce** and commerce with other nations in exchange for a ban on export taxes. **11** **Federalists** favored the new Constitution. The *Federalist Papers* attempted to allay the fears of the Constitution's critics. **Anti-Federalists** argued that the Constitution would lead to aristocratic **tyranny** or an overly powerful central government that would limit personal freedom. To gain support for ratification, the Federalists promised to add a bill of rights to the Constitution. By 1790, all of the states had ratified the Constitution.

LO5 **Summarize the Constitution's major principles of government, and describe how the Constitution can be amended.** **12** The Constitution incorporates the principle of limited government: government can do only what the people allow it to do. This principle rests on the concept of popular sovereignty—the people create the government. Under the principle of **federalism,** the national government shares powers with the states. By **separating the powers** of the national government and establishing a system of **checks and balances,** the framers ensured that no one branch—legislative, executive, judicial—can exercise exclusive control. **13** An amendment to the Constitution can be proposed either by a two-thirds vote in each chamber of Congress or by a national convention called at the request of two-thirds of the state legislatures. Ratification of an amendment requires either approval by three-fourths of the state legislatures or by three-fourths of special conventions called in each state.

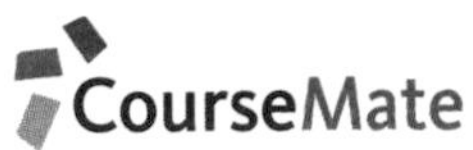

Find more practice tests and study tools for this chapter on CourseMate.

interstate commerce Trade that involves more than one state. *34*

Madisonian Model The model of government devised by James Madison, in which the powers of the government are separated into three branches: executive, legislative, and judicial. *39*

Mayflower Compact A document drawn up by Pilgrim leaders in 1620 on the ship *Mayflower.* The document stated that laws were to be made for the general good of the people. *24*

rule of law A basic principle of government that requires those who govern to act in accordance with established law. *37*

Second Continental Congress The congress of the colonies that met in 1775 to assume the powers of a central government and to establish an army. *27*

separation of powers The principle of dividing governmental powers among the executive, the legislative, and the judicial branches of government. *39*

Shays' Rebellion A rebellion of angry farmers in western Massachusetts in 1786, led by former Revolutionary War captain Daniel Shays. This rebellion and other similar uprisings in the New England states emphasized the need for a true national government. *31*

three-fifths compromise A compromise reached during the Constitutional Convention by which three-fifths of all slaves were to be counted for purposes of representation in the House of Representatives. *33*

tyranny The arbitrary or unrestrained exercise of power by an oppressive individual or government. *36*

unicameral legislature A legislature with only one chamber. *29*

veto power A constitutional power that enables the chief executive (president or governor) to reject legislation and return it to the legislature with reasons for the rejection. This prevents or at least delays the bill from becoming law. *39*

Quiz Answers: 1. False; 2. False; 3. d; 4. c; 5. True

CHAPTER IN REVIEW 3 *Federalism*

KEY TERMS

block grant A federal grant given to a state for a broad area, such as criminal justice or mental-health programs. ***65***

categorical grant A federal grant targeted for a specific purpose as defined by federal law. ***65***

competitive federalism A model of federalism devised by Thomas R. Dye in which state and local governments compete for businesses and citizens, who in effect "vote with their feet" by moving to jurisdictions that offer a competitive advantage. ***67***

confederal system A league of independent sovereign states, joined together by a central government that has only limited powers over them. ***55***

concurrent powers Powers held by both the federal and the state governments in a federal system. ***50***

cooperative federalism The theory that the states and the federal government should cooperate in solving problems. ***60***

devolution The surrender or transfer of powers to local authorities by a central government. ***62***

division of powers A basic principle of federalism established by the U.S. Constitution, by which powers are divided between the federal and state governments. ***53***

dual federalism A system of government in which the federal and the state governments maintain diverse but sovereign powers. ***58***

expressed powers Constitutional or statutory powers that are expressly provided for by the Constitution. ***53***

federal mandate A requirement in federal legislation that forces states and municipalities to comply with certain rules. If the federal government does not provide funds to the states to cover the costs of compliance, the mandate is referred to as an *unfunded* mandate. ***49***

federalism A system of shared sovereignty between two levels of government—one national and one subnational—occupying the same geographic region. ***62***

fiscal federalism The allocation of taxes collected by one level of government (typically the national government) to another level (typically state or local governments). ***65***

implied powers The powers of the federal government that are implied by the expressed powers in the Constitution, particularly in Article I, Section 8. ***53***

QUIZ

1. **True or False: One of the reasons a federal form of government is well suited to the United States is our country's large size.**
2. **The ability of each state to enact whatever laws are necessary to protect the health, morals, safety, and welfare of its people are called _____ powers.**
   a. police
   b. expressed
   c. implied
   d. inherent
   e. enumerated
3. **True or False: The Tenth Amendment to the Constitution gives numerous powers to the national government.**
4. **The model in which every level of government is involved in implementing a policy is sometimes referred to as _____ federalism.**
   a. fiscal
   b. new
   c. picket-fence
   d. competitive
   e. dual
5. **True or False: By giving or withholding federal grant dollars, the federal government has been able to exercise control over matters that traditionally have been under the control of state governments.**

© ROBYN BECK/AFP/GETTY IMAGES

SUMMARY & OBJECTIVES

LO1 Explain what federalism means, how federalism differs from other systems of government, and why it exists in the United States. ***1*** The United States has a federal form of government, in which governmental powers are shared by the national government and the states. For a system to be truly federal, the powers of both the national units and the subnational units must be specified and limited. Alternatives to **federalism** include a **unitary system** and a **confederal system.** In a unitary system, any subnational government is a "creature of the national government." Subnational governments exercise only those powers given to them by the national (central) government. In a confederal system, the central government exists and operates only at the direction of the subnational governments. ***2*** The Articles of Confederation failed because they did not allow for a sufficiently strong central government. The framers of the Constitution, however, were fearful of tyranny and a too-powerful central government. The appeal of federalism was that it retained state powers and local traditions while establishing a strong national government capable of handling common problems. Federalism has been viewed as well suited to the United States for several reasons, but it also has some drawbacks.

LO2 Indicate how the Constitution divides governing powers in our federal system. ***3*** The Constitution delegates certain powers to the national government and also prohibits the national government from exercising certain powers. The national government possesses three types of powers: **expressed, implied,** and **inherent.** The Constitution expressly enumerates twenty-seven powers that Congress may exercise, such as the power to coin money and the power to regulate interstate commerce. The Constitution's **"necessary and proper" clause** is the basis for implied powers. Thus, Congress has the power to make all laws "necessary and proper" for the federal (national) government to carry out its responsibilities. The national government also enjoys certain inherent powers—powers that governments must have simply to ensure the nation's integrity and survival. ***4*** The Tenth Amendment to the Constitution states that powers that are not delegated to the national government by the Constitution, nor prohibited to the states, are "reserved" to the states or to the people. In principle, each state has the ability to regulate its internal affairs and to enact whatever laws are necessary to protect the health, safety, morals, and welfare of its people. These powers of the states are called **police powers. Concurrent powers** can be exercised by both the state governments and the federal government. ***5*** The Constitution also contains provisions relating to interstate relations. The full faith and credit clause, for example, requires each state to honor every other state's public acts, records, and judicial proceedings. The Constitution's **supremacy clause** asserts that national laws are supreme. National government power takes precedence over any conflicting state action.

LO3 Summarize the evolution of federal-state relationships in the United States over time. ***6*** Two early Supreme Court cases, *McCulloch v. Maryland* (1819) and *Gibbons v. Ogden* (1824), played a key role in establishing the constitutional foundations for the supremacy of the national government. The nation's struggle over slavery also took the form of a dispute over states' rights versus national supremacy. ***7*** The relationship between the states and the national government has evolved through several stages since the Civil War. The model of **dual federalism,** which prevailed until the 1930s, assumes that the states and the national government are more or less equals, with each level of government having separate and distinct functions and responsibilities. The model of **cooperative federalism,** which views the national and state governments as complementary parts of a single governmental mechanism, grew out of the need to solve the pressing national problems caused by the Great Depression. The 1960s and 1970s saw an even greater expansion of the national government's role in domestic policy, but the massive social programs undertaken during this period also precipitated greater involvement by state and local governments. The model in which every level of government is involved in implementing a policy is sometimes referred to as **picket-fence federalism.**

LO4 Describe developments in federalism in recent years. ***8*** Starting in the 1970s, several administrations favored a shift from nation-centered federalism to state-centered federalism. One of the goals of the **"new federalism"** was to return to the states certain powers that had been exercised by the national government since the 1930s. During and since the 1990s, many Supreme Court decisions have had the effect of enhancing the power of the states. ***9*** The federal government and the states now seem to be in a constant tug-of-war over federal regulation, federal programs, and federal demands on the states. Decisions made about welfare reform, educational funding, same-sex marriages, health-care reform, homeland security, and the economic crisis have involved the politics of federalism and have not always reflected clear-cut partisan divisions.

LO5 Explain what is meant by the term *fiscal federalism.* ***10*** To help the states pay for the costs associated with implementing policies mandated by the national government, the national government gives back some of the tax dollars it collects to the states—in the form of **categorical** and **block grants.** The states have come to depend on grants as an important source of revenue. By giving or withholding federal grant dollars, the federal government has been able to exercise control over matters that traditionally have been under the control of state governments. ***11*** Sometimes state and local governments engage in competitive federalism by offering lower taxes or more services.

Find more practice tests and study tools for this chapter on CourseMate.

inherent powers The powers of the national government that, although not always expressly granted by the Constitution, are necessary to ensure the nation's integrity and survival as a political unit. Inherent powers include the power to make treaties and the power to wage war or make peace. ***53***

necessary and proper clause Article I, Section 8, Clause 18, of the Constitution, which gives Congress the power to make all laws "necessary and proper" for the federal government to carry out its responsibilities; also called the elastic clause. ***53***

New Deal A program ushered in by the Roosevelt administration in 1933 to bring the United States out of the Great Depression. The New Deal included many government-spending and public-assistance programs, in addition to thousands of regulations governing economic activity. ***60***

new federalism A plan to limit the federal government's role in regulating state governments and to give the states increased power to decide how they should spend government revenues. ***61***

picket-fence federalism A model of federalism in which specific policies and programs are administered by all levels of government—national, state, and local. ***60***

police powers The powers of a government body that enable it to create laws for the protection of the health, morals, safety, and welfare of the people. In the United States, most police powers are reserved to the states. ***54***

preemption A doctrine rooted in the supremacy clause of the Constitution that provides that national laws or regulations governing a certain area take precedence over conflicting state laws or regulations governing that same area. ***61***

secession The act of formally withdrawing from membership in an alliance; the withdrawal of a state from the federal Union. ***58***

supremacy clause Article VI, Clause 2, of the Constitution, which makes the Constitution and federal laws superior to all conflicting state and local laws. ***55***

unitary system A centralized governmental system in which local or subdivisional governments exercise only those powers given to them by the central government. ***50***

Quiz Answers: 1. True; 2. a; 3. False; 4. c; 5. True

CHAPTER IN REVIEW 4 *Civil Liberties*

KEY TERMS

bill of attainder A legislative act that inflicts punishment on particular persons or groups without granting them the right to a trial. *72*

civil liberties Individual rights protected by the Constitution against the powers of the government. *72*

commercial speech Advertising statements that describe products. Commercial speech receives less protection under the First Amendment than ordinary speech. *81*

double jeopardy The prosecution of a person twice for the same criminal offense; prohibited by the Fifth Amendment in all but a few circumstances. *89*

due process clause The constitutional guarantee, set out in the Fifth and Fourteenth Amendments, that the government will not illegally or arbitrarily deprive a person of life, liberty, or property. *73*

due process of law The requirement that the government use fair, reasonable, and standard procedures whenever it takes any legal action against an individual; required by the Fifth and Fourteenth Amendments. *73*

establishment clause The section of the First Amendment that prohibits Congress from passing laws "respecting an establishment of religion." Issues concerning the establishment clause often center on prayer in public schools, the teaching of fundamentalist theories of creation, and government aid to parochial schools. *74*

exclusionary rule A criminal procedural rule requiring that any illegally obtained evidence not be admissible in court. *89*

***ex post facto* law** A criminal law that punishes individuals for committing an act that was legal when the act was committed. *73*

free exercise clause The provision of the First Amendment stating that the government cannot pass laws "prohibiting the free exercise" of religion. Free exercise issues often concern religious practices that conflict with established laws. *74*

***Lemon* test** A three-part test enunciated by the Supreme Court in the 1971 case of *Lemon v. Kurtzman* to determine whether government aid to parochial schools is constitutional. To be constitutional, the aid must (1) be for a clearly secular purpose; (2) in its primary effect, neither advance nor inhibit religion; and (3) avoid an "excessive government entanglement with religion." The Lemon test has also been used in other types of cases involving the establishment clause. *77*

libel A published report of a falsehood that tends to injure a person's reputation or character. *82*

QUIZ

1. An order requiring that an official bring a specified prisoner into court and show the judge why the prisoner is being kept in jail is known as _____.

a. a writ of *habeas corpus*
b. a bill of attainder
c. probable cause
d. the exclusionary rule
e. double jeopardy

2. True or False: The U.S. Supreme Court incorporated the protections guaranteed by the national Bill of Rights against the actions of state governments at the time the Bill of Rights was ratified in 1791.

3. True or False: The U.S. Supreme Court has held that it is not a violation of the First Amendment's establishment clause for public schools to include the recitation of prayers in their morning exercises as long as the prayers are nondenominational.

4. The First Amendment has been interpreted by the U.S. Supreme Court to protect _____.

a. libel
b. obscenity
c. symbolic speech
d. all speech
e. slander

5. True or False: Under the U.S. Supreme Court's ruling in *Roe v. Wade* (1973), the right of a woman to terminate her pregnancy is absolute.

© AP PHOTO/MATT YORK

SUMMARY & OBJECTIVES

LO1 Define the term *civil liberties*, explain how civil liberties differ from civil rights, and state the constitutional basis for our civil liberties.

1 **Civil liberties** are legal and constitutional rights that protect citizens from government actions. While civil rights specify what the government *must* do, civil liberties are limitations on government action, setting forth what the government *cannot* do. **2** The Bill of Rights (the first ten amendments to the Constitution) sets forth most of our civil liberties. Other safeguards to protect citizens against an overly powerful government, such as the **writ of *habeas corpus*,** are specified in the original Constitution. For many years, the courts assumed that the Bill of Rights limited only the actions of the national government, not those of the states. Over time, the United States Supreme Court began using the **due process clause** of the Fourteenth Amendment to say that the states could not abridge a civil liberty that the national government could not abridge. In other words, the Court has incorporated most of the protections guaranteed by the Bill of Rights into the liberties protected under the Fourteenth Amendment.

LO2 List and describe the freedoms guaranteed by the First Amendment and explain how the courts have interpreted and applied these freedoms.

3 The First Amendment prohibits government from passing laws "respecting an establishment of religion, or prohibiting the free exercise thereof." The first part of this amendment is referred to as the **establishment clause;** the second part is known as the **free exercise clause.** Issues involving the establishment clause include prayer in the public schools, the teaching of evolution versus creationism, and government aid to parochial schools. The Supreme Court has ruled that the public schools cannot sponsor religious activities and has held unconstitutional state laws forbidding the teaching of evolution in the schools. Some aid to parochial schools has been held to violate the establishment clause, while other forms of aid have been held permissible. ***4*** The free exercise clause does not necessarily mean that individuals can act in any way they want on the basis of their religious beliefs. The Supreme Court has ruled consistently that the right to hold any belief is absolute. The right to practice one's beliefs, however, may have some limits. The free exercise of religion in the workplace was bolstered by Title VII of the Civil Rights Act of 1964, which requires employers to accommodate their employees' religious practices unless such accommodation causes an employer to suffer an "undue hardship." ***5*** Although the Supreme Court has zealously safeguarded the right to free speech under the First Amendment, at times it has imposed limits on speech in the interests of protecting other rights. These rights include security against harm to one's person or reputation, the need for public order, and the need to preserve the government. ***6*** The First Amendment freedom of the press generally protects the right to publish a wide range of opinions and information. Over the years, the Supreme Court has developed various guidelines and doctrines to use in deciding whether freedom of speech and the press can be restrained.

LO3 **Discuss why Americans are increasingly concerned about privacy rights.** ***7*** The Supreme Court has held that a right to privacy is implied by other constitutional rights guaranteed in the Bill of Rights. The government has also passed laws ensuring the privacy rights of individuals. The nature and scope of this right, however, are not always clear. ***8*** In 1973, the Supreme Court held that the right to privacy is broad enough to encompass a woman's decision to terminate a pregnancy, though the right is not absolute throughout pregnancy. Since that decision, the Court has upheld restrictive state laws requiring counseling, parental notification, and other actions prior to abortions. The issue of "partial-birth" abortion has been particularly controversial. ***9*** The Supreme Court upheld the states' rights to ban physician-assisted suicide in situations involving terminally ill persons, but it did not hold that state laws permitting physician-assisted suicide were unconstitutional. Americans continue to be at odds over this issue. ***10*** Since the terrorist attacks of September 11, 2001, Americans have debated how the United States can address the need to strengthen national security while still protecting civil liberties, particularly the right to privacy. Various programs have been proposed or attempted, and some have already been dismantled after public outcry. Many civil libertarians point out that trading off even a few civil liberties, including our privacy rights, for national security is senseless. These liberties are at the heart of what this country stands for. Other Americans believe that we have little to worry about. Those who have nothing to hide should not be concerned about government surveillance or other privacy intrusions undertaken by the government to make our nation more secure against terrorist attacks.

LO4 **Summarize how the Constitution and the Bill of Rights protect the rights of accused persons.** ***11*** Constitutional safeguards provided for criminal defendants include the Fourth Amendment protection from unreasonable searches and seizures and the requirement that no warrant for a search or an arrest be issued without **probable cause;** the Fifth Amendment prohibition against **double jeopardy** and the protection against **self-incrimination;** the Sixth Amendment guarantees of a speedy trial, a trial by jury, a public trial, the right to confront witnesses, and the right to counsel at various stages in some criminal proceedings; and the Eighth Amendment prohibitions against excessive bail and fines and against cruel and unusual punishments. The Constitution also provides for the writ of *habeas corpus*—an order requiring that an official bring a specified prisoner into court and show the judge why the prisoner is being kept in jail.

Find more practice tests and study tools for this chapter on CourseMate.

Miranda* warnings** A series of statements informing criminal suspects, on their arrest, of their constitutional rights, such as the right to remain silent and the right to counsel; required by the Supreme Court's 1966 decision in *Miranda v. Arizona*. ***89

obscenity Indecency or offensiveness in speech, expression, behavior, or appearance. Whether specific expressions or acts constitute obscenity normally is determined by community standards. ***82***

probable cause Cause for believing that there is a substantial likelihood that a person has committed or is about to commit a crime. ***89***

school voucher An educational certificate, provided by the government, that allows a student to use public funds to pay for a private or a public school chosen by the student or his or her parents. ***78***

seditious speech Speech that urges resistance to lawful authority or that advocates the overthrowing of a government. ***81***

self-incrimination Providing damaging information or testimony against oneself in court. ***89***

slander The public utterance (speaking) of a statement that holds a person up for contempt, ridicule, or hatred. ***82***

symbolic speech The expression of beliefs, opinions, or ideas through forms other than speech or print; speech involving actions and other nonverbal expressions. ***79***

writ of *habeas corpus* In order that requires an official to bring a specified prisoner into court and explain to the judge why the person is being held in prison. ***72***

Quiz Answers: 1. a; 2. False; 3. False; 4. c; 5. False

CHAPTER IN REVIEW 5 *Civil Rights*

KEY TERMS

affirmative action A policy calling for the establishment of programs that give special consideration, in jobs and college admissions, to members of groups that have been discriminated against in the past. *112*

busing The transportation of public school students by bus to schools physically outside their neighborhoods to eliminate school segregation based on residential patterns. *98*

civil disobedience The deliberate and public act of refusing to obey laws thought to be unjust. *99*

civil rights The rights of all Americans to equal treatment under the law, as provided for by the Fourteenth Amendment to the Constitution. *95*

civil rights movement The movement in the 1950s and 1960s, by minorities and concerned whites, to end racial segregation. *99*

***de facto* segregation** Racial segregation that occurs not as a result of deliberate intentions but because of past social and economic conditions and residential patterns. *98*

***de jure* segregation** Racial segregation that occurs because of laws or decisions by government agencies. *98*

equal protection clause Section 1 of the Fourteenth Amendment, which states that no state shall "deny to any person within its jurisdiction the equal protection of the laws." *95*

feminism The belief in full political, economic, and social equality for women. *102*

fundamental right A basic right of all Americans, such as First Amendment rights. Any law or action that prevents some group of persons from exercising a fundamental right is subject to the "strict-scrutiny" standard, under which the law or action must be necessary to promote a compelling state interest and must be narrowly tailored to meet that interest. *96*

glass ceiling An invisible but real discriminatory barrier that prevents women and minorities from rising to top positions of power or responsibility. *104*

quota system A policy under which a specific number of jobs, promotions, or other types of placements, such as university admissions, must be given to members of selected groups. *113*

rational basis test A test (also known as the "ordinary-scrutiny" standard) used by the Supreme Court to decide whether a discriminatory law violates the equal protection clause of the Constitution. Few laws evaluated under this test are found invalid. *96*

reverse discrimination Discrimination against those who have no minority status. *113*

QUIZ

1. **True or False: A law based on a suspect classification, such as race, is subject to the ordinary-scrutiny standard by the courts.**
2. **The Supreme Court ____ the separate-but-equal doctrine in *Brown v. Board of Education of Topeka* (1954).**
   a. established
   b. overturned
   c. upheld
   d. justified
   e. adopted
3. **True or False: The 1964 Civil Rights Act made it illegal to interfere with anyone's right to vote in any election held in this country.**
4. **____ is an invisible but real discriminatory barrier that prevents women from rising to top positions of power or responsibility.**
   a. Feminism
   b. Affirmative action
   c. The glass ceiling
   d. Suffrage
   e. Sexual harassment
5. **True or False: The "Don't ask, don't tell" policy grants same-sex couples most of the benefits of marriage.**

© MARK PETERSON/REDUX

SUMMARY & OBJECTIVES

LO1 Explain the constitutional basis for our civil rights and for laws prohibiting discrimination. ***1*** **Civil rights** are the rights of all Americans to equal treatment under the law, as provided for by the Fourteenth Amendment. The **equal protection clause** of the Fourteenth Amendment has been interpreted by the courts to mean that states must treat all persons in an equal manner and may not discriminate unreasonably against a particular group or class of individuals. The U.S. Supreme Court has developed various standards for determining whether the equal protection clause has been violated. In addition, Section 5 of the Fourteenth Amendment provides a legal basis for civil rights legislation.

LO2 Discuss the reasons for the civil rights movement and the changes it caused in American politics and government. ***2*** The equal protection clause was originally intended to protect the newly freed slaves from discrimination after the Civil War. By the late 1880s, however, southern states had begun to pass a series of segregation ("Jim Crow") laws. In 1896, the Supreme Court held that a law did not violate the equal protection clause if separate facilities for blacks equaled those for whites. The **separate-but-equal doctrine** justified segregation for nearly sixty years. ***3*** In the landmark case of *Brown v. Board of Education of Topeka* (1954), the Supreme Court held that segregation by race in public education violated the equal protection clause. One year later, the arrest of Rosa Parks for violating local segregation laws spurred a boycott of the bus system in Montgomery, Alabama. The protest was led by the Reverend Dr. Martin Luther King, Jr. In 1956, a federal court prohibited the segregation of buses in Montgomery, marking the beginning of the **civil rights movement.** ***4*** Civil rights protesters in the 1960s applied the tactic of nonviolent **civil disobedience** in actions throughout the South. In response, Congress passed a series of civil rights laws, including the Civil Rights Act of 1964 (which forbade discrimination on the basis of race, color, religion, gender, and national origin), the Voting Rights Act of 1965, and the Civil Rights Act of 1968. ***5*** Today, the percentages of voting-age blacks and whites registered to vote are nearly equal. Political participation by African Americans has increased, as has the number of African American elected officials. African Americans have achieved high government office, including secretary of state. In 2008, Barack Obama became the first African American elected president of the United States.

LO3 Describe the political and economic achievements of women in this country over time and identify some obstacles to equality that women continue to face. ***6*** The struggle of women for equal treatment initially focused on **suffrage**—the right to vote. In 1920, the Nineteenth Amendment was ratified, granting voting rights to women. **Feminism**—the belief in full political, economic, and social equality for women—shaped a new movement that began in the 1960s. Although women remain underrepresented in politics, increasingly women have gained power as public officials. Following the 2006 elections, a woman was chosen as Speaker of the House of Representatives for the first time. Women have mounted serious campaigns for president or vice president, and several women have held cabinet posts. Four women have been appointed to the Supreme Court. ***7*** In spite of federal legislation to promote equal treatment of women in the workplace, they continue to face various forms of discrimination, including a wage gap and a lingering bias that has been described as the **glass ceiling.** ***8*** The prohibition of gender discrimination has been extended to prohibit **sexual harassment.** Court decisions and legislation have expanded the remedies available to its victims.

LO4 Summarize the struggles for equality that other groups in America experience. ***9*** Hispanics, or Latinos, constitute the largest ethnic minority in the United States. Each year, the Hispanic population grows by nearly 1 million people. A disproportionate number of Hispanic families live below the poverty line. Hispanic leaders tend to attribute the low income levels to language problems, lack of job training, and continuing immigration. ***10*** Asian Americans have also suffered from discriminatory treatment. Immigration was restricted by the Chinese Exclusion Act of 1882. During World War II, most of the West Coast Japanese American population was evacuated to internment camps. ***11*** The Europeans arriving in the New World brought with them diseases that caused a severe decline in the Native American population. In 1789, Congress designated the Native American tribes as foreign nations so that the government could sign land and boundary treaties with them. In the early 1830s, boundaries were established between lands occupied by Native Americans and those occupied by white settlers. In the 1880s, the U.S. government changed its policy to one of assimilation. Reservations were reduced dramatically, and schools were established to teach American Indian children to speak English and to practice Christianity. Native Americans had no civil rights under U.S. laws until 1924. In the 1960s, some Native Americans formed organizations to strike back at the U.S. government and to reclaim their heritage, including their lands. New legislation passed in the 1980s and the 1990s allowed gambling on reservation lands and promoted Native American languages. ***12*** Persons with disabilities first became a political force in the 1970s. The Americans with Disabilities Act (ADA) of 1990 is the most significant legislation protecting the rights of these Americans. It includes a requirement that all public buildings and services be accessible to persons with disabilities. Supreme Court decisions and congressional legislation continue to define the scope of the ADA. ***13*** Until the late 1960s and early 1970s, gay men and lesbians tended to keep quiet about their sexual preferences because exposure usually meant facing harsh consequences. In the decades following the launch of the gay power movement, sodomy laws were repealed or invalidated. Many states have laws prohibiting discrimination against gay men and lesbians in at least some contexts, including housing, education, banking, employment, or public accommodations. Same-sex marriage is legal in several states, and public support for gay rights continues to rise.

LO5 Explain what affirmative action is and why it has been so controversial. ***14*** **Affirmative action** gives special consideration, in jobs or college admissions, to members of groups that have been discriminated against in the past. It has been tested in court cases involving claims of **reverse discrimination.** The Supreme Court has held that any government affirmative action program that uses racial classifications as the basis for making decisions is subject to "strict scrutiny," which means that to be constitutional, a discriminatory law or action must be narrowly tailored to meet a compelling government interest. ***15*** Some states have banned affirmative action or replaced it with alternative policies. Some affirmative action programs have been deemed unconstitutional by the courts.

separate-but-equal doctrine A Supreme Court doctrine holding that the equal protection clause of the Fourteenth Amendment did not forbid racial segregation as long as the facilities for blacks were equal to those for whites. The doctrine was overturned in the *Brown v. Board of Education of Topeka* decision of 1954. ***97***

sexual harassment Unwanted physical contact, verbal conduct, or abuse of a sexual nature that interferes with a recipient's job performance, creates a hostile environment, or carries with it an implicit or explicit threat of adverse employment consequences. ***105***

sit-in A tactic of nonviolent civil disobedience. Demonstrators enter a business, college building, or other public place and remain seated until they are forcibly removed or until their demands are met. The tactic was used successfully in the civil rights movement and in other protest movements in the United States. ***99***

suffrage The right to vote; the franchise. ***101***

suspect classification A classification, such as race, that provides the basis for a discriminatory law. Any law based on a suspect classification is subject to strict scrutiny by the courts—meaning that the law must be justified by a compelling state interest. ***96***

Quiz Answers: 1. False; 2. b; 3. False; 4. c; 5. False

CHAPTER IN REVIEW 6 *Interest Groups*

KEY TERMS

direct technique Any method used by an interest group to interact with government officials directly to further the group's goals. *131*

free rider problem The difficulty that exists when individuals can enjoy the outcome of an interest group's efforts without having to contribute, such as by becoming members of the group. *123*

independent expenditures An expenditure for activities that are independent from (not coordinated with) those of a political candidate or a political party. *133*

indirect technique Any method used by interest groups to influence government officials through third parties, such as voters. *133*

interest group An organized group of individuals sharing common objectives who actively attempt to influence policymakers. *120*

labor force All of the people over the age of sixteen who are working or actively looking for jobs. *127*

lobbying All of the attempts by organizations or by individuals to influence the passage, defeat, or contents of legislation or to influence the administrative decisions of government. *131*

lobbyist An individual who handles a particular interest group's lobbying efforts. *131*

material incentive Practical benefits from joining an interest group, such as discounts, subscriptions, or group insurance. *123*

pluralist theory A theory that views politics as a contest among various interest groups—at all levels of government—to gain benefits for their members. *124*

political action committee (PAC) A committee that is established by a corporation, labor union, or special interest group to raise funds and make contributions on the establishing organization's behalf. *132*

public-interest group An interest group formed for the purpose of working for the "public good." Examples of public-interest groups are the American Civil Liberties Union and Common Cause. *125*

purposive incentive A reason to join an interest group—satisfaction resulting from working for a cause in which one believes. *123*

rating system A system by which a particular interest group evaluates (rates) the performance of legislators based on how often the legislators have voted with the group's position on particular issues. *133*

right to work laws Laws that ban unions from collecting dues or other fees from workers that they represent but who have not actually joined the union. *128*

QUIZ

1. **True or False: The difficulty that exists when individuals can enjoy the outcome of an interest group's efforts without having to contribute is called the free rider problem.**
2. **True or False: According to the pluralist theory of American democracy, politics is a contest among various government institutions.**
3. **Interest groups *do not* ____.**
   a. help bridge the gap between citizens and government
   b. help raise public awareness and inspire action on various issues
   c. serve as another check on public officials to make sure they are carrying out their duties responsibly
   d. enable citizens to explain their views on policies to public officials
   e. compete for public office
4. **True or False: The most common interest groups are those that promote private interests.**
5. **Direct lobbying techniques include ____.**
   a. running "issue ads"
   b. staging demonstrations
   c. offering "expert" testimony before congressional committees
   d. mobilizing constituents
   e. developing rating systems

© AP PHOTO/ALASTAIR GRANT

SUMMARY & OBJECTIVES

LO1 Explain what an interest group is, why interest groups form, and how interest groups function in American politics. ***1*** An **interest group** is an organization of people sharing common objectives who actively attempt to influence government policymakers through direct and indirect methods. The right to form interest groups and to lobby the government is protected by the First Amendment. Interest groups may form—and existing groups may become more politically active—when the government expands its scope of activities. Interest groups also come into existence in response to a perceived threat to a group's interests, or they can form in reaction to the creation of other groups. The term *disturbance theory* has been used to describe this kind of defensive formation of groups. *Entrepreneurial theory* focuses on the importance of the leaders who establish viable organizations and their significance to the group's survival. **Purposive incentives, solidary incentives,** and **material incentives** are among the reasons people join interest groups. ***2*** Interest groups (a) help bridge the gap between citizens and government; (b) help raise public awareness and inspire action on various issues; (c) often provide public officials with specialized and detailed information that may be useful in making policy choices; and (d) serve as another check on public officials to make sure that they are carrying out their duties responsibly. The **pluralist theory** of American democracy views politics as a contest among various interest groups that compete at all levels of government to gain benefits for their members.

LO2 Indicate how interest groups differ from political parties. ***3*** Although interest groups and political parties are both groups of people joined together for political purposes, they differ in several ways. Interest groups focus on a handful of key policies; political parties are broad-based organizations that must attract the support of many opposing groups and consider a large number of issues. Interest groups are usually more tightly organized than political parties, and they are often financed through contributions or dues-paying memberships. Interest groups may try to influence the outcome of elections, but unlike parties, they do not compete for public office.

LO3 Identify the various types of interest groups. ***4*** The most common interest groups are those that promote private interests. These groups seek government policies that benefit the economic interests of their members. Other groups, sometimes called **public-interest groups,** are formed with the broader goal of working for the "public good," though there is no such thing as a clear public interest in a nation of more than 300 million diverse people. In reality, all lobbying groups represent special interests. ***5*** Business has long been well organized for effective action. There are umbrella organizations that include small and large corporations and businesses, and **trade organizations** that support policies that benefit specific industries. Interest groups representing labor have been some of the most influential groups in the nation's history, though the strength and political power of labor unions have waned in the last several decades. One reason for this decline is the continuing fall in the proportion of the nation's workforce employed in sectors such as manufacturing and transportation that have always been among the most heavily unionized. Another reason is the general political environment and the existence of **right-to-work laws.** Public employee unions, however, have grown in both numbers and political clout in recent years. ***6*** Most professions that require advanced education or specialized training have organizations to protect and promote their interests. These groups are concerned mainly with the standards of their professions, but they also work to influence government policy. Many groups work for general agricultural interests at all levels of government, and producers of various specific farm commodities have formed their own organizations. Groups organized for the protection of consumer rights were very active in the 1960s and 1970s, and some are still active today. ***7*** Americans who share the same race, ethnicity, gender, or other characteristic often have important common interests and form identity interest groups. Ideological interest groups, such as Club for Growth, are organized to promote a shared political perspective. Environmental groups range from traditional organizations to more radical groups. ***8*** Numerous interest groups focus on a single issue, such as abortion. Efforts by state and local governments to lobby the federal government have escalated in recent years.

LO4 Discuss how the activities of interest groups help to shape government policymaking. ***9*** Interest groups operate at all levels of government and use a variety of strategies to steer policies in ways beneficial to their interests. Sometimes interest groups attempt to influence policymakers directly, but at other times they try to exert indirect influence on policymakers by shaping public opinion. Lobbying and providing election support are two important **direct techniques** used by interest groups to influence government policy. ***10*** **Lobbying** refers to all of the attempts by organizations or individuals to influence the passage, defeat, or contents of legislation or to influence the administrative decisions of government. Interest groups often become directly involved in the election process. Groups provide campaign support for legislators who favor their policies and urge their members to vote for candidates who support the views of the group. Federal laws have allowed corporations, labor unions, and special interest groups to raise funds and make campaign contributions through **political action committees (PACs).** ***11*** Interest groups also try to influence public policy through third parties or the general public. Indirect techniques include advertising and other promotional efforts designed to shape public opinion, **rating systems,** issue advocacy through **independent expenditures,** mobilizing constituents, going to court, and organizing demonstrations.

LO5 Describe how interest groups are regulated by government. ***12*** The Federal Regulation of Lobbying Act of 1946 was very limited and contained many loopholes. In 1995, Congress passed the Lobbying Disclosure Act. This legislation reformed the 1946 act in several ways, particularly by creating stricter definitions of who is a lobbyist. The number of registered lobbyists nearly doubled in the first few years of the new legislation. In the wake of lobbying scandals in the early 2000s, additional lobbying reform efforts were undertaken. The Honest Leadership and Open Government Act of 2007 increased lobbying disclosure and placed further restrictions on the receipt of gifts and travel by members of Congress paid for by lobbyists and the organizations they represent.

Find more practice tests and study tools for this chapter on CourseMate.

solidary incentive A reason to join an interest group— pleasure in associating with like-minded individuals. ***123***

trade organization An association formed by members of a particular industry, such as the oil industry or the trucking industry, to develop common standards and goals for the industry. Trade organizations, as interest groups, lobby government for legislation or regulations that specifically benefit their groups. ***126***

Quiz Answers: 1. True; 2. False; 3. e; 4. True; 5. c

CHAPTER IN REVIEW 7 Political Parties

KEY TERMS

coalition An alliance of individuals or groups with a variety of interests and opinions who join together to support all or part of a political party's platform. ***150***

dealignment Among voters, a growing detachment from both major political parties. ***147***

electorate All of the citizens eligible to vote in a given election. ***151***

majority party The political party that has more members in the legislature than the opposing party. ***150***

minority party The political party that has fewer members in the legislature than the opposing party. ***150***

national convention The meeting held by each major party every four years to select presidential and vice-presidential candidates, write a party platform, and conduct other party business. ***153***

national party chairperson An individual who serves as a political party's administrative head at the national level and directs the work of the party's national committee. ***153***

national party committee The political party leaders who direct party business during the four years between the national party conventions, organize the next national convention, and plan how to obtain a party victory in the next presidential elections. ***153***

party activist A party member who helps to organize and oversee party functions and planning during and between campaigns. ***151***

party identifier A person who identifies himself or herself as being a supporter of a particular political party. ***151***

party platform The document drawn up by each party at its national convention that outlines the policies and positions of the party. ***153***

party ticket A list of a political party's candidates for various offices. In national elections, the party ticket consists of the presidential and vice-presidential candidates. ***153***

patronage A system of rewarding the party faithful and workers with government jobs or contracts. ***152***

political party A group of individuals who organize to win elections, operate the government, and determine policy. ***142***

precinct A political district within a city, such as a block or a neighborhood, or a rural portion of a county; the smallest voting district at the local level. ***153***

primary A preliminary election held for the purpose of choosing a party's final candidate. ***149***

QUIZ

1. **True or False: The Democratic Party emerged in 1828, when Andrew Jackson ran against John Quincy Adams and won the presidency.**

2. **Abraham Lincoln was the first president elected under the _____ Party banner.**
   a. Federalist
   b. National Republican
   c. Republican
   d. Whig
   e. Reform

3. **True or False: After the election of 1896, the Republicans established themselves in the minds of many Americans as the party that knew how to manage the nation's economy, and they remained dominant in national politics until the onset of the Great Depression.**

4. **The party in the electorate consists of _____.**
   a. local and state organizations, as well as the national party organization
   b. party identifiers and party activists
   c. the state party chairpersons and the national party chairperson
   d. the national party committee and the congressional campaign committees
   e. all of the party's candidates who now hold public office

5. **The two-party system continues to thrive in the United States _____.**
   a. even though election laws tend to favor third parties
   b. because members of the House of Representatives are elected from multimember districts
   c. because of the winner-take-all feature of the electoral college system for choosing the president
   d. because of dealignment
   e. because third-party candidates are not allowed to run for president

© PHOTO BY JOHN MOORE/GETTY IMAGES

SUMMARY & OBJECTIVES

LO1 Summarize the origins and development of the two-party system in the United States. ***1*** Two major political factions—the Federalists and Anti-Federalists—were formed even before the Constitution was ratified. After ratification, the Federalist Party supported a strong central government that would encourage the development of commerce and manufacturing. Opponents of the Federalists referred to themselves as Republicans. The Jeffersonian Republicans favored a more limited role for government. After the Jeffersonian Republicans won the presidency and control of Congress in 1800, the Federalists never returned to power and eventually went out of existence, resulting in what could be considered a **realignment** of the party system. In the mid-1820s, however, the Republicans split into two groups. Supporters of Andrew Jackson called themselves Democrats. They appealed to small farmers and the growing class of urbanized workers. The other group, the National Republicans, had the support of bankers, business owners, and many southern planters. As the Democrats and the Whigs competed for the presidency during the 1840s and 1850s, the **two-party system** as we know it today emerged. ***2*** By the mid-1850s, the Whig **coalition** had fallen apart, and most northern Whigs were absorbed into the new Republican Party, which opposed the extension of slavery. The founding of the Republican Party led to a new realignment. When the former Confederate states rejoined the Union after the Civil War, the Republicans and Democrats were roughly even in strength, although the Republicans were more successful in presidential contests. After the realigning election of 1896, however, the Republicans established themselves in the minds of many Americans as the party that knew how to manage the nation's economy, and they remained dominant in national politics until the onset of the Great Depression. **3** The realigning election of 1932 brought Franklin D. Roosevelt to the presidency and the Democrats back to power at the national level. (The elections of 1860 and 1896 are also considered to represent **realignments.** The popular support for and relative strength of the parties shifted.) From the 1960s through the 1980s, however, conservative Democrats in Congress sided with the Republicans on most issues. In time, these conservative Democrats were replaced by conservative Republicans. The result of this "rolling realignment" was that the two major parties were now fairly evenly matched.

realignment A process in which the popular support for and relative strength of the parties shift and the parties are reestablished with different coalitions of supporters. ***143***

solidarity Mutual sympathy among the members of a particular group. ***151***

third party In the United States, any party other than one of the two major parties (Republican and Democratic). ***156***

two-party system A political system in which two strong and established parties compete for political offices. ***155***

ward A local unit of a political party's organization, consisting of a division or district within a city. ***153***

LO2 Describe the current status of the two major parties. **4** Individuals with similar characteristics tend to align themselves more often with one or the other major party. Such factors as race, age, income, education, marital status, and geography all influence party identification. In 2000, the two major parties were closely matched in terms of support. By 2006 the Republican Party had lost points in popularity relative to the Democrats, but within one year of Obama's inauguration, the Democratic advantage had vanished. **5** A key characteristic of recent politics has been the extreme partisanship of party activists and members. Ideological uniformity has made it easier for the parties to maintain discipline in Congress, while compromise with the other party is seen as a form of betrayal. Another political development is the growth in the number of independent voters, reflecting a **dealignment** in the party system.

LO3 Explain how political parties function in our democratic system. **6** Political parties link the people's policy preferences to actual government policies. They also recruit and nominate candidates for political office, which simplifies voting choices. Parties help educate the public about important current political issues, and they coordinate policy among the various branches and levels of government. The "out party" does what it can to influence the "in party" and its policies, and to check the actions of the party in power. Political parties also balance competing interests and arrange compromises among different groups. Parties coordinate campaigns and take care of a large number of tasks that are essential to the smooth functioning of the electoral process.

LO4 Discuss the structure of American political parties. **7** Each of the two major political parties consists of three components. The party in the **electorate** is the largest component, consisting of **party identifiers** (those who identify themselves as being members of a **political party**) and **party activists** (party members who help to organize and oversee party functions and planning). Generally, people belong to a political party because they agree with many of its main ideas and support some of its candidates. **8** Each major party has a nationwide organization with national, state, and local offices. Neither party is a closely knit or highly organized structure. Much of the public attention that the party receives comes at the **national convention,** which is held every four years during the summer before the presidential elections. Delegates to the convention nominate the party's presidential and vice-presidential candidates, and they adopt the **party platform.** The national party organization includes a **national party committee,** a **national party chairperson,** and congressional campaign committees. **9** The third component of the two major parties is the party in government, which consists of all of the party's candidates who have won elections and now hold public office. The party in government helps to organize the government's agenda by convincing its own party members to vote for its policies.

LO5 Describe the different types of third parties and how they function in the American political system. **10** The United States has a two-party system in which two major parties, the Democrats and the Republicans, dominate national politics. The first major political division between the Federalists and the Anti-Federalists established a precedent for a two-party system that has been perpetuated for several reasons. **11** Third parties have traditionally found it extremely difficult to compete with the major parties for votes. American election laws tend to favor the major parties, and the rules governing campaign financing also favor the major parties. There are also institutional barriers that prevent third parties from enjoying electoral success, such as the single-member district and the winner-take-all feature of the electoral college system for electing the president. Finally, because third parties normally do not win elections, Americans tend not to vote for them. **12** Throughout American history, third parties have competed for influence in the nation's two-party system. There are many different kinds of third parties. An issue-oriented party is formed to promote a particular cause or timely issue. An ideological party supports a particular political doctrine or a set of beliefs. A splinter party develops out of a split within a major party. This split may be part of an attempt to elect a specific person. **13** Third parties have brought many political issues to the public's attention. They can also influence election outcomes. Third parties provide a voice for voters who are frustrated with and alienated from the Republican and Democratic parties.

Find more practice tests and study tools for this chapter on CourseMate.

Quiz Answers: 1. True; 2. c; 3. True; 4. b; 5. c

CHAPTER IN REVIEW 8 Public Opinion and Voting

KEY TERMS

agents of political socialization People and institutions that influence the political views of others. *164*

biased sample A poll sample that does not accurately represent the population. *168*

gender gap The difference between the percentage of votes cast for a particular candidate by women and the percentage of votes cast for the same candidate by men. *182*

grandfather clause A clause in a state law that had the effect of restricting the franchise (voting rights) to those whose ancestors had voted before the 1860s; one of the techniques used in the South to prevent African Americans from exercising their right to vote. *175*

literacy test A test given to voters to ensure that they could read and write and thus evaluate political information; a technique used in many southern states to restrict African American participation in elections. *165*

media Newspapers, magazines, television, radio, the Internet, and any other printed or electronic means of communication. *168*

peer group Associates, often close in age to one another; may include friends, classmates, co-workers, club members, or religious group members. Peer group influence is a significant factor in the political socialization process. *168*

political socialization The learning process through which most people acquire their political attitudes, opinions, beliefs, and knowledge. *164*

poll tax A fee of several dollars that had to be paid before a person could vote; a device used in some southern states to prevent African Americans from voting. *175*

public opinion The views of the citizenry about politics, public issues, and public policies; a complex collection of opinions held by many people on issues in the public arena. *164*

public opinion poll A numerical survey of the public's opinion on a particular topic at a particular moment. *168*

push poll A campaign tactic used to feed false or misleading information to potential voters, under the guise of taking an opinion poll, with the intent to "push" voters away from one candidate and toward another. *173*

random sample In the context of opinion polling, a sample in which each person within the entire population being polled has an equal chance of being chosen. *169*

sample In the context of opinion polling, a group of people selected to represent the population being studied. *168*

QUIZ

1. Political socialization usually begins ____.

a. when an individual is settled in an occupation
b. when adolescents have friends who influence their attitudes and beliefs
c. in high school
d. during early childhood
e. when a person is eligible to vote

2. True or False: A straw poll is a nonscientific poll; there is no way to ensure that the opinions expressed are representative of the larger population.

3. For many decades, African Americans were effectively denied the ability to exercise their voting rights by ____.

a. methods such as literacy tests and the grandfather clause
b. exit polls and push polls
c. registration and residency requirements
d. methods such as black primaries and the minimum voting age
e. the "Motor Voter Law"

4. True or False: Among the factors affecting voter turnout, education appears to be the most important.

5. Which of the following statements is accurate?

a. For established voters, party identification is one of the most important and lasting predictors of how a person will vote.
b. Voters' rarely base their decisions more on the perceived character of the candidates rather than on their qualifications or policy positions.
c. Historically, social issues have had the strongest influence on voters' choices.
d. *Gender gap* is a term used to describe the differences in the campaign styles of male and female candidates.
e. Socioeconomic factors do not influence how people vote.

© GEORGE FREY/LANDOV

SUMMARY & OBJECTIVES

LO1 Explain what public opinion is and how it is measured. ***1*** **Public opinion** is the sum total of a complex collection of opinions held by many people on issues in the public arena. Public officials learn about public opinion through election results, personal contacts, interest groups, and media reports. The only relatively precise way to measure public opinion is through the use of public opinion polls.

LO2 Describe the political socialization process. ***2*** Most people acquire their political attitudes, opinions, beliefs, and knowledge through a complex learning process called **political socialization,** which begins in childhood and continues throughout life. Most political socialization is informal. The strong early influence of the family later gives way to the multiple influences of school, peers, television, co-workers, and other groups. People and institutions that influence the political views of others are called **agents of political socialization.** ***3*** The family's influence is strongest when children clearly perceive their parents' attitudes. Education also strongly influences an individual's political attitudes. From their earliest days in school, children learn about the American political system. They also learn citizenship skills through school rules and regulations. Generally, those with more education have more knowledge about politics and policy than those with less education. The **media** also have an impact on political socialization. Television continues to be a leading source of political and public affairs information for most people. Opinion leaders, major life events, **peer groups,** economic status, and occupation may also influence a person's political views.

LO3 Summarize the history of polling in the United States, and explain how polls are conducted and how they are used in the political process. ***4*** A **public opinion poll** is a numerical survey of the public's opinion on a particular topic at a particular moment, as measured through the use of **samples.** Early polling efforts often relied on **straw polls.** The opinions expressed in straw polls, however, usually represent an atypical subgroup of the population, or a **biased sample.** Over time, more scientific polling techniques were developed. To achieve the most accurate results possible, pollsters use **random samples,** in which each person within the entire population being polled has an equal chance of being chosen. If the sample is properly selected, the opinions of those in the sample will be representative of the opinions held by the population as a whole. Nevertheless, how a question is phrased can significantly affect how people answer it. Polling questions also sometimes reduce complex issues to questions that simply call for "yes" or "no" answers. Any opinion poll contains a **sampling error.** Today, polling organizations frequently conduct polls through telephone interviews, while some pollsters use prerecorded messages that solicit responses. Others specialize in Internet surveys. ***5*** Polling is used extensively by political candidates and policymakers to learn which issues are of current concern to Americans. Many journalists base their political coverage during campaigns almost exclusively on poll findings, though the media sometimes misuse polls. News organizations also use exit polls to give an early indication of the outcome of elections, but there have been problems with the reliability of exit polls in some recent elections. One tactic in political campaigns is to use **push polls,** which ask "fake" polling questions that are actually designed to "push" voters toward one candidate or another.

LO4 Indicate some of the factors that affect voter turnout, and discuss what has been done to improve voter turnout and voting procedures. ***6*** Some historical restrictions on voting, including religion, property ownership, and tax-payment requirements, disappeared early on in the history of the republic. Restrictions based on race and gender continued, however. The Fifteenth Amendment to the Constitution (1870) guaranteed suffrage to African American males. Yet, for many decades, African Americans were effectively denied the ability to exercise their voting rights. Today, devices used to restrict voting rights, such as the **poll tax, literacy tests,** the **grandfather clause,** and **white primaries,** are explicitly prohibited by constitutional amendments, by the Voting Rights Act of 1965, or by court decisions. The Nineteenth Amendment (1920) gave women the right to vote, and the Twenty-sixth Amendment (1971) reduced the minimum voting age to eighteen. ***7*** Some restrictions on voting rights, such as registration, residency, and citizenship requirements, still exist. Most states also do not permit prison inmates or felons to vote. Attempts to improve voter turnout and voting procedures include simplifying the voter-registration process, conducting voting by mail, updating voting equipment, and allowing early voting. ***8*** Just because an individual is eligible to vote does not necessarily mean that the person will actually go to the polls on Election Day. Voter turnout is affected by several factors, including educational attainment, income level, age, and minority status.

LO5 Discuss the different factors that affect voter choices. ***9*** Several factors influence voters' choices. For established voters, party identification is one of the most important and lasting predictors of how a person will vote. Voters' choices often depend on the perceived character of the candidates rather than on their qualifications or policy positions. When people vote for candidates who share their positions on particular issues, they are engaging in policy voting. Historically, economic issues have had the strongest influence on voters' choices. ***10*** Socioeconomic factors also influence how people vote. These factors include educational attainment, occupation and income level, age, gender, religion and ethnic background, and geographic region. A person's political ideology is another indicator of voting behavior.

CourseMate

Find more practice tests and study tools for this chapter on CourseMate.

sampling error In the context of opinion polling, the difference between what the sample results show and what the true results would have been had everybody in the relevant population been interviewed. ***170***

Solid South A term used to describe the tendency of the southern states to vote Democratic after the Civil War. ***183***

straw poll A nonscientific poll; a poll in which there is no way to ensure that the opinions expressed are representative of the larger population. ***168***

vital center The center of the political spectrum; those who hold moderate political views. The center is vital because without it, it may be difficult, if not impossible, to reach the compromises that are necessary to a political system's continuity. ***184***

voting-age population The number of people residing in the United States who are at least eighteen years old. ***178***

vote-eligible population The number of people who are actually eligible to vote in an American election. ***179***

white primary A primary election in which African Americans were prohibited from voting. The practice was banned by the Supreme Court in 1944. ***175***

Quiz Answers: 1. d; 2. True; 3. a; 4. True; 5. a

CHAPTER IN REVIEW 9 Campaigns and Elections

KEY TERMS

Australian ballot A secret ballot that is prepared, distributed, and counted by government officials at public expense; used by all states in the United States since 1888. ***189***

campaign strategy The comprehensive plan for winning an election developed by a candidate and his or her advisers. The strategy includes the candidate's position on issues, slogan, advertising plan, press events, personal appearances, and other aspects of the campaign. ***199***

caucus A meeting held to choose political candidates or delegates. ***193***

closed primary A primary in which only party members can vote to choose that party's candidates. ***196***

Credentials Committee A committee of each national political party that evaluates the claims of national party convention delegates to be the legitimate representatives of their states. ***198***

delegate An official meeting of a political party to choose its candidates. Nominating conventions at the state and local levels also select delegates to represent the citizens of their geographic areas at a higher-level party convention. ***193***

direct primary An election held within each of the two major parties—Democratic and Republican— to choose the party's candidates for the general election. Voters choose the candidate directly, rather than through delegates. ***195***

elector A member of the electoral college. ***191***

electoral college The group of electors who are selected by the voters in each state to elect officially the president and vice president. The number of electors in each state is equal to the number of that state's representatives in both chambers of Congress. ***191***

general election A regularly scheduled election to choose the U.S. president, vice president, and senators and representatives in Congress. General elections are held in even-numbered years on the Tuesday after the first Monday in November. ***189***

independent expenditure An expenditure for activities that are independent from (not coordinated with) those of a political candidate or a political party. ***203***

loophole A legitimate way of evading a certain legal requirement. ***203***

nominating convention An official meeting of a political party to choose its candidates. Nominating conventions at the state and local levels also select delegates to represent the citizens of their geographic areas at a higher-level party convention. ***193***

QUIZ

1. **A candidate must win at least ____ electoral votes, cast by the electors, to become president through the electoral college system.**
   a. 100
   b. 270
   c. 435
   d. 535
   e. 538
2. **True or False: The electoral college system is primarily a winner-take-all system, in which the candidate who receives a majority of popular votes becomes president.**
3. **True or False: Primary elections were designed to take nominations out of the hands of the party bosses, and indeed, the most important result of the primary system has been to dramatically reduce the power of elected and party officials over the nominating process.**
4. **A(n) ____ is a person selected to represent the people of one geographic area at a political party convention.**
   a. lobbyist
   b. candidate
   c. elector
   d. delegate
   e. poll watcher
5. **True or False: In the context of political campaigns, a *battleground state* is a state where voters are not clearly leaning toward either major candidate leading up to the elections.**

© AP PHOTO/MORRY GASH

SUMMARY & OBJECTIVES

LO1 Explain how elections are held and how the electoral college functions in presidential elections. ***1*** **General elections** are regularly scheduled elections held in even-numbered years in November. During general elections, the voters decide who will be the U.S. president, vice president, and senators and representatives in Congress. General elections are also held to choose state and local government officials. Since 1888, all states have used the **Australian ballot**—a secret ballot that is prepared, distributed, and counted by government officials. ***2*** An election board supervises the polling place and the voting process in each precinct. **Poll watchers** from each of the two major parties typically monitor the polling place as well. ***3*** In presidential elections, citizens do not vote directly for the president and vice president; instead, they vote for **electors** who will cast their ballots in the **electoral college.** Each state has as many electoral votes as it has U.S. senators and representatives; there are also three electors from the District of Columbia. ***4*** The electoral college is a **winner-take-all system** because, in nearly all states, the candidate who receives the most popular votes in the state wins all of that state's electoral votes. To be elected through this system, a candidate must win at least 270 electoral votes, a majority of the 538 electoral votes available.

LO2 Discuss how candidates are nominated. ***5*** The methods used by political parties to nominate candidates have changed over time, and have included **caucuses** and **nominating conventions.** Today, candidates who win **primary elections** go on to compete against the candidates from other parties in the general election. In a **direct primary,** which can be either **closed** or **open,** voters cast their ballots directly for candidates. ***6*** Most of the states hold presidential primaries, beginning early in the election year. These indirect primaries are used to choose **delegates** to the national nominating conventions. In some states, delegates are chosen through a caucus/

convention system instead of through primaries. In late summer, each political party holds a national convention. Convention delegates adopt the official party platform and nominate the party's presidential and vice-presidential candidates.

LO3 **Indicate what is involved in launching a political campaign today, and describe the structure and functions of a campaign organization.** ***7*** To run a successful campaign, the candidate's campaign staff must be able to raise funds, get media coverage, produce and pay for political ads, schedule the candidate's time effectively with constituent groups and potential supporters, convey the candidate's position on the issues, conduct research on the opposing candidate, and persuade the voters to go to the polls. Because political party labels are no longer as important as they once were, campaigns have become more candidate-centered. Professional **political consultants** now manage nearly all aspects of a presidential candidate's campaign. Most candidates have a campaign manager who coordinates and plans the **campaign strategy.**

LO4 **Describe how the Internet has transformed political campaigns.** ***8*** Today, the ability to make effective use of the Internet is essential to a candidate. Barack Obama took Internet fund-raising to a new level during his 2008 presidential bid. The Obama campaign attempted to recruit as many supporters as possible to act as fund-raisers who would solicit contributions from their friends and neighbors, sparing Obama much of the personal fund-raising effort that consumes the time of most national politicians. ***9*** Microtargeting, a technique that involves collecting as much information as possible about voters in a database and then filtering out various groups for special attention, was pioneered by the George W. Bush campaign in 2004. In 2008, microtargeting was supplemented with behavioral targeting. This technique uses information about people's online behavior to tailor the advertisements that they see. ***10*** In his presidential campaign, Obama also took Web-based organizing to a new level. He used existing sites such as Facebook, his videos were on YouTube, and his own Web site racked up more than a million members. The Obama campaign was also able to create local support groups in towns and counties across the country.

LO5 **Summarize the laws that regulate campaign financing and the role of money in modern political campaigns.** ***11*** Campaign-financing laws enacted in the 1970s provide public funding for presidential primaries and general elections, limit presidential campaign spending of candidates receiving federal funds, require candidates to file periodic reports with the Federal Election Commission, and limit individual and group contributions. ***12*** Two major **loopholes** in the campaign-financing laws involved **soft money** and **independent expenditures.** The Bipartisan Campaign Reform Act (BCRA) of 2002 addressed these concerns to a certain extent. There were constitutional challenges to the new law, and issue advocacy groups soon attempted to exploit loopholes in BCRA by establishing 527 committees and 501(c)4 organizations. In 2010, the Supreme Court took a major step toward freeing up corporate funding of political advertisements. ***13*** Many groups routinely donate money to candidates from both parties so that, regardless of who wins, the groups will have access to the officeholder. Access is important for those who want to influence policymaking.

LO6 **Describe what took place during recent presidential elections and what these events tell us about the American electoral system.** ***14*** The 2000 presidential elections were the first since 1888 in which the electoral college system gave Americans a president who had not won the popular vote. Democrat Al Gore won the popular vote by 540,000 votes, but after the disputed vote in Florida was resolved, George W. Bush had a majority of electoral votes. In 2004, Bush edged out the Democratic challenger, John Kerry, by a mere thirty-five electoral votes and a 2.5 percentage vote margin of popular votes. In 2008, however, Democrat Barack Obama's popular-vote margin over John McCain was about 7.2 percentage points. Obama won approximately 52.9 percent of the popular vote and 365 electoral votes.

CourseMate

Find more practice tests and study tools for this chapter on CourseMate.

office-block ballot A ballot (also called the Massachusetts ballot) that lists together all of the candidates for each office. ***189***

open primary A primary in which voters can vote for a party's candidates regardless of whether they belong to the party. ***196***

party-column ballot A ballot (also called the Indiana ballot) that lists all of a party's candidates under the party label. Voters can vote for all of a party's candidates for local, state, and national offices by making a single "X" or pulling a single lever. ***189***

political consultant A professional political adviser who, for a fee, works on an area of a candidate's campaign. Political consultants include campaign managers, pollsters, media advisers, and "get out the vote" organizers. ***199***

poll watcher A representative from one of the political parties who is allowed to monitor a polling place to make sure that the election is run fairly and to avoid fraud. ***190***

primary election An election in which voters choose the candidates of their party, who will then run in the general election. ***194***

soft money Campaign contributions not regulated by federal law, such as some contributions that are made to political parties instead of to particular candidates. ***203***

special election An election that is held at the state or local level when the voters must decide an issue before the next general election or when vacancies occur by reason of death or resignation. ***189***

winner-take-all system A system in which the candidate who receives the most votes wins. In contrast, proportional systems allocate votes to multiple winners. ***191***

Quiz Answers: 1. b; 2. False; 3. True; 4. d; 5. True

CHAPTER IN REVIEW 10 Politics and the Media

KEY TERMS

citizen journalism The collection, analysis, and dissemination of information online by independent journalists, scholars, politicians, and the general citizenry. *224*

electronic media Communication channels that involve electronic transmissions, such as radio, television, and the Internet. *211*

issue ad A political advertisement that focuses on a particular issue. Issue ads can be used to support or attack a candidate. *217*

managed news coverage News coverage that is manipulated (managed) by a campaign manager or political consultant to gain media exposure for a political candidate. *219*

mass media Communication channels, such as newspapers and radio and television broadcasts, through which people can communicate to mass audiences. *211*

negative political advertising Political advertising undertaken for the purpose of discrediting an opposing candidate in the eyes of the voters. Attack ads are one form of negative political advertising. *217*

personal attack ad A negative political advertisement that attacks the character of an opposing candidate. *217*

podcasting The distribution of audio or video files to a personal computer or a mobile device, such as an iPod. *225*

political advertising Advertising undertaken by or on behalf of a political candidate to familiarize voters with the candidate and his or her views on campaign issues; also advertising for or against policy issues. *216*

print media Communication channels that consist of printed materials, such as newspapers and magazines. *211*

sound bite A brief televised comment, lasting for only a few seconds, that captures a thought or a perspective and has an immediate impact on the viewers. *215*

spin A reporter's slant on, or interpretation of, a particular event or action. *219*

spin doctor A political candidate's press adviser, who tries to convince reporters to give a story or event concerning the candidate a particular "spin" (interpretation, or slant). *219*

QUIZ

1. **True or False: The war in Iraq has been called the first "television war."**

2. **_____ during the 1952 presidential campaign.**
   a. The infamous "daisy girl" issue ad was aired
   b. Televised debates between the candidates first took place
   c. Political advertising first appeared on television
   d. Personal attack ads were first used
   e. The first political blog appeared

3. **Candidates' campaign managers and political consultants have shown increasing sophistication in creating newsworthy events for journalists to cover, an effort commonly referred to as _____.**
   a. citizen journalism
   b. twittering
   c. podcasting
   d. managed news coverage
   e. blogging

4. **True or False: Modern talk radio took off in the 1930s, after Franklin D. Roosevelt held his first "fireside chats" on radio, and politicians realized the power of that medium.**

5. **_____are online activists who support the candidate but are not controlled by the candidate's organization.**
   a. Netroots groups
   b. The mass media
   c. The Wild West of the media
   d. Podcasters
   e. Spin doctors

© KEVIN LAMARQUE/REUTERS /LANDOV

SUMMARY & OBJECTIVES

LO1 Explain the role of a free press in a democracy. ***1*** The **mass media** include the **print media** (newspapers and magazines) and the **electronic media** (radio, television, and the Internet). The media play a vital role in our political lives, and a free press is essential to the democratic process. If people are to cast informed votes, they must have access to a forum in which they can discuss public affairs fully and assess the conduct and competency of their officials. The concept of freedom of the press has been applied to print media since the adoption of the Bill of Rights. Such freedoms were not, however, immediately extended to other types of media as they came into existence. ***2*** What the media say and do has an impact on what Americans think about political issues, but the media also reflect what Americans think about politics. By helping to determine what people talk and think about, the media help set the political agenda. Of all the media, television has the greatest impact. Television is the primary news source for most Americans, but the limitations of the TV medium significantly affect the scope and depth of news coverage.

LO2 Summarize how television influences the conduct of political campaigns. ***3*** Candidates for political office spend a great deal of time and money obtaining a TV presence through political ads, debates, and general news coverage. Televised **political advertising** consumes at least half of the total budget for a major political campaign. Candidates often use **negative political advertising,** including **personal attack ads** (which attack the character of an opposing candidate) and **issue ads** (which focus on flaws in an opponent's positions on issues). Televised debates are now a routine feature of presidential campaigns. Television debates provide an opportunity for voters to find out how candidates differ on issues and allow candidates to capitalize on the power of television to improve their images or point out the failings of their opponents. ***4*** Candidates' campaign managers and political consultants have become increasingly sophisticated in creating newsworthy events for the media to cover, an effort commonly referred to as **managed news coverage.** Each candidate's press advisers also try to convince reporters to give a story or event a **spin** that is favorable to the candidate.

LO3 Explain why talk radio has been described as the Wild West of the media.
5 Modern talk radio took off in the United States during the 1990s. The growth of talk radio was made possible by the Federal Communications Commission's repeal of the fairness doctrine in 1987. Talk-show hosts do not attempt to hide their political biases; if anything, they exaggerate them for effect. No journalistic conventions are observed. ***6*** Those who think that talk radio is good for the country argue that talk shows, taken together, provide a great populist forum. Others are uneasy because they fear that talk shows empower fringe groups, perhaps magnifying their rage. Prominent hosts have had great fun organizing potentially disruptive activities. Those who claim talk-show hosts go too far ultimately have to deal with the constitutional issue of free speech.

LO4 Describe types of media bias and explain how such bias affects the political process. ***7*** The media are frequently accused of having a liberal bias. A number of media scholars suggest that even if many reporters hold liberal views, these views are not reflected in their reporting. Media bias against losers, however, may be playing a role in shaping presidential campaigns and elections. The media use the winner-loser framework to describe events throughout the campaigns. ***8*** The expansion of the media universe to include cable channels and the Internet has increased the competition among news sources. News directors select programming they believe will attract the largest audiences and garner the highest advertising revenues. Competition for viewers and readers has become even more challenging in the wake of a declining news audience. Many journalists believe that economic pressure is making significant inroads on independent editorial decision making. Today's news culture is in the midst of change as news organizations are redefining their purpose and increasingly looking for special niches in which to build their audiences.

LO5 Indicate the extent to which the Internet is reshaping news and political campaigns. ***9*** The Internet is now a major source of information for many people. All major newspapers are online, as are transcripts of major television news programs. In addition, there has been a virtual explosion of blogs in recent years. Blogs are offered by independent journalists, various scholars, political activists, and the citizenry at large. Many blogs are political in nature, both reporting political developments and discussing politics. Taken as a whole, the collection, analysis, and dissemination of information online by the citizenry is referred to as **citizen journalism.** Another nontraditional form of news distribution is **podcasting.** Still another relatively new Internet technology is Twitter, a method for sending short messages to large numbers of people. ***10*** The use of the Internet is an inexpensive way for candidates to contact, recruit, and mobilize supporters, as well as disseminate information about their positions on issues. Having an Internet strategy has become an integral part of political campaigning. Candidates typically hire Web managers to create a well-designed Web site to attract viewers, manage their email, and track their credit-card contributions. The Web manager also hires bloggers to promote the candidate's views, arranges for podcasting of campaign information, and hires staff to monitor the Web for news about the candidates and to track online publications of netroots groups— online activists who support the candidate but are not controlled by the candidate's organization. ***11*** Citizen videos have also changed the traditional campaign. A candidate can never know when a comment that he or she makes may be caught on camera by someone with a cell phone or digital camera and published on the Internet for all to see. This 24/7 exposure also makes it difficult for the candidates to control their campaigns.

Find more practice tests and study tools for this chapter on CourseMate.

Quiz Answers: 1. False; 2. c; 3. d; 4. false; 5. a

CHAPTER IN REVIEW 11 Congress

KEY TERMS

apportionment The distribution of House seats among the states on the basis of their respective populations. *232*

appropriation A part of the congressional budgeting process that involves determining how many dollars will be spent in a given year on a particular set of government activities. *249*

authorization A part of the congressional budgeting process that involves the creation of the legal basis for government programs. *249*

cloture A method of ending debate in the Senate and bringing the matter under consideration to a vote by the entire chamber. *242*

conference committee A temporary committee that is formed when the two chambers of Congress pass differing versions of the same bill. The conference committee, which consists of members from both the House and the Senate, works out a compromise form of the bill. *246*

conference report A report submitted by a congressional conference committee after it has drafted a single version of a bill. *246*

congressional district The geographic area that is served by one member in the House of Representatives. *233*

continuing resolution A temporary resolution passed by Congress when an appropriations bill has not been passed by the beginning of the new fiscal year. *251*

entitlement program A government program (such as Social Security) that allows, or entitles, a certain class of people (such as elderly persons) to receive special benefits. Entitlement programs operate under open-ended budget authorizations that, in effect, place no limits on how much can be spent. *249*

filibustering The Senate tradition of unlimited debate undertaken for the purpose of preventing action on a bill. *241*

first budget resolution A budget resolution, which is supposed to be passed in May, that sets overall revenue goals and spending targets for the next fiscal year, which begins on October 1. *251*

fiscal year A twelve-month period that is established for bookkeeping or accounting purposes. The government's fiscal year runs from October 1 through September 30. *250*

gerrymandering The drawing of a legislative district's boundaries in such a way as to maximize the influence of a certain group or political party. *234*

instructed delegate A representative who mirrors the views of the majority of his or her constituents. *235*

QUIZ

1. **True or False: The distribution of seats in the House of Representatives among the states on the basis of their respective populations is called gerrymandering.**

2. **Which of the following best describes a whip in Congress?**
   a. The party leader elected by the majority party in the House or in the Senate
   b. The presiding officer in the House of Representatives
   c. The member of the majority party with the longest continuous term of service in the Senate
   d. A member who assists the majority or minority leader in the House or in the Senate in managing the party's legislative preferences
   e. The presiding officer in the Senate

3. **A ____ committee is formed for the purpose of achieving a compromise between the House and the Senate on the exact wording of a legislative act when the two chambers have passed differing versions of the same bill.**
   a. conference
   b. standing
   c. rules
   d. select
   e. joint

4. **To end a filibuster, ____ senators must vote for cloture.**
   a. sixteen
   b. fifty-one (a majority of the entire membership)
   c. sixty (three-fifths of the entire membership)
   d. one hundred
   e. twenty-six

5. **True or False: As soon as a bill is introduced in either the House or the Senate, it is sent to the floor of the chamber for debate.**

MARK WILSON/GETTY IMAGES

SUMMARY & OBJECTIVES

LO1 Explain how seats in the House of Representatives are apportioned among the states. ***1*** The Constitution provides for the **apportionment** of House seats among the states on the basis of their respective populations, though each state is guaranteed at least one seat. Every ten years, the 435 House seats are reapportioned based on the outcome of the census. ***2*** Each representative to the House is elected by voters in a **congressional district.** Districts must contain, as nearly as possible, equal numbers of people. This principle has come to be known as the **"one person, one vote" rule. Gerrymandering** occurs when a district's boundaries are drawn to maximize the influence of a certain group or political party.

LO2 Describe the power of incumbency. ***3*** If a member of Congress wants to run for reelection in the next congressional elections (representatives are elected every second year and senators are elected every six years), that person's chances are greatly enhanced by the power that incumbency brings to a reelection campaign. ***4*** Incumbent legislators enjoy several advantages over their opponents. They benefit from name recognition, access to the media, congressional franking privileges, and lawmaking power. They also have professional staffs both in Washington, D.C., and in their home districts. A key advantage is their fund-raising ability. Most incumbents in Congress are reelected.

LO3 Identify the key leadership positions in Congress, describe the committee system, and indicate some important differences between the House of

Representatives and the Senate. **5** The Constitution provides for the presiding officers of both the House and the Senate, and each chamber has added other leadership positions as it has seen fit. The majority party in each chamber chooses the major officers of that chamber, controls debate on the floor, selects committee chairpersons, and has a majority on all committees. **6** Chief among the leaders in the House of Representatives is the **Speaker of the House,** who has a great deal of power. Other leaders include the **majority and minority leaders,** and the **whips.** **7** The vice president of the United States is the president of the Senate, and senators elect another presiding officer, the president pro tempore (pro tem), who is ordinarily the member of the majority party with the longest continuous service in the Senate. The real power in the Senate is held by the majority leader, the minority leader, and their respective whips. **8** Most of the actual work of legislating is performed by the committees and **subcommittees** in the House and in the Senate. The permanent and most powerful committees are the **standing committees.** Before any bill can be considered by the entire House or Senate, it must be approved by a majority vote in a standing committee. **9** Because of its large size, the House requires more rules and formality than the Senate. The House **Rules Committee** proposes time limits on debate for most bills. The Senate normally permits extended debate. The use of unlimited debate to obstruct legislation is called **filibustering,** which may be ended by invoking **cloture.** The House originates bills for raising revenues and may impeach federal officials. The Senate has the power of advice and consent on presidential appointments and treaties and may convict federal officials of impeachable offenses. Senators typically enjoy more prestige and access to the media than do members of the House, and they have more opportunities to engage in national leadership.

LO4 Summarize the specific steps in the lawmaking process. **10** After a bill is introduced by a member of Congress, it is sent to a standing committee. A committee chairperson will typically send the bill on to a subcommittee, where public hearings might be held. After a **markup session,** in which changes may be made to the bill, the bill goes to the full committee for further action. The bill may be reported to the full chamber, or, if it lacks sufficient support, it may not make it out of the committee. **11** After a bill is reported, it is scheduled for floor debate. In the House, the Rules Committee plays a major role in the scheduling process. The Senate brings a bill to the floor by "unanimous consent." After floor debate, which rarely changes anybody's mind, votes are taken on the legislation. When the House and Senate pass differing versions of the same bill, a **conference committee** with members from both chambers is formed to produce a compromise bill. The **conference report** is sent to each chamber for a vote. If the bill is approved by both chambers, it is sent to the president. The president has ten days to sign the bill or veto it (with a two-thirds majority vote in both chambers, Congress can override the president's veto). If the president does nothing, the bill becomes law unless Congress has adjourned before the ten-day period expires. In that case, the bill dies in what is called a **pocket veto.**

LO5 Identify Congress's oversight functions and explain how Congress fulfills them. **12** One of the most important functions of Congress is its oversight of the executive branch and its many departments and agencies. Congress can rein in the power of the executive bureaucracy by choosing not to provide the money necessary for the bureaucracy to function or by refusing to fund government programs. **13** Congress also has the authority to investigate the actions of the executive branch, the need for certain legislation, and even the actions of its own members. It has the power to impeach and remove from office federal officials. **14** The Senate confirms the president's nominees for the Supreme Court, other federal judgeships, and members of the cabinet.

LO6 Indicate what is involved in the congressional budgeting process. **15** The congressional budgeting process involves **authorization** (creating the legal basis for government programs) and **appropriation** (determining how many dollars will be spent in a given year on a particular set of government activities). **16** The budgeting process begins when the president submits a proposed federal budget for the next **fiscal year.** In the **first budget resolution,** Congress sets overall revenue goals and spending targets. The **second budget resolution** sets "binding" limits on taxes and spending. Whenever Congress is unable to pass a complete budget by the start of the fiscal year, it passes **continuing resolutions,** which enable the executive agencies to keep doing whatever they were doing the previous year with the same amount of funding.

Find more practice tests and study tools for this chapter on CourseMate.

majority leader The party leader elected by the majority party in the House or in the Senate. *239*

malapportionment A condition in which the voting power of citizens in one district is greater than the voting power of citizens in another district. *233*

markup session A meeting held by a congressional committee or subcommittee to approve, amend, or redraft a bill. *245*

minority leader The party leader elected by the minority party in the House or in the Senate. *239*

minority-majority district A district in which minority groups make up a majority of the population. *234*

"one person, one vote" rule A rule, or principle, requiring that congressional districts have equal populations so that one person's vote counts as much as another's vote. *234*

pocket veto A special type of veto power used by the chief executive after the legislature has adjourned. Bills that are not signed die after a specified period of time. *246*

Rules Committee A standing committee in the House of Representatives that provides special rules governing how particular bills will be considered and debated by the House. The Rules Committee normally proposes time limits on debate for any bill. *241*

second budget resolution A budget resolution, which is supposed to be passed in September, that sets "binding" limits on taxes and spending for the next fiscal year. *251*

Speaker of the House The presiding officer in the House of Representatives. The Speaker has traditionally been a longtime member of the majority party and is often the most powerful and influential member of the House. *238*

standing committee A permanent committee in Congress that deals with legislation concerning a particular area, such as agriculture or foreign relations. *240*

subcommittee A division of a larger committee that deals with a particular part of the committee's policy area. Most standing committees have several subcommittees. *241*

trustee A representative who serves the broad interests of the entire society, and not just the narrow interests of his or her constituents. *235*

whip A member of Congress who assists the majority or minority leader in the House or in the Senate in managing the party's legislative preferences. *239*

Quiz Answers: 1. False; 2. d; 3. a; 4. c; 5. False

CHAPTER IN REVIEW 12 *The Presidency*

KEY TERMS

cabinet An advisory group selected by the president to assist with decision making. Traditionally, the cabinet has consisted of the heads of the executive departments and other officers whom the president may choose to appoint. *273*

chief diplomat The role of the president in recognizing and interacting with foreign governments. *261*

chief executive The head of the executive branch of government. In the United States, the president. *258*

chief of staff The person who directs the operations of the White House Office and who advises the president on important matters. *274*

commander in chief The supreme commander of a nation's military force. *259*

diplomat A person who represents one country in dealing with representatives of another country. *261*

executive agreement A binding international agreement, or pact, that is made between the president and another head of state and that does not require Senate approval. *269*

Executive Office of the President (EOP) A group of staff agencies that assist the president in carrying out major duties. Franklin D. Roosevelt established the EOP in 1939 to cope with the increased responsibilities brought on by the Great Depression. *274*

executive order A presidential order to carry out a policy or policies described in a law passed by Congress. *267*

executive privilege An inherent executive power claimed by presidents to withhold information from, or to refuse to appear before, Congress or the courts. The president can also accord the privilege to other executive officials. *272*

head of state The person who serves as the ceremonial head of a country's government and represents that country to the rest of the world. *259*

kitchen cabinet The name given to a president's unofficial advisers. The term was coined during Andrew Jackson's presidency. *274*

National Security Council (NSC) A council that advises the president on domestic and foreign matters concerning the safety and defense of the nation; established in 1947. *275*

Office of Management and Budget (OMB) An agency in the Executive Office of the President that assists the president in preparing and supervising the administration of the federal budget. *275*

patronage The practice of giving government jobs to individuals belonging to the winning political party. *261*

QUIZ

1. In his role as _____, the president leads the nation's armed forces.
a. chief diplomat
b. commander in chief
c. chief executive
d. chief legislator
e. head of state

2. In his role as _____, the president engages in ceremonial activities as a personal symbol of the nation.
a. chief diplomat
b. commander in chief
c. chief executive
d. chief legislator
e. head of state

3. True or False: An executive agreement is a pact between the president and other heads of state.

4. True or False: Constitutionally, Congress and the president share the power to declare war.

5. True or False: Congress has the advantage over the president in dealing with a national crisis, in setting foreign policy, and in influencing public opinion.

© MIKE THEILER/EPA /LANDOV

SUMMARY & OBJECTIVES

LO1 List the constitutional requirements for becoming president. ***1*** Article II of the Constitution sets forth relatively few requirements for becoming president. A person must be a natural-born citizen, at least thirty-five years of age, and a resident within the United States for at least fourteen years.

LO2 Explain the roles that a president performs while in office. ***2*** The president has the authority to exercise a variety of powers. Some of these are explicitly outlined in the Constitution, and some are simply required by the office. In the course of exercising these powers, the president performs a variety of roles. The president is the nation's **chief executive**—the head of the executive branch—and enforces laws and federal court decisions. The president leads the nation's armed forces as **commander in chief.** As **head of state,** the president engages in ceremonial activities as a personal symbol of the nation. As **chief diplomat,** the president directs U.S. foreign policy and is the nation's most important representative to foreign governments. The president has become the chief legislator, informing Congress about the condition of the country and recommending legislative measures. As political party leader, the president chooses the chairperson of his or her party's national committee and exerts political power within the party by using presidential appointment and removal powers.

LO3 Indicate the scope of presidential powers. ***3*** The Constitution gives the president specific powers, such as the power to negotiate **treaties,** to grant reprieves and pardons, and to **veto** bills passed by Congress. The president also has inherent powers—powers that are necessary to carry out the specific responsibilities of the president as set forth in the Constitution. ***4*** Several presidents have greatly expanded the powers of the president. Congress has come to expect the president to develop a legislative program. The president's political skills, the ability to persuade others, and the strategy of "going public" play a large role in determining the administration's success. Since the 1930s, the president has been expected to be actively involved in economic matters and social programs. ***5*** The president's executive authority has been enhanced by the use of **executive orders** and

signing statements, and the ability to make **executive agreements** has enhanced presidential power in foreign affairs. As commander in chief, the president can respond quickly to a military threat without waiting for congressional action, and since 1945, the president has been responsible for deciding if and when to use nuclear weapons.

LO4 Describe advantages enjoyed by Congress and by the president in their institutional relationship. ***6*** The relationship between the president and Congress is arguably one of the most important institutional relationships in American government. Congress traditionally has had the advantage in this relationship in the areas of legislative authorization, the regulation of foreign and interstate commerce, and some budgetary matters. The president has the advantage over Congress in dealing with a national crisis, in setting foreign policy, and in influencing public opinion. ***7*** The relationship between Congress and the president is affected by their different constituencies, their different election cycles, and the fact that the president is limited to two terms in office. The relationship between Congress and the president is also affected when government is divided, with at least one house of Congress controlled by a different party than the White House.

LO5 Discuss the organization of the executive branch and the role of cabinet members in presidential administrations. ***8*** The fifteen executive departments are an important component of the executive branch. The heads of the departments are members of the president's **cabinet.** The president may appoint other officials to the cabinet as well. Some presidents have relied on the advice of their cabinets, while other presidents have preferred to rely on the counsel of close friends and associates (sometimes called a **kitchen cabinet**). President Obama's response to the need to seek advice has been to centralize the advisory function within the White House Office by appointing a number of "czars." Each of these czars has responsibility for a certain policy area. ***9*** Since 1939, presidents have had top advisers and assistants in the **Executive Office of the President (EOP)** who help carry out major duties. The EOP is subject to frequent reorganizations at the discretion of the president. Some of the most important agencies in the EOP are the **White House Office** (which is headed by the **chief of staff**), the **Office of Management and Budget** (which assists the president in preparing the proposed annual budget), and the **National Security Council** (which is the president's link to his or her key foreign and military advisers). In recent years, the responsibilities of the vice president have grown immensely, and the vice president has become one of the most important of the president's advisers.

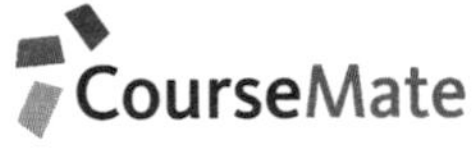

Find more practice tests and study tools for this chapter on CourseMate.

press secretary A member of the White House staff who holds news conferences for reporters and makes public statements for the president. ***274***

signing statement A written statement, appended to a bill at the time the president signs it into law, indicating how the president interprets that legislation. ***267***

treaty A formal agreement between the governments of two or more countries. ***262***

veto A Latin word meaning "I forbid"; the refusal by an official, such as the president of the United States or a state governor, to sign a bill into law. ***263***

Watergate scandal A scandal involving an illegal break-in at the Democratic National Committee offices in 1972 by members of President Nixon's reelection campaign staff. Before Congress could vote to impeach Nixon for his participation in covering up the break-in, Nixon resigned from the presidency. ***272***

White House Office The personal office of the president. White House Office personnel handle the president's political needs and manage the media. ***274***

Quiz Answers: 1. b; 2. e; 3. True; 4. False; 5. False

CHAPTER IN REVIEW 13 The Bureaucracy

KEY TERMS

adjudicate To render a judicial decision. In regard to administrative law, the process in which an administrative law judge hears and decides issues that arise when an agency charges a person or firm with violating a law or regulation enforced by the agency. ***293***

bureaucracy A large, complex, hierarchically structured administrative organization that carries out specific functions. ***281***

bureaucrat An individual who works in a bureaucracy. As generally used, the term refers to a government employee. ***281***

civil service Nonmilitary government employment. ***292***

enabling legislation A law enacted by a legislature to establish an administrative agency. Enabling legislation normally specifies the name, purpose, composition, and powers of the agency being created. ***292***

government corporation An agency of the government that is run as a business enterprise. Such agencies engage in primarily commercial activities, produce revenues, and require greater flexibility than that permitted in most government agencies. ***289***

independent executive agency A federal agency that is not located within a cabinet department. ***285***

independent regulatory agency A federal organization that is responsible for creating and implementing rules that regulate private activity and protect the public interest in a particular sector of the economy. ***288***

iron triangle A three-way alliance among legislators, bureaucrats, and interest groups to make or preserve policies that benefit their respective interests. ***294***

issue networks Groups of individuals or organizations—which consist of legislators and legislative staff members, interest group leaders, bureaucrats, the media, scholars, and other experts—that support particular policy positions on a given issue. ***295***

legislative rule An administrative agency rule that carries the same weight as a statute enacted by a legislature. ***292***

neutral competency The application of technical skills to jobs without regard to political issues. ***294***

partisan politics Political actions or decisions that benefit a particular party. ***285***

privatization The transfer of the task of providing services traditionally provided by government to the private sector. ***298***

QUIZ

1. The major service organizations of the federal government are the _____.
a. executive departments
b. independent executive agencies
c. independent regulatory agencies
d. government corporations
e. issue networks

2. The _____ is an independent regulatory agency.
a. Department of Labor
b. U.S. Postal Service
c. Federal Trade Commission
d. Central Intelligence Agency
e. U.S. Citizenship and Immigration Services

3. True or False: The Federal Bureau of Investigation (FBI) is an independent executive agency.

4. True or False: The U.S. Postal Service is a government corporation.

5. True or False: Federal bureaucrats holding top-level positions are part of the civil service and obtain their jobs through the Office of Personnel Management.

AP PHOTO/MANUEL BALCE CENETA

SUMMARY & OBJECTIVES

LO1 Describe the size and functions of the U.S. bureaucracy. ***1*** The **bureaucracy** is a large, complex administrative organization. Government **bureaucrats** carry out the policies of elected government officials. In the federal government, the head of the bureaucracy is the president of the United States, and the bureaucracy is part of the executive branch. The reason the federal bureaucracy exists is that Congress, over time, has delegated certain tasks to specialists. ***2*** The federal government that existed in 1789 had only three departments and about fifty employees. Today, the federal government has about 2.8 million employees. Together, the local, state, and federal levels of government employ about 16 percent of the civilian labor force.

LO2 Discuss the structure and basic components of the federal bureaucracy. ***3*** The executive branch of the federal government includes four major types of bureaucratic structures: executive departments, independent executive agencies, independent regulatory agencies, and government corporations. ***4*** The fifteen executive departments, which are directly accountable to the president, are the major service organizations of the federal government. Each department was created by Congress as the perceived need for it arose, and each manages a specific policy area. Each department head is appointed by the president and confirmed by the Senate. **Independent executive agencies** are federal bureaucratic organizations that have a single function. Sometimes agencies are kept independent because of the sensitive nature of their functions; at other times, Congress created independent agencies to protect them from **partisan politics. Independent regulatory agencies** are responsible for a specific type of public policy. Their function is to create and implement rules that regulate private activity and protect the public interest in a particular sector of the economy. **Government corporations** are businesses that are owned by the government. They provide a service that could be handled by the private sector, and they charge for their services. A number of intermediate forms of organization exist that fall between a government corporation and a private one.

LO3 Indicate when the federal civil service was established and explain how bureaucrats get their jobs. ***5*** Federal bureaucrats holding top-level positions are appointed by the president and confirmed by the Senate. The list of positions that are filled by appointments is published after each presidential election in a booklet that summarizes about eight thousand jobs. The rank-and- file bureaucrats—the rest of the federal bureaucracy—are part of the **civil service.** They obtain their jobs through the Office of Personnel Management (OPM), which was created by the Civil Service Reform Act of 1978. The OPM recruits, interviews, and tests potential government workers and makes recommendations to agencies as to which persons meet relevant standards. The 1978 act also created the Merit Systems Protection Board to oversee promotions and employees' rights. The idea that the civil service should be based on a merit system dates back more than a century, when the Civil Service Reform Act of 1883 established the principle of government employment on the basis of merit through open, competitive examinations.

LO4 Explain how regulatory agencies make rules and how issue networks affect policymaking in government. ***6*** Regulatory agencies are sometimes regarded as the fourth branch of government because of the powers they wield. They can make **legislative rules** that are as legally binding as laws passed by Congress. When they are engaging in **rulemaking,** agencies must follow certain procedural requirements, and they must make sure that their rules are not "arbitrary and capricious." ***7*** Bureaucrats in federal agencies are expected to exhibit **neutral competency,** which means that they are supposed to apply their technical skills to their jobs without regard to political issues. One way to understand the bureaucracy's role in policymaking is to examine **iron triangles**—alliances among legislators, bureaucrats, and interest groups to make or preserve policies that benefit their respective interests. In some policy domains, there are less structured relationships among experts who have strong opinions and interests regarding the direction of policy. These **issue networks** are able to exert a great deal of influence on legislators and bureaucratic agencies.

LO5 Identify some of the ways in which the government has attempted to curb waste and improve efficiency in the bureaucracy. ***8*** The government has made several attempts to reduce waste, inefficiency, and wrongdoing. Federal and state governments have passed laws requiring more openness in government. Other laws encourage government employees to report any waste and wrongdoing that they observe, and Congress has passed laws to protect **whistleblowers.** To improve efficiency, virtually every federal agency has had to describe its goals and methods for evaluating how well those goals are met. President Obama has created the position of a chief performance officer who works with other economic officials in an attempt to increase efficiency and eliminate waste in government. Another idea for reforming government bureaucracies is **privatization,** which means turning over certain types of government work to the private sector.

Find more practice tests and study tools for this chapter on CourseMate.

rulemaking The process undertaken by an administrative agency when formally proposing, evaluating, and adopting a new regulation. ***294***

whistleblower In the context of government employment, someone who "blows the whistle" (reports to authorities) on gross governmental inefficiency, illegal activities, or other wrongdoing. ***296***

Quiz Answers: 1. a; 2. c; 3. False; 4. True; 5. False

CHAPTER IN REVIEW 14 The Judiciary

KEY TERMS

administrative law The body of law created by administrative agencies (in the form of rules, regulations, orders, and decisions) in order to carry out their duties and responsibilities. ***307***

appellate court A court having appellate jurisdiction. An appellate court normally does not hear evidence or testimony but reviews the transcript of the trial court's proceedings, other records relating to the case, and attorneys' arguments as to why the trial court's decision should or should not stand. ***310***

case law The rules of law announced in court decisions. Case law includes the aggregate of reported cases that interpret judicial precedents, statutes, regulations, and constitutional provisions. ***307***

civil law The branch of law that spells out the duties that individuals in society owe to other persons or to their governments, excluding the duty not to commit crimes. ***307***

common law The body of law developed from judicial decisions in English and U.S. courts, not attributable to a legislature. ***304***

concurring opinion A statement written by a judge or justice who agrees (concurs) with the court's decision, but for reasons different from those in the majority opinion. ***312***

conference In regard to the Supreme Court, a private meeting of the justices in which they present their arguments concerning a case under consideration. ***312***

constitutional law Law based on the U.S. Constitution and the constitutions of the various states. ***306***

criminal law The branch of law that defines and governs actions that constitute crimes. Generally, criminal law has to do with wrongful actions committed against society for which society demands redress. ***307***

dissenting opinion A statement written by a judge or justice who disagrees with the majority opinion. ***312***

diversity of citizenship A basis for federal court jurisdiction over a lawsuit that arises when (1) the parties in the lawsuit live in different states or when one of the parties is a foreign government or a foreign citizen, and (2) the amount in controversy is more than $75,000. ***308***

federal question A question that pertains to the U.S. Constitution, acts of Congress, or treaties. A federal question provides a basis for federal court jurisdiction. ***308***

judicial review The power of the courts to decide on the constitutionality of legislative enactments and of actions taken by the executive branch. ***316***

QUIZ

1. ____ law is the body of law enacted by legislatures.
   a. Constitutional
   b. Statutory
   c. Administrative
   d. Case
   e. Common

2. True or False: Most of the U.S. Supreme Court's work is as an appellate court. It has original jurisdiction only in rare instances.

3. When the Supreme Court has reached a decision in a case, the chief justice, if in the majority, assigns the task of writing ____ to one of the justices.
   a. oral arguments
   b. the Court's opinion
   c. a dissenting opinion
   d. a concurring opinion
   e. a writ of *certiorari*

4. True or False: The House of Representatives appoints federal judges with the advice and consent of the Senate.

5. True or False: Through its power of judicial review, the federal judiciary can decide on the constitutionality of legislative enactments and of actions taken by the executive branch.

SUMMARY & OBJECTIVES

LO1 Summarize the origins of the American legal system and the basic sources of American law. ***1*** The American legal system evolved from the **common law** tradition that developed in England over hundreds of years. A cornerstone of the English and American judicial systems is the practice of deciding new cases with reference to previous decisions, or **precedents.** This practice forms a doctrine called ***stare decisis,*** which theoretically obligates judges to follow the precedents established in their jurisdictions.

2 **Primary sources of American law** include constitutions (**constitutional law**); laws enacted by legislatures (**statutory law**); rules, regulations, orders, and decisions of administrative agencies (**administrative law**); and the rules of law announced in court decisions (**case law**). ***3*** **Civil law** spells out the duties that individuals in society owe to other persons or to their governments. **Criminal law** has to do with wrongs committed against the public as a whole. ***4*** Before a court can hear and decide a particular case, it must have **jurisdiction.** To bring a lawsuit before a court, a person must have **standing to sue,** and the issue must be a **justiciable controversy.** In addition to these basic judicial requirements, both the federal and the state courts have established procedural rules that apply in all cases.

LO2 Delineate the structure of the federal court system. ***5*** The federal court system includes the U.S. district courts, the U.S. courts of appeals, and the United States Supreme Court. The district courts are **trial courts;** they have jurisdiction over cases involving **federal questions** and over cases involving **diversity of citizenship.** There is at least one federal district court in every state, and there is one in the District of Columbia. Currently, there are ninety-four judicial districts. The U.S. courts of appeals are **appellate courts** that hear cases on review from the U.S. district courts located within their respective judicial circuits, and in many cases appeals from decisions made by federal administrative agencies (bypassing the district courts). There are thirteen federal courts of appeal, one of which (the Court of Appeals for the Federal Circuit) has national jurisdiction over certain types of cases. The United States Supreme Court has some original jurisdiction, but most of the Court's work is as an appellate court. The Supreme Court may take appeals of decisions made by the U.S. courts of appeals as well as appeals of cases decided in the state courts when federal questions are at issue. ***6*** To bring a case before the Supreme Court, a party may request that the Court issue a **writ of *certiorari*.** The Court will not issue a writ unless at least four of the nine justices approve. If the Supreme Court grants cert., it will typically hear **oral arguments,** after which the justices discuss the case in **conference.** When the Court has reached a decision, the justices explain their reasoning in written **opinions.**

LO3 Indicate how federal judges are appointed. ***7*** Federal judges are appointed for life by the president and confirmed by the Senate. The Senate Judiciary Committee holds hearings on judicial nominees and makes its recommendation to the Senate, where it takes a majority vote to confirm a nomination. **Senatorial courtesy** is a practice that gives home-state senators of the president's party some influence over the choice of nominees for district courts (and, to a lesser extent, the U.S. courts of appeals). Presidents have attempted to strengthen their legacies by appointing federal judges with political and philosophical views similar to their own. The process of nominating and confirming federal judges often involves political debate and controversy.

LO4 Explain how the federal courts make policy. ***8*** In the United States, judges play an important policymaking role. Federal judges can decide on the constitutionality of laws or actions undertaken by the other branches of government through the power of **judicial review.** Moreover, when a court interprets a law or a constitutional provision and applies that interpretation to a specific set of circumstances, the court is essentially "making the law" on that issue. ***9*** One issue that is often debated is how the federal courts should wield their policymaking power. Activist judges believe that the courts should actively use their powers to check the other two branches of government to ensure that they do not exceed their authority. Restraintist judges generally assume that the courts should defer to the decisions of the other branches, because members of Congress and the president are elected by the people, whereas federal judges are not.

LO5 Describe the role of ideology and judicial philosophies in judicial decision making. ***10*** There are numerous examples of ideology or policy preferences affecting Supreme Court decisions. However, judicial decision making, particularly at the Supreme Court level, can be very complex. The Court must consider any number of sources of law, and at times, the Court may also take demographic data, public opinion, and foreign laws into account. The approaches justices take toward the interpretation of law (strict versus broad construction) or toward constitutional interpretation (original intent versus modernism) are also important in determining why justices decide as they do.

LO6 Identify some of the criticisms of the federal courts and some of the checks on the power of the courts. ***11*** Policymaking by unelected judges in the federal courts has important implications in a democracy. Critics, especially on the political right, frequently accuse the judiciary of "legislating from the bench." ***12*** There are several checks on the courts, however. Supreme Court justices traditionally have exercised a great deal of self-restraint in decision making. The judiciary is also constrained by its lack of enforcement powers and by potential congressional actions in response to court decisions. The American public continues to have a high regard for the Supreme Court and the federal courts generally.

Find more practice tests and study tools for this chapter on CourseMate.

judiciary The courts; one of the three branches of government in the United States. ***304***

jurisdiction The authority of a court to hear and decide a particular case. ***307***

justiciable controversy A controversy that is not hypothetical or academic but real and substantial; a requirement that must be satisfied before a court will hear a case. *Justiciable* is pronounced jus-*tish*-a-bul. ***308***

opinion A written statement by a court expressing the reasons for its decision in a case. ***308***

oral argument A spoken argument presented to a judge in person by an attorney on behalf of her or his client. ***312***

precedent A court decision that furnishes an example or authority for deciding subsequent cases involving identical or similar facts and legal issues. ***304***

primary source of law A source of law that establishes the law. Primary sources of law include constitutions, statutes, administrative agency rules and regulations, and decisions rendered by the courts. ***306***

senatorial courtesy A practice that allows a senator of the president's party to veto the president's nominee to a federal court judgeship within the senator's state. ***313***

standing to sue The requirement that an individual must have a sufficient stake in a controversy before he or she can bring a lawsuit. The party bringing the suit must demonstrate that he or she has either been harmed or been threatened with a harm. ***308***

stare decisis A common law doctrine under which judges normally are obligated to follow the precedents established by prior court decisions. Pronounced *ster*-ay dih-*si*-sis. ***305***

statutory law The body of law enacted by legislatures (as opposed to constitutional law, administrative law, or case law). ***306***

trial court A court in which trials are held and testimony taken. ***308***

writ of *certiorari* An order from a higher court asking a lower court for the record of a case. *Certiorari* is pronounced sur-shee-uh-*rah*-ree. ***311***

Quiz Answers: 1. b; 2. True; 3. b; 4. False; 5. True

CHAPTER IN REVIEW

15 Domestic Policy

KEY TERMS

action-reaction syndrome For every government action, there will be a reaction by the public. The government then takes a further action to counter the public's reaction—and the cycle begins again. ***339***

agenda setting Getting an issue on the political agenda to be addressed by Congress; part of the first stage of the policymaking process. ***328***

Blue Dog Coalition A caucus that unites most of the moderate-to-conservative Democrats in the House of Representatives. ***332***

cap-and-trade A method of restricting the production of a harmful substance. A cap is set on the volume of production, and permits to produce the substance can then be traded on the open market. ***336***

Congressional Budget Office (CBO) An agency established by Congress to evaluate the impact of proposed legislation on the federal budget. ***333***

Corporate Average Fuel Economy (CAFE) standards A set of federal standards under which each manufacturer must meet a miles-per-gallon benchmark averaged across all cars or trucks that it sells. ***334***

domestic policy Public policy concerning issues within a national unit, such as national policy concerning health care or the economy. ***327***

easy-money policy A monetary policy that involves stimulating the economy by expanding the rate of growth of the money supply. An easy-money policy supposedly will lead to lower interest rates and induce consumers to spend more and producers to invest more. ***338***

economic policy All actions taken by the national government to smooth out the ups and downs in the nation's level of business activity. ***337***

Federal Open Market Committee (FOMC) The most important body within the Federal Reserve System. The FOMC decides how monetary policy should be carried out by the Federal Reserve. ***337***

fiscal policy The use of changes in government expenditures and taxes to alter national economic variables. ***337***

global warming An increase in the average temperature of the Earth's surface over the last half century and its projected continuation. ***334***

greenhouse gas A gas that, when released into the atmosphere, traps the sun's heat and slows its release into outer space. Carbon dioxide (CO2) is a major example. ***334***

QUIZ

1. The first stage of the policymaking process is ____.
   a. policy implementation
   b. policy formulation
   c. issue identification and agenda setting
   d. policy evaluation
   e. policy adoption

2. True or False: Medicaid is a joint federal-state program that provides health-care subsidies to low-income persons.

3. During the 2009 health-care debate, Republicans and the Blue Dog Coalition were opposed to a proposal for ____, a government-sponsored insurance plan.
   a. an individual mandate
   b. a reconciliation act
   c. a personal mandate
   d. a public option
   e. cap-and-trade

4. Sources of renewable energy include____.
   a. greenhouse gas
   b. wind
   c. coal
   d. natural gas
   e. nuclear power

5. True or False: Congress makes decisions about monetary policy several times each year.

© KEVIN LAMARQUE/REUTERS /LANDOV

SUMMARY & OBJECTIVES

LO1 Explain what domestic policy is and summarize the steps in the policymaking process. ***1*** Public policy can be defined as a plan or course of action taken by the government to respond to a political issue or to enhance the social or political well-being of society. **Domestic policy** consists of public policy concerning issues within a national unit. ***2*** Public policy is the end result of a **policymaking process** that involves several phases. First, a problem in society must be identified as an issue that can be solved politically, and then the issue must be included on the political agenda. The next stage involves the formulation and adoption of specific plans for achieving a particular goal. The final stages of the process focus on the implementation of the policy and evaluating its success. Each phase of the policymaking process involves interactions among various individuals and groups.

LO2 Discuss the issue of health-care funding and recent legislation on universal health insurance. ***3*** Health care in the United States is expensive, and almost 42 million Americans have no health-care insurance. ***4*** The federal government pays for health care in a variety of ways. It buys health insurance for its employees, and members of the armed forces, veterans, and Native Americans receive medical services provided directly by the government. Most federal spending on health care is accounted for by **Medicare** and **Medicaid.** Medicaid is a joint federal-state program that provides health care subsidies to low-income persons. Another program, the **State Children's Health Insurance Program (SCHIP),** covers children in families with incomes that are modest but too high to qualify for Medicaid. Medicare is the federal government's health-care program for persons over the age of sixty-five. Medicare is now the government's second-largest domestic spending program, after Social Security. Medicare costs are expected to soar as millions of "baby boomers" retire over the next two decades. ***5*** In many countries, the government is responsible for providing basic health-care insurance to everyone through **national health insurance.** The plan that the United States adopted in major health-care reform legislation in 2010, however, provides a larger role for the private sector. Congress considered several proposals for reforming the way we pay for health care, though they had common features. Employer-provided health insurance would continue to be a large part of the system. Medicaid would continue. A new Health Insurance Exchange would allow individuals and small employers to shop for plans. Insurance companies would not be allowed to deny anyone coverage. An **individual mandate** would require most individuals to obtain coverage or pay a penalty. House legislation called for a **public option,** which drew opposition from Republicans and conservative Democrats in the House of Representatives (the **Blue Dog Coalition**). It was also rejected by the Senate. ***6*** After two different health-care reform bills had passed the House and the Senate, House Speaker Nancy Pelosi and President Obama were able to find enough votes in the House to pass the Senate's bill; thus no conference committee action was necessary. A second **reconciliation** act amending the Senate bill in several ways was then passed in both chambers. After the health-care bills were signed by the president, attorney generals in twenty states challenged the constitutionality of the individual mandate. Republicans made repeal of the health-care reform legislation part of their platform for the 2010 elections.

LO3 Summarize the issues of energy independence, global warming, and alternative energy sources. ***7*** A priority for the Obama administration, energy policy is important because of two problems. One problem is our reliance on imported oil. Many of the nations that export oil are not particularly friendly to the United States. In response to a spurt in oil prices in the 1970s, the federal government imposed Corporate Average Fuel Economy (CAFÉ) standards on cars and trucks sold in the United States. In 2009, President Obama issued higher fuel efficiency standards. ***8*** A second reason energy policy is important has to do with the problem of global warming. Most climatologists believe that **global warming** is the result of human activities, especially the release of **greenhouse gases** into the atmosphere. A rise in global temperatures could cause seawater to expand and polar ice to melt, causing sea levels to rise. Rainfall patterns are expected to change, and increases in extreme weather are likely. ***9*** Efforts to combat global warming include turning away from energy that depends on burning carbon, which releases greenhouse gases into the environment, and turning to sources of **renewable energy,** including solar power, hydropower, and wind energy. New nuclear power plants may also be constructed in the near future. The chief proposal to respond to global warming was known as **cap-and-trade.** Under this Democratic plan, the government would establish a "cap" for carbon dioxide emissions. Major emitters would need permits, which they could buy and sell, or trade, on the open market. Over time, the cap would decline, resulting in a reduction in emissions. So far, cap-and-trade legislation has not had enough support in Congress to pass.

LO4 Describe the two major areas of economic policymaking. ***10*** **Economic policy** is the responsibility of the national government. **Monetary policy** involves changing the amount of money in circulation to affect interest rates, credit markets, the rate of inflation, the rate of economic growth, and the rate of unemployment. Monetary policy is under the control of the Federal Reserve System (the Fed), an independent regulatory agency. The Fed and its **Federal Open Market Committee** make decisions about monetary policy several times each year. ***11*** **Fiscal policy** involves changes in government expenditures and taxes to alter national economic variables, including the rate of unemployment, labor force participation rates, and the rate of economic growth. Typically a lag exists between the government's decision to make a change in fiscal or monetary policy and the point at which the economy begins to feel the effects of a policy change. ***12*** The government raises revenues to pay its expenses by levying taxes on business and personal income and through borrowing. When the federal government spends more than it receives, it has to finance this shortfall. Typically, it borrows. Every time there is a federal government deficit, there is an increase in the total accumulated **public debt.** Historic legislation passed by Congress in 2008 and 2009 involved hundreds of billions of dollars in additional spending, contributing to a net public debt that will rise by trillions of dollars.

Find more practice tests and study tools for this chapter on CourseMate.

individual mandate In the context of health-care reform, a requirement that all persons obtain health-care insurance from one source or another. Those failing to do so would pay a penalty. ***332***

Keynesian economics An economic theory proposed by British economist John Maynard Keynes that is typically associated with the use of fiscal policy to alter national economic variables. ***338***

Medicaid A joint federal-state program that provides healthcare services to low-income persons. ***330***

Medicare A federal government program that pays for health-care insurance for Americans aged sixty-five years or over. ***330***

monetary policy Actions taken by the Federal Reserve Board to change the amount of money in circulation so as to affect interest rates, credit markets, the rate of inflation, the rate of economic growth, and the rate of unemployment. ***337***

national health insurance A program, found in many of the world's economically advanced nations, under which the central government provides basic health-care insurance coverage to everyone in the country. Some wealthy nations, such as the Netherlands and Switzerland, provide universal coverage through private insurance companies instead. ***331***

policymaking process The procedures involved in getting an issue on the political agenda; formulating, adopting, and implementing a policy with regard to the issue; and then evaluating the results of the policy. ***327***

public debt The total amount of money that the national government owes as a result of borrowing; also called the *national debt.* ***340***

public option In the context of health-care reform, a government-sponsored health-care insurance program that would compete with private insurance companies. ***332***

reconciliation A special type of legislation not subject to filibuster in the Senate. A reconciliation act must deal only with taxes or spending and in principle should reduce the federal budget deficit. ***333***

renewable energy Energy from technologies that do not rely on extracted resources, such as oil and coal, that can run out. ***335***

State Children's Health Insurance Program (SCHIP) A joint federal-state program that provides health-care insurance for low-income children. ***331***

Quiz Answers: 1. c; 2. True; 3. d; 4. b; 5. False

CHAPTER IN
REVIEW 16 Foreign Policy

KEY TERMS

coalition An alliance of nations formed to undertake a foreign policy action, particularly a military action. A coalition is often a temporary alliance that dissolves after the action is concluded. *356*

Cold War The war of words, warnings, and ideologies between the Soviet Union and the United States that lasted from the late 1940s through the early 1990s. *351*

colonial empire A group of dependent nations that are under the rule of a single imperial power. *350*

containment A U.S. policy designed to contain the spread of communism by offering military and economic aid to threatened nations. *351*

Cuban missile crisis A nuclear stand-off that occurred in 1962 when the United States learned that the Soviet Union had placed nuclear warheads in Cuba, ninety miles off the U.S. coast. The crisis was defused diplomatically, but it is generally considered the closest the two Cold War superpowers came to a nuclear confrontation. *352*

détente French word meaning a "relaxation of tensions." Détente characterized the relationship between the United States and the Soviet Union in the 1970s, as the two Cold War rivals attempted to pursue cooperative dealings and arms control. *352*

deterrence A policy of building up military strength for the purpose of discouraging (deterring) military attacks by other nations; the policy of "building weapons for peace" that supported the arms race between the United States and the Soviet Union during the Cold War. *352*

foreign policy A systematic and general plan that guides a country's attitudes and actions toward the rest of the world. Foreign policy includes all of the economic, military, commercial, and diplomatic positions and actions that a nation takes in its relationships with other countries. *347*

interventionism Direct involvement by one country in another country's affairs. *350*

iron curtain A phrase coined by Winston Churchill to describe the political boundaries between the democratic countries in Western Europe and the Soviet-controlled Communist countries in Eastern Europe. *351*

isolationism A political policy of noninvolvement in world affairs. *349*

Marshall Plan A plan providing for U.S. economic assistance to European nations following World War II to help those nations recover from the war; the plan was named after George C. Marshall, secretary of state from 1947 to 1949. *351*

QUIZ

1. True or False: The Department of State is, in principle, the government agency most directly involved in foreign policy.

2. The nation's founders and early presidents believed that _____ was the best way to protect American interests.

a. interventionism
b. containment
c. isolationism
d. deterrence
e. mutually assured destruction

3. During the Cuban missile crisis, the United States and _____ came close to a nuclear confrontation.

a. the Soviet Union
b. Pakistan
c. Iran
d. North Korea
e. Cuba

4. True or False: In 2001, following the 9/11 terrorist attacks, the U.S. military attacked al Qaeda camps in Iraq and the ruling Taliban regime that harbored those terrorists.

5. True or False: Israel and its Arab neighbors have had long-running conflicts, but they have never escalated into war.

© AP PHOTO/ANDY WONG

SUMMARY & OBJECTIVES

LO1 Discuss how foreign policy is made and identify the key players in this process. ***1*** Foreign policy includes all of the economic, military, commercial, and diplomatic positions and actions that a nation takes in its relationships with other countries. American foreign policy has been shaped by the principles of **moral idealism** and **political realism.** ***2*** The president oversees the military, guides defense policies, and represents the United States to the rest of the world. The Department of State is responsible for diplomatic relations with other nations and with multilateral organizations. The Department of Defense establishes and carries out defense policy and protects our national security. Other agencies, including the National Security Council and the Central Intelligence Agency, are also involved in U.S. foreign relations. Congress has the power to declare war and the power to appropriate funds to equip the armed forces and provide for foreign aid. The Senate has the power to ratify treaties. A few congressional committees are directly concerned with foreign affairs.

LO2 Summarize the history of American foreign policy through the years. ***3*** Early U.S. leaders sought to protect American interests through **isolationism.** After the Spanish-American War of 1898, which marked the first step toward **interventionism,** the United States acquired a **colonial empire** and was acknowledged as a world power. ***4*** When World War I broke out, the U.S. initially adopted a policy of **neutrality,** and after the war, returned to a policy of isolationism until the attack on Pearl Harbor in 1941. After World War II ended in 1945, the wartime alliance between the U.S. and the Soviet Union began to deteriorate. Many Americans considered Soviet attempts to spread Communist systems to other countries a major threat to democracy. The Truman Doctrine and the **Marshall Plan** marked the beginning of a policy of **containment.** ***5*** During the **Cold War,** the U.S. and the Soviet Union engaged in an arms race that was supported by a policy of **deterrence,** and out of that policy came the theory of **mutually assured destruction (MAD).** In 1962, the U.S. and the

Soviet Union came close to a nuclear confrontation during the **Cuban missile crisis.** The collapse of the Soviet Union in 1991 altered the framework and goals of U.S. foreign policy.

LO3 Identify the foreign policy challenges presented by terrorism and the consequences of the "Bush doctrine" with respect to Iraq. ***6*** Terrorist attacks have occurred with increasing frequency during the past three decades. After the attacks on September 11, 2001, the U.S. military, supported by a **coalition** of allies, attacked al Qaeda camps in Afghanistan and the ruling Taliban regime that harbored those terrorists. ***7*** In 2002, President George W. Bush described Iraq as a regime that sponsored terrorism and that sought to develop **weapons of mass destruction.** He enunciated a doctrine under which the United States was prepared to strike "preemptively" at Iraq. ***8*** The invasion of Iraq in 2003, in what was a **preventive war** rather than a **preemptive war,** succeeded in deposing the Iraqi dictator, Saddam Hussein. ***9*** In 2005, Iraqi voters chose a new government in the first free elections for half a century, but Iraq appeared to be drifting toward interethnic civil war. A "surge" of U.S. troops in 2007 and counterinsurgency tactics helped to improve the situation. In 2010, U.S. combat forces left Iraq.

LO4 Describe the principal issues dividing the Israelis and the Palestinians and the solutions proposed by the international community. ***10*** Following the 1948 Arab-Israeli war, a large number of Palestinians—Arab residents of the Holy Land—were forced into exile. The aftermath of another war in 1967 gave rise to the **Palestine Liberation Organization (PLO),** a nonstate body committed to armed struggle against Israel. The West Bank of the Jordan River and the Gaza Strip fell under Israeli control, and the Palestinians living in these areas became an occupied people. Palestinian terrorist attacks on Israel and Israeli settlements in the occupied territories have impeded any efforts toward peace. ***11*** The international community has been in agreement on several principles for settling the conflict. Lands seized in the 1967 war should be granted to the Palestinians, who could organize their own independent nation-state there. In turn, the Palestinians would have to recognize Israel's right to exist and take concrete steps to guarantee Israel's security. In 1993, Israel and the PLO met officially for the first time in Oslo, Norway. A major result of the **Oslo Accords** was the establishment of a Palestinian Authority, under Israeli control, on the West Bank and Gaza Strip. Further attempts to reach a settlement collapsed in acrimony. ***12*** In 2007, Gaza was taken over by Hamas, a radical Islamist party that refuses to recognize Israel. The Palestinian Authority again became an effective government on the West Bank, however, and in 2010, peace talks were restarted.

LO5 Outline some of the actions taken by the United States to curb the threat of nuclear weapons. ***13*** The pursuit of nuclear technology in North Korea and Iran is of major concern to the United States. Neither weapons inspections nor talks that have included China, Japan, North Korea, Russia, South Korea, and the United States have resolved the issue of North Korea's nuclear ambitions. North Korea conducted nuclear tests in 2006 and 2009, and in 2009 it tested a long-range missile as well. ***14*** Iran has made considerable progress in many aspects of its nuclear program, and, like North Korea, has been openly hostile to the U.S. The United Nations has imposed sanctions on Iran in an attempt to curb its nuclear ambitions. In 2009, a round of talks involving Britain, China, France, Germany, Iran, Russia, and the United States was begun to discuss Iran's nuclear program. Some observers see the talks as a way for the Iranians to play for time as they develop their nuclear capabilities.

LO6 Discuss China's emerging role as a world leader. ***15*** China may be destined to challenge American global supremacy. China has one of the fastest-growing economies in the world and a population of 1.3 billion. Congress has granted China **normal trade relations status,** and many Americans are concerned that low-cost imports from China are preventing the U.S. economy from enjoying a vigorous recovery. Although China has not shown ambitions to acquire more territory or become militarily aggressive, it has expressed a desire to take control of the island of Taiwan, a former Chinese province that has functioned since 1949 as if it were an independent nation.

Find more practice tests and study tools for this chapter on CourseMate.

Monroe Doctrine A U.S. policy, announced in 1823 by President James Monroe, that the United States would not tolerate foreign intervention in the Western Hemisphere, and in return, the United States would stay out of European affairs. ***349***

Moral idealism In foreign policy, the belief that the most important goal is to do what is right. Moral idealists think that it is possible for nations to cooperate as part of a rule-based community. ***347***

mutually assured destruction (MAD) A phrase referring to the assumption, on which the policy of deterrence was based, that if the forces of two nations are equally capable of destroying each other, neither nation will take a chance on war. ***352***

neoconservatism A philosophy of foreign policy based on moral idealism. Neoconservatives support the use of economic and military power to bring democracy and human rights to other countries. ***356***

neutrality A position of not being aligned with either side in a dispute or conflict, such as a war. ***350***

normal trade relations (NTR) status A trade status granted through an international treaty by which each member nation must treat other members at least as well as it treats the country that receives its most favorable treatment. This status was formerly known as *most-favored-nation status.* ***362***

Oslo Accords The first agreement signed between Israel and the PLO; led to the establishment of the Palestinian Authority in the occupied territories. ***359***

Palestine Liberation Organization (PLO) An organization formed in 1964 to represent the Palestinian people. The PLO has a long history of terrorism but for some years has functioned primarily as a political party. ***358***

political realism In foreign policy, the belief that nations are inevitably selfish, and that we should seek to protect our national security regardless of moral arguments. ***347***

preemptive war A war launched by a nation to prevent an imminent attack by another nation. ***356***

preventive war A war launched by a nation to prevent the possibility that another nation might attack at some point in the future; not supported by international law. ***356***

Soviet bloc The group of Eastern European nations that fell under the control of the Soviet Union following World War II. ***350***

weapons of mass destruction Chemical, biological, or nuclear weapons that can inflict massive casualties. ***356***

Quiz Answers: 1. True; 2. c; 3. a; 4. False; 5. False

CHAPTER IN REVIEW 17

California's People, Economy, and Politics

KEY TERMS

Constitution of 1849 California's first constitution was copied from constitutions of other states and featured a two-house legislature, a supreme court, and an executive branch including a governor, lieutenant governor, controller, attorney general, and superintendent of public instruction, as well as a bill of rights. Only white males were allowed to vote. ***370***

Constitution of 1879 California's second constitution retained the basic structures of the Constitution of 1849 but added institutions to regulate railroads and public utilities and to ensure fair tax assessments. Chinese were denied the right to vote, own land, or work for the government. ***372***

"hourglass economy" Tendency of California economy to include many people doing very well at the top, many barely getting by at the bottom, and fewer and fewer in the middle; symptomatic of California's vanishing middle class. ***383***

Progressives Members of an anti-machine reform movement that reshaped the state's political institutions between 1907 and the 1920s. ***374***

Silicon Valley Top area for high-tech industries; located between San José and San Francisco. ***379***

Southern Pacific Railroad Railroad company founded in 1861; developed a political machine that dominated California state politics through the turn of the century. ***371***

Workingmen's Party Denis Kearney's anti-railroad, anti-Chinese organization; instrumental in rewriting California's constitution in 1879. ***372***

QUIZ

1. **In the 1880's the largest landowner in California was ________.**
   a. the state government
   b. the federal government
   c. the Southern Pacific railroad
   d. Native American tribes
   e. William Randolph Hearst
2. **The ________ introduced direct democracy which allowed the voters to amend the Constitution and create laws through initiative and referenda.**
   a. Progressives
   b. Grangers
   c. Workingmen's Party
   d. Republicans
   e. Tea Party
3. **True or False: As of 2010, California's Constitution of 1879 had been amended 27 times.**
4. **True or False: As of 2010, nearly 27 percent of the state's population was foreign born.**
5. **The gap between wealthy and poor in California is most evident in**
   a. education and health care
   b. housing and education
   c. food and education
   d. housing and health care
   e. food and housing

JEFF KRAVITZ/FILM MAGIC/GETTY IMAGES

SUMMARY & OBJECTIVES

LO1 List some of the key events in California's road to statehood. ***1*** The colonization of California began in 1769 with the first Spanish missions and outposts. European diseases and other disasters reduced the Native American population to about 100,000 by 1849. ***2*** When Mexico and the United States went to war in 1846, Yankees in California declared independence from Mexico. Gold was discovered in 1948, and the influx of '49ers drove the non-native population to 264,000 by 1852. ***3*** The **Constitution of 1849** was based on earlier state constitutions. The constitutional convention petitioned Congress for statehood, which was promptly granted. Chinese, African Americans, and Native Americans had almost no rights. A few hundred men came to own most of the farmland.

LO2 Describe the impact railroads had on California's state government. ***4*** The **Southern Pacific Railroad** connected California with the rest of the country through a transcontinental link completed in 1869. ***5*** The Southern Pacific became the dominant railroad in the state, eventually owning 11 percent of California's land. Its political machine controlled both the Republican and Democratic parties. ***6*** During a depression in the 1870s, Irish immigrants founded the **Workingmen's Party,** which blamed economic difficulties on the railroad and the Chinese. Small farmers organized the Grange movement, and the two groups were able to call a second constitutional convention and write the **Constitution of 1879.** This document sought to regulate the railroads and other businesses and to keep the Chinese from voting or owning land. The railroad soon gained control of the agencies created to regulate it, however.

LO3 Point out the key changes introduced by the Progressives. ***7*** A growing middle class objected to the railroad machine and called for "good government." In 1910, these **Progressives** elected Hiram Johnson as governor and took over the legislature. ***8*** The progressives sought to weaken party bosses through primary elections. City and county positions became nonpartisan. Direct democracy was introduced—the initiative, the referendum, and the recall election. Over the years, as a result of constitutional initiatives, the state constitution became increasingly long and complex.

LO4 Summarize how the Great Depression and World War II changed California's population and ethnic landscape. ***9*** The California unemployment rate hit 33 percent in the Great Depression of the 1930s, but more than a million people still moved into the state. Many were whites who displaced Mexican farm workers, with resulting racial tensions. Labor unrest peaked in the 1930s. President Roosevelt's New Deal strengthened the Democratic Party, but the Republicans continued to win the larger number of elections. ***10*** World War II (U.S. involvement 1941–1945) brought 500,000 new defense jobs and an economic boom. More than 100,000 Japanese Americans were interned in prison camps during the war. Water projects begun in the 1930s fueled a boom in the Central Valley.

LO5 Explain the factors that influenced postwar political party shifts. ***11*** In 1958, the Democrats gained control of both the legislature and the governorship for the first time in the Twentieth Century. Under Governor Pat Brown, the state completed the California Water Project, a state highway network, and a higher education system. These projects were expensive. ***12*** With the election of Ronald Reagan as governor in 1966, the voters turned back to the Republicans. Democrat Jerry Brown, who succeeded Reagan, was a social liberal but avoided spending on infrastructure. Anti-tax Proposition 13, passed in 1978, solidified the anti-spending consensus. After Brown, Republicans held the governorship for sixteen years. Democrats, however, elected a majority of the state's congressional representatives after 1960. ***13*** Throughout these years, the state's population continued to grow, largely as a result of immigration from Latin America and Asia. Racial tensions troubled the state's politics, but the increasing clout of minorities provided some balance.

LO6 Discuss how economic, demographic, and technological changes have impacted California politics. ***14*** If California were an independent nation, its economy would be the eighth largest in the world. ***15*** California is the nation's leading farm state, providing nearly half of the vegetables, fruits, and nuts and a quarter of the dairy products consumed nationally. Labor relations, environmental issues, and overuse of the state's water supply are political issues involving agriculture. ***16*** While California's industries are diverse, a few stand out. These include the defense industry, which boomed for years but suffered large job losses at the end of the Cold War. California is the world's leader in the entertainment industry in Los Angeles and high-tech industry in **Silicon Valley.** ***17*** Since the "dot-com bust" of 2000, the state has experienced hard times. Shortages of electricity after 2000 led to a major crisis. Recession, expanded state spending, and tax cuts led to a state budget crisis and the recall of Democratic governor Gray Davis in 2003. After a brief economic resurgence, the Great Recession that began in 2007 led to a new budget crisis—and unpopularity for Republican governor Arnold Schwarzenegger. ***18*** In 2010, 27 percent of the state's population was foreign born. The state has about three million illegal immigrants. Non-Hispanic whites are no longer a majority of the state's population. ***19*** The gap between rich and poor in California is among the largest in the United States and is growing. California now exhibits an **"hourglass economy"** with many rich and poor, but fewer in the middle. ***20*** While California was traditionally divided between a liberal north and a conservative south, current regional divisions seem to be between a liberal coast and conservative inland areas.

Find more practice tests and study tools for this chapter on CourseMate.

Quiz Answers: 1. c; 2. a; 3. False; 4. True; 5. d

CHAPTER IN REVIEW 18

California's Political Parties and Direct Democracy

KEY TERMS

bonds Subject to voter approval, state and local governments can borrow money by issuing bonds, which are repaid (with interest) from the general fund budget or from special taxes or fees. ***398***

central committee Political party organizations at county and state levels; weakly linked to one another. ***390***

closed primary Election of party nominees in which only registered party members may participate. ***390***

constitutional amendments May be placed on the ballot by a two-thirds vote of the legislature or through the initiative process; must be approved by a simple majority of the voters. ***398***

cross-filing Election system that allowed candidates to win the nomination of more than one political party; eliminated in 1959. ***389***

direct democracy Progressive reforms giving citizens the power to make and repeal laws (initiative and referendum) and to remove elected officials from office (recall). ***388***

general elections Statewide elections held on the first Tuesday after the first Monday of November in even-numbered years. ***388***

initiative Progressive device by which people may put laws and constitutional amendments on the ballot after securing the required number of voters' signatures. ***397***

legislative initiatives Propositions placed on the ballot by the legislature rather than by citizen petition. ***398***

nonpartisan elections Progressive reform that removed party labels from ballots for local and judicial offices. ***389***

open primary Voters may cast their ballots for any listed candidate for an office irrespective of the voters' party affiliation; the top two vote winners proceed to a runoff in the general election; instituted by a 2010 ballot measure to take effect in 2012. ***390***

preprimary endorsement Political parties' designation of preferred candidates in party primary elections, thus strengthening the role of party organizations in selecting candidates; banned by state law until 1990. ***389***

primary elections Elections to choose party nominees; held in June of even-numbered years. ***388***

recall Progressive reform allowing voters to remove elected officials by petition and majority vote. ***394***

QUIZ

1. Reform legislators replaced party conventions with ________, in which registered voters of each party chose the nominee.
   a. general elections
   b. primary elections
   c. nonpartisan elections
   d. caucuses

2. True or False: In California, the state central committee is the highest-ranking body in each party.

3. True or False: Democratic candidates have won eight of the last thirteen gubernatorial elections in California.

4. Much of California's ________ is dictated by past ballot measures rather than the legislature or the governor.
   a. constitution
   b. civil rights legislation
   c. immigration law
   d. state budget
   e. tax code

5. Total spending for proposition campaigns in any given year now averages ________.
   a. \$300 thousand
   b. \$3 million
   c. \$30 million
   d. \$300 million
   e. \$3 billion

ROBYN BECK/AFP/GETTY IMAGES

SUMMARY & OBJECTIVES

LO1 Summarize the impact the Progressives had on political parties. ***1*** In California, party organizations are weak, and the electorate itself often makes policy. The Progressives weakened the parties to eliminate the railroad political machine, and in so doing elevated candidate personalities, the media, and campaign finance over the parties. The Progressives also introduced **direct democracy**—the initiative, referendum, and recall. ***2*** In 1909, Progressive legislators replaced party conventions with **primary elections,** in which the voters of each party choose nominees. Primary winners face the nominees of other parties in the **general election.** This system ended the machine's control of nominations. ***3*** The Progressives also replaced the party column ballot with separate balloting for each office. **Cross-filing** permitted candidates to receive the nomination of two or more parties, weakening the control of each party. Judges, school board members, and local government officials were now chosen in **nonpartisan elections,** which weakened the parties at the local level. Party leaders tried to regain control by making **preprimary endorsements,** but these were outlawed. Democratic legislators eliminated cross-filing in 1959, however.

LO2 Explain the structure and support systems of political parties. ***4*** The Republicans and the Democrats easily qualify for the ballot under current laws, but **third parties** find the process harder. Today, four such parties are qualified: the American Independent, Green, Libertarian, and Peace and Freedom parties. California voters choose their party when they register to vote. Almost a fifth of the voters "decline to state" a party. Under the **closed primary** system, voters in the past could only vote in a party primary if they were registered with that party. Since 2002, decline-to-state or independent voters can participate in most party primaries. Republicans were the dominant party until the 1930s and since then have continued to win many elections despite the Democratic edge in registration. ***5*** The state **central committee** is the highest-ranking body in each party. All party candidates and officeholders are members, along with county chairpersons. Additional members are elected or appointed. Counties also have central committees. ***6*** In 1990, the United States Supreme Court overturned the ban on preprimary endorsements, but voters often pay little attention to such endorsements. ***7*** Caucuses and clubs have dominated the parties. These include the conservative California Republican Assembly and the liberal California Democratic Council. Democrats tend to be sympathetic to the poor and immigrants; concerned about health care, education, and the environment; in favor of gay rights, gun control, and abortion rights; and supportive of tax increases to provide public services. Republicans are likely to oppose these views and to worry about big government and high taxes. ***8*** The Democrats are stronger among blacks, Latinos, city dwellers, and union members. Asian Americans tend to vote Democratic, except for Vietnamese and Chinese Americans. The Republican Party does better with whites, suburbanites, rural voters, older, more affluent voters, and Christian conservatives. Straight-ticket voting has become more common in recent years.

LO3 Describe the different forms of direct democracy. ***9*** Using the **recall,** voters can remove officeholders between scheduled elections. Recalls are easier in California than elsewhere. Other states that have the provision require more signatures and most require corruption or malfeasance by the officeholder (any reason suffices in California). Nevertheless, recalls are rare in the state. A major exception was the recall of Governor Gray Davis in 2003 and his replacement by movie star Arnold Schwarzenegger. ***10*** A **referendum** allows the voters to nullify acts of the legislature. Referenda have been relatively rare. ***11*** The **initiative** allows citizens to make policy themselves by passing a new law or constitutional amendment. To put a measure on the ballot, sponsors of a law must collect a number of signatures equal to 5 percent of the votes cast for the position of governor in the last election. Constitutional amendments require 8 percent. Signatures must be gathered within 150 days. Californians have voted on a wide variety of initiatives. ***12*** The legislature can also place initiatives on the ballot through **legislative initiatives.** Voter approval is also required to amend the constitution or issue bonds.

LO4 Discuss the pros and cons of ballot propositions. ***13*** Even the most grassroots-driven initiatives cost half a million dollars to qualify and millions more for a successful campaign. Initiatives are therefore sponsored by well-funded interest groups, not ordinary voters.
14 Politicians may advance initiatives to further their careers or to shape public policy. Governor Schwarzenegger, for example, attempted to use initiatives to bypass the legislature, with mixed results. Marketing firms may encourage interest groups to consider initiatives on which the firms can work. ***15*** Still, almost every ballot contains grass-roots driven initiatives, many of which challenge corporate interests. ***16*** Because self-interested sponsors draft initiatives, they are often poorly worded. Flaws are often resolved only in state and federal courts. Initiatives can constrain the power of elected officials, especially the power to set the state's budget. The voters themselves believe that there are too many initiatives, but they also strongly support the principle of direct democracy.

Find more practice tests and study tools for this chapter on CourseMate.

referendum Progressive reform requiring the legislature to place certain measures before the voters, who may also repeal legislation by petitioning for a referendum. ***396***

third party In the United States, any party other than one of the two major parties (Republican and Democratic). ***389***

Quiz Answers: 1. b; 2. True; 3. False; 4. d; 5. d

CHAPTER IN REVIEW 19

California Elections, Campaigns, and the Media

KEY TERMS

absentee ballots Voters who prefer not to vote at their polling places or who are unable to vote on Election Day may apply to their county registrar of voters for an absentee ballot and vote by mail. ***407***

direct mail Modern campaign technique by which candidates communicate selected messages to selected voters by mail. ***414***

Fair Political Practices Commission (FPPC) This independent regulatory commission monitors candidates' campaign finance reports and lobbyists. ***412***

independent expenditures An expenditure for activities that are independent from those of a political candidate or a political party. ***412***

political action committee (PAC) A committee that is established by a corporation, labor union, or special interest group to raise funds and make contributions on the establishing organization's behalf. ***411***

Political Reform Act of 1974 Initiative requiring officials to disclose conflicts of interest, campaign contributions, and spending; also requires lobbyists to register with the FPPC. ***412***

register to vote Citizens who are over eighteen years of age and who are not incarcerated or in a mental institution are eligible to sign up to vote by completion of a registration form. Nearly 30 percent of those eligible to register in California do not do so and thus cannot participate in elections. ***406***

voter turnout The proportion of eligible and/or registered voters who actually participate in an election. When turnout is high, the electorate is usually more diverse and liberal; when it is low, the electorate is usually older, more affluent, and more conservative. ***406***

QUIZ

1. **True or False: Those between the ages of 18 and 24 are most likely to vote.**
2. **True or False: African Americans remain the most under-represented of California's racial minorities.**
3. **True or False: Several initiatives attempting to limit the amount of money that individuals and groups can contribute to campaigns were invalidated by the courts on the grounds that they limited free speech.**
4. **True or False: Since 1909, the focus of political campaigns has shifted from political parties to individual candidates.**
5. **True or False: The majority of Californians get their news and information about state politics from newspapers.**

SUMMARY & OBJECTIVES

Find more practice tests and study tools for this chapter on CourseMate.

LO1 Summarize the profile of California voters and factors involved in nonparticipation. ***1*** The California ballot requires voters to make decisions about many elective positions and propositions, and citizens often find it difficult to choose. Party labels, campaigns, and the media help. ***2*** Citizens eighteen or older are eligible to vote unless they are institutionalized. Nearly 23.4 million Californians are eligible to vote, but only 17 million register and as few as 8 million actually vote in some elections. Almost half of those voting do so by mail using **absentee ballots.** ***3*** Latinos, African Americans, and Asian Americans are less likely to vote. ***4*** Those who participate most are white, older, more affluent, often homeowners, and better educated.

LO2 Describe where political candidates come from, how representative they are of the population, and which groups are underrepresented. ***5*** Most candidates start at the bottom and work their way up. Staff members of elected officials and wealthy individuals may skip such apprenticeships. In the past, most candidates were well-off white men, but better organization, term limits, and redistricting have helped more women and minorities win.

LO3 Explain where the money comes from for political campaigns and the laws that regulate campaign financing. ***6*** Weak parties mean that candidates must promote themselves. Interest groups, businesses, and wealthy individuals provide the money. Much financing comes from **political action committees (PACs).** Increasingly, wealthy candidates have funded their own campaigns. ***7*** The **Political Reform Act of 1974** required public disclosure of all donors and expenditures. The courts have invalidated some campaign finance initiatives on free speech grounds. In 2000, Proposition 34 set higher contribution limits than previous measures. It also set voluntary spending limits for candidates. There is no limit on how much candidates can contribute to their own campaigns. ***8*** Consequences of Proposition 34 include larger contributions to the parties and huge **independent expenditures** by interest groups.

LO4 Discuss how campaigning in California differs from other states, the challenges faced by candidates, and how the recall election of 2003 changed the rules for typical campaigning. ***9*** Campaign contributors expect their money to buy immediate access and long-term influence. ***10*** TV advertising accounts for up to 80 percent of all spending for statewide races. ***11*** Most candidates for legislative and local offices rely on **direct mail.** ***12*** The high costs of campaigns benefit incumbents. ***13*** Campaigns today use the Internet to recruit volunteers and send direct e-mail. ***14*** The Gray Davis recall campaign was unusually brief—75 days. The importance of fundraising and TV was an advantage to Arnold Schwarzenegger.

LO5 Indicate the role each form of media plays in California politics. ***15*** Almost everything Californians know about politics comes from the media, which until the 1950s was dominated by a few family-owned newspapers. ***16*** These newspapers, founded in the 19th century were often conservative and supporters of the Southern Pacific Railroad. In the 1970s, most newspapers became part of corporate chains with more professional editors and reporters. Newspapers have become less influential. ***17*** TV is the major political news source for most Californians, yet most stations minimally cover state politics. Major controversies and technological advances have improved coverage in recent years.

Quiz Answers: 1. False; 2. False; 3. True; 4. True; 5. False

20 California Interest Groups

CHAPTER IN REVIEW

QUIZ

1. True or False: Public interest groups are regularly among the state's largest contributors.
2. True or False: Lobbyists are referred to as members of the "third house," alongside the assembly and senate.
3. True or False: When a group questions the legality of legislation, they have the option of litigation.
4. True or False: The Progressive Reform Act of 1909 requires politicians to report their assets, disclose contributions, and declare how they spend campaign funds.
5. True or False: Local governments often act like interest groups by lobbying state government and hiring contract lobbyists.

SUMMARY & OBJECTIVES

Find more practice tests and study tools for this chapter on CourseMate.

LO1 Discuss how the power of interest groups has evolved in California.
1 **Interest groups** are organizations formed to protect and promote the shared objectives of their members by influencing public policy. ***2*** Agriculture has always been strong. Banking and high-tech industries are now among the most powerful.

LO2 Describe the various types of interest groups. ***3*** Economically oriented groups often have small memberships but a great deal of money, whereas public interest groups often have large memberships but little money. ***4*** Every major corporation in the state is represented in Sacramento. ***5*** Important professional associations include the California Medical Association, the California Association of Realtors, and the Consumer Attorneys of California. Teachers' organizations represent professionals but also act as labor unions. The labor movement is relatively strong in California. ***6*** **Demographic groups** are based on characteristics that distinguish their members, such as their ethnicity, gender, or age, and usually have an interest in overcoming discrimination. ***7*** **Single-issue groups** seek specific resolutions of specific questions. Abortion and tax rates are examples. ***8*** **Public interest groups** seek no private gain, and include consumer, environmental, and good government groups.

LO3 Explain the techniques used by interest groups and who they target.
9 Groups must persuade the legislature, executive branch, courts, and sometimes voters. ***10*** The attempt to influence legislators is called **lobbying.** Today's lobbyists rely on subject-matter expertise, but money is crucial. Lobbyists spend close to $2 million per year per legislator. ***11*** Between 1977 and 2006, the number of registered lobbyists in Sacramento more than doubled. Most represent a particular interest, but others are *contract lobbyists* who work for several clients simultaneously. Long-term lobbyists became more powerful when term limits eliminated senior legislators with countervailing knowledge. ***12*** Some poorly funded groups rely on their own members to lobby. Efforts by ordinary citizens have special credibility with legislators, but well-funded groups have learned to mimic grass-roots efforts by forming front groups. ***13*** Savvy groups also lobby the executive branch. Groups may lobby the general public to create popular support for their causes. ***14*** Most groups try to further their cause by helping sympathetic candidates win election through financial contributions or volunteers. ***15*** Campaign contributors claim their money merely buys them access to decision makers, but several scandals have featured explicit trade of money for votes. ***16*** Interest groups also employ **litigation** to reverse laws or decisions they oppose. ***17*** Direct democracy gives interest groups the chance to make policy by promoting their proposals through initiatives and referenda. Only broad-based or well-financed groups have the resources to collect the necessary signatures or to pay for expensive campaigns. ***18*** Interest groups are also major players in opposing initiatives that might harm their interests.

LO4 Summarize how interest groups are regulated. ***19*** Allegations of corruption led to the Political Reform Act of 1974. The law regulates politicians and compels lobbyists to register and file campaign and donation-related reports. The **Fair Political Practices Commission (FPPC)** monitors these activities. ***20*** Well-funded economic interest groups have staying power. Public interest and demographic groups, however, sometimes prevail due to their strength in numbers.

Quiz Answers: 1. False; 2. True; 3. True; 4. False; 5. True

KEY TERMS

contract lobbyist Individual or company that represents the interests of multiple clients before the legislature and other policy-making entities. ***430***

demographic groups Interest groups based on race, ethnicity, gender, or age; usually concerned with overcoming discrimination. ***426***

direct democracy Progressive reforms giving citizens the power to make and repeal laws (initiative and referendum) and to remove elected officials from office (recall). ***433***

economic groups Interest groups with sizable financial stakes in the political process who seek to influence legislators and other public policymakers. ***424***

interest groups An organized group of individuals sharing common objectives who actively attempt to influence policymakers. ***423***

litigation Interest group tactic of challenging a law or policy in the courts to have it overruled, modified, or delayed. ***433***

lobbying Interest group efforts to influence political decision makers, often through paid professionals (lobbyists). ***428***

Proposition 22, the California Defense of Marriage Act (2000) A ballot initiative that declared marriage an act between a man and a woman. ***427***

Proposition 22, the Local Taxpayers, Public Safety and Transportation Act (2010) An initiative that keeps the state government from taking local government funds dedicated by the voters for public safety. ***428***

Proposition 34 An initiative setting contribution limits for individuals and PACs; commonly circumvented through independent expenditures. ***435***

public interest groups Interest groups that purport to represent the general good rather than private interests. ***427***

single-issue groups Organized groups with unusually narrow policy objectives; not oriented toward compromise. ***427***

CHAPTER IN REVIEW 21

The Legislature: The Perils of Policy Making

KEY TERMS

bicameral legislature Organization of the state legislature into two houses: the forty-member senate (elected for four-year terms) and the eighty-member assembly (elected for two-year terms). ***440***

Citizens Redistricting Commission Enacted by the voters in Proposition 11 (2009), this commission will assume responsibility for determining the boundaries of state legislative districts and Board of Equalization districts. ***441***

conference committee Committee of senate and assembly members that meets to reconcile different versions of the same bill. ***452***

ghost voting When legislators cast electronic votes in place of assembly members who are not at their posts; this practice is against the law. ***453***

gut-and-amend The process of removing the original provisions from a bill and inserting new, unrelated content. ***452***

legislative analyst Assistant to the legislature who studies the annual budget and proposed programs. ***449***

legislative committees Small groups of senators or assembly members who consider and make legislation in specialized areas such as agriculture or education. ***451***

legislative counsel Assists the legislature in preparing bills and assessing their impact on existing legislation. ***449***

logrolling A give-and-take process in which legislators trade support for each other's bills. ***453***

president pro tem Legislative leader of the state senate; chairs the Rules Committee; selected by the majority party. ***447***

Proposition 11, the Voters FIRST Initiative (2008) An initiative that placed legislative redistricting in the hands of a fourteen-member citizens commission instead of the state legislature. ***442***

Proposition 140 A 1990 initiative limiting assembly members to three 2-year terms and senators and statewide elected officials to two 4-year terms and cutting the legislature's budget. ***443***

redistricting Adjustment of legislative district boundaries by the state legislature to keep all districts equal in population; done every ten years after the national census. ***441***

Reynolds v. Sims A 1964 U.S. Supreme Court decision that ordered redistricting of the upper houses of all state legislatures by population instead of land area. ***441***

QUIZ

1. California's Constitution fixed the number of senators at _________ members and the assembly at _________ members.

a. 50/120
b. 40/80
c. 27/78
d. 30/90

2. Constitutional amendments may be submitted by the legislature for voter approval after receiving:

a. an absolute two-thirds majority in the assembly.
b. an absolute majority in the senate.
c. an absolute majority in both houses.
d. an absolute two-thirds majority in both houses.

3. True or False: Every ten years, the state legislature redraws district boundaries to have the same number of people in each district based on census figures.

4. True or False: Democrats have controlled the California assembly speakership for all but four years since 1959.

5. Which legislative support agency provides fiscal expertise, reviewing the annual budget and assessing programs that affect the state's coffers?

a. Legislative Analyst's Office
b. Legislative Counsel
c. Joint Committee
d. Budget Committee

JUSTIN SULLIVAN/GETTY IMAGES

SUMMARY & OBJECTIVES

LO1 Summarize the evolution of California's legislature, including the impact of reapportionment and term limits. ***1*** With the governor, the legislature sets the budget and funds programs. Yet partisanship often leaves it tied up in knots. ***2*** Senators serve four-year terms (half the body is elected every two years), and assembly members serve two-year terms. Formerly, the assembly was elected on the basis of population, and senators by county. Los Angeles County, with 35 percent of the state's residents in 1965, had only one senator. ***3*** In 1964, the United States Supreme Court ordered all states to apportion senate seats by population. In 1966, voters created a full-time legislature. Lawmakers now meet more than 200 days per year. As of 2010, members' base salary is $95,291, the highest in any state. Lawmakers also receive perks. ***4*** So that districts remain equal in population, after each census the legislature undertakes **redistricting** to redraw assembly, senate, and U.S. congressional district boundaries. ***5*** Past redistricting has been bipartisan, but in 1991 Governor Pete Wilson vetoed a plan that favored the Democrats. The state Supreme Court then drafted a new plan. ***6*** In 2001, the legislature agreed to a plan that benefited incumbents by making most districts either highly Democratic or highly Republican. This enhanced partisanship in the legislature. ***7*** Proposition 77 in 2005, endorsed by Governor Schwarzenegger, would have given redistricting powers to a panel of retired judges. Voters rejected it, but in 2008 they approved Proposition 11, which gives redistricting to an independent commission after the 2010 census. ***8*** Today's legislators are more professional than in the past, and there are more women and minority group members. ***9*** **Proposition 140** in 1990 established **term limits** that limited executive branch officers and senators to two four-year terms and assembly members to three two-year terms. ***10*** Lawmakers try to maximize their time in office by serving all available terms in the assembly and then switching to the senate. Lobbyists and bureaucrats have no term limits and have gained power. Leaders of the two houses have lost clout. **11** California voters have twice refused to amend the rules on term limits.

LO2 Characterize the role of leaders and staff members in the legislature.

12 The assembly is the more hierarchical house. The **Speaker of the assembly** controls the flow of legislation, committee chairs and assignments, and vast campaign funds. The majority party chooses the Speaker in a closed caucus. Before term limits, Speakers often held their posts for long periods. Since 1996, Speakers have served between one and three years. **13** The most powerful senator is the **president pro tem,** elected by the majority party. Power lies in the **Rules Committee,** which is chaired by the president pro tem and controls committee assignments and the flow of legislation. Presidents pro tem enhance their power by raising large sums and dispensing it to fellow members. **14** The full-time legislature required a larger support staff, but Proposition 140 cut back staff numbers. Staff in the capital work on legislation, while district staff members help constituents with problems. Committees have staff with subject-matter expertise. **15** Staff members employed by party caucuses nominally work on legislation but are actually political operatives. Neutral staff members include the **legislative analyst,** who reviews the budget and assesses the fiscal impact of proposed programs. The **legislative counsel** writes legislation and examines the impact of proposed laws on existing ones. The **state auditor** reviews existing programs.

LO3 Explain how a bill becomes a law through both the formal and informal process.

16 The legislature can submit constitutional amendments and bond measures to the voters if the measures receive the votes of two-thirds of the full membership of both houses (an absolute two-thirds vote). Laws that take effect immediately on the governor's signature and veto overrides also require an absolute two-thirds vote. Regular laws that take effect the following January require absolute majorities. **17** Assembly members are limited to 50 proposals and senators to 65. The senate or assembly Rules Committee decides which **legislative committees** receive the bill. More than half of all bills die in committee; others are amended. Members of the majority party chair almost all committees. **18** Only if a bill receives a positive recommendation from all of its committees is it likely to go to the whole body. After any amendments, the bill goes to a vote. If it passes, it is sent to the other house. Bills can be amended by completely replacing the original and addressing a different topic instead. This is called **gut-and-amend.** **19** If the two houses pass different versions of a bill, the versions must be reconciled by a **conference committee.** Senate members are appointed by the Rules Committee, assembly members by the Speaker. If the two houses approve the conference results, the bill goes to the governor. It becomes law if the governor signs it or takes no action within twelve days. The governor may veto it, and veto overrides are next to impossible. **20** There are so many bills that lawmakers must rely on staff, committee, or leadership recommendations. In **logrolling,** members agree to support each other's bills. Assembly members have been known to cast the votes of other members by clicking their electronic devices. This **ghost voting** is illegal. **21** Pressure from public opinion and interest groups is crucial to shaping legislation.

LO4 Provide examples of the role personal power plays within the legislature.

22 Threats are part of the legislative process. To send a message to the executive, key legislators may block appointments by the governor. The threat of an initiative can shape legislation.

Find more practice tests and study tools for this chapter on CourseMate.

Senate Rules Committee A five-member committee consisting of the senate president pro-tem and two other members from each party in the senate; assigns chairs and committee appointments; functions as the gatekeeper of most senate legislation. *447*

speaker of the assembly Legislative leader of the assembly; selected by the majority party; controls committee appointments and the legislative process. *446*

state auditor An assistant to the legislature who analyzes ongoing programs. *449*

term limits Limits on the number of terms that officeholders may serve; elected executive branch officers and state senators are limited to two 4-year terms, and assembly members are limited to three 2-year terms. *443*

Quiz Answers: 1. b; 2. d; 3. True; 4. True; 5. a

CHAPTER IN REVIEW 22

California Law: Courts, Judges and Politics

KEY TERMS

collegiality Deferential behavior among justices as a way of building consensus on issues before the court. ***464***

Commission on Judicial Appointments Commission to review the governor's nominees for appellate and supreme courts; consists of the attorney general, the chief justice of the state supreme court, and the senior presiding judge of the courts of appeal. ***461***

Commission on Judicial Performance State board empowered to investigate charges of judicial misconduct or incompetence. ***462***

courts of appeal Three-justice panels that hear appeals from lower courts. ***459***

district attorney Chief prosecuting officer elected in each county; represents the people in cases against the accused. ***463***

judicial activism Making policy through court decisions rather than through the legislative or electoral process. ***466***

Judicial Council Chaired by the chief justice of the state supreme court and composed of twenty-one judges and attorneys; makes the rules for court procedures, collects data on the courts' operations and workload, and gives seminars for judges. ***464***

plea bargaining Reaching an agreement between the prosecution and the accused; the former gets a conviction, and the latter agrees to a reduced charge and lesser penalty. ***463***

Proposition 8 (Victims' Bill of Rights) A 2009 California initiative to amend the state constitution and restrict marriage to opposite-sex couples. ***466***

public defender County officer representing defendants who cannot afford an attorney; appointed by the county board of supervisors. ***463***

runoff election Election in which the top two candidates in a nonpartisan primary for trial court judge or local office face each other. ***461***

superior courts Lower courts in which criminal and civil cases are first tried. ***459***

supreme court California's highest judicial body; hears appeals from lower courts. ***460***

"three strikes" A 1994 law and initiative requiring sentences of twenty-five years to life for anyone convicted of three felonies. ***469***

QUIZ

1. **True or False: California's judges have no term limits.**
2. **Members of the district courts of appeal and the state supreme court attain office:**
   a. through selection by conference committees.
   b. through selection by the house judicial committee.
   c. through general elections.
   d. through gubernatorial appointment.
   e. through presidential appointment.
3. **Each year, about 10,000 petitions are filed with the supreme court, of which about ________ are chosen for consideration.**
   a. 200
   b. 500
   b. 900
   d. 1,200
   e. 5,000
4. **True or False: The Commission on Judicial Appointments often rejects nominees with heavily partisan backgrounds.**
5. **True or False: Of the 9,552,781 cases filed in California's trial courts in 2007, a little over half were criminal cases.**

SUMMARY & OBJECTIVES

PAUL SAKUMA/GETTY IMAGES

LO1 Explain the three levels of the California court system and how judges are appointed and fired. ***1*** Courts are political because their judgments are choices between public policy alternatives. ***2*** The California court system is the largest in the nation, with more than 2,000 judicial officers. ***3*** **Superior courts** in each county are trial courts, handling misdemeanors, felonies, civil suits, divorces, and juvenile cases. They also operate small claims courts. Losers may appeal to one of the six district **courts of appeal.** Ultimately, parties may petition for review by the seven-member state **supreme court.** Its decision is final unless a federal issue allows the matter to be appealed to the United States Supreme Court. ***4*** Technically, superior court judges are elected, but most actually gain office through appointment by the governor when a sitting judge leaves office. Judges must run for office when their terms expire, but almost always win. If no candidate wins a majority in the primary election, the two candidates with the most votes face each other in a **runoff election** in November. Superior court judges serve six-year terms and have no term limits. ***5*** Justices in the courts of appeal and the supreme court are always appointed by the governor. Appointees must be approved by the **Commission on Judicial Appointments,** which consists of the attorney general, the chief justice of the supreme court, and the senior presiding justice of the courts of appeal. At the next gubernatorial election, appointed justices go before the voters, who check "yes" or "no" on retaining the justice. Terms are for twelve years. ***6*** Incumbent justices routinely won reelection without controversy until the 1960s. In 1986, three liberal supreme court justices were swept from office, the only ones so removed in California history. ***7*** Judges can also be removed or censured by the **Commission on Judicial Performance,** which has members appointed by the supreme court, the governor, and the legislature.

LO2 Describe the work of the courts and the appeals process, including the role of the supreme court. ***8*** California's constitution guarantees the right to a jury trial for criminal and civil cases, but if both parties agree, a judge alone may hear the case. In criminal cases, the **district attorney,** an elected official, handles the prosecution. Defendants who cannot afford a lawyer are provided with a court-appointed attorney—in larger counties, the **public defender.** Most cases never go to trial but are settled by **plea bargaining,** which results in an agreement on a penalty. Civil suits are often settled before trial as well. Only 17 percent of California's attorneys are non-white. ***9*** Most appeals are refused. Appeals courts do not review the facts of a case, but whether the procedures were fair. The state supreme court reviews all death penalty cases. ***10*** The supreme court accepts only about 1 percent of the petitions filed with it. Attorneys for the two sides file written briefs and then make oral arguments, where they are questioned by the justices. In conference, the justices vote in order of seniority with the chief justice voting last. Draft opinions may circulate among the justices for months. **Collegiality** is needed to build consensus on issues.

LO3 Summarize the role of the chief justice and point out some of the more controversial decisions made by the supreme court, including rulings in which initiatives approved by voters were overturned. ***11*** The chief justice is also administrative head of the California court system. This includes overseeing supreme court staff and assigning cases to specific appellate courts. He or she is chair of the 21-member **Judicial Council,** which includes 14 judges appointed by the chief justice, four attorneys appointed by the state bar association, and one member from each house of the legislature. The council makes rules for court procedures, collects data on court operations and workload, and gives seminars for judges. ***12*** The courts are important in California because the constitution is long and complicated, requiring interpretation. ***13*** Long dominated by liberals, the supreme court turned to the right in 1986 when three liberal justices, including Chief Justice Rose Bird, were defeated. Bird and the court majority had consistently reversed death sentences. Today, only one serving justice was appointed by a Democratic governor. Still, the court is only moderately conservative. It tends to be pro-business and pro-prosecution, but anti-abortion activists have campaigned against retention of some justices. ***14*** The court usually avoids judicial activism but will take controversial positions, such as approving state-funded abortions. ***15*** The court will overrule decisions of voters. In 2008, the court overruled a 2002 initiative banning same-sex marriage. Opponents then succeeded in passing **Proposition 8,** which again restricted marriage to opposite-sex couples—this time through a constitutional amendment, overruling the justices.

LO4 Discuss the supreme court's past rulings on crime and the impact of the three strikes initiative. ***16*** Crime was a major political issue in the 1980s and 1990s. Today's court affirms most death sentences, but law-and-order advocates condemn the long delays before sentences are carried out. ***17*** In 1994, the voters approved the **"three-strikes"** initiative that requires anyone convicted of three felonies to serve a sentence of 25 years to life. The law reflected the view that judges were "soft on crime." The three-strikes law quickly increased the state's prison population. Crime rates have fallen since 1992, and crime is no longer a top political issue. Despite increased funding, California's prisons are severely overcrowded, which has led to intervention by the federal judiciary.

Find more practice tests and study tools for this chapter on CourseMate.

Quiz Answers: 1. True; 2. d; 3. a; 4. False; 5. False

CHAPTER IN REVIEW 23

The Executive Branch: Coping with Fragmented Authority

KEY TERMS

attorney general California's top law enforcement officer and legal counsel; the second most powerful member of the executive branch. ***485***

Board of Equalization Five-member state board, elected by district, that oversees the collection of sales, gasoline, and liquor taxes. ***487***

civil service system System for hiring and retaining public employees on the basis of their qualifications or merit. ***488***

controller Independently elected state executive who oversees taxing and spending. ***486***

director of finance Officer primarily responsible for preparation of the budget. ***476***

executive order Ability of the governor to make rules that have the effect of laws; may be overturned by the legislature. ***478***

general veto Power to reject an entire bill or budget; overruled by an absolute two-thirds vote of both houses. ***478***

governor California's highest-ranking executive officeholder; elected every four years. ***474***

insurance commissioner Elected executive who regulates the insurance industry. ***487***

item veto Power to delete or reduce the budget within a bill without rejecting the entire bill absolute two-thirds vote of both houses is required to override. ***477***

lieutenant governor Chief executive when the governor is absent from the state or disabled; succeeds the governor in case of death or other departure from office; casts a tiebreaking vote in the senate; is independently elected. ***485***

Proposition 58 Set broad spending limits on state government and required a "rainy day" fund. ***482***

Proposition 187 Initiative reducing government benefits for illegal immigrants; parts were declared unconstitutional in 1995. ***479***

Proposition 209 A 1996 initiative that eliminated affirmative action in California. ***479***

Proposition 227 A 1998 initiative limiting bilingual education to no more than one year. ***479***

secretary of state Elected state executive who keeps records and supervises elections. ***485***

special session Legislative session called by the governor. ***478***

superintendent of public instruction Elected state executive in charge of public education. ***486***

treasurer Elected state executive responsible for state funds between collection and spending. ***487***

Quiz Answers: 1. False; 2. True; 3. True; 4. True; 5. False

QUIZ

1. **True or False: Jerry Brown is California's first governor to be elected to three terms in office.**
2. **True or False: No other formal power is more important than the governor's budgetary responsibility.**
3. **True or False: An absolute two-thirds majority from each house is necessary to overturn item vetoes.**
4. **True or False: The attorney general is usually considered the second most powerful member of the executive branch.**
5. **True or False: California's bureaucracy is the largest of the fifty states on a per capita basis.**

SUMMARY & OBJECTIVES

Find more practice tests and study tools for this chapter on CourseMate.

LO1 Explain both the formal and informal powers of the governor. ***1*** The **governor** is California's most powerful public official, who shapes the budget and makes key executive and judicial appointments. ***2*** The state budget is a year-round task for the governor and the appointed director of finance. The legislature can disregard the governor's budget recommendations but often goes along with them. The governor has the power to reduce or eliminate spending on items through an **item veto.** ***3*** The **general veto** lets the governor reject non-appropriations measures in their entirety. The legislature can overturn either type of veto with an absolute two-thirds vote of both houses, which is difficult to obtain. ***4*** The governor can call a special session of the legislature, which must then discuss only the specific business proposed by the governor, and can issue an **executive order,** which looks similar to legislation. ***5*** Today, 99 percent of state employees are selected through a merit system. The governor fills about 2,500 key positions in the executive departments and cabinet agencies. Except for personal staff, these appointees must be approved by the state senate. If one of the other elected executive officers resigns, the governor's nominee must be approved by majorities in both houses of the legislature. The governor fills vacant judicial positions and may name hundreds of judges during his or her term in office. ***6*** A popular governor can exercise considerable informal power, including securing the passage of initiatives.

LO2 Describe the role of the other major members of the executive branch. ***7*** Other elected executive officials serve four-year terms, and all run independently. ***8*** The **lieutenant governor** fills in for the governor if the top executive is disabled or out of the state. If the governor leaves office, the lieutenant governor becomes governor. ***9*** The **attorney general** is the second most powerful member of the executive branch. He or she oversees law enforcement, acts as legal counsel to state agencies, represents the state in important cases, and renders opinions on proposed and existing laws. ***10*** The **secretary of state** keeps records and supervises elections. ***11*** The **superintendant of public instruction** heads the Department of Education. ***12*** The state's "money officers" are the **controller,** the **treasurer,** and the **Board of Equalization.** ***13*** The **insurance commissioner** oversees the state's insurance industry.

LO3 Summarize the makeup and tasks of the bureaucracy and how it is administered. ***14*** Most state workers are hired and fired through the state's civil service system, designed to insulate them from political influences and make them more professional. ***15*** Departments and agencies are run by administrators who are political appointees.

24 Taxing and Spending: Budgetary Politics and Policies

CHAPTER IN REVIEW

QUIZ

1. **True or False: The treasury and finance committees guide budget proposals through the legislative process.**
2. **True or False: The personal income tax is the fastest-growing component of state revenue.**
3. **True or False: Health and human services programs receive the second-largest share of the state budget.**
4. **True or False: Of the major state allocation categories, the budgets for prisons and corrections have declined the most in recent years.**
5. **True or False: California's state budget has been cut in recent years, even though the state's population has grown.**

Find more practice tests and study tools for this chapter on CourseMate.

SUMMARY & OBJECTIVES

LO1 Explain California's budgetary process and the role of each group of participants. ***1*** States are supposed to operate with balanced budgets, but this has been difficult in California. Following a recession, the 2003 budget faced a revenue deficit of $21 billion, which helped lead to the recall of Governor Gray Davis. Matters improved for a short while but the governor and legislature faced huge budget gaps in 2008, 2009, and 2010, resulting in a drastically cut budget of $83 billion in 2010–2011. Voters strongly favor budget cuts in general, but do not provide majority support for cutting in any specific policy area. ***2*** The governor frames the budget before it goes to the legislature and refines it thereafter through the item veto. In the summer and fall, the governor's director of finance works with department heads to create a first draft for the governor. ***3*** In the legislature, the budget submitted in January is examined by the legislative analyst and in the appropriations and budget committees in each house. Sections of the budget may then be farmed out to other committees. In April, the work of the various committees is combined. Negotiations among the **Big Five** shape the final decisions. Passage requires support by an absolute two-thirds majority in both houses. ***4*** The public can shape taxes and expenditures through initiatives and referenda. **Proposition 13** cut property taxes by 57 percent. ***5*** The courts may become involved if the legality of various budget provisions is questioned.

LO2 Summarize the main sources of revenue used to fund the state's budget. ***6*** The largest sources of revenue for the general fund budget are personal income tax, sales tax, and bank and corporation taxes. Counties collect property tax to fund local governments. ***7*** **Sales tax** supplies 31.8 percent of the state's tax revenues. ***8*** The **personal income tax** rate varies from 1 to 10.3 percent, depending on a person's income , and is the fastest-growing component of state revenue. ***9*** **Bank and corporation tax** provides about 9.9 percent of state revenues. **User taxes** are levied on gasoline and cigarettes. ***10*** The state borrows money by issuing bonds. Per capita indebtedness is well above the national average. The state also collects charges for services, such as state park fees and concessions.

LO3 Indicate the major areas of spending addressed in the state budget. ***11*** Outlays for public education, health and welfare, higher education, and prisons account for nearly 90 percent of the general fund. Much spending is determined by formulas rather than by legislative discretion. ***12*** Public schools get the largest share of state expenditures. Still, California ranks forty-sixth among the states in per capita expenditures. The student-teacher ratio is forty-ninth, and the state ranks near the bottom in student performance tests. ***13*** A fourth of public school students do not have English as their first language, compared to 9 percent nationally. Charter schools have been proposed as an alternative to a "broken system." ***14*** Higher education exceeds 11 percent of the general fund. The share of the budgets of higher education provided by the state has fallen substantially. ***15*** Health and human services were about 25 percent of the general fund in 2010. Programs include Medi-Cal (health care for the poor), Supplemental Security Income (for the elderly and disabled), and CalWORKS (welfare). California has about a quarter of the nation's welfare recipients. ***16*** The **"three strikes" law** added more than 43,000 long-term inmates to the prison system from 1994 to 2004. Growth in the prison population has forced the building of many new prisons.

KEY TERMS

bank and corporation tax Tax on the profits of lending institutions and businesses; the third most important source of state revenue. ***498***

Big Five The governor, assembly speaker, assembly minority leader, senate president pro tem, and senate minority leader, who gather together informally to thrash out decisions on the annual budget and other major policy issues. ***495***

personal income tax A graduated tax on individual earnings; the largest source of state revenues. ***497***

Proposition 13 (Jarvis-Gann initiative) A 1978 measure that cut property taxes. ***496***

Proposition 58 A 2004 proposition that set broad spending limits on state government and required the state to gradually set aside up to 3 percent of all revenues in a "rainy day" fund. ***500***

Proposition 98 A 1988 initiative awarding public education a fixed minimum percentage of the state budget. ***501***

Proposition 227 A 1998 initiative limiting bilingual education to no more than one year. ***502***

sales tax Statewide tax on most goods and products; local governments receive a portion of this tax. ***497***

three strikes law A 1994 measure requiring sentences of twenty-five years to life for anyone convicted of three felonies. ***504***

user taxes Taxes on select commodities or services "used" by those who benefit directly from them; e.g., gasoline and cigarette taxes. ***498***

Quiz Answers: 1. False; 2. True; 3. True; 4. False; 5. True

CHAPTER IN REVIEW 25 Local Government in California

KEY TERMS

at-large elections Local elections in which all candidates are elected by the community as a whole rather than by districts. *513*

board of supervisors Five-member governing body of counties, usually elected by district to four-year terms. *510*

bonds Subject to voter approval, state and local governments can borrow money by issuing bonds, which are repaid (with interest) from the general fund budget or from special taxes or fees. *516*

charges for services Local government fees for services such as sewage treatment, trash collection, building permits, and the use of recreational facilities; a major source of income for cities and counties since the passage of Proposition 13 in 1978. *520*

charter A document defining the powers and institutions of a California city or county. *510*

charter city or county A local government that drafts its own structures and organization through a document like a local constitution (also known as a "home-rule" charter), subject to voter approval. *510*

cities Local governments in urban areas, run by city councils and mayors or city managers; principal responsibilities include police and fire protection, land-use planning, street maintenance and construction, sanitation, libraries, and parks. *512*

city council Governing body of a city; members are elected at large or by district to four-year terms. *512*

city manager Top administrative officer in most California cities; appointed by the city council. *512*

consolidation The merger of cities, school districts, or special districts; usually requires voter approval. *518*

contracting for services Smaller cities contract with counties or other cities to provide services they cannot efficiently provide themselves. *518*

council–manager system Form of government in which an elected council appoints a professional manager to administer daily operations; used by most California cities. *515*

councils of government (COGs) Regional planning organizations. *518*

counties Local governments and administrative agencies of the state, run by elected boards of supervisors; principal responsibilities include welfare, jails, courts, roads, and elections. *509*

county executive Top administrative officer in most California counties; appointed by the board of supervisors. *510*

QUIZ

1. ________ is unique among California's local governments because it operates as both a city and a county.
- a. San Bernardino
- b. Santa Barbara
- c. San Francisco
- d. Los Angeles

2. Thirty-eight California cities use some form of ________.
- a. district election
- b. at-large election
- c. charter election
- d. runoff election

3. True or False: Median turnout in local elections which are held separately from state and national elections is less than 30 percent.

4. True or False: In 2010, voters approved Proposition 22 banning state borrowing from local governments.

5. What is the biggest expenditure for cities?
- a. schools
- b. welfare
- c. public safety
- d. garbage collection
- e. street repair

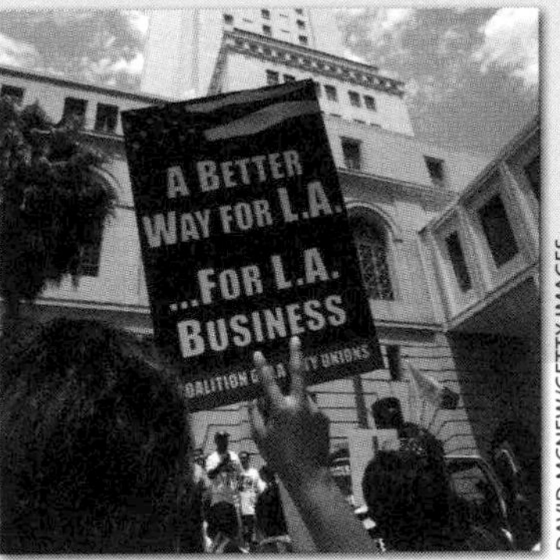

DAVID MCNEW/GETTY IMAGES

SUMMARY & OBJECTIVES

LO1 Describe the structure of California's counties and cities, and how they are established. ***1*** Local governments are created by state law. ***2*** **Counties** are both local governments and administrative arms of the state. As local governments, they provide police and fire protection, maintain roads, perform services for unincorporated areas, operate transit systems, and keep records. For the state, they oversee elections, operate courts, administer the welfare system, and collect some taxes. Counties are governed by a five-member **board of supervisors,** elected by districts to staggered four-year terms. The board usually hires a county executive. Voters also elect a sheriff, district attorney, tax assessor, and other officials to four-year terms in nonpartisan elections. ***3*** Fourteen counties have **charters** that allow them to set their own governmental structures. San Francisco is unique in that it is both a city and county. It therefore has a **mayor.** ***4*** **Cities** are established when citizens petition for **incorporation.** A county's **local agency formation commission (LAFCO)** reviews the request. If LAFCO approves, residents vote on incorporation. ***5*** Most cities are **general law cities** operating under the state's default rules. A five-member **city council,** with members elected for four-year terms, appoints a **city manager** who in turn appoints department heads. Some cities have obtained charters to customize their structures. Cities are responsible for police and fire protection, sewage treatment, garbage disposal, parks and recreation, streets, libraries, and land-use planning.

LO2 Explain who controls California's cities, and how they are elected. ***6*** Larger cities with charters may choose to have more than five council members or a stronger mayor. ***7*** In most cities, council members are chosen citywide in **at-large elections** on non-partisan ballots. At-large elections can make it difficult for minority group members to win. ***8*** As a result, some cities have returned to **district elections.** In most cities, candidates that get the most votes win even if they don't have a majority. In many larger cities, if no candidate has a majority in the primary, the top two finishers compete in a runoff election. San Francisco has **instant runoff voting,** in which voters rank candidates in order of preference. ***9*** About a third of California cities hold elections on dates different from the date of state and national elections. This reduces turnout. County elections always coincide with state and national voting. ***10*** The costs of city and county races have risen since the 1980s, and many cities and counties now have local campaign finance laws. ***11*** In most cities, the post of mayor is largely ceremonial, with executive authority in the hands of the city manager—the **council-manager system.** Several of the state's largest cities, however, have adopted strong-mayor systems. ***12*** While retaining the city manager, many cities have begun to elect their mayors directly.

LO3 **Identify other forms of local government in California and the services that they provide.** ***13*** California has almost a thousand **school districts,** created and overseen by the state and governed by elected boards. Building repairs and the construction of new schools are funded by bonds, which were hard to pass after Proposition 13 required two-thirds support by the voters. In 2000, the required margin was reduced to 55 percent. **Special districts** provide a single service such as transit, fire protection, or sewage. Their boards may be elected or appointed. ***14*** Cities that are too small to provide certain services efficiently may address the problem by **contracting for services** from counties, other cities, or private businesses. ***15*** Twenty urban areas have **councils of government (COGs)** to coordinate plans. These bodies cannot force their plans on the local governments. In contrast, such state-created agencies as the Metropolitan Water District have great power.

LO4 **Discuss the ways in which direct democracy is used in local politics.** ***16*** The initiative, referendum, and recall are used even more at the local level than the state level. Voters must approve charter amendments, tax increases, and bonds. Other than school bonds, a supermajority of two-thirds is required for bonds and new taxes. ***17*** Measures to control growth are among the most popular initiative topics.

LO5 **Summarize how local governments raise and spend money, and the initiatives that have affected revenues.** ***18*** The **property tax** was the largest source of local revenue until **Proposition 13,** which cut property taxes by 57 percent. Many cities thereafter introduced **charges for services** such as sewage treatment, trash collection, and recreational facilities. The sales tax returns 2 percent of the state's basic 8.25 percent to local governments. Some governments tax other items, for example hotel rooms. Many cities now prefer retail businesses to housing or industry because of the resulting sales taxes. This is called the **fiscalization of land use.** ***19*** More than half of county revenues come from the state and federal governments, but this money must be spent on required programs. Counties spend 95 percent of their budgets on state-mandated services. Some local governments have flirted with bankruptcy, and the city of Vallejo actually did go bankrupt in 2008. ***20*** During recent budget crises, the state has seized income that previously went to local governments. In 2004, the state took property tax revenue from **redevelopment agencies** to balance its budget. **Proposition 1A** in 2004 was supposed to block such raids, but in 2009, the state diverted about $4 billion in property taxes to its own uses. Cities and counties responded in 2010 with Proposition 22 banning state borrowing from local governments and won voter approval.

CourseMate

Find more practice tests and study tools for this chapter on CourseMate.

district elections Elections in which candidates are chosen by only one part of the city, county, or state. ***513***

fiscalization of land use Cities and counties, when making land-use decisions, opt for the alternative that produces the most revenue. ***520***

general-law city or county A city or county whose powers and structure of government are derived from state law. ***512***

incorporation Process by which residents of an urbanized area form a city. ***512***

instant runoff voting Voters rank candidates in order of preference. If no candidate wins a majority, the candidate with the fewest votes is eliminated and those votes are assigned to the voters' second choice—and so on until one candidate attains a majority. ***514***

local agency formation commission (LAFCO) A county agency set up to oversee the creation and expansion of cities. ***512***

mayor Ceremonial leader of a city, usually a position that alternates among council members, but in some large cities is directly elected and given substantial powers. ***510***

property tax A tax on land and buildings; until the passage of Proposition 13 in 1978, the primary source of revenues for local governments. ***519***

Proposition 1A A 2004 ballot measure designed to prevent the state from taking revenues from local governments in times of fiscal stress. ***521***

Proposition 13 A 1978 initiative that cut property taxes by 57 percent and limited their future growth. It also created a requirement that local tax increases must pass by a two-thirds majority. ***519***

Proposition 22, the Local Taxpayers, Public Safety and Transportation Act (2010) An initiative that keeps the state government from taking local government funds dedicated by the voters. ***521***

runoff election When no candidate receives more than 50 percent of the vote in a nonpartisan primary for trial court judge or local office, the top two candidates face each other in a runoff. ***514***

school districts Local governments created by states to provide elementary and secondary education; governed by elected school boards. ***516***

special districts Local government agencies providing a single service such as fire protection or sewage disposal. ***516***

term limits Limits on the number of terms that officeholders may serve. Local elected officials are usually limited to two or three 4-year terms. ***519***

Quiz Answers: 1. c; 2. a; 3. True; 4. True; 5. c

CHAPTER IN REVIEW 26

State–Federal Relations: Conflict, Cooperation, and Chaos

KEY TERMS

congressional delegation Members of the House of Representatives and Senate representing a particular state. ***530***

Environmental Protection Agency (EPA) Federal government body charged with carrying out national environmental policy. ***534***

federalism A system of shared sovereignty between two levels of government—one national and one subnational—occupying the same geographic region. ***536***

grants-in-aid Payments from the national government to states to assist in fulfilling public policy objectives. ***536***

Quiz Answers: 1. d; 2. c; 3. True; 4. True; 5. d

QUIZ

1. **California has ________ members in the U.S. House of Representatives.**
   a. 46
   b. 38
   c. 23
   d. 53
2. **Only on the question of ________ have most members of California's delegation voted the same way.**
   a. immigration
   b. desert protection
   c. offshore oil drilling
   d. foreign trade
3. **True or False: Illegal immigrants make up as much as 90% of the farming workforce.**
4. **True or False: The EPA's new national policy on higher gasoline mileage and lower emissions by 2017 is based on California's standards.**
5. **Federal financial assistance to California's state and local treasuries amounted to about ________ in fiscal year 2010.**
   a. $4 billion
   b. $83 billion
   c. $275 billion
   d. $653 billion

MARK RALSTON/AFP/GETTY IMAGES

SUMMARY & OBJECTIVES

LO1 Describe the relationship California has had with the nation's recent presidents. ***1*** California and the national government have differed on issues such as environmental protection and offshore oil drilling. On issues such as workplace conditions, officials have worked well together. California has often confronted issues earlier than the rest of the nation. ***2*** President Bill Clinton funneled discretionary funds to California, and his policies were largely in tune with those of the state. President George W. Bush was more remote, visiting the state infrequently. His administration refused to intervene during the 2001 energy crisis. Electing a Republican governor changed little. California is reliably Democratic in presidential races, so campaigns invest few resources here. Candidates do come to raise funds, however—California is the top donor state for both parties. President Barack Obama has been sensitive to the role of technology in California, called for extension of the $74 billion research and development tax credit, and embraced California's strict rules on automobile exhaust emissions. On the other hand, the Obama administration has been willing to compensate California for only a fraction of the hundreds of millions of dollars spent on the incarceration of illegal immigrants awaiting transport to their home countries. And California was unsuccessful in wresting any of the $4.35 billion in Obama's "Race to the Top" education improvement funds at a time when public education has been gasping for support.

LO2 Explain the power California has within Congress and the conflicts that divide its representatives. ***3*** California has 53 members in the U.S. House, dwarfing the delegation of every other state. When Republicans controlled the House before the 2006 elections, California Republicans chaired a record six House committees. ***4*** The 2006 Democratic takeover propelled California's Nancy Pelosi into the position of Speaker of the House. Political party fortunes took a turn in 2010 when the Republicans captured control of the House and increased their minority in the Senate. As of 2011, California Republicans were poised to gain at least three chairmanships, and Kevin McCarthy was elected majority whip. **5** After the 2010 elections, Democrats had a 34–19 margin in U.S. House seats. The delegation contains seven Latinos, four African Americans, and three Asian Americans; nineteen women are members, and both of California's U.S. senators are women. **6** In contrast to many other states, California's **congressional delegation** rarely presents a united front on the issues. **7** The Auburn Dam controversy is an example. Republicans and farmers supported the proposed dam; environmentalists and Democrats opposed it. While California representatives fought among themselves over this issue, bipartisan blocs in other states brought home the bacon.

LO3 Summarize California's responsibility in fighting terrorism. **8** Between 2002 and 2010, the Governor's Office of Homeland Security distributed more than $1.3 billion in federal funds for state and local equipment and training, and the state has also absorbed major security obligations without federal funding. **9** The initial formula used to distribute homeland security aid was drastically biased against California, which in 2004–2005 was dead last in per capita allocations. Work by California Republicans in the House and Senator Feinstein produced a better formula, raising California's per capita ranking to twenty-first in 2006–2007. Since then, the Obama administration has promised to review the funding formula in recognition of high-risk states such as California, but serious economic issues have prevented the development of new legislation.

LO4 Discuss the impact of immigration on California. **10** Hostility to immigration has grown in California. In 1980, 15.1 percent of the state's population was foreign-born; in 2010 the figure was 27 percent. The national numbers for those years were 6.2 and 12.1 percent. The state may contain as many as three million illegal immigrants. **11** Experts are divided on whether immigration helps or hurts the economy. It is certain, however, that the labor of illegal immigrants is essential to the state's agriculture. **12** While the federal government controls immigration policy, many of its costs are borne by the states. These include large sums for health care, education, and prisons.

LO5 Identify some of the issues involved in California's relationship with the EPA. **13** Many in California have resisted, on economic grounds, measures against air pollution brought by the Environmental Protection Agency (EPA). **14** The state has led the nation in addressing automobile emissions, however. California has regularly received EPA approval for emission standards that go beyond national requirements. In 2005, however, the Bush administration's EPA refused to approve a California request that the state be allowed to regulate emissions as greenhouse gases. California and sixteen other states sued; they won in court, but it was the arrival of the Obama administration that actually changed federal policy. Obama's EPA announced it would adopt California's standards nationally in 2017.

LO6 Indicate how California has worked with the federal government to deal with the issue of water. **15** Rights to water in the Colorado River have pitted California against other states. California has exceeded its share of this water. In 2000, representatives from seven states agreed to a formula that would allow California to reduce its excess consumption over a fifteen-year period. The matter was settled without federal intervention. **16** Through CalFed, California and the federal government have worked together to improve the system of supplying water from the Sacramento-San Joaquin Delta. Both levels of government have provided funding. CalFed must contend with a three-way tug-of-war over water between farmers, environmentalists, and urban consumers. In 2007, in reaction to a long drought, a federal judge reduced deliveries of water to Southern California by 25 percent so that water could be used to save endangered species.

LO7 Point out some of the issues involved in sharing resources between California and the federal government.
17 **Federalism** refers to the relationship between state governments and the national government. The national government supplied about $653 billion to state and local governments in fiscal year 2010. Most of this came in the form of grants-in-aid. Formerly, California received a disproportionate share of federal grants-in-aid, in part due to defense work. Today, however, the state ranks thirty-seventh in per capita grant receipts.
18 California has an above-average percentage of citizens in poverty and a huge immigrant population, both of which argue for more federal support than the state currently receives.

Find more practice tests and study tools for this chapter on CourseMate.